180 Holes

114°2'E
22°43'E

WORLD'S No. 1

MISSION HILLS
GOLF CLUB

Mission Hills, located only 30 minutes north of the Shenzhen/Hong Kong border, spans over 3,500 acres. Currently Asia's largest with 5 courses, the additional 5 courses to open in 2003/4 will make it the world's largest golf complex with 180 holes.

Chairman's Message

"My ambition to make Missions Hills the No.1 golf complex in the world with 180 holes of championship courses designed by world golfing legends from five continents is being realized"

Dr. David S.H. Chu, LL.D.,JP.
Chairman Mission Hills Group

Dr. Chu with 1995 World Cup Champion - US Team.
The 1st International golf tournament in China

*T*iger Woods was hosted by
Mission Hills in his inaugural
visit to China in November 2001
for the Mission Hills Tiger Woods
China Challenge

TIGER WOODS

MISSION HILLS
TIGER WOODS
China Challenge
Nov 2001

1998 Johnnie Walker Super Tour

2003 will witness the inaugural Dynasty Cup. Based on the Ryder Cup format, the matches will see the best Japanese Team taking on the best of Asia Team with Mission Hills honored as the host club for the first three competitions.

Jack Nicklaus

"I am very proud of my contribution to golf
in China and am honored that my World Cup
Course has been so well received"

World Cup
Course

Jumbo Ozaki

"Playing through these canyons of dense vegetation provides a very peaceful, natural experience"

Canyon
Course

Ernie Els

"This course has a great mix of terrain that visually ties together with brilliant bunkering and landscaping and is challenging from head to toe".

Savannah Course

Vijay Singh

"The look and feel of this course is new to China but very similar to our Tournament Players Club where I live and often play-It feels like my home away from home"

New Valley
Course

Greg Norman

"I look forward to the challenge of creating the toughest course in China- I feel this task fits our vision and design sensibilities quite well".

Greg Norman Course

David Duval

"As a big fan of traditional design, I intend to create a challenging, straight forward course that evokes the atmosphere of the great courses of past eras"

David Duval
Course

Annika Sorenstam

"The views within and out of this property are outstanding ! With the elevation change from some tees I intend to create not just one but a few of the most commanding golf views in China".

Annika Sorenstam
Course

Jose Maria Olazabal

"With a property and project this unique, the ability to build an outstanding design is a given- my desire is to bring an equally unique vision and individuality creates a course that stirs the soul"

Jose Maria Olazabal
Course

David Leadbetter

"I intend to integrate the atmosphere of a learning center into my design- a course that not only makes you but teaches you to think".

Photo by Richard Castka

David Leadbetter Course

*M*ission Hills as an international resort provides one of the largest and highest quality sporting centres. A "state-of-the-art" gymnasium, traditional Chinese acupuncture, foot reflexology, spa, snooker, children's nursery/playground and the world renowned David Leadbetter Golf Academy are amongst the vast array of leisure facilities provided. The resort also has a 450-room hotel, conference facilities and 15 F&B outlets featuring international cuisine and bars.

USD *400* *million*
world of facilities

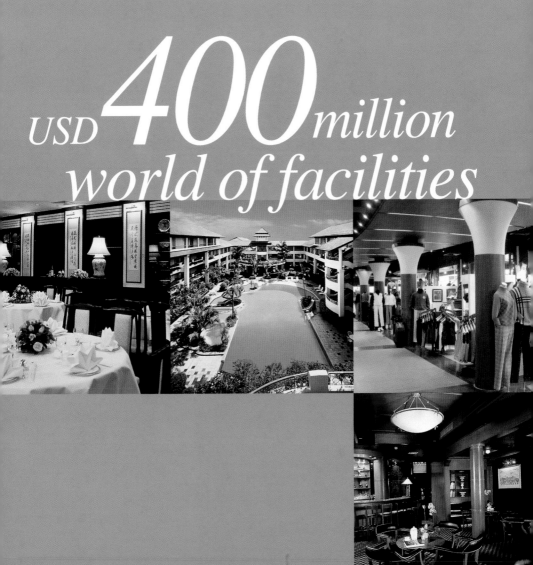

Tennis Centre

Mission Hills provides one of the largest tennis centres with 50 floodlight courts and a stadium court with a seating capacity of 3000. Mission Hills has also hosted many international tournaments.

Country Club

Mission Hills Country Club has complemented the operations of Mission Hills Golf Club and Resort and transformed the whole complex into an integrated family resort. Members enjoy facilities on sport, leisure, wining and dinning in a relaxed environment.

Mission Hills has established the first exclusive Leadbetter Academy in China since March, 2002. This world class teaching academy provides a dedicated 9 hole course, 2 full-length grass tee driving ranges, a 2-tier covered floodlit range and 4 short game practice area.

MISSION HILLS
David Leadbetter
Golf Academy

DAVID
LEADBETTER
GOLF
ACADEMY®

MISSION HILLS
GOLF CLUB

Presents

The World of
Professional Golf
2003

Mark H. McCormack

An IMG PUBLISHING Book

An IMG PUBLISHING Book

First published 2003
© IMG Operations, Inc. 2003

Designed and produced by Davis Design

ISBN 1-878843-37-0

Printed and bound in Hong Kong.

Contents

Foreword

It is a special pleasure to welcome and introduce Mission Hills Golf Club as the sponsor of *The World of Professional Golf 2003*.

Readers of previous editions of this golf annual will recognize the name of Mission Hills, which opened in 1994 in Shenzhen, China, and now includes a five-star resort, 50 floodlit tennis courts, and a world-class residential development. Mission Hills has been a contributor to global golf and a pioneer in the growth and promotion of the sport in China since its inception.

Mission Hills was the host of the World Cup in 1995, and of the final of the Johnnie Walker Super Tour in 1998. In 2001, on the same weekend that China entered the World Trade Organization, Mission Hills hosted the first visit to China by Tiger Woods for an exhibition, and will host the first-ever Dynasty Cup in 2003.

Presently, there are five signature golf courses and a David Leadbetter Golf Academy within this spectacular golfers' paradise. The golf courses, all designed by renowned professionals, are the World Cup Course (designed by Jack Nicklaus), Stadium Course (Nick Faldo), Canyon Course (Jumbo Ozaki), Savannah Course (Ernie Els) and New Valley Course (Vijay Singh).

By 2004, there will be a total of 10 golf courses at Mission Hills — two or three of which will open in 2003, thus bringing together an astounding total of 180 holes on the same property, the largest collection in the world — with the new designs to be done by David Duval, David Leadbetter, Greg Norman, Jose Maria Olazabal and Annika Sorenstam.

This annual is about the world of professional golf, and in 2002 Mission Hills announced its intention to be the world's No. 1 golf destination. We are happy to be able to share in the promotion of the success of Mission Hills, because the growth of golf at all levels always has been very important to our company. IMG has enjoyed a great relationship with Mission Hills. It is a world-class facility which continues to demonstrate its commitment to the game.

Mark H. McCormack

Mark H. McCormack
January 2003

1. The Year in Retrospect

For several reasons, 2002 could be referred to as the Golf Year of the Women. No one dominated like Annika Sorenstam. One year after winning eight tournaments and taking Player of the Year honors by a mile, Sorenstam bettered her own mark, winning 11 times on the LPGA Tour — two victories short of the record set by Mickey Wright in 1963 — and 13 times worldwide. Sorenstam won more than half of the tournaments she entered (13 of 25), a record that hadn't been touched since the middle 1940s by Byron Nelson and Ben Hogan.

"That's incredible," Meg Mallon said of Sorenstam's accomplishments. "You wouldn't say that about Tiger Woods. Golf just doesn't allow that anymore. It's pretty exciting in this era."

Sorenstam set many LPGA records in 2002, including lowest 54-hole total (195), lowest 54-hole total in relation to par (21 under) and largest margin of victory (11 strokes). She set an all-time record scoring average of 68.70, as well as breaking the LPGA single-season earnings record with $2,863,904 ($2,997,812 worldwide) and all-time earnings records for women. In May she became the first woman golfer in history to earn $9 million; in July she reached $10 million; and by the end of November, her career earnings eclipsed $11 million, finally reaching $11,170,368.

Even Tiger Woods showed deference to Sorenstam. "If you look at the numbers, that's when you appreciate what she's done. She performed at the highest level for the longest period of time. That's what makes her year a very, very special year."

Sorenstam finished in the top three 17 times in her 23 LPGA starts. Only three times in 25 starts worldwide did she finish lower than seventh, which means she had a chance to win on virtually every Sunday she competed. Her 42 career victories passed Babe Zaharias and tied Sandra Haynie for eighth on the all-time list.

At 32 years of age, as Ron Sirak noted in *Golf World*, Sorenstam has a realistic chance to catch Patty Berg, whose 60 victories are the third best ever. The 82 wins by Mickey Wright and 88 by Kathy Whitworth are probably unrealistic.

Sorenstam is on a run now — 24 LPGA victories (26 worldwide) over the last three seasons — that compares favorably with the other great runs in history. Nelson won 26 times in 1944-45, Hogan won 30 times from 1946 through 1948, and Woods won 22 times (30 times worldwide) in three years beginning in 1999. Wright won an astounding 44 times from 1961 through 1964.

"It's kind of scary when you think about it," Juli Inkster said. "Annika did things in the past two years nobody thought was possible. When she got things rolling she was untouchable."

After a record-setting performance in 2001, Sorenstam set her goals even higher. "I know inside what I'm capable of," she said. "I play golf because I love it, and I set goals for myself and not for anybody else. Last year was a wonderful year, but I was determined to prove that I could do it again, or even better. I knew I wasn't there yet, and I figured that if I worked out harder and longer, I would see some better results. That's what happened this year."

ANNIKA SORENSTAM

EVENT	POSITION
Australian Ladies Masters	1
Takefuji Classic	1
Ping Banner Health	2
Welch's/Circle K Championship	T-7
Kraft Nabisco Championship	1
The Office Depot	2
Chick-fil-A Charity Championship	T-58
Aerus Electrolux USA Championship	1
Asahi Ryokuken International	T-3
Kellogg-Keebler Classic	1
McDonald's LPGA Championship	3
Evian Ladies Masters	1
ShopRite Classic	1
U.S. Women's Open	2
Sybase Big Apple Classic	3
Weetabix Women's British Open	MC
Compaq Open	1
Williams Championship	1
Safeway Classic	1
Samsung World Championship	1
Mobile Tournament of Champions	T-4
Sports Today CJ Nine Bridges Classic	T-5
Cisco World Ladies Match Play	T-17
Mizuno Classic	1
ADT Championship	1

If there was a downside to Sorenstam's season it was the fact that she only won one of the four majors: the Kraft Nabisco Championship. Se Ri Pak won the McDonald's LPGA Championship, one of her five wins of the year. Pak also had 17 top-10s, solidifying herself at age 23 as the No. 1 challenger for the future. A member of the old guard, Juli Inkster, won the U.S. Women's Open in a thrilling come-from-behind, final-round duel with Sorenstam. Inkster had two LPGA victories in 2002, which matched the count of another of the usual challengers, Karrie Webb. Webb won the fourth major of the year, the Weetabix Women's British Open. She also had a third victory for the year in the AAMI Women's Australian Open.

While Sorenstam was setting records on the LPGA Tour, another woman, Suzy Whaley, was also making history. Whaley, a club professional in Connecticut, became the first woman since Zaharias to qualify for a PGA Tour event. Zaharias did it in 1938 when she qualified for the Los Angeles Open. Whaley did it in 2002 when she won the PGA's Connecticut sectional championship, playing from tees 10 percent shorter than the men's, and earned a spot in the 2003 Greater Hartford Open. It took Whaley a few months to decide whether or not to accept the spot, where she must play from the same tees as the men, but in October she informed the PGA Tour that she would, indeed, tee it up in Hartford.

"I took a long time to make this decision," Whaley said. "It's a lot longer than I'm used to playing, but I'm going to do it anyway. I'm going to do it the best I possibly can, and that's going to have to be good enough. I understand the historical implications of this decision and the importance it has for women golfers."

The PGA Tour couldn't have been more accommodating. "I think it'll be neat," Davis Love said. "It's going to be long for her, but I think it will be great for her, and great for the tour."

PGA Tour spokesman Bob Combs said, "We said all along that if Suzy chose to play we'd be delighted to welcome her as a contestant. We look forward to having her in the field at next year's event."

All the stories couldn't be like Suzy Whaley's. The biggest golf story of the year was a gender fight away from the golf courses between a man who wasn't a very good golfer and a woman who didn't play the game at all.

Marcia Chambers wrote a feature in the April issue of *Golf for Women* magazine which centered on the single-gender nature of the membership at Augusta National Golf Club. How, Chambers wondered, could the most recognized golf club in America host the Masters Tournament, the most watched golf event of the year, while remaining male only?

The article might have had little impact, except that Christine Brennan, a columnist for *USA Today*, had been wondering the same thing as part of her ongoing campaign on behalf of women in sports. Brennan did not attend the 2002 Masters, although she had been there previously, had raised questions in a press conference with Masters chairman Hootie Johnson, and had already written about it several times.

Continuing her protest from afar, Brennan turned to a contact from her Olympics coverage, the chief executive officer of the United States Olympic Committee and a relatively new member of Augusta National. Lloyd Ward broke a long-standing rule by speaking to a member of the media about the club. Ward, an African-American, told Brennan that he would be working to try to bring in a female member. Little else was said about the issue during the Masters week, and for the weeks immediately following, but Brennan's column had caught the attention of one Martha Burk.

On June 12, Johnson received a letter from Burk, the leader of the National Council of Women's Organizations, an umbrella organization for 160 women's groups including the National Organization for Women, the Women's Defense Fund and the National Abortion Rights Action League. The letter, which was sent without any preliminary contact, stated in part, "We know that Augusta National and the sponsors of the Masters do not want to be viewed as entities that tolerate discrimination against any group, including women ... We hope that you will take action so this is not an issue when the tournament is staged next year."

Enraged by what he perceived as bullying, Johnson took slightly less than a month to respond to Burk's letter, but when he did, he made a splash. "I found your letter's several references to discrimination, allusions to the sponsors and your setting of deadlines to be both offensive and coercive," Johnson wrote in a letter he made public. "I hope you understand why any further communication between us would not be productive."

Accompanying the letter was a three-page public statement, a break from tradition for any Augusta National chairman. The most provocative parts of the statement read: "Our membership alone decides our membership, not any outside group with its own agenda. ... We will not be bullied, threatened, or intimidated. ... We do not intend to become a trophy in their display case. There may come a day when women will be invited to join our membership, but that timetable will be ours and not at the point of a bayonet."

Johnson also stated, "We are not unmindful of the good work undertaken by Dr. Burk's organization in global human rights, Social Security reform, reproductive health, education, spousal abuse and workplace equity, among others. We are therefore puzzled as to why they have targeted our private golf club."

Burk came back swinging. Her first jab was aimed at CBS, the network that carries the Masters. "I think if I were in charge at CBS, I'd take a hard look at how this is going to look to my consumers," Burk said. "I'm going to be talking to them about airing something that is clearly underwriting discrimination."

CBS Sports president Sean McManus responded that, "CBS will broadcast the Masters again in 2003."

Burk then set her sights at the individual club members and the sponsors of the Masters. "I think we talk to individual members we can identify," Burk said. "And we talk to the corporations they represent. I think we try to find out who is paying their dues. I think we ask the public how they feel about executives of these corporations being members of a club that discriminates against women. We point out to the sponsors that they have corporate policies against discrimination and that it would enhance the image of their companies to reaffirm that stand in public."

Augusta members from former U.S. Senator Sam Nunn to Jack Nicklaus were asked to comment, but few chose to voice an opinion. Nunn restated the club's policy of having the chairman speak on all club matters, and Nicklaus said, "As members we're restricted from discussing any club policies outside the grounds of the club."

Nicklaus added a caveat. "I sympathize greatly with the diversity issue, or I wouldn't have the record I have as it relates to my clubs," he said. "Every club I have has minorities. My first members at Muirfield we had Anglo-Saxon, Jewish, African-American, Japanese, Korean, Australian and German. There was no woman to start with, but a couple of years later we added a woman. Now we have six or seven women members. This controversy puts me in very difficult position, because I can't discuss the club policies. I'm just a member. Augusta is not my deal."

When the sponsors — Coca Cola, Citigroup and IBM — were pressured by Burk, Johnson took the unprecedented step of doing without his own sponsors. "As we predicted several weeks ago, the National Council of Women's Organizations has launched a corporate campaign against the Masters Tournament and Augusta National to immediately invite women to join our club," Johnson said. "Accordingly, we have told our media sponsors that we will not request their participation in the 2003 Masters. This year's telecast will be conducted by the Masters Tournament."

Burk's frustration began to show when she said, "They can run it without sponsors for a year or two, but it can't go on forever."

She may have misunderstood the economics of the Masters and the wealth, power and occasional obstinacy of the Augusta National membership. According to estimates, the club generates an average of $21 million per year from sources other than television, and the net worth of the approximately 300 members is more than the gross national product of many countries. They might run the Masters Tournament commercial free for many, many years if they so chose.

Burk continued her campaign. She appeared on talk shows and news programs ranging from "This Week" on ABC to "The Best Damn Sports Show Period" on Fox Sports, and the dust-up between Burk and Johnson made shows ranging from "Meet the Press" to "Breakfast with Frost." *The New York Times* printed many stories and even two editorials that suggested that Tiger Woods should boycott the 2003 Masters and forgo a chance to become the first in history to win in three consecutive years. *The Times* came under intense scrutiny when they declined to publish (but later relented) two columns in the sports section that took views differing from the editorial positions.

By year's end only two Augusta National members had resigned, and no player voiced any plans to boycott the tournament. Still, Burk promised to be a visible presence throughout the spring. "There's only one end to this story," she said. "It doesn't matter what they do or when they do it; we are always going to be in the picture."

TIGER WOODS

EVENT	POSITION
Mercedes Championships	T-10
Telstra Hyundai New Zealand Open	T-6
AT&T Pebble Beach National Pro-Am	T-12
Buick Invitational	T-5
WGC Accenture Match Play	T-33
Genuity Championship	2
Bay Hill Invitational	1
The Players Championship	T-14
Masters Tournament	1
Verizon Byron Nelson Classic	3
Deutsche Bank - SAP Open	1
Memorial Tournament	T-22
U.S. Open Championship	1
British Open Championship	T-28
Buick Open	1
PGA Championship	2
WGC NEC Invitational	4
WGC American Express	1
Disney Golf Classic	3
The Tour Championship	T-7
Dunlop Phoenix	8
PGA Grand Slam	1
Target World Challenge	2

Fortunately, the war of words took place after the 2002 Masters, so there were no protests as Tiger Woods strolled to his second consecutive Masters title. Woods shot 12-under-par 276 and won by three strokes over Retief Goosen. The best player in the world carved his way around the newly lengthened Augusta National course like a skilled surgeon performing a routine operation. The only thing he didn't do was whistle a tune as he walked up the 18th fairway.

A month after winning for the third consecutive year in Orlando at the Bay Hill Invitational, Woods came into the Masters rested and prepared. He shot 70 in the opening round to trail Davis Love by three, then came back on a rain-soaked Friday and played 10 holes in one under par before the rain and darkness stopped play. Saturday was when he won it. He was up at 4:30 a.m. and played 26 holes in eight under par to come from six strokes behind Vijay Singh to take a share of the lead into the final round. It was a position from which he had never lost a major championship, and this year's Masters would be no exception.

It was over in four holes. Woods split the first fairway and made a par while Goosen, the co-leader, hooked his tee shot and made a bogey. Woods birdied the par-five second to extend the lead to two, then made another birdie from six feet at the third. By that time they could have taken Woods' 42-long green jacket out of the closet. And they could forget the saying that the tournament doesn't start until the back nine on Sunday.

At the sixth, Woods missed the green by about three feet, but chipped in from 25 feet for his third birdie of the day while Goosen continued to go in the wrong direction. He bogeyed the 11th to fall five strokes behind.

Els was four back through 12 holes. Realizing Woods wasn't going to make a mistake, Els took out his driver on the 13th tee. Six swings and two penalty strokes later, Els walked off the green with an eight.

"The thing about Tiger is, he's the only leader you know won't falter," Phil Mickelson said after finishing third, four strokes behind. "When other guys are up there, you know that if you can just stay around, there's a good chance they might come back two or three shots. Tiger doesn't ever seem to do that. You know that you have to go after him to make birdies to catch him, which is why I think we saw guys making aggressive plays and making bogeys and doubles because of it."

That's what they used to say about Nicklaus.

Tiger's father, Earl Woods, had a slightly different view. "The more he wins, the easier it becomes for him," Woods said. "He's just like a forest fire coming at you, and you don't have anything to stop it. He knows how to lead, and he knows how to come from behind. He knows how to apply pressure."

They said that about Nicklaus, too.

After Woods' 2002 season, where he added an even more efficient U.S. Open title to his record along with three other PGA Tour titles (a total of five), a victory on the PGA European Tour and the PGA Grand Slam, and a near-miss at the PGA Championship (his first runner-up finish in a major), a lot more comparisons were drawn between Woods and Nicklaus.

"Jack, and I'm sure Tiger, just believe they are miracle workers," said Tom Weiskopf, who competed against Nicklaus in his prime. "They do the things they do because they believe they can."

When Woods won the U.S. Open at the Bethpage State Park Black Course in New York while leading wire-to-wire, he became the first man since Nicklaus in 1972 to win the first two major championships of the season. Just as in Jack's day, talk turned to the Grand Slam. "I would never deny that Jack Nicklaus is the greatest player who ever lived," Gary Player said. "But Jack was never this dominant."

Johnny Miller agreed. "You look at Bobby Jones; what he did was amazing," Miller said. "Then you look at Nicklaus, and that was amazing too. But when you look at Tiger, there's nothing like it in history."

Sergio Garcia, one of the young players attempting to mount a challenge to Woods, wondered if there was anything the rest could do to stop him. "I never saw Nicklaus in his prime, but I'll tell you one thing, Tiger is unbelievable," Garcia said. "If he's leading by four or five, he doesn't need to play too hard, so he doesn't. If he needs to play a little harder, he does. He's able to do whatever it takes."

The most shocking score of the year was the 81 by Woods in the wind and rain of the third round of the British Open. Playing seven groups ahead of the leaders, Woods had all but two of his holes in the teeth of the storm. He went from two to 11 strokes behind, and his chances of the Grand Slam in 2002 were ended. Even 65 in the final round only brought Woods back to a tie for 28th place.

But for that, and the unlikely charge by Rich Beem in the final round of the PGA Championship, where Woods was second by one stroke, and all four major championships for the year might have been his.

Still, Woods led the World Money List for a record fifth consecutive year with $8,292,188, which was his second highest total behind his record $11,034,530 in 2000. And Woods continued to dominate the Official World Golf Ranking, extending his record to 176 consecutive weeks as No. 1 in the world.

Woods, age 26, ended the year with eight professional major championships (plus three U.S. Amateur victories) and 34 PGA Tour career victories. He was still far short of Nicklaus' record of 18 professional majors and two U.S. Amateur titles, but at his current pace he could pass Nicklaus in eight or nine years. The record for PGA Tour career victories is 82 by Sam Snead, and Woods could exceed that by keeping at his pace for nine or 10 more years.

"I would be very surprised if he doesn't break my records," Nicklaus said. "Very surprised. At the rate he's going, it's not such an awfully long haul."

ERNIE ELS

EVENT	POSITION
Bell's South African Open	T-13
Dunhill Championship	9
Johnnie Walker Classic	4
Heineken Classic	1
WGC Accenture Match Play	T-17
Genuity Championship	1
Dubai Desert Classic	1
Bay Hill Invitational	T-9
The Players Championship	T-44
Masters Tournament	T-5

Worldcom Classic	T-19
Compaq Classic of New Orleans	MC
Verizon Byron Nelson Classic	T-4
Memorial Tournament	T-13
Buick Classic	T-39
U.S. Open Championship	T-24
Canon Greater Hartford Open	T-10
Barclays Scottish Open	T-50
British Open Championship	1
The International	T-4
PGA Championship	T-34
WGC NEC Invitational	T-15
Omega European Masters	T-23
Linde German Masters	T-23
WGC American Express	T-23
Dunhill Links Championship	72
Cisco World Match Play	1
The Tour Championship	T-13
Nedbank Golf Challenge	1
Ernie Els Invitational	T-8

The only major where Woods never contended on Sunday was the British Open at Muirfield, which was won by my No. 2 pick for Player of the Year, Ernie Els. Nobody had a better early-season run than Els. He won on three continents in five weeks, picked up two more titles in Britain, and then won the Nedbank Golf Challenge at home in South Africa, bringing his year-end victory total to six.

In any year outside the Woods era, a six-victory season that included one major championship would be hailed as extraordinary. For Els it was simply second best. He won the Genuity Championship by opening up an eight-shot lead through three rounds, then hanging on while Woods made a charge up the leaderboard. Els also won Heineken Classic and the Dubai Desert Classic on the PGA European Tour, and he won his fourth Cisco World Match Play title, bringing him to within one of the record of five wins held by Gary Player and Seve Ballesteros. But the British Open victory, his third major championship title, made his year.

He took a share of the lead at Muirfield in the second round, then held it alone after surviving the toughest weather test of the season with 72, one over par, on Saturday. By all rights Els should have won the British Open in the regulation 72 holes. He led by one stroke over Thomas Levet, Steve Elkington and Stuart Appleby through 15 holes. When he walked off the 16th green, Els trailed by one. Chipping escapades that looked more like actor Ray Romano at Pebble Beach led to a double bogey. Els steadied himself with a birdie at the 17th to join a four-way playoff, which he won five holes later with a deft up-and-down from a bunker at the 18th.

Feeling relief as much as joy, Els admitted that in this era it might have been his last chance at a major championship. "I've been after this for 10 years," he said. "If I hadn't gotten it this year, I don't think I would have made it."

After he won the Genuity Championship in March, Els admitted to battling some inner demons in recent years. "I used to be a great frontrunner," Els said. "Then this little voice started coming into my head, this little guy inside me that made me defensive, almost scared." At Muirfield, he admitted that the little voice was back. "I'm never going to get rid of him," he said. "I mean, this week I had a chance a couple of times to break away and the little guy just kept sitting on my shoulder. Every time I tried to shoo him away I made a mistake. It was difficult, but I'm proud of myself for getting through this one."

Not the words you would expect from a player ranked third in the world who finished the year with over $6 million in worldwide earnings, second only to Woods. Els also finished tied for fifth in the Masters, and made a respectable showing with a tie for 24th at the U.S. Open. Still, in the age of Woods, Els wasn't sure how he stacked up. "I can't ever get to Tiger's level of intensity," he said. "But if we're going to be going at each other for the next 10 years, and I hope we do, I can try to get closer to his level, and I think I am. If there's going to be a rivalry, it can't have the same result every time, can it?"

PHIL MICKELSON

EVENT	POSITION
Bob Hope Chrysler Classic	1
Phoenix Open	T-23
AT&T Pebble Beach National Pro-Am	MC
Buick Invitational	MC
WGC Accenture Match Play	T-33
Honda Classic	T-11
Bay Hill Invitational	T-3
The Players Championship	T-28
BellSouth Classic	3
Masters Tournament	3
Worldcom Classic	3
Compaq Classic of New Orleans	T-9
Verizon Byron Nelson Classic	T-17
MasterCard Colonial	T-23
Memorial Tournament	T-9
Buick Classic	T-25
U.S. Open Championship	2
Canon Greater Hartford Open	1
British Open Championship	T-66
The International	MC
Buick Open	T-29
PGA Championship	T-34
WGC NEC Invitational	T-9
WGC American Express	T-23
Buick Challenge	3
The Tour Championship	T-5
Target World Challenge	10

Phil Mickelson, who found himself in the all-too-familiar position of losing to Woods throughout most of the year, could have uttered those same words. At both the Masters and the U.S. Open Mickelson contended with one round to play, but failed to close. He remained without a victory in the major championships, even though he won twice on the PGA Tour at the Bob Hope Chrysler Classic and the Canon Greater Hartford Open (events where Woods was not in the field). He remained No. 2 on the World Ranking, and he finished third on the world money list with $4.7 million. For those reasons, Mickelson is third on my Player of the Year list.

He finished third in the Masters and second in the U.S. Open. But then there was the five-putt at The Players Championship which dropped him out of the lead, and the questionable shot from the trees at the 16th at Bay Hill, a gamble that had some wondering about Mickelson's strategic thinking and speculating about his need to feel the rush of the challenge.

Mickelson added fuel to the speculation that he might enjoy the gamble more than the victory when he said, "I'm not going to change my style of play. I get criticized for it, but the fact is that I play my best when I play aggressive, when I attack, when I create shots. That's what I enjoy about the game, that challenge."

He went on to justify his go-for-broke style by pointing to his record. "I have won more tournaments than anybody playing the game right now other than Tiger Woods," Mickelson said. "And I haven't seen anybody step up to the plate and challenge Tiger the way I have winning the 1998 Mercedes, winning the 2000 Tour Championship, winning the 2000 and 2001 San Diego championships (Buick Invitational) head-to-head with him. He's the best player in the game and I am not going to back down from him. I see these guys wilt and it's unbelievable to me that they haven't been able to play their best golf when he's in contention.

"The fact is that if I change the way I play golf, one, I won't enjoy the game as much, and, two, I won't play to the level I have been playing. So I won't ever change. Not tomorrow, Sunday, at Augusta or the U.S. Open, not at any tournament."

Mickelson birdied the first hole of the final round at the Masters, but did not seriously challenge, and he pulled to within two strokes of Woods in the final round of the U.S. Open, but never got closer.

"I think it would be much more difficult if I had never been in contention," Mickelson said. "I love to compete for these championships, and to be a part of it, to have a shot at the end is a very wonderful experience. It would be much more difficult had I not even had a shot at it. But it doesn't take away the disappointment, or the feeling of another lost opportunity."

RICH BEEM

EVENT	POSITION
Sony Open in Hawaii	T-54
Bob Hope Chrysler Classic	MC
Phoenix Open	MC
Buick Invitational	T-30
Nissan Open	MC
Touchstone Energy Tucson Open	MC
Genuity Championship	4

Honda Classic	MC
The Players Championship	T-44
Shell Houston Open	MC
BellSouth Classic	T-25
Worldcom Classic	MC
Greater Greensboro Chrysler Classic	WD
Compaq Classic of New Orleans	T-14
Verizon Byron Nelson Classic	T-39
MasterCard Colonial	WD
Kemper Insurance Open	2
Buick Classic	MC
FedEx St. Jude Classic	T-54
Advil Western Open	T-78
Greater Milwaukee Open	T-24
John Deere Classic	MC
The International	1
PGA Championship	1
WGC NEC Invitational	T-6
Linde German Masters	T-94
WGC American Express	T-49
Valero Texas Open	T-67
Invensys Classic at Las Vegas	T-37
Disney Golf Classic	T-47
The Tour Championship	T-26
Holden Australian Open	T-2
PGA Grand Slam	4
Target World Challenge	16

Rich Beem won twice in 2002, holding off a charging Steve Lowery to capture The International title, then holding off an even more aggressive Tiger Woods to win the PGA Championship. Beem won his first major title by hitting solid shots under the pressure of a final round where Woods was making four birdies in a row to finish. Calmly, coolly, Beem hit an eight iron into the 16th green and rolled in a 25-footer for birdie, then hit solid shots to the 17th and 18th greens for the victory.

"I didn't know if I had what it took to win," Beem admitted, as he answered questions with the Wanamaker Trophy by his side. "Obviously I found out today that I do, and I'm actually still surprised at myself for it. I mean, I'm elated beyond belief, but this time I found out where to put the pressure. I know how to control myself a little better."

With a common-man flair and a refreshing frankness that made him the darling of the year's final major, Beem became the hit of the year, and earned the fourth spot on my list.

RETIEF GOOSEN

EVENT	POSITION
Mercedes Championships	T-14
Bell's South African Open	T-5
Dunhill Championship	T-2

Johnnie Walker Classic	1
Dimension Data Pro-Am	1
WGC Accenture Match Play	T-17
Honda Classic	T-30
Bay Hill Invitational	T-15
The Players Championship	T-14
BellSouth Classic	1
Masters Tournament	2
Canarias Open de Espana	T-8
Benson and Hedges International	T-19
Deutsche Bank - SAP Open	T-60
Volvo PGA Championship	MC
Buick Classic	T-25
U.S. Open Championship	MC
Smurfit European Open	T-2
Barclays Scottish Open	T-14
British Open Championship	T-8
TNT Open	T-31
Buick Open	T-14
PGA Championship	T-23
WGC NEC Invitational	T-11
Omega European Masters	T-43
Linde German Masters	T-23
WGC American Express	2
Dunhill Links Championship	T-35
Cisco World Match Play	T-5
Telfonica Open de Madrid	T-7
The Tour Championship	T-9
Volvo Masters Andalucia	T-34
Nedbank Golf Challenge	T-4
Target World Challenge	11

Fifth on my list for 2002 is Retief Goosen, owner of one of the most impressive stretches in golf. From the time to he won the 2001 U.S. Open, through his second-place finish at the Masters, Goosen won six titles in 24 starts, and went from a player with tons of untapped potential to a two-time European Order of Merit winner.

After capturing his first European Order of Merit in 2001, Goosen won the Johnnie Walker Classic in Australia by a record eight strokes after shooting 63 on Saturday to open up a whopping 13-shot lead. That prompted Sergio Garcia to say, "What Retief is doing is possible, but you have to be playing perfect golf."

Goosen wasn't perfect throughout the rest of 2002, but he was good. He had another early victory in the Dimension Data Pro-Am in South Africa, then a win at the BellSouth Classic in Atlanta made him one of the favorites to challenge Woods at the Masters, which he did, finishing second in the first major championship of the year. He also finished second in the WGC American Express Championship, and tied for second in the Dunhill Championship and the Smurfit European Open.

Those finishes moved him to No. 5 in the World Ranking, and he finished the year at seventh on the World Money List with $3.8 million.

SERGIO GARCIA

EVENT	POSITION
Mercedes Championships	1
Sony Open in Hawaii	T-40
Johnnie Walker Classic	3
Nissan Open	T-13
WGC Accenture Match Play	T-9
Genuity Championship	T-33
Bay Hill Invitational	T-9
The Players Championship	T-4
Masters Tournament	8
Worldcom Classic	T-19
Canarias Open de Espana	1
Verizon Byron Nelson Classic	MC
MasterCard Colonial	MC
Memorial Tournament	73
Buick Classic	T-12
U.S. Open Championship	4
Canon Greater Hartford Open	T-20
British Open Championship	T-8
The International	18
PGA Championship	T-10
WGC NEC Invitational	T-58
WGC American Express	7
Cisco World Match Play	2
The Tour Championship	28
Volvo Masters Andalucia	T-7
Dunlop Phoenix	2
Nedbank Golf Challenge	6

Rounding out the top six in my players of the year is Sergio Garcia, who continued to dazzle the golf world with his flamboyant play and infectious smile. Garcia won the first tournament of the year on the PGA Tour when he took David Toms to a playoff in the Mercedes Championships, then overpowered the defending PGA champion with a birdie on the first extra hole.

It looked as though Garcia would be a multiple winner in both Europe and America, but while he contended at almost every big event of the year, he only won once more. But it was a good one, the Canarias Open de Espana, or Spanish Open. It wasn't a major championship, but winning in his home country was the next best thing.

Garcia was the only player to finish in the top 10 in all four majors — eighth at the Masters, fourth at the U.S. Open, tied for eighth at the British Open and tied for 10th at the PGA Championship — and he was the closest challenger to Tiger Woods after three rounds of the U.S. Open at Bethpage.

Ranked fourth in the world when the season ended, Garcia finished the year eighth in the world in money earned with over $3.4 million, all before his 24th birthday.

Honorable mentions go to Vijay Singh, who won twice, once in the spring at the Shell Houston Open and again at the season-ending Tour Championship, and to David Toms, who didn't win, but who followed up his great 2001 season with a playoff loss at the Mercedes Championships, seconds at the MasterCard Colonial and Buick Challenge, and a third at the Tour Championship. Singh won over $4.3 million for the year to finish fourth on the World Money List, and Toms walked away with over $4 million, the fifth best in the world.

It says a lot when someone like Singh can have two victories, two top-10 finishes in major championships (seventh at the Masters and eighth at the PGA) and two other top-fives and only make honorable mention on my year-end list, but that's the way the world of professional golf has evolved since the coming of Woods. No longer is a two-win season considered a crowning accomplishment. Eighteen players on the PGA Tour won for the first time in 2002, and by the end of the year a majority of golf fans probably couldn't name half of them. Woods made anything short of a multiple-win season and a major victory seem like a failure. He set a bar that would not only change the game, but changed the way the general public measured success in the sport.

The downside of the Woods-dominated era is that a lot of good golf gets overlooked. Justin Rose won four times in 2002. Padraig Harrington won three. Colin Montgomerie, Adam Scott, Bernhard Langer and Michael Campbell all had really good years, but their achievements were overshadowed by Woods' dominance.

It's hard to predict how long Woods will continue to play at such a dominant level. "Of course, Tiger has all the ingredients to do it, every single one," Gary Player said. "But he's still got to do it. So many things can go wrong. Great players — Palmer, Watson, Seve — they all stopped (winning majors) in their early 30s."

All we can do is enjoy being around to witness it.

The Royal Bank of Scotland Group

Presents

The Major Championships

2. Masters Tournament

The first was a coronation ceremony, full of sweeping social implications. The second was a shoot-out where the best played their best and the outcome was uncertain until the end. This time, Tiger Woods made it look easy.

The No. 1 player in the world joined an elite club on a warm April Sunday in Augusta, Georgia, becoming only the third (following Jack Nicklaus and Nick Faldo) to successfully defend his title in the Masters Tournament. He didn't do it by shattering tournament records, nor did he electrify the crowds with late birdies to fend off challengers. This one was utilitarian ... professional ... some would say boring. Woods worked his way around the landscape of Augusta National Golf Club like a predator drone over a war zone. Any target in his sights was annihilated with dispassionate efficiency.

He was patient, methodical and head-and-shoulders above the rest of the field. So complete was his domination of this major championship that the first questions he was asked afterward weren't about how it felt to join Nicklaus, Faldo, Jimmy Demaret, Sam Snead, Gary Player and Arnold Palmer a winner of three or more Masters, because to make those comparisons would be to somehow equate Woods with the Demarets of the world. Nor did it seem appropriate to ask how he felt being the youngest (age 26) player to win seven majors. That somehow implied finality, as if this were the last major title he would ever own. The questions were not about the records Woods had set, but the ones he might break. And the question on everybody's mind was: Could he win the Grand Slam?

"I've won four (majors) in a row before," he said. "It would be great to do it in one year, just because it would be something different."

No one else could have gotten away with describing the Impregnable Quadrilateral (known in common parlance as the Grand Slam) as "something different." Then again, no one else could wake up at 4:30 on a Saturday morning trailing in the Masters by six strokes, play 26 mud-caked holes in eight under par, leave Saturday night with a share of the lead, then rip the heart out of the competition in the first three holes of the final round. That's how Woods did it, playing the middle 27 holes in eight under par, then cruising to the finish after jumping out to a four-stroke lead on Sunday.

His scores were 70-69-66-71–276, 12 under par on the newly lengthened and demonstrably tougher Augusta National, and the final margin of victory was three over Retief Goosen. It was really not that close. Once Woods came back on Saturday morning to finish his rain-delayed second round, this one was his. He made 19 birdies, 46 pars and seven bogeys for the week, nothing record-breaking, just good enough to win. He hit 75 percent of the greens in regulation, 69 percent of the fairways and averaged 293.75 yards off the tees.

Most of the early talk was about the 300 additional yards and new tees Augusta National had added. The opening hole was so much longer that the bunker on the right (which had become little more than an aiming point for most long hitters) was now so far away 80 percent of the field couldn't reach it with their drives. The seventh hole was pushed back an additional 45 yards. The ninth, a par-four that had become little more than a driver and a short iron, had been lengthened by 30 yards, bringing "Hogan's ledge," the only level spot of ground on the fairway and the spot where Ben Hogan tried to place his tee shot every time, back into play. When you took the ricochet off the hill into account, the 30 additional yards on the ninth played more like 50 yards.

The 10th had been moved beyond the limits of logic. From the new tee the par-four measured 500 yards, and if players couldn't carry the ball 290 yards with a draw, it played even longer. The 11th was lengthened by 35 yards, the 13th was moved back an additional 25 yards (onto property the National had purchased from its neighbor, Augusta Country Club).

The biggest change came at the 18th, where the tee was moved back an additional 60 yards. Already a narrow driving hole, the new tee had players like Greg Norman lamenting, "It's like trying to hit it up a gnat's arse." The final hole took its toll through the week. During the opening round only eight players hit six iron or less into the green, and on Sunday the final 10 players played the 18th in four over par. It was the hardest green to hit all week (only 32 percent found the green in regulation), and the average score was 4.321 for the four days, making the 18th the toughest hole on the course. "It was certainly easier last year when I hit lob wedge into that green every day," Padraig Harrington said. "It's quite steep up that hill. It's not like you're hitting four iron from a flat piece of ground. There's no water on the hole, but it still bites."

The design changes had at least one of the desired effects. The scoring average for the week jumped from 72.493 in 2001, when the course measured 6,985 yards, to a whopping 73.445 on the new 7,270-yard layout. But anyone who thought they had Tiger-proofed the course by adding extra yards didn't understand the game.

"You want to Tiger-proof a course? Move everybody up to the ladies' tees," said Tiger's father, Earl Woods. "Eliminate the rough completely. Cut the greens to eight or nine on the Stimpmeter, and I'll guarantee you, Tiger won't win. But this course plays right into his hands."

Players agreed with that assessment. "They said they Tiger-proofed the thing," Colin Montgomerie said. "If they want to do that, they should make it shorter. The tees were on the tips. They have played right into his hands."

"Look at the leaderboard and try to find a short hitter," Nick Price said. "Kind of backfiring on everyone, isn't it?"

And Jeff Sluman, who spoke for the distance-challenged, summed up the problem nicely when he said, "The days of Larry Mize and Ben Crenshaw winning this thing are over."

When the final scores were tallied, the only players in the top 10 who weren't considered long hitters were Jose Maria Olazabal (fourth, five strokes behind Woods) and Miguel Angel Jimenez (tied for ninth, nine back). Everyone else played the long ball.

Woods proved to be the best, not only by hitting the ball farther and hitting more greens than everyone, but also by crawling into the other players' heads. His presence proved intimidating, a fact his nearest competitors acknowledged.

"The thing about Tiger is, he's the only leader you know won't falter," Phil Mickelson said after yet another near-miss. Mickelson finished in third place, four behind Woods. "When other guys are up there, you know that if you can just stay around, there's a good chance they might come back two or three shots. But Tiger doesn't ever seem to do that. So, with that being the case, you know that you have to go after him to make birdies to catch him, which is why I think we see guys taking aggressive plays and making bogeys and doubles."

Tied with Goosen at the start of the final round, Woods hit a perfect tee shot then watched as Goosen snap-hooked his shot into the ninth fairway. Woods parred; Goosen bogeyed. The lead was one.

Ernie Els and Mickelson both birdied the first hole to move to within three strokes and give some early hope to those who wanted a down-to-the-wire finish. But Woods went about his business, rolling in a birdie at the par-five second, then another from six feet at the short par-four third. He parred the fourth, and then recovered from an errant tee shot at the fifth, but three-putted for bogey. At the sixth, Woods missed the green by about three feet, but chipped in from 25 feet for his third birdie of the day.

Goosen continued to head in the wrong direction with a disappointing par at the second hole followed by a bogey at the fourth and another at the par-five eighth. When he bogeyed the 11th to fall five strokes back, the defending U.S. Open champion and winner of six events in his last 24 starts was like a punch-drunk fighter trying to make it to the bell. "Do I get the green pants for finishing second?" he joked.

Els hung around at four strokes behind through 12 holes, but realizing Woods wasn't going to make a mistake, he took a driver out of the bag at the 13th, a hole where he had hit a three wood off the tee all week. The result was a disastrous hook into the trees on the far side of Rae's Creek. To compound his mistake, Els ignored his caddie (who thought Els should chip out sideways). Instead he tried to play through a gap in the trees. The ball hit a limb and bounded about 30 yards sideways before rolling into the water. "The second shot was the mistake," Els said. "I don't know what it is about professional golfers. I thought I had a shot."

He dropped and hit a seven-iron fourth shot from 194 yards that hit on the greenside of the bank, but rolled back into the creek again. Another drop, a chip and two putts later, Els walked away with an eight. His chances were over.

Vijay Singh was around for a while as well. He had been the leader in the clubhouse when play was suspended on Friday thanks to rounds of 70 and 65. The even-par 72 on Saturday didn't hurt him much. Singh was still only two strokes behind with 18 holes to play. The gap widened to three on the first nine, but Singh felt he could make a second-nine run. Instead, he bogeyed the 11th, bogeyed the 14th, then hit his second shot in the creek at the 13th, but managed to salvage par. At the par-five 15th, Singh hit a poor tee shot, laid up short of the water, then chunked an 82-yard wedge shot about 10 yards short of the green and into the water. He hit another wedge that landed on the front of the green and promptly spun back into the pond. Another wedge shot, and another ball in the water (this time over the green), and Singh walked away with a quadruple-bogey nine.

Mickelson avoided any big numbers, but he didn't make any small ones either. He followed birdies at the first two holes with bogeys at the third and fourth. He birdied the sixth to pull within four, but bogeyed the seventh (while Woods was chipping in for birdie at the sixth). Six behind with 11 holes to play, Mickelson finished with 10 pars, one birdie and the resigned attitude of someone who had been there too many times.

"It was probably possible today, but it would have taken an incredible round and a lot of good breaks," Mickelson said. "I don't feel like it was a missed opportunity, per se. Every tournament, every major is an opportunity, and throughout the four days I played very solid golf, but I didn't have that explosive spurt to vault me up the leaderboard, which you have to have here at Augusta. Even though I did not win, this was a very fun and enjoyable week. Today I thought I was very lucky to be able to play in the final round of the Masters, play the back nine and be on the leaderboard, and play this game for a living."

Mickelson sounded like someone who had survived a five-car pile-up. But Woods had that effect on people. As Goosen said, "He's the best player. He was never really in any trouble, and no one was putting any pressure on him. I think he was just cruising in, not taking any chances out there. He was just hitting to the safe sides on every hole. He didn't have to do anything but par in on the back nine. You just know Tiger is not going to make any mistakes."

He didn't, finishing with a par on the 18th for 71 and the three-stroke victory. This one was like watching a Ferrari race a pack of minivans. All he had to do was keep the motor running.

At the time, the hot topic among the press and the players was Johnson's decision to oust the elder statesmen from the Masters field. One of the qualifying criteria for the Masters Tournament was its lifetime invitation to past champions. While few of the over-60 crowd had made the 36-hole cut in recent outings, the presence of players like Gay Brewer, Tommy Aaron, Charles Coody, Gary Player, Billy Casper, Doug Ford and Arnold Palmer made the early rounds unique and provided an air of nostalgia. But Johnson treated this particular tradition like a trespasser. In letters to Casper, Ford and Brewer, Johnson characterized their recent Masters records as "not indicative of active participation, and in keeping with the spirit of the intent of the founders, we believe that the 2001 Masters should be your final one as a player."

They could come to the practice rounds, play in the par-three contest, and attend the champions' dinner, but that was it. Come Thursday morning, they should be watching from the verandah. Casper's feelings were hurt, but he came anyway. So did Ford, who had withdrawn early in six of his last eight appearances, leaving after only one hole in 2001. Brewer, the 1967 champion, was so devastated he stayed home. "I told Gay, 'You're making a mistake; you should go,'" Casper said. "He didn't want to hear it."

None of the older players wanted to be put in the position of getting a similar letter. Charles Coody said that 2003 would be his last Masters. "Nobody wants to go out there and embarrass himself," Coody said. "I think most players, if left to their own devices, are going to make the right decision about when to stop playing. Regardless of what happened, I had always planned to stop playing here when I turned 65. Next year was going to be my last year anyway."

Arnold Palmer — who many believed made the Masters the most popular tournament in golf and one of only two past champions who are full-fledged members of the club (the other is Jack Nicklaus) — stated on Thursday afternoon that he would be retiring from the Masters on Friday. "Tomorrow will be it," Palmer said. "I don't want to get a letter."

The course changes had made it tough for the 72-year-old Palmer. He had to hit a three wood into the first green, and couldn't get home on the 18th with his two best shots. "I guess there are some things in life that are inevitable, and I guess I'm facing that right now," he said. "I'm not any different than most people. I like to think there are a couple more good rounds in my body, and maybe there are. But certainly I haven't shown up here, and I think enough of this golf tournament, the people that are playing it, and the people that run it, to say, 'Hey, I don't need to be here.' Like I said, I'm like most people. I hit a couple of shots today that I got encouraged about and, hell, I can't wait to get to the practice tee and see if I can hit a few and see if I can make it work. I guess that's what keeps me going, the love of the game. But as far as playing is concerned, it's over."

After his final press conference at the Masters, Palmer walked back to the clubhouse with his head slightly bowed. He felt a tug on his waist. When he turned and looked, he saw Tiger Woods standing there. "How'd you do?" Palmer asked. Woods answered by giving Palmer a heartfelt embrace.

Other than the departure of one of the most beloved figures in all of sports, the first couple of days weren't too exciting. At 8 a.m. on Thursday, Sam Snead hit his last ceremonial tee shot at the Masters, a low push that nailed a patron in the nose and broke his glasses. Snead never saw the ball or the man he hit. He knelt down, picked up his tee, waved to the crowd, and shuffled back to the cart that would wheel him to the clubhouse. This was another ceremony that was over, and everyone knew it. Six weeks later, just four days shy of his 90th birthday, Snead died in Hot Springs, Virginia.

Almost two hours after Sam hit the first ceremonial first shot, Mark Brooks birdied the second hole to become the first player under par. At 1:43 p.m., Adam Scott signed for 71 and posted the first under-par round of the tournament. He would be one of 21 players who would finish in red figures on Thursday. Davis Love went the lowest, shooting 67. Angel Cabrera and Sergio Garcia shot 68s, while Mickelson, Goosen and Padraig Harrington shot 69s.

"This is a place we all prepare for," Love said. "We are all ready for it, and it doesn't matter if it's Cabrera, Love, Nick Price or anybody. We are all ready for this week. It's just nice to catch it on a calm day, especially with the weather predictions of rain."

Those last words would prove to be prophetic, although Love didn't know it at the time. Weather would play a key role in this championship.

Cabrera was an unlikely contender. Playing in only his third Masters (he missed the cut in 2000 and finished tied for 10th in 2001), the long-hitting Argentine had only one bogey in his four-under-par round. "I came in with a lot of confidence," said the winner of the 2001 Argentine Open. "The more you play here, the more you get to know the course and the more you understand it."

He was a dark horse, but with a top-10 finish in only his second trip to Augusta, no one was ready to completely count Cabrera out. When asked about his good play and the play of other international contestants, the Argentine shrugged. "It's not a surprise," he said. "Golf is going around the world. If you look at what's happening over the past year with the South Africans, particularly with Goosen, or with Michael Campbell, there are players of absolute quality who are winning around the world. You only have to look to my Argentine compatriot, Jose Coceres, who won twice last year."

Garcia was another example of the game's international homogeny. Garcia was as well known in Madison, Georgia, as he was in Malaga, Spain, and he made no bones about his goals of winning both the U.S. and European money titles in the same year. If Cabrera's opening 68 was mildly surprising, Garcia's 68 was as expected as the coming of spring.

"Last year was very unfortunate, the way I missed the cut," Garcia said. "I've always said it; in major championships, you've got to play well, but you've got to be a little lucky. Unfortunately, I don't think I've been really lucky in this tournament, so I haven't really contended. I'm looking forward to doing it this year. You know, if my putter behaves a little, I think that I should have a good chance the way I'm hitting the ball."

Woods wasn't quite so brash, but then again, he didn't have to be. He was the defending champion and someone everyone expected to have a "good chance." With 70, he was right there after the first round. "You've just got to keep hanging in there," he said. "It's not one of those type of golf courses where you can just turn it on here and make a few birdies, no big deal. You've still got to keep plugging along. That's what I did."

When the sun set on Thursday and the clouds started rolling in from the west, the leaderboard looked like this:

Davis Love	67	Ernie Els	70
Angel Cabrera	68	Tiger Woods	70
Sergio Garcia	68	Jose Maria Olazabal	70
Phil Mickelson	69	Chris DiMarco	70
Padraig Harrington	69	Vijay Singh	70
Retief Goosen	69	Miguel Angel Jimenez	70
Nick Price	70	Adam Scott	71
Justin Leonard	70	Brad Faxon	71
Jesper Parnevik	70	Greg Norman	71
Darren Clarke	70	Tom Watson	71
Scott Verplank	70		

The skies opened with rain on Friday and the course played as long and wet as it possibly could. While it wasn't the wettest Masters on record, it was one of the muddiest days anyone could recall when play was not suspended. Compounding matters was the decision by the tournament committee to forgo lift-clean-and-place rules, a decision that drew the ire of many players.

"Even my umbrella had standing water," Stewart Cink said. "It was pretty much over the line unplayable. When you have standing water on the greens, that's above and beyond what we should do in a major championship."

Mild-mannered players such as Steve Stricker and Fred Couples drew stares of shock after raising their voices to tournament officials (both later apologized). "It was a joke, to tell you the truth," Stricker said. "There was no place to take the ball. Maybe they saw what was coming on radar, and I guess they wanted to get it in. The main guy (meaning the head rules official) wasn't even on the course. He must have been in the clubhouse eating bacon and eggs or something."

David Toms called it, "the wettest golf course where they haven't allowed us to play lift, clean and place. You almost had to drop it in the rough on several holes to get relief."

The venting went on. "The eighth hole should be renamed (from Yellow Azalea) to 'A River Runs Through It,'" said Couples.

Brad Faxon said, "If this was the PGA Tour, we wouldn't have played. It was bordering on laughable. You couldn't take a drop. Everybody hit shots out of casual water because there was no place to go."

"Every hole, if you didn't hit the high spots, you were taking a drop," Robert Allenby said.

Said David Duval, "Maybe you could have carried a mat around with you. I don't know ... what's wrong with going on Monday or Tuesday? I don't think anybody would leave."

And Vijay Singh said, "I went out to the driving range and was waiting for the call to come that it was going to be delayed, but surprisingly there was none."

Singh went on to say that he wasn't a very good wet weather player, but you wouldn't have known it from the round he carved out of the mud on Friday. When play was called at 5:07 p.m. (with 37 players still on the course) Singh held a four-stroke lead by virtue of a seven-under-par 65. He shot one-under 35 on the first nine before going on a tear that included birdies at the 12th, 13th, 17th and 18th and an eagle at the 15th for a six-under 30.

"I wasn't really thinking about shooting a number out there," Singh said. "My wife asked me last night, 'What would be a good number for you?' I said, 'A 68 would be a great number for me.' I thought about it after I finished, and I said, 'Man, that's a great score I shot out there.'"

The birdies were infectious in Singh's group. Thomas Bjorn set a tournament record by starting the day with five consecutive birdies. "A couple of times a year, you get on a streak like that," Bjorn said. "But hardly ever at the start of a round, and never on a course like this. It was almost too easy."

Bjorn finished with 67 for a three-under 141 total. "Today was nice, good, proper golf," Bjorn said in spite of the weather. "I got what I deserved, and that was important."

Garcia also thought he got what he deserved. He finished with a birdie on the sloppy 18th to shoot 71 and go into the weekend at five-under-par 139. "After playing so well yesterday, I would have liked to be a little better," Garcia said. "I really felt like I could have shot another 69 or 68 today and been right up there. But it's still pretty decent. I think I want it as badly as anybody else. It's just the same old thing: Just go out there, be as patient as you can be, try to play the best you can, and if you get momentum and make a couple of birdies, keep yourself out of trouble and hit the ball the way you want to, that's what you've got to do. That's what I'm going to try to do this weekend."

He had a little catch-up work ahead of him. Singh's 65 had everyone singing his praises. "It's strong," Garcia said. "More than anything I think the 30 on the back was quite sweet. He must have played really good and putted well, and probably everything just went his way."

When asked whether there were any more 65s out there, Garcia wouldn't commit. "It all depends on how the wind reacts," he said. "If the wind starts blowing, you know how tricky it gets on this golf course. I mean, maybe a guy can just go at it and start doing really good things and everything seems to go his way, maybe shoot a 65 or so, but I don't see many coming. Even with the greens as soft as they are, the course is still playing long. It's still not easy to score."

When the rain finally subsided and the second round was finished, the leaderboard was shaped up for a great weekend.

Vijay Singh	65 - 135	Phil Mickelson	72 - 141
Retief Goosen	67 - 136	Thomas Bjorn	67 - 141
Ernie Els	67 - 137	Miguel Angel Jimenez	71 - 141
Jose Maria Olazabal	69 - 139	Chris DiMarco	71 - 141
Angel Cabrera	71 - 139	Nick Faldo	67 - 142
Tiger Woods	69 - 139	Davis Love	75 - 142
Padraig Harrington	70 - 139	Jesper Parnevik	72 - 142
Sergio Garcia	71 - 139		

The third round was well underway by the time the second-round scores were tallied. Another deluge in the wee hours of Saturday morning made completing the day look unlikely. Augusta National's staff went to work to cover mud-caked areas with pine straw and sweep standing water off the greens, but it was still a wet and muddy affair with a distinct aroma reminiscent of bull droppings wafting through Amen Corner. When asked about the odiferous conditions on Saturday, an Augusta National spokesman said the rain had dredged up some naturally decaying grass. "I think somebody brought their pet cow," Faldo said.

The smell didn't bother Woods. He made two birdies in the closing holes of his second round, and seven more birdies (along with one bogey) in the afternoon 18. He didn't miss a fairway, but he did catch a couple of "mud balls" as he called them. When he missed a green, his putting saved him. And it was his putting that elevated Woods' confidence as the day went on.

"I've made my share of par putts," Woods said after he finished with a birdie at the 18th late in the afternoon to shoot 66. "I have always said that it's a better feeling making a big par putt than it is making a birdie. This morning, I made a lot of par putts. I made about a 10-footer on 11 starting out. I made about a four-footer on 14. On 17, I made a 10-footer again. And today, I made about an eight-footer on 14 for par. These are things you have to do in order to keep the momentum in the round going. I seem to have been successful at it so far."

Asked when he started looking at the leaderboards, Woods said, "Right away. I'm always looking. You always want to know. I'm naturally kind of curious."

A lot of other guys were looking too. After Woods made birdie at the 18th to get to 11-under-par 205, Goosen hit his tee shot right on the final hole and made bogey to shoot 69 for the day and 205 for the tournament. "I cut it into the trees and had to chip it out," Goosen said of his stumble at the last. "It's playing really long."

That bogey had a bigger psychological impact than the one shot on the scorecard. It gave Woods a share of the lead, a position from which he had never faltered in a major and from which he was 22-2 since turning professional. "Tiger is going to be the guy to beat," Goosen said. "I can't hit it the way Tiger hits it; I'm going to be 30 yards behind him tomorrow. But I'm just going to have to really try and get it in there close and try to put pressure on him. I'll play the course as well as I can play it."

Mickelson tried to remain upbeat and positive, but at four strokes back after his 68, even he knew it was a long shot. "If I do get that low round tomorrow, it very well may be enough," he said. "And that's the best that I could hope for right now, with the quality of the leaderboard, with Tiger up there, Vijay and Retief playing as well as he is. Those guys are not going to come back. I'm going to have to catch them, and I'm hoping that if I can get a good low round, it will be enough."

Tied with Mickelson and Els at 209, Garcia also tried to put a good face on the situation, but even the effervescent Spaniard had a hard time spinning this one in a positive light. "I feel a little disappointed, because I really feel like I should be at least two or three shots better," Garcia said after a third-round 70. "But, you know, that's the way it goes. Sometimes, some weeks, it doesn't matter how good a putt you hit; it doesn't want to go in the hole. So, I just keep trying, and that's what I'm going to do tomorrow."

Inevitably, the Woods question came up, and Garcia handled it with typical aplomb. "It's always harder when he's four shots in front of you, there's no doubt," he said. "But it's not impossible. That's what I mean. If he were eight in front, then I'll say that it's tough, but the guys at seven under and six under, if they can shoot maybe 64 or so, they still have a chance. So, I'm going to go out there tomorrow and try to give it a run."

As positive as those words sounded, Garcia delivered them with the enthusiasm of a soldier at the Alamo. Even Singh, a former Masters winner, had a hard time ginning up enthusiasm for the final round. "Obviously Tiger is playing very well, he likes this golf course, and he's defending champion and he's right up there," Singh said. "I'm not going to go out there worrying about trying to beat him. I'm going to go out there and try to play my game and focus on what I'm doing. If I play good enough and putt well enough, I think I have a good chance of winning. If that's not good enough, then, you know, you can't do anything about it.

"You've got numbers one, two, three, four and five in the World Ranking up there, so it's going to be a real battle. Anybody who gets hot tomorrow has got a very good chance of winning."

With one round to go, the leaderboard shaped up like this:

Tiger Woods	66 - 205		Jose Maria Olazabal	71 - 210
Retief Goosen	69 - 205		Thomas Bjorn	70 - 211
Vijay Singh	72 - 207		Padraig Harrington	72 - 211
Phil Mickelson	68 - 209		Angel Cabrera	73 - 212
Sergio Garcia	70 - 209		Chris DiMarco	72 - 213
Ernie Els	72 - 209		Mike Weir	71 - 214

Woods and Goosen teed off at 1:56 p.m. on Sunday, and by 3 p.m. it was all but over. "It's like Nicklaus and Palmer," Love said as a way of explaining the Tiger-effect. This time three of the world's top 10 players crumbled with big numbers, and none of the others could mount anything approaching a charge. Woods was able to stroll home.

"He's playing great golf and we're not putting it to him," Love said. "There are guys who can do it, but they aren't doing it. I heard someone say something's going on with him that's not going on with us."

Price, who spent a couple of years in the 1990s as the player to beat, agreed that Woods' presence on an Augusta leaderboard was like seeing bicycle racer Lance Armstrong coming up in your mirror. "This golf course is perfect for him," Price said. "It's like Jack Nicklaus in his day. Jack loved this course. When you hit it high and long, it's a huge difference. He had a two-club advantage over almost everyone and he is playing great golf."

"It's tough to play with Tiger," Olazabal said. "The guy is the best player in the world, and he's not going to give you any room to maneuver, so all you have to do is play your best."

As Tiger continued to climb the leaderboard, those aiming for him repeatedly shot themselves in the foot. Mickelson followed his two early birdies with two consecutive bogeys. Garcia had five bogeys and shot 75. Els played the 13th like an amateur and finished with 73. Goosen never recovered from his slow start, while Singh saw his chances drown with the three balls he plunked into the water at the 15th.

Woods did exactly what he had to do to win. "I just stayed away from trouble and big numbers," he said.

"I think you know when he gets there he's going to play steady golf," Faxon said. "Knowing you have to play mistake-free, that gets you out of your own rhythm and your own game. He's very impressive."

Adam Scott, the young Australian who has drawn plenty of comparisons to Woods, knows that there is a distinct difference between Tiger and the rest of the world. "It's hard coming down the last nine holes in a major," Scott said. "Everything has to go your way in these things, and you have to go around and make no mistakes. That's what Tiger does, and he's better than anyone else at it. It's a simple fact."

Woods tried to downplay all the comparisons to Nicklaus, and all the records, and all the hoopla about his potential Grand Slam this year. "It would be nice to win as many majors as Jack did," he said. "That would be great. But if it doesn't happen, it doesn't happen. I think the thing I keep saying to myself every year is that I want to become a better player at the end of the year than I was at the beginning. If I can keep doing that year after year, I'll have a pretty good career."

That might have been the understatement of the decade. As Padraig Harrington said with his typical Irish wit, "I think he can build his game up now. He's good enough that he just picks his game up the weeks that he needs it. But the gap is closing now. He didn't win by 15, did he?"

No Woods didn't. But he still went home wearing the green jacket.

3. U.S. Open Championship

Despite a little rain, a lot of rough and the longest course in U.S. Open Championship history, Tiger Woods had another grand week as he defeated Phil Mickelson by three strokes to win his second major title of the year. It was the first time in 30 years that a player had won the first two majors of the year (the last being Jack Nicklaus in 1972), which prompted a slew of questions about a possible Grand Slam, a sweep of the four major championships, with the British Open and PGA Championship to come.

"Well, it's certainly do-able," Woods said. "Because, I've done it before." Woods won four consecutive majors over two years (2000-2001), which he considered as important a milestone as the calendar Grand Slam. But, as he said, "To win all four in a calendar year would just be something different, because at one time in my house, there were all four major championships (trophies) right there. No one else in the world had them but me. That was a very special time in my life. Hopefully I can do it again."

He felt better about the one-month interval between the U.S. and British Opens than he did having to wait seven months between his 2000 PGA Championship and the 2001 Masters Tournament. "I think the buildup will certainly be a lot easier than what I had to deal with going to Augusta in 2001," he said. "Going seven months and dealing with that question at every single tournament I played in — this time the majors are in back-to-back months. I think that will be a lot easier."

It seemed like having to answer the same question a hundred times was the only tough part of the game for Woods. This time he led wire-to-wire at the first U.S. Open ever to be held on a public golf course (since Pebble Beach and Pinehurst are deemed resort courses), but it wouldn't have mattered if New York's Bethpage State Park Black Course on Long Island was a public park or a privately owned playground. There was only one player who could tame this 7,214-yard beast.

"This one was hard fought," Woods said after closing with 72 for a three-under-par 277 total. He was the only player under par on the par-70 layout. "From what I've been told, this is obviously the longest (course in Open history), but it's also the narrowest U.S. Open course I've ever played. The widest fairway is 28 yards wide. On top of that, you have three holes playing 490-plus yards as par-fours. That's not a whole lot of room to work with. It made for a difficult test all week. You just couldn't slap it around and play poorly and contend for this championship. You had to play well, and I was able to do that the entire week."

The USGA billed this one as the "People's Open," a public park setting with a blue-collar flavor set against the backdrop of suburban New York City. But it was also a course where the USGA took a lot of heat for their over-the-top setup. When it rained on Friday and the tees were pushed back, the players let their displeasure be known.

Ernie Els, holder of two U.S. Open titles and one of the longest players in the game, thought the setup was a travesty. "A guy who hits it 265 yards right down the middle? No chance," Els said. "This is a great golf course, one of the best to ever host a U.S. Open, but what they did to it was horrible."

Not only did the USGA narrow the fairways more than normal, they sped up the greens to the point of ridiculous. On Thursday they were running at a 12 on the Stimpmeter, and by Sunday morning, after a good, soaking rain, they were running at 15. When asked if they were faster than the greens at August National, Els said, "No, they're way faster." But the biggest criticism came when the USGA refused to modify their setup when the weather turned cold and rainy. That was when half the field couldn't reach the fairways on some par-fours.

"That's the way we set it up, and we can't let the elements dictate to us where we're going to put the tees," said Tom Meeks, the USGA director of competitions. "I know the PGA Tour often times will go forward on tees when they get a weather forecast that calls for a lot of rain or a lot of wind. We don't do that. I'm not saying we're right and the PGA Tour is wrong, but that's our philosophy."

A lot of players took issue with that philosophy. "The setup was just not very intelligent," Nick Price said. "If it's going to rain all day, move some of the tees up so at least we have a way to get around the golf course. They're taking all the fun out of the game. If all it takes is to hit the ball a mile, then the same guys are going to win all the time. Maybe that's what they want."

When Scott McCarron was asked if the USGA erred in its setup, he quipped, "It depends on what you call an error. If they wanted us to shoot 76 or 77, they did a great job."

John Cook, who missed the cut by one stroke on a day when the scoring average was up to 76.478, said, "It was long before, but not to the point where anybody was eliminated. Today they eliminated half the field."

And Scott Verplank called the setup "poor," adding, "I'm a USGA member, and I've won an Amateur. I've been a big supporter and I really like Tom Meeks, but they should be embarrassed. They've caved in to the whole technology scare, the idea that you have to hit the ball straight and forever to play the game. I wish I could hit it like Tiger Woods does, but I can't. I'm pretty straight and not very long, and when you have three or four holes where you can't reach the fairway, that's pushing it."

Everyone wished they could hit like Tiger Woods at one point or another during the week. Jesper Parnevik said, "I think Earl (Woods, Tiger's father) picked this course." It was a perfect venue for a player who hits the ball long, high and straight, and who is strong enough to recover from thick, wet rough, which is where Woods really won this one. He missed 15 fairways all week and played those holes in one under par. Mickelson, his nearest challenger, missed 15 fairways as well, but played those holes in five over. Sergio Garcia, another contender until the final round, and the man who played in the final twosome with Woods, was six over for the 20 holes where he failed to find the fairway.

The fact that Woods only won by three strokes was somewhat misleading. He led Garcia by one after the first round, and extended the lead to three on the rainy Friday. An even-par 70 on Saturday gave him a four-shot edge over Garcia and a five-shot cushion over Mickelson going into the final round, which had everyone believing that this was another fate accompli.

Woods was 23-2 when he held the 54-hole lead, and he had never lost a major when he was playing in the final group.

Woods three-putted the first two holes for bogeys to let Mickelson and Garcia climb to within two, but that was as close as anyone got. Garcia fell away with some iron shots that flew the greens and landed in the high rough, and Mickelson, who got to within two again with a birdie at the par-five 13th, bogeyed the 16th and 17th after Woods two-putted for birdie at the 13th right behind him. That gave Woods enough of a margin to bogey both the 16th and 18th and still win by three.

"I never saw Nicklaus in his prime, but I'll tell you one thing, he's unbelievable," Garcia said afterward. "If he's leading by four or five, he doesn't need to pull too hard, so he doesn't. If he needs to play a little harder, he does. He's able to do whatever it takes."

Did he make any mistakes? Pull any wrong clubs? Try any wrong shots? "None," Woods said.

How about mental mistakes? How far back did he have to go to remember making a mental error in a major? "I don't know," Woods said. "Sorry, I really don't."

And was this Woods' best ball-striking round ever at a major (he missed two fairways and three greens in the final round). "In the final round of a major, yes," he said. "I really didn't mis-hit a shot today. I may have put the ball in a spot I didn't want to put it in, but I hit it flush. I really hit the ball clean today. To do that in the final round of a major championship, hit it that clean, that flush ... it wasn't easy, but I was able to do it."

He picked up his eighth professional major championship, moving past Harry Vardon, Bobby Jones, Gene Sarazen, Sam Snead and Arnold Palmer on the all-time major win list, and into a tie for fifth place with Tom Watson. Nicklaus was age 30 when he won his eighth. Woods was 26.

"Is that what it is?" Woods said with a smile. "That's not bad. Not bad at all."

The only reason Woods didn't lead from the very start is that he had a late tee time on Thursday. That gave Mickelson and Garcia a couple of chances to see their names atop the leaderboard. Mickelson was the first to reach the coveted spot. Teeing off on the 10th hole (the first time the USGA used split tees for a U.S. Open), Mickelson birdied the long par-four 10th and the equally difficult 11th for a quick two-under-par lead. A bogey at the 12th and a double bogey at the 15th brought Mickelson back to the field, but he still finished with 70.

"You don't know where your birdies are going to come out here," Mickelson said. "You just kind of hope you get a few of them in the course of a day. It's one of the most difficult tests of golf that I've played in an Open, one of the most difficult setups that the Open has ever had. Over par will most likely win."

Mickelson wasn't quite right on that last count. He finished even par for the week, which would have won by two had it not been for Woods.

Garcia teed off in the first round on No. 1, and got into red numbers with a near chip-in from 60 feet at the par-five fourth. He then birdied the fifth when his eight-iron approach stopped six feet from the hole. But he followed that up with a bogey at the sixth when his seven-iron approach found the greenside bunker. Garcia blasted to 12 feet and missed the par putt. Then he played steady par golf for five holes before hitting driver, six iron to 20 feet and making the putt for birdie at the 12th, a 499-yard par-four, the longest in U.S. Open history. Six pars to finish gave Garcia the early lead with 68.

"The conditions were as easy as they can get, or close to it," Garcia said. "There wasn't a lot of wind, and the greens were softer than yesterday. But still it's playing really hard. I think these greens are the fastest I've ever seen in my life. It's hard, but it's what you expect from this tournament. You've got to realize it's going to be difficult. You've got to realize that one or two under par or even par is always going to be a good round. That's the main goal. You get a couple of birdies early on, and you try to hold on to it and try to get another chance. More than anything you don't want to get too greedy."

Garcia's score was posted before Woods teed off, and the 68 held through most of the afternoon. But the signs of how the week would progress came early and often. Woods missed only three fairways and never had a par putt of more than 12 feet. He drove it well, hitting driver on the first, fourth, seventh, ninth, 10th, 12th, 13th and 16th holes. He birdied the second and ninth, and bogeyed the sixth to turn in 34. Then he birdied the 13th and 14th to take sole possession of the lead for the first time. A bogey at the 16th dropped him back into a tie with Garcia, but he made up for it at the 18th. After hitting a nine iron from 153 yards, he made the eight-footer for birdie. At 6:25 p.m. on Thursday, Woods took the first-round lead with 67. He would never relinquish it.

"I think the only time I putted better than this was at Augusta," Woods said. "It's always nice to have the first-round lead, because it's easier to keep the momentum going, rather than playing poorly and somehow having to go find it on the range, put it together, and somehow go and compete. The years that I've shot under par (in the opening round) I've really played well, and I was able to continue that for the rest of the event."

Some players who had nice rounds were completely overlooked. Billy Mayfair played exceptionally well, and was noticed by absolutely no one. He shot 69 and was only two strokes behind Woods, but the odds of Mayfair winning were higher after the opening round than they were before the day started.

Never known for his length, Mayfair's round could be summed up quite simply: He didn't miss a fairway. Not one. In the U.S. Open, that usually goes a long way. "A long hitter has an advantage if they can knock it in the fairway, but if not, they may not have an advantage like some other places," Mayfair said. "I think Tiger, when he won at Pebble Beach, there were a few times he missed the fairway, but he was so far up, it didn't matter. But you can't do that here at Bethpage. No chance."

Mayfair hadn't shown up on anyone's radar prior to his opening 69. Coming into the event, he had only posted one top-10 finish all year. But he had an explanation. "I love courses where you have to make a lot of pars," he said. "Pars are good scores, and this definitely a great golf course for that. My biggest key was that I hit every fairway. You keep the ball in play out here, and you're going to give yourself a good chance to score."

Jeff Maggert, another less-than-long but always-in-the-fairway player, shot 69 as well after struggling throughout much of the first half of the year. "I know this is not a tournament where you shoot seven or eight birdies a round," he said. "I want to be patient, just drive the ball in the fairway. I felt if I could just keep the ball in the fairway this week, I could keep it around par."

But Maggert was under no illusions. "Today is early," he said. "If I'm sitting here talking to you Saturday afternoon, it will be a different story. There's a ton of holes to be played, and they're all very difficult. If you get off your game for a little bit out there, you can run into a mess of bogeys."

Dudley Hart, who also shot 69, concurred with that assessment. "You have to roll with the punches," Hart said. "It's a long day playing 18 holes on this golf course. I sure don't want to play 19 or 20. I think I missed two fairways today, and if I can do that all week, I'll be elated."

With the books closed on round one, the leaderboard looked like this:

Tiger Woods	67	Stewart Cink	70
Sergio Garcia	68	Nick Faldo	70
K.J. Choi	69	Padraig Harrington	70
Dudley Hart	69	Franklin Langham	70
Jeff Maggert	69	Steve Lowery	70
Billy Mayfair	69	Phil Mickelson	70

Friday was miserable. It rained from sunup until sundown and the temperature never climbed above 60. The only conditions were a cold drizzle or an even colder downpour, but the players who went out early had a distinct advantage. The course was wet and soft, but the greens weren't holding water in the morning the way they were in the afternoon.

"The course is so long and the rough is so thick and so wet that you can't advance the ball anywhere," McCarron said. "It was tough before, but you had just enough to get through it. Now your club doesn't want to go through it at all. It just twists in your hands."

At the 10th and 11th upwards of 50 players couldn't reach the fairways with their tee shots. "Some of us are debating whether or not we want to come back tomorrow," Brad Faxon said.

Some didn't have that option. Among those that missed the cut were winners of two of the four major championships in 2001. David Duval opened with 78 and finished with a double bogey and a triple bogey to shoot 11-over-par 151 and miss the weekend by one stroke. When asked about the course, Duval quipped, "Would I sleep in my car to play this course in the morning? Maybe under my car."

That was more than Retief Goosen had to say. Goosen shot 79 and 75 and became the first defending U.S. Open champion to miss the cut since his fellow countryman Ernie Els did it in 1995. None too pleased by his performance, Goosen blew past the media without comment on Friday and would only say, "I'm disappointed," as he hurriedly changed his shoes and headed for the airport. "But I guess I'll live on. Nobody died."

That was literally true, but as Jim Carter said, "This course rips your heart out. You can manage yourself in the rain with staying dry, but the bad shots really are magnified by this golf course, and the weather magnifies it more."

One player didn't seem to have any trouble with the rough or the weather. After missing the first fairway, Woods ripped a pitching wedge from the high stuff that stopped four feet from the hole. He rolled that putt in for birdie. On the second hole his approach stopped two feet from the hole, and he tapped that in for another birdie. At the par-five fourth he hit his second shot just short of the green but in the wet, gnarly grass. A flop shot with a lob wedge rolled seven feet past the hole, and at 9:50 a.m. Woods made that putt to reach six under, the lowest score relative to par anyone would reach the rest of the week.

He gave a couple of strokes back, bogeying the eighth when his three iron found the greenside bunker and the 10th when he bunkered his five-iron approach, but he got another birdie at the 18th when, for the second day in a row, his approach shot never left the flag. This time it was an eight iron that stopped 18 feet below the hole. When the putt went in, Woods chased it and pointed at the hole to the thunderous roar of the New York gallery.

"They aren't quiet, I'll tell you that," Woods said of the crowd. "If I don't have a hearing problem, I might have one by the end of the week. You come to the tee boxes, and they scream right in your ear. Eventually you don't hear it anymore because it's so loud."

As for how he felt about the weather, Woods shrugged. "You know that everyone had to deal with it," he said. "You go out and play. You just plod along. It's going to be a tough day, it's going to be a wet day, and it's going to be a long, slow one. You just go out and try to stay out of trouble.

"Growing up in Southern California, obviously we didn't get a whole lot of this, but when we did, I used to love to go out and play in it. I loved to play in bad weather, because we didn't get any of it. The only hard part was trying to convince my mom that I could go out and play without catching a cold."

No rants, no complaints, no grumbles about the rough, the tees, the water or the greens. Woods simply went about his business, posted 68 and walked away at five-under-par 135 and holding a three-shot lead over Padraig Harrington, who had scores of 70 and 68.

The loudest gripes came in the afternoon when the rain was at its heaviest and the course was borderline unplayable. Of those who vented their frustrations, none was more pointed in his criticism than Garcia, who pointed his comments at both the USGA and at Woods. "If Tiger Woods had been out there I think it would have been called," he said of the weather conditions. "There was a moment when not even the squeegees were going to help. I really felt like we probably should have taken a 40-, 45-minute break. Don't get me wrong, it wasn't easy this morning, but it was almost impossible this afternoon. So I'll say it was three or four shots easier.

"If you get the luck of getting the good side of the draw, like somebody seems to do in these kinds of tournaments, and you're the best player in the world, and you make a lot of putts, everything works. It's tough to beat a guy when things are going like that. When he's out there and he's getting good breaks when he needs them and making good putts when he needs them, it's even harder."

All this was uttered after Garcia shot 74 in a round that included two birdies, four bogeys and a double bogey. He also had a run-in with the spectators who took issue with Garcia's maddening pre-shot re-gripping routine. The minimum number of re-grips was a dozen in the second round. At times the ritual exceeded 30. On the 16th fairway when the waggles pushed the limits of absurdity, the crowd started counting re-grips out loud. Garcia backed off and gave the fans a one-finger salute.

"The people have to realize that we're trying as hard as we can out there, and sometimes they make some stupid comments," Garcia said. "I would like to see some of those comments made to some of the other players, too. It feels like they don't make those comments to the bigger guys, and maybe they're afraid of them or something."

Thomas Bjorn just shook his head when he heard Garcia's comments. "The only thing wrong with Sergio is his mouth," Bjorn said. "He's going to become one of the greatest players who ever lived. But he lets himself down by saying things that should never be said."

Victor Garcia pulled his son aside for a chat afterwards. "I told him he had made a mistake," the father said, but the stern conversation appeared a little more demonstrative than that. "He was wrong about Tiger and the scoring conditions. Right away he was sorry. At 22, you say things you don't say at 26. The important thing is that he learned and that it is rectified."

Garcia would make amends on Saturday, but not before falling seven shots behind Woods. The closest challenger at the halfway mark was Harrington, who equaled Woods' 68 in the tough conditions and had no trouble with the weather. "I think it was a good day to play well," he said. "What I mean by that is I think there was a vast difference from playing well and playing average on any particular hole today. Obviously, it wasn't too windy; if you hit the fairways and good iron shots, the greens were soft enough that you could leave yourself a chance at a birdie. If you were slightly askew, you could end up double-bogeying the hole. A lot of players played well and shot in the high 70s. I played well and had quite a difference in shots."

Because of his "difference in shots," Harrington drew the honor of playing with Woods on Saturday, a turn of events he neither cherished nor dreaded. It was what it was. "I think over the years, looking at guys who have been paired with Tiger on Saturdays and Sundays of major tournaments, it tends to have a negative effect on the players that he's paired with," Harrington said. "I've seen many of my friends in the game who have shot 77, 78 when they're paired with Tiger, so it's obviously very difficult."

Harrington had a little experience on that front. In 2001 he was paired with Woods in the third round of the U.S. Open at Southern Hills. "Neither of us were in contention, but at least it gives me some idea of what the goings-on around him are," he said. "I think the first thing I noticed was there were like 30 photographers on the second fairway trying to get pictures of him. There can be a distraction factor, but I've seen it before. It's going to be there tomorrow, so I should expect it.

"It's not going to be easy playing with Tiger, but if I play well with him, I'll play with him for two days. I've got to think of 36 holes, but 36 under that pressure is going to be hard."

Davis Love knew exactly how hard it was going to be. Love had been there before, and he'd come up short too often when Woods was in the lead. He, better than most, knew what the weekend was going to be like. At 142 and tied with Garcia, Love knew that things were likely to change substantially in the 36 holes to come.

"It looks like Tiger is holing a lot of putts and hitting a lot of fairways and we're just going to have to do the same," he said. "But if you go back through U.S. Open history, I bet there have only been a few where the leader after the first and second day had the winning score. You can't chase scores. And you can't change your strategy. You've got to hit it in the fairway, hit it on the green, and hope to make putts. This course is so hard, there are no holes where you can say, 'I'm going to change my plan and get aggressive.' Today half the field couldn't get to some of the fairways, but you can't change. Everybody is going to have some tough holes. And you've got to expect that he's not going to keep that pace up on this kind of golf course."

It sounded like wishful thinking. With two rounds to go, everybody was playing catch-up. The leaderboard looked like this:

Tiger Woods	68 - 135	Jeff Maggert	73 - 142
Padraig Harrington	68 - 138	Shigeki Maruyama	67 - 143
K.J. Choi	73 - 142	Billy Mayfair	74 - 143
Sergio Garcia	74 - 142	Phil Mickelson	73 - 143
Davis Love	71 - 142		

Early Saturday Garcia put a note of apology in Woods' locker. All was forgiven between the two players. Garcia's relationship with the New York fans was something different. He went about rehabilitating himself by smiling and waving as fans continued to chide him. "Wagglepuss," was the most common name Garcia heard. Others counted the re-grips even louder, while one shouted, "Hey, Sergio, give me the finger, you hack." More than once a New Yorker would become fed up with Garcia's interminable pre-shot waggle and say, "Hit it while we're young!" Through it all, the affable Spaniard smiled, waved and even joked with the gallery.

The strategy worked. Garcia won over the galleries with his charm, and he beat the golf course that had brutalized him a day before. A driver and nine iron on the first hole stopped six feet below the hole, and Garcia made the putt for birdie to get off to a good start. He bogeyed the par-three third after his five iron found the bunker, but he got it back quickly at the par-five fourth with a drive, a three iron and two putts from 40 feet for birdie. Another birdie at the eighth from 14 feet and Garcia was two under for the day and back to even par for the tournament.

He gave another one back on the 10th when he hit his tee shot into the rough and had to hack his ball back in play, but he electrified the crowds when his nine iron at the 14th stopped five inches from going in the hole. Another birdie from 20 feet at the 16th and the Garcia reclamation project was complete. As he stood on the 18th tee the crowd was yelling, "Come on, Sergio. Last group with Tiger!"

A par at the final hole did, indeed, put Garcia in the final twosome with Woods. His 67 put him at one-under-par 209 for the week. There just might be a showdown after all, or so Garcia hoped.

"I get more intimidated by the four shots (behind Woods) than I do with Tiger," he said. "I think that four shots, the way he's playing, is going to be difficult, but if I'm able to start well and put some pressure on him, you never know what's going to happen. But I don't think I'm intimidated by him. I'm respectful of his game and his persona, but other than that, we're two human beings trying to put a little ball in the hole. If I shoot a good number and win, great. If he plays well and wins, great. If I shoot 150, I'm not going to care. I'm just going to enjoy the moment. I'm going to have as much fun as I can have and we'll see."

Even though the course was ripe for scoring on Saturday (Nick Faldo shot the low round of the day with 66), Woods appeared to struggle with his swing early. He bogeyed the fifth and 11th holes and failed to make any birdies in his first 14 holes, including missing both the par-fives. Finally, at the 15th, Woods hit a six iron from the fairway that stopped 12 feet below the hole, and he made the putt for his first birdie of the day. Then on the par-three 17th he hit a six iron to eight feet and made his second birdie. It was a utilitarian even-par 70, one of the highest scores of those who would start the final round in the top 10, but still good enough for Woods to carry a four-stroke lead into the final round.

"Today was a long day," Woods said. "It seemed like I was over par for most of the day, but I hung in there. I saw the guys making a run at me, and I just tried to keep hanging in there. My intensity didn't change. I kept doing the same thing. Trying to keep the ball in play however I can. Some of the shots I played to get in the fairway weren't very good, but they were in the fairway.

"I'm very happy now. Somehow I hung in there. Even though the other players made a run and played some great rounds of golf, I look at the leaderboard and actually I increased my lead."

The lead was four over Garcia and five over Mickelson and Maggert, who both shot 67s. Everyone expected Mickelson to be somewhere near the top. Almost nobody expected the same from Maggert.

"I just tried to play aggressive," Maggert said. "I knew Tiger was going to have probably an easy time today. He had an opportunity to shoot a low score today, and if he would have done that, we would have been in a very difficult situation tomorrow. But it looks like he struggled a little bit with his game today, and there are some players that shot some good scores to kind of put themselves back into it with a chance to win. Tomorrow is going to be a similar situation."

Calling a five-shot deficit to Woods being "back into it with a chance to win," might have been a little optimistic, but everyone agreed that Woods had failed to put substantial distance between himself and the rest of the field. Mickelson summed it up perfectly when he said, "The last thing on my mind was trying to get in contention to win this tournament. Even if I got it back on track, if Tiger goes out and shoots three or four under par, it wouldn't have made any difference."

Woods had a chance to put this one out of reach, and he failed to do it. Saturday afternoon he hit balls until dark, even though he had, indeed, increased his lead by shooting even par. With one round to go, the leaderboard at the U.S. Open had a familiar feel to it.

Tiger Woods	70 - 205	Billy Mayfair	68 - 211
Sergio Garcia	67 - 209	Padraig Harrington	73 - 211
Phil Mickelson	67 - 210	Nick Faldo	66 - 212
Jeff Maggert	68 - 210	Justin Leonard	68 - 212
Robert Allenby	67 - 211		

The galleries were pulling for the underdogs on Sunday, with their favorite being Mickelson, who had started the week 0-39 in major championship play. From the moment he arrived on the first tee until he holed his final putt, the crowds never stopped cheering. On every tee, they sang "Happy Birthday." They chanted, "Let's go Mick-el-son" a variation on the Yankees cadence that regularly filled the Bronx.

"It was an experience playing with Phil today," Maggert said after it was over. "I've never seen a crowd behind a player more in a round of golf than the crowds were today. It was amazing."

Mickelson didn't disappoint. After charging back on Saturday with 67 to get within five shots of the lead, he hit a driver and sand wedge to four feet on the first hole on Sunday and rolled in the putt to an uproarious ovation.

The decibel level increased as Woods hit a three wood and pitching wedge to 35 feet on the first hole and three-putted for bogey. When Woods missed a two-footer for par at the second, the crowd went nuts. Mickelson was back in contention, and they were with him every step of the way.

Garcia also moved to within two strokes with routine pars on the first and second, but bogeys on the third, seventh and ninth dropped him out of the running. He turned in 38 and went into the final nine trailing Woods by six. Another bogey at the 12th sealed Garcia's fate. He would birdie the 14th before adding one more bogey at the last for 74 and a fourth-place finish.

"I had the chance," Garcia said. "Unfortunately, I didn't get it going at the beginning. You miss a couple of putts at the beginning, and you miss a couple of good opportunities for birdie, and everything seems to be tougher. The hole seems to be smaller. But I tried and I gave it my best shot. I hung in there and gave it my best shot. It was pretty tough, but it made me mature. It made me mentally tougher. I've just got to keep hanging in there and give myself as many opportunities as I can. If I do that, eventually one is going to come, and as soon as the first one comes, then everything seems a little easier."

That's what Mickelson said 40 majors ago. This time Mickelson was the only player to challenge Woods on the final nine. Bogeys at the fifth and sixth holes dropped him to four behind. Then Mickelson hit a six iron on the par-three eighth to 35 feet. When that putt fell, you could have heard the roar across the course.

Woods certainly heard it one hole behind. But as has happened too many times to count, Woods elevated his game when he needed. He split the fairway with a three wood on the seventh and hit a seven-iron approach to 15 feet. When that putt fell, Woods had kept his four-shot edge.

Mickelson cut the margin to three with a driver and nine iron to four feet at the 11th, and then cut it to two when he hit a deft wedge shot to six feet and made the putt for birdie at the par-five 13th. But that was as close as he got.

Woods hit a perfect drive on the 12th, and a perfect approach for a routine two-putt par. Then on the 13th, after seeing that Mickelson had made birdie, Woods hit driver off the tee, even though his caddie was warning him that the fairway ended 350 yards downrange. Woods' ball stopped 10 yards shy of the rough, and he hit a perfect two iron to the center of the green to set up a two-putt birdie.

Mickelson imploded down the stretch, driving the ball in the fairway bunker at the 16th and making a bogey and three-putting the 17th for another bogey and a round of 70. That gave Woods the room he needed. Even though he hit a nine iron into the bunker for a bogey at the 16th and three-putted the 18th for another bogey, Woods cruised in with 72 and a three-stroke win.

Mickelson was gracious in defeat and thankful for all the support he had in the final round. "I don't know if it's the proudest event I've ever played, but I will say this was not a disappointing day," Mickelson said. "The people of New York gave me one of the most incredible experiences I've had in this game."

Even so, Woods walked away the winner. And it didn't take long for Woods to be asked about Muirfield and the next leg in his quest for another four in a row. "Right now I could care less about that," he said. "I want to celebrate this one. This one was hard fought. This was tough. It's going to be awhile before I start working on my links game."

No one doubted that when the time came, Woods would be ready with whatever game the situation and conditions required. "I didn't give it much thought until I needed to either," Jack Nicklaus said of his 1972 run that ended, ironically, at Muirfield. "Tiger will do the same. He'll enjoy this a little bit before he moves on."

4. British Open Championship

It was on to Muirfield, home of the Honourable Company of Edinburgh Golfers, for Tiger Woods to bid for the third trick of the modern professional Grand Slam in the British Open Championship.

Since its birth in 1934, only four other men had won the Masters Tournament and then the U.S. Open Championship in the same year, and only three of those had gone to the British Open. Craig Wood won both in 1941, but war raged across Europe and the British Open had been suspended after 1939 and not revived until 1946.

Ben Hogan won both in 1951 and didn't bother with the British Open, but two years later he won both again, went to Carnoustie, shot a better score in each round, and won by four strokes.

Arnold Palmer tried next, but Kel Nagle edged him by one stroke at St. Andrews in 1960, and by striking coincidence, it was at Muirfield in Scotland that Jack Nicklaus arrived in 1972 after winning the Masters and U.S. Open. But as Nagle had done to Palmer, Lee Trevino denied Nicklaus his British Open and ended Jack's attempt for the Slam.

Thirty years had passed since that day, and yet time hadn't changed much. Just as Nicklaus failed, so did Woods. Only Hogan had won all three. Unlike Palmer, Nicklaus and Woods, he could not have won the fourth — the PGA Championship — because the PGA's last two rounds were played on the same dates as the British Open's qualifying rounds, which everyone had to play, including Bobby Locke, the defending champion.

Through 2002, no one had won all four in the same year, although Woods had held all four trophies at the same time. He had won the two Opens and the PGA in 2000 and added the 2001 Masters, but he hadn't won all four in the same year.

Bobby Jones had set the four-championship standard in 1930 by winning both Opens and both the U.S. and British Amateurs. As professional golf had developed through the latter part of the 20th century, Jones's Slam became next to impossible. The professional Slam, on the other hand, is definitely within reach. Since Hogan's year, the schedules avoided conflicts.

Comparing the 1972 and 2002 British Opens, there were certain similarities and certain differences. First of all, the course. Both men played the same course, and since Muirfield ranks among the best of all, the best player should have the advantage — provided he plays his game. While Nicklaus did indeed play his game, he was beaten by Trevino, who at that time was as good as anybody.

Woods, though, didn't play his game; he beat himself by shooting 81 in nasty weather during the third round. The championship went instead to Ernie Els, who won a playoff from Frenchman Thomas Levet and Australians Steve Elkington and Stuart Appleby. All four played Muirfield in 278 strokes and then moved onto a scheduled four-hole playoff, a situation that had never happened before. Through its 131-year history, the British Open had seen many playoffs but none had involved four men.

Both Elkington and Appleby played the four holes in one over par and were eliminated, and when Levet bogeyed the extra hole, Els saved his par and won the championship.

It was fitting in a way, because Els had attracted international notice at Muirfield 10 years earlier, when, as a 22-year-old, he shot 279 and tied for sixth place. Nick Faldo shot 272 and won his third British Open.

Els shot 66, 69, 70 and 74 that year. In 2002, at the age of 32, he shot 70, 66, 72 and 70, just one stroke under his 1992 total, but no one scored lower. Woods, on the other hand, had played three rounds in 10 under par, closing with 65 in the fourth, but his 81 in the third cost him all those 10 strokes. A player is only as good as his last tournament, and Woods didn't play well enough to win. Els played better. Instead of winning the third trick of his Grand Slam, Woods shot 284 and tied for 28th place, six strokes out of first. He'd gone as far as he would go in 2002.

While Woods had proved his consistency, Els had been an enigma. He had climbed to prominence by winning the 1994 U.S. Open, beating Colin Montgomerie and Loren Roberts in an extra-hole playoff at Oakmont Country Club outside Pittsburgh, and three years later won his second U.S. Open, once more outplaying Montgomerie at Congressional Country Club near Washington, D.C.

His successes, though, mingled with a number of failures. Leading the 1995 PGA Championship by three strokes going into the last round, Els shot 72 and stood aside while Elkington beat Montgomerie in a one-hole playoff at Riviera Country Club in Los Angeles. One year later he reached the final holes of the British Open with only pars remaining to tie Tom Lehman for first place at Royal Lytham and St. Annes. Instead, he bogeyed the 16th and 18th and finished two strokes behind.

Four years later Els opened the 2000 British Open by shooting 66 at St. Andrews, but in the end finished second to Woods, as he had done a few weeks earlier at Pebble Beach in the U.S. Open. It must be said, though, that Els placed that high only because David Duval collapsed completely over the last seven holes at St. Andrews, and Miguel Angel Jimenez blundered through the final two holes at Pebble Beach.

Furthermore, second place didn't mean he threatened to win. He finished eight strokes behind Woods at St. Andrews and 15 strokes behind him at Pebble Beach.

No wonder, then, that for a time Els seemed obsessed with Woods, apparently giving up the fight by saying that whenever he played a good round, Woods played better, and suggesting he probably wasn't good enough to beat him, hardly the attitude of a champion.

Even though he won at Muirfield, Els hadn't ended doubt completely, because he hobbled at the end.

One stroke ahead with three holes to play, he nearly threw it all away on the 16th, a 185-yard par-three with a hassock-like green. He pulled his tee shot left, played a shoddy recovery that scooted off the front, chipped on, two-putted, and slumped off in fourth place.

He caught up by birdieing the 17th and finished with a routine par four on the home hole, setting up the playoff over the first, 16th, 17th and 18th.

After three holes Els had fallen one stroke behind Levet, tied with Elkington and Appleby. Els parred the 18th, all the rest bogeyed, and he and Levet moved on to sudden death. Playing the 18th once more, Levet bogeyed again and Els played a stunning recovery from a greenside bunker, saved his par four, and won.

This was a rewarding moment, since, except for his double bogey on the 16th, he had played remarkably well throughout the championship. For example, shooting 66 in the second round, Els birdied seven of the first nine holes and went out in 29, one stroke short of the British Open record set by Denis Durnian over the first nine at Royal Birkdale in 1983.

The next day Els shot 72 while Woods struggled to 81. The weather, of course, had been foul, and Els stumbled out in 40 strokes, but when it eased late in the day, he played the second nine in 32.

Els had often played well in the British Open, although never well enough to win. He had tied for second in 1996 and 2000, for third in 2001 and for sixth in both 1992 and 1993. Other than his missed cut in 1989, he had never placed below a tie for 28th.

Now in the midst of a busy and successful year — he had played in 21 tournaments and won twice on the European Tour and once in the United States — he arrived at Muirfield ready for his 12th British Open, his second at Muirfield.

Not much had changed over the last 10 years, although both the fourth and 13th holes, two of the four par-threes, had been lengthened.

Muirfield's strength lies not in its length but in the challenges of its design. Set up in two concentric circles, the first nine, which makes up the outer ring, runs clockwise; the second nine, the inner ring, flows counter-clockwise. When the wind blows — and it usually does — it comes at you from every direction over the course of a round.

Its fairways, while not generous, weren't overly tight, but the rough remained as deep and punishing as always. Every blade of grass that has ever grown on that ancient ground is still there. It is never cut; it grows lush and strong, bends over, eventually dies, and new grass grows in its place. Playing a shot from that rough challenges any golfer's skills. It can rip the club from a player's hands, and it gobbles golf balls, as Gary Evans found to his cost.

With a chance to win late in the fourth round, Evans pulled his second shot into the rough left of the 17th fairway, and even though what seemed half the population of East Lothian searched for it, they couldn't find it. Evans finished one stroke out of the playoff.

It caught Woods as well with his opening shot of the first round, although he saved his par four.

Woods teed off at 9:01 a.m. Thursday, grouped with Justin Rose, the 21-year-old South African-born Englishman, and the effervescent Shigeki Maruyama, Japan's gift to good humor and good manners. After winning the Verizon Byron Nelson Classic, Maruyama stood on the 18th green and boxed the compass, bowing to the galleries to the north, east, south and west.

It was only realistic to believe that Woods would give those two a lesson in course management, but in one of the game's twists, Woods finished with the highest score. He shot 70 while both Rose and Maruyama, along with 10 others, shot 68.

Duffy Waldorf shot 67 and shared first place with Carl Pettersson, a burly Swede who lived in North Carolina and commuted to the European Tour, and David Toms, who had given a course-management lesson to Phil Mickelson in winning the 2001 PGA Championship.

Muirfield played about as easy as it could. The weather had been fair Monday, with clear skies and warm temperatures, but clouds had moved in Tuesday and carried over to Wednesday, bringing occasional rains that softened the greens and lowered temperatures.

Thursday began warmer, and by mid-day the clouds had drifted off, the temperature climbed to the high 60s, and the scores dropped. At the end of the day, 37 men had broken Muirfield's par of 71, and 22 of them had shot in the 60s.

Among those a stroke off the lead, Des Smyth was closing in on his 50th birthday and 44-year-old Sandy Lyle, the 1985 British Open champion, had found his game after years of struggle.

Phil Mickelson was among them as well, and so were 45-year-old Nick Price, eighth in the U.S. Open, Soren Hansen of Denmark, who would be in it to the end, Thomas Bjorn, another Dane who had tied for second at St. Andrews in 2000, and Steve Jones, the 1996 U.S. Open champion, who would have joined the leaders had he not missed a putt from five feet on the home hole.

After shooting 69, Padraig Harrington remarked, "There's not a hole out there you couldn't birdie if you were playing well. The toughest job is selecting the club for the tee shot."

Perhaps, but strange things happened nonetheless.

Hacking his way through the rough, Bjorn scored threes on 11 holes, three of them on the opening holes, all for birdies, yet beat par by only three strokes.

Still, he did better than David Duval, the defender, and Shingo Katayama, who were with him. Both shot 72. Duval played every bit as well as Bjorn, yet had none of Bjorn's luck. Aside from seldom holing a putt, his pitch to save par on the 16th hit the flagstick and caromed yards away. Instead of the three that seemed likely, Duval bogeyed. He'd had a similar incident early in the year, when his approach to the 16th at Bay Hill, in Florida, ricocheted off the flagstick into a pond.

Putting for a birdie on one side of the 10th, Faldo gave his ball too much punch, rolled it completely across the green and almost into a bunker. His next shot was a chip. He shot 73.

Then there was Levet on the ninth. He ripped a drive into the right rough, hacked across the fairway into the left rough, spent several minutes finding his ball, walked ahead to check the lay of the land, then lost it again. A frantic search found it before his time had run out, and he saved a par five.

While all this was going on, most of the gallery's interest centered around Woods, whose day hadn't begun well. Setting himself for his opening drive, he heard a camera click. Stepping away, he said something to the photographer, then drove into the right rough.

Setting himself once again, he heard another click. That was enough. Officials escorted the photographer off the grounds. That settled, Woods pulled out his 60-degree wedge, took a mighty whack as if scything hay, and somehow chopped the ball to the fairway, pitched to six feet and saved a par four. Speaking of his shot from the rough, Woods claimed, "I don't know how I did that."

From there on, he agonized through a frustrating day. The putts that usually fell for him either grazed the lip or stopped inches short. He birdied only the fifth, a par-five, and the 11th, a par-four, and dropped strokes on the sixth, where he three-putted from 20 feet, and the 10th, where once again he drove into deep rough.

At 70, he lay only three strokes behind the leaders, and with three rounds to play, no one ahead of him began counting his winnings. Peculiar things could happen, of course, but while Toms, the current PGA champion, could become a serious threat, Waldorf and Pettersson didn't have the background.

Still, they stood among the leaders, which Montgomerie couldn't say.

Montgomerie had been a mournful figure in many British Opens. He had begun beautifully at Lytham in 2001, but after following an opening par with a pair of birdies here at Muirfield, he played shabby golf.

By the time he reached the ninth he had gone from two under to one over, courtesy of a double-bogey six on the eighth, but he birdied there and finished the first nine at even par. Still even par going to the 14th, he hacked his ball from the rough into a pot bunker and took another six on a par-four hole, bogeyed the 18th as well, shot 74, and stepped off the final green realizing that with another such round he wouldn't survive the cut.

These were the first-round leaders:

David Toms	67	Jean-Francois Remesy	68
Duffy Waldorf	67	Steve Jones	68
Carl Pettersson	67	Len Mattiace	68
Des Smyth	68	Nick Price	68
Sandy Lyle	68	Phil Mickelson	68
Shigeki Maruyama	68	Stephen Ames	68
Justin Rose	68	Soren Hansen	68
Thomas Bjorn	68		

When he left Muirfield Thursday evening, it seemed likely Montgomerie would have to shoot in the 60s Friday to advance to the weekend.

"I'll try to rally, of course," he said. "I came here full of expectation, but it was no good. It will be very difficult now."

To the contrary; it was easy.

Playing the game his army of supporters felt sure he could, Montgomerie swept around in 64 strokes and leaped from 106th place into a tie for ninth.

Montgomerie's exceptional round set the tone for a day of low scoring. Of the 153 men who finished the second round, 69 either broke or matched par — about 45 percent of the field — 39 shot in the 60s, 19 shot 70, and 11 more shot 71.

Els raced through the first nine in 29 strokes, shot 66, and jumped to the top of the standings, tied at 136 with Maruyama, Harrington, Waldorf and Bob Tway. The 1986 PGA champion, Tway, Mark Calcavecchia, the 1989 British Open champion, and Levet shot 66s as well.

With Muirfield yielding all those sub-70 scores, the field bunched so tightly that 16 men stood within two strokes of one another. Other than the five sharing first place, three more had tied for sixth, and eight others tied for ninth.

Pettersson stayed among the leaders with 70, and at 137 shared sixth place with Smyth and Hansen.

Meantime, Woods made his move. With an opening 70, he had stood four strokes out of the lead, tied for 23rd place with Els, Tway and 12 others, but he shot 68 in the second round, and lay poised only two strokes off the lead, sharing ninth place with the dangerous Bjorn, Levet, Price, Montgomerie, Mark O'Meara, Stephen Ames and young Englishman Ian Poulter.

While they advanced, others fell back. Toms, who had shared first place at 67, opened with a double-bogey six, went out in 39, shot 75 and dropped to 43rd place. Both Jones and Rose shot 75 and at 143 dropped from fourth into a tie for 50th, and Mickelson played worse. He double-bogeyed both the first and 14th, shot 76, and at 144 barely survived the cut.

Showing no spark at all, Duval added 71 to his first-round 72 and sat close to the bottom of the standings, seven strokes off the lead. He would not repeat as champion.

While the field didn't ravage Muirfield, the rush of low scoring surprised nearly everyone, because the weather had worsened. Unlike Thursday's pleasant day, an intermittent rain fell much of Friday before the skies cleared toward late afternoon. The wind had shifted overnight as well and picked up strength.

Darren Clarke felt perplexed. "Today it's not so nice and the pins are more difficult, and yet the scoring is better," he said. "I'm surprised."

Montgomerie's 64 ranked as the second lowest score ever shot during a British Open at Muirfield. Isao Aoki had shot 63 in 1980, the year Tom Watson won his third Open. Alterations to the course, however, meant that Montgomerie's 64 stood as the new record.

Monty had nearly finished when Els teed off shortly after one o'clock. He began with four consecutive threes, three for birdies. Even though the first hole played into the wind, Els reached it with a two iron and a four iron that settled within perhaps 12 feet, followed with a four iron and sand wedge to 15 feet on the second, then a two iron and sand wedge to eight feet on the third.

Playing his driver for the first time, Els hit the fifth fairway, played a four iron short of the green, rolled the ball close, and holed for still another birdie. Four under now. Short of the sixth with his second? No problem; he chipped in — his fifth birdie in six holes.

A pitch to the eighth braked inside five feet, and he reached the ninth with his second and two-putted for his 29. He had played the first nine with seven threes and only two fours, both for birdies. He had shot 70 in the first round, and now he stood eight under par for 27 holes.

His great run had ended, though. Distracted on the 10th tee, he stepped away from his ball, then drove into the rough. While he salvaged a par four, something had been lost. He missed fairways, missed greens and holed nothing. He came back in 37, shot his 66, and at six under par, climbed into first place while Maruyama, Harrington, Waldorf and Tway still had holes to play.

Maruyama, meanwhile, survived a rocky start, driving into the rough on the first, the only fairway he missed all day, and losing a stroke. He recovered quickly and played beautifully through the remaining holes. At the end he had missed only the first fairway and had hit 15 greens. Equally important, he had given up only two bogeys in 36 holes.

With better luck, Woods would have bettered Maruyama's score, even though he didn't play as well.

While Woods had been expected to challenge for the championship, Tway and Smyth ranked as total surprises. Smyth considered himself lucky to have started. Arriving at Edinburgh from Geneva Monday, he had rented a car and driven to Muirfield. Too tired to play more than nine holes, he putted a little, then climbed into his car to wait for a friend. Tilting the seat back, he slung one foot over the steering wheel, propped the other on the dashboard, and fell asleep for about 15 minutes. He awoke with a stiff back that felt worse Tuesday morning.

When physical therapists told him he had put pressure on a nerve and shouldn't play, he skipped a practice round Wednesday but went out Thursday and shot 68, then followed with 69 Friday. With 137 for 36 holes, he tied for sixth place, one stroke off the lead.

Still, he held no illusions. "I'm in for the weekend," Smyth glowed. "My next ambition is to stay among the top 15 and get an exemption for next year. Anything else is a bonus."

Among the late starters, Tway had only one blemish in his round. Bunkered on the sixth, he bogeyed, ending a string of three straight birdies, but he made up for it by reaching the ninth green with two three woods and scoring his fourth birdie. Out in 33, he came back in 33 as well, birdieing the 11th and 17th, and with 66 took a share of first place.

Perhaps even more satisfying, he had made the cut, his first since 1991.

Many others hadn't. The cut fell at 144, two over par, and caught Jose Maria Olazabal, the winner of two Masters tournaments, along with John Daly and Tom Lehman, the 1995 and 1996 British Open champions, and, sadly, Watson, the winner of five British Opens.

These were the second-round leaders:

Ernie Els	66 - 136	Colin Montgomerie	64 - 138
Shigeki Maruyama	68 - 136	Nick Price	70 - 138
Padraig Harrington	67 - 136	Stephen Ames	70 - 138
Duffy Waldorf	69 - 136	Thomas Levet	66 - 138
Bob Tway	66 - 136	Mark O'Meara	69 - 138
Carl Pettersson	70 - 137	Tiger Woods	68 - 138
Des Smyth	69 - 137	Thomas Bjorn	70 - 138
Soren Hansen	69 - 137	Ian Poulter	69 - 138

Before most of Saturday's gallery of more than 35,000 spectators arrived, Justin Leonard and Rose had cruised around Muirfield in 68 strokes, an improvement over their respective rounds of 72 and 75 Friday. Gratifying, certainly, but they foundered in 27th place, hopelessly out of the chase. After signing their scorecards, Rose wandered to the clubhouse and Leonard putted for a while, then left for his room in Greywalls, the hotel alongside Muirfield's ninth hole.

Then things began stirring; the longer they sat, the higher they climbed. When they struck their first shots shortly after 10 o'clock, they lay buried in 50th place. By day's end, they had climbed into a third-place tie at 213, five strokes behind Els at 208, and three behind Hansen at 210. The men who had begun the day so far ahead had run into hard times.

While Rose and Leonard snuggled indoors, storm clouds scudded overhead, wind whipped in across open water, temperatures dropped, rain fell, and scores rose. Battered by wind, rain and cold, the late starters struggled through a miserable day, one of the worst within memory. The wind bore in from the north at a steady 25 miles an hour and gusted much stronger, driving the rain sideways with such force, every drop felt like it had been shot from a dart gun. Temperatures fell so low fans suspected that the shadowy land mass across the Forth was not the east neuk of Fife but the North Pole.

Thus ended the quest for the Grand Slam.

Woods shot 81, and fresh off shooting 64 on Friday, Montgomerie erupted to 84, both bizarre scores.

It should be understood, though, that these were trying conditions. Forced to battle through weather that would ordinarily keep them indoors, golfers wrapped themselves in sweaters and waterproof suits, hid behind umbrellas, and did the best they could. It wasn't always enough. Ten men shot in the 80s, and just four scored in the 60s. Close to extinction with 144 over the first 36 holes, both Elkington and Peter Lonard matched the 68s of Leonard and Rose, the best of the day, and became contenders. Five others shot 70, most notably Appleby, who would be heard from later, and another nine shot 71. Every one of them had teed off before 10 o'clock, when conditions were livable.

Like all those near the top after 36 holes, and consequently late starters, Els had played through the worst conditions. But while Scottish weather can be appalling, it is changeable. As Ernie turned for home, the wind died, the rain stopped, the waterproofs came off, and scoring improved. Els, for example, stumbled through the first nine in 40 but came back in 32 and shot 72, the best of those who began late. One stroke behind the five 36-hole co-leaders, Hansen shot 73 and passed all of them except Els.

Maruyama shot 75 and fell into a third-place tie, Harrington shot 76 and settled into a tie for 10th, Waldorf shot 77 and fell to 14th, and Tway shot 78 and dropped to 23rd.

Leonard and Rose, meanwhile, shared third place with Maruyama, Bjorn, Smyth, Scott McCarron, a 37-year-old American playing in only his second British Open, and Sergio Garcia, who shot 71.

Absurd happenings became commonplace. Waldorf shot 45 on the first nine, yet came back in 32, unreeling a string of five consecutive threes followed by a two.

Strangest of all was the collapse of Woods. He opened the third round by driving into the rough, failed to reach the green with his second, and bogeyed. While one lost stroke seemed insignificant at the time, he lost another at the fourth and was off on a wild ride that would ruin his dream of the Slam.

Woods had built his game around sound planning, control of his shots, avoiding mistakes and holing putts. Playing through the worst of the day's weather, his plan was useless. Not only did he lose control of the ball's flight, he had little control on the greens; the wind constantly blew putts off line. At 219 for 54 holes, he sank to 67th place, and in truth, everyone ahead breathed easier.

The 20-stroke difference between Montgomerie's second-round 64 and his third-round 84 matched the record for the greatest difference in scoring from one round to the next for the British Open. R.G. French had shot 71 in the second round in 1938 and followed with 91 during the storm.

While Woods and Montgomerie were playing themselves out of the championship, Els, Smyth and Harrington took turns claiming the lead.

Harrington went ahead first, birdieing the first hole and moving to seven under par. After both Smyth and Els fumbled at the start, he held a clear two-stroke lead, but a blundering five on the par-three fourth hole dropped him into a tie with Els, who had just started. Harrington followed with four more bogeys, went out in 41, shot 76, and dropped to 10th.

Maruyama birdied the first hole as well and went seven under, but he took six on the second, went out in 40, and shot 76, tied for third.

The struggle through most of the day centered around Smyth and Els.

Smyth had come into the Open with no great expectations and no intention of battling young lions who consistently belted the ball 50 yards past him. Yet here he was, bundled against the cold in a heavy jacket and woolen cap, outplaying men nearly half his age.

Paired with Pettersson, not yet 25, Smyth bunkered his opening drive, three-putted, double-bogeyed, and played the first nine in 38, two over par. Five holes later, faced with a 20-footer to take the lead, Smyth rolled it in and dropped to four under, one stroke in front.

By then Els had gone out in 40 and fallen from six under to two under, but he picked up strokes on the 11th and 13th with putts so perfectly gauged that, had his target been a painted circle, they would have stopped in the exact center.

Smyth finally broke on the last two holes. Mis-playing shots and missing putts, he bogeyed both. Back in 36, he shot 74 and 211.

Now Els took charge. A par on the 15th, then a five iron to five feet on the 16th. The putt fell; four under now and back in front. Two big shots to the 17th green and another birdie.

Five under par once more and two strokes clear of the field, Els drilled a drive down the 18th fairway, played a five iron to the front of the green, and got down in two. After his labored start he could go into the last round with a slight cushion.

These were the third-round leaders:

Ernie Els	72 - 208	Des Smyth	74 - 211
Soren Hansen	73 - 210	Shigeki Maruyama	75 - 211
Justin Leonard	68 - 211	Steve Elkington	68 - 212
Justin Rose	68 - 211	Peter Lonard	68 - 212
Sergio Garcia	71 - 211	Thomas Levet	74 - 212
Scott McCarron	72 - 211	Padraig Harrington	76 - 212
Thomas Bjorn	73 - 211		

The weather had eased from Saturday's miserable conditions, the morning overcast cleared, the sun shone bright, sweaters came off, and scores dropped. At the end, 36 players had rounds in the 60s and another 13 had broken par 71. Only 25 of the 83 starters failed either to break or match par 71.

Montgomerie and Toms, both of whom shot in the 80s Saturday, teed off at 7:45 and sprinted around in two hours and 40 minutes. Both shot 75. Montgomerie's 297 beat only Toms, whose 298 placed him last.

Woods played every shot for all he could squeeze from it, sped around in

65, and posted 284, even par, but not nearly good enough to catch up. Playing for pride, he had given all he had to give on the off chance he might frighten the leaders and by some miracle steal the championship. But he had started too far behind. Still, when he holed his last putt and took off his cap to shake hands with Jeff Maggert, who had played alongside him, the gallery cheered as if he had pulled it off.

Playing directly behind Woods, Pierre Fulke matched his 284 by shooting 65 as well, and a few pairs later Australian Peter O'Malley shot his own 65.

Starting an hour before Els and Hansen, who teed off at 2:30, Appleby shot his 65 later in the day, scorching the second nine with a closing 30. Polishing off with birdies on the 15th, 17th and 18th, he flirted with a 28, but he missed birdies from three feet on the 13th and from almost as close on the 16th.

About an hour after Woods had finished, the fans had the feeling they might be cheering the first English champion since Faldo in 1992, because Gary Evans had been tearing into Muirfield. If not for a wild drive on the home hole, he might have made it a five-man playoff.

Out in 31, Evans kept his streak alive by holing a huge putt on the 10th, and ended this remarkable run with a pitch to 12 feet and his eighth birdie on the 11th. He had gone from one over par to six under, leading the championship.

He still had seven hard holes to play, and try as he might he couldn't pick up another stroke. His round reached its climax on the 17th, where he felt he could reach the green with his second shot and set up a certain birdie, or perhaps an eagle three. His drive split the fairway, but he yanked a fairway wood into Muirfield's impossible rough. The ball burrowed into the grass and couldn't be found. Dropping another, he played a good shot to the green, and against all logic holed a putt from at least 40 feet to save par.

Still six under with only the home hole left, Evans was spent. He hit shots into the right rough, into the left grandstand, and holed a desperate 10-footer to save a bogey five. Stepping off the green, he took off his cap and wiped his forehead, emotionally exhausted. He had put scores of 65 and 279 on the board. It was up to the others to match it. His had been a gallant effort, but again, it wasn't good enough.

With Muirfield yielding, the field grew tightly bunched. At one stage, nine men had closed within one stroke of one another, but one by one they fell back until only four remained.

Hansen had begun two strokes behind Els and made up no ground at all. Harrington reached six under par by birdieing the 17th, but bogeyed the 18th and fell to five under, one too many. Scott Hoch shot 66 but needed something better. Peter O'Malley had started too far back for his 65 to catch up. Retief Goosen needed something better than his 67. Garcia's closing 69 left him two strokes behind. Perhaps his age had caught up, but Smyth shot 73, one of the day's higher rounds. And Leonard shot 70 and Rose 72, far too many. There would be neither a Swedish, nor an American, nor an Irish, nor a Spanish, nor an English champion.

Until the very end it seemed equally unlikely we would see a French champion, for after a promising first nine of 33, Levet had stalled. He had birdied the second and third, Muirfield's shortest par-four holes, and added another at the ninth. Four under now, he played a series of frustrating par holes until the 17th. After a useful drive, Levet ripped a two iron to the back of the green, and from a ridiculous range holed for an eagle three. At six under, he had caught Appleby, who had just finished.

For a time at least, a Japanese golfer appeared destined to become champion. Beginning three strokes behind Els, Maruyama surrendered the almost obligatory bogey on the first, but he followed by birdieing four of the next five holes. When he added another at the ninth he had gone out in 32, four under par and five under for 63 holes. He had caught up, for Els, playing four groups behind, had made no headway.

Apparently overwhelmed realizing the British Open lay within reach, Maruyama lost his touch. He three-putted the 10th, parred the 11th, then drove into the right rough of the 12th, missed the green, played a sloppy chip, and bogeyed once more. Four under now, he three-putted the 13th; he was finished.

Maruyama had been paired with Elkington, who had struggled to make the field. No longer exempt, he'd had to go through a qualifying round, then played the first two rounds at Muirfield in 144 and barely made the cut. He bounced back by shooting 68 in the third round, and now had moved into position to win.

Putting had never been Elkington's strength, otherwise he probably would have won the British Open in 72 holes, because he played such steady golf on the way to his 66. Six under par, Elkington had caught Appleby and Levet at 278; now they would wait for Els.

Ernie had birdied the ninth and moved to six under as well, but this looked like the beginning of a runaway sprint to the championship.

Els stepped onto the 10th tee just one of a bunch within a stroke of one another, but quickly opened a gap. His seven-iron approach ran about six inches off the back of the 10th green, but he holed the putt. Seven under now, he hit the 11th green from the rough and parred, then birdied the 12th and slipped eight under.

Since neither Appleby, Levet nor Elkington stood better than five under par, although still with holes to play, Els' birdie on the 12th moved him three strokes ahead. He could play the last six holes in even par and win with strokes to spare.

Nothing came easy; he bunkered his tee shot to the little 13th. A terrific pitch inside a foot saved par, but one hole later he drove into a new fairway bunker and bogeyed. Seven under now, but Appleby had finished by then, and now Els' lead had shrunk to one stroke. A steady par on the 15th, still one ahead, and then he stepped onto the 16th tee.

Throughout the day, Els had tended to pull his irons, and here his tee shot settled left of the green at the base of a downgrade. Facing what looked to be a simple pitch-and-run up a slope to the flagstick, he bladed the shot, double-bogeyed, and rather than leading by one stroke, strode to the 17th tee trailing by one. He had thrown away three strokes and faced the probability that once again he had bungled a great chance to win something of importance. Now he would have to birdie one of the last two holes, and the 17th would be easier than the 18th.

He ripped into a drive, flew a four iron to the green, left his first putt dangerously short, but holed the second. Six under, he had caught up. On to the final hole.

Avoiding the two fairway bunkers, Els drove with an iron, played a five iron to the back of the green within holing distance, and once again left the putt short. When the ball stopped rolling, he hung his head, disgusted. Then he holed it.

After he checked and signed his scorecard, he joined Levet, Elkington and Appleby to settle the championship.

The playoff became just as tense as the finish. Elkington bogeyed the first, birdied the 17th, bogeyed the 18th by missing another makeable putt, and stepped aside. Appleby bogeyed the 16th, birdied the 17th, bogeyed the 18th, and joined him. Els, meanwhile, parred every hole, and Levet birdied the 16th, bogeyed the 18th, and at even par, joined Els for sudden death on the 18th.

All Els' years of struggle came down to one dangerous 449-yard hole. If he failed here, he might never regain the confidence he'd need to win another championship.

Here Levet made a mistake; going with a driver, he ran his ball into a fairway bunker. Now Els looked as if he had won, but once again he pulled an iron shot that dived into the left greenside bunker.

Shaken, Els still had the resolve to play the shot of his life. With only his left foot in the sand and his right bent at an awkward angle over the bank outside, Els popped the ball out and ran it within about three feet of the hole. Levet had a putt for a matching par, but he missed.

When Els' putt fell, he smiled for the first time that day, secure in knowing that after five lean years, he had finally won another of the game's great challenges.

Summing it all up later, Els said, "I've been after this for 10 years. If I hadn't got it this year, I don't think I'd have made it. I've had a fabulous time, but it's been very hard."

5. PGA Championship

Not since 1991, when John Daly waved a towel over his head as he walked down the final fairway at Crooked Stick, has there been a more improbable major champion than Rich Beem. With a Joe Six-pack background and disarming honesty and good cheer, this former cell phone salesman was supposed to crash when Tiger Woods made another major championship charge in the PGA Championship at Hazeltine National Golf Club in Chaska, Minnesota, outside Minneapolis.

Any guy who had a book written about him entitled *Bud, Sweat, and Tees* wasn't supposed to make an eagle and two birdies in the final nine holes to squelch Woods' bid for another triple major victories year. Beem was supposed to put up a good fight, then lose to Tiger, either in regulation or in a thrilling three-hole playoff.

Even though Woods finished the tournament birdie-birdie-birdie-birdie, Beem parlayed a little late-round magic of his own, hitting a 271-yard seven wood on the 11th hole to within seven feet of the hole. It was the shot that would define the championship, a go-for-broke rip that set up a straightforward eagle and a three-stroke lead for Beem.

Only four holes earlier, Beem had been faced with a 260-yard second shot over water to the par-five seventh. "What do you think?" Beem's caddie asked. "Well," Beem said, "we haven't backed off all week. Why start now?" He didn't back off on the seventh or 11th, or later on the 16th when he ripped the seven wood into the center of the fairway, then hit a nine iron over Lake Hazeltine to within 35 feet of the hole. When that putt fell, Beem could coast home.

When Beem found the fairway and the green on the 18th, it was over. A three-putt bogey didn't matter. Beem had done what Phil Mickelson, David Duval, Sergio Garcia, Ernie Els, Colin Montgomerie and Retief Goosen had been unable to do: He took the best Tiger Woods had to give, and he beat him.

"I didn't miss a shot coming in," Woods said. "I was on 15, and I said, just get the ball in play and let's make a four here. From there we were walking down the fairway and I told (caddie) Stevie (Williams), 'If we birdie in, we'll win the tournament. Let's suck it up and get it done.'"

Woods laid up on the par-five 15th, then hit a wedge from 55 yards to eight feet for his first birdie. Then he hit a three iron and eight iron on the difficult 16th to 10 feet and made that. On the par-three 17th he hit a seven iron to 10 feet and made his third birdie in a row. By this time the air was electrified. Woods was surely going to overtake Beem and snuff out all challenges for his third major title of the year and the ninth of his career.

Even though he hadn't led after 54 holes (Woods trailed Justin Leonard by five on Sunday morning), and had never won a major championship he hadn't led after three rounds, everyone thought Woods would come back to take this one. On the 18th he hit a three wood off the tee into the center of the fairway and a seven-iron approach that never left the flag. The ball stopped four feet from the hole, and Woods made the putt for his fourth birdie in a row, a 67 and a nine-under-par 279.

Surely, that would be enough, at least for a playoff. It was one thing for a player like Beem, who chugged Pepto Bismol before teeing off every day and who told the media on Saturday, "I don't have any expectations of winning," to make a good game of it, but to actually fend off a charge by the world's best player in the final round of a major was something quite different. Beem had even said the night before, "To win a major, you have to have something special, and I don't know if I have it." With three holes left, the tournament was his to win or lose.

That's when he hit the nine iron over the lake and onto the 16th green, an improbable shot on the toughest hole Hazeltine National had to offer. On Thursday Daly made 11 on the 16th, and Beem's playing companion, third-round leader Leonard, hit his approach in the hazard right before Beem stepped up to his shot. Beem had even predicted the outcome of this situation on Saturday. "If I have a one- or two-stroke lead going into 16, that will probably be one of the hardest shots I'll ever hit," he said.

Beem held a two-stroke lead at that point, as Woods had just birdied the 17th. He steadied himself over the 35-footer and rolled it into the center of the cup like a man who had been leading majors for years. "I know I told you yesterday that I would puke on that hole," Beem said. "But I was probably as committed to that shot at 16 as I've been to any shot I've ever hit."

Beem punched the sky when his putt for birdie fell. The crowd erupted. Even other players watching in the locker room let out a hoot or two. "When he made that putt on 16, I thought I was going to jump in the water," Rocco Mediate said. "It's great for the game. The guy, six years ago he was selling cell phones, and now he's about to win a major championship. It's beautiful."

The finish wasn't too shabby, either. As Beem put it: "What can I say? It was unbelievable. At 17, I hit a seven iron just exactly where I was trying to, just right in the middle of the green, and I knew I could get it up the hill from there. Then I took my time on 18, just took a deep breath, and whacked that sucker right down the middle. When I found out that I had a two-stroke lead, I didn't want to get too aggressive and knock it over the green, so I thinned a little eight iron on the front edge and managed to three-jingle it down there. Yay. Yay, me."

He was that way all week, speaking to the golf world as if he were chatting with his buddies over an adult beverage with a hockey game playing in the background. "I was working up in Seattle at the Magnolia Hi-Fi Buy making seven dollars an hour for about a year, and watched Paul Stankowski win the (1996) BellSouth Classic," Beem said. "That kind of fired me up about playing golf again. I didn't have much success on the mini-tours, and decided to go back to El Paso Country Club where I worked for the better part of two and a half years until the head pro, Cameron Doan, came in one day and said, 'Rich, you have two choices. Either you're going to quit here and go play golf for a living, or you're just going to have to quit.' I really wasn't a very good assistant pro. I finished eighth at Q-school in 1998, and here I am, still at it. I can't believe it."

Neither could anyone else. Beem did his best Jennifer Lopez impression after the two-footer for bogey on the 18th fell in — arms in the air, head to the sky, shaking his hips to the *K.C. & the Sunshine Band* tune that was playing in his mind. It had been a long, strange trip, but Rich Beem was, at the end of it all, a major championship winner. As he put it: "Don't that beat all?"

The course was supposed to be geared for long-hitters, which had a number of pros shaking their heads before their planes landed in Minnesota. It was the third major championship venue of the year to undergo renovations, including adding a few hundred yards here and there. The only major venue that didn't undergo a facelift in 2002 was Muirfield, because as R&A Secretary Peter Dawson said, "We're very happy with the challenge this course presents." At 7,360 yards, the new-and-improved Hazeltine was the longest major championship course of the year and the third longest in PGA Championship history. "It's not a cow pasture any more," Paul Azinger said.

The "cow pasture" comment was a reference to the 1970 U.S. Open played at Hazeltine where Dave Hill, who had just shot 69 to move into contention on Friday, was asked what he thought about the course. Hill, never one to hold back his true feelings, said, "If I had to play this course everyday for fun, I'd find another game. The only things missing are 80 acres of corn and a few cows. They ruined a good farm when they built this course." When asked what he would recommend the members at Hazeltine do to their pride-and-joy, Hill said, "Plow it up and start over again. The man who designed this course had the blueprints upside down."

At first they were furious. Then the members at Hazeltine stepped back and reevaluated their course, realizing that, while harsh, some of the criticism was well-founded. They brought in course designer Rees Jones, and the results were impressive. "I think Hazeltine is an excellent example of what we should do," Phil Mickelson said. "It is really a wonderful setup, testing all the elements of a player's game. I hope the courses we use in the future will continue to do the same."

British Open champion Ernie Els called it, "A ball striker's dream," and went on to say, "It's a big, long, championship golf course. If you're on your game, you should have a good week."

Any harping about the added distance was muffled in the opening round when two of the straightest but less-than-long-hitting players set the pace. After a three-hour rain delay that softened the course and brought with it winds that swirled at 10 to 15 miles an hour, Jim Furyk and Fred Funk charged out of the gate with four-under-par scores of 68 to share the early first-round lead.

Furyk was in first. He started on the second nine with a bogey at the 13th after hitting a three iron through the green and failing to save par from the high rough. A birdie at the difficult 16th brought him back to even par and bolstered his confidence. "I actually started playing when the wind started kicking up a bit," Furyk said. On the first nine he had four birdies on the first, second, sixth and seventh holes, the first coming when he hit an eight-iron approach to six feet. Then he hit an eight iron from the fairway at the second hole to 10 feet and made that for birdie. On the sixth he hit eight iron again, this time to 25 feet and made the birdie. "The eight iron was looking pretty good," he said. On the seventh he found the fairway again and hit a sand wedge to six feet and made the putt for the four-under-par 68 total.

As for his prospects for the rest of the week, Furyk was noncommittal.

"It's going to be weather dependent," he said. "If the wind keeps blowing real hard and everything dries out, I can see even par being a good score. If it rains more and guys are able to get a little more aggressive with some iron shots, then I could see more under par winning, like 10 or 12 under. But it's going to depend on the weather."

Co-leader Funk agreed. "This is the kind of course where you have to work the ball into the fairway," Funk said. "Depending on the way the wind is blowing, you've got to feed the ball into the right trajectory and the right ball flight to get it to hold the fairways."

Funk did a good job of working his ball on Thursday. After spending the rain delay stretching in the fitness trailer, Funk started out with six pars before hitting a pitching wedge into the par-five seventh and making a 12-footer for birdie. At the par-five 11th, he laid up 65 yards from the green and hit a wedge to seven feet for his second birdie of the day, which he followed with another birdie at the par-five 15th. The only bogey came at the 13th, where he said, "I hit a five iron that was three feet from being perfect, but it kicked into the rough, and the kind of lies you get here are not very good around the greens." He made another birdie at the 16th after hitting a seven iron to 25 feet and making the putt. Then at the par-three 17th he hit a four iron to 20 feet and made that for his fifth birdie of the day to go with one bogey.

"It was probably my best putting round of the year," Funk said. "I was trying to kill time on the 18th, so I added up how many putts I had and I thought, well, if I make this, that will be only 24 for the day, so that was a pretty good day. I can't remember having 24 putts in a long, long time, regardless of how many greens I hit or missed."

Woods was another who putted well. Good thing. Woods only hit seven fairways in the first round, and described his driving as "Blue, not very good. No matter what I tried to do I just seemed to get out of rhythm. I got the club stuck behind me and would flip it left or hang onto it and hit it right."

Woods' round started at 8:35 a.m. when he split the middle of the 10th fairway with a two iron. Just as he stepped off the tee the horn sounded, suspending play for lightning in the area. When the round resumed at 11:30 a.m., Woods seemed to have lost touch with his driver. "It was frustrating," he said. "Overall I hit the ball pretty good except for my driver."

He started with a birdie at the 11th after laying up with a three wood and chipping to a foot. On the 12th he made an eight-footer for birdie, but on the 18th his wayward drive cost him. Woods flew an eight-iron shot over the green from the rough and failed to get up and down for his first bogey. He bogeyed the next hole (the first) after pulling another drive. A birdie at the par-three fourth, and a number of scrambling pars were it for the day. Woods finished with 71.

Beem didn't finish on Thursday. Play was called at 8:36 p.m. because of darkness. Weather would hamper play for the rest of the week. When it became too dark to see, Beem was one over par through 15 holes and in the sights of exactly no one. He came back at 7 a.m. on Friday and finished at even-par 72, in a 16-way tie for 22nd place with Ernie Els and Charles Howell, among others.

Nobody paid a lick of attention. The only upstart dark horse creating any buzz after the first round was England's Justin Rose, who shot 69. Rose was a three-time winner on three different continents in 2002, a far cry from the teenager who had missed 21 consecutive cuts in his rookie season. Now he was a contender to be taken seriously. The fact that his opening 69 was his first competitive round on American soil only added to the deliciousness of the story. Throw in the fact that Rose still carried the boyish good looks that made him the darling of the 1998 British Open and a quiet charm that bordered on courtly, and you had a newsworthy event, even though the young Englishman never led at any point in the opening round.

"It's been a windy sort of roller coaster for me," Rose said of his pre-21st-birthday career. "I don't really regret the way things have turned out, because I think all of the bad experiences I went through really toughened me up, made me learn a lot about myself, made me realize I've got to practice hard and give the game a lot of respect. But also, each time I had a chance to make the cut, I did feel a real sense of pressure upon myself to make that first cut. Learning to deal with that helped me when I had a chance to win my first tournament. Although there were bad times, I think they did stand me in good stead for playing better golf in the future."

Those quotes led the English papers on Friday as the United Kingdom pinned its hopes on a tall, skinny kid from Hampshire.

But the week was young. When the first-round scores were finally tallied, the leaderboard looked like this:

Jim Furyk	68	Steve Lowery	71
Fred Funk	68	Angel Cabrera	71
Retief Goosen	69	Vijay Singh	71
Peter Lonard	69	Tiger Woods	71
Justin Rose	69	Padraig Harrington	71
Bernhard Langer	70	Nick Faldo	71
Lee Janzen	70	Greg Norman	71
Mark Calcavecchia	70	David Duval	71
Davis Love	70	Chris Riley	71
Jeff Sluman	70	Adam Scott	71
Tom Lehman	71		

Weather was the big story again on Friday, just as it was in the 1991 U.S. Open at Hazeltine when a lightning strike killed one spectator and injured five others. There were no deaths reported during the 2002 PGA Championship, because golf officials — and Minnesotans — had learned their lesson. At 6:35 p.m. the horn sounded for the second time in two days and play was suspended with 45 players still on the golf course.

Among those with holes to complete was tournament leader and 46-year-old short-hitting Fred Funk, a man who became an instant hero on Friday with fist pumps and gyrations that would have made both Tiger Woods and Elvis Presley proud. Funk played 13 holes in three under par on Friday. Starting on the 10th, he birdied his first and fourth holes (Nos. 10 and 13) to take possession of the lead. He added a third birdie at the par-five 15th, and a fourth at the par-five third before rushing and missing his par putt on the par-three sixth in an attempt to finish before play was called.

"It was exciting," Funk said of his round. "I was playing a lot better tee-to-green than yesterday, and I felt like I could really get things going. I was really enjoying the moment. I wanted to relish the fact that I was in the lead at the PGA in the second round, and I wanted to keep it going. It's just bad timing that I could not finish the round. That was the biggest disappointment. Obviously, everybody would have loved to have finished tonight and have our 36 holes done, but that happens."

Beem, Goosen, Leonard and Mark Calcavecchia all got their 36 holes completed on Friday, and each finished the day with six-under-par 138 totals, leaving them one behind Funk, but as the leaders among those who had completed the two rounds. The hottest of those leaders was Beem, who shot a course-record-tying 66 on Friday, a round that included a 50-foot chip-in and birdies from under trees and behind port-a-potties.

"I didn't hit it particularly well today, but my putting has been unbelievable," Beem said. "I've made virtually everything I've looked at for 36 holes. That certainly helps in any tournament, especially in the majors when the greens are as good as you can possibly get."

Beem carried low expectations into the weekend, just as he did when he arrived at the beginning of the week. "Coming down the stretch just kind of tells you what kind of intestinal fortitude you have," Beem said. "This weekend, it's going to be completely different, so I don't know exactly what's going to happen. But it's going to be fun, unless I shoot 90; then it won't be fun."

Of the players closest to Funk when the sun fell blow the prairie, Goosen had to be the favorite. He was the reigning Order of Merit winner in Europe, holder of six titles in 14 months, and the runner-up in the Masters. He was also the only player near the top of the leaderboard to have won a major in the last five years. If anyone out of this group was going to challenge for the title, good money went Goosen's way.

"I know I can play under pressure," the soft-spoken South African said. "Obviously, winning the U.S. Open last year has given me a lot more confidence. I'm really looking forward to the weekend."

But Goosen knew that the player everyone was watching wasn't among the leaders, or even among those who were a shot or two back. "Tiger is not finished yet," he said. "He could still lead by the end of the day if he gets it going. You know, really, the only chance the other players have got is when he's not really in contention, like he was last year at my U.S. Open. He never really shaped up during the whole week. I think everybody is sort of still looking where he is and keeping an eye on it, just trying to stay ahead."

One of the biggest surprises was Calcavecchia, who was fresh off a disqualification for signing an incorrect scorecard after rounds of 80 and 75 at The International and a spectacular fall at the British Open on that infamous Saturday. "In a nutshell, I'm not usually a good summer player," Calcavecchia said. "I usually do okay through April and then seem to go on about a three-month vacation. Why, I don't know. I wish I could tell you."

What he could tell you was why he was able to shoot 80 one week and 70-68 in major championship conditions the next. "I'm probably one of the streakiest players on tour," he said. "But I'm also streaky bad, which isn't a good thing. I'm emotional. I'm aggressive. When I'm swinging good, I just go right at it, which works on a lot of occasions when the ball is going the direction I want it to go. I just aim at everything and I can make a lot of birdies and get on one of those rolls.

"On the other hand, that probably backfires a little bit when I'm not swinging good, because I just have a hard time aiming in the middle of the greens in certain situations. I'm like 'what the hell. I'm swinging bad, but I need to make birdies; I've got to go at the pin.' It's just in my nature. Thank God there are some good streaks in there to offset the bad ones."

Funk played the final five holes of the second round one over par in a cold wind on Saturday morning. That dropped him into a tie with Beem, Leonard, Goosen and Calcavecchia. With two rounds finally in the books, and the third round underway, the leaderboard for the weekend shaped up like this:

Rich Beem	66 - 138	Charles Howell	73 - 141
Retief Goosen	69 - 138	Kenny Perry	68 - 141
Mark Calcavecchia	68 - 138	Robert Allenby	66 - 142
Fred Funk	70 - 138	Steve Lowery	71 - 142
Justin Leonard	66 - 138	Peter Lonard	73 - 142
Pierre Fulke	68 - 140	Bernhard Langer	72 - 142
Tiger Woods	69 - 140	Adam Scott	71 - 142
Chris Riley	70 - 141	Justin Rose	73 - 142
Jim Furyk	70 - 141	Soren Hansen	69 - 142

The rain blew out overnight on Friday, but the wind that moved the system to the east hung around and made things miserable for the golfers on Saturday. It peaked in the afternoon at 35 miles an hour, but the swirling gusts throughout the day sent scores skyrocketing. The field averaged 75.87 for the day, making it the toughest third round in PGA Championship history. Pat Perez shot 85, and Howell shot 80. Furyk, the first-round co-leader, who normally grinds his way through windy conditions, shot 76, while Pierre Fulke, just two back at the start of the round, shot 78.

One of the biggest surprises was the seven-over-par 79 shot by Goosen, the second-round co-leader. "The wind hurt me like it did Tiger at Muirfield," Goosen said. "Every time I missed a green I was dead. I couldn't make a putt. It's unfortunate, but it's one of those rounds."

Only four players broke par, which made Leonard's 69, the lowest score of the day, far and away the best performance of the tournament. He did it by pulling his hat down tight on his head, keeping his ball flight low and straight, and working for every par he made.

Leonard drove the ball well all day, and didn't let the few fairways he missed cost him. The only bogey came at the fifth hole when he missed his drive right, hit a nine iron in front of the green, then hit a great chip to four feet but missed the putt. He made up for it with a birdie at the par-five seventh, which he played safely and smartly, driving it away from the water, laying up, pitching to 10 feet, and rolling the putt in the hole.

On the second nine Leonard judged the wind perfectly while the rest of the field struggled. He hit a seven iron to four feet at the 10th and made birdie, and played the par-five 15th just as he had the seventh, safely driving away from trouble and hitting a wedge from 40 yards to five feet.

The shot of the round, however, came at the 16th. With the wind whipping off Lake Hazeltine, Leonard hit a perfect tee shot into the center of the fairway, then hit a seven iron to a foot for his final birdie of the day.

"I don't know if I've ever been in a zone, or if there is a zone," Leonard said. "I strung together some really good golf shots right in a row, starting with the chip at 14. I felt like from there through to 18 I didn't miss a shot. If that's a zone, then I was in it, but again, I'm not real sure on that zone thing. I enjoy playing in difficult conditions, and today this course played extremely difficult."

Leonard's 207 total, nine under par, gave him a three-stroke lead over Beem, a four-shot edge over Funk and a five-shot cushion over Woods. Then in a statement that said what everyone was thinking, Leonard said, "Tiger is probably the one to watch. The person I watch is usually the one closest to me, but, you know, I'm human, so obviously I'm going to look and see how Tiger's doing."

Beem never entered the equation. The only time people paid much attention to him on Saturday was when they thought he violated a rule on the 15th green when he brushed away some sand from the putting surface with his hat. As it turned out, he was just having a little fun with the rules official.

"I kind of got the best of him," Beem said with a smile. "I was off the green. When you're off the green, you can touch the line of your putt, you can sweep debris off the green with a towel, with basically anything you want. I was off the green, and instead of trying to sweep everything with my hand, I did it with my hat. I knew that was going to raise a few eyebrows, but I knew the rules, and I didn't think twice about it. But I knew it was going to get the attention of a bunch of folks, and it did. Mission accomplished, I guess."

Despite his slightly mischievous behavior, Beem shot 72 and got into the final pairing with Leonard, but even he didn't take himself too seriously. "If I go to bed tonight thinking about being in the final group in a major, I'm not going to get any sleep no matter how many pills I take," he said. As for the Pepto Bismol he would be downing before his final round, Beem said, "Instead of one swig, I'll probably take a couple, and I'll probably do it in the locker room so nobody sees how big a swig. But I think it's going to be more than one."

Everyone laughed and went on their way. This would be a showdown between Leonard, a tough-as-nails closer known for his gritty Sunday performances, and Woods, five strokes back. With one round to play, the PGA Championship was shaping up nicely.

Justin Leonard	69 - 207	Rocco Mediate	70 - 215
Rich Beem	72 - 210	Jose Coceres	72 - 215
Fred Funk	73 - 211	Steve Lowery	73 - 215
Tiger Woods	72 - 212	Peter Lonard	75 - 217
Mark Calcavecchia	74 - 212	Jim Furyk	76 - 217
Chris Riley	72 - 213	Retief Goosen	79 - 217

Bob Sansevere, a columnist for the *St. Paul Pioneer Press*, summed it up best. "Let's be honest here," Sansevere wrote. "Everyone knew Justin Leonard actually carried a five-shot lead into the final round of the PGA Championship. It didn't really matter that Rich Beem was three strokes behind and Fred Funk was four back. Who among us seriously believed Rich Beem could win? And Fred Funk? Come on. You fall into a funk. A funk doesn't fall into a win at the PGA Championship."

This was supposed to be a showdown between Woods and Leonard, and if Leonard showed any signs of weakness, Woods was supposed to pounce with a flurry of birdies. Both those things came true: Leonard did collapse, and Woods did come on strong with a five-under-par 67 that included a four-birdie finish. What wasn't expected was the "nothing to lose" 68 by Beem.

Leonard's troubles started early. He bogeyed the second, and Beem birdied the third to cut the lead to one. Beem then tied the lead with another birdie at the par-four fourth when he hit what he called "a perfect six iron in there and made it."

On the seventh Beem had that exchange with his caddie where he said, "We haven't backed down all week. Why start now?" He didn't back down, hitting a three wood right onto the front edge of the green and two-putting from 50 feet for his third birdie. Leonard birdied the seventh as well, and the two remained tied at nine under.

Leonard's wobbly wheels finally fell off at the eighth when he hit one ball in the hazard, dropped, hit a mediocre pitch and a haphazard putt. When he tapped in for a double bogey, the lead was gone. He would end up shooting 77, the highest score of any player who started the final round in the top 40. "It was a bad day to play poorly," he said. "Sure, you're nervous, but that was no excuse to shoot whatever I shot today."

Beem bogeyed the eighth after finding the greenside bunker, but he kept the lead by one over Leonard and Woods, who birdied the fourth, sixth and seventh holes to reach seven under. By all indications, this would be a second-nine shoot-out, only Beem had replaced Leonard as Woods' foil.

They went to the second nine with Beem leading by one. That's when Beem hit the first shot that would move him from a sideshow to a champion. Of the par-five 11th, he said, "I knew we could get there, so I just went after a big drive and got it." Then, faced with 248 yards to the front edge of the green and 271 to the hole, Beem ripped a seven wood that stopped seven feet from the hole. He made that eagle just as Woods made one of only two mistakes he would make all day.

After hitting his approach shot to 15 feet on the 13th and looking at what could have been his fourth birdie of the day, Woods hit his first putt uncharacteristically long, then pushed the second putt. A three-putt bogey gave Beem a four-stroke lead.

"I just made a mistake on 13. I didn't trust myself on the read," Woods said. "I knew from the practice rounds that putt has been fast, every practice round I played. The greens were slow today, and I kept telling myself this putt is not as fast as it looks, blah, blah, blah. I went ahead and hit it the way I thought the greens were running, and it fooled me. Second putt was just blocked. It was a bad putt."

It was followed by a bad tee shot at the 14th. "I just got over on the top of it and I hit a pull left. I compounded the problem by putting myself behind the trees in the rough," Woods said.

While Tiger was making bogey at the 14th, Beem was making another birdie at the 13th to go to 11 under. "It was the same exact number we had on four, so it was a perfect six iron. Hit it in there about eight feet and made it," he said.

The lead was six was five holes to play before Tiger went on his birdie tear. Beem bogeyed the 14th and parred the 15th before the knockout birdie at the 16th.

"Rich played well," Woods said afterward. "He's been playing well, and I guess he just got up there, trusted his game, believed in himself, and he hit some good shots coming in."

Beem had his shirttail out after he accepted the Wanamaker Trophy, but no one seemed to mind. "Yesterday, I didn't know if I had what it took to win," he said. "Obviously, I found out today that I do."

6. The Players Championship

To call Craig Perks an unlikely winner of The Players Championship would be an understatement. When Perks, a 35-year-old native of New Zealand, teed off at the TPC at Sawgrass in Ponte Vedra Beach, Florida, he wasn't even the best-known Kiwi in the field. That distinction went to Michael Campbell, and for good reason. Perks had only managed to break into the top 10 on the PGA Tour four times in his career. His last victory had come in 1995 on the Hooters Tour. This was a guy who missed over half the cuts on the Buy.com Tour in the four years he played there. Were it not for his dogged persistence at the Tour's year-end qualifying tournament, Perks might have been getting ready for the weekly Buy.com Tour event instead of playing in the final group at the PGA Tour's showcase tournament.

Then there was the finish itself. A harrowing final hour saw Perks play three of the toughest finishing holes in golf in three under par, and needing only one putt to do so. He chipped in twice, missed a water hazard by less than a foot, missed two putts that measured 18 inches at best, hit only four fairways the entire final round, made seven bogeys in his first 15 holes, and made only two pars between the fourth and 18th holes, one of which came at the 18th, which Perks played in a fashion that NBC television analyst Johnny Miller described as "absolutely nutty."

Nutty or not, the results spoke for themselves. Perks, who started the round one stroke behind third-round leader Carl Paulson, shot an adventurous even-par 72 for an eight-under-par 280 total, and became the first to make The Players Championship his first PGA Tour victory. Tiger Woods called it "unbelievable," and Stephen Ames who finished second, two strokes behind Perks, said it was "miracle stuff."

Perks just called it the fruits of a lot of hard labor. "I've worked hard since I came to this country in 1985 for this moment," he said. "I just think the hard work and perseverance has paid off."

Persistence had little to do with the final frenetic minutes of this championship. After Ames posted 67 for a 282 total, and Perks missed his second 18-incher for par at the 15th, it looked as though Ames would win this one from the comfort of the locker room. Then on the par-five 16th Perks hit the shot that started it all.

"I think I had about 208 yards," Perks said. "It was a four iron. It was actually a bit more into the wind, out of the left. It started a little bit further right than I wanted it to, but I hit it solid enough to hold its line. I was concerned that it would go over the green more than I thought about missing it to the right. I mean, it was pretty close, no question, maybe five, six feet."

The ball carried the bulkhead on the front right portion of the green by no more than a foot, then stopped in the rough five feet from the right edge of the water. His effective target area for the line he took with that 208-yard four iron was a three-foot circle.

"I'm aggressive by nature, and I wasn't going to back away from that flag," he said. "With the wind down and left I felt like I could kind of cut it in there. It barely carried. The rough being so difficult kind of helped me on that hole."

His ball stopped in the rough rather than rolling forward into the water. From there Perks played a nine iron back in his stance and chipped in for an eagle three. "I felt comfortable over that chip," he said. "Obviously when it went in it was pretty mind-boggling. I really just tried to control my emotions knowing that, you know, the 17th is right there."

He had immediately gone from one stroke down to Ames to holding a one-stroke lead with two holes to play. But the two holes in question were the 17th and 18th at the TPC at Sawgrass.

On the island 17th, the most dramatic and sinister short hole in golf, Perks found the center of the green. "I really, really hit a good shot there," he said. "That's exactly where I was aiming." He was left with a downhill 20-footer for birdie, a slippery putt that could have easily run three or four feet by the hole. When it went in, the crowd surrounding the 17th erupted. "When that thing went in, that's the hardest I've had to work to remain composed," he said. "I knew that now I had a little breathing room knowing that a (bogey) five would be in."

All Perks needed was a bogey on the final hole to win by one stroke. With that being the case, the smart play would have been to hit an iron off the tee. As Miller told the television audience, "he could hit two seven irons out there and still make five." But Perks chose a less conventional route. When the driver came out of the bag, Miller called it "absolutely nutty," an opinion shared by most amateur and expert observers. "He brings all kinds of trouble into play that's totally unnecessary," Miller said.

Ames had eaten with his family, signed autographs, tipped the locker room attendants and emptied his locker by the time Perks reached the 18th tee. Only then did he decide to go out to the range and hit a few balls, just in case. "I heard this big roar when Craig chipped in on 16," Ames said. "Then he makes birdie on 17, then he chooses the wrong club on 18. I thought it was the wrong club, anyway. Everybody would agree he chose the wrong club off the tee."

Adding to the perplexing process was the fact that Perks admitted he "couldn't find the planet" with his driver all day. With water on the left, rough and trees on the right, hitting a club that had been so uncooperative seemed almost Van de Veldeian in its absurdity. Everyone thought it was a mistake, except Perks. "I knew I could make five from the right rough, and I didn't want to become conservative off the tee, so I took an aggressive line," he said. "I really just wanted to finish in style. My thought on 18 was, I am always going to hit driver."

Perks pushed his driver away from the water and into a cluster of trees right of the fairway. But the nuttiness continued. As he was walking up to the ball Perks turned to his caddie and said, "I could just chip out and play for five."

The caddie looked at the situation and said, "Why don't you move these people aside and see what you've got?"

What Perks had was a 190-yard shot out of the rough, under a tree, down the cart path, with bunkers and grandstands on his right and water on his left. "When I started to walk up there I said, 'Man, if I can get this thing along the cart path, there's no way if it's running along the cart path the rough is going to stop it. Then I'll have a 50- or 60-yard shot, and I can make five from there,'" Perks said. "There was just this one tree that was actually leaning a little from left-to-right that really swayed my decision. If that tree wasn't there, I definitely would have hit that shot along the cart path low and up there 30, 40 yards short of the green."

Miller told the television viewers, "If he tries this shot, it will be the dumbest decision in the history of professional golf, even dumber than taking driver off the tee."

After four or five minutes of analyzing his situation, common sense prevailed and Perks chose to chip back to the fairway. "I didn't, you know, want to get myself further in trouble," he said. "I knew that if I could chip out and get it in the fairway, I could still make five. The other part was that it was a tough chip getting back to the fairway. I was on pine needles with water facing me, and there's the rough. I think the smart play was to chip it out. I mean, maybe if I'd had to make four to win, I might have tried to gamble. But knowing that five was going to do it, then it made the decision a little bit easier."

His second shot found the fairway, but the trouble wasn't over yet. Armed with a seven iron, Perks hit his third shot right over the flag, over the green and into the rough on the small embankment behind. A double bogey definitely remained in the equation.

"When I walked down there, I actually had a decent lie," Perks said. "I've hit a lot of good shots out of the rough this week. The wind was back into it, and the green wasn't nearly as burned out and crusted as a lot of them were. I figured I'd hit the shot 100,000 times before. Certainly not in this situation, but that's where the hard work has paid off. When the thing landed I said, 'I've won,' because I knew that it wasn't going to go any more than a foot past."

The ball was rolling slowly when it fell in the hole for par, a final round of 72 and a 280 total and the most unlikely ending in The Players Championship history.

So compelling were the final moments that they overshadowed a week filled with rain delays, missed opportunities, wild leaderboard shifts, great putts, poor putts and five-putts. The winner might not have been a household name, but when it was over everyone agreed. This was a tournament that no one would forget.

As had happened often during this tournament, weather played a big role. One year before, rain had forced Woods to stay until Monday to finish the final round and take home the crystal trophy. This time the rain came on Thursday, forcing a two and a half hour delay and providing a distinct advantage to those who teed off after the water softened the course and the storm winds died down.

When darkness fell and play was halted at 6:38 p.m. on Thursday, seven players were in the clubhouse at three under par, but three others were five under with a few holes left to play. Robert Allenby, Jeff Sluman, Mark Calcavecchia, David Toms, Stuart Appleby and Brian Gay drew the short straw on Thursday, playing early when the course was hard, dry and fast and the wind was swirling in from the west at 20 miles an hour. The fact that they were able to shoot 69s was a testament how well they handled adversity. Scott Hoch summed it up for the leaders when he said, "I feel like Tiger Woods."

Calcavecchia, who held the outright lead for a while at four under, fell back into the pack at three under when he three-putted for bogey at the 17th. Still, he wasn't complaining about being the co-leader in the clubhouse, even though 74 of the 148 players in the field didn't finish. "It was a tough day," Calcavecchia said. "On a day like today, you just need to chip and putt well, which is just how you're going to get it around without doing anything drastic, keeping it out of the water and whatnot."

After the rain, things changed dramatically. "Obviously, after the rain came, the greens got a lot softer, so it really gave you an opportunity if you hit a good drive off the tee," said Appleby, who teed off in weather he called "a hurricane" but finished in the relatively calm afternoon. "You could really compensate and attack the flags out there. That's what I did the last four or five holes. I made some good putts and hit some good shots."

When everyone went home on Thursday night, Phil Mickelson, Chris DiMarco and Hoch were tied at five under at varying points on the second nine. Mickelson had to finish eight holes on Friday morning, DiMarco had seven holes to play, and Hoch was on the 13th when the horn sounded. The next morning they teed off at 7 a.m. and made good use of the cool, calm conditions. Mickelson had a career-low 64 to lead, while DiMarco added one more birdie to his round to finish at 66. Hoch played the last five holes in even par for 67 to finish alone in third. Nick Faldo and David Duval shot 68s to tie for fourth, and 10 players were tied with 69s when the first round was completed.

It was hard to keep up with the leaderboard for the first three rounds, because Thursday's round carried over until Friday, which forced a dozen players to finish their second rounds on Saturday morning. Throw in more rain and a lot of wind, and the scores became more erratic than the weather.

Mickelson, who jumped into the lead on Friday morning with a birdie at the ninth (his 18th) to finish at eight under, lost his momentum in the afternoon and finished with what he termed "a pretty good 75." That dropped Mickelson back to five-under-par 139 and in a tie for third place with Calcavecchia and Perks.

"It seemed like it was an up-and-down day," Mickelson said. "But I started the day at five under, and I finished the day at five under 25 holes later. I was very pleased with that. As the round wore on and as the wind started to swirl and it became very difficult, I felt like I did a good job of keeping the 75 where it was. It could have easily slid away. I made some good up-and-downs and made a birdie coming in on 16. So I wasn't disappointed in the round at all. I think I put myself in a good position heading into the weekend."

Mickelson also made some comments concerning his style of play that had come under criticism the week before at the Bay Hill Invitational, where Mickelson took what many considered an unnecessary gamble at the par-five 16th. That aggressive play resulted in a bogey, which cost Mickelson a chance of winning the tournament. "I won't ever change my style of play," Mickelson said. "I get criticized for it, but the fact is I play my best when I play aggressive, when I attack, when I create shots. That's what I enjoy about the game, the challenge. If I were to change my style of play, I wouldn't perform at the same level, nor would I enjoy the game as much. So to win 20 tournaments the way I have, I have had to do it the way that brings out my best golf, and my best golf comes out when I play aggressive and play with creativity."

He creatively played himself a shot out of the second-round lead, as Carl Paulson finished Friday with his second consecutive 69 for a 138 total, and Sluman came back Saturday morning to shoot a second straight 69 as well.

Paulson, who started the week 20 victories behind Mickelson — with zero — found himself in the lead by taking a very different approach than the left-hander. "I was playing too aggressive early," Paulson said, referring to his bogey on the par-five 11th after hitting his second shot in the water. "I went back to just trying to get it in the fairway and take an extra club and hitting it as easy as I could with the wind blowing around. I was just waiting for good stuff to happen and trying to stay away from the bad stuff. If I made a mistake, the goal was not to compound it with another mistake."

Two different approaches, two different players, two different results, but it was only the halfway mark. As co-leader Sluman put it, "Usually if you make the cut at a tournament you have a chance to win. It's probably no more apparent than here."

The third round was full of surprises. The players no one expected to contend played solid, steady golf to move into position going into the final 18 holes, and the experienced players everyone expected to make their moves played like amateurs.

The first star to fall off the leaderboard was arguably the hottest player coming into the week and certainly the most fatigued. Ernie Els had won three times on three continents in five weeks and had spent over 100 hours in the air in the previous 30 days. He had flown from South Africa (where he won), to Miami (where he won), to Dubai (where he won), to Orlando (where he finished tied for ninth). The two-hour drive to Ponte Vedra Beach proved to be the last straw. Els started the third round with a triple bogey, and things got progressively worse from there.

"I made a six on the next hole, so I was four over after two holes," Els said. "Now, I'm just trying to break 80."

Els did manage that task, making a birdie at the eighth (his 17th) and lipping out for birdie at the ninth (his last) for 79. "I was never really there," he said. "One minute I hit a bad tee shot, the next I'm eight over. I played a hell of a back nine just to shoot 79. Nothing went right. It was the craziest of days."

Craig Stadler thought the day was crazy with a capital "C". Stadler started the day at 141 and was paired with Woods, the defending champion. On the second nine, Stadler made a run at the lead with birdies at the 11th and 12th holes followed by a four iron to the par-three 13th that went into the hole for a one, only the fourth ace on that hole in The Players Championship history. He parred the 14th, then birdied the 15th to get to six under and within striking distance. Three pars coming in and Stadler would be in the hunt going into the final round.

Instead Stadler bogeyed the par-five 16th after missing the fairway. He hit his tee shot into the lake on the 17th and walked away with a double bogey. To finish, he pull-hooked his tee shot into the water on the 18th and made a triple-bogey seven for an even-par 72 day and a 215 total, eight strokes behind the leaders.

"I felt bad for him," Woods. "You feel bad for any player who goes through a stretch like that. He was playing so well. It was tough to watch."

Stadler summed up the day as succinctly as possible. "It was the good, the bad, and the ugly out there for me," he said. "That's about all you can say."

Those were the same feelings Mickelson had after his Saturday performance. Mickelson, who was playing in the final group with leaders Paulson and Sluman, hung around the lead, two strokes behind, through the first nine holes, then missed the green at the 10th and chipped to within 10 feet. Rather than coaxing the 10-footer for par somewhere near the hole, Mickelson stuck to his aggressive play and gunned the putt six feet past. Then his bogey putt rolled three feet by. The putt for double bogey zipped four feet past, his triple bogey effort hit the low side of the hole and lipped out to two feet. Mickelson tapped in his fifth putt for quadruple bogey and never contended again.

"I just couldn't get the ball in the hole," Mickelson said.

"After he missed the fourth one, Jeff and I were trying to figure out how many he had putted," Paulson said. "We were just watching him and he was putting it back and forth. By the time we figured it out, he had tapped in."

Both Paulson and Sluman turned their backs and walked to the 11th tee without saying anything. "I wouldn't want anybody patting me on the back if I five-putted," Paulson said.

Paulson had plenty of pats on the back after his round. He gunned a birdie putt at the first almost 10 feet past the hole, then made the par putt coming back to calm his nerves. He hit three wood into the fairway at the par-five second and ripped a four iron from 240 yards to within a foot of the hole. He tapped in for eagle, followed by a steady diet of pars through the remainder of the first nine.

Just before Mickelson's putting fiasco, Paulson made his first bogey at the 10th when he missed the green with a six iron, chipped to eight feet, and missed that putt for par. He made up for the mistake with a birdie from 50 feet at the 12th. Another birdie from eight feet at the 14th moved Paulson (who was so unknown the Jacksonville newspaper ran his name next to a photograph of Dennis Paulson, another PGA Tour player who didn't make the cut) to nine under par and into sole possession of the lead.

"It was great," Paulson said. "There were a couple of times when I got a little nervous, but I handled the pressure and executed the shots pretty much like I was trying to. I stuck to my game plan and didn't get overly aggressive out there. I just waited for my chances, so it was nice. It was fun. I am going to come out tomorrow and try to play the same way, which is not overly aggressive. I don't know if anybody else has told you this, but it's getting firm out there, and this is a tough, tough golf course."

Paulson would be in the final pairing on Sunday for the first time with another player who was a stranger to late afternoon tee times. Perks shot 69 for a 208 total, one more than Paulson, but two less than Sluman and Rocco Mediate.

"I'm going to try not to think about it," Perks said. "It's only human nature, when you're in the last group on Sunday, to think about winning, about what would happen if you won, or how you'd win, or whatever. But I have done a good job of just staying in the present and in the now and concentrating on each shot, because one bad shot can kill you out here. I think if your mind starts to wander a little bit, it can get away from you pretty fast."

As for playing in the final group with Paulson, with whom he had played on the Buy.com Tour, Perks had no illusions about the way the day would shape up. "No matter if it was Tiger Woods or Carl Paulson (in the final group), I would be nervous anyway," he said. "But I think knowing that we're both in the same boat and we're both trying to win a very, very prestigious golf tournament, it will be a little easier than it would be with the pandemonium of playing with Tiger, Phil, Ernie or somebody like that."

Ames started the final round eight strokes behind at one under par and was 11 groups ahead of Paulson and Perks. There was no pressure and no gallery to speak of, just a sunny Florida day in which to post a good number and see what happened. Ames did just that, starting out strong with birdies at the second, fifth and ninth to get to four under par. Then at the 10th he had the good fortune of watching his playing companion, Dudley Hart, play first from the back of the green.

"That's when I started seeing the changes in the greens," Ames said. "I just watched Dudley hit his chip that was barely crawling down the hill and it went three feet past."

Ames had a 30-footer, which he barely touched. The ball kept rolling and fell in for his fourth birdie of the day. He made his fifth birdie at the 11th. When his wedge shot to the 12th stopped three feet from the hole and he made that putt, Ames was in the lead.

Ames fell out of the top spot just as quickly with a three-putt bogey at the 13th. "I was on the wrong side of the slope," he said. But he made up for it at the 15th when he hit a driver and nine iron 12 feet below the hole and rolled in the putt for his seventh birdie of the day. The round ended on a slightly down note when Ames three-putted the 18th for bogey, but his 67 was the second best score of the day (Rich Beem posted 66 in the early morning hours), and his 282 total gave the rest of the field a target score.

Paulson had trouble from the early going, but not with his long game. On the first hole he split the fairway, hit his approach to five feet, rolled in the birdie for a two-shot lead, and marched to the second tee like he had been there a hundred times before. But on the second, something happened. He forgot the strategy that had gotten him into the lead and began trying to play defensively. Instead of playing to win, he played not to lose.

"It just wasn't happening," Paulson said. And the explanation was, indeed, just that simple. He missed two greens on the first nine and failed to get up and down both times. Throw in one three-putt, and he turned in 38. On the second nine he hit every green in regulation, but three-putted three times for 39. What had been a one-shot lead and the chance of a lifetime, turned into a final-round 77 and a tie for fourth place at 284.

Mediate shot 73 to finish at 283, one stroke behind Ames. Sluman made a momentary run, pulling into a share of the lead with five holes to play. But he faltered on the final four holes, shooting 74 for a 284 total. The next run came from Hoch, who also gained a share of the lead with three holes to go, but couldn't finish. Hoch's 72 left him tied with Sluman, Paulson, Sergio Garcia and Billy Andrade.

That left only Perks.

7. Ryder Cup

England was coming back to life that September Monday morning, and Birmingham Airport was bustling with the start of a new week. There were the casual-clad tourists shoving top-heavy baggage carts, and neat, orderly businessmen in ties and with briefcases heading for important conferences, and echoing in the background were announcements over the public address system. Suddenly, one line of businessmen erupted in cheers, and chants of "Eur-ope! Eur-ope!" boomed through the airport.

"What was that all about?" one asked.

"Padraig Harrington," another said. "He just went that way to catch his plane back to Ireland."

This wasn't just any Monday. This was after the Ryder Cup, and Harrington didn't really have to fly. He was walking on air. So were his 11 teammates, somewhere else. Harrington had helped Europe to a surprising upset of the favored Americans in the 34th Ryder Cup Matches, possibly the most historic of all.

This was the 2001 Ryder Cup, but just two weeks before it could be played, the world changed. The day would be known as 9/11 — September 11. That was the day terrorists hijacked four airliners and crashed two of them into the World Trade Center in New York, one into the Pentagon and, in a foiled attempt, one into a field in Western Pennsylvania. Some 3,000 people died. The Ryder Cup was postponed a year, still at the DeVere Belfry, Sutton Coldfield, outside Birmingham, England.

These were the same teams, same uniforms, same captains and even the same logo on merchandise. But the world in general had been scarred. Security had been tightened everywhere, and that included sporting events. At the Belfry, security was airport-tight behind metal detectors, baggage searches and ominous-looking police carrying sidearms and submachine guns.

This Ryder Cup was also far different from the ones of the past two decades in another way. It would be known more for what didn't happen. There were none of the petty controversies that, depending on one's view, had either spiced or marred the event. This one was about as peachy as the ones in the old days when the U.S. beat Great Britain-Ireland routinely and almost no one paid attention. This was a time of sympathy for a wounded America, and so this Ryder Cup, contested as hard as any, had great care for good sportsmanship.

The goodwill was so good, in fact, that the closest this Ryder Cup came to friction were two episodes so small they weren't even flaps, they were merely ripples.

One developed when Tiger Woods came out early on the final practice day. Many fans, expecting him later, didn't get to see him and were miffed. The tabloids tried to puff it up into an incident, but it fizzled quickly.

The other ripple centered on the Brabazon Course's short par-four 10th, with its long, narrow green protected by water in front and trees to the right. In three previous Ryder Cups, practically everyone could drive it from the forward tee, at about 270 yards. At something over 300 from the back tee, it took a deep breath and a lot of nerve for a guy to go for it. The Americans were loaded with big guns, so European captain Sam Torrance decided to spike them. He opted for the deeper tee, turning the hole into an iron lay-up and a pitch for all but the absolute boldest. The problem arose when Torrance hinted he might use the forward tee if his players asked him.

This got American captain Curtis Strange's attention. "My only question is that my team has to prepare," Strange said. "So if the tees go up one day, and they haven't practiced there, then something is not right."

Torrance apologized, and assured Strange it was just a slip of the tongue.

Torrance made a few other adjustments to the course. He had the greens rolling at 10 feet on the Stimpmeter — slower than the Americans were accustomed — and he eased the rough around the greens, thus foiling the flop shot, a favorite on the American tour. "There's nothing untoward out there," Torrance said. "I've tried to set it up to suit the European players."

Whether it was layout, strategy or inspiration, the Europeans won, 15½ to 12½, their biggest victory since 1985. Torrance's layout surely helped, especially at the defused 10th, but it was the underdog Europeans simply outplaying the Americans. The European win barely dented the overall American record — 24-8-2 since the Ryder Cup started in 1927. More to the point, since Great Britain-Ireland became Europe in 1979, the U.S. is only 6-5-1. And in the last nine Ryder Cups, it's Europe, 5-3-1.

They said it was a stroke of genius when Torrance "front-loaded" his singles lineup — putting big guns Colin Montgomerie, Sergio Garcia and Bernhard Langer up front. Maybe so. But when it came to great strokes, what about his first move? That was pairing Montgomerie and Langer in the team matches from the start. Hindsight makes that an easy call, of course. Monty and Bernhard went 2-0-1. This seemed to have been a preemptive move. Here were the two oldest, most experienced Europeans — Langer, 45, with nine Ryder Cups behind him, and Monty, 39, with five. They were still playing well. So with their skill, stability and experience, Torrance might have gotten more out of them by pairing them with rookies. But Montgomerie had been complaining of a bad back, and Langer had some difficulties. What if their problems arose? Then two matches might be lost. But if they were paired together, then Europe would lose only one. Is this what Torrance had in mind? Well, when it came to revealing strategy, Torrance's answers were mostly a twitch of a smile under that heavy mustache.

And so over three days in September 2002, these things played out at the Belfry. Montgomerie was beaming like the sun breaking through the highland mists. He seemed inspired by the chance to play us-against-them against the Americans. All he did was play in all five matches and go 4-0-1, the leading point-winner in the matches, lifting his lifetime record to 16-7-5. In the three matches in which he played his own ball, he had 16 birdies and only two bogeys.

At the other extreme came Woods, the No. 1 player in the world. He started 0-2 and finished 2-2-1 — for a 5-8-2 record in his two Ryder Cups. David Toms (3-1-1) and Scott Verplank (2-1-1), two of the three American rookies, played like veterans, and the four European rookies did nothing gaudy, unless you count Niclas Fasth getting the half point that tied for the cup and Paul McGinley holing the putt on the 18th that won it.

And finally, there was the most telling fact of all. After battling back to an 8-8 tie in team play, the Americans went kaput in their specialty, winning only two of the 12 singles matches.

Torrance, exercising another captain's choice, had opted to begin this Ryder Cup with best-ball (fourball) matches, and his men stunned the Americans with three knockout punches, sweeping the first three matches neat as you please. His lineup included Lee Westwood, one-time heir apparent to the European Tour gone badly sour. In 18 starts this year, he missed eight cuts and his finishes were out of sight. Torrance, uncannily, figured that a dose of the frisky Garcia was what Westwood needed, and he was right. "We're both laid-back guys, and I tried to get into Lee's head and relax him," Garcia said. Maybe that was the answer — Garcia's free spirit letting the old Westwood emerge. They went out in the second match of the morning and came back first with a hefty 4-and-3 win over David Duval and Davis Love.

Garcia, unable to resist the temptation, became the first to go for the green at the short par-four 10th. His ball came down short, in the water. He dropped, wedged on, watched Westwood make a bogey, then holed his putt for a salvaged par, halving the hole to preserve the 1-up lead with the Americans, who had stuck to their lay-up strategy. And what did Torrance think of Garcia risking the lead with that tee shot?

"It was fourball," Torrance said. "Foursomes (alternate shot), I might give him a wee smack on the wrists."

Westwood and Garcia sprinted from the 12th. Over the next four holes, Westwood birdied from seven feet, Garcia from 20, and Westwood from 16 to notch the 4-and-3 win.

In the first match of the day, Woods and Paul Azinger — to use stroke play for a measure here — combined for a nine-under-par 63, and lost. That's because Darren Clarke and Thomas Bjorn shot 10 under. It was one of the great matches ever in the best-ball. Neither side bogeyed. Clarke was devastating. He birdied the first three holes on putts of eight, eight and three feet for a win and two halves. The Americans led briefly on Woods' birdie from 30 feet at the eighth, and that was it. "Nine under will win 95 out of 100 matches," Azinger said. "But it just didn't win this time."

It would take a great act to upstage Garcia and Westwood, and that's exactly what the Monty and Bernhard Show was against Scott Hoch and Jim Furyk. They halved the first hole, and it was all but over. "So that's the kind of day it is with best ball," Hoch said. "You've got to go out and birdie. You can't expect to win anything from off the course." Montgomerie and Langer were putting demons. They made four birdies apiece. Langer holed from 20, 10, 10 and 20 feet, and Monty from 25, eight, 12 and 12. It added up to a 4-and-3 win and a 3-0 European lead.

The stunned Americans needed the cavalry. And up rode Phil Mickelson, the smooth left-hander best known for not having won a major title, and Toms, a Ryder Cup rookie and a relative unknown until he won the 2001 PGA Championship. They turned back Harrington and Fasth — but barely — in the last best-ball match of the morning. Harrington's putt for a tie on the 18th lipped out, and the Americans, who led all the way, took a 1-up win. Mickelson did his share, but it was Toms who defied the supposed rookie pressure. He was uncanny with his irons and putter. He took five of the six holes they won on birdie putts of three, eight, 15, 25 and two feet.

Strange might not have been breathing easier, but at least he could breathe again with that 3-1 fragment. But the news wasn't good for the Americans. The Europeans had won the best ball in the past two Ryder Cups, and now the first day of this one.

"I still don't believe they're better in best ball," Strange said.

Strange had said all of his players would see action before Sunday's singles, and he made good on that promise immediately. The four men who sat out Friday morning went out in the afternoon foursomes (alternate shot). He led off with a new pairing — Hal Sutton, the slumping veteran, and Verplank, the Ryder Cup rookie and captain's choice. He paired Mark Calcavecchia with Woods and Stewart Cink with Furyk, and left Mickelson and Toms together.

The juggled lineup paid off in the first match, but not easily. Sutton and Verplank seesawed against Clarke and Bjorn until the 16th, where Verplank fired a stunning approach to two feet, setting up Sutton for a winning birdie. Then they won, 2 and 1, when the Europeans bogeyed the 17th. It was more than just a point to Strange, though. He was pleased for Sutton. "He didn't play great," Strange said, "but he gutted it out like Hal Sutton does."

Strange's feel-good glow disappeared in the next match, where he found his big gun, Woods, was still mysteriously silent.

Woods and Calcavecchia were all-square with Garcia and Westwood through the 10th, then Woods missed par putts of four and two feet and Calcavecchia left a shot in the bunker. That's three losing bogeys in four holes. They went down, 2 and 1.

Garcia, playing second fiddle to Woods in golf's youth movement, admitted to no particular pleasure in his second win over him in the same day. "It's not about Sergio Garcia and Tiger Woods," said Garcia, age 22 and sounding 42. "It's about Europe against the USA."

The media continued to press the question, and Garcia couldn't resist a little dig. "It must be hard to be the No. 1 player in the world," Garcia said, "and not have such a good record in the Ryder Cup."

"Actually," Woods said, "it was one of the most fun matches I've ever had. I had so much fun. I had three buddies in the group, and we were all talking together all day."

Cink and Furyk won three straight holes on two birdies and a par from the 10th and rolled over Harrington and McGinley, 3 and 2, cutting Europe's lead to a point at 4-3.

Europe nearly got the point back, but the Montgomerie-Langer team got hit with a three-birdie blitz by Mickelson down the stretch. Set up by Toms, Mickelson dropped a three-footer at the 15th, holed from the fringe at the 16th, and got a conceded two-footer at the 17th. A tie in bogeys at the 18th halved the match and brought the U.S. to within a point, 4½-3½, after the first day.

"The rookies — not the rookies, but the guys that haven't had that much (Ryder Cup) experience," Woods said. "They were our backbone today."

Most observers thought it was just a question of time before the Americans woke up. The time came promptly on Saturday morning.

Strange sent Mickelson and Toms out together for the third straight match, this time in alternate shot, and they paid off again. They ran their record to 2-0-1 with a 2-and-1 win over Pierre Fulke and Phillip Price, both seeing their first action. Said Strange, "I expected them to be my best team from the get-go." They were 1 down, then won three straight from the 13th on two European bogeys and Mickelson's crushing three wood to three feet at the par-five 15th for a conceded eagle. The Ryder Cup was tied at 4½.

Then came the news Strange was waiting to hear — Woods had shown up. Well, that's a relative term. It was effective golf, but it wasn't exactly sparkling golf. Woods and Love, in the final match out in the morning, beat the stumbling twosome of Clarke and Bjorn, 4 and 3. It was only Woods' second alternate shot win in six tries. The Americans made only three birdies, the last one being Woods' winning seven-footer at the 15th. Woods blamed the slowness of the greens. "I put more on my stroke and still can't get it to the hole," he said. "Either play long and putt downhill, or put the 'Arnold' stroke on it (charge the putt)." The Europeans made one birdie, but lumbered to three bogeys. Well, a win is a win, and the Americans led this Ryder Cup for the first time, 5½-4½. But not for long.

In an even less sparkling display, Westwood and Garcia rang up their third point in three outings with a 2-and-1 win over Cink and Furyk. They took the lead at the fourth hole on a par, and two birdies and three bogeys later, they had re-tied the match.

Then it was Monty and Bernhard again in the last alternate shot match, and they put Europe ahead with a 1-up win. "Mentally, it was very important to win the game," Langer said. "It would not have been much fun, having been 2 up and coming into 18 and even losing the match or tying it." The two Scotts, Verplank and Hoch, battled back from 2 down on Verplank's 35-footer at the 11th and Hoch's three-footer at the 15th for birdies. And Montgomerie came barreling through yet again. He had made the two earlier birdies from six and 10 feet off Langer's strong iron play. The next came on Langer's seven-iron shot to five feet behind the pin at the 17th. He ranked it among the best shots of his career. Monty first conceded a short par putt to Hoch, then holed the five-footer Langer had left him for a birdie. "The whole team wanted to play with this guy," Monty said, "and I was the lucky one." A half in pars at the 18th did the trick, and the Europeans led, 6½-5½.

For all of the so-so play in alternate shot Saturday morning, the afternoon's best-ball turned into a wild shootout. A staggering 66 birdies — including concessions — were made in the four matches. Only two bogeys were made, and both decided matches.

Take the opening match. Duval made five birdies and Calcavecchia three for a 1-up victory over Fasth (five birdies) and Jesper Parnevik (two). And what a show. The Americans were 2 down going to the 10th tee. Duval, abandoning the American strategy, went for the green and made it. Jesper Parnevik stepped up and pulled out an iron for a lay-up. The crowd roared "No-o-o-o!" They wanted to see him go for it. Seduced by the excitement, Parnevik dropped the iron and pulled his driver. Then the crowd groaned. Parnevik's tee shot hit the bank and trickled back into the water. Now Fasth had to play cautiously. He laid up off the tee. Unbelievably, he dropped a simple wedge approach short into the water. That was the beauty of the 10th. Did Parnevik, with a 2-up lead, really have to try to match Duval, or was it simply bravado? Whichever, it might have cost the Europeans the match. For now their lead was down to one hole. And that also disappeared at the 13th when Calcavecchia put his approach stiff to the pin and birdied. The match was all-square for the first time since the first hole. Duval birdied the 14th, and the Americans were on their way to the 1-up win that tied the Ryder Cup.

Not to worry. Montgomerie was up next. But what's this? Without Langer? This was the pair that had won 2½ of a possible three points. Langer, 45, now had 23 career points, just two behind Nick Faldo's record 25. Now he had no chance to tie him in this Ryder Cup. Had Torrance gone daft, breaking up this combination? No, it was Langer's choice.

"I didn't feel I should be playing five rounds," Langer said. "I've had a bit of an injury, which I woke up with Thursday morning. I couldn't turn my head very well to the left. And it was actually a question to even play yesterday morning (Friday). If I'm out there 10 hours again today, I probably wouldn't be in shape for tomorrow. So I told Sam to give me a little bit of a rest. I'm the oldest guy on the team, and I think it was the wisest thing to do."

No matter. Just give Montgomerie a partner and off he goes. This time it was Harrington, and they took the lead at the second hole and stayed there for a 2-and-1 win over Mickelson and Toms. Montgomerie was dropping putts all over the place, notching five of their eight birdies, four of them for winners. Europe now went back into the lead. Once again — not for long.

Woods and Love teamed up again for another win this day. And after nine birdies — seven by Woods — it was a par by Love at the 18th that beat Garcia and Westwood, 1 up. It was one of the great battles of the week, and it was never drawn finer than at the tempting 10th. Both Garcia and Westwood went for the green, and Woods and Love, two of the biggest hitters in the game, stubbornly stuck to the American plan and laid up off the tee. Garcia just missed the green, but stayed dry. Westwood hit it about 30 feet from the pin. Woods and Love hit their short pitches, but neither could birdie. Westwood two-putted for a birdie and a 1-up lead. Said Love, "It wasn't a percentage play. I'll take Tiger Woods at a hundred yards over hitting it over the lake." Said Woods, "For me, driver is too much and three wood — even my best one — I don't know if I can clear the trees. My game plan was to give ourselves two looks at it. We did that. Unfortunately, we didn't make the putts."

Even so, each side led for short stretches, neither by more than 1 up, and it came down to the last two holes. At the 17th, Garcia hit the green in two, and missed on his eagle try. Love chipped in from the fringe for a birdie. Garcia was three feet from tying him. He missed. The match was all-square going to the 18th. All four players had birdie chances. Love two-putted for a par, Garcia bogeyed, and Westwood faced a three-footer for a tying par. He missed. This was one of only two bogeys in the best-ball. The Ryder Cup was tied at 7½.

The day came down to the final best-ball match. This was another see-saw battle, Clarke and McGinley against Hoch and Furyk. The Americans made 10 birdies, the Europeans nine. They each shot a best-ball of 63. But it was decided on the final hole by a bogey. The Americans were 1 up on Hoch's fourth birdie, a 12-footer at the 17th. But at the 18th, Clarke and both Americans all missed the green and bogeyed. McGinley, the Irish rookie, hit a good drive and fired a long iron to 30 feet. His first putt stopped on the edge of the hole. He tapped in for a winning par, a halved match — and an 8-8 tie going into the singles.

Now it was time for a history lesson. The Americans could reflect on their superiority in singles. In the past seven Ryder Cups alone, beginning with the European breakthrough year of 1987, the Americans were 6-1 in singles. The Europeans would try to raise the spirit of that one lone win, Oak Hill, 1995, when they trailed by 9-7 going into the singles and rolled over the Americans, 7½-4½, to take the cup by a point.

"What is history?" Bjorn asked. "Oak Hill? We won the singles at Oak Hill. It can be done. If we can win in America with a team that was underdogs there, we can win singles here."

Strange and Torrance had released their order of play for the singles. With the teams tied 8-8 going into Sunday, the order looked like disaster for someone. Could you believe? — Torrance was making a wild do-or-die charge coming out of the gate, sending out his big guns, Montgomerie, Garcia, Clarke and Langer, first through fourth. This immediately was dubbed "front-loading." Strange took the opposite approach. He put his biggest guns, Mickelson and Woods, at the end, playing them 11th and 12th, as insurance in case the Europeans would get that far.

"Now, having seen the order," a golf writer asked, "are you a little concerned that the match could conceivably be over before your two best players have had a chance to make a difference?"

Strange looked at the guy as though he were daft.

But one man's fantasy turned into Strange's nightmare. The question turned into prophecy. By the time the Ryder Cup got to Mickelson and Woods, it was over.

Strange saw Torrance's front-loading as a bid for the crowd. "He wants to get the spectators involved early," Strange said. "He wants to get momentum early and hopefully that will feed over into the back end of his field."

Strange had his strategy planned a year ago. If the United States was well ahead after the team matches, he would have two, maybe three of his top players up front. And if not, "Then, coming in, if it's on the line, you certainly have to have a couple of horses there," he said. It all hinged on Woods. "If the Ryder Cup is on the line," Strange said, "that's the guy you have to have go last."

Torrance's lineup took everybody by surprise, including his own team. After the cup was safe in European hands, Parnevik revealed that he and his teammates were delighted at the singles order. In contrast, he recalled the 1999 Ryder Cup and the sinking feeling he and Montgomerie got when they saw the singles lineup. "Monty and I looked at each other ... and said, 'Where are we going to get the points?'" Parnevik said. It was just the opposite this time. "Everybody on the team just knew we were going to win," he said. "And it wasn't one of those wishful 'I hope we're going to win.' It was, 'We know we're going to win.'"

That's called confidence, and no one felt it more than Montgomerie when he finally found his name in the pairings. "I came out and was looking for my name at (match) seven, eight or nine, where I usually play," he said, "and I couldn't see my name because it was 'Monty' instead of 'Montgomerie.'"

Torrance had jotted it in at the top of the lineup. Leading off? So be it. And can you believe the opponent he drew? — Scott Hoch, whom he had already beaten twice in team matches the past two days. In Hoch's only other Ryder Cup, in 1997, Montgomerie conceded him a 15-foot par putt on the final hole, but it was for a ceremonial halve in the final singles match after Europe had already wrapped up the cup. So Monty was 2-0-1 overall against him in three outings. He made it 3-0-1 in short order this time. He took the lead for good on Hoch's bogey at No. 5, and then starting holing everything — a 30-footer here, a nine-footer there and a 15-footer there. Montgomerie took the 13th with a four-wood second shot to inches, and closed Hoch out at the 14th with his sixth birdie of the day — against no bogeys. He left Hoch muttering to himself.

"He's got my number," Hoch said. "And my hat's off to him. I told him, I don't want any part of him over here, but come on back to the States and we might play another match."

So Montgomerie finished as the leading point-winner in this Ryder Cup — 4½ points out of the possible 5. He was a terror. In the three matches in which he played his own ball he had 16 birdies and only two bogeys. He raised his lifetime record to 16-7-5. For a man with a sore back and a wounded ego, how can this be?

"You like to think that major championships are more important, but I've always liked team competition," Montgomerie said, "and I've always thrived on that competition."

But how to explain the rest of the Europeans? When the singles got underway, the Americans needed 14 points for a tie that would retain the cup. The Europeans needed 14½ to take it back. They wasted no time.

The fifth match out came back second in a hurry, and if the win wasn't an upset, the score surely was — Harrington over Calcavecchia, 5 and 4. Said Calcavecchia, "He was 4 under and I was 1 over. That pretty much says it all." Actually, Harrington had four birdies — one a 50-foot putt at the ninth — and one bogey, and Calcavecchia had nary a birdie and four bogeys. That made it Europe, 10-8.

And now the crowd sensed victory. The thunder echoed around the Belfry, first here, then there. It was like the footsteps of the giant in Jack and the Beanstalk booming across the land.

Next, Bernhard Langer made it 11-8 with a 4-and-3 romp over the slumping Hal Sutton in the fourth match. "Not bad for the old man on the team," someone offered. Langer gave his little grin. "I have to take that, I guess," he said. A tough question went to Sutton: How would he be feeling if he were the American captain? "Uptight," Sutton said. "Just like I'm sure Curtis is."

David Toms delayed the inevitable briefly, taking a 1-up victory over Garcia, who had a 2-up lead going to No. 10 and then decided to go for the tempting green. He carried the water, but ended up on the bank, and from there hit a poor chip. He parred the hole. Toms laid up off the tee, pitched to 10 feet, and made the birdie to cut Garcia's lead to one hole. Toms' birdie at the 11th squared things, for one hole. Then it was Garcia's turn, and he went 1 up with a birdie at the 12th. Toms refused to stay put, though. Garcia chopped up the par-three 14th and conceded Toms a winning birdie that squared the match. Toms then took the lead for good with another birdie at the 15th, and took the 1-up win when Garcia caught water at the 18th. Toms had completed an outstanding record for a rookie or anyone else — 3-1-1 — and cut Europe's lead to two points, at 11-9, and that was as close as the Americans would get.

Darren Clarke and David Duval hooked up like a couple of bulldogs and battled all-square over the last seven holes, and they finished that way for a halve each. Thomas Bjorn took the lead with a birdie at No. 5 and was never threatened in a 2-and-1 win over Stewart Cink, and Europe edged a point closer, 12½-9½.

Scott Verplank birdied No. 1 — the first American to win the first hole in singles — and then eagled the par-five third and led all the way in a 2-and-1 win over Lee Westwood. Verplank, running his rookie record to 2-1-1, thus cutting the Europeans back to a two-point lead, 12½-10½.

The stage next belonged to Price, a 35-year-old rookie from Wales. Torrance's brinkmanship in the order of play put Price, No. 119 in the world, up against the formidable Mickelson, ranked No. 2. Little was expected of Price. In fact, *The Times* of London, handicapping the field for the singles, strained to be polite to him.

"Steady and solid," *The Times* wrote, "but possibly out of his depth in the Ryder Cup context. In his favor, the Welshman has often played well at the Belfry, and may justify his place."

Strange had put Mickelson next to last, looking for some late muscle. Instead, it was Mickelson getting muscled. They started out as the 11th match, but were over early and the eighth match coming in. They halved the first four holes, and Price took the lead at the fifth on Mickelson's bogey. Price, who made no bogeys, rang up five birdies, including a breathtaking 22-footer from above the hole at the par-four 16th to close out Mickelson, 3 and 2. The gallery exploded in a roar. Europe, with four matches to go, was now within a point of locking up the cup, 13½-10½.

The Europeans came within an eyelash in the next match. Fasth led Azinger from the second hole, and was 2 up until he missed the 16th green and bogeyed. That left him a hole to the good and set the stage for a stunning finish. Fasth did his part, hitting the fairway at the daunting 18th, then firing his approach to the green, some 30 feet above the hole. Azinger also hit the fairway, but put his approach into the bunker at the left of the green. He was looking at a tough par, and maybe a bogey. But Azinger, who came back from cancer, was not to be counted out. Who could forget the 1993 Memorial Tournament, when he was caught in a deep greenside bunker and somehow splashed out and right into the hole to win. Here he was again, hanging by a thread. And pow! He blasted the ball out and into the hole for a birdie. Azinger miraculously had won the hole and denied Fasth the thrill of winning the cup in his first year. But the half did move Europe within a half-point of it, at 14-11.

Very well. That let another rookie do it. Enter Ireland's McGinley, a man of charm and modest accomplishments. In 18 European events this season, his only single-digit finishes were ties for fifth and sixth, and he missed five cuts. The Times of London had pretty much dismissed him.

"One of Sam Torrance's biggest doubts coming into the contest," *The Times* wrote. "McGinley has at least been able to get some competitive experience before the final day."

And McGinley would hole the pressure putt that would win the Ryder Cup.

It was McGinley against Furyk, the man with the loopy swing. Furyk led from the second by as much as two holes, but every time he had a chance to pull away, he would bogey. "I made some poor decisions at the eighth, 10th and 13th," Furyk said. He played them in a double bogey and two bogeys, and lost all three. But he was able to cling to the lead because McGinley threw in a couple of bogeys of his own. Eventually, in the mounting pressure, someone had to make a move. It was McGinley.

At the par-five 17th, Furyk missed his birdie putt from about 14 feet, but McGinley got his from 12 to square the match. It was the first time since the second hole that Furyk wasn't leading. Now the 18th would do it. Or would it? McGinley pulled his approach wide left of the green. But he pitched on to about nine feet below the hole. Then he made the putt of his life. Europe hoisted the Ryder Cup.

"To have the opportunity to hole the putt was magnificent," McGinley said. "And to actually hole it was magnificent. What more can I say? Thank you very much."

McGinley, in this Ryder Cup debut, was 0-1-2. That's undistinguished by any standard, but that second tie made him a champion. Until he dropped that putt, the Ryder Cup, arithmetically, was still up for grabs. What followed was mere epilogue, and awkward epilogue at that. There were still two meaningless matches out.

The No. 11 match, Love vs. Fulke, was embarrassingly awkward thanks to Garcia, whose playfulness slopped over. When McGinley clinched the cup for Europe with that pressure putt, Garcia went cavorting gleefully down the 18th fairway. Meanwhile, Love and Fulke were waiting to hit their shots. It was ceremonial, but they did want to finish. They were all-square coming to the 18th. Fulke offered to concede the match. Love declined. They hit their tee shots. Then waiting for Garcia to run out of glee, they finally decided to pick up and halve the match.

Woods and Parnevik in the final match were also in the ceremonial stage. Woods went 2 up on the first nine but couldn't stay there, and finally broke in front with a birdie at the 17th. And at the 18th, after three-putting for a bogey, he conceded Parnevik's four-foot putt for a winning par and a halved match.

Europe officially had the Ryder Cup. Let the questions begin. First, would Strange get blistered in the press for his bottom-heavy order against Torrance's front-loaded lineup?

"I haven't been asked about it, but I will be," Strange said in the closing news conference. "Sam did one remarkable job today. And I mean by that he took a hell of a gamble front-loading his team like he did. It turns out to be smart."

Torrance didn't dwell on it. "Apart from my marriage and the birth of my children, without doubt this is the proudest moment of my life," he said. He praised his team, but he singled out one for special treatment. "There are 12 guys here," Torrance said, "but we were led by the infamous Colin Montgomerie, who was magnificent all week.

"Bad heart, bad back — and he'll have a bad head tomorrow."

8. Cisco World Match Play

There was a very special home winner of the Cisco World Match Play Championship in 2002. Not that Ernie Els is British, far from it. He is a proud South African but also a man of the world. He has homes in Johannesburg and George in South Africa, in the United States in Orlando, Florida, and on Paradise Island in the Bahamas. But for almost half the year Els lives in England, on the Wentworth estate in Virginia Water, southwest of London.

It is perhaps here that Els and his family feel most at home when away from their homeland. Els enjoys the English summer sporting season, going to watch tennis at Wimbledon or to cricket matches in his off weeks. More especially it was here that his daughter, Samantha, was born in 1999 and his son, Ben, just over a week before the World Match Play began.

It was also in the clubhouse at Wentworth that he celebrated, with considerable gusto, his British Open Championship victory at Muirfield in July. The silver claret jug stood proudly in the bar all week of the World Match Play.

By beating Sergio Garcia 2 and 1 in the final, Els gave himself more reasons for celebrating. It was his fourth victory in the tournament but his first since 1996, when he won for the third year in a row. Only Gary Player and Seve Ballesteros, with five each, have held the title more often. "After the third one I wanted to try and catch Gary and Seve, but after I lost to Vijay (Singh) the next year I've struggled to get back into the final," Els said. "If I can, I'll be back next year to try and equal the record."

Els also became the first player since Mark O'Meara in 1998 to win the British Open and the World Match Play in the same year. "What more can you ask for in one year?" Els said. "I've won a major championship, the Open, which was always the ultimate dream in golfing terms.

"To have a son in the same year is wonderful. We have a great family and we have always been happy at Wentworth. It is nice to have a good club to look after you. It means even more to win this tournament now we've lived here for a few years."

What Els shares from his countryman Player, and Ballesteros, is a knack for winning 36-hole matches. It is the classic distance, testing a player's mettle over a full day, and Els has now won 15 of his 19 matches in the event. If the length of the matches provides opportunities for recovery that 18-hole matches do not, it was not that sort of week for Els. He never trailed in any of his three matches over 100 holes.

In this, the 39th edition of the World Match Play, Els needed to play at such an exceptional standard to prevail against a field that included five of the top eight players on the World Ranking. In only one match did a player ranked higher lose, but rarely did the player who was expected to win find it an easy matter to accomplish. This was no more evident than in the top match in the first round, which became the longest in the history of the event.

Michael Campbell finally defeated Nick Faldo at the 43rd hole after the pair had to come back on the following morning to complete the match.

Darkness had forced the marathon encounter to be suspended overnight after the sixth of the extra holes in the playoff. The pair had already played the four usual playoff holes — the first, second, 17th and 18th — before setting out again.

"On the second tee we both decided that would be the last hole," Campbell said. "It was hard to read the putts by then." When Faldo's birdie putt for victory lipped out, he turned to the referee and shaped a 'T' (for timeout) with his hands. Campbell gave a sweeping cut-off gesture.

The match was suspended nine hours and five minutes, including a half-hour lunch break, after it began. "That was an honest day's work at the office," Faldo said, "but I need a breather now." The Englishman also had to resume his first-round match the following morning in 2000 against Darren Clarke. He ended up losing at the 40th hole in a match that equaled the event's then-longest encounter.

In 2001, Faldo, the two-time former champion, lost 9 and 8 to Padraig Harrington in the first round and was determined not to make such an ignominious departure again. Yet Campbell led for much of the day, with Faldo missing a number of short putts in the morning on greens that had more nap than usual after rain earlier in the week.

The drama increased after Campbell went two up with three to play. At the 16th he had a five-footer for the match but pulled it. Faldo, having charged his first putt, still needed to hole out from four feet to continue the match. Campbell then had chances at the 17th and 18th but somehow Faldo survived.

At the first two extra holes Faldo had the better chances to finish it, but after that it became more a matter of attrition as the light faded. "I had Nick by the short and curlies," Campbell said, "but that's gone. I just want to go home and get something to eat now." When they resumed the following morning, it was at the 17th hole, which with out-of-bounds down the left-hand side is never the most welcoming of tee shots at any time. It was cold and wet, but Campbell found the green at the par-five in two and holed from 10 feet for the winning birdie.

It meant so much to Campbell to beat Faldo that he went back to shake his hand for a second time on the green. "I wanted to make the most of it," Campbell said. "He was a big hero of mine. I used to watch on television in New Zealand and I've read lots of books on him. Over the last few years, through a mutual friend, I got quite close to Nick and played a lot of practice rounds with him.

"You have to prod him a bit for advice, but he has changed a lot in the last few years. His character shows more and his game is coming back. He has the body of a 25-year-old, he is getting his length back, and he still has one of the best short games in the world. There is no reason why he should not be on the next Ryder Cup team."

Justin Rose, making his debut in the event at the age of 22, almost took his match against Vijay Singh into extra holes but for a missed four-footer on the last green. Hitting the putt with a little more speed, hoping it would hold the line, Rose was shocked when the ball lipped out.

Rose trailed from the moment Singh, the two-time major champion, birdied the fifth. At lunch, and again with 10 holes to play, Rose was three down but battled back superbly, holing from six feet at the 17th to take the match to the last. Singh pulled his second shot next to the grandstand and could not chip close enough to guarantee a par.

Rose was just off the back of the green in two and elected to chip with his three wood, a Tiger Woods-inspired shot, but left it those four feet short. "To take three to get down from the fringe was a shame, but what can you do?" Rose said. "I enjoy the situation when it comes down to the end and it would have been good to get back to all square."

Singh was impressed by the youngster who had won four times around the world earlier in the season. "He has a beautiful golf swing," he said. "He shouldn't change it, but focus on keeping doing what he is already doing. He has a lot of potential. He could be a future star."

Harrington, last year's losing finalist, booked his place in the quarter-finals by beating Canadian Mike Weir 4 and 3. "I wasn't playing very well, but it is better to be lucky, and I got the breaks when it mattered," Harrington said.

Unlike when he led throughout the entire Ryder Cup, Montgomerie trailed as early as the second hole against Fred Funk, the only American in the field. However, it was a momentary blip and Monty was soon in command and ran out a 3-and-2 winner. "Fred seems to enjoy himself on the greens and you are always conscious that a good putter is a dangerous opponent," Montgomerie said. "I was lucky that he missed a couple of crucial putts that gave me the advantage."

Montgomerie, the 1999 champion, had little luck in meeting Els in the quarter-finals. There was a suggestion that following his British Open triumph and having just become a father for the second time, Els' mind might not be on the job at hand. How wrong that theory proved as Els, who had turned 33 on the day before, won 6 and 5.

Montgomerie's day could be summed up by the fact that his (approximate) 65 in the morning was good enough only to be four down against Els. "Bloody hell," sighed the Scot. "I was delighted only to be four down."

The South African was awarded a round of 60 for the first 18 holes, a record for the event, beating the 61s of Montgomerie and Harrington. In match play it is often misleading to speak of scores, for the circumstances are very different. In this round, only two longish putts were conceded, a 15-footer for an eagle at the fourth when he won the hole to go three up and a six-footer for a par at the 12th when Montgomerie had already won the hole.

Otherwise Els relentlessly hit brilliant approach shots and holed putt after putt. "Everything in my bag, up to the three wood, was very good," Els said. "To be 12 under against one of the best players in the world is a great feeling." At the 18th he left himself a 30-footer for an eagle that would have given him 59. "Even though it would not be a real 59, it was still special to have a putt to break 60."

In the match as a whole, Els produced three eagles and 11 birdies in 31 holes of outstanding golf. Though the sun came out after lunch, following a miserable morning, neither Els nor Montgomerie were quite at their best. Even so, Els finished 15 under par, equaling the record set by Sandy Lyle in 1986 and equaled by Montgomerie in 2000.

Els is used to getting the upper hand against Montgomerie, with two U.S. Opens and a final of the World Match Play on one side of the ledger and a playoff defeat at Sun City, when Monty was just glad to get out of the country alive, on the other. "At the end I wanted to say to Colin that for some reason he brings out the best in me," Els said, "but I didn't think it was the right time."

A meeting with Els' compatriot, Retief Goosen, in the semi-finals did not materialize because the world's No. 4 golfer was beaten by Singh, the world's No. 8. Singh, who was troubled by a shoulder injury, trailed for much of the morning, but after leveling the match at lunch, soon went three up in the afternoon and secured a 4-and-3 victory.

For Campbell, it turned into a very special day, for after seeing Faldo, he then went on to defeat the defending champion, Ian Woosnam. This was the New Zealander's first appearance in the event, but his opponents had combined for five World Match Play titles as well as seven major championships.

His match against Woosnam was far swifter than that against Faldo. Not only did he win 3 and 2, but the 34 holes occupied barely five and a half hours. While Campbell continued to play steadily, Woosnam was a bit in and out and went four down after 15. The Welshman, however, won two of the last three holes before lunch and then three of the first four of the afternoon. He birdied the second, put his approach at the third to three inches and eagled the fourth, but led for only one hole and a few errors crept in again on the second nine.

Campbell had a three-footer to finish the match at the 16th, the same hole where he could have seen off Faldo the day before, but this time he avoided the nine additional holes. "I am feeling good about my game and comfortable with my fitness, but it is hard mentally to maintain your focus over such a long time," said Campbell after playing 77 holes in two days.

Garcia was the fourth seed to be given a bye into the quarter-finals and his opponent, Harrington, revealed he was plagued by a regripping problem, something the young Spaniard had only just conquered himself. Harrington said it was not nearly to the same extent as Garcia reached, but it was a distraction. "The regripping in itself is not a problem," Harrington said. "But it is if you are aware of it. I am probably regripping only once or twice, which is probably normal, but I am distracting myself with it at the moment."

Perhaps it was at the root of Harrington's problem with the 17th hole, which had an inordinately huge impact on the match that Garcia won 2 and 1 after being four down after 16 holes in the morning. The Irishman went out of bounds on the 17th once in the first round, when he only needed to play the hole once, and twice against Garcia.

On the first occasion it sparked a run of four holes in a row for the Spaniard, and on the second it ended the match after Harrington had birdied the previous two holes to keep the match going. With Faldo's match held over to that morning, Harrington's defeat completed the set of an Englishman, a Scot, a Welshman and an Irishman all departing the event on the same day.

Garcia had to rally again in the semi-finals where he faced Campbell. Despite all his extra golf compared to his opponent, Campbell started the sprightlier and was three up after six holes. "I wouldn't say I have had a bad start, but the guys I've been playing have gone crazy at the beginning,"

Garcia said. As if to prove his point, the par-five fourth was halved in eagles. "But as long as you don't get five or six down, you can come back because they are long matches."

A poor drive at the 17th in the morning from Campbell brought Garcia back to even, and it was not until the 12th hole in the afternoon that the Spaniard edged in front for the first time. He won the next as well, and though Campbell took the 15th with a par, Garcia birdied the next and put a sudden end to the match at the 17th with a typical display of brilliance. Campbell hit a superb second shot onto the green at the par-five, but Garcia then chipped in for his eagle from 30 yards short of the green. "I was just hoping to get a four," Garcia said, "but five feet from the hole I thought it had a chance and it went."

Els found it hard to recapture his brilliance of the day before, but his semi-final opponent, Singh, was not at his best either. He handed the South African a dream start by bogeying the first three holes. Els was soon four up after five, and though Singh clawed his way back to only one behind, Els won the 16th and 17th to be three up at lunch.

The pair had met in two finals, Els winning in 1996 and Singh ending the South African's run of victories in 1997. With his second shot to the first hole after lunch, Singh pulled his five wood into the trees and hit a woman, who was attended by a nearby St. John's Ambulance. With Singh going four down and then five down at the fifth, it looked as if the Fijian was entering terminal territory. Els had pulled his tee shot at the short fifth into a bunker and won the hole by holing out with his recovery shot.

Singh got a hole back with a birdie at the eighth and received some help from Els when the South African three-putted from off the green at the 11th and drove into a ditch in the trees at the par-five 12th. At the uphill 13th, which begins the long march back to the clubhouse, Els put his seven-iron second shot to 15 feet and holed the putt to restore a three-up lead, the eventual winning margin.

"Neither of us played as well as yesterday," Els said. "We just couldn't get the putts in the hole, but I was solid from tee to green. Sergio is a good friend of mine. He has a lot of energy and that will keep me going tomorrow."

With Player and Ballesteros among their golfing ancestors, the Els-Garcia final was a fitting one and the match took on the characteristics of both players' previous encounters. Els was never behind and took an early lead which Garcia, at age 22 the youngest finalist ever, attempted to haul back.

Over the first 12 holes the only impression the Spaniard could make was with an eagle at the fourth. Els went out in 30 and added a birdie at the 11th and an eagle at the 12th, set up by a wondrous two iron from the right trees and 225 yards from the hole. He then was five up.

Even given his previous deficits, this was Garcia's greatest challenge, both numerically and because the placid South African is usually such a good front-runner. Some players overpower opponents by the force of their personality, and in time, Garcia, impetuous but brilliant, will be one of them. Els is merely relentless. The mistakes were few, but poor drives at the 15th and 16th did hand two holes back to Garcia.

Three down at lunch, Garcia needed a quick start, and the first birdie of the week at the first hole was the perfect start. Another at the sixth brought him back to one down, but then came too many destructive shots at the wrong times. When he pushed his drive at the seventh into a ditch, it set a pattern for the afternoon. He lost the hole and then birdied the eighth, but pushed his drive at the ninth into the trees to fall two behind again.

A long putt for a birdie on the short 10th put Els three up and apparently coasting. Not so. Bunkered with his drive, Els lost the 13th and then the short 14th when his par putt from above the hole from four feet lipped out. "It was a terrible stroke and I really felt down then," Els said. "I felt the match could really turn around then. Match play is such a crazy game."

The match could not have been be more delicately poised. The 15th was halved in pars, but there was to be a tame end. Garcia pulled his drive at the 16th into the trees and, attempting to hack out left-handed, put it in a ditch. One more hack and he conceded the hole.

The next was a similar story. The Spaniard hooked his drive and, though he got a kind bounce off a tree, he was blocked out for his second around the dogleg. His next did not bend and ended deep in the trees on the right. It looked hopeless, but Garcia would not give up. He somehow got it out, and then pitched to a foot for a conceded five. But with Els on the green in three and with two putts for the match, Garcia offered his hand.

"It was great fun but Ernie played the best today," Garcia said. Els marveled at his opponent's spirit. "In 10 years' time I expect him to be close to a career grand slam," he said. "Today I made the fewer mistakes, but he will never show you that he is scared of you. He is not going to back down. He is very positive and likes to let you know it. That's why I think he will go a long way."

9. American Tours

If 2002 proved anything it is that the U.S. PGA Tour is really two tours. There is the tour that is dominated by Tiger Woods, and there is the one that produced 18 first-time winners. This year only served to highlight the broadening chasm between the truly big events and the second tier.

A case-in-point was the Buick Challenge, an autumn event in Pine Mountain, Georgia, once called the Southern Open, hosted at Callaway Gardens, a beautiful little park on the way to absolutely nowhere. This was the last year of the Buick Challenge. The economics of golf had reached a point where small-market events at such venues as this couldn't attract the television ratings and the galleries needed to stay alive. Despite praise from past champions such as David Toms, Davis Love and Chris DiMarco and regular appearances by players such as David Duval, Nick Price and Phil Mickelson, the Buick Challenge couldn't make it in today's environment because they couldn't attract one player: Tiger Woods.

At the Buick Challenge, Jonathan Byrd joined such notables as John Rollins, Bob Burns, Ian Leggett, Luke Donald and Spike McRoy as a first-time winner, and even the most ardent golf fans had a hard time caring. Even stories such as Matt Gogel coming back to win at Pebble Beach after losing a seven-shot lead to Woods a few years ago or Craig Perks hitting only seven fairways in the final round and scrambling to make The Players Championship his first victory were considered yawners by year's end. If Woods wasn't in the field, and if the world's best weren't on the leaderboard, the PGA Tour had a hard time mustering much interest.

This shouldn't come as a big surprise. The PGA Tour has become a victim of its own success. Not a week goes by that world-class golf isn't played somewhere. The PGA Tour now runs from the first week in January through the middle of November, with unofficial events rolling through the holidays. If you count the British Open and the Ryder Cup, the tour held two simultaneous events six times in 2002.

The Reno-Tahoe Open (won by a fellow named Chris Riley) ran at the same time as the WGC NEC Invitational (won by Craig Parry, with Woods, Love, Mickelson and Rich Beem finishing in the top 10). Leggett won the Touchstone Energy Tucson Open the same week the world's best were in Carlsbad, California, at the WGC Accenture Match Play. Spike McRoy won the BC Open while Ernie Els was throwing his hat in triumph at the British Open, and while Woods was holding off Retief Goosen in the WGC American Express Championship, K.J. Choi was beating Glen Day, John Morse and Rodney Pampling in the Tampa Bay Classic.

While the market isn't completely saturated, it is certainly showing signs of backwater runoff. Golf fans, just like golf pros, have a burnout point. They must pace themselves for the marathon that is today's PGA Tour schedule, which means that events such as the SEI Pennsylvania Classic and Valero Texas Open aren't going to garner much attention and enthusiasm.

While there have always been conflicting events between the American, European and other tours, we are now seeing a growth in conflicts between events sanctioned by the PGA Tour. Where this will lead is anyone's guess, but if current trends are any indication, American golf fans can expect more, not less, golf from the American tours, and a continually growing gap between the top and second-tier tournaments.

Meanwhile Tiger Woods just keeps on rolling. In 18 weeks on the PGA Tour, Woods won five times (including two major championships) and completed the year with 13 top-10 finishes. He won his fourth consecutive Vardon Trophy with a scoring average of 68.56, a fifth consecutive PGA Tour money title with $6.9 million in earnings, and remained in the top spot in the World Ranking for the fifth consecutive year.

The rising tide of Tiger has raised all ships. Jay Williamson, who finished 125th on the PGA Tour money list and secured the final exempt spot for the 2003 season, won $515,445 in 2002. In 1996, the year Woods turned professional, that same amount would have put Williamson among the top 40 money winners.

Money is only one indicator. Players are continuing to work harder because of Woods, and the overall scoring is showing it. Byrd shot 27-under-par 261 the week he won the Buick Challenge. That was the lowest 72-hole total of the year. Phil Mickelson had the lowest score relative to par for the year (30 under at the Bob Hope Chrysler Classic), while six players shot 61s at varying points in 2002. Phil Tataurangi, another of the year's first-time winners, shot the low final round of the year when he posted 62 at the Invensys Classic at Las Vegas.

What does the future hold? It's anyone's guess, but as long as Woods keeps elevating the bar, you can expect golf to continue to grow.

U.S. PGA Tour

Mercedes Championships—$4,000,000
Winner: Sergio Garcia

Sergio Garcia outlined his lofty goals at the start of the year. "I want to win the money titles on the U.S. Tour and the European Tour together," Garcia said, and with two 10-foot birdie putts in back-to-back trips down the par-five 18th hole, he got off on the right foot, winning the $1 million first prize at the season-opening Mercedes Championships on the Plantation Course at Kapalua, Hawaii.

"I'm leading the money list," Garcia said after nailing the last 10-footer to beat David Toms in a playoff after they had tied a 274, 18 under par. "When I get old I can say to my nephews, 'I was the money leader — for at least one week.'"

It took a nine-under-par 64 and help from Toms on the last hole of regulation for Garcia to be able to make that claim on a day when six players found the top of the leaderboard and the brutal Pacific winds that had driven players nuts for three days died down to a mild zephyr.

The Spaniard drove the green on the downhill 398-yard sixth hole for a birdie, then came within a foot of a double eagle at the par-five ninth. His tap-in eagle gave him a share of the lead with 54-hole leader Kenny Perry. One hole later, Garcia snagged the lead outright with a 12-foot birdie putt.

Chris DiMarco made a brief appearance at the top when he tied Garcia, but 38 on the second nine dropped DiMarco into a tie for fifth place with Mark Calcavecchia and Scott McCarron at 278. Ahead of them were Perry in third place at 275 after shooting 69, and Jim Furyk in fourth with 277 following his 65. Scott Verplank, who shared Saturday's overnight lead with Perry, stayed at the top for four holes until an errant tee shot, a looming canyon and an ugly double bogey at the fifth dropped him off the pace. Verplank shot 73 for a 279 total.

When Toms, who started the final round one stroke back, moved to the top of the leaderboard with a cluster of steady pars, he appeared to be the favorite to win. There hadn't been many occasions when Toms had failed to slam the door on all comers when he held a lead, especially the 2001 PGA Championship and Compaq Classic in New Orleans.

The last hole of regulation looked similar to the 2001 PGA Championship, when Toms chose to lay up on the 72nd hole and won with a deft wedge shot and a steady putter. This time he had no choice. The 633-yard, par-five 18th wasn't reachable for even the longest hitters, an elite group to which Toms did not belong. Toms hit a wedge 10 feet behind the hole, leaving him a birdie putt to win. With a slight rain blowing in from the south, Toms hit what looked to be a good putt. It rolled right to the edge of the hole before stopping a half turn short.

"I felt like I was going to make it," said Toms, who finished with 67. "I was convinced I was going to make it and I was going to win the tournament right there. I was shocked that I left it short. When I looked up halfway, I thought it was in."

Toms' shock was compounded by the knowledge that his best chance had just slipped away. With the playoff starting at the 18th and Garcia carrying a membership card to the Big Hitter's Club, Toms knew he wasn't the favorite. "That's not a medium hitter's hole," he said. "And I'm a medium hitter."

That assessment proved correct. Toms hit driver and three wood to the 142-yard mark. His nine-iron third shot stopped 30 feet away, where par was the only reasonable score he could make. Garcia, however, hit his three-wood second shot 30 yards short of the green. He hit his chip 10 feet beyond the hole and made the putt for the win. "He played great," Toms said. "I had a chance to win. I had a real good chance."

Sony Open in Hawaii—$4,000,000
Winner: Jerry Kelly

Still in search of his first PGA Tour victory after six seasons and a string of near-misses, Jerry Kelly stood on the par-five 18th needing birdie or better to avoid a playoff and win the Sony Open in Hawaii. Two perfect swings later, Kelly was in the middle of the green with an eagle putt. He two-putted for his first victory.

"You put in years of hard work and it comes down to those two shots right there," Kelly said. "I knew what I had to do to get the job done." The Wisconsin native found himself tied on the final hole with an old nemesis. John Cook, who had come from behind to beat Kelly the previous year at the Reno-Tahoe Open, caught him again in Hawaii. Cook made three birdies between the 10th and 16th holes to gain a share of the lead. A ringing cell phone during his swing disrupted Cook on the 17th and caused him to push his tee shot into a greenside bunker. He made a bogey to fall one stroke back. A birdie on the par-five 18th by Cook gave him 69 for a 13-under-par 267 total.

Kelly came to the 18th at 13 under and needing a birdie to win. "I just didn't want Reno to happen again to me," he said. "I wasn't going to do the things that let someone else win. I wanted to win the tournament." He did just that by splitting the fairway with a three wood, then ripping a three iron from 245 yards to the back portion of the green, some 45 feet from the hole. With all the pressure on him, Kelly then rolled his first putt to within a foot and tapped in for his first PGA Tour victory with even-par 70 and a 266 total.

"I've wanted to win for a long time," Kelly said. "This feels great."

Cook recalled the cell phone incident at the 17th with regret. "At that point in time with the perfect club in my hand ... I don't know how that happens. It was the point of no return," Cook said. He had nothing but good things to say about the champion. "Jerry had worked hard," Cook said. "He deserved to win."

Jay Don Blake had the low final round, finishing with 65 for a 269 total and third place alone. That was one stroke better than Matt Kuchar, Charles Howell and David Toms, who gained a share of the lead through five holes. An errant tee shot on the sixth cost Toms a double bogey, and he never recovered, finishing with 72 for a 270 total.

That had been Kelly's problem before this week. Throughout the 2001 season, where he posted two runner-up finishes and held the lead at The Players Championship going into the final round, Kelly had a final-round scoring average of 71.36, which ranked 136th on the PGA Tour. That same score in Hawaii would have put Kelly in second place behind Cook. But his 70 gave Kelly his first win.

Bob Hope Chrysler Classic—$4,000,000
Winner: Phil Mickelson

On a sunny Sunday afternoon in the California desert, Phil Mickelson added his name to the distinguished list of 20-event winners on the PGA Tour when he almost holed an 80-yard lob wedge shot to defeat David Berganio on the first extra hole of the Bob Hope Chrysler Classic. Mickelson's 20th career victory came after the big left-hander took five months off to spend time with his family.

"I've played golf for 30 years, so it's not like I'm going to forget how," Mickelson said after shooting eight-under-par 64 to finish the five-round event at 30-under-par 330, then making one more birdie on the playoff hole to dispense with Berganio.

In the throes of competition, Mickelson didn't forget a thing. He birdied the final three holes of regulation to reach 30 under, including one on the 18th from the rough. "Yeah, it was a great shot," Mickelson said of the flop shot he hit to within five feet of the hole to set up the final birdie of regulation. For a while it looked as if that might be enough for the win.

Berganio, looking for his first PGA Tour victory, didn't give up. He birdied two of the final three holes in regulation, including the 18th, to force the playoff. Back on the 18th for the playoff, however, it was all Mickelson. After laying up 80 yards short of the green, Mickelson watched as Berganio hit a four iron into the water. "I was trying to hit a hard cut to the right portion of the green," Berganio said. "I just chunked it."

Berganio made a great recovery after his drop, giving himself a decent putt for par. But Mickelson ended the suspense with a full lob wedge that landed three inches in front of the hole, jumped just past the pin and spun back to within four inches of the hole.

"I felt like, during my time off, I became more consistent from 130 yards in, and more efficient," Mickelson said. "That's why I'm excited to have won the tournament, because what I've specifically worked on paid off. I'm pleased that I shot eight under and very pleased to have won. To have won 20 times and to play golf, which is what most people do on vacation, as my job is great."

Berganio could do little more than shake his head and congratulate the champion. "You can't count Phil out because of his short game," Berganio said. "He knew exactly what he was doing and he just did it. He's a great player, obviously, and it showed right there."

Berganio had 66, six under par, in the final round for his 330 total. Fourth-round leader Cameron Beckman shot a closing 69 for a 332 total to tie for third with Briny Baird, who finished with 64. Jerry Kelly, one week removed from his first PGA Tour victory, shot 67 for a 333 total and fifth place.

Phoenix Open—$4,000,000
Winner: Chris DiMarco

In early September of 2001, Chris DiMarco vowed to prove his critics, most notably, Ryder Cup captain Curtis Strange, wrong. Strange passed on DiMarco as a captain's pick despite his consistent play. Determined to prove Strange wrong, DiMarco beat David Duval in a playoff in October to win the Buick Challenge, then came into 2002 with strong showings in Hawaii and the California desert. Four weeks into the new golfing year, DiMarco won his third career title when he defeated Kenny Perry by one shot at the Phoenix Open.

DiMarco opened up a four-shot lead in the early holes of the final round after John Daly, who temporarily shared the top spot, missed fairways left and right and played seven holes in five over par.

But Daly's wasn't the only seesaw round. DiMarco led by four shots with eight holes to play before hitting his tee shot under a mesquite tree on the 11th. The result was a double bogey and the beginning of a downward slide. He followed that with a bogey at the 12th from the fairway bunker, and another bogey at the 13th when his tee shot found the water.

Perry gained the lead and looked to open up a two-shot advantage at the 13th until he missed an 18-inch putt. "That really killed me," Perry said. "I missed a gimme." The putt would prove crucial as DiMarco clawed his way back into the lead with a near ace at the par-three 16th. The birdie knotted DiMarco and Perry at 17 under par.

Both players found trouble on the 17th, but DiMarco saved par from the back fringe while Perry three-putted for bogey. That proved to be the difference. DiMarco hit a three wood safely into the middle of the 18th fairway and found the green with his approach. Two putts later, DiMarco signed for 69 and a 267 total to win by one stroke.

"To be on top, and then all of a sudden your world falls, it makes you dig deep and learn a lot about yourself," DiMarco said. "I've won by six strokes, and I've birdied the 18th to force a playoff. This one was one you had to hold on to."

Kaname Yokoo closed with 64 to pull into a tie for second at 268 with Perry, who shot 70. It was Yokoo's best career finish on the PGA Tour. As happy as the Japanese golfer was with his performance, Perry was equally disappointed with his. It was the third time in 2002 that Perry had played in the final group and come away winless. "Pitiful," he said. "I just didn't get it done."

Daly regrouped from his disastrous middle stretch to close with 70 for a 269 total and a share of fourth place with Lee Janzen, who finished with 64.

AT&T Pebble Beach National Pro-Am—$4,000,000
Winner: Matt Gogel

It was two years in the making, but Matt Gogel finally had his day of atonement at Pebble Beach. In 2000, Gogel was leading the AT&T Pebble Beach National Pro-Am by seven strokes with seven holes to play when Tiger Woods went on a back-nine tear that included an eagle and three birdies. Gogel shot 40 on the inward half that afternoon and lost by two. Two years later, Gogel trailed by four going into the final round and shot 69 in the Monterrey Peninsula breeze to win by three with a 274 total, 14 under par.

But for every winner in golf there has to be a loser, and Gogel's redemption came at a price. This time the hard-luck kid left broken on the Pacific boulders was PGA Tour rookie Pat Perez. Rounds of 66, 65 and 70 gave Perez a comfortable cushion going into the final round. He led by four strokes over Lee Janzen and Gogel. Memories of Gogel's earlier demise didn't bother the leader, especially considering that Tiger Woods had failed to break 70 in the first three rounds and Phil Mickelson had missed the cut. It's one thing to lose seven shots to Tiger; it's quite another to buckle under pressure from Andrew Magee and Phil Tataurangi. Perez felt good about his chances. He was driving well, hitting a lot of greens and making enough putts on the bumpy Pebble Beach greens.

Perez was undone by a second-nine 39 and a final 76 that included four penalty shots. After having his lead whittled away on the first nine, Perez regained possession of the top spot with a birdie on the 13th. After a perfect drive on the 14th, Perez chose a three wood for his second shot on the par-five hole, a questionable decision given the prevailing headwind. His chances of reaching the green were slim but Perez said, "With that pin I wanted to be as close as I could get. I didn't want to hit a seven iron in there and have to get up in the wind. Who knows where it might go?"

It probably wouldn't have gone out of bounds, which is where Perez's three wood ended up. Ahead, Gogel, who did, indeed, hit a seven iron for his third shot at the 14th, holed a 15-foot putt for birdie. When Perez walked away with a double-bogey seven, he went from leading by one to trailing Gogel by two.

Perez clawed his way back again by making birdies at the 15th and the difficult 17th to regain a one-shot lead after Gogel three-putted the 17th. All Perez needed was a par to ensure a tie and a playoff (assuming Gogel didn't make an eagle at the 18th). A birdie on the par-five would lock up a win.

His decision on the 18th tee was easy. A day before, Perez had vowed to "go after all the pins and try to make all the birdies I can." He drew his driver out of the bag as though he were pulling a sword from a stone. The resulting shot ended up out of bounds. "I figured par would win," he said, although he was wrong on that count. Gogel made birdie on the 18th. "All that changed in about 30 seconds. I found my ball was out of bounds, Gogel made birdie, and the crowd went crazy. It was a long walk back to the tee."

Perez's only hope was to make three with his second ball for a par. When his three-wood second shot sailed into the ocean, all hope drowned with it. He finished with an eight, and lost by three.

"Sometimes ignorance is bliss," Gogel said on Saturday night as a way of explaining his loss to Woods two years earlier and the emotions Perez might go through. "Pat certainly has a lot on his side," Gogel said. "I was that way in 2000. And then I kind of got spooked a little bit, and Tiger made a great run. On the maturity side, I feel like I understand the situation now. I can execute my game a little better."

Gogel also learned another lesson from his loss to Woods. After holing the birdie to win, Gogel hung around the scorer's trailer to console Perez, just as Woods did for him. "Tiger made the effort to come into the trailer and I was feeling pretty low," Gogel said. "I know Pat feels bad. He'll learn from it."

Maybe, but Perez was inconsolable immediately after his round. "Matt said he went through it," Perez said. "But he didn't make eight on the last hole, either. I will always remember that last hole. Always. Nothing good is coming out of this week."

Buick Invitational—$3,600,000
Winner: Jose Maria Olazabal

On a week when the Century Club of San Diego, the folks who run Torrey Pines, hoped to impress the U.S. Golf Association and lock up a future U.S. Open with their new and improved 7,563-yard re-designed South Course, one of the shortest drivers proved that the key to victory still lies on the greens. Jose Maria Olazabal had been working on his swing for the better part of two years trying to hit more fairways when it counted. The results of that work showed on the weekend at Torrey Pines. After shooting 71 and

72 and making the cut with no room to spare, Olazabal went on a tear, shooting 67 and 65 on the weekend to edge out Mark O'Meara and J.L. Lewis by one stroke.

"I've put a lot of work into my swing," the 36-year-old Spaniard said. "You know that in this game you have to go backward in order to go forward and that's what happened to me last year. I was just trying to fix certain things. I'm getting closer. My goal is to get my swing better and more consistent, so I can trust it under pressure. That will be the first step forward for me, to give myself more chances to win."

His chance to win at Torrey Pines came early on Sunday when he birdied three of the first six holes to shoot four-under-par 32 on the first nine. Birdies at the 13th, 14th and 15th moved Olazabal to 13 under par. His only bogey of the round came, not as a result of his sometimes erratic driver, but on the par-three 16th when a gust of wind blew his tee shot into a greenside bunker.

Then came the most dramatic shot of the day. After laying up on the 551-yard final hole, Olazabal almost holed a wedge shot for an eagle. The tap-in gave Olazabal a seven-under-par 65 and a share of the lead at 275. He then had to wait almost an hour as the third-round leaders — O'Meara, Lewis and Jerry Kelly — played the final holes.

O'Meara bogeyed the 17th to fall to 11 under, but came back with a birdie at the 18th to shoot 70 and finish one stroke behind. John Daly also closed with 70 to finish fourth at 277.

That left only Lewis, who birdied the 17th to gain a share of the lead and needed only a par at the last to force a playoff. He made a critical error on his second shot, hitting a six iron too close to the pond guarding the front of the green and leaving himself with a delicate wedge shot over water. He hit the shot 40 feet beyond the hole, left his first putt eight feet short, and never touched the hole with his second putt. The three-putt bogey for 70 dropped Lewis into a tie for second with O'Meara at 276.

"I choked," Lewis said. "I just embarrassed myself. What can I say? You've got to be able to handle the pressure and come through in the clutch. I've done it before, but I didn't do it today. Hopefully I'll be able to handle the nerves better next time. I've choked before, and I'm sure it may happen again. On some of those holes I showed some heart. But if you can't handle the pressure, you've got to do something else."

Tiger Woods came back from 77 on Friday to shoot 69 and 66 on the weekend and finish tied for fifth with Rory Sabbatini and Bob Estes at 278, but the real winners were Olazabal and Torrey Pines. "Imagine if you play this course with U.S. Open rough and firmness," Olazabal said. "It's going to be a monster course. It's a great track. It doesn't give you many chances."

Nissan Open—$3,700,000
Winner: Len Mattiace

Louis Mattiace didn't make the trip to California to watch his son play the Nissan Open. There didn't seem to be any need. Len was 34 years old, a grown man who had traveled the PGA Tour for eight seasons on his own, and he had teed it up in 219 tournaments without bringing home a title. He would be home in Ponte Vedra Beach, Florida, in a few weeks for The Players Championship anyway, so Louis didn't think the cross-country trip was necessary. He didn't even cancel his Sunday afternoon game at the TPC of Sawgrass with his buddies.

After the round, Louis came into the grill room just in time to watch Len line up the one-footer he needed to shoot 68 and win at Riviera Country Club. Tears hit the table before the putt hit the hole. The bartender closed the doors and the PGA Tour bought drinks for the house. On his 220th try, Louis Mattiace's son had finally won a tournament.

Back in Los Angeles, Len held things together a little better. After rolling in the one-footer for a 15-under-par 269 total and a one-shot win over Scott McCarron, Brad Faxon and Rory Sabbatini, Mattiace signed his scorecard, consoled McCarron, who missed three six-footers on the final three holes, and answered questions with quiet professionalism. Then Rich Lerner from The Golf Channel asked about Len's mother, Joyce, who died of lung cancer in 1998. "Tight family," Mattiace said. "She's the reason I kept going." Asked when he finally recovered from losing his mom, Mattiace smiled through the tears and said, "What year is this?"

Mattiace offered kind words for McCarron, who led by one going into the final round, then extended the lead to three strokes with seven holes to play. McCarron missed a six-footer for par on the 16th and another six-footer for birdie on the 17th, followed by a three-putt from the fringe on the 18th for 71 to lose by one. "I wouldn't wish that on anyone," Mattiace said. "You don't want to see anyone make a mistake like that."

McCarron took it well. "That was my tournament to win," he said, "and I didn't get it done. Basically, I've got to laugh at myself." Referring to the decision to putt from the fringe at the 18th instead of chip, he said, "Maybe in hindsight a playoff was better. But if you try to chip it out of that stuff, there's no way to stop the ball on the green. I hit the ball great all week, but my short game let me down a little bit. I didn't putt that well."

Faxon had the same sentiments. Regarded as one of the best putters, Faxon missed birdie putts of eight and 12 feet on the last three holes. When another 12-footer for birdie on the 18th came up an inch short, Faxon bent over and pulled his hair. He finished with 68.

The champion putted just well enough. His only mistake on Sunday came at the 12th when he failed to save par from the greenside bunker. Other than that, his 68 seemed like it came from a man who had a cupboard full of trophies.

"You see guys winning out here for the first time, and you think how nice it would be to do that," Mattiace said. "There are times when you ask yourself whether you'll ever win. Growing up, this is all I ever wanted as a kid. Not winning is not so bad. There are so many good things out here. We have a nice life out here, even not winning. I'm very lucky. But winning, finally winning, it's a better feeling than I ever imagined. We live this every day. You can touch it, smell it. That last putt, a one-footer. I just didn't want to whiff it, top it or chunk it. And now that I've done it, I'd like to win more."

WGC Accenture Match Play—$5,500,000
Winner: Kevin Sutherland

Anything can happen in match play. That's the accepted adage. In four years as the PGA Tour's only match-play contest, the WGC Accenture Match Play has affirmed this. Anything and everything has happened, including victories by such long-shots as Steve Stricker, Jeff Maggert and, in 2002, Kevin Sutherland, the 62nd-ranked player in the field of 64.

With a 1-up victory over Scott McCarron, Sutherland became the fourth upset victor in as many years. Maggert, the inaugural winner, was ranked 24th when he defeated Andrew Magee, Darren Clarke was the 19th seed when he upset Tiger Woods, and Steve Stricker was ranked 55th when he and Pierre Fulke squared off in the final. Only five of the 16 different players who have made it to the finals of this single-elimination event have been ranked in the top 20. None other than Woods has been ranked in the top 10.

This time the three top-ranked players in the world exited Wednesday night. The 64th-ranked Australian Peter O'Malley, who was so confident that his week would be a short one he brought a shopping list from home, took down No. 1-ranked Woods. "I had a few things to do while I was here," O'Malley said. "The clothing is less expensive here than at home. My wife gave me a list of things she wanted me to pick up."

Phil Mickelson, the second-ranked player in the field, also made an early exit at the hands of John Cook. Cook became annoyed early in the match when Mickelson failed to concede any short putts, even though Cook was giving plenty of short ones to Mickelson. That changed on the 11th when Cook chose not to concede a two-footer. Mickelson missed the putt, lost the hole and ultimately the match 3 and 2. "That was the turning point," Cook said.

Sutherland came from behind to force extra holes in his opening match with David Duval. Two birdies on the last two holes, plus another birdie on the second extra hole moved Sutherland along to victory. "You go back to that match, and if I hadn't made those birdies I'm home on Wednesday and it looks like a bad week," Sutherland said. "To parlay that five days later into me winning the tournament is just amazing. To think about all the things that went right for me this week is amazing. And I mean everything went right."

After taking down Duval, Sutherland eliminated Paul McGinley 2 and 1 on Thursday, then surprised everyone again by having his way with Jim Furyk, winning his quarter-final match 4 and 3. Another 1-up victory in the semi-finals against reigning PGA champion David Toms moved Sutherland into the final.

McCarron had his own adventures through the bracket. A hole-in-one on Wednesday helped McCarron make quick work of Colin Montgomerie, whose scowl deepened with each passing hole. Not only was Montgomerie a little slow with his congratulatory handshake after McCarron's ace, the Scot intimated that he might call it quits in America. "I'm on my last legs over here," Montgomerie said. "I don't need this anymore. Why not concentrate on playing in Europe where people like and respect me? Why not be near my family?"

He got his wish on Wednesday afternoon when McCarron won 2 and 1. McCarron then beat Mike Weir 1 up to advance to the third round against Sergio Garcia. Garcia had beaten Lee Janzen 3 and 2, and taken his friend Charles Howell to the mat on the final hole. But McCarron eliminated the Spaniard 1 up. Then McCarron trounced Tom Lehman 3 and 2, moving to the semi-finals against Paul Azinger. That match went down to the wire. All-square on the 18th and a week removed from the mile of putts he missed to lose the Nissan Open at Riviera, McCarron ended things with a round-house 30-footer for birdie on the 18th. "Long putter or not, that putt was in all the way," Azinger said. Then, shaking his head at the prospect of a Sutherland-McCarron final, Azinger summed up the feelings of most in attendance. "People are going to be upset," he said. "But you only have to put up with it once a year."

The underdog 36-hole final turned out to be riveting golf once you got over the fact that neither of the guys participating had much television cache. Sutherland rolled in a putt on the final hole for par to win 1 up after McCarron caught a flier with his approach. For Sutherland, a winless seven-year veteran, the finish was the happiest moment of his life. He had to agree: Anything can happen in match play.

Touchstone Energy Tucson Open—$3,000,000
Winner: Ian Leggatt

With players like Heath Slocum, Spike McRoy, Kenneth Staton and David Peoples on the final-round leaderboard, the Conquistadors, organizers of the Touchstone Energy Tucson Open, were praying for any one with a name they recognized to step forward. Local favorite Andrew Magee was tied for second with one round to play, but he made bogeys early and often. So did Brandel Chamblee, who was only one shot back going into the final round. Chamblee and Magee both shot 75s and finished tied for 25th. The only hope the Conquistadors had left was Loren Roberts, and he almost came through.

Roberts started the final round tied with Chamblee and Magee, one stroke behind Peoples and Greg Kraft. Roberts made four straight birdies from the eighth through the 11th holes to gain a share of the lead with Canadian journeyman Ian Leggatt. Then Roberts' putter began to falter. He missed four birdie putts inside of 20 feet in the last six holes, and made one late bogey to finish with 66 and a 270 total. He tied for second place with Peoples, who shot 67.

They were two strokes shy of Leggatt, who tied his career low with a final-round 64 for a 268 total, 20 under par. The former speed skater was in shock when asked what the victory meant. "It hasn't sunk in yet," Leggatt said. "I'll be able to fix my schedule now. We're expecting a baby in May, and with my exempt situation, I can maybe take two or three weeks off."

A 10-year tour regular in South Africa, Asia, Canada and Australia, Leggatt had been on and off the U.S. PGA Tour since the mid-1990s. He had to qualify again after finishing 133rd on the 2001 money list. Rather than wilt under the Sunday pressure, Leggatt came through like a seasoned winner, getting up-and-down from a greenside bunker for birdie at the 17th and making another spectacular save from a bunker at the 18th for par to secure the victory.

"My stats might not reflect it," Leggett said, "but I've always been a pretty good bunker player." He was also a "pretty good" speed skater as a teenager. "But it wasn't an Olympic sport back then," he said. "It was a bit of a dead end. It's not a sport you do for the rest of your life."

With their new champion — the third player in a row to call Tucson his first career win — the Conquistadors were left, once again, to explain how tough it is to attract attention and a quality field to an event that is contested the same week as the WGC Accenture Match Play. Fortunately for them, many of the players came to their defense.

"There's incredible talent all the way down the line," said Fred Funk, who finished tied for fourth with Staton at 271. "I played with Steve Jones, a U.S. Open winner. Craig Stadler's here. He's a Masters champion. You have a lot of great players here, a lot of guys who are unbelievably good, guys you're going to hear about. The winning score, whether Tiger Woods is here or not, would be the same because anybody can get hot. Obviously the depth is not as strong, but the quality of the golf is there."

Leggatt proved that. He shot 68, 71 and 65 before closing with the 64. "I was playing well around the world," he said. "I was making money and never in dire straits where I was dead broke. I had confidence in my game. My problem was that I couldn't get by the second stage of tour school. When I finally did, I felt I was on my way."

Genuity Championship—$4,700,000
Winner: Ernie Els

It had to be like a recurring nightmare. There Ernie Els stood with an eight-stroke lead. And there was Tiger Woods, charging again. The last time this scenario materialized Els was on the short end of the 1998 Johnnie Walker Classic in Thailand, where an eight-stroke lead wasn't enough. This time, at Doral's Genuity Championship, a supposed second-tier event viewed as a warm-up for events like The Players Championship and the Masters, Els found himself in the fight of his career, leading by eight with 18 to play, then watching as Woods methodically dismantled that lead with birdie after birdie.

Els ultimately prevailed, but not without conjuring up the memories of the loss in Thailand and the other runner-up finishes he's been forced to accept when Woods is in the field. "I used to be a great front-runner," Els said. "Then this little voice started coming into my head, this little guy inside me that made me defensive, almost scared. Things that happened today, it might have gone the other way if I had listened and thought negatively. It isn't a question of motivation. It's attitude. After all, if you get down, it's not because you don't want it or don't care. But I told that little guy today, let's be friends."

The conversation worked, and Woods' putter ran cold after narrowly missing an eagle at the par-five 12th that would have pulled him into a tie for the lead. He parred the final six holes for 66, missing several putts inside 15 feet in the process, for a 15-under-par 273 total. Els had two 66s on his card, one on Thursday to give him the first-round lead and the second on Saturday when the winds exceeded 30 miles an hour. That second 66 (the lowest score of the day by three) gave Els his eight-shot cushion.

Els tried to put the negative thoughts behind him. A few bad breaks in the early going on Sunday — a downhill lie from the back bunker on the sixth, a squirting lie from the second cut of rough on the eighth, a downhill lie in the thick rough beside the green on the 10th and a sidehill lie with his feet in the sand on the 14th — had Els wondering if he were somehow cursed. "This would have been a bitter pill to swallow if I had lost," he said.

But Els didn't lose. Pars on the final two holes for 72 were good enough for a 271 total and a two-stroke victory. "Ernie earned it," Woods said after failing to maintain his charge through the final six holes. "But my game is progressing."

That's what scares Els and the rest of the players on tour. "I can't ever get to Tiger's level of intensity," Els said. "But if we're going to be going at each other for the next 10 years, and I hope we do, I can try to get closer to his level, and I think I am. That's why the way this turned out might have been a blessing in disguise, the way I hung in there. It was not a comfortable feeling gradually losing that big lead, but if there's going to be a rivalry, it can't have the same result every time, can it?"

Els smiled at that last comment, knowing he might have slipped by with a win even though he didn't have his best game. Then he offered a closing comment on the man he finally beat. "I tell you, that guy is special," Els said. "Tiger is special."

Honda Classic—$3,500,000
Winner: Matt Kuchar

It took 17 weeks and a lot of second guessing, but Matt Kuchar finally won his first professional event at the Honda Classic. The 1997 U.S. Amateur champion, who turned down millions in endorsements in order to stay in college at Georgia Tech, shot a final-round 66 in a hot Coral Springs, Florida, for a two-stroke win over Brad Faxon and Joey Sindelar.

"I wasn't sure it would happen as soon as it did," Kuchar said. "I knew it would happen. I always dreamed and knew that I would win, and that I would win a lot, but I wasn't sure that it would happen this soon. What a great feeling! To come out on top, to play all week and to come out as a champion. Wow. It hasn't happened to me a whole lot, so the times it does, it's outstanding."

Kuchar was the darling of amateur golf after winning his U.S. Amateur title. In his first trip to the Masters, he delighted the galleries by remaining on the leaderboard through much of the weekend. He finished tied for 21st and earned a return trip. He then stunned everyone with an equally impressive U.S. Open performance where he was only two shots off the lead on Saturday. Kuchar finished a respectable 14th at The Olympic Club, and everyone assumed his days as an amateur were over. But he passed up the endorsement opportunities to remain in college, even though he never won another title as an amateur.

"I've always known it was the right decision," he said. But even after taking a job as an investment banker, Kuchar longed for the week-in and week-out competition of the tour. "I wanted nothing more than to be out there," he said. "I needed to go full time, see if I could be around with the best players in the world. I was happy to make something special out of something that maybe wasn't. That's cool."

He proved he could in Florida. Trailing Sindelar by two strokes going into the final round, Kuchar saw his deficit grow to four through nine holes. Then he remembered the advice his college coach, Bruce Heppler, gave him before teeing off on Sunday. "Go play golf," Heppler said. "Add it up at the end, and if you win, that's great." Kuchar rallied with four consecutive birdies on the second nine. He gained a share of the lead with a 12-footer on the par-four 13th, then took the lone spot atop the leaderboard with a tap-in birdie on the par-five 14th. Another birdie at the par-five 16th extended the lead to two, and a solid six-footer to save par on the 18th sealed the win.

"When that putt dropped, the rush of excitement I felt, I haven't felt that since the U.S. Amateur," he said. That putt, Kuchar's 23rd of the day and his eighth in the final eight holes, was good enough for a second consecutive score of 66, a 19-under-par 269 total, a $630,000 winner's check and the praise of his fellow competitors. "It's going to be a big day for him," Sindelar said. "It's going to change his golf life. You think of what he's been through, being Mr. Everything there for a couple of years. I'm sure it was painful for him to go through that."

After the interviews were over and the sun had long since set, Kuchar picked up a phone message in the locker room from Greg Norman. "Congratulations," the note said. "Welcome to the club. It's about bloody time."

Bay Hill Invitational—$4,000,000
Winner: Tiger Woods

With records mounting so fast it's almost impossible to keep track, Tiger Woods added another to his long list when he completed the "triple-triple," becoming the first player to win three different PGA Tour events three times in a row. This feat was accomplished with a four-stroke victory at the Bay Hill Invitational. Woods added Arnold Palmer's tournament to the hat trick, matching his three-peat records at Jack Nicklaus' Memorial Tournament and the WGC NEC Invitational.

This time Woods not only set another record, he gave an object lesson in why he's the best player in the world. After limping in with a 74 Saturday, Woods carried a one-shot lead over Len Mattiace into the final round. Fourteen players, including Phil Mickelson, Sergio Garcia, Vijay Singh and Ernie Els, were within three strokes. "There were so many guys with a chance to win," Woods said. "A lot of different things could have happened."

What did happen was instructive. Woods continued to struggle with his control, hitting his tee shot in the bunker on the sixth hole and his approach shot from there into the water fronting the green. He walked away with bogey at the same time Mickelson was rolling in a 25-footer for birdie up ahead at the eighth. Another 10-footer for birdie by Mickelson at the 10th gave him the lead. Woods limped along, but holed an eight-footer for par on the eighth to remain within two shots.

Woods regained the lead when he got up-and-down for birdie at the par-five 12th at the same time Mickelson flubbed a chip and made bogey from behind the green at the 14th. Then Mickelson made a decision that would hound him for weeks. After pulling his drive into the trees right of the 16th fairway, Mickelson chose to try for the green on the par-five hole, even though he had a 180-yard carry over water to a hard green with a flagstick on the front. Mickelson also had a questionable lie with trees all around him.

"It wasn't easy, but it wasn't impossible," Mickelson said. "I didn't have a shot back to the fairway," he said, although many questioned that conclusion. "I would have loved to pitch out, but I didn't have a shot. More than likely it was going to get stuck short in the high grass. The only shot I felt I had was to go at the green. That was the only opening, to go right at the majority of the trees and try to put it on the back part of the green or in the back bunker. Rather than be in the rough and have a shot over water I couldn't stop, I went for the green. I had to catch it a little thin to get underneath the branches. I caught it a little too thin. I don't feel like the play was bad. I just didn't execute it."

Mickelson's shot never had a chance. It squirted left and skipped off the water once before disappearing, along with his chances. He finished with three bogeys to shoot 71 for a 280 total. That tied him for third place with Mattiace, Rocco Mediate and John Huston.

A day before, while in the throes of his 74, Woods pushed his tee shot on the 16th into a similar spot. When asked what distance he had to the pin, Woods said, "I didn't get a number. You can't hit the green from there." He pitched out and made par on Saturday.

On Sunday Woods pulled his tee shot on the 16th, and once again, he didn't get a number to the pin. He played his second shot to the 100-yard marker, then hit wedge over the water to eight feet. When the putt for birdie fell in, Woods had a commanding lead he wouldn't relinquish.

Woods finished with two pars for 69, a 13-under-par 275 total, and a four-shot margin over Michael Campbell, who chipped in for birdie at the 18th to shoot 71 for a 279 total. "It was quite a fight out there," Woods said. "I tried to hang in there and give myself a lot of looks at birdie and not make any bogeys. You needed to play smart, and I was able to do that."

The Players Championship—$6,000,000
Winner: Craig Perks

See Chapter 6.

Shell Houston Open—$4,000,000
Winner: Vijay Singh

Despite stacking up top-10 finishes like buckets of range balls, Vijay Singh, the hardest working man in golf, arrived in Houston, Texas, a little annoyed at the fact that he hadn't won in America since the 2000 Masters. There were back-to-back 2001 wins in Singapore and Malaysia, and his 14 runner-up finishes on the PGA Tour in 2001 led the league, beating Phil Mickelson by one and Tiger Woods by five. Singh also finished fourth in earnings in 2001. But a victory eluded him and, with his 40th birthday and another trip to Augusta looming, Singh wanted to remedy that problem.

"To say that just because you reach a certain age you can't compete, I don't believe that," Singh said after shooting a tournament record 22-under-par 266 total and running away with the Shell Houston Open by six strokes. "That's just an excuse. Maybe it comes from laziness, I don't know. But with the equipment now, and all the progress that's been made in the areas of nutrition and fitness, of course you can keep up with these kids if you put your mind to it. You have to make that commitment, though, because it's that tough on the PGA Tour. It's tougher every year."

Singh put his mind to it and racked up an impressive victory as a reward. "I still love what I do out here," Singh said after a final-round 68 moved him well ahead of second-place finisher Darren Clarke, who shot 71 for a 272 total. "When I was 37," Singh said, "I decided if I wanted to keep doing it, I would work at least as hard each year on my game, and twice as hard each year as I did the previous year on my conditioning. If some guys want to go the other way, to lie around and relax, that's fine."

After blasting a bunker shot into the hole for birdie on the 16th on Friday, Singh took the lead at The Woodlands and never let go. When the dust settled, Singh had carded 23 birdies and only two bogeys, the last coming on the 14th hole on Saturday. He cruised in on Sunday, never letting Clarke within three shots of his lead. The lead extended to five strokes when Singh barely missed an eagle putt at the 15th and tapped in for birdie while Clarke bogeyed the 17th. It ended with a six-shot margin of victory; the biggest margin since Jackie Burke won in Houston by six in 1952. The total score of 266 shattered the 22-year-old record of 18-under-par 270 held by Curtis Strange.

"You always get antsy when you don't win," Singh said. "It's just a matter of how you handle it. Last year I got a little antsy, and this year I just decided to concentrate on playing. Today I wanted to play a solid round of golf, and that's what I did. It had been almost two years. I was wondering when the next one would come. This one couldn't be at a better time, two weeks before the Masters."

Another Masters champion, Jose Maria Olazabal, showed his game was in shape for a return trip to Augusta when he shot a closing 70 for a 273 total and sole possession of third place, two shots clear of Jay Haas and Shigeki Maruyama. It was Olazabal's sixth top-10 finish of the season.

BellSouth Classic—$3,800,000
Winner: Retief Goosen

It was hard to tell which was the bigger story at the BellSouth Classic: Retief Goosen grinding his way to another victory or Phil Mickelson losing again. There was no doubt that Goosen added an exclamation point to his worldwide performance of the previous 10 months, starting with his U.S. Open win and including a European Order of Merit title. His final-round 70 for a 272 total was a textbook example of posting solid numbers and letting the field take its best shot. In the end, it was good enough for a four-stroke victory over Jesper Parnevik and a five-shot margin over Mickelson.

"I think it's great coming here and winning again the States," Goosen said as he hoisted his sixth trophy in his last 24 events. "It's really a confidence builder for me. People will know me a little better now."

Playing in the final pairing with Mickelson, Goosen started with a two-stroke lead and promptly went bogey, double bogey. At the fourth tee Goosen trailed Mickelson by two, and it looked as if Mickelson, the world's No. 2 player, would enter the Masters with a come-from-behind victory. But over the next four holes, Goosen holed a wedge shot for an eagle at the fourth, saved par from a buried lie in the fairway bunker at the fifth, made a solid birdie at the sixth and saved par from the pine straw at the seventh. When Mickelson three-putted for bogey on the eighth, the tournament was effectively over. Goosen played the final 15 holes in five under par.

Mickelson looked like the player to beat throughout most of the week. He led on Thursday with an error-free 65, then retained a share of the lead on Friday after a 68 left him tied with Steve Elkington. Two three-putt greens on the second nine on Friday were a bad omen. On Saturday, he played flawless golf on the first nine, then bogeyed the par-five 10th. After driving the green on the par-four 13th, Mickelson rolled his first putt to within three feet. He then lipped out his second and third putts. His fourth putt found the hole, and Mickelson walked away with a bogey.

"Phil has got to be more patient," Elkington said after witnessing the spectacle. "That's how you win majors."

"The greens were very greasy," Mickelson said in explaining what happened. "It's hard to give the ball enough steam to hold its line without risking it running eight feet by. I had made them all through the round up to that point and went ahead and gave it an aggressive roll rather than trying to trickle it in."

When Mickelson's second shot on the par-five 18th found the water on Sunday, many were left to wonder if the tournament that was supposed to be a warm-up for the Masters had somehow foretold the outcome we could expect one week later.

Masters Tournament—$5,000,000
Winner: Tiger Woods

See Chapter 2.

WorldCom Classic—$4,000,000
Winner: Justin Leonard

No one could remember how long it had been since a PGA Tour player won without making a birdie on the final day. "When you get to Walter Hagen let me know," Justin Leonard said as the search continued into the night and long after Leonard and his new bride, Amanda, were on their way back to Dallas with the WorldCom Classic trophy stored with the luggage and the tartan winner's jacket hanging neatly in the cabin.

Leonard was believed to be the first to win the post-Masters party-turned-golf-tournament at Hilton Head Island, South Carolina, or any other PGA Tour event for that matter, without a single birdie on the final day. Fortunately, he made just enough birdies in the three previous days to eke out a victory. Equally fortunate was the fact that he said, "Yes, dear," when Amanda asked him to play at Hilton Head so she could enjoy the yachts and the parties instead of going back to Texas. "It's like spring break this week after final exams last week at the Masters," he said.

Maybe it was the parties at the Quarterdeck, a local haunt beneath the lighthouse and overlooking the harbor that did it, but Leonard's previous record at Harbour Town smelled like day-old fish dredged from the bottom of the boats that lined Calibogue Sound. Despite the fact the golf course seemed well-suited for his shotmaking, Leonard's previous best finish had been a tie for 30th.

That all changed this time around. With early rounds of 67, 64 and 66, Leonard set a 54-hole scoring record and carried a two-shot lead into the final round. When Cameron Beckman, the man closest to Leonard at the end of the third round, made double bogey on the third hole, the lead was four with 15 holes to play. Leonard seemed to be coasting toward victory.

But the cruise control got stuck on the way to victory circle. Birdies that had come by the oyster-bucket-full on Thursday, Friday and Saturday were nowhere to be found on Sunday. When the wind picked up, Leonard found himself struggling to stay ahead. He made 12 straight pars from some unseemly locations before finally hitting the wall literally on the 13th. There, after draining par putts of 15, 12 and 30 feet, Leonard ran out of luck when his ball ricocheted off one of Pete Dye's many retaining walls guarding the small greens at Harbour Town. Leonard made bogey. He made another at the 14th when a two-foot putt hit the lip and spun out. "I was mad at myself when I missed that putt," he said.

Meanwhile, Buy.com Tour graduate Heath Slocum came to play in the final round. Armed with a new belly putter, Slocum birdied the fifth, sixth and 12th holes to pull within one stroke. When he rammed home a birdie putt at the 14th, he shared the lead. Ten minutes later, when Leonard missed his short putt, Slocum found himself alone atop the leaderboard.

The sensation didn't last long. With Leonard returning to his par-making form, Slocum pulled his tee shot in the waste bunker that lines the 16th fairway. His next shot stayed in the bunker, and his third shot rolled 40 feet past. Three putts and one double bogey later, Slocum was back in second place, where he finished. "I don't think it was the pressure," he said. "I stepped up there and committed to my target. I don't miss it left often, but I did there. Except for the 16th I played extremely well. I'm pleased with how I played."

Phil Mickelson had another typical week, playing brilliantly for two days and setting a 36-hole scoring record, then shooting 72 and 71 on the weekend to finish alone in third at 272, one better than Bernhard Langer.

Leonard played solidly on the final three holes, making pars each step of the way for a final-round 73, a 270 total, and the distinction of being the first man since the PGA Tour began keeping statistics in 1983 to win without a birdie in the final round. "I just hit some good shots and played really solid those last three holes," he said. Not good enough to make birdies, just good enough to win.

Greater Greensboro Chrysler Classic—$3,800,000
Winner: Rocco Mediate

At least there's no pollen in Phoenix. That's what Mark Calcavecchia was saying on Sunday in Greensboro, North Carolina, when he found himself transported back to his last victory, the 2001 Phoenix Open where he shot a PGA Tour-record 256 total. The victim of Calcavecchia's birdie barrage that week was Rocco Mediate, who played in the final group and finished alone in second place eight shots back. "Not many people can say that they got beat by the lowest score in history," Mediate said. "I did. That's what happened in Phoenix."

In the Greater Greensboro Chrysler Classic 14 months later, the two players found themselves paired again, only this time the conditions and the outcome were different. While Mediate, who has never suffered from allergies, had no problem with the pollen, Calcavecchia was miserable. "My eyes were so fogged over from sneezing and itching and watering that I couldn't even see," Calcavecchia said.

Those were not the words of a winner. Calcavecchia, who led after the first two rounds with scores of 65 and 69, trailed Mediate by two when the final round began. He shot even-par 72 between sneezing fits on Sunday, and lost to Mediate by three strokes. "Aside from the pollen and those excuses, Rocco played great," Calcavecchia said. "He drove it great, and on the three fairways he missed he made two pars and a birdie. I was pretty much toast."

A birdie on the second hole moved Calcavecchia within a shot, and after another birdie from five feet on the fourth, while Mediate was making bogey from the front fringe, the two were tied. Four holes later it was all but over. Calcavecchia missed his tee shot left on the fifth, then missed the green and failed to get up and down. Mediate also missed the fairway, but he caught a great lie and hit an eight iron to 10 feet and made birdie. With his two-shot lead restored, Mediate played aggressively off the tee on the sixth and made another birdie when his wedge approach rolled to within three feet. Calcavecchia, who played an iron off the tee, made par and fell three behind. Then on the seventh, Calcavecchia yanked his tee shot while in the throes of a sneezing fit. "All that pollen nearly killed me," he said. He recovered and had a putt for par, which he missed as a woman in the gallery began sneezing in his backstroke.

It was that kind of week for Calcavecchia, who tied a 13-year-old PGA Tour record for fewest putts in a tournament with 93. He shot a closing 72 for a 275 total, while Mediate bettered par by a shot, 71, for an aggregate 272 and his first win since the 2000 Buick Open. "Today it was just survival," Mediate said. "I just kept going forward and that's what's most satisfying to me. Overall the game's good, but I needed everything today."

"The better player won today," Calcavecchia said. "I'll look at it that way and sit back and say I made a bunch of miraculous saves around the greens. Finishing second isn't too bad."

Compaq Classic of New Orleans—$4,500,000
Winner: K.J. Choi

It seemed ironic that on a week when chefs were blackening redfish on the range and steaming etouffee in the locker room, the winner of the Compaq Classic of New Orleans spent the week searching for Korean kimchee. K.J. Choi became the first Korean to win a PGA Tour event when he shot five-under-par 67 in the sweltering Louisiana heat for a 271 total. That was four strokes better than Geoff Ogilvy and Dudley Hart, and five clear of John Cook, Chris DiMarco, Mike Sposa and Dan Forsman.

The fact that Choi bogeyed the final hole was academic. He had this one in hand early, and removed all doubt with two of the best pressure shots anyone can remember. The first came on the 16th hole when Choi hit a wedge from 124 yards that hung on the lip of the hole for a tap-in birdie. Then he chipped in for another birdie at the difficult 17th to move to 18 under par, five clear of his nearest competitor. The final bogey was meaningless.

"This is a special win," said Choi, who speaks no English, through a translator. "When I first came to America in 2000, I had a 10-year plan. First was to keep my card so that every year I would have a chance to win. Then was the goal of winning. This win may seem easy, but it was very strategically laid out, although it came sooner than expected."

Forsman led with 65 after the first day. Choi, who shot 68 on Thursday, came back with a 65 of his own on Friday to take a one-shot lead into the weekend. The round was capped by one of the most impressive shots of the week that wasn't the wedge Choi hit on Sunday. With the wind howling, Choi hit a four iron from 198 yards to within six inches on the difficult par-four 18th.

A 71 in difficult conditions on Saturday gave Choi a one-shot advantage over Bryce Molder and John Rollins. When asked how he would reflect on leading his first PGA Tour event with one round to play, a smiling Choi said, "Tonight I will pray, I will eat well, I will sing some religious songs (Choi is a Baptist) and I will have a good sleep."

All those things paid off. With the field making birdies all around him, Choi held himself together remarkably well. Phil Mickelson, who started the day six shots back, birdied four of his first six holes to pull within two shots before Choi took his first swing. But Mickelson played the final nine in even par and faded. Cook, David Toms and Mike Sposa shot 31s on the front to pull within a couple of shots of Choi at various times during the round, and Hart and DiMarco went out in 32.

At varying times during his first nine holes, Choi had 11 players within three shots of his lead. Choi's 34 on the first nine kept all comers at bay, and his 33 on the second nine slammed the door. When the shot on the 16th almost found the hole, Choi said, "I felt I had the tournament under control." Indeed he did.

Verizon Byron Nelson Classic—$4,800,000
Winner: Shigeki Maruyama

One look at Shigeki Maruyama's face will tell you how he stands and what kind of shot he's just hit. Nothing is left to the imagination. At the Verizon Byron Nelson Classic, leading Ernie Els by four strokes going into the final round, Maruyama ran the gambit. There was the happy Maruyama, the one who held it together pretty well for 10 holes until Tiger Woods started making a charge; the concerned Maruyama, who chewed his tongue and furrowed his brow; the shocked Maruyama, who stood wide-eyed with his mouth agape as a kid from Oregon named Ben Crane made birdie after birdie to pull to within two; and the relieved Maruyama, who put his hand on his chest and broke out in an ear-to-ear grin when the final putt for par fell on the 18th and the Japanese star realized he had his second career PGA Tour victory.

"I wish I could speak more English," Maruyama said through a translator after closing with 68 for a 266 total and a two-stroke win over Crane. "I could make you all laugh harder."

Maruyama wasn't laughing when his game abandoned him in the middle of the final round. Clinging to a three-shot lead, he pulled a short approach on the 11th into the water and walked away with a bogey on the second easiest hole on the course. Then he missed the green at the 12th and had to make a 12-footer for par. His birdie putt at the 13th missed the hole by four feet, and he had to make a slippery sidehill shot to save par. At that point, he heard the roars from up ahead and checked the scoreboard to see what had happened. It was Woods, who had made three birdies in a row to pull within four shots of the lead.

"I almost fell over," Maruyama said. He salvaged par at the 14th after missing yet another green, then regrouped, hitting the middle of the greens at the 15th and 16th to keep his lead intact.

Woods ran out of holes, closing with two pars to shoot 65 and finish third at 270. Els wasn't making any moves, and David Toms, who shot 66, started too far back. That left Crane, a two-time Buy.com Tour winner who was so new to the scene that he had to introduce himself to Els when the two found themselves paired on Sunday.

Crane birdied the 16th to pull within three shots of the lead and into sole possession of second place. He would have been happy to finish there until a curling 25-footer for birdie at the par-three 17th found the hole on its last turn. Crane leapt in the air and raised his hands and eyes to the sky while Maruyama watched in stunned silence on the tee. "When I saw Ben make that putt on 17, I nearly fainted," Maruyama said.

He came even closer to fainting after his own tee shot at the 17th headed straight for the bank and looked destined for the water. Miraculously, the ball stayed on the bank in the rough, and Maruyama, who had displayed a deft touch all day, got up and down for the most important par of the tournament.

Up ahead Crane was too pumped up to swing on the 18th tee. He walked faster than normal, picked a line quicker than at any other time in the previous two hours, and swung so hard Els was amazed that his playing partner's shoes didn't fly off. The ball soared right into the trees. Crane punched out, then almost holed a wedge shot. "I didn't know Shigeki was leading," Crane said. "I don't look at boards, so I obviously couldn't think about putting the heat on him."

He applied the pressure anyway, making a gutsy par at the last hole for 65 and a 268 total. But Maruyama hung tough, driving the ball in the fairway and finding the center of the green. With Byron and Peggy Nelson watching from their traditional spot behind the final green, Maruyama calmly two-putted, placed his hand over his heart and broke into his familiar smile.

Later that night he donned a cowboy hat and hoisted his son Sean into his arms while his wife, Mizuho, brushed moisture from her eyes. Some moments require no translation.

MasterCard Colonial—$4,300,000
Winner: Nick Price

Anyone caught in a time capsule for the last 10 years might have believed they hadn't missed much if they woke up and saw the Sunday leaderboard at the MasterCard Colonial. There was Nick Price, the No. 1 player in the world and a dominant force a decade ago, with a commanding four-shot lead in Ft. Worth, Texas. Not far down the list was Tom Watson, a major champion with plenty of game left in the early 1990s.

But this wasn't 1992. It was 2002. Tom Watson was riding golf carts every week on the Senior PGA Tour and Nick Price was stuck in the middle of that dearth between a player's 40th birthday and the golden parachute that comes at age 50. Price was 45 and four years removed from his last PGA Tour victory when he teed off at Colonial. "I've always been blessed with desire," Price said. "But there have been moments of doubt."

Those doubts dissipated when Price shot 69 and 65 in the first two rounds. He followed it up with 66 on Saturday to take a five-stroke lead over Kenny Perry into the final round.

Watson, the oldest man ever to win the Colonial title at age 48, also shot 66 on Saturday, thrilling the crowds and rekindling a little confidence and desire. At 52 years old, he entered the final round six stroke back. "I figured I needed a 65 to win," Watson said. "It turned out that wouldn't have been good enough, but it was fun. I feel like I can play with the kids on this course, where you don't have to hit driver off every tee, and where I have 24 years of experience. I have a lot of good memories here."

Watson shot 69 on Sunday and finished alone in seventh place. His magic number of 65 would have left him alone in second, four shots from catching Price. That's because Price played like he was young again, shaping shots and making putts in the same fashion that propelled him to the top spot in the world. Before this week, Price was noted as the answer to a trivia question: Who was the last player before Tiger Woods to win two major championships in a row? It was Price, who won the British Open and the PGA Championship in 1994. He also won the Colonial in 1994. Those memories came flooding back as he teed off on Sunday with a commanding lead.

"I've had six or seven chances to win in the last two years, and for some rhyme or reason something always seemed to go wrong," he said. "I've certainly tossed a few away."

For a few fleeting moments he thought this might be another of those throwaway days. Birdies on the first and second holes increased his lead, then he endured a little slippage, hitting his first putt on the fifth hole on a heartbeat and running it eight feet past the hole, leading to a bogey. He made another bogey at the sixth when his tee shot plugged in the face of a bunker. When his tee shot on the seventh sailed right into the rough, Price decided this was the defining moment of his 40s. He marched down the fairway and had a little chat with himself. "I said, 'I'm not going to make any more mistakes,'" he said. "'That's it. I'm just going to make birdies and pars.' And I did. Sometimes you just reach deep down."

He recovered on the seventh and played the eighth, ninth and 10th holes with solid pars. "Then I made a 35-footer for birdie on 11, and I figured maybe this is my day," Price said. He followed that bomb with birdies on the 12th and 14th to extend his lead to five. That's where it remained. Price finished with 67 for a 267 total. Perry shot 67 to finish tied for second with David Toms at 272.

"It feels like it's been 10 years," Price said. "I didn't think this day was going to come. That self-doubt has been cast away now. This one I didn't really expect."

Memorial Tournament—$4,500,000
Winner: Jim Furyk

The biggest news out of Dublin, Ohio, was that 12 players were within three strokes of the lead with nine holes to play at the Memorial Tournament and none of them were named Tiger Woods. The three-time defending champion shot 66, but his earlier lackluster rounds of 74, 70 and 72 ruled out any chance of making it four in a row. Woods finished tied for 22nd place.

With Woods out of contention, there was no shortage of players ready to take over the tournament he had won the previous three years. Bob Tway and Stewart Cink were two of them. Tway shot 65, 71 and 68, while Cink regrouped from a early-season slump to shoot 66, 70 and 69 for a share of the lead. Shigeki Maruyama was three strokes back after recovering from an opening 74 with rounds of 66 and 67, leaving him tied with Ernie Els going into the final round. John Cook was four off the pace, while Jim Furyk was five shots back.

When Cink and Tway struggled, the field opened up. It was a birdie race to the finish. David Duval, who struggled to make the cut after an opening 75 and started the day seven shots back, came through with a blistering run that gave him an early share of the lead. He hit a three wood to tap-in range for eagle on the fifth, then rolled in a 20-footer for birdie on the 12th to reach seven under for his round. Three holes of missed opportunities, including a three-putt bogey at the 13th, a pushed iron shot at the 14th and a failed up-and-down for birdie at the par-five 15th, killed Duval's rally. He finished with 66 for a tie for fourth place and his first top-10 finish of the year.

Winless 10-year veteran David Peoples also sniffed the top of the leaderboard for a few moments after a birdie at the 12th, but a bogey at the 14th and missed birdie chances dropped Peoples into a tie for second with John Cook at 276.

Harrison Frazar was the next player to mount a charge. Like Duval, he was coming off a crippling round of 75 (Frazar's came in the third round), and with nothing to lose, he attacked the pins early. With four birdies in his first five holes on the second nine, Frazar took a share of the lead. He had a chance to take the outright lead on the par-five 15th, but he missed an 18-inch putt. Frazar never recovered. A closing round of 67 for a 277 total earned him a share of fourth with Maruyama, Vijay Singh, Duval and Tway.

The only player who could mount a sustained charge was Furyk, who let his wedge do most of the talking. After pulling a four wood into the water on the par-five fifth hole, Furyk made a great save, his second par save of the day. That set the tone for the remainder of his round. On the 12th hole, after missing the green long, Furyk hit a downhill curling chip that rattled the pin and fell in for birdie. Three holes later he did it again, this time holing a bunker shot for eagle to take the lead. His closing 65 and 274 total were good enough for a two-stroke victory over Cook and Peoples.

"I started looking at the leaderboard and realized it was a close race," Furyk said. "I got from one down to three up pretty quickly. It was pretty exciting." He was also pretty fortunate. Neither of his holed wedge shots trickled into the edge of the hole. "Both those balls weren't exactly dying in the hole," he said. "They hit the pin pretty hard. But you need some breaks to win golf tournaments."

Kemper Insurance Open—$3,600,000
Winner: Bob Estes

The Kemper Insurance Open would have loved to have Tiger Woods, David Duval and Phil Mickelson, but all three, along with Sergio Garcia, Vijay Singh, Ernie Els, David Duval and David Toms, chose to skip the week in suburban Washington, D.C. Even Jim Furyk took a pass.

"It's difficult to get guys to come and play here," said Fred Couples, who made one his limited appearances of the year at the TPC of Avenel. "Part of it is that it's a tough part of the schedule. I know a lot of guys play the two events in Texas, play the Memorial, take this week off, and then play Westchester next week to get geared up for the U.S. Open. And another part is that guys don't like the golf course. It was rock hard the first couple of years we played here, and I think that left a bad taste in some guys' mouths."

That wasn't a problem when the tournament was held across the street at Congressional Country Club, site of the 1997 U.S. Open. In those days the Kemper, not the Buick Classic at Westchester, was the warm-up event for the U.S. Open. Because of the move to a questionable golf course with one hole (the 13th) that Nick Price describes as "the worst par-five on the planet," the field at the Kemper is mostly relegated to the lesser lights.

"It's been a real struggle, but that's how it is out here when you have a great field every week," the eventual winner, Bob Estes, said. "Whether it's Tiger or Phil or David Duval or anyone else, you always have to play good to beat these guys." All the guys Estes mentioned were not there. One of the few players with any star power to grace the grounds at Avenel was Greg Norman, who, playing on his seventh sponsor's exemption of the season, shot 67 and 65 and took a one-shot lead into the weekend. "I don't feel 47 years old," Norman said. "And I certainly still think I can win. If I didn't, I wouldn't be out here."

Norman might not have felt 47, but he played like it on the weekend, shooting 74 and 73 to finish tied for 13th place. That left Bob Burns and Estes, two utilitarian pros with solid games. Tied at the top at 10-under-par 203 with 18 holes to play, they marched out in the hopes of making a game of it. One birdie on the "worst par-five on the planet" and 17 pars later, Estes hoisted the trophy and collected the $648,000 first-place check.

Rich Beem made a charge at the lead, getting to 11 under par and sharing the top spot with Estes through 16 holes. A bogey at the par-three 17th dropped Beem back to two under on his round and 10 under for the week. That's where he finished, at 274, alone in second place. Burns finished one over on his round and tied with Steve Elkington for third at 275, while Jonathan Kaye and Justin Leonard, one of only three players in the top-10 on the money list to play the Kemper, tied for fifth at 276.

Buick Classic—$3,500,000
Winner: Chris Smith

For some, the Buick Classic was a warm-up week, a chance to get accustomed to New York temperatures and fine-tune their games before traveling 30 miles south to Long Island for the U.S. Open. As Stewart Cink put it, "The only way to prepare for competitive golf is to play competitive golf." But for Chris Smith, this was it. Smith wouldn't be going to Bethpage since he failed to qualify for the U.S. Open. This, his sixth tournament in a row, was all he had left.

He made the most of it. With rounds of 66, 69, 67 and a closing one-under-par 70, the 33-year-old Smith picked up his first PGA Tour victory by two strokes over David Gossett, Pat Perez and Loren Roberts. "It's an awesome feeling," Smith said. "I've struggled all year, so this is great."

Smith missed the cut in the first three events of his six-in-a-row stretch, then finished tied for 56th in the Memorial Tournament before finding the magic with his putter and carding a seventh-place finish at the Kemper Insurance Open. "The funny thing is, I feel like I've played better and haven't gotten the job done," Smith said.

Not getting the job done had nothing to do with Smith's length. He entered the week tied for fifth place in driving distance and holds the record for the longest drive ever hit in a PGA Tour competition (427 yards in the 1999 Honda Classic). On Sunday at Westchester he hit a 290-yard five wood on the 11th hole over water. He hit only four of 14 fairways in the final round, the biggest one coming at the par-four 15th when he drove it 305 yards around the dogleg. His eight iron stopped 12 feet from the hole, and he rolled in his 18th birdie of the week to take a one-shot lead.

Perez, known best for his collapse at the 2002 AT&T Pebble Beach National Pro-Am, chipped in from 20 feet for a birdie on the 16th to reach 11 under and draw even with Smith. Perez's stint atop the leaderboard was short-lived. He three-putted from seven feet on the 17th to fall one back. When Smith rolled in a 10-footer for birdie at the 16th, the lead was two. That's where it ended. Smith finished with two pars for a closing round of 70 and a 272 total. Perez, who couldn't stop complaining about the pin locations on Sunday — "Ludicrous," he said. "I can't believe where they put the pins. There's no way I should have lost this tournament." — finished with 70 for a 274 total. That tied Perez with Gossett, who made six birdies and six bogeys on Sunday. "I had too many unforced errors," the 23-year-old said. "Still, I'm making progress, especially in my putting. That's what had been holding me back. I'm pleased with myself that I didn't throw in the towel."

So is Smith, who became the first Buy.com Tour player to earn a battle-field promotion, only to lose his card and be back in the minors in 2000. Now he's exempt for two years. "I don't know when I'll play again," he said. "I might not ever play again ... just kidding. I'm going to take a break, and reassess my schedule."

U.S. Open Championship—$5,500,000
Winner: Tiger Woods

See Chapter 3.

Canon Greater Hartford Open—$4,000,000
Winner: Phil Mickelson

Whoever said caddies aren't worth what they're paid needed to eavesdrop on the conversation between Phil Mickelson and his caddie, Jim "Bones" MacKay, during the closing holes of the Canon Greater Hartford Open. With his boss standing in the middle of the 13th fairway tied for the lead with Davis Love and Jonathan Kaye at 12 under par, MacKay did everything in his power to ensure that Mickelson didn't take another in what had become a long list of unnecessary gambles. Standing at the 240-yard mark, the conversation went like this:

MacKay: "If there was no wind I would still think that three iron is a marginal carry. But we've definitely got some wind. You can feel it now. If we hit three iron, we've got to go at that second tower on the right."

Mickelson: "You're not thinking three wood are you?"

MacKay: "No, I'm thinking about hitting a three iron up the right side, trying to land on the very right-hand part of the green."

Mickelson: "How about if I go between the pin and the TV tower?"

MacKay: "It's still going to be almost as much of a carry as if you went at the flag."

Mickelson then sighed and waggled the three iron for a moment before snipping: "You're basically saying to lay up into a four-yard area."

MacKay: "Well, then we play right of the green and get up and down."

Mickelson: "I've got to think this is enough. It's warm. If I bust a draw, turn it over ..."

MacKay: "We've got a 10 mile-per-hour wind straight into us. If we had a two iron in the bag, it would be a good two. But we just have the three. You can hit that just right of the green. That'll be perfect."

Mickelson, after addressing the ball then backing off: "I don't like that play because I feel like I'm trying to draw it into a four-yard area that's pulling it to the right. If I'm not going to go at the green, let me just not go at the green and use the slope. Otherwise let me take three wood. I think three iron is enough to go right at it."

MacKay, forcefully: "Just go to the right."

Mickelson: "Okay."

He hit three iron into the collection area right of the green, chipped to four feet and made the birdie. Love and Kaye made pars, and Mickelson had a one-shot lead. Emboldened by his lead, and fired up by the cheers of the clearly partisan crowd, Mickelson went on to hit a 108-yard wedge shot on the 18th hole to within two feet. He made that putt (even though he had missed a two-footer for par on the eighth), and finished with a six-under-par 64 for the day and a 14-under-par 266 for the week. Then Mickelson went to the putting green and waited.

"I fully expected to be in a playoff," he said. "If you give Davis and Jonathan that 18th hole again, they're going to make birdie seven times out of 10."

Not this time. Love missed a 25-footer, and Kaye missed from 13 feet. "I didn't hit a good putt," Kaye said. "It hopped up in the air right after I hit it."

Love made no such excuses. "I got better every day," he said. "I just got a little unfortunate."

Love shot 67 to Kaye's 70. Both finished at 267, one more than Mickelson, who became the first repeat winner in Hartford.

"To be the first one to win it twice is something very special, but there's nothing greater than the feeling walking up 18 and feeling the support from the fans," Mickelson said. "To close the deal and birdie the last hole the way I did is the most rewarding feeling a player can achieve."

While Mickelson was uttering these words, MacKay sat silently in the back of the room with a smile on his face. He too had one of the most rewarding feelings one can achieve.

FedEx St. Jude Classic—$3,800,000

Winner: Len Mattiace

Len Mattiace didn't even check the leaderboard before teeing off on Sunday. What was the point? He had played well in Memphis, but not that well. It didn't matter how far back he was. He knew he needed to post a career round and hope for the best. He never considered winning. "I didn't look at the leaderboards because I didn't feel I needed to," Mattiace said. "I knew I just needed to keep making birdies."

Which is exactly what he did, making a total of seven, five on the second nine, in a bogey-free final round of 64 for an 18-under-par 266 total. Only on the 18th green did Mattiace check the status. "I looked at the board on the 18th and saw I had a two-shot lead at that time," Mattiace said. "Then I just tried to two-putt."

His 64 was the lowest round of the day, but it didn't automatically ensure a victory. Third-round leader Glen Hnatiuk imploded with a closing 77, but there were still a couple of golfers on the course who had a chance. One of them was Notah Begay, who, coming off an injured back, had posted solid rounds in the 60s all week. Begay started the day four shots behind Hnatiuk, but jumped into the fray when a birdie at the par-three 14th tied him with Mattiace. That lead was short-lived. On the 15th Begay followed a poor tee shot with a pulled approach that flew long, left and into the lap of a fan. After a drop, Begay chipped through the green and failed to hole his second chip for par. He finished with 69 for a 268 total and third place.

A few moments later, Mattiace's caddie talked him out of hitting a six iron to the green from 175 yards at the 17th and into a seven iron. The shot stopped pin high, 15 feet from the hole, and Mattiace rolled in the curling putt for his final birdie of the day. "Jim (Walker, his caddie) was right again," Mattiace said.

The only other player with a chance was Tim Petrovic, who needed to sink a 35-footer for birdie at the 18th to tie for the lead. The putt never had a chance, and Petrovic finished with 68 on the day and a 267 total, good enough for sole second place, but one more than he needed to have a shot at his first win.

While Petrovic was putting, Mattiace was doing something he had never done before: hitting balls and thinking about a possible playoff. "It was pretty nerve-racking," he said. "I'm not used to this."

He is getting used to winning. After a decade of disappointments, Mattiace's victory was his second of 2002 and the second in his career. "It's a great feeling to win for the second time this year and to win here," he said. "A lot of guys know this is a special tournament for a special charity, St. Jude Children's Hospital. So, I'm just so happy with the way I played over the weekend."

Advil Western Open—$4,000,000
Winner: Jerry Kelly

A week that began with a grand disappointment ended with cheers, roars and tears from fans in the heartland. The disappointment came when Tiger Woods fell ill and withdrew from the Advil Western Open, a turn of events that left tournament officials scrambling to remain upbeat. Five days later every one was ecstatic as local favorite Jerry Kelly, a native of nearby Madison, Wisconsin, shot a seven-under-par 65 on Sunday for a 269 total and a two-shot victory over Davis Love.

The entire state of Wisconsin didn't make the 60-mile trek across the Illinois border to Cog Hill; it just seemed like it. With cheers that echoed through the pines, Kelly quickly realized he held home advantage, even though he entered the final round trailing Robert Allenby by three. But Allenby, who is normally a steady front-runner, struggled to 75 for a 276 total. That left the door open for Kelly, who grabbed the lead with birdies on three of his first five holes. Once he reached the top of the leaderboard, he never left.

Love provided the most consistent challenge. He started the final round only two back of Allenby, and when his 10-footer for birdie on the par-three 14th found the hole, Love joined Kelly in the top spot at 16 under par.

The tie was short-lived. Just as happened in 2001 when Love finished second, the final four holes were his undoing. He hit a perfect drive on the 16th, but flew the green with his approach, landing in high rough on the short side of the pin. From there the ball could have gone anywhere. Fortunately for Love, the chip stopped eight feet from the hole and he was able to salvage par.

One hole later things fell apart. A pulled tee shot left Love with a terrible lie in the rough with trees obstructing his line. To complicate matters further, a group of inebriated spectators chose that moment to question Love's ability to hold a lead. "Some people are just overdoing it," Love said. "They're yelling before you hit and screaming after you hit. They're not supposed to yell at players, they're not supposed to give players advice, and they're not supposed to tell players what to do and interfere in their games."

Love's second shot on the 17th rolled behind the green, and he had a few words with the offending patrons before pointing them out to security personnel, who promptly escorted them off. "I said something back there," Love said. "I don't like doing that, but it gets worse every year. It's really gone overboard this year since the U.S. Open."

After a great recovery to three feet, Love lipped out his par putt and settled for a bogey at the same time Kelly was rolling in a birdie at the 15th to move to 19 under par. That putt and a recovery from the trees on the 16th for a par sealed the victory for Kelly. Love tapped in for par at the 18th for 66, a 270 total and his second consecutive runner-up finish at the Western Open. "The incident on 17 didn't affect my play," Love said. "I just started too far back and ran into a buzz saw."

Kelly, who would have never considered himself a buzz saw even in the days when he was the hatchet man on the University of Hartford hockey team, soaked up the noise on Sunday, especially as he walked down the 18th fairway with his second win of the season secured. He got a standing ovation as he walked onto the green, and after he tapped in his par putt for the victory, Kelly pumped his fists twice and gave the crowd an ovation of his own.

Greater Milwaukee Open—$3,100,000
Winner: Jeff Sluman

The demons of yesteryear prowled through Jeff Sluman's noggin on the hot Milwaukee Sunday. One year before, he had gone into the final round at Brown Deer Park as the leader and favorite to win his second Greater Milwaukee Open. Friends and family drove from Chicago to watch. Sluman sent them all home in a slump with a lackluster final round of 72 and tie for 10th place. This year he hoped things would be different.

He shot 64 on Thursday and 63 on Saturday, but Sluman's lead was only two shots over Steve Lowery. That was about as deep as this field got. Only three players in the top 30 on the PGA Tour money list were there, and no one in the top 15 on the World Ranking made the trip. Sluman missed two of his last three fairways, but hung on to win, shooting a three-under-par 68 for a 261 total and a four-shot margin over Lowery and Tim Herron.

"I had a lot of friends and family up from Chicago again to cheer me on," Sluman said. "After feeling like I disappointed them last year, I was certainly glad to get it done this year."

There were a couple of shaky moments. Sluman parred the first hole and bogeyed the second, not the kind of start he had hoped for given the low scores that Brown Beer Park had yielded all week. Then he came alive, birdieing four straight holes to move to three under on his round through the first nine.

Lowery pulled back to within two strokes with a birdie at the 10th, but that's as exciting as this got. The big man from Alabama three-putted for bogey on the 11th and Sluman was free to cruise home with a win. "That's not a good time to three-putt," Lowery said. "I think if I could have knocked it in there and made birdie, made him think about it for a few holes, it might have been different. But he got that one right back and he never seemed to look back after that. He played real well with the lead. He drives the ball in the fairway and doesn't make mistakes to hurt himself."

Lowery seemed nonplused by the loss, perhaps because the second-place finish was his best of the season. "I've been going through a divorce for about a year," he said. "It's coming to an end, and it's wearing on me. Milwaukee was the place where I put the house fire behind me. Maybe it will be the place I put the divorce behind me, too."

Lowery's Orlando home burned in 1999, and he played miserably throughout the summer until shooting a closing 61 in Milwaukee and finishing fourth. He followed that up with two of his best years as a professional before the divorce crippled his 2002 season. He could only hope this showing would have a similar affect.

Herron didn't feel bad about his second-place finish either. "I won't have too much pressure to get on the road to keep my card," he said. His wife, Ann, was expecting their first child in a week. "I love playing here," he said. "People enjoy watching golf here, which is fun. This has the feel of a Midwest golf course. It's an old-style golf course, and that's why I like it."

Sluman likes it, too, even though he's not too sure how long he can continue to hold out in a game where the young guns keep getting longer and straighter. "The older you get, the more you understand about yourself," the 44-year-old winner said. "I think I'm doing pretty well for a guy who couldn't make his college golf team his senior year. None of the guys who were ahead of me then are out here. I've been out there 18 years. This is my sixth win. It has been a very good career so far.

"But every year I say it. I don't know how much longer I've got out here. I've been lucky. I've had no major injuries. My swing is fundamentally very, very sound. There's a little life in the old war-horse. I'm not ready to hang them up yet."

B.C. Open—$2,100,000
Winner: Spike McRoy

Robert McRoy, Sr. mounted a old Western dinner bell behind his Huntsville, Alabama, home over a decade ago, much to the chagrin of his neighbors who thought the "Rocket City" had become far too civilized for such displays. But McRoy didn't plan on ringing the bell every night when the rations were ready. According to his son, Robert Jr., known to everyone as

Spike, "Every win I have, my dad gets a golf plaque and he puts it on the post. We have a big gathering at the house. The family will come over and some friends of mine, and we'll ring the bell and enjoy life."

The bell rang many times on a sultry July Sunday, although none of the neighbors needed to be told what had happened. When Spike McRoy came from seven shots back to win the B.C. Open, the whole town celebrated. The final putt had barely fallen when a local sports bar put out a sign that read "Spike Wins!"

No one was more surprised by the victory than McRoy himself. After rounds of 70, 65 and 69, he trailed Shaun Micheel by seven shots. All he could hope for was a solid round and, hopefully, a top-five finish. McRoy accomplished the first part, playing the first 12 holes in six under par, then capping the bogey-free final round with a curling 35-footer for birdie on the 18th to reach 19-under-par 269.

At the time that put McRoy in a tie with Micheel. The tie didn't last long. Moments after McRoy rolled in his final birdie, Micheel bogeyed the par-three 14th to lose the lead for the first time since the second round. An eight-foot birdie putt at the 16th gave Micheel another temporary share of the lead, but he bogeyed the par-three 17th after hitting his tee shot over the green. Needing a birdie at the 18th to force a playoff, Micheel pushed his tee shot and made another bogey for a closing 74 and a 271 total. That final bogey allowed Fred Funk, who shot a final-round 67, to slip into second place with 270. Micheel finished tied for third with Glen Day, Robert Gamez, Brian Henninger and Cliff Kresge.

"It's just a funny game like that, you know?" McRoy said as he watched Micheel's collapse from a television in the press room. "It's so hard to put four solid rounds together, whether you're at Bethpage, the hardest golf course I've ever seen, or a scorable course like this. The most miserable thing about this is that I'm watching a buddy of mine that's not having a good day. Here we are, we're battling it out for a golf tournament. Shaun's a great dude and we've played a lot of golf together, so it's tough to watch him struggle."

Even with the empathy he felt for his friend, McRoy had to admit that "winning takes care of a lot of problems." As for the bell and the plaque to be nailed to the post along with those for his wins in the Alabama Open, two Hooters Tour and two Buy.com Tour events, McRoy couldn't wait to get home for the celebration. "It's going to be great to see that plaque go up there," he said. "I know my dad will be very proud."

John Deere Classic—$3,000,000
Winner: J.P. Hayes

When a professional golfer hits 61 out of 72 greens, shoots a course-record 61, sets a tournament record with a 22-under-par 262 total, and toys with the competition in the final two rounds only to pull away and win by four, you might believe this was another Tiger Woods victory. Throw in the fact that the professional hit 17 or 18 greens and squashed any challengers with a closing 67 and you would certainly figure this guy was someone whose name you might recognize.

But it wasn't Woods, Mickelson, Garcia, Duval or Els who struck the ball with such precision and threw out more birdies than there are wrinkles on Craig Stadler's shirts. The victor of the week in Silvis, Illinois, was none other than John Patrick Hayes, a 36-year-old Wisconsin native who goes by J.P. and who came to the John Deere Classic with only one career victory in a decade of trying. With a rumpled shirt and clueless expression, Hayes could have been confused for a local club pro who had accidentally stumbled into the field at the John Deere Classic until you checked the numbers the walking scorer kept putting beside his name.

The 61 on Friday moved him to 14-under-par 138. That was only good enough for a tie atop the leaderboard with Fred Funk. A 67 on Saturday moved Hayes into another tie at the top with Robert Gamez, who won twice as a rookie before discovering the Las Vegas nightlife. Before the 2002 season, Gamez hadn't broken into the top 10 since 1999. His last win had been the 1994 Casio World Open in Japan, and his best finish in 2001 was a tie for 11th at the Bob Hope Chrysler Classic, a bleak performance for one of the most promising young players of the late 1980s.

A recent move to Orlando, where Gamez vowed to work on his game and on controlling his nocturnal impulses, seemed to have paid off. Gamez had posted three top-five finishes prior to his good play at the John Deere Classic, where he put together three steady rounds of 65, 64 and 66 to join the final twosome on Sunday.

The trip back from Edinburgh — one where Duffy Waldorf lost his luggage and, for the third year in a row, Stuart Cink lost his golf clubs — kept the field at Silvis devoid of any top-billed names. The highest ranked player in the field was Funk, who came in slotted at 32nd in the world, followed by Pat Perez (35th), Charles Howell (44th), Rich Beem (45th), Cameron Beckman (47th) and John Huston (48th). By Sunday none of those players were in contention, and none had put together the kind of ball-striking performance Hayes displayed under pressure.

He started out par-birdie to extend his lead to four shots (Gamez started bogey-par), and from there all Hayes had to do was hit fairways and greens, which he did with great precision. "I felt good from the start," Hayes said. "I got off to a good start and, with Robert struggling from the start, it gave me more confidence."

Gamez limped in with 71 for a 266 total, which was good enough for second place, a spot he hadn't seen in a while and one he wasn't too disappointed in finding. "What can I say?" Gamez asked. "He just played better than I did."

"I kind of surprised myself a little bit in that I never really missed a golf shot today," Hayes said afterward. "Every shot I hit was pleasing to the eye. I don't think I have ever gone that many holes or played a tournament with that few bogeys. It was a pretty steady week."

The closing 67 set the tournament record. And the $540,000 winner's check was also very pleasing.

The International—$4,500,000
Winner: Rich Beem

Rich Beem was on a roll. If he parred the 18th at Castle Pines on Sunday, he would shoot a bogey-free 63 and set a single-day tournament record of 19 points in the modified-Stableford format of The International. Even though he started the day three points off the lead, his stellar play had put Beem in the lead by 10 points with five holes to play, a comfortable cushion, or so he thought. The only player who could catch him was Steve Lowery, who appeared to be on a run.

Walking up the 18th fairway, Beem heard a roar from behind him on the 17th. It was the kind of roar usually reserved for a hole-in-one. But the 17th was a par-five, so that hadn't happened. With CBS on-course reporter David Feherty walking alongside him, Beem turned and held up three fingers. "Did Lowery make three?" he asked.

Feherty paused and put a hand to his headset to make sure he was getting the right information. He shook his head and held up two fingers. "No, Lowery made two," he said.

"Ree-ally," Beem said, somewhat stunned. Suddenly what had appeared to be a comfortable lead was the tightest race of the year. "The more nervous I got, the better I seemed to swing," he said.

Beem hit his second shot into the middle of the 18th green, then coaxed his birdie putt to within two feet. When he made the par, all he could do was wait. "It was the longest 10 minutes of my life," he said. And it ended with the longest two seconds, the time Lowery's birdie putt at the 18th hung on the lip before everyone realized it wasn't going to fall in.

The double eagle at the 17th had given Lowery 43 points. Beem had finished the tournament with 44. A birdie by Lowery at the 18th and the tournament would be his. "I hit a good putt at 18 that just didn't break," he said.

Thus ended an event CBS announcer Jim Nantz called, "the greatest chase I've ever seen," and one J.P. Hayes, a good friend of Beem, called, "the most exciting golf tournament you're ever going to watch."

That might have been a stretch, but there was no doubt Lowery and Beem were producing some of the best golf of the season. It started when Beem, who had no points on Friday and 15 on Saturday, kept the birdies coming in the final round. He held a commanding lead at the turn and seemingly put the tournament out of reach when he made an 18-footer for eagle on the 17th to reach 44 points.

Lowery had other plans. He took off his shoes and put on his rain pants to play a shot from a pond on the 14th, which paid off with an up-and-down birdie, and he eagled the par-four 15th when he flew a gap wedge in the hole from 127 yards. The only hiccup in what was shaping up to be a record-setting performance was a three-putt bogey from 50 feet on the 16th. When Lowery's second putt on the 16th failed to find the hole and, seconds later, Beem's eagle at the 17th rolled into the center of the cup, the tournament looked to be over. Then the unthinkable happened.

From the center of the fairway Lowery hit a perfect six iron. "The ball took off and my caddie said, 'If that's not good, there is no good,'" Lowery said. "I was thinking the same thing." What neither Lowery nor his caddie nor anyone else watching was thinking was that the six-iron shot would take two hops and fall into the hole.

"I was watching from the clubhouse and thinking it was a replay of some other year," Beem's father, Larry, said. "I'm thinking, this is fiction, this can't be real. When he left that putt on the lip at 18, I thought it was going to back in the hole. Heck, he dunked a couple of them, wouldn't this one back in?"

The putt did not back in, and when it stayed on the lip, Lowery fell to his knees. Beem, standing behind the 18th green, fell into the arms of his wife, Sara, then walked down to 18, shook Lowery's hand and took the flag off the flagstick and put it in his pocket. "It seemed appropriate," he said later. "This was unbelievable."

Buick Open—$3,300,000
Winner: Tiger Woods

Tiger Woods normally takes off the week before a major championship, a schedule that has served him well in his career. This time he chose to warm up for the PGA Championship by playing the Buick Open at Warwick Hills in suburban Detroit.

Solid putting pulled Woods through to a victory even though he opened the weekend by hitting his first tee shot of the third round out of bounds and struggled to find greens in a dismal (by his standards) one-under 71. The 63 he shot on Friday gave Woods room for a few loose shots, and he carried a one-shot lead over Esteban Toledo into the final round.

The lead quickly increased to two when Woods made up for his double bogey Saturday at the first hole with a birdie from five feet. Toledo, a former professional boxer from Mexico, didn't let the pressure of playing with the best player in the world get to him. He came back with a solid birdie putt from 20 feet on the fourth hole to cut Woods' lead back to one. When Woods pulled an eight-footer at the fifth and walked away with a bogey, Toledo found himself sharing the top spot at 15 under par.

Woods answered by draining a 30-footer for birdie at the sixth, a putt that prompted the right-fisted uppercut that has become Woods' trademark. Toledo wasn't going away. He and Woods both birdied the seventh hole to keep the fight alive. Toledo bogeyed the ninth when he pulled a five-footer that caught the left edge of the hole and spun out, but he came charging back with a birdie on the 10th to bring Woods' margin to one shot again.

In every one of Woods' 32 previous career victories there was a moment when he needed to hit a shot, when the pressure was on and he had to produce. This time the shot was the final-round tee shot at the par-three 11th. He hadn't played the par-threes particularly well all week, and his swing still wasn't firing on all cylinders. If Toledo could birdie and draw even with seven holes to play, anything was possible. The challenger hit a good shot inside 20 feet to give himself a chance. Then Woods made the swing that won the tournament for him, a laser iron that never left the flag. When the ball fell to earth, it stopped one foot from the hole. Toledo missed his birdie putt, and Woods tapped in his birdie to take a two-shot lead.

From there Toledo was forced to fire at all the pins. "I had to try to make birdies," he said. That strategy cost him. At the par-five 13th, Toledo went for a left-tucked pin with his second shot and missed the green to the left, leaving himself a tricky pitch from the rough. He tried to hit a flop shot close to the hole, but the ball squirted out of the thick grass, ran all the way across the green, and plopped in a pond. Toledo's birdie effort turned into a bogey, and the tournament was all but over.

Woods made a routine birdie on the 13th to open a three-shot lead with five holes to play. Bogeys by Toledo at the 14th and 15th ended any pretense of drama. Even a double bogey by Woods at the par-three 17th, after he pushed a tee shot and attempted the same flop shot that had cost Toledo four holes earlier, didn't spoil the moment. Woods made a par on the 18th to shoot 70 for a 17-under-par 271 total. That would have left him tied for 14th at the Buick Open a year ago. This time around it was good enough for a four-stroke victory.

Toledo made one more bogey on the 18th, which proved costly. He fell into a tie for second at 275 with Fred Funk, Mark O'Meara and Brian Gay. "I had to birdie the 13th," Toledo said. "That was the key to the tournament, and I pulled it."

Woods saw another key to the tournament, which he hoped to carry forward to the PGA Championship. "I won this tournament two ways," he said. "The first two days I hit the ball great, and in the last two rounds I made every putt I looked at. If I can combine those two things, I'll be in great shape for next week."

PGA Championship—$5,500,000
Winner: Rich Beem

See Chapter 5.

WGC NEC Invitational—$5,500,000
Winner: Craig Parry

It was a new venue and a new victor for the NEC Invitational, the second event in the World Golf Championships schedule. It was moved from the Firestone Country Club in Akron, Ohio, a course that been a PGA Tour staple for 40 years, to Sahalee Country Club in Sammamish, Washington, where golf comes somewhere below cappachino on the priority scale. And there was a new winner, a 5-foot-6 fireplug of a man named Craig Parry who shot a final-round, six-under-par 65 for a 268 total and a four-stroke victory.

Three-time defending champion Tiger Woods, who had played Firestone like he owned it, failed to mount a final-round charge, shooting 68 for a 273 total and sole possession of fourth place. Woods shared the lead through 16 holes of the third round, but made a costly error when he chose the wrong club at the par-three 17th.

"It was a nice, smooth five iron," Woods said of the shot that wound up short and left of the green. "Stevie (Williams, his caddie) talked me out of a five and into a six. What ticks me off is that I had the final say-so, and I didn't trust my own gut instincts. Just keep the loft open on it, hold it open and just put it right in the middle of the green. It's just a stupid play, and it cost me a shot."

Woods never seriously contended after that.

Parry entered the final round tied with fellow Australian Robert Allenby, who looked to be the favorite. Parry had won 19 times worldwide, but had never scratched a victory in America, while Allenby had become a consistent winner on the PGA Tour. "I've had Tom Lehman go birdie-birdie to beat me at Colonial," Parry said. "Phil Mickelson chipped in for an eagle on the 16th at the Byron Nelson one year. I think he beat me by a shot. Nick Price was the hottest golfer in the '90s, and he got me down at the Honda."

He didn't mention the 1992 Masters where he held a three-shot lead with 16 holes to play before three-putting his way to a tie for 13th. "I felt like I had to hit it a foot to make birdie," he said of his ongoing putting woes. "It's tough. You're speaking with your wife and say you're playing good and she sees four over and two over on the board."

All that changed with a new putter he put into play the week before the PGA Championship, and a new attitude he assumed after watching Rich Beem stare down Tiger Woods. "I wasn't focused 100 percent on the shot at hand," he said. "I watched Rich, and saw that the shot he tried to play, he played. I thought, 'Why can't you do that?'"

He certainly hadn't done it for most of the year. Parry came into the event having missed his last five cuts. The way he qualified for the field was through a victory in January in New Zealand with Woods in the field. "If Tiger doesn't play in New Zealand, I'm not here," he said.

Parry made the best of this opportunity on Sunday, distancing himself from the field with consecutive birdies at the second, third and fourth to open a three-shot lead. He made solid par saves at the seventh and eighth, before rolling in a curling birdie putt at the ninth. "When I was three birdies up, that put enough pressure on the other guys," he said.

Allenby shot a solid 69 on Sunday, but fell well shy of the margin he needed, while Fred Funk came in with 68 to tie for second at 272. Still, five birdies into the final round and sitting on a comfortable four-shot lead, Parry refused to let his emotions show until his second shot on the par-five 18th found the center of the green. Then he smiled, waved and allowed himself a moment's joy before two-putting for birdie and a closing 65.

"I'm very lucky at the moment," Parry said. "Hopefully, I'll have a little more confidence in my golf game, knowing I can finish the job off. I always knew it was just a matter of time."

Reno-Tahoe Open—$3,000,000
Winner: Chris Riley

Inspiration comes in many forms. Chris Riley, a former University of Nevada-Las Vegas golf star, playing in front of a home state crowd at the Reno-Tahoe Open, found his spark of confidence in the encouraging words he received from Tiger Woods. They were paired in the third round of the PGA Championship where Riley held his own, matching Woods' 72 for the day. "It was an incredible last Saturday playing with Tiger," Riley said. "He told me, 'Chris, you are going to win.' That's how smart the guy is."

Eight days later Riley two-putted from eight feet on the first playoff hole to defeat Jonathan Kaye and claim his first career title. "This is something you dream about," Riley said. "The state of Nevada was pulling for me all week. It was a great match today. We were back and forth. I never had the lead until the end."

Despite the inspiration from Woods and the confidence he gained from his third-place finish at the PGA Championship, Riley needed help from Kaye. The two were tied for the lead with Steve Flesch at 204 through 54 holes, but Kaye held a one-shot lead with two holes to play before bogeying the par-five 17th. Another chance slipped away when Kaye missed an eight-foot birdie putt at the 18th that would have given him the victory. "It was in the heart of the hole with three inches to go," Kaye said. "I hit a good putt, but it just wasn't meant to be. The golf gods weren't with me today."

Riley parred the 17th, but hit his drive into the rough on the final hole. He chopped a seven iron out and onto the front fringe, leaving the ball 75 feet from the hole. Under normal circumstances this would have been a tough up-and-down. With the pressure of his first victory on the line, it was nearly impossible. But Riley hit the shot of his life, a deft running chip that grazed the edge of the hole before stopping two feet past. He made his putt for par and a closing 67. Both he and Kaye signed for totals of 271 before trotting back to the 18th tee for overtime.

The playoff wasn't nearly as dramatic as regulation. This time Riley found the fairway, and Kaye missed his drive to the right. Playing first, Kaye found the greenside bunker with his approach, and Riley hit his second shot eight feet left of the flag. From there Riley easily two-putted for par, while Kaye blasted out to five feet, but missed his par effort.

"This has been hard work for me over my whole career," Riley said. "I've never really won anything, but I've always competed hard, and I finally kicked the door down."

Air Canada Championship—$3,500,000
Winner: Gene Sauers

There was no more improbable story in 2002 than Gene Sauers' one-stroke victory in the Air Canada Championship. Sauers hadn't won since 1989 and hadn't competed regularly on any tour in over six years. He played in the Buy.com event in Odessa, Texas, the week before his win, and wasn't sure he was in the field until he got a call at his Savannah, Georgia, home on Monday informing him that his seventh-alternate status had earned him a spot in the tournament. On Tuesday he flew to Vancouver, but his luggage (including his golf clubs) never made it out of Atlanta. He was finally re-united with his clubs on Wednesday night, and hit his first tee shot of the tournament without ever seeing the golf course.

Sauers bogeyed the first hole, but things got progressively better after that. He had scores of 69, 65 and 66 for a one-shot lead going into the final round, his best showing on tour in over a decade.

"If I could have found a job where I could make 50 to 80 grand a year, I would have taken it," Sauers said of his frustrations. "I kind of got tired with the game. I wasn't happy out here. I was hitting it in the rough, and you can't play golf out of the rough. It really got frustrating, but I didn't have anything to do, so I kept on struggling, working on my game."

For his 40th birthday he armed himself with new irons, a new driver and a new attitude. "I've been hitting the ball good for the last couple of months and I was just hoping for this opportunity," he said.

After starting his final round with six straight pars, Sauers settled in with a birdie on the 584-yard, par-five seventh. He stayed in red figures for the day with par saves out of the sand on the eighth and ninth, the latter coming when he made a curling 15-footer. A key birdie on the par-five 12th kept Sauers atop the leaderboard, but he had company.

Steve Lowery, who started the day two shots back and played two groups ahead of Sauers, birdied the 12th and 15th holes to gain a share of the lead, but he gave it back with a bogey from the bunker on the par-three 16th. Lowery had another chance to put pressure on Sauers when he hit his approach on the 18th to within eight feet. The putt hit the edge of the hole and spun out. Lowery had to settle for a final round of 68 and a total of 270.

That left it up to Sauers, who hadn't made a bogey since the opening round. After his birdie at the 12th, he reeled off five straight pars before hitting his approach shot 30 feet from the hole on the 18th, but on the wrong level of the two-tiered green. The putt was a tricky left-to-right downhill breaker. A few minutes earlier Craig Barlow had left the same putt on the top tier and had to make a three-footer to keep from four-putting. Now Sauers needed to two-putt to win.

"I knew he was going to have to make one of the best two-putts of his life to win," said Lowery, who was waiting behind the 18th green for the possible playoff.

Sauers did just that, trickling the putt over the front of the crest and watching as it gained speed and fed toward the hole. He barely missed his birdie putt and the ball rolled a mere three feet below the hole. "That's the hardest two-putt I've ever had to make," he admitted. "I told myself, 'Don't leave it up top.' Then again, I could have putted it off the green."

He did neither, and when the three-footer found the hole, he took home $630,000, more money than he had ever earned in a season. "I didn't have a chance to make many birdies," he said. "But a couple of the putts I did make were clutch. The last three holes I started to get a little nervous, and I tried to do my yoga breathing again. I told myself, 'It's just a game.'"

Bell Canadian Open—$4,000,000
Winner: John Rollins

You had to give Neal Lancaster the benefit of the doubt. After what he had just been through it's a wonder he knew his own name, much less the name of the man whose spectacular final-hole collapse he had just emulated.

"I guess I know how Jean-Claude van Damme feels now, or whatever his name is," Lancaster said after making double bogey on the last hole to blow a two-shot lead in the Bell Canadian Open. He was referring to Jean Van de Velde, who made triple bogey on the final hole at Carnoustie to blow a three-shot lead at the 1999 British Open. Van de Velde (not to be confused with the French action film star, van Damme) lost in a three-way playoff with Paul Lawrie and Justin Leonard.

Leonard made a return cameo as the third wheel in another unlikely play-off, this time featuring Lancaster and John Rollins, a winless 27-year-old Virginian. Rollins won, landing an iron in the middle of the 18th fairway and hitting a seven iron from 163 yards to 20 feet before draining the birdie putt, but even he didn't believe what had happened until after it was over.

"I thought I was going to be in a tie for second, a great week," Rollins said. After making a great par-saving putt on the 18th to shoot seven-under-par 65 and finish with a 272 total, Rollins kicked off his shoes and called his wife from the locker room. There was no need to stay loose or warm. "Loose for what?" he would ask.

Lancaster seemed on cruise control, entertaining the galleries with his humor. — "Ava Gardner is also from Smithfield (North Carolina). She's dead, but she's still bigger than me." "I thought about being a garbage man as a kid. He came on Tuesdays and Thursdays, so I figured he only worked two days a week." "Seven-thirty a.m. ain't no time to play golf. Only time you play golf then is when you can't get a tee time, or when you have a wife to get away from." — and puffing on cigarettes he brought from home, while he put together enough solid shots to get to 18 under par through 71 holes. A two-shot cushion with one hole to play should have been enough.

"I got a little quick, and then I choked," Lancaster said as a way of describing what transpired next. He hit his drive in the middle of the fairway, but his caddie noticed that Lancaster hadn't smoked a cigarette in the last four holes. Every second he went without nicotine was a second Lancaster cut off his pre-shot routine.

He only had a seven iron left to the green, but he pulled it almost 40 yards left of the target, over a bunker and into the rough. His third shot rolled into a valley, leaving him an uphill 40-footer for par. Laughing at his own misfortune to keep from letting his true emotions show, Lancaster then ran the first putt four feet past the hole. The second putt, the one for bogey and the win, never had a chance.

"One lousy swing, really, on that seven iron, and I was cooked," he said. "Hadn't bogeyed but one hole all week, the first hole on Friday, and that didn't count because I was barely awake. Embarrassing is what it is. I gave it away. I blew it."

Leonard, who had no idea he was in a playoff until tour officials found him in the locker room, missed the green with his approach in the playoff but chipped to within five feet. Lancaster hit his second shot in the bunker he had missed during regulation. This time his third shot stopped 30 feet from the hole, and he missed his par putt before Rollins removed all doubt by draining the 20-footer for birdie.

"Don't think they'll be having a 'Neal Lancaster Day' in Smithfield, not after this thing," Lancaster said. "What I'd like to do is crawl under a rock. Tell you what I need, though. I need a cigarette."

SEI Pennsylvania Classic—$3,300,000
Winner: Dan Forsman

Nobody gave Dan Forsman much of a chance. Only moments before teeing off in the second round of the SEI Pennsylvania Classic, the 44-year-old Forsman handed an envelope to John Andrews of the PGA Tour. In it was an application to the second stage of qualifying school. Forsman had missed the application deadline once in 2000, then dropped to 128th on the money list and found himself without a full-time job. "It's an error you don't forget," he said. "A humbling one at that."

He wouldn't make the same mistake in 2002.

Billy Andrade looked to be the player with the best chance at winning after an opening 66 followed by rounds of 68 and 68 for a two-shot lead. He extended the lead through nine holes on Sunday when he went on a four-birdie run to get to 15 under par for the tournament.

Defending champion Robert Allenby made a run, reeling off six birdies in his first 12 holes to get to 13 under and take second place. Andrade, who had struggled with his swing throughout the summer (missing the cut at all four majors), hit an errant tee shot out of bounds on the par-four 10th. The resulting double bogey dropped Andrade back to 13 under and into a tie with Allenby.

Forsman had earlier rounds of 73, 68 and 64. He made birdies on the third, fifth and 10th holes to get to 11 under and within striking distance of the leaders. He hadn't won in a decade — the 1992 Buick Open to be exact — so his chances probably were considered slim at best. It was a good showing, and one that might keep him in the top 125 on the money list and out of qualifying.

Then Forsman birdied the 15th to pull within one shot of the leaders. That's when he started taking himself seriously. "I didn't look at the leaderboard," he said. "I knew I was keeping pace with the leaders. I felt if I could knock it on the 18th green, maybe something crazy would happen."

Allenby, who had played flawless golf through 14 holes, missed the fairway at the par-five 15th and made bogey. Then at the par-three 17th, a hole he had aced on Saturday, Allenby hit what he thought was a perfect shot, but the ball plugged in the bunker short of the green, and he had no shot. The resulting bogey was the one that killed him. "The only thing I'm disappointed in was my shot into 17," Allenby said afterward. "I hit a perfect shot but it came up short and I had no second shot."

Allenby was playing two groups ahead of Forsman and three ahead of Andrade, so he knew he needed an eagle at the 18th to have any chance at a win. He reached the green in two, but his eagle putt came up two inches short. He tapped in for birdie and a final round of 65 for a 271 total. That, he thought, wouldn't be good enough.

Twenty minutes later, Forsman hit a three-wood shot from the first cut of rough along the left edge of the 18th fairway. The ball squirted past the right greenside bunker and came to rest 25 feet from the hole. When he looked at the putt, Forsman had a good feeling.

"Instinctively, when you look up, you judge the speed of the ball and think, okay, that looks good," he said. "I had a sense in my heart that it was going to be a good putt."

When the putt fell for his closing 65, the crowd erupted, and Forsman threw his arms in the air. For the first time in four days of competition, Forsman held the outright lead at 270.

Andrade could have tied with a birdie at the 18th or won with an eagle, but another wayward tee shot right found the fairway bunker and Andrade's chances were sunk. He had to lay up to the 200-yard marker, and his third shot stopped 20 feet from the hole. It was a makeable putt, but Andrade left it 12 inches short. He had to tap in for par, a score of 69 and a tie for second at 271 with Allenby.

"There are a couple of holes out here where you have to hit the fairway," Andrade said. "They are the 10th, 15th and 18th, and I didn't do that. Long story short, second place sucks."

But winning makes a world of troubles go away. After signing his scorecard and watching Andrade's putt come up short, Forsman was walking toward the clubhouse when he saw John Andrews approaching him with the white envelope in his hand. "I thought you might want this back," Andrews said. As for the future of the check that was in that envelope, Forsman couldn't have been clearer. "That one," he said, "is getting framed."

Tampa Bay Classic—$2,600,000
Winner: K.J. Choi

K.J. Choi liked firsts. He enjoyed being the first Korean to earn a PGA Tour card in 1999, and he liked being the first former power lifter ever to successfully play professional golf. He certainly enjoyed being the first Korean ever to win a PGA Tour event in 2002 when he captured the Compaq Classic of New Orleans. Then, in late September, he set another record — this time for the largest margin of victory of the year when he won the Tampa Bay Classic by seven strokes over Glen Day.

"Things happen for a reason," Choi said after shooting 17-under-par 271 and capturing his second title of the year. He missed playing in Ireland by virtue of his 31st position on the money list (the top 30 played in the WGC American Express Championship). "The alternative was to come here and play this tournament. Maybe it was lucky that happened."

Luck had little to do with Choi's play on the Copperhead Course at the Westin Innisbrook Resort. He opened with a course- and tournament-record 63 and never relinquished the lead. By sundown on Saturday, after two consecutive rounds of 68, Choi held a five-shot lead over Pat Perez and a six-shot edge over Glen Day.

Day cut the margin to three on Sunday with four consecutive birdies on the sixth through ninth holes. A bogey on the 10th after clipping a tree with his approach doused Day's chances. "I made the turn thinking, 'You're playing good, stick to the routine and let whatever happens, happen,'" Day said after finishing with 69 for a 10-under-par 274 total. "At the first of the week I said 12 under would win. Obviously I was wrong. K.J. played really well."

Choi made one birdie on the first nine, then capped his day with birdies at the 11th and 14th to shoot a closing 68 for a 267 total, 17 under par, and extend the final margin to seven. "When I first started out the day I did feel some pressure, an uneasiness to be honest," Choi said. "But as the holes went by, I felt much more comfortable. I just said to myself, 'I'll take it one hole at a time.'"

As for what was happening in Ireland at the WGC event, Choi smiled and said, "It would have been good if Tiger Woods was here. I can learn from him. But it would not have mattered who was here, I would have continued to play my game."

The tour's youngest player cashed his first official check in Tampa as well. Ty Tryon, age 18, came back after missing all summer with mononucleosis and tonsillitis to shoot 73-65-72-75–285 and finish tied for 41st. The $8,620 check he received wasn't going to make Tryon's season, but he viewed it as a good start to a comeback. "I've got official money, and I'm pretty happy about that," he said. "It's a lot better than where I left off. Of course I'd rather have been healthy and not have missed the whole summer, but I feel that maybe next year I'll be more ready. I'll be a little older, more refined."

Valero Texas Open—$3,500,000
Winner: Loren Roberts

Conventional wisdom says that 47-year-olds can't win on the PGA Tour these days. A few of the over-40 crowd took exception to that and attempted to prove their point at the Valero Texas Open. Loren Roberts (age 47) won with a closing 64 that included four birdies in the final six holes. His 19-under-par 261 total was good enough for a three-stroke win over Fred Funk (45) and Fred Couples (42). J.L. Lewis (42) and Joel Edwards (40) finished tied for fifth, while Bob Tway (43) shot 267 and finished tied for 10th. Garrett Willis (28), who shared second place with Funk and Couples, was the only young player even close.

"This could be the sweetest victory of my career," Roberts said. "I feel like I really turned the calendar back a little bit."

He did it the same way he captured his previous seven titles, being patient, making pars, and letting his putter heat up when the time was right. This time it happened on the second nine on Sunday after Roberts lost the lead to Funk, who went on a mid-round tear with birdies at the 11th, 12th and 13th holes to reach 17 under par. Couples soon joined him with birdies at the 13th through 16th.

Both Funk and Couples shot closing 64s, but gave strokes back in the homestretch. Funk bogeyed the 380-yard 16th after a poor approach left him with a 40-footer for birdie. He three-putted for his only bogey of the day. "That was disappointing," Funk said. This was Funk's fourth runner-up finish of the year, a trend that had him more than a little frustrated. "I want to win so bad," he said.

Couples also wanted to break a three-year winless streak. His miscue came at the par-three 17th where he hit a six iron over the green, chipped long, then missed his 20-footer for par. "I would have loved to make par there and put a little more pressure on Fred at the time, and then, obviously, Loren."

While all this was happening, Roberts continued to make pars and build momentum. He parred the ninth through the 12th before starting his birdie surge at the 13th. Another birdie at the par-five 14th put him in a tie atop the leaderboard. Then, after a par at the 15th, he closed the deal with birdies at the 16th and a solid 13-footer for birdie at the 17th.

"The putt at 17 was probably the best shot I hit all week," Roberts said. "I wanted to focus in and make that putt, and I hit it right in the middle of the hole."

Not surprisingly, Roberts needed only 111 putts for the week. What was surprising was that he was using a new putter. "It's only the sixth putter I've had in my career," said the man known as the Boss of the Moss. "Some guys have six putters in one week out here."

Roberts knows at least one tournament he'll be playing in years to come. "I love San Antonio," he said. "I like playing here. I've had some good success on this golf course, and I suspect I'll be coming here until I'm on the senior tour."

Michelob Championship at Kingsmill—$3,700,000
Winner: Charles Howell

Charles Howell doesn't drink. Never has and probably never will. At age 23 he hasn't been eligible to partake of adult beverages for long, but even so the Augusta, Georgia, native and Oklahoma State graduate never gave alcohol a thought as he was growing up on the golf course. "No time," he said. He was too busy honing a golf swing that would launch the ball huge distances from a body that was only slightly thicker than one of his golf shafts.

So it was easy to forgive the lad with the chiseled chin when he grimaced after taking a swing of the ceremonial drink-of-choice for the winner of the Michelob Championship at Kingsmill. The beer might have tasted bitter, but the victory that led up to it couldn't have been sweeter.

Trailing Brandt Jobe by three at the start of the final round, Howell put on a shotmaking display, bombing drives and hitting laser approaches, the kind of ball-striking that made him a shoo-in for Rookie of the Year in 2001 and a name that continued to pop up when the "Who's going to challenge Tiger?" question came up. He made up his deficit in four holes, hitting his approach to within two feet at the first, two-putting for birdie at the par-five third and tapping in from two inches after a monster six-iron approach at the par-four fourth.

"I was just enough in contention to get nervous, but I was just enough out of contention to get hacked off at myself for not being way ahead," Howell said. "For my first win, this couldn't have been a better scenario."

A bogey at the fifth caused Howell to "talk to myself in foreign tongues." The chat worked. On the par-five seventh, he hit a drive 345 yards, easily flying a bunker at the 295-yard mark. That left him with a soft nine-iron approach to the par-five, a shot he left 15 feet below the hole. When he made the putt for eagle, he knew this tournament could be his. "That was a pretty big turning point," he said.

The second big turning point came at the 15th, another reachable par-five for someone of Howell's length. He pulled his approach long and left, leaving a testy pitch. He made a great up-and-down for birdie to recapture the lead.

Billy Mayfair, who started the final round two shots behind Jobe, made up the deficit with three quick birdies, but ran into a buzz saw at the par-four 14th when he drove his ball into the rough and failed on three attempts to get out. His triple-bogey seven on the hole dropped Mayfair out of contention. He finished with a final round of 73 for a 274 total and fifth place.

Jobe was another story. He also birdied the par-five 15th to gain a share of the lead with Howell at 14 under par. Jobe found trouble at the 16th when his nine-iron approach fell two feet from perfect and the ball rolled back down an embankment. Instead of having a short birdie putt, Jobe had a tough up-and-down, which he failed to convert. The bogey dropped him one shot back with two holes to play.

Jobe's score hadn't been posted when Howell reached the 18th tee. He thought he needed one more birdie, so, as he had done all day, he hit a tee shot 320 yards in the middle of the fairway. His three-quarter wedge was pulled a little, but he still had only a 15-footer for birdie. The putt didn't fall, but by that point it didn't matter. Jobe drove into the rough on the 18th and made another bogey to finish the day with 72 and in a tie for second with Scott Hoch at 272.

For Howell the questions about when this enormous talent would finally find the winner's circle were finally answered. His closing 67 and 270 total wasn't the best this tournament had ever seen, but it was certainly good enough. "After a while you start asking yourself, 'When is it going to happen?'" Howell said. "I know that ideally you're not supposed to, but it starts to get in your head a little bit. Now that I've won, it's hard to put into words. I don't think it's sunk in yet."

Invensys Classic at Las Vegas—$5,000,000
Winner: Phil Tataurangi

When you've been on a stretcher beside the 17th tee with an oxygen mask strapped to your face and the prospect of a career-ending heart attack, the pressure of a one-shot final-round lead is nothing. So says New Zealander Phil Tataurangi, who didn't actually have a heart attack at the 2001 Air Canada Championship.

"Supraventricular tachycardia," he says with the fluidity of a cardiologist or of someone who suffers from the disease. In Tataurangi's case, it's the latter. "My heart would go into a panic," he said describing the condition that led his heart rate to jump to 190 beats per minute one afternoon in Vancouver. He collapsed after hitting his tee shot on the 17th at the Air Canada Championship and underwent a procedure to open his arteries in Dallas later that summer.

No one would have guessed that a five-round marathon in the Invensys Classic at Las Vegas would be the spot where Tataurangi would pick up his first victory after eight years of struggle on the PGA Tour. But a 10-under-par 62 in the final round for a 330 total can make up for a lot of ills, even those that most laymen can't pronounce. Still, even Tataurangi couldn't believe the final result.

"I didn't think for one minute that I was going to win the golf tournament today," he said. "No way did I start the day thinking I had a chance to win. Not even when I finished. No way."

That wasn't being pessimistic, just realistic. Tataurangi was one of seven players tied for 12th place at 268 through four rounds, five strokes behind leader David Duval, who was looking like the man who won the 2001 British Open. As if Duval and the five shots weren't enough, players like Jeff Sluman, Stuart Appleby and Jim Furyk, who had won in Las Vegas three of the last seven years, stood between Tataurangi and the lead.

"As driven and motivated as I am, what gives me the most satisfaction is seeing how good I can be," Tataurangi said. "Today I was pretty good."

He was more than pretty good. Five birdies on the first nine, followed by five more in the first seven holes of the second nine, and two routine pars coming in qualified as spectacular on a day when this journeyman needed to make a good check just to keep his playing privileges for next year. "I worked hard to get in a situation like this, and I wasn't going to throw it away," Tataurangi said.

Tataurangi never looked at the leaderboard until he had tapped in for a 29-under-par 330 total. Then he saw that Furyk, who had held a three-shot lead on the first nine, had made three bogeys to fall a shot back, while Appleby and Sluman were also one behind. Duval returned to his disturbing and all-too-familiar form on Sunday, shooting 71 on a course Appleby described as "a realistic par 67" to fall into a tie for sixth at 334.

Furyk could still force a playoff with a birdie at the 18th, but he pulled his nine-iron approach over a bunker and near the edge of a pond. He finished two shots back. That left only Sluman and Appleby. Sluman also missed the green and failed to chip in. Appleby hit his approach to 12 feet and had what appeared to be a good run at birdie. But he pushed the putt and had to settle for a closing 66 and a tie for second with Sluman at 331.

"I really wanted that one at 18," Appleby said. "I just lost my momentum on the front nine. You just can't get stuck, and I got stuck on the front nine."

Sluman was equally disappointed, but more reflective about the outcome. "I said yesterday that somebody would have to come out and shoot 10 under, and that's what happened," he said. "I really can't complain. I did all the things you were supposed to do. Phil just did one thing better. He won the shoot-out."

Tataurangi didn't know how much he had won, even after being handed the oversized cardboard check for $900,000. "I've never played the game to make a lot of money," he said. He knew that the win secured his PGA Tour card for the next two years, and that the move up to 33rd on the money list probably secured him an invitation to next year's Masters.

Disney Golf Classic—$3,700,000
Winner: Bob Burns

With a solid closing round of seven-under-par 65 for a total of 263, Bob Burns became the 16th first-time winner on the PGA Tour in 2002, a record number of first-timers. Burns distinguished himself among the others who cashed winner's checks for the first time in 2002. He was the only first-time winner to hold off a charging Tiger Woods.

Burns played like a veteran, not someone who last won at the 1998 Buy.com Tour Championship in Mobile, Alabama. After wrestling the lead away from

Chris DiMarco with a 10-foot birdie putt on the 11th (Burns' fifth birdie of the day), he solidified his lead with a 15-footer for birdie at the 13th, followed by a unlikely 30-footer for birdie at the 14th. Suddenly Burns held a two-stroke lead with four holes to play.

Four pars should do it. But the pressure was greater than normal. The crowd had let him know that something was happening up ahead. Woods was making one of his familiar Sunday moves. Five birdies on the first nine got things rolling. Woods could have easily shot 28. He missed two eagle putts inside 15 feet.

The charge continued after he hit his second shot from the rough on the 13th to within four feet for another birdie. At the 14th he made a 35-footer for birdie. Pars on the 15th and 16th slowed the momentum slightly, but Woods was still the favorite. All he needed to do was birdie the final two holes. As she watched her son walk off the 17th tee, Kultida Woods checked the scoreboard and asked, "Has Burns ever won before?" When informed that he had not, Mrs. Woods opined, "It might be tough if he sees Tiger up there."

Indeed it was, especially after Woods hit a nine iron to three feet on the 17th and made the putt for another birdie. The electricity in the air could have lit the Magic Kingdom, but Woods continued his quest. One more birdie was all he thought he needed.

His seven-iron approach to the 18th stopped six feet below the hole. It looked as though the improbable would, indeed, come true. Woods pulled the putt, walking after the ball and slapping the head of his putter after making the stroke. He knew he had blown his chance with his 63 for a 265 total. "I felt like if I could get to 10 under for the day I'd have a good chance," Woods said. "As it ended up, it probably wouldn't have been good enough."

Burns parred the 15th and 16th, then stood on the 17th tee — the most demanding driving hole on the final nine — knowing he needed a par-par finish to win. "I was pretty nervous until hitting my tee shot on 17," he said. "Once I got it over the water, I thought I could get it to the house."

Woods knew it was over too. Sitting in a lounge chair on the putting green near the big screen television, Woods watched as Burns prepared to hit his tee shot on the 17th. "This is the tournament right here," he said. When Burns' shot sailed over the water, landing perfectly in the center of the fairway, and the winless 30-year-old snatched his tee off the ground and marched down the fairway, Woods couldn't hold back a smile. "Oh, he pured it," Woods said. "Good for him."

Burns parred the 17th and 18th and won by one over DiMarco and by two over Woods. "Thankfully, it was only 72 holes," he said. "Give Tiger nine more and he would have had it."

Buick Challenge—$3,700,000
Winner: Jonathan Byrd

With all the first-time winners on the PGA Tour in 2002, it was no longer a surprise to find a name no one recognized atop the leaderboard. What was eyebrow-raising was the way in which 24-year-old rookie Jonathan Byrd became the 17th first-time champion of the year at the Buick Challenge in Callaway Gardens, Georgia.

Byrd came within two strokes of the PGA Tour's all-time scoring record, shooting 63 on Sunday for a 27-under-par 261 total. He also passed David Toms, a major championship winner, but Byrd was loaded with a bundle of talent. According to his caddie, Mike Carrick, who carried the bag for Tom Kite for 21 years, "Jonathan has the length that Tom never had. He's young, but he's really smart as far as golf course management goes. Just raw talent, Jonathan has more. He hits the ball farther and swings better. Tom's wedge play is better, but we're working on that."

As for his heart, that became apparent in the early going on Sunday when Byrd made the best swing of the week, or as he put it, "the best swing ever in competition," on the par-three fifth hole. "A perfect five iron," he said. "The shot, the flight, everything was great." The ball stopped five feet from the hole and Byrd made birdie to join Toms in the lead.

At the par-five seventh Byrd caught the kind of break that made everyone think this was his day. His tee shot drifted right, but hit a spectator on the shoulder, bouncing back into the fairway. The person Byrd hit turned out to be his fiancée. "She took one for the team," Byrd said with a smile.

The analogy wasn't that far off. Hitting his betrothed kept the ball from going in the pines, and Byrd was able to carve a three wood onto the green for yet another birdie.

Toms rallied back with birdies at the seventh and ninth to reach 21 under and regain a share of the lead, but, as Toms said, "that's when Jonathan took it deep on me." Byrd reached the par-five 11th with a three wood and hit a 25-foot eagle putt that never left the center of the hole. He then birdied the short par-four 12th and made a curling 40-footer for birdie at the 13th. At that point, fate seemed to be on his side.

"I was like, 'Wow, this is great!'" Byrd said. On the 14th he made another 25-footer for birdie that momentarily hung on the lip before falling in.

If Toms wasn't dejected enough, the 15th put an exclamation point on the kind of day it would be. Byrd hit a huge drive down the right side of the fairway, which left him a perfect five-wood distance to the well-guarded green on the par-five. He never thought about laying up short of the water. The ball stopped in the middle of the green, 50 feet from the hole. When that putt also fell for an eagle, Byrd momentarily started thinking about a possible 59. Toms just thought about second place, finishing with 65 for a 262 total.

A bogey coming in when Byrd missed the 16th green opened the door a little, but not far enough. Toms failed to convert any of his birdie putts on the final three holes, and Byrd cruised in with a one-shot victory. Phil Mickelson, who missed enough short putts throughout the week to last a season, finished third at 265 after matching Byrd's final-round 63.

Tour Championship—$5,000,000
Winner: Vijay Singh

The best thing about this rendition of the season-ending Tour Championship was the prize money, an additional $5 million on the line to 30 guys who already had won at least $1.8 million each for the year. There was little good to be said for the golf course — the historic East Lake Club in Atlanta which had hosted two previous Tour Championships and would become the permanent home of the event starting in 2004. Torrential rains made it play more like East Mud Puddle, or as Ernie Els called it, "7,000 yards of ground under repair."

Even with greens so soft they looked and sounded like sponges, 12 under par was the best anyone could muster. That came from a man who had played well at East Lake in the past. Vijay Singh, who finished runner-up to Hal Sutton in 1998 and third to Phil Mickelson in 2000, vowed to avenge his previous defeats. Longer and stronger after committing himself to a new workout regimen, Singh followed through on that promise with the best weekend and the best week, shooting 65 and 67 on Saturday and Sunday for a 268 total and a two-stroke victory over Charles Howell.

"Look out," Singh said, playfully displaying his bulging biceps. "I'm not done yet. My workouts have elevated my ability to repeat my swing. Charles is 23, and I'm hitting it with him all day, by him quite a few times. That tells you something — I'm almost twice his age and hitting it as long as he is."

That proved critical in a week when roll was nonexistent and even the longest hitters found themselves pulling out three and four irons for their approaches. It was fitting that the duel to the finish would come from two very long, very accurate ball-strikers who aren't known for their short-game prowess. Singh shot the low round of the week (65) twice, on Thursday and Saturday, and Howell was the only player in the field who finished with four rounds in the 60s.

In the end Singh's accuracy was too much to handle. Leading by three going into the final round, Singh put this one away by hitting 16 of the final 18 greens. Even a couple of four-footers that slid by the hole couldn't undo the Fijian.

"No doubt you're going to have to do something early, on the first four or five holes, if you're going to catch somebody from three behind," Howell said. "It would have taken a 63 to beat him, and that's a hard score to come by." Howell shot 66 and finished alone in second at 270, while David Toms was a distant third at 273.

Tiger Woods struggled with his tee shots throughout the week, which meant he didn't get to put his hands on the ball as often from the rough as Singh and Howell did from the fairway. That made a big difference in the end, as Woods finished at 276 for the week. Still, he was not too displeased.

"I hit the ball almost as good as I did in 2000," Woods said. "I just didn't hit it as close. I fired at a lot of flags in 2000, because I knew I wasn't going to short-side myself. This year I was more conservative. Nonetheless, six wins worldwide, that's not too bad."

Indeed it isn't. Nor was the $900,000 Singh collected for winning the grand finale. "This is a good springboard," he said. "I'm ready to make another charge."

Southern Farm Bureau Classic—$2,600,000
Winner: Luke Donald

The purse might not have been as large as that at the Tour Championship in Atlanta, but 300 miles east of East Lake, the Southern Farm Bureau Classic was no less about money.

Calculators were plentiful throughout the week as players on the bubble ran through all the calculations, figuring what they needed to shoot and how they needed to finish in order to avoid the grind of qualifying. They also watched the Weather Channel. It hadn't stopped raining in Mississippi for almost a month. Any more rain and the event could be cancelled.

That was exactly what happened when a deluge hit on Sunday. By Monday morning, PGA Tour officials announced that the course was unplayable and the event would be shortened to 54 holes. Luke Donald, a promising youngster from England, was declared the winner. His 66-68-67–201 total was a model of consistency, and the $468,000 he picked up for the one-stroke victory over Dean Pappas moved Donald to 58th on the season-ending money list.

"Winning this tournament turned a good year into a great year," Donald said. "I would have loved to have won the tournament in 72 holes, but there is nothing we could do about that. I'm just happy I was the leader in the clubhouse after three rounds."

The odd-man-out was Brad Elder, who came into the week 173rd in earnings and needing a win to avoid going back to qualifying. Scores of 65 and 67 gave Elder a two-stroke lead, but a third-round 71 dropped him into third place at 203.

"I should have played better on Saturday," Elder said. "I can't think about it. There are going to be other days I can play golf. It's not just these last days that are going to make or break my career."

Spoken like a man in search of a positive thought.

Donald won the tournament, but the big winner in the tournament-within-a-tournament was Jay Williamson, a 35-year-old winless professional who birdied four out of his last six holes on Saturday to jump into a tie for fifth with 205 total. The $85,150 he earned ($2,000 less than Fred Funk and Jeff Sluman earned for finishing tied for 25th in the Tour Championship) pushed Williamson from 127th to 125th place on the money list, exactly what he needed to keep his card for next year.

"It's like 99 cents on the dollar," Williamson said. "It's significantly better than 126th because I'll be able to set my schedule. It's amazing that it can come down to the way it did today, but you've got to cut it off somewhere. I just feel fortunate that I'm on the good side."

Special Events

CVS/pharmacy Charity Classic—$1,200,000
Winners: Dudley Hart and Chris DiMarco

Former college teammates Dudley Hart and Chris DiMarco high-fived each other like they were back at the University of Florida, but then again, they had reason to celebrate. When Hart rolled in a breaking 25-footer for birdie on the second extra hole, the team of Hart and DiMarco had completed a spectacular comeback to win the CVS/pharmacy Charity Classic in Barrington, Rhode Island.

It was the third time Hart had birdied the 18th hole in a 40-minute span. The first time, Hart and DiMarco were trailing Stewart Cink and David Toms by one stroke when Hart made an eight-footer for birdie to reach 20-under-par 122 to send the event to extra holes.

Still, Cink and Toms held the hot hand. Even though they missed a birdie putt at the last hole, they shot a tournament-record 14-under-par 57 to reach 20 under for the 36-hole event. Hart and DiMarco had been tied for the lead with defending champions Mark Calcavecchia and Nick Price after an opening round of 60. It didn't take long for them to fall behind Cink and Toms. Hart's birdie putt at the 18th gave the team of former Gators a nine-under-par 62.

Both teams parred the 18th in the playoff the first time through, then Cink made a seven-footer for birdie the next time, only to watch as Hart matched it with a six-footer of his own. The third time down the 18th Hart ended it with his 25-footer for birdie. Cink could have halved the hole, but his 16-footer stayed on the high side, and this one was over.

"To make a putt on 18 to get into the tie shows you something about the person," DiMarco said about his partner. "And I knew he was going to make that putt on the third playoff hole."

Steve Elkington and Craig Stadler had the second-lowest score of the second round when they combined for 59. That left them tied for third place with David Duval and Peter Jacobsen at 124. Calcavecchia and Price made nine straight pars on the back nine to finish alone in fifth at 125.

Fred Meyer Challenge—$1,075,000
Winners: Scott McCarron and Brian Henninger

Although a pair of Ryder Cup teammates tried to make it close, the team of Scott McCarron and Brian Henninger led the Fred Meyer Challenge in Aloha, Oregon, from the opening shot. McCarron and Henninger shot 22-under-par 122 to win by two strokes, but it was never that close.

With a 12-under-par 60 in the first round, Henninger and McCarron took a two-shot lead over Casey Martin and Notah Begay. David Toms and Stuart Cink were another shot back after 63 the first day. Also at 63 were the teams of Charles Howell and Matt Kuchar, Jack and Gary Nicklaus, and Tom Wargo and Bob Gilder.

Cink and Toms, who were Ryder Cup rookies together in 2002, made a run at the lead on the second day. They combined for 61 for a 124 total, but that was as close as anyone would get to the winners. McCarron and Henninger put this one away with a 10-under-par 62.

Wargo and Gilder shot their second consecutive 63 to finish tied for third with Howell and Kuchar, and the Nicklaus team. Martin and Begay shot 65 to finish tied for sixth with Craig Stadler and Steve Elkington, and Dudley Hart and David Duval.

UBS Warburg Cup—$3,000,000
Winner: United States

Gary Player gained some personal revenge by trouncing opposing captain Arnold Palmer in their singles match during the final day of the UBS Warburg Cup, but it didn't matter. Unlike 2001 when the United States squad rallied after Palmer's victory over Player, this time the Americans didn't need Palmer's point. They led 5½ to 6½ going into the 12 singles matches and made quick work of the Rest of the World team on Sunday, winning eight singles matches to retain the trophy.

On a blustery final day at Sea Island, Georgia, the U.S. lost only three matches, the first coming when Player beat Palmer 6 and 5, and the second when Barry Lane defeated Scott Hoch 1 up. Lane, who was making his debut in this over-40, Ryder Cup-style competition, called the week "wonderful" and said, "I played lovely all day. I had maybe two bad shots, but it's always tough when it's as windy as it was today."

Temperatures barely inched above 40 degrees the final day, which should have played into the hands of the Rest of the World squad, which was full of players accustomed to inclement conditions. That was evident when Ian Woosnam handed Tom Kite the third U.S. defeat of the day, 3 and 2.

But unlike the year before at Kiawah Island when the U.S. trailed in seven of the 12 singles matches at the halfway point, this one was never in question. Curtis Strange got things rolling for the Americans by defeating fellow Ryder Cup captain Sam Torrance 4 and 3.

Paul Azinger was next with a 4-and-3 victory of his own over Bernhard Langer. Azinger won his match in the same flamboyant style he displayed in the Ryder Cup, holing a bunker shot at the 15th to close out Langer. "Paul played fantastic, and whenever he's in a bunker you know he's either going to hole it or get it very close," Langer said. "The Ryder Cup proved that. He's one of the greatest bunker players ever."

Tom Lehman was 3-0 for the week and capped things off with a 2-and-1 victory over Eduardo Romero, while Hale Irwin moved the Americans within a half point of retaining the cup with a 2-and-1 win over Rodger Davis. That left it up to Fred Funk to clinch the title. But Funk lost the final three holes to Isao Aoki to halve his match, which gave the Americans a 12-9 lead. That insured that the U.S. would retain the cup, even if the Rest of the World team won the remaining matches.

Raymond Floyd secured the victory with a 2-and-1 win over Seiji Ebihara, and Bob Gilder added another point for good measure when he beat Stewart Ginn 1 up. The only other scratch the Rest of the World team would make on the board came when Denis Durnian halved with Tom Watson in the final match of the day.

"The United States simply played better than us, and they deserve the victory," Player said. "But it makes us feel good when golf is played is such a spirit."

Palmer also acknowledged the good spirit of these matches. "I'm very pleased and proud and happy that we were able to retain the UBS Warburg Cup," Palmer said. "I think what we accomplished with the camaraderie and competition says it all."

Hyundai Team Matches—$1,200,000
Winners: Rich Beem and Peter Lonard
    Dana Quigley and Allen Doyle
    Lorie Kane and Janice Moodie

After falling two down through two holes to defending champions Fred Couples and Mark Calcavecchia, the team of Rich Beem and Peter Lonard rallied with birdies on all four of the par-three holes at St. Regis Monarch Resort in Dana Point, California, to win the PGA Tour portion of the Hyundai Team Matches 2 and 1.

"I thought it was going to be a very humiliating and short day," Lonard said of the situation after Couples rolled in birdie putts on the first two holes. "Then we birdied the third hole and won after it looked like they were going to win that one, too."

After squaring the match at the fifth, Beem and Lonard never trailed again. "Peter made most of (the birdies)," Beem said. "But I contributed a few. We complemented each other very well."

The same could be said of Lorie Kane and Janice Moodie who combined for nine birdies and no bogeys in their 3-and-2 win over Juli Inkster and Dottie Pepper. "I usually like the end of the year and the beginning of the year," said Kane, who successfully defended her title with Moodie from 2001. "Maybe it has something to do with my being Canadian. If you look at my record overall, you'll see that I usually have a lull during the summer months."

Although Moodie ended it with a five-footer for birdie at the 16th hole, the Scot admitted that this win was a true team effort. "Lorie started well and I made my share of birdies," she said. "We just had them on different holes. That's something you have to do in match play."

In the senior division, defending champions Dana Quigley and Allen Doyle successfully held on to their title when Quigley chipped in for a birdie from behind the 17th green to end things against Jim Thorpe and John Jacobs 2 and 1.

"Our goal was to win last year so they'd have to invite us back again this year," Doyle said. "So it looks like we made that our goal again this year."

Callaway Golf Pebble Beach Invitational—$300,000
Winner: Mark Brooks

With the same precision that made him a major championship winner and a runner-up in the U.S. Open in 2001, Mark Brooks systematically picked apart the Del Monte, Spyglass and Pebble Beach courses in the Callaway Golf Pebble Beach Invitational. Brooks shot 16-under-par 272 to win by three strokes over Jeff Gove.

A second-round 65 gave Brooks a one-shot lead over Duffy Waldorf going into the weekend. He followed that up with 68 on Saturday to extend the lead to two. A closing 69 at Pebble Beach was all he needed. Gove shot 66 in the final round to take second at 275, while Waldorf shot 72 the final day to finish in a tie for third with Loren Roberts at 277.

Roger Maltbie hung up his broadcasting microphone for a week and had a good showing, posting 68, 69, 71 and 70 to finish fifth at 278, one clear of Brett Quigley and Matt Gogel.

Franklin Templeton Shootout—$2,250,000
Winners: Lee Janzen and Rocco Mediate

The Franklin Templeton Shootout at Tiburon Golf Club in Naples, Florida, came down to one swing. Watching from the 18th fairway as Matt Kuchar and David Gossett rolled in a birdie putt on the final green to get to 30-under-par 186 and tie the lead, Lee Janzen and Rocco Mediate knew what they needed to do. "I wanted to hit a great shot, get it as close as I could, make birdie, and win the tournament, no playoff," Janzen said.

He did all of the above with one well-struck eight iron from 157 yards that stopped three feet from the hole. "I knew he was going to do something silly there," Mediate said of his partner and former college teammate. "I had a feeling he was going to hit it to about five or six feet."

Janzen exceeded his partner's expectations, firing his approach straight at the left-tucked flag. It was the shot they needed at exactly the right time. Playing with Janzen and Mediate, John Huston and Jeff Maggert eagled the 17th hole to get to within one stroke of the lead, then rolled in a 20-footer at the 18th to join Kuchar and Gossett at 186. That was good enough for a share of the lead for the 30 seconds it took Janzen to line up the three-footer and roll it into the hole for birdie and a 31-under-par 185 total.

"Lee hit it pretty awesome in there," Maggert said. "They knew they had to make birdie there to have a chance to win, so that was a pretty impressive shot."

Maggert and Huston finished tied for second with Kuchar and Gossett, who came from five shots back on the final day with 56 in the scramble format. Although it was one off the tournament record, and one away from forcing a playoff, Kuchar was pretty happy with his team's play. "It would have been something to birdie every single hole today, but 16 under is awfully good," he said.

Just not quite good enough. "It just doesn't happen that often," Mediate said. "You don't get the chance to win. You might play a bunch together, but to win, it's kind of cool."

PGA Grand Slam of Golf—$1,000,000
Winner: Tiger Woods

How impressive was Tiger Woods' victory in the PGA Grand Slam of Golf? In addition to setting a couple of tournament records and winning the event for the fifth straight time, Woods' 17-under-par 127 would have beaten the best-ball score of the other three players in the field. He won by 14 strokes over Justin Leonard and Davis Love, and shot a tournament- and course-record 61 in the second round, tying his personal best for a single tournament round.

"Unbelievable," said PGA champion Rich Beem, who brought up the rear of this four-man event at Poipu Bay in Kauai, Hawaii. "What a phenomenal round Tiger played. It was a lot of fun watching him. It's amazing how when somebody gets on a roll how much fun it is to watch. Everything clicks. The golf ball was just going right at the target all day."

Woods birdied six of the first eight holes in the second round, ending all doubt about the eventual outcome. By the time he walked to the 10th tee after having shot 30 on the front, Woods held an eight-shot lead. The only remaining questions were: Could he shoot 60, and how big would the margin of victory be?

"I needed to go out and play a good solid front nine and I just got on a roll," Woods said. "I was surprised by a couple of shots I hit out there. I really couldn't miss a shot today. Every shot I hit was right in the middle of the clubface. I was making shots, aiming my shots, and I was knocking down my putts. It's a lot of fun when it works out that way."

He shattered the previous tournament scoring record of 12 under (which Woods set in 2001), and his 14-stroke victory was the widest margin in the history of the event, more than doubling the old margin of five shots set back in 1982.

"I enjoyed watching Tiger's round," Love said afterward. "It was one of the better rounds I've seen in a long time."

Target World Challenge—$3,800,000
Winner: Padraig Harrington

When Tiger Woods is playing in the final group, no lead seems safe. That's what Padraig Harrington found out after carrying a six-stroke lead into the final round of the Target World Challenge presented by Williams, a charity event benefiting the Tiger Woods Foundation at Sherwood Country Club in Thousand Oaks, California. Harrington birdied the first two holes to extend the lead to eight, then watched it all but evaporate as Woods put together one of his familiar final-round charges.

"I knew Tiger would come at me," Harrington said. "I heard someone say on No. 13, 'Oh, Tiger is in his head.' I'm thinking, 'He's been in there all day.'"

Woods cut the eight-shot lead down to three through 11 holes with a barrage of birdies, but Harrington, who had been on a tear one day earlier, rolled in a birdie putt at the 12th to restore a four-shot lead with six holes to play. This one seemed to be in hand.

Then on the 14th Harrington made the one mistake he couldn't afford to make. After driving his ball in ground under repair, he chose not to take a drop because of the angle he would have at the green from the drop area. From a questionable lie, Harrington pulled his approach left of the green, over a cart path, through a fence and out of bounds. His fourth shot was also left, but the ball stayed on a hillside beside the green. From there, Harrington hit a flop shot to five feet and rolled in the putt for a double bogey.

Woods missed an 18-footer for birdie, or the two would have left the 14th green tied. As it was, Harrington held on to a one-shot lead, but the advantage seemed to go to Woods.

That momentum swung back in Harrington's direction at the par-five 16th when, from the center of the fairway, Woods pulled a three-iron approach into the trees 40 yards left of the green. With no backswing, he punched out, missed the green with his fourth shot, then chipped in for par. Harrington birdied, which extended the lead to two shots with two holes to play. "I would have rather had a three-shot lead with two holes to play," Harrington said.

Woods birdied the 17th to cut the lead to one, but that was as close as he would get. Needing a birdie at the 18th to force a playoff, Woods pushed his approach and made bogey. Harrington held on, finishing with one-under-par 71 for a 268 total and a two-shot victory over Woods, who finished with 67.

"I had a pretty good shot at it," Wood said. "I had two bad swings, and that cost me."

Once his second shot found the 18th green, Harrington found that he could breath again. "Three putts to win?" he said. "Yes, I was breathing quite comfortably then."

WGC EMC World Cup—$3,000,000
Winner: Japan

Even though they started the final round with a three-shot lead over Phil Mickelson and David Toms, the Japanese team of Shigeki Maruyama and Toshimitsu Izawa needed some help from the Americans to win their first WGC EMC World Cup title. The Japanese team shot 36-under-par 252, but had to rely on a double bogey by the Americans at the 18th for the victory on the Nicklaus Course at Vista Vallarta in Puerto Vallarta, Mexico.

"We were aiming for 36 under at the beginning," Maruyama said. "We knew there was going to be one team that would be chasing us, and it was the Americans."

The Americans birdied the first two holes of the final alternate-shot round, and they took the lead for the first time all week at the par-four 13th when Toms rolled in a birdie putt of five feet to get to 35 under while Japan followed their birdie at the 12th with an unseemly double bogey at the 13th after Maruyama hit his approach long and Izawa chipped across the green and into the rough.

Toms and Mickelson birdied the 16th, which looked to be enough to close out the victory. The lead was two with two holes to play. A par at the 17th made a U.S. victory even more of a certainty. But Mickelson hit the tee shot at the 18th into the rough, leaving Toms with a difficult approach, one he tried to get too close to the hole.

"I was trying to keep the face open so it wouldn't shoot left on me. I hit a bad shot. Looking back, I should have hit a sand wedge over the trees, but I just didn't think the shot through."

After much deliberation, Mickelson took a drop and hit a pitch shot six feet long. When Toms' putt for bogey slipped by the hole, the lead was gone.

Meanwhile the Japanese were birdieing the 17th to regain a one-shot lead with one to play. On the 18th, Maruyama hit a perfect approach that stopped three feet from the hole. When Izawa rolled the birdie putt in the hole, the margin of victory was extended to two.

"It's been quite a few years since Japan has won the World Cup," Maruyama said. "I'm very happy now."

Not as happy were the Americans, who wondered how on earth they had shot themselves in the foot like that. "We played very well this week and gave ourselves a shot at it and put ourselves in a position to win with a couple of holes to go," Mickelson said. "The last hole certainly was a disappointing way for us to finish, given that we fought so hard yesterday and today to get back in the tournament."

Office Depot Father-Son Challenge—$1,000,000
Winners: Craig and Kevin Stadler

The father-son team of Craig and Kevin Stadler played brother-in-law golf in the final moments of the Office Depot Father-Son Challenge at Paradise Island in the Bahamas. Trailing by one with one hole to play, Kevin made an eight-footer for birdie to force a playoff with Hale and Steve Irwin. One hole later, Craig made a 30-footer for birdie to end the event in the Stadlers' favor.

Both the Stadlers and the Irwins played extremely well, each team making eight birdies in the final nine holes. "We were tied after nine, then made eight birdies on the back nine and still almost lost it outright," Craig said. "That just ain't right."

The Irwins birdied their first eight holes of the back nine, but missed a 15-footer on the 18th that would have won it in regulation. As it was, both teams shot 12-under-par 60 in the second round for a two-day total of 24-under 120.

Five-time winners Raymond Floyd and his son Raymond Jr. also shot 60 in the second round, but finished two shots out of the playoff and tied for third with Johnny and John Miller. Gary and Wayne Player shot 64 and 61 to finish tied for fifth with Myatt and Hubert Green, and Dave and Dave Stockton, Jr.

Buy.com Tour

While rain dripped from the magnolias and peppered the green tin roof of the clubhouse, 32-year-old Patrick Moore sat and tried to come to grips with what had just happened. The night before he had gone to bed in another cheap motel (this one in Prattville, Alabama) as the overnight leader in the Buy.com Tour Championship. Now, after a decade of greasy diners, Monday morning qualifiers and mini-tours nobody could remember, Moore was a three-time winner on the Buy.com Tour.

He rubbed his finger over the white plastic PGA Tour card with his name embossed below the logo and tried to control his emotions. "It's just amazing how life can change so quickly," he said. "This is the culmination of 10 years of hard work turned into six months of good golf."

Moore only had to play four holes on that rainy Sunday in Alabama, the last four holes of his third round. He birdied three of them for a six-under-par 66 and a two-stroke lead over Steve Alker. That was where the season ended. When rain flooded most of the golf course, officials called off the Buy.com Tour Championship after 54 holes, making Moore the winner with a 10-under-par 206 total. He climbed to the top spot on the year-end money list, earned Player of the Year honors, and was the first player of the 2002 season to earn a "battlefield promotion" onto the PGA Tour. A week later he would miss the cut in his debut at the Southern Farm Bureau Classic, but for a few, brief moments in the Alabama rain, Moore felt as if he were a man of destiny.

"I've stayed in cheap motels and eaten in restaurants that I probably had no businesses being in," Moore said. Those eateries were scattered all across the globe as Moore spent the better part of his 20s hopping around the Asian and African tours in an attempt to find a golfing home. He had been a four-time runner-up in Canadian Tour events, but the University of North Carolina graduate came up short every time he attempted to earn his way to the PGA Tour.

That all changed in 2002. He qualified for a spot in the Buy.com Richmond Open in May, and earned a spot on the tour for the rest of the year when he won the event. Four weeks later, Moore became the first multiple winner of the year when he took the Lake Erie Charity Classic. By the final week of the season he led the tour in scoring average (69.86), was second in birdies per round (4.17) and putts per green hit (1.735), and was in the top 10 in every statistical category. The one stat that mattered most was the money title. "You work so hard for so long, to finally get here ... it's just hard to believe," he said.

Moore's nearest challenger was another multiple winner. Arron Oberholser won the Samsung Canadian PGA Championship in June and the Utah Classic in early September. He finished tied for fifth in the Tour Championship, three strokes behind Moore, but by then the pressure was off. Oberholser won $319,883 for the year and earned his tour card by a comfortable margin.

Jason Gore won twice, taking the Oregon Classic and the Albertson's

Boise Open in consecutive weeks to finish sixth for the year, while Cliff Kresge won both the Virginia Beach Open and Hershey Open in a playoff. Before earning his tour card for finishing fifth on the money list, Kresge was best known for falling into a pond while lining up a putt at the 2000 qualifying tournament. "When I went under the water, I thought about taking a big gulp and not coming back up," he said. Fortunately, he dried himself off and continued to play.

PGA Tour veteran Doug Barron (who played the regular tour from 1997 through 2001) didn't win on the Buy.com circuit in 2002, but his four runner-up finishes were enough to push him into third place on the money list. Two-time Australian Open champion Aaron Baddeley didn't win either. But three consecutive top-five finishes in October pushed the 21-year-old Australian from 35th on the money list to 10th and earned him a spot on the PGA Tour.

Baddeley wasn't the only Australian to qualify. Gavin Coles not only won the Jacob's Creek Open (co-sponsored with the Australasian Tour), he became the second Australian and the shortest man (at 5-foot-4) to earn a 2003 PGA Tour card.

There were some heart-tugging comebacks this year as well. Darren Stiles, who was diagnosed with cancer in 1989 at age 16, won the Knoxville Open in June and finished ninth on the money list. While inspirational, that story paled in the light of the saga of Todd Barranger. A player on the PGA Tour in 1994, Barranger was diagnosed with testicular cancer in 1995 and underwent extensive treatment. He returned to golf in 1996 and won the Thailand Open, but had failed to make it back to the PGA Tour. In 2001 he was perched in the precarious 15th spot on the money list entering the final week of the season, but shot 85 in the opening round of the Tour Championship and fell out of the top 15. This year he was back in the 15th spot on the money list, but he shot 65 in the opening round to take the lead after the first 18 holes. He followed it with rounds of 73 and 74 and was three over par when play was called on Sunday, but that was still good enough to hold on to the 15th and final qualifying spot.

Some big names graced the leaderboards throughout the year, but they weren't always what they seemed. At the State Farm Open in September the names Miller and Stockton were on top of the boards. But it wasn't Johnny Miller and Dave Stockton; it was their sons, Andy Miller and Dave Stockton, Jr. Miller, a Monday qualifier, won the event in a playoff over Stockton. "It was like turning back the clock with Miller and Stockton on the leaderboard," Miller said. Unfortunately, that would be Miller's only moment in the sun. He finished with year with just over $103,000, 45th on the money list and $100 behind another famous golfing name — Haas (not Jay but Hunter). Stockton did a little better, finishing the season with $110,154 and in 40th place on the list.

Gary Hallberg won the Northeast Pennsylvania Classic, coming from seven shots back in the final round to set a comeback record for the Buy.com Tour. It was Hallberg's first victory in a decade (the last coming in the 1992 Buick Challenge), but it was also the only bright spot of his season. In 21 events, Hallberg only made $106,317. He finished 42nd on the money list.

Canadian Tour

For a while this year it appeared that the Canadian Tour had become a home for former U.S. Amateur standouts still battling the burdens of high expectations. Names from the past like Scott, Kuehne and Quinney consistently showed up on Canadian Tour leaderboards throughout the year, and the highly touted Americans took a few steps toward the stardom they were all supposed to attain.

The Texas Classic in Houston in early March was a microcosm for the season. Few were watching as Steve Scott, the former University of Florida All-American who lost to Tiger Woods in a playoff in the 1996 U.S. Amateur, shot 69 in the final round to beat former Amateur champions Hank Kuehne (1998) and Jeff Quinney (2000) by one stroke.

Afterward all three spoke like war-weary soldiers. "Even when I missed putts in the final round, I told myself to stay patient and hang in there," Scott said. He also had to answer the usual questions about finishing second to Woods in the most thrilling recent U.S. Amateur final, and how the two players' careers had taken divergent paths since that day in Oregon. Before the end of 1996 Woods was on his way to becoming the best player in the world while Scott's career sunk like a stone. "I'm not sure this win will put that to rest," Scott said. "But it should help. Of course I still wish I could have won (the Amateur), but finishing second is something that I will always be known for. Hopefully this win will push it further back in people's minds."

For a few moments after Scott finished speaking the only sounds were a few birds chirping in the distance, and a thickly accented Texas voice that said, "Yeah, right."

Quinney tried to sound upbeat after the loss, but it was obvious he still struggled in the spotlight, even one this dim. "Things just didn't go my way," he said. "But hats off to Steve. He's a good player who stepped up when he needed to. I'd like to get another chance at him over the next few weeks."

He would, indeed, get another shot at him throughout the rest of the season. Quinney, who struggled with his confidence and with the pressures of the limelight after winning the U.S. Amateur and returning to Arizona State as the top-ranked player in the country, had become something of a fixture on the Canadian Tour, heading north from his Eugene, Oregon, home after being bumped from the second stage of the 2001 qualifying tournament.

Two weeks after losing in Texas, Quinney won his first professional title in Arizona at the Scottsdale Swing. He shot 23-under-par 265 at McCormick Ranch and won $16,000. That was a week after Kuehne broke through with his first win of the year at the Texas Challenge.

"I don't think we're that dominant," Quinney said. "Each one of us just seems to be playing good golf right now. We've proven ourselves at the highest level of competition as amateurs, so maybe that has something to do with it. But to go three-for-three is surprising."

Quinney might have been surprised, but Kuehne, who still looked like the same swaggering bald Texan who was supposed to challenge Woods, talked like a man who had never lost a step. "Most people know if anyone can make birdies, it's me," Kuehne said. "I just need to limit my mistakes."

At the same time Woods was accepting his third straight Bay Hill Invitational trophy, Kuehne collected $16,000 for his win the Circle C Ranch in Austin, one week after 1999 U.S. Amateur champion Matt Kuchar took home $630,000 in his first victory on the PGA Tour in Coral Springs.

Their rise continued through the summer. Quinney won again in June at the Bay Mills Open in Michigan, and Kuehne won the Telus Quebec Open the second week in August. In between, players like Jimmy Walker, Rob McMillan and Derek Gillespie all picked up titles. Mike Grob won the Ontario Open and Iain Steel won in Vancouver. Scott Hend won the Victoria Open and Alex Quiroz picked up his first title in the MTS Classic in Winnipeg.

But this was the year of the amateurs from days gone by. Kuehne won the money title and earned spots in the Air Canada Championship and Bell Canadian Open while Quinney and Scott finished second and third. Kuehne and Quinney also earned exemptions to the finals of the U.S. qualifying tournament.

"It feels like a big weight has been lifted off of me," Kuehne said. "This is what I've worked for all year. Any time you can skip a week of q-school, not to mention get into the PGA Tour events up here, that's huge."

Neither Kuehne nor Quinney advanced to the PGA Tour, however. Kuehne finished tied for 128th in the qualifying finals, while Quinney suffered a herniated disk, shot a pair of 80s, and finished tied for 157th.

South American Tour

When the final amounts were tallied in early December, Argentine Rafael Gomez was alone at the top. Gomez won his first Tour de las Americas Order of Merit title going away, earning $55,986 in 11 events and eclipsing his nearest challenger, Paraguay's Marco Ruiz, by more than $20,000.

Gomez got the year off to a fast start, winning the Corona Caribbean Open and then American Express Costa Rica Open in February despite miserable conditions and over-par scores. He was one of the few players to post a round in the 60s, shooting 69 in the second round. Things got worse on the weekend. Gomez shot 73 and 74 in awful weather, while Ruiz shot 69 and 76. Both finished at five-over-par 289, and Gomez won in a playoff.

Between the two victories came a runner-up finish in the TLA Los Encinos Open where Gomez shot a closing 68 to finish two shots behind American Roland Thatcher. The week after his win in Costa Rica, Gomez tied for third in the Tikal Trophy Guatemala. Those four top-five finishes catapulted Gomez to the top of the Order of Merit, a position he never relinquished.

Paraguay's Pedro Martinez (not to be confused with the Boston Red Sox pitcher) won the LG Panama Masters the first week in March by shooting three consecutive rounds of 67 for a 12-under-par 272 total, but Gomez had another good week to finish tied for 14th. He followed that with a share of 12th in the TLA Players Championship in Acapulco. Even though Roberto Coceres won the event, Gomez's Order of Merit lead continued to widen.

Jesus Amaya made a mid-season run, winning back-to-back-to-back events in the Medellin Open, Serrezuela Masters, and capping off the run with a four-shot victory in the CANTV Venezuela Open. Amaya, a native Colombian, finished the year with $31,438 in 11 starts, good enough to take the fourth-place spot on the Order of Merit behind Gomez, Ruiz and Argentine Gustavo Acosta.

The season ended on a familiar note. Angel Cabrera, a veteran of world golf, won the Argentina Open by four shots over Jose Coceres, and became the first successful defending champion of the event since Miguel Fernandez won back-to-back titles in 1987 and 1988.

"This is a great moment," Cabrera said after firing rounds of 70, 62, 68 and 69. "There is always an enormous amount of prestige that goes with winning this championship, particularly this year with the high level of players in the field."

10. European Tours

If the PGA European Tour season felt like a carryover from 2001, it was because so many of the players who broke onto the scene a year ago continued without missing a beat. For 11 months starting in June 2001 and extending through the Masters in April 2002, the second-hottest player in the game (behind You-Know-Who) was Retief Goosen, the quiet South African who won the 2001 U.S. Open and earned his first European Order of Merit title a year ago. Goosen did it again in 2002, winning the Order of Merit with over €2.3 million in earnings.

Goosen won the Johnnie Walker Classic in Australia in January, the Dimension Data Pro-Am in South Africa in February, the BellSouth Classic in Georgia in April, and he finished second to Tiger Woods in the Masters, prompting him to give one of the best one-liners of the year. "Do I get the green pants?" Goosen asked the Masters committeeman after his runner-up finish. He didn't, but he did get a boatload of cash for his efforts, earning $3.8 million worldwide for the year. Goosen barely edged out Padraig Harrington for Europe's money title. The difference between first and second on the year's Order of Merit list was less than €25,000.

It was also a great year for Goosen's compatriot and friend Ernie Els. Although Goosen once played in the shadow of Els, in 2001 it was Els who seemed lost in the darkness. He had finished second in three of the four majors in 2000, but on occasion seemed to be a victim of self-doubt and conflicted loyalties. All that changed in 2002 when Els began working with Belgian sports psychologist Jos Vanstiphout.

While Vanstiphout doesn't sugarcoat anything with any of his clients (including Goosen and Thomas Levet), with Els he was particularly brutal. "Ernie has all the talent, but he doesn't think he is the best, so he isn't," Vanstiphout said. "I tell him this, which is what he needs to hear. The average person tries to please everyone. I'm not that way. With me there is only black and white."

Those black-and-white sessions bore fruit early. Els won the Heineken Classic in Australia in early February and the Dubai Desert Classic in early March. He won in Miami the week before going to Dubai, holding off Tiger Woods in the Genuity Championship at Doral, but still sounded like someone dealing with deep psychological scars. "I used to be a great front-runner," Els said. "Then this little voice started coming into my head, this little guy inside me that made me defensive, almost scared. It isn't a question of motivation. It's attitude. After all, if you get down, it's not because you don't want it or don't care. But I told that little guy, let's be friends."

The "little guy" was back in full force in July at Muirfield when Els lost what appeared to be a comfortable lead in the British Open with a double bogey at the 16th. He rallied with a birdie at the 17th and ultimately won in a playoff, but afterward he admitted that the "little guy" had been screaming in his backswing throughout most of the day. "I'm never going to get rid of him," Els said. "I mean, this week I had a chance a couple of times to break away and the little guy just kept sitting on my shoulder. Every time

I tried to shoo him away, I made a mistake. It was difficult, but I'm proud of myself for getting through this one."

Nevertheless, Els proceeded to win for the fifth time of the year at the Cisco World Match Play, then won his sixth at the Nedbank Golf Challenge in South Africa, where the $2 million first prize elevated him to $6.2 million worldwide, second only to Woods.

This was also a breakout year for Justin Rose, when potential was finally realized and past demons exorcised. Rose, who once missed 21 consecutive cuts, was the first player on any tour to win four times worldwide in 2002. Rose won twice in South Africa, once in Japan and a fourth time on his native soil when he came from behind to win the Victor Chandler British Masters. He also had top-five finishes at the Barclays Scottish Open and the TNT Open.

After winning the Mercedes Championships in Hawaii in January, Spain's Sergio Garcia stated his long-term goals. "I want to win the money titles on the U.S. Tour and the European Tour together (in the same year)," Garcia said. While he didn't achieve either of those goals, he did finish the year in sixth place on the European Order of Merit with €1.4 million in 11 starts, and 12th on the U.S. money list with $2.4 million. He won the Canarias Open de Espana in April, and had over $3.4 million in worldwide earnings.

The year ended in an unusual fashion as the Volvo Masters Andalucia was called due to darkness, and Colin Montgomerie and Bernhard Langer were declared co-winners. Montgomerie finished fourth on the Order of Merit and Langer took 19th place. "I agree that it was very appropriate that we share this wonderful trophy," Montgomerie said after the tie was declared. "I think that it's also appropriate that in a Ryder Cup year, with a victory for Europe, that my partner and I should share this trophy. It's good for the pair of us to be victorious again."

PGA European Tour

Bell's South African Open—£500,000
Winner: Tim Clark
See African Tours chapter.

Dunhill Championship—£500,000
Winner: Justin Rose
See African Tours chapter.

Johnnie Walker Classic—A$2,700,000
Winner: Retief Goosen
See Australasian Tour chapter.

Heineken Classic—A$2,000,000
Winner: Ernie Els
See Australasian Tour chapter.

ANZ Championship—A$1,750,000
Winner: Richard Johnson
See Australasian Tour chapter.

Caltex Singapore Masters—US$900,000
Winner: Arjun Atwal
See Asia/Japan Tours chapter.

Carlsberg Malaysian Open—US$1,000,000
Winner: Alastair Forsyth
See Asia/Japan Tours chapter.

Dubai Desert Classic—€1,644,544
Winner: Ernie Els

The golf season is often a long series of ups and downs with various players showing streaks of brilliance for a couple of weeks along the way. The full measure of a season usually isn't clear until after the PGA Championship in August. With that in mind, the best way to describe Ernie Els' winter was to simply state the facts. In two months he won three times on three continents and asserted himself as the hottest early season player of the year so far.

The third of those wins came the first week in March at the Dubai Desert Classic where Els birdied the second, third, ninth, 10th and 16th holes on Sunday for a score of 69 to reach 16-under-par 272 and win by four strokes over Niclas Fasth.

"So far, so good," Els said of his hard-charging start to the year. He was a cumulative 50 under par for the three wins — the others were the Heineken Classic in Australia and Genuity Championship in the United States — a performance the notably understated Els called, "a really good start." He went on to say, "I'm really enjoying it. I always felt I was in control today from tee to green and it was a comfortable win in the end."

Els had a three-shot lead going into the final round thanks to a shot at the par-five 18th that Els called "one of the three best shots of my career." It was a three iron from the sand and scrub well left of the fairway that sailed 230 yards under one tree and over another before stopping 30 feet from the hole. "I reckon there was a 30 percent chance of success with that shot," Els said. He made the putt for eagle to shoot 67 and give himself the cushion over Fasth with one round to go.

On Sunday Els gave up shots on the first and fourth holes while Fasth was making eagle at the third and birdie at the seventh to pull into a share of the lead. Fasth gave the lead back just as quickly as he got it. He hit a terrible tee shot on the eighth that led to a triple-bogey eight. Another birdie at the 13th pulled Fasth to within two, but a bogey at the 16th while Els was making birdie settled things for good. The lead was four with two holes to play. That was how it ended, as Fasth shot 70 for a 276 total.

"The turning point was definitely the eighth, because Niclas was right up there and putting a lot of pressure on me," Els said. He was the only player to post four rounds under 70.

Qatar Masters—€1,713,903
Winner: Adam Scott

Living up the potential everyone in the golf world expected, Australian Adam Scott won his second PGA European Tour title in as many seasons when he shot a closing 67 to win the Qatar Masters by six strokes over Nick Dougherty and Jean-Francois Remesy. Scott's 19-under-par 269 total won €285,651, but it was worth more than that in confidence for the youngster.

"I think winning for the second time is harder than winning for the first," he said. Scott picked up his first European win as a rookie at the Alfred Dunhill Championship in 2001. "I said at the start of the year that I would like to have a multiple-win season in Europe, so this is a great way to start. Now I can really go and dig in my heels."

Scott thrilled the galleries in the small Arab nation with shots that put this one away early. After holing a four iron from 200 yards for an eagle on the second day en route to a 66 (his lowest score of the week), Scott did it again on Sunday, holing a wedge from 133 yards on the 634-yard, par-five ninth for eagle to extend his lead to six, which is where it would remain. He had just birdied the eighth after starting the day with a three-shot lead, when the wedge at the ninth took one hop and spun back into the cup. That's when Scott knew this was going to be his day, his week and his tournament.

"I didn't put any pressure on myself today," he said. "Maybe if someone had gotten off to a hot start, then I would have felt pressure, but no one did, and I felt comfortable and relaxed. But the conditions were difficult with the wind, which made it hard for someone to come from the pack."

Dougherty shot 69 on Sunday to finish at 275, while Remesy shot 70. The only score lower than Scott's 67 in the final round came from Joakim Haeggman, who shot 66 to move into a six-way tie for fourth at 277.

Madeira Island Open—€550,000
Winner: Diego Borrego

The PGA European Tour finally played an event in Europe the last week in March, but it was without their leading money winners. Most of Europe's best were in Ponte Vedra Beach, Florida, trying (unsuccessfully) to break a European winless drought at The Players Championship. While Goosen, Garcia, Montgomerie, Langer and Els were struggling there, Spain's Diego Borrego was battling the gusting Mediterranean winds to win the Madeira Island Open, his first victory in seven years.

Borrego started the last round four strokes behind fellow Spaniard Ivo Giner and Holland's Maarten Lafeber, but he knew the windy conditions would make for a difficult day.

"I stuck to the plan. I just hit fairways and greens and two-putted," Borrego said. After a three-putt bogey on the first hole, Borrego had four birdies and 13 pars to shoot 69 for a seven-under-par 281 total. "When I saw the leaderboard on the 15th, I said to my caddie that now is the chance to win the tournament. That hole was the key because I birdied it and knew I would win from there."

That prediction was almost premature. Giner, who battled in the wind throughout most of the day, was even par for the day and seven under for the week walking up the final fairway. A par on the 18th would send him to extra holes. But Giner's eight-iron approach landed well short of the green, and his chip shot stopped four feet from the hole. When he missed the four-footer for par, Giner fell back into a tie with Lafeber. Both shot one-over-par 73 on Sunday to finish the week at 282. "It hurts," Giner said after missing the final putt.

Giner's pain was Borrego's pleasure, as the Spaniard, who was in danger of losing his tour card after the 2001 season, won €91,660 and a two-year exemption in Europe.

Algarve Open de Portugal—€750,000
Winner: Carl Pettersson

There wasn't a cloud on the horizon on Saturday, and after a brief but heavy shower on Sunday morning, the sky was clear and blue. But no one played golf. The Algarve Open de Portugal was shortened to 36 holes, not because of rain or lightening or course conditions, but because of wind.

That left two players tied at two-under-par 142, even though they arrived at their scores by different routes. David Gilford, the 36-year-old former Ryder Cup player, put together solid rounds of 70 and 72, while 24-year-old Carl Pettersson, a native of Sweden who resides in North Carolina and considers himself a North Carolinian, shot 66 on Thursday to take a four-shot lead, but played into the teeth of the wind on Friday and ballooned to 76.

Then the trouble started. Wind speeds peaked at 50 miles an hour on Saturday, which led officials to shorten the tournament to 54 holes. When the rain came and the wind picked up again on Sunday, they were forced to end the event after 36 holes and cut the purse by 25 percent.

When the wind calmed down enough, Pettersson and Gilford trotted back to the 18th hole for a playoff. Both found the fairway on the uphill par-four. After Pettersson hit a six iron to the center of the green, Gilford hit his six iron long and right into thick rough. The Englishman then chipped long and missed his 25-footer for par. That gave Pettersson two putts for the win, which he negotiated without much trouble.

"I've never felt pressure like I did in the playoff, knowing I had two putts to win," Pettersson said. "I am normally very calm under pressure, but I was shaking a bit today. I had a tricky one uphill, but that was okay as I didn't want to leave myself a short one downhill."

Like everyone else, Pettersson would have liked to play all four days, but he would take the win any way he could get it. "One of my goals this season was to win," he said. "It's a shame the tournament had to be shortened to

36 holes, but winning was a goal and now I've achieved it. I'm extremely happy."

The Seve Trophy—€2,400,000
Winner: Great Britain and Ireland

The singles match between team captains Seve Ballesteros for the Continentals and Colin Montgomerie for Great Britain and Ireland was a highlight of the week of The Seve Trophy. Montgomerie shot an approximate 74 on a wet, cold Druid's Glen course in Ireland, while Ballesteros shot about 79. In the end Ballesteros, as he had done countless times throughout the years, found a way to win the match. In the process he received three free drops, hit two shots left-handed, chopped out sideways and backwards three more times, and needed only 26 putts to beat Montgomerie 1 up.

"It was amateur hour out there," Montgomerie said. "I did not play well, but Seve is just amazing. Just when you think you're going to win a hole, you end up losing it."

In the end Seve's efforts were not enough. With Jesper Parnevik, Bernhard Langer and Sergio Garcia choosing to skip the event, the Continentals were handicapped from the start, and it showed. In the first two days the GB&I team earned 10 points. They only needed 13½ to win back the cup, and with the weather getting uglier by the minute, Montgomerie's team looked to be in control.

Ballesteros tried to set the tone by winning the first match against Montgomerie, but his victory carried little weight and even less momentum. Darren Clarke quickly righted things on Sunday with a 4-and-3 victory over Thomas Bjorn. The Continentals took the next two points when Miguel Angel Jimenez, sporting a new red hairstyle that gave him a distinct clown look, beat Paul Casey 4 and 3 just moments before Robert Karlsson beat Paul Lawrie 1 up to inch the Continentals within two points of a tie.

Ireland's Paul McGinley righted things for GB&I when he beat Mathias Gronberg 4 and 3. Minutes later Lee Westwood beat Raphael Jacquelin 3 and 2. That gave GB&I 13 points and ensured at least a tie. When Padraig Harrington beat Jose Maria Olazabal 3 and 2, the GB&I team had the 14 points it needed to win.

"This was very much a team effort," Montgomerie said. "Obviously there is a personal pride involved within the team, but overall we needed 13½ points and we got that in the end. It was a harder battle than we thought, and the Europeans actually won the singles, the only series they won. But at the same time we had enough of a lead to cope, and I thank all the team members who came through. Everybody got at least a point, and that's a true team effort."

"It was not easy under the conditions," Ballesteros said. "Everyone played very well and we tried our best. I guess the British and Irish team played a little bit better, and perhaps they were a little bit more lucky."

Canarias Open de Espana—€1,722,000
Winner: Sergio Garcia

When Sergio Garcia plays in his home country, there's never a dull moment. From the moment the 22-year-old Spaniard teed off in the Canarias Open de Espana, the crowds were enthusiastically behind him. They even cheered when he made a couple of putts on the practice green.

Garcia didn't disappoint his boisterous fans, although he did turn what should have been a final-round victory lap into a battle down the stretch. After opening up a five-stroke lead with scores of 67, 68 and 67, Garcia increased the lead to seven shots after a birdie at the opening hole on Sunday and an eagle at the par-five second. Garcia made things interesting with bogeys at the fourth and sixth and a double bogey at the 12th after hitting a ball in the water. One more bogey at the 13th and Garcia's lead had slipped to a single stroke.

The closest pursuer at the time was Carl Pettersson, the winner of the Algarve Open de Portugal. Pettersson made five birdies in his first 14 holes to draw within a shot of the lead. Then at the 15th he drove into the fairway bunker and attempted a sand shot over water with a three iron. It never had a chance. Pettersson made a double bogey.

"I had to go for it," Pettersson said. "I don't play to finish second or third. If there is a chance to win, I will go for it. Obviously I'm a little disappointed, because I had gotten it to one shot behind. I knew Sergio would play well coming in, but I'm pleased I gave him something to think about, at least for a little while."

Moments after Pettersson made his double bogey, Garcia rolled in a birdie putt at the 14th and the lead was back to four. Pettersson finished with two more bogeys for 72 and a 281 total, enough for a share of fourth place, but as he said, "a little disappointing."

Garcia closed with pars to shoot 73 and 275 for the week. The margin of victory turned out to be four strokes over Emanuele Canonica. Greg Owen was third, five behind. But for a couple of hours at least, it was a lot closer than that.

"I knew what I had to do and I knew that I was in control," Garcia said. "Even though it didn't look like it for a while, I knew if I kept hitting good shots, be patient and play smart, that everything was going to be fine and that is what happened. I'm very happy. It's always great to win your home Open. It's something I've been looking forward to doing."

Novotel Perrier Open de France—€2,000,000
Winner: Malcolm Mackenzie

In a true testament to the fact that dogged persistence eventually pays, England's Malcolm Mackenzie, a 20-year winless veteran of the PGA European Tour, battled a late bout of nerves to hold off Trevor Immelman and win the Novotel Perrier Open de France by one stroke. It was Mackenzie's 509th start and his first victory.

"This changes my life," the 40-year-old said. "I went back to (qualifying) school twice in the last three years, but I kept trying and kept going and it was worth it. This proves you should never give up. Just don't ever give in, ever."

Those were words Mackenzie muttered to himself more than once in the final round. After 65 gave him a one-shot lead over Immelman, Mackenzie hoped for a strong start on Sunday, but he didn't get it. "It could have been a lot worse," he said. "I up-and-downed it on the first and second holes for bogey, so I wasn't that disheartened. At the third I hit a great bunker shot to make a birdie and after that I played superb."

After 14 holes he held a three-shot lead. Then nerves took over. For three straight holes Mackenzie made unforced errors that resulted in bogeys. "At 15 it all fell apart," he said. "I lost it a little there and went in the water, then up-and-downed it again for a (bogey) five. On 16 I left a four-footer for par short of the cup, which was nerves more than anything. Then on 17 I dropped a shot again, but I had a bad lie in the fairway. Then it all came down to 18."

At the 514-yard par-five Mackenzie knew that a birdie would win it, but a par would mean a playoff. He boomed a tee shot to within 200 yards of the island green. Then he had a chat with his caddie.

"Should I go for the green?" Mackenzie asked.

"Absolutely," caddie Rob Wooler said. "Smooth two iron."

That's what Mackenzie hit. The ball landed in the middle of the green and he two-putted for 72 and a 14-under-par 274 total, and a long-awaited one-stroke victory.

"After the 17th I thought I was going to mess up the last hole as well," Mackenzie said. "I thought I was losing it altogether, but managed to find some reserves and hit the shot of my life. That is what it comes down to in the end, having a chance. If you don't have a go, you might never get the chance again. I've waited long enough, so I had a go."

Immelman also shot 72 to finish the day where he started — one stroke back and alone in second place. "When you finish second you always say I could have or should have, but it is tough," he said. Mackenzie agreed. After 20 winless years, nobody had to tell him how tough this game can be.

Benson and Hedges International Open—€1,766,171
Winner: Angel Cabrera

It was a wild finish that saw six players within striking distance in the final hour and the ultimate winner of the Benson and Hedges International Open sealing the victory with a deft up-and-down for par on the final hole. Those final two shots, struck by Argentine Angel Cabrera, were good enough for a final-round 69 and a 10-under-par 278 total, one stroke better than third-round leader Barry Lane and two clear of Padraig Harrington, Colin Montgomerie and Michael Campbell.

"To win a big tournament such as this is great, really great, and I hope this can be the start of a really good season for me," Cabrera said.

Something good certainly happened to him at the De Vere Belfry in Sutton Coldfield. With Lane struggling in the wind, Cabrera took a chance at the short par-four 10th by attempting to drive the green. His ball cleared the water and landed in the right fringe, and he made an easy birdie to move to 10 under par and into sole possession of the lead.

That lead vanished just as quickly on the 11th when Cabrera pushed his drive into a fairway bunker. He couldn't reach the green with his second shot and failed to save par. That dropped him into a six-way tie for the lead with Lane, Harrington, Montgomerie and Campbell.

Montgomerie dropped off the pace when he attempted to drive the 10th green. His ball found the water, and the Scot fell back to eight under with a bogey. That was where he would finish. One birdie and one more bogey (at the difficult par-four 18th) for a 69 dropped Montgomerie into a tie for third at 280.

Cabrera parred the six holes from the 12th through 17th, then caught another great break at the 18th. After pulling his two-iron approach into the gallery, he received a free drop from a woman's purse. The lie was perfect, and Cabrera pitched to within two feet of the hole. He calmly rolled the final putt into the hole for the par and the win. "Wonderful," the winner said. "The lie was perfect, and I hit a really very good shot."

Deutsche Bank - SAP Open—€2,700,000
Winner: Tiger Woods

After shooting 65 on Saturday to take a one-shot lead into the final round of the Deutsche Bank - SAP Open, Colin Montgomerie provided a little insight into his thinking. "You're not going to beat Tiger Woods mentally," Montgomerie said. "You're not going to beat him physically. You are not going to beat him by out-driving him. You are not going to beat him with putting, chipping or iron play. The only way to beat Tiger Woods is by shooting a lower score than he does. You just want to add up the scores and be ahead of him. Normally, if you can do that, you're making a speech."

That sounded simple enough in theory. Practice was another matter.

Montgomerie entered the final round hoping to make a statement as well as a speech. The Scot had never won a tournament when Woods was in the field. Playing head-to-head with him, Montgomerie hoped to end that streak and prove that even the greatest could be beaten. There was one problem: No one had figured out how to shoot a lower number than Woods at the St. Leon-Rot course. Every time Woods had played in Heidelberg, he came away the winner.

This was no exception. Even though Montgomerie extended his one-stroke margin to three shots with quick birdies at the first and second holes, Woods failed to lie down, making an eagle at the third while Montgomerie was making his third birdie in a row. Woods then birdied the 10th and 11th to gain a share of the lead. When Montgomerie bogeyed the 13th, Woods held the lead outright.

Montgomerie battled back with a birdie at the 15th to gain another share of the top spot, which he hoped would be enough. Pars on the 16th, 17th and 18th gave Montgomerie a closing 69 and a 268 total. Woods parred the 16th and 17th as well, but he missed the green at the 18th and chipped to four feet. He needed the final putt to shoot 68 and force a playoff, which he did.

It took three extra holes (all of them the 18th) to determine the winner.

On the third pass down the tough par-four, Woods hit his approach to the center of the green while Montgomerie, who found the sand off the tee, attempted a tough approach but failed to clear the water. The two-putt par by Woods was enough.

"Montgomerie played so well," Woods said. "He's a true champion, and he fought all the way. It was a lot of fun and a great battle."

Volvo PGA Championship—€3,172,280
Winner: Anders Hansen

With a final round of 70 in dreary, cold conditions, Anders Hansen finished the impossible, shooting a tournament-record 19-under-par 269 on the famed West Course at Wentworth and becoming the first player to make the Volvo PGA Championship his first PGA European Tour victory.

The 31-year-old Dane did it in style, setting a 54-hole scoring record of 17-under-par 199 to take a five-stroke lead into the final round. There were more than a few scribes scrambling for their media guides. While Hansen wasn't completely anonymous (he did finish third earlier in the year at the French Open), his five seasons on the PGA European Tour had been uneventful and at times disappointing. He came out of the University of Houston as one of the players to watch. Hansen had not only struggled to crack the top of the leaderboard throughout his first years on tour, he had trouble differentiating himself from fellow Dane Soren Hansen, to whom he is not related. "Fifteen percent of all Danes are called Hansen," Anders said.

But none of those other Hansens have their name in the Wentworth record book, which is where Anders found himself all weekend. He was a model of poise on Sunday even with Colin Montgomerie and Eduardo Romero in pursuit. A birdie at the short second hole opened up a six-shot lead, but Hansen gave the shot back with a bogey at the third. He didn't let anyone nibble into the lead, however. He birdied the fourth to maintain a five-shot edge, then bogeyed the 12th before birdieing the 14th, bogeyed the 15th before a final birdie on the 17th.

It was a boring round, the kind you might expect from someone who had been there a dozen times before. No wonder Hansen was thrilled by the outcome.

"This is the biggest moment of my career," he said. "Hopefully I can go on to further successes. My goal was to get to the Open Championship and I've done it. I feel fantastic. I have been playing well all year. Who knows? Maybe soon I'll win again."

Montgomerie finished with 67, and his 14-under-par 274 left him tied for second with Romero and two clear of Michael Campbell, Carlos Rodiles and Nick Faldo.

Montgomerie was one of the first players to congratulate Hansen, and his words afterward summed up the event for everyone. "I know what it's like to stand here with this trophy, and I just want to congratulate one of the up-and-coming stars of the European Tour for his win and his record-setting total," Montgomerie said. "Well done Anders."

Victor Chandler British Masters—€1,976,275

Winner: Justin Rose

It's hard to think of Justin Rose as being only 21 years old. So much has happened in such a short time, but the fresh-faced Englishman couldn't legally drink until early in the 2002 season. He first burst onto the scene when he finished fourth in the 1998 Open at Royal Birkdale, won by Mark O'Meara but also remembered for the final-hole eagle Rose produced when he hit a wedge in the hole from the rough. Then he turned professional, and things went downhill. Who could forget the 21 consecutive missed cuts?

When Rose tapped in for par at the final hole to complete a 65-65 weekend and post a 19-under-par 269 total in the Victor Chandler British Masters, it seemed equally hard to believe that he was the first player of the year to win four worldwide professional titles. He also won the Dunhill Championship and the Nashua Masters in South Africa and The Crowns tournament in Japan before earning his first victory on his home soil.

This time he came from three strokes behind third-round leader Phillip Price, but joined the hunt early with birdies on the first two holes of the final round. Two more birdies on the fifth and seventh holes pushed Rose past Price. He still trailed Ian Poulter, who had made four consecutive birdies starting at the fifth hole.

From the 10th tee forward it was a battle between Rose and Poulter, who not only were friends but housemates for the week. Poulter lived in nearby Milton, and he invited Rose to bunk at his place during the tournament. Little could either of them have known that they would be battling for the title.

Rose birdied the 11th to pull within one, and both players birdied the 12th. When Poulter bogeyed the 13th they were tied. At the 14th the advantage appeared to swing in Rose's direction. After his approach shot stopped 10 feet from the hole, Rose watched as Poulter hit his ball in a greenside bunker. Things changed quickly. Poulter blasted his ball out of the sand and into the hole for a birdie. Rose, seemingly nonplused by the affair, drained the 10-footer and gave his friend a high-five as they walked on to the 15th tee.

That's the way this match played out. These were friends first, competitors second. "It captured how we were enjoying what happened," Rose said. "After Ian holed the bunker shot and I holed the putt to follow him in, we were chatting and saying we had never had so much fun on the golf course. We were playing golf for all the right reasons."

On the 16th Rose went ahead for good when Poulter three-putted for bogey from the fringe. Both players parred the 17th. At the 18th Rose missed a birdie putt then had to watch as Poulter attempted a 10-footer that would have tied them. The birdie putt slid low, Poulter had 68 for a 270 total, and Rose had his fourth title of the year.

"The other three victories this year have been in far and distant places," Rose said. "Although they were special, it's fantastic to win one on my home soil." He also said he felt fortunate to get away without having to go to extra holes. "Ian is such a great competitor," Rose said. "He plays with so much heart and determination that you never know what is coming next from him."

Compass Group English Open—€1,252,816
Winner: Darren Clarke

Darren Clarke would like for the Compass Group English Open to be re-named the Darren Clarke Slump Buster, but he's not holding his breath. The 33-year-old Clarke was too busy celebrating his first victory of the year and his third English Open title in four years to worry about the fact that he had only had two other top-10 finishes all season and was coming off an abysmal tie for 76th at the previous week's Victor Chandler British Masters.

"Probably this is more satisfying than the other victories because I have been playing well recently without being able to put a score on the board," Clarke said. "I led from start to finish and that says an awful lot about my game. I feel very comfortable at the moment."

The only time Clarke didn't feel comfortable was at the end of the third round when he was angry at himself for making a bogey at the par-five 17th that dropped him into a tie with Raphael Jacquelin at 203. "I hit the ball great all day tee to green," he said late on Saturday, "until I got to 17. Then I over-hit my third shot and made bogey. This is definitely a tournament I should have in the bag already."

He put it in the bag on the first nine on Sunday when, playing in rain and wind, he made five straight pars before two birdies at the sixth and seventh gave him a two-shot edge over Jacquelin and Phillip Price. Five holes later Clarke put this one away.

Because of a brutal wind, players were struggling to make par at the 547-yard, par-five 12th hole. But Clarke overpowered the hole, reaching the green with a driver and five iron, then making an 18-foot putt for eagle and a five-shot lead. He was able to play the remaining six holes in even par without being seriously challenged.

Clarke's final-round 68 and 17-under-par 271 was three clear of Soren Hansen, who finished with 70, and five better than Jacquelin and Price.

"I felt great today and was pleased with the way I handled myself," Hansen said. "But it was tough today with the wind howling and the rain coming in sideways. It was easy to make mistakes, but Darren didn't, so all the credit to him."

Clarke was ready to accept any credit offered him. "It feels very good to go out and play the way I played and win," he said. "I'm swinging well and hitting it where I want to most of the time. This is certainly very satisfying."

Great North Open—€935,760
Winner: Miles Tunnicliff

Two weeks before traveling to Northumberland to play in the Great North Open, journeyman pro Miles Tunnicliff was at his mother's deathbed. "Two day before she died, she told me to win a tournament," an emotional Tunnicliff recalled.

That was a tall order. Tunnicliff had never won in 13 years on the PGA European Tour and was ranked 284th on the Order of Merit at the halfway mark in the season. But Tunnicliff told his mother that he would win one for her. "I had to get out there and try to win," he said.

On a windswept day when no one else broke 70, Tunnicliff did just that, shooting three-under-par 69 at the De Vere Slaley Hall Course for a nine-under-par 279 total and a four-stroke victory over Sven Struver.

For a brief moment it looked as though Tunnicliff would be unable to keep his promise. He entered the final round tied with Struver and David Gilford, but quickly dropped to one back with a bogey from the sand on the first hole. Tunnicliff righted things on the third when he holed a 30-footer for birdie to reclaim a share of the lead. And he extended that lead with chip-in birdies at the fifth and eighth to take a three-shot lead.

A bogey at the ninth while Struver was making his second consecutive birdie at the 11th dropped the lead to two, but Tunnicliff righted things again with a birdie of his own at the 11th while Struver bogeyed the 12th. That four-shot lead held up throughout the rest of the round.

"I was going for the flags on the back nine," Struver said. "I had to, because I knew he was doing well up front, but I couldn't achieve it, couldn't get close enough to put any real pressure on him."

Tunnicliff wasn't sure additional pressure would have mattered. "What happened to my mother made me dig a little bit more and try a little bit harder," he said. "She gave me quite a bit of positive strength. She was positive right to the end, so I just took as much from that out on the course this week as I could."

Murphy's Irish Open—€1,600,000
Winner: Soren Hansen

Soren Hansen didn't like being the second-best Hansen on the PGA European Tour. "It is strange to follow Anders," Hansen said, referring to Anders Hansen, another Dane who won his first title at the Volvo PGA Championship earlier in the year. The two are not related, but that hasn't cut down on the confusion. "Before it was always me doing something and Anders catching up afterward," Soren said. "This time it was different after Anders won the Volvo PGA."

Not to be outdone, Soren Hansen won his first career title by making an eagle on the final hole of regulation to shoot 68 and 14-under-par 270 total for the week at the Murphy's Irish Open. Then he endured a four-hole four-man playoff before making another birdie at the par-three 17th to secure the title.

"The last few weeks I have been playing so well I thought it was just a matter of time," the 28-year-old Hansen said. "I played well the first two days, but in the third and fourth rounds I was struggling but hanging in there. I got the birdies at the right time, and I played some cracking golf from the 15th."

It was the 18th the earned him a spot in the playoff. Hansen boomed a drive on the 507-yard par-five, then hit a pitching wedge from 160 yards to within six feet of the hole, converting the putt for eagle to tie Darren Fichardt, Richard Bland and Niclas Fasth. "I knew I needed eagle at the last," Hansen said, "and I got it."

He didn't do as well the next time he came down the 18th (the first hole of the playoff), but fortunately neither did any of the other players. Hansen boomed another tee shot and had a short iron to the par-five, but this time he pulled his approach and the ball squirted off the green and into the water. After a penalty drop he almost chipped in for birdie, but had to settle for par.

Bland and Fasth also missed the green with their second shots, and both failed to get up and down for birdie. That left only Fichardt, who hit the green in two and needed only two putts from 15 feet to win. There was a collective gasp from the gallery when Fichardt rolled his first putt three feet past the hole, and a roar when he missed the comeback putt for birdie.

The second time down the 18th everyone made birdie except Bland, who pulled his tee shot into the trees and failed to recover. He shook the hands of the other players, then watched as the remaining three players walked to the first tee to continue the playoff.

This time it was Hansen who had the best chance. His approach on the 409-yard par-four stopped 12 feet from the hole, and after Fichardt and Fasth missed their birdie efforts, Hansen had a chance to end things. But his birdie putt lipped out.

One hole later Hansen settled things with a four iron to the 222-yard, par-three 17th that stopped 10 feet below the hole. When the putt fell in Hansen was €226,660 richer, and at least as well known as Anders. "I thought the playoff was over on the first hole," he said. "But Darren and Richard both missed, and then I grabbed my chance."

Smurfit European Open—€3,102,816
Winner: Michael Campbell

The amateur hour that was the final four holes of the Smurfit European Open gave new meaning to the term "winning ugly." So horrendous was the play of Michael Campbell and Padraig Harrington in the waning moments of the tournament that it was easy to forget the good play that got them into the final group at The K Club outside Dublin.

Campbell shot 68, 71 and 70 the first three days to share the third-round lead with Harrington, who also had been consistent with rounds of 72, 69 and 69. With birdies at the ninth, 12th and 13th holes, Campbell reached 10 under par for the tournament and opened up a four-shot lead. That lead was extended to five when Harrington bogeyed the 14th. That was when things got really ugly.

Campbell bogeyed the 15th while Harrington birdied. That cut the lead to three. Then Campbell found the water at the par-five 16th and made six. Harrington, trying to mount a comeback, tried to reach the green in two with a five wood but also found the water. He managed to save par to cut the lead to two, but he took his failure to make birdie badly. Muttering to himself, Harrington missed a three-footer for par at the 17th that would have pulled him within one as Campbell was chopping around for another bogey.

Two shots clear with one hole to play, Campbell kept his streak alive by hitting yet another approach into the water at the par-five 18th to finish with his second six in three holes. Harrington, knowing that a birdie would probably win, and an eagle would ensure the victory, played a six iron at the flag rather than safely hitting to the center of the green. He pulled the shot and his ball also found the water.

Harrington managed to save par, but it didn't matter. Campbell had run out of holes just in time. His 73 and six-under-par 282 was one better than Harrington, Bradley Dredge, Paul Lawrie and Retief Goosen, who had been finished over an hour and was in a car on his way to Dublin when he heard there might be a playoff.

"I feel gutted," said Harrington, who also shot 73. "I kept on being given chances, and it looked as if I had another down at the last. I had thought there was no point in hitting to the middle of the green and seeing if I could win a playoff. Michael got so much ahead he saw the winning post and started to bleed. Certainly, I had a good chance to win the tournament, and I'm gutted."

Campbell said, "I was cruising along with four holes to play and I said, 'This is it, I've got the trophy in one arm.' But unfortunately, it wasn't in the other. I think my emotions got too far ahead of myself and I made some ridiculous mistakes. You're taught not to think ahead, but I was doing just that. Obviously, I'm elated that I won, but disappointed with the way I finished."

Barclays Scottish Open—€3,438,770
Winner: Eduardo Romero

Either way it was going to be a memorable week. Either 28-year-old Fredrik Jacobson would hold onto the lead he'd had since late Friday afternoon and make the Barclays Scottish Open his first PGA European Tour victory after five runner-up finishes or Eduardo Romero, at three days shy of his 48th birthday, would become the third oldest winner in tour history.

This time age and guile prevailed over youth as the Argentine shot 70 on Sunday for an 11-under-par 273 total, then birdied the first hole of a playoff to beat Jacobson. "It has always been my dream to win in Scotland," Romero said. "When I look at the lochs and mountains, I think of home, and it means a lot to me to win here. The Scottish people are fantastic."

The Scots felt the same way about Romero, who received thunderous applause as he made one putt after another on the long and soggy Loch Lomond course. "This win is perhaps more important for me than the others because I'm 48 years old next week. I'm not old, but compared to some of the young players here, I could be their father."

After bogeys at the second and third holes, Romero ground out birdies at the seventh, 12th and 15th to get to 11 under and within one stroke of the lead. That's when Romero noticed a little wobble in Jacobson. "I could see his hands were shaking as he was chipping and putting," Romero said.

Only a couple of free drops on the 16th allowed Jacobson to hold onto the lead. After driving the ball far left, he received a drop from some tractor tire prints, then proceeded to hit his approach into a bank two feet from a water hazard, where he received another drop for an embedded ball. From there Jacobson chipped to eight feet and coaxed the par putt into the hole.

He wasn't so fortunate at the 17th. After both players hit the green in regulation, Romero two-putted for par, but Jacobson stabbed at his first putt and pulled it three feet past the hole. He missed that one too.

"When I made the par at 16 I thought that might be a sign that this was my day," Jacobson said. "But I just made a terrible three-putt at 17, which was not the place to do something like that."

Both players parred the 18th to finish at 273, with Jacobson shooting 71, before heading back to the tee for the playoff. Romero ended things early when, from the center of the fairway, he hit a pitching wedge nine feet under the hole and rolled in the birdie putt.

"This is a very, very special moment because all my family is here," Romero said. "I played really well this week and I concentrated really well. My game was perfect."

Jacobson couldn't say the same. "That was the best chance I have ever had to win a tournament," he said. "I had it pretty much in control, but just over the last three or four holes I got very nervous. I didn't see much of the back nine to be honest. It was all kind of a fog."

British Open Championship—€6,080,102
Winner: Ernie Els

See Chapter 4.

TNT Open—€1,800,000
Winner: Tobias Dier

It was a lot more fun to talk about the 10 first-round birdies and the course-record 60 that equaled a PGA European Tour scoring record than to recount the six closing pars on Sunday. But it was the latter that won the TNT Open for 35-year-old German Tobias Dier.

"I didn't really think about the way it was going in the final round," Dier said. "I just tried to keep on playing solid golf, hitting the greens and seeing how the putter worked."

It worked well enough, just as it had all week. After opening with his 60 (the lowest score of the year and the lowest first-round score in tour history), Dier set 36- and 54-hole scoring records with consecutive 67s. Still, he only held a three-stroke lead over Padraig Harrington going into the final round.

Dier made 10 straight pars to start the final round, then showed his only signs of cracking when he hooked his tee shot into the trees at the 11th and walked away with a bogey. The setback was temporary. One hole later Dier extended his lead when he made a 12-footer for eagle at the par-five 12th.

The only pressure came when Jamie Spence, playing well ahead, closed with an eagle at the par-five 18th to shoot 65 and post 264, one stroke off the lead. Dier knew he needed to par in when he stepped onto the 13th tee. And that's what he did, shooting 69 for a 17-under-par 263 total.

"If somebody had told me I was going to win before the start of the week, I would have told them to dream on, because I wasn't playing well," Dier said. "But I led from the first moment I stepped on the golf course this week, so in a way it felt normal for me to be up there. Anybody else up there would have been a strange feeling, so I thought I had better try to keep it up there. Now, it's a fairy tale for me."

Spence finished alone in second place, his best finish of the year, and one he wasn't at all displeased with. "I really like it here," Spence said. "Because par had been reduced from previous years (from 72 to 70), I thought that 15 under would be a really good score. I've beaten that by one shot, and I'm delighted with my week."

Harrington finished with 68 for a 265 total and a tie for third with Peter Lonard, who got within one stroke of the lead before bogeying the 16th to close with 67.

Volvo Scandinavian Masters—€1,900,000
Winner: Graeme McDowell

There's nothing like winning in your fourth professional start to boost your confidence. Ireland's Graeme McDowell didn't need much of a build-up. People had been comparing him to Tiger Woods ever since McDowell beat Woods' college scoring average with a 69.6 per round average for four years at the University of Alabama-Birmingham. The fact that the Ulsterman won the Volvo Scandinavian Masters in fewer starts than Woods had when he won his first title only bolstered the talk.

Woods wasn't in the field in Kungsangen as McDowell closed with 67 for a 14-under-par 270 total and a one-stroke victory, but that didn't mean this one was easy. The youngster started the final round tied with Jeff Sluman, and never held the lead outright until the final putt fell. By then Sluman had bogeyed the final hole to drop two off the pace, and Trevor Immelman, who came to the 18th tee tied at the top of the leaderboard, was shaking his head and wondering what hit him.

After Sluman made bogey to shoot 69 for the day and 272 for the week, it was up to Immelman and McDowell, with Immelman holding a distinct advantage. McDowell, who hadn't missed a fairway on the second nine, pushed his tee shot on the 18th under the lip of a bunker. He had no way to advance the ball and was lucky to be able to hit it backward. After blasting back to the fairway, McDowell still hadn't lost his turn. He had to play his third shot before Immelman hit his second. The seven-iron third shot looked for a moment as if it might go in. It stopped two feet from the hole, and McDowell made an easy par.

Shaken by the miraculous recovery he had just seen, Immelman flew his eight iron long and right and into the rough. He chipped to eight feet, but missed the par putt. Both Immelman and McDowell finished with 67, but Immelman had a 271 total and McDowell who walked away the winner.

"I've never been happier," McDowell said. "To win in the fashion I did is an incredible thing. I never dreamed I would do this well in my first six or seven weeks. This is the highlight of my life."

Celtic Manor Resort Wales Open—€1,753,869
Winner: Paul Lawrie

A year ago in the Celtic Manor Wales Open, Paul Lawrie lost in a playoff to Paul McGinley after the event was shortened to 36 holes due to foul weather. The weather was equally bad this time around, so Lawrie did his best to be leading outright at the end of each round, just in case.

He succeeded on Friday, shooting a course-record 65 in the worst of the rain and wind to take a two-shot lead into the weekend. Lawrie never trailed again, shooting 70-70 on Sunday (Saturday's round was cancelled and players were required to play 36 holes the final day) for a 16-under-par 272 total and a five-stroke win over John Bickerton.

Even though the number of holes was in question, the outcome was never in doubt. Lawrie extended his lead to four shots when he holed a lob wedge for eagle from 101 yards at the par-four fourth in the final round. He two-putted for birdie at the par-five fifth to move five ahead, then ran and hid from the rest of the field with birdies at the eighth and 10th. The three bogeys in the final five holes were meaningless, and the rest of the field knew it.

"I was never going to catch Paul," said Bickerton, who also closed with 70 after shooting 73 in the morning. "He was hot today, and played lovely golf, but it was nice to hang on at the end for second. I'm delighted."

Mikko Ilonen birdied the final hole to shoot 70-70 on the final day as well. He finished alone in third at 278 and couldn't have been happier. "This was certainly my best finish," he said. "I really needed this, and I pulled it off when I needed to. I can go on from here and secure my tour card."

Lawrie also felt great about pulling one off when he needed to. "It was nice to come back and win this time," he said. "I played well last year and didn't win. This time I putted a lot better. When you're coming on and off the course because of the weather, it's difficult to keep your focus and concentration, but I did that very well."

Then Lawrie tried to put to rest the notion that he is a bad-weather champion, even though all three of his victories had come in miserable conditions. "I think it's a coincidence that I seem to play well in bad weather," he said. "I'm as capable of playing in beautiful sunshine as I am in bad weather, but I do seem to win tournaments when it's unpleasant."

North West of Ireland Open—€350,000
Winner: Adam Mednick

With Europe's best in Minnesota for the PGA Championship, it was fitting that the PGA European Tour event held over the same week would be won by a Bethesda, Maryland, native who once caddied at Augusta National. Adam Mednick, a 35-year-old former caddie and journeyman who makes his home in Sweden, played 23 holes in seven under par on Sunday to capture the North West of Ireland Open by five shots over Andrew Coltart and Costantino Rocca.

He won by coming out strong and finishing the rain-delayed third round with a flurry of three birdies in the last five holes to shoot 69. Nobody else broke par in the third round, and 23 players shot 80 or higher. Mednick played his first 13 holes on Saturday in 40 mile-an-hour winds like everyone else. Unlike other players, Mednick played those holes even par. That would prove to be the difference. His strong finish on Sunday morning after play resumed moved him to within a shot of Italy's Massimo Florioli, but the momentum had clearly shifted.

A birdie at the second hole gave Mednick a share of the lead. When he hit the par-five fifth in two and two-putted from 20 feet, the lead was his for good. Four more birdies and two meaningless bogeys later, Mednick closed with 68 and a 281 total for his first victory since winning five times on the European Challenge Tour.

"It has been a fantastic week," Mednick said. "This win means so much to me because I was on the borderline for getting into tournaments, and I haven't had many starts this year. Now I can play my season exactly the way I want to, and next year as well."

Coltart had the best round on Sunday, finishing with 67 for a 286 total and a share of second with Rocca, who shot even-par 72 on Sunday. "I am starting to hole some putts, and that makes a big difference," Coltart said. "I'm delighted with the way I putted this week."

Florioli shot 76 in the final round and was six over for the 22 holes he played on Sunday.

Diageo Scottish PGA Championship—€1,590,759
Winner: Adam Scott

There are a lot of ways of proving a point. For Adam Scott the best way to show that he belonged in the field at the WGC NEC Invitational was by shooting a final-round 63 to run away with the Diageo Scottish PGA Championship. In the process, the youngster from Australia shot the lowest closing round of the year on the European Tour (63), the lowest 72-hole total (262) and the year's largest margin of victory (10 shots over Raymond Russell).

"It's important to play my way back into the top 50 (in the World Ranking)," Scott said afterward. "I feel like I should be up there."

He proved his point, playing the par-fives on the Gleneagles Centenary Course (site of the 2014 Ryder Cup), in 22 under par for the week. The 22-year-old started the final round five shots ahead of Russell, and ran away from any contenders by shooting 31 on the first nine to extend the lead to eight. It grew to 10 before the round was over.

"The reason for me to come here was to win," said the winner of the Qatar Masters. That quote was uttered in Scotland, but was aimed where the top players from Europe were competing in the World Golf Championship event. "It is important for me to win in Britain and on the Continent of Europe under different conditions. The other times I've won in hot weather. This week was different. It was testing, especially Friday (when the wind blew and the temperature never got above 50), so I can draw a lot of confidence from that."

Ryder Cup captain Sam Torrance finished alone in third at 273 after a closing round of 67, while Scott Gardiner birdied the final hole to shoot 72 and finish fourth at 276.

BMW International Open—€1,800,000

Winner: Thomas Bjorn

Thomas Bjorn was annoyed. It had been 18 months since he had beaten Tiger Woods at the Dubai Desert Classic, and since that weekend Bjorn's and Woods' games had been heading in opposite directions. Woods won three majors after losing to Bjorn. The Dane hadn't scratched a victory, and had fallen to 27th on the Order of Merit and 34th in the World Ranking. It was an untenable situation as far as Bjorn was concerned, one he hoped to rectify with a victory in a familiar setting.

Paired with local favorite Bernhard Langer for all four rounds, Bjorn blazed his way through the field at the BMW International Open in Munich, taking the lead on Friday with 64 and never letting go. He led by two after a 66 on Saturday, then matched Langer shot-for-shot in the early going before pulling ahead for good with birdies at the eighth and ninth to shoot 32 on the first nine and extend his lead to three strokes.

Langer tried to apply some pressure, chipping in for par twice and rolling in four birdies to only one bogey in the first nine holes. He lost ground. Bjorn made four birdies without any bogeys. Bjorn made his first bogey on the 10th to cut the lead back to two, but he bounced back and restored the margin with birdies at the 11th and 12th. Langer made his last birdie at the 11th.

Bjorn tacked on one more birdie for good measure at the 18th, but by then the outcome was certain. He finished with his second consecutive round of 66 for a 24-under-par 264 total and a four-shot victory over Langer and England's John Bickerton, who also shot 66 on Sunday.

"I went out this morning to play as aggressive as I had all week and attack the course, because I knew I needed to shoot a number," Bjorn said. "Down the stretch it was in my control, and I knew if I didn't make any mistakes the tournament was mine."

Bjorn turned to a pivotal moment in the first nine when he started feeling that the tournament truly was his for the taking. "The key moment in the round was when Bernhard holed a long putt (for birdie) on the ninth, and I rolled mine in after him. That kept the momentum going my way. At that point I felt the tournament was going to go my way."

It was Langer's third runner-up finish in this, the only German tournament he hasn't won in his career. "I played with Thomas all four rounds and he played very well all week," Langer said. "He looked comfortable with his swing, especially with the short game. He didn't miss many putts at all. Every time I made a birdie, he seemed to hit back with one of his own. But I will come back next year and try to win this tournament to complete the set."

Omega European Masters—€1,500,000

Winner: Robert Karlsson

It isn't often that a player can bogey the last two holes and still win comfortably, but that was where Robert Karlsson found himself at the Omega European Masters. Karlsson was able to enjoy the beautiful Swiss scenery and smell the edelweiss for the final half hour of this one. He bogeyed the 17th and 18th holes on Sunday to shoot 71 and finish at 14-under-par 270, but it didn't matter. He held a six-stroke lead with two holes to play. The closing bogeys only cut his winning margin to four over Trevor Immelman and Paul Lawrie.

Karlsson led wire-to-wire, but it wasn't the runaway the final few holes might suggest. Rounds of 65, 66 and 68 put him two shots ahead of Emanuele Canonica going into the final round. Barry Lane and Lawrie were three back on Sunday morning, but when Karlsson bogeyed the second, third and fourth holes, it was anyone's tournament.

Lane moved into a temporary share of the lead, but Karlsson reasserted himself with a birdie at the eighth while Lane was bogeying the ninth. The Englishman never contended again, slipping into a tie for 13th after a dreadful quadruple bogey at the short 16th.

The next challenger was Lawrie, who pulled within a shot of the lead before picking the wrong club for his approaches on three of the five closing holes. He bogeyed all three and shot 72 for a 274 total. Immelman never mounted much of a charge, also finishing with 72 and a share of second.

That left Karlsson alone at the top. He expanded his lead with birdies at the 11th, 13th and 15th, with the one at the 13th coming from a deft chip-in from high grass behind the green. The lead was six when he came to the 17th tee, so the final two bogeys were meaningless.

When he accepted the trophy and the €250,000 winner's check, Karlsson dedicated the win to his former sports psychologist, Dr. Bengt Stern, who died on Friday.

"I got the message Friday afternoon, and I felt I wanted to do this for him," Karlsson said. "He has been a very important person in my career. One of the most important things he got me to understand was that if I am playing badly, it is only actually a thought; it doesn't have to be the truth. If you are playing badly on the golf course, it is only a feeling and it is important to realize I am not my feelings. I am Robert."

Linde German Masters—€3,000,000
Winner: Stephen Leaney

After Paul Casey shot a course-record 62 on Saturday to take a two-shot lead at the Linde German Masters, Stephen Leaney knew he needed to go for broke on Sunday to have any chance at winning. He did exactly that, shooting 67 to jump past Casey and hold off challenges from Alex Cejka, Ian Woosnam and Nick Dougherty. When the final putt fell, Leaney shot 22-under-par 266 for the week and eked out a one-shot win over Cejka.

It was Leaney's fourth career title and it came at a perfect time. The €500,000 first-place check moved him to 10th on the Order of Merit, which got him in the WGC American Express Championship at Mount Juliet in Ireland. He wasn't thinking about future opportunities. The leaderboard was too packed and things were too close to worry about anything but the present.

Leaney battled nerves in the early going. He drove into the bunker on the first hole and made a great save for par, then hit a perfect seven iron to three feet and rolled in the putt for birdie at the second. That calmed him down a little. Another birdie at the fourth got him into a good rhythm, and when he made two more birdies at the seventh and eighth, Leaney started to believe that the tournament might be his.

Casey struggled, making three early bogeys and never contending again. He finished with 71 for 268 total and in a three-way tie for third with Woosnam and Dougherty. That left only Leaney and Cejka, who were playing together.

Leaney took a two-shot lead when his fifth birdie of the day found the hole at the 10th. After that, he cruised in with eight straight pars, hitting the middle of every green and two-putting for pars. If he was going to lose, someone was going to have to beat him.

Cejka made a good run, but he pulled his approach with a pitching wedge at the final hole to douse any chances he had of forcing a playoff. After a poor chip, Cejka had to make a 20-footer for par for 68 to hold on to second place at 267. "I am more happy because I achieved my goal of playing all four rounds under 70," Cejka said. "I knew I needed to get close at the last, but I pulled my shot. I was nervous." Then I holed a good 20-footer to finish second."

Leaney admitted to battling nerves as well. "I really was quite nervous starting off the day," he said. "I wasn't sure how I was going to play, and I got a really bad lie in the bunker on the first, right under the lip. But I managed to get that up and down and that set the tone for the round. The key shot came at the 16th, because it's a very hard hole. I hit a great four iron, and once I hit that green, I knew I was going to make enough good swings coming home.

"It's just great to win again. This is a major golf tournament on what I think is a very difficult course. To shoot those scores is pretty satisfying."

WGC American Express Championship—€5,645,078
Winner: Tiger Woods

Since the World Golf Championships were created to showcase the world-wide game, it seemed fitting that winner of the first WGC event played in Ireland would be the world's No. 1 golfer. Also fitting was the record-setting performance Tiger Woods put together en route to winning his sixth WGC event out of only 12 that have been contested. He led wire-to-wire on the Mount Juliet course in County Kilkenny and didn't make a bogey until the last hole of the championship. Still, the tournament was closer than many expected, thanks to a late charge by a European favorite.

Woods looked unbeatable through three rounds. A pair of 65s followed by 67 on Saturday gave him a five-stroke edge. What was supposed to a victory march turned out to be a grueling match as South African Retief Goosen, last year's Order of Merit winner, strung together some of the best shot-making of the year and surged to within one stroke of Woods. Over a six-hole stretch on the second nine, Goosen posted four birdies and an eagle, the latter coming at the par-five 17th after a laser three-iron shot stopped two feet from the hole.

Woods said he was "very aware" of the charge. "We were on the 16th green and knew somebody had stiffed it on 17 because of the roar," Woods said. "This roar was a little louder than normal, so I figured it had to be Goosen. And when we were on the tee, he buried the putt."

Woods knew he needed to answer, but when his tee shot found the rough, the rumblings in the gallery increased. The leader then laid up in the right rough, leaving himself a tough short iron shot from a questionable lie. "It was pretty gnarly, into the grain and sitting down on top of that," Woods said. "I knew that was probably going to be the shot of the tournament."

He punched a short iron through the high grass, and the ball squirted onto the green some 18 feet below the hole. When that putt fell, the tournament that shouldn't have been close was close no longer. Woods punched the air when that birdie fell. He was 26 under par at that point. No one was going to catch him. A bogey on the last hole, where Woods was distracted by a cameraman then shoved a four-iron approach and missed a four-footer for par, spoiled the bogey-free tournament. He finished with 66 for a 263 total, 25 under par, and one ahead of Goosen, who had closed with 62.

"I was hot," Woods said in describing his feelings at the moment. "The most important shot of the week and he gets the happy finger. I'm hot at him and I'm hot at myself for blocking that putt. Maybe if I'd had a one-shot lead, I would have settled down a little more. But with two shots, subconsciously, I got a little hotter."

Woods was a different kind of hot throughout most of the week, but he had to be. With normal Irish winds nowhere on the horizon, temperatures in the balmy 70s, and greens that were described as "the best in Europe," conditions were ripe for scoring, which is exactly what the best players in the world did. The field averaged 69.5 for the week, and 56 of 64 players finished under par.

Woods shot a course-record 65 on Thursday, matched it on Friday, then watched it get pulverized on Sunday when Goosen and Sergio Garcia both shot 62s. To illustrate how low the scoring was, Bob Estes shot four rounds in the 60s and lost by nine strokes.

"Everyone was shooting lights out," Goosen said. "I knew I had to shoot something very low to have a chance. Obviously that's one of the best rounds I've played. I've had a couple of good ones before, but this was great. Unfortunately, it wasn't enough in the end."

Woods was a little surprised the ending was as close as it was. "You had to keep making birdies, because it wasn't playing hard at all," he said. "I knew somebody was going to make a run, somebody would shoot a low number. But I didn't figure it to be that low. You go out and shoot 66, you think you've got one."

In the end he did get one, the 34th PGA Tour victory of his career.

Dunhill Links Championship—€5,124,000
Winner: Padraig Harrington

He had been there plenty of times this season, but when Padraig Harrington found himself one stroke out the lead with two holes to play at St. Andrews, Scotland, in the Dunhill Links Championship, a sense of calm came over him. Never mind that Harrington had yet to win in 2002. The fact that he and his European teammates captured the Ryder Cup the week before had

Harrington dancing on clouds all week. It seemed fitting that he would nail an 18-foot birdie putt on the 18th hole at the Old Course for a closing 69 and share of the lead at 19-under-par 269. Then he holed an eight-footer for birdie on the second playoff hole and watched as Eduardo Romero missed from four feet.

"Even though I was a stroke behind with two to play I was feeling positive, and I made a couple of great putts, first to get into the playoff and second to win," Harrington said. "These last two weeks have easily been the best back-to-back weeks in my life, even if I had finished last here that would still have been the case."

Instead of finishing last, Harrington won on two fronts. He and his partner, J.P. MacManus, won the pro-am portion of the event as well, shooting 37 under par to beat Romero and his partner, Neil Crichton, by six shots.

Harrington played all four rounds at the three links courses (Carnoustie, Kingsbarns and St. Andrews) under 70, opening with two 66s, then closing with a 68-69 weekend, capped by the curling 18-footer at the last. Romero missed an eight-footer at the 18th that would have won in regulation, finishing with 69, then seemed to regain the advantage at the second playoff hole when he hit his approach to four feet. Harrington, who was eight feet away, made his birdie first to apply just enough pressure, and Romero pushed his putt to end things.

Colin Montgomerie shot 63 on Sunday, including a bogey at the final hole to tie for third with Sandy Lyle and Vijay Singh at 271. "I'm disappointed," Montgomerie said afterward. "I wanted that course record (62 by Curtis Strange), but my drive at the last landed in a seeded divot and I caught it a touch heavy. Still, I can't complain about a 63. It's still a very good score."

Another player who wasn't complaining was Ernie Els, even though he withdrew before teeing off on Sunday morning. Els got an emergency call in his hotel room. His wife, Liezl, had just gone into labor. Els and his father (who was his amateur partner for the week) flew immediately to London where they arrived just in time to witness the birth of the Els' first son.

Trophee Lancome—€1,450,736
Winner: Alex Cejka

When he won three times in 1995, the 24-year-old, smooth-swinging Alex Cejka appeared to be on his way to stardom on the PGA European Tour. No one would have expected that it would be seven more years before the Czech-born German would win again. At 31, hardened by the near-misses, Cejka broke the drought by shooting 68 on a beautiful Sunday in Paris to win the Trophee Lancome by two strokes.

"I've been waiting since 1995, and it's been a long seven years," Cejka said after his closing 68 for a 12-under-par 272 total to finish two clear of Spain's Carlos Rodiles. "It doesn't seem like seven years, but then again, sometimes it seems like 25 years. I've been second or third plenty of times, but there was always someone ahead of me. It can sometimes be cruel."

The game can sometimes be cruel, but it can also be generous, which it was in the last hour of the final round. Cejka hadn't lost the lead since his opening 64, but that lead was threatened late Sunday when five players —

Rodiles, Simon Dyson, Paul Eales, Ian Garbutt and Steen Tinning — all tied Cejka for the lead at 10 under par with nine holes to play. Cejka made a birdie at the 10th to regain sole possession of the lead, then caught the break of the tournament at the 15th.

His tee shot flared to the right and landed in a dense cluster of trees. It was not only possible but also highly probable that Cejka would not have a play at the green or even a shot back to the fairway. When he got to the ball, he found that he had a perfect opening to the green. He salvaged a par four with ease, and went on to birdie the 16th to reach 12 under and take a two-shot lead into the final two holes. Two solid pars later, Cejka could erase the bad memories of the last seven years.

"It was hard work at times, but I put in a lot of hard work in that time and stayed patient when things weren't going so well," Cejka said. "I needed a bit of luck as well, as all winners do, and I got that, but I also tried not to make any stupid mistakes. It worked to perfection."

Cisco World Match Play—£1,000,000
Winner: Ernie Els

See Chapter 8.

Telefonica Open de Madrid—€1,400,000
Winner: Steen Tinning

Two weeks after his 40th birthday, Sweden's Steen Tinning was wondering what you had to do to earn any respect. After all, he had just shot a course-record 62 on Saturday to pull within one stroke of third-round leader Padraig Harrington in the Telefonica Open de Madrid, and he was in the midst of a solid final round when he glanced up at the leaderboard and saw six names at the top. Brian Davis, Bradley Dredge, Paul Lawrie, Harrington, Adam Scott and Tinning all shared the lead with nine holes to play.

Good money was on Davis, who had looped the tournament into his honeymoon. Six birdies, one eagle and a solid par save from the bunker at the 18th gave Davis 63 for the final day and an early lead in the clubhouse of 266. That lead stood for about 10 minutes, the time it took Andrew Coltart to make his second 15-foot birdie putt in a row on the 18th to shoot 64 and match Davis's total. For an hour, the two men stood at 18 under par, waiting and watching to see if a playoff would ensue, and, if so, who else might join them.

Harrington fell away, posting 72 to finish tied for seventh at 269, while Dredge shot 64 to vault to 267. All eyes were on Scott, the young Australian who already had two wins on the year and the low 72-hole total of the year set at Gleneagles at the Diageo Scottish PGA Championship. Scott birdied the 12th and 14th to get to 18 under par before making what appeared to be the back-breaker at the 16th, a 20-foot putt that got him to 19 under.

One hole later, things turned around again. Tinning, who continued to march along unheralded at 18 under, hit a seven iron to five feet and made birdie at the par-three, while Scott pushed his nine iron right of the green and failed to get up and down. Now Tinning held a one-shot lead with one hole to play. If Tinning made bogey at the 18th, there would be a four-way playoff. If Scott made birdie and Tinning made par, the two of them would go to a playoff.

Neither scenario came into play. Tinning hit a superb eight iron into the center of the green and two-putted from 15 feet, while Scott hit his approach to the back of the green and missed his birdie effort. Scott finished with 68 and a 266 total, in a three-way tie for second, while the old man, Tinning, took home the title and the €233,300 first-place check with his closing 67 and 265 mark.

Italian Open Telecom Italia—€1,100,000
Winner: Ian Poulter

In what was otherwise a boring rain-shortened week, the Italian Open Telecom Italia offered some last-minute fireworks that saw the lead change three times over the final three holes before England's Ian Poulter claimed the title with a 19-under-par 197 total.

On paper that's the way it should have been. Poulter led from the first hole on Thursday, and his course-record 11-under-par 61 set the tone for the rest of the week. After a complete washout on Friday, Poulter came back on Saturday with 67, which kept his lead at one stroke over Lawrie, who shot 64 in the second round.

Lawrie birdied the first hole on Sunday, and they were tied for the next 14 holes. At the par-three 16th both players found the bunker with their tee shots. Poulter blasted out to five feet and made par, while Lawrie missed from a similar length and made bogey. Poulter's lead was one with two holes to play.

Not for long. On the par-five 17th, Lawrie had to lay up with his second shot, but Poulter tried to go for the green. He failed, hitting a tree 150 yards out. Both players reached the green in three, but Lawrie made a 15-footer for birdie, while Poulter three-putted for bogey. Now Lawrie had a one-shot lead.

That lasted about five minutes, which was the time it took Lawrie to hit his tee shot on the 18th dead right, out of bounds 60 yards off the fairway. Poulter found the fairway and the green, and made an uphill four-footer for birdie to win by two, as Lawrie could manage no better than a double-bogey six on the final hole. Poulter finished with 69 for a 19-under-par 197 total while Lawrie shot 70 for a 199 total.

"It got interesting towards the end," Poulter said afterward. "Really, it was unbelievable. As soon as he made bogey at 16, I was one up with two to play. I hit a great shot at 17. He missed the fairway and had to lay up. I thought here is my opportunity, but I hit the tree. Funny things happen. I three-putted, and he rolled in a birdie. All of a sudden I've gone from a great position to being one behind with one to play. Unfortunately, Paul hit it too far right on the 18th. I didn't even know there was out of bounds over there, and I don't think he did either. I crushed my drive down there and had perfect yardage for a nine iron. I knew I had to hit it close, and I did.

"It was awesome to go out there and do it. It was a tremendous advantage to play as well as I did on the first day, and if I had let it go, I would have been upset."

Upset was the word Lawrie was groping for afterward. "I don't know what happened to be honest," he said. "I thought I made a pretty good swing, and it came off at an unbelievable angle right out of bounds. I would have bet my house on making a four up the last, but there you go. Disappointed is not the word. I don't know how to describe it."

Volvo Masters Andalucia—€3,136,700
Winners: Bernard Langer and Colin Montgomerie

It wasn't what one might term a "masterful" finish to the year, but the Volvo Masters Andalucia did, indeed, end, just not to anyone's satisfaction. The only winner proved to be darkness, which forced the event to be called after 72 holes of regulation and two playoff holes. The winners were Bernard Langer and Colin Montgomerie, both of whom shot three-under-par 281 totals. When a winner couldn't be determined before darkness fell, the first draw on the PGA European Tour since 1986 was called. Montgomerie had a flight scheduled to Asia for the TCL Classic, and Langer was off to Sea Island, Georgia, for the UBS Warburg Cup. So the European season ended with a fizzle and a kiss-your-sister tie.

There might have been time for a third extra hole in the playoff had a demonstrative Montgomerie not been summoned to the television compound with rules official John Paramour for a conference. The subject was an incident that occurred on the 10th green when Montgomerie harrumphed around a missed putt, forcefully planting his putter head into the turf some nine inches behind the ball. The ball moved, but it wasn't clear from the pictures whether Montgomerie's putter head had cause the ball to move.

"While the ball certainly moved, I concluded that, because his club touched the ground so far from the ball and he had not taken his stance, Colin was not at address as it happened," Paramour said. "The only doubt I had was whether he touched the ball to cause it to move. The pictures were inconclusive on that, as two-dimensional images invariably are."

Montgomerie was asked about the incident at the 12th tee, and he and Paramour had an animated discussion at that point. Later, after Montgomerie bogeyed the 18th hole to fall into a tie with Langer, the Scot showed his anger in the scorer's tent. He felt he shouldn't have been told of the possible infraction during the round. "Colin made his feelings known to us," Paramour said. "But he calmed down when it was explained to him that he had to be told so he could have the chance to modify his tactics and strategy."

That wasn't the end of it. After signing for a final-round 70 (Langer shot 67) Montgomerie went to the television compound with Paramour to view the incident in slow-motion replay. "I had to give Colin the opportunity to call a penalty on himself if he felt that was appropriate," Paramour said. "We watched it. Then I asked Colin a simple question: 'Did you touch the ball?' When he answered in the negative, I said, 'Let's go for a playoff.' When Montgomerie confirmed he had not touched the ball, the incident simply went away."

That might have been the case had someone birdied either of the two playoff holes to determine a winner. But by the time the two players reached the 18th green for a third time, it was too dark. A short discussion ensued, and everyone agreed to end this one in a tie.

"There was no way we could continue," Langer said. "It was really getting ridiculous. There were two options: come back in the morning, which would have provided an anticlimax to this great championship, or share the victory. I think we both agreed it was the appropriate thing to do."

"There was no way we could play," Montgomerie said. "When Ken Schofield came on the radio with that suggestion, Bernhard very quickly took off his hat and I took mine off, and we shook hands. I agree that it was very appropriate that we did share this wonderful trophy. I think that it's also appropriate that in a Ryder Cup year, with a victory for Europe, that my partner and I should share this trophy. It's good for the pair of us to be victorious again."

BMW Asian Open—US$1,500,000
Winner: Padraig Harrington

See Asia/Japan Tours chapter.

Omega Hong Kong Open—US$700,000
Winner: Fredrik Jacobson

See Asia/Japan Tours chapter.

Challenge Tour

Eight years after winning the British Amateur, Lee James secured his card for the 2003 PGA European Tour by finishing the season as No. 1 on the Challenge Tour. James achieved the feat despite missing 10 weeks at the end of the season with a hand injury.

James' success began in the first event of the season when he won the Sameer Kenya Open in February and he followed that with victories in the Clearstream International Luxembourg Open in June and then the Talma Finnish Challenge in August. At the end of that month James hurt his left hand while playing from heavy rough at the North West of Ireland Open, an event sanctioned by both the European PGA Tour and Challenge Tour.

"I couldn't take the club past the horizontal," James said, "and I couldn't lift a plate or hold a cup of tea. I did not touch a club for eight weeks." James led the money list by about €60,000 when the injury struck, but held on to his No. 1 position when he made his comeback for the Grand Final. With a total of €121,531, James stayed ahead of Jean-Francois Lucquin by just under €20,000.

"It is a great honor to finish as the No. 1," said James. "I have been waiting five years to get on the European PGA Tour and now I can't wait to play."

James turned professional after playing in the Walker Cup in 1995 and won for the first time on the Challenge Tour the following year. Lucquin, who almost won the Lancome Trophy on the main circuit when he was invited to the Paris tournament, was twice the French Amateur champion, but also served an apprenticeship on the Challenge Tour before his improved play in 2002 led to his victory at the Panalpina Banque Commerciale du Maroc Classic.

Another former Amateur champion, Iain Pyman, who has played extensively on the main tour since he turned professional in 1993, won twice, at the Golf Challenge in Germany and the BMW Russian Open. Matthew Blackey also returned to the European Tour by winning back-to-back in September at the Formby Hall Challenge in England and the Telia Grand Prix in Ireland.

Ireland's Peter Lawrie, who missed four of the first five cuts, secured his card by finishing second in the penultimate event of the season and then the following week winning the Grand Final with a brilliant final-round 65 at Golf du Medoc in Bordeaux. France's Julien Van Hauwe needed to finish in the top two at the event to gain his card and finished second, four strokes behind Lawrie but four ahead of those in third place, to gain the 15th spot on the money list.

The others to gain their PGA European Tour cards from the top 15 were: Simon Hurd, John Morgan, Simon Wakefield, Gary Birch and Benn Barham, all from England; Belgium's Nicolas Vanhootegem and Nicolas Colsaerts; Gustavo Rojas from Argentina; and Sweden's Fredrik Widmark.

11. Asia/Japan Tours

Familiar names and faces dominated the scene during the Japan Tour's slimmed-down 2002 season. Only six players won for the first time in the 29 tournaments played between mid-March and early December and not a one was Japanese. Instead those victories were scored by two Australians, a New Zealander, a South Korean, an American and young English star Justin Rose, who already had won on other world tours. Among them, only David Smail, an experienced 32-year-old New Zealander, made a consequential impact, winning the Japan Open Championship and the lucrative Casio World Open. Otherwise, the most omnipresent were players who have been the top competitors on the Japan Tour in recent years.

Toru Taniguchi led the way in 2002. The 32-year-old Taniguchi, who had ventured onto the international scene on occasion and held the 48th position in the World Ranking at year's end, topped the victory list with four titles and, after second- and fifth-place finishes the previous two seasons, led the money standings for the first time with earnings of ¥140,182,600. His closest pursuer was Nobuhito Sato, the only other player to win more than twice during the year. Two of Sato's three victories came in significant events — the Match Play and the Tour Championship — and he held the money lead until Taniguchi won for the fourth time in mid-October.

Toshimitsu Izawa, the No. 1 player in 2001, went without a victory and finished 14th on the Japan money list and 50th in the World Ranking. Shingo Katayama, the money leader in 2000 and runner-up in 2001 and the other Japanese player with a high (47th) World Ranking, jumped into third place when he won the season-ending Nippon Series. Nostalgia had its place, too, as two of the country's all-time greats came up with victories in 2002. At age 55, the incredible Masashi (Jumbo) Ozaki won for the 94th time on the Japan Tour, capturing the ANA Open for the eighth time in 30 years, and Tsuneyuki (Tommy) Nakajima, now 48 and winless since 1995, secured his 45th and 46th victories at the Diamond Cup and the rich Visa Taiheiyo Masters.

Besides the aforementioned Smail, Katayama and Nakajima, three other players posted pairs of victories. Kenichi Kuboya won the Japan PGA Championship and Munsingwear KSB Cup back to back; Hawaiian Dean Wilson, a three-time winner and No. 3 on the money list in 2001, added two more titles and placed fourth in 2002, and Yasuharu Imano scored consecutive victories in the NST Niigata Open and Aiful Cup in mid-summer. Nine of the year's titles went to overseas players — South Korean Hur Suk-ho, American Christian Pena, Australians Scott Laycock and Brendan Jones in addition to Smail, Wilson and Rose.

At least three of the 2002 winners were to be playing most of their golf elsewhere in 2003. Wilson, Laycock and Kuboya earned playing privileges on the PGA Tour in America at the rugged 108-hole qualifying tournament in early December in California.

The Asian PGA's Davidoff Tour continued to chug along with 18 tournaments and — most remarkably — no player winning more than one. The winners included such familiar names as Thongchai Jaidee, Arjun Atwal and Charlie Wi.

Sergio Garcia of Spain made a visit and won the Kolon Cup Korean Open, and the Europeans returned late in the year for events that strangely mark the beginning of their 2003 Order of Merit race. Colin Montgomerie won in the TCL Classic, then in official 2003 PGA European Tour co-sponsored events, Padraig Harrington won the BMW Asian Open and Fredrik Jacobson won the Omega Hong Kong Open.

Asian PGA Davidoff Tour

Johnnie Walker Classic—A$2,700,000
Winner: Retief Goosen

See Australasian Tour chapter.

London Myanmar Open—US$200,000
Winner: Thongchai Jaidee

The Davidoff Tour's 2002 season got under way the second week of February with the London Myanmar Open at Yangon Golf Club, and it looked like anyone's tournament. Clustered atop the leaderboard in the first round were a Swede, a couple of Thais, a couple of Americans and a local from Myanmar. At the end, however, it was the veteran versus the rookie, and finally, it was the veteran winning out.

Fittingly, what started like a scramble ended like one, with Thailand's Thongchai Jaidee, the No. 1 player in Asia, beating the rookie, American Ed Loar, with a par on the first playoff hole.

"I'm very lucky to win," said Thongchai, after Loar just missed a winning birdie putt at the 72nd hole and then bogeyed the first extra hole. In a tournament that saw a swarm of players leading and challenging, Thongchai shot 69-70-69-69, and Loar shot 65-71-70-71. They tied at 277, 11 under par at the Yangon Golf Club.

Loar, 24, a left-hander, got his career off to an electrifying start, shooting 65 to tie Sweden's Olle Nordberg, an Asian veteran, for the first-round lead. "I'm enjoying my experience in Asia," said Loar, and little wonder. His round included two improbable birdie putts, a 40-footer at No. 4 and a 20-footer at the 17th. Nordberg and Loar enjoyed a three-stroke cushion over Thailand's Suthep Bunpimuck, who would fade badly, and a four-stroke lead over Myanmar's surprising Aung Win, who would not.

Win became the surprise of the tournament. Why? First, because he used to be a waiter, which doesn't square with a crack golfer. And then he shot 67 in the second round to leap to a one-stroke lead over Loar and Indian star Arjun Atwal. But Win, 28, was not accustomed to the fast lane. He recalled trying to keep his scorecard. "My hands were trembling," he said. He got a good boost from the home crowd, and even more of one from Loar, who blew his lead with three straight bogeys on the back nine. Win's story was too good to last, and it didn't. But he held together admirably and finished tied for sixth.

Lurking in the wings, meanwhile, was Thongchai. But he would have to get past the par-fives. He bogeyed the 12th in the first round, and double-bogeyed it in the second and still shot 70. "I need to make my move tomorrow," Thongchai said. This he did, with 69 in the third round, to get within two of the leaders, Atwal, who shook off a sore back and shot 70, and Loar, who again creaked on the back nine, dropping three strokes over his last three holes, also for 70.

In the mad dash of the final round, victory stayed just beyond Loar's eager fingertips. His last good chance for a debut victory ended when his birdie putt at the final hole died just short. And he would say, "I had my chances, but I didn't take advantage of the par-fives." It was the reverse for Thongchai. "I thought I didn't have a chance," he said. "The turning point was on 17, when I birdied the hole despite driving into the hazard." He hacked the ball out, then fired a 210-yard five iron to 15 feet and holed the putt. "But when Edward failed to birdie 17 and 18 to allow me to get into the playoff, I was confident of finishing the job," he said. And he did.

Hero Honda Masters—US$300,000
Winner: Harmeet Kahlon

India's Harmeet Kahlon, 31, faithful to his sports psychologist's teaching that a bird in hand is worth two in the bush, was all set when his first victory as a professional came within reach.

"I knew nothing about my position until hitting my drive off the 18th tee," Kahlon said. "I could make out a certain buzz around my group, but I didn't want to think it." He remembered what his psychologist preached: Concentrate on the task at hand rather than on the results. He did, and the result was that after the three veterans who were tied for the lead at the final turn became undone, he kept his head, salvaged a bogey at the 18th, and broke through with the Hero Honda Masters at the DLF Golf and Country Club in New Delhi.

And he did it thanks to three Davidoff Tour veterans, who cleared a path for him down the final nine. India's Arjun Atwal, the defending champion, bogeyed the 16th and 18th. Thailand's Prayad Marksaeng pulled his second shot into the rough on the final hole and couldn't get up and down. And Sweden's Daniel Chopra double-bogeyed the 13th and 16th. Atwal (70) tied for fifth, and Chopra (72) for seventh. Marksaeng closed with 72 and tied for second, a stroke off the lead, with Thailand's Thammanoon Sriroj (67) and Korean rookie James Oh, 19, whose 65 was the day's best.

At the start of the tournament, it didn't seem there would be much room for someone who hadn't won yet. Atwal burst into the first-round lead with a six-under-par 65. But he stumbled coming out of the gate in the second round, going five over par through the fifth hole. Three birdies over the final four holes kept him afloat with a 74. Meanwhile, Indian veteran Jeev Milkha Singh, a four-time winner, rode a hot putter to a 65 to take the 36-hole lead. He dropped birdies all over the place — a five-footer, a couple from 10, two from 15, one from 30. But he blew to 76 in the third round and was out of the picture, giving way to India's Vijay Kumar, who posted a par 71 to tie Marksaeng through 54 holes. This is when Kahlon finally made his appearance. A one-under 70 tied him for third with South Africa's Craig Kamps, a stroke off the lead. It was anybody's tournament.

Kahlon announced his presence in the final round with a 25-foot birdie putt on the first hole. He read the greens very well through the day, suffering only one three-putt, a bogey at the fifth, and he bogeyed the par-three eighth from a buried lie in a bunker. But he birdied the ninth from 20 feet. He ignored the pressure from the veterans and stuck to the business at hand. He birdied the 13th with a tricky five-footer, then saved par from the bushes at the 17th. Then it seemed it was all over at the 18th. He missed the green to the left and bogeyed. But he had his victory. "It was like destiny," Kahlon said, winning on 69-68-70-70–277. "The reality has yet to sink in, but I'm delighted that I've finally broken through."

Caltex Singapore Masters—US$900,000
Winner: Arjun Atwal

"I expected to win, the way I was playing this year," Arjun Atwal was saying. "But I didn't expect to win so quickly." Not in the third event, late in February, and certainly not this easily. "But I'll take it," he said.

Who wouldn't, the way he outran the field in the Caltex Singapore Masters. Atwal, 28, edged into the lead in the third round, then raced away for a five-stroke victory, becoming the first Indian to win on the PGA European Tour (the tournament was jointly sponsored with the Davidoff Tour). The win healed some fresh, harsh wounds for Atwal, a rookie on the European Tour. A week earlier, he was leading the Hero Honda Masters with three holes to play, but stumbled and finished fifth. The week before that, in the season-opening London Myanmar Open, he led with nine holes to play and finished fourth. A man can learn to doubt himself over something like that.

The Singapore Masters was highlighted by a stirring by Nick Faldo. A six-time winner of majors, Faldo was the only one who mounted any kind of challenge in the final round. He made four birdies in succession from the 11th, but lost some steam when he turned a birdie chance into a par at the par-five 15th, needing two to escape a bunker. He dropped a shot at the 17th for a closing 70 and finished third.

Atwal resolved a lot of doubt in the third round with a seven-birdie, two-bogey 67 at the par-72 Laguna National Golf and Country Club at Singapore. That carried Atwal, a three-time winner on the Davidoff Tour, into the lead when Australian left-hander Nick O'Hern, who led the first two rounds, bogeyed the last two holes of the third. O'Hern disappeared with a final-round 76.

Atwal, while touring Laguna National in 70-69-67-68 for a 14-under-par total of 274, couldn't help but remember his previous two failures.

"I just need to hang in there," he said. "If it doesn't happen, it doesn't

180 洞 *Holes*

On the Road to
World No. 1

www.missionhillsgroup.com

happen. I'm not going to expect anything from tomorrow's round. I'm playing well. I just want to stick to my game plan and keep hitting solid shots
and putts ..."

Which is what he did. He started the final round with a one-stroke lead,
but was never pushed the rest of the way, cruising the course without a
bogey. He played the front in three-under-par 33 to up his lead to four
strokes, then birdied the 11th to get to five.

"I just felt very comfortable with the way I was hitting the ball, and I
knew if I hung in there I would be okay, and this was the perfect week to
peak," Atwal said, tending toward the transcendental. "That was my game
plan — to not get into the situation itself, just stay in the present and make
sure I hit the ball well."

Carlsberg Malaysian Open—US$1,000,000

Winner: Alastair Forsyth

Alastair Forsyth was on autopilot for a while in the grueling heat and hu-
midity, but he turned the Carlsberg Malaysian Open, co-sponsored by the
Davidoff and PGA European Tours, into one for the books. The 26-year-old
Scot was not only playing on a sponsor's invitation, and not only led or
shared the lead all the way, he went into the pressure cooker of a sudden-
death playoff and emerged with his first victory as a professional.

It looked like a bit too much pressure for a while late in the final round.
Forsyth, who lost his European Tour card the year before, seemed to be in
good shape. He started the final round with a two-stroke lead. Then came
the shakes — or the heat — just after he headed for home. He dropped three
strokes in a five-hole span, and for the first time in the tournament, he
trailed. In fact, he trailed Australian Stephen Leaney by two strokes with
three holes to play. Things didn't look good for Forsyth. Leaney was a
seasoned three-time European Tour winner.

"I had a sore head from the 13th hole onwards, and it's been like that
every day," Forsyth said. "When I bent down to put my tee in the ground
or mark my ball, I thought my head was going to burst. It was horrific. But
when I birdied 16 and 17, it eased the pain."

The heat at Royal Selangor, near Kuala Lumpur, had Forsyth reeling in
near heat exhaustion back in the first round, when he ran off eight birdies.
"The last couple holes were a real struggle," he said. "I didn't know where
I was. My head was spinning and my legs were like jelly." But he held
together for an eight-under-par 63, and added 65, 69 and 70 to tie at 17-
under 267 with Leaney, who had only one bogey in the tournament. Leaney
closed with 67 to catch Forsyth, and Alex Cejka came within a hole of
winning outright and an inch of joining the playoff. Cejka was leading by
a stroke coming to the 18th, but he hit his tee shot into the trees and his
approach into the rough, and from there he needed a par to tie for the
playoff. But his par putt from six feet stopped an inch short.

So it was Forsyth and Leaney in the playoff, and Leaney left his approach
50 feet short of the cup. Forsyth coolly holed a 15-foot birdie putt for the
win.

"I felt I had the tournament in my hands on the 16th green," Leaney said.

"But Alastair birdied the 16th and 17th. He showed some guts coming down the stretch."

"To lose it and win it again was unbelievable," said Forsyth. "It's really hard for me to explain the winning feeling." He'll find the words. The win was worth, among other things, a two-year exemption on the European Tour.

Casino Filipino Philippine Open—US$175,000
Winner: Rick Gibson

There wasn't a great deal of suspense at the Casino Filipino Philippine Open. Could amateur Angelo Que, for example, make the cut? He could and he did, and not only made the cut, he bounced back from a 78 in the storm-whipped third round to tie for seventh. Could anybody beat the famous Wack Wack course at Manila in those brutal winds, when the high 70s and even mid-80s were the scores of the day? Yes, but only one. American Robert Jacobson managed a one-under-par 68, the only score in the 60s, and it boosted him to a runner-up finish. So much for suspense.

Meanwhile, back at the tournament, the name was Canadian but it was strictly a case of home-cooking when Rick Gibson, leading by six going into the final round, ran off with a wire-to-wire victory, winning by four. Why home-cooking? Because Gibson, 40, had lived in Manila for the past 13 years, and played most of his career in Asia, mostly on the Japanese Tour. He topped the old Asian Tour money list in 1991.

The only question here was who would finish second? Gibson, who had a different pursuer each day, led by a stroke through the first two rounds. The third round was the killer — for everyone else. The winds came up with a fury over Wack Wack, blowing games and hopes all over the place. Jacobson shot that 68, a small miracle considering that the only other under-par round was 71 by Korea's Kang Wook-soon. There were 46 players at 75 through 79, and 17 players at 80 through 85, one of them the Philippines' ace, Frankie Minoza, with 81.

The wind hurt Gibson, too. He suffered three bogeys on the front nine, but birdied the 13th and 14th and posted a one-over 73, and saw his lead balloon from one shot to six, this over Korea's Anthony Kang (73), Thailand's Chawalit Plaphol (74) and the Philippine's Tony Lascuna (75). American Greg Hanrahan, one behind after the second round, blew to an 81.

In the first round Gibson, blessed with a sharp short game, ran off three birdies from the fourth, and all told logged six birdies and two bogeys for a one-under 68 for a one-stroke lead over Korea's Kim Sang-ki and Que, the amateur. Minoza, always a threat, was in a crowd at 70. Defending champion Felix Casas, also of the Philippines, shot 81 and was on his way to missing the cut. In the second round, Gibson birdied the 16th and 17th for 69 and the halfway lead by a stroke, this time over Hanrahan, who shot 68. Then came the third round and the wind, and it was all over.

Royal Challenge Indian Open—US$300,000
Winner: Vijay Kumar

Vijay Kumar, a 33-year-old former caddie, came into the Royal Challenge Indian Open with nothing but a chance and a lot of hope, and left it having to make travel plans. Now, he said, with his first Davidoff Tour title safely in his pocket, he would schedule six or seven events a year in Asia.

"I have no sponsor, so I wasn't playing more events in Asia," said the 33-year-old former caddie. "But now I can invest some of the money I've won in myself."

Kumar ended up with that pleasant scheduling dilemma after pulling away from Canadian Rick Gibson going through the final turn and racing off for a two-stroke victory. Kumar opened the tournament with a two-under-par 70, four behind Singapore's Mardan Mamat and Mexico's Pablo Del Olmo. Both fell away with 73 and 74, respectively, in the second round, when Kumar took the lead for good, posting 66-68-71 for a 13-under-par 275 total at Delhi Golf Club.

Kumar leaped into the lead with a six-birdie, no-bogey 66 in the second round, and was almost bogey-free in the third round as well, but dropped a shot at the par-five 18th. He settled for a three-stroke lead going into the final round, with the veteran Canadian Rick Gibson, winner of the Casino Filipino Philippine Open, lurking just behind.

Gibson had his chance in the final round. Kumar parred the first four holes comfortably, and Gibson pulled within two with a birdie at No. 3. Then Kumar seemingly started to unravel. He three-putted from 40 feet at the fifth, and missed from the fringe at the sixth. The two straight bogeys dropped him back into a tie with Gibson. But he came through when he had to.

When Gibson missed from the fringe at the ninth and bogeyed, Kumar was ahead by one, and was off and running. He birdied the 10th, firing a five iron to four feet, birdied the 14th with a 13-footer and the 16th from 15 feet.

Kumar called the victory a dream come true, leaving Gibson to be more eloquent. "He showed lots of character and steel," Gibson said. "He played well just when he needed to, pulled off some great shots just when I would have a chance."

SK Telecom Open—US$400,000
Winner: Charlie Wi

On paper, it looks like a comfortable two-stroke victory. On the fairways and greens of Lakeside Country Club in Seoul, it was more like an old Wild West shootout. Charlie Wi, a Los Angeles-based Korean, started the final round with a four-stroke lead, and seemed on his way. Before he knew it, he was in a dogfight and had to come from behind over the closing holes to take his second straight SK Telecom Open.

"This is unbelievable," said Wi. He had to outrun Kevin Na, a promising 18-year-old Korean out of Los Angeles, who turned professional in 2001, and then had to outduel former World and Australian Amateur champion Kim Felton, 27, over the final two holes.

"I stayed very focused under pressure, and my swing held up so well," Wi said. He certainly did that. Wi shot 67-69-67-69–272, 16 under par. He took the lead in the third round and was up by a healthy four strokes over Na, Felton and Korean Kim Tae-hoon going into the final round. Scratch Tae-hoon. He was quickly on his way to a closing 76. Wi then led by five through the fifth hole. But Na and Felton turned up the heat, and they were tied at 14 under with four holes to play. Felton played the front nine in four under and birdied the 11th, and Na birdied five out of six holes from No. 8.

Then Na was out of the chase. He bogeyed the 15th, and it was a two-man race. Felton, in his third year on the Davidoff Tour, edged into a one-stroke lead at the 16th, holing a 35-foot putt for a birdie. But he hooked his tee shot at the par-four 17th, and almost made a sensational par out of the rough, but he just missed his 15-footer and had to settle for a bogey. While Felton was stumbling at the 17th, Wi was making birdie at the 16th, holing a 10-footer to retake the lead. Wi then birdied the 18th from 20 feet for a 69 to lock up what looked like a two-stroke win.

American Robert Jacobson seemed to be on his way to an excellent Davidoff rookie year, opening with a seven-birdie 66 for a one-stroke lead. But he shot 74 in the second round. Na took over in the second with the best round of his young career, a 65. "The plan was to just make the cut today and try and make a move on Day Three," said Na, who was playing on a sponsor's invitation after failing to win his card at the Asian PGA Qualifying School earlier in the year. Na moved to the United States at the age of eight and won a number of junior titles. Another bright Korean youngster emerged in this tournament. Jae An, a 14-year-old amateur, missed the cut, but stamped himself as a comer with rounds of 74 and 76.

Maekyung LG Fashion Open—US$350,000
Winner: Lee Seung-yong

For those who like the cliché "Youth must be served," consider that it became painfully real for Thai star Thammanoon Sriroj at the Maekyung LG Fashion Open. Think of a veteran shooting 69-66-66-68–269 and losing — to a teenage amateur.

But that's what happened when Lee Seung-yong, a mere 18, absolutely exploded down the final backstretch for a seven-under-par 65 to become only the second amateur to win on the Davidoff Tour. The first — Korea's Kim Dae-sub, now a pro — was in the field with him and tied for 14th.

Lee, who is known as Eddie, played the par-72 Nam Seoul Country Club in 70-64-69, and was five, one, and two strokes off the lead, respectively. Thammanoon was leading him by one with five holes to play. Then Lee put on one of the most dazzling shows ever seen on the Davidoff Tour. He birdied the 14th and 15th, eagled the par-five 16th, and birdied the 17th. He made his only bogey of the day at the 18th, but that merely reduced his winning margin to one.

"I felt very confident today, and sensed that I could win," Lee said, "but it took a really great finish."

He may be young, but he has a gift for understatement. Somehow, going five under across four holes seems a bit more than great.

Thammanoon, seeking his fifth Davidoff title, tried his best to turn the kid back, getting birdies at the 14th and 16th. And his closing 68 was hardly a surrender. Lee was just too hot.

Lee didn't come as a total surprise to those who pay attention to amateur golf. Lee, who has lived in New Zealand since he was five, has an outstanding amateur record. A New Zealand national team player, he won the New Zealand Amateur Open in 2001 and was runner-up in the 2002 season. He tied for 19th on the PGA European Tour's Heineken Classic in Australia this year.

Lee was hardly noticed at first. Korea's Kang Wook-soon, a seven-time Davidoff winner, shot a stunning 65 to take the first-round lead — stunning because he bogeyed the last two holes. But a 71 in the second round was enough to knock him back into the field, after America's Ahmad Bateman, with 66, and Korea's Park Do-kyu, with 67, tied at 133 after two rounds. Then it was Thammanoon, moving into position with a 66 for a two-shot lead over Lee heading into the final round. And then it was Lee, the kid, having his day.

In a way, this was youth being served on a grand scale. There were 21 amateurs in the Maekyung field, and in addition to Lee, six others made the cut, and one tied for 21st and two others for 27th.

Mercuries Masters—US$300,000
Winner: Tsai Chi-huang

After about a four-month summer break, the Davidoff Tour resumed in the third week of August, and it was a tough time for some at the Mercuries Masters. Players such as South African Justin Hobday, Taiwan's T.C. Chen and Scotland's Simon Yates missed the cut, and defending champion Daniel Chopra of Sweden made it just exactly on the number. If these were surprises, consider that Taiwan's Tsai Chi-huang, hardly a big name, ran off with the tournament by five strokes.

It didn't look that easy to start with. Tsai, age 33, had won twice in Taiwan years earlier, but he was not even close to being tournament-tough. The Mercuries Masters was his first tournament on the Davidoff Tour this year. The highly regarded Chopra opened with 75 at a time when it was looking like American Week on Taiwan Golf and Country Club's par-72 Tamsui Course. Aaron Meeks, age 37, from Las Vegas, looking for his first win on the Davidoff Tour, staked an early claim with an impressive eight birdies and just one bogey for a seven-under-par 65. That gave him the first-round lead by three strokes over Tsai and Australian Kim Felton.

Six of the top nine places after the second round were occupied by Taiwanese golfers, led by Lu Wen-teh, age 39, the only player to win the Mercuries Masters twice in its 16-year history. Lu, who won in 1994 and 1996, before it became part of the Davidoff Tour, matched Meeks' tournament-low 65 for a 10-under 134 total. That put him a stroke ahead of Meeks, who shot 70. As the tournament rolled along, the challengers — almost to a man — drifted into the 70s, clearing the way for Tsai. And he jumped at his chance.

Not that Tsai was thoroughly accustomed to doing what one has to do to win. He had only two victories in his career — the 1997 Taiwan Open and the 1998 ROC PGA Championship. But he marched along like a real veteran. In the third round, he posted six birdies against two bogeys for 68 and a two-stroke lead over Lu.

Only two players could take some of the spotlight away from Tsai in the final round. Filipino Marciano Pucay had the shot of the day, a hole-in-one at the 215-yard 10th (he had 74 and tied for 40th), and India's Jyoti Randhawa, who was playing in his first tournament since suffering a broken collarbone in March. He closed with 69 and tied for 15th. Apart from them, it was all Tsai. He posted a no-bogey 69 — the only man in the field to shoot all four rounds in the 60s. He finished at 14-under-par 274 for a five-stroke win over Lu. The surprising Tsai had closed out in style.

Shinhan Donghae Open—US$400,000
Winner: Hur Suk-ho

When the guys are sitting around talking about favorite golf holes, Hur Suk-ho won't have any trouble finding his. Hands down, it's the par-five 18th at Jae Il Country Club in Seoul. From a double eagle in the first round to a pair of birdies in the playoff, that's where Hur scored his first Davidoff Tour victory, taking the Shinhan Donghae Open. Equally to his credit, in between, he led all the way.

"I thought I could have shot a better score in the final round," Hur confessed, "but I was a bit nervous." The 28-year-old Korean won in the toughest way for a first-timer. Playing the par-72 course in 65-67-72-72, he knew he had very little margin for error. His biggest lead was by two strokes through the third round. And that evaporated when he shot par in the final round and got caught at 12-under 276 by Scotland's Simon Yates, who closed with 69.

The 18th was the playoff hole. The first time, they both birdied it. The second time, Hur rolled in a six-footer for another birdie and the victory. It was another playoff frustration for the Thai-based Yates. In the 2001 SK Telecom Open, he lost in a three-way playoff.

Hur, who had won in Japan earlier in the year, came to the late summer still looking for his first Davidoff Tour victory. He didn't know it at the time, of course, but he got a fingernail-grip on the win in the first round when he holed out his approach for a double-eagle two at the 18th and the tournament-best 65 (tied later by Yates and Korea's Kim Tae-hoon). Hur also had an eagle and three birdies plus one bogey for the one-stroke lead over a crowd at 66. There were two surprises in the second round: For one, Hur was able to hang on to the lead. For the other, the cut came in at par 144, and India's Arjun Atwal, the Davidoff Tour Order of Merit leader, missed by five shots.

The real test for Hur came in the final round. He shot 35 on the first nine and seemed to be comfortably on his way. Oops, he lost his tee shot at the 10th and took a double-bogey six. Then coming down the stretch, he knew what he had to do. Yates finished ahead of him and was the leader in the clubhouse at 12 under.

"It was windy out there and I lost control of my tee shot at the 10th," Hur said. "But I just told myself to hang in there."

Kolon Cup Korean Open—US$350,000
Winner: Sergio Garcia

Sergio Garcia added Asia to his victory list with a tougher-than-it-seemed win in the Kolon Cup Korean Open. And if Garcia didn't know Korea's Kang Wook-soon before, he must have felt as if he had known him all his life afterward. Garcia racked up his third victory of the season, but had to hold off a gritty Kang to do it. The way Kang hung on while the rest of the field faded, his name must mean "bulldog."

Garcia, famed for his youthful free spirit, breezed around Seoul's Hanyang Country Club, playing the par-72 course in 67-65-66-67 for a hefty 23-under-par 265. His total was the tournament record and lowest four-round total on the Davidoff Tour this year. But Garcia needed some clutch play down the stretch to lock up the win. He beat Kang by three, and Kang was a whopping seven shots clear of his nearest rivals.

Garcia was out of the lead only in the first round, and only by one stroke. Kang and three others shared the lead at 66. After that, it was all Garcia. This was his third victory of the year, following one each on the U.S. PGA Tour and the PGA European Tour.

This one was wide open for the first round. Garcia started with a quick bump, a bogey on his third hole (he started at No. 10), but he snapped back. He posted four birdies and an eagle three on the par-five sixth, his 15th hole. Then he got down to business. But so did Kang. The tournament essentially turned into match play.

Second round: Garcia opened with three straight birdies and did not drop a shot the rest of the way. His seven-under 65 lifted Garcia into the lead at 12 under, one ahead of Kang. "I'm happy with my game," Garcia said. "I played real solid, and I hope it will keep going at the weekend." Sharp iron play did the trick. His longest birdie putt was from 18 feet, at the 11th. Kang bogeyed his second hole, but bounced back for four birdies and an eagle for 67. The spread was on. Korea's K.J. Choi was third, two strokes behind Kang.

Third round: Garcia ran off four straight birdies from the 11th, and was bogey-free until the 18th. That slip gave him 66. Kang matched him and stayed one stroke behind.

Fourth round: Going out, the never-say-die Kang drew even when Garcia bogeyed the third. Garcia birdied the fourth, sixth and eighth. Kang almost stayed with him. He also birdied the sixth and eighth, but bogeyed the seventh, and Garcia had a two-stroke lead through the turn. Kang simply refused to wilt. He birdied the 10th to pull within one.

The 11th hole was where the tournament was all but decided. Kang bogeyed, and Garcia birdied and led by three. The gritty Kang birdied the 16th, but all that did was dent Garcia's lead. Garcia himself closed in style, getting his sixth birdie of the day at the 18th, and sticking another pin in his map of the world, adding Asia to his previous conquests in Europe, North America and Africa.

Volvo China Open—US$500,000
Winner: David Gleeson

David Gleeson figured he has to play catch-up with his Australian pals, who were out making names for themselves. If his assessment was correct, he took a giant step in the Volvo China Open, leading from wire-to-wire and finishing with a gritty performance in blustery winds to score his first victory on the Davidoff Tour.

Gleeson, 24, solved the tricky winds for a one-under-par 71 in the final round, holding off a fiercely determined Pablo Del Olmo of Mexico. Gleeson racked up a 16-under-par 272 total at the Shanghai Silport Golf Club, beating Del Olmo by a stroke.

You could almost hear a sigh of relief from Gleeson, who came up in golf at the same time as Adam Scott, Aaron Baddeley, Geoff Ogilvy and Brett Rumford. "I'm still way behind them," Gleeson said. "Ogilvy is playing on the U.S. Tour, Rumford had kept his card on the European Tour, and Scott and Baddeley are multiple winners. When we were playing on the same level, yeah, I could beat them. And I did, sometimes. But they took off pretty quick."

There was nothing slow about Gleeson at Shanghai. He took the lead with 65 in the first round and added 67 in the second, to hold a one-stroke lead at the end of each day. He shot 69 in the third round and was tied by South Africa's James Kingston, who posted a tournament-low 64. "Shooting 64 to be right up there with David is even more pleasing," Kingston said, "and the fact that it was on a reasonably windy day made the jump in the field even bigger." Kingston couldn't keep the heat on, however, and slipped to a third-place finish with 73 in the final round.

Early on, Gleeson faced a challenge. He bogeyed the seventh hole and found himself out of the lead, a stroke behind Kingston. This might have been fatal to the spirit of a guy who had come so far, but Gleeson snapped back with birdies at the next two holes to regain the lead.

Del Olmo, who started four strokes off the lead, figured he would need 66 to win, and as things turned out, he was right. He closed to within a stroke, but then two-putted from four feet for a bogey at the 16th, and his chances died. He closed with 68 and a 273 total. Gleeson was home free.

"I've won small events on the Malaysian Tour, but I haven't won a tournament this big since the Australian Amateur in 1996," Gleeson said. "I wasn't really thinking about winning this tournament until the 17th tee. I was trying not to mess up."

Acer Taiwan Open—US$300,000
Winner: Danny Chia

Danny Chia got into the Acer Taiwan Open on a sponsor's invitation. Against high winds and high scores, he made the cut after opening with 76. Coming into the final round, he was seven shots off the lead. So a high finish and a good paycheck were the most he could hope for. Imagine his surprise — and everyone else's — when the leader, Taiwan's Hsieh Yu-shu, came apart and bogeyed four of the last five holes. And so Chia, 29, found himself with his first Davidoff Tour victory and the biggest paycheck of his young career.

Chia, also the first Malaysian to win on the tour, knew how Hsieh felt. "I used to have problems containing my emotions when I'm in contention," he said, "but I'm a lot calmer now." For sure. Ignoring that seven-shot deficit, he birdied the sixth, ninth, 12th and 18th, and didn't drop a shot, wrapping up scores of 76, 70, 77 and 68 for a hefty three-over-par 291 total on the par-72 Sunrise club.

Hsieh could have forced a playoff with a birdie at the final hole, but he bogeyed instead and shot 77, leaving Chia the winner by two over him and Taiwan's Lin Chie-hsiang (66).

"I beat myself out there," Hsieh said. "I have been wanting to win this tournament for almost 20 years. I felt great after the first few holes, but after 15 holes, it was getting tight and I started to look at the scoreboard after every stroke. I had no idea it could be so scary."

Before that, the tournament was up for grabs. Myanmar's Kyi Hla Han, former Asian No. 1, shot a three-birdie, three-bogey par 72 in heavy winds for a share of the lead with Australian Kim Felton and American Clay Devers. Chia was tied for 19th with his 76. Against the persistent winds in the second round, Chia climbed to a share of third place behind Taiwan amateur Kao Bo-song (70), who would finish as low amateur, tied for ninth. The third round was Hsieh's time. And then it passed.

Chia took up golf after going to the driving range with his businessman father, and Jack Nicklaus was his idol. He had a good amateur career and won a number of mini-tour events, but his previous best in four years on the Davidoff Tour was a sixth in the 2002 Casino Filipino Open. Nerves had been a big problem, but there's nothing like pressure to toughen a guy. There was playing in the World Cup and also working on the psychological side of golf.

"It helped tremendously," Chia said. "I didn't crack today."

Macau Open—US$250,000
Winner: Zhang Lian-wei

The casual golf fan might think it's a fluke when a golfer from China, a country so new to the game, can win a professional event. If so, note that when China's Zhang Lian-wei scored his first Davidoff Tour victory in the 2001 Macau Open the field included such notables as John Daly and Lee Westwood. And then in this tournament, Zhang came up against the famed Nick Price — literally. Zhang rallied to tie Price with a birdie on the final hole, then dueled him over five extra holes before taking his second Davidoff Tour title.

Unaccustomed as Zhang was at making victory speeches, he did all right with this one. "This was the toughest victory of my career," he said. "I felt like I was swimming against the current. It is the first time I have played a five-hole playoff. It was very difficult, as Nick Price is such a tough competitor."

Price was foiled by Macau Golf Club's 18th green. "I hit good putts on the 18th, and they all missed," he said. "I hit a poor putt at the end for par, but it's just as well. I'm not sure we could have continued."

Zhang thought so, too. "It was getting dark," he said. And he suffered another doubt. "Things were starting to tighten up," he said. He meant himself, squandering a two-shot lead on the second nine with bogeys at the 13th and 14th. "I felt that it was slipping away," he admitted. "I was a little bit nervous."

It had been a long road. Price shot a five-under-par 66 in the first round to take a one-shot lead over Rafael Ponce of Ecuador. Zhang, at even-par 71, was 15 men back. Myanmar's Zaw Moe (66) and Sweden's Stephen Lindskog (67) tied for the second-round lead, one shot ahead of Price (71) and four ahead of Zhang, who moved up to sixth place with 69. Said Price, "I think I used up most of my putts yesterday." Said Zhang, "I am still in it, but I will have to shoot low."

The race shaped up in the third round. Lindskog took the lead with 70, Zhang moved to within a stroke with his 67, and Price slipped to third with another 71.

In the fourth round, Zhang, Price and Lindskog were tied at six under par with two holes to play. Price took the lead with a 35-foot birdie putt at the par-four 17th. Then Zhang birdied the 18th from 25 feet for 70, and the puzzled Price lipped out from 20 feet for 69, and they were tied at seven-under 277. Lindskog parred in for 72 and slipped to a tie for third.

Then it was back to the 18th, the playoff hole, and Zhang and Price had to play it five times with darkness closing in. Both missed winning birdie chances, and then on the fifth trip, Zhang got his par, and Price overshot the green and missed his par putt from six feet.

"I had two putts from one direction and two from another, but they all went different ways," Price said. "That green was like trying to read Cantonese."

TCL Classic—US$1,000,000
Winner: Colin Montgomerie

There was Colin Montgomerie, about mid-summer, saying he might quit. Then in the Ryder Cup, Monty led the European charge after saying he might not play because of a bad back. He then shared a win with Bernhard Langer when they tied in the Volvo Masters. A week later in mid-November, Monty took his first victory in Asia, outrunning Thai star Thongchai Jaidee for a two-stroke victory in the TCL Classic, the first $1 million tournament in China.

"It shows my peers I'm still here, and I'm still competitive at the highest level," Montgomerie said. Not that anyone doubted him. Monty, who didn't drop a shot over the last 41 holes, trailed Thongchai by two strokes going into the final round and raced past him for a two-stroke win at the par-72 Harbour Plaza Golf Club at Dongguan. Montgomerie took his first lead on the first nine in the fourth round, then came home in five-under-par 67 against Thongchai's 71. He wrapped up the title with rounds of 70-68-67-67—272, 16 under par.

Thongchai, age 33, who led off the year by winning the Myanmar Open, was playing his 36th start. "I have played too much golf," he said. He perked up in the second round when five birdies in an eight-hole stretch lifted him to 67 and a three-stroke lead. Montgomerie birdied three of the last five holes and joined a tie for second, three strokes back. It became the Thongchai-and-Montgomerie Show in the third round. Montgomerie saw six putts burn the cup and stay out down the last six holes, but 67 left him in a good humor. "Five under with missing the last six putts is a good score," he said. Thongchai shot 68 and led by two. "I was a little bit excited on the first couple of holes and bogeyed the second," Thongchai said. "But I settled down after that."

Montgomerie took the lead for the first time in the final round, dropping a 25-foot birdie putt at the eighth. He went two ahead with a birdie at the 10th. Thongchai battled back and tied him with birdies at the 14th and 15th, then slipped at the 16th, three-putting from 40 feet for a bogey. Both birdied the 17th, and then Thongchai's chances died when he missed the 18th green and bogeyed. "I really enjoyed playing with Colin," Thongchai said. "It was a great experience, so I am not too disappointed."

BMW Asian Open—US$1,500,000
Winner: Padraig Harrington

When last seen (unless one counts the Dunhill Links Championship in October), Padraig Harrington, the smiling Irishman, was helping the Europeans win the Ryder Cup in England. When next seen, in mid-November, he was in Taiwan, plucking the BMW Asian Open, US$1.5 million plum of the Orient and the opening event on the 2003 European Tour international schedule. Harrington had just finished No. 2 on the 2002 European Order of Merit and, though still in the same year, was off and running for the next. And out of failure, came success — sort of.

"I played badly in the last three events because I was trying to win the merit list and wasn't focused enough to win the individual events," said Harrington, ranked No. 8 in the world. "This week, I came out here just looking to win this, and thankfully, I did." He did so by charging back into the lead in the final round and surviving a shaky finish to beat India's fast-closing Jyoti Randhawa by one stroke. Harrington, who led the first round, played the Ta Shee Golf Club in 66-70-68-69–273, 15 under par.

Randhawa, seven off the pace after the third round, fell a stroke short with an eight-under-par 64 in the fourth round. "I could have made two more birdies on the back nine, but I missed four-foot putts," Randhawa said. "I guess the pressure got to me a bit." Randhawa's charge was the only real threat to Harrington.

The next nearest were three shots back tied for third, and these included Holland's Maarten Lafeber, who fought off jet lag to shoot a pair of 66s to take the halfway lead by four over Harrington. "Hopefully, I will win," Lafeber said. "The last couple months I've been up there a bit. But what can you do, you can't force it." He still led through the third round — with Harrington closing to within a shot — but a 73 in the final round took him out of the picture.

It was a picture of Harrington's making. One shot behind Lafeber at the start of the final round, Harrington streaked to four birdies in his first seven holes. He bogeyed the ninth, but got the stroke back with a birdie at the 10th. He stumbled dangerously down the stretch, though. He was leading by two with three holes to play when he drove into the water at the 16th. He scrambled to a par, however, holing an eight-foot putt. Then he bogeyed the 17th, missing the green and chipping badly. And at the par-three 18th, he missed the green again, and his chip was 10 feet short.

"The last couple holes, I was thinking that pars would be good enough," Harrington said. "Obviously, when you get into that frame of mind, you struggle to make pars." He faced one final struggle — a double-breaking 10-foot putt on the final hole. He closed like winner.

Omega Hong Kong Open—US$700,000
Winner: Fredrik Jacobson

"My ambition was to win two tournaments in Europe this year," said Sweden's Fredrik Jacobson. With December coming on, he was still looking for his first career victory in seven years on the PGA European Tour. "But the season ran out at the Volvo Masters," he added, "so I came to Asia hoping to win here and last week in Taiwan. Well, I got half of what I wished for."

Indeed. Jacobson, 28, missed by a mile in the BMW Asian Open a week earlier, the first of two co-sponsored Asian-European Tour events. He was just moving along here in the Omega Hong Kong Open, then surged into the lead down the final stretch to win by two strokes over fellow Swede Henrik Nystrom and Argentina's Jorge Berendt.

The victory was exceedingly sweet for him. "It's a big relief to win a tournament after so many near-misses," said Jacobson, who was six times a runner-up, including the Barclays Scottish Open this year. This time he came out of the pack and got within a stroke going into the final round, shooting 68, 65 and 63 at the par-69 Hong Kong Golf Club. Then he closed with 64, the lowest finish in the field, for a 260 total.

The earlier leaders took turns disappearing. India's Amandeep Johl took the lead with 63 in the first round, then finished 48th. The second round ended in a seven-man logjam. Stephen Dodd, a big-hitting Welshman, was the only one of them still in the picture at the end. Interestingly, after 36 holes, Jacobson was nowhere in sight.

Taiwan amateur Lo Shih-kai, at age 13, became the youngest player ever in a European event. Lo, who got in by winning the Hong Kong Amateur, opened with 73 that included two bogeys, a double bogey and a triple bogey. "I was a bit nervous," he said. Another 73 in the second round cost him the cut.

Jose Maria Olazabal labored in the final round for 73 and a tie for 56th. "For the first time in my career, I actually gave up on the front nine," Olazabal said. "I'm going to have a long break now." And Nick Faldo, trying to make a comeback at age 46, tied for 11th at 10 under.

Dodd, enjoying his first lead ever in a European event, still shared it through the third round. But he would have been the solo leader except for bogeys at the 16th and 18th. The stumble eventually cost him the tournament. "It was disappointing to finish like that," Dodd said. It would be worse in the final round.

Jacobson, starting a stroke off the lead, made his move with a bogey-free 30 on the first nine. With his only bogey of the day at the 11th, he slipped a stroke behind Dodd. Then came the decisive stretch. Jacobson birdied the

12th and 14th, and Dodd bogeyed the 15th and 18th. A 68 dropped him to joint fourth. And Jacobson revealed the secret to breaking that runner-up jinx. "I didn't watch any scoreboards this time," Jacobson said.

Volvo Masters of Asia—US$500,000
Winner: Kevin Na

Kevin Na, a 19-year-old Davidoff Tour rookie, won the inaugural and season-ending Volvo Masters of Asia. A California-based Korean, Na came bashing through with 66 in the final round to take the championship by two strokes. He gave most of the credit to his caddie — who also happened to be his father.

Things didn't look promising when Na shot 71 in the third round. "I was three back, but my dad said that we still had a chance," Na said. "He said if I shot 66 in the final round, I would win."

And that was what Na did, wrapping rounds of 69, 66, 71 and the closing 66 for a 272 total, 16 under at the par-72 Kota Permai Golf and Country Club in Malaysia. That gave him the victory over four veterans — South Africa's Craig Kamps, who led the first two rounds and shared the third-round lead with India's Arjun Singh, and Korea's Anthony Kang and Scotland's Simon Yates. India's Jyoti Randhawa finished 32nd, winning US$3,933, which lifted him to No. 1 on the Asian money list.

Youth had been nibbling at the veterans for some time, and now the Davidoff Tour had another teenage winner for the year. Eddie Lee, an 18-year-old Korean — like Na — rallied down the final round and took the Maekyung Classic in May.

Na started the final round tied for sixth, three strokes off the lead. He could only hope that his father was right. He made three birdies and a bogey on the first nine. Then he erupted for four consecutive birdies from the 10th that gave him the lead, and he parred in from the 14th. He missed an eight-foot birdie putt at the 18th. "At worst, I thought, I'll be in a playoff," Na said. "But Arjun still had to play 17, which is not an easy hole to birdie, and the pin on 18 was tucked as well."

Arjun was out in 33, but labored coming in. He bogeyed the 10th and 11th, then recovered and birdied the 12th and 14th to tie Na. He two-putted from four feet to bogey the 15th, dropped out of the lead, and couldn't make up the ground. At the 16th, he left his birdie try short. He saved par at the tough 17th after missing the green, and then needed a birdie at the par-five 18th to force a playoff with Na. "I hit a bad drive into the bunker," said Singh, "but my approach found its way into the trap." He came out to three feet, and missed that, too, and slipped out of solo second place and into a tie.

Na cruised in like a veteran. "I aimed for a lot of pins, but when I needed not to, I made sure I had pars," he said. "Things went according to plan. I thought I had a chance of winning this season, and it was a matter of capitalizing on the opportunities."

This victory was also vindication. He'd had an outstanding junior career in the United States, and there were critics who said he was turning professional too soon. "I thought it was a risky decision," Na conceded. "But I saw it as a shortcut. I think I'm doing well."

Japan Tour

Token Corporation Cup—¥100,000,000
Winner: Toru Taniguchi

It turned out to be a harbinger of things to come when Toru Taniguchi erupted with a blistering finish and captured the season-opening Token Corporation Cup tournament in mid-March. Nine months later, the 34-year-old Taniguchi was crowned the year's leading money winner. More about that through the season. At the Kedoin Golf Club, Taniguchi resided in a 16th-place tie going into the final round, then exploded with a course-record-tying 61 that wiped out his six-stroke deficit and gave him a two-shot victory with his 16-under-par 272.

Kiyoshi Murota had the lead twice — after the first and third rounds — but faded to a tie for fifth Sunday when he could manage just 71. He shared the top spot at 67 Thursday with two other 2001 winners — American Dean Wilson and Toshimitsu Izawa, the previous season's leading money winner. Tateo Ozaki shot 67 Friday and moved a stroke ahead of Izawa, Murota (70s) and Chen Tze-chung (68) before Murota reclaimed the lead with 68–205, a stroke ahead of Chen (69) and Hirofumi Miyase (66).

Taniguchi put together a flawless round Sunday. He piled up 11 birdies to go with seven pars for the 61 that equaled the low at Kedoin and matched the all-time 18-hole record. Miyase took the runner-up spot with 68–274 and Taichi Teshima tied Chen for third at 275.

Dydo Drinco Shizuoka Open—¥100,000,000
Winner: Kiyoshi Murota

Kiyoshi Murota made amends for his faltering finish in the season-opening Token Corporation Cup when the Japan Tour moved on to Hamaoka and the Shizuoka Country Club for the Dydo Drinco Open. The 47-year-old veteran, who had scored his fourth career victory after a seven-year drought the previous November against a strong international field in the Casio World Open, seized the lead at Shizuoka in the third round and went on to a two-stroke victory with 69 for a 276 total, 12 under par.

Toru Taniguchi carried his scoring touch over from his victorious finish in the Token Cup. Making 19 birdies in his last 36 holes of play, Taniguchi fashioned a 65 in the opening round of the Dydo Drinco tournament and shared first place with Australia's David Smail and American Peter Teravainen. Murota trailed by two at that point, then cut his deficit in half with a 68–135 Friday, moving within a stroke of co-leaders Hiroyuki Fujita (67-67) and Lin Ken-chi of Taiwan (69-65).

Strong winds puffed up the scores Saturday and Murota's par 72 for 207 put him in front by a stroke over Zhang Lian-wei, China's first international player of note, whose 69 matched the day's best scores. The victory did not come easily for Murota Sunday. In fact, he trailed Korea's Kim Jong-duck at one time early in the round, but birdies at the 11th and 12th holes pushed him back in front and he finished steadily for the 69 and two-stroke victory over Kim and 55-year-old Masashi Ozaki, who closed with 67.

Tsuruya Open—¥100,000,000
Winner: Dean Wilson

Dean Wilson, who became the latest of a half-dozen, little-known Americans to achieve stardom in Japan in the last decade or so when he won three times and finished third on the 2001 Japan money list, added to his winning record in the Land of the Rising Sun. He won the Tsuruya Open when the circuit resumed after a month-long hiatus in late April. The Hawaii-born player finished 69-68 to grab a two-shot victory at Sports Shinko Country Club at Kawanishi, Hyogo Prefecture. His 11-under-par 273 gave him a two-stroke margin over Toru Taniguchi and his fifth title in Japan.

The opening round belonged to Hiroyuki Fujita, Kazumasa Sakaitani and Katsumasa Miyamoto, who won his first of four tour victories there in 1998. They shot 67s. Wilson was among 10 players who shot 69. Fujita followed Friday with a five-birdie 66 for 133 that gave him a two-stroke margin over Sakaitani and three over Wilson, who shot 67. Miyamoto fell back with 72.

Wilson produced a solid but unspectacular 69 Saturday — three birdies and a lone bogey at the 11th — to move in front with 205. Fujita shot 74 and dropped into a four-way tie for second at 207 with Miyamoto (68), Azuma Yano (69) and Jeev Milkha Singh (70). Taniguchi provided Wilson's biggest challenge Sunday. Just back from Augusta where for the first days he was the playing partner of Arnold Palmer in his 46th and final Masters, Taniguchi shot 67 for 275 and threatened Wilson's lead until the American birdied the 16th hole to open his final two-stroke margin. Miyamoto finished at 276.

Chunichi Crowns—¥120,000,000
Winner: Justin Rose

Thanks to its swollen purse and active recruiting pursuit abroad, the Chunichi Crowns tournament has successfully imported a wide variety of strong international players over its 43-year history and many of them have rewarded the sponsor with victories. The title list includes major winners Greg Norman, Seve Ballesteros, Davis Love and Darren Clarke. Young Justin Rose joined the overall group in 2002, becoming the first English winner of the Chunichi Crowns with his five-stroke victory at Nagoya Golf Club at Togo, Aichi Prefecture.

The victory of the 21-year-old Rose was the season's first wire-to-wire performance and his first win in Japan. Rose had earlier wins in Europe and South Africa that verified the credentials he had shown with his fourth-place finish as a 17-year-old amateur in the 1968 British Open but that had been questioned with his subsequent slow start as a professional.

Rose had his first of two sizzling rounds that iced the victory when he opened with 64, but he had to share first place with Kazumasa Sakaitani, a little-known player who had first gotten attention as an early contender the previous week in the Tsuruya Open. Although he shot 70 Friday, the young Englishman retained his share of the lead, then with Dean Wilson, who shot 70-64 coming off his Tsuruya triumph the previous Sunday.

Rose's other hot round, 63, rocketed him four strokes into the lead Saturday. He had seven birdies in the unflawed round on the par-70 course and his four-shot margin was over collegiate amateur Yusaku Miyazato (66-201). Wilson shot 69 and slipped six behind at 203 with Katsunori Kuwabara. Rose was never threatened Sunday. He had a pair of birdies and a 14th-hole bogey for 69 and a 14-under-par 266, an easy five strokes ahead of runner-up Prayad Marksaeng of Thailand, who closed with 67 for 271. Wilson matched Rose's 69 and took third at 272.

Fujisankei Classic—¥140,000,000
Winner: Nobuhito Sato

It had been a frustrating spell of more than a year for Nobuhito Sato after he had come very close to the money title of the Japan Tour in 2000. A four-time winner, Sato had finished a close third in the final standings. But he lost his touch in 2001, going without a victory and plunging to 18th on the money list. His troubles continued in early 2002, his finishes ranging from 10th place to a missed cut in the first four events. The 31-year-old got back on track at the Fujisankei Classic, but not without a struggle. After nearly giving it away on the final day, Sato managed to eke out a tie in regulation and defeated Australian Scott Laycock in the subsequent playoff.

Sato took the lead at the par-71 Kawana Hotel golf course in the second round with 70 after his opening 67 was one of 17 scores in the 60s, the best being the 65s of Katsumi Kubo and Lin Keng-chi. At 137, Sato stood two strokes in front of Lin (74) and Takenori Hiraishi (68-71), and he remained in the top spot Saturday. He had six birdies and three bogeys for 68–205, holding a one-stroke advantage over American Gregory Meyer and just two over Lin, Toru Suzuki and Hidemasa Hoshino.

Sailing along on Sunday, Sato suddenly took three bogeys on the first four holes after the turn, but birdied the 14th and 17th holes to salvage a 71 and overtake Laycock, who had shot 67 for his 276. The playoff went two holes before Sato won with a par.

Japan PGA Championship—¥110,000,000
Winner: Kenichi Kuboya

Kenichi Kuboya landed his first major title on the Japan Tour — the Japan PGA Championship — and did it in style with a playoff birdie in an over-time duel with the formidable Shingo Katayama, first and second on the circuit's money list the two previous seasons. Kuboya's only two previous victories on the tour had come in 1997.

Both players had trailed the leaders at KOMA Country Club in Nara Prefecture going into the final round of the 69th playing of the championship. In fact,

Katayama had begun the tournament with 73 and Kuboya with 74 as Richard Backwell and Hideyuki Sato led with 69s. They were still out of serious contention after the second round when the amazing Masashi Ozaki, a six-time winner of the PGA Championship, shared the lead with Toru Taniguchi, 2001's No. 1 player, and Mamoru Osanai at 140.

Osanai followed with 69 Saturday for 209, remaining in a tie for the lead but then with Hur Suk-ho, a little-known player from South Korea, as Ozaki slipped two back with 71–211. A pair of 68s that day moved Kuboya within three strokes of the lead and Katayama to 213, four back.

Katayama took the clubhouse lead Sunday when he shot the day's best round, 66, for a nine-under-par 279, and Kuboya joined him at that score shortly thereafter with a 67 to force the playoff. At the second extra hole — the par-five 17th — Kuboya nearly holed a bunker shot and tapped in for the winning birdie after Katayama missed his birdie attempt from eight feet.

Munsingwear Open KSB Cup—¥120,000,000
Winner: Kenichi Kuboya

Kenichi Kuboya, who had gone nearly five years before adding a victory to his record with his overtime triumph in the Japan PGA Championship, went to the other extreme, putting the Munsingwear Open KSB Cup title back to back with it the following May weekend at Kagawa's Ayutaki Country Club course. Extra holes again, this time four of them before Kuboya subdued Todd Hamilton and Yoshimitsu Fukuzawa, became the season's first double winner and took over the top spot on the money list.

Although within close range of the lead, Kuboya never was in front until the three-man deadlock was forged Sunday. He opened with 66, which left him two strokes behind Tomoaki Ueda, a qualifier playing in his first event of the year. Five men shot 65, including defending champion Dinesh Chand and Thailand's Prayad Marksaeng, who followed with 69 Friday and moved into a share of the lead with American Dean Wilson, the Tsuruya Open winner in April. Wilson, a five-time winner in Japan, had rounds of 66 and 68 for his 134, chipping in for an eagle on the 18th green. Kuboya shot 70–136.

Wilson had first place to himself after his third-round 68 for 202, again eagling the last hole, that time with a tap-in after the 32-year-old Hawaii native nearly holed out his second shot on the par-five hole. Kuboya remained two back with a matching 68, but had second place to himself. Wilson's game disintegrated Sunday. While he was stumbling to a 77, Kuboya, Hamilton and Fukuzawa were assembling the deadlock at 11-under-par 273. Kuboya shot 69 while the other two produced 66s. In the playoff, Fukuzawa bowed out at the second extra hole when Kuboya and Hamilton both made birdies. The Japanese pro then took his second consecutive victory with another birdie at the 18th hole after the American, a seven-time winner in Japan but without a title since 1998, bogeyed the hole.

Diamond Cup—¥100,000,000
Winner: Tsuneyuki Nakajima

Matter-of-factly, a relieved and delighted Tsuneyuki (Tommy) Nakajima remarked, "It's been a long time." Yes, it had — a little more than seven years, in fact, since Nakajima, one of Japan's most successful and best known players ever, had posted a victory early in the 1995 season, the 45th of his spangled career. Nakajima had made some strong passes at victory in the ensuing years but didn't break through for No. 46 until the Japan Tour visited the Sayama Golf Club at Iruma for the Diamond Cup tournament. There the 47-year-old broke from a three-way tie after 54 holes to score a two-stroke victory with a 19-under-par 269.

Nakajima lingered just off the pace in the opening rounds. Japan's Tomohiro Kondo and Shinichi Yokota shared the first-day lead with American Christian Pena at 64 as low scoring abounded. Kondo, the former Japan amateur champion in his third season on the Japan Tour, came back with 65 Friday, and his 129 gave him a two-stroke lead over Pena (67) and three on Yokota (68) and Hirofumi Miyase (67-65). With rounds of 67 and 66, Nakajima trailed by four.

On Saturday, Pena managed only 70 and was overtaken by Nakajima and South Korea's Hur Suk-ho, who shot 68s for their 201s. A four-birdie back nine sparked Nakajima to his four-under round, and he put away the victory on the second nine Sunday. After an even-par 36 on the first nine, Nakajima birdied four of the next five holes and parred in for the winning 68–269. Kondo, Miyase and Pena tied for second place at 271.

JCB Classic Sendai—¥100,000,000
Winner: Toru Suzuki

Maybe Tsuneyuki Nakajima ought to travel back and forth from tournament sites by himself. At the JCB Classic Sendai, he shared the ride to and from Omotezao Kokusai Golf Club with Toru Suzuki and dispensed some advice to his friendly adversary en route. Exactly how much it helped is hard to say, but the fact of the matter was that Suzuki wound up facing and defeating Nakajima in a playoff, the fourth in five weeks on the Japan Tour. The win, Suzuki's first since the 2000 Casio World Open and sixth of his career, prevented Nakajima from notching a consecutive victory to go with his drought-ending win the previous Sunday in the Diamond Cup.

Nakajima and Christian Pena, protagonists in the title run at the Diamond Cup, remained contentious at the JCB Sendai. Perhaps inspired by his near-miss at Sayama, Pena jumped off fast at Omotezao, firing a seven-under-par 64 that gave him a piece of first place with unheralded Satoshi Oide. Nakajima started with a 67 and wound up tied for the lead when he shot 65 Friday for 132. Pena had 68.

Suzuki and Kenichi Kuboya, the leading money winner, took over the top spot Saturday. Kuboya spurted from 11th place with a seven-birdie 64, while Suzuki also went without a bogey in shooting 65 for his 201. Pena trailed by one after a 70 and Nakajima slipped back with 71. Scoring conditions were less than ideal Sunday and Nakajima's 68, the day's best round and one of only two under 70, put his 271 on the board. Suzuki, who had suffered three bogeys on the first nine, rallied coming in, forcing a playoff when he made his fourth birdie with a 12-footer on the final green for 70 and his 271.

In the playoff, after both men parred the first extra hole, Nakajima bogeyed the next one to turn the victory over to Suzuki and his par.

Tamanoi Yomiuri Open—¥90,000,000
Winner: Toru Taniguchi

Toru Taniguchi took a different route to his second victory of 2002 in the Tamanoi Yomiuri Open. When he opened the season by winning the Token Corporation Cup, Taniguchi staged a remarkable rally from a six-stroke deficit entering the final round. At Yomiuri Country Club at Nishinomiya, Taniguchi grabbed the first-round lead and never trailed as he became the year's second double winner. He won by two strokes with his 18-under-par 270, scoring the fifth victory of his 10-year career.

Playing "not to make big mistakes" in a damp and windy first round, Taniguchi did just that and more, shooting a bogey-free, seven-under-par 65. Hirofumi Miyase birdied his last three holes and joined Taiwan's Lin Kengchi in the runner-up spot at 64. The next day, Miyase capped his round with an eagle and two birdies for 68 and finished the day in a first-place tie with Taniguchi, who banged out 69 for his 134.

Taniguchi clearly established himself as the man to beat Saturday when he strung together three birdies twice in a round of 67 and moved three strokes in front with 201. Miyase slipped into a four-way tie for third at 205 with Shinichi Yokota, Daisuke Maruyama and Takashi Kamiyama when he shot 71 as Hiroyuki Fujita rode a 65 into second place at 204. On Sunday, Taniguchi again went without a bogey on his card for 69 and the two-stroke victory. Maruyama, with 66, and Satoru Hirota, with 65, tied for second place with 272s.

Mizuno Open—¥100,000,000
Winner: Dean Wilson

Americans had enjoyed unusual success in the Mizuno Open over the last decade, winning four of the eight stagings of the tournament prior to the 2002 event, and Dean Wilson continued the trend. The Hawaii-born player posted his second victory of the season in the Mizuno in late June, his five-under-par 67 in the final round giving him a one-stroke victory over Kiyoshi Miyazato. It was Wilson's sixth victory in Japan, coming two months after he won the Tsuruya Open.

Hirofumi Miyase, a contender in several events earlier in the season and a two-time winner in 2000, got off to another strong start at Setonaikai Golf Club at Kasaoka. He opened with 66 and shared the first-round lead with Hidemasa Hoshino, then moved in front alone by a shot in Friday's round. He scored a 69 for 135, which put him a stroke ahead of Toshimitsu Izawa, the 2001 money leader, and two in front of Toru Taniguchi, the current No. 1 man. Wilson was then five strokes off the pace with 71-69.

Bad weather moved in Saturday and Wilson made the best of it. His 70 — two birdies, no bogeys — matched the day's best score and jumped him a stroke in front of the field with 210. Miyazato fared well, too, his 71 moving him into a second-place tie with Taniguchi, who shot 74 for his 211. Miyase struggled to a 77 and dropped two off the pace. Though rainy, conditions and scoring improved Sunday and Wilson needed his 67 to stave off Miyazato in what turned out to be a two-man battle for the title. Wilson prevailed when he birdied two of the final four holes to edge the second-year pro with his 11-under-par 277. His 20-footer at the 17th gave him a two-shot cushion that he needed at the end. Taniguchi, bidding for his third win of the year, mustered only a 71 and tied for third with 282 with Hajime Meshiai.

Japan Tour Championship Iiyama Cup—¥120,000,000
Winner: Nobuhito Sato

For the third week in a row, the tournament winner already had a 2002 title in the bag. In the two previous weeks, it was Toru Taniguchi and Dean Wilson. In the rich Japan Tour Championship Iiyama Cup, the victory was claimed by Nobuhito Sato, who had scored a hard-fought overtime win in early May in the Fujisankei Classic. This time, Sato came up with brilliant closing round to run away with a six-stroke victory and jump past Taniguchi into first place on the Japan Tour money list.

Sato was a deserving winner in the third Tour Championship. He, Taniguchi and Kenichi Kuboya shot 67s in the opening round at the Hourai Country Club at Nishinasuno and led the field. Sato took a three-stroke lead with a six-birdie 66 Friday for 133, but wasn't certain of his position until the next morning when a late-afternoon thunderstorm prevented 47 players from completing their rounds Friday. Kuboya, the season's first two-time winner with his back-to-back victories in the PGA Championship and Munsingwear KSB Cup, shot 69 for 136 and second place. Taniguchi (71) and Toshimitsu Izawa were threats at 138.

Kuboya turned the tables on Sato Saturday. He shot 67 with an eagle, four birdies and a bogey and slipped a stroke ahead of Sato, who lost the lead when he double-bogeyed the par-three 17th. Sato took a 71 for 204, and Taniguchi remained in the thick of things with his own 67 for 205. On Sunday, though, Sato didn't give anybody a chance. He scorched the field with an eight-under-par 64 for 268. Kuboya held onto second place despite a 71, finishing two shots ahead of David Smail of New Zealand. With a par round, Taniguchi wound up in a four-way tie for fourth place, picking up a good check, but not big enough to retain his No. 1 position on the money list.

Juken Sangyo Open Hiroshima—¥90,000,000
Winner: Hur Suk-ho

It was mid-July before the Japan Tour had a first-time professional winner. That distinction went to South Korea's Hur Suk-ho, when he won the Juken Sangyo Open at Hiroshima impressively by three strokes. Justin Rose, the

Chunichi Crowns victor, had not won before in Japan but had other earlier victories on his record. Though an unfamiliar name in just his second season in Japan, Hur had signaled his ability twice earlier in the season when he shared third-round leads twice and finished a shot out of the playoff for the Japan PGA Championship.

Third time was the charm for the South Korean. Hur was never more than a stroke out of the lead all week on the Hachihommatsu course of Hiroshima Country Club. In Thursday's first round he shot 64, not good enough to lead but it put him just a stroke behind tour rookie Hideto Tanihara, 23, who lives in the Hiroshima Prefecture and had a supportive gallery. Tanihara's 63 tied the course record. He took 10 more strokes in his second round and dropped to fifth in the standings as Hur, with 70, and tour-non-winner Mitsuhiro Tateyama, with 65-69, took over the lead at 134.

Yet another winless veteran, Tetsuji Hiratsuka, had his moments of glory Saturday. He rang up seven birdies for 65 and moved into first place at 204. Hur shot 71 and David Smail 70 to settle in a stroke back at 205, and Brendan Jones moved into contention with 69–206. Among the leaders, only Hur retained his firepower Sunday. The South Korean produced 69 for 274 total, while Hiratsuka faded with 77, Smail shot 73 to tie for third, and Jones took 76 and dropped into a tie for 15th.

Sato Foods NST Niigata Open—¥50,000,000
Winner: Yasuharu Imano

Yasuharu Imano does not win very often, but when he does, he does it with resounding finishes. In 1999, he fired a final-round 65 to win the Chunichi Crowns. A year later, he rang up the same score the last day to win the Mizuno Open. Two very unproductive years followed for Imano before he came up with another of his blazing finishes. He whipped up a six-under-par 66 on the closing Sunday of the Sato Foods NST Niigata Open to capture his third title going away to a four-stroke victory margin. He was 18 under par at 270.

The 29-year-old Imano had an even better round the second day to put himself in position to win. After opening with 70 and sitting far down the standings behind leaders Katsumasa Miyamoto and Katsuya Nakagawa, Imano jumped into a first-place tie with an solid, eight-under-par 64 at Nakamine Golf Club in Toyoura. He and Australian Craig Jones (67-67) were at 134, one stroke ahead of Miyamoto (69), and rookie Koushi Yokoyama and Kazuhiko Hosokawa, who both shot 67-68.

Miyamoto regained the lead with 68 for a 203 total, stringing together five birdies in the course of the round. That moved him a shot ahead of Imano (70) and Hosokawa (69) going into the last day. That belonged to Imano, who piled up seven birdies and took a lone bogey in putting together the victorious 66. Miyamoto shot 71, but finished second, one stroke in front of Jones (69) and 1997 champion Hosokawa.

Aiful Cup—¥120,000,000
Winner: Yasuharu Imano

Yasuharu Imano made it two in a row at the Aiful Cup tournament, but his route to the victory was in striking contrast to those in his three previous wins. No hot final round this time. Imano had to survive a shaky back nine Sunday to pull out a one-stroke triumph and become the season's second back-to-back winner. "Around the 13th hole, I started thinking about winning and my knees and back started creaking," said Imano in describing his struggle to a par 72 that barely got him in one stroke ahead of Toshimitsu Izawa.

Imano had taken a three-stroke lead into the final round after leading from the start. Fresh from his four-shot victory in the NST Niigata Open, Imano blitzed the field with a course-record 64, jumping off to a one-shot lead over Masanori Kobayashi and Katsunori Kuwabara. It rained Friday, forcing 21 players to complete their rounds the next morning, but the wet weather didn't faze Imano. He widened his lead to three strokes with a six-under-par 66 for 130. Hiroaki Iijima (70-63) and China's Zhang Lian-wei (68-65) were at 133.

Imano started slowly Saturday with two early bogeys, but an eagle at the fifth hole put him back on track. He went on to a second straight 66 and went a remarkable 20 under par at 196 to retain his three-stroke margin. Naomichi Ozaki took over second place with 64–199, and Izawa was another shot back after shooting 66. Imano absorbed two bogeys on his struggling back nine Sunday that led to the 72, but Izawa fell a stroke short with his 69. Ozaki dropped back with a par round himself and his older brother, Tateo, picked off a share of third place with Tetsuji Hiratsuka at 270.

Imano was the fifth double winner of the season.

Sun Chlorella Classic—¥120,000,000
Winner: Christian Pena

Christian Pena's three years in Japan finally bore fruit at the Sun Chlorella Classic when the American scored his maiden professional victory. Pena did it the hard way, surviving a three-man playoff against Naomichi Ozaki and Australian Brendan Jones at Sapporo Bay Golf Club after carrying a two-stroke lead into the final round.

Pena, a University of Arizona graduate, was a contender from the opening gun. He shot 67 the first day, joining a six-player group trailing leader Brad Andrews by two strokes. Veteran Hideki Kase, 42, whose most recent of three tour victories came in the 1996 Nikkei Cup tournament, surprised with a nine-under-par 63 Friday and seized the lead by a stroke with his 133. Pena and Ozaki repeated their opening 67s and Jones (66-68) joined them in the runner-up spot at 134.

The American remained hot Saturday, shooting a 66–200 to grab the two-stroke lead over Ozaki (68) and Kase (69), three over Tsuneyuki Nakajima. Then, on Sunday, Pena shot 69 for 269 and was overtaken by Ozaki (67) and Jones (65). The playoff ended quickly when Pena birdied the par-five 18th, the first playoff hole. "I've worked hard for this moment," exclaimed

Pena. "I admit I was a little nervous standing over that birdie putt."

Hisamitsu-KBC Augusta—¥100,000,000
Winner: Nobumitsu Yuhara

Perhaps Nobumitsu Yuhara drew inspiration from the victory of Tsuneyuki Nakajima earlier in the season. Nakajima had gone seven years without a win before capturing the Diamond Cup in early June. The 45-year-old Yuhara was a six-time winner on the Japan Tour, but the last victory had come in 1992 in the Yonex Open. The dry spell ended for Yuhara at the Hisamitsu-KBC Augusta tournament, although dry spell is a bit of a misnomer, since the soaking effects of the fringes of Typhoon Rusa had a big influence on the outcome. The bad weather forced cancellation of Saturday's third round, and Yuhara and Masashi Shimada carried the lead into the final round. Yuhara then survived a stumbling finish to eke out a one-stroke victory over five other players at Keya Golf Club in Shima.

Yuhara and Shimada forged the leadership tie Friday after two little-known players — Kazuhiro Shimizu and Tomonori Takahashi — had a day of glory atop the standings with 67s. Both Yuhara and Shimada had 68-69 rounds to finish the day a shot ahead of Katsunori Kuwabara, Toshimasa Nakajima and Christian Pena, who had just notched his first Japan victory the previous Sunday. After sitting out the Saturday deluge, Yuhara took control of first place over the first 14 holes Sunday. He eagled the par-five 13th and birdied the 14th to open a three-stroke lead, but admitted, "I got in a bit of a panic at the end." He bogeyed two of the final four holes, but his 72–209, seven under par, was just enough to edge Pena, Toshimasa Nakajima and Kuwabara, who also shot 72s and split second-place money with Zhang Lian-wei and Shigemasa Higaki, who had final-round 70s.

Japan PGA Match Play—¥80,000,000
Winner: Nobuhito Sato

It's not exactly a kiss of death, but drawing a high seed for the Japan PGA Match Play in recent years hasn't been of much help. Most of the favorites have gone by the boards in the early rounds and a top-ranked player hasn't taken the title since Tsuneyuki Nakajima won for the third time in 1992. Nobuhito Sato reversed that trend in 2002 although, despite being the leading money winner as the championship began, he was just the fourth seed. With his 5-and-4 victory over lightly regarded Tomohiro Kondo in the 36-hole title match, Sato became the first player with three wins on his 2002 record and enhanced his lead in the money race.

Virtually all the other top players went out early. Yasuharu Imano and Kenichi Kuboya, both double winners in 2002, lost in the opening round, and Dean Wilson, the defending champion, Toshimitsu Izawa, the No. 1 player in 2001, and Toru Taniguchi, the other two-time victor in 2002, were ousted the next day.

Meanwhile, Sato was advancing to the semi-finals with wins over Shinichi Yokota, 1 up; Tetsuji Hiratsuka, 5 and 4, and David Smail, 1 up. Kondo reached that level with victories over Toru Suzuki, 2 up; Wilson, 1 up, and Kiyoshi Murota, 2 and 1. Kondo sprang another surprise in the semi-finals when he eliminated Shingo Katayama, 1 up, while Sato, after blowing a three-hole advantage over Hirofumi Miyase, birdied the 19th to reach the championship match. After winning three of his four matches on the 18th hole and the other on the 17th, Kondo ran out of luck in the 36-hole final at the Nidom Classic course at Tomakomai in Hokkaido. The victory was the ninth in the career of the 32-year-old Sato.

Suntory Open—¥100,000,000
Winner: Shingo Katayama

The first eight months of the season had been disappointing for Shingo Katayama, a leader for the previous two seasons. The biggest blow had come when he lost to Kenichi Kuboya in a playoff for the PGA Championship in May. His game came around decisively when he defended his 2001 victory in the Suntory Open. He produced four rounds in the 60s and scored a four-stroke victory with his 15-under-par 269.

For three rounds, though, the focus was on Yasuharu Imano's quest for his third win of the season. Imano, who won the Niigata Open and the Aiful Cup back-to-back in mid-summer, was in first place the first three days. On Thursday, he opened with 65 and was tied with Hiroyuki Fujita atop the standings. Then, he took the lead by himself with 70–135 on Friday, with Katayama (68-68) and Keiichiro Fukabori (70-66) just one stroke back. Fujita shot 72 and dropped to fourth place.

Katayama shot his third straight 68 Saturday and climbed into a tie for the lead with Imano, who shot 69 for his 204. Fujita (68) and Fukabori (69) were at 205. Katayama established his victory run early in Sunday's round. He birdied three straight holes, starting at the second, and rolled to a bogey-free 65 that provided the four-stroke victory, the 11th on the career record of the colorful, 29-year-old pro. Imano shot 69 for 273 and shared second place with Koki Idoki, who closed with 67.

ANA Open—¥100,000,000
Winner: Masashi Ozaki

Masashi (Jumbo) Ozaki continues to defy the aging process. Just when it seems that his last victory on the Japan Tour was the end of an astonishing run of triumphs, the brilliant Ozaki resurfaces with another win and adds to a record that might never even be approached. Nine months beyond his 55th birthday, just when it appeared his triumph in the 2000 Sun Chlorella Open would be the final one, Ozaki won for the 94th time on the Japan Tour, a tight, one-stroke triumph in the ANA Open, a tournament at which he had achieved victory seven other times over the previous 30 seasons. Throwing in a variety of other wins, the ANA title in 2002 was his 113th. No wonder he forsook the senior circuits.

Ozaki's path to the ANA victory was impeded only in the opening round, when he shot 67 but, with Masanori Kobayashi and Satoshi Higashi, trailed

Jun Kikuchi by a stroke. Ozaki then went ahead to stay Friday. He shot 66 for 133 and moved three strokes in front of Kikuchi (70), Toshimitsu Izawa and Takashi Kanemoto (69-67s). Through two rounds, Masashi didn't have a bogey and the first one didn't come until the 14th hole Saturday. He went on to a 69 for 202, his lead then just one over Hiroyuki Fujita (66) and two ahead of younger brother Tateo (66) and Toru Taniguchi (67).

Fujita pushed his elder to the end. He actually edged a stroke in front at the 13th hole, but gave that advantage back at the 16th. Masashi went ahead to stay when he birdied the 17th and parred the 18th for 69 and the winning total of 17-under-par 271. Fujita finished at 272, and Tsuneyuki Nakajima continued his strong season with a 66 in the final round that elevated him into third place at the end.

Acom International—¥120,000,000
Winner: Toru Taniguchi

It rained on Toru Taniguchi's parade, but didn't affect his march to his third victory of the 2002 Japan Tour season. Taniguchi led the weather-shortened Acom International from the start and held off the final-round bid of Zhang Lian-wei, China's first international player of note, to add a victory in Japan to nearly a dozen titles he had accumulated since 1994 on other circuits in Asia. It was the second Acom victory in three years for the 34-year-old Taniguchi and sixth of his career. He and Nobuhito Sato were then the tour's only three-time winners of the year.

Despite rounds of 64 and 63 on the par-71 Ishioka Golf Club, Taniguchi had only a two-stroke lead when play was completed Friday evening. Jun Kikuchi kept close on his heels with a 65-64 start, and Zhang was at 130 after matching Taniguchi's 63 that day. Heavy rain inundated the course overnight and tournament directors cancelled the Saturday round, deciding on a 54-hole event finishing Sunday. Kikuchi faded badly with 75 the last day, but Zhang kept the pressure on Taniguchi until Toru established his one-stroke margin with a birdie at the 16th hole and parred in to a 70–197. Zhang shot 68–198, and Tsuneyuki Nakajima made a late run and finished third with 66–199.

Georgia Tokai Classic—¥120,000,000
Winner: Toru Taniguchi

Not even an open week on the schedule could slow down Toru Taniguchi. When play resumed on October 10 with the Georgia Tokai Classic at Miyoshi, Taniguchi staged a strong finish to nail his second consecutive victory on the Japan Tour and his fourth of the season. The ¥24 million winner's check vaulted him past Nobuhito Sato into the No. 1 spot on the year's money list. His career record then sported seven titles.

Taniguchi started out in the hole, though. He shot 72 in the opening round and trailed leader Satoru Hirota, a journeyman pro, by six strokes. It was the first time the 29-year-old Hirota topped a leaderboard during his eight years on the tour. And the last time, at least for that week. The stars shone

Friday. Sato (70-69) and Shingo Katayama (68-71) took over the lead at 139 as Hirota struggled to 76. Taniguchi moved into contention with 69, joining seven others at 141. One of those players — Nozomi Kawahara — jumped into first place Saturday when he shot 68 for 209, and Taniguchi (69) joined Masashi Ozaki (69) and Sato (71) a stroke off the lead.

Despite the strong company surrounding him atop the standings, non-winner Kawahara acquitted himself well Sunday despite a triple bogey at the 11th hole, but it was Taniguchi's day. He came up with a four-under-par 68 at Miyoshi Country Club, finishing 10 under par at 278, two strokes ahead of Kawahara (71) and Myanmar's Zaw Moe (68). Sato and Katayama tied for fourth at 281.

Japan Open—¥120,000,000
Winner: David Smail

David Smail did something few visiting players have done in recent decades. He won the Japan Open in mid-October, just the third non-Japanese winner of the country's national championship since 1978. The 32-year-old New Zealander did it in style, shooting a final-round 67 and winning by four strokes with his nine-under-par 271. Tied for the lead going into the final round at Shimonoseki Golf Club, Toyoura, Smail lived up to his assessment of the situation: "Playing in the Japan Open is always tough. This is my fourth time here and I realize that to win you need to be mentally tough."

For two days, it didn't appear that Smail would have an opportunity to win his first Japanese title and, in this case, its important bonus — a five-year exemption on the Japan Tour — as Nobuhito Sato dominated. Sato, intent on regaining the lead in the money race, fired an opening eight-under-par 62 that equaled the Open's 18-hole record in relation to par. That put him three strokes in front of the field with Noboru Fujiiko and South Korea's Kim Jong-duck next at 65. Despite a wild and woolly round Friday that led to 71, Sato retained the lead at 133, one stroke ahead of Kim and namesake Hideyuki Sato. Nobuhito had five birdies, four bogeys and a double bogey in the round. Smail, who had opened in a 36th-place tie with 71, improved by five strokes with 66, advancing within four strokes of the lead.

He claimed a half-share of it in drizzly weather Saturday when he shot 67 for 204, deadlocking the South Korean, who shot 70. Sato shot 72 to slip a stroke behind, and Yasuharu Imano, a two-time 2002 winner, entered the picture with 67–206. Nobody else was closer than 209. It rained through Sunday's round as well, but it didn't faze Smail, particularly when Kim, a three-time winner in Japan, couldn't keep up with him. The South Korean shot 71, but still took the runner-up slot as Katsunori Kuwabara and Katsuya Nakagawa produced 67s and tied for third at 276. Sato faded with 72 and tied for fifth with Masashi Ozaki at 277.

Bridgestone Open—¥110,000,000
Winner: Scott Laycock

Australian Scott Laycock defied the odds at the Bridgestone Open and became the second straight first-time winner on the Japan Tour at the end of October. Laycock surely was the underdog going into the tournament's final round, since he was tied for the lead with leading money winner Toru Taniguchi and had several other players of higher repute close behind. He responded with a 71 that was just good enough for him to edge Taniguchi and fast-closing Shingo Katayama by a stroke with his 16-under-par 272 at Sodegaura Country Club, Chiba. He, New Zealand's David Smail (Japan Open) and England's Justin Rose (Chunichi Crowns) were three of just four first-time winners of the season.

Laycock never trailed in the tournament. He began with 66, which put him in a three-way tie for the lead with Katayama and Hisayuki Sasaki. Taniguchi was one of four players just a stroke back. Laycock repeated the 66 Friday and opened a two-stroke lead over Taniguchi, who shot his second 67 for 134. Gunning for his fifth win of the season, Taniguchi overtook Laycock with 67 in Saturday's third round in cold, wet weather, putting seven birdies with two bogeys. Laycock bounced back from an early bogey with four birdies, but left several putts short.

At 201, those two players stood four strokes ahead of the field going into the final round and it was basically a duel Sunday. Laycock led much of the round, dropped back into a tie when he bogeyed the 14th, but came back with a birdie at the par-five 16th and held on for the victory. Taniguchi shot 72, and Katayama made his run for his second 2002 victory with 67.

Philip Morris Championship—¥200,000,000
Winner: Brendan Jones

It seemed like a rerun. Substitute one Australian player for another, fatten the purse and the Philip Morris Championship seemed like the Bridgestone Open all over again. Just as Scott Laycock did the previous week, Brendan Jones, his countryman from Down Under, led from wire to wire and fended off one of the Japan Tour's finest players, in his case to capture the Philip Morris Championship, one of the two richest events of the year. As with Laycock, it was the first win in Japan for Jones and extended a Southern Hemisphere domination of the winners' circle that began three Sundays earlier with the initial victory on the circuit of New Zealand's David Smail.

The biggest challenge for the 27-year-old Jones at the ABC Golf Club in Tojo was Yoshimitsu Izawa, the previous year's leading money winner who was trying for his first 2002 victory, although Shingo Katayama carried over his strong finish in the Bridgestone into the first round of the Philip Morris. He and Jones both opened with 65s and shared the lead with Fiji's Dinesh Chand. Izawa shot 66 in each of the first two rounds, finishing on Friday in a deadlock with Jones (67) at 134.

The long-hitting Jones remained hot Saturday, worked up another 67 and took a two-stroke lead over Izawa (69) with his 199 total. Katayama shot 68 and trailed by four in third place. Even though posting 70, his highest score of the week, Jones set a tournament record with his 19-under-par 269, a shot under Ryoken Kawagishi's 270 in 1999. Izawa also scored 70 Sunday to finish second, three strokes better than Dean Wilson and Hiroyuki Fujita, who shared third place.

Mitsui Sumitomo Visa Taiheiyo Masters—¥150,000,000
Winner: Tsuneyuki Nakajima

Tsuneyuki (Tommy) Nakajima put the capper on his finest season in nearly a decade when, 15 years after winning the prestigious Mitsui Sumitomo Visa Taiheiyo Masters, he did it again. Nakajima, four times the Japan Tour's leading money winner in the 1980s, had ended a seven-year victory drought earlier in the 2002 season with a win in the Diamond Cup tournament and had quite a few high finishes in a rewarding comeback year.

His mid-November win on the Taiheiyo Club's Gotemba course was fraught with difficulty, not the least of which was the heavy cold and sore back he was nursing. The 48-year-old veteran also had to contend with three international young guns and a countryman just back from a successful season on the U.S. PGA Tour. Nakajima's experience prevailed at the end as he held off the challenges in the final round, shooting 70 for 16-under-par 272 to eke out a one-stroke victory, the 47th of his brilliant career.

An open week created by the cancellation of the long-time Ube Kosan Open did not blunt the momentum of Philip Morris winner Brendan Jones, who began the Taiheiyo Masters with 65. That put him two strokes in front of Hidemichi Tanaka, playing in his first Japan Tour event of the season after retaining his American playing privileges with a 92nd-place finish on the PGA money list. Nakajima started with 69, then climbed to within a stroke of leader Jones with 66. Jones shot 69–134 Friday.

Sparked by a 20-foot eagle putt at the par-five sixth and a birdie on the next hole, Nakajima surged two strokes in front Saturday with a five-under-par 67 for 202. Tanaka matched the 67 and took over the runner-up spot at 204, one stroke in front of Taichi Teshima and young Australian star Aaron Baddeley. Still within range, too, were Shingo Katayama at 205 and Jones, two-time 2002 winner Dean Wilson and Justin Rose, the 22-year-old winner of the Chunichi Crowns in early May, all at 207.

As things turned out, the outcome hinged on the final hole Sunday. Nakajima had built his lead to four strokes early in the round, but a two-shot swing at the 15th and a Tanaka birdie at the 16th sliced it to one as they played the par-five 18th. Tanaka, who said later, "I didn't want to play just for a playoff," went for the green in two from 240 yards and put the ball in the front-guarding pond. Nakajima then strategically laid up, pitched on the green and two-putted for his 70 and the triumph. Tanaka still salvaged a par for 69–273, and Baddeley chipped in for an eagle at the 18th to attain a 69 and finish third at 274. Rose and Katayama tied for fourth at 275, and young American Charles Howell also closed with a 69 that put him in seventh place at 277.

Dunlop Phoenix—¥200,000,000
Winner: Kaname Yokoo

The Dunlop Phoenix tournament had its usual complement of world-class stars in the Japan Tour's best field of the season, but when all was said and done the title was in the hands of a Japanese professional who didn't play well enough in his season in America to retain full playing privileges on the PGA Tour. Amid the likes of Tiger Woods, defending champion David Duval, European Ryder Cuppers Sergio Garcia, Darren Clarke, Lee Westwood and Thomas Bjorn, and young English star Justin Rose, Kaname Yokoo hammered out a one-stroke victory in the season's second and last ¥200 million tournament with a final-round 69 and a 15-under-par total of 269. It was the fourth and most important victory in Japan for the 30-year-old Yokoo, who finished 130th on the PGA Tour money list and did not try to qualify for the 2003 season. If he goes to America, his conditional status should get him into about half of the year's tournaments.

Clarke blasted off on a damp Thursday with 64, seizing a two-stroke lead over Yokoo, Rose and Tsukasa Watanabe. Garcia and the Ozaki brothers, Masashi and Naomichi, were in a five-player group at 67. Yokoo then took the lead for good Friday with a blazing, bogey-free 65 for 131 and a four-stroke advantage over Rose (69), Garcia (68) and Zaw Moe of Myanmar (67). Clarke shot 72 and fell into a four-man group at 136.

It wasn't that easy the rest of the way for Yokoo. Although he shot a respectable 69 Saturday for 200, Yokoo saw three strokes of his lead disappear as Irishman Clarke bounced back with 65 for 201. Moe had 68 for 203, Garcia was at 204, and Rose and Duval at 205. When both Clarke and Moe faltered Sunday, the steady Yokoo built enough of a lead that he withstood a late charge by Garcia, who birdied four of the last six holes for 66–270. Yokoo had a two-shot cushion when he played and bogeyed the 72nd hole for his second straight 69, 269 total and the victory. Woods, making his third visit to Japan, never challenged. Plagued by faulty putting, Tiger finished six strokes back in eighth place thanks to a closing 67.

Casio World Open—¥140,000,000
Winner: David Smail

It took David Smail four years to win his first tournament in Japan, then just six weeks to put another victory on his Japan Tour record. The New Zealander became the seventh multiple winner of the season when he powered his way to a two-stroke triumph in the rain-abbreviated Casio World Open to go along with his maiden win in the Japan Open Championship in mid-October. He snatched the title away from Australia's Brendan Jones, who had also broken the victory ice earlier in the fall at the Philip Morris tournament.

Both players had opened strongly with 68s and were just a shot off the pace of co-leaders Tsukasa Watanabe and Kazuhiko Hosokawa in a field usually sprinkled with a few stars from overseas but devoid of anybody of international note this time. Jones then took the lead Friday, firing a six-under-par 30 on the incoming nine for 64–132 and a three-stroke lead. Tateo

Ozaki, seeking his first win in two years, moved into second place with 66–135, and Smail shared third place at 136 with Hajime Meshiai, Smail repeating his first-round 68 and Meshiai duplicating Ozaki's 66.

Heavy weather arrived Saturday morning, forcing a suspension of play with only two threesomes off the first tee and eventually a cancellation of the round. Smail came out with the hot hand Sunday, made up his four-shot deficit and eagled the final hole for 64–200 and the two-stroke victory over Jones, who finished with 70 for 202. Watanabe wound up in third place at 205 after a 66, one stroke ahead of Ozaki.

Nippon Series JT Cup—¥100,000,000
Winner: Shingo Katayama

When Shingo Katayama captured the money championship in 2000, his victory in the Nippon Series JT Cup in the next-to-last event that season played a key role. He clinched the title with another win in the finale in Okinawa. Katayama won the Nippon Series again in 2002 and it rewarded him with a move into the No. 3 position on the money list. He never trailed at Tokyo's Yomiuri Country Club and raced to a nine-stroke victory, by three shots the biggest margin of the season.

Only 20 players teed it up in the Series, for which only the season's winners and top money-earners qualify. A half-dozen of the eligibles, including No. 2 money winner Nobuhito Sato and two-time winner Dean Wilson, skipped the event to go to America to compete in the PGA Tour qualifier that week. It's doubtful whether their presence would have made any difference in the outcome. Katayama was solid all four days. He and Masashi Ozaki tied the course record with 62s in the opening round. He then went in front to stay Friday when he birdied four of the last six holes for 66–128 and a one-shot lead over South Korean Kim Jong-duck, who had a sparkling 65 to go with his first-round 64. Ozaki shot 71 and slipped into a third-place tie at 133 with David Smail, coming off his Casio Open win the previous week.

Katayama broke it wide open with a second 66 to go 16 under par at 194. That staked him to a six-stroke margin as Kim went two over par with 72 and dropped to third place as Masashi shot 67 for 200. Katayama set up the 66 early as he ran off four birdies in a row starting at the fourth hole. On Sunday, he allowed no challenges by shooting a comfortable 67 for his 19-under-par 261, his second victory of the season and 12th of his career. It was by far the lowest 72-hole score of the year.

Asia/Japan Okinawa Open—¥100,000,000
Winner: Hiroyuki Fujita

After a two-season hiatus, the Okinawa Open was reborn in the final days of December as the jointly sanctioned first tournament on the 2003 schedules of both the Japan and Asian PGA Tours, much as the Kirin Open operated for many years before its demise in 2002. Ironically, the winner of the revived Okinawa event was Hiroyuki Fujita, who already had scored victories on both circuits, two on the Asian Tour and the Sun Chlorella on the 2001 Japan Tour. Fujita broke from a five-way tie to win with a closing 67 for a 14-under-par 202 in the rain-shortened event at Okinawa's Southern Links Golf Club.

While Fujita was reveling in the victory and the three-year exemption it gave him on the Japan Tour, American Ted Purdy was dealing with his second major disappointment in two weeks. Purdy, who had opened the tournament on a rain-plagued Thursday with a seven-under-par 65 and the lead and had shared it with Fujita (67-68), Tateo Ozaki (71-64), Tomohiro Kondo (66-69) and Tetsuji Hiratsuka (68-67) on Sunday morning, had come to Japan for the tournament after failing by a single stroke to qualify for the PGA Tour in the U.S. The 29-year-old Purdy's 65 gave him a one-shot lead over Kondo, the 2002 Japan Match Play runner-up, and two over Fujita and three other players when the first round was completed Friday.

Bad weather continued through Friday and Saturday, and the second round extended into Sunday morning when the five-man deadlock at 135 was confirmed. Fujita was near perfect Sunday. He birdied the first three holes and was never seriously threatened on his way to his three-stroke victory. Purdy's title hopes died when he four-putted the 10th hole, but he rallied to 70 for a 205 total and tied for second with 22-year-old amateur Yusaku Miyazato, who closed with 67.

12. Australasian Tour

The Australasian Tour had a rollicking start with an appearance by Tiger Woods, playing in the Telstra Hyundai New Zealand Open while on a visit to the homeland of his friend and caddie Steve Williams.

Visiting heads of state, not to mention touring rock stars, don't get as much coverage as Woods received while at Paraparaumu Beach. Woods was accustomed to the attention, although the distractions were unsettling to others, including some of his fellow competitors. That was no fault of Woods, of course, and it was interesting that one of the golfers to make the best of the situation was Australia's Craig Parry, one of Tiger's neighbors from Isleworth Country Club in Windermere, Florida.

Parry won by one stroke over New Zealand's Michael Campbell. Later, Parry achieved one of the more significant victories of the year by an Australian when he won the NEC Invitational, one of the World Golf Championship events in the United States.

New Zealand's Craig Perks also won on the U.S. PGA Tour at The Players Championship, and Australian Stephen Leaney won on the PGA European Tour in the Linde German Masters. Two Australians — Stuart Appleby and Steve Elkington — were in the British Open Championship playoff (along with Frenchman Thomas Levet) which was won by South Africa's Ernie Els.

Three of the early-year events were co-sponsored by the European Tour and two were indicative of what was to come. South Africa's Retief Goosen, winner of the 2001 European Tour of Merit, got off to a great start with his eight-stroke victory, which was a record for the Johnnie Walker Classic, held at Lake Karrinyup. Goosen went on to lead the European money list again, while also winning in South Africa and the United States, and he was second to Woods in the Masters Tournament.

Next, Els took the first of his six worldwide victories in the Heineken Classic, winning by five strokes at Royal Melbourne. In addition to the British Open, Els won the Dubai Desert Classic on the European Tour, the Genuity Championship in the United States, his fourth Cisco World Match Play Championship in England, and wrapped up the year with the $2 million first prize from the Nedbank Golf Challenge in his homeland.

The third of Australasian/European Tour events was the ANZ Championship, which was won by Sweden's Richard Johnson. Then, the Australasian Tour settled into its routine and after that there were three players who had two victories each. Terry Price won the Volvo Trucks Golf Klassik and the New South Wales Open. Andre Stolz won the Queensland PGA Championship and the Victorian Open. At the year's end Peter Lonard won the Australian PGA Championship (sharing the title with Jarrod Moseley after the event ended in darkness) and the MasterCard Masters.

The week before the tie in the Australian PGA, there was the most controversial incident of the year, when the first round of the Holden Australian Open was cancelled because conditions were such that the greens became too fast. "They played with the snake that is Victoria and they've been bitten," said Appleby, the defending champion. "If they had kept on like this, the cut would have been 15 over, no problem."

The winner of the Holden Australian Open was Victoria's Steve Allan, who came through in the clutch with 68 in the year's biggest event to win his first-ever Australasian Tour title. Allan's 12-under-par 268 total held up while stars such as Parry, Aaron Baddeley and U.S. PGA champion Rich Beem were on his trail. Robert Allenby also challenged in the middle of the final round. The veterans had nothing but praise for Allan. "He hit the ball very hard and very straight," Beem said. "And he putted brilliantly. He definitely has the game to do well on the U.S. Tour."

Lonard not only shared a victory because of darkness, but also needed a playoff to win the second title. His triumph in the year-ending MasterCard Masters came after Lonard posted 66 in the final round to reach the extra holes against Adam Scott and Gavin Coles. He won on the second playoff hole.

Telstra Hyundai New Zealand Open—NZ$1,000,000
Winner: Craig Parry

Coming to the home country of his caddie, Steve Williams, and as part of his mission to spread his golf to all points on the globe, Tiger Woods played in his first Telstra Hyundai New Zealand Open in 2002. The media circus that followed was unlike anything the island nation had ever seen. Every step Woods took while visiting Paraparaumu Beach was televised and written about as if it were epic news. Visiting heads of state didn't get as much coverage. But after six years of traveling internationally as the No. 1 golfer in the world, Woods was accustomed to the attention.

What he wasn't accustomed to was the poor putting he displayed throughout his visit to New Zealand. While he remained in contention until the final round through outstanding ball-striking, Woods' struggles on the greens cost him a chance at the title. On Sunday he almost drove the first green, but missed a short birdie putt. Then he four-putted the second green for a double bogey. He reached three of the four par-fives in two, but could only manage a final-round 69 and a tie for sixth at five-under-par 279.

With Woods out of contention, the focus turned to a four-way down-to-the-wire duel between Australians Craig Parry and Stephen Leaney, and New Zealanders Michael Campbell and Steve Alker. Through 63 holes the four were tied for the lead at eight under par.

Parry birdied the 10th to break the logjam, but Leaney knotted things again at nine under with a birdie at the 11th. Parry blew an opportunity to pull ahead at the 12th after hitting the par-five in two, then missing a two-footer for birdie. Alker and Campbell joined the lead again after both hit the 12th in two and two-putted for their birdies.

The tie was broken again when Parry birdied the 13th to move to 10 under, but Campbell joined him with a birdie at the 15th. Then it was Campbell's turn to take the lead. With a brilliant iron shot, the New Zealander birdied the par-three 16th to get to 11 under.

Campbell appeared to be in control after Parry missed a six-footer for birdie at the 17th. Things changed quickly again. Campbell, playing one group behind Parry, hit his second shot at the 17th into the grandstands and made a double bogey, while Parry hit a perfect three-wood second shot into the par-five 18th. With a routine two-putt birdie, Parry shot a final-round 68 for an 11-under-par 273 total and an improbable two-shot lead.

Campbell had one last go at forcing a playoff. He reached the 18th green in two and had a 10-footer for eagle to tie him. The putt slipped by the hole and Campbell had to settle for a final-round 69 and second place at 274. Leaney and Alker finished tied for third at 275, while Australian amateur Adam Groom shot 67 to finish alone in fifth at 277.

Johnnie Walker Classic—A$2,700,000
Winner: Retief Goosen

It's hard to stay focused when you know you can shoot 80 and still win. Not a lot of professionals have that problem, but Retief Goosen did as he tried to cope with his 13-stroke lead going into the final round of the Johnnie Walker Classic. "I think it probably would have been easier to play if I had had a two-shot lead out there, because then you can attack," Goosen said. He instead had the largest 54-hole lead in PGA European Tour history after playing golf his fellow competitors described as "unworldly." Goosen simply said, "You have such a big lead, and in a way it's difficult to play."

Playing wasn't really much of a concern in the final round. The tournament was ostensibly over Saturday night after the 2001 U.S. Open champion shot a nine-under-par 63, a score not seen at Lake Karrinyup Country Club since 1974, when Gary Player was in his prime and the course was 300 yards shorter. This was not a day when birdies were flying. The average score for the field was 73.6. Thongchai Jaidee, trailing by one at the halfway mark and Goosen's closest challenger when the third round began, shot 78. Pierre Fulke, who would finish as runner-up, shot 74. Goosen made nine birdies, no bogeys, hit every fairway, and looked invincible.

"He doesn't seem to be playing the same golf course as the rest of us," said Sergio Garcia, who shared second place with Ernie Els after the third round. "What Retief is doing is possible, but to do it you have to be playing perfect golf."

So what did the quiet South African have to say for himself after such a perfect performance? "Hopefully, I'll hang on," he said.

The media interview room erupted in laughter at that response, but Goosen smiled. That was about as demonstrative as he got. "All I can do is keep concentrating and not get ahead of myself," he continued. "That was probably the best round I've ever played, given the conditions and the way the course was set up. I'm seeing every shot so well and holing a lot of putts. I would have to give myself 10 out of 10 today."

Sunday he started out with a six instead of a 10, as in a double bogey at the par-four first, something Goosen hadn't seen all week. When Els birdied the opening hole, the lead was down to 10. "I have no idea what happened," the winner said. "Suddenly it was a three-shot swing." Not that anyone noticed. Goosen could have given Els five strokes a side and still come out on top.

"Today was just hit a green, hit a fairway, two-putt and get out of there," Goosen said, which is exactly what he did, posting 73 in a final round that was more coronation than competition. The final margin was eight strokes over Fulke, who had a closing 66 for a 282 total.

Goosen was the only player who finished double digits under par at 14-under 274. While that didn't break any scoring records, his streak of four victories and 13 top-10 finishes in 16 tournaments since his breakthrough victory at the U.S. Open was the best in Europe by a mile.

Heineken Classic—A$2,000,000
Winner: Ernie Els

In what would prove to be the launching pad for an unforgettable season, Ernie Els returned to victory early in 2002 with a comfortable five-stroke win in the Heineken Classic. He led wire-to-wire after opening with a course-record-tying 64 at Royal Melbourne (a record that lasted one day), then cruising in with a three solid rounds of 69 for a 17-under-par 271 total. In all its years of hosting professional events, Royal Melbourne had never given up a lower 72-hole total, and Els couldn't have been happier to be back in a winning frame of mind.

"I want to win, then I want to win again and again and again," Els said. "I've never had trouble winning until last year. But 2000 was really the start of it, to be honest. I played really well in a lot of events and finished second and third all the time. That was hard to take. My problem wasn't a lack of effort or practice. I worked harder last year than at any time in my career, but I was practicing the wrong things. And overdoing it. I ended up playing 'golf swing' rather than golf. I'd be on the course thinking about any number of things and forgetting why I was out there — to shoot the lowest score I could. The end result was that I looked and felt good on the range, but couldn't take that feeling to the golf course."

The only serious challenge this week came from David Howell, who climbed to within two shots of Els before finishing five shots back and tied for second with Peter Fowler and Peter O'Malley at 276. Other than that, the biggest highlight of the week was the course-record 62 shot on Friday by New Zealand's Richard Lee.

"I can't believe it," said Lee, who was looking at missing the cut after opening with 75. His weekend wasn't much better. Scores of 71 and 74 left Lee in a five-way tie for 14th place at 282. "It might be the best round ever played here, but I'm not the best player to play here," he said.

That title belonged to Els, at least this week. "I've been lucky," the two-time U.S. Open champion said. "I had a lot of success early in my career. I was used to that. So I expected it all the time. I was a winner in my own mind. Then, when I couldn't win, I couldn't understand it. I was a bit spoiled to be honest. I won't make that mistake again.

"Golf is a strange old game. You get your highs and your lows. I feel like I am getting into my highs. I feel I have a lot of golf left."

ANZ Championship—A$1,750,000
Winner: Richard Johnson

A new format for both the European and Australasian Tours produced a first-time winner when Sweden's Richard Johnson earned 11 points in the final round of the ANZ Championship to take the first Stableford event contested there in over a decade. Johnson shot a metal score of 68 on Sunday to finish the week with 46 points and a two-point victory over Australians Craig Parry and Scott Laycock.

Third-round leader Andre Stolz finished alone in fourth with 43 points, while Scotland's Stephen Gallacher gave back a few points on Sunday with a metal score of 74 that dropped him to fifth with 39 points. Sixth place went to Ian Garbutt, who shot a tournament-low 64 on Sunday for a 19-point day and a 38-point week, while first-round leader Jonathan Lomas followed up his 20-point opening day with one point, nine points and seven points to finish seventh. Thomas Levet and Greg Turner rounded out the top 10 with 36 points apiece, 10 behind Johnson, who was ecstatic with his win.

"This means so much to me," the 25-year-old Johnson said. "This is my third year on tour, and it just keeps getting better and better each year. When I hit the last putt, my life just changed, because now I am a winner. We'll just have to see what happens next."

In addition to playing well, Johnson had some help. Laycock and Parry both held the lead at varying points in the final round, but Laycock bogeyed the 17th to drop a point, and Parry missed a par putt at the 18th which would have given him a share of the lead.

"I missed some real good opportunities on the back nine," Laycock said after missing birdie putts on the 13th, 14th and 16th. "You just can't afford to let those chances go at this level."

Parry was a little more animated in venting his displeasure with the outcome. "I have to be careful, because if I talk about it, I think I'll swear," Parry said. "It is so frustrating. I played pretty well, but that's just the way it goes."

Johnson felt the same way. "Things happen in golf," he said. "This week it was my time."

New South Wales Masters—A$100,000
Winner: Steve Collins

With his second birdie at the 18th hole at Longyard Golf Club in a 40-minute span, Steve Collins won the New South Wales Masters in a playoff over Leigh McKechnie. Collins birdied the final hole of regulation to shoot 68 and reach 20-under-par 268. Leading by one at the start of the day, Collins saw his lead slip away when McKechnie made six birdies and one bogey en route to 67. McKechnie held the hot hand all weekend after 64 on Saturday moved him into the final group. But he fell one birdie short as Collins rolled in the winning putt on the first hole of the playoff.

Scott Hend finished in third at 269 with 65, a score that was equaled by Paul Davenport, who finished fourth at 270. Second-round leader Brad Andrews, who looked unbeatable when he started the week with scores of 63 and 69, cooled off over the weekend, but still managed to shoot 71 and 68 for 271 total and fifth place. That was one shot better than first-round leader David Armstrong, who had 62 but followed with rounds of 72, 67 and 71.

Jacob's Creek Open—A$1,000,000
Winner: Gavin Coles

Australia's Gavin Coles won his first professional title at the Jacob's Creek Open, a co-sponsored event between the Australasian PGA Tour and U.S. Buy.com Tour. It was also the first time American Bryce Molder played in Australia. While a second-place finish was a good showing for the former No. 1 college player from Georgia Tech, Molder was anything but happy. "I gave it away," Molder said. "I had it and I couldn't close."

Even though Coles led after three days, Molder charged ahead with two birdies on the first nine at the Kooyonga Resort. Another birdie at the 14th to reach 11 under gave Molder a comfortable two-stroke edge with two holes to play. A bogey at the 15th cut the margin to one, and another bogey after a pulled approach at the 16th dropped Molder back into a tie with Coles. A third consecutive bogey at the 17th gave Coles the outright lead.

Molder needed a birdie at the 18th to force a playoff, but for the fourth hole in a row, he pulled his approach shot, found the rough, and made bogey. A 73 dropped Molder into second place at seven-under-par 281, two behind Coles, who survived on a steady diet of pars on the second nine for a 279 total. Peter Fowler, who also reached 11 under early in the final round before making five straight bogeys, finished third at 282, while veterans Stephen Leaney and Peter O'Malley finished tied for fourth at 285.

Holden Clearwater Classic—A$1,000,000
Winner: Peter O'Malley

The Buy.com/Australasian Tour experiment proved to be nothing if not extreme. It produced the shortest winner in either tour's history when 5-foot-4 Gavin Coles won the Jacob's Creek Open, and the highest ranked winner in Buy.com Tour history when Peter O'Malley, the 65th ranked player in the world, cruised to victory at the Holden Clearwater Classic.

It was an easy week for O'Malley, who made two bogeys in 72 holes (the last coming at the 10th on Friday) and posted four rounds in the 60s for a five-stroke victory over Brad Ott. The closing 68 was about as flawless a round as O'Malley, who eliminated Tiger Woods from the Accenture Match Play Championship, could remember playing. "The last nine holes is probably as good as I've ever played," O'Malley said. "I didn't miss a shot. I hit every shot where and how I wanted to hit it. Certainly that was very pleasing. I came out for these two weeks and achieved what I wanted to do."

He needed a win or a second place to earn exemptions into the British and U.S. Opens, which he got with ease on Sunday. Joel Kribel, who started the final round one shot back, struggled early with five bogeys and a double bogey to shoot 76. He finished the week at eight-under-par 280 and in a tie for fifth with Andrew McLardy and Nick O'Hern.

That left the door open for Ott, who started the final round five shots back and equaled O'Malley's 68 to take second. Rich Barcelo finished third with 69 for a 277 total, while Alex Cejka closed with 70 for 279 and fourth place.

Scenic Circle Hotels Dunedin Classic—A$100,000
Winner: Gareth Paddison

In a final round full of birdies, New Zealander Gareth Paddison had the hottest hand when he needed it. Paddison, who trailed Brad Andrews by one stroke going into the final round, shot a seven-under-par 64 on Sunday for a 17-under-par 267 total and a three-stroke victory in the Scenic Circle Hotels Dunedin Classic.

Paddison was the only player in the field to post four rounds in the 60s. His opening 66 put him two shots behind Andrews, and 69 on Friday moved him only one off the pace. He and Andrews traded 68s on Saturday, while Andrew Bonhomme made a run by shooting 63 to tie Paddison at 203.

Bonhomme shot 71 on Sunday to finish tied for third with Tony Carolan, who saved the best score of the tournament for the final day, when he closed with 62 for a 274 total. Kim Felton finished alone in fifth at 275, while Wayne Smith shot 68 to finish in a six-way tie for sixth.

No one got close to Paddison, who made up his one shot deficit to Andrews on the second hole and never looked back. Andrews shot his second consecutive 68 on Sunday to finish alone in second at 270. "I felt great all day," Andrew said, "but Gareth made too many putts."

Volvo Trucks Golf Klassik—A$100,000
Winner: Terry Price

It was a down-to-the-wire finish, but when the final putt fell Terry Price's three-under-par 70 in the final round proved to be good enough for a one-stroke victory in the Volvo Trucks Golf Klassik in New South Wales. Price barely edged out a hard-charging Brad Kennedy, who closed with 65 for a 276 total, good enough for second place, but one more than he needed to match Price's 275.

Third-round leader David van Raalte finished alone in third at 277 after only managing a 73 final round. It was Raalte's first round in the 70s and it came at an inopportune time. He was the only player in the top 10 who didn't break par on the last day.

Rick Schmidt shot 69 to finish tied for fourth with Jason Dawes and Steve Collins at 279, while David Diaz and Adam Le Vesconte finished one more shot behind, sharing seventh at 280.

South Australian PGA Championship—A$100,000
Winner: Richard Ball

Richard Ball capped a magnificent week with 68 in the South Australian PGA Championship. It was Ball's highest score of the week, not that it mattered. The 64 and 65 he shot on Friday and Saturday at the Vines Resort all but locked up his victory. His lead was six with 18 holes to play, and Ball showed no signs of folding. When he tapped in for 68, the total was 20-under-par 264 and the margin of victory was five.

Adrian Percey was the closest challenger. Percey posted four rounds in the 60s and showed flashes of brilliance throughout the week, but he never led and never came close on Sunday. His 269 left him alone in second place, one shot clear of Chris Downes, who led on Thursday after 63 and held on to a one-shot lead at the halfway mark with 67. Downes fell back on Saturday when he shot 71, but recovered with 69 on Sunday to barely edge out a charging Euan Walters.

Walters shot 64 on Sunday to move to 272 and into a three-way tie for fourth with Gary Simpson and Brad Andrews. Craig Warren, Westley Rudel, Adam Fraser and Craig Carmichael tied for seventh at 273.

Western Australian PGA Championship—A$100,000
Winner: Kim Felton

With the home crowd firmly in his corner, Perth's Kim Felton closed with six birdies on the final 10 holes to reach 17-under-par 263 and force a playoff with David Diaz, who had led the Western Australian PGA Championship since the first round. Diaz held a four-shot lead going into the final round, having lit up the scoreboard with rounds of 64, 67 and 63. But a ho-hum 69 on Sunday gave Felton a chance.

The 26-year-old took full advantage, making six birdies and one bogey for a final round of 65.

Both players were nervous on the playoff hole (the par-four 17th), and both missed the green with their approach shots. Felton chipped to six feet, while Diaz rolled his chip to within four feet of the hole. The advantage seemed to be in Diaz's favor until Felton rolled in his putt for par. With the pressure on, Diaz missed his par putt, handing the victory to the former Australian amateur champion.

Marcus Cain of Queensland finished alone in third at 268, one clear of Leigh McKenzie and Adrian Percey. David Bransdon and Michael Wright shared sixth at 270, with David Armstrong and Adam Crawford one more back and sharing eighth.

Queensland PGA Championship—A$100,000
Winner: Andre Stolz

In a birdie-fest that had everyone wondering just how low the scores would go, Andre Stolz shot his second consecutive 68 in the final round of the Queensland PGA Championship to take the title by two shots over third-round leader Paul Sheehan. Stolz shot a staggering 22-under-par 266 for the week. It was just enough.

Sheehan was 20 under through three rounds after flirting with history on Saturday with an 11-under-par 61. He took a two-shot lead into the final round, but the birdie well ran dry on Sunday. Sheehan could only manage

72 in the final round, which left him two shy of victory.

Stolz, who held the lead at the halfway point after rounds of 64 and 66, came back with his second 68 on Sunday for the win. Sheehan finished alone in second place at 268, while Anthony Summers shot 70, 66, 65 and 70 to finish alone in third at 271.

Victorian PGA Championship—A$100,000
Winner: Craig Carmichael

With the best score on Sunday and the best weekend total by three shots, Craig Carmichael overcame a seven-stroke deficit after two rounds to win the Victorian PGA Championship in a playoff. Carmichael, a former milkman, shot 66 for a 10-under-par 278 total, then birdied the first extra hole to defeat Craig Jones, who closed with 70 and a par in the playoff.

It was Carmichael's first professional victory and a great start to the autumn (spring Down Under) 2002 Australasian season. Despite 69 on Saturday, Carmichael entered the final round trailing third-round leader Steve Bowditch by five shots. Seven players, including Jones, stood between Carmichael and the lead when the day began, but a blistering bogey-free 66 gave Carmichael the clubhouse lead at 278. Bowditch fell away early with three bogeys and a double bogey. He closed with 75 for a 282 total and in a five-way tie for sixth.

That left Jones as the only man with a chance to win outright. He held his own at two under par for the day and 10 under for the week, but a missed birdie opportunity at the 18th spoiled his chance to take home the top spot in regulation.

In the playoff, Carmichael continued the attacking style that had worked so well for him on the weekend. He hit a perfect six iron to the par-three 18th that stopped six feet from the hole. Jones left his tee shot 20 feet from the flag and missed the putt. When Carmichael's birdie putt fell (his seventh of the day), the victory was his. "It's unbelievable," he said. "This is a great way to start the season."

Victorian Open—A$100,000
Winner: Andre Stolz

It took a final round of 68 and two extra holes, but when the birdie putt fell on the second playoff hole, 30-year-old Andre Stolz had his second victory in five months and seemed poised to make a run at the top 10 on the Australasian Order of Merit.

This one required a great deal of fortitude as well as a boatload of weekend birdies. Despite 65 on Saturday, Stolz trailed third-round leader Andrew Bonhomme by four shots. New South Wales' David Bransdon was one shot further back after a stunning 63 on Saturday, 10 shots less than his opening score.

Sunday's shoot-out saw Stolz, Bransdon and Bonhomme battling for the lead. Bransdon was the first to post a number, finishing with 67 for an eight-under-par 274 total. Stolz matched that total when he shot 68. That left only

Bonhomme, who struggled with his control. When the final putt on the 18th wouldn't fall, the Queenslander finished with 73 for a 275 total, one more than he would need to make the playoff.

Victoria's Michael Light shot 68 on Sunday to finish alone in fourth place, while reigning Volvo China Open champion David Gleeson shot 68 on Sunday to finish tied for fifth with Andrew Webster, Craig Carmichael, Scott Hend and Marc Leishman at 278.

Both Stolz and Bransdon parred the first playoff hole, and both found the fairway their second time through the 18th. But Stolz hit his approach to within four feet, while Bransdon pulled his second shot and missed an 18-footer for birdie. When Stolz's putt fell, he had his second victory of the year, the first coming at the Queensland PGA Championship in June.

Queensland Open—A$100,000
Winner: Andrew Buckle

Sometimes the breaks have to go your way. No one knows that better than 20-year-old Andrew Buckle, who won his professional debut with an 11-under-par 277 total at the Queensland Open that included a 351-meter tee shot that found the 10th green on Sunday and a fortuitous bounce off a handheld sign on the final green.

Buckle came charging out of a crowded field on the final day with large drives and a gallery-pleasing swagger that drew the bulk of the spectators at Ipswich Golf Club to his side. He trailed Paul Sheehan by two when the final round began, but the youngster made his presence known when he pulled out the driver on the 351-meter par-four 10th and promptly drove the green. The crowd noise let all challengers know that Buckle wasn't going away quietly.

Only moments before, veteran Peter Senior had drawn to within a shot of the lead with two front-nine birdies, but an errant tee shot that landed out of bounds on the short 10th cost Senior a double bogey. When Buckle tapped in for a birdie to take a one-shot lead, the roar could have been heard in Sydney.

Buckle added to his lead with another birdie at the 17th. The margin was two with one hole to play, but the leaders were behind him. Anything was possible going into the final hole. The final break and the final sign that this was, indeed, Buckle's week came when his approach to the 18th green drifted right and nailed a "Quiet Please" sign being held by a marshal. The ball, which was bound for three-foot-high rough, ricocheted onto the green, and Buckle two-putted for a par and the win.

Sheehan finished one back at 278 and in a three-way tie for second with Ryan Haller and Craig Warren, who was a surprise addition to the three after finishing with three straight birdies to jump from 11th to one stroke out of the lead.

New South Wales Open—A$200,000
Winner: Terry Price

Always considered one of the best ball-strikers on the Australasian circuit, Terry Price was also known as an underachiever, a player who made a good living on tough golf courses, but not a winner. That criticism made Price's victory at the New South Wales Open even sweeter. Trailing by two at the start of the final round, Price closed with a two-under-par 70 on the difficult Horizons Resort course for a nine-under-par 279 total and a five-stroke victory.

Price did it through steady play and great ball-striking, the trademark of his game. What was somewhat surprising was the abysmal play of the third-round leaders. Tony Carolan and Jon Riley, who were tied for the lead going into the final round, shot 76 and 79 respectively and dropped down the leaderboard. Jason Norris, who assumed an early share of the final-round lead when Carolan and Riley began their descent, couldn't capitalize either, shooting 73 to finish at 284 and in a five-way tie for second with Andre Stolz, Adam Groom, Wayne Grady and New Zealand's Mahal Pearce.

The second happiest player of the week (behind Price) was 20-year-old amateur Richard Moir, who finished in 10th place and earned a spot in the Holden Australian Open.

Holden Australian Open—A$1,500,000
Winner: Steve Allan

Despite challenges by a two-time Australian Open champion, a World Golf Championships winner and one of the three major championship winners of the year, Victoria's Steve Allan came through with a clutch 68 to win his first Australasian Tour title in the year's biggest event. Allan was thrilled when his 12-under-par 204 total held up in the shortened Holden Australian Open, especially with players like Aaron Baddeley, Craig Parry and U.S. PGA champion Rich Beem on his trail.

The 29-year-old Allan led after 27 holes, but he admitted to feeling the pressure of playing the final round with Beem and Parry. "I think I got ahead of myself a couple of times out there," he said. "I looked up at the leaderboard on the 13th and noticed that I was three shots clear and thought, 'Whoa, this is all right.'"

He had already birdied the 11th and 12th holes when he decided that things were all right, but he added one more birdie at the 14th for good measure. That proved to be just enough, as Baddeley came charging from behind with a final round of 65 that included a bogey at the 11th and a near-miss for eagle at the 18th that would have forced a playoff.

The only other serious challenge came when Robert Allenby made four consecutive birdies in the middle of the round to pull even with Allan. But bogeys at the 13th and 15th dropped Allenby back to nine under, which is where he finished. Allenby tied for sixth with Adam Crawford and Charles Howell at 279.

Gavin Coles finished alone in fifth at 278, while Beem and Parry shared second with Baddeley. But neither the American PGA champion nor the

Australian two-time winner found his stride on Sunday. Beem had three bogeys in a round of 73, while Parry missed enough makeable putts to run away with the tournament. His final chance at a playoff was dashed when he hit his tee shot into a bunker at the 18th.

Even though they didn't play well, both veterans had nothing but praise for Allan. "He hits the ball very hard and very straight," Beem said. "And he putted brilliantly. He definitely has the game to do well on the U.S. Tour."

In one of the most unusual situations of the season on any tour, this championship was shortened to 54 holes after Thursday's round was cancelled because the greens got too fast.

Australian PGA Championship—A$1,000,000
Winners: Peter Lonard and Jarrod Moseley

In a scene oddly reminiscent of the tie between Colin Montgomerie and Bernhard Langer that ended the PGA European Tour season, dimming light and a decision not to bring players back for a Monday finish resulted in the first tie on record on the Australasian Tour. After 27 grueling holes on Sunday in a week that was frequently interrupted by thunderstorms, Peter Lonard and Jarrod Moseley remained tied at 17-under-par 271. When the tie could not be broken after one extra hole, the players huddled with tour officials and agreed to share the title and the prize money.

It was an anticlimactic end to what had otherwise been an outstanding final round. Moseley completed nine holes of the third round in the early hours of Sunday morning and opened up a five-shot lead, but by the time the leaders reached the 11th tee the lead had disappeared. Play was briefly suspended again when a thunderstorm rolled in, and after it resumed, Lonard, who had fought back into a share of the lead, bogeyed the 11th and 13th and missed a short birdie putt on the 17th, but Moseley was unable to completely slam the door. He parred the final seven holes to finish at 17 under. That might have been enough were it not for the monster 50-footer for birdie Lonard made on the 18th hole to force the playoff.

With daylight dwindling, both players hustled back to the 18th where they both made par. Daylight was gone. They had played 28 holes and weathered another rain delay, and no one thought it was prudent to come back on Monday, so the decision was made.

Stuart Appleby finished alone in third place at 274, while Greg Norman closed with a 32 on his final nine to finish alone in fourth at 275.

MasterCard Masters—A$1,250,000
Winner: Peter Lonard

One week after deciding to declare a tie with Jarrod Moseley when darkness fell on the Australian PGA Championship, Peter Lonard found himself in another playoff, this time with Adam Scott and Gavin Coles to decide the winner of the season-ending MasterCard Masters.

There would be no tie this time around. Lonard got into the playoff by virtue of a spectacular final nine on Sunday that included a 25-foot birdie at the 12th followed by birdies at the 13th, 14th and 15th to give him a score of 66 and a total of nine-under-par 279.

Coles looked to be the one to beat. Poised at 10 under par through 10 holes, he ran into controversy at the 11th when he stood on the edge of a bunker to play his fourth shot at the par-four. Coles slipped and partially fell into the bunker, which was distracting enough. But he also had to deal with the fact that his putter hit his ball while he was falling. After consulting with Adam Scott, who was in the group, and with several of the spectators nearby, officials ruled that Coles' ball had not moved, and therefore it was not a penalty. He missed the par putt and tapped in for bogey, but was clearly distracted by the episode.

"It definitely distracted me," he said. "It mucked up my momentum, and I was still thinking about it on the next tee."

Coles finished the round with seven pars for a 279 total and a share of the lead with Lonard.

Scott struggled early on Sunday with bogeys at the first and fifth holes, but he scraped his way back into a share of the lead with birdies at the par-five second, the seventh and the par-five 14th. He, too, closed out with 279, but his otherwise consistent ball-striking abandoned him in the playoff. On the first extra hole (the 18th) Scott pushed his approach shot, then flubbed his chip. When his par putt missed on the low side of the hole, Scott was eliminated from the playoff.

Lonard and Coles marched back to the 17th where they both made pars. Then on the 18th again, Lonard found the green with his approach and calmly two-putted, while Coles missed the green to the left and failed to get up and down.

"I'm not really sure how this happened," the winner said after donning the gold jacket and hoisting the crystal globe trophy. "After nine holes I really thought I had no chance."

Robert Allenby finished in fourth, only one shot out of the playoff after a five-birdie run in the final 11 holes. He missed birdie putts on the 17th and 18th that would have won the tournament for him. If only one had fallen, Allenby would have joined the playoff as the player with the hottest hand, but he had to settle for fourth at 280, one clear of Adam Crawford, Craig Parry and Richard Green.

13. African Tours

Despite the worldwide gains of South African golfers, only a few of the events on the Southern African Tour rose in prominence in 2002. Among them was the Dunhill Championship, a co-sponsored event with the PGA European Tour that produced a winner both continents could claim. Justin Rose, who came to prominence at the 1998 British Open when he was a teenager finishing fourth and winning the hearts of the British faithful, is an Englishman who was born in Johannesburg. That made his wins at the Dunhill Championship and the Nashua Masters doubly special.

South Africans themselves had a good year in their homeland. Retief Goosen won the Dimension Data Pro-Am as part of his continued great play around the world, and Ernie Els capped off the best season of his career with a $2 million win at the Nedbank Golf Challenge.

It was a season of firsts and a year of resurrections. To say that 21-year-old Nicholas Lawrence was star-struck after winning the Southern Africa Tour Championship would have been an understatement. "Is Tiger Woods playing?" Lawrence asked after learning that his win had earned him a spot in the field at the WGC NEC Invitational. When told that Woods would be in the event, Lawrence said, "Oh my word, I'm going to be playing in the same tournament as Tiger Woods."

Chris Williams wasn't quite as giddy as Lawrence, but when he birdied the final two holes to win the Telkom PGA Championship, the Englishman was as thrilled as anyone could be, and rightfully so. The victory put Williams in an elite club of professionals who hold two South African PGA titles. The other members are Bobby Locke, Gary Player and Ernie Els. Williams did something even those great players couldn't do. He won his two PGA Championship titles 17 years apart. "I was really nervous," Williams said. "But the closer I got to the finish, the better it got for me. Memories of my last win came flooding back."

Speaking of comebacks, Hennie Otto, once nicknamed "Wild Thing" for his volatile temper and aggressive play, made a spectacular recovery after back surgery in 2001 threatened to cripple his career. Otto won the Limpopo Industrelek Classic, and in what could be described as the biggest victory of his career, overcame a late bogey and avoided disaster to win the Nashua Masters, the second playing in 2002 of that event. "I've got a whole new focus on life and golf," Otto said. "Now it's just a matter of getting rid of the bad habits so I can focus on being a better golfer."

In a surprise ending to the season, Michiel Bothma won the Telkom PGA Championship after final-round leader Mark Murless called a penalty on himself and made two double bogeys in his final four holes. Both players finished regulation at 273, and Bothma won on the second playoff hole, after Murless grounded his putter at the 13th and backed away after his ball had moved. Calling a one-shot penalty on himself, Murless missed the putt and made his first double bogey of the tournament, but not the last he would make before the end of the day. "The penalty rattled me," Murless said. "But I had a big lead and just couldn't close it out."

Els had no such issues. After celebrating his first British Open title and the birth of his first son, the big South African superstar won the richest title at the Nedbank Golf Challenge. For Els and for the Southern Africa tour, it was the perfect way to end the year.

Bell's South African Open—£500,000
Winner: Tim Clark

Third-round leader Tim Clark never felt comfortable during the final 18 holes of the Bell's South African Open, but that didn't slow him down. Clark shot a seven-under-par 65 on a sunny Sunday in Durban to take the title by two strokes over a charging Steve Webster of England.

As far as Clark was concerned, the most impressive thing about his 19-under-par 267 was how he held it together even though he never felt like his game was at its best. "Even the birdies weren't enough to make me feel comfortable," he said.

Those birdies included a string of four straight that Clark reeled off after a three-putt bogey at the 11th allowed Webster to draw level. Webster shot 64 for a 271 total and was clearly playing the best golf on the final day. But he ran out of holes and had to settle for second place, three strokes clear of third-place finishers James Kingston and Jonathan Lomas.

Welshman David Park also shot 64 for a 276 total and a tie for fifth with England's Simon Dyson, Scotland's Alastair Forsyth and local favorite Retief Goosen. Ernie Els, the other South African in the field who drew great crowds all week, got off to a slow start with 73. He finished with rounds of 69, 68 and 69 for a 279 total and a tie for 13th.

Dunhill Championship—£500,000
Winner: Justin Rose

The potential was finally realized. Four years after he burst onto the scene by finishing fourth at the 1998 British Open at Royal Birkdale as a 17-year-old, and three years removed from the 21 consecutive missed cuts that made him the poster boy for turning professional too early, Justin Rose broke through with a come-from-behind victory at the Dunhill Championship in Johannesburg. Rose shot 65 on Sunday for a 20-under-par 268 total, which was enough for a two-stroke win over third-round leader Martin Maritz, Mark Foster and Retief Goosen.

Rose started the final round trailing by three and tied for fourth with Ernie Els (who shot 63 on Saturday and looked to be the man who would challenge for the title), Roger Wessels and Paul McGinley. Rose made up ground quickly, then held off a late surge by Maritz, who ran into trouble on the first nine, but made two eagles and a birdie in his final five holes to shoot 71.

The shot of the tournament came at the 17th, when Rose hit a five iron to the par-three hole that almost went in before stopping two feet from the hole. "It was the best five iron I've ever hit, to be honest," Rose said. The birdie gave him the lead for good. He followed it up with another birdie at the par-five 18th, a hole he failed to birdie in 2001 in a one-stroke loss to Adam Scott. This time Rose felt like fate was on his side.

"My tee shot (at 18) ended up in the same spot as Adam's did last year, so I took it as a good omen," he said. "I decided just to set myself up for a chip-and-putt finish like he did."

Retief Goosen also shot 65 to finish in the tie for second place. McGinley finished at 17-under-par 271 and in a three-way tie for fifth with Mark Mouland and Anthony Wall. Els finished ninth.

Telkom PGA Championship—R1,000,000
Winner: Chris Williams

With birdies on the final two holes, England's Chris Williams joined an elite group of professionals who hold two South African PGA titles. The other members are Gary Player, Ernie Els and Bobby Locke. But Williams did something even those great players couldn't do. He won his two PGA Championship titles 17 years apart.

The 1985 champion got off to a slow start at the Woodhill Country Club, shooting 74 on Thursday to fall eight shots off the pace. He made up a lot of ground the next day when his hot putter lifted him to an eight-under-par 64. A 65 on Friday gave Williams a three-shot lead with 18 holes to play.

He wasn't as hot on the final day as he had been earlier in the week, but Williams was still good enough, posting birdies on the final two holes for a closing round of 68, a 17-under-par 271 total and a two-stroke victory over Hennie Otto, who shot 67.

"It was no surprise that Hennie came back at me," Williams said. "But the birdie on 17 gave me the confidence going into the 18th. I was really nervous throughout the final nine holes, but the closer I got to the finish, the better it got for me. Memories of my last win came flooding back."

American Bruce Vaughan shot 67 to climb into a share of third at 274 with Martin du Toit, who shot 65. Mark McNulty also shot 65 on Sunday, which was good enough to push the Zimbabwean into a four-way tie for fifth at 12-under-par 276 with Andrew McLardy, Tjaart van der Walt and Tim Clark. Martin Maritz and Grant Muller rounded out the top 10. Both South Africans finished at 11-under-par 277.

Dimension Data Pro Am—R2,000,000
Winner: Retief Goosen

Retief Goosen had a lot to celebrate. Not only was he the reigning U.S. Open champion, he was also the holder of the European Order of Merit title and one of the hottest players in the world. Then, on his 33rd birthday, he was given another reason to celebrate as he won the Dimension Data Pro-Am.

Goosen led wire-to-wire after opening with 63 and following with rounds of 70, 69 and a closing 66 to win by three over Scotland's Scott Drummond, who stayed close all week. Drummond trailed by three after the opening round, but drew level with Goosen after 67 on Friday. They remained tied atop the leaderboard after both players posted 69s on Saturday. That led to a Sunday showdown that wasn't finished until the final putt fell.

"Scott played really well," Goosen said. "He kept coming back at me, and he holed a lot of putts. He only made one mistake and that was at the seventh."

Drummond led by one at that point, but he pulled the wrong club for his approach into the well-guarded green. The result was a double bogey, while Goosen, who picked the perfect club, made birdie for a three-shot swing in one hole.

The Scot didn't go away quietly. He was within one shot of Goosen at the par-three 13th when the South African hit a mediocre tee shot to 40 feet. Then, in a moment that sealed the tournament, Goosen made the 40-footer for birdie to take a two-stroke lead.

"I made a big putt there, but Scott then holed about a 60-footer at the next," Goosen said, but the lead remained three as Goosen made a birdie of his own at the 14th. Another birdie from 20 feet at the 15th extended the lead to three with one hole to play. "The 17th was the key birdie," Goosen said. "It was nice to have a three-shot lead playing the last, which is a par-five. It was good just to need a two-putt for the win."

That's exactly what he did, making par for a 268 total, three clear of Drummond and five ahead of Jaco Van Zyl. Tjaart van der Walt was alone in fourth at 14-under-par 274, followed by David Park at 275 and Michael Kirk at 276.

Nashua Masters—R1,000,000
Winner: Justin Rose

In a stiff wind that sent scores soaring, Justin Rose showed a discipline and patience beyond his years as he fired a steady two-under-par 68 final round for a 15-under-par 265 total and a one-stroke victory in the Nashua Masters. In the process he outlasted four other players with whom he shared the third-round lead at 197. In the blustery conditions only Rose and Titch Moore managed to break par on Sunday.

"I think the course showed its real teeth today," Rose said. "It was a lot more difficult in the wind."

In addition to Rose and Moore, Scott Drummond, Richard Sterne and James Kingston shared the third-round lead. All battled the wind pretty effectively for the first five holes, but that changed at the sixth. Drummond and Kingston made bogey, while Sterne made double bogey. When Rose sank a 20-footer for birdie, the tone of the round was set.

"I think the turning point was really at the sixth," Rose said. "I enjoyed a two-shot turnaround there over my playing partners and managed to get away."

He followed up the birdie at the sixth with two more at the seventh and eighth to take a three-shot lead into the final nine. Another birdie at the 12th was flanked by bogeys at the 11th and 13th. From there he parred in, making one last spectacular shot at the 17th from a greenside bunker to save par and the lead.

"The other key today was the bunker shot at 17," he said. "I thought I had a two-shot lead when in fact it was one, so I was very happy to save par."

Moore, who was the first-round leader after a course-record-tying 62, parred the final three holes to shoot 69 for the day and 266 for the week. That was good enough for second place, one better than a hard-charging Andre Cruse, who closed with 63. Stern, who had only recently turned 20 years old, shot 71 to finish at 267, tied for fourth with Tim Clark and Grant Muller. Sean Pappas shot 64 on Sunday to finish tied for sixth with Drummond, Ashley Roestoff and Mark Murless at 268.

With the exception of Drummond, who is Scottish, and Rose, who was born in Johannesburg but is English, eight of the top 10 were native South Africans. But it was Rose, the country's adopted son, who entered the final weeks of the season as the only multiple winner (he also won the Dunhill Championship). "It's really great," Rose said. "I'm having my best results in South Africa."

Southern Africa Tour Championship—R2,000,000
Winner: Nicholas Lawrence

To say that 21-year-old Nicholas Lawrence was star-struck would have been an understatement. "Is Tiger Woods playing?" Lawrence asked after learning that his maiden victory in the Southern Africa Tour Championship earned him a spot in the field at the WGC NEC Invitational. When told that Woods would be in the event, Lawrence said, "Oh my word, I'm going to be playing in the same tournament as Tiger Woods."

But Lawrence displayed maturity beyond his years as he ground his way around the Leopard Creek Golf Club in 14-under-par 274 for the week, good enough for a one-stroke victory over Tim Clark and Bruce Vaughan.

Lawrence started the final round with a one-stroke lead, but struggled with his swing on the first nine. "When I stood on the first tee my hands were shaking," he admitted. "I struggled with my swing all day, but I just kept plugging away."

The lead swung back and forth between Lawrence, Clark and Vaughan all day, but momentum seemed to shift in Clark's favor when he made a crucial 15-footer for par at the 16th after Lawrence was in with a bogey. That gave Clark a one-shot lead with two holes to play.

That lead lasted one hole. On the 17th Clark found the fairway bunker with his tee shot and couldn't reach the green with his approach. His third shot with a wedge skidded across the green and into the back rough, from which he failed to get up and down. The result was a double bogey. When Lawrence tapped in for par, his one-shot lead was restored.

Playing smart golf, Lawrence laid up short of the water on the par-five 18th, wedged his third shot safely into the center of the green and two-putted for par. If Clark or Vaughan were going to take this one to extra holes, they would have to do it with birdies. Both men left their birdie efforts short at the last, and just like that, Lawrence was the winner.

"I'm dumbstruck," he said. "I can't believe what's happened. It hasn't sunk in yet." Then the rookie offered words of consolation to the veteran Clark. "I couldn't believe what happened at 17," Lawrence said. "When Tim was two shots clear of me, I thought he was going to run away with the tournament. But after 17 I thought, 'Gosh, I can win this tournament.' My heart goes out to Tim. He really gave it everything out there."

Royal Swazi Sun Open—R500,000
Winner: Andrew McLardy

Through the first five holes of the final round, it appeared as if Andrew McLardy's three-year victory drought would continue. Despite shooting 63 on Saturday, McLardy trailed Nic Henning by two strokes going into the final round. When he started out on Sunday with five straight pars, it looked like another good week but no trophy for McLardy.

Then McLardy came within inches of a one on the par-three sixth, and his fortunes changed. "I almost made a hole-in-one," he said. "That kind of upped the confidence a bit."

He tapped in for a birdie at the sixth and followed it up with birdies at the seventh, eighth and ninth to snatch sole possession of the lead. "I was 16 under through the first nine and knew that I just needed to keep it together over the back," he said.

He did better than that. At the short par-five 12th, he hit driver and seven iron to four feet and made that putt for eagle. Then, at the par-five 17th, he made a 60-footer for another eagle. A routine two-putt par at the 18th gave McLardy a bogey-free 64 and a 20-under-par 268 total. That was good enough for a two-stroke victory over Henning, who finished with 68.

James Loughnane also shot 68 to finish alone in third place at 272, four clear of Bradford Vaughan and Marc Cayeux.

It was McLardy's first win since the 1998 Kalahari Classic, and it came at just the right time. He lost his exempt status in 2001. In addition to the R79,000 winner's check, this victory gave him a two-year exemption. "I'm thrilled," he said. "I was pleased with my consistency this week. And the two eagles came as quite a surprise."

Stanbic Zambia Open—R927,362
Winner: Marc Cayeux

Thanks to some spectacular play early in the week, Marc Cayeux could cruise home with 70 on an overcast Sunday in Lusaka to take his fifth career title with relative ease. The 24-year-old finished the week at 22-under-par 270 to win the Stanbic Zambia Open by two strokes, but it was never really close.

Early rounds of 69, 66 and 65 gave the Zimbabwean a three-shot lead going into the final round, and he was never threatened. Andre Cruse came on strong with three late birdies to close with 66 and get to within two of Cayeux when the leader three-putted the 17th for bogey, but that was as close as this ever got. Cruse finished tied for second with Richard Sterne at 272, while England's Simon Hurd, Simon Wakefield and Kariem Baraka finished tied for fourth at 274.

"I am very, very happy with this victory," Cayeux said. "In 1998, the win here was my first professional victory. Four years down the line, this tournament is so much bigger, and this victory means I am one step closer to earning my European Tour card for next year. My first course of action is to defend my title at the FNB Botswana Open. After that, it's off to Europe."

FNB Botswana Open—R268,380
Winner: Hendrik Buhrmann

After a flurry of birdies and a closing round of 66, it came down to a two-putt par at the 18th. That was all Hendrik Buhrmann needed to capture the FNB Botswana Open, even though he didn't know it at the time. Buhrmann parred the final hole for a 19-under-par 194 total in the 54-hole event, then had to watch as Brett Liddle stood over a birdie putt. When Liddle missed his birdie try, he had to make a three-footer for par to force a playoff. When that putt didn't go in, Buhrmann had his first title in eight years.

"It is almost sad to have waited this long to win again," Buhrmann said after collecting his first trophy since the 1994 Nashua Challenge. "I am extremely pleased with my victory. It's a great way to start your season, even if I am a little late. This win is the result of hard work and lots of faith. I really feel blessed right now."

It was also the result of Liddle's putter cooling off on the second nine. Liddle shot 29 on the first nine and took a three-shot lead into the final nine holes. But he could only manage a 36 on the back. Meanwhile, Buhrmann holed a wedge shot for eagle at the 14th to regain the lead. He added one more birdie at the 16th, but missed what he thought was a crucial birdie putt at the 18th.

"It was frustrating when I missed that putt at the last," Buhrmann admitted. "Fortunately I remained calm through the final couple of holes, which is not usual for me. I think that is what made the difference today."

Liddle's three-putt at the 18th left him with 65 for the day and a 195 total, two clear of Doug McCabe and five ahead of Shane Pringle. Still, Liddle couldn't help being dejected. With a three-shot lead with nine to play, he thought he should have won.

"Brett played superb," Buhrmann said. "He was really on fire through the front nine. I struggled with my chipping and just saw him pull away from me. It was such a relief for me when I hit that sand wedge in the hole for two at 14. That's when I knew I was still in with a chance."

Limpopo Industrelek Classic—R225,000
Winner: Hennie Otto

Hennie Otto was just glad to be able to walk around the Pietersburg Golf Club. Winning his second Limpopo Industrelek Classic was a bonus.

Only eight months before teeing off in the final round of this tournament with a one-stroke lead, Otto was lying in a hospital bed after having two disks fused together. The pain was unbearable and his career as a golfer was in question. That made the final-round 69 and the one-stroke victory over Des Terblanche even more special.

Otto and Terblanche had been there before. The two had battled in the last group of the final round for this title in 1999. Back then Otto came out on top. This time it was a little closer, but the results were the same. "This was a lot closer than 1999," Otto said. "There was a lot more pressure. But having been here before, I knew what I had to do."

Terblanche added to the pressure with a birdie on the first hole to erase Otto's one-shot overnight lead. But Otto birdied three of the next four holes to regain the lead. Another birdie at the 10th gave him a three-shot margin.

"I knew a two-stroke lead wasn't going to be enough on the back nine," Otto said. "When I made the birdie at 10 I started to relax a little."

He might have relaxed too early. A three-putt at the 11th cut the lead back to two, but Terblanche was unable to capitalize. On the 12th, the challenger hit his tee shot in the water and made a double bogey. When Otto tapped in for par, the lead was four.

"That's when I turned to my caddie and said, 'Right, let's just slot into cruise control, make our pars and go home,'" Otto said. "I knew it was up to Des to catch me, and he almost did."

Terblanche birdied the 13th and 14th to get to within two. When Otto three-putted for bogey at the 16th, the lead was only one. But that was as close as it would get. Both players hit the green at the 17th and 18th, and although Terblanche had a reasonable run at birdie on the final green, he missed it low. Both players shot 69 in the final round, but Otto finished with a 14-under-par 202 total, while Terblanche took home second place with 203.

"I didn't go out and play for many birdies," Otto said. "I just played for pars and let the birdies come themselves."

This was a new style for the player who was once called "Wild Thing" for his aggressive style and volatile temper. But the surgery repaired more than Otto's back. "I've got a whole new focus on life and golf," he said. "Now it's just a matter of getting rid of the bad habits so I can focus on being a better golfer."

Royal Swazi Sun Classic—R200,000
Winner: James Kingston

With an eight-birdie, no-bogey final round, James Kingston came from four shots back to win the Royal Swazi Sun Classic by one stroke over Keith Horne and Bobby Lincoln in Mbabane. Kingston shot 64 on Sunday to reach 12-under-par 204 and overtake leader Lincoln and hold off a hard-charging Horne with two late birdies for a closing 64.

Consecutive rounds of 70 on the first two days left Kingston four shots back with a half-dozen players ahead of him. He got off to a quick start with a flurry of early birdies, followed by five solid pars, before ending with two birdies on the final two holes for his eight-under-par 64 total. After he made his final putt and signed his card, Kingston waited to see if Horne or Lincoln could birdie the final hole to force a playoff. When neither player found the hole, Kingston threw his arms in the air and celebrated his victory.

Lincoln finished the day with 69 for a 205 total, and Horne closed with 66. Steve Basson also shot 66 in the final round for a 206 total and a share of fourth place with Marc Cayeux. Nic Henning was alone in sixth at 207 after finishing the week with 65, while Brett Liddle shared seventh with Ulrich van den Berg at 208.

Vodacom Golf Classic—R200,000
Winner: Ashley Roestoff

It took a couple of extra holes and an uncharacteristic mistake by the most consistent player of the week, but when the final putt fell at Royal Johannesburg, Ashley Roestoff had his first victory of the season. Roestoff took a two-stroke lead into the final round after opening with consecutive 67s, but he failed to make some crucial birdie putts on the final day, which allowed his nearest challenger, England's Chris Williams, to join him at the top of the leaderboard.

Williams opened with a pair of 68s by missing only three greens in the first 36 holes. He continued his great ball-striking in the final round, closing with 69 to shoot 11-under-par 205. Meanwhile Roestoff failed to convert birdie putts on three of the last four holes and closed with 71 to send this one to extra holes.

Both players parred the first playoff hole. Then on the 17th, Williams made a mistake, pushing his approach into the rough and failing to get up and down. It was the first green he had missed since the 11th hole of regulation, and it proved costly. Roestoff two-putted for par and the victory.

Richard Sterne and Jaco Van Zyl finished tied for third place at 207, while Brett Liddle and Keith Horne shared fifth at 208. Vaughn Groenewald, who started the final round one shot out of the lead, skied to a 74 on Saturday to fall into a tie for seventh with Craig Kamps at 209.

Bearing Man Highveld Classic—R200,000
Winner: Titch Moore

In a week when birdies were prevalent and everyone wondered how low the scores would ultimately go, Titch Moore proved that consistency was still the key to victory. Moore didn't have the lowest final round or the lowest round of the tournament, but he did put together three solid numbers in what turned out to be a runaway victory at the Bearing Man Highveld Classic.

Moore opened with 64, which wasn't the best score of the day. That honor belonged to Hanno de Weerd, who shot 63 to take a one-shot lead. But de Weerd shot 69 on Saturday to fall back, while Moore put together a 65 to take command. He led by three over Ashley Roestoff going into the final round.

On Sunday, with the winds calm and the course dry and firm, the possibility of someone breaking 60 was discussed. While no one reached golf's magic number, Tyrol Auret improved his position by shooting 62 to get into a tie for fourth with Ulrich van den Berg and Ryan Reid at 204. Auret was near the bottom of the pack after opening with 75, but he fought his way back with 67 on Saturday before closing with the 10-under-par 62, the low round of the tournament.

Roestoff also had a good run of birdies in the final round. He finished with

65, which propelled him past de Weerd and into second place at 201. But that was five shots shy of Moore, who finished his consistent week with 67 for a 20-under-par 196 total and an easy victory.

Wayne Bradley shot 66 to finish at 205 and alone in seventh, two shots clear of Brett Liddle, who also shot 66 in the final round to finish alone in eighth with a 207 total.

Platinum Classic—R500,000
Winner: Titch Moore

For the second time in four weeks, Titch Moore put together three consistent ball-striking rounds that resulted in another victory for the veteran. The first win came in early October at the Bearing Man Highveld Classic. This time it was at the Platinum Classic at Mooi Nooi Golf Club, where Moore shot 65, 66 and 67 and breezed to a five-stroke victory over Scotland's Doug McGuigan.

The 19-under-par 198 total was worth R79,000 and gave him a four-week earnings total of over R100,000. But unlike his earlier win, this time Moore led wire-to-wire. His 65 on Friday gave him a share of the first-round lead with McGuigan, and his 66 on Saturday moved him three clear of the field.

McGuigan shot 68 on Saturday and 70 in the final round to drop to five back. He finished alone in second place at 203, but never contended for the title. Des Terblanche made a run at second in the final round, adding 68 to his earlier scores of 67 and 69, but he fell one short of his goal, finishing in third at 204, one behind McGuigan, but one clear of Grant Muller. Sean Farrell rounded out the top five by matching Moore's final-round 67 for a 206 total.

Telkom PGA Championship—R1,250,000
Winner: Michiel Bothma

In a bizarre ending, Michiel Bothma was the surprise winner of the Telkom PGA Championship after leader Mark Murless called a penalty on himself and made two double bogeys in his final four holes. Both players finished regulation at 15-under-par 273, and Bothma won on the second playoff hole, but that was only part of the drama.

Murless led from the opening day, shooting 64 in the first round and following it up with scores of 68 and 72 to remain atop the leaderboard at 204 with one round to play. He seemed to be in control, especially after his nearest challengers — Mark McNulty and Simon Hurd — hit shots out of bounds at the 11th hole during the final round and took double bogeys. Bothma, who started the final round one-shot back, had fallen five off the pace. Murless seemed to have this one wrapped up.

Then at the 13th the leader stood over a three-footer for par, grounded his putter, and backed away. The ball had moved. He replaced the ball to its original position and called a one-shot penalty on himself. Shaken, Murless missed the three-footer and tapped in for a double bogey.

He still held a three-shot lead, but that evaporated when his tee shot found the water at the par-three 16th. When Bothma rolled in his second birdie in a row at the 16th, what had once been a five-shot Murless lead had become a one-shot deficit. Bothma assumed the lead at 15 under with two holes to play.

But Murless wasn't out of it yet. He birdied the par-five 17th to draw even at 15 under par. That's where they finished. Both players parred the 18th in regulation, then parred it again in the playoff.

The third time through the 18th, both players hit their approach shots on the back of the green, leaving 50-footers for birdie. Murless played first and ran his putt six feet past. Bothma lagged his birdie effort to within a foot. When Murless missed his par, Bothma tapped in the one-footer for par and the win.

"It's unbelievable," Bothma said afterward. "I wish the incident on 13 had never happened. I would never want that to happen to any player, even if it meant a victory for me."

Murless was disheartened by the turn of events, but he wasn't ready to blame the penalty at the 13th. "I got a huge lead and couldn't close the door," he said. "But life goes on. I'm glad Michiel won it. He deserved it."

Nashua Masters—R1,000,000
Winner: Hennie Otto

The last time here, Hennie Otto threw his golf clubs into the lagoon after losing the Nashua Masters. This time around, the 26-year-old kept his cool and his golf clubs, finishing as the only player under par. His one-under-par 279 was good enough for a two-stroke victory over an international contingent that included Ireland's Gavin McNeil and Ciaran McMonagle, South Africa's Roger Wessels and Zimbabwean Mark McNulty.

"I still don't like this golf course," Otto said. "But fortunately the clubs I have now float."

Trailing McNulty by three and Wessels by one at the beginning of the day, Otto made the fewest mistakes when other players were giving back shots. McNulty was the first to fall away. He made two early bogeys on the front nine and never recovered, finishing with 74 for a 281 total. Wessels took advantage and assumed a one-shot lead over Otto through 12 holes. At the 13th, Wessels pulled his tee shot on the par-three into an unplayable lie. A penalty, a poor chip and two putts later, Wessels walked off the green with a double bogey. Just like that, Otto had a one-stroke lead.

Otto gave back the lead at the 16th when he found the water with his second shot and made bogey. But Wessels couldn't take advantage. He also hit a ball in the water at the 16th and finished with a bogey. Both players parred the final two holes, and Otto walked away with the victory.

"I thought I had lost it at 16," Otto said. "I said to my caddie, 'We've just given away the tournament.' I hit a four iron from 212 yards downwind. You could throw a stone that far. Then I took a drop and it landed in a divot, which really got me angry. I took my six at the 16th and left. Normally, I would have made seven on the next par-three, but I made two good putts for par and we snuck in for the win."

Nedbank Golf Challenge—US$4,060,000
Winner: Ernie Els

Ernie Els set a course record at Sun City in the final round of the Nedbank Golf Challenge and, in the process, won the biggest prize in golf by a whopping eight strokes over Colin Montgomerie.

"I don't know what it is," Els said. "It's just one of those things. You get into the zone or something and everything goes right."

That was a pretty good summation of Els' year. In addition to three early season wins, the big South African won his first British Open title in July, and he and his wife had their first son in the autumn. He then won the Cisco World Match Play and capped the year with his 28th consecutive under-par round, a bogey-free, nine-under-par 63.

With birdies at the second, third and ninth holes, Els opened up a six-shot lead over Chris DiMarco. He extended that lead with birdies at the 10th and 12th, followed by an incredible closing stretch that included birdies at the 14th, 15th, 17th and 18th to run away from the field. His 21-under-par 267 total was worth $2 million.

With Els setting a pace no one could match, the rest of the field was playing for second place. Montgomerie moved ahead of DiMarco in that race when the big Scot made an eagle at the par-five 10th. He followed with three more birdies, including one at the 18th, to shoot 31 on the second nine for a closing 67 and a 275 total. Under any other circumstances Montgomerie's 65-67 weekend would have been the news of the week, but with Els setting the course on fire, the Scot's score was only good enough to edge DiMarco out of second by three strokes. Retief Goosen and Jim Furyk finished tied for fourth at 281.

Vodacom Players Championship—R2,000,000
Winner: Mark McNulty

With 50 victories and a professional career in its 30th year, Mark McNulty felt comfortable making a prediction before the final round of the Vodacom Players Championship. "This one is going to come down to the final nine holes," McNulty said.

The 49-year-old's prognostication proved to be right on the money. With nine holes to play, McNulty was tied for the lead with Darren Fichardt, and both were watching American Scott Dunlap light up the leaderboard like an early Christmas tree. Dunlap made six consecutive birdies starting at the ninth and finished with 64 to post an early 275 total. With the wind picking up in the final hours, that number in the clubhouse looked pretty good, but McNulty still felt confident. "It was for me to win or lose today," he said. "When the wind came up on the back nine, I knew it would be tough."

McNulty played steady golf, using irons off all but one of the tees on the final nine holes at Royal Cape Golf Club. The strategy worked. He made two birdies and no bogeys, while Fichardt hit his driver six times and made three consecutive bogeys starting at the 12th.

"I stuck to my game plan all week," McNulty said. "That was to try and eliminate mistakes and not go for shots which were out of my repertoire. It was all a case of strategy. I said to Darren afterward that I couldn't believe he hit driver all over the place. I just couldn't believe it. Darren's a good player, but he just makes some critical errors."

McNulty made no mistakes coming in, closing with 70 for a 16-under-par 272 and his 51st career victory.

"I was chuffed with myself for playing the back nine under par," McNulty said. "It's a wonderful thrill to win my 51st tournament here. I've won (the Players Championship) at Royal Johannesburg and at Royal Durban, but never at Royal Cape until now. This is something special."

Dunlap's 64 was good enough to move the American into second place at 275, while Fichardt dropped into a tie for third with Hennie Otto at 277.

Hassan II Trophy—US$490,000
Winner: Santiago Luna

Age is just a state of mind, or so says Santiago Luna. One month after celebrating his 40th birthday, Luna ripped up the Red Course at Royal Dares-Salam in Morocco with rounds of 69, 70, 69 and 70 for a 14-under-par 278 and a four-stroke victory in the Hassan II Trophy. It was Luna's second victory in the event (the first coming in 1998), and he finished second to Joakim Haeggman in 2001.

"This is one of my favorite courses, and I am sure if they played the Moroccan Open here I could win it," Luna said after never being seriously challenged for this title. Steve Lowery finished second at 281 after a 73-70 weekend. That was two shots better than the defending champion. Haeggman shot 75 for a 283 total and a tie for third place with Olivier Edmond.

"This course has been my friend each time I've played, and it brings to an end a wonderful year — unbelievable for a player like me," Luna said. "I've only missed two cuts, and this win is just a brilliant feeling.

"It must be because I'm now in my 40s, I'm thinking better on the course. Who knows what next year will bring? All I know is that it's almost 2003 and I'll still be playing."

Ernie Els Invitational—R200,000
Winner: Louis Oosthuizen

Less than year after leaving his Ernie Els Foundation scholarship to join the professional ranks, Louis Oosthuizen made the 36-hole event named after his mentor his first professional victory. With rounds of 66 and 64, Oosthuizen won the Ernie Els Invitational by four shots over Des Terblanche.

Terblanche led by one after the first round, but a closing 69 dropped him to second at 10-under-par 134, three clear of third-place finisher Ulrich van den Berg and four ahead of Ian Hutchings, Alan McLean and Richard Sterne. Sterne matched Oosthuizen's 64 in the second round after opening with 74, while the tournament's namesake, Els, shot 72 and 68 to finish tied for eighth.

The win earned Oosthuizen R25,000, the largest check of his young career.

14. Senior Tours

The winners didn't change much on the U.S. Senior PGA Tour. Hale Irwin won yet another money title, taking home over $3 million and four tournament victories. Irwin also had 18 top-five finishes, and never finished over par in any of the 27 events he played. Bob Gilder had back-to-back victories twice, winning four tournaments and taking second on the money list with $2.3 million. Bruce Fleisher had another good year, winning once and finishing third with $1.86 million. Tom Kite and Doug Tewell put up good numbers all year. Kite won three times and was fourth with $1.6 million, and Tewell won twice and was fifth with $1.5 million.

Even though many of the names were the same, the attitude among the over-50 crowd was much more accommodating than it had been in years past. With CNBC taking a pass on future television coverage and many of the sponsorships in limbo, the older generation dug deep and found that they had some salesmanship left in them. Leading the charge were a couple of fresh faces.

Bruce Lietzke had been out less than one full year and his impact was already being felt. Lietzke had always been a fan favorite on the PGA Tour, a regular guy who never took the game or himself too seriously, and who looked more like an accountant who played every other weekend than someone who made his living on the golf course. Of course, a lot of accountants played more rounds per year than Lietzke did when he was on the regular tour. "I still love to fish and spend time with my family," Lietzke said. "But I'll probably play more out here (on the senior tour) than I did the last few years on the regular tour."

Lietzke was seventh with $1.5 million and won three times in 2002, and each time he made the spectators feel like they were part of the process. "We're out here to entertain," he said. At one point during Lietzke's win at the SAS Championship in Cary, North Carolina, a gallery member said, "How 'bout hooking one here," as Lietzke prepared to hit his tee shot. "I can't," Lietzke said. "How 'bout you hooking one for me." He pulled the fan under the ropes and gave him a driver, stopping the action before the amateur could actually take a swing, but making his point. This was about having fun. Leave the serious stuff for the youngsters taking on Tiger Woods week in and week out.

That attitude was contagious. John Jacobs, long a believer in the entertainment value of the Senior PGA Tour, stepped up in 2002. He also won once and had four runner-up finishes, including a thrilling down-to-the-wire duel with Jim Thorpe in the year's first major championship, The Countrywide Tradition. "People came out here for a show," Jacobs said. "I'm going to give them what they came to see."

Thorpe was also a convert. "We've got to entertain folks," Thorpe said. "That means we've got to quit the whining and get the job done."

There also was the addition of a man whose name was both an acronym and an appropriate description for his demeanor. Frank Urban Zoeller, "Fuzzy" as he was known to everyone, joined the seniors in early 2002 and had an immediate impact on galleries. Joking and engaging the fans just as he did throughout his days on the PGA Tour, Zoeller made the Senior PGA Championship his first win on his new tour, and he was back to his same old self afterward. "Man, you don't win for a while and you forget," he said. "Sort of like sex, I guess; once you get back in contention, you remember what you're supposed to do."

The winners of the other two major championships were Don Pooley in the U.S. Senior Open and Australian Stewart Ginn in the Ford Senior Players Championship.

On the European Seniors Tour, Delroy Cambridge and Japan's Seiji Ebihara each won three times, and Denis Durnian won twice. Noboru Sugai was the winner of the Senior British Open.

Ebihara, who was the leading money winner in Europe, returned to Japan for a fourth victory in the year. Isao Aoki won once in the United States and once in Japan, and Aoki and Ebihara were both members of the UBS Warburg Cup team.

U.S. Senior PGA Tour

MasterCard Championship—$1,500,000
Winner: Tom Kite

He looked like the Tom Kite of old, displaying a putting stroke as solid and precise as his swing, and a short game to complement the accurate iron shots he continued to hit well into his 53rd year. "I've hit the ball quite nicely for the past couple of years," Kite said after a final-round 67 and a six-shot victory over John Jacobs in the MasterCard Championship in Hawaii. "If I can get a putting stroke that will even come close to matching that, it should be a good year."

He certainly got the year off to a good start, birdieing seven of the last 14 holes on Sunday after shooting a course-record 63 on Friday. In between he had a five-birdie 69 on a blustery Saturday where winds peaked at 40 miles an hour. That opened up a five-shot lead for Kite with 18 holes to play. From there he put it on cruise control, hitting laser irons to 17 of the final 18 greens and employing a more upright putting stance that allowed him to see the line better and make a more consistent stroke.

"I've been trying to make it more of an arm-and-shoulder stroke, instead of arm and hands," Kite said. "I told my caddie, 'I think I've found something with my putting stroke.' I've got a stroke now to go with my ball striking."

The only time the stroke failed him was on the first hole of the final round when he ran his birdie putt well past the hole and missed the par putt coming back. Other than that, it was a flawless week. Through nine holes on Sunday Kite had a five-shot lead over Walter Hall and a six-shot margin over Jacobs.

Only once did anyone make a game of it, and that was only for an instant when Jacobs had one of the rarest animals in golf: an albatross. It happened on the par-five 10th, a downhill, downwind, 566-yard hole that most players had reached in two. Jacobs caught a perfect drive that caught the hill and wind and bounded down the fairway some 377 yards. He only had an eight iron left to the pin, which he struck beautifully. The ball hit on the front of the green and released 30 feet back to the hole where it fell in for a two.

"Geez, what a thrill," Jacobs said. "I've never seen one. I've never made one. I didn't know they existed."

That pulled Jacobs to within three, but he never got closer. Kite's seven birdies included a final one at the 18th for 67 and a 17-under-par 199 total. He was the only player to post three rounds in the 60s, and his six-shot margin of victory over Jacobs was one shy of an all-time Senior PGA Tour record.

"This is a great start," Kite said. "Hopefully it will just lead into a great year."

Royal Caribbean Classic—$1,450,000
Winner: John Jacobs

Hours before Tom Brady and the New England Patriots put on a Super Bowl show for the ages, golf fans were treated to a final-round senior showdown that was as entertaining as it was competitive. That's because burly, cigar-chomping John Jacobs not only won the Royal Caribbean Classic in Key Biscayne, Florida, by one shot, he kept the gallery and the television audience entertained along the way.

Football fans were impressed too. Jacobs looks like an old linebacker. At 6-foot-2 and a broad-shouldered 225 pounds, with a Cohiba cigar never far from his lips, Jacobs looked (and dressed) like a guy who had spent 10 years chasing quarterbacks before taking a job as the teaching professional on a cruise ship. He handed out cigars and advised the gallery on when to press an opponent in a two-dollar Nassau. He joked about his own clothes and the attire of others, as well as the over-serious nature of some of his fellow competitors. "You've got to really work hard to be an ass out here," he said. "But some guys do it."

Jacobs wasn't one of them. He joked his way into a two-shot lead after making his seventh birdie of the day on the 14th during Sunday's final round of the rain-shortened 36-hole event. From there he knew what he needed. He told his caddie (and the viewers at home), "All we need is four pars coming in to win."

After the round he called that comment "the kiss of death." Then he said, "I should have never looked at the scoreboard."

Isao Aoki was in at 10-under-par 134 after rounds of 70 and 64, and Tom Watson was making a run as well, holding at 10 under with two holes to play. Bruce Fleisher looked like he would get in at 10 or 11 under, as former Florida club pro Jay Overton, who qualified on Monday and led the tournament after an opening 65, was struggling to break 70. All Jacobs needed was four simple pars and the tournament would be his.

He left birdie putts on the 15th and 16th dead in the hole, but short. Then on the par-three 17th he hit his shot safely into the center of the green, but left his third birdie putt in a row short. This time he didn't recover. Jacobs' par putt slid low and he tapped in for bogey. Now his lead was just one with one hole to play.

By all rights he should have hit a three wood off the tee on the 18th. "That's the worst hole to have to make par on," he said later. "You're back on the tee in that chute and the fairway looks about 15 feet wide."

Jacobs decided against playing it safe. He had gotten into the lead by being aggressive and that's how he would finish, regardless of the outcome. "I'm going to go down smoking," he said. That was almost how things worked out. Jacobs pushed his tee shot into a palm tree, onto a cart path and into the water hazard right of the fairway. He then took a drop into a questionable lie some 288 yards from the green.

"I think the Good Lord wanted me to go over there and get a bad drop to see if I had any guts," Jacobs said. "Then I hit the best three wood I've ever hit in my life. For me, from where I was, to get the ball where I did was a miracle."

Where he got it was right in front of the green. From there, Jacobs hit the best chip of his life to two feet and coaxed the putt in for 66 and an 11-under-par 133 total, one better than Aoki, Watson and Fleisher, and two ahead of Overton and Tom Kite.

"I know one thing," Jacobs said after taking more than a few bows on the 18th green. "If you're in a position to win, you had better give it your best shot. If you don't, you're not going to win."

ACE Group Classic—$1,500,000
Winner: Hale Irwin

This one was a throwback to the early 1980s with names golf fans recognized and final-round go-for-broke drama that overshadowed the so-so real estate course that hosted the ACE Group Classic in Naples, Florida. Fuzzy Zoeller played in his second senior event. Ben Crenshaw played in his first. The fact that they finished 22nd and 43rd didn't matter. The marquee value of having recognizable stars on the senior circuit outweighed their ability to contend.

What helped push this rendition of the Naples tournament over the top was the final-round duel between a couple of guys this tour has longed for since Arnold Palmer and Jack Nicklaus stopped winning senior events. It came down to the 17th hole on Sunday. Hale Irwin, the winningest player in Senior PGA Tour history and a man who continues to make periodic appearances on major championship leaderboards, had caught second-round leader and Hall of Famer Tom Watson.

Irwin played the way he always does, consistent and conservative, hitting fairways and greens and making a minimum number of mistakes. Watson continued to strike the ball like a man who won eight majors. His putting was the only question mark. Rounds of 64 and 66 gave Watson a two-shot edge going into the final round, but then his putter soured. By the 17th on Sunday, he had let Irwin (who shot 68 and 64 the first two days) tie for the lead with a 10-foot birdie putt on the 16th.

"I knew No. 16 was going to be a big hole," Irwin said. "I know he has the advantage at 17. With his length and the way he could hit the ball, the (par-five) 17th was right in his wheelhouse, so I had to do something at 16."

Irwin was right about Watson's length at the 17th. He hit a perfect tee shot that left him with 235 yards to the flag. Irwin was well short and had to lay up to water guarding the green. The shot of the tournament came when Watson pulled his five-wood second shot. The ball never had a chance. It splashed in the pond and disappeared along with Watson's chances of victory.

"I wanted him to go for that shot," Irwin said. "I wanted him to have that pressure of going for the green in two. It's not an easy shot, what he was trying to do. For him, it's well within his range. It's still a tough shot. He just didn't hit it the way he wanted."

Watson explained it this way. "I hit it about 10 yards left of where I wanted to hit it. I was trying to put the pressure on Hale. He's back there in a safe position. I'm in a risky position right there, and I don't play the risky shot very well."

Irwin birdied the 17th. Watson bogeyed. The lead was two with one hole to play. But Irwin hit a fairway bunker with his tee shot on the 18th and had to lay up short of the green on the par-four. His third shot stopped four feet below the hole, and when Watson made a six-footer for birdie, Irwin had to convert the four-footer for the win.

"When Tom made his six-footer, that four-footer became a little nerve-wracking," Irwin admitted. "It's kind of fun because you still have the nerves, you still have the anxiety, you still have the adrenaline rush."

And you still have the name recognition to make people care about whether or not a four-footer goes in. Irwin made the putt for a closing 68 and 54-hole total of 200, one clear of Watson, who shot 71, and two ahead of Jim Dent and Jim Thorpe, but the event was more than just another Irwin victory. There was a new attitude and some fresh contenders on the senior tour.

This time, things might be different.

Verizon Classic—$1,500,000
Winner: Doug Tewell

After more than a quarter-century of playing professional golf with marginal success (four wins in 26 years on the PGA Tour), Doug Tewell had no illusions about reaching star status as a senior. All he wanted was a little respect. "I've won two senior majors and three other tournaments now," Tewell said after a 69 earned him a one-stroke victory over Hale Irwin at the Verizon Classic at the TPC of Tampa Bay in Lutz, Florida. "And I'm struggling to get people to remember my name. But if I keep winning, maybe at least people will pronounce my name correctly."

His name is pronounced "Tool" like the hammer he used to nail the door shut on all challengers in the final round. Tewell, who trailed second-round leader Bruce Fleisher by three shots at the start of the day, got out of the blocks with four birdies in his first seven holes. He was helped by Fleisher and Tom Kite (who was one shot back at the start of the final round), both of whom struggled early in the final 18 holes.

Tewell set the tone for the day with a 50-footer for birdie at the first hole followed by birdies at the fifth and sixth. "I've been on myself pretty hard after the first three events because I thought I had played pretty well," Tewell said. "But I haven't putted well. After making that 50-footer for birdie on the first hole, I started thinking this just might be my day."

Those thoughts were reinforced after Tewell made a difficult 20-footer from the fringe for birdie at the 12th. "That putt was huge," he said. "To knock it in from off the green, I could have knocked that thing six or seven feet by the hole coming off that hill. I have to kind of give Dana Quigley an assist. The ball rolled over his coin and it kind of veered it back into the left edge of the cup. Those are the kinds of things that happen when you win."

Opponents hitting balls in the water are among the other kinds of things that happen when you win. Tewell got two more assists before the round was out from Kite and Fleisher. Kite hit balls in the water on the 12th and 14th and walked away with double bogeys on both holes. He never recovered, finishing with 75 for a six-under-par 207 total. Fleisher held on only after Tewell made bogeys at the 16th and 18th, but his attempt at a comeback came to an end when he hit a three iron from 195 yards on the 18th that sailed right and found the water.

"Pretty ugly," Fleisher said in describing his final-round 75, which left him tied for third with Dave Stockton at 206. "I never felt comfortable all day, and I hit the ball very poorly. I've got no excuses."

Tewell agreed that the finale wasn't the prettiest in senior tour history. "It wasn't a textbook finishing round," he said after tapping in for bogey on the 18th for a final round of 69 and a 203 total, one better than Irwin, who closed with 66. "But under the circumstances, this course can be tough coming down the stretch. I feel very fortunate."

Audi Senior Classic—$1,700,000
Winner: Bruce Lietzke

Nothing rattles Bruce Lietzke. To look at him on the golf course you would never know if he was 10 under par or 10 over. He's always the same smiling, affable fellow who never takes his golf or himself too seriously. "Winning is great, but it isn't the most important thing for me," Lietzke said after coming from five strokes back on Sunday to win the Audi Senior Classic. "My family and friends are more important."

Lietzke looked more like a tourist soaking up the Naucalpan, Mexico, sunshine than someone grinding his way back from an opening 75. "I think the weather had an effect," he said. "I had a bad day on Friday, but it was windy on Friday. On the weekend it was calm and sunny, and I hit it close."

He followed his 75 with a six-under-par 66, which put him a handful of shots behind Ed Dougherty (71-65). Gary McCord (74-66) and Bruce Fleisher (72-66) also stood between Lietzke and the lead. But Lietzke never seemed rattled. He rolled in a birdie from 10 feet at the fourth and two-putted for birdie at the par-five eighth to shoot 34 on the first nine. If that was good enough, fine. If it wasn't good enough, that was fine, too.

It turned out to be good enough. Dougherty struggled, making early bogeys from which he never recovered. He shot 75 in windless conditions to fall into a five-way tie for fourth with Jose Maria Canizares, Danny Edwards, Dana Quigley and Bruce Fleisher at 211. Fleisher, who had a dismal Sunday the week before in Tampa, faired no better in this final round. After gaining a temporary share of the lead on the first nine when Dougherty faltered, Fleisher made a couple of bogeys of his own and finished with 73.

McCord moved into a share of the lead with two holes to play, but bogeyed the 16th and left a birdie putt on the 17th one inch short of the hole. He closed with 69 and finished tied for second with Hale Irwin, who had another strong final-round showing by shooting 67 for a 209 total.

"My short game and putting aren't sharp right now," McCord said. "I haven't been playing, and I haven't been practicing much."

Lietzke has never played or practiced much, but that didn't stop him from winning 13 times on the PGA Tour and three times since joining the senior ranks in the autumn of 2001. He pulled this one out by hitting a wedge close for birdie on the par-five 11th, then adding another one with a close wedge shot on the 12th. He scrambled for par from the bunker on the 14th, then added his final birdie of the day with a 12-foot effort at the 17th.

"I had been looking at the leaderboard on the last four or five holes," he said. "I thought if I could make two birdies on the last five I could win. I just made one, but still won."

His closing 67 was good enough for an eight-under-par 208 and a one-stroke victory. "I dearly love to win," Lietzke said. "While it's not the most important thing in my life, it is pretty cool."

SBC Senior Classic—$1,450,000
Winner: Tom Kite

Once more the superstars of yesteryear made a bid to put their games (and their tour) back on track by thrilling galleries with one quality shot after another on a sunny Sunday in Valencia, California. Tom Kite, the winner of the SBC Senior Classic, summed it up for everyone in one word: "Wow."

That was all he needed to say. Even though the playoff — a two-man, two-hole affair that ended with some shoddy putting by Tom Watson — provided a lukewarm ending, the play in regulation that forced these two aging warriors into overtime was well worth the price of admission.

Round one was nothing to write home about. Kite shot 74, Watson 72, on a day when no one broke 70 and only two players (Tom Purtzer, 70, and Gil Morgan, 71) broke par. Kite and Watson both broke 70 on Saturday, each shooting 69, which gave Watson a one-shot lead going into the final day.

Birdies were rare creatures all week. Kite gained the lead with birdies at the ninth and 12th, then gave it right back with a double bogey at the 13th. "I lost my concentration," Kite said. "I pushed my tee shot into the rough. It was practically a shank."

None of that mattered in the end. The show was the final hole, where four players came down to the wire trying to force a playoff or win the event outright. When it was over, two still stood and two went home, but the final 15 minutes made everyone forget about the missed putts and shanked tee shots they had seen earlier in the week.

Gil Morgan was first. In the penultimate group, Morgan hit a three wood to the par-five 18th that looked like it was going in the hole for a two. When the ball stopped less than two feet behind the hole, Morgan tapped in for an eagle and a closing round of 70. That put him at 213 for the week.

"In 27 years in the game, that might have been the best shot under the circumstances I've ever seen," said Purtzer, who played with Morgan.

Purtzer got up and down from the front bunker at the 18th for a birdie to shoot 69 and join Morgan at 213. Now there was a three-way knot at the top of the leaderboard. Watson needed to birdie at the last hole to join Purtzer and Morgan at 213. Kite, who parred the 17th to remain three under, needed to birdie the final hole to win outright.

Kite hit his second shot on the par-five through the green, leaving himself 25 feet from the first cut of fringe. Watson bailed out left and had a 45-foot chip.

First to play, Watson hit a nine iron that scooted on the ground before running straight for the hole. It caught the left edge of the cup then dove in the hole for an eagle, a 71 and 212 total, prompting Watson to run across the green with his arms in the air, reminiscent of his dance after chipping in at the 17th at Pebble Beach to beat Jack Nicklaus in the U.S. Open.

All of a sudden Kite went from leading to trailing by one. He had to get up and down to force a playoff. The first putt he hit from the fringe rolled eight feet past the hole, but Kite steadied himself and made a great comeback putt for birdie and 69 to join Watson at 212.

"Those are two of the best up-and-downers, two guys with some of the best short games in the world, not just on our tour, but anywhere," Purtzer said. "I expected both of them to get up and down."

Morgan expected the same. "I went from the penthouse to the outhouse pretty quickly," he said.

After the 15-minute thrill ride, the playoff proved anticlimactic. Watson missed a five-footer for birdie on the first playoff hole, then missed an equally short putt for par on the second extra hole, allowing Kite to two-putt for the win.

"Personally, it's a great thrill to go head-to-head with Tom Watson," Kite said. "He's such a great player and champion, and you know you are in for a battle all the way."

Toshiba Senior Classic—$1,500,000
Winner: Hale Irwin

With every additional win, Hale Irwin breaks his own record. He became the winningest player in Senior PGA Tour history two years ago. Three months shy of his 57th birthday, Irwin added a 34th victory to that moniker with a record-setting 17-under-par 196 total in the Toshiba Senior Classic for a five-stroke victory over defending champion Allen Doyle in Newport Beach, California.

I've played well all year," Irwin said. "If I can keep this up, I think I can have a banner year. I'm trying to keep my game simple. I've got a whole lot of variables going on, so I'm trying to stick with the basics."

Those basics included rounds of 67 and 64 for a three-shot lead over

Doyle and Larry Nelson with 18 holes to play. Nelson cut the lead to two with a birdie at the first hole, but he quickly faded, finishing with 73 for a 207 total and a share of 15th place. Doyle got within two when Irwin bogeyed the fifth, but the winner made up for his mistake with a six-footer for birdie at the sixth, a three-foot putt for birdie at the seventh and a 25-footer that found the hole at the eighth for his third consecutive birdie. It was never close after that.

"I put some space between myself and the others when it got close," said Irwin, who finished with 65. "I kind of hit another gear. You have to be hungry enough to finish. He finished equally strong with birdies at the 15th, 16th and 18th to run away from the field. Doyle never had a round over 68, but never made a serious challenge for the title, either.

"I've played so well over the last four tournaments," said Irwin, who finished first, second, tied for second and first in four consecutive weeks. "I've putted very well and am driving the ball well. If I can keep this up and not burn myself out, I feel pretty good about things."

As for bucking the previous senior trend of winning from age 50 to 54, then falling into obscurity after turning 55, Irwin showed some of the fiery competitiveness that made him one of the greatest grinders in the history of the game. "I think sometimes when somebody says I can't do something it gives me a little more incentive," he said. "I don't feel age is a barrier to success. Certainly, when you get older, that hurdle gets a little harder to get over, but at this point I feel good. I don't accept that premise."

Siebel Classic in Silicon Valley—$1,400,000
Winner: Dana Quigley

With a Massachusetts accent that sounds more at home on the docks of Gloucester than the links of Monterrey, Dana Quigley summed up a brutal week in Silicon Valley with one line: "I told my wife, 'these conditions are good for me.'" He was right. In miserable conditions, Quigley holed a 12-footer for birdie on the final hole to win the Siebel Classic in San Jose, California.

Friday was cool and windy, and Saturday was downright cold. The wind stopped on Sunday, but the rain came down in buckets, forcing players to put on extra layers and hope for the best. "I was a lot more comfortable today than in that wind," Quigley said. "I've learned to be a mudder. I've got a horrible, choppy little golf swing, and if I put on a lot of clothes, I've still got a horrible, choppy little golf swing. The cold doesn't bother me."

Quigley and Bob Gilder started the final round one stroke behind Jay Sigel, who had the most consistent first two days with scores of 68 and 73. Quigley and Gilder both shot 67s on Friday and 75s on Saturday. Those Saturday numbers were actually pretty good. The field averaged 77.429 for the day, the highest single-round scoring average since the third round of the 1998 Las Vegas Senior Classic, when the field averaged 78.079 in a gale. It was the first time in seven years that no one broke par on a full-field senior event.

Sunday wasn't quite as bad, but it was far from good. Only two players broke 70 — John Jacobs (68) and Hale Irwin (67) — and only nine players broke par, while eight shot 80 or higher. Orville Moody had a career-high 92.

Sigel did a little better than Moody, but not much. He made triple-bogey seven on the fourth hole and never recovered, finishing with 79 to fall into a tie for 18th.

Fuzzy Zoeller, who started the final round two strokes behind Sigel and one back of Quigley and Gilder, moved to the top of the leaderboard with four birdies on the first nine to get to four under. But he bogeyed the 12th and 14th holes to fall back into a tie with Quigley.

Gilder's final round was more inconsistent than the weather. He birdied the first four holes, then followed it up with four bogeys over the next 12 holes. A final birdie from 30 feet at the 17th moved him within one of Quigley, but that was as close as he would get.

Afterward Gilder admitted that the conditions got to him. "I played in this stuff in high school, but I'd forgotten," he said. "I don't go out in this kind of weather unless somebody really pokes me these days."

Quigley came to the last hole tied with Zoeller, and both had makeable putts for birdie. Quigley had been in the rough with his tee shot and hit his approach to 12 feet. Zoeller, looking for his first victory as a senior, had a 15-footer for birdie, but the ball disappeared in the hole and spun out.

"I did get a big chunk of the hole," Zoeller said. "I swallowed my tongue twice when it went in and out of there. I haven't been in the hunt for a while, so that was great. My nerves were fine. It's a good feeling to know for next time."

That set up Quigley's 12-footer for a closing round of 70, a 212 total, and a one-stroke victory. "I thought par might be a pretty good score today," Quigley said. "Pretty boring, huh?"

Emerald Coast Classic—$1,450,000
Winner: Dave Eichelberger

When the weather is iffy, every shot counts. That's why the seven iron Dave Eichelberger hit on the par-three eighth hole in the first round of the Emerald Coast Classic proved to the critical swing of the tournament. The ball took one hop on the 190-yard hole and fell into the cup for an ace. Doug Tewell parred the eighth in the first round. That two-stroke swing would prove to be the difference, as Eichelberger carried a two-shot lead into the final round, which was cancelled when a violent storm blew through Milton, Florida.

"I might have figured it would be my week," Eichelberger said. "Something unusual seems to happen in my wins. Picking up two shots, that was the difference."

Eichelberger parlayed the ace into 65 on Friday, a score he matched on Saturday without replicating the hole-in-one. Tewell shot 63 on Saturday after 69 on Friday. That put him two back, but with momentum clearly in his favor.

He stayed close during the first nine on Sunday as Eichelberger bogeyed the first hole, then birdied the fourth. But at 1:47 p.m., with Eichelberger standing in a greenside bunker on the 11th hole, lightening forced a suspension of play. Two hours and an inch and a half of rain later, the round was cancelled and Eichelberger was declared the winner.

"It's unfortunate to get close and not have an opportunity," Tewell said. "But if the course is unplayable, it is unplayable. You trust officials to make the right decisions, and I feel they did."

It was Eichelberger's first victory since August of 1999 and the first of his career in a rain-shortened event. "The win almost makes your whole season," he said. "It's been almost three years since I've won. Every time you win, you wonder if you're ever going to win again. It feels pretty good. This should hold me for a while, but I'm wondering what's in store now that I've come around. I've never won two in a row."

Liberty Mutual Legends of Golf—$2,505,000
Winner: Doug Tewell

In an interesting twist to the golf adage, Doug Tewell won the Liberty Mutual Legends of Golf by driving for dough. Hitting 41 of 42 fairways for the week (14 for 14 in the final 18 holes), Tewell played to his strength and finished with an 11-under-par 205 that bettered Bobby Wadkins by a single stroke.

"I guess that's something people know me for," Tewell said when asked about his driving accuracy. "It's something I never think about." His only missed fairway was on the seventh hole on Friday, a slight hook into the light rough, "no big deal," as Tewell put it. "My visualization and my ability to look at the target is so good with the driver right now," he said. "Sometimes my caddie wants me to putt with the driver, too."

He putted fine with the putter, shooting 69 and 66 in the opening rounds before his final-round 70. In the process, Tewell hit 47 out of 50 greens in regulation. "That's my golf game," he said. "I try not to make a lot of mistakes, and I don't make a lot of mistakes."

It was hard to pick the best drive he hit all week, but the best putt was never in question. On the 13th hole on Sunday, trailing Stewart Ginn by a shot, Tewell rolled a 10-footer for birdie into the center of the hole. Ginn then missed from eight feet to save par. Suddenly the tide had turned and Tewell went from trailing by one to holding a one-shot lead.

On the next tee box, Tewell put an exclamation point on his day by hitting his shot to the par-three 14th within a foot of the hole. The tap-in birdie gave him a two-shot lead. Wadkins, who charged with four birdies including one on the 18th to shoot 66, pulled to within a shot, but no one got closer. Tewell hit fairways and greens from the 15th through 18th and made the victory look routine.

"I knew what I had to do to beat him," said Ginn, who closed with 72 for a 208 total and a share of third with Bob Gilder. "I went for it. I didn't back off. If he makes birdies, he makes birdies. You've got to golf your own golf ball."

Tewell golfed his golf ball perfectly in this one. "I felt some butterflies in my stomach coming down the stretch," the winner said. "But my caddie told me that butterflies fly in formation, so I guess it worked out okay."

The Countrywide Tradition—$2,000,000
Winner: Jim Thorpe

Jim Thorpe thought he probably had enjoyed the good life too much to be considered a serious contender for golf's major titles. The potential Thorpe had shown in his 30s had given way to age, and Thorpe viewed his playoff with John Jacobs at The Countrywide Tradition in Superstition Mountain, Arizona, the first senior major of the year, as a lifetime second chance.

"Just wonderful," Thorpe said after closing with three straight rounds of 70 for a 277 total, then rolling in a six-footer for birdie on the first extra hole to beat Jacobs. "I felt John or I or anyone could have taken control of the tournament, but we couldn't do it. But you know what? I think it's great for golf when it's not a runaway."

Jacobs, another self-described good-timer who played 25 years in Asia and "knew every bartender from Saigon to Shanghai," held a one-shot lead going into the final round, but struggled with his driver. He hit only five fairways on Sunday, but scrambled for pars every time he got in trouble. He did the same thing on the par-five finishing hole when, leading by one, he hooked his tee shot into a horrible sidehill lie. He contemplated hitting his second shot left-handed before settling on a chop-punch with a wedge. The ball squirted across the fairway and into the right rough. From there Jacobs hacked a pitching wedge on the green, then drained a 15-footer for par and 71, punching the air with his big fist when the ball disappeared.

"It was one of the best pars of my career," Jacobs said. But it wasn't quite good enough. "I wasn't thinking about winning the tournament. I was thinking that I was not going to let this hole beat me." Thorpe hit his third shot from 120 yards to three feet and made the short birdie putt to take the tournament to extra holes.

Back on the 18th both players laid up with their second shots, but Thorpe missed the fairway. He had a delicate third shot from 65 yards, which he hit to six feet. Jacobs found the fairway in the playoff and had a four-footer for birdie. But when Thorpe made his birdie putt, Jacobs hit his putt too firmly and the ball never took the break.

"Believe me," Jacobs said, "it wasn't because I was nervous. It just didn't go in. If I was nervous, I wouldn't have made the other one on the last hole. Look, we had fun out there. That's what this tour should be about."

Jacobs' putt wasn't the only missed opportunity on the 18th. Bruce Summerhays shot 68 on Sunday, but missed a five-footer on the 72nd hole that would have allowed him to join the playoff. Summerhays tied for third with Bob Gilder at 278.

Bruno's Memorial Classic—$1,400,000
Winner: Sammy Rachels

As a former club professional in the Dixie Section of the PGA and a five-time winner of that section's championship, Sammy Rachels felt right at home in Birmingham, Alabama. He was equally comfortable with the 12-hole stretch that started on the 13th hole in Saturday's second round and ended on the sixth hole of Sunday's finale, which Rachels played in 10 under par. That was good enough to propel Rachels to the title at the Bruno's Memorial Classic.

This one was a lot more lucrative than the club pro tournaments Rachels won while selling sweaters and booking tee times at Defuniak Springs Country Club. Rachels beat another former club pro, Dana Quigley, on the second hole of a playoff to take home the $210,000 first-place check, which Rachels' wife, Pia, took off his hands. "It's our 35th wedding anniversary," Rachels said. "She asked for this, and it was special to be able to do it for her."

After an opening round of 70, Rachels went on a birdie barrage, making four birdies in the last six holes of Saturday's round and four on the first six holes Sunday. That gave him a comfortable three-shot cushion. He parred the final eight holes of regulation — a stretch that allowed Quigley, who trailed by one at the start of the final round, to catch up with birdies on his final three holes.

"I didn't have to deal with any adversity out there," Rachels said. "I don't know what I would have done if I had. There was nothing for me to think about other than keeping things going and don't mess up. I didn't even know about Dana until I was on the 17th hole. I looked over there (at the leaderboard) and said, 'Where'd he come from?'"

Quigley shot 66 on Sunday to Rachels' 67. Both signed for 17-under-par 201 totals before marching back to the 18th tee for the playoff.

Rachels knew that pars wouldn't get it done in the playoff. Both players reached the par-five 18th in two shots, but Rachels had the best chance. His 25-foot eagle putt stopped one revolution short of going in. He tapped in and watched as Quigley made a three-footer.

At the 17th, Rachels won when his six iron to the par-three stopped 10 feet from the hole. Quigley had a 30-footer for birdie that never had a chance. When Rachels' birdie putt (his second of the playoff and sixth of the day) found the hole, the winner punched the sky and waved to the fans who were shouting.

Larry Nelson finished alone in third place after 70 and a 202 total, while Hale Irwin continued his streak of top-five finishes with a 203 total and fourth place. Neither had a chance of joining the playoff, and that suited the winner just fine. "It just doesn't get any better than this," Rachels said as he hugged Pia and presented her with his anniversary gift.

TD Waterhouse Championship—$1,600,000
Winner: Bruce Lietzke

It's not often that a player wakes up at 2:00 a.m. on a Sunday knowing he's going to win a golf tournament, but that's what happened to Bruce Lietzke in Kansas City, Missouri. On two occasions in the wee hours of Sunday morning, Lietzke, who normally has no trouble sleeping on a lead, awoke to the sound of thunder. The final blast, which jarred the hotel room, made Lietzke think he would win the TD Waterhouse Championship without ever taking a swing.

Rain cancelled the final round of the tournament, and Lietzke, who pulled two shots ahead of Larry Nelson by shooting an eight-under-par 64 on Saturday for a 133 total, was declared the winner.

"It's not quite the kind of victory you want to celebrate," Lietzke said. "You want to putt out on 18, hug your wife, kiss your mom, shake hands with your caddie and grab the trophy. This is different." The trophy presentation was made in a small room in the basement of the clubhouse as rain continued to pelt the already soaked Tiffany Greens Golf Club.

It might not have been the ceremony he had in mind or the kind of victory Lietzke wanted to celebrate, but it was one he could chalk up to thinking ahead. After trailing Ed Dougherty, John Schroeder and Bob Eastwood by one shot on Friday, Lietzke spent a few extra minutes watching the weather channel. "I had seen what the forecast was for the weekend," he said. "I can remember making a mental note to play well on Saturday."

He did just that, birdieing three of his first five holes. He birdied the ninth to go out in 32. On the second nine his putter really got hot, and he made four more birdies, including a 30-footer on the 18th to shoot 64 and take his two-stroke lead back to the hotel.

"The bad news is I don't have a chance to catch Bruce," Nelson said. "The good news is, nobody else has a chance to catch me."

Instinet Classic—$1,500,000
Winner: Isao Aoki

One day after virtually guaranteeing that either he or Jim Thorpe would win the Instinet Classic, John Jacobs tried to put a philosophic spin on things. "Some days you putt well, and some days you putt bad," Jacobs said. "If we putted good all the time, we would always win. Today, I putted terrible."

Isao Aoki, on the other hand, putted well and won, coming from two strokes back on the final day to shoot 65 and run away with the title by four in Princeton, New Jersey. "I knew that if I putted well I would have a chance," Aoki said, playing on the same theme as Jacobs. "I have been putting better the last couple of weeks, especially this week."

Thorpe, who shot 65 and 69 the first two days, led Jacobs by one stroke with Aoki and Allen Doyle two back going into Sunday. That lead remained intact when everyone in contention birdied the first hole. Thorpe's game fell apart after that. On the fourth hole he looked like an 18-handicapper, sculling a wedge through the green for a bogey. He followed that up with bogeys at the sixth, ninth, 14th and 18th, limping in with 75 for a 209 total and a tie for eighth.

Aoki pulled ahead with birdies at the third and fourth, but Jacobs, who hit the par-five third in two shots, stayed close. He missed his eagle opportunity, but birdied the third and the sixth to gain a temporary share of the lead. Then Jacobs three-putted the seventh to fall out of the lead, and three-putted again at the par-four 10th to fall two back.

The 10th proved to be the pivotal hole and an indicator of how everyone's day would go. Moments before Jacobs three-putted, Aoki pulled his tee shot into a tree, and the ball fell 198 yards from the green. His second shot hit another tree, and the Japanese star had 96 yards left to the hole on the par-four. He hit his third shot to three feet and made the putt for par. From there he birdied the 12th, 13th, 16th and 17th to pull away.

Jacobs birdied the 18th to shoot 70 and take second place at 205, but he knew it was over after the 10th. "Isao's whole round turned around after that hole," he said.

"It was a very important hole," Aoki said after signing for a 201 total and collecting his $225,000 winner's check, his first in almost four years. "Every time I participate in a tournament my aim is to win, but I didn't expect this to happen. I have been swinging the club well and making good shots, but my problem was my putting. This week my putting was very good."

Farmers Charity Classic—$1,500,000
Winner: Jay Sigel

One rotator cuff operation is enough to make a golfer in his 50s contemplate hanging up his cleats. Two shoulder surgeries in two years at age 56 and 57 are a surefire prescription for forced retirement. But Jay Sigel, age 58, never gave up. He came to the professional game late, turning pro at age 50 after winning two U.S. Amateur titles, and he felt certain that he still had what it took.

He proved that point in Ada, Michigan, when he shot a final-round 67 for a 13-under-par 203 total and a two-stroke victory in the Farmers Charity Classic. "Everything fell into place," Sigel said. "This has to be my best victory as senior."

His final round included two eagles, the first coming when he holed a flop shot from 20 yards at the par-five seventh, and the second coming when he overpowered the 518-yard, par-five 17th with a driver and five iron. In between he made a couple of crucial 15-footers, first at the 12th to save par, then at the 14th for birdie to pull away from Morris Hatalsky.

Sigel entered the final round tied for the lead with Rodger Davis, who shot 68-67 and was looking for his first win as a senior. But Davis fell short, even though he had a brief look at the lead after Sigel bogeyed the third. "He made one bogey at the third hole and then wouldn't allow another mistake," Davis said of Sigel's final round. The Australian finished with 70 and took third at 206, one shot more than Hatalsky, who birdied the final three holes to shoot 68.

Sigel seemed overwhelmed by the victory and what it meant at this stage in his career. "It's nice to come through," he said. "It's been so long. Winning is what we are here for, and dealing with what you've got at the moment is what has always been intriguing to me."

NFL Golf Classic—$1,300,000
Winner: James Mason

The tiny town of Dillard, Georgia, would have to get through the summer with one less teaching pro, but none of the citizens seemed to mind. They were too busy spreading the good news, sticking their heads in the door of the local Waffle House and asking, "Did you hear about James Mason?"

It was not the famous British actor that had the town of Dillard in such a flutter, but a local teaching pro, a pudgy 51-year-old with glasses and a fondness for knickers that made him look like an early '80s version of Billy

Casper. Mason had done what only seven others before him had been able to accomplish: He qualified for a Senior PGA Tour event on Monday (or in this case Tuesday, since Monday was Memorial Day) and walked away the winner on Sunday in the NFL Golf Classic in Clifton, New Jersey.

"It hasn't totally sunk in yet," Mason said after making an unlikely par on the last hole to shoot 69 and win by two over Morris Hatalsky, Bruce Fleisher and Dave Eichelberger. "The only thing I know for sure is that I don't have to Monday qualify anymore."

The victory carried a one-year exemption on the senior tour, an exemption that had Mason's wife, Suzie, in tears. "We were spending a lot of money," Mason said. "I kept saying we would scrape and scrape whatever we could, because I knew I had the game. To do this is just phenomenal."

Mason led after the first day when he shot a bogey-free 65 to take a one-shot edge over Eichelberger. He showed signs of inexperience and pressure on Saturday, though, shooting 73 to fall two shots behind Jay Sigel and John Bland. Sigel was looking for his second straight win after coming back from shoulder surgery, and Bland was trying to break a six-year winless streak.

Sigel and Bland played like local teaching pros on Sunday and Mason looked like the veteran. Sigel never got going and finished with 74 for a 210 total and a share of fifth place. Bland did even worse, shooting 77 for a 213 total and a tie for 10th.

Mason made an eagle from the fairway on the par-four second when he holed a wedge shot from 104 yards, then made a birdie on the sixth when he holed a bunker shot. "Playing six holes and holing one from the fairway and another out of the bunker, you may go the whole year and never do that," Mason said. "I guess maybe Lady Luck was with me all the way around."

He built a three-shot lead with three holes to play, but gave one back when he missed the fairway and bogeyed the 16th. Then he missed the green at the par-three 17th and had to make a five-footer to save par.

On the par-five 18th, Mason pushed his tee shot into the trees. Ignoring the advice of his local caddie, who told him to punch it back in play, Mason chose to hook a five iron into the 10th fairway and hope he had a shot at the green. From there he hit an eight iron over water and onto the green, where he two-putted for the two-shot victory. "I felt if I could get it airborne I would be okay," he said.

Mason looked like a man who had just won the lottery. "You don't know how hard it is to Monday qualify," he said. "I can't describe it. Hopefully my wife and I will have some time to talk about it and reflect about it. We have arrived."

Senior PGA Championship—$2,000,000
Winner: Fuzzy Zoeller

Larry Nelson summed up the consensus of the over-50 crowd when he said of Firestone Country Club's South Course in Akron, Ohio, "This place will make you look like a fool."

It was no small irony that one of the game's breeziest clowns, a man whose name is both an acronym and an appropriate moniker, would be the only man under par for the four days of the Senior PGA Championship. Fuzzy Zoeller whistled and sang songs to himself as he strolled around the soggy Firestone layout in 68 on Sunday to finish with a two-under-par 278 total and a two-stroke victory over third-round leader Bobby Wadkins and three-time past champion Hale Irwin.

Zoeller did it by making the fewest mistakes during a week when big numbers were the rule. The field averaged 74.26 for the week, the second highest average of the year and the highest by far for a week where weather was not a factor. How tough was it? According to Gary McCord, who finished with 290, "I missed one fairway yesterday and three fairways today, and I shot seven over on those four holes. That's pretty much the story."

It's also what made Zoeller's performance so outstanding. Trailing Wadkins by a shot going into the final round, Zoeller made one recovery after another, getting up and down for pars on the 13th, 14th and 17th holes to complete his two-under-par performance and capture his first title as a senior. None was more impressive than his par save at the 13th where Zoeller drove into shin-high rough, hacked the ball back into deeper rough after hitting a tree, then hit a wedge shot to 10 feet and made the putt for par.

"It seemed like every time I was out today, my putter saved me," Zoeller said. "The putts at 13 and 14 were crucial. Those are the things that happen when you win tournaments."

Wadkins, who closed with 71, agreed with Zoeller's assessment. "Fuzzy is a competitor," he said. "I was seeing somebody do his job today. He hit a bad tee shot at the 13th, then a bad second shot. He caught a break when it hit the tree and came down in the light rough. Then he got up and down for par. Not having won for a while, if he makes double bogey there, it's a different ball game."

It has been almost 16 years since Zoeller last won a tournament, a fact he pretended not to know. "Has it been that long really?" he said, then laughed. "It's been 16 years, but in my mind I knew I still had it. I could do it."

After the par saves at the 13th and 14th, Zoeller said he fought his only bout with nerves on the par-three 15th when he hit a three iron into the center of the green and two-putted for par. "The only time I was nervous was on 15," he said. "After I hit the putt there, I knew I was fine. I knew that was a very, very big putt. That made it a heck of a lot easier for me the rest of the way."

It didn't seem easier. His tee shot at the 17th went low and left and nestled into the high rough. He then hit a low screamer left of the green, chipped to eight feet and made another par-saving putt. That allowed him to cruise up the 18th with a two-shot lead. He hit the final fairway and green and two-putted for a comfortable win.

"What's pressure?" Zoeller asked when it was over. "It's just a word in the dictionary. Yes, I would have loved to have won the first week or two I was out here, but it didn't happen. That's the difference between a professional and an amateur golfer. The professional has the patience to wait."

BellSouth Senior Classic at Opryland—$1,600,000
Winner: Gil Morgan

There's an old country song that extols the virtues of comfortable surroundings. Gil Morgan isn't much of a country crooner, but he could certainly relate to the lyrics after shooting a five-under-par 67 on Sunday at Opryland in Nashville, Tennessee, for a three-stroke victory at the BellSouth Senior Classic. Morgan had won this event once before, and he had never finished out of the top five.

"Obviously this has been a great golf course for me," Morgan said. "I always seem to play well here. It sets up well for my shot."

Trailing Jay Sigel by a stroke going into the final round, Morgan got off to a fast start. He birdied the first hole to pull into a tie for the lead, then pulled away after Sigel three-putted for bogey at the second. Bruce Fleisher and Morris Hatalsky made a run when Morgan three-putted for bogey at the fifth, but he quickly regained the lead with an eagle at the par-five sixth. He birdied the 10th to retain the lead, then extended it with a short birdie at the 14th. Another bogey at the 15th gave Fleisher a glimmer of hope, but Morgan slammed the door with birdies at the 16th and 17th.

The closing 67 gave Morgan a 14-under-par 202 total and a comfortable winning margin of three strokes over Fleisher, Mike McCullough and Dana Quigley. Hatalsky and Leonard Thompson finished tied for fifth at 206, while Sigel finished with 76 for a 210 total.

"That's unbelievable," Morgan said. "I thought surely one of those guys would take charge out there and come on up to 12 or 13 under at least, but nobody did."

Greater Baltimore Classic—$1,450,000
Winner: J.C. Snead

He never held the outright lead until the final putt fell, but when the Greater Baltimore Classic was over, 61-year-old J.C. Snead looked skyward and pointed to the clouds. This one was for his uncle. Snead, who hadn't won in over six years, could only think of Sam Snead, who died three weeks before, as he capped an improbable comeback by scrambling for par at the final hole, making a breaking 10-footer for a closing 70 and a 13-under-par 203 total. That was good enough for a one-stroke victory over John Mahaffey, Doug Tewell and Bobby Wadkins.

"It was only 10 feet, but it seemed like it was a mile," Snead said of the last putt. "The problem with having that putt is that I didn't know where to hit it. It looked like it could go either way. To be honest, I couldn't believe I made it. I've never been that good a putter."

He had to make it to avoid a playoff with Mahaffey, Tewell and Wadkins, all of whom were in the clubhouse at 204. Wadkins had started the day five shots back of second-round leader Rodger Davis, but he came soaring up the leaderboard with a closing 66 to be the first in the clubhouse at 204. Tewell was next. He fell behind early when Davis made birdies on the first four holes, and Tewell played the first four holes one over. But Tewell came back with birdies at the fifth, seventh and ninth holes, then inched closer to the lead with two more birdies at the 11th and 12th. He added two more birdies at the 16th and 17th to get to 13 under. A birdie on the par-five finishing hole would have propelled Tewell to victory, but instead he missed a short putt for par. The bogey gave him a final-round 67.

Snead shot 64 on Saturday, his best score since 1996, and entered the final round tied for the lead with Davis at 11-under-par 133. But Davis jumped out to a three-shot lead with his barrage of early birdies. Snead and Mahaffey birdied the seventh hole while Davis bogeyed, then Snead knotted things at the top again when he made a birdie at the 12th.

The two were tied when they got to the 18th, but Davis hit his tee shot out of bounds right, and made a double bogey for his 72. All Snead needed was a par to win. He laid up with his second shot, but hit his wedge approach long and into the back bunker. After blasting out to 10 feet, he made the dramatic and, in his words, "unlikely" putt to win. "I just tried to play it inside right," Snead said. "It was absolutely the right speed for that putt. Any harder and it probably would have lipped out."

When it was over, Snead invoked the memory of his late uncle. "I thought about it this week," Snead said. "I thought that it would be nice if I won for Sam."

U.S. Senior Open—$2,500,000
Winner: Don Pooley

This one was worth watching, which was extraordinary, given how dreary the Senior PGA Tour television ratings had been throughout most of the year. Then the USGA stepped in and showed the tour how things should be done. The only thing, it seems, you need to get people interested in senior golf is a final U.S. Senior Open round featuring an everyman grinder against a Hall of Famer, a six-birdie, five-shot comeback, five playoff holes and a knee-knocking, 10-foot birdie putt to finally settle things. Mix all that together with a Caves Valley Golf Club in Owings Mills, Maryland, that had every television viewer saying "Wow," and the result was the best senior golf tournament in more than a decade.

The champion was Don Pooley, a journeyman professional with two regular tour victories (the last coming in the 1987 Memorial), an on-again, off-again bad back, big broad shoulders and a face that bore a resemblance to Western movie legend Randolph Scott.

The challenger, whose six back-nine birdies captivated the golf fans, was eight-time major champion Tom Watson.

Other players included Tom Kite, who finished at 277, and Ed Dougherty, who finished fourth at 278, but this was match play from the 10th hole onwards, with Pooley and Watson hitting one great shot after another, neither man backing down or showing the slightest hint of succumbing to the pressure.

Pooley closed regulation with the kind of play that's supposed to win U.S. Opens. He made 14 straight pars after the fifth hole for a final round of 70 and a 10-under-par 274 total. Watson put together one of the rounds that made him the No. 1 player in the world in the late 1970s and early 1980s. He reeled off six birdies in eight holes to reach 13 under par and gain a share of the lead with three holes left. Then Watson bogeyed the 16th after an errant tee shot, but came back with a birdie at the 17th.

He made a great up-and-down par on the final hole for 67, but had to watch as Pooley stood over a birdie putt that would have won in regulation. When Pooley missed the birdie putt on the 72nd hole, the advantage appeared to be in Watson's favor. With a three-hole aggregate score playoff (modeled after the British Open format and adopted by the USGA for its senior championship in 1999), Watson clearly held the hot hand.

Both players recovered from poor tee shots to par the 16th. Then Pooley hit the shot of the tournament on the 17th. After hitting his approach in a greenside bunker on the short side of the hole, Pooley hit a terrific blast to two feet to salvage par. Watson also parred the 17th, then the 18th. Once again Watson had to watch as Pooley stood over a birdie putt that would end the tournament. This one was from six feet, and after Pooley backed away from the putt twice, he missed it right.

"It wasn't that I was nervous," Pooley said, "My thoughts weren't where I wanted them. My mind was going places it shouldn't have been going."

With both players tied after the three extra holes, the format went to sudden death. On the 77th hole Pooley broke his string of 17 straight pars with a 10-foot birdie to win.

"To win the U.S. Senior Open as my first senior event, it doesn't get any better than that," Pooley said. "I think this is as good as it gets this side of heaven. I've been in contention in the majors on the regular tour a few times, and I didn't handle it as well as I did today. This is as good as I've played under this kind of pressure. It was a great thrill playing with Tom Watson, whom I have great admiration for. He usually beats me."

Watson, who beat Jack Nicklaus in down-to-the-wire major championship duels in both the U.S. and British Opens, didn't like the view from the losing end. "I feel like Lighthouse Harry Cooper," Watson said. "I feel like Jug McSpaden to Byron Nelson. I feel like Phil Mickelson to Tiger Woods. It's not a lot of fun to finish second."

But it's a heck of a lot of fun to win, especially when it's your first time out. "All week I thought I could win the tournament," Pooley said. "I was just full of positive thoughts."

AT&T Canada Senior Open—$1,600,000
Winner: Tom Jenkins

Sometimes a little rest and relaxation is just what the doctor ordered, especially when you're over 50. That's what 54-year-old Tom Jenkins discovered in LaSalle, Ontario, after spending much of the early part of the week in bed trying to fight off a cold before playing in the AT&T Canada Senior Open. The strategy worked. Jenkins shot a career-low, 18-under-par 195 to win by three shots over Walter Morgan, Bruce Lietzke and Morris Hatalsky.

"Practice is obviously overrated," Jenkins said of birdieing five of the final nine holes for a closing 64. "I didn't hit a ball until the pro-am on Thursday. I guess that's what my body needed. When I came out Friday my mind was fresh, my timing was back and my putter felt great."

He needed all of the above on a week when pars were losing ground fast.

Jenkins shot a career-low 63 on Friday and a respectable 68 on Saturday, but only held a share of the lead with Hatalsky, who shot 67 and 64. Lietzke was one stroke back after shooting 62 on Saturday, and Walter Morgan, who became the youngest player in Senior PGA Tour history to break his age, shot a Tour-record-tying 60 to climb to within two strokes of the lead. Morgan missed an 18-footer to shoot 59, but there was some controversy after video evidence suggested that he whiffed a tap-in putt at the 17th after his birdie effort stopped one revolution short. Morgan insisted that he had not intended to strike the ball and it was not a stroke. Officials took Morgan at his word.

Sunday was another birdie-fest, led by Lietzke, who made three birdies in the first eight holes then took the lead with a 10-foot birdie putt at the ninth. He extended that lead to two shots with an eagle at the par-five 10th.

Jenkins birdied the 10th to remain within striking distance, but had to play catch-up to his former teammate from the University of Houston. He did just that with three consecutive birdies to regain a one-shot lead. Then Jenkins hit the putt that he claims was the key to the tournament, a downhill 15-footer for par on the 14th he poured into the center of the hole.

"That's probably what won the tournament for me right there," Jenkins said. "You're trying to keep the wheels from coming off. It was a tricky little downhill putt. Once you get things rolling you don't want to give one back. That can be a sick feeling."

Lietzke bogeyed the 15th, which extended Jenkins' lead. Jenkins finished with 64 for his 195 total, and at 198 were Lietzke (66), Morgan (65) and Hatalsky (67). "My downfall really was not making birdies after the 10th hole," Lietzke said. "It certainly wasn't because my mindset changed."

Jenkins' mindset certainly changed after the win. "I'll have to adopt Canada after this," he said. "In my career I haven't won that much, so every win is breathtaking and exciting. It's a great feeling to accomplish what you set out to do."

Ford Senior Players Championship—$2,500,000
Winner: Stewart Ginn

Question: What happens when a native Australian who lives in Kuala Lumpur, Malaysia, and who bears a resemblance to Steven Spielberg shoots 66 in Dearborn, Michigan? Answer: Stewart Ginn wins his first U.S. tournament at the Senior PGA Tour's final major event — the Ford Senior Players Championship.

It was the 13th time a senior player made his first victory a major title, and the third time it happened in 2002. (Don Pooley won at the U.S. Senior Open and Fuzzy Zoeller won at the Senior PGA Championship.)

The newly crowned champion skipped the press conference in order to catch a trans-Pacific flight back home. "I've got 14 hours to Taipei and then another four or five hours through to Kuala Lumpur," Ginn said as he hurriedly changed his shoes after coming from four strokes back to beat Mike McCullough, Hubert Green and Jim Thorpe by a single shot.

Ginn's 14-under-par 274 total was marked by opening and closing 66s and two rounds of 72 and 70 in the middle. But none of that was on Ginn's mind late Sunday afternoon. "All I want to do is get home and spend time with my wife," he said. "And give the kids a ring and say 'Hi.'"

Ginn was four strokes behind McCullough and three behind Green when the day began, but he made up ground quickly with four consecutive birdies starting at the 10th. That moved him to 14 under par, which is where he stayed thanks to a great par-saving putt at the 16th after hitting his tee shot in the trees and his approach into a greenside bunker. That par save gave him the confidence he needed to add one more birdie at the 17th from 12 feet. "When I holed at No. 17 and made up-and-down at 16, I thought this was my week," he said.

Ginn missed the green again at the 18th. This time he failed to save par, but it didn't matter. He held a two-shot lead, so the final bogey only shortened his margin of victory. "All we could do was hope he blew up," Green said after posting 70 for a share of second place at 275. "He shouldn't worry about bogeying 18. I won two majors with bogeys on 18 with two-shot leads."

Ginn's only worry seemed to be making his flight back home. "To win here for the first time gives me a lot of satisfaction," he said. "I'm not a star, or whatever. I don't profess to be. I'm just happy to play the game and enjoy what I do. I know I can play; I know I can win. I'm just happy to be able to finally win one."

SBC Senior Open—$1,450,000
Winner: Bob Gilder

Even Bob Gilder didn't like his chances at the end of regulation. After a course-record 63 on Saturday at the Harborside International Golf Club in Chicago gave Gilder a three-shot lead at the SBC Senior Open, he saw that lead slip away as Hale Irwin came charging in with a final-round 66 to match Gilder's 12-under-par 204 total and force a playoff.

"It's hard to follow those kinds of scores," Gilder said of teeing off on Sunday after shooting 63 on Saturday. "You go out and think, 'Well, I birdied this hole yesterday and now I'm doing worse.' But you can't think that way. I'd been coming over the ball a bit and adjusted my set-up on the range. That's something that's tough to do when you're playing."

Gilder closed with 71 to finish regulation tied with Irwin, who had the hot hand after seven birdies on Sunday. Bruce Fleisher also had a seven-birdie 66 on Sunday to finish third at 206, one clear of Rodger Davis but two more than he needed to join the playoff.

On his way back to the par-five 18th for the playoff, Gilder knew he was at a disadvantage. He hadn't birdied the final hole in regulation (Irwin had), and he was struggling with the new set-up. Irwin had already won three times in 2002. Gilder needed something special to happen to have any chance at his first victory of the year.

He never expected what came next. Both players pushed their tee shots into the same fairway bunker on the first playoff hole. Both hit second shots right. Irwin's ball hit the cart path before bounding up a hill and landing in waist-high rough. Gilder's ball hit the cart path as well, but he caught a break. His ball steered clear of the deepest rough.

Irwin was the first to play his third shot, which he almost whiffed. Grass stuck to the shaft of his club and he almost fell down as he whacked at the ball. Then, in what appeared to be a mild fit of temper, Irwin hurried his fourth shot from the deep stuff. The ball bounded out of the rough, but caught the cart path again, bounced across the fairway and landed in a lake. After a drop, Irwin played his sixth shot onto the green and had a 12-footer for double bogey.

Gilder could finally relax. He played his third shot safely into the center of the green and two-putted for par and the win.

"I felt bad for Hale, but I also felt good," Gilder said. "I hate to see that happen to someone, no matter who it is, because you wouldn't want it to happen to you."

FleetBoston Classic—$1,500,000
Winner: Bob Gilder

For the second week in a row Bob Gilder found himself a playoff, and for the second week in a row he found himself saying, "Anything can happen. That's what is great about this game."

The previous week Gilder was a fortunate recipient of some sloppy play and a bad bounce off the cart path by Hale Irwin, who had charged from behind to catch Gilder at the end of regulation. Irwin then chopped it around before losing to Gilder's par on the first extra hole. This time, in the Fleet-Boston Classic in Concord, Massachusetts, Gilder made a blunder to make the playoff possible, then rallied on the third extra hole to beat John Mahaffey.

Rounds of 66 and 67 gave Gilder a one-shot edge over Jim Thorpe going into the final round, a lead he maintained throughout most of the day. When Gilder hit a seven iron to 12 feet on the 170-yard, par-three 17th and drained the putt for birdie to get to 14 under par, he thought it was over. At that point his lead was one shot over Thorpe (who was playing in the group with Gilder) and Mahaffey (who finished two groups ahead with 65 for a 13-under-par 203 total). The par-five 18th was the third easiest hole on the course. Playing without a single bogey all week, Gilder knew he was likely to birdie the last hole.

"I figured one, maybe both of them, would birdie," Mahaffey said.

Gilder drove in the left rough and laid up short of the green. He then hit a nine iron from 132 yards through the green and into the high rough. From there he chipped out long and missed his par putt, finishing with 70 for a 203 total.

Thorpe hit his third shot to three feet. All he needed to do was make the short one for a birdie to win. Instead, he hit the putt four feet past the hole and missed the par putt coming back. That bogey left Thorpe with a final round of 70 and in a tie for third with Dave Eichelberger at 204.

"The putt just exploded," Thorpe said. "I guess that's what you call choking."

"I thought I had it won," Gilder said. "Then I thought Jimmy was going to win it. I really didn't expect him to miss that putt."

Gilder got two more chances at the 18th. The first time through with Mahaffey, both players made par. They both parred the 17th as well, which took them to a third extra hole. This time, Gilder hit driver and four wood to the front edge of the green and chipped to eight inches for a tap-in birdie. Mahaffey couldn't get close with his second shot, and his third shot stopped 30 feet from the hole. "I don't have a club for that shot," Mahaffey said. "I guess I'm getting too old."

Lightpath Long Island Classic—$1,700,000
Winner: Hubert Green

It was as even a match-up as you could get in the Lightpath Long Island Classic in Jerico, New York. Hubert Green and Hale Irwin entered the final round tied for the lead at 131. Green shot 67-64 the first two days; Irwin shot 64-67. They both shot 68 on Sunday to finish regulation tied at 14-under-par 199. Then they tied the next six playoff holes before Green finally ended the day with a long birdie putt on the par-three 18th.

"We were out here a long time," Green said. "I knew we would finish first and second, or second and first as we were playing 18, so that's when the playoff really started."

It was the second playoff in three weeks for Irwin, and the results weren't much better this time around. At the SBC Senior Open, Irwin made up five shots on Bob Gilder with a barrage of birdies, then lost the playoff when he hit a bunker, a cart path, waist-high rough and a lake on the same hole. This time Irwin kept his ball in play, but he couldn't make the putter work for him.

On the fifth extra hole it looked as though Irwin would win when his approach landed 15 feet from the hole and Green had his second shot in the greenside bunker 60 feet away. But Green blasted his bunker shot to within two feet, and Irwin missed his birdie effort. One hole later, Green ended it with a downhill 12-footer on the 167-yard 18th. It was the fourth time the two had played the final hole and the first time either of them had made birdie.

"Hubert played very well, better than he's played in a long time," Irwin said. "That's good to see."

What wasn't good for Irwin to see was the way regulation ended. After taking the lead on the eighth hole and extending it to two shots on the back nine, Irwin watched as Green made a two-footer for birdie at the 16th to pull within a shot. Still, things favored Irwin. He held a one-shot lead with the par-five 17th and the par-three 18th ahead.

But things changed suddenly at the 17th. With a lob wedge in his hand from 60 yards away, Irwin made a rare mistake, pulling the ball into a greenside bunker and failing to get up and down. The bogey could have cost him the outright lead and could have lost it for him in regulation if Green had been able to convert his birdie from 12 feet. Green missed the putt at the 17th, but a par was good enough for a tie at 14 under par.

"That was a mental lapse," Irwin said of his poor wedge shot at the 17th. "I just didn't hit it hard enough. That was a terrible play. That's when I gave it to him. The tournament was mine when I was two up."

Green agreed. "When Hale made birdie at 15, I thought it was over," he said. "I knew I was in trouble. You're not talking about Joe Gump here."

Once regulation ended, Green liked his chances. Irwin was 0-3 in playoffs, including the debacle two weeks before. This time it became a marathon of pars. Irwin missed the green on the 18th the final time through, and his chip was long, setting up Green for the winning birdie.

"I felt like Hale was going to get up and down," Green said. "I hit it hard enough and knew the last four or five feet were straight at the hole, so I just had to wait."

3M Championship—$1,750,000
Winner: Hale Irwin

It was only a matter of time. Hale Irwin already had two victories on the year and six top-five finishes, including playoff losses in two of the previous three tournaments, when he arrived at the TPC of Twin Cities in Blaine, Minnesota, for the 3M Championship. With the way he was playing, everyone knew that Irwin was destined to win again. The only question was, when?

He answered that question in emphatic fashion, winning his third full-field title of the year at an event he has owned like few others. In seven Minnesota appearances Irwin has three wins, a second place and two thirds. He was never out of the final-round lead in this one, and at one point on Sunday he was up by as many as five strokes over second-round co-leader James Mason. Hubert Green birdied three of the last four holes to shoot 67 and close to within three of Irwin, but no one got any closer. Irwin had fired a bogey-free 68 for a 12-under-par 204 total, three better than Green and four better than Mason and Doug Tewell.

"It's nice to have Hubert's name under mine this week on the final board," Irwin said after losing to Green in a six-hole playoff the week before. "Last week I played well from tee to green but was putting terribly. This week my putting came around. I made some nice long putts, but I made all the three-, four-, five- and six-footers that I haven't been making."

Two of those six-footers came at the seventh and eighth holes, where Irwin made back-to-back birdies to pull away from Mason, who bogeyed the eighth. Another birdie at the 10th gave Irwin a three-shot lead.

"Then it's a situation where I just don't do anything stupid and make pars," he said. "I force somebody to make up three shots to catch me."

While making up shots on Irwin was possible, it wasn't probable, as most of the other players knew. "Hale's not known to be kind out here and give any strokes away," Green said. "He doesn't have a reverse in his machine."

"I just want to keep getting better," Irwin said after collecting his 35th victory as a senior. "The money and the trophies will follow, but it's trying to be the best you can be that matters. I approach each year with the idea I can do these things. I don't buy into being 57 years old and over the hill. I've never accepted anything less than my best effort, so staying motivated is not an issue."

In 20 competitive rounds in Minnesota at this event (which had been staged on two different courses with three different title sponsors), Irwin had posted 18 under-par rounds for a combined 81-under-par total. Just like his record number of senior victories, no one was close to equaling that.

"I take great pride in what I've accomplished," Irwin said. "Right now, I'm playing as well as I have in a long, long time. But all I want to think about and do is try to get better."

Uniting Fore Care Classic—$1,500,000
Winner: Morris Hatalsky

Park City, Utah, isn't a big golf town, never has been, and despite the best efforts of developers who keep putting golf courses at the bases of the ski slopes, it probably never will be. The youthful spectators, who usually ride to the annual Senior PGA Tour event on their mountain bikes, view the Uniting Fore Care Classic as a good excuse for a summer picnic. Even appearances by Tom Watson and Arnold Palmer failed to generate a great deal of enthusiasm.

So the Senior PGA Tour tried a new format, a modified-Stableford system that rewarded aggressive play and lots of birdies. They got what they hoped for, just not from the player they had expected. Morris Hatalsky, a four-time winner on the PGA Tour who quit playing in his 40s to build and run a golf course in his native North Carolina, made seven birdies in the final 18 holes for a 42-point total and a 12-point victory over Jay Sigel. Hatalsky, who played on a sponsor's exemption as a non-exempt rookie, never cracked a smile as he birdied the final hole for his final two points of the tournament.

"Considering the way the year started, this is way beyond my expectations," Hatalsky said in a bone-dry voice that never hinted at excitement. "I had no idea how this year was going to go. When I started out, it was to get prepared for Q-school. Now I'm very happy, exceedingly happy."

Hatalsky started the final round tied with John Jacobs. Both had 30 points after Jacobs put on a spectacular putting display on Saturday that led to 24 points on the day, the largest single-day point total of the tournament. The format should have benefited the long-hitting Jacobs. With five points awarded for eagles and two for birdies, Jacobs' ability to reach all four par-fives at the Park Meadows Country Club and overpower many of the par-fours should have given him the upper hand. But the format also severely penalized bogeys and higher. A bogey was minus one point and a double bogey or higher was minus three. Jacobs had five bogeys and a double on Sunday and finished alone in seventh with 28 points.

"This is about the fourth or fifth time I've played bad on Sunday here," Jacobs said. "I think there's a jinx up here or something. Sometimes you try too hard and it backfires."

Tom Watson started the final day only four points out of the lead, but he never contended. Three bogeys on the front nine had Watson moving in the wrong direction. He finished with no points on Sunday and in a tie for 10th. "It wasn't my day on the greens," Watson said. "In fact, it was pretty lousy."

It was anything but a lousy day for the winner. Hatalsky put the tournament out of reach when he made a 35-footer for birdie on the 13th, then followed it up with another lengthy birdie putt at the 15th. "I have no idea how to react," Hatalsky said afterward. "The other four times I won I really did break down and cry. There's got to be something wrong with me."

Allianz Championship—$1,850,000
Winner: Bob Gilder

It had been 20 years since Bob Gilder had three victories in a season, but that thought never entered his mind as he stood over the four-footer for par on the 54th hole of the Allianz Championship. The day had been too tough, the competition too tight for Gilder to let his mind wander in those final moments. When the final putt fell, Gilder walked away with a final-round 67, a 200 total and a one-stroke victory over second-round leader John Bland. A half hour later he remembered how long it had been since he had won three times.

"It's hard to explain, hard to believe myself even right now that I've won three times this year," Gilder said. "Somehow I've been able to focus on the job I needed to do and not what everybody else is doing."

Staying focused on his own game was tough on this Sunday in West Des Moines, Iowa. By the time the final twosome made the turn it was a two-man race. "It became like match play out there," Bland said. He started the final round with a two-shot lead after a hole-in-one on Saturday propelled him to a nine-under-par 63. But Bland couldn't keep the streak alive on Sunday. Gilder birdied the first two holes of the final round, and the two were neck-and-neck for the rest of the round.

"It's always difficult to get yourself back up after a round like that," Bland said. "I think if you look at it, guys who shoot 63, 62, 61 very seldom come back with 70 or better the next round. It takes a lot out of you."

Bland made two birdies of his own on the eighth and 10th to claw back ahead, but Gilder birdied the 11th and 13th to take a one-shot lead. Bland then made a six-footer for birdie at the 15th to knot things at the top again. Both players missed birdies at the 16th before Bland, who was still muttering to himself about his putting as he played the 17th, hit a wayward five iron from the fairway that proved to be the difference in the tournament. "I pushed it right and the ball never came back," Bland said.

He chipped long and two-putted for bogey while Gilder hit the green with his second shot and two-putted from 18 feet for par.

Bland never gave up. Both players drove in the rough on the 18th and both missed the green. Bland chipped to six feet and made his par putt, putting the pressure on Gilder, who had chipped to four feet and needed the final putt to win. "I thought, let's just take it," Gilder said.

He did just that, canning the four-footer for the win.

Kroger Senior Classic—$1,500,000
Winner: Bob Gilder

Bob Gilder has a lot of explaining to do to his friends and family. "They've been on me lately asking, 'Where have you been? You've never been this good before,'" Gilder said after winning his fourth title of the year, his fourth in seven weeks and his second in a row at the Kroger Senior Classic in Maineville, Ohio. "I might have played this good over a period of time, but I've never had this much success."

None of the wins was easy. Two of his previous three victories came in playoffs, one against Hale Irwin, the all-time winningest player on the Senior PGA Tour, and the third was a neck-and-neck duel to the finish with John Bland, which had come just seven days prior to his final-round showdown at the TPC at River's Bend.

This time the victim was Tom Jenkins, who started the final round seven shots behind Gilder (who led after 36 holes with scores of 66 and 65). Jenkins shot a course-record 10-under-par 62 on Sunday, the best round of his career, to take the lead at 16-under-par 200. Gilder, playing four groups behind Jenkins, made a four-footer for birdie at the 17th to regain a share of the lead. When Gilder parred the 18th for 69 and 200, the two went back to the 18th for a playoff.

Jenkins had an opportunity to end things on the first extra hole, but his 20-footer for birdie stopped one revolution short. He hit his approach to the second extra hole (the par-four 10th) 12 feet behind the hole. Gilder, after making another knee-knocking three-footer for par on the first extra hole, hit a pitching wedge to the 10th from 106 yards. His ball stopped a foot away. Jenkins' birdie effort slid below the hole, and Gilder tapped in for the victory.

"When you shoot 62 you can't do much better," Jenkins said. "It's disappointing to get close and not win, but if you told me this morning I'd finish second and lose in a playoff, I'd have taken it. This will keep me coming back with more determination."

Gilder felt as though he couldn't do much better either. "Life is pretty good right now," the winner said. "I'm in a daze. I am in a zone. I'm worn out mentally, but I'm fortunate I'm hitting it as good as ever. I'm thinking down the middle and at the flagstick, and it's a wonderful feeling to have."

RJR Championship—$1,600,000
Winner: Bruce Fleisher

When Bruce Fleisher finally broke out of his 36-week winless slump, he did it in style. Even though the Clemmons, North Carolina, weather was dreary and the Senior PGA Tour's leading money winner and all-time winningest player, Hale Irwin, was in hot pursuit, Fleisher hit 16 of 18 greens on Sunday for a closing round of 67 and a Senior PGA Tour 54-hole scoring record of 19-under-par 191. He also equaled the all-time 18-hole record on Friday when he shot 10-under-par 60, a score that Irwin thought put this one away early.

"I though the 60 could win the tournament if he played respectably the last two days," Irwin said. "He did that."

Irwin matched Fleisher birdie for birdie in the final two rounds, but trailed by five when the final putt fell. His 196 left him alone in second, two ahead of Don Pooley and five clear of Larry Nelson, Mike McCullough and Ed Dougherty.

It only got close for a few moments in the final round. Fleisher three-putted twice in the opening nine holes for his first two bogeys on the week, and Irwin, after getting angry at himself for missing a short putt at the fourth, reeled off three straight birdies at the seventh, eighth and ninth to pull to within three.

"You never stop worrying that Hale is going to come up on you, because he's going to come," Fleisher said. "He's just one of these premier athletes that defy gravity. I marvel at his game when I play with him."

But Fleisher let his worries distract him, and as he was driving to the course on Sunday morning, his wife Wendy told him so. "I was making excuses, saying I was tired," Fleisher said. "She said, 'Grow up, that's what you're out here for, to win.' I wasn't really trying to talk myself out of winning, but I was nervous, uncomfortable."

Fleisher collected himself and his game just in time on Sunday. He made a great par save from 20 yards short of the 12th green to remain three ahead, then extended the lead to five with birdie putts of 10 and six feet on the 13th and 14th. That's the way things stayed until the end when Fleisher two-putted for par on the 18th.

"I can smile now, but do you ever get comfortable out there?" Fleisher asked rhetorically. "Maybe with a five-shot lead on the last hole. That's about the only time. Now I'm drinking wine, boys. I've earned it."

SAS Championship—$1,700,000
Winner: Bruce Lietzke

If he had any lingering doubts about whether the Prestonwood Country Club in Cary, North Carolina, suited his consistent fade, Bruce Lietzke got his answer during the second round of the SAS Championship when he shot a course-record 63. "I'm starting to change my mind about this not being a fader's golf course," Lietzke said. "I've just got too much proof otherwise to deny that now."

The proof was in the putting on Sunday, as Lietzke, who started the final round one shot behind Andy North, made birdie putts on the seventh and eighth holes to take the lead, then held onto that lead by making a crucial eight-footer for par at the 15th after chipping from the deep rough. "That up-and-down at 15 kept my momentum going," he said.

He closed with another birdie from 11 feet at the 18th to shoot 67 in the final round for a 16-under-par 202 total and waltz in with a four-shot victory over Sammy Rachels, Gil Morgan and Tom Watson.

North, who had never led going into the final round of a senior event, made two quick bogeys, then birdied the seventh to regain a temporary share of the lead with Lietzke. Once Lietzke made his birdie on the eighth, North never saw the lead again. On the 16th, he hit his tee shot into a lake well right of the fairway and made triple bogey to finish with 76 and a 210 total.

"I was nervous teeing off, but he had to sleep on the lead," Lietzke said of North's collapse. "It's tougher to sleep on a lead, and Andy hasn't been there for a while. Tom and I were able to call upon more recent memories of tournament play and competition to help us get through days like this. It's kind of a learning curve for Andy."

Watson might have had more experience, but it didn't seem to help. "My talent today was not good enough to get the ball very close to the hole or make any long putts," Watson said. "I didn't make too many mistakes, but I was 20 or 25 feet all day. I knew Bruce was going to have to make some mistakes and he wasn't in the mistake-making mode today. He's not missing too many greens when he's swinging like he did today."

Watson's caddie, Bruce Edwards, even employed a little gamesmanship by keeping Lietzke, an avid Dallas Cowboys fan, apprised of the 44-13 loss the Cowboys suffered to the Philadelphia Eagles. "I was pretty obnoxious when the Cowboys were good," Lietzke said. "I probably got what I deserved."

Turtle Bay Championship—$1,500,000
Winner: Hale Irwin

It wasn't a planned strategy, but after it was over Hale Irwin figured the best place to end his 0-5 playoff streak was Hawaii. Irwin arrived at the Turtle Bay Resort with five victories on the Islands. He was also a three-time champion of the Turtle Bay Championship, so there was no better place for Irwin to chalk up his first playoff win.

"This is a nice one to get down for a lot of reasons," Irwin said after rolling in an eight-foot birdie putt on the first extra hole to beat Gary McCord and win his sixth Hawaiian title. "My playoff record is not exemplary. I don't know why. It just isn't."

That's the only thing non-exemplary on Irwin's record. At 57, the win was his fourth of the season, locking up the money title and assuring Irwin another Player of the Year award. Every win breaks his all-time Senior PGA Tour record for most victories. This was win number 36. He also inched closer to becoming the first senior in history to win over $3 million in a single season. The $225,000 first-place check gave Irwin a year-to-date total of $2,829,041.

"I guess you could call Hawaii a second home," he said. "It certainly is a primary home for my golf game with the successes I've had here. It's just fantastic."

Irwin and McCord were paired together all three days, and both shot 69s on Friday. Irwin edged into the lead by a single shot with 69 on Saturday to McCord's 70. Sunday was a little tougher with the winds gusting at upwards of 25 miles per hour, but both played brilliantly. Irwin birdied the first and ninth holes and made scrambling par saves on the third, fourth, 14th and 17th before lipping out an eight-foot birdie putt at the 18th that would have ended things in regulation.

McCord birdied the seventh, eighth and ninth to tie Irwin for the lead, then parred in as well. Both players finished at eight-under-par 208, as Irwin shot 70 and McCord, 69. "The front nine was okay, but then the back nine I just couldn't get the ball close to the hole," McCord said. "I was relying on 40-foot birdie putts, but the stroke was pretty good today, much better than it's been all year."

The only time the stroke failed McCord was during the playoff when he missed a 20-footer for birdie before Irwin ended things. "He doesn't make any mistakes," McCord said of Irwin. "I hadn't been there in a while, and I couldn't pressure him and couldn't go out in front of him."

Napa Valley Championship—$1,300,000
Winner: Tom Kite

His putter abandoned him in the final round, but Tom Kite played well enough tee to green to compensate for his putting lapses and capture his third title of the year at the Napa Valley Championship. Kite shot an even-par 72 on Sunday (the highest final-round for a winner all year), but his 204 total was good enough for a one-stroke victory over Bruce Fleisher and Fred Gibson.

"I putted very well the first two days, but for some reason I didn't trust my stroke today," Kite said afterwards. After consecutive rounds of 66, he went to bed Saturday night with a two-shot lead over Allen Doyle. Kite extended that lead with a birdie at the first hole, and he increased the margin to four with another birdie at the 10th. But the putter abandoned him after that. A three-putt bogey at the 13th was followed by five straight pars to finish. The big boost came at the 14th when Kite hit his approach shot in the greenside bunker, then blasted to within a foot of the hole to save par. From there he hit fairways and greens and made routine two-putts.

Meanwhile Gibson and Fleisher made impressive last-minute runs. Gibson, who started the final round seven shots back, charged to within a stroke of the lead with birdies at the third and fourth and consecutive eagles at the par-five ninth and par-five 10th. But just as quickly, Gibson fell back with two bogeys at the 11th and 12th. He recovered with a three-foot birdie putt on the 18th hole to finish with 66 for an 11-under-par 205 total, one shot away from a playoff.

"I never thought about winning," Gibson said. "I just wanted to have a good finish to end the year. I was just so relieved that I was able to play well before I went home."

Fleisher did think about winning, and he had plenty of opportunities to do just that. He made three birdies between the 13th and 16th to draw within a shot of Kite, but missed short birdie efforts on the 17th and 18th, including a six-footer on the final green that would have forced a playoff.

"I'm a little disappointed," Fleisher said after signing for 67. "I hit it close a lot but I just couldn't convert. When I got to 18, I thought I'd have to make a birdie to force him to make birdie."

Kite knew who was moving up and how he stood in relation to the rest of the field. He also knew that steady pars down the stretch would get the job done. "I was watching the leaderboard all day," he said. "The par save on 14 was big. From that point on, every shot was a quality shot."

SBC Championship—$1,450,000
Winner: Dana Quigley

Even with six Senior PGA Tour victories under his belt and one win so far in 2002, Dana Quigley still had trouble battling nerves as he stood on the 17th tee on Sunday in San Antonio with a two-shot lead in the SBC Championship. "I was choking really bad up there," Quigley admitted.

He didn't show it. Quigley had taken a one-shot lead into the final round after shooting a seven-under-par 64 on Saturday. Vicente Fernandez was in second place, and Tom Watson and Gil Morgan trailed by three. Quigley extended his lead to two shots with three birdies in the first 13 holes on Sunday, and he maintained that lead through the 16th. That's when the nerves kicked in.

Negative thoughts started creeping into his head as he stood over his second shot at the dogleg-left 17th. He had missed the fairway to the right (only the second fairway he had missed all day), and he knew that an aggressive play could prove disastrous. "I didn't want to hit it over the green and out of bounds," Quigley said. "I was just going to make my five and move on." He laid up well short of the green, pitched to 22 feet and two-putted for a bogey.

That gave Quigley a one-shot lead over Bob Gilder, who charged from six strokes back at the start of the final round with six consecutive birdies starting at the third hole. Gilder then parred the ninth before adding another birdie at the 10th. The only blemish of the day — one that proved costly — was a bogey at the par-four 12th. Gilder quickly recovered with a birdie at the 13th and another at the par-five 15th, but it was too little, too late. He finished with 64 for an 11-under-par 202, then had to watch and wait to see how Quigley handled the pressure.

After the bogey at the 17th, Quigley stood on the 198-yard par-three 18th at Oak Hills Country Club with a lot of negative thoughts going through his head. Three decades before he had needed a par on the final hole to win the Rhode Island Par-Three Championship, but he three-putted and lost by a shot. "I said to myself, 'Man, don't do that again,'" Quigley said.

He made a great swing with a four iron and the ball landed safely in the middle of the green. Quigley then rolled his 18-footer to within 10 inches of the hole, and he tapped in for a par, a closing 69, a 201 total and his second victory of the year.

"This is absolutely the high point of the season for me," he said afterward.

Gilder finished alone in second, one shot ahead of Fernandez, who shot 70 for a 203 total, and three clear of Watson, who also had 70.

"This was the kind of round you want to have on the last day," Gilder said of his closing 64. "It just wasn't working the first couple of days. I think that if I didn't bogey the 12th I'd have been in a bit better shape and I might have threatened him a little bit."

Senior Tour Championship at Gaillardia—$2,500,000
Winner: Tom Watson

No one had to be reminded of Tom Watson's past. No one needed to hear about the days as a boy when Watson shoveled snow in Kansas City in order to practice or the times he fought the wind to win five British Open titles. No one had to be told who was the best bad-weather player on the Senior PGA Tour. They could see it from the smile on Watson's face that kept getting broader as the conditions in Oklahoma City worsened.

The weather was so bad at the Senior Tour Championship that Lee Trevino donned a trench coat over his rainsuit, and the pro shop at Gaillardia Golf and Country Club sold out of ski caps. The 30-degree temperatures and chilling rain might have eliminated a lot of players from contention. "I think a lot of guys felt it was a little bit too cold," Watson said after shooting five-under-par 67 for a 274 total and a two-stroke victory over Gil Morgan. "But this is my kind of weather."

Watson proved his point throughout the week. As the weather worsened, his scores improved. On Thursday, with play suspended due to rain, he shot 74. When the cold wind blew in on Friday and Saturday, he came back with rounds of 67 and 66 to tie Morgan for the lead at 207. When the cold rain returned on Sunday, Watson held off Morgan, who shot 69, by making three birdies on the first nine and two on the second nine.

"The first round really was not a bad round of golf," Watson said of his opening 74. "I had a lot of opportunities for birdies that round which I didn't make. Even though I shot 74, I was hitting the ball well. I figured if I could just start making a few putts, I would get back in the golf tournament."

He did just that, rolling in critical putts in the final nine holes to seal the victory. With Morgan matching him birdie-for-birdie on the front nine, Watson moved into the lead when he rolled a curling 20-footer into the hole for birdie at the 12th, a putt he described as "the best shot of the day."

Then Morgan, who had hit every fairway and green in the first 12 holes, contracted a case of the pushes. His tee shots on the 14th, 15th and 16th flew well right. He recovered on the 14th and 15th, getting up and down from some awkward spots for par, but his luck ran out at the 16th. He missed the fairway, chipped out, hit a four iron to 22 feet, and missed the putt for par.

"The bogey at 16 really hurt," Morgan said. "I just didn't feel like I played as well as he did coming down the stretch, and that was the biggest difference."

It was a vindication for Watson, who finished second five times in 2002, including a playoff loss to Don Pooley at the U.S. Senior Open. "I blame some of my second-place finishes this year on my putting woes," Watson said. "But I made my share of putts this weekend. I pulled a couple of putts early today, but I had mis-read them, and the ball went right in the hole. That's when I said, 'Well, maybe today is going to be my day.' And it sure as heck was."

Putting might have been one factor, but the weather and Watson's ability to handle it proved to be the biggest difference. "The weather might have been hostile to some players, but to me it wasn't," he said. "I was very comfortable. Keep your hands from getting cold and you'll be okay. I know one thing: I probably wouldn't have been out following people around. I felt sorry for people walking out there."

Senior Slam—$600,000
Winner: Fuzzy Zoeller

Unlike the PGA Grand Slam, where Tiger Woods beat the best-ball score of the other three competitors, the Senior Slam, which pitted the four major winners from the Senior PGA Tour, was a nail-biter. Fuzzy Zoeller came out on top, shooting 71 in the second round of the two-day event at Superstition Mountain, Arizona, to edge Don Pooley by one stroke. Zoeller's six-under-par 138 total was worth $300,000, but this check didn't come easily.

An opening 67 gave Zoeller a three-shot lead over Pooley and Stewart

Ginn, but by the time the foursome made the turn, Ginn, winner of the Ford Senior Players Championship, had clawed his way into a share of the lead. Zoeller pulled back ahead with a birdie at the 10th, but he fell back with a bogey at the 11th. Ginn made two bogeys in the next three holes to fall two behind, but Pooley pulled into a share of the lead with a birdie at the 11th.

Pooley also gave a shot back when he hit his tee shot on the par-three 15th into the front bunker and failed to get up and down. Zoeller never lost the lead after that, even though Pooley had opportunities at the 17th and 18th to make birdie, but failed to convert.

"I had some opportunities and I didn't capitalize on them," Pooley said. He finished with 69 to take second, while Ginn matched Zoeller's closing 71 to finish third three shots back. Jim Thorpe, who qualified for the event by winning The Countrywide Tradition at Superstition Mountain, couldn't find the magic again. He finished last in the field of four.

But as Zoeller aptly pointed out when it was over, "We're all winners. Everybody out here won." He went on to say, "When you play against the best, it brings out the best in everybody. You've got four major winners here, so it's a win-win for everybody. It's just that somebody has to finish first."

That somebody turned out to be Zoeller. "This is a great feeling," he said. "It's a great way to end the year."

European Seniors Tour

Royal Westmoreland Barbados Open—€203,197
Winner: Peter Townsend

It was a extensive dry spell for Peter Townsend. Long a leading player in Britain and elsewhere in Europe with Walker and Ryder Cup credentials to prove it, Townsend had not won in almost a quarter century before taking the title in the Royal Westmoreland Barbados Open, the season opener on the European Seniors Tour. In fact, the 56-year-old Englishman had toiled without victory into his sixth season in the senior circuit before the breakthrough in the Caribbean in mid-March. He closed with a two-under-par 70 at Royal Westmoreland Golf Club to edge second-round leader Guillermo Encina, a first-year player from Chile, by a stroke with his 212.

Encina, trying to match the 1995 feat of John Bland by winning in his first start on the European Seniors Tour, had been in front for two days. The 50-year-old professional from Santiago opened the tournament with a four-under-par 68, staking himself to a two-shot lead over Tommy Horton, who won the inaugural at Westmoreland in 2000, and was three in front of Americans David Oakley, John Grace and Jerry Bruner, and Townsend. Encina shot 72 Saturday and retained his two-stroke margin, but it was Townsend then in the runner-up spot after his second 71 as Horton slipped to 76. Malcolm

Gregson (75-70) and Bernard Gallacher (72-73) shared third place.

Three strokes lost on two holes in the middle of the final round spoiled Encina's bid, although he had a 16-foot birdie putt that he missed on the final hole to force a playoff. Townsend, who had six birdies in shooting the 70, conceded that "all I could think about coming down the last few holes was the two-year-exemption for winning a tournament." When Encina missed the final birdie try, Townsend had his first win since the 1978 season, when he won tournaments in Morocco, Zambia and Baranquilla, and that 24-month perk.

Tobago Plantations Seniors Classic—€201,716
Winner: Steve Stull

Steve Stull did in his second start what Guillermo Encina just missed doing the week before in his first, capturing the Tobago Plantations Seniors Classic at the second and last stop of the Caribbean kickoff of the new season. In so doing, Stull became the eighth first-time winner in the last 10 senior tour events dating back into the 2001 season. Stull outplayed Scotland's John Chillas on the final nine holes, carded 69 and won the inaugural Tobago Seniors by three strokes with his 11-under-par 205.

The victory may have come just in time for Stull, who had led the qualifying for the 2002 tour by 10 strokes. "I have to admit that I needed the money," said the Richland, Washington, resident. "I've been doing this off my own back for the last three or four years and ... I wondered if my stock account would hold up."

Stull was never out of the lead. Out in 32, he shot 68 the first day and led by a shot over Chillas, Tony Jacklin, Bernard Gallacher, David Ojala and Denis Durnian, the No. 2 money winner in 2001. Chillas, the professional at Stirling Golf Club in Scotland who was also playing just his second tournament on the European Seniors Tour, joined Stull at the top Saturday with a five-under 67. The American shot 68 for his 136 and the two had just a one-shot lead over Australian Simon Owen, who shot a course-record 65. Stull wrapped up the title with birdies at the 12th, 16th and 17th holes Sunday. Chillas shot 72 for 208, dropping into a second-place tie with New Zealand's Barry Vivian, who closed with 70.

AIB Irish Seniors Open—€310,000
Winner: Seiji Ebihara

When action resumed after a two-month lapse, the victory pattern changed drastically. After Peter Townsend and Steve Stull scored maiden wins in March in the Caribbean, Japan's Seiji Ebihara, a new grandfather, successfully defended his title in the AIB Irish Seniors Open in County Limerick. Ebihara, who posted three victories in 2001 — the Irish Seniors and Microlease Jersey Seniors Masters in Europe and the N. Cup Senior Open in Japan — came from a shot off the pace with a final-round 70 and won by two strokes over Denis Durnian. He finished at eight-under-par 208.

So taken with the warm reception he had received in Ireland, the Japanese professional, a protégé of his country's famed Isao Aoki, gave a sizable portion of his prize purse to Irish children's charities. "I love it over here in Ireland," said Ebihara, 53, through his interpreter-daughter, Akiko, who is also his caddie. "The people are so warm and friendly."

Ebihara set up the victory with a blazing 66 in Friday's first round, running off six consecutive birdies on the back nine. That gave him a two-shot lead over Ireland's Denis O'Sullivan and Americans John Grace and Hank Woodrome. Bruce Fleisher, the U.S. Senior Tour star who won the 2000 Irish Open, managed just 74 and was never in contention.

Scotland's Mike Miller fired 67 Saturday and climbed into first place at 137 when Ebihara shot 72 for 138, a score matched by Ireland's Joe McDermott. The Scot couldn't maintain the pace Sunday, though, taking a triple bogey on the sixth hole and shooting 76 to fall into a sixth-place tie at the end. Ebihara's challenge instead came from Durnian, who closed with 69 for 210.

Flanders Nippon presents Legends in Golf—€170,000
Winner: Gary Wintz

Gary Wintz had a tough decision on his hands — continue his rookie-year quest for success on the European Seniors Tour in the Flanders Nippon presents Legends in Golf in Belgium or accept the proffered spot in the field of the prestigious and lucrative Senior PGA Championship on the American circuit.

"When I heard I had gotten into the PGA, my first inclination was to go back to the States," explained the Daytona Beach, Florida, professional. "But then, after realizing that I had won less than 2,000 pounds in my first two starts, I knew I had to stay here and try to improve my position on this tour."

Good decision, Gary. He proceeded to win the Legends in Golf, his first seniors title, in sensational fashion, exhilarating for him but devastating for Nick Job. Leading Wintz by a shot playing the final hole, the Englishman overshot the green with his approach and failed to save par. Wintz arched a nine-iron shot three feet from the cup and knocked in the winning birdie putt for 69 and the one-shot victory with his 11-under-par 205.

Job, the professional at London's Richmond Golf Club, had taken a one-stroke lead in Saturday's second round when he fired a flawless, course-record 64 at the Nippon Flanders Golf Club at Hasselt, ringing up eight birdies and 10 pars for his 135. He missed only two greens over the first 36 holes and described the 64 as "just about a perfect round of golf." Wintz shot his second 68 for 136 and had a share of the lead until he three-putted the 18th green. Japanese newcomer Dragon Taki and American Hank Woodrome, who shared the first-day lead with 67s, fell from contention with 75s. Taki bounced back Sunday with 67 and tied for third place with David Creamer at 209.

Microlease Jersey Seniors Masters—€155,110
Winner: Delroy Cambridge

Delroy Cambridge atoned for a near-miss the previous year when he marched to a two-stroke victory in the Microlease Jersey Seniors Masters in mid-June. An errant tee shot by the long-hitting Jamaican knocked him out of a three-way playoff in 2001, but in his return to Jersey's La Moye Golf Club, Cambridge outplayed Seiji Ebihara, the defending champion and second-round leader, and local favorite Tommy Horton, another former winner of the event, down the stretch. He closed with 67 for an 11-under-par 205.

Ebihara at 135 and Horton at 136 had led the field into the final round with Cambridge trailing by three. The Japanese professional, who already had a 2002 title in his bag — the AIB Irish Seniors Open — could muster no better than 73 Sunday, and Horton, the first-round leader with 66, was headed for a similar fate with an outgoing 39 on his 61st birthday. Cambridge did little on the first nine, but came alive after the turn. He posted birdies at the 11th and 13th holes, three-putted the par-five 16th for par, but birdied the last two holes to wrap up the victory.

"When I came to La Moye last year, I didn't know much about playing links golf, but I seem to be a quick learner," noted Cambridge afterward.

Horton found his game too late, but climbed into a second-place tie with Ian Mosey when he came home with 32 for 71–207. Ebihara shot 73 and tied for fourth with John Morgan.

Lawrence Batley Seniors Open—€196,893
Winner: Neil Coles

Old age just can't seem to catch up to Neil Coles. The remarkable Englishman defied the rigors of life once again when he won the Lawrence Batley Seniors Open, breaking his own record as the oldest winner ever on any established circuit in the world, set two years earlier in the Microlease Jersey Seniors Masters.

Coles was just three months shy of his 68th birthday when he birdied the fifth extra hole to land the Lawrence Batley title, his 15th on the senior tour and 46th since his first professional victory 46 years earlier. Nobody is even a close second. For instance, the oldest winner ever in the U.S. was Mike Fetchick on the Senior PGA Tour in 1985 and he was "just" 63 the day he won at Hilton Head Island. "This is very exciting for me at my age," confessed Coles. "Time does tend to creep up on you, but I always thought I could win again if my back stood up."

Coles overtook second-round leader David Creamer the last day, shooting 70 to fellow Englishman Creamer's 73, missing the chance to win outright in regulation when he bogeyed the 17th and parred the par-five 18th. American Steve Stull was already in with his 209 after a 68, setting up the three-way playoff. Stull went out when he bogeyed the fourth extra hole, before Coles ended it with his five-foot birdie at the next hole.

Coles had come from six strokes off the pace and Stull was eight back after Alberto Croce of Italy, the 1995 Lawrence Batley victor, opened with 66 and led Creamer by a shot. Both Coles and Stull moved up with 67s before Creamer took the lead Saturday with 69 for 136 in his unsuccessful bid for his second European Seniors Tour title.

Wales Seniors Open—€773,385
Winner: Seiji Ebihara

History repeated itself at the Wales Seniors Open, the richest tournament on the European Seniors Tour. Just as in 2001, Japan's Seiji Ebihara became the first multiple winner of the season when he rolled to a three-stroke victory at Royal St. David's in Harlech the first weekend of July, two months after his playoff triumph in the AIB Irish Seniors Open. He closed with a three-under-par 66 to pull away from the field after sharing the second-round lead with Nick Job and 66-year-old Bob Charles, whose spangled record includes victories in both the British Open and Senior British Open. Ebihara finished at four-under-par 203 on the par-69 course.

In posting his fourth European win in 14 months, the Japanese professional was in contention from the first day, when he and three others — Job, Noel Ratcliffe of Australia and Denis Durnian, the defending champion — trailed leaders Christy O'Connor, Jr. and American Jay Horton by a stroke. He then followed his 68 with a two-under 69 Saturday and moved into a three-way tie for the lead with Charles and Job at 137. The New Zealand left-hander shot 67, Job 69.

Ebihara came out firing Sunday as he took command of the tournament. Birdies at the second, sixth, eighth and ninth holes helped him to an outgoing 34 and two more at the 11th and 12th widened his lead to five strokes. He dropped shots at the 13th and 16th before wrapping up the victory with his seventh birdie at the 17th hole. O'Connor closed with 66 to join Durnian (68) in the runner-up slot at 206. Making one of his strongest showings on the circuit, Tony Jacklin tied for fourth with Ian Stanley of Australia, while Job dropped to sixth place with 71–208 and Charles tumbled to a ninth-place tie when he shot 73 for 210.

The Mobile Cup—€195,357
Winner: Bernard Gallacher

"I feel as if something massive has just been lifted off my shoulders." Those were the relieved and happy words of Bernard Gallacher after he ended a frustrating string of 62 non-victories since joining the European Seniors Tour in 1999 with a decisive, four-stroke win in the inaugural Mobile Cup at Stoke Park Club in England. The renowned Scotsman, the long-time professional at the famed Wentworth Club who won 13 times and played on eight Ryder Cup teams in his distinguished career on the regular European Tour, broke open a tight battle with Delroy Cambridge, the Microlease Jersey Seniors Masters winner, in the final round.

Gallacher, whose best previous showings on the senior circuit were four third-place finishes, shot 66 for his 12-under-par 201, capping his ride at the top of the leaderboard all week. On Friday, he shared the top spot with Cambridge and New Zealander Barry Vivian at four-under 67, then stood alone following Saturday's round after posting 68 for 135, taking a one-stroke lead over England's John Morgan. Cambridge shot 70 and was joined in third place by Australians Bob Shearer and Ian Stanley, who took only 29 strokes on the incoming nine.

The three-time Ryder Cup captain opened with birdies on the first two holes Sunday to take the lead and distance himself from Morgan. But Cambridge mounted his challenge with an eagle at the par-five fifth hole and overtook Gallacher with a birdie at the ninth. They swapped the lead on the early holes of the incoming nine before Gallacher made birdies at the 15th and 17th holes for the 66 and the four-stroke victory. Cambridge shot 68 for 205. Morgan had 70 and placed third at 206.

"There were times when I would sit around and wonder if I would ever win, so you can imagine how great this feels now," said Gallacher afterward. "I've been desperate to win since I came out here, so I'm absolutely delighted. A 66 is a great score on a course as difficult as this, but it could easily have been two shots better. I missed two three-foot putts. But that's what seniors do, I suppose."

Senior British Open—€736,714
Winner: Noboru Sugai

Every major championship in golf has had its share of surprise champions and the Senior British Open is no exception. Unheralded Japanese professional Noboru Sugai certainly fit that description in 2002 at Royal County Down, although he accomplished the feat in impressive fashion as he led from start to finish and racked up a two-stroke victory on a windy July weekend in Northern Ireland. The 52-year-old Sugai, joining Bob Verwey (1991), John Fourie (1992) and Tom Wargo (1994) as underdog winners, built a five-stroke lead over the first 36 holes with consecutive 67s, then battled the wind and rain with 73-74 over the final two days for his victorious three-under-par 281. He was the first Japanese winner of the circuit's premier tournament and the first wire-to-wire Senior Open winner since Gary Player in 1988.

Sugai, who had only two victories during his career on the Japan Tour and a 2001 triumph on Japan's Senior Tour, had American Hall-of-Famer Tom Watson on his heels the first two days. The Tokyo professional had five birdies and a bogey in his opening 67 as he led Russell Weir by one and John Chillas and Peter Kerr by two, as Watson, after eagling his first hole, settled for 70. Sugai widened his lead to five with his second 67 Friday, but then had Watson in second place and joked, "I need a 20-stroke lead. I'll be looking over my shoulder."

Despite two double bogeys on Saturday, Sugai managed the 73 and extended his lead to six strokes with his 207. Canadian John Irwin moved into second place with 74–213, Chillas (77) and John Bland (73) tied for third at 214, and Watson slipped to 215 with his 76, his bid to add the Senior British Open title to his five British Open victories gone.

Irwin, another lightly regarded professional in the field, mounted the only challenge to Sugai in Sunday's final round. The Japanese player opened the door when he bogeyed the seventh and double-bogeyed the eighth to finish with the 74, but Irwin lost his last chance for a playoff when he bogeyed the final hole for 70 and 283, the only other player under par for the distance. Watson tumbled far down the standings when he closed with 79.

De Vere PGA Seniors Championship—€318,955
Winner: Seiji Ebihara

The Japanese influence continued when the circuit returned to England for the De Vere PGA Seniors Championship as Seiji Ebihara solidified his first-place position on the Order of Merit with his third victory of the season. Ebihara achieved the victory at De Vere Carden Park with record decisiveness, running away from the field to a 10-stroke final margin in the second of back-to-back 72-hole major events, one week after countryman Noboru Sugai won the Senior British Open. Ebihara was 21 under at 267.

Little wonder the rout. Starting at the 16th hole in the opening round, Ebihara made nothing worse than pars over the remaining 57 holes. He posted 69 that first day and trailed leader Mike Ferguson, the Australian brother-in-law of the late Payne Stewart, by three strokes. The Japanese professional moved into a delayed tie for the lead with Ferguson Friday. He shot 67–136 and the Australian finished his round of 70 the next morning after darkness halted play Friday.

The tournament turned into a two-man race Saturday as Ebihara shot 65 and bolted to a three-shot lead at 15-under-par 201. American George Burns, a tournament winner in America in his younger days, had a 66 for 204, but Ferguson lost serious ground with 72, winding up in a tie for third with John Chillas and Ian Mosey at 208.

Ebihara never slowed down Sunday. He ran off six birdies and 12 pars for the 66 that broke the all-time winning margin record held by Tommy Horton, who twice scored nine-stroke victories in 1997 and 1998. In addition, the 267 set a new PGA Seniors and Seniors Tour record, also by a stroke. Kel Nagle won the 1975 championship with 268. Burns managed just 73 Sunday and finished in a runner-up tie at 277 with fellow American Steve Stull (66), who won the season's second event in Tobago.

Bad Ragaz PGA Seniors Open—€230,000
Winner: Dragon Taki

Dragon Taki, who gained his reputation in Japan for his prowess in long-driving contests rather than on the Japan Tour, followed his better-known countrymen Noboru Sugai and Seiji Ebihara to victory on successive weeks on the European Seniors Tour, but in quite different fashion — a three-hole playoff after an overnight downpour abbreviated the Bad Ragaz PGA Seniors Open to 36 holes.

Taki, who became the sixth first-time winner on the 2002 circuit, had fired a blazing, seven-under-par 63 Saturday after opening with 67. That put him in a deadlock atop the bunched field with Irishman Denis O'Sullivan, a four-time winner on the senior circuit. O'Sullivan had 64 after starting with 66, which put him in a eight-player group a shot behind first-round leaders John

Chillas and David Good. Both Taki and O'Sullivan had bogey-free rounds Saturday, Taki holing a 40-footer at the 17th hole for his final birdie.

When heavy rains inundated the Switzerland course Saturday night, tournament officials cancelled the final round and set up a three-hole playoff to settle matters. Taki won it easily with three pars as the Irishman bogeyed all three holes. It was just the second playoff of the 2002 season.

Travis Perkins Senior Masters—€352,878
Winner: Ray Carrasco

Californian Ray Carrasco had come close just one time in his three-and-a-half years on the European Seniors Tour, so it made sense when he admitted "it didn't even cross my mind that I would win when I arrived here" for the Travis Perkins Senior Masters at the storied Wentworth Club in England. At week's end, Carrasco, whose history of success in tournament golf was a long string of victories on America's mini-tours after two fruitless seasons on the U.S. PGA Tour, had his first important victory in the books, posting a 10-under-par 206 on Wentworth's Edinburgh course for a one-stroke triumph.

What made the win even more meaningful was that it came in a head-to-head battle against Seiji Ebihara, the tour's leading money winner and three-time victor in 2002. "It's particularly special because it was Seiji I defeated coming down the stretch," said the 55-year-old Carrasco, the eldest of 15 children who bought his first clubs with earnings from delivering newspapers. His triumph ended a run of three successive victories on the circuit by pros from Japan and made Carrasco the seventh first-time winner of the season.

Carrasco and Ebihara were in the picture from the start. The American, playing in the day's first group, shot a six-under-par 66 Friday and shared the lead with Maurice Bembridge and Denis Durnian, while Ebihara shot 67 despite a triple bogey on his card. Scoring was higher in general Saturday and Carrasco's 71 and Ebihara's 70 put them in a tie for the lead going into the final round.

The battle came down to the final hole Sunday. After Ebihara pulled within a stroke with birdies at the 16th and 17th holes, Carrasco dropped a five-foot birdie putt for 69 after the Japanese professional lipped out a 20-footer in his bid to force a playoff. David Good shot 68 and finished third at 208. Ryder Cupper Eamonn Darcy, making his senior debut, endured back trouble and finished far back in the field after a closing 79.

De Vere Hotels Seniors Classic—€234,654
Winner: Brian Jones

It was getting so that, with regard to victory, if you had a previous win on your record, don't apply for another at the next tournament site. At the De Vere Hotels Seniors Classic at England's Slaley Hall course, the eventual victor had arrived with a winless EST record for the eighth time in the first 13 events. It was Australian Brian Jones at the De Vere Classic, a rookie on the circuit, and he joined the seven other first-time winners in fine style, running away to a nine-under-par 207 and a seven-stroke victory over Tommy Horton, the tour's all-time money and wins leader.

Jones had not fared well earlier in his first season on the senior tour, finishing in the top 20 just once in his previous eight starts. But he had his "A" game going at windy Slaley Hall the first two rounds. On Friday he mustered a 70 and shared the top spot with Albanian-American Agim Bardha, the barber-turned-professional from Detroit who missed the 2001 season while recovering from prostate cancer. With winds still whistling at a 30 mph clip, Jones carved out a 68 Saturday and moved to a four-stroke lead over Horton and five over Mike Miller of Scotland.

With 69 Sunday, the product of four birdies and a bogey early in the round, Jones opened the seven-shot final margin as Horton could work up just a par 72. In a way, Jones was carrying on Japanese domination of that segment of the senior circuit, since he enjoyed his greatest success earlier in his career on the Japan Tour, where he won 10 of the 20 titles on his record. "I thought I played really well in the wind we had during the first two rounds and I did just what I had to do," said Jones. "It's fantastic to win again."

GIN Monte Carlo Invitational—€220,949
Winner: Terry Gale

Unlike the three most recent winners, Terry Gale had a victory on his record. But it was six years after his victory in the 1996 Senior PGA Championship at The Belfry when he grabbed his second title at the GIN Monte Carlo Invitational in early September.

It took a two-shot swing on the final hole to make it happen for the 56-year-old Australian, who owns 26 victories from his campaigning on the Australasian and Far East Tours in his younger days. Trailing England's Keith MacDonald by a stroke as they played the 54th hole, Gale wedged to six feet and, after MacDonald overshot the green and bogeyed, rolled in the winning birdie putt for 68 and 197, 10 under on the par-69 Monte Carlo Golf Club course.

It had been Gale's tournament to lose after the first day, when he blew up a storm of a 62 and jumped off to a four-stroke lead over MacDonald, with whom he played all three rounds. Gale produced the 62, the lowest score of the season matching the tour's all-time record 18-hole number, with seven birdies on the last 10 holes following eight pars. MacDonald caught up in the second round when he birdied his last three holes for 63 as Gale shot 67. Their 129s set a new all-time tour record by a stroke and put them four shots in front of third-place Jerry Bruner.

MacDonald led from the start in the Saturday final round when he birdied the opening hole and went three shots in front with birdies at the third and seventh. But he gave shots back at the 10th, 16th and tragically the 18th for his 69–198. Sympathized Gale, "I hate to win that way. Keith didn't deserve to lose like he did." Spain's Manuel Pinero shot 66 and tied Bruner for third at 201.

Bovis Lend Lease European Senior Masters—€356,871
Winner: Delroy Cambridge

Jamaican Delroy Cambridge became the second multiple winner of the 2002 season when he came from a shot off the pace with a final-round 68 to win the Bovis Lend Lease European Senior Masters at England's respected Woburn Golf and Country Club. With his second victory of the year, the long-hitting Cambridge joined Seiji Ebihara, a three-time winner, in the two-or-more category for the year.

Cambridge did what the venerable Neil Coles was on the verge of doing. The 67-year-old Coles, who won the Lawrence Batley in June and was just two weeks shy of his 68th birthday, carried a one-stroke lead into the final round, but could manage only a one-over-par 73 and tied for fourth place with Ross Metherell and David Good.

Cambridge, who had started the second round three strokes behind leader American David Oakley (66), moved into a runner-up tie Saturday when he shot 70 for 139. He joined Alan Tapie (71-68) and Eamonn Darcy (68-71), who returned to action for his second senior start after missing a month with back trouble. Coles took the lead with 71-67–138.

In Sunday's finale, Cambridge, the Microlease Jersey Seniors Masters winner in June, played the incoming nine in three under to put away the victory, his third EST title. Ebihara might well have landed his fourth win. He had moved into the hunt with three early birdies, but put two drives in the bushes and took an eight on the par-four eighth hole. He did well the rest of the way and rescued a 68 to deadlock Darcy (70) for second place at 209. Darcy started fast with birdies on two of the first three holes, but could do nothing to advance further after that.

Charles Church Scottish Seniors Open—€240,165
Winner: Denis Durnian

Denis Durnian's initial victory of the year in the Charles Church Scottish Seniors Open, though late in coming, had an extra reward. His powerful, six-stroke triumph at the Roxburghe Golf Club assured his year-end finish in second place on the Order of Merit. With that position, he earned a return visit to America in November for the international UBS Warburg Cup competition at Sea Island, Georgia, along with points leader Seiji Ebihara.

A frequent contender during the season — nine top-10 finishes — Durnian lingered a stroke off the pace of Denis O'Sullivan, who opened the late September tournament with 66. The remarkable Neil Coles also shot 67 in Friday's round. Durnian ran off five birdies and a three-putt bogey for 68 Saturday and stepped a stroke ahead of Coles (69) with his nine-under-par 135. O'Sullivan slipped to 71–137, standing third, a shot ahead of defending champion David Oakley, who moved into contention with 67.

It came up windy and wet for Sunday's final round, but Durnian wasn't fazed by it. He carved out a 71 and, with no challenges afoot, his margin swelled to six at the end over Coles (76), Martin Gray (71), Alan Tapie (73) and Tommy Horton (70). After a steady outgoing nine, Durnian had three birdies and two bogeys coming in.

Of his second tour victory — the first was in the 2001 Wales Seniors Open — Durnian said, "That's probably the best I have played all season. In fact, it might be the best I have played since I joined the Seniors Tour a couple of years ago."

Daily Telegraph/Sodexho Seniors Match Play—€159,760
Winner: Delroy Cambridge

Following a two-week break, a select 32 members of the European Seniors Tour showed up in Spain for the Daily Telegraph/Sodexho Seniors Match Play, and Delroy Cambridge was the winning survivor at week's end after five grueling rounds in four days at the new Flamingos Golf Club. Cambridge matched Seiji Ebihara's title collection for the season when he defeated Northern Ireland's Eddie Polland in the final match, 1 up, for his third victory of the season and fourth in his two years on the circuit.

It was a tough defeat for Polland, the former Ryder Cupper, whose only victories in six EST seasons came in 1999. Polland battled back from two- and three-hole deficits over the first 14 holes and went to the 18th hole all square with the powerful Jamaican. He got a bad break when his dead-center tee shot wound up in a divot. His approach then squirted over the green into a hazard, and when he left it in the bunker on his next shot after Cambridge nailed his second 10 feet from the cup, he conceded the hole and match.

Cambridge rolled to easy victories in the first two rounds, taking David Good and Ian Mosey by 5-and-4 scores, while Polland nipped John Irwin, 1 up, the first day and Priscillo Diniz, 3 and 2, in the second round. The surprising Brian Evans, a club professional in Portugal who got into the field on a sponsor invitation, gave Cambridge a tough match in the quarter-finals before losing the last two holes.

Polland ousted Antonio Garrido, 3 and 2, then advanced to the championship match when Denis O'Sullivan, who had eliminated top-seeded Denis Durnian the day before, three-putted the final green. A birdie at the 17th hole gave Cambridge his semi-final victory over Nick Job.

Tunisian Seniors Open—€158,363
Winner: Denis O'Sullivan

Denis O'Sullivan almost ran out of tournaments. The Irishman had made several serious runs at victories during the season when the circuit reached its next-to-last stop — the Tunisian Seniors Open in late October — but had not been able to add a 2002 victory to his four earlier victories since joining the tour in 1998. O'Sullivan rectified that at Port El Kantaoui Golf Club. With birdies on four of the last seven holes in Saturday's final round, he climbed past John Morgan, posted a four-under-par 68 and registered a two-stroke victory with his 204.

Australian Noel Ratcliffe, another multiple winner on the EST in earlier seasons without a 2002 victory, had the upper hand over the first two rounds. He shared the lead the first day with Scotland's Mike Miller at 67, a shot in front of Craig Defoy, Steve Stull, Denis Durnian and O'Sullivan. A 66 in the second round put him in front alone at 133, but O'Sullivan matched the 66 and trailed by just a shot.

Morgan, who was two back, grabbed the early lead the last day, leading by two strokes at the turn before O'Sullivan turned up the heat. O'Sullivan notched birdies at the 12th, 14th, 15th and 17th, the latter off a spectacular wedge shot over a tree to two feet. That birdie gave him the lead for the first time and he added a shot to the margin with a par to Morgan's bogey at the final hole. Morgan had 69–204. Ratcliffe finished third at 205 behind the two players whom he had been helping with their games earlier in the week. "I think I am going to have to buy him a present," quipped O'Sullivan.

Estoril Seniors Tour Championship—€240,000
Winner: Denis Durnian

Appropriately, the season-ending Estoril Seniors Tour Championship produced one of the year's most exciting finishes and a victory for one of the season's outstanding performers. Denis Durnian, the most dominant player over the final stretch of the season, picked off his second victory of the season at Portugal's Quinta da Marinha in a tense duel with Ireland's Eamonn Darcy, who was completing his injury-shortened rookie season. It was Durnian's third circuit victory, which like his first in 2001 was decided by playoff, and enhanced his No. 2 position on the final Order of Merit listing.

Durnian and Darcy were in contention from the start. Durnian and John Chillas opened with three-under-par 68s and Darcy was just a shot back at the end of Friday's round. Durnian retained a share of first place Saturday, firing another 68 for 136. Mike Miller joined him with 69-67 rounds. Darcy was then tied for third with Delroy Cambridge, another star of the late season, at 138.

The battle came down to the final green. Durnian and Darcy were tied for the lead and Darcy gave Durnian an opening when he missed the green and bogeyed, but Durnian three-putted from 18 feet to send the decision to extra holes. Cambridge missed a chance to join them when his 25-foot birdie bid at the 54th failed to drop. The playoff ended quickly and sadly for Darcy. He drove into the trees and, when he broke a branch with a practice swing, knew he had incurred a two-stroke penalty. With that, he conceded the victory to Durnian, who sympathized, "I can't think of a worse way to lose. It's the sort of thing that only happens in your worst nightmares."

Japan Senior Tour

Castle Hill Open—¥30,000,000
Winner: Namio Takasu

Namio Takasu, who had meager success with just a pair of victories in secondary events during his career on the regular Japan Tour, picked up his first victory on the Japan Senior Tour in the season-opening Castle Hill Open in late May. It took extra holes to do it as Takasu prevailed in a three-man overtime battle against Toshiki Matsui and Norihiko Matsumoto.

Takasu's hopes were not promising after a first-round 74. It left him five strokes behind leader Toru Nakamura, whose 69 had staked him to a one-stroke lead over Hisao Inoue and Shuichi Sano. Undaunted, Takasu surged into the lead with 67 the second day for 141, slipping a stroke in front of Nakamura (74), Inoue (72), Matsumoto (73-69), Takayoshi Nishikawa (72-70) and Toshiharu Morimoto (71-71).

Takasu shot 71 Sunday for a four-under-par 212 at Castle Hill Country Club, and Matsui (68) and Matsumoto (70) matched that total to bring about the playoff.

Asahi Ryokken Cup—¥10,000,000
Winner: Hisao Inoue

A week later, the season's second tournament played out with the same scenario — another three-man playoff. That time, Hisao Inoue came out the victor, defeating defending champion Noboru Sugai and Tetsuhiro Ueda in the overtime test at Ito Golf Club.

As was the case with Namio Takasu, the previous playoff winner, Inoue began the tournament well off the pace, shooting 71 in the opening round of the 36-hole event. That put him four strokes in the hole behind Motomasa Aoki, whose 67 gave him a one-shot lead over Taiwanese star Hsieh Min-nan and two over Sugai and Tadao Furuichi.

Inoue came back with 67 in Sunday's final round to catch Ueda (68) and Sugai (69) at 138 and mandate a playoff. Aoki shot 73 for 140 and fifth place, a stroke behind Hsieh (71).

Aderans Wellness Open—¥60,000,000
Winner: Yukio Noguchi

Play resumed on the circuit six weeks later with the Aderans Wellness Open at Nakajo Golf Club and a first-time winner was crowned. Yukio Noguchi picked up his initial title with a solid performance over the 54 holes as he chalked up a three-stroke victory with his 12-under-par 204.

Noguchi was just a stroke off the lead the first day, sharing a five-way tie for second behind leader Kimpachi Yoshimura. Fujio Kobayashi, the career wins leader on the Japan Senior Tour with 11 titles, headed the runner-up group that also included Koji Okuno, Tadami Ueno and Toru Nakayama. Yoshimura skied to 76 Saturday, and Noguchi took over first place with a sparkling 66 for 134. Kenjiro Iwama also shot 66 and moved into second place at 135. Shoichi Sato also passed all of the first-day contenders with 68–137.

Noguchi's 70 on Sunday produced the three-shot victory as Katsuji Hasegawa fired the week's best round of 65 to jump from 20th place into the runner-up slot with 207. Iwama shot 73 for 208.

Fancl Senior Classic—¥60,000,000
Winner: Katsunari Takahashi

Katsunari Takahashi made the biggest move toward the money title when he successfully defended his championship at the Fancl Senior Classic at Susono Country Club, Shizuoka, in late August. The Fancl was one of Takahashi's two victories during the 2001 season, which, in turn, followed his initial two seniors wins in 2000. The three-stroke victory gave Katsunari a ¥15 million check, which, by itself, turned out to be enough to give him the No. 1 position on the final money list. Only the six 54- and 72-hole events counted in those standings.

Hiroshi Ishii was the first-round leader at Susono with a four-under-par 68 on a rainy Friday. He led Tadanao Takeshita, Dragon Taki and Terry Gale of Australia by two strokes, and Takahashi opened with 71. When Takahashi followed with 70 for 141, he moved into the lead by two strokes over Koji Okuno (73-70) and three over Teruo Nakamura, Hisao Inoue, Yasuo Tanabe and Takeshita.

Another 70 on Sunday wrapped up the victory for Takahashi. Nakamura also shot 70 to finish second, and Yoshitaka Yamamoto climbed into third place with 68 for 215.

HTD Senior Classic—¥10,000,000
Winner: Noboru Sugai

Noboru Sugai captured his third title when he came from five strokes back in the final round of the 36-hole HTD Senior Classic and picked off a one-stroke victory. His closing 65 and 137 total edged first-round co-leader Tadao Nakamura by that single stroke at Mitsui Kanko Iris Golf Club in Hokkaido. Sugai had won twice on the 2001 tour.

Nakamura shared the first-round lead with Hisao Inoue, the Asahi Ryokken Cup winner in June, with their five-under-par 67s. Koichi Uehara shot 68 that Saturday, three others had 70s, among them Seiichi Kanai, the 10-time Senior Tour winner, and Sugai began with 72.

Inoue shot 72 Sunday and took third place behind Sugai and Nakamura.

Japan PGA Senior Championship—¥30,000,000
Winner: Chen Tze-ming

Talk about first impressions. Chen Tze-ming (or T.M. Chen, as he is known in the United States), the Taiwanese veteran of the Asian golf wars, made a rare and his initial appearance of the season at the Japan PGA Senior Championship in early October and left the rest of the field in a shambles. Chen led from wire-to-wire at Caledonian Golf Club and wound up with a 10-stroke victory at a dazzling 21-under-par 267 in one of the circuit's most important events. It was his first win on the Japan Senior Tour.

Chen put it away the third day with the lowest round of the season — a nine-under-par 63. He had opened with 68 to lead Takayoshi Nishikawa by one stroke and 10 others by two. Another 68 in the second round Thursday widened the margin to two, then over Takeru Shibata, who followed a 72 with 66 for 138. Teruo Nakamura (69) was at 139, Seiji Ebihara and Moto-masa Aoki at 140.

The 63 rocketed Chen 11 strokes ahead of the field Friday. He was at 199, Shibata (72) and Kiyoshi Hinata (69) at 210. A 68, his fourth straight round in the 60s, completed the rout. Nakamura shot 65 Saturday to claim second place at 277, as Shibata finished third with 69–279.

PGA Philanthropy Biglayzac Senior—¥30,000,000
Winner: Seiji Ebihara

Seiji Ebihara displayed the game that carried him to the No. 1 position on the European Seniors Tour earlier in the year when he rolled to a five-stroke victory in the PGA Philanthropy Biglayzac Senior tournament two weeks after returning to the country from his three-victory season in Europe. The 53-year-old from Chiba took command of the tournament in the third round and went on to a five-stroke win, his third on the Japan Senior Tour.

Ebihara had to shake off a slow start at Biglayzac Country Club. He shot 74 the first day and trailed the three leaders — Fujio Kobayashi, Toru Naka-yama and Yoshimi Watanabe — by six strokes, lodged in a tie for 28th position in the standings. Haruo Yasuda, who also started with 74, vaulted into a first-place tie at three-under-par 141 Friday with Koji Okuno and Chen Tze-ming, fresh from his victory in the Japan PGA Championship. Yasuda shot 67, Okuno 68, and Chen 70.

Ebihara moved up to 11th place with 70–144, then took over the lead Saturday with 67–211, a shot in front of Yasuda, Okuno and Chen, all of whom had 71s. Ebihara never faltered Sunday, came up with a 68, and finished five ahead of Yasuda and Chen (72s). He was nine-under-par at 279.

Japan Senior Open Championship—¥50,000,000
Winner: Takaaki Fukuzawa

Takaaki Fukuzawa stood up to the challenges of several players with superior credentials as he became a dark horse winner of the Japan Senior Tour's most prestigious event — the Japan Senior Open Championship — the first weekend of November. Fukuzawa, a 50-year-old rookie whose record was devoid of any tour victories, battled through the final three rounds against the hugely successful Isao Aoki and Seiji Ebihara, currently the top Japanese senior player, to post a one-stroke victory at Abiko Golf Club.

Those three men dominated the race after Motomasa Aoki began a roller coaster ride with a leading 67 Thursday. (He followed with 80-69-69 and tied for fifth.) Fukuzawa claimed the lead Friday with his 69-71–140, and Isao Aoki and Ebihara took up the chase, Aoki with 70-71–141 and Ebihara with 71-70–141. All three players shot 71s Saturday and carried that status into the final round, Fukuzawa at 209, Aoki and Ebihara at 210. When Fukuzawa and Aoki matched scores for the third day in a row — 70s in the final round — Fukuzawa had his first senior victory.

Takanosu Senior Open—¥10,000,000
Winner: Takashi Miyoshi

Six days after losing in a playoff to Toru Nakamura in the one-day Teruo Sugihara Senior, Takashi Miyoshi landed his first victory on the Japan Senior Tour, scoring a one-stroke triumph in the Takanosu Senior Open at Takanosu Golf Club.

Miyoshi put up a pair of four-under-par 68s to win the title by the single stroke over Mitsuo Iwata, who had rounds of 69 and 68. Yurio Akitomi, who led the first day with 67, skied to 78 Sunday. Yasuzo Hagiwara finished third with 69-69–138.

N. Cup Senior Open—¥15,000,000
Winner: Isao Aoki

Isao Aoki enjoyed his best season of the new century in 2002, at home and abroad. After picking up his ninth victory on the U.S. Senior PGA Tour at the Instinet Classic during another full season of play in America, the 60-year-old Aoki returned home in October, finished second to Takaaki Fukuzawa in the Japan Senior Open and captured the season-ending N. Cup Senior Open on the par-73 Central Golf Club course in late November. It was his sixth senior title in Japan to go with his four consecutive Senior Open titles in the mid-1990s and the now-defunct Senior Grand Slam in 1995.

Aoki seized the N. Cup lead the first day with a five-under-par 68, standing one stroke ahead of Koichi Uehara and three in front of five others — Toru Nakayama, Kikuo Arai, Shigeru Kawamata, Wataru Horiguchi and Mitsuhiro Kitta. Aoki shot 71 Sunday for 139 and won by two strokes when runner-up Uehara, a two-time winner on the Senior Tour, took a 72. Nakayama finished in a four-way tie for third with Seiji Ebihara, Fujio Kobayashi and Katsuji Hasegawa.

15. Women's Tours

In 2001 Annika Sorenstam won eight tournaments including four in a row and one major, shot a record-setting 59, and set an all-time scoring average for women's golf. Her accomplishments were overshadowed in golf by what Tiger Woods accomplished and in the world at large by the terrorist attacks of September 11. This year there were no such distractions, and Sorenstam's performance was the most dominant in golf and perhaps the best of the year in all of sports.

Her year went like this: win, win, second, tie for seventh, win, second, tie for 58th, win, tie for third, win, third, win, win, second, third, missed cut, win, win, win, win, tie for fourth, tie for fifth, tie for 17th, win, win. That's 25 tournaments and 13 victories worldwide, 11 on the LPGA Tour.

Not that anyone should have been surprised by Sorenstam's dominance. She believes that a 54 is not only possible, it's in her future. "You can birdie every hole," she said, calling her goal "54 vision." That sort of singular focus and devotion to task led Sorenstam to push herself in every aspect of the game. "When I am on the golf course I want to win every time out," she said. "I would like to win all the majors. I want to see how much better I can get. That's what drives me today. The older I get, the more I understand that importance of golf in my life. I realize how much more there is to the game than just hitting shots. It is a way of life for me."

Sorenstam didn't win every time out and she only won one major title, but she decided that no record was untouchable. She won her fifth money title, which placed her second on the all-time list behind Kathy Whitworth's eight, and she broke her own single-season earnings title with $2,863,904. Her record scoring average from 2001 went down as well. Sorenstam averaged 68.7 strokes per round in 2002, breaking her own record by almost a full stroke. Most impressive, however, was that her 42 career LPGA victories placed her tied for eighth, at age 32, with Sandra Haynie on the all-time victories list.

The only blemish on Sorenstam's 2002 record was that she only won one of the year's majors, the Kraft Nabisco Championship in March. The other three majors went to Sorenstam's nearest challengers. Se Ri Pak, who had five victories for the year, won in Delaware when she beat Beth Daniel in the McDonald's LPGA Championship. Hall of Famer Juli Inkster came from behind to beat Sorenstam in the U.S. Women's Open. It was Inkster's fourth major title in three years. Karrie Webb won the final major, the Weetabix Women's British Open, on a windswept day in Scotland. She finished the year with three victories.

It was also a breakout year for players like Laura Diaz, who won twice, and Cristie Kerr, who broke her long winless drought with a victory in California. Rachel Teske had another multiple win season, winning twice and finishing ninth on the money list, and Carin Koch finished eighth without a victory.

With all those records being broken and earnings marks being set, one might assume that women's golf was healthier than ever. Just below the surface, trouble continues to plague the women's game. The LPGA has a long way to go. While Sorenstam's winnings were an all-time high, Jenny Lidback, who finished 100th on the money list, won only $61,557.

"I don't really have the one answer to the question of how to make the LPGA grow," Sorenstam said. "We as players have to work together and understand we are all part of the product we are trying to sell. We are an entertainment vehicle, and we have to put the fans first. What I can do to best help the tour, I think, is to simply be myself. When people see me play, I want them to see how much I enjoy the game. And when they come out, I want to hit as many great shots as I can to entertain them and make them want to come back again and again, and make them want to tell their friends to come out and see us.

"I love this game, and I love the LPGA. And I hope my love for it benefits the entire tour."

Nevertheless, the LPGA continues to lead the world of women's golf, attracting most of the best players from around the globe. On their home circuits, Yuri Fudoh, age 25, was the leading money winner in Japan for the third consecutive year and won four tournaments. The only players to win more than once on the 12-event Evian Ladies European Tour were, with two victories, Iben Tinning and (no surprise) Sorenstam.

U.S. LPGA Tour

Takefuji Classic—$900,000
Winner: Annika Sorenstam

No one was shocked when Annika Sorenstam birdied four of her last seven holes to tie Lorie Kane at the end of regulation. Nor were there any gasps of disbelief when Sorenstam rolled in a four-footer for birdie on the first playoff hole to win the Takefuji Classic in Hawaii. It was Sorenstam's second victory in as many weeks, making her two-for-two in 2002. Sorenstam won eight times in 2001 and appeared to be riding a wave of momentum into the New Year.

"I'm overwhelmed and super happy," the Swede said after hitting an 81-yard wedge shot to four feet and rolling in the final birdie putt for the victory. "I can't believe it worked out the way it did."

She might have been the only person who couldn't believe it. A week after defeating Karrie Webb in a playoff in the Australian Ladies Masters, Sorenstam won over Kane with some of the most impressive iron shots of the week. Her four birdies on the 12th, 13th, 15th and 16th holes were all from inside 20 feet.

"I think today is a true test of what Annika can do given the opportunity," Kane said. "Top players like Annika rise to the occasion and never really have a doubt in their mind. They assume that every hole they have a shot.

I'm disappointed that I did not win, but there are 26 more weeks in the year, and I will be looking to stay where I am and keep building from here."

Sorenstam shot 64 and 66 in the opening rounds, but trailed Kasumi Fujii by three shots and Kane by one when the three teed off on Sunday. For a while it appeared that this would not be the Swede's week. A string of pars saw her fall three shots behind Kane after the first nine.

Fujii received a two-shot penalty on the third hole when she brushed aside sand from the fringe, a violation of the rules since neither her ball nor the sand were on the green. "I tried to forget about the penalty," Fujii said. "But it was still on my mind." She triple-bogeyed the fifth and finished with 72 for an 11-under-par 199 total.

That left Sorenstam and Kane to battle it out. "I didn't feel good about my game this week," Sorenstam said. "But on the back nine, things just totally turned around. I made four great birdies and the momentum turned."

Kane couldn't buy a putt in the final nine holes. She made 11 straight pars coming in, missing one opportunity after another. On the 54th hole, she had a chance to win outright, but her 20-foot birdie putt hit the lip of the hole, spun all the way around, and came back toward her. The dejected tap-in par was a bad sign. A while later, it was over. Sorenstam finished with 66 for her 196 total while Kane closed with 67.

"Of course I know what I've done in the past," Sorenstam said. "But it's a new year. My expectations are very high. I was very, very happy about last year, but I believe I can be better this year."

She certainly got off to a good start.

Ping Banner Health—$1,000,000
Winner: Rachel Teske

This was supposed to be Annika Sorenstam's tournament to win. She was the hottest player in golf, winning her first two events of the year and seemingly marching toward a third in a row when she entered the final round in Phoenix, Arizona, at the Ping Banner Health with a four-stroke lead. This was where Sorenstam carded her historic 59 in 2001. The last round appeared little more than a formality.

A cold wind, a cool putter and a steely six-footer on the second playoff hole by Rachel Teske upset Sorenstam's romp through the ranks of the LPGA. When regulation play ended, Sorenstam had taken 76 blows on Sunday, 33 of those with the putter, and bogeyed the final two holes to lose her lead. Rather than waltzing out of Arizona with her third straight victory, she was heading back to the 18th for a playoff, one Teske had no idea she had made until the final moments.

"Even coming up 18, I thought I was two shots behind Annika," the affable Australian said. "I just had no idea. I didn't expect to get into a playoff. My caddie was still hanging around the scorer's tent, and I thought it was a bit odd, because he usually shoots off. I was having a chat, and he said, 'Annika has got to get up and down to win.' That's when I realized."

As had happened throughout the day, Sorenstam's putt for par on the 18th didn't come close. "Today my first putts were not even close," she said. "I didn't leave it two, three feet short. I left it four feet left, four feet right.

I didn't have a chance. The feel was just off."

That feeling remained off during the playoff. Teske's surprise at having to play more golf showed on the 18th when she hit one of her worst shots of the day into a fairway bunker. From there she flew her approach into the back bunker. This seemed to give Sorenstam the advantage. The Swede split the fairway with a four wood and hit her approach to 14 feet. Teske blasted out to two feet and made par, while Sorenstam's birdie putt never had a chance of going in.

On the 17th, the second playoff hole, Teske hit an eight iron to six feet while Sorenstam's approach stopped 14 feet behind the hole. Teske felt good about her chances at that point. She had birdied the 17th less than an hour before. Sorenstam had bogeyed the hole in regulation. This time Sorenstam's birdie effort stopped short. Teske's did not. She rolled the birdie putt into the center of the hole to cap the victory. It was Teske's third career playoff win to go with one loss. The loss came to Sorenstam in the 2000 Jamie Farr Classic, but she also beat Sorenstam in extra holes at the 1999 Betsy King Classic. While she birdied the last two holes of regulation for 71 and the 281 tie and one of two playoff holes for the victory, everyone, including Teske, agreed that this one was a gift.

"I threw it away," Sorenstam said, referring to her double bogey on the opening hole, her bogey-bogey finish and the putts missed throughout the day. "Rachel played very steady. She was there at the right time. But I normally don't finish bogey-bogey. I normally don't shoot 76 on Sunday. I don't make double bogeys. If you play golf, you know what it's like. You have good days, and you have bad days."

Sorenstam's bad day turned out to be Teske's good one.

Welch's/Circle K Championship—$800,000
Winner: Laura Diaz

With all the questions swirling about when and if she would ever win, Laura Diaz was glad she didn't back into her first one. "As much as it's been talked about — all of my seconds, no victories yet — I'm relieved," Diaz said after sinking a three-footer on the final hole of the Welch's/Circle K Championship in Tucson, Arizona, to beat Juli Inkster by one stroke. "The question was always, 'When are you going to get a victory?' I've got a victory. The question is over."

Not only is it over, Diaz answered it with an exclamation mark. Trailing Inkster by two shots going into the final round, Diaz bogeyed the first two holes to fall four back. She hung tough with birdies at the third, fourth and fifth. "I didn't look at it as if I were two over," she said. "I was still 12 under." The three-birdie binge moved her to 15 under and within a shot of Inkster.

Even with Diaz coming back strong, Inkster had plenty of chances to pull away. She birdied the third to keep her four-shot edge, but bogeyed the fourth as Diaz was rolling in her birdie. Inkster repeated the trend on the second nine when she followed her birdie at the 10th with a bogey at the 11th.

"I take pride in being a pretty good front-runner," Inkster said. "The last two days I just couldn't get anything going. I felt like I was always trying to kick-start myself, so I'm very disappointed."

When Diaz rolled in another birdie at the 12th, the two players were tied at 16 under. Another birdie from six feet by Diaz at the par-five 13th, and she held the lead outright for the first time all week. The lead remained intact throughout the next four holes, despite some close calls. On the 15th, Inkster's 18-foot birdie putt disappeared only to come back out of the hole. "I don't have any idea how it didn't stay down," Inkster said.

When the two players arrived at the short par-five 18th, Diaz led by one, and Inkster knew she needed an eagle. When her second shot landed 20 feet from the hole, she felt she had her chance. Diaz hit her approach 35 feet beyond the hole and rolled her first putt to three feet. Inkster had to make her eagle putt to force a playoff.

The putt never hit the hole. Diaz rolled her three-footer into the cup, and it was all over. Diaz had rounds of 67, 67, 68 and 68 for a 270 total, while Inkster finished with 71 for her 271 total.

"Winning is a big goal for the year," Diaz said. "But not just winning once. Winning more than once. I have a long-term goal of the Hall of Fame. To do that I have to win a number of times."

The magic number of victories for Hall of Fame induction is 27. You can't get there until you win once. After four years and four runner-up finishes, Diaz finally took that first step.

Kraft Nabisco Championship—$1,500,000
Winner: Annika Sorenstam

The only thing missing was a yellow brick road. Annika Sorenstam decided early on Sunday to put on ruby red slippers for her final-round showdown against Karrie Webb and her childhood idol Liselotte Neumann. "I figured today was the day I had to go low," Sorenstam said. "If I'm not afraid to wear them, then I'm not afraid to play."

It takes courage to set standards, be they fashion trends like the day-glow red Nike golf shoes or golf statements like becoming the first player to successfully defend her title at the Kraft Nabisco Championship in Rancho Mirage, California, since Sandra Post did it in 1978 and 1979. "I told my caddie last year that I wanted to have my name on the Wall of Champions," Sorenstam said. "Now I'll see it double."

That double-take was made possible by a final-round 68 delivered in typical Sorenstam fairways-and-greens style. She missed birdie putts on the first four holes, which left an opening for Neumann, who moved ahead with a six-foot birdie putt at the third. Sorenstam remained steady, rolling in a birdie at the fifth to regain a share of the lead, then holing a 10-footer for birdie at the sixth to take the lead outright. She never lost it.

Neumann, looking for her first win since 1998, put up a good fight. After making six on the par-five 11th (the easiest hole on the course), the elder Swede had a chat with herself behind the 12th tee box. Whatever she said paid off. Neumann made birdies at the 12th and 13th to pull within one.

Sorenstam had her game on auto-pilot. A two-putt from 50 feet on the 15th kept the momentum in her favor, and when she rolled her birdie putt on the last hole two feet past, she decided not to mark her ball and wait for Neumann's 15-foot birdie effort.

"I didn't want to mark it and look at it for 10 minutes," Sorenstam said. "It would probably be four feet by the time I hit it, and that's not what I wanted."

She rolled in the two-footer for a four-under-par 68 and a 280 total, then stood on the side of the green while Neumann lined up her 15-footer to tie. When that putt slid by the hole, Sorenstam had her third victory of the year and her second straight Nabisco title.

"Boy, that was close," Neumann said. "I think I played really good golf today. I was fighting. If someone had asked me, 'Do you think 69 is going to be good enough?' I would have said, 'Yes.' But Annika was one step better today. She hit it a bit closer."

She did not, however, hit it longer than Neumann, who spent most of the off-season working with a trainer to improve her distance and accuracy. "I spent a lot of time in the gym," she said. "We had plenty of time off, so I got myself a trainer and really dedicated myself to getting in better shape. I looked at my stats from last year and realized I was 124th in driving distance and 136th in accuracy. That's a terrible combination. So I decided to get stronger and more balanced, and that way be able to hit the ball longer and straighter."

The results were obvious. Neumann hit the ball 16 yards longer than her average last season, closed with 69 for a 281 total, and carded her best finish in over two years.

The other member of the final threesome, Webb, had no trouble with distance, but her accuracy was another matter. It was the first time Webb and Sorenstam had been paired together in the final group of a major, but the much-anticipated fireworks never materialized. Instead, Webb missed four of her first seven greens and never made a birdie until the 16th hole. She finished with 72 for a 284 total. "I didn't feel I was playing all that bad," Webb said. "I thought I was capable of running off some birdies, but it was the 16th hole before I got one. By then I was out of holes."

Sorenstam won this one the same way she won so many of her titles in 2001 — steady, consistent, mistake-free play. "That's her strength," Neumann said. "She plays like that every day, seven days a week. That's what makes her so good."

The Office Depot Hosted by Amy Alcott—$1,000,000
Winner: Se Ri Pak

It was a see-saw finish, and despite some last minute sputters, Se Ri Pak held on and denied Annika Sorenstam her third victory of the year and her second consecutive come-from-behind win in The Office Depot Hosted by Amy Alcott in Tarzana, California. A year ago, Sorenstam came from 10 strokes behind to overtake Pat Hurst, then beat Mi Hyun Kim in a playoff. This time neither Pak nor Sorenstam played all that well, but Pak's three-shot cushion at the beginning of the final round proved to be enough to put her on top.

After consecutive rounds of 68, where her putter saved her on more than a few occasions, Pak's shaky ball-striking caught up with her on Sunday. She bogeyed the second and third holes to let Sorenstam pull to within a stroke.

The 31-year-old Swede then tied her with a birdie at the fourth hole. Another birdie at the par-five fifth and Sorenstam found herself alone atop the leaderboard for the first time all week.

Pak scraped her way into a tie at the top with birdies on the fifth and sixth, then Sorenstam's putter began showing signs of wear. She missed a short par putt on the par-three eighth to give Pak the lead outright.

When Pak drained a 15-footer for birdie at the 13th, she had a two-shot cushion again. Sorenstam made a tough eight-footer for par on the 13th after leaving her birdie effort woefully short, but her putting troubles continued at the par-three 16th when she missed the green short, chipped to within three feet, then missed the par putt. Pak made a 10-footer for birdie at the 16th to regain her original three-shot lead.

The tide turned once more on the 17th when Sorenstam made a curling 15-footer for birdie while Pak went off with a bogey after missing the green to the right. That cut the lead to one.

Sorenstam played her approach first and hit the ball long and left, leaving herself 30 feet for birdie. Pak got closer, but not by much, leaving her approach 20 feet below the hole. If Sorenstam made her putt and Pak missed, they would head back out for extra holes.

The putt looked good, but Sorenstam hit it too hard and the ball rolled three feet beyond the hole. All Pak needed was a two-putt, which she got when she rolled her 20-foot birdie attempt one revolution short of the hole. She tapped in for a one-over-par 73 and a 54-hole total of 209. Sorenstam shot 71, but fell one stroke short.

"Playing with Annika was great," Pak said. "Then she caught up, but I didn't want to think about that. She's really a consistent player, so I knew she wouldn't back off easily. But I was not going to give my trophy away."

While Sorenstam wanted a different outcome, she praised the winner's play. "I think Se Ri has been in the shadows, and we should give her all the credit she deserves," Sorenstam said. "For me it was all about Sunday and the last group, where we played great golf and it was a great crowd. I would lead and then she would lead. It was a great performance."

Longs Drugs Challenge—$900,000

Winner: Cristie Kerr

It took five and a half years and 50 fewer pounds, but 24-year-old Cristie Kerr finally lived up to all the potential she showed as a teenager by shooting eight-under-par 280 to win her first professional title at the Longs Drugs Challenge in Lincoln, California. Kerr came under heavy criticism after turning professional straight out of high school, then struggling through mood swings and bouts of temper on the golf course in her first couple of seasons. But in recent years she underwent a makeover, working out religiously and losing over 50 pounds.

"I wanted to change my image, change the way I felt about myself," Kerr said. "Everything has its own way of falling into place, and no matter how eager you are to change the events that happen, things have to evolve over time. I came out on tour so early I wasn't ready to win. It took me being more independent, me handling my own money, me losing 50 pounds to get there."

She got there in spite of herself. Leading by five strokes on a sunny Sunday and seemingly on cruise control for her first victory, Kerr started struggling early with bogeys on the fifth and seventh holes to drop two shots to Korea's Hee-Won Han. A birdie at the 11th kept Kerr ahead by three, but she nearly threw the tournament away at the par-three 15th. She pulled a five iron 40 yards off line on the short hole, and the ball landed in a water hazard that shouldn't have been in play.

After taking time to compose herself, Kerr hit her third shot onto the green and two-putted for a double-bogey five. Han then birdied the 16th hole to evaporate what had seemed like a comfortable cushion. Kerr and Han walked to the 18th tee tied for the lead at eight under par.

Now it was Han's turn to make a mistake. She hooked her drive on the final hole so badly that it ended up in the glove compartment of a golf cart. After taking a drop onto some wood chips, Han pushed her four-iron second shot into the rough short and right of the green. She chipped on and missed her 20-footer for par.

Kerr regrouped after leaving her approach shot to the 17th some 50 feet short of the hole. When she almost holed the putt, she got a boost of confidence. That confidence carried over to the 18th where she split the fairway with a tee shot, then hit a seven-iron approach into the center of the green. She two-putted from 18 feet for the victory.

"I've never experienced anything as difficult as those last three holes," Kerr said after tapping in for a three-over-par 73. "I got a few gray hairs out there today."

Han finished alone in second at 281 after the bogey at the 18th gave her 70 for the day, while Heather Bowie shot a closing 71 to finish tied for third with Jane Crafter at 282.

As for having the weight of all the expectations removed, Kerr was philosophic beyond her years. "This is my sixth year on tour and it's a tough way to grow up," she said. "But I've learned so much about myself as a person, and I've done all the right things to become the best player I can be. I knew it would pay off eventually. I'm just glad those two putts today on 18 turned out the way they did."

Chick-fil-A Charity Championship—$1,250,000
Winner: Juli Inkster

After a couple of dry years, the LPGA's Atlanta stop, the Chick-fil-A Charity Championship, resumed its waterlogged reputation. The course was flooded for two days, forcing officials to short the event to 36 holes.

That suited Juli Inkster just fine. Coming back from an extended vacation after the Kraft Nabisco Championship, Inkster was just the kind of grinder who could overcome the conditions. "I've been out here forever," the 41-year-old said. "I should know how to handle it."

She handled it well, making an eagle on the final hole to shoot 12-under-par 132 and win by two strokes over first-round leader Kelly Robbins. As if the sloppy conditions weren't enough, Inkster had to wait almost 48 hours between her rounds. That gave her time to regroup after missing a few makeable putts in the first round. Her ball-striking was superb. She hit every fairway in her opening score of 66 and missed only two fairways on the second day for 66 again. Inkster had short iron approaches on most of the par-fours and she reached three of the four par-fives in regulation strokes.

After reaching 10 under par with a birdie at the 16th on Sunday, Inkster laced a drive on the par-five 18th, then hit a five wood to six feet. When that putt fell for eagle, she knew she had won. She pumped her fist and waved her visor in celebration.

Robbins wasn't so fortunate. Rust from her own layoff (she too hadn't played since the Nabisco) showed in her errant tee shots. After an opening 64, she struggled to find the fairway in the second round. Were it not for a birdie-birdie-eagle finish, Robbins risked falling out of the top five. As it was, the eagle putt at the 18th gave her a final round of 70 for a 134 total and sole possession of second place.

"I couldn't find my swing," Robbins said. "I thought I would play better today. Don't get me wrong, I'll take another second, but I'd like to do a little better at one of these."

Karrie Webb made a temporary appearance atop the leaderboard after making an eagle at the par-five sixth and a birdie at the seventh to get to nine under par. Her game went south on the second nine. Bogeys at the 10th and 11th started the slide. When the dust settled, Webb shot 39 for the nine holes and finished tied for ninth at 138.

Laura Diaz finished alone in third at 135 after a solid 69, while Se Ri Pak and Grace Park both shot 136 to tie for fourth.

Aerus Electrolux USA Championship—$800,000
Winner: Annika Sorenstam

The last time they had been in the same situation the result was a playoff and the largest comeback victory in LPGA history. This time things were a lot tighter, but the outcome was the same. Annika Sorenstam came from behind to beat Pat Hurst when Hurst made a mistake on the final hole. A year ago the event was the Office Depot, and Sorenstam made up 10 strokes on Hurst in the final round. This time it was the Aerus Electrolux USA Championship in Nashville, Tennessee — the invitational tournament run by country singer Vince Gill and his wife Amy Grant — and Hurst's third-round lead was only one shot. But the result was the same: Sorenstam smiled and hoisted the trophy, and Hurst hung her head and held back tears.

Unlike a year ago, Hurst didn't totally collapse in this final round. She and Sorenstam traded birdies for most the day, swapping the lead back and forth four times before they ran out of holes.

The turning point was the 18th, a reachable par-five. Sorenstam, who played two groups ahead of Hurst, left her second shot in the front fringe. She chipped to four feet and made the uphill putt for birdie to shoot 64 and 17-under-par 271 for the week.

Moments later Hurst birdied the 17th hole to reach 17 under. All she needed was a par on the 18th to go to a playoff. A birdie would win outright. After a good drive, Hurst chose a three wood from 199 yards. From the moment the ball came off the clubface she knew it was right. Hurst's ball hit the bank on the right side of the green and bounded into the water.

Now Hurst needed to save par to send the tournament into overtime. She sculled her wedge shot across the green, leaving a 25-footer for par, which never had a chance. The bogey gave Hurst a final round of 66 for a 272 total.

Flushed and fighting tears, Hurst tried to put a good face on the outcome. "I was in complete control all day, and I felt like I could do it (reach the 18th green in two). That's why I did it," she said. "But what can you do? Annika shot 64. She played great. Hats off to her."

Sorenstam was thrilled with how she played. "I did everything I could," she said. "Sometimes that means a lot to me. Winning is great and everything, but I did everything I could today. If Pat would have birdied 18, I still would've been happy. Sometimes you can only do so much."

Asahi Ryokuken International—$1,250,000
Winner: Janice Moodie

According to Scotland's Janice Moodie, the best way to beat the world's hottest player is to open up a huge early lead, then run away from the field with enough birdies to deflate any potential challengers.

That's exactly what Moodie did at Mount Vintage Plantation in North Augusta, South Carolina, in this second rendition of the Asahi Ryokuken International. "I've been feeling a bit of urgency," Moodie said. "For the last few months I've been hitting it great and not scoring. I figured if I stayed patient I would play my way out of it."

She did just that in the soggy slop of a rain-soaked course 15 miles from Augusta National. Saturday rains caused play to be suspended and everyone had to come back on Sunday morning. At the time Moodie — by virtue of earlier rounds of 70 and 66 — was two strokes ahead of Laura Davies and four ahead of Annika Sorenstam. The 28-year-old Glasgow native birdied two out of five holes in the wee hours of Sunday morning to double her advantage over Davies and move six ahead of Sorenstam with 18 holes to play.

Then Moodie slammed the door with a birdie from five feet on the first hole of the final round and another birdie from 12 feet on the third hole. Davies and Sorenstam didn't score a birdie in the first five holes.

The challengers tried to claw their way back into contention. Davies hit her second shot at the par-five sixth to four feet and made the putt for eagle, while Sorenstam birdied the fifth, sixth and seventh holes. Moodie bogeyed the seventh to see her lead shrink to three shots over Davies and five over Sorenstam. That was as close as anyone got.

Another birdie from five feet on the par-three seventh gave Moodie a four-shot edge and allowed her to play to the center of the greens for the remainder of the round. Her lead was nine with two holes to play, so the double bogey she made at the 17th didn't matter. A round of 70 gave her a 15-under-par 273 total, enough for a seven-stroke victory over Davies and an eight-shot margin over Sorenstam and Rosie Jones.

"I tried, but Janice played really solid," Sorenstam said. "She won the tournament outright, as you can see. I gave it a run, but it didn't work out this time."

Moodie admitted to feeling a little heat with Sorenstam around, even though the LPGA Tour's leading money winner never got within a handful of shots. "Obviously you're going to be intimidated playing with the best in the world," Moodie said. "I look at what Annika does and just try to emulate it, especially her putting. She's a good friend. But it's my second victory, and that says, 'You're good, you can do it.'"

Corning Classic—$1,000,000
Winner: Laura Diaz

The question of who would challenge the foreign LPGA contingent continued to nag many an American golfer. For her part, Laura Diaz made a bid for that title in Corning, New York, when she became the first native New Yorker to win the Corning Classic and the first American-born female golfer to notch multiple wins in 2002.

She led wire to wire after opening with a six-under-par 66 and following it up with two consecutive 69s. Rosie Jones, a three-time winner of the Corning Classic, was in hot pursuit after a Saturday round of 67 left her one shot off the pace. That margin was erased early on Sunday when Jones birdied the second hole to draw even with Diaz.

The tie didn't last long. Diaz birdied the par-three third after almost making an ace. Another bogey by Diaz at the fourth hole gave Jones another temporary share of the lead, but Diaz birdied the sixth to go in front for good. Jones fell to two back after a bogey at the eighth.

The ninth hole proved to be the turning point of the tournament. Italy's Silvia Cavalleri had charged up the leaderboard and was within a shot as Diaz stood on the ninth tee, and Jones, who was playing with Diaz, was two behind. But Diaz opened the door when she pushed her tee shot into the trees. An attempt at a punch-out produced a near-top. The ball only advanced to the thick rough. She then hit a poor sand wedge just short of the green. Needing to get up and down for bogey, Diaz hit a perfect chip with a pitching wedge from 30 feet that hit the flag and fell in for a par.

"It's a par, so I normally I wouldn't talk about it," Diaz said afterward. "But it was definitely a highlight. I was frustrated after a bad tee shot and a couple of other bad shots to get to the green. Fortunately, I was able to chip it in. It was great. You like them better when they're for birdie, but they're a little sweeter when they're to save par."

Eight more routine pars and a final birdie at the par-five 18th were enough to give Diaz the victory. She shot 70 for a 14-under-par 274 total and a two-stroke victory over Jones, who couldn't have been more complimentary of America's next great hope. "She's really getting comfortable and confident," Jones said. "She has a lot of passion."

Cavalleri finished tied for third with Marnie McGuire at 277 after closing with 70 of her own. The Italian seemed to be on a roll when she sank a 12-footer for birdie at the eighth to move within a shot of the lead. But a missed three-footer for par at the 13th, followed by a four-footer at the 14th that stayed out of the hole doused Cavalleri's chances.

Michele Redman also contended, reaching 11 under with an eagle and two birdies on the first nine, but she fell back when she also missed a three-foot par putt at the 13th. Redman finished at 279 and in a tie for sixth with Beth Bauer and Pamela Kerrigan.

Kellogg-Keebler Classic—$1,200,000
Winner: Annika Sorenstam

On Thursday afternoon before the first round of the Kellogg-Keebler Classic in Aurora, Illinois, Annika Sorenstam was asked what she thought the winning score would be. "Somewhere in double digits under par," she said.

Two days later Sorenstam proved herself correct as Danielle Ammaccapane, Mhairi McKay and Michele Redman all shot 10 under par to finish tied for second behind Sorenstam. What the 31-year-old Swede never could have imagined was that the double-digit number she mentioned on Thursday would start with a "2."

Sorenstam continued her romp through the LPGA by tying an all-time scoring record of 21-under-par 195 and routing the field in this first-year event. Her 11-stroke margin of victory was the largest of the year by four, and three strokes shy of another all-time record.

"I said 'double digits,' but I could not have expected 21 under," Sorenstam said. "I was right, but I didn't know it was going to be 20-something."

She got things rolling with a course-record 63 on Friday, then followed it with 67 on Saturday to take a five-shot lead over Ammaccapane into the final round. Things got a little tighter as Sorenstam got off to a slow start on Sunday. But when Ammaccapane almost aced the 130-yard, par-three eighth, Sorenstam answered by making a 20-footer for birdie on the same hole, her first of the day.

That got things rolling. Sorenstam birdied four of the next six holes to run and hide from the rest of the field. She had a chance on the 18th to break the all-time 54-hole scoring record (also 21 under par set by Wendy Ward at the 2001 Wendy's Championship), but an 18-footer for birdie at the 18th curled just past the hole.

"I hit a lot of lips today instead of the bottom of the cup," Sorenstam said. "I think that was the difference in the first few holes. Then I rolled in that nice birdie putt on eight. After that it just turned. To shoot 65 on Sunday, I'll take that any day. It would have been nice to shoot one or two better, but this was a sweet win anyway."

Ammaccapane had no illusions about contending for the title. "I really wasn't playing to win," she said. "I was playing to finish second because I didn't see Annika coming back." A 71 for Ammaccapane for a 206 total was only good enough for a share of second place, as McKay shot 70 and Redman shot 68 to reach double digits under par. Unfortunately they were all double digits away from victory.

McDonald's LPGA Championship—$1,500,000
Winner: Se Ri Pak

It was a duel steeped in symbolism — young versus old, history's past against the game's future, aging American dominance against new Asian dominance — and like the steady movement of a clock, it soon became evident that as romantic as the past might seem, it must give way to the passage of time.

Then there was the golf, which was pretty darned good. Se Ri Pak (age 24) trailed Beth Daniel (45) by four strokes at the start of the final round of the McDonald's LPGA Championship in Wilmington, Delaware. Pak was trying to become the youngest woman in history to capture all four major championships, while Daniel, already in the Hall of Fame, was trying to become the oldest woman to win a major.

The course was hard and fast with rough that gobbled up any errant shots. Only three players — Pak, Daniel and Karrie Webb — were under par after three rounds. By the end of the fourth day that number would be two. (Webb shot 74 to finish tied for fourth with Juli Inkster at 285.) It was no surprise that two of the most accurate ball-strikers and patient players in the game were battling it out in tough conditions. The only question was one of putting. Daniel, who went to the long putter years ago, could go through streaks where she couldn't make a tap-in, while Pak, the consummate grinder, could get streaky hot or streaky cold on the greens.

The final day started like a purist's dream. Daniel hit every fairway and every green for the first four holes. Pak was equally accurate and consistent, finding fairways and greens and birdieing the second hole to cut the lead to three.

The first signs of how the day would shape up came at the fourth hole, when Daniel hit her approach to four feet then watched as Pak hit her second shot to within one foot. Pak tapped in for birdie, but Daniel's shaky putting stroke reared its ugly head. The four-footer never hit the hole.

Pak played first at the par-three fifth and hit her tee shot safely in the middle of the green. When Daniel hit, she immediately yelled, "Get in the bunker!" The ball did, indeed, find the bunker. Daniel avoided the perils of the rough, but to no avail. She blasted out long and left, then chipped up and two-putted for a double bogey. Fortunately she only lost one shot as Pak three-putted for bogey. But the damage was done. What had looked like a comfortable lead had dwindled to a single shot and Daniel was struggling.

The true turning point came at the 10th, when Daniel's approach landed in the middle of the green but the ball rolled down a ridge and ended up 20 feet off the putting surface. Daniel bogeyed, and Pak had one of the rare birdies on the hole after skipping a wedge to within tap-in range. The tide had turned and it would never turn back.

Daniel struggled the rest of the round, limping in with 40 on the second nine for 77 on the day and a 282 total. Pak was on cruise control, missing only one fairway and two greens in the final round for 70 and a 279 total for a three-shot victory.

"It was really hard out there this week," Pak said. "I was really, really tired each day and asleep by nine every night. This golf course, something can happen anytime, anywhere. It was pretty tough mentally."

Daniel called the day "lousy," then bemoaned the fact that Babe Zaharias' record (the oldest major champion winner at age 42) was still secure. "I think the ghost of the Babe stepped on my ball," she said. Even Daniel had to admit that Pak won the tournament as much as she lost it. "She did everything she needed to do to win this golf tournament," Daniel said. "She hit fairways and greens and made putts. And I did none of that."

Pak surpassed Mickey Wright, who was the youngest to win all four majors at age 25. "This is the most special tournament," Pak said afterward. "I didn't push myself at all. I was swinging solid and putting great. I just did my best and I had a great score."

Evian Masters—$2,100,000
Winner: Annika Sorenstam

See Evian Ladies European Tour section.

Wegmans Rochester LPGA—$1,200,000
Winner: Karrie Webb

In a year when everyone was asking if anyone could beat Annika Sorenstam, the former world No. 1, Karrie Webb, had one answer: Not so fast. Webb captured her first victory of the season with a come-from-behind win at the Wegmans Rochester LPGA, shooting a closing 68 to bolt past a sputtering Mi Hyun Kim.

Kim, who had been the model of consistency all week with rounds of 69, 67 and 67, had a five-shot lead with one round to play and a four-shot lead with six holes left. Webb played in the final group, but she hadn't been quite as consistent. An opening 64 gave the Australian a four-shot lead, but a pair of lackluster 72s put her in a five-shot deficit.

Kim helped Webb out with bogeys on the 13th and 16th holes, the latter coming after her fifth wayward tee shot of the day found the high rough and she was unable to reach the green in two. Webb helped herself with two birdies on the first nine (along with one bogey) and a curling 12-footer for birdie at the 16th that turned the tide in her favor. When Webb's putt fell, Kim walked off the green staring at the sky and muttering to herself in Korean.

Weather was also a factor, and Webb played it to her advantage. The wind gusted up to 20 miles an hour at times, and Kim, who hits high, towering approaches and a lot of woods, struggled to overcome the elements. "I needed a little bit of wind to help me and I got my wish," Webb said. "Once I had that, I knew I had to step up to the plate and I did it. If I was going to play reasonably well, I knew the wind would make her think a little bit more and maybe not feel as comfortable as she probably did yesterday."

The 17th was a prime example. Kim hit a mile-high three-wood approach to the par-five and the wind pushed the ball right and into the rough. From there she had to stab a chip 20 feet by the hole. Her birdie putt narrowly missed. Webb played two knockdown shots to the front of the green, chipped to 10 feet and made the birdie. Heading to the 18th tee, the two were tied.

The wind knocked Kim's approach down on the 18th as well, leaving her 30 feet off the front edge of the green. Webb hit the green, but had a 30-footer for birdie. When Kim chipped to eight feet, Webb knew the tournament was in her hands. But a poor putt left her with a four-footer for par.

That's when a little strategy came into play. Rather than mark her ball and allow Kim to putt, Webb elected to finish, rolling her four-footer right in the heart for a 276 total, forcing Kim to make an eight-footer to tie.

"I didn't want to have a four-footer if she made it, and I think she probably would have made it if I had marked," Webb said. "Then my putt would have looked like it was about eight feet instead of four feet. I would have marked it in any other situation. I wanted to put it in the hole and put the pressure back on her."

Kim's eight-footer never had a chance.

"I did not have confidence," Kim said afterward. "I don't know why. I couldn't sleep last night. I got maybe two hours. Maybe I was thinking too much."

Webb felt no pressure, and that was the difference. "I never thought I didn't have a chance of winning," the winner said. "Sometimes you think three shots with three holes to go you might not really have much of a chance, but I've always played the last three holes on this course pretty well."

ShopRite Classic—$1,200,000
Winner: Annika Sorenstam

Annika Sorenstam had never heard of Vince Lombardi when she came to Atlantic City for the ShopRite Classic, but she certainly lived by one of the old coach's most notable quotes. Winning, it seemed, was a habit, one Sorenstam indulged in with much delight.

This time she won by three strokes, jumping past second-round leader Juli Inkster and outracing fellow Swede Carin Koch to the finish line with 67 and a 201 total. Sorenstam won her sixth tournament in only her 12th start of the year by hitting fairways and greens and outpacing one of the toughest closers in the game. "Every time I looked up, Annika was right down the middle," Inkster said. "And I only hit 10 greens today. You're not going to win a tournament hitting only 10 greens."

You might win one with three birdies in your first five holes from inside 10 feet. That's the way Sorenstam's final round started when she hit it close on the third, fourth and fifth and walked to the sixth tee at 10 under and moving up quickly. Two more birdies on the second nine were all she needed, even though Kate Golden, one of the few players who has charged from behind to beat Sorenstam (shooting 63 to make up six shots and win last year's State Farm Classic), had a two-shot lead with five holes to play. Bogeys on four of the last five holes dropped Golden to 71 and into a tie for second with Inkster and Koch at nine-under-par 204.

"I would have loved to win," Golden said. "But this is my second-best finish on tour, so I'm happy."

So was Sorenstam, who took command with a tap-in birdie at the 16th and finished with solid pars for her 201 total and another in a long line of victories. "The confidence is there," Sorenstam said. "Maybe I shouldn't ask the question why it's happening, but I'm sure enjoying this."

U.S. Women's Open—$3,000,000
Winner: Juli Inkster

Turn about was fair play in Juli Inkster's book. One week before, Annika Sorenstam had come from behind and snatched a victory away from Inkster at the ShopRite Classic on a tough windswept course in Atlantic City. It only seemed fair that Inkster would return the favor.

But this was the U.S. Women's Open, the most prestigious and important women's golf tournament by a mile, and Sorenstam was the best player in the world by an equally large margin. When she entered the final round with a two-shot lead, everyone assumed Sorenstam would do what she had done all year — close out the win by three, four, five, maybe 11 strokes. Not many folks gave Inkster much of a chance. Despite fond memories of Prairie Dunes and Hutchinson, Kansas (Inkster won the first of her three U.S. Amateur titles there), and a fan following that would make Kansas State basketball coaches green with envy, spotting Sorenstam two shots was like giving Marian Jones a 10-yard head start. By all rights, it should have been over.

But somebody forget to give Inkster the "you are supposed to lose" memo. Pumping her fists and whipping the fans into a frenzy, Inkster relied on a spotless short game to make up for a few spotty swings she made during the week. So bad was the swing that Inkster made a midnight call to her instructor, Mike McGetrick, Saturday night.

"Mike videotaped Saturday's round and saw that she was getting her weight too far forward," Inkster's husband, Brian, said. "He told her to get her weight back on her heels and to make a better turn going away from the ball to get the weight back."

The lesson worked, but it was still the putter that made the difference. Inkster stuck her tee shot on the par-three second hole to within five feet, and drained a bomb to save par from the fringe at the fourth after chipping out from the rough. Then she chipped in from 40 feet at the sixth for another birdie. Suddenly, she was tied for the lead.

"When Juli birdied the second hole, the look on her face ... I knew Annika was going to have to shoot under par to win," said Shani Waugh, who was in the group with Inkster and witnessed the fan enthusiasm when the putts started to fall.

Sorenstam knew something was happening, too. The roars from up ahead let her know that her lead was gone. Then on the seventh, another mammoth roar. Inkster rolled in a 25-footer from just off the fringe for birdie and the place erupted. Inkster got into the action, pumping her fists and waving to the crowd. It was a spectacle not seen in women's golf in years.

Sorenstam never gave up. She played just as consistently as she had all week, but the putter was the difference. Inkster needed only 105 putts for the week, a whopping 18 less than Sorenstam. "That was definitely the difference," Sorenstam said. "My strength has always been hitting the ball well. I hit a lot of fairways and greens. Juli must have figured out the greens, especially today."

That became evident on the par-three 15th, where Inkster pulled her tee shot badly and had to take a drop off some television cables. After chipping 15 feet long, she drained another par-saving putt, pumped her fist and whipped the partisan crowd into another frenzy. Sorenstam had just made a nine-footer of her own on the 14th to pull to within one, but she too missed the 15th green and hit a brilliant chip to five feet, but the putter abandoned her. She missed and Inkster had a two-shot lead with three to play.

The drama wasn't over yet. Inkster made another putt, this one from 12 feet for birdie at the 16th to increase the margin to three. That's when Johnny Miller, broadcasting for NBC, said, "This is the best putting round I've ever seen in a major for a man or woman."

Inkster's luck ran out at the 17th when she made bogey. That left the margin at two shots with one hole to play. Sorenstam had to make an eagle at the last. She hit driver on the par-five for the first time all week and the ball found the rough. Her wedge third shot was well right of the hole and it was over. Inkster had done what no woman had ever done, shooting 66 in the final round of a U.S. Open to win. Her 276 total was one of only two scores under par.

"I did everything I could do," Sorenstam said after tapping in for a final round of 70 and a two-under-par 278 total. "I think I played great golf. Juli played excellent. She really outplayed me. There was nothing I could do. I gave it all I had, and I'm happy about that."

Not as happy as Inkster, who did a high-five run-through on her way to the scorer's tent. "I'm 42 years old," she said. "I'm already in the Hall of Fame. Everybody asks me, 'Why do you continue to play?' I play because I love to play, and how can you not love to do what I did today? When I made that putt at 16, my heart was pumping so hard it was fantastic. That's why I work so hard at my game."

Jamie Farr Kroger Classic—$1,000,000
Winner: Rachel Teske

It seems like the best players in the world bring out the best in Rachel Teske. Earlier in the year she rallied from five shots down with 18 holes to play to catch Annika Sorenstam and then win the Ping Banner Health Classic in a playoff. Three months later at the Jamie Farr Kroger Classic in Sylvania, Ohio, Teske did it again, this time coming from one back to overtake Karrie Webb and Beth Bauer and win the event by two shots.

She did it with almost flawless ball-striking, hitting every fairway and every green. Her only bogeys came at the eighth and 10th holes as a result of three-putts on each green. Other than that, her final-round 66 was as perfect as a round of golf could be.

"I'm back on track and played so solid all day," Teske said. She birdied three of the first seven holes to jump out in front by one shot over Bauer and two over Webb. Then she lost the lead with the three putts at the eighth and 10th before regaining it for good with a 10-footer for birdie at the 11th and another 15-footer for birdie at the 12th. She made her sixth birdie at the 15th when her approach stopped 10 feet below the hole and the putt rolled straight in. Then at the 16th, she sealed the victory with another 15-footer for birdie, this one a curling right-to-left breaker that fell in the high side of the hole after she provided the necessary body English. Routine pars on the 17th and 18th were good enough for the closing 66 and a 12-under-par 270 total, two shots better than Bauer and three ahead of Webb and Laura Diaz.

Webb got out of the box slowly, bogeying the first three holes before rallying with four birdies on the back nine for a final round of 70, while Bauer made nine straight pars coming in for 69.

"I guess there aren't many people who can say they've come back against Annika and Karrie," Teske said. "It's a great feeling. It should give me even more confidence going forward."

Giant Eagle Classic—$1,000,000
Winner: Mi Hyun Kim

Mi Hyun Kim is shorter than Emilee Klein's driver — a fact the diminutive Korean sometimes forgets. "I saw a picture in the newspaper of Kelly Robbins and me. I didn't realize how short I am!" the 4-foot-11 Kim said. But she felt 10 feet tall when she hit a seven-wood shot to within four feet of the pin on the 53rd hole of the Giant Eagle Classic in Vienna, Ohio. That shot set up the final birdie, the one that would put her over the top and into the winner's circle after a series of disappointing second places, including losses to Karrie Webb and Annika Sorenstam where Kim held commanding leads going into the final 18 holes.

This time she trailed going into the final round. Robbins, another player who had not seen the winner's circle of late, led by one shot after rounds of 64 and 68. The nearest player to the final twosome was Grace Park, who started the day six shots back.

It felt like match play from the beginning, which should have worked to Robbins' advantage given her length. "I didn't like it, because she's a very long player," Kim said. "Every time she was playing a short iron, I'd have to hit a long iron or a fairway wood. But it seemed like every time I hit it closer."

Robbins held a two-shot advantage at the turn and continued to lead by two after both players parred the 10th. Then at the 11th, the tables turned. Kim hit her approach shot into the green with a seven iron that never left the flag. The ball stopped two feet from the hole. Then Robbins, who was 60 yards ahead, hit a fat sand wedge that found the front bunker. She blasted out to six feet, but missed her par effort. When Kim rolled the short birdie putt in the center of the hole, they were tied.

They both made pars over the next five holes, leaving things knotted until Kim hit her miracle seven-wood shot at the 17th. "I knew the way things were going for both of us that one or two shots were going to make the difference," Robbins said. "Neither of us were doing too much out there until Kimmy hit one close."

It was a shot Kim knew well and felt comfortable hitting. "Before that shot I had a lot of confidence," she said. "I knew how I had to hit the ball. Every time my shot had hooked back a little bit because I was on a little hill. I aimed a little to the right side of the pin, and it came back."

On the final hole both players hit the fairway, but once again Robbins was in different zip code than Kim. The Korean hit a five wood to the green, while Robbins had a seven-iron approach. The difference in the last hole illustrated the difference in the tournament. Kim hit her five wood to within 15 feet, while Robbins hooked her seven iron left of the green and into the gallery. After a drop, Robbins almost chipped in for birdie, leaving the ball a foot beyond the hole. Kim got a little anxious and ran her birdie putt three feet by, but nailed the par putt coming back.

"I hit a strong first putt," Kim said. "I was a little nervous."

Nerves didn't show when she rolled the second putt in the center of the hole for a closing 69 and a 14-under-par 202 total. Robbins finished with 71 for a 203 total, three strokes better than Park, who closed with 67.

It was Robbins' second loss of the year while holding the lead going into the last day. She dropped to 4-8 when protecting a final-round lead and 0-6 when that lead was only one shot. "I'm obviously disappointed, because any time you go into the final round of a tournament with a one-shot lead, you like to play well enough to win," Robbins said. "I just couldn't get the ball close enough. Any time you can finish second you've hit a lot of good shots, but I was licking my chops hoping for something better. I feel a little short-changed."

Kim understood perfectly. "Finishing second is really no fun," she said. "Today was fun."

Sybase Big Apple Classic—$950,000
Winner: Gloria Park

Under normal circumstances a 63 is cause for celebration, or at the very least a little praise and a pat on the back. At least that's what Gloria Park thought after shooting eight-under-par 63 on Saturday to earn a share of the lead with Annika Sorenstam (71-66-64) going into the final round of the Sybase Big Apple Classic in New Rochelle, New York. What Park didn't expect was the fight she had with her father, Steven.

It seemed the father was unhappy with the fundamentals of his daughter's putting, even though the daughter (age 22, and in search of her second LPGA victory) had leapt past stalwarts like Karrie Webb and Kelli Kuehne to earn a spot in the final pairing with the best female player in the world. The father-daughter spat carried over into the wee hours of the night. "I cried for two hours," Park said. "I really couldn't sleep."

Neither could the father, who kept the door to his daughter's adjacent room locked so she wouldn't hear him pacing. A fog delay helped both, as Park caught a few extra winks in her car thanks to a two-hour roll back, and Steven spent a few extra minutes in the hotel room pondering his mistake.

All was forgiven late Sunday afternoon as the young Korean put on a stoic display of shot-making. Park jumped ahead of Sorenstam quickly with a birdie at the par-five first hole, and extended the lead to two with another birdie at the par-five third. It was Sorenstam who seemed rattled early, frustrated by a putter that wouldn't cooperate. When Park hit a nine iron to three feet on the ninth and made the birdie putt, her lead was three over Hee-Won Han and four over Sorenstam.

The tide turned early on the back nine when Park bogeyed the 11th while Sorenstam and Han birdied. Suddenly the lead was one over Han and two over Sorenstam. Park and Han both birdied the 12th, and Han birdied the 13th to gain a share of the lead while Sorenstam three-putted for bogey to fall four behind.

Sorenstam rallied in the end with birdies at the 16th and 17th, and when both Han and Park bogeyed the 17th, the lead was back to one. But that was as close as the world's No. 1 woman golfer got. Her birdie effort at the 18th, which would have allowed her to join a playoff, slipped just below the hole. She shot a closing round of 70 (the highest in the final group) for a 13-under-par 271 total, one more than she needed for a chance at her seventh victory of the year.

"I had a good chance and hit a great putt that hole, but that wasn't the shot that lost it," Sorenstam said. "I had chances all day." But it was not her day, and Sorenstam accepted that with the grace of a champion. "They played excellent, both of them," she said. "Gloria made a lot of putts early, and Han never showed any fear."

Park and Han parred the final hole and headed back to the 18th for the playoff. They had finished with 14-under-par 270 totals, Park shooting 69 and Han, 67. Park won when her 100-yard wedge shot stopped six feet from the hole and she made the putt for birdie.

Then the tears came from both father and daughter. Steven was the first person onto the green to hug his daughter and to apologize for the turmoil of the previous night. "Sometimes he gets really cranky," the winner said. But not on Sunday night. There's nothing like a victory to smooth family tensions.

Wendy's Championship for Children—$1,000,000
Winner: Mi Hyun Kim

Say one thing for Mi Hyun Kim: She makes it interesting. Six weeks after blowing a five-shot lead to Annika Sorenstam and two weeks after coming from one back on the final day to beat Kelly Robbins, Kim did a little of both, double-bogeying the 17th to blow a lead, then salvaging par from the bleachers to hold off Hee-Won Han and win her second title of the year at the Wendy's Championship for Children in Dublin, Ohio.

"Golf is a difficult game," Kim said after the dust settled and she collected her $150,000 winner's check. "Nobody knows who's going to win."

This time Kim started the final round with a three-shot lead after rounds of 68 and 67. She maintained that lead through 16 holes on Sunday before pushing a five iron on the 148-yard, par-three 17th into the water. After a debate with LPGA officials about where to drop, Kim went back to the tee and hit another five iron. This one came up 12 feet short of the hole. She missed the 12-footer and came away with a double bogey. The lead was one.

"After Mi Hyun put the ball in the water, I got excited," Han said. "I was anxious to make another birdie at the next hole."

Maybe a little too anxious. Han found the rough with her tee shot on the 18th and had to chop her ball out in front of the green some 45 feet from the hole.

Meanwhile Kim's adventures continued. She hit one of her longest drives of the day in the middle of the final fairway, but her seven-iron approach sailed dead right into the grandstands. After receiving relief, Kim hit a deft chip from 45 feet that carried a small collection area and stopped three feet from the hole.

"After Mi Hyun put the chip close to the hole at 18, I knew she would win," Han said.

Kim rolled the three-footer in the center of the hole for 73 and an eight-under-par 208 total, good enough for a one-shot victory over Han (who closed with 70) and a two-shot edge over Danielle Ammaccapane (73-65-70).

"Every time I play in Ohio, I play good," Kim said. "When I play here I have a little bit of confidence."

Asked if she had learned the lessons of winning and losing after blowing the earlier lead to Sorenstam then beating Robbins in a down-to-the-wire finish, the Korean didn't mince words. "No," she said. "I still worry."

Weetabix Women's British Open—E1,580,110
Winner: Karrie Webb

See Evian Ladies European Tour section.

Bank of Montreal Canadian Women's Open—$1,200,000
Winner: Meg Mallon

When Meg Mallon awoke on Sunday morning and looked out her hotel window, she knew what kind of day it was going to be. "I saw the conditions and I just knew that it was going to be difficult," she said. "I knew that nobody was going to come from behind and shoot a low number to come back."

It was a tough day in Vaudreuil-Dorion, Quebec, at the Bank of Montreal Canadian Women's Open, with wind gusts blowing shots all over and players fighting to stay somewhere near the top of the leaderboard.

Trailing Catriona Matthew by one shot after three rounds, Mallon prevailed by making the least number of mistakes. Her one-over-par 73 was enough to give Mallon a four-under-par 284 total and a three-shot victory over Matthew, Michelle Ellis and Michele Redman.

Matthew, a native of Scotland and no stranger to severe weather conditions, birdied the first hole of the day to open up a two-shot lead, then looked unflappable after making 10 straight pars. But one swing and one gust of wind were all it took to derail her chances.

At the 344-yard, par-four 12th hole, Matthew hit her tee shot into a driving wind, and the ball sailed right and landed in a bush. She took a drop from an unplayable lie, but still had no shot at the green. All she could do was advance the ball back to the fairway. Her fourth shot, again into the teeth of the wind, landed short of the green. She then chipped to five feet and had to back away from the ball three times because of wind gusts before finally jabbing at the putt. Her double-bogey putt never hit the hole.

"I was just hitting a little four wood that I didn't hit that bad," Matthew said. "I got it turning left, and it went with the wind and ended up in the bushes. That 12th hole really threw me, and the last holes it was tough to try to make birdies. You were just trying to make pars."

Even pars were tough to come by. Mallon made birdie on the 11th to get to within one of the lead, then took a one-shot lead after the debacle at the 12th, even though the American hit both a tree and a spectator's forehead en route to a bogey of her own on that hole.

"I couldn't let myself think about winning," Mallon said. "I knew how difficult the holes were coming up. It was a matter of not making anything bigger than a bogey."

Mallon made another bogey coming in, but Matthew made more, closing with 77 to drop to 287. Se Ri Pak closed with 75 to finish at even-par 288 and alone in fifth place, while Gloria Park and Charlotta Sorenstam both finished at 289 for the week and shared sixth.

Only two players broke par for the day — Canadian Lorie Kane, who finished at 290 and tied for eighth, and Marisa Baena, who tied for 11th at 291. Both shot 71.

Eight players shot 80 or higher on Sunday, and the players who finished in the top 10 combined for 33 bogeys, four double bogeys and one triple. "It was brutal," Mallon said. But it was a win nonetheless.

First Union Betsy King Classic—$1,200,000
Winner: Se Ri Pak

Se Ri Pak has a knack for winning in style. In her first two victories of the 2002 season she came from behind in the final round to fend off challenges from some of the best in the world. In late August she picked up her fourth title of the year and 16th of her career when she birdied the last four holes to shoot a course-record 63 at the Berkleigh Country Club in Kutztown, Pennsylvania, and a tournament-record 21-under-par 267 to win the First Union Betsy King Classic by three shots.

On the final 18 holes Pak had two bogeys, six pars, nine birdies and an eagle. The victim of this eruption was Australian Michelle Ellis, who carried a two-shot lead into the final round, only to see it evaporate early. Ellis made bogeys on two of her first three holes, but so did Pak. Both players parred the fourth, then Pak holed a 30-foot chip for eagle at the par-five fifth and never looked back. Ellis shot 74 and finished tied for sixth at 275 with Joanne Morley and Danielle Ammaccapane, while Pak was off to the races.

"It was important to par the fourth hole," Pak said. "Then the eagle got me back on track. I still don't think this is my best for the season, but each day I swing the club better. My swing feels good right now."

Angela Stanford had the best week of her career, finishing with 66 for a 270 total and second place, two shots clear of Karrie Webb, who closed with 69.

"I just wanted to take it one swing at a time," Stanford said. "I feel a lot better about my career now, and I can just go out there and play as well as I could. I figured as long as I was making birdies I had a chance."

Any other week that might have been the case, but with Pak making birdies by the bushel on Sunday, this one was out of reach early. In addition to breaking the tournament record of 18 under par (set by Annika Sorenstam in 1996), Pak's 267 was also the best 72-hole tournament score of the year, beating Sorenstam's 19-under-par 269 at the Evian Masters.

"It was just a great week," Pak said. "I just feel really good right now."

State Farm Classic—$1,100,000
Winner: Patricia Meunier-Lebouc

Amid the backdrop of final qualifying for the Solheim Cup, a European veteran and member of the victorious 2000 team out-dueled Mi Hyun Kim and a charging Se Ri Pak at the State Farm Classic. Patricia Meunier-Lebouc of France had won five times in Europe, but the victory in Springfield, Illinois, was her first LPGA title.

"This year has not been easy for me," the 29-year-old said of her transition to the American tour. "I've worked so hard and had to let it go and just make the score happen."

The score that happened was a final-round 67 for an 18-under-par 270 total, two better than Kim and Pak, and three clear of Beth Bauer, Laura Davies and Emilee Klein.

Meunier-Lebouc had played well all week, leading after an opening 64 and holding the advantage with 67 on Friday. On Saturday it looked as though she would have a rough weekend. Her even-par 72 was the highest third-round score of any player in the top 10, and while Meunier-Lebouc retained a share of the lead, she allowed a dozen players back into contention. Among those who rose on the leaderboard was Kim, who shot 68 on Saturday to share the lead at 193.

Determined not to let one lackluster round spoil her chances, Meunier-Lebouc came out firing on Sunday, hitting her irons at the hole and rolling in a lot of early birdies. She needed them. Kim made four birdies on the first nine, the last coming at the ninth to take a one-shot lead, but Meunier-Lebouc wrestled back a share of the top spot with a 25-foot birdie putt at the 13th.

Kim bogeyed the 14th, which put the Frenchwoman on top. She remained there after both players birdied the par-five 15th. Beth Bauer, who played herself back into contention with 65 on Saturday, gained a temporary share of the lead when she too birdied the 15th. But Bauer hit her tee shot on the 163-yard, par-three 16th into the water and took a double bogey to drop from contention.

Meunier-Lebouc made steady pars on the 16th, 17th and 18th, while Kim struggled, recovering from greenside bunkers on the 16th and 17th but failing to get up and down for par after missing the green again at the 18th. "I was mad at the course," the Korean said after finishing with 69 for a 272 total.

"She played so well, which was good for me," Meunier-Lebouc said of playing with Kim. "At least I was with her and we were just fighting both together. It was much better for us to be together."

The low score of the day came from Pak, who crept up the leaderboard with 65 and finished tied for second with Kim at 272, but the big winner who didn't win was Klein, who earned the 10th spot on the Solheim Cup team with four rounds in the 60s and a tie for third place at 15-under-par 273. "This feels as good as a win," Klein said. "I've worked so very hard this week, and this just proves hard work pays off."

Williams Championship—$1,000,000
Winner: Annika Sorenstam

What does the best female golfer in the world do as a warm-up for the Solheim Cup? If you're Annika Sorenstam, you put a new driver in your bag and win your ninth worldwide event of the year.

"This is shaping up to be my best season ever," Sorenstam said after going low on Sunday with 65 for a 199 total to beat Lorie Kane by four shots at the Williams Championship in Tulsa, Oklahoma. "I'm thrilled with the way I played today. I made a few mistakes, but I bounced back quickly."

In addition to the new driver (a Callaway Great Big Bertha II she picked up the week before), Sorenstam experimented with a new/old putting grip, going back to the cross-handed style she used two years ago. "I know you're not supposed to fix something that isn't broken, but it's okay to try," Sorenstam said. "If it doesn't work, leave it. But if you see the results right away, and I did, it is fantastic."

Sorenstam made only one bogey on Sunday, but closed strong with birdies on the 17th and 18th to pull away from Kane. The two players hit approaches inside five feet on the par-three 17th, but Kane had to putt first and missed. When Sorenstam's putt fell in, she pumped her fist and got the crowd into it.

"She hit a great tee shot, but I hit a great shot myself," Sorenstam said. "I knew that if I made that putt I'd have a three-shot lead going into 18. I felt really comfortable after making it."

Another birdie at the 18th was merely academic. Kane put up a good fight, but she was no match for the best in the game. "Anytime you can play a final round with the No. 1 player in the world, you're doing things right," Kane said. "Still, I think I could have won if I'd put some pressure on Annika early on." Kane missed birdie opportunities on the first two holes. "But I'm happy with the way I finished."

The Canadian's closing 69 gave her a seven-under-par 203 total, one better than third-place finishers Joanne Mills and Cristie Kerr. Meg Mallon, another Solheim Cup stalwart, had the low round on Sunday, shooting 64 to tie for fifth with Beth Bauer at 206. "I was upset over playing so poorly on the first day," said Mallon, who opened with 74. "It was just a lack of knowledge of this course."

As for Sorenstam, the putting grip might change again in a few weeks, but the driver is definitely staying. "I'm probably carrying the ball 10 yards farther, but also now getting some roll," she said. The statistics bore that out. Sorenstam averaged 284.5 yards per drive for the week, almost 20 yards longer than her season average. "This week I hit some drives I couldn't believe. Now I know how Tiger Woods feels when he's 40 yards ahead of other players. It makes the course a lot shorter."

Safeway Classic—$1,000,000
Winner: Annika Sorenstam

There comes a moment in every epic event when you know that you're witnessing history. With Annika Sorenstam's 2002 season it wasn't so much a moment as a process, with each victory building the story throughout the year. She added one more chapter to that story at the Safeway Classic when she won her third title in a row and her 10th worldwide victory of the year.

"When you sit and add them all up, I'm really amazed by what I've done," Sorenstam said after shooting 17-under-par 199 to defeat Texan Kate Golden by one stroke.

Everyone else was amazed as well. Sorenstam, who stuck with her cross-handed putting style for the second week in a row, shot a course-record 62 at Portland, Oregon's Columbia Edgewater Country Club on Saturday to open a three-shot lead over Golden. But Golden wasn't about to give up. In September of 2001, Golden came from six shots back to beat Sorenstam in the final round of the State Farm Classic. Anther good final round this year would at least make things interesting.

Golden made a move with three early birdies, but things didn't get close until the second nine. Sorenstam birdied the 10th, then Golden birdied the 11th and 12th while Sorenstam's putter cooled. On the par-five 15th, Sorenstam hit her second shot in a greenside bunker, then blasted out long and missed her birdie try. The gap was narrowing.

At the 15th Sorenstam missed the green again and failed to get up and down. Golden missed a birdie of her own at the 15th, which would have tied her for the lead. Sorenstam's advantage was a single stroke with three holes to play. "I felt really comfortable after 10," Sorenstam said. "I thought I could play it safe for a while. But that didn't last long."

On the 18th, Sorenstam split the middle of the fairway and hit a perfect approach to 11 feet. Golden played the hole equally well, hitting her shot to 10 feet. If Sorenstam missed and Golden made, they would move on to extra holes. But Sorenstam removed all doubt when she drained the 11-footer for birdie and a final round of 68.

She raised her hands to the gallery, who understood the significance of what they were witnessing. Even Golden tipped her hat to Sorenstam. The Texan made her 10-footer to cut the margin of victory to one, but the win still went to the Swede.

Solheim Cup
Winner: United States

Team match play is about momentum, and even though the United States trailed Europe by two points at the end of the second round in the biannual Solheim Cup at Interlachen Country Club in Minneapolis, team captain Patty Sheehan knew the momentum had shifted in her squad's favor.

"We felt things starting to change on Saturday afternoon, and we were confident that we could get it done," Sheehan said. "We felt that being two points down was a victory for us, because the U.S. team has been a lot farther back than that in the past going into Sunday's singles."

Sheehan was right, and she had history on her side. Not only had the Europeans never won a Solheim Cup in America, the U.S. held a total advantage of 47½ to 28½ in singles matches. Nobody knows exactly why Americans dominate the singles competitions, but the numbers don't lie. In the past six meetings, America held a 14-point lead in Solheim singles.

Sheehan stuck to the strategy she had been plotting for months, putting veteran Juli Inkster out first on Sunday and Rosie Jones out as the anchor. Inkster, who won a point on Saturday after losing one on Friday, lost the first hole of her match against Raquel Carriedo, but squared the match on the second hole and never trailed again. Getting the crowd behind her — as she always does — Inkster put the first point on the board by defeating Carriedo 4 and 3.

Laura Diaz, the fiery Solheim rookie, drummed Paula Marti 5 and 3 to square the matches at 10 points each. But the momentum was clearly moving in the Americans' favor. Even a win by Denmark's Iben Tinning over Kelli Kuehne (who went 0-4 in her Solheim debut) couldn't turn the tide. When Emilee Klein sank the winning putt to upset heavily favored veteran Helen Alfredsson 2 and 1, the Americans squared the matches at 11 points apiece. They would never trail again.

Kelly Robbins was the next player to post a victory, winning 5 and 3 over Sweden's Maria Hjorth to put the U.S. up 12-11. It might as well have been 12-0 at that point. The wind was out of Europe's sails.

Meg Mallon beat Laura Davies 3 and 2. When asked why the Americans played so well in singles, Mallon said, "Because we have to. You're playing for your team and your country, and I think Juli (Inkster) and I really get into that. We play hard and stay within ourselves."

The biggest surprise came two matches later when Wendy Ward took Annika Sorenstam to the final hole and had a six-footer to win the match. Even though she missed the short putt, a split between the world's No. 1 player and the No. 56 player was like a win for the U.S. "I felt like if I could take her to 18, I would have done my job," Ward said. "That's what Patty expected of me, to take it to the end."

Rosie Jones sealed the victory with a 3-and-2 win over Karine Icher of France for the requisite 14½ points.

Carin Koch, the hero of the 2000 Solheim Cup, kept her unblemished Solheim record intact by halving her match with American Beth Daniel, but the 7-0-1 record didn't mean much when it was over. "We lost the cup," Koch said. "That's all that matters."

Patty Sheehan did cartwheels across the 18th green when it was finally over. "I'm lucky I didn't pull a groin," the 45-year-old said. With the Solheim Cup firmly in hand, she wouldn't have been too upset even if she had.

Samsung World Championship—$775,000
Winner: Annika Sorenstam

Not since Nancy Lopez did it in 1978-79 had any woman won 17 tournaments in a two-year stretch until Annika Sorenstam did it in 2001-02. Her six-shot victory at the Samsung World Championship in Vallejo, California, her ninth LPGA win and her 11th worldwide victory of the year put Sorenstam in the league of legends and had her setting her eye on that one line in the LPGA Media Guide that continued to nag at her.

It's found on page 346 in small print, one line that doesn't jump out unless you're someone like Sorenstam. It's underneath a photo of Mickey Wright from the early 1960s and beneath the statistics that show Wright had 13 major titles and 82 career wins. "In 1964," the line reads, "her 13 victories is a record that may never be touched."

With 11 wins by the first weekend in October, Sorenstam hoped to erase that line. The Samsung event was Sorenstam's fourth victory in a row, and gave her two more wins at this point in the season than Juli Inkster, Karrie Webb and Se Ri Pak combined.

She won by shattering another tournament record, this time shooting 66-67-68 and closing with 65 for a 22-under-par 266 total, good enough to run away from second-place finisher Cristie Kerr.

"I don't believe you should limit yourself," Sorenstam said. "That's what keeps me going forward. I think I can improve in every area of my game. You should be able to birdie every hole and shoot 54. So why should you limit yourself? Sky's the limit."

If there was ever a doubt about this one, it was answered on the first hole on Sunday when Sorenstam, who started the day tied with Kerr, made a birdie while Kerr pushed a tee shot out of bounds and made a double bogey. A bogey by Kerr at the second hole extended the margin to four. Birdies by Sorenstam at the fifth, seventh and ninth kept the lead at four, and an eight-foot birdie putt at the 13th followed by another birdie from 10 feet at the 15th extended the margin to six. Sorenstam made her last birdie on the 18th hole, even though the victory was never in doubt.

"I think I'm playing better now than ever before," the winner said. "I wanted to beat my record from last year, and here I am."

Kerr remained alone in second place after closing with 71 for a 272 total. "I just got off to a terrible start," she said. "I struggled with my swing early. But in that situation you can either fight or give up, and you saw what I did. I had to play tip-top golf today and I didn't do it. But I didn't give up either. I was fortunate to make some putts coming down the stretch and was able to finish second. I didn't ever say to myself, 'I'm playing for second.' You always think you have a chance to win, but at some point you realize that you're not going to."

That's a realization a lot of people have had when they came up against Sorenstam. "She's just phenomenal," Inkster said. "Other players, if they win once or twice, they've had a great season. But Annika, she keeps doing it. She never gets tired of winning."

Mobile Tournament of Champions—$750,000
Winner: Se Ri Pak

It's hard to feel sorry for someone with nine LPGA victories in a season, 11 worldwide wins for the year and 17 in the past 48 months, but that is what Se Ri Pak said she felt for Annika Sorenstam after the former beat the latter in the Mobile Tournament of Champions in Alabama. Not that Sorenstam was looking for sympathy, but with a record-tying 13 single-season victories within her reach, having a spoiler like Pak take a big one away late in the year stings more than usual.

"I don't think she likes me," Pak said after closing with 66 for a four-stroke win over Carin Koch and Catriona Matthew. Sorenstam finished five shots back after a closing round of 70. "I feel sorry for her," Pak said, "but I was hungry for a win too."

Koch held the lead after each of the first three days, posting her best score of the year on Thursday when she shot 10-under-par 62. But the numbers got progressively higher from there. Friday's 66 was still good enough for a comfortable lead, but Saturday's 70 was a bad sign. Koch still held a three-shot lead, but her game was headed in the wrong direction.

Pak played the way she always played — consistently making great strikes and riding the wave of a sometimes-streaky putter. Her 65-70-67 scores put her within sight of the lead and in the final group with Koch.

Koch birdied the second hole, but bogeyed the third to drop a shot to Pak. Pak eagled the fourth, and Sorenstam, who shot 66-70-66 the first three days, started to march up the board with birdies at the third and fifth. Every player on the course knew where Sorenstam stood. She was the name everyone watched.

"I saw her score on the front nine," Pak said. "I knew that Annika was going to be the one to start firing on the back nine. Annika was right behind, so I knew I had to play well."

Koch held onto the lead until the 14th hole when Pak rolled in a birdie putt to tie her. When Pak made another birdie at the 15th, the lead was hers for good.

Sorenstam trailed by two with three holes to play, but didn't get up and down for birdie on the easiest hole on the course, the par-five 16th, after pushing her second shot into a questionable lie. "I had a four wood to the 16th green and just missed it right," she said. "I could have still gotten up and down for birdie and birdied the last two. I'm disappointed in the way I played."

Sorenstam bogeyed the 18th, but by then it didn't matter. Pak birdied the 16th and 17th before parring the 18th to shatter the tournament record of 16-under-par she set only a year ago when she won this event.

"After last year, I think I know how to play this golf course, especially since I won the tournament," Pak said. "I have a lot of confidence, so I played well again."

Koch was disappointed as well. "I knew if I could shoot three or four under and get it to 20 or 21 under, someone would have to go low. I didn't feel like I played as bad as my score, but I didn't play great. If three or four putts drop, that makes a big difference. I've just got to work on my swing so that it's a little more consistent under pressure. It's not quite there now."

Sports Today CJ Nine Bridges Classic—$1,500,000
Winner: Se Ri Pak

Only one player managed to break par for the three rounds of the Sports Today CJ Nine Bridges Classic on the windswept Jeju Island of South Korea. The fact that it was homegrown Se Ri Pak surprised no one.

Pak closed with an even-par 72 for a 213 total and a six-stroke victory over Carin Koch. It was the first time Pak had ever played an LPGA event in her home country, and it might have been the only venue in the world where Pak had a decided advantage over Annika Sorenstam, who was making a bid to win a record 13 tournaments in a season.

"There's always a lot of pressure coming back to Korea to play golf," Pak admitted. She's more recognized in her home country than the Korean Prime Minister, and the crowds cheered every step she took. Her photo was on the front page of every newspaper in Korea, and her appearance led every newscast for the week.

"Because it's an LPGA event, it's different than the other times I played in Korea," Pak said. "But I think I controlled myself well. I just freed my mind and it feels really good to win."

The victory was never in doubt. The warmest day was 45 degrees and the wind and rain made it seem much colder throughout most of the week. Pak shot the low round of the tournament on Friday when she opened with 65. Only one other player, Jackie Gallagher-Smith, broke 70 (by shooting 69), and the field averaged 75.1 for the day.

Saturday was even worse. Pak shot 76 and didn't lose ground on a day when no one broke par and the lowest score was 73 posted by Annika Sorenstam. The highest score was 89, and 41 players failed to break 80. "I've never played in anything like it," Sorenstam said.

The sun finally came out on Sunday, but the wind picked up and the temperature dropped even lower. Gallagher-Smith, the only person within striking distance of Pak at four back, ballooned to 85. Koch, who shot 70 and 76 the first two days, shot 73 in the tough conditions to move into second place at 219, but nobody challenged Pak. Her 72 was one of her best rounds of the year, given the conditions.

"It was tougher today than yesterday," said Sorenstam, who finished tied for fifth after closing with 76 for a 222 total. "The wind was a little stronger and the temperature was much lower. So it was quite a tough day."

Cisco World Ladies Match Play—¥107,100,000
Winner: Grace Park

See Japan LPGA Tour section.

Mizuno Classic—¥138,990,000
Winner: Annika Sorenstam

See Japan LPGA Tour section.

ADT Championship—$1,000,000
Winner: Annika Sorenstam

It was only fitting that Annika Sorenstam would come from behind to win the ADT Championship at Trump International in West Palm Beach, Florida.

What better way to add an exclamation point to her season than with a 13-under-par 275 total and a three-shot victory in the season-ending event? And what better way to end the season than with a fantastic second-nine duel with third-round leader Rachel Teske?

"I'm at a loss for words," Sorenstam said afterward. "I gave it all I had. I came to win."

Winning was no guarantee this week, especially with Teske carrying a one-shot lead into the final round. Known among her peers as "Pesky Teske," the Australian had proven herself to be a great front-runner and a formidable challenger to Sorenstam. Teske won the Ping Banner Health Classic earlier in the year in a playoff against Sorenstam after trailing the world's No. 1 going into the final round. No one expected Teske to go away quietly.

By the fourth hole Sorenstam had erased the one-shot deficit and drawn even with Teske and Karrie Webb at 10 under par. Webb fell away with a sloppy bogey at the sixth and a tee shot that found the water on the short par-four seventh and led to a double bogey. That left Teske and Sorenstam alone to battle for the title.

Sorenstam took the upper hand with birdies on the sixth and ninth to carry a three-shot lead into the final nine. But Teske rallied at the 10th. After laying up perfectly on her second shot, she hit a wedge into the par-five that never left the flag. One skip later, the ball hit the flag and fell in for an eagle. Teske had clawed back to within one.

Two holes later Sorenstam showed some uncharacteristic sloppiness of her own, flubbing a chip on the par-five 12th, then pushing a par putt that never hit the hole. The bogey left the two tied with six holes to play.

Sorenstam pulled back into the lead with a birdie at the 14th, but the key to her round came at the 16th, the toughest hole on the course. After driving the ball in the right rough, Sorenstam played a low punch that rolled through the green and against the high grass bordering the fringe. She used her four wood to putt the ball from the awkward lie and it barely missed the hole. The tap-in par gave Sorenstam the confidence she needed to finish strongly.

On the par-three 17th, Sorenstam hit a perfect seven iron to five feet, and she rolled the birdie putt in the center of the hole to move to 13 under. Teske, playing one group behind, rolled in a 10-footer for birdie at the difficult 16th, but Sorenstam's lead remained one stroke. The unlikely par at the 16th was the difference.

Teske, knowing she needed at least one more birdie, pushed her five-iron tee shot at the 17th. The ball bounded off an embankment and into the water. She walked away with a double bogey, and Sorenstam cruised home with a par at the 18th for 68 and a comfortable three-stroke win.

It was Sorenstam's 11th LPGA victory of the season (the most since Mickey Wright won 13 in 1963) and her 13th worldwide in just 25 starts, the best winning percentage since Wright won 10 times in 17 starts in 1961.

Webb limped in with 74 for sole possession of third place at 281, while Patricia Meunier-Lebouc continued to acclimate herself well to the LPGA Tour by finishing with three consecutive 71s for a 282 total and fourth place.

Evian Ladies European Tour

Australasian Ladies Masters—A$750,000
Winner: Annika Sorenstem
See Australian Women's Tour section.

AAMI Women's Australian Open—A$500,000
Winner: Karrie Webb
See Australian Women's Tour section.

Ladies Tenerife Open—€200,000
Winner: Raquel Carriedo

Having battled through the high winds for three rounds in the Ladies Tenerife Open, Spain's Raquel Carriedo took advantage of the calm on the final day to claim her fourth Ladies European Tour victory. Carriedo, first on the money list in 2001, had maintained her lead in the third round despite 77 as scoring soared in the winds.

But a final round of 71, to finish four over par, left Carriedo one ahead of England's Johanna Head. Carriedo's advantage was greater than that for most of the day, particularly after she holed out with a wedge shot for an eagle on the 313-yard eighth hole. She was three clear with two holes to play before finishing bogey-bogey. Finding a bunker with her second shot at the 18th, she made sure of the bogey rather than try for the par.

"I was very nervous out there, especially coming down the last," said Carriedo, who secured her place on the European Solheim Cup team. "I started off very well and made some solid pars out there, and when I made the eagle, it pushed my confidence up a lot. Then I was just thinking make pars and pars to get in. But on the 17th I hit the wrong club and thought it's not finished yet. It's never easy, but I am very happy now."

Head, who was suffering from a neck injury, made six birdies in nine holes around the turn, but hoping to birdie the 18th to set a target score, she three-putted. Marine Monnet from France and Germany's Elisabeth Esterl shared third place at eight over par after a grueling week in the wind.

Ladies Irish Open—€165,000
Winner: Iben Tinning

A hole-in-one during the final round of the Ladies Irish Open was not good enough to give victory to Sweden's Maria Boden. The rookie holed her five iron at the 153-yard eighth hole, but did not even get into a playoff at Killarney. Instead, Iben Tinning beat Suzann Pettersen at the first extra hole to claim her first victory in her seventh year on tour.

The 28-year-old from Copenhagen made the early running, but Pettersen made up ground as she birdied the 11th and 15th holes, while Tinning bogeyed both. The pair were tied at two under par and both birdied the 17th, Pettersen missing from six feet for an eagle, before both bogeyed the last. Tinning, the cousin of Steen Tinning, a winner on the men's European Tour, could not get up and down from a bunker, while Pettersen three-putted.

In the playoff, Pettersen played a brilliant recovery after putting her drive at the 18th on the fourth fairway, but once again three-putted from 30 feet to lose to a par.

"I can't believe it," said Tinning, who lost in a playoff to Sophie Gustafson at the 1998 Ladies Irish Open. "This has always been a big goal for me and, to be honest, it's come as a bit of a surprise because my putting hasn't been so good lately. This will mean a lot to the people of Denmark, and I hope that people will focus on us a lot more instead of just our boys."

Boden finished one shot behind while four players tied for fourth place at one over par, including Corinne Dibnah from Australia, England's Trish Johnson and Kirsty Taylor, and Spain's Marina Arruti.

La Perla Italian Open—£117,000
Winner: Iben Tinning

Denmark's Iben Tinning won for the second consecutive week, adding the La Perla Italian Open to her Irish crown. Tinning beat Italy's Silvia Cavalleri by one stroke in a tense battle in the final round at Poggio dei Medici in Tuscany.

Cavalleri began the day one stroke ahead, but Tinning overtook her with a three-under-par 70 to close at 14 under. At the first hole, a two-shot swing meant the Italian was leading by three before Tinning birdied four of the next six holes to forge ahead.

Coming home Tinning made nine straight pars to secure the second win of her career. "To be honest, I'm stunned," said Tinning, the first back-to-back winner on the Ladies European Tour since Sandrine Mendiburu in 1999. "It's a nice habit to have really, no wins in seven years then two come along at once. I really can't understand it, the win last week was brilliant, and this week, it's even better."

New Zealander Gina Scott finished in third place at nine under par, with Australian Karen Lunn in fourth place after a course-record 64 in the third round.

Ladies Open of Costa Azul—€70,000
Winner: Kanna Takanashi

A Canadian television documentary team chose the right week to follow Japan's Kanna Takanashi at the Ladies Open of Costa Azul. Takanashi, 32, claimed her first-ever victory with a one-stroke win over Scotland's Julie Forbes.

Forbes scored a fine 68 in the blustery conditions in the final round, but

Masters Tournament

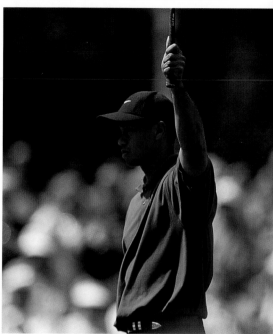

Starting the fourth round in a tie for the lead, Tiger Woods shot 71 to win by three strokes.

Masters chairman Hootie Johnson helped Woods into his green jacket after Tiger's second consecutive Masters victory and the third of his career.

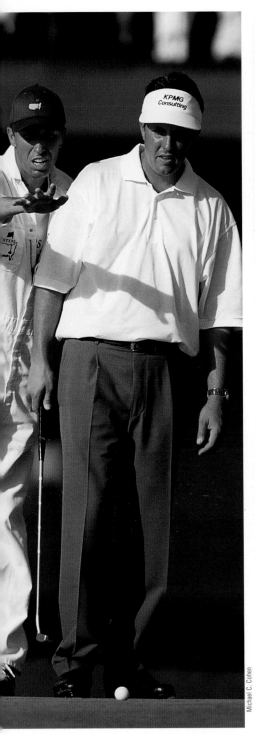

Jose Maria Olazabal took fourth alone.

Phil Mickelson was third, as in 2001.

Retief Goosen fell to second place.

Michael C. Cohen

Vijay Singh shot 65 to lead after 36 holes.

Ernie Els shared fifth place.

Michael C. Cohen

Padraig Harrington's best round was 69 the first day and he tied Els, six strokes behind.

Leading wire-to-wire, Tiger Woods won his second U.S. Open and eighth USGA title.

Michael C. Cohen

Phil Mickelson applied the pressure.

Jeff Maggert stayed close for four days.

Sergio Garcia let his emotions show.

Scott Hoch advanced with a final 69.

Nick Faldo was a crowd favorite.

British Open

With his left foot in the sand, and his right foot bent at an angle, Ernie Els played out to four feet for the playoff victory in the British Open.

Els won despite his struggles in the final round and a four-man, four-hole playoff.

Steve Elkington bogeyed twice in the playoff.

Thomas Levet took Els to the end.

Stuart Appleby missed at the 11th, but closed with 65.

Gary Evans holed from 40 feet at the 17th.

Tiger Woods struggled to 81.

PGA Championship

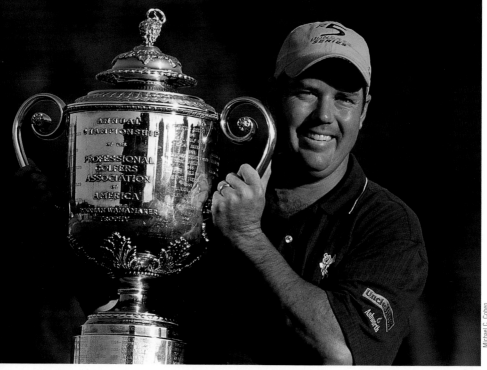

Michael C. Cohen

Unexpectedly, it was Rich Beem raising the trophy at the conclusion of the PGA Championship.

Michael C. Cohen

Beem holed for an eagle at the 11th following a great seven-wood shot from 271 yards.

Michael C. Cohen

Tiger Woods was one stroke short.

Michael C. Cohen

Chris Riley was third with four solid rounds.

Michael C. Cohen

Justin Leonard shot 77 Sunday and fell back.

Michael C. Cohen

Fred Funk enjoyed the spotlight.

Michael C. Cohen

Mark Calcavecchia collapsed with 74-74.

U.S. PGA Tour

Despite his two PGA Tour victories, Phil Mickelson was still burdened by his lack of success in the major championships. He was second in the U.S. Open and third in the Masters.

Vijay Singh finished by winning the Tour Championship, to go with the Shell Houston Open.

David Toms was fourth on the U.S. money list.   Ernie Els won $6.2 million worldwide.

Justin Leonard won at Heritage.

Charles Howell claimed his first victory.

Jim Furyk took the Memorial title.

Retief Goosen had three worldwide wins. Sergio Garcia won in U.S., Spain, Asia.

Michael C. Cohen

Fred Funk earned $2.7 million worldwide.

Scott Halleran/Getty Images

Jerry Kelly had two U.S. victories.

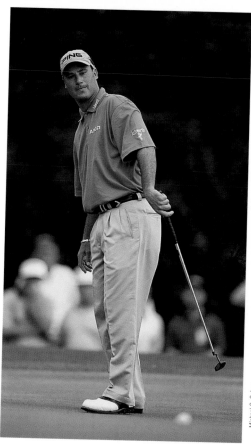

Michael C. Cohen

Chris DiMarco was the Phoenix champion.

Michael C. Cohen

Jeff Sluman won at Milwaukee.

Shigeki Maruyama won in Dallas.

Len Mattiace had two victories.

Nick Price topped the Colonial.

Davis Love made over $2.5 million.

K.J. Choi won in New Orleans, Tampa.

Scott Hoch played well in U.S., British Opens.

Robert Allenby was 20th on U.S. money list.

Craig Parry took the NEC title.

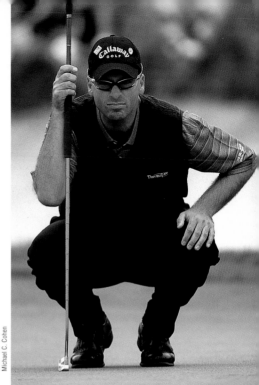

Rocco Mediate won at Greensboro.

David Duval did not have a victory.

The Players Championship

In his first try, Craig Perks had a prestigious win in The Players with an eagle-birdie-par finish.

Stephen Ames shot 67 but was two back.   Rocco Mediate took third place.

could not quite catch Takanashi, who finished the 36-hole event at five under par after rounds of 69 and 70. Her final round contained seven birdies, a bogey and two double bogeys.

One shot further back in third place were England's Nicola Moult and New Zealander Lynnette Brooky. Sweden's Nina Karlsson made a costly visit to the water at the final hole when she was tied for the lead and finished tied for fifth place.

"I am shaking now, I have even got goose bumps," said Takanashi. "I was very nervous out there today, I have never seen so many television people, including my guys. Standing over that last putt, I was just thinking playoff-win-playoff-win, and I made it."

Caja Duero Open de Espana—€250,000
Winner: Karine Icher

Karine Icher held firm to her lead to win the Caja Duero Open de Espana by one stroke from local favorite Raquel Carriedo at Salamanca. It was a third career win for the 23-year-old Frenchwoman after she won twice in her rookie season in 2001.

Icher led by two strokes going into the final round over Carriedo and New Zealand's Lynette Brooky, but the Spaniard birdied the first two holes to draw even. With Icher dropping shots at the third and seventh, Carriedo went three ahead with a birdie at the ninth.

Icher birdied the 11th before Carriedo restored her three-shot advantage at the next. At the short 13th, Carriedo bogeyed and Icher holed from off the green for a birdie for a two-shot swing. Carriedo then also bogeyed the 14th, and Icher hit a nine iron to three feet at the 17th for the winning birdie.

"It was an unbelievable day," Icher said. "Raquel played so well today and I felt the pressure early on. I was thinking about playing for second or third place. But when I holed out on the 13th, and she made a couple of bogeys, that was the break I needed. I made a good par save on the 15th and that was another key moment, and on the 17th, that shot was almost perfect."

Icher closed with 71 to finish at 11 under par, while Carriedo had 70. Brooky finished three behind the winner, sharing third place with Paula Marti, who equaled the best round of the week with 67.

Evian Masters—US$2,100,000
Winner: Annika Sorenstam

On a steaming hot day beside Lake Geneva in the foothills of the Alps, Annika Sorenstam showed again why she is untouchable as the best woman golfer in the world. The Evian Masters brings together the leading players from both the LPGA and European Tours, and Sorenstam won for the second time in three years.

Holding a four-stroke lead going into the last day, thanks to 65 in the third round, Sorenstam was briefly pulled back to two ahead when Mi Hyun Kim made three birdies in a row from the third. But Sorenstam soon rallied, and with birdies at the third, seventh and 10th, she was five in front.

The eventual winning margin was four shots over Kim and Maria Hjorth, who sprung out of the pack with 64 using a "belly" putter. Sorenstam closed with 69, her highest score of the week, to be 19 under par, a new tournament record. Laura Diaz, after a final round of 65, and Se Ri Pak, winner of the LPGA Championship the week before, shared fourth place at 14 under. Vicki Goetze-Ackerman took sixth place.

This was the 31-year-old Sorenstam's second European Tour win of the season and the sixth worldwide. It was her 44th career win and ensured her place on the European Solheim Cup team.

"My goal was to win here for many reasons," said Sorenstam. "I love this event. It is like the women's Masters. This is a first-class event, with a first-class field, and I have achieved my goal. I couldn't feel any better. I am determined to keep improving, and with the way I am playing now, I really feel like a better player, scoring-wise at least.

"You cannot always measure success in wins. The way I look at the game, I am playing better, striking the ball better, and I'm making more putts, and that is what I am looking for."

Open de France Dames Credit Mutuel Nord—€275,000
Winner: Lynnette Brooky

New Zealand's Lynnette Brooky swept away the opposition to win the Open de France Dames Credit Mutuel Nord with an eagle and four birdies in her closing round of 66 in Arras. It was a second victory for the 34-year-old from Wellington, following her win in the Austrian Open in 1998.

Brooky finished at 16 under par and left some of the European Tour's brightest young talents in her wake. She won by five strokes over Spain's Paula Marti, who closed with 68, and seven over two-time winner Iben Tinning and two Frenchwomen, Marine Monnet and Karine Icher. All three players had final rounds of 70 after sharing second place with Marti after 54 holes, three behind Brooky.

Tinning birdied the opening hole, but Brooky was always in command after her eagle at the fourth hole. Her birdie at the 18th gave her the lowest score of the day and brought her run of tournaments without a three-putt to five in a row.

"I wasn't really nervous out there, I just thought to myself, do what you have to do," said Brooky. The Kiwi admitted there were a few mental scars to get over after her win in Austria four years earlier. "I went to a psychic and she said to me, 'I can't see you winning again.' I also went to a psychiatrist who reckoned the problem stemmed from my last win in Austria.

"What I actually said then was I would like to 'Spank' the sponsors at the presentation, and I scared myself because Trish (Johnson) and Laura (Davies) were in the ceremony and they were falling over themselves laughing, and I automatically thought to myself, 'I don't want to do that again.'"

P4 Norwegian Masters—£220,000
Winner: Laura Davies

Laura Davies continued her record of winning every year since she turned professional in 1985 by winning the P4 Norwegian Masters in Oslo. To do so the 38-year-old Englishwoman needed two extra holes to defeat the diminutive Spaniard Ana Larraneta.

Larraneta, a 29-year-old from Pamplona, caught Davies with a final-round 68, while Davies could only manage 73 to tie at five under par. Larraneta had an eagle and two birdies to set the clubhouse target, but Davies bogeyed the 17th to fall back into a playoff. "It's going to be like David and Goliath. I'm going to have to look up at this big, tall girl and I'll be so nervous," laughed Larraneta.

Larraneta, whose previous best finish was fifth place, holed a six-foot putt at the 18th to make sure the first extra hole was halved in pars. When the hole was played again, Davies hit a wedge to five feet, and after the Spaniard's birdie effort came up just short, she holed the putt and punched the air after the 64th win of her career.

"I've managed to keep my record going of winning every year," Davies said. "I'm not a big fan of playoffs. I could have won a bit earlier, but the bogey at 17 didn't help. I hit a good tee shot and it just bounced straight back into the ditch, and it was always a bogey from there. Ana played those two extra holes very well and I knew that anything could happen in the playoff."

France's Marine Monnet and Karine Icher tied for third place at four under par. Icher led by one stroke before bogeying two of the final three holes, and Monnet had a chance to make the playoff but missed from six feet at the 18th. Australia's Shani Waugh equaled the course record of 66, set by England's Samantha Head during the first round, to share fifth place with Sophie Gustafson.

"This is definitely the best week of my life," Larraneta said. "When I finished at five under, it just felt so good, especially after yesterday's 78. Laura was so nice to me in the playoff, she was truly the best, so professional, and she made me feel so relaxed. I didn't do anything wrong in the playoff. I had a chance to make birdie the second time, but the putt just jumped.

"But it was such a proud moment for me. You always dream of being up there with a chance to win, and I had to pinch myself in the presentation standing next to Laura, Karine Icher and Marine Monnet. I was thinking, 'How good is this?'"

Weetabix Women's British Open—€1,580,110
Winner: Karrie Webb

Karrie Webb, the Australian from Ayr in Queensland, grew up in a town where it seldom falls below 80 degrees and rarely rains. Just down the coast from Scotland's original Ayr, where it rarely gets above 80 degrees and is seldom not raining, Webb won the Weetabix Women's British Open.

Webb came from three strokes behind the lead to clinch victory with a flawless round of 66. The Ailsa course at Turnberry demanded a variety of shot-making skills all week, and in the damp conditions on the final day, the most authoritative striker of the ball in the women's game prevailed. Webb, who earned €249,000, won by two strokes over Spain's Paula Marti and another Australian, Michelle Ellis. Catrin Nilsmark, Jenny Jung, Candie Kung and Jenny Rosales all shared fourth place two shots further back.

This was the third time Webb had won the British Open, the title becoming the first of her career in 1995 at Woburn, and she won again at Sunningdale in 1997. Now that the event is a major championship on the LPGA Tour, having replaced the du Maurier Classic, it was Webb's sixth major title — at 27, she was the second youngest to reach that mark — and meant she became the first player to achieve the LPGA "Super Career Grand Slam" of victories in five different majors.

Webb claimed her victory at the same venue where Greg Norman won the British Open in 1986. "I really enjoyed playing at Turnberry," she said. "There have been a lot of great champions in the men's Open here, so it is fantastic. I have won the British Open before, but now it is a major it is even more special.

"This was one of the best rounds I can remember," Webb added. "I shot 66 to win my first major, the du Maurier, but I then birdied four of the last five holes. This was a more solid round with a lot of good iron shots and I made the putts."

Webb birdied the third, fifth and sixth holes to draw even with the leaders, Carin Koch and Rosales. A pair of 15-foot birdie putts at the 10th and 12th put her two ahead and the lead was extended when Marti dropped a shot at the 13th.

The Spaniard recovered the shot with a four at the par-five 14th, but after Webb survived her only awkward moment at the 16th, she was safe. A ditch runs in front of the green and the pin was at the front of the putting surface. Webb's second shot appeared to have fallen back into the hazard but stayed up on the bank. Her chip did not promise a certain par, but she then holed from 20 feet to avoid dropping a stroke.

She got to 15 under with a birdie four at the 17th, where Marti also had a birdie, while Ellis birdied three of the last four holes. "I love Webby to bits and to finish second to her is awesome," said Ellis. "Her ability to pull it off consistently under the gun is why she is so successful."

Marti, a 22-year-old from Barcelona with three wins in less than two seasons as a professional, produced her best finish in a major after a closing 69. She was the only player to break 70 in all four rounds. She also secured her place on the European Solheim Cup team. "It's a dream come true to finish second and, finally, I have enough points to make the team, so that's another dream come true," Marti said.

"When I came here the first day I thought, okay, top five will be really good. It was tough out there today, I can tell you. I just told myself to be patient and, as you can see, I made seven pars in a row. I knew I was putting good and playing good and I knew the birdies were coming. There were a couple of putts that I hit really good that didn't go in, like on 15 and 16, but that's golf. But I'll take second place, I'm happy with that. I never did it before, shoot four rounds in the 60s."

Compaq Open—€537,555
Winner: Annika Sorenstam

A week after missing the cut in the Weetabix Women's British Open, Annika Sorenstam returned to business as usual by winning the Compaq Open at Vasatorps in Helsingborg, Sweden. It was Sorenstam's eighth victory of the year worldwide and was achieved by four strokes over Sophie Gustafson, with Spain's Ana Belen Sanchez taking third place three more strokes behind.

Sorenstam was not really challenged during the final round. She led by six strokes after 54 holes, but her nearest pursuer, Laura Davies, struggled on the course after having her passport and laptop computer stolen from her hotel. Sorenstam closed with 70 after rounds of 67, 66 and 68 and finished at 271, 17 under par. Gustafson scored a final-round 66, while Sanchez had 68.

"It was a nice week at the office," said Sorenstam after turning the final round into a parade in front of her home supporters. "It was much better than last week. The game is getting back to its best. But I've spent so much time on the range that I have lost a little feeling with my putting, but that's golf, and it keeps you on your toes."

Wales WPGA Championship of Europe—€661,600
Winner: Asa Gottmo

Sweden's Asa Gottmo claimed her first-ever title at the Wales WPGA Championship of Europe, but the main interest at Royal Porthcawl was in the Solheim Cup qualifying. Gottmo, a 31-year-old from Kalmar, scored 71 in the final round to win by two over compatriot Maria Hjorth, whose second place was good enough to claim an automatic place on the European team for the match against the Americans.

Hjorth finished one stroke ahead of Kirsty Taylor, but the real drama came when Iben Tinning holed her putt at the 18th to share 10th place with Laura Davies and Elisabeth Esterl. Tinning earned two qualifying points, which put her even with Hjorth with 125 points for seventh place on the qualifying table. The original formula was for seven players to qualify automatically and five to be picked as wild cards by captain Dale Reid.

As it was impossible to separate Hjorth and Tinning, both were deemed to have qualified, along with Annika Sorenstam, Raquel Carriedo, Karine Icher, Paula Marti, Sophie Gustafson and Suzann Pettersen. Reid then chose Davies, Helen Alfredsson, Carin Koch and Mhairi McKay as her wild cards.

Gottmo, who was aided by the demise of overnight leader Johanna Head, was not concerned with the qualifying and cruised to victory at seven under par. "I'm delighted," said Gottmo. "At the start of the day I thought I needed 10 under, but 71 was enough and I am so thrilled.

"The Solheim Cup didn't matter to me today. I knew other players would be thinking about that, but I just played my own game today and didn't worry about the rest. This course suited me all week. I love links golf, as I hit the ball low.

"It's been hard for me during my career, as I have finished in the top 10 so many times, and trying make the next step was always difficult. But I have looked at other players who have been on tour for a long time, like Raquel Carriedo, and if she could do it, so could I, and I have now."

Solheim Cup
Winner: United States

See U.S. LPGA Tour section.

Biarritz Ladies Classic—€165,000
Winner: Sophie Gustafson

Sophie Gustafson finished the European season with a victory in a playoff at the Biarritz Ladies Classic. Gustafson beat Scotland's Mhairi McKay at the first extra hole, but both players only got into the playoff after the misfortune of Riikka Hakkarainen. She led for much of the final round and was one ahead coming to the 18th, where her approach plugged in a green-side bunker.

Hakkarainen ended up with a double bogey and fell back into third place alongside Helen Alfredsson. Gustafson had set the clubhouse target at 10 under par after a final-round 64, which included an eagle at the third hole and a double bogey at the 14th.

McKay joined her with 66, but missed the chance to win when she was unable to convert a 12-footer on the 18th. In the playoff, Gustafson holed from eight feet for a birdie, which the Scot could not match from four feet. "It's so great to have finally won again," said Gustafson, who also secured the 2002 stroke average trophy with a 70.59 average. "It's been an up-and-down year and this is a great way to close out the season."

Spain's Paula Marti won the money list title from Maria Hjorth and Gustafson, while Annika Sorenstam won the players' vote for their own Player of the Year by only one vote over both Marti and Iben Tinning. England's Kirsty Taylor wrapped up the Bill Johnson Rookie of the Year trophy after finishing 24th on the money list.

Princess Lalla Meriem Cup
Winner: Johanna Head

Johanna Head of England posted a five-stroke victory in the Princess Lalla Meriem Cup in Rabat, Morocco, winning for the second time in her career. Head shot rounds of 75, 68, 69 for a 212 total, seven under par, for the victory over runner-up Rebecca Hudson, a former British Curtis Cup player who carded a final-round 72 in her first professional event. Head, who received $11,000, previously won the 1999 Malaysian Open.

Japan LPGA Tour

Daikin Orchid Ladies—¥60,000,000
Winner: Kasumi Fujii

Kasumi Fujii, who scored her first victory on the Japan LPGA Tour in the second tournament of the 2001 season, put her second title on the books even earlier in the year in 2002. Fujii, playing in her seventh season, survived a late challenge from Mikino Kubo and captured the season-opening Daikin Orchid Ladies tournament in early March in Okinawa. Her final-round 72 gave her an eight-under-par 208 and a one-stroke victory over Kubo and Junko Omote at Ryukyu Country Club.

Fujii had assumed the tournament lead with her second straight 68 in the second round, a shot in front of Kubo. Both had trailed by one stroke after the first round, in which Toshimi Kimura, fifth on the 2001 money list, and Kozue Azuma had opened with 67s. Twice during the final round, Fujii dropped back into a tie with Kubo, but Kubo lost a playoff opportunity when she bogeyed the 18th hole for a matching 72 to that of Fujii and 209. Defending champion Yuri Fudoh tied for sixth place at 211.

Promise Ladies—¥60,000,000
Winner: Mayumi Inoue

It took five years, but Mayumi Inoue picked up her first victory in Japan and did it in fine fashion when the circuit moved into the meat of its schedule more than a month after the Daikin opener. The 27-year-old Hyogo native led from wire-to-wire and held off one of the tour's long-time stars in the final round to post a one-stroke victory at Tomisato Golf Club in Chiba.

Inoue ran off three birdies over the last five holes in Friday's first round for 69 and a one-shot margin over five other players, including Kaori Higo, the money runner-up in 2001. Toshimi Kimura, Rie Murata, Hisako Ohgane and Yuri Kawanami also shot 70s. Inoue followed with 71–140 Saturday and maintained her one-stroke lead, again over five players, Higo and Michiko Hattori, the No. 1 player on the 1998 tour, among them.

Inoue had never before led going into a final round and it was a struggle all the way. Hattori went in front on the second nine, but gave back a stroke at the 15th, and Inoue broke from a tie with Hattori and Yu-Cheng Huang with back-to-back birdies at the next two holes for 71 and the one-shot victory at five-under-par 211. Hattori also shot 71 for 212, and Huang dropped back into a three-way tie for third at 213 with Higo and Hsiu-Feng Tseng.

Saishunkan Ladies Hinokuni Open—¥60,000,000
Winner: Ai-Yu Tu

Taiwan's Ai-Yu Tu compiled a very impressive record in the 1980s and early 1990s, acquiring 57 victories in a brilliant career, but she hit a dead end after winning that 57th title in the Tohato Ladies in 1993. She went nine years without winning before capturing No. 58 in the Saishunkan Ladies Hinokuni Open at the age of 47. Tu emerged from a pack of contenders on the final day to snatch a one-stroke victory with her one-under-par 215 at Kumamoto Kuukou Country Club in Kumamoto.

The scores were high throughout the weekend at Kumamoto. Ayako Okamoto, another veteran ace, joined Harumi Sakagami and Fumiko Muraguchi in the first-round lead at 71 and remained in front Saturday with 73–144, tied there with Kyoko Ono (72-72), Shiho Ohyama (73-71) and Chieko Amanuma (73-71). Ai-Yu Tu, who had opened with 75, came back with 71 and trailed by two strokes entering the final round. The veteran then fashioned one of the two lowest scores of the week, a 69, to put away the long-sought victory. Ono and Ohyama shot 72s and finished second at 216 with Mikino Kubo (70), her second runner-up finish in the first three 2002 events.

Katokichi Queens—¥60,000,000
Winner: Chieko Nishida

One-stroke victories continued to be the order of the week at the Katokichi Queens tournament. The season's fourth tournament was decided just as were the earlier three events by one stroke, the winner this time Chieko Nishida, who had three victories during the preceding 10 seasons.

Orie Fujino had put together a pair of two-under-par 70s and led the tournament the first two days, by two strokes after 36 holes. The runner-up was Michiko Hattori, making her second run of the season at a victory. Hattori matched the day's best score of 68 for her 142. Chihiro Nakajima (72-71) was third at 143, and Nishida (73-71) was in a four-way deadlock with Kaori Higo, Nayoko Yoshikawa and Kaori Harada at 144.

Only Nishida among the leaders challenged Fujino Sunday. She eventually sank a three-footer on the final green for 71 and 215 total, just enough to edge the two-day front-runner by a stroke when Fujino faltered to 76 for 216. Rena Yamazaki, Mineko Nasu and Mikiyo Nishizuka tied for third at 217.

Nichirei Cup World Ladies—¥60,000,000
Winner: Yuri Fudoh

Maybe Yuri Fudoh had been waiting for a serious challenge. Though never finishing out of the top 10, the talented Japanese player didn't really take a strong run at any of the first four titles on the 2002 schedule. She came alive at the fifth stop — the Nichirei Cup World Ladies tournament — perhaps egged on by the visiting presences of Karrie Webb and Laura Davies, two of the game's top international stars, at Tokyo's Yomiuri Country Club in early May. Fudoh, the tour's leading money winner the two previous years, never trailed and withstood a charge by Webb over the weekend in registering a three-stroke victory, the 12th of her relatively brief career. Eleven came in the 2000s.

Fudoh began brilliantly, making two eagles on her way to a 65, her career-best score. It gave her a two-stroke lead over Mineko Nasu and Toshimi Kimura. Webb, the two-time defending champion, opened with 69. Fudoh widened her lead to five strokes on a rainy Friday, shooting 69 for 134. Webb had 70 and joined Kimura (72), Chikako Matsuzawa (70-69) and Rie Murata (71-68) in the runner-up slot at 139.

It was Webb's turn to shoot 65 Saturday, and when Fudoh shot 70, the two were tied at 204 and four strokes in front of the rest of the field going into the final round of the year's first 72-hole event. The Australian started fast Sunday and went in front with three consecutive birdies on the first nine, but Fudoh countered with five birdies and had it easy at the finish as Webb bogeyed the 15th and 16th holes and closed with 70. Fudoh closed with 67 for 271, a 17-under-par total that set a tour record for 72-hole events. Webb had 70 for 274. Chieko Amanuma finished third at 278.

Vernal Ladies—¥100,000,000
Winner: Mikino Kubo

Mikino Kubo had a lot of overtime work to do before rejoining the winners at the Vernal Ladies tournament. Kubo, who hadn't won since scoring her initial victory in the 1996 Miyagi TV Cup, battled Toshimi Kimura through seven playoff holes before taking the title with a two-putt par.

The 29-year-old player, who already had two 2002 runner-up finishes on her record, almost let the Vernal get away from her, too. She had moved into a share of the lead with Taiwan's Yun-Jye Wei at the end of the second round at 138. Mikino had 71-67 and Wei 72-66, the latter her best round ever. Kubo took just 10 putts in her career-best 31 on the second nine.

On Sunday, though, both of them floundered, Wei shooting 77 and Kubo taking 75. Meanwhile, Kimura was firing a 67, and Rena Yamazaki, a third-season player, joined them at 213 with her 72. Yuri Fudoh and Ikuyo Shiotani missed the playoff by a stroke. Yamazaki exited when she couldn't match the birdies of the other two on the first extra hole. Then, after duplicating scores on the next five holes, Kimura, a seven-time winner on the circuit, blinked with a bogey at the seventh. The ¥18 million first prize in the richest of the early season events jumped Kubo into first place on the tour's money list.

Chukyo TV Bridgestone Ladies—¥50,000,000
Winner: Shin Sora

Shin Sora's chip-in on the final hole of the Chukyo TV Bridgestone Ladies tournament frustrated Mikino Kubo's bid for two wins in a row in late May. That shot from the edge of the 18th green gave South Korean Sora, who, like Kubo, had won her only previous-to-2002 victory in 1996, a closing 67 and a one-stroke victory over the tour's leading money winner. Her 212 was four under par.

Strong winds swept the Ishino course of Chukyo Golf Club in the opening round as Kubo and four others — Hsiao-Chuan Lu, Kumi Yamashita, Yukiyo Haga and Shiho Ohyama — shared the lead with 71s. Ohyama slipped a stroke in front on her 25th birthday Saturday, shooting 70–141 with an eagle on her card. Kubo posted another 71 for 142. At that point, Sora was four off the pace. Finishing ahead of the Saturday leaders with her dramatic 21-foot chip at the 18th, Sora didn't watch as Kubo played the last hole. Kubo fell one stroke short with her 71–213, and Ohyama had 73 for 214 and third place.

Kosaido Ladies Golf Cup—¥60,000,000
Winner: Orie Fujino

Even though she had just conjured up a six-under-par 66 in the final round of the Kosaido Ladies Golf Cup, Orie Fujino saw little reason to stick around until the tournament was over. After all, she had begun the day 11 strokes off the lead. It was well that she stayed, because she wound up being the winner in the biggest come-from-behind performance in the history of the Japan LPGA Tour. The victim was Toshimi Kimura, who just two weeks earlier had fallen in a seven-hole playoff in the Vernal Ladies. This time, she tumbled into a tie with Fujino and lost in overtime again, in this case to a birdie on the second extra hole.

Kimura, a veteran with seven victories, had been rolling toward an eighth the first two days. She had 13 birdies in the first two rounds as she opened a three-stroke lead the first day and widened the gap on Saturday with 68 for 135. That put her four strokes in front of Michiko Hattori and seven ahead of all the rest. Fujino shot 70 that day after putting herself in jeopardy of missing the cut with 76 Friday. On Sunday, she started with a bogey before the turnaround to the 66 and the long wait for the playoff. Meanwhile, Kimura was crashing to 77 and the fatal deadlock. Hattori in particular failed to take advantage of the opportunity, shooting 75 and finishing in a tie for third with Mihoko Takahashi at 214.

Resort Trust Ladies—¥50,000,000
Winner: Kozue Azuma

That old saying in golf — "You can't beat an injured player" — rang true at the Resort Trust Ladies tournament as Kozue Azuma, nursing a sore leg, became the Japan LPGA season's second first-time winner. And she waited nine years for number one to come. "It wasn't exactly winning golf that I played out there today. I hurt my leg last week and didn't think I'd play well," she said. Azuma played just well enough to get into a playoff at Grandee Naruto Golf Club, Tokushima, and win it on the first playoff hole.

Azuma loitered just off the lead the first two days. Aki Takamura, the 2001 champion, who also was ailing, in her case with a bad shoulder, began her title defense with 68 and a one-stroke lead over Kaori Harada, then yielded the top spot to money leader Mikino Kubo Saturday. Kubo posted a pair of 70s for a one-stroke lead over Azuma (70-71), Harada (69-72), Michie Ohba (71-70) and frustrated Toshimi Kimura (73-68), taking her third serious shot at a title in four weeks. No one shot better than 71 among the contenders Sunday. Both Azuma and Ohba shot 72s to bring on the playoff, and Azuma ended it quickly when she chipped in for a birdie on the first extra hole.

Sharing the gallery and media interest, Kumiko Kaneda, a 12-year-old junior high school student, shot 75-74–149 and became the youngest player ever to qualify for the final round of a Japanese Tour event. She shot 78 Sunday for 227, tying for 47th place. Two professionals finished below her in the standings.

We Love Kobe Suntory Ladies Open—¥60,000,000
Winner: Takayo Bandoh

Playoffs continued to be the fashion in late spring. For the third consecutive week and the fourth time in five tournaments, the winner was decided in overtime in the We Love Kobe Suntory Ladies Open, one of the few 72-hole events on the circuit. The victor was Takayo Bandoh, who had gone five seasons since winning her previous and first title at age 22. Her victim was second-year professional Hiroko Yamaguchi, the third-round leader, who won the Sankyo Open in 2001.

Michie Ohba, who lost in the previous Sunday's playoff, and money leader Mikino Kubo, who faltered on the final holes and missed that playoff by a stroke, started strongly at Yokawa's Japan Memorial Golf Club, sharing first place with Yu-Cheng Huang with six-under-par 66s. The Taiwan player came back with another solid round Friday. She shot 67 for 133 and jumped five strokes in front of Ohba (72), Yamaguchi (69-69), Woo-Soon Ko (70-68) and persistent contender Toshimi Kimura (69-69). Bandoh, with 70-69, joined four others, including Kubo, at 139

Huang slumped to 77 Saturday, opening the door for Yamaguchi, who shot her third straight 69 for 207 and took a two-stroke lead over amateur Ai Miyazato. Huang was at 210 and Bandoh was three strokes further behind after a 74. However, Bandoh produced a five-birdie 67 Sunday for 280 and overtook Yamaguchi, who closed with 73. Yamaguchi slipped on the first playoff hole, and Bandoh, who was just 19 when she joined the tour in 1994, picked up the victory with a two-putt par.

Apita Circle K Sankus Ladies—¥50,000,000
Winner: Mihoko Takahashi

Another bid for back-to-back victories fell just short as the third first-time winner of the 2002 season was crowned at the Apita Circle K Sankus tournament in Nakatsugawa. Mihoko Takahashi tasted her first victory when she edged Takayo Bandoh by one stroke with a seven-under-par 209 in late June.

Bandoh, fresh from victory in the Suntory Open, spurted in front in Thursday's opening round on the U Green Nakatsugawa Golf Club with a four-under-par 68, one stroke better than the scores recorded by Rie Murata and

Kaori Yamamoto. Bandoh "persevered pretty well" in posting 71 Saturday and retaining her one-shot margin. Midori Yoneyama, the defending champion, (70-70) and Murata (71) were the runners-up, with Takahashi another stroke back with Kasumi Fujii, the Daikin Orchid winner, and Yamamoto. Takahashi had rounds of 70 and 71.

When she could do no better than a one-under-par 71, Bandoh had to settle for second place at 210, as Takahashi came up with a six-birdie 68 that included three birdies on the incoming nine.

Belluna Ladies Cup—¥60,000,000
Winner: Orie Fujino

Orie Fujino became the first multiple winner of the 2002 Japan LPGA Tour season when she put the Belluna Ladies Cup alongside the Kosaido Golf Cup on her record the first week of July at Kanra. The Belluna victory was more easily achieved as Fujino rolled to a two-stroke triumph at Obatago Golf Club, registering a 10-under-par 206.

Hsiao-Chuan Lu, the Golf 5 winner in 2001, launched a bid for her second victory on the circuit with a six-under-par 66 Friday. She made her sixth birdie of the bogey-free round at the last hole to stand one stroke ahead of Natsuko Noro at day's end. Fujino, who settled for 71 Friday, vaulted into the lead Saturday when she fired a sparkling 66 of her own. An eagle at the fourth hole and a run of three birdies in the middle of the second nine highlighted the round.

At 137, Fujino had a stroke on Taiwan's Yu-Cheng Huang (67) and Hsiu-Feng Tseng (68) and Noro (71) as Lu slipped into a four-way tie for fifth with her 73–139.

Fujino needed a stout finish Sunday when she faltered on the early holes, and she had the stuff to do it. She racked up an eagle at the 15th hole amid two birdies on the final six holes for 69 and the 206. Tseng shot 70 Sunday and finished second, one stroke in front of Noro.

Toyo Suisan Ladies Hokkaido—¥50,000,000
Winner: Chihiro Nakajima

Chihiro Nakajima scored her first victory in four years when she overcame veteran Ok-Hee Ku in a playoff at the Toyo Suisan Ladies Hokkaido tournament. The two had wound up deadlocked at 208 after 54 holes at Sapporo Kitahiroshima Prince Golf Club. The playoff, which Nakajima won on the first extra hole, turned out to be the final extra-hole event of the season.

Ku and Kasumi Fujii, the Daikin Orchid winner in March, opened the Toyo Suisan with course-record, five-under-par 67s. Nakajima shared third place with Orie Fujino, coming off her Belluna Cup victory the previous Sunday, with Masaki Maeda and Aki Takamura one stroke off the pace. Nakajima climbed into first place Saturday with 70–138, two shots in front of Mihoko Takahashi, whose 69 was the day's best score. Ku slipped to 141 after a 74, and Fujino to 142 following a 75.

Nakajima repeated her 70 Sunday, and the 45-year-old Ku, winner of 19 circuit titles over the years, caught up with 67 for her 208. It was a two-player race, as Fujii and Takahashi tied for third at 211.

Golf 5 Ladies—¥50,000,000
Winner: Ikuyo Shiotani

Ikuyo Shiotani proved again that she hasn't lost her winning touch when she squeezed out a one-stroke victory in the Golf 5 Ladies tournament at the end of July. The 40-year-old Shiotani has registered 19 victories over two decades in Japan, though her best years came in the early and mid-1990s when she led the money list in 1992 and 1995. She had won No. 18 just a year ago and was a contender on several occasions in between the last two wins.

Shiotani opened the Golf 5 at Mizunami Country Club at Gifu with a two-under-par 70 and trailed leader Hikaru Kobayashi by three strokes. Then she overhauled Kobayashi the second day as they reversed scores for 137 totals and had two-stroke margins on Yuri Fudoh and Masaki Maeda. Shiotani had birdied three of the first five holes en route to a day's best round. She repeated the fast start Sunday with birdies on the first four holes and fattened her lead to six strokes with an eagle at the 10th hole. The 27-year-old Kobayashi, winless in five years, nearly caught her at the end, though, as Shiotani stumbled a bit over the last eight holes. She finished with 68 for 206, and Kobayashi came up just short with 70–207. Only Mikiyo Nishizuka at 209 was even in range with her third-place finish.

Vernal Open—¥80,000,000
Winner: Yuri Fudoh

Yuri Fudoh began her run toward a third consecutive money title in Japan when she successfully defended the Vernal Open title that marked one of her five victories in 2001. As in that previous year, Fudoh made the Vernal Open her second win of the season. It boosted her victory total to 13 in her seven-year professional career, all since late in 1999. Orie Fujino — Kosaido and Belluna Cups — was the only other multiple winner at that point on the 2002 circuit.

Fudoh put the Vernal Open away with a potent finish. In fact, she began the tournament with a par-72 round that left her far behind South Korean veteran Young-Me Lee, who opened with six birdies, an eagle and a 65, three strokes ahead of runner-up Mayumi Hirase. Scoring rose drastically Saturday, enabling Yun-Jye Wei to take the lead with a pair of 70s, as Lee skied to 78 and Hirase shot 75. Fudoh also had 70 and moved into a fourth-place tie with Shin Sora and Mayumi Murai, one stroke back of Ae-Sook Kim and Ai Kikuchi.

Fudoh was the only player to break 70 Sunday. She had five birdies in a seven-hole stretch starting at the 10th hole as she breezed into the lead and raced to a five-stroke victory with her 68 for 210 total. Runner-up honors went to Chieko Amanuma and Hsiao-Chuan Lu, who both shot 70s for 215.

NEC Karuizawa 72—¥60,000,000
Winner: Akiko Fukushima

Akiko Fukushima, who won her first tournament on the Japan LPGA Tour as a 20-year-old in 1994, added a 15th to her sparkling record at the NEC Karuizawa 72, which she had won in 1996. The talented Fukushima, who has played most of her golf in America since 1999 but had been out of action much of the season with a broken toe, rallied from a two-stroke deficit in the final round to post her first win in two years in Japan. She fired a blazing six-under-par 66 and won by four strokes with her 202 on the North Course of the Karuizawa 72 Golf Club.

Fukushima was never far behind in the early going. Taiwan's Yun-Jye Wei, finishing her first full year in Japan, and little-known Atsuko Ueno led the way Friday with 67s, with Fukushima among seven players at 68. The course record fell Saturday as another Taiwan player, Yu-Cheng Huang, rang up seven birdies for 65 and slipped two strokes into the lead at 134. Fukushima shot another 68 and wound up in a second-place tie at 136 with Yuri Fudoh, already a two-time winner in 2002, and Toshimi Kimura, a two-time runner-up earlier in the year.

Fukushima overtook Huang early in the last round and went in front to stay when she made her third birdie of the round at the fifth hole. Four more birdies followed as Fukushima rolled to the victory in just her third appearance this season in Japan. Masaki Maeda shot 65 Sunday and jumped into a second-place deadlock with Woo-Soon Ko (69) at 206.

New Caterpillar Mitsubishi Ladies—¥60,000,000
Winner: Kaori Higo

Little had been heard from Kaori Higo in the early months. For good reason. Higo, playing in her 14th season though just 33 years old, underwent an appendectomy in June and didn't get her full strength back for quite some time. By the time of the New Caterpillar Mitsubishi Ladies at the end of August, though, she was fit enough to march to victory. As the winners had done in the two preceding tournaments, Higo came from just off the lead in the final round and won easily. Her final-round 68 and seven-under-par 212 on the par-73 Daihakone Country Club course put her three strokes in front of Toshimi Kimura and second-round leader Woo-Soon Ko at the finish. It was her 16th victory and first of the year after winning three times in 2001.

The first round was déjà vu for Taiwan's Yun-Jye Wei. For the second week in a row, the 22-year-old Wei wound up in the lead the first day. She shot 70 in a steady rain, one better than the efforts of Kyoko Ono, Mitsuko Kawasaki and Nobuko Kizawa. Difficult conditions continued Saturday as Ko, a 38-year-old South Korean from Pusan, took the lead with 73-70–143, one stroke ahead of Higo, who posted a pair of one-under-par 72s.

Higo took command early Sunday. She made six birdies and took a lone bogey on the first eight holes to establish her big lead and protected it with 10 pars the rest of the way. Kimura tied a tour record with nine birdies as she shot 67 to tie with Ko (72) at 215.

Yonex Ladies Open—¥60,000,000
Winner: Yuri Fudoh

Not unexpectedly, Yuri Fudoh became the first player to reach the three-victory plateau with her successful defense of the Yonex Ladies Open title at Niigata's Yonex Country Club. The 25-year-old Fudoh, who had won her other 2002 titles decisively, was even more emphatic at Yonex. The Kumamoto native steamrollered the opposition with a final-round 68 that built a seven-stroke victory margin with her 15-under-par 201. Fudoh's win total grew to 14 in her seven seasons on tour.

Not only did Fudoh lead from the start, but she shot the best score of her career — an eight-under-par 64 — in the opening round to get herself off and running. Kaori Higo, coming off her Caterpillar Mitsubishi win the previous Sunday, shot 66, and Ikuyo Shiotani, the Golf 5 winner, was at 67. Continuing her bogey-free run Saturday, Fudoh fired a 69 for 133 and advanced four strokes ahead of Higo (71), Shiotani (70) and Michiko Hattori (69).

The only blotch on Fudoh's cards came when she three-putted the first hole for her lone bogey at the start of Sunday's final round, but she rang up five birdies the rest of the way as she rolled to the easy triumph. Higo birdied the last two holes for 71 and second place at 208. Shiotani (73), Woo-Soon Ko (70), Yuka Sakaguchi (69) and Yuka Shiroto 66) shared third place at 210.

Fujisankei Ladies Classic—¥60,000,000
Winner: Ok-Hee Ku

Veterans continued to enjoy their resurgent days as they moved into September and to Fujizakura Country Club for the Fujisankei Ladies Classic. South Korea's Ok-Hee Ku, 45, joined 47-year-old Ai-Yu Tu and 39-year-old Ikuyo Shiotani in the 2002 winner's circle there, scoring her first victory in two years and the 20th in her two decades of campaigning in Japan. Ku came from two shots back with a final-round 67 to score a three-stroke victory with her 10-under-par 206.

Midori Yoneyama, young enough to be Ku's daughter, held the lead for two days in rainy weather. The 25-year-old Yoneyama, the 1999 rookie of the year who has four victories on her record, including back-to-back wins in 2001, launched her bid for another with a 67 Friday, taking a one-stroke lead over Kasumi Fujii, the Daikin Orchid winner in March. Despite some putting problems on the damp greens, Yoneyama widened her margin to two strokes with a one-under-par 70 for 137 Saturday. Ku recovered from a first-round 73 with 66 and moved into second place at 139 with Fujii (71).

Yoneyama's one-over-par 72 Sunday was no match for the day's lowest round. Ku produced the solid 67 for the victory.

Japan LPGA Championship Konica Cup—¥70,000,000
Winner: Ok-Hee Ku

Ok-Hee Ku became the first and, as it turned out, only winner of consecutive tournaments in the 2002 season and she couldn't have picked a better time to double up. The victory that came on top of the Fujisankei was the Japan LPGA Championship Konica Cup, a prized major which the South Korean had first won in 1992 among her 20 victories in Japan over more than 20 years. The win was a tight one, Ku prevailing by a stroke with a closing 73 and five-under-par 283 total on the Rokko course of the Taiheiyo Club in Yokawa.

Fresh from the Fujisankei victory, Ku opened with 68 in the PGA Championship, holing two long putts in a three-birdie streak in the middle of the round. Toshimi Kimura, who stuck around to the end and finished second in the championship for the second straight year, shot 69 and shared the runner-up slot with Mikiyo Nishizuka. Orie Fujino, who already had two 2002 wins in the bag, took the spotlight Friday. She had the day's best round of 67 and moved into a one-shot lead at 137 over Kimura (69). Ku shot 71 and was third at 139.

Fujino retained her one-shot margin Saturday, matching four birdies with four bogeys for 72–209 as Ku climbed a stroke closer with 71–210. Kimura was another stroke back at 211 with Nishizuka. Things did not look promising for Ku as she bogeyed three of the first six holes, but she fought back with two birdies and soared into the lead when she holed a 50-foot putt and Fujino knocked two balls in the water at the 12th and took a quadruple-bogey eight. It came down to the final hole, where Ku dropped a 20-foot birdie putt for her 73 to edge Kimura, who also shot 73 Sunday and nosed out Nishizuka. Fujino dropped into a fourth-place tie at 286 with Woo-Soon Ko.

Munsingwear Ladies Tokai Classic—¥60,000,000
Winner: Kasumi Fujii

Kasumi Fujii had exclusive company after she won the Munsingwear Ladies Tokai Classic in late September. It was her second victory of 2002 and only three other players — Yuri Fudoh, the leading money winner, Orie Fujino and Ok-Hee Ku — had accomplished multiple triumphs in the current campaign. Fujii's previous victory was in the Daikin Orchid opener in March. This time, Fujii, trailing by two strokes, needed a rally the last day, shot 69 and won by two over Kyoko Ono, the second-round leader, with her 12-under-par 204.

Fujii had yielded the lead to Ono Saturday after opening on top with 66, one stroke in front of Ono and Michiko Hattori. Ono came back with a 66 of her own Saturday, taking a two-stroke lead when Fujii followed with 69 for 135. Junko Yasui (67) and Yuriko Ohtsuka (69) were at 137. Fujii's strong finish gave her the third victory of her seven-year career.

Miyagi TV Cup Dunlop Ladies Open—¥60,000,000
Winner: Mihoko Takahashi

For the third week in a row, the Japan LPGA Tour had a second-time winner. In this case in the Miyagi TV Cup Dunlop Ladies Open, the victor, Mihoko Takahashi, had scored her maiden triumph earlier in the season in the Apita Circle K Sankus tournament, assuring her of her finest season ever. Takahashi shot a final-round 69 and won by two strokes over Woo-Soon Ko with her five-under-par 211. It was Ko's third runner-up finish in seven tournaments.

Orie Fujino, seeking her third title of the year, and Kaori Harada shared the first-round lead with Takahashi at 70, with four others, including British star Laura Davies, at 71. Saturday came up soggy, but Taiwan's Hsiu-Feng Tseng managed a 69 and went ahead with her 140, a stroke ahead of Kotomi Akiyama and two in front of Takahashi. Woo-Soon Ko was another shot back. Tseng could do no better than 74 Sunday and dropped into a three-way tie for third at 214 with Young-Me Lee and Nobuko Kizawa.

Japan Women's Open—¥70,000,000
Winner: Woo-Soon Ko

Players from other nations have won a decent share of the tournaments on the Japan LPGA Tour over the years, but the native daughters had kept the national championship in Japanese hands for more than a decade — until 2002. South Korean veteran Woo-Soon Ko brought that streak to an end with a record-breaking performance. Her 14-under 278 on the par-73 Hakone Country Club course was the lowest total since the Japan Women's Open was established as a 72-hole event in 1982.

The victory was not surprising. Ko had been a frequent contender through the season and had just posted her third runner-up finish of the year the week before in the Miyagi TV Cup tournament. She was the third South Korean winner in 2002, preceded by Shin Sora and double victor Ok-Hee Ku, who captured the circuit's other major title in September — the Japan LPGA Championship. The Open gave Ko a special reward — a three-year exemption on the tour.

The championship had an international flavor all week. Lorena Ochoa, the highly touted, 20-year-old rookie from Mexico, had center stage for two days. Ochoa, playing on a special invitation from the organizers, shot "perhaps the best round of my career" the first day. Her record eight-under-par 65 gave her a two-stroke lead over non-winner Junko Omote, and Ochoa remained on top after shooting 72 for 137 in rough weather Friday. Omote closed within a stroke with 71–138, and Yu-Cheng Huang moved into third place with 70–139. Huang duplicated the 70 for 209 Saturday and jumped a shot in front of Ochoa (73) and Kayo Yamada (69).

Ko moved into contention Saturday, shooting 69 for 211, setting up her run to the title Sunday. A hot stretch in the middle of the final round — an eagle followed by three birdies over the next four holes — pushed the South Korean to 67, the day's best round, and a two-stroke victory over Huang, her only serious competition Sunday. It was her seventh win in Japan. Ochoa, money leader Yuri Fudoh and Yuka Shiroto tied for third at 285, six strokes behind the winner.

Sankyo Ladies Open—¥60,000,000
Winner: Toshimi Kimura

It had been a frustrating year for Toshimi Kimura. She had finished second four times, two of those when she lost in playoffs, in one case a seven-hole marathon in the Vernal Ladies and the other when she blew a four-stroke lead in the final round of the Kosaido Golf Cup. It wasn't a case of not having experienced victory, either. She had seven on her record. Finally, in mid-October at the Sankyo Ladies Open, Kimura captured her eighth, parlaying a fiery second round into a two-stroke victory with a nine-under-par 207 total.

Yu-Cheng Huang and Hsiu-Feng Tseng, two Taiwanese pros who were non-winners but frequent contenders during the season, made another run in the Sankyo, opening in first place with 68s, one stroke ahead of Suntory winner Takayo Bandoh. Then Kimura rocketed through the field with a course-record-matching 65 at Akagi Country Club and seized a two-stroke lead with her 135. Kasumi Fujii shot 67 for 137, the runner-up position. Kimura rang up eight birdies and a bogey.

Kimura yielded the lead briefly in the early going Sunday, but two birdies righted the ship and her par 72 produced the three-shot victory. Fujii had 73 for 210 total, taking second place, one stroke ahead of four others, including Kyoko Ono, who had a hole-in-one en route to her 68–211.

Fujitsu Ladies—¥60,000,000
Winner: Chihiro Nakajima

For the fourth time in six weeks, a two-time winner was crowned. Chihiro Nakajima, who had scored a playoff victory in July in the Toyo Suisan Hokkaido tournament, eked out a one-stroke triumph in the Fujitsu Ladies at the Tokyu Seven Hundred Club with her 12-under-par 204.

Her final-round 70 enabled her to come from two strokes off the pace Sunday and edge Hsiu-Feng Tseng and Kyoko Ono.

Nakajima and Tseng traded course-record-tying 65s the first two days. Nakajima's seven-under-par round came Thursday and gave her a one-stroke advantage over Mayumi Hirase and a two-shot edge over five other players, including Tseng. The Taiwanese pro, in her 10th season in Japan, holed 13-foot putts on the final two greens for her 65 Saturday and the two-shot margin over Nakajima (69). Ono fired a 66 and climbed into a third-place tie with Akiko Fukushima and Mayumi Murai five strokes off the lead at 137.

Nakajima was not particularly sharp Sunday, absorbing three bogeys to go with her five birdies for the 70, but a run of four of the birdies at the end of the first nine was decisive.

Hisako Higuchi Classic—¥60,000,000
Winner: Kasumi Fujii

Although it only brought her within hailing distance of Yuri Fudoh in the race for leading money winner, Kasumi Fujii's victory in the Hisako Higuchi Classic put her level with Fudoh in number of titles for the year at three apiece. Fujii never trailed at the Taiheiyo Club, Minori, and eased to a three-stroke victory with her seven-under-par 209. She had only one other win before 2002 in her seven-year career.

Fujii, Akiko Fukushima and Mayumi Hirase shot 68s in the opening round, but only Fujii was able to follow up respectably the second day. While Fukushima, the seasoned veteran and NEC Karuizawa 72 winner, stumbled to a shocking 78 and Hirase was struggling to 73, Fujii repeated her 68 and soared to a five-stroke lead over Hirase and Ikuyo Shiotani, the Golf 5 winner in July.

Fujii let her margin dwindle to two strokes at one point in the final round, but finished steadily with 73 for the three-shot victory. Hirase took second place with 71–212, and Fudoh kept Fujii from chopping a big piece of her money lead by shooting 68, the day's best round, and tying for third at 213.

Cisco World Ladies Match Play—¥107,100,000
Winner: Grace Park

Grace Park produced her most impressive and perhaps her most difficult victory since capturing the 1998 U.S. Women's Amateur as a freshman at Arizona State when she outlasted Japan's Midori Yoneyama in the championship match of the Cisco World Ladies Match Play at Narita Golf Club. Much of the potential drama was drained from the tournament by a series of early round upsets before the two finalists battled through 22 holes at the end.

The three top-ranked stars in the 32-player field drawn from the U.S. and Japan LPGA Tours were surprise victims the first two days. Defending champion Annika Sorenstam, nearing the end of her sensational season, and Se Ri Pak, the brilliant South Korean with five 2002 titles to her credit, went out in the first round. Sorenstam lost to Chieko Amanuma, the lowest seeded of the 16 players from the Japan LPGA circuit, 2 and 1, while Takayo Bandoh ousted Pak, 1 up. Park won her first match against Mikino Kubo easily, 4 and 3. Then in her next two matches she eliminated Australian star Karrie Webb in the rain-drenched second round, 1 up, and Yuri Fudoh, the dominant player on the Japan LPGA Tour, 6 and 5.

Meanwhile, Yoneyama, 26, didn't have exactly an easy path to the semi-finals. Winless in 2002 and 15th ranked among the Japanese players in the field, Yoneyama advanced with 1-up victories over Mi Hyun Kim and Lorie Kane, both of whom were having strong seasons in America, and a 4-and-3 defeat of veteran Kelly Robbins. In the semi-finals, Park took out Sweden's Carin Koch decisively, 5 and 4, but Yoneyama had to birdie her last three holes to take a 19-hole victory over Hee-Won Han of South Korea.

Yoneyama just missed a long birdie putt at the 18th hole for the win in the championship match and a two-footer at the second extra hole before bowing to the 23-year-old Park two holes later when Park sank a 12-foot birdie putt. It was her third official victory on the LPGA Tour.

Mizuno Classic—¥138,990,000
Winner: Annika Sorenstam

Normally, the odds are clearly against a player successfully defending a title on any of the world's professional tours. Not when the person trying to repeat happens to be somebody of the caliber of Annika Sorenstam. That was the situation when the joint LPGA Tours of Japan and America wrapped up their two-week stand in the Asian country with the Mizuno Classic in mid-November and defender Sorenstam rolled to her 10th — 12th world- wide — win of the season. Her two-stroke victory was over Grace Park, the South Korean who had won the Cisco World Ladies Match Play the previous week.

Clearly, in LPGA records, she matched 10-win seasons posted by Kathy Whitworth and Carol Mann in 1968, but counting her non-LPGA victories during the season in Australia and Sweden, Sorenstam was within a win of the all-time record 13 of Mickey Wright in 1963.

Mi Hyun Kim, who won twice during the summer in the United States, grabbed the first-round lead, running off a six-birdie string on her way to a seven-under-par 65 at Seta Golf Course in Otsu City. It gave her a one- stroke lead over Grace Park, compatriot Gloria Park and Japan's Chieko Amanuma. Sorenstam, Amanuma's surprise victim at Narita in the Match Play, opened with 69. She then took command of the tournament with a 65 of her own in the second round, finishing eagle-birdie on the two closing par-fives for her 134 total and a one-shot margin over Grace and Gloria Park, who had 69s. Se Ri Pak (69) and Akiko Fukushima (68) were next at 137. On Sunday, Sorenstam, fighting a cold and talking in a whisper after- ward, birdied those last two holes for 67–201 and the two-stroke victory over Grace Park (68–203). Sorenstam also had an eagle and a birdie on the other two par-fives on the first nine to offset a double bogey at the par-three fifth. Pak closed with 67 to take third place at 204, and Gloria Park shot 71 to grab fourth position with 206.

Itoen Ladies—¥60,000,000
Winner: Yuri Fudoh

With the American visitors from the LPGA Tour gone after their two weeks in Japan, Yuri Fudoh got back to her business of monopolizing things on the Japan Tour. Fudoh all but eliminated any doubts that she would finish No. 1 on the money list for the third year in a row when she came from three strokes behind in the final round of the Itoen Ladies and posted a one-shot victory over Akiko Fukushima at Great Island Club, Chonan.

Fudoh and Kasumi Fujii, also a three-time 2002 winner and the only player with even a remote chance of catching her in the money race, began the tournament with 65s and the co-lead, two shots ahead of Kaori Higo and Woo-Soon Ko, who also owned 2002 victories. On Saturday, Fukushima claimed first place with a 65 of her own, running off an eagle and five birdies as she strengthened her bid for a second 2002 victory with her 133. Junko Yasui shot 66 for 135 and shared second place with Fujii, who had 70. With 71, Fudoh was another stroke back at 136 with Ko (69).

Fukushima could only muster a par round Sunday, and Fudoh slipped ahead of her to win by a single stroke with her 68 for 204. It was her fourth victory of the year and 15th of her seven-year career. Fujii and Ko took the next two spots in the final standings with final-round 71s. Although it merely jumped her to fifth place, Midori Yoneyama created a stir Sunday when she matched a Japan LPGA Tour record with nine birdies en route to 66.

Daio Seishi Elleair Ladies Open—¥80,000,000
Winner: Hiromi Kobayashi

To state correctly that Hiromi Kobayashi won her first tournament in Japan in four years when she took the Daio Seishi Elleair Ladies Open gives a bit of a false impression of ineptness. Kobayashi has been playing the U.S. LPGA Tour since 1990, her action in Japan limited to the fall after her return from America each year. Up to the late stages of the 1998 season, Kobayashi landed four titles in the United States to go with nine in Japan. Her 14th that year was in the LPGA Japan Classic, a strong-field official event on both tours, and the 2002 Elleair Ladies Open was her 15th.

Kobayashi led all the way at Elleair Golf Club, Saita, but her first-round start of 66 was a bit overshadowed by a flood of holes-in-one. Three, tying a Japan LPGA Tour record, were shot that day — by Chikako Matsuzawa, Toshimi Kimura and Hiroko Yamaguchi, who parlayed hers into a 67 and second place. Kobayashi expanded her lead to four strokes when she fired a bogey-free 69 for 135. Midori Yoneyama, the losing finalist in the Cisco World Match Play, shot 67 and tied for second at 138 with Misayo Fujisawa. The shocker that day was the departure of leading money winner Yuri Fudoh, who shot 76-72–148 and missed the cut for the first time in three seasons.

Kobayashi's two-under-par 70 in Sunday's final round wrapped up a two-stroke victory at 205 over fast-closing Yun-Jye Wei, who shot 67 and edged Yoneyama for second place by a stroke.

Japan LPGA Tour Championship—¥60,000,000
Winner: Woo-Soon Ko

Woo-Soon Ko and Yuri Fudoh were both title winners in the Japan LPGA Tour's finale and last 72-hole major event — the third LPGA Tour Championship at Hibiscus Golf Club, Miyazaki. Ko, who had won the Japan Women's Open, another major, earlier in the season, took the Tour Championship with a 10-under-par 278, winning by two strokes. Fudoh finished in third place at 281 to wrap up her third straight money title.

For two days, Kasumi Fujii kept alive her chances of winning her fourth tournament of the season and overtaking Fudoh in the run for No. 1. Knowing she needed to win the Tour Championship and its ¥15 million first-place check to do that, Fujii produced a 68 in the opening round and led by one stroke over Mihoko Takahashi. Her bid just about disappeared Friday even though she followed with 70–138 to up her margin to two. Fudoh fell seven strokes behind her with 74 for 146, but virtually clinched the money title simply by making the cut, as she had failed to do the previous week.

The tables turned for Fujii Saturday. She took a 74 for 212 and Woo-Soon Ko assumed the lead with 67–207. Kaori Higo, the defending champion who, like Ko, was seeking her second 2002 victory, moved into second place with 69–209, and Fudoh moved within a stroke of Fujii with 68 for 213. Ko protected her lead and its two-stroke margin with one-under-par 71 Sunday for the 278. Higo matched the 71 to take second place with her 280, and Fudoh wrapped up her third outstanding season with 68 to climb into third place at 281.

Fujii, who shot 72–284, took second place on the money list with ¥82,647,102, and the winner's check of ¥15 million jumped Ko into third place on the money list with ¥73,083,748. Fudoh's final total was ¥95,690,917.

Australian Women's Tour

Educom ALPG Players' Championship—A$100,000
Winner: Paula Marti

After two wins in her rookie season in Europe, Spain's Paula Marti started her 2002 campaign in the perfect manner by winning the Educom ALPG Players' Championship at the Horizons Resort in New South Wales. The tournament did not count on either the European or U.S. LPGA circuits, but gave the 22-year-old from Barcelona a nice boost in confidence for the season ahead.

Marti won by beating Australia's Karen Pearce in a three-hole playoff after the pair had tied at three-under-par 216 for 54 holes. Both shot rounds of 72, one under par, in the final round after Marti had opened with scores of 68 and 76, while Pearce had two rounds of 72. The first two holes of the playoff were halved in pars before Pearce three-putted on the 18th hole for a bogey.

England's Diane Barnard scored a final-round 67 to jump into third place, one shot behind and alongside Holland's Judith Van Hagen, who bogeyed the last hole to fall out of the playoff.

"Winning here gives me a whole load of confidence," Marti said. "After this, I feel I am capable of anything. My whole season revolves around getting into the Solheim Cup team. It would be a dream come true to represent Europe and to have the chance to beat the Americans on home turf."

Australasian Ladies Masters—A$750,000
Winner: Annika Sorenstam

Annika Sorenstam won her first tournament of the season at the Australasian Ladies Masters by denying Karrie Webb's attempt to win the event for the fifth consecutive year. Two of the best players in the women's game ended up in a playoff at Royal Pines and it took four holes before the Swede prevailed.

In the opening event on the Evian Ladies European Tour, Webb shared the lead with Elisabeth Esterl going into the final round. Sorenstam, who had scored 64 in the second round, was three strokes back. By the turn, Esterl had dropped off the pace and it looked as if Webb, leading by two, would take her fifth title. But Webb dropped shots at the 10th and 13th, while Sorenstam reached 10 under par with a birdie at the par-three 14th.

Webb then fell behind by three-putting the 16th for a bogey, but responded with a 10-foot birdie putt at the 17th and closed out with 72 to Sorenstam's 69. The first three holes of the playoff were halved in pars, but then Webb missed the fairway on the fourth extra hole. While Sorenstam put her second shot to 15 feet, Webb was still 45 yards short of the green and took three to get down.

"I knew how much it would mean for Karrie to win and win five in a row," said Sorenstam. "I wouldn't say I'm apologetic, but I understand how much it would mean to her. When you come into a playoff and for the fourth time, it's a bit of luck and this time it was my turn.

"I was three shots behind this morning, so I was chasing and I had nothing to lose and it came down to a playoff. It was exciting. The slogan early in the week said, 'The Main Event,' so there we were. It couldn't have been any better. I enjoyed the whole week."

"It just wasn't there today," Webb said. "I started off pretty well, but it was just one of those days where I struggled right from the go.

"Maybe there was a little tension there, the whole week I've had to think about a lot of things in my game and I just didn't do it today. I love that kind of pressure but it doesn't have any bearing on the way I played. I've had pressure like that before and risen to the occasion. It was one of those things that wasn't meant to be."

Australian Michelle Ellis took third place, two shots out of the playoff, while Laura Davies, who scored the best round of the day, 66, tied for fourth at seven under par with Sweden's Helen Alfredsson and the younger of the Sorenstam sisters, Charlotta.

AAMI Women's Australian Open—A$500,000
Winner: Karrie Webb

A week after losing a playoff, Karrie Webb beat Norway's Suzann Pettersen at the first extra hole to win the AAMI Women's Australian Open at Yarra Yarra. Webb birdied the par-five 18th hole in the playoff when she holed a fast, eight-foot downhill putt after Pettersen, the European Rookie of the Year in 2001, came out of a greenside bunker to 20 feet but could only make a par.

"I thought, 'Not again,'" said Webb. "But hats off to Suzann. She played really well today. She hung in there and made some great birdies coming down the stretch. I gave myself a couple of opportunities, but couldn't make them. But I was obviously very happy to make that last putt in the playoff.

"It feels great to win; to lose two playoffs would have been disappointing, so I am glad I won this week. I only just found out that Suzann is 20 years old, and knowing that, we will definitely have to look out for her. She didn't falter coming down the stretch and gave herself a great eagle chance at the last to win the tournament."

Both players started the final round five strokes clear of the field and closed with rounds of 69 to finish at 10 under par. Webb moved three clear at the turn and again after 12 holes, but then Pettersen birdied the 13th and 16th. She saved par with a long putt at the 17th and then hit a four iron to 20 feet at the 18th. With Webb only parring the hole, Pettersen just missed the eagle putt for victory, but the birdie put her in the playoff.

"I gave myself a chance and that was nice," said Pettersen. "I kept it going all the way and had a birdie on the last. Karrie is a great player and she is really a good putter."

Becky Morgan from Wales closed with 71 to tie for third place with Australian Michelle Ellis at two under par, while defending champion Sophie Gustafson from Sweden was fifth.

South African Women's Tour

Vodacom SA Ladies Players Championship—R150,000
Winner: Mandy Adamson

The opening event on the South African Women's Tour provided Mandy Adamson with her seventh home victory, but only after Adamson made a big comeback against Laurette Maritz at Parkview in Johannesburg.

Adamson, 30, closed with 70 to finish at three under par, but at one point in the final round Maritz had led by four strokes. Maritz just missed a birdie putt at the 18th to draw even and Adamson two-putted. Cherry Moulder finished third, six strokes behind the winner, with Sweden's Eva-Lotta Stromlid a further stroke back.

Kyocera-Mita South African Women's Open—R100,000
Winner: Mandy Adamson

Mandy Adamson won for the second consecutive week, taking the title in the Kyocera-Mita South African Women's Open for the third time. Adamson added to her victories in 1995 and 1997 with a five-stroke win thanks to rounds of 69, 68 and 68 for a 205 total, eight under par at Devonvale in Cape Town. Adamson had double-bogeyed the first hole, but five birdies between the fourth and 13th put her safely clear of the field. South African rookie Morgana Robbertze, after a closing 67, shared second place with Annerie Wessels, while Carina Vagner, Cecilie Lundgreen and Andrea Hirchhorn tied for fourth.

Telkom Ladies Classic—R140,000
Winner: Riikka Hakkarainen

Finland's Riikka Hakkarainen birdied the last three holes at Randpark in Johannesburg to win the Telkom Ladies Classic. It was the 24-year-old Hakkarainen's first professional victory and was achieved with three rounds of 70 to finish at six-under-par 210 and by two strokes over Cecilia Ekelundh and Amanda Moltke-Leth, with Mandy Adamson and Eva-Lotta Stromlid sharing fourth place.

Nedbank Ladies South African Masters—R125,000
Winner: Mandy Adamson

Mandy Adamson ended the South African circuit as she began it by winning the Nedbank Ladies South African Masters for her third victory in four tournaments. After 64 in the second round, Adamson closed with 71 to be 12 under par and win by one stroke over Norway's Cecilia Lundgreen. Denmark's Amanda Moltke-Leth was one stroke further back in third place, and Eva-Lotta Stromlid of Sweden was fourth after a closing 65.

"It was marvellous to have so many overseas players on the tour, which really added to the prestige and the competitiveness of our circuit," said Adamson. South Africa's Michelle de Vries had a double eagle at the ninth hole and an eagle on the 14th in her closing 76.

APPENDIXES

Official World Golf Ranking
(As of December 31, 2002)

Ranking		Player	Country	Points Average	Total Points	No. of Events	00/01 Points Lost	2002 Points Gained
1	(1)	Tiger Woods	USA	15.72	660.24	42	-697.41	+684.00
2	(2)	Phil Mickelson	USA	7.72	378.17	49	-427.93	+375.52
3	(4)	Ernie Els	SAf	6.84	389.48	54	-364.73	+377.78
4	(6)	Sergio Garcia	Spn	6.19	321.97	52	-274.60	+303.35
5	(10)	Retief Goosen	SAf	6.16	369.72	60	-278.50	+356.12
6	(7)	David Toms	USA	6.02	331.13	55	-279.53	+278.33
7	(11)	Padraig Harrington	Ire	5.63	276.09	49	-199.16	+233.74
8	(8)	Vijay Singh	Fiji	5.53	326.38	59	-318.76	+309.20
9	(5)	Davis Love	USA	4.82	221.72	46	-225.11	+175.72
10	(14)	Colin Montgomerie	Sco	4.39	228.24	52	-192.84	+201.57
11	(15)	Jim Furyk	USA	4.18	204.91	49	-194.64	+189.60
12	(20)	Chris DiMarco	USA	4.18	242.45	58	-212.43	+212.99
13	(29)	Nick Price	Zim	4.14	169.82	41	-161.20	+182.61
14	(34)	Angel Cabrera	Arg	3.70	186.53	45	-144.42	+164.54
15	(3)	David Duval	USA	3.68	169.29	46	-231.90	+74.06
16	(13)	Bernhard Langer	Ger	3.58	179.05	50	-173.15	+112.87
17	(40)	Justin Leonard	USA	3.51	199.96	57	-163.96	+209.09
18	(27)	Michael Campbell	NZl	3.48	180.85	52	-187.38	+198.50
19	(80)	Eduardo Romero	Arg	3.47	138.64	40	-75.22	+151.82
20	(45)	Charles Howell	USA	3.46	211.05	61	-86.86	+198.63
21	(279)	Rich Beem	USA	3.42	215.72	63	-57.89	+244.10
22	(21)	Scott Hoch	USA	3.40	156.60	46	-172.11	+115.61
23	(9)	Darren Clarke	NIr	3.38	179.09	53	-240.15	+137.69
24	(18)	Bob Estes	USA	3.35	174.08	52	-146.92	+129.43
25	(22)	Robert Allenby	Aus	3.33	203.27	61	-201.21	+172.59
26	(30)	Rocco Mediate	USA	3.30	145.24	44	-150.84	+152.10
27	(79)	Jerry Kelly	USA	3.20	194.91	61	-125.66	+222.56
28	(33)	Kenny Perry	USA	3.11	161.88	52	-133.90	+154.56
29	(63)	Shigeki Maruyama	Jpn	3.03	160.72	53	-120.21	+174.83
30	(51)	Scott McCarron	USA	2.81	148.95	53	-130.98	+160.25
31	(145)	Craig Parry	Aus	2.79	159.08	57	-73.23	+175.53
32	(43)	Stuart Appleby	Aus	2.74	169.60	62	-125.31	+146.51
33	(16)	Scott Verplank	USA	2.73	142.16	52	-187.33	+100.95
34	(91)	Fred Funk	USA	2.73	177.25	65	-105.61	+188.42
35	(24)	Thomas Bjorn	Den	2.70	140.40	52	-177.52	+114.30
36	(42)	Steve Lowery	USA	2.66	148.99	56	-133.05	+132.85
37	(162)	Justin Rose	Eng	2.65	156.64	59	-75.58	+178.10
38	(48)	Jose Maria Olazabal	Spn	2.62	154.71	59	-153.40	+173.99
39	(38)	Niclas Fasth	Swe	2.61	122.64	47	-100.65	+105.85
40	(49)	Adam Scott	Aus	2.58	154.92	60	-97.23	+144.06
41	(188)	K.J. Choi	Kor	2.57	149.25	58	-61.64	+164.34
42	(56)	Paul Lawrie	Sco	2.57	133.44	52	-84.29	+106.79
43	(119)	Peter Lonard	Aus	2.52	161.12	64	-84.91	+175.62
44	(85)	Chris Riley	USA	2.51	148.07	59	-81.18	+140.69
45	(61)	Jeff Sluman	USA	2.51	157.96	63	-117.47	+149.45
46	(37)	Shingo Katayama	Jpn	2.49	129.66	52	-125.49	+96.14
47	(12)	Mike Weir	Can	2.47	118.60	48	-205.40	+73.30
48	(44)	Brad Faxon	USA	2.44	126.83	52	-151.28	+143.60
49	(17)	Toshimitsu Izawa	Jpn	2.38	107.32	45	-128.49	+52.02
50	(48)	Toru Taniguchi	Jpn	2.38	135.77	57	-127.77	+136.43

( ) Ranking in brackets indicates position as of December 31, 2001.

Ranking		Player	Country	Points Average	Total Points	No. of Events	00/01 Points Lost	2002 Points Gained
51	(155)	Len Mattiace	USA	2.26	130.85	58	-93.13	+165.54
52	(105)	John Cook	USA	2.23	111.45	50	-80.30	+120.08
53	(65)	Loren Roberts	USA	2.17	108.28	50	-101.07	+118.35
54	(23)	Tom Lehman	USA	2.14	100.52	47	-153.49	+82.30
55	(167)	Alex Cejka	Ger	2.10	103.09	49	-40.45	+102.60
56	(72)	Dean Wilson	USA	2.05	94.52	46	-62.48	+81.38
57	(26)	Mark Calcavecchia	USA	2.05	98.33	48	-159.87	+79.97
58	(482)	Tim Clark	SAf	2.04	81.78	40	-32.72	+105.93
59	(402)	Jonathan Byrd	USA	1.96	96.28	49	-16.28	+101.13
60	(160)	Anders Hansen	Den	1.96	103.98	53	-58.17	+112.15
61	(174)	Stephen Leaney	Aus	1.94	103.05	53	-54.50	+116.62
62	(19)	Jose Coceres	Arg	1.94	77.42	40	-115.06	+25.84
63T	(238)	Bradley Dredge	Wal	1.93	100.28	52	-34.06	+101.76
63T	(408)	John Rollins	USA	1.93	104.14	54	-29.37	+119.62
65	(70)	Robert Karlsson	Swe	1.93	86.68	45	-58.06	+70.98
66	(101)	Nick Faldo	Eng	1.91	80.41	42	-68.06	+89.90
67	(66)	Kevin Sutherland	USA	1.89	109.46	58	-112.04	+116.78
68	(25)	Paul Azinger	USA	1.86	74.39	40	-124.63	+55.96
69	(62)	Dudley Hart	USA	1.85	94.58	51	-90.33	+88.97
70	(67)	John Huston	USA	1.84	84.65	46	-93.48	+98.85
71	(130)	Tsuneyuki Nakajima	Jpn	1.83	76.70	42	-38.43	+64.77
72	(31)	Stewart Cink	USA	1.80	102.80	57	-153.31	+78.02
73	(474)	Phil Tataurangi	NZl	1.79	96.76	54	-20.42	+108.40
74	(50)	Billy Andrade	USA	1.79	103.87	58	-116.99	+96.72
75	(87)	Ricardo Gonzalez	Arg	1.78	78.27	44	-59.88	+67.88
76	(75)	Peter O'Malley	Aus	1.78	97.78	55	-81.10	+91.94
77	(77)	Ian Poulter	Eng	1.77	99.38	56	-72.19	+79.60
78	(192)	Steve Elkington	Aus	1.77	78.08	44	-36.94	+84.45
79	(102)	Thomas Levet	Frn	1.70	95.21	56	-60.65	+76.97
80	(133)	David Smail	NZl	1.70	100.06	59	-51.14	+89.47
81	(32)	Jesper Parnevik	Swe	1.69	89.68	53	-142.08	+74.57
82	(68)	Ian Woosnam	Wal	1.69	76.09	45	-70.12	+57.89
83	(110)	Fredrik Jacobson	Swe	1.69	84.44	50	-50.01	+73.57
84	(128)	Chris Smith	USA	1.66	99.36	60	-66.37	+107.48
85	(206)	Matt Kuchar	USA	1.66	74.48	45	-46.31	+92.96
86	(507)	Pat Perez	USA	1.64	76.96	47	-37.71	+106.70
87	(41)	Kirk Triplett	USA	1.63	83.07	51	-111.34	+55.07
88	(58)	Billy Mayfair	USA	1.62	97.45	60	-98.86	+75.93
89	(100)	Bob Tway	USA	1.60	91.16	57	-77.04	+87.70
90	(52)	Steve Flesch	USA	1.60	102.11	64	-126.88	+90.12
91	(69)	Rory Sabbatini	SAf	1.59	77.99	49	-84.63	+74.75
92	(54)	John Daly	USA	1.54	90.76	59	-93.91	+60.39
93	(55)	Steve Stricker	USA	1.54	64.53	42	-81.16	+57.89
94	(590T)	Luke Donald	Eng	1.53	61.39	40	-14.14	+69.97
95	(304)	Bob Burns	USA	1.53	90.37	59	-29.16	+93.35
96	(175)	Soren Hansen	Den	1.53	88.73	58	-51.99	+92.35
97	(253)	Craig Perks	NZl	1.50	90.18	60	-66.88	+121.50
98	(78)	Scott Laycock	Aus	1.49	85.09	57	-68.68	+62.49
99	(140)	Matt Gogel	USA	1.49	77.33	52	-66.44	+85.79
100	(35)	Paul McGinley	Ire	1.49	81.74	55	-114.41	+36.13

( ) Ranking in brackets indicates position as of December 31, 2001.

Ranking		Player	Country	Points Average	Total Points	No. of Events	00/01 Points Lost	2002 Points Gained
101	(224)	Dan Forsman	USA	1.47	73.74	50	-36.63	+76.42
102	(176)	Trevor Immelman	SAf	1.45	97.34	67	-55.57	+102.05
103	(118)	Nobuhito Sato	Jpn	1.45	86.70	60	-72.78	+84.96
104	(104)	Lee Janzen	USA	1.44	83.44	58	-78.95	+86.48
105	(90)	Paul Casey	Eng	1.44	70.39	49	-41.78	+54.04
106	(59)	Hidemichi Tanaka	Jpn	1.43	81.50	57	-76.57	+65.35
107	(153)	Stephen Ames	T&T	1.43	76.98	54	-72.75	+95.47
108	(194)	Hiroyuki Fujita	Jpn	1.40	78.39	56	-35.69	+70.63
109	(53)	Pierre Fulke	Swe	1.39	57.14	41	-92.73	+64.09
110	(73)	Masashi Ozaki	Jpn	1.39	70.94	51	-69.59	+57.04
111	(148)	David Peoples	USA	1.37	82.19	60	-59.43	+83.33
112	(113)	Joel Edwards	USA	1.36	79.07	58	-65.98	+71.41
113	(122)	Cameron Beckman	USA	1.35	75.36	56	-65.53	+69.89
114	(159)	Carl Pettersson	Swe	1.34	75.21	56	-42.41	+79.83
115	(47)	Frank Lickliter	USA	1.34	78.77	59	-118.73	+56.78
116	(151)	Mark O'Meara	USA	1.32	62.00	47	-46.47	+63.60
117	(185)	Kaname Yokoo	Jpn	1.32	77.66	59	-49.04	+81.25
118	(233)	Gary Evans	Eng	1.30	76.70	59	-37.68	+77.51
119	(112)	Greg Norman	Aus	1.28	51.21	40	-52.65	+53.07
120	(103)	Jeff Maggert	USA	1.25	68.83	55	-76.17	+71.57
121	(88)	Brian Gay	USA	1.25	82.56	66	-77.46	+65.05
122	(163)	Barry Lane	Eng	1.25	73.64	59	-42.19	+68.37
123	(134)	Tim Herron	USA	1.23	72.43	59	-58.67	+67.64
124	(250)	Steen Tinning	Den	1.22	49.86	41	-25.94	+50.52
125	(125)	Greg Owen	Eng	1.21	67.51	56	-60.90	+60.79
126	(71)	Taichi Teshima	Jpn	1.18	66.36	56	-68.28	+31.02
127	(182)	Jay Haas	USA	1.18	54.37	46	-42.90	+58.37
128	(131)	Geoff Ogilvy	Aus	1.16	72.08	62	-57.88	+68.92
129	(60)	Phillip Price	Wal	1.16	59.02	51	-92.05	+44.89
130	(931)	S.K. Ho	Kor	1.15	45.81	40	-8.56	+53.00
131	(317)	Yasuharu Imano	Jpn	1.14	61.81	54	-27.08	+66.28
132	(106)	Katsumasa Miyamoto	Jpn	1.13	58.56	52	-55.27	+42.03
133	(268)	Brandt Jobe	USA	1.12	65.13	58	-35.56	+68.44
134	(481)	Andre Stolz	Aus	1.12	44.67	40	-15.82	+51.90
135	(144)	J.P. Hayes	USA	1.11	52.16	47	-47.87	+50.04
136	(99)	Mark Brooks	USA	1.11	65.45	59	-63.83	+50.83
137	(74)	Mathias Gronberg	Swe	1.10	46.40	42	-68.63	+28.41
138	(298)	Zhang Liang-wei	Chi	1.09	47.00	43	-19.32	+47.87
139	(138)	Jonathan Kaye	USA	1.09	66.46	61	-68.49	+63.65
140	(302)	Ian Leggatt	Can	1.08	62.85	58	-35.80	+73.85
141	(116)	Richard Green	Aus	1.08	56.29	52	-59.34	+47.51
142	(453)	Ben Crane	USA	1.07	53.70	50	-20.41	+64.58
143	(89)	Duffy Waldorf	USA	1.07	57.73	54	-81.16	+64.73
144	(275)	Jarrod Moseley	Aus	1.06	63.77	60	-31.37	+65.61
145	(171)	Joey Sindelar	USA	1.06	60.55	57	-48.80	+61.01
146	(81)	Tom Pernice Jr.	USA	1.06	67.73	64	-72.16	+42.15
147	(97)	Fred Couples	USA	1.02	40.98	40	-58.01	+43.34
148	(107)	David Gossett	USA	1.01	60.82	60	-45.31	+51.71
149	(154)	Brian Davis	Eng	1.01	54.62	54	-44.62	+46.53
150	(39)	Joe Durant	USA	1.01	52.46	52	-116.08	+26.74

( ) Ranking in brackets indicates position as of December 31, 2001.

Ranking		Player	Country	Points Average	Total Points	No. of Events	00/01 Points Lost	2002 Points Gained
151	(181)	Esteban Toledo	Mex	1.01	68.60	68	-52.11	+62.62
152	(445)	Kim Jong-duck	Kor	0.99	46.74	47	-15.00	+50.56
153	(115)	David Howell	Eng	0.99	51.58	52	-58.72	+34.67
154	(117)	Steve Webster	Eng	0.99	57.50	58	-57.94	+42.97
155	(242)	Kenichi Kuboya	Jpn	0.99	55.40	56	-36.53	+58.13
156	(203)	John Bickerton	Eng	0.98	57.87	59	-41.50	+58.05
157	(296)	Heath Slocum	USA	0.97	54.41	56	-26.67	+62.43
158	(290)	Katsunori Kuwabara	Jpn	0.97	51.47	53	-26.06	+51.04
159	(92)	Mark McNulty	Zim	0.97	42.67	44	-56.67	+37.11
160	(173)	Chad Campbell	USA	0.96	54.71	57	-29.09	+49.60
161	(172)	Briny Baird	USA	0.96	61.15	64	-49.62	+61.56
162	(149)	Glen Day	USA	0.95	56.79	60	-51.55	+51.13
163	(340)	Brendan Jones	Aus	0.94	51.64	55	-12.67	+49.17
164	(132)	Harrison Frazar	USA	0.94	49.66	53	-54.20	+48.83
165	(313)	Carlos Rodiles	Spn	0.93	45.70	49	-21.93	+47.88
166	(254)	Rodney Pampling	Aus	0.93	59.55	64	-37.82	+62.46
167	(146)	Aaron Baddeley	Aus	0.93	45.47	49	-36.57	+41.72
168	(770)	Gene Sauers	USA	0.93	37.11	40	-7.83	+42.22
169	(189)	Neal Lancaster	USA	0.92	61.97	67	-41.44	+50.56
170	(57)	Miguel A. Jimenez	Spn	0.91	52.93	58	-84.23	+28.92
171	(36)	Hal Sutton	USA	0.91	47.12	52	-131.19	+22.23
172	(276)	Jim Carter	USA	0.91	51.62	57	-40.34	+62.72
173	(197)	Tom Byrum	USA	0.89	44.42	50	-37.55	+43.14
174	(83)	Andrew Coltart	Sco	0.89	54.00	61	-72.50	+41.12
175	(480)	Nick Dougherty	Eng	0.88	40.50	46	-17.63	+49.52
176	(421)	David Gilford	Eng	0.87	39.88	46	-17.08	+46.18
177	(209)	J.L. Lewis	USA	0.86	53.44	62	-50.66	+62.19
178	(123)	Skip Kendall	USA	0.85	54.67	64	-70.97	+48.40
179	(142)	J.J. Henry	USA	0.85	53.64	63	-44.19	+38.05
180	(111)	Carlos Franco	Par	0.84	49.55	59	-61.08	+44.60
181	(28)	Lee Westwood	Eng	0.84	42.78	51	-158.98	+35.43
182	(137)	Nick O'Hern	Aus	0.83	44.69	54	-52.97	+41.93
183	(370)	Maarten Lafeber	Hol	0.83	50.35	61	-24.95	+55.39
184	(234)	Tomohiro Kondou	Jpn	0.82	39.40	48	-20.64	+35.09
185	(1202T)	Graeme McDowell	NIr	0.82	32.73	40	-4.69	+37.42
186	(199)	Craig Stadler	USA	0.82	34.35	42	-34.08	+39.46
187	(386)	Stephen Allan	Aus	0.80	49.83	62	-19.15	+51.87
188	(357)	Christian Pena	USA	0.80	32.95	41	-18.10	+34.62
189	(95)	Robert Damron	USA	0.80	44.05	55	-60.65	+26.86
190T	(76)	Andrew Oldcorn	Sco	0.80	36.03	45	-51.36	+19.82
190T	(114)	Greg Chalmers	Aus	0.80	51.24	64	-70.51	+45.73
192	(606)	Gavin Coles	Aus	0.80	31.81	40	-8.73	+35.30
193	(86)	Warren Bennett	Eng	0.78	43.83	56	-40.22	+25.40
194	(147)	Brent Geiberger	USA	0.78	42.09	54	-45.99	+38.80
195	(294)	Pat Bates	USA	0.78	35.79	46	-18.05	+34.23
196T	(396)	Robert Gamez	USA	0.77	37.90	49	-18.61	+39.85
196T	(325)	Jean F. Remesy	Frn	0.77	41.76	54	-25.30	+47.28
198	(141)	Naomichi Ozaki	Jpn	0.77	43.29	56	-55.81	+41.29
199	(120)	Raphael Jacquelin	Frn	0.77	44.81	58	-55.43	+28.87
200	(158)	Olin Browne	USA	0.77	48.65	63	-50.76	+41.56

( ) Ranking in brackets indicates position as of December 31, 2001.

Age Groups of Current Top 100 World Ranked Players

Under 25	25-28	29-30	31-32	33-34	35-36	37-38	39-42	Over 43
				Els				
				Goosen				
			Mickelson	DiMarco				
			Harrington	Cabrera				
			Furyk	Campbell				
			Duval	Clarke	Toms			N.Price
			Beem	Maruyama	B.Estes		Singh	Langer
			Allenby	Lawrie	Kelly		Montgomerie	Romero
			Appleby	Izawa	Parry		Mediate	Hoch
	Woods		Bjorn	Taniguchi	Olazabal		K.Perry	Funk
	T.Clark		K.J.Choi	D.Wilson	Lonard		Lowery	Sluman
	Rollins		Weir	Leaney	Mattiace	Love	Faxon	Cook
Garcia	Poulter	Leonard	Cejka	R.Karlsson	Mayfair	McCarron	Calcavecchia	Roberts
Howell	Jacobson	Fasth	A.Hansen	D.Hart	Flesch	Verplank	Coceres	Lehman
Rose	Perez	C.Riley	Tataurangi	R.Gonzalez	Daly	Sutherland	Azinger	Faldo
Scott	Sabbatini	Katayama	Smail	Levet	Stricker	Andrade	Huston	Nakajima
Byrd	Donald	Dredge	Laycock	C.Smith	Perks	O'Malley	Elkington	Woosnam
Kuchar	S.Hansen	Cink	Gogel	Burns	McGinley	Parnevik	Triplett	Tway

2002 World Ranking Review

Major Movements

	Upward				Downward		
	Net Points	Position				Net Points	Position
Name	Gained	2001	2002	Name		Lost	2001 2002
Rich Beem	186	279	21	David Duval		158	3 15
Charles Howell	112	45	20	Mike Weir		132	12 47
K.J. Choi	103	188	41	Lee Westwood		123	28 181
Justin Rose	103	162	37	Hal Sutton		109	36 171
Craig Parry	102	145	31	Darren Clarke		102	9 23
Jerry Kelly	97	79	27	Joe Durant		89	39 150
John Rollins	90	408	63	Jose Coceres		89	19 62
Phil Tataurangi	88	474	73	Scott Verplank		86	16 33
Jonathan Byrd	85	402	59	Mark Calcavecchia		79	26 57
Fred Funk	83	91	34	Paul McGinley		78	35 100
Eduardo Romero	77	80	19	Toshimitsu Izawa		76	17 49
Tim Clark	73	482	58	Stewart Cink		75	31 72

Highest-Rated Events of 2002

	Event	Top 5	Top 15	Top 30	Top 50	Top 100	World Rating Points
		No. of World Ranked Players Participating					**World Rating Points**
1	PGA Championship	5	15	30	50	98	821
2	British Open Championship	5	15	29	47	86	765
3	U.S. Open Championship	5	15	30	48	75	745
4	Masters Tournament	5	15	30	50	67	725
5	The Players Championship	5	15	28	48	78	745
6	WGC NEC Invitational	5	15	30	50	67	719
7	WGC Accenture Match Play	5	15	28	48	64	714
8	WGC American Express	5	15	30	49	60	692
9	Bay Hill Invitational	5	9	20	33	56	551
10	Verizon Byron Nelson Classic	4	10	18	25	53	496
11	MasterCard Colonial	2	9	18	28	59	472
12	Buick Classic	4	11	18	30	50	462
13	Memorial Tournament	4	7	14	28	52	461
14	The Tour Championship	5	11	21	28	30	450
15	Volvo PGA Championship	1	4	7	11	25	180
16	Nissan Open	2	7	17	31	53	438
17	Genuity Championship	4	10	14	23	41	395
18	Phoenix Open	1	5	13	26	48	372
19	WorldCom Classic	3	5	13	24	44	366
20	Canon Greater Hartford Open	3	7	12	21	35	352
21	Mercedes Championships	3	8	14	22	27	336
22	Buick Challenge	1	6	14	23	42	345
23	The International	3	6	14	20	42	345
24	BellSouth Classic	1	9	14	22	38	349
25	Buick Open	3	6	13	20	35	341
26	Disney Golf Classic	1	6	15	24	45	335
27	Shell Houston Open	1	5	13	22	42	329
28	AT&T Pebble Beach Pro-Am	2	7	10	19	32	320
29	Bob Hope Chrysler Classic	2	4	9	20	39	319
30	Barclays Scottish Open	2	3	9	17	41	284
31	Advil Western Open	0	5	13	17	41	289
32	Dunhill Links Championship	2	5	9	15	31	253
33	Compaq Classic New Orleans	2	4	9	12	36	276
34	Honda Classic	1	6	10	17	31	272
35	Linde German Masters	2	4	9	15	28	233
36	Invensys Classic Las Vegas	0	4	9	18	44	268
37	Sony Open in Hawaii	1	4	9	16	36	255
38	Deutsche Bank SAP Open	2	5	8	12	25	220
39	Buick Invitational	2	4	6	13	30	250
40	Volvo Masters Andalucia	1	5	7	14	27	215

World Golf Rankings 1968-2002

Year	No. 1	No. 2	No. 3	No. 4	No. 5
1968	Nicklaus	Palmer	Casper	Player	Charles
1969	Nicklaus	Player	Casper	Palmer	Charles
1970	Nicklaus	Player	Casper	Trevino	Charles
1971	Nicklaus	Trevino	Player	Palmer	Casper
1972	Nicklaus	Player	Trevino	Crampton	Palmer
1973	Nicklaus	Weiskopf	Trevino	Player	Crampton
1974	Nicklaus	Miller	Player	Weiskopf	Trevino
1975	Nicklaus	Miller	Weiskopf	Irwin	Player
1976	Nicklaus	Irwin	Miller	Player	Green
1977	Nicklaus	Watson	Green	Irwin	Crenshaw
1978	Watson	Nicklaus	Irwin	Green	Player
1979	Watson	Nicklaus	Irwin	Trevino	Player
1980	Watson	Trevino	Aoki	Crenshaw	Nicklaus
1981	Watson	Rogers	Aoki	Pate	Trevino
1982	Watson	Floyd	Ballesteros	Kite	Stadler
1983	Ballesteros	Watson	Floyd	Norman	Kite
1984	Ballesteros	Watson	Norman	Wadkins	Langer
1985	Ballesteros	Langer	Norman	Watson	Nakajima
1986	Norman	Langer	Ballesteros	Nakajima	Bean
1987	Norman	Ballesteros	Langer	Lyle	Strange
1988	Ballesteros	Norman	Lyle	Faldo	Strange
1989	Norman	Faldo	Ballesteros	Strange	Stewart
1990	Norman	Faldo	Olazabal	Woosnam	Stewart
1991	Woosnam	Faldo	Olazabal	Ballesteros	Norman
1992	Faldo	Couples	Woosnam	Olazabal	Norman
1993	Faldo	Norman	Langer	Price	Couples
1994	Price	Norman	Faldo	Langer	Olazabal
1995	Norman	Price	Langer	Els	Montgomerie
1996	Norman	Lehman	Montgomerie	Els	Couples
1997	Norman	Woods	Price	Els	Love
1998	Woods	O'Meara	Duval	Love	Els
1999	Woods	Duval	Montgomerie	Love	Els
2000	Woods	Els	Duval	Mickelson	Westwood
2001	Woods	Mickelson	Duval	Els	Love
2002	Woods	Mickelson	Els	Garcia	Goosen

(*The World of Professional Golf* 1968-1985; World Ranking 1986-2002)

Year	No. 6	No. 7	No. 8	No. 9	No. 10
1968	Boros	Coles	Thomson	Beard	Nagle
1969	Beard	Archer	Trevino	Barber	Sikes
1970	Devlin	Coles	Jacklin	Beard	Huggett
1971	Barber	Crampton	Charles	Devlin	Weiskopf
1972	Jacklin	Weiskopf	Oosterhuis	Heard	Devlin
1973	Miller	Oosterhuis	Wadkins	Heard	Brewer
1974	M. Ozaki	Crampton	Irwin	Green	Heard
1975	Green	Trevino	Casper	Crampton	Watson
1976	Watson	Weiskopf	Marsh	Crenshaw	Geiberger
1977	Marsh	Player	Weiskopf	Floyd	Ballesteros
1978	Crenshaw	Marsh	Ballesteros	Trevino	Aoki
1979	Aoki	Green	Crenshaw	Ballesteros	Wadkins
1980	Pate	Ballesteros	Bean	Irwin	Player
1981	Ballesteros	Graham	Crenshaw	Floyd	Lietzke
1982	Pate	Nicklaus	Rogers	Aoki	Strange
1983	Nicklaus	Nakajima	Stadler	Aoki	Wadkins
1984	Faldo	Nakajima	Stadler	Kite	Peete
1985	Wadkins	O'Meara	Strange	Pavin	Sutton
1986	Tway	Sutton	Strange	Stewart	O'Meara
1987	Woosnam	Stewart	Wadkins	McNulty	Crenshaw
1988	Crenshaw	Woosnam	Frost	Azinger	Calcavecchia
1989	Kite	Olazabal	Calcavecchia	Woosnam	Azinger
1990	Azinger	Ballesteros	Kite	McNulty	Calcavecchia
1991	Couples	Langer	Stewart	Azinger	Davis
1992	Langer	Cook	Price	Azinger	Love
1993	Azinger	Woosnam	Kite	Love	Pavin
1994	Els	Couples	Montgomerie	M. Ozaki	Pavin
1995	Pavin	Faldo	Couples	M. Ozaki	Elkington
1996	Faldo	Mickelson	M. Ozaki	Love	O'Meara
1997	Mickelson	Montgomerie	M. Ozaki	Lehman	O'Meara
1998	Price	Montgomerie	Westwood	Singh	Mickelson
1999	Westwood	Singh	Price	Mickelson	O'Meara
2000	Montgomerie	Love	Sutton	Singh	Lehman
2001	Garcia	Toms	Singh	Clarke	Goosen
2002	Toms	Harrington	Singh	Love	Montgomerie

World's Winners of 2002

U.S. PGA TOUR

Mercedes Championships	Sergio Garcia
Sony Open in Hawaii	Jerry Kelly
Bob Hope Chrysler Classic	Phil Mickelson
Phoenix Open	Chris DiMarco
AT&T Pebble Beach National Pro-Am	Matt Gogel
Buick Invitational	Jose Maria Olazabal
Nissan Open	Len Mattiace
WGC Accenture Match Play	Kevin Sutherland
Touchstone Energy Tucson Open	Ian Leggatt
Genuity Championship	Ernie Els (2)
Honda Classic	Matt Kuchar
Bay Hill Invitational	Tiger Woods
The Players Championship	Craig Perks
Shell Houston Open	Vijay Singh
BellSouth Classic	Retief Goosen (3)
Masters Tournament	Tiger Woods (2)
WorldCom Classic	Justin Leonard
Greater Greensboro Chrysler Classic	Rocco Mediate
Compaq Classic of New Orleans	K.J. Choi
Verizon Byron Nelson Classic	Shigeki Maruyama
MasterCard Colonial	Nick Price
Memorial Tournament	Jim Furyk
Kemper Insurance Open	Bob Estes
Buick Classic	Chris Smith
U.S. Open Championship	Tiger Woods (4)
Canon Greater Hartford Open	Phil Mickelson (2)
FedEx St. Jude Classic	Len Mattiace (2)
Advil Western Open	Jerry Kelly (2)
Greater Milwaukee Open	Jeff Sluman
B.C. Open	Spike McRoy
John Deere Classic	J.P. Hayes
The International	Rich Beem
Buick Open	Tiger Woods (5)
PGA Championship	Rich Beem (2)
WGC NEC Invitational	Craig Parry (2)
Reno-Tahoe Open	Chris Riley
Air Canada Championship	Gene Sauers
Bell Canadian Open	John Rollins
SEI Pennsylvania Classic	Dan Forsman
Tampa Bay Classic	K.J. Choi (2)
Valero Texas Open	Loren Roberts
Michelob Championship at Kingsmill	Charles Howell
Invensys Classic at Las Vegas	Phil Tataurangi
Disney Golf Classic	Bob Burns
Buick Challenge	Jonathan Byrd
Tour Championship	Vijay Singh (2)
Southern Farm Bureau Classic	Luke Donald

SPECIAL EVENTS

CVS/pharmacy Charity Classic	Dudley Hart/Chris DiMarco (2)
Fred Meyer Challenge	Brian Henninger/Scott McCarron
Ryder Cup	Europe
UBS Warburg Cup	United States
Hyundai Team Matches	Rich Beem (3)/Peter Lonard
Callaway Golf Pebble Beach Invitational	Mark Brooks

Franklin Templeton Shootout — Lee Janzen/Rocco Mediate (2)
PGA Grand Slam of Golf — Tiger Woods (7)
Target World Challenge — Padraig Harrington (3)
WGC EMC World Cup — Shigeki Maruyama (2)/Toshi Izawa
Office Depot Father-Son Challenge — Craig/Kevin Stadler

BUY.COM TOUR

Louisiana Open — Steve Alker
Arkansas Classic — Jace Bugg
BMW Charity Pro-Am at The Cliffs — Charles Warren
Virginia Beach Open — Cliff Kresge
Richmond Open — Patrick Moore
SAS Carolina Classic — Zoran Zorkic
Northeast Pennsylvania Classic — Gary Hallberg
Samsung Canadian PGA Championship — Arron Oberholser
Lake Erie Charity Classic — Patrick Moore (2)
Knoxville Open — Darron Stiles
Hershey Open — Cliff Kresge (2)
Dayton Open — Jason Buha
Fort Smith Classic — Todd Fischer
Price Cutter Charity Championship — Patrick Sheehan
Omaha Classic — Jay Delsing
LaSalle Bank Open — Marco Dawson
Preferred Health Systems Wichita Open — Tyler Williamson
Permian Basin Open — Tag Ridings
Utah Classic — Arron Oberholser (2)
Oregon Classic — Jason Gore
Albertson's Boise Open — Jason Gore (2)
State Farm Open — Andy Miller
Bank of America Monterey Peninsula Classic — Roland Thatcher (2)
Gila River Classic at Wild Horse Pass Resort — David Branshaw
Hibernia Southern Open — David Morland
Buy.com Tour Championship — Patrick Moore (3)

CANADIAN TOUR

Panama Open Panasonic — Mario Tiziani
Texas Classic — Steve Scott
Texas Challenge — Hank Kuehne
Scottsdale Swing at McCormick Ranch — Jeff Quinney
Scottsdale Swing at Eagle Mountain — Jimmy Walker
Michelin Ixtapa Classic — Pablo Del Olmo
Barefoot Classic — Rob McMillan
Myrtle Beach Barefoot Championship — Derek Gillespie
Lewis Chitengwa Memorial Championship — Chris Wisler
Bay Mills Open — Jeff Quinney (2)
Ontario Open Heritage Classic — Mike Grob
Greater Vancouver Classic — Iain Steel
Victoria Open — Scott Hend
Telus Edmonton Open — Matt Daniel
MTS Classic — Alex Quiroz
Telus Quebec Open — Hank Kuehne (2)
Greater Toronto Open — Chris Locker
Casino de Charlevoix Cup — Pete Bousquet/Jean-Louis Lamarre

SOUTH AMERICAN TOUR

Corona Caribbean Open — Rafael Gomez
TLA Los Encinos Open — Roland Thatcher
American Express Costa Rica Open — Rafael Gomez (2)
Tikal Trophy Guatemala — Sebastian Fernandez
LG Panama Masters — Pedro Martinez
TLA Players Championship Acapulco Fest — Roberto Coceres

Medellin Open	Jesus Amaya
Serrezuela Masters	Jesus Amaya (2)
CANTV Venezuela Open	Jesus Amaya (3)
Argentina Open	Angel Cabrera (2)

PGA EUROPEAN TOUR

Dubai Desert Classic	Ernie Els (3)
Qatar Masters	Adam Scott
Madeira Island Open	Diego Borrego
Algarve Open de Portugal	Carl Pettersson
The Seve Trophy	Great Britain & Ireland
Canarias Open de Espana	Sergio Garcia (2)
Novotel Perrier Open de France	Malcolm Mackenzie
Benson and Hedges International Open	Angel Cabrera
Deutsche Bank - SAP Open	Tiger Woods (3)
Volvo PGA Championship	Anders Hansen
Victor Chandler British Masters	Justin Rose (4)
Compass Group English Open	Darren Clarke
Great North Open	Miles Tunnicliff
Murphy's Irish Open	Soren Hansen
Smurfit European Open	Michael Campbell
Barclays Scottish Open	Eduardo Romero
British Open Championship	Ernie Els (4)
TNT Open	Tobias Dier
Volvo Scandinavian Masters	Graeme McDowell
Celtic Manor Resort Wales Open	Paul Lawrie
North West of Ireland Open	Adam Mednick
Diageo Scottish PGA Championship	Adam Scott (2)
BMW International Open	Thomas Bjorn
Omega European Masters	Robert Karlsson
Linde German Masters	Stephen Leaney
WGC American Express Championship	Tiger Woods (6)
Dunhill Links Championship	Padraig Harrington
Trophee Lancome	Alex Cejka (2)
Cisco World Match Play	Ernie Els (5)
Telefonica Open de Madrid	Steen Tinning
Italian Open Telecom Italia	Ian Poulter
Volvo Masters Andalucia	Bernhard Langer/Colin Montgomerie

CHALLENGE TOUR

Sameer Kenya Open	Lee James
Panalpina Banque Commerciale du Maroc Classic	Jean-Francois Lucquin
Tessali Open del Sud	Simon Wakefield
Izki Challenge de Espana	Fredrik Widmark
Austrian Golf Open	Markus Brier
Nykredit Danish Open	Ed Stedman
Aa Saint Omer Open	Nicolas Vanhootegem
Galeria Kaufhof Pokal Challenge	Alex Cejka
Clearstream International Luxembourg Open	Lee James (2)
Open des Volcans	Scott Kammann
Golf Montecchia - PGA Triveneta Terme Euganee International Open	Wolfgang Huget
Volvo Finnish Open	Thomas Norret
Golf Challenge	Iain Pyman
Charles Church Challenge Tour Championship	John Morgan
Talma Finnish Challenge	Lee James (3)
BMW Russian Open	Iain Pyman (2)
Skandia PGA Open	Thomas Besancenez
Rolex Trophy	Simon Hurd
Formby Hall Challenge	Matthew Blackey
Telia Grand Prix	Matthew Blackey (2)

Fortis Bank Challenge Open   Didier de Vooght
Challenge Tour Grand Final   Peter Lawrie

ASIAN PGA DAVIDOFF TOUR

London Myanmar Open	Thongchai Jaidee
Hero Honda Masters	Harmeet Kahlon
Caltex Singapore Masters	Arjun Atwal
Carlsberg Malaysian Open	Alastair Forsyth
Casino Filipino Philippine Open	Rick Gibson
Royal Challenge Indian Open	Vijay Kumar
SK Telecom Open	Charlie Wi
Maekyung LG Fashion Open	*Lee Seung-yong
Mercuries Masters	Tsai Chi-huang
Shinhan Donghae Open	Hur Suk-ho (2)
Kolon Cup Korean Open	Sergio Garcia (3)
Volvo China Open	David Gleeson
Acer Taiwan Open	Danny Chia
Macau Open	Zhang Lian-wei
TCL Classic	Colin Montgomerie (2)
BMW Asian Open	Padraig Harrington (2)
Omega Hong Kong Open	Fredrik Jacobson
Volvo Masters of Asia	Kevin Na

JAPAN TOUR

Token Corporation Cup	Toru Taniguchi
Dydo Drinco Shizuoka Open	Kiyoshi Murota
Tsuruya Open	Dean Wilson
Chunichi Crowns	Justin Rose (3)
Fujisankei Classic	Nobuhito Sato
Japan PGA Championship	Kenichi Kuboya
Munsingwear Open KSB Cup	Kenichi Kuboya (2)
Diamond Cup	Tsuneyuki Nakajima
JCB Classic Sendai	Toru Suzuki
Tamanoi Yomiuri Open	Toru Taniguchi (2)
Mizuno Open	Dean Wilson (2)
Japan Tour Championship Iiyama Cup	Nobuhito Sato (2)
Juken Sangyo Open Hiroshima	Hur Suk-ho
Sato Foods NST Niigata Open	Yasuharu Imano
Aiful Cup	Yasuharu Imano (2)
Sun Chlorella Classic	Christian Pena
Hisamitsu-KBC Augusta	Nobumitsu Yuhara
Japan PGA Match Play	Nobuhito Sato (3)
Suntory Open	Shingo Katayama
ANA Open	Masashi Ozaki
Acom International	Toru Taniguchi (3)
Georgia Tokai Classic	Toru Taniguchi (4)
Japan Open	David Smail
Bridgestone Open	Scott Laycock
Philip Morris Championship	Brendan Jones
Mitsui Sumitomo Visa Taiheiyo Masters	Tsuneyuki Nakajima (2)
Dunlop Phoenix	Kaname Yokoo
Casio World Open	David Smail (2)
Nippon Series JT Cup	Shingo Katayama (2)
Asia/Japan Okinawa Open	Hiroyuki Fujita

AUSTRALASIAN TOUR

Telstra Hyundai New Zealand Open	Craig Parry
Johnnie Walker Classic	Retief Goosen
Heineken Classic	Ernie Els
ANZ Championship	Richard Johnson
New South Wales Masters	Steve Collins

Jacob's Creek Open	Gavin Coles
Holden Clearwater Classic	Peter O'Malley
Scenic Circle Hotels Dunedin Classic	Gareth Paddison
Volvo Trucks Golf Klassik	Terry Price
South Australian PGA Championship	Richard Ball
Western Australian PGA Championship	Kim Felton
Queensland PGA Championship	Andre Stolz
Victorian PGA Championship	Craig Carmichael
Victorian Open	Andre Stolz (2)
Queensland Open	Andrew Buckle
New South Wales Open	Terry Price (2)
Holden Australian Open	Steve Allan
Australian PGA Championship	Peter Lonard (2)/Jarrod Moseley
MasterCard Masters	Peter Lonard (3)

AFRICAN TOURS

Bell's South African Open	Tim Clark
Dunhill Championship	Justin Rose
Telkom PGA Championship	Chris Williams
Dimension Data Pro-Am	Retief Goosen (2)
Nashua Masters	Justin Rose (2)
Southern Africa Tour Championship	Nicholas Lawrence
Royal Swazi Sun Open	Andrew McLardy
Stanbic Zambia Open	Marc Cayeux
FNB Botswana Open	Hendrik Buhrmann
Limpopo Industrelek Classic	Hennie Otto
Royal Swazi Sun Classic	James Kingston
Vodacom Golf Classic	Ashley Roestoff
Bearing Man Highveld Classic	Titch Moore
Platinum Classic	Titch Moore (2)
Telkom PGA Championship	Michiel Bothma
Nashua Masters	Hennie Otto (2)
Nedbank Golf Challenge	Ernie Els (6)
Vodacom Players Championship	Mark McNulty
Hassan II Trophy	Santiago Luna
Ernie Els Invitational	Louis Oosthuizen

U.S. SENIOR PGA TOUR

MasterCard Championship	Tom Kite
Royal Caribbean Classic	John Jacobs
ACE Group Classic	Hale Irwin
Verizon Classic	Doug Tewell
Audi Senior Classic	Bruce Lietzke
SBC Senior Classic	Tom Kite (2)
Toshiba Senior Classic	Hale Irwin (2)
Siebel Classic in Silicon Valley	Dana Quigley
Emerald Coast Classic	Dave Eichelberger
Liberty Mutual Legends of Golf	Doug Tewell (2)
The Countrywide Tradition	Jim Thorpe
Bruno's Memorial Classic	Sammy Rachels
TD Waterhouse Championship	Bruce Lietzke (2)
Instinet Classic	Isao Aoki
Farmers Charity Classic	Jay Sigel
NFL Golf Classic	James Mason
Senior PGA Championship	Fuzzy Zoeller
BellSouth Senior Classic at Opryland	Gil Morgan
Greater Baltimore Classic	J.C. Snead
U.S. Senior Open	Don Pooley
AT&T Canada Senior Open	Tom Jenkins
Ford Senior Players Championship	Stewart Ginn
SBC Senior Open	Bob Gilder

FleetBoston Classic	Bob Gilder (2)
Lightpath Long Island Classic	Hubert Green
3M Championship	Hale Irwin (3)
Uniting Fore Care Classic	Morris Hatalsky
Allianz Championship	Bob Gilder (3)
Kroger Senior Classic	Bob Gilder (4)
RJR Championship	Bruce Fleisher
SAS Championship	Bruce Lietzke (3)
Turtle Bay Championship	Hale Irwin (4)
Napa Valley Championship	Tom Kite (3)
SBC Championship	Dana Quigley (2)
Senior Tour Championship at Gaillardia	Tom Watson
Senior Slam	Fuzzy Zoeller (2)
Hyundai Team Matches	Dana Quigley (3)/Allen Doyle

EUROPEAN SENIORS TOUR

Royal Westmoreland Barbados Open	Peter Townsend
Tobago Plantations Seniors Classic	Steve Stull
AIB Irish Seniors Open	Seiji Ebihara
Flanders Nippon presents Legends in Golf	Gary Wintz
Microlease Jersey Seniors Masters	Delroy Cambridge
Lawrence Batley Seniors Open	Neil Coles
Wales Seniors Open	Seiji Ebihara (2)
The Mobile Cup	Bernard Gallacher
Senior British Open	Noboru Sugai
De Vere PGA Seniors Championship	Seiji Ebihara (3)
Bad Ragaz PGA Seniors Open	Dragon Taki
Travis Perkins Senior Masters	Ray Carrasco
De Vere Hotels Seniors Classic	Brian Jones
GIN Monte Carlo Invitational	Terry Gale
Bovis Lend Lease European Senior Masters	Delroy Cambridge (2)
Charles Church Scottish Seniors Open	Denis Durnian
Daily Telegraph/Sodexho Seniors Match Play	Delroy Cambridge (3)
Tunisian Seniors Open	Denis O'Sullivan
Estoril Seniors Tour Championship	Denis Durnian (2)

JAPAN SENIOR TOUR

Castle Hill Open	Namio Takasu
Asahi Ryokken Cup	Hisao Inoue
Aderans Wellness Open	Yukio Noguchi
Fancl Senior Classic	Katsunari Takahashi
HTD Senior Classic	Noboru Sugai (2)
Japan PGA Senior Championship	Chen Tze-ming
PGA Philanthropy Biglayzac Senior	Seiji Ebihara (4)
Japan Senior Open Championship	Takaaki Fukuzawa
Takanosu Senior Open	Takashi Miyoshi
N. Cup Senior Open	Isao Aoki (2)

U.S. LPGA TOUR

Takefuji Classic	Annika Sorenstam (2)
Ping Banner Health	Rachel Teske
Welch's/Circle K Championship	Laura Diaz
Kraft Nabisco Championship	Annika Sorenstam (3)
The Office Depot Hosted by Amy Alcott	Se Ri Pak
Longs Drugs Challenge	Cristie Kerr
Chick-fil-A Charity Championship	Juli Inkster
Aerus Electrolux USA Championship	Annika Sorenstam (4)
Asahi Ryokuken International	Janice Moodie
Corning Classic	Laura Diaz (2)
Kellogg-Keebler Classic	Annika Sorenstam (5)
McDonald's LPGA Championship	Se Ri Pak (2)

Wegmans Rochester LPGA	Karrie Webb (2)
ShopRite Classic	Annika Sorenstam (7)
U.S. Women's Open	Juli Inkster (2)
Jamie Farr Kroger Classic	Rachel Teske (2)
Giant Eagle Classic	Mi Hyun Kim
Sybase Big Apple Classic	Gloria Park
Wendy's Championship for Children	Mi Hyun Kim (2)
Bank of Montreal Canadian Women's Open	Meg Mallon
First Union Betsy King Classic	Se Ri Pak (3)
State Farm Classic	Patricia Meunier-Lebouc
Williams Championship	Annika Sorenstam (9)
Safeway Classic	Annika Sorenstam (10)
Solheim Cup	United States
Samsung World Championship	Annika Sorenstam (11)
Mobile Tournament of Champions	Se Ri Pak (4)
Sports Today CJ Nine Bridges Classic	Se Ri Pak (5)
Hyundai Team Matches	Lorie Kane/Janice Moodie (2)
ADT Championship	Annika Sorenstam (13)

EVIAN LADIES EUROPEAN TOUR

Ladies Tenerife Open	Raquel Carriedo
Ladies Irish Open	Iben Tinning
La Perla Italian Open	Iben Tinning (2)
Ladies Open of Costa Azul	Kanna Takanashi
Caja Duero Open de Espana	Karine Icher
Evian Masters	Annika Sorenstam (6)
Open de France Dames Credit Mutuel Nord	Lynnette Brooky
P4 Norwegian Masters	Laura Davies
Weetabix Women's British Open	Karrie Webb (3)
Compaq Open	Annika Sorenstam (8)
Wales WPGA Championship of Europe	Asa Gottmo
Biarritz Ladies Classic	Sophie Gustafson
Princess Lalla Meriem Cup	Johanna Head

JAPAN LPGA TOUR

Daikin Orchid Ladies	Kasumi Fujii
Promise Ladies	Mayumi Inoue
Saishunkan Ladies Hinokuni Open	Ai-Yu Tu
Katokichi Queens	Chieko Nishida
Nichirei Cup World Ladies	Yuri Fudoh
Vernal Ladies	Mikino Kubo
Chukyo TV Bridgestone Ladies	Shin Sora
Kosaido Ladies Golf Cup	Orie Fujino
Resort Trust Ladies	Kozue Azuma
We Love Kobe Suntory Ladies Open	Takayo Bandoh
Apita Circle K Sankus Ladies	Mihoko Takahashi
Belluna Ladies Cup	Orie Fujino (2)
Toyo Suisan Ladies Hokkaido	Chihiro Nakajima
Golf 5 Ladies	Ikuyo Shiotani
Vernal Open	Yuri Fudoh (2)
NEC Karuizawa 72	Akiko Fukushima
New Caterpillar Mitsubishi Ladies	Kaori Higo
Yonex Ladies Open	Yuri Fudoh (3)
Fujisankei Ladies Classic	Ok-Hee Ku
Japan LPGA Championship Konica Cup	Ok-Hee Ku (2)
Munsingwear Ladies Tokai Classic	Kasumi Fujii (2)
Miyagi TV Cup Dunlop Ladies Open	Mihoko Takahashi (2)
Japan Women's Open	Woo Soon-Ko
Sankyo Ladies Open	Toshimi Kimura
Fujitsu Ladies	Chihiro Nakajima (2)
Hisako Higuchi Classic	Kasumi Fujii (3)

Cisco World Ladies Match Play	Grace Park
Mizuno Classic	Annika Sorenstam (12)
Itoen Ladies	Yuri Fudoh (4)
Daio Seishi Elleair Ladies Open	Hiromi Kobayashi
Japan LPGA Tour Championship	Woo-Soon Ko (2)

AUSTRALIAN WOMEN'S TOUR

Educom ALPG Players' Championship	Paula Marti
Australasian Ladies Masters	Annika Sorenstam
AAMI Women's Australian Open	Karrie Webb

SOUTH AFRICAN WOMEN'S TOUR

Vodacom SA Ladies Players Championship	Mandy Adamson
Kyocera-Mita South African Women's Open	Mandy Adamson (2)
Telkom Ladies Classic	Riikka Hakkarainen
Nedbank Ladies South African Masters	Mandy Adamson (3)

Multiple Winners of 2002

PLAYER	WINS	PLAYER	WINS
Annika Sorenstam	13	Yasuharu Imano	2
Tiger Woods	7	Juli Inkster	2
Ernie Els	6	Shingo Katayama	2
Se Ri Pak	5	Jerry Kelly	2
Seiji Ebihara	4	Mi Hyun Kim	2
Yuri Fudoh	4	Woo-Soon Ko	2
Bob Gilder	4	Cliff Kresge	2
Hale Irwin	4	Ok-Hee Ku	2
Justin Rose	4	Kenichi Kuboya	2
Toru Taniguchi	4	Hank Kuehne	2
Mandy Adamson	3	Shigeki Maruyama	2
Jesus Amaya	3	Len Mattiace	2
Rich Beem	3	Rocco Mediate	2
Delroy Cambridge	3	Phil Mickelson	2
Kasumi Fujii	3	Colin Montgomerie	2
Sergio Garcia	3	Janice Moodie	2
Retief Goosen	3	Titch Moore	2
Padraig Harrington	3	Chihiro Nakajima	2
Lee James	3	Tsuneyuki Nakajima	2
Tom Kite	3	Arron Oberholser	2
Bruce Lietzke	3	Hennie Otto	2
Peter Lonard	3	Craig Parry	2
Patrick Moore	3	Terry Price	2
Dana Quigley	3	Iain Pyman	2
Nobuhito Sato	3	Jeff Quinney	2
Karrie Webb	3	Adam Scott	2
Isao Aoki	2	Vijay Singh	2
Matthew Blackey	2	David Smail	2
Angel Cabrera	2	Andre Stolz	2
Alex Cejka	2	Noboru Sugai	2
K.J. Choi	2	Mihoko Takahashi	2
Laura Diaz	2	Rachel Teske	2
Chris DiMarco	2	Doug Tewell	2
Denis Durnian	2	Roland Thatcher	2
Orie Fujino	2	Iben Tinning	2
Rafael Gomez	2	Dean Wilson	2
Jason Gore	2	Fuzzy Zoeller	2
Hur Suk-ho	2		

World Money List

This list of the 400 leading money winners in the world of professional golf in 2002 was compiled from the results of men's (excluding seniors) tournaments carried in the Appendixes of this edition. This list includes tournaments with a minimum of 36 holes and four contestants and does not include such competitions as skins games, pro-ams and shootouts.

In the 37 years during which World Money Lists have been compiled, the earnings of the player in the 200th position have risen from a total of $3,326 in 1966 to $448,752 in 2002. The top 200 players in 1966 earned a total of $4,680,287. In 2002, the comparable total was $251,869,685.

The world money list of the International Federation of PGA Tours was used for the official money list events of the U.S. PGA Tour, PGA European Tour, PGA Tour of Japan, Davidoff Asian PGA Tour, Southern Africa Tour and PGA Tour of Australasia. The conversion rates used for 2002 for other events and other tours were: Euro = US$0.95; British pound = US$1.52; Japanese yen = US$0.00804; South African rand = US$0.095; Australian dollar = US$0.54; Canadian dollar = US$0.65.

POS.	PLAYER, COUNTRY	TOTAL MONEY
1	Tiger Woods, USA	$8,292,188
2	Ernie Els, South Africa	6,260,746
3	Phil Mickelson, USA	4,706,971
4	Vijay Singh, Fiji	4,306,139
5	David Toms, USA	4,077,239
6	Padraig Harrington, Ireland	4,076,728
7	Retief Goosen, South Africa	3,850,363
8	Sergio Garcia, Spain	3,471,317
9	Rich Beem, USA	3,379,646
10	Chris DiMarco, USA	3,177,930
11	Jerry Kelly, USA	3,039,389
12	Justin Leonard, USA	3,009,453
13	Colin Montgomerie, Scotland	2,856,124
14	Charles Howell, USA	2,815,167
15	Jim Furyk, USA	2,765,750
16	Shigeki Maruyama, Japan	2,754,794
17	Fred Funk, USA	2,737,737
18	Davis Love, USA	2,581,160
19	Nick Price, Zimbabwe	2,562,363
20	Jeff Sluman, USA	2,472,080
21	K.J. Choi, Korea	2,441,174
22	Rocco Mediate, USA	2,333,176
23	Robert Allenby, Australia	2,328,992
24	Len Mattiace, USA	2,291,564
25	Michael Campbell, New Zealand	2,276,081
26	Jose Maria Olazabal, Spain	2,239,541
27	Bob Estes, USA	2,217,100
28	Scott McCarron, USA	2,072,964
29	Chris Riley, USA	2,032,979
30	Brad Faxon, USA	1,973,415
31	John Rollins, USA	1,956,565

POS.	PLAYER, COUNTRY	TOTAL MONEY
32	Loren Roberts, USA	1,932,547
33	Kenny Perry, USA	1,928,598
34	Steve Lowery, USA	1,915,553
35	Eduardo Romero, Argentina	1,891,502
36	Peter Lonard, Australia	1,888,147
37	Stuart Appleby, Australia	1,834,737
38	Craig Parry, Australia	1,808,188
39	John Cook, USA	1,745,095
40	Darren Clarke, N. Ireland	1,682,772
41	Scott Hoch, USA	1,677,673
42	Phil Tataurangi, New Zealand	1,664,295
43	Craig Perks, New Zealand	1,656,293
44	Bernhard Langer, Germany	1,598,697
45	Justin Rose, England	1,591,939
46	Kevin Sutherland, USA	1,575,029
47	Angel Cabrera, Argentina	1,573,329
48	Adam Scott, Australia	1,519,559
49	Jonathan Byrd, USA	1,462,713
50	Pat Perez, USA	1,451,726
51	Billy Andrade, USA	1,446,957
52	John Huston, USA	1,429,053
53	Matt Kuchar, USA	1,427,906
54	Chris Smith, USA	1,391,094
55	Dudley Hart, USA	1,379,830
56	Lee Janzen, USA	1,377,740
57	Mark Calcavecchia, USA	1,338,759
58	Toru Taniguchi, Japan	1,320,621
59	Thomas Bjorn, Denmark	1,319,243
60	Dan Forsman, USA	1,305,790
61	Stephen Ames, Trinidad & Tobago	1,295,787
62	Ian Leggatt, Canada	1,282,548
63	Steve Elkington, Australia	1,279,736
64	Paul Lawrie, Scotland	1,266,012
65	David Peoples, USA	1,243,774
66	Scott Verplank, USA	1,217,022
67	Bob Burns, USA	1,199,802
68	Steve Flesch, USA	1,196,491
69	Bob Tway, USA	1,160,399
70	Tom Lehman, USA	1,145,355
71	Toshi Izawa, Japan	1,113,596
72	Stewart Cink, USA	1,112,962
73	Trevor Immelman, South Africa	1,106,850
74	Matt Gogel, USA	1,103,626
75	Mark O'Meara, USA	1,100,132
76	Luke Donald, England	1,088,205
77	Jonathan Kaye, USA	1,082,803
78	Joel Edwards, USA	1,077,651
79	Stephen Leaney, Australia	1,071,202
80	Nobuhito Sato, Japan	1,057,824
81	Shingo Katayama, Japan	1,043,520
82	Tim Clark, South Africa	1,026,752
83	Niclas Fasth, Sweden	1,026,728
84	Rory Sabbatini, South Africa	1,023,499
85	Anders Hansen, Denmark	1,010,668

POS.	PLAYER, COUNTRY	TOTAL MONEY
86	Geoff Ogilvy, Australia	1,003,356
87	David Duval, USA	992,982
88	Jesper Parnevik, Sweden	986,680
89	Brandt Jobe, USA	972,479
90	Mike Weir, Canada	959,240
91	Soren Hansen, Denmark	958,003
92	J.L. Lewis, USA	957,182
93	Bradley Dredge, Wales	955,893
94	J.P. Hayes, USA	955,271
95	Tim Herron, USA	954,917
96	Ian Woosnam, Wales	954,859
97	Alex Cejka, Germany	946,296
98	Cameron Beckman, USA	927,161
99	Brian Gay, USA	926,735
100	Ben Crane, USA	926,576
101	Duffy Waldorf, USA	922,503
102	Paul Azinger, USA	919,926
103	Hidemichi Tanaka, Japan	919,764
104	Nick Faldo, England	911,469
105	Thomas Levet, France	891,068
106	Jeff Maggert, USA	888,979
107	Billy Mayfair, USA	864,745
108	Heath Slocum, USA	864,615
109	Glen Day, USA	859,930
110	Kirk Triplett, USA	848,773
111	Kaname Yokoo, Japan	844,780
112	Chad Campbell, USA	825,474
113	David Gossett, USA	823,717
114	Rodney Pampling, Australia	823,168
115	Ian Poulter, England	820,782
116	Briny Baird, USA	817,514
117	Jim Carter, USA	815,946
118	Neal Lancaster, USA	813,230
119	Robert Gamez, USA	807,892
120	Craig Stadler, USA	807,622
121	Gary Evans, England	804,274
122	Fredrik Jacobson, Sweden	797,434
123	Tim Petrovic, USA	797,206
124	Fred Couples, USA	792,703
125	Peter O'Malley, Australia	791,840
126	Mark Brooks, USA	791,671
127	Joey Sindelar, USA	790,750
128	Steve Stricker, USA	789,713
129	David Smail, New Zealand	789,407
130	Dean Wilson, USA	787,300
131	Esteban Toledo, Mexico	781,963
132	Gene Sauers, USA	767,072
133	Paul Casey, England	766,276
134	Tsuneyuki Nakajima, Japan	745,851
135	Frank Lickliter, USA	740,460
136	Harrison Frazar, USA	733,195
137	Jay Haas, USA	722,782
138	Ricardo Gonzalez, Argentina	716,225
139	Hiroyuki Fujita, Japan	702,029

POS.	PLAYER, COUNTRY	TOTAL MONEY
140	Barry Lane, England	689,500
141	Robert Karlsson, Sweden	685,116
142	John Daly, USA	683,685
143	Greg Chalmers, Australia	679,352
144	Kenichi Kuboya, Japan	679,276
145	Brendan Jones, Australia	676,734
146	Carlos Franco, Paraguay	668,946
147	Carl Pettersson, Sweden	668,279
148	John Bickerton, England	667,974
149	Notah Begay, USA	661,526
150	Skip Kendall, USA	653,594
151	Tom Pernice, Jr., USA	645,110
152	Shaun Micheel, USA	641,450
153	Spike McRoy, USA	630,269
154	Greg Norman, Australia	628,420
155	Yasuhara Imano, Japan	620,719
156	Tom Byrum, USA	620,280
157	Olin Browne, USA	619,978
158	Andrew Magee, USA	616,785
159	Scott Laycock, Australia	608,275
160	John Senden, Australia	603,963
161	Paul McGinley, Ireland	587,842
162	Brent Geiberger, USA	582,592
163	Per-Ulrik Johansson, Sweden	576,438
164	Peter Jacobsen, USA	575,873
165	David Berganio, Jr., USA	573,151
166	J.J. Henry, USA	569,875
167	Carl Paulson, USA	568,924
168	Paul Stankowski, USA	565,294
169	Glen Hnatiuk, Canada	558,940
170	Jarrod Moseley, Australia	554,927
171	Masashi Ozaki, Japan	548,785
172	S.K. Ho, Korea	541,796
173	Pat Bates, USA	537,284
174	Maarten Lafeber, Netherlands	530,134
175	Craig Barlow, USA	528,569
176	Nick Dougherty, England	527,048
177	Pierre Fulke, Sweden	526,197
178	Jean Francois Remesy, France	516,574
179	Lee Westwood, England	515,467
180	Jay Williamson, USA	515,445
181	Steve Allan, Australia	511,800
182	David Frost, South Africa	511,145
183	Greg Owen, England	507,849
184	Alastair Forsyth, Scotland	500,469
185	Steen Tinning, Denmark	499,424
186	Phillip Price, Wales	495,906
187	Jay Don Blake, USA	495,066
188	Miguel Angel Jimenez, Spain	494,680
189	Dean Pappas, South Africa	494,404
190	Kent Jones, USA	489,879
191	Brian Davis, England	473,597
192	Carlos Rodiles, Spain	468,652
193	Richard Green, Australia	465,657

POS.	PLAYER, COUNTRY	TOTAL MONEY
194	Mike Sposa, USA	463,418
195	Zhang Lian-wei, China	461,041
196	Brett Quigley, USA	458,172
197	Kenneth Staton, USA	453,816
198	Katsunori Kuwabara, Japan	453,471
199	Bob May, USA	452,778
200	Paul Gow, Australia	448,752
201	Graeme McDowell, N. Ireland	448,500
202	Frank Nobilo, New Zealand	447,324
203	Malcolm Mackenzie, England	444,931
204	Garrett Willis, USA	444,483
205	Tomohiro Kondou, Japan	443,272
206	Jyoti Randhawa, India	435,633
207	Andrew Coltart, Scotland	435,271
208	Kim Jong-duck, Korea	427,971
209	Aaron Baddeley, Australia	427,828
210	Joe Durant, USA	427,217
211	David Gilford, England	425,836
212	Bryce Molder, USA	420,092
213	Steve Webster, England	417,429
214	Paul Goydos, USA	411,035
215	Hirofumi Miyase, Japan	409,520
216	Naomichi Ozaki, Japan	408,540
217	Peter Fowler, Australia	407,800
218	Sandy Lyle, England	407,307
219	Mathew Goggin, Australia	405,855
220	Emanuele Canonica, Italy	403,745
221	Jamie Spence, England	399,599
222	Patrick Moore, USA	399,104
223	Tobias Dier, Germany	398,572
224	Joakim Haeggman, Sweden	395,214
225	Robert Damron, USA	391,867
226	John Riegger, USA	390,675
227	Sam Torrance, Scotland	386,382
228	Mike Heinen, USA	384,894
229	Raphael Jacquelin, France	382,078
230	Christian Pena, USA	382,007
231	Santiago Luna, Spain	381,277
232	Tommy Armour, USA	379,191
233	Ignacio Garrido, Spain	377,539
234	Brian Henninger, USA	372,914
235	Brandel Chamblee, USA	372,263
236	Nick O'Hern, Australia	370,322
237	Rolf Muntz, Netherlands	367,771
238	Thongchai Jaidee, Thailand	366,420
239	Brad Elder, USA	362,892
240	Corey Pavin, USA	362,012
241	Tom Scherrer, USA	356,657
242	Richard S. Johnson, Sweden	355,986
243	Simon Dyson, England	355,917
244	Toru Suzuki, Japan	350,822
245	Cliff Kresge, USA	346,635
246	Dennis Paulson, USA	344,121
247	Charlie Wi, Korea	340,191

POS.	PLAYER, COUNTRY	TOTAL MONEY
248	Soren Kjeldsen, Denmark	339,019
249	Tetsuji Hiratsuka, Japan	335,563
250	Grant Waite, New Zealand	332,947
251	Katsumasa Miyamoto, Japan	331,799
252	Mathias Gronberg, Sweden	330,713
253	Roger Chapman, England	325,177
254	Tripp Isenhour, USA	323,740
255	Hal Sutton, USA	320,002
256	Arron Oberholser, USA	319,883
257	Jose Coceres, Argentina	316,360
258	Andrew Oldcorn, Scotland	315,367
259	Bart Bryant, USA	313,570
260	Richard Bland, England	310,000
261	Woody Austin, USA	307,348
262	Kiyoshi Miyazato, Japan	306,606
263	Steve Alker, New Zealand	305,413
264	Jeff Gove, USA	303,852
265	Kiyoshi Murota, Japan	301,306
266	Todd Fischer, USA	297,343
267	Henrik Nystrom, Sweden	296,874
268	Darren Fichardt, South Africa	296,310
269	Gavin Coles, Australia	291,951
270	Henrik Bjornstadt, Norway	290,535
271	Raymond Russell, Scotland	290,191
272	Warren Bennett, England	288,965
273	David Howell, England	285,947
274	David Lynn, England	282,195
275	Brian Bateman, USA	281,421
276	Jeff Brehaut, USA	280,335
277	Anthony Wall, England	272,542
278	Jerry Smith, USA	269,953
279	Zaw Moe, Myanmar	269,579
280	Matt Peterson, USA	266,543
281	Prayad Marksaeng, Thailand	265,149
282	Ian Garbutt, England	265,051
283	Donnie Hammond, USA	263,366
284	Doug Barron, USA	262,543
285	Jonathan Lomas, England	254,094
286	Taichi Teshima, Japan	252,080
287	Tommy Tolles, USA	250,506
288	David Morland, Canada	247,563
289	Arjun Atwal, India	244,626
290	Patrik Sjoland, Sweden	244,288
291	Mark Pilkington, Wales	242,604
292	Nobumitsu Yuhara, Japan	242,280
293	Jason Gore, USA	241,940
294	Shinichi Yokota, Japan	240,545
295	Lin Keng-chi, Taiwan	240,431
296	Michael Clark, USA	239,422
297	Franklin Langham, USA	238,461
298	Robin Freeman, USA	232,386
299	Tatao Ozaki, Japan	232,093
300	Todd Barranger, USA	231,166
301	Steve Pate, USA	230,808

POS.	PLAYER, COUNTRY	TOTAL MONEY
302	Daisuke Maruyama, Japan	229,460
303	Marco Dawson, Germany	227,590
304	Edward Fryatt, England	225,823
305	Roger Wessels, South Africa	224,901
306	Darron Stiles, USA	222,845
307	Greg Kraft, USA	222,614
308	Shigemasa Higaki, Japan	220,847
309	David Carter, England	220,785
310	Hajime Meshiai, Japan	219,101
311	Tsukasa Watanabe, Japan	218,040
312	Mark Roe, England	217,606
313	Miles Tunnicliff, England	217,413
314	Mamoru Osanai, Japan	216,901
315	Mark McNulty, Zimbabwe	215,505
316	Jamie Donaldson, Wales	214,117
317	Jean-Francois Lucquin, France	212,062
318	Marc Farry, France	207,859
319	Hideki Kase, Japan	207,843
320	Sven Struver, Germany	207,217
321	Jason Buha, USA	204,938
322	Kelly Gibson, USA	204,184
323	Koki Idoki, Japan	203,590
324	Brett Wetterich, USA	203,034
325	Greg Turner, New Zealand	201,371
326	Patrick Sheehan, USA	201,231
327	Gary Orr, Scotland	201,183
328	Rick Gibson, Canada	199,916
329	Mikael Lundberg, Sweden	199,063
330	Kazuhiko Hosokawa, Japan	197,794
331	David Park, Wales	197,672
332	Martin Maritz, South Africa	197,661
333	James Kingston, South Africa	197,437
334	Jarmo Sandelin, Sweden	195,985
335	Jim Gallagher, Jr., USA	195,633
336	Mikko Ilonen, Finland	194,464
337	Stephen Gallacher, Scotland	191,680
338	Hsieh Chin-sheng, Taiwan	191,077
339	Todd Hamilton, USA	190,719
340	Jason Caron, USA	190,683
341	Stephen Gangluff, USA	190,184
342	Marten Olander, Sweden	189,007
343	Jay Delsing, USA	187,583
344	Tag Ridings, USA	187,494
345	John Morse, USA	186,881
346	Nozomi Kawahara, Japan	185,420
347	Kenneth Ferrie, England	184,771
348	Brian Watts, USA	181,957
349	Ted Purdy, USA	181,224
350	Lee Porter, USA	179,396
351	Dinesh Chand, Fiji	178,899
352	Charles Warren, USA	177,294
353	Diego Borrego, Spain	176,265
354	Russ Cochran, USA	176,111
355	Kevin Na, Korea	175,288

POS.	PLAYER, COUNTRY	TOTAL MONEY
356	Fredrik Andersson, Sweden	174,946
357	Anthony Painter, Australia	174,864
358	Stephen Dodd, Wales	173,482
359	Thammanoon Sriroj, Thailand	171,121
360	Paul Eales, England	170,982
361	Scott Dunlap, USA	169,640
362	Steve Jones, USA	169,315
363	Michael Long, New Zealand	169,048
364	David Drysdale, Scotland	168,511
365	Gordon Brand, Jr., Scotland	168,487
366	Jeev Milkha Singh, India	167,383
367	Peter Baker, England	166,644
368	Omar Uresti, USA	166,620
369	Curtis Strange, USA	166,207
370	Miguel Angel Martin, Spain	165,741
371	Gregory Meyer, USA	165,344
372	Eric Meeks, USA	165,027
373	Gary Emerson, England	164,921
374	Mark Foster, England	164,661
375	Stuart Little, England	164,417
376	Takenori Hiraishi, Japan	164,023
377	Jean Hugo, South Africa	161,605
378	Klas Eriksson, Sweden	161,114
379	Brent Schwarzrock, USA	160,673
380	Keiichiro Fukabori, Japan	159,681
381	Paul Claxton, USA	158,946
382	Katsuyoshi Tomori, Japan	158,644
383	Simon Yates, Scotland	158,173
384	Hidemasa Hoshino, Japan	157,101
385	Matthew Cort, England	156,905
386	Scott Gardiner, New Zealand	156,097
387	Christopher Hanell, Sweden	155,108
388	Jorge Berendt, Argentina	155,006
389	Markus Brier, Austria	154,977
390	Jess Daley, USA	154,675
391	Andrew McLardy, South Africa	153,403
392	Brett Rumford, Australia	152,731
393	Dicky Pride, USA	151,906
394	Marcel Siem, Germany	151,693
395	Jason Hill, USA	150,860
396	Andrew Pitts, USA	150,345
397	Hank Kuehne, USA	149,713
398	Adam Mednick, Sweden	148,464
399	Jun Kikuchi, Japan	147,834
400	Des Smyth, Ireland	147,729

World Money List Leaders

YEAR	PLAYER, COUNTRY	TOTAL MONEY
1966	Jack Nicklaus, USA	$168,088
1967	Jack Nicklaus, USA	276,166
1968	Billy Casper, USA	222,436
1969	Frank Beard, USA	186,993
1970	Jack Nicklaus, USA	222,583
1971	Jack Nicklaus, USA	285,897
1972	Jack Nicklaus, USA	341,792
1973	Tom Weiskopf, USA	349,645
1974	Johnny Miller, USA	400,255
1975	Jack Nicklaus, USA	332,610
1976	Jack Nicklaus, USA	316,086
1977	Tom Watson, USA	358,034
1978	Tom Watson, USA	384,388
1979	Tom Watson, USA	506,912
1980	Tom Watson, USA	651,921
1981	Johnny Miller, USA	704,204
1982	Raymond Floyd, USA	738,699
1983	Seve Ballesteros, Spain	686,088
1984	Seve Ballesteros, Spain	688,047
1985	Bernhard Langer, Germany	860,262
1986	Greg Norman, Australia	1,146,584
1987	Ian Woosnam, Wales	1,793,268
1988	Seve Ballesteros, Spain	1,261,275
1989	David Frost, South Africa	1,650,230
1990	Jose Maria Olazabal, Spain	1,633,640
1991	Bernhard Langer, Germany	2,186,700
1992	Nick Faldo, England	2,748,248
1993	Nick Faldo, England	2,825,280
1994	Ernie Els, South Africa	2,862,854
1995	Corey Pavin, USA	2,746,340
1996	Colin Montgomerie, Scotland	3,071,442
1997	Colin Montgomerie, Scotland	3,366,900
1998	Tiger Woods, USA	2,927,946
1999	Tiger Woods, USA	7,681,625
2000	Tiger Woods, USA	11,034,530
2001	Tiger Woods, USA	7,771,562
2002	Tiger Woods, USA	8,292,188

Career World Money List

Here is a list of the 50 leading money winners for their careers through the 2002 season. It includes players active on both the regular and senior tours of the world. The World Money List from this and the 36 previous editions of the annual and a table prepared for a companion book, *The Wonderful World of Professional Golf* (Atheneum, 1973) form the basis for this compilation. Additional figures were taken from official records of major golf associations, although shortcomings in records-keeping outside the United States in the 1950s and 1960s and a few exclusions from U.S. records during those years prevent these figures from being completely accurate, although the careers of virtually all of these top 50 players began after that time. Conversion of foreign currency figures to U.S. dollars is based on average values during the particular years involved.

POS.	PLAYER, COUNTRY	TOTAL MONEY
1	Tiger Woods, USA	$40,982,742
2	Ernie Els, South Africa	32,850,041
3	Davis Love, USA	26,793,298
4	Hale Irwin, USA	26,578,229
5	Vijay Singh, Fiji	26,416,402
6	Colin Montgomerie, Scotland	26,414,538
7	Nick Price, Zimbabwe	26,174,502
8	Phil Mickelson, USA	24,380,888
9	Bernhard Langer, Germany	23,865,706
10	Greg Norman, Australia	23,565,730
11	Fred Couples, USA	21,835,406
12	Masashi Ozaki, Japan	21,097,777
13	Scott Hoch, USA	20,350,856
14	David Duval, USA	19,538,807
15	Mark Calcavecchia, USA	18,815,576
16	Nick Faldo, England	18,789,872
17	Tom Kite, USA	18,690,009
18	Raymond Floyd, USA	18,580,135
19	Tom Lehman, USA	18,247,364
20	Gil Morgan, USA	17,989,384
21	Mark O'Meara, USA	17,706,250
22	Jose Maria Olazabal, Spain	17,384,522
23	Ian Woosnam, Wales	16,857,664
24	Lee Trevino, USA	16,810,586
25	Tom Watson, USA	16,593,414
26	Isao Aoki, Japan	16,463,588
27	Jim Furyk, USA	15,739,528
28	Larry Nelson, USA	15,565,002
29	David Frost, South Africa	15,526,396
30	Justin Leonard, USA	15,272,288
31	Hal Sutton, USA	14,959,499
32	Jeff Sluman, USA	14,834,654
33	Jim Colbert, USA	14,718,163
34	Paul Azinger, USA	14,643,670
35	Payne Stewart, USA	14,617,674
36	David Toms, USA	14,461,430
37	Brad Faxon, USA	14,394,458

POS.	PLAYER, COUNTRY	TOTAL MONEY
38	Naomichi Ozaki, Japan	13,614,048
39	Darren Clarke, N. Ireland	13,568,046
40	John Cook, USA	13,416,582
41	Sergio Garcia, Spain	13,413,992
42	Corey Pavin, USA	13,411,747
43	Steve Elkington, Australia	13,409,275
44	Jesper Parnevik, Sweden	13,060,666
45	Lee Westwood, England	13,054,768
46	Dave Stockton, USA	12,913,611
47	Bob Charles, New Zealand	12,759,105
48	Loren Roberts, USA	12,684,426
49	Graham Marsh, Australia	12,636,822
50	Retief Goosen, South Africa	12,548,085

These 50 players have won $908,997,221 in their careers.

Senior World Money List

This list includes official earnings from the world money list of the International Federation of PGA Tours, U.S. Senior PGA Tour, European Seniors Tour and Japan Senior Tour, along with other winnings in established unofficial events when reliable figures could be obtained.

POS.	PLAYER, COUNTRY	TOTAL MONEY
1	Hale Irwin, USA	$3,332,304
2	Bob Gilder, USA	2,696,137
3	Bruce Fleisher, USA	1,929,134
4	Doug Tewell, USA	1,924,068
5	Tom Watson, USA	1,917,593
6	Tom Kite, USA	1,914,905
7	Dana Quigley, USA	1,723,722
8	Jim Thorpe, USA	1,625,778
9	Bruce Lietzke, USA	1,557,676
10	Bobby Wadkins, USA	1,451,336
11	Allen Doyle, USA	1,434,171
12	Morris Hatalsky, USA	1,391,044
13	Gil Morgan, USA	1,380,901
14	Hubert Green, USA	1,315,725
15	Don Pooley, USA	1,305,456
16	Tom Jenkins, USA	1,294,872
17	John Jacobs, USA	1,290,157
18	Stewart Ginn, Australia	1,284,555
19	Fuzzy Zoeller, USA	1,274,031
20	Larry Nelson, USA	1,258,224
21	Dave Stockton, USA	950,735
22	Mike McCullough, USA	933,760
23	Ed Dougherty, USA	908,960

POS.	PLAYER, COUNTRY	TOTAL MONEY
24	Sammy Rachels, USA	879,537
25	Isao Aoki, Japan	877,156
26	Jay Sigel, USA	872,346
27	John Bland, South Africa	852,361
28	Walter Hall, USA	800,792
29	Gary McCord, USA	779,960
30	Rodger Davis, Australia	773,895
31	Tom Purtzer, USA	772,756
32	Wayne Levi, USA	763,447
33	Jim Dent, USA	674,511
34	Dave Eichelberger, USA	672,607
35	Jose Maria Canizares, Spain	647,620
36	Mike Hill, USA	641,326
37	J.C. Snead, USA	633,955
38	Vicente Fernandez, Argentina	625,566
39	George Archer, USA	618,692
40	Tom Wargo, USA	566,940
41	John Mahaffey, USA	555,416
42	Walter Morgan, USA	546,679
43	Bruce Summerhays, USA	539,460
44	Seiji Ebihara, Japan	538,262
45	Jim Colbert, USA	529,252
46	Dale Douglass, USA	528,712
47	Gibby Gilbert, USA	449,566
48	Jim Ahern, USA	448,417
49	James Mason, USA	443,996
50	Dick Mast, USA	440,601
51	Bob Charles, New Zealand	438,596
52	Lee Trevino, USA	437,138
53	Raymond Floyd, USA	420,218
54	Jim Albus, USA	409,161
55	Mike Smith, USA	404,445
56	Hugh Baiocchi, South Africa	395,242
57	Graham Marsh, Australia	393,725
58	John Schroeder, USA	389,320
59	Andy North, USA	381,434
60	Terry Dill, USA	365,110
61	Denis Durnian, England	355,162
62	Larry Ziegler, USA	350,248
63	Ted Goin, USA	349,780
64	Gary Player, South Africa	349,724
65	Jay Overton, USA	345,903
66	Lanny Wadkins, USA	338,824
67	Fred Gibson, USA	331,718
68	Charles Coody, USA	328,454
69	Leonard Thompson, USA	328,373
70	Rocky Thompson, USA	325,869
71	Butch Sheehan, USA	321,682
72	Bob Eastwood, USA	302,629
73	Jack Spradlin, USA	297,627
74	Steven Veriato, USA	291,700
75	Jim Holtgrieve, USA	291,629
76	Jerry McGee, USA	255,603
77	R.W. Eaks, USA	245,705

POS.	PLAYER, COUNTRY	TOTAL MONEY
78	Terry Mauney, USA	243,107
79	Danny Edwards, USA	241,742
80	Christy O'Connor, Jr., Ireland	236,235
81	Dan O'Neill, USA	216,311
82	Ben Crenshaw, USA	213,428
83	Howard Twitty, USA	206,890
84	Katsunari Takahashi, Japan	205,226
85	David Graham, Australia	203,240
86	Mark McCumber, USA	200,561
87	Arnold Palmer, USA	191,096
88	Joe Inman, USA	183,700
89	Delroy Cambridge, Jamaica	178,960
90	Mark Pfeil, USA	174,090
91	Dave Barr, Canada	164,884
92	Noboru Sugai, Japan	161,034
93	Roy Vucinich, USA	160,175
94	David Eger, USA	154,510
95	John Morgan, England	153,691
96	Steve Stull, USA	149,377
97	Chi Chi Rodriguez, Puerto Rico	142,135
98	Bobby Walzel, USA	141,329
99	Doug Johnson, USA	139,788
100	Eamonn Darcy, Ireland	125,466

Women's World Money List

This list includes official earnings on the U.S. LPGA Tour, Evian Ladies European Tour and Japan LPGA Tour, along with other winnings in established unofficial events when reliable figures could be obtained.

POS.	PLAYER, COUNTRY	TOTAL MONEY
1	Annika Sorenstam, Sweden	$2,997,812
2	Se Ri Pak, Korea	1,722,281
3	Juli Inkster, USA	1,204,349
4	Karrie Webb, Australia	1,119,080
5	Mi Hyun Kim, Korea	1,049,993
6	Grace Park, Korea	881,943
7	Laura Diaz, USA	873,790
8	Rachel Teske, Australia	793,212
9	Carin Koch, Sweden	793,197
10	Lorie Kane, Canada	785,520
11	Yuri Fudoh, Japan	769,355
12	Rosie Jones, USA	722,412
13	Cristie Kerr, USA	685,393
14	Michele Redman, USA	666,849
15	Kasumi Fujii, Japan	664,483
16	Hee-Won Han, Korea	612,747
17	Woo-Soon Ko, Korea	587,585

POS.	PLAYER, COUNTRY	TOTAL MONEY
18	Catriona Matthew, Scotland	567,394
19	Kelly Robbins, USA	547,372
20	Toshimi Kimura, Japan	533,501
21	Mhairi McKay, Scotland	533,209
22	Janice Moodie, Scotland	524,238
23	Beth Bauer, USA	500,909
24	Laura Davies, England	494,456
25	Maria Hjorth, Sweden	494,444
26	Beth Daniel, USA	480,618
27	Meg Mallon, USA	463,731
28	Gloria Park, Korea	460,630
29	Akiko Fukushima, Japan	427,541
30	Orie Fujino, Japan	417,094
31	Mikino Kubo, Japan	410,700
32	Michelle Ellis, Australia	407,960
33	Kelli Kuehne, USA	405,799
34	Danielle Ammaccapane, USA	396,280
35	Ok-Hee Ku, Korea	387,793
36	Shani Waugh, Australia	381,632
37	Midori Yoneyama, Japan	373,329
38	Patricia Meunier-Lebouc, France	354,175
39	Mihoko Takahashi, Japan	350,621
40	Yu-Chen Huang, Taiwan	343,398
41	Jenny Rosales, Philippines	342,887
42	Kaori Higo, Japan	339,774
43	Liselotte Neumann, Sweden	312,417
44	Dorothy Delasin, USA	309,885
45	Heather Bowie, USA	289,995
46	Vicki Goetze-Ackerman, USA	278,166
47	Jeong Jang, Korea	276,820
48	Emilee Klein, USA	274,236
49	Sophie Gustafson, Sweden	267,004
50	Ikuyo Shiotani, Japan	261,742
51	Candie Kung, Taiwan	261,044
52	Natalie Gulbis, USA	259,310
53	Kate Golden, USA	259,143
54	Wendy Doolan, Australia	258,713
55	Yun-Jye Wei, Taiwan	254,578
56	Kyoko Ono, Japan	254,117
57	Hiromi Kobayashi, Japan	252,429
58	Leta Lindley, USA	252,051
59	Chihiro Nakajima, Japan	246,465
60	Pat Hurst, USA	237,682
61	Helen Alfredsson, Sweden	236,346
62	Hsiu-Feng Tseng, Taiwan	235,632
63	Donna Andrews, USA	229,825
64	Ji-Hee Lee, Korea	226,336
65	Takayo Bandoh, Japan	226,182
66	Chieko Amanuma, Japan	224,143
67	Angela Stanford, USA	221,857
68	Paula Marti, Spain	219,781
69	Joanne Morley, England	215,861
70	Kris Tschetter, USA	215,235
71	Karen Stupples, England	214,760

POS.	PLAYER, COUNTRY	TOTAL MONEY
72	Jill McGill, USA	204,941
73	Silvia Cavalleri, Italy	191,557
74	Charlotta Sorenstam, Sweden	189,687
75	Jackie Gallagher-Smith, USA	187,180
76	Wendy Ward, USA	186,592
77	Mayumi Hirase, Japan	182,921
78	Betsy King, USA	169,808
79	Michiko Hattori, Japan	168,112
80	Kim Saiki, USA	167,016
81	Yu Ping Lin, Taiwan	166,259
82	Mikiyo Nishizuka, Japan	160,499
83	Hiroko Yamaguchi, Japan	158,290
84	Kozue Azuma, Japan	158,124
85	Kaori Harada, Japan	157,777
86	Junko Omote, Japan	156,672
87	Brandie Burton, USA	152,704
88	Shiko Ohyama, Japan	149,752
89	Shin Sora, Korea	147,499
90	Kayo Yamada, Japan	146,508
91	Barb Mucha, USA	146,283
92	Yuka Shioto, Japan	146,032
93	Becky Morgan, Wales	144,967
94	Dawn Coe-Jones, Canada	142,921
95	Michie Ohba, Japan	142,380
96	Joanne Mills, Australia	142,313
97	Mayumi Inoue, Japan	139,261
98	Karine Icher, France	136,266
99	Young-Me Lee, Korea	133,687
100	Moira Dunn, USA	133,652
101	Fuki Kido, Japan	132,534
102	Tracy Hanson, USA	132,478
103	Sherri Steinhauer, USA	131,373
104	Marnie McGuire, New Zealand	131,041
105	Johanna Head, England	130,249
106	Asa Gottmo, Sweden	129,394
107	Masayo Fujisawa, Japan	128,103
108	Amy Fruhwirth, USA	126,161
109	Nancy Scranton, USA	125,863
110	Natsuko Noro, Japan	123,096
111	Rena Yamazaki, Japan	122,630
112	Chieko Nishida, Japan	122,484
113	Catrin Nilsmark, Sweden	121,924
114	Suzanne Strudwick, England	121,811
115	Tammie Green, USA	121,413
116	Stephanie Keever, USA	121,015
117	Iben Tinning, Denmark	120,211
118	Tina Barrett, USA	119,059
119	Masaki Maeda, Japan	117,967
120	Rie Murota, Japan	117,422
121	Hsiao-Chuan Lu, Taiwan	117,058
122	Kristal Parker-Manzo, USA	116,953
123	Aki Takamura, Japan	116,693
124	Ai-Yu Tu, Taiwan	116,041
125	Becky Iverson, USA	114,738

American Tours

Mercedes Championships

Plantation Course, Kapalua, Maui, Hawaii
Par 36-37–73; 7,263 yards

January 3-6
purse, $4,000,000

		SCORES			TOTAL	MONEY
Sergio Garcia	73	69	68	64	274	$720,000
David Toms	69	66	72	67	274	432,000
(Garcia defeated Toms on first playoff hole.)						
Kenny Perry	68	67	71	69	275	275,000
Jim Furyk	67	72	73	65	277	196,000
Mark Calcavecchia	72	66	71	69	278	150,000
Chris DiMarco	67	72	68	71	278	150,000
Scott McCarron	71	72	69	66	278	150,000
Scott Verplank	67	69	70	73	279	130,000
Brad Faxon	71	71	69	69	280	120,000
Bob Estes	70	70	71	70	281	105,000
Tiger Woods	68	74	74	65	281	105,000
David Duval	67	71	72	72	282	92,000
Joel Edwards	69	71	71	72	283	88,000
Retief Goosen	69	71	77	67	284	83,500
Mike Weir	63	74	74	73	284	83,500
Davis Love	69	72	78	68	287	77,500
Tom Pernice, Jr.	70	70	75	72	287	77,500
Cameron Beckman	67	73	75	73	288	73,000
Justin Leonard	70	72	75	71	288	73,000
Joe Durant	73	73	74	69	289	69,000
Frank Lickliter	66	74	77	72	289	69,000
Robert Allenby	74	72	71	73	290	64,000
Scott Hoch	72	75	73	70	290	64,000
Shigeki Maruyama	72	75	72	71	290	64,000
Steve Stricker	71	70	79	71	291	60,000
Jesper Parnevik	74	75	72	71	292	57,000
Hal Sutton	75	73	76	68	292	57,000
John Cook	72	69	78	74	293	55,000
David Gossett	74	78	72	72	296	54,000
Robert Damron	69	73	85	71	298	52,500
Jeff Sluman	74	76	78	70	298	52,500
Garrett Willis	77	80	74	73	304	51,000

Sony Open in Hawaii

Waialae Country Club, Honolulu, Hawaii
Par 35-35–70; 7,060 yards

January 10-13
purse, $4,000,000

		SCORES			TOTAL	MONEY
Jerry Kelly	66	65	65	70	266	$720,000
John Cook	66	62	70	69	267	432,000
Jay Don Blake	69	67	68	65	269	272,000
Matt Kuchar	68	69	66	67	270	165,333.34
Charles Howell	72	62	66	70	270	165,333.33
David Toms	68	67	63	72	270	165,333.33

	SCORES				TOTAL	MONEY
Tommy Armour	68	70	68	65	271	112,333.34
David Peoples	72	68	66	65	271	112,333.34
Stephen Ames	67	67	66	71	271	112,333.33
K.J. Choi	68	65	69	69	271	112,333.33
Joel Edwards	70	66	68	67	271	112,333.33
Jim Furyk	69	66	64	72	271	112,333.33
Luke Donald	69	67	66	70	272	75,000
Brad Elder	68	64	70	70	272	75,000
Fred Funk	68	65	69	70	272	75,000
Chris Riley	65	67	68	72	272	75,000
Pat Perez	68	67	70	68	273	54,133.34
Hidemichi Tanaka	70	69	69	65	273	54,133.34
Bob Burns	69	69	67	68	273	54,133.33
Brad Faxon	68	67	67	71	273	54,133.33
Scott Hoch	68	66	69	70	273	54,133.33
Jeff Sluman	69	66	67	71	273	54,133.33
Jonathan Byrd	67	68	72	67	274	33,714.29
Hiroyuki Fujita	70	70	67	67	274	33,714.29
Kenny Perry	65	70	69	70	274	33,714.29
Dean Wilson	74	66	67	67	274	33,714.29
Robert Allenby	69	66	67	72	274	33,714.28
Brian Gay	68	69	67	70	274	33,714.28
Frank Lickliter	68	68	67	71	274	33,714.28
Michael Allen	70	65	72	68	275	23,250
Briny Baird	72	66	67	70	275	23,250
John Huston	68	66	70	71	275	23,250
Greg Kraft	70	67	68	70	275	23,250
Andrew Magee	68	72	68	67	275	23,250
Corey Pavin	69	66	71	69	275	23,250
Mike Sposa	71	67	65	72	275	23,250
Esteban Toledo	68	72	64	71	275	23,250
Jay Haas	68	68	73	67	276	18,400
Tom Lehman	70	66	70	70	276	18,400
Cameron Beckman	67	67	72	71	277	16,000
Steve Elkington	69	69	70	69	277	16,000
Sergio Garcia	71	66	69	71	277	16,000
Bob May	70	70	69	68	277	16,000
Scott Dunlap	71	66	69	72	278	11,560
Bob Heintz	70	67	71	70	278	11,560
Tim Herron	71	68	64	75	278	11,560
Ian Leggatt	71	67	71	69	278	11,560
Peter Lonard	70	68	69	71	278	11,560
Len Mattiace	68	67	72	71	278	11,560
Loren Roberts	71	68	68	71	278	11,560
Chris Smith	69	67	71	71	278	11,560
Chad Campbell	71	65	75	68	279	9,520
Lee Porter	71	66	72	70	279	9,520
Stuart Appleby	70	69	68	73	280	9,080
Rich Beem	68	69	69	74	280	9,080
Joe Durant	68	69	71	72	280	9,080
Brent Geiberger	70	70	70	70	280	9,080
Jesper Parnevik	66	71	72	71	280	9,080
John Riegger	70	70	69	71	280	9,080
Jim Carter	69	69	70	73	281	8,520
Jess Daley	72	68	70	71	281	8,520
David Gossett	69	68	75	69	281	8,520
David Ishii	70	70	72	69	281	8,520
Gary Nicklaus	69	70	73	69	281	8,520
John Rollins	69	70	70	72	281	8,520
Phil Tataurangi	67	72	71	71	281	8,520

	SCORES				TOTAL	MONEY
Richard Zokol	71	67	73	70	281	8,520
Fred Couples	70	70	69	73	282	8,120
David Sutherland	70	68	75	69	282	8,120
Dudley Hart	72	68	74	69	283	7,920
Shigeki Maruyama	70	66	74	73	283	7,920
Brent Schwarzrock	72	68	71	72	283	7,920
Tom Scherrer	70	69	77	68	284	7,760

Bob Hope Chrysler Classic

PGA West, Palmer Course: Par 36-36–72; 6,950 yards
Bermuda Dunes CC: Par 36-36–72; 6,927 yards
Tamarisk CC: Par 36-36–72; 6,881 yards
Indian Wells CC: Par 36-36–72; 6,478 yards
La Quinta, California

January 16-20
purse, $4,000,000

	SCORES					TOTAL	MONEY
Phil Mickelson	64	67	70	65	64	330	$720,000
David Berganio, Jr.	69	66	65	64	66	330	432,000
(Mickelson defeated Berganio on first playoff hole.)							
Briny Baird	67	67	68	66	64	332	232,000
Cameron Beckman	67	67	64	65	69	332	232,000
Jerry Kelly	64	69	65	68	67	333	160,000
Chris DiMarco	67	69	64	67	67	334	116,857.15
Charles Howell	65	67	71	66	65	334	116,857.15
Brandel Chamblee	63	67	68	66	70	334	116,857.14
Justin Leonard	70	66	64	67	67	334	116,857.14
Deane Pappas	66	68	63	67	70	334	116,857.14
Kenny Perry	69	64	68	62	71	334	116,857.14
Kirk Triplett	64	69	64	67	70	334	116,857.14
Scott McCarron	68	65	68	67	67	335	77,333.34
Ian Leggatt	69	69	65	64	68	335	77,333.33
John Senden	64	65	69	67	70	335	77,333.33
Chad Campbell	66	70	68	67	65	336	60,000
Jay Haas	63	68	68	63	74	336	60,000
J.P. Hayes	65	68	69	68	66	336	60,000
J.L. Lewis	68	68	68	67	65	336	60,000
Bob May	69	68	67	66	66	336	60,000
Fred Couples	69	66	70	67	65	337	40,000
John Huston	65	72	68	66	66	337	40,000
Rodney Pampling	66	72	67	66	66	337	40,000
Steve Pate	70	68	65	67	67	337	40,000
Loren Roberts	70	67	64	66	70	337	40,000
Craig Stadler	70	66	64	67	70	337	40,000
Fred Funk	70	63	70	67	68	338	29,000
Per-Ulrik Johansson	68	69	65	68	68	338	29,000
Rocco Mediate	66	70	70	64	68	338	29,000
Jeff Sluman	67	68	67	67	69	338	29,000
John Daly	69	67	65	72	66	339	21,733.34
David Gossett	70	70	68	64	67	339	21,733.34
David Peoples	70	68	66	68	67	339	21,733.34
Glen Hnatiuk	64	72	67	71	65	339	21,733.33
Geoff Ogilvy	74	69	64	66	66	339	21,733.33
Phillip Price	65	69	68	66	71	339	21,733.33
Heath Slocum	64	68	70	71	66	339	21,733.33
David Toms	72	68	66	67	66	339	21,733.33
Duffy Waldorf	66	67	64	68	74	339	21,733.33

	SCORES					TOTAL	MONEY
Stephen Ames	67	71	65	68	69	340	16,800
Brad Elder	66	68	71	70	65	340	16,800
Bob Burns	70	67	68	69	67	341	13,600
Ben Crane	69	69	70	66	67	341	13,600
Greg Kraft	67	65	69	71	69	341	13,600
Joey Sindelar	68	68	70	68	67	341	13,600
Scott Verplank	69	69	67	65	71	341	13,600
Grant Waite	67	66	70	69	69	341	13,600
Olin Browne	69	67	69	70	67	342	10,320
David Duval	69	68	68	67	70	342	10,320
Tom Pernice, Jr.	72	67	65	68	70	342	10,320
Steve Stricker	69	67	65	66	75	342	10,320
Jay Don Blake	73	66	67	69	68	343	9,190
Carlos Franco	73	68	68	66	68	343	9,190
Brian Gay	70	65	68	72	68	343	9,190
J.J. Henry	67	69	69	66	72	343	9,190
Mark O'Meara	65	72	69	66	71	343	9,190
Kevin Sutherland	73	66	66	68	70	343	9,190
Esteban Toledo	69	69	68	69	68	343	9,190
Mike Weir	66	68	67	69	73	343	9,190
Pete Jordan	69	72	66	66	71	344	8,760
Neal Lancaster	70	69	68	67	70	344	8,760
Stuart Appleby	68	69	70	68	70	345	8,520
Peter Jacobsen	67	67	71	69	71	345	8,520
Tim Petrovic	66	70	70	69	70	345	8,520
John Rollins	72	69	66	65	73	345	8,520
Steve Jones	66	68	71	70	71	346	8,240
Skip Kendall	66	70	70	68	72	346	8,240
Steve Lowery	69	73	67	64	73	346	8,240
Jonathan Byrd	69	70	66	69	73	347	8,080
Glen Day	69	69	68	68	74	348	8,000

Phoenix Open

TPC of Scottsdale, Scottsdale, Arizona
Par 35-36–71; 7,089 yards

January 24-27
purse, $4,000,000

	SCORES				TOTAL	MONEY
Chris DiMarco	68	64	66	69	267	$720,000
Kenny Perry	69	65	64	70	268	352,000
Kaname Yokoo	70	66	68	64	268	352,000
John Daly	68	65	66	70	269	176,000
Lee Janzen	74	67	64	64	269	176,000
Duffy Waldorf	65	65	67	73	270	144,000
Per-Ulrik Johansson	67	68	65	71	271	134,000
Brent Geiberger	68	67	67	70	272	100,000
John Huston	70	70	66	66	272	100,000
Jeff Maggert	70	66	66	70	272	100,000
Rodney Pampling	68	68	71	65	272	100,000
Rory Sabbatini	67	64	70	71	272	100,000
Vijay Singh	66	65	72	69	272	100,000
Kevin Sutherland	66	68	70	68	272	100,000
Brandel Chamblee	71	66	67	69	273	68,000
Rocco Mediate	72	67	65	69	273	68,000
Craig Perks	68	66	69	70	273	68,000
Cameron Beckman	67	67	69	71	274	54,000
Fred Funk	69	68	71	66	274	54,000

	SCORES				TOTAL	MONEY
Tom Lehman	66	69	71	68	274	54,000
Billy Mayfair	69	68	69	68	274	54,000
Scott Verplank	69	65	67	74	275	44,800
Michael Clark	72	67	70	67	276	35,600
Skip Kendall	66	66	74	70	276	35,600
Frank Lickliter	71	66	72	67	276	35,600
Phil Mickelson	72	66	70	68	276	35,600
Steve Stricker	72	69	67	68	276	35,600
Matt Gogel	72	66	71	68	277	24,933.34
Tim Herron	72	68	67	70	277	24,933.34
Steve Lowery	74	67	68	68	277	24,933.34
Paul Azinger	70	67	67	73	277	24,933.33
Stewart Cink	71	69	70	67	277	24,933.33
Steve Flesch	64	72	68	73	277	24,933.33
Charles Howell	68	69	66	74	277	24,933.33
Davis Love	72	69	68	68	277	24,933.33
Mike Weir	67	70	73	67	277	24,933.33
Bob Burns	70	66	72	70	278	18,800
Jim Furyk	69	68	71	70	278	18,800
Deane Pappas	68	71	70	69	278	18,800
Dan Forsman	70	70	70	69	279	15,600
Len Mattiace	68	69	70	72	279	15,600
Geoff Ogilvy	73	66	71	69	279	15,600
Craig Stadler	69	69	68	73	279	15,600
Grant Waite	69	67	74	69	279	15,600
Jim Carter	67	70	71	72	280	10,835.56
Fred Couples	68	71	67	74	280	10,835.56
Andrew Magee	69	69	72	70	280	10,835.56
Scott McCarron	75	66	68	71	280	10,835.56
Mike Sposa	71	66	73	70	280	10,835.56
Luke Donald	73	66	72	69	280	10,835.55
Shigeki Maruyama	70	67	75	68	280	10,835.55
Jose Maria Olazabal	69	69	73	69	280	10,835.55
Esteban Toledo	70	69	72	69	280	10,835.55
Pat Bates	70	68	72	71	281	9,080
Paul Casey	72	67	70	72	281	9,080
Brian Gay	68	69	72	72	281	9,080
Glen Hnatiuk	67	70	77	67	281	9,080
Brandt Jobe	70	71	67	73	281	9,080
Matt Kuchar	66	71	74	70	281	9,080
Jay Don Blake	70	68	74	70	282	8,680
Glen Day	72	67	71	72	282	8,680
Edward Fryatt	68	71	73	70	282	8,680
Donnie Hammond	69	70	73	70	282	8,680
Briny Baird	72	69	67	75	283	8,440
David Gossett	71	70	70	72	283	8,440
David Sutherland	72	69	71	73	285	8,320
Jay Williamson	72	69	69	76	286	8,240
Harrison Frazar	71	67	74	76	288	8,120
Nick Price	71	69	74	74	288	8,120
Bob Tway	74	66	71	78	289	8,000

AT&T Pebble Beach National Pro-Am

Pebble Beach GL: Par 36-36–72; 6,799 yards
Spyglass Hill GC: Par 36-36–72; 6,855 yards
Poppy Hills GC: Par 36-36–72; 6,833 yards
Pebble Beach, California

January 31-February 3
purse, $4,000,000

	SCORES				TOTAL	MONEY
Matt Gogel	66	72	67	69	274	$720,000
Pat Perez	66	65	70	76	277	432,000
Lee Janzen	68	67	70	73	278	232,000
Andrew Magee	69	70	67	72	278	232,000
Jose Maria Olazabal	70	71	71	68	280	146,000
Jerry Smith	67	69	72	72	280	146,000
Phil Tataurangi	67	72	70	71	280	146,000
Mathew Goggin	69	72	68	72	281	112,000
Paul Goydos	72	70	67	72	281	112,000
Kent Jones	70	71	70	70	281	112,000
Vijay Singh	69	71	70	71	281	112,000
Charles Howell	71	71	68	72	282	84,000
Tim Petrovic	70	71	70	71	282	84,000
Tiger Woods	70	73	71	68	282	84,000
Todd Fischer	71	73	71	68	283	60,000
Steve Flesch	73	67	69	74	283	60,000
Jesper Parnevik	67	72	70	74	283	60,000
Brett Quigley	70	73	69	71	283	60,000
John Rollins	67	77	68	71	283	60,000
Rory Sabbatini	69	72	72	70	283	60,000
Brent Schwarzrock	64	75	70	74	283	60,000
Todd Barranger	72	70	68	74	284	43,200
Fred Couples	69	68	72	75	284	43,200
Dan Forsman	69	73	71	72	285	32,400
Tom Lehman	71	70	71	73	285	32,400
Len Mattiace	72	73	71	69	285	32,400
Phillip Price	70	70	73	72	285	32,400
Kevin Sutherland	69	73	72	71	285	32,400
Kevin Wentworth	73	71	72	69	285	32,400
Jim Furyk	71	71	73	71	286	26,600
Dudley Hart	69	71	72	74	286	26,600
Jeff Brehaut	72	73	69	73	287	21,657.15
Craig Stadler	69	72	73	73	287	21,657.15
Pete Jordan	68	73	73	73	287	21,657.14
Skip Kendall	72	70	71	74	287	21,657.14
Rodney Pampling	70	69	73	75	287	21,657.14
Chris Smith	75	69	68	75	287	21,657.14
Esteban Toledo	71	75	70	71	287	21,657.14
Olin Browne	69	71	75	73	288	13,421.54
Paul Claxton	68	76	71	73	288	13,421.54
Trevor Dodds	74	71	71	72	288	13,421.54
Brad Faxon	69	72	74	73	288	13,421.54
Robin Freeman	69	75	71	73	288	13,421.54
Tim Herron	71	70	73	74	288	13,421.54
Tripp Isenhour	74	68	69	77	288	13,421.54
Brandt Jobe	73	71	70	74	288	13,421.54
Matt Kuchar	68	72	76	72	288	13,421.54
Tom Pernice, Jr.	72	68	73	75	288	13,421.54
John Senden	72	73	71	72	288	13,421.54
Ben Crane	74	67	75	72	288	13,421.53
Neal Lancaster	72	69	75	72	288	13,421.53
Paul Azinger	74	72	70	73	289	9,190

	SCORES				TOTAL	MONEY
Robert Gamez	71	72	70	76	289	9,190
Bradley Hughes	77	67	70	75	289	9,190
Scott McCarron	70	70	73	76	289	9,190
Jim McGovern	74	68	74	73	289	9,190
Corey Pavin	74	73	69	73	289	9,190
David Sutherland	69	73	74	73	289	9,190
Mike Weir	74	71	71	73	289	9,190
David Frost	73	72	71	74	290	8,680
Donnie Hammond	74	68	73	75	290	8,680
Craig Perks	70	71	72	77	290	8,680
Paul Stankowski	71	72	71	76	290	8,680
Ronnie Black	73	73	69	76	291	8,360
Jay Don Blake	72	69	71	79	291	8,360
Jeff Quinney	70	72	73	76	291	8,360
Jay Williamson	71	73	72	75	291	8,360
Tom Byrum	71	72	73	76	292	8,120
Shaun Micheel	69	71	75	77	292	8,120
Jay Delsing	70	74	72	77	293	7,960
Steve Scott	76	69	71	77	293	7,960
Gabriel Hjertstedt	71	72	72	79	294	7,840

Buick Invitational

Torrey Pines Golf Course, La Jolla, California
South Course: Par 36-36–72; 7,607 yards
North Course: Par 36-36–72; 6,647 yards

February 7-10
purse, $3,600,000

	SCORES				TOTAL	MONEY
Jose Maria Olazabal	71	72	67	65	275	$648,000
J.L. Lewis	68	67	71	70	276	316,800
Mark O'Meara	67	69	70	70	276	316,800
John Daly	69	70	68	70	277	172,800
Bob Estes	75	66	71	66	278	131,400
Rory Sabbatini	70	66	71	71	278	131,400
Tiger Woods	66	77	69	66	278	131,400
Jerry Kelly	73	67	66	73	279	104,400
Chris Riley	66	73	71	69	279	104,400
John Rollins	70	67	71	71	279	104,400
Lee Janzen	70	72	69	69	280	86,400
Vijay Singh	69	71	71	69	280	86,400
Greg Chalmers	70	73	75	63	281	65,520
Fred Funk	72	70	67	72	281	65,520
Jay Haas	68	68	76	69	281	65,520
John Senden	72	65	75	69	281	65,520
Jay Williamson	65	72	70	74	281	65,520
K.J. Choi	69	69	69	75	282	48,600
Luke Donald	65	75	74	68	282	48,600
Chris Smith	68	74	69	71	282	48,600
Phil Tataurangi	75	67	71	69	282	48,600
Brian Bateman	73	68	69	73	283	31,590
Mark Brooks	73	67	73	70	283	31,590
Paul Casey	72	67	74	70	283	31,590
Ben Crane	71	69	73	70	283	31,590
Mathew Goggin	64	76	72	71	283	31,590
Kent Jones	68	67	72	76	283	31,590
Peter Lonard	75	65	75	68	283	31,590
Rodney Pampling	73	67	70	73	283	31,590

	SCORES				TOTAL	MONEY
Steve Allan	70	72	73	69	284	21,394.29
Fulton Allem	71	66	76	71	284	21,394.29
Rich Beem	69	72	72	71	284	21,394.29
Tripp Isenhour	73	68	73	70	284	21,394.29
Paul Goydos	68	75	73	68	284	21,394.28
Bob May	71	71	77	65	284	21,394.28
Shaun Micheel	70	71	72	71	284	21,394.28
Jim Carter	71	70	71	73	285	17,280
Grant Waite	74	68	74	69	285	17,280
Bob Burns	69	71	71	75	286	14,760
Danny Ellis	73	69	72	72	286	14,760
Neal Lancaster	69	73	74	70	286	14,760
Bernhard Langer	72	68	70	76	286	14,760
Brian Watts	71	70	71	74	286	14,760
Jeff Brehaut	72	68	74	73	287	9,524.58
Tim Herron	70	67	76	74	287	9,524.58
Michael Allen	69	69	78	71	287	9,524.57
Stephen Ames	75	65	73	74	287	9,524.57
David Berganio, Jr.	69	74	71	73	287	9,524.57
Jay Don Blake	71	72	72	72	287	9,524.57
Scott Dunlap	69	74	72	72	287	9,524.57
Steve Elkington	73	70	75	69	287	9,524.57
Steve Flesch	70	68	78	71	287	9,524.57
David Frost	67	76	72	72	287	9,524.57
Skip Kendall	68	71	74	74	287	9,524.57
Lee Porter	68	72	72	75	287	9,524.57
Joey Sindelar	71	67	75	74	287	9,524.57
Kevin Sutherland	70	72	73	72	287	9,524.57
Harrison Frazar	74	69	72	73	288	7,920
Jeff Gove	71	72	74	71	288	7,920
Peter Jacobsen	68	73	74	73	288	7,920
Craig Perks	74	64	74	76	288	7,920
Esteban Toledo	75	67	72	74	288	7,920
Kaname Yokoo	70	71	74	74	289	7,704
Dan Forsman	71	72	71	76	290	7,452
Jeff Maggert	72	68	76	74	290	7,452
Steve Pate	72	67	73	78	290	7,452
Matt Peterson	68	75	74	73	290	7,452
Brett Quigley	75	66	72	77	290	7,452
Tommy Tolles	68	75	75	72	290	7,452
Bart Bryant	69	72	77	73	291	7,020
Greg Kraft	72	69	75	75	291	7,020
Brad Lardon	69	74	76	72	291	7,020
Jesper Parnevik	73	70	73	75	291	7,020
Tim Petrovic	69	72	77	73	291	7,020
Mike Sposa	71	72	75	73	291	7,020
Russ Cochran	72	70	74	76	292	6,624
John Cook	70	71	74	77	292	6,624
Richie Coughlan	70	70	74	78	292	6,624
Michael Long	70	73	73	76	292	6,624
Hidemichi Tanaka	73	70	73	76	292	6,624
Ian Leggatt	74	67	78	74	293	6,336
Michael Muehr	75	66	75	77	293	6,336
Jeff Sluman	68	72	74	79	293	6,336
Doug Barron	73	65	77	79	294	6,084
Jason Hill	68	71	78	77	294	6,084
Mike Hulbert	76	67	71	80	294	6,084
Shigeki Maruyama	75	67	79	73	294	6,084
Brian Henninger	73	70	76	77	296	5,904
Brent Schwarzrock	71	71	83	73	298	5,832

Nissan Open

Riviera Country Club, Pacific Palisades, California
Par 35-36–71; 6,987 yards

February 14-17
purse, $3,700,000

	SCORES				TOTAL	MONEY
Len Mattiace	69	65	67	68	269	$666,000
Brad Faxon	67	67	68	68	270	276,266
Scott McCarron	69	65	65	71	270	276,266
Rory Sabbatini	69	68	65	68	270	276,266
Toru Taniguchi	66	67	67	71	271	148,000
Chris DiMarco	68	70	66	68	272	123,950
Charles Howell	68	71	64	69	272	123,950
Per-Ulrik Johansson	70	68	68	66	272	123,950
Fred Couples	72	68	68	66	274	96,200
Fred Funk	69	68	69	68	274	96,200
Brian Gay	71	67	68	68	274	96,200
Jose Maria Olazabal	66	71	70	67	274	96,200
Sergio Garcia	73	67	67	68	275	74,000
Billy Mayfair	69	69	71	66	275	74,000
J.J. Henry	69	67	71	69	276	61,050
John Rollins	71	69	67	69	276	61,050
Bob Tway	67	68	72	69	276	61,050
Lee Westwood	69	68	70	69	276	61,050
Cameron Beckman	69	71	66	71	277	46,435
Bob Estes	69	69	71	68	277	46,435
Paul Stankowski	69	69	72	67	277	46,435
Scott Verplank	69	68	67	73	277	46,435
Mark Calcavecchia	70	70	70	68	278	32,005
Jim Carter	71	68	70	69	278	32,005
Glen Hnatiuk	69	72	69	68	278	32,005
David Peoples	66	70	69	73	278	32,005
Pat Perez	71	69	70	68	278	32,005
Loren Roberts	69	70	68	71	278	32,005
Tommy Armour	67	69	73	70	279	24,050
Edward Fryatt	69	71	68	71	279	24,050
Jerry Kelly	72	66	68	73	279	24,050
Rocco Mediate	69	69	69	72	279	24,050
Jesper Parnevik	65	69	73	72	279	24,050
Mark Brooks	71	68	73	68	280	19,980
Tom Lehman	70	69	69	72	280	19,980
Vijay Singh	71	70	71	68	280	19,980
Robert Allenby	73	66	73	69	281	13,729
Stephen Ames	71	71	69	70	281	13,729
Briny Baird	71	71	67	72	281	13,729
Olin Browne	70	69	72	70	281	13,729
Stewart Cink	70	71	69	71	281	13,729
Michael Clark	68	72	69	72	281	13,729
John Daly	70	69	72	70	281	13,729
Carlos Franco	69	72	69	71	281	13,729
Jim Furyk	70	71	71	69	281	13,729
Dennis Paulson	69	71	72	69	281	13,729
Jeff Sluman	70	69	73	69	281	13,729
David Sutherland	68	71	71	71	281	13,729
Hidemichi Tanaka	69	72	66	74	281	13,729
Paul Azinger	69	69	70	74	282	8,924
Pat Bates	72	68	71	71	282	8,924
Scott Hoch	68	72	70	72	282	8,924
Peter Lonard	71	71	71	69	282	8,924
Kenny Perry	70	72	67	73	282	8,924

	SCORES				TOTAL	MONEY
Billy Andrade	66	73	72	72	283	8,251
Greg Chalmers	69	73	72	69	283	8,251
Bradley Hughes	71	71	70	71	283	8,251
Andrew Magee	73	67	70	73	283	8,251
Bob May	71	69	70	73	283	8,251
Matt Peterson	75	67	69	72	283	8,251
Kenneth Staton	71	70	69	73	283	8,251
Kirk Triplett	73	69	72	69	283	8,251
Ben Crane	70	72	71	71	284	7,844
Tom Pernice, Jr.	71	70	73	70	284	7,844
John Senden	71	69	73	71	284	7,844
John Cook	71	69	71	74	285	7,659
Craig Perks	71	71	72	71	285	7,659
Steve Flesch	69	71	72	74	286	7,511
J.P. Hayes	74	67	72	73	286	7,511
K.J. Choi	69	73	70	75	287	7,289
Neal Lancaster	70	71	73	73	287	7,289
Esteban Toledo	67	72	72	76	287	7,289
Kaname Yokoo	72	70	74	71	287	7,289
Russ Cochran	69	70	71	78	288	6,956
Jay Haas	71	71	73	73	288	6,956
Matt Kuchar	71	68	76	73	288	6,956
Paul McGinley	71	70	76	71	288	6,956
Michael Muehr	73	68	72	75	288	6,956
Scott Simpson	71	68	75	76	290	6,734
Bob Burns	72	70	73	78	293	6,660
David Duval	67	69	70		WD	

WGC Accenture Match Play

La Costa Resort and Spa, Carlsbad, California
Par 36-36–72; 7,002 yards

February 20-24
purse, $5,500,000

FIRST ROUND

Peter O'Malley defeated Tiger Woods, 2 and 1.
Nick Price defeated Angel Cabrera, 2 and 1.
Scott Verplank defeated Frank Lickliter, 3 and 2.
Bob Estes defeated Stuart Appleby, 1 up.
Davis Love defeated Phillip Price, 2 and 1.
Paul Azinger defeated Jesper Parnevik, 1 up.
Vijay Singh defeated Toru Taniguchi, 3 and 2.
Niclas Fasth defeated Michael Campbell, 2 and 1.
Sergio Garcia defeated Lee Janzen, 3 and 2.
Charles Howell defeated Stewart Cink, 4 and 3.
Mike Weir defeated Paul Lawrie, 3 and 2.
Scott McCarron defeated Colin Montgomerie, 2 and 1.
Ernie Els defeated Jeff Sluman, 4 and 3.
Tom Lehman defeated Hal Sutton, 2 and 1.
Matt Gogel defeated Darren Clarke, 2 and 1.
Steve Lowery defeated Scott Hoch, 5 and 4.
John Cook defeated Phil Mickelson, 3 and 2.
Lee Westwood defeated Shingo Katayama, 3 and 2.
Adam Scott defeated Bernhard Langer, 2 and 1.
Brad Faxon defeated Kenny Perry, 7 and 6.
Retief Goosen defeated Billy Mayfair, 4 and 3.
Jose Maria Olazabal defeated Justin Leonard, 1 up.
Chris DiMarco defeated Steve Stricker, 3 and 2.

Mark Calcavecchia defeated Jerry Kelly, 3 and 2.
Kevin Sutherland defeated David Duval, 20 holes.
Paul McGinley defeated Joe Durant, 5 and 4.
Jim Furyk defeated Billy Andrade, 20 holes.
Toshimitsu Izawa defeated Pierre Fulke, 4 and 3.
David Toms defeated Rory Sabbatini, 1 up.
Rocco Mediate defeated John Daly, 5 and 4.
Steve Flesch defeated Padraig Harrington, 3 and 2.
Kirk Triplett defeated Robert Allenby, 3 and 2.

(Each losing player received $27,500.)

SECOND ROUND

Nick Price defeated O'Malley, 2 and 1.
Estes defeated Verplank, 20 holes.
Azinger defeated Love, 1 up.
Fasth defeated Singh, 3 and 2.
Garcia defeated Howell, 1 up.
McCarron defeated Weir, 1 up.
Lehman defeated Els, 19 holes.
Gogel defeated Lowery, 20 holes.
Cook defeated Westwood, 1 up.
Faxon defeated Scott, 3 and 2.
Olazabal defeated Goosen, 1 up.
Calcavecchia defeated DiMarco, 2 and 1.
Sutherland defeated McGinley, 2 and 1.
Furyk defeated Izawa, 3 and 1.
Toms defeated Mediate, 1 up.
Flesch defeated Triplett, 3 and 2.

(Each losing player received $55,000.)

THIRD ROUND

Estes defeated Price, 1 up.
Azinger defeated Fasth, 20 holes.
McCarron defeated Garcia, 1 up.
Lehman defeated Gogel, 4 and 3.
Faxon defeated Cook, 3 and 2.
Olazabal defeated Calcavecchia, 2 up.
Sutherland defeated Furyk, 4 and 3.
Toms defeated Flesch, 1 up.

(Each losing player received $85,000.)

QUARTER-FINALS

Azinger defeated Estes, 2 and 1.
McCarron defeated Lehman, 4 and 3.
Faxon defeated Olazabal, 20 holes.
Sutherland defeated Toms, 3 and 2.

(Each losing player received $175,000.)

SEMI-FINALS

McCarron defeated Azinger, 1 up.
Sutherland defeated Faxon, 1 up.

PLAYOFF FOR THIRD-FOURTH PLACE

Faxon defeated Azinger, 19 holes.

(Faxon received $450,000; Azinger received $360,000.)

FINAL

Sutherland defeated McCarron, 1 up.

(Sutherland received $1,000,000; McCarron received $550,000.)

Touchstone Energy Tucson Open

Omni Tucson National Resort, Tucson, Arizona
Par 36-36–72; 7,109 yards

February 21-24
purse, $3,000,000

		SCORES			TOTAL	MONEY
Ian Leggatt	68	71	65	64	268	$540,000
David Peoples	67	68	68	67	270	264,000
Loren Roberts	65	70	69	66	270	264,000
Fred Funk	65	71	67	68	271	132,000
Kenneth Staton	69	69	69	64	271	132,000
Cameron Beckman	70	67	68	67	272	84,562.50
Russ Cochran	67	69	68	68	272	84,562.50
Greg Kraft	69	68	66	69	272	84,562.50
Shigeki Maruyama	70	66	68	68	272	84,562.50
Spike McRoy	67	71	70	64	272	84,562.50
Heath Slocum	69	67	64	72	272	84,562.50
Chris Smith	70	65	69	68	272	84,562.50
Bob Tway	67	67	69	69	272	84,562.50
Paul Stankowski	73	65	67	68	273	57,000
Jonathan Byrd	73	64	68	69	274	51,000
Chad Campbell	71	68	68	67	274	51,000
Paul Goydos	67	72	68	67	274	51,000
Tom Byrum	70	67	69	69	275	36,514.29
Edward Fryatt	69	68	71	67	275	36,514.29
Mike Sposa	70	66	69	70	275	36,514.29
Duffy Waldorf	71	68	67	69	275	36,514.29
Miguel Angel Jimenez	67	70	65	73	275	36,514.28
Bob May	71	65	69	70	275	36,514.28
Craig Parry	69	69	67	70	275	36,514.28
Michael Allen	64	71	71	70	276	21,015
Brandel Chamblee	65	67	69	75	276	21,015
Bob Heintz	66	70	68	72	276	21,015
Glen Hnatiuk	69	69	67	71	276	21,015
Peter Lonard	68	69	70	69	276	21,015
Andrew Magee	66	70	65	75	276	21,015
Dicky Pride	69	71	65	71	276	21,015
Chris Riley	70	68	67	71	276	21,015
Scott Simpson	69	66	70	71	276	21,015
Hidemichi Tanaka	71	67	69	69	276	21,015
Jim Carter	72	67	68	70	277	12,940.91
K.J. Choi	68	72	67	70	277	12,940.91
Brian Gay	69	68	72	68	277	12,940.91
Dudley Hart	70	70	66	71	277	12,940.91
Bradley Hughes	72	67	67	71	277	12,940.91
Tripp Isenhour	71	66	69	71	277	12,940.91
Steve Jones	67	72	67	71	277	12,940.91

		SCORES			TOTAL	MONEY
Jonathan Kaye	70	68	73	66	277	12,940.91
Esteban Toledo	70	68	70	69	277	12,940.91
Tommy Tolles	69	67	69	72	277	12,940.91
Dan Forsman	68	69	67	73	277	12,940.90
Tim Clark	69	70	71	68	278	8,505
Ben Crane	69	68	72	69	278	8,505
John Huston	66	70	69	73	278	8,505
Lee Porter	72	65	74	67	278	8,505
Paul Casey	70	68	69	72	279	7,236
Donnie Hammond	69	69	73	68	279	7,236
Tim Herron	70	69	68	72	279	7,236
Pete Jordan	68	71	69	71	279	7,236
Len Mattiace	67	73	71	68	279	7,236
Aaron Baddeley	70	68	66	76	280	6,780
Olin Browne	69	71	68	72	280	6,780
Bob Burns	69	70	71	70	280	6,780
Phil Tataurangi	68	69	73	70	280	6,780
Willie Wood	69	67	70	74	280	6,780
David Berganio, Jr.	66	73	72	70	281	6,510
Brent Geiberger	70	70	73	68	281	6,510
Gary Nicklaus	68	70	70	73	281	6,510
Jerry Smith	67	72	72	70	281	6,510
Brian Claar	68	70	72	72	282	6,300
Jeff Gove	72	68	70	72	282	6,300
Scott Watkins	69	68	73	72	282	6,300
Jeff Brehaut	68	70	72	73	283	6,150
Carlos Franco	70	69	69	75	283	6,150
Han Lee	68	72	70	74	284	5,970
Michael Long	68	72	72	72	284	5,970
Steve Pate	68	66	76	74	284	5,970
Dennis Paulson	68	68	76	72	284	5,970
Mathew Goggin	72	66	73	75	286	5,820

Genuity Championship

Doral Golf Resort & Spa, Blue Course, Miami, Florida
Par 36-36–72; 7,125 yards

February 28-March 3
purse, $4,700,000

		SCORES			TOTAL	MONEY
Ernie Els	66	67	66	72	271	$846,000
Tiger Woods	67	70	70	66	273	507,600
Peter Lonard	70	67	70	70	277	319,600
Rich Beem	69	68	72	70	279	225,600
Angel Cabrera	72	70	71	67	280	159,330
Steve Elkington	67	71	74	68	280	159,330
Craig Perks	71	68	70	71	280	159,330
Nick Price	69	69	75	67	280	159,330
Vijay Singh	66	73	70	71	280	159,330
Jesper Parnevik	71	67	72	71	281	126,900
Paul Azinger	69	72	71	70	282	108,100
Justin Leonard	67	70	72	73	282	108,100
Pat Perez	69	69	75	69	282	108,100
Fred Funk	68	72	71	72	283	86,950
Craig Parry	68	72	71	72	283	86,950
Steve Allan	66	73	71	74	284	63,802.50
Briny Baird	69	66	78	71	284	63,802.50
Ian Leggatt	71	67	73	73	284	63,802.50

		SCORES			TOTAL	MONEY
Len Mattiace	70	69	74	71	284	63,802.50
Tom Scherrer	71	71	69	73	284	63,802.50
Steve Stricker	71	72	73	68	284	63,802.50
David Toms	67	74	75	68	284	63,802.50
Mike Weir	70	71	73	70	284	63,802.50
Brian Bateman	71	71	74	69	285	35,563.34
Stewart Cink	67	74	74	70	285	35,563.34
Brian Gay	74	70	71	70	285	35,563.34
Ben Crane	71	73	69	72	285	35,563.33
Robert Damron	68	73	73	71	285	35,563.33
Brent Geiberger	69	70	75	71	285	35,563.33
Jay Haas	70	70	73	72	285	35,563.33
Skip Kendall	67	70	77	71	285	35,563.33
Shigeki Maruyama	67	72	74	72	285	35,563.33
Stuart Appleby	68	70	73	75	286	25,380
Luke Donald	68	75	72	71	286	25,380
Sergio Garcia	73	70	71	72	286	25,380
Paul Gow	73	69	71	73	286	25,380
Greg Norman	71	73	71	71	286	25,380
Stephen Ames	70	74	72	71	287	21,150
Lee Janzen	68	71	77	71	287	21,150
Geoff Ogilvy	78	65	76	68	287	21,150
Bob Burns	71	73	72	72	288	14,877.64
Erik Compton	71	70	78	69	288	14,877.64
Neal Lancaster	71	71	76	70	288	14,877.64
Steve Lowery	73	71	72	72	288	14,877.64
Billy Mayfair	69	75	71	73	288	14,877.64
Chris Smith	68	74	74	72	288	14,877.64
Brian Watts	69	73	74	72	288	14,877.64
Greg Kraft	66	75	74	73	288	14,877.63
David Peoples	70	73	71	74	288	14,877.63
Bob Tway	68	71	75	74	288	14,877.63
Grant Waite	72	68	75	73	288	14,877.63
Tommy Armour	67	72	71	79	289	10,798.25
Jay Don Blake	70	73	69	77	289	10,798.25
Charles Howell	69	72	73	75	289	10,798.25
Spike McRoy	69	75	70	75	289	10,798.25
Lee Porter	67	72	77	73	289	10,798.25
Joey Sindelar	71	71	76	71	289	10,798.25
Mike Sposa	69	73	75	72	289	10,798.25
Duffy Waldorf	69	72	78	70	289	10,798.25
Paul Claxton	70	71	73	76	290	10,246
Carlos Franco	69	73	72	76	290	10,246
Dudley Hart	69	74	76	71	290	10,246
James Driscoll	72	72	73	74	291	9,917
David Gossett	69	73	76	73	291	9,917
Andrew Magee	68	74	77	72	291	9,917
Shaun Micheel	67	76	79	69	291	9,917
Greg Chalmers	69	71	78	74	292	9,447
Brandel Chamblee	70	73	77	72	292	9,447
Chris DiMarco	65	79	75	73	292	9,447
J.J. Henry	68	76	77	71	292	9,447
Rodney Pampling	74	70	76	72	292	9,447
Jerry Smith	72	72	78	70	292	9,447
Brandt Jobe	70	72	75	76	293	9,024
Tom Pernice, Jr.	73	69	79	72	293	9,024
Hal Sutton	69	74	76	74	293	9,024
Edward Fryatt	72	70	79	73	294	8,695
John Huston	70	73	80	71	294	8,695
Per-Ulrik Johansson	69	75	75	75	294	8,695

	SCORES				TOTAL	MONEY
Brent Schwarzrock	70	74	74	76	294	8,695
Tim Petrovic	68	72	80	75	295	8,460
Deane Pappas	69	74	78	75	296	8,366
Brad Elder	71	71	83	73	298	8,272
John Rollins	73	70	81	75	299	8,178

Honda Classic

TPC at Heron Bay, Coral Springs, Florida
Par 36-36–72; 7,268 yards

March 7-10
purse, $3,500,000

	SCORES				TOTAL	MONEY
Matt Kuchar	68	69	66	66	269	$630,000
Brad Faxon	65	70	69	67	271	308,000
Joey Sindelar	68	67	66	70	271	308,000
Billy Andrade	68	70	67	67	272	144,666.67
J.L. Lewis	68	68	68	68	272	144,666.67
Brett Quigley	70	66	67	69	272	144,666.66
Rodney Pampling	67	67	71	68	273	117,250
Peter Jacobsen	71	67	68	68	274	101,500
John Riegger	63	69	72	70	274	101,500
Brett Wetterich	68	66	68	72	274	101,500
Joe Durant	71	67	69	68	275	63,350
Carlos Franco	70	69	66	70	275	63,350
Brent Geiberger	70	69	68	68	275	63,350
Skip Kendall	66	74	67	68	275	63,350
Peter Lonard	70	65	71	69	275	63,350
Phil Mickelson	70	66	68	71	275	63,350
Chris Riley	69	68	67	71	275	63,350
Brent Schwarzrock	72	66	67	70	275	63,350
Kenneth Staton	68	69	71	67	275	63,350
Mike Weir	68	65	67	75	275	63,350
Angel Cabrera	70	70	68	68	276	31,966.67
Greg Chalmers	69	71	68	68	276	31,966.67
Joel Edwards	66	72	69	69	276	31,966.67
Danny Ellis	66	68	72	70	276	31,966.67
Tim Herron	69	67	69	71	276	31,966.67
John Senden	71	65	70	70	276	31,966.67
Mark Calcavecchia	72	67	70	67	276	31,966.66
Fred Couples	68	70	67	71	276	31,966.66
Jerry Kelly	69	70	65	72	276	31,966.66
Woody Austin	70	70	66	71	277	19,495
Briny Baird	72	67	71	67	277	19,495
Luke Donald	68	68	72	69	277	19,495
Stephen Gangluff	72	66	65	74	277	19,495
Retief Goosen	71	66	72	68	277	19,495
Dudley Hart	67	68	69	73	277	19,495
Davis Love	69	71	69	68	277	19,495
Kenny Perry	67	70	69	71	277	19,495
Lee Porter	72	65	68	72	277	19,495
David Toms	72	68	70	67	277	19,495
Brian Bateman	70	70	70	68	278	13,300
Per-Ulrik Johansson	67	69	72	70	278	13,300
Bernhard Langer	68	71	70	69	278	13,300
Frank Nobilo	71	68	69	70	278	13,300
Geoff Ogilvy	69	68	70	71	278	13,300
Mike Sposa	68	68	71	71	278	13,300

	SCORES				TOTAL	MONEY
Fulton Allem	67	70	70	72	279	9,222.50
Olin Browne	68	69	71	71	279	9,222.50
Chad Campbell	71	69	70	69	279	9,222.50
Robert Damron	67	70	70	72	279	9,222.50
Brian Gay	71	67	74	67	279	9,222.50
J.J. Henry	65	72	69	73	279	9,222.50
Neal Lancaster	68	68	71	72	279	9,222.50
Brenden Pappas	68	71	69	71	279	9,222.50
Michael Allen	67	71	72	70	280	8,015
Paul Casey	68	66	73	73	280	8,015
Jeff Gove	70	67	71	72	280	8,015
Bob Heintz	65	70	72	73	280	8,015
Tim Clark	71	68	68	74	281	7,735
John Daly	69	70	70	72	281	7,735
Chris DiMarco	67	70	72	72	281	7,735
Mike Hulbert	70	69	70	72	281	7,735
Michael Clark	69	70	72	71	282	7,455
Harrison Frazar	71	69	70	72	282	7,455
John Rollins	71	69	69	73	282	7,455
Chris Smith	73	67	71	71	282	7,455
Ben Crane	73	67	70	73	283	7,105
Gene Fieger	70	70	67	76	283	7,105
John Huston	69	70	71	73	283	7,105
Craig Perks	70	69	73	71	283	7,105
Tim Petrovic	69	70	72	72	283	7,105
Jay Williamson	72	66	71	74	283	7,105

Bay Hill Invitational

Bay Hill Club & Lodge, Orlando, Florida
Par 36-36—72; 7,239 yards

March 14-17
purse, $4,000,000

	SCORES				TOTAL	MONEY
Tiger Woods	67	65	74	69	275	$720,000
Michael Campbell	72	68	68	71	279	432,000
John Huston	67	71	70	72	280	192,000
Len Mattiace	73	66	68	73	280	192,000
Rocco Mediate	69	70	71	70	280	192,000
Phil Mickelson	69	71	69	71	280	192,000
Harrison Frazar	69	70	71	71	281	129,000
Jose Maria Olazabal	71	68	70	72	281	129,000
Angel Cabrera	67	70	72	73	282	100,000
Ernie Els	70	67	72	73	282	100,000
Sergio Garcia	68	71	70	73	282	100,000
Scott Hoch	71	68	70	73	282	100,000
Pat Perez	70	69	69	74	282	100,000
Peter Lonard	71	72	72	68	283	76,000
Stewart Cink	68	71	71	74	284	60,000
John Daly	67	71	71	75	284	60,000
Retief Goosen	71	73	69	71	284	60,000
Jerry Kelly	70	69	74	71	284	60,000
Steve Lowery	71	70	73	70	284	60,000
Rodney Pampling	68	72	72	72	284	60,000
Vijay Singh	69	71	69	75	284	60,000
Stephen Ames	69	71	73	72	285	41,600
David Duval	71	70	72	72	285	41,600
Kenny Perry	72	69	76	68	285	41,600

	SCORES				TOTAL	MONEY
Robert Allenby	69	71	71	75	286	32,666.67
Paul Azinger	69	72	73	72	286	32,666.67
Paul McGinley	74	68	68	76	286	32,666.66
Cameron Beckman	70	69	73	75	287	28,400
Greg Chalmers	71	72	74	70	287	28,400
Matt Kuchar	72	73	68	74	287	28,400
David Berganio, Jr.	72	73	75	68	288	21,733.34
Bernhard Langer	72	71	76	69	288	21,733.34
Davis Love	72	72	75	69	288	21,733.34
Billy Andrade	74	69	74	71	288	21,733.33
Chad Campbell	70	70	68	80	288	21,733.33
Brad Faxon	76	70	70	72	288	21,733.33
Steve Flesch	67	75	75	71	288	21,733.33
Shigeki Maruyama	70	70	71	77	288	21,733.33
Frank Nobilo	75	71	69	73	288	21,733.33
John Cook	70	74	75	70	289	15,600
Per-Ulrik Johansson	69	72	71	77	289	15,600
Sandy Lyle	73	73	73	70	289	15,600
Scott McCarron	69	67	72	81	289	15,600
Duffy Waldorf	73	73	68	75	289	15,600
Bob Estes	70	73	72	75	290	12,040
Corey Pavin	72	71	74	73	290	12,040
David Peoples	73	73	69	75	290	12,040
Joey Sindelar	75	71	68	76	290	12,040
Fred Funk	74	72	76	69	291	9,691.43
Tim Herron	74	71	73	73	291	9,691.43
Justin Leonard	76	69	71	75	291	9,691.43
Frank Lickliter	70	75	72	74	291	9,691.43
Craig Parry	72	72	73	74	291	9,691.43
Paul Stankowski	70	72	76	73	291	9,691.43
Lee Janzen	73	73	69	76	291	9,691.42
Niclas Fasth	72	70	76	74	292	8,920
Jeff Maggert	75	68	74	75	292	8,920
Mark O'Meara	73	73	74	72	292	8,920
Craig Perks	76	70	70	76	292	8,920
Jeff Sluman	72	68	74	78	292	8,920
Kaname Yokoo	68	77	71	76	292	8,920
Peter Jacobsen	71	73	80	69	293	8,600
Tom Lehman	69	71	75	78	293	8,600
Mathew Goggin	76	70	73	75	294	8,400
Tripp Isenhour	75	71	70	78	294	8,400
Curtis Strange	69	72	77	76	294	8,400
Fulton Allem	72	74	74	75	295	8,200
Kent Jones	71	75	74	75	295	8,200
Mark Calcavecchia	72	72	76	76	296	8,040
Charles Howell	71	69	74	82	296	8,040
Kirk Triplett	72	74	72	79	297	7,920
Paul Goydos	73	72	78	75	298	7,800
D.A. Weibring	67	75	78	78	298	7,800
*Bubba Dickerson	72	72	75	80	299	

The Players Championship

TPC at Sawgrass, Stadium Course,
Ponte Vedra Beach, Florida
Par 36-36–72; 7,093 yards

March 21-24
purse, $6,000,000

	SCORES				TOTAL	MONEY
Craig Perks	71	68	69	72	280	$1,080,000
Stephen Ames	74	69	72	67	282	648,000
Rocco Mediate	71	70	69	73	283	408,000
Billy Andrade	73	69	70	72	284	226,200
Sergio Garcia	70	72	71	71	284	226,200
Scott Hoch	67	77	68	72	284	226,200
Carl Paulson	69	69	69	77	284	226,200
Jeff Sluman	69	69	72	74	284	226,200
John Huston	73	69	73	70	285	168,000
Nick Price	74	71	71	69	285	168,000
Robert Allenby	69	73	72	72	286	138,000
Michael Campbell	72	68	74	72	286	138,000
Jerry Kelly	69	76	74	67	286	138,000
Jim Furyk	71	72	71	73	287	102,000
Retief Goosen	71	71	72	73	287	102,000
Jeff Maggert	72	72	71	72	287	102,000
Shigeki Maruyama	72	72	69	74	287	102,000
Tiger Woods	71	72	70	74	287	102,000
Steve Stricker	69	74	71	74	288	78,000
David Toms	69	72	70	77	288	78,000
Mike Weir	70	73	68	77	288	78,000
Thomas Bjorn	74	72	75	68	289	55,700
Carlos Franco	75	69	72	73	289	55,700
Padraig Harrington	70	72	77	70	289	55,700
Bernhard Langer	75	71	72	71	289	55,700
Steve Lowery	69	73	71	76	289	55,700
Chris Riley	71	74	74	70	289	55,700
Stuart Appleby	69	74	75	72	290	38,212.50
K.J. Choi	71	75	73	71	290	38,212.50
David Duval	68	75	72	75	290	38,212.50
Tim Herron	71	73	74	72	290	38,212.50
Tom Lehman	73	71	74	72	290	38,212.50
Phil Mickelson	64	75	75	76	290	38,212.50
Bob Tway	74	68	77	71	290	38,212.50
Scott Verplank	71	75	73	71	290	38,212.50
Angel Cabrera	71	72	73	75	291	26,437.50
Glen Day	71	75	73	72	291	26,437.50
Chris DiMarco	66	75	74	76	291	26,437.50
Brad Faxon	71	73	74	73	291	26,437.50
Tom Kite	72	71	79	69	291	26,437.50
Bob May	73	70	73	75	291	26,437.50
Jose Maria Olazabal	73	73	71	74	291	26,437.50
Craig Stadler	71	72	72	76	291	26,437.50
Rich Beem	72	74	80	66	292	18,648
Ernie Els	76	69	79	68	292	18,648
Bob Estes	70	74	78	70	292	18,648
Harrison Frazar	73	71	71	77	292	18,648
Justin Leonard	72	74	72	74	292	18,648
Briny Baird	71	74	74	74	293	14,430
Jim Carter	74	72	73	74	293	14,430
Brandel Chamblee	74	69	78	72	293	14,430
Nick Faldo	68	73	72	80	293	14,430
Jay Haas	71	71	74	77	293	14,430

	SCORES				TOTAL	MONEY
Dudley Hart	71	72	72	78	293	14,430
Frank Lickliter	76	70	73	74	293	14,430
Loren Roberts	72	71	73	77	293	14,430
Mark Brooks	72	70	74	78	294	13,440
Jonathan Kaye	72	72	77	73	294	13,440
Craig Parry	72	73	72	77	294	13,440
Joel Edwards	70	72	75	78	295	13,080
Charles Howell	71	74	78	72	295	13,080
Kenny Perry	73	71	76	75	295	13,080
Steve Elkington	74	68	77	77	296	12,600
Brian Gay	69	76	80	71	296	12,600
J.L. Lewis	74	70	71	81	296	12,600
Colin Montgomerie	70	76	72	78	296	12,600
Scott Simpson	72	72	76	76	296	12,600
Neal Lancaster	73	71	75	78	297	12,240
Mark Calcavecchia	69	70	73	86	298	11,940
David Gossett	69	72	78	79	298	11,940
Len Mattiace	71	75	71	81	298	11,940
Tom Pernice, Jr.	70	75	78	75	298	11,940
Esteban Toledo	73	72	78	76	299	11,640
Robert Damron	74	71	80	75	300	11,520
David Frost	71	75	75	82	303	11,400

Shell Houston Open

TPC at The Woodlands, The Woodlands, Texas   March 28-31
Par 36-36–72; 7,018 yards   purse, $4,000,000

	SCORES				TOTAL	MONEY
Vijay Singh	67	65	66	68	266	$720,000
Darren Clarke	69	65	67	71	272	432,000
Jose Maria Olazabal	71	68	64	70	273	272,000
Jay Haas	67	70	69	69	275	176,000
Shigeki Maruyama	68	71	66	70	275	176,000
Brandt Jobe	70	66	69	72	277	129,500
Justin Leonard	70	68	69	70	277	129,500
Tom Pernice, Jr.	71	70	67	69	277	129,500
Adam Scott	72	67	67	71	277	129,500
Jim Carter	65	73	68	72	278	104,000
J.P. Hayes	67	68	71	72	278	104,000
Fred Funk	71	70	67	71	279	88,000
John Huston	70	73	68	68	279	88,000
Briny Baird	70	71	67	72	280	72,000
Nick Price	68	71	69	72	280	72,000
Scott Verplank	67	70	72	71	280	72,000
Tom Byrum	70	70	70	71	281	54,133.34
Frank Nobilo	70	70	70	71	281	54,133.34
Greg Chalmers	69	72	66	74	281	54,133.33
Fred Couples	68	71	68	74	281	54,133.33
Rory Sabbatini	69	71	66	75	281	54,133.33
David Toms	69	72	67	73	281	54,133.33
Stephen Ames	71	71	68	72	282	33,714.29
Rodney Pampling	70	71	68	73	282	33,714.29
Loren Roberts	70	71	70	71	282	33,714.29
Hal Sutton	72	67	74	69	282	33,714.29
Chris DiMarco	69	73	72	68	282	33,714.28
Jerry Kelly	71	68	70	73	282	33,714.28

	SCORES				TOTAL	MONEY
Greg Norman	70	68	68	76	282	33,714.28
Chris Riley	67	70	71	75	283	27,200
Chad Campbell	69	74	67	74	284	24,800
Luke Donald	71	68	71	74	284	24,800
Paul Stankowski	72	68	66	78	284	24,800
Geoff Ogilvy	71	65	75	74	285	18,109.10
Robert Allenby	68	72	69	76	285	18,109.09
Brian Bateman	67	72	73	73	285	18,109.09
Pat Bates	71	71	70	73	285	18,109.09
David Duval	75	67	68	75	285	18,109.09
Kent Jones	71	72	71	71	285	18,109.09
Shingo Katayama	68	72	73	72	285	18,109.09
Skip Kendall	72	69	72	72	285	18,109.09
Dennis Paulson	72	69	69	75	285	18,109.09
Heath Slocum	70	73	72	70	285	18,109.09
Phil Tataurangi	72	69	73	71	285	18,109.09
Tommy Armour	72	70	71	73	286	11,440
Woody Austin	71	70	71	74	286	11,440
Bob Burns	68	74	71	73	286	11,440
Mike Heinen	70	73	71	72	286	11,440
Len Mattiace	72	69	74	71	286	11,440
David Peoples	71	72	69	74	286	11,440
K.J. Choi	72	70	75	70	287	9,472
Russ Cochran	71	71	70	75	287	9,472
Glen Day	70	71	74	72	287	9,472
Kevin Sutherland	72	70	74	71	287	9,472
Bob Tway	71	71	73	72	287	9,472
Michael Allen	71	69	72	76	288	8,960
Jeff Brehaut	70	72	68	78	288	8,960
Colin Montgomerie	72	71	74	71	288	8,960
Craig Parry	74	69	69	76	288	8,960
Jay Williamson	72	70	73	73	288	8,960
Miguel Angel Jimenez	69	73	73	74	289	8,680
J.L. Lewis	68	73	73	75	289	8,680
Michael Clark	70	72	74	74	290	8,480
Ian Leggatt	70	73	70	77	290	8,480
Esteban Toledo	66	73	75	76	290	8,480
Andrew Magee	69	74	71	77	291	8,280
Jerry Smith	70	70	71	80	291	8,280
Robert Thompson	70	73	72	77	292	8,120
Grant Waite	72	71	78	71	292	8,120
Pete Jordan	70	73	74	77	294	8,000

BellSouth Classic

TPC at Sugarloaf, Duluth, Georgia
Par 36-36–72; 7,293 yards

April 4-7
purse, $3,800,000

	SCORES				TOTAL	MONEY
Retief Goosen	68	66	68	70	272	$684,000
Jesper Parnevik	66	69	76	65	276	410,400
Phil Mickelson	65	68	71	73	277	258,400
Scott McCarron	67	72	71	68	278	182,400
John Rollins	66	70	72	71	279	144,400
Bob Tway	67	71	69	72	279	144,400
Dudley Hart	66	72	70	72	280	127,300
Phil Tataurangi	71	64	76	70	281	106,400

		SCORES			TOTAL	MONEY
K.J. Choi	70	68	70	73	281	106,400
Steve Flesch	68	68	72	73	281	106,400
Padraig Harrington	69	65	73	74	281	106,400
Glen Day	68	71	72	71	282	74,480
David Toms	68	68	74	72	282	74,480
Skip Kendall	71	69	71	71	282	74,480
Dennis Paulson	71	68	70	73	282	74,480
Thomas Bjorn	66	70	69	77	282	74,480
Colin Montgomerie	69	70	70	74	283	57,000
Zach Johnson	68	71	69	75	283	57,000
Mike Weir	67	70	69	77	283	57,000
Hidemichi Tanaka	69	68	74	73	284	47,500
Glen Hnatiuk	69	72	69	74	284	47,500
Matt Kuchar	69	74	70	72	285	42,560
Bob May	74	70	71	71	286	38,000
Chris DiMarco	69	73	69	75	286	38,000
Rich Beem	70	69	76	72	287	25,523.34
Kenny Perry	72	71	72	72	287	25,523.34
David Frost	72	67	75	73	287	25,523.34
Jim Carter	73	68	73	73	287	25,523.34
Jess Daley	70	71	73	73	287	25,523.33
Shaun Micheel	68	68	77	74	287	25,523.33
Andrew Magee	72	70	72	73	287	25,523.33
Luke Donald	73	68	71	75	287	25,523.33
Bo Van Pelt	71	72	69	75	287	25,523.33
Jeff Sluman	68	69	74	76	287	25,523.33
Kent Jones	68	73	69	77	287	25,523.33
Steve Elkington	64	69	73	81	287	25,523.33
Franklin Langham	74	69	76	69	288	18,240
Paul Stankowski	70	70	73	75	288	18,240
Peter Lonard	67	75	74	73	289	14,060
Jay Don Blake	71	69	75	74	289	14,060
Deane Pappas	71	73	72	73	289	14,060
Vijay Singh	69	69	76	75	289	14,060
Frank Lickliter	71	71	72	75	289	14,060
Stuart Appleby	68	70	75	76	289	14,060
Lee Westwood	72	70	71	76	289	14,060
Frank Nobilo	66	74	73	76	289	14,060
Brad Faxon	72	69	69	79	289	14,060
John Huston	71	70	78	71	290	10,146
Matt Peterson	71	72	74	73	290	10,146
Grant Waite	70	74	74	73	291	9,094.67
Edward Fryatt	68	75	74	74	291	9,094.67
Pat Perez	74	69	72	76	291	9,094.67
Craig Parry	68	71	75	77	291	9,094.67
Jonathan Kaye	73	68	73	77	291	9,094.66
J.J. Henry	68	72	74	77	291	9,094.66
Ian Leggatt	66	74	77	76	293	8,626
Hal Sutton	72	71	72	78	293	8,626
Steve Allan	72	70	79	73	294	8,436
Brian Bateman	70	72	76	76	294	8,436
Billy Andrade	71	71	74	78	294	8,436
Paul Claxton	73	71	73	78	295	8,246
Miguel Angel Jimenez	71	72	73	79	295	8,246
Bart Bryant	70	74	78	75	297	8,094
Briny Baird	73	69	71	84	297	8,094
Adam Scott	69	74	79	76	298	7,942
Richard Zokol	71	73	73	81	298	7,942
Jerry Smith	71	70	79	79	299	7,790
Tommy Armour	74	69	75	81	299	7,790

	SCORES				TOTAL	MONEY
Brett Wetterich	70	72	78	84	304	7,676
Brian Watts	71	70	79	85	305	7,600

Masters Tournament

Augusta National Golf Club, Augusta, Georgia
Par 36-36–72; 7,270 yards

April 11-14
purse, $5,000,000

	SCORES				TOTAL	MONEY
Tiger Woods	70	69	66	71	276	$1,008,000
Retief Goosen	69	67	69	74	279	604,800
Phil Mickelson	69	72	68	71	280	380,800
Jose Maria Olazabal	70	69	71	71	281	268,800
Ernie Els	70	67	72	73	282	212,800
Padraig Harrington	69	70	72	71	282	212,800
Vijay Singh	70	65	72	76	283	187,600
Sergio Garcia	68	71	70	75	284	173,600
Angel Cabrera	68	71	73	73	285	151,200
Miguel Angel Jimenez	70	71	74	70	285	151,200
Adam Scott	71	72	72	70	285	151,200
Chris DiMarco	70	71	72	73	286	123,200
Brad Faxon	71	75	69	71	286	123,200
Thomas Bjorn	74	67	70	76	287	98,000
Nick Faldo	75	67	73	72	287	98,000
Davis Love	67	75	74	71	287	98,000
Shigeki Maruyama	75	72	73	67	287	98,000
Colin Montgomerie	75	71	70	71	287	98,000
Paul McGinley	72	74	71	71	288	81,200
Darren Clarke	70	74	73	72	289	65,240
Jerry Kelly	72	74	71	72	289	65,240
Justin Leonard	70	75	74	70	289	65,240
Nick Price	70	76	70	73	289	65,240
Mark Brooks	74	72	71	73	290	46,480
Stewart Cink	74	70	72	74	290	46,480
Tom Pernice, Jr.	74	72	71	73	290	46,480
Jeff Sluman	73	72	71	74	290	46,480
Mike Weir	72	71	71	76	290	46,480
Robert Allenby	73	70	76	72	291	38,080
Charles Howell	74	73	71	73	291	38,080
Jesper Parnevik	70	72	77	72	291	38,080
John Daly	74	73	70	75	292	32,410
Bernhard Langer	73	72	73	74	292	32,410
Billy Mayfair	74	71	72	75	292	32,410
Craig Stadler	73	72	76	71	292	32,410
Fred Couples	73	73	76	72	294	26,950
Rocco Mediate	75	68	77	74	294	26,950
Greg Norman	71	76	72	75	294	26,950
David Toms	73	74	76	71	294	26,950
Steve Lowery	75	71	76	73	295	26,950
Kirk Triplett	74	70	74	77	295	26,950
Tom Watson	71	76	76	72	295	26,950
Scott Verplank	70	75	76	75	296	20,720
Lee Westwood	75	72	74	76	297	19,600
Bob Estes	73	72	75	78	298	18,480

Out of Final 36 Holes

Michael Campbell	74	74	148
Kevin Sutherland	78	70	148
Tom Lehman	76	72	148
Rory Sabbatini	73	75	148
Paul Azinger	75	73	148
Larry Mize	74	74	148
Joe Durant	74	74	148
*Michael Hoey	75	73	148
David Duval	74	74	148
Scott McCarron	75	73	148
Mark Calcavecchia	79	70	149
Mark O'Meara	78	71	149
Lee Janzen	74	75	149
Toshimitsu Izawa	73	76	149
Matt Kuchar	73	77	150
*Bubba Dickerson	79	71	150
Tom Kite	77	73	150
Shingo Katayama	78	72	150
Jim Furyk	73	77	150
Billy Andrade	75	75	150
Kenny Perry	76	74	150
Toru Taniguchi	80	70	150
Steve Stricker	75	76	151
Niclas Fasth	76	75	151
Scott Hoch	76	75	151
Fuzzy Zoeller	75	77	152
Raymond Floyd	79	74	153
Jose Coceres	74	79	153
Sandy Lyle	73	81	154
Tim Jackson	76	78	154
*Robert Hamilton	77	77	154
Ian Woosnam	77	78	155
Seve Ballesteros	75	81	156
Tommy Aaron	79	78	157
Ben Crenshaw	81	77	158
Gary Player	80	78	158
Stuart Appleby	80	79	159
*Chez Reavie	74	86	160
Charles Coody	82	84	166
Arnold Palmer	89	85	174
Frank Lickliter			WD

(Professionals who did not complete 72 holes received $5,000.)

WorldCom Classic

Harbour Town Golf Links, Hilton Head Island, South Carolina — April 18-21
Par 36-35–71; 6,916 yards — purse, $4,000,000

	SCORES				TOTAL	MONEY
Justin Leonard	67	64	66	73	270	$720,000
Heath Slocum	67	68	66	70	271	432,000
Phil Mickelson	65	64	72	71	272	272,000
Bernhard Langer	71	65	68	69	273	192,000
Davis Love	62	69	72	71	274	146,000
Billy Mayfair	65	68	72	69	274	146,000
Scott Verplank	67	68	72	67	274	146,000

		SCORES			TOTAL	MONEY
Angel Cabrera	66	67	70	72	275	120,000
Glen Hnatiuk	68	71	66	70	275	120,000
Mark Calcavecchia	68	70	73	65	276	92,000
Len Mattiace	70	68	66	72	276	92,000
Frank Nobilo	72	69	69	66	276	92,000
Jeff Sluman	73	66	65	72	276	92,000
Craig Stadler	69	68	69	70	276	92,000
Carlos Franco	68	67	72	70	277	66,000
David Frost	65	71	71	70	277	66,000
Jim Furyk	70	65	73	69	277	66,000
Tom Lehman	71	69	72	65	277	66,000
Billy Andrade	64	71	72	71	278	45,142.86
Woody Austin	72	68	68	70	278	45,142.86
Ernie Els	71	67	73	67	278	45,142.86
Sergio Garcia	70	72	66	70	278	45,142.86
Nick Price	69	71	70	68	278	45,142.86
Cameron Beckman	70	63	67	78	278	45,142.85
Charles Howell	68	71	66	73	278	45,142.85
Esteban Toledo	69	69	69	72	279	32,000
Jay Don Blake	70	66	72	72	280	28,400
Robert Damron	70	71	69	70	280	28,400
Tim Herron	70	72	68	70	280	28,400
Greg Norman	66	69	72	73	280	28,400
Mike Sposa	67	73	71	69	280	28,400
Jose Coceres	69	72	68	72	281	20,320
Bob Estes	73	67	72	69	281	20,320
Brad Faxon	71	70	69	71	281	20,320
Steve Flesch	67	70	72	72	281	20,320
Per-Ulrik Johansson	69	67	71	74	281	20,320
Corey Pavin	67	74	69	71	281	20,320
John Riegger	71	69	69	72	281	20,320
Chris Riley	68	73	67	73	281	20,320
Chris Smith	69	71	68	73	281	20,320
Bob Tway	70	65	70	76	281	20,320
David Edwards	72	70	69	71	282	12,870
Peter Jacobsen	69	69	72	72	282	12,870
Brandt Jobe	72	68	71	71	282	12,870
Steve Jones	67	72	69	74	282	12,870
Neal Lancaster	70	65	70	77	282	12,870
Ian Leggatt	70	69	76	67	282	12,870
Carl Paulson	70	69	70	73	282	12,870
David Sutherland	69	69	72	72	282	12,870
Pat Bates	68	69	71	75	283	9,450
Greg Chalmers	74	68	64	77	283	9,450
Dan Forsman	70	69	74	70	283	9,450
Jay Haas	71	71	72	69	283	9,450
Dudley Hart	71	67	74	71	283	9,450
J.P. Hayes	70	72	70	71	283	9,450
Lee Porter	70	71	73	69	283	9,450
Garrett Willis	71	69	70	73	283	9,450
Chad Campbell	70	65	74	75	284	8,840
Brandel Chamblee	70	69	73	72	284	8,840
Matt Gogel	69	71	73	71	284	8,840
Scott Hoch	72	69	73	70	284	8,840
Stephen Ames	71	70	73	71	285	8,480
Russ Cochran	70	72	70	73	285	8,480
Glen Day	71	71	68	75	285	8,480
Fred Funk	71	71	71	72	285	8,480
Tom Scherrer	68	72	72	73	285	8,480
Lee Janzen	65	67	73	81	286	8,240

		SCORES			TOTAL	MONEY
John Cook	72	70	72	73	287	8,080
Steve Lowery	67	73	70	77	287	8,080
Doug Tewell	69	70	73	75	287	8,080
Bob Burns	69	72	73	74	288	7,840
Paul Gow	71	71	71	75	288	7,840
Geoff Ogilvy	70	72	76	70	288	7,840
Jonathan Kaye	70	70	72	78	290	7,680
Hidemichi Tanaka	69	73	69	81	292	7,600

Greater Greensboro Chrysler Classic

Forest Oaks Country Club, Greensboro, North Carolina
Par 36-36–72; 7,062 yards

April 25-28
purse, $3,800,000

		SCORES			TOTAL	MONEY
Rocco Mediate	68	67	66	71	272	$684,000
Mark Calcavecchia	65	69	69	72	275	410,400
Jonathan Byrd	72	71	69	66	278	220,400
Chad Campbell	67	72	66	73	278	220,400
Jim Gallagher, Jr.	67	73	70	69	279	144,400
Carl Paulson	68	70	73	68	279	144,400
Stephen Ames	71	69	72	68	280	118,433.34
K.J. Choi	71	69	69	71	280	118,433.33
Robert Gamez	67	67	73	73	280	118,433.33
Pat Bates	71	67	73	70	281	91,200
Jonathan Kaye	69	72	66	74	281	91,200
Paul Stankowski	66	74	71	70	281	91,200
Kevin Sutherland	71	68	75	67	281	91,200
Stuart Appleby	70	73	68	71	282	64,600
Edward Fryatt	71	69	72	70	282	64,600
Lee Porter	67	71	71	73	282	64,600
Chris Riley	74	70	69	69	282	64,600
Loren Roberts	68	72	71	71	282	64,600
Matt Gogel	73	68	68	74	283	47,690
Brandt Jobe	72	70	70	71	283	47,690
Jerry Kelly	69	70	71	73	283	47,690
Duffy Waldorf	71	70	74	68	283	47,690
Jay Haas	69	70	77	68	284	32,028.58
Jim Furyk	69	72	71	72	284	32,028.57
Dudley Hart	70	72	71	71	284	32,028.57
Frank Nobilo	71	70	71	72	284	32,028.57
Dennis Paulson	73	68	70	73	284	32,028.57
David Peoples	70	70	73	71	284	32,028.57
Mike Sposa	69	71	69	75	284	32,028.57
Bob Heintz	70	69	72	74	285	22,087.50
John Huston	71	66	71	77	285	22,087.50
Kent Jones	70	74	73	68	285	22,087.50
Shaun Micheel	69	72	72	72	285	22,087.50
Brett Quigley	69	73	73	70	285	22,087.50
Heath Slocum	72	69	73	71	285	22,087.50
Phil Tataurangi	68	67	73	77	285	22,087.50
Willie Wood	69	71	71	74	285	22,087.50
Tim Clark	71	70	73	72	286	15,960
Carlos Franco	70	74	68	74	286	15,960
Paul Goydos	68	75	75	68	286	15,960
Steve Jones	69	71	76	70	286	15,960
Geoff Ogilvy	73	67	74	72	286	15,960

	SCORES				TOTAL	MONEY
John Senden	70	71	74	71	286	15,960
Briny Baird	72	70	75	70	287	12,160
Russ Cochran	69	71	74	73	287	12,160
John Rollins	74	69	74	70	287	12,160
Bo Van Pelt	68	76	70	73	287	12,160
Michael Allen	70	69	78	71	288	9,667.20
Bart Bryant	72	68	73	75	288	9,667.20
Trevor Dodds	72	72	73	71	288	9,667.20
Mathew Goggin	71	70	75	72	288	9,667.20
Tom Scherrer	70	72	75	71	288	9,667.20
Tom Byrum	70	72	73	74	289	8,841.34
Paul Claxton	72	69	73	75	289	8,841.33
Joel Edwards	71	70	72	76	289	8,841.33
Luke Donald	72	68	76	74	290	8,512
Brian Gay	73	71	71	75	290	8,512
Tripp Isenhour	69	72	75	74	290	8,512
Skip Kendall	70	73	72	75	290	8,512
Neal Lancaster	72	72	72	74	290	8,512
Tim Herron	71	71	71	78	291	8,208
John Maginnes	72	70	76	73	291	8,208
John Riegger	71	73	74	73	291	8,208
Steve Elkington	71	73	78	70	292	8,018
Stephen Gangluff	71	73	70	78	292	8,018
J.L. Lewis	75	67	75	76	293	7,904
Paul Azinger	71	73	76	74	294	7,828
Harrison Frazar	70	73	80	72	295	7,752
Jim Carter	71	71	78	76	296	7,638
Eduardo Herrera	72	72	79	73	296	7,638
Jeff Maggert	72	72	76	77	297	7,524

Compaq Classic of New Orleans

English Turn Golf & Country Club,
New Orleans, Louisiana
Par 36-36–72; 7,116 yards

May 2-5
purse, $4,500,000

	SCORES				TOTAL	MONEY
K.J. Choi	68	65	71	67	271	$810,000
Dudley Hart	68	71	69	67	275	396,000
Geoff Ogilvy	70	67	71	67	275	396,000
John Cook	74	67	69	66	276	177,187.50
Chris DiMarco	72	66	70	68	276	177,187.50
Dan Forsman	65	69	72	70	276	177,187.50
Mike Sposa	72	68	68	68	276	177,187.50
Nick Price	74	67	70	66	277	139,500
Tim Clark	68	67	75	68	278	112,500
Phil Mickelson	73	66	71	68	278	112,500
Bryce Molder	69	67	69	73	278	112,500
David Toms	69	69	71	69	278	112,500
Scott Verplank	69	69	73	67	278	112,500
Rich Beem	67	70	74	68	279	83,250
Steve Stricker	69	70	71	69	279	83,250
Duffy Waldorf	73	66	75	66	280	63,128.58
Olin Browne	72	68	70	70	280	63,128.57
Chad Campbell	72	72	70	66	280	63,128.57
Joel Edwards	74	68	71	67	280	63,128.57
Steve Elkington	70	71	69	70	280	63,128.57

	SCORES				TOTAL	MONEY
Charles Howell	71	72	68	69	280	63,128.57
John Rollins	68	69	68	75	280	63,128.57
Fulton Allem	70	69	72	70	281	37,012.50
Bob Estes	70	71	75	65	281	37,012.50
Fred Funk	71	71	71	68	281	37,012.50
Peter Lonard	76	67	66	72	281	37,012.50
Scott McCarron	74	67	70	70	281	37,012.50
Tom Scherrer	74	69	68	70	281	37,012.50
Kenneth Staton	73	71	70	67	281	37,012.50
Kirk Triplett	71	72	72	66	281	37,012.50
Stephen Ames	68	74	69	71	282	27,900
Bart Bryant	69	73	67	73	282	27,900
Stewart Cink	68	72	72	70	282	27,900
Jonathan Byrd	69	75	69	70	283	21,768.75
Jim Carter	70	71	74	68	283	21,768.75
David Frost	72	69	74	68	283	21,768.75
Bob Heintz	69	72	72	70	283	21,768.75
Billy Mayfair	73	71	71	68	283	21,768.75
Shaun Micheel	69	70	71	73	283	21,768.75
Michael Muehr	71	69	74	69	283	21,768.75
Chris Riley	71	72	70	70	283	21,768.75
Bubba Dickerson	70	70	75	69	284	14,875.72
J.P. Hayes	71	72	74	67	284	14,875.72
Matt Peterson	72	68	77	67	284	14,875.72
Bob Burns	70	74	70	70	284	14,875.71
Jeff Maggert	69	70	69	76	284	14,875.71
Brett Quigley	72	68	69	75	284	14,875.71
Brent Schwarzrock	73	70	70	71	284	14,875.71
Billy Andrade	70	66	71	78	285	10,822.50
Steve Flesch	71	67	73	74	285	10,822.50
Brandt Jobe	72	68	72	73	285	10,822.50
Frank Nobilo	71	72	71	71	285	10,822.50
Rodney Pampling	75	67	68	75	285	10,822.50
Craig Perks	76	68	70	71	285	10,822.50
Paul Stankowski	73	71	70	71	285	10,822.50
David Sutherland	70	73	71	71	285	10,822.50
Steve Allan	71	71	74	70	286	9,990
Michael Allen	71	70	71	74	286	9,990
Per-Ulrik Johansson	68	72	74	72	286	9,990
Dennis Paulson	72	72	73	69	286	9,990
Brett Wetterich	73	70	68	75	286	9,990
Brian Bateman	70	72	75	70	287	9,540
J.J. Henry	70	69	77	71	287	9,540
John Huston	74	69	75	69	287	9,540
Pete Jordan	71	70	73	73	287	9,540
Jesper Parnevik	71	70	72	74	287	9,540
Tommy Armour	74	68	75	71	288	8,820
Jeff Brehaut	74	70	73	71	288	8,820
Jess Daley	71	73	76	68	288	8,820
Joe Durant	69	72	78	69	288	8,820
Jeff Gallagher	68	76	74	70	288	8,820
Kent Jones	72	71	71	74	288	8,820
Skip Kendall	70	73	68	77	288	8,820
Blaine McCallister	73	69	75	71	288	8,820
Scott Simpson	70	71	75	72	288	8,820
Bob Tway	74	70	67	77	288	8,820
Grant Waite	69	75	71	73	288	8,820
Brandel Chamblee	72	71	70	76	289	8,235
Brad Lardon	73	68	73	75	289	8,235
Jeff Sluman	72	72	68	78	290	8,100

	SCORES				TOTAL	MONEY
Tommy Tolles	72	69	75	76	292	8,010
Mike Standly	73	69	76	78	296	7,920

Verizon Byron Nelson Classic

TPC Four Seasons Resort Las Colinas:
Par 35-35–70; 7,017 yards
Cottonwood Valley Golf Course:
Par 35-35–70; 6,846 yards
Irving, Texas

May 9-12
purse, $4,800,000

	SCORES				TOTAL	MONEY
Shigeki Maruyama	67	63	68	68	266	$864,000
Ben Crane	68	67	68	65	268	518,400
Tiger Woods	71	65	69	65	270	326,400
Ernie Els	69	70	64	69	272	211,200
David Toms	68	68	70	66	272	211,200
Jim Carter	65	67	71	70	273	166,800
Steve Stricker	69	66	70	68	273	166,800
Robert Allenby	69	69	67	69	274	120,000
Cameron Beckman	70	65	66	73	274	120,000
David Frost	66	72	68	68	274	120,000
Frank Lickliter	64	70	70	70	274	120,000
Nick Price	64	71	69	70	274	120,000
Loren Roberts	67	68	68	71	274	120,000
Duffy Waldorf	71	67	66	70	274	120,000
David Duval	66	70	72	67	275	84,000
Justin Leonard	67	69	71	68	275	84,000
Franklin Langham	68	67	71	70	276	67,200
Phil Mickelson	69	64	71	72	276	67,200
Jesper Parnevik	71	68	70	67	276	67,200
Tim Petrovic	72	66	70	68	276	67,200
Scott Simpson	71	65	70	70	276	67,200
Fred Funk	67	69	70	71	277	46,080
Brian Henninger	67	68	71	71	277	46,080
Bryce Molder	63	70	72	72	277	46,080
Paul Stankowski	67	65	72	73	277	46,080
Bob Tway	69	70	70	68	277	46,080
Chris DiMarco	69	68	70	71	278	31,950
J.P. Hayes	69	70	72	67	278	31,950
Lee Janzen	64	69	70	75	278	31,950
Per-Ulrik Johansson	65	69	73	71	278	31,950
Peter Lonard	69	66	74	69	278	31,950
Carl Paulson	70	67	71	70	278	31,950
John Rollins	69	65	75	69	278	31,950
Esteban Toledo	64	70	73	71	278	31,950
Billy Andrade	68	68	73	70	279	24,180
Steve Flesch	65	73	71	70	279	24,180
Brent Geiberger	69	69	73	68	279	24,180
Phil Tataurangi	68	68	72	71	279	24,180
Rich Beem	68	67	73	72	280	18,240
Chad Campbell	69	68	71	72	280	18,240
Dudley Hart	68	70	72	70	280	18,240
John Huston	68	66	77	69	280	18,240
Jeff Maggert	66	67	73	74	280	18,240
David Peoples	71	67	69	73	280	18,240
Craig Perks	68	69	69	74	280	18,240

	SCORES				TOTAL	MONEY
Mike Sposa	68	70	71	71	280	18,240
Michael Allen	69	69	70	73	281	13,184
J.J. Henry	71	67	73	70	281	13,184
Brett Wetterich	67	72	68	74	281	13,184
Woody Austin	71	67	70	74	282	11,488
Davis Love	71	68	73	70	282	11,488
Len Mattiace	68	70	72	72	282	11,488
Billy Mayfair	67	71	75	69	282	11,488
Michael Muehr	71	68	74	69	282	11,488
Scott Verplank	68	71	72	71	282	11,488
Craig Barlow	66	73	70	74	283	10,704
Joe Durant	63	71	76	73	283	10,704
Matt Gogel	71	68	76	68	283	10,704
Andrew Magee	69	70	70	74	283	10,704
Tom Scherrer	65	72	75	71	283	10,704
Jeff Sluman	69	70	73	71	283	10,704
Scott Dunlap	70	67	74	73	284	10,176
Bob Estes	67	69	74	74	284	10,176
Brian Gay	68	67	75	74	284	10,176
David Gossett	64	71	79	70	284	10,176
Deane Pappas	66	73	72	73	284	10,176
J.C. Anderson	68	70	73	74	285	9,552
Tom Byrum	70	68	73	74	285	9,552
Tim Clark	70	68	76	71	285	9,552
Steve Lowery	68	69	76	72	285	9,552
Scott McCarron	70	69	71	75	285	9,552
Kenny Perry	69	69	70	77	285	9,552
Kenneth Staton	68	71	74	72	285	9,552
Hidemichi Tanaka	71	68	70	76	285	9,552
Garrett Willis	68	69	74	77	288	9,120
Michael Connell	66	73	76	76	291	8,976
Paul Gow	70	69	78	74	291	8,976
Craig Stadler	71	68	80	73	292	8,832

MasterCard Colonial

Colonial Country Club, Ft. Worth, Texas
Par 35-35–70; 7,080 yards

May 16-19
purse, $4,300,000

	SCORES				TOTAL	MONEY
Nick Price	69	65	66	67	267	$774,000
Kenny Perry	70	66	69	67	272	378,400
David Toms	71	71	64	66	272	378,400
Dudley Hart	73	65	70	65	273	206,400
Davis Love	70	70	67	67	274	163,400
Phil Tataurangi	70	69	66	69	274	163,400
Tom Watson	68	72	66	69	275	144,050
Stuart Appleby	70	71	71	64	276	120,400
Jonathan Byrd	73	67	68	68	276	120,400
Steve Flesch	68	67	70	71	276	120,400
Esteban Toledo	67	67	72	70	276	120,400
Billy Andrade	68	70	70	69	277	79,242.86
Olin Browne	69	72	69	67	277	79,242.86
Frank Lickliter	67	72	70	68	277	79,242.86
Vijay Singh	68	70	70	69	277	79,242.86
Hal Sutton	69	68	71	69	277	79,242.86
Joel Edwards	67	71	69	70	277	79,242.85

	SCORES				TOTAL	MONEY
Bob Tway	67	68	71	71	277	79,242.85
Cameron Beckman	71	69	70	68	278	53,965
Justin Leonard	70	68	69	71	278	53,965
Shigeki Maruyama	72	67	69	70	278	53,965
Scott Verplank	67	70	72	69	278	53,965
Bob Estes	65	72	72	70	279	38,270
John Huston	70	70	71	68	279	38,270
Peter Jacobsen	72	68	69	70	279	38,270
Tom Lehman	71	67	71	70	279	38,270
Phil Mickelson	73	70	69	67	279	38,270
Chad Campbell	72	68	71	69	280	29,240
Jerry Kelly	69	71	72	68	280	29,240
Scott McCarron	70	70	69	71	280	29,240
Jesper Parnevik	69	72	70	69	280	29,240
Corey Pavin	68	71	69	72	280	29,240
Briny Baird	71	71	70	69	281	24,295
Bob Burns	68	68	72	73	281	24,295
Stewart Cink	72	69	69	71	281	24,295
Matt Gogel	69	71	73	69	282	20,693.75
Steve Jones	67	73	70	72	282	20,693.75
Peter Lonard	68	70	69	75	282	20,693.75
Mike Weir	71	68	73	70	282	20,693.75
Mark Brooks	68	71	73	71	283	15,480
Chris DiMarco	72	71	71	69	283	15,480
Steve Elkington	74	68	72	69	283	15,480
Jay Haas	69	74	72	68	283	15,480
Brandt Jobe	67	72	69	75	283	15,480
Steve Lowery	67	75	72	69	283	15,480
David Peoples	72	71	71	69	283	15,480
Loren Roberts	70	73	67	73	283	15,480
Luke Donald	73	69	69	73	284	10,588.75
David Frost	72	67	73	72	284	10,588.75
David Gossett	74	69	71	70	284	10,588.75
Lee Janzen	69	72	74	69	284	10,588.75
Per-Ulrik Johansson	68	73	73	70	284	10,588.75
Jeff Maggert	68	74	72	70	284	10,588.75
John Rollins	70	73	69	72	284	10,588.75
Joey Sindelar	68	71	74	71	284	10,588.75
Brent Geiberger	72	68	76	69	285	9,675
Skip Kendall	68	71	74	72	285	9,675
Carl Paulson	68	72	74	71	285	9,675
Pat Perez	72	66	74	73	285	9,675
Tom Pernice, Jr.	72	69	72	74	287	9,460
Brandel Chamblee	69	73	72	74	288	9,245
Jose Coceres	70	68	73	77	288	9,245
Ian Leggatt	70	69	74	75	288	9,245
Billy Mayfair	70	73	71	74	288	9,245
Glen Day	69	67	77	77	290	9,030
K.J. Choi	69	72	69	81	291	8,901
Rodney Pampling	72	71	73	75	291	8,901
Brian Gay	70	66	78	78	292	8,729
J.J. Henry	72	71	75	74	292	8,729
Paul Stankowski	72	69	74	79	294	8,557
Duffy Waldorf	71	71	74	78	294	8,557
Neal Lancaster	71	72	77	76	296	8,428

Memorial Tournament

Muirfield Village Golf Club, Dublin, Ohio

Par 36-36–72; 7,221 yards

May 23-26

purse, $4,500,000

	SCORES				TOTAL	MONEY
Jim Furyk	71	70	68	65	274	$810,000
John Cook	73	69	65	69	276	396,000
David Peoples	69	74	65	68	276	396,000
David Duval	75	69	67	66	277	169,650
Harrison Frazar	70	65	75	67	277	169,650
Shigeki Maruyama	74	66	67	70	277	169,650
Vijay Singh	69	67	72	69	277	169,650
Bob Tway	65	71	68	73	277	169,650
Billy Andrade	72	72	67	67	278	117,000
Stewart Cink	66	70	69	73	278	117,000
Jerry Kelly	71	71	68	68	278	117,000
Phil Mickelson	73	66	70	69	278	117,000
Ernie Els	70	71	69	69	279	87,000
Brad Faxon	71	69	70	69	279	87,000
John Rollins	72	69	68	70	279	87,000
Tim Clark	77	64	68	71	280	72,000
Skip Kendall	73	66	68	73	280	72,000
Justin Leonard	69	65	72	74	280	72,000
Rocco Mediate	70	73	68	70	281	58,500
Heath Slocum	73	66	69	73	281	58,500
Jeff Sluman	69	70	71	71	281	58,500
Fred Funk	72	70	69	71	282	43,200
John Huston	73	70	71	68	282	43,200
Tom Lehman	68	73	71	70	282	43,200
Craig Stadler	73	69	70	70	282	43,200
Tiger Woods	74	70	72	66	282	43,200
Robert Allenby	70	73	72	68	283	31,950
Charles Howell	70	76	67	70	283	31,950
Steve Lowery	73	72	68	70	283	31,950
Jeff Maggert	72	67	74	70	283	31,950
Corey Pavin	73	69	72	69	283	31,950
Stuart Appleby	67	73	71	73	284	22,860
Paul Azinger	73	68	69	74	284	22,860
Cameron Beckman	72	70	69	73	284	22,860
K.J. Choi	71	74	71	68	284	22,860
David Gossett	70	72	69	73	284	22,860
Lee Janzen	73	68	70	73	284	22,860
Matt Kuchar	74	72	67	71	284	22,860
Peter Lonard	73	71	70	70	284	22,860
Len Mattiace	71	73	71	69	284	22,860
Mike Weir	74	68	72	70	284	22,860
Olin Browne	70	71	71	73	285	16,650
J.L. Lewis	75	70	68	72	285	16,650
Frank Lickliter	69	72	70	74	285	16,650
Tim Herron	74	69	71	72	286	13,545
Steve Jones	74	70	68	74	286	13,545
Billy Mayfair	71	72	72	71	286	13,545
Tom Pernice, Jr.	68	73	72	73	286	13,545
Glen Day	72	69	74	72	287	10,902.86
Joel Edwards	75	68	73	71	287	10,902.86
Rodney Pampling	75	69	72	71	287	10,902.86
Dennis Paulson	74	72	70	71	287	10,902.86
Scott Verplank	72	68	74	73	287	10,902.86
Briny Baird	75	70	67	75	287	10,902.85

	SCORES				TOTAL	MONEY
Brett Quigley	71	71	68	77	287	10,902.85
Robert Damron	72	73	74	69	288	10,125
Andrew Magee	72	74	71	71	288	10,125
Mark O'Meara	76	68	71	73	288	10,125
Chris Smith	75	69	71	73	288	10,125
Jose Coceres	70	73	74	72	289	9,720
David Edwards	73	69	72	75	289	9,720
Matt Gogel	73	73	71	72	289	9,720
Carl Paulson	75	69	74	71	289	9,720
Kenny Perry	74	68	74	73	289	9,720
Jay Don Blake	76	69	75	70	290	9,315
Chad Campbell	76	69	72	73	290	9,315
Geoff Ogilvy	75	70	72	73	290	9,315
Toru Taniguchi	74	68	75	73	290	9,315
Kevin Sutherland	73	71	71	77	292	9,090
Garrett Willis	73	69	73	79	294	9,000
Jack Nicklaus	71	74	71	79	295	8,910
Paul Stankowski	75	71	74	76	296	8,820
Sergio Garcia	75	70	77	75	297	8,730
Bubba Dickerson	74	72	78	76	300	8,640
Carlos Franco	74	71	78	79	302	8,550

Kemper Insurance Open

TPC at Avenel, Potomac, Maryland
Par 36-35–71; 7,005 yards

May 30-June 2
purse, $3,600,000

	SCORES				TOTAL	MONEY
Bob Estes	65	69	69	70	273	$648,000
Rich Beem	68	68	69	69	274	388,800
Bob Burns	68	66	69	72	275	208,800
Steve Elkington	70	67	69	69	275	208,800
Jonathan Kaye	69	69	69	69	276	136,800
Justin Leonard	72	67	67	70	276	136,800
Harrison Frazar	69	66	72	70	277	116,100
Chris Smith	70	72	68	67	277	116,100
Olin Browne	70	70	69	69	278	93,600
Bart Bryant	72	70	66	70	278	93,600
Duffy Waldorf	67	68	70	73	278	93,600
Jay Williamson	66	71	67	74	278	93,600
Brian Gay	66	69	73	71	279	65,520
Glen Hnatiuk	69	71	70	69	279	65,520
Franklin Langham	63	72	70	74	279	65,520
Bryce Molder	67	69	73	70	279	65,520
Greg Norman	67	65	74	73	279	65,520
Stuart Appleby	71	71	66	72	280	46,944
Tim Clark	68	73	66	73	280	46,944
Chris DiMarco	66	71	72	71	280	46,944
Andrew Magee	67	68	70	75	280	46,944
Bob May	68	67	69	76	280	46,944
Craig Barlow	67	67	73	74	281	29,610
Joe Durant	67	69	73	72	281	29,610
Hank Kuehne	69	69	70	73	281	29,610
J.L. Lewis	71	71	68	71	281	29,610
Blaine McCallister	70	68	71	72	281	29,610
Shaun Micheel	68	69	72	72	281	29,610
Craig Parry	71	71	68	71	281	29,610

		SCORES			TOTAL	MONEY
Willie Wood	66	68	72	75	281	29,610
Pat Bates	73	68	72	69	282	20,880
Luke Donald	68	69	74	71	282	20,880
Wayne Grady	73	69	71	69	282	20,880
Charles Howell	70	66	74	72	282	20,880
Dennis Paulson	71	70	66	75	282	20,880
Phil Tataurangi	67	72	71	72	282	20,880
Dan Forsman	70	71	71	71	283	16,200
Stephen Gangluff	69	69	74	71	283	16,200
Jose Maria Olazabal	70	70	73	70	283	16,200
Brenden Pappas	69	71	68	75	283	16,200
Joey Sindelar	68	68	77	70	283	16,200
Tommy Armour	69	69	70	76	284	11,583
Mark Brooks	69	67	77	71	284	11,583
Tom Byrum	68	74	68	74	284	11,583
Fred Couples	72	69	69	74	284	11,583
Brent Geiberger	73	69	72	70	284	11,583
J.P. Hayes	68	73	69	74	284	11,583
Mike Sposa	72	69	70	73	284	11,583
Kirk Triplett	71	67	68	78	284	11,583
Jay Don Blake	71	70	75	69	285	8,616
Paul Claxton	71	71	72	71	285	8,616
Scott Dunlap	69	71	70	75	285	8,616
Mathew Goggin	71	69	69	76	285	8,616
Donnie Hammond	69	72	71	73	285	8,616
Miguel Angel Jimenez	69	70	71	75	285	8,616
Mark Calcavecchia	71	67	72	76	286	8,136
Deane Pappas	68	70	73	75	286	8,136
Tommy Tolles	71	70	72	73	286	8,136
Kent Jones	68	72	71	76	287	7,992
Michael Clark	73	67	72	76	288	7,848
Gary Nicklaus	70	71	76	71	288	7,848
John Senden	67	74	77	70	288	7,848
Carlos Franco	70	68	73	78	289	7,632
Brian Henninger	69	71	77	72	289	7,632
Grant Waite	72	69	75	73	289	7,632
Tim Herron	69	71	81	69	290	7,380
Brett Quigley	73	66	77	74	290	7,380
Jerry Smith	68	72	73	77	290	7,380
Hidemichi Tanaka	67	72	81	70	290	7,380
Woody Austin	72	69	71	79	291	7,128
Jeff Brehaut	71	71	80	69	291	7,128
Brian Watts	66	74	78	73	291	7,128
Russ Cochran	73	66	78	76	293	6,984
Mike Hulbert	72	70	77	75	294	6,912
Glen Day	72	69	79	75	295	6,804
David Hutsell	68	72	76	79	295	6,804

Buick Classic

Westchester Country Club, Harrison, New York
Par 36-35–71; 6,722 yards

June 6-9
purse, $3,500,000

		SCORES			TOTAL	MONEY
Chris Smith	66	69	67	70	272	$630,000
David Gossett	66	67	70	71	274	261,333.34
Pat Perez	67	70	67	70	274	261,333.33

	SCORES				TOTAL	MONEY
Loren Roberts	64	68	71	71	274	261,333.33
Stewart Cink	67	69	71	68	275	133,000
Ian Leggatt	69	68	67	71	275	133,000
Jerry Kelly	65	70	70	71	276	112,875
Tom Lehman	68	72	68	68	276	112,875
Stephen Ames	70	71	66	71	278	94,500
Jim Furyk	68	69	74	67	278	94,500
Peter Lonard	71	68	69	70	278	94,500
Brad Faxon	69	71	70	69	279	66,500
Sergio Garcia	68	70	70	71	279	66,500
Len Mattiace	69	70	72	68	279	66,500
Bryce Molder	71	66	71	71	279	66,500
David Toms	70	68	68	73	279	66,500
Mike Weir	70	71	70	68	279	66,500
Woody Austin	69	69	74	68	280	42,600
Jose Coceres	68	68	71	73	280	42,600
Brent Geiberger	68	75	69	68	280	42,600
Craig Parry	67	75	69	69	280	42,600
Kevin Sutherland	73	69	67	71	280	42,600
Hal Sutton	71	68	67	74	280	42,600
Phil Tataurangi	69	70	70	71	280	42,600
Fred Funk	69	73	71	68	281	25,593.75
Brian Gay	68	70	72	71	281	25,593.75
Retief Goosen	67	72	70	72	281	25,593.75
Paul Gow	68	73	68	72	281	25,593.75
Skip Kendall	70	72	70	69	281	25,593.75
Phil Mickelson	69	70	71	71	281	25,593.75
Michael Muehr	65	76	68	72	281	25,593.75
Mike Sposa	69	70	72	70	281	25,593.75
Angel Cabrera	69	73	71	69	282	18,491.67
K.J. Choi	72	67	73	70	282	18,491.67
Dudley Hart	73	65	74	70	282	18,491.67
Frank Nobilo	69	70	74	69	282	18,491.67
Briny Baird	70	70	68	74	282	18,491.66
Cameron Beckman	73	65	73	71	282	18,491.66
Fred Couples	68	72	70	73	283	13,650
Steve Elkington	67	71	71	74	283	13,650
Ernie Els	68	69	72	74	283	13,650
Shaun Micheel	69	68	73	73	283	13,650
Joey Sindelar	72	71	68	72	283	13,650
Duffy Waldorf	72	71	70	70	283	13,650
Jay Williamson	69	72	72	70	283	13,650
J.J. Henry	71	68	70	75	284	9,922.50
Glen Hnatiuk	73	70	70	71	284	9,922.50
Lee Janzen	73	69	70	72	284	9,922.50
Bo Van Pelt	70	71	71	72	284	9,922.50
Jim Carter	67	72	73	73	285	8,442
Brandel Chamblee	70	71	73	71	285	8,442
John Rollins	67	75	72	71	285	8,442
Bob Tway	71	71	71	72	285	8,442
Richard Zokol	73	70	70	72	285	8,442
Fulton Allem	71	69	70	76	286	7,910
Luke Donald	73	68	70	75	286	7,910
Brad Elder	68	74	71	73	286	7,910
Steve Flesch	73	70	71	72	286	7,910
Davis Love	71	69	72	74	286	7,910
Jeff Gove	71	72	71	73	287	7,595
Scott Hoch	70	69	74	74	287	7,595
Corey Pavin	70	72	73	72	287	7,595
Kenneth Staton	74	67	73	73	287	7,595

	SCORES				TOTAL	MONEY
Paul Azinger	69	74	73	72	288	7,210
Jonathan Byrd	75	67	70	76	288	7,210
David Frost	69	72	71	76	288	7,210
Neal Lancaster	69	70	73	76	288	7,210
Franklin Langham	71	71	74	72	288	7,210
Jeff Maggert	72	71	67	78	288	7,210
Brett Quigley	75	68	74	71	288	7,210
Toshimitsu Izawa	72	70	74	73	289	6,895
Brett Wetterich	72	68	73	76	289	6,895
Robert Allenby	67	75	75	73	290	6,615
Pat Bates	69	72	74	75	290	6,615
Mark Brooks	69	74	75	72	290	6,615
Greg Chalmers	74	68	72	76	290	6,615
Miguel Angel Jimenez	73	70	70	77	290	6,615
Billy Mayfair	70	71	72	77	290	6,615
Jay Haas	70	73	78	71	292	6,265
Jonathan Kaye	71	70	77	74	292	6,265
Gary Nicklaus	71	70	77	74	292	6,265
Adam Scott	72	71	77	72	292	6,265
Danny Ellis	73	69	77	77	296	6,090

U.S. Open Championship

Bethpage State Park, Black Course, Farmingdale, New York June 13-16
Par 35-35–70; 7,214 yards purse, $5,500,000

	SCORES				TOTAL	MONEY
Tiger Woods	67	68	70	72	277	$1,000,000
Phil Mickelson	70	73	67	70	280	585,000
Jeff Maggert	69	73	68	72	282	362,356
Sergio Garcia	68	74	67	74	283	252,546
Nick Faldo	70	76	66	73	285	182,882
Scott Hoch	71	75	70	69	285	182,882
Billy Mayfair	69	74	68	74	285	182,882
Tom Byrum	72	72	70	72	286	138,669
Padraig Harrington	70	68	73	75	286	138,669
Nick Price	72	75	69	70	286	138,669
Peter Lonard	73	74	73	67	287	119,357
Robert Allenby	74	70	67	77	288	102,338
Justin Leonard	73	71	68	76	288	102,338
Jay Haas	73	73	70	72	288	102,338
Dudley Hart	69	76	70	73	288	102,338
Shigeki Maruyama	76	67	73	73	289	86,372
Steve Stricker	72	77	69	71	289	86,372
Luke Donald	76	72	70	72	290	68,995
Steve Flesch	72	72	75	71	290	68,995
Charles Howell	71	74	70	75	290	68,995
Thomas Levet	71	77	70	72	290	68,995
Mark O'Meara	76	70	69	75	290	68,995
Craig Stadler	74	72	70	74	290	68,995
Jim Carter	77	73	70	71	291	47,439
Darren Clarke	74	74	72	71	291	47,439
Chris DiMarco	74	74	72	71	291	47,439
Ernie Els	73	74	70	74	291	47,439
Davis Love	71	71	72	77	291	47,439
Jeff Sluman	73	73	72	73	291	47,439
Jason Caron	75	72	72	73	292	35,639

	SCORES				TOTAL	MONEY
K.J. Choi	69	73	73	77	292	35,639
Paul Lawrie	73	73	73	73	292	35,639
Scott McCarron	72	72	70	78	292	35,639
Vijay Singh	75	75	67	75	292	35,639
Shingo Katayama	74	72	74	73	293	31,945
Bernhard Langer	72	76	70	75	293	31,945
Stuart Appleby	77	73	75	69	294	26,783
Thomas Bjorn	71	79	73	71	294	26,783
Niclas Fasth	72	72	74	76	294	26,783
Donnie Hammond	73	77	71	73	294	26,783
Franklin Langham	70	76	74	74	294	26,783
Rocco Mediate	72	72	74	76	294	26,783
Kevin Sutherland	74	75	70	75	294	26,783
Hidemichi Tanaka	73	73	72	76	294	26,783
Tom Lehman	71	76	72	76	295	20,072
David Toms	74	74	70	77	295	20,072
Kenny Perry	74	76	71	74	295	20,072
Jean Van de Velde	71	75	74	75	295	20,072
Robert Karlsson	71	76	72	76	295	20,072
Frank Lickliter	74	76	68	78	296	16,294
Craig Bowden	71	77	74	74	296	16,294
Tim Herron	75	74	73	74	296	16,294
Jose Maria Olazabal	71	77	75	73	296	16,294
Harrison Frazar	74	73	75	75	297	14,764
Ian Leggatt	72	77	72	76	297	14,764
Jesper Parnevik	72	76	69	80	297	14,764
Corey Pavin	74	75	70	78	297	14,764
Brad Lardon	73	73	74	78	298	13,988
John Maginnes	79	69	73	78	299	13,493
Greg Norman	75	73	74	77	299	13,493
Bob Tway	72	78	73	76	299	13,493
Andy Miller	76	74	75	75	300	12,794
Jeev Milkha Singh	75	75	75	75	300	12,794
Paul Stankowski	72	77	77	74	300	12,794
Spike McRoy	75	75	74	77	301	12,340
Angel Cabrera	73	73	79	77	302	12,000
Brad Faxon	75	74	73	80	302	12,000
Kent Jones	76	74	74	79	303	11,546
Len Mattiace	72	73	78	80	303	11,546
John Daly	74	76	81	73	304	11,083
Tom Gillis	71	76	78	79	304	11,083

Out of Final 36 Holes

Mark Calcavecchia	74	77	151
John Cook	74	77	151
Ben Crane	75	76	151
David Duval	78	73	151
Brian Gay	75	76	151
Lucas Glover	74	77	151
Steve Haskins	74	77	151
Matt Kuchar	76	75	151
Colin Montgomerie	75	76	151
Peter O'Malley	75	76	151
Tom Pernice, Jr.	75	76	151
Todd Rose	71	80	151
Kirk Triplett	73	78	151
Stewart Cink	70	82	152
Jim Gallagher, Jr.	75	77	152
Per-Ulrik Johansson	78	74	152

	SCORES		TOTAL
*Taichiro Kiyota	73	79	152
Steve Lowery	70	82	152
Craig Perks	76	76	152
Phil Tataurangi	74	78	152
Mike Weir	78	74	152
*Ricky Barnes	78	75	153
Mark Brooks	75	78	153
Greg Chalmers	72	81	153
Jose Coceres	77	76	153
Ken Duke	76	77	153
Scott Dunlap	75	78	153
Jim Furyk	73	80	153
Brent Geiberger	75	78	153
John Huston	75	78	153
Lee Janzen	76	77	153
Tom Kite	80	73	153
Scott Verplank	75	78	153
Jimmy Walker	77	76	153
Stephen Ames	77	77	154
Billy Andrade	72	82	154
Jay Don Blake	74	80	154
Bob Estes	81	73	154
Kelly Gibson	77	77	154
Retief Goosen	79	75	154
Steve Jones	74	80	154
Paul McGinley	75	79	154
Jim McGovern	75	79	154
Ben Portie	77	77	154
Andrew Sanders	77	77	154
Hal Sutton	77	77	154
Woody Austin	79	76	155
Michael Campbell	72	83	155
Pete Jordan	76	79	155
Jerry Kelly	76	79	155
*Ryan Moore	76	79	155
Michael Muehr	77	78	155
Joey Sindelar	76	79	155
Michael Allen	77	79	156
David Frost	75	81	156
Blaine McCallister	77	79	156
Mario Tiziani	76	80	156
Paul Azinger	75	82	157
Olin Browne	76	81	157
Trevor Dodds	77	80	157
Craig Parry	79	78	157
Steve Pate	82	75	157
Pat Perez	76	81	157
Adam Scott	77	80	157
Kaname Yokoo	78	79	157
Joe Durant	81	77	158
Matt Gogel	78	80	158
Paul Gow	76	82	158
Paul Goydos	80	78	158
Jerry Haas	80	78	158
George McNeil	79	79	158
David Howell	78	81	159
Charles Raulerson	78	81	159
Tony Soerries	84	76	160
Michael Clark	83	80	163
Hale Irwin	82	81	163

	SCORES				TOTAL
Darrell Kestner	77	86			163
Scott Parel	82	83			165
Heath Slocum	83	82			165
Adam Speirs	80	85			165
*Derek Tolan	78	88			166
Wayne Grady	84	83			167
Felix Casas	82	92			174
Toshimitsu Izawa	80				WD

(Professionals who did not complete 72 holes received $5,000.)

Canon Greater Hartford Open

TPC at River Highlands, Hartford, Connecticut
Par 35-35–70; 6,820 yards

June 20-23
purse, $4,000,000

	SCORES				TOTAL	MONEY
Phil Mickelson	69	67	66	64	266	$720,000
Jonathan Kaye	65	67	65	70	267	352,000
Davis Love	68	64	68	67	267	352,000
Scott Verplank	65	70	63	71	269	192,000
Jim Carter	67	69	66	68	270	152,000
Joel Edwards	68	71	68	63	270	152,000
Dan Forsman	68	70	69	64	271	124,666.67
Skip Kendall	65	72	67	67	271	124,666.67
Scott Hoch	67	66	66	72	271	124,666.66
Ernie Els	69	70	69	64	272	100,000
David Frost	72	68	67	65	272	100,000
Jeff Gove	73	64	68	67	272	100,000
Pat Bates	70	71	64	68	273	72,800
Mathew Goggin	66	70	70	67	273	72,800
Tim Herron	65	72	66	70	273	72,800
Kenny Perry	70	71	64	68	273	72,800
Hidemichi Tanaka	64	70	68	71	273	72,800
Billy Andrade	70	70	69	65	274	58,000
Briny Baird	65	67	73	69	274	58,000
Mark Calcavecchia	68	70	68	69	275	41,714.29
Sergio Garcia	69	67	69	70	275	41,714.29
Frank Nobilo	69	69	71	66	275	41,714.29
Brett Quigley	64	71	70	70	275	41,714.29
Peter Lonard	66	68	70	71	275	41,714.28
Steve Pate	66	70	66	73	275	41,714.28
Kaname Yokoo	65	68	71	71	275	41,714.28
Steve Allan	66	73	67	70	276	27,800
Robin Freeman	69	70	70	67	276	27,800
Paul Gow	73	66	64	73	276	27,800
Kent Jones	70	68	69	69	276	27,800
Len Mattiace	70	64	73	69	276	27,800
Kirk Triplett	66	70	69	71	276	27,800
Notah Begay	67	72	69	69	277	21,133.34
Charles Howell	71	69	72	65	277	21,133.34
Stewart Cink	69	72	67	69	277	21,133.33
Edward Fryatt	72	68	68	69	277	21,133.33
David Peoples	69	65	70	73	277	21,133.33
Vijay Singh	70	71	66	70	277	21,133.33
Jay Don Blake	72	68	69	69	278	14,416
Olin Browne	72	64	70	72	278	14,416

		SCORES			TOTAL	MONEY
Michael Clark	69	72	67	70	278	14,416
Chris DiMarco	70	66	71	71	278	14,416
Danny Ellis	71	67	70	70	278	14,416
Glen Hnatiuk	66	71	69	72	278	14,416
Mike Hulbert	70	69	69	70	278	14,416
Tim Petrovic	71	68	68	71	278	14,416
Joey Sindelar	68	70	71	69	278	14,416
Grant Waite	69	68	68	73	278	14,416
James Driscoll	69	72	67	71	279	9,872
John Huston	69	71	71	68	279	9,872
Peter Jacobsen	67	69	70	73	279	9,872
Tom Pernice, Jr.	68	71	72	68	279	9,872
Chris Riley	70	66	70	73	279	9,872
Steve Elkington	70	71	72	67	280	9,000
Robert Gamez	70	69	71	70	280	9,000
Dudley Hart	72	68	72	68	280	9,000
Tripp Isenhour	69	67	72	72	280	9,000
Brandt Jobe	67	70	73	70	280	9,000
Frank Lickliter	68	72	67	73	280	9,000
Corey Pavin	67	74	72	67	280	9,000
Esteban Toledo	74	64	72	70	280	9,000
Fulton Allem	71	69	69	72	281	8,640
Tommy Armour	70	69	68	75	282	8,400
Brian Bateman	73	68	69	72	282	8,400
Brad Faxon	74	66	69	73	282	8,400
Dicky Pride	68	73	69	72	282	8,400
John Riegger	71	70	72	69	282	8,400
Craig Barlow	70	69	68	76	283	8,160
Brad Elder	72	68	72	72	284	8,000
Billy Mayfair	71	70	71	72	284	8,000
Joe Ogilvie	70	69	74	71	284	8,000
Willie Wood	69	72	74	71	286	7,840
Brian Henninger	72	69	68	78	287	7,680
Miguel Angel Jimenez	69	71	71	76	287	7,680
Carl Paulson	68	66	81	72	287	7,680
Deane Pappas	67	72	77	72	288	7,520

FedEx St. Jude Classic

TPC at Southwind, Memphis, Tennessee
Par 36-35–71; 7,006 yards

June 27-30
purse, $3,800,000

		SCORES			TOTAL	MONEY
Len Mattiace	69	68	65	64	266	$684,000
Tim Petrovic	65	68	66	68	267	410,400
Notah Begay	66	65	68	69	268	258,400
David Toms	68	68	65	68	269	182,400
Jim Carter	68	67	67	68	270	133,475
David Howser	66	70	70	64	270	133,475
Tripp Isenhour	72	65	64	69	270	133,475
Matt Kuchar	66	66	67	71	270	133,475
Robert Allenby	72	67	66	66	271	95,000
Pat Bates	68	63	69	71	271	95,000
Robert Gamez	70	64	69	68	271	95,000
Neal Lancaster	70	67	64	70	271	95,000
Justin Leonard	66	66	71	68	271	95,000
Tom Byrum	73	63	69	67	272	64,600
Jason Hill	68	66	70	68	272	64,600

	SCORES				TOTAL	MONEY
Glen Hnatiuk	65	65	65	77	272	64,600
Steve Pate	67	68	69	68	272	64,600
Loren Roberts	69	68	66	69	272	64,600
Robert Damron	68	68	72	65	273	37,723.64
Glen Day	70	68	68	67	273	37,723.64
Stephen Gangluff	69	69	69	66	273	37,723.64
Tim Herron	72	65	68	68	273	37,723.64
Shaun Micheel	72	68	66	67	273	37,723.64
Boo Weekley	67	68	75	63	273	37,723.64
Garrett Willis	66	72	68	67	273	37,723.64
David Edwards	70	69	64	70	273	37,723.63
Jay Haas	67	64	73	69	273	37,723.63
Mike Heinen	70	67	65	71	273	37,723.63
Kevin Sutherland	70	68	66	69	273	37,723.63
Brian Bateman	68	68	68	70	274	24,130
Bob Estes	69	69	66	70	274	24,130
Donnie Hammond	70	66	67	71	274	24,130
Ian Leggatt	71	67	64	72	274	24,130
Paul Claxton	73	67	63	72	275	20,045
Brian Gay	69	70	68	68	275	20,045
Nick Price	68	71	70	66	275	20,045
Chris Riley	72	67	67	69	275	20,045
Steve Flesch	69	67	68	72	276	16,340
David Gossett	71	65	68	72	276	16,340
Bob May	68	69	72	67	276	16,340
Tommy Tolles	71	68	69	68	276	16,340
Kirk Triplett	69	67	69	71	276	16,340
Briny Baird	70	70	68	69	277	11,856
Cameron Beckman	69	67	70	71	277	11,856
Jess Daley	68	70	69	70	277	11,856
Joel Edwards	73	63	71	70	277	11,856
Edward Fryatt	67	69	69	72	277	11,856
Jim McGovern	73	66	68	70	277	11,856
Ted Tryba	68	68	73	68	277	11,856
Brian Henninger	74	65	71	68	278	9,253
Greg Kraft	68	70	68	72	278	9,253
Spike McRoy	68	71	67	72	278	9,253
Kenneth Staton	71	66	71	70	278	9,253
Paul Azinger	73	66	68	72	279	8,626
Rich Beem	67	68	67	77	279	8,626
Frank Nobilo	72	64	73	70	279	8,626
John Riegger	66	68	74	71	279	8,626
John Senden	68	70	67	74	279	8,626
Grant Waite	70	68	69	72	279	8,626
Doug Barron	67	67	70	76	280	8,284
J.J. Henry	71	69	71	69	280	8,284
Sean Murphy	68	70	65	77	280	8,284
Robin Freeman	70	67	68	76	281	7,942
Jim Gallagher, Jr.	69	70	74	68	281	7,942
J.L. Lewis	68	71	68	74	281	7,942
David Peoples	71	67	73	70	281	7,942
Matt Peterson	72	67	70	72	281	7,942
Dicky Pride	70	70	72	69	281	7,942
Jerry Pate	69	70	73	71	283	7,676
David Morland	69	68	70	77	284	7,562
Mike Sposa	72	68	72	72	284	7,562
Brenden Pappas	71	68	71	77	287	7,410
Carl Paulson	69	69	72	77	287	7,410
Paul Goydos	72	68	71	77	288	7,296
John Daly	66	70	79	74	289	7,220

Advil Western Open

Cog Hill Golf & Country Club, Lemont, Illinois
Par 36-36–72; 7,073 yards

July 4-7
purse, $4,000,000

	SCORES				TOTAL	MONEY
Jerry Kelly	67	69	68	65	269	$720,000
Davis Love	67	70	68	66	271	432,000
Brandt Jobe	69	69	69	66	273	272,000
John Cook	67	66	72	69	274	192,000
Stuart Appleby	70	65	71	69	275	135,600
Neal Lancaster	68	68	67	72	275	135,600
Peter Lonard	71	71	68	65	275	135,600
Chris Riley	70	70	66	69	275	135,600
Duffy Waldorf	70	70	66	69	275	135,600
Robert Allenby	69	67	65	75	276	100,000
Bob Estes	66	70	68	72	276	100,000
Nick Price	73	68	66	69	276	100,000
Steve Stricker	74	67	71	65	277	80,000
Scott Verplank	67	69	70	71	277	80,000
David Frost	67	73	66	72	278	64,000
John Riegger	74	69	66	69	278	64,000
Vijay Singh	68	67	72	71	278	64,000
David Toms	68	73	70	67	278	64,000
Bob Tway	70	72	65	71	278	64,000
Briny Baird	71	69	70	69	279	44,960
Jonathan Byrd	67	68	75	69	279	44,960
Luke Donald	68	70	71	70	279	44,960
Paul Gow	69	68	70	72	279	44,960
John Senden	71	70	66	72	279	44,960
Stephen Gangluff	69	70	74	67	280	33,600
Brent Geiberger	73	68	72	67	280	33,600
Tom Byrum	68	71	72	70	281	24,981.82
Joe Durant	68	68	73	72	281	24,981.82
Joel Edwards	69	71	72	69	281	24,981.82
David Gossett	65	73	71	72	281	24,981.82
J.J. Henry	70	70	71	70	281	24,981.82
Bradley Hughes	68	74	70	69	281	24,981.82
Jonathan Kaye	71	70	71	69	281	24,981.82
John Rollins	73	68	73	67	281	24,981.82
Rory Sabbatini	71	70	70	70	281	24,981.82
Jess Daley	74	67	67	73	281	24,981.81
Lee Janzen	72	67	70	72	281	24,981.81
Greg Chalmers	71	72	69	70	282	17,200
Steve Elkington	71	67	72	72	282	17,200
Carl Paulson	71	68	72	71	282	17,200
Joey Sindelar	69	70	69	74	282	17,200
Mike Weir	71	72	68	71	282	17,200
Steve Allan	72	71	71	69	283	11,688
Cameron Beckman	73	66	71	73	283	11,688
Tim Clark	70	71	73	69	283	11,688
Steve Flesch	73	69	69	72	283	11,688
Carlos Franco	71	71	72	69	283	11,688
Harrison Frazar	71	68	71	73	283	11,688
Brian Gay	69	73	70	71	283	11,688
Rocco Mediate	69	68	74	72	283	11,688
Shaun Micheel	69	70	71	73	283	11,688
Loren Roberts	71	72	68	72	283	11,688
Tommy Armour	74	68	68	74	284	9,216
Glen Day	69	72	72	71	284	9,216

	SCORES				TOTAL	MONEY
Steve Lowery	70	71	70	73	284	9,216
Jeff Sluman	70	71	71	72	284	9,216
Kevin Sutherland	75	65	68	76	284	9,216
Glen Hnatiuk	71	72	71	71	285	8,880
Skip Kendall	74	69	72	70	285	8,880
Geoff Ogilvy	70	72	67	76	285	8,880
Bob Burns	73	70	70	73	286	8,480
Chad Campbell	72	70	72	72	286	8,480
Justin Leonard	69	72	70	75	286	8,480
Blaine McCallister	69	72	73	72	286	8,480
Michael Muehr	71	72	70	73	286	8,480
Bo Van Pelt	73	69	72	72	286	8,480
Grant Waite	70	72	73	71	286	8,480
Matt Gogel	70	70	69	78	287	8,000
Frank Nobilo	71	70	78	68	287	8,000
Craig Perks	71	72	72	72	287	8,000
Tom Pernice, Jr.	69	72	76	70	287	8,000
Mike Sposa	71	72	69	75	287	8,000
Craig Barlow	70	71	77	70	288	7,600
Scott Dunlap	73	70	73	72	288	7,600
Franklin Langham	68	70	75	75	288	7,600
Heath Slocum	72	71	72	73	288	7,600
Jerry Smith	71	72	74	71	288	7,600
Rich Beem	71	72	74	73	290	7,280
Jeff Gove	73	70	72	75	290	7,280
Bryce Molder	71	72	74	73	290	7,280
Notah Begay	68	74	74	75	291	7,080
Bubba Dickerson	72	71	76	72	291	7,080
Robert Damron	75	68	76	73	292	6,960
Scott McCarron	69	72	76	76	293	6,880
Mark Brooks	73	69	77	76	295	6,800
Ben Crane	71	72	72	81	296	6,720

Greater Milwaukee Open

Brown Deer Park Golf Course, Milwaukee, Wisconsin
Par 36-35–71; 6,759 yards

July 11-14
purse, $3,100,000

	SCORES				TOTAL	MONEY
Jeff Sluman	64	66	63	68	261	$558,000
Tim Herron	68	66	65	66	265	272,800
Steve Lowery	66	65	64	70	265	272,800
Kenny Perry	64	70	67	65	266	148,800
Greg Chalmers	67	66	65	69	267	113,150
J.P. Hayes	68	69	63	67	267	113,150
Joey Sindelar	69	68	65	65	267	113,150
Tommy Armour	63	67	71	67	268	93,000
Kirk Triplett	66	64	67	71	268	93,000
Skip Kendall	68	67	69	65	269	80,600
Chris Smith	67	70	64	68	269	80,600
Chad Campbell	66	66	71	67	270	60,760
Robert Damron	69	63	71	67	270	60,760
Dan Forsman	69	63	69	69	270	60,760
Mathew Goggin	70	69	67	64	270	60,760
Steve Stricker	65	72	66	67	270	60,760
Kelly Gibson	65	70	71	65	271	40,565.72
Grant Waite	70	66	70	65	271	40,565.72

	SCORES				TOTAL	MONEY
Kaname Yokoo	68	71	67	65	271	40,565.72
Bart Bryant	70	67	71	63	271	40,565.71
Jess Daley	67	67	68	69	271	40,565.71
Scott Hoch	69	64	70	68	271	40,565.71
Bob May	68	67	66	70	271	40,565.71
Rich Beem	69	70	69	64	272	27,280
David Berganio, Jr.	69	70	68	65	272	27,280
Hidemichi Tanaka	68	67	68	69	272	27,280
Mark Calcavecchia	70	67	68	68	273	22,010
Glen Day	66	70	70	67	273	22,010
Robert Gamez	71	68	69	65	273	22,010
Brandt Jobe	68	67	70	68	273	22,010
Bo Van Pelt	64	68	78	63	273	22,010
Pat Bates	70	67	70	67	274	16,430
Joe Durant	69	68	67	70	274	16,430
Brian Henninger	70	69	68	67	274	16,430
Glen Hnatiuk	69	70	68	67	274	16,430
Shigeki Maruyama	65	70	69	70	274	16,430
Bryce Molder	65	71	67	71	274	16,430
David Peoples	66	67	67	74	274	16,430
Brett Quigley	74	63	68	69	274	16,430
Russ Cochran	69	70	67	69	275	12,710
J.J. Henry	67	69	69	70	275	12,710
Matt Peterson	70	67	71	67	275	12,710
Ben Crane	70	69	69	68	276	10,230
Jim Gallagher, Jr.	67	71	69	69	276	10,230
Mike Heinen	66	69	71	70	276	10,230
Joe Ogilvie	68	67	69	72	276	10,230
Steve Pate	68	69	70	69	276	10,230
Robin Freeman	69	68	70	70	277	7,633.75
Donnie Hammond	69	70	68	70	277	7,633.75
Neal Lancaster	70	67	70	70	277	7,633.75
Larry Mize	71	68	69	69	277	7,633.75
Gene Sauers	71	66	69	71	277	7,633.75
Mike Springer	66	72	70	69	277	7,633.75
Craig Stadler	70	68	67	72	277	7,633.75
Phil Tataurangi	70	66	71	70	277	7,633.75
Michael Clark	67	72	68	71	278	6,944
Paul Claxton	70	65	74	69	278	6,944
James Driscoll	69	66	74	69	278	6,944
Bradley Hughes	66	68	73	71	278	6,944
Corey Pavin	68	71	70	69	278	6,944
*Jon Turcott	66	73	71	68	278	
Woody Austin	73	66	71	69	279	6,603
Brent Geiberger	66	69	73	71	279	6,603
David Gossett	66	72	72	69	279	6,603
Jason Hill	68	69	70	72	279	6,603
Charles Howell	69	68	71	71	279	6,603
Mario Tiziani	71	65	69	74	279	6,603
Michael Bradley	67	71	73	69	280	6,293
Carlos Franco	68	65	71	76	280	6,293
Geoff Ogilvy	70	67	68	75	280	6,293
Richard Zokol	70	67	71	72	280	6,293
Danny Ellis	71	68	70	72	281	6,107
Jerry Smith	70	69	71	71	281	6,107
Brian Bateman	67	67	72	76	282	5,859
Ronnie Black	67	71	72	72	282	5,859
Brandel Chamblee	70	68	73	71	282	5,859
Jeff Gove	69	69	71	73	282	5,859
Paul Goydos	68	71	71	72	282	5,859

	SCORES				TOTAL	MONEY
Michael Muehr	70	69	70	73	282	5,859
Lucas Glover	70	69	74	70	283	5,549
Frank Nobilo	69	69	75	70	283	5,549
Deane Pappas	64	72	74	73	283	5,549
Fred Wadsworth	71	68	70	74	283	5,549
Brad Elder	69	69	75	72	285	5,332
Andrew Magee	69	69	74	73	285	5,332
D.A. Weibring	66	73	75	71	285	5,332

B.C. Open

En-Joie Golf Club, Endicott, New York
Par 37-35–72; 6,974 yards

July 18-21
purse, $2,100,000

	SCORES				TOTAL	MONEY
Spike McRoy	70	65	69	65	269	$378,000
Fred Funk	71	66	66	67	270	226,800
Glen Day	67	69	67	68	271	94,710
Robert Gamez	68	68	69	66	271	94,710
Brian Henninger	67	69	70	65	271	94,710
Cliff Kresge	72	67	70	62	271	94,710
Shaun Micheel	65	65	67	74	271	94,710
Eduardo Herrera	69	68	67	68	272	65,100
Paul Gow	67	66	67	73	273	58,800
John Rollins	71	69	65	68	273	58,800
Dennis Paulson	69	72	66	67	274	50,400
Hidemichi Tanaka	71	66	67	70	274	50,400
Notah Begay	70	69	67	69	275	37,100
Greg Chalmers	69	66	73	67	275	37,100
Kevin Johnson	67	68	70	70	275	37,100
Carl Paulson	69	69	69	68	275	37,100
Matt Peterson	68	69	66	72	275	37,100
Tommy Tolles	69	68	69	69	275	37,100
Pat Bates	72	69	68	67	276	24,570
Kelly Gibson	70	68	68	70	276	24,570
Donnie Hammond	67	70	70	69	276	24,570
Brandt Jobe	72	67	65	72	276	24,570
Hank Kuehne	76	63	69	68	276	24,570
Dan Pohl	69	71	71	65	276	24,570
Steve Allan	69	67	68	73	277	15,356.25
Paul Claxton	65	69	73	70	277	15,356.25
Glen Hnatiuk	69	69	72	67	277	15,356.25
Tripp Isenhour	65	70	68	74	277	15,356.25
Joe Ogilvie	65	70	70	72	277	15,356.25
Tom Scherrer	69	71	71	66	277	15,356.25
Joey Sindelar	69	70	67	71	277	15,356.25
Mike Springer	70	71	68	68	277	15,356.25
Jess Daley	71	69	68	70	278	10,860
David Edwards	72	68	67	71	278	10,860
Scott Gump	69	71	70	68	278	10,860
John Morse	69	70	65	74	278	10,860
David Peoples	67	69	68	74	278	10,860
Bo Van Pelt	70	65	73	70	278	10,860
Brian Wilson	66	72	68	72	278	10,860
Michael Clark	68	69	71	71	279	7,560
Erik Compton	68	72	70	69	279	7,560
James Driscoll	71	67	69	72	279	7,560

	SCORES				TOTAL	MONEY
Carlos Franco	72	66	75	66	279	7,560
Robin Freeman	70	70	70	69	279	7,560
Dicky Pride	68	71	72	68	279	7,560
Heath Slocum	71	70	70	68	279	7,560
Phil Tataurangi	70	65	72	72	279	7,560
Michael Allen	74	67	72	67	280	5,171.25
Jeff Gove	73	66	72	69	280	5,171.25
J.P. Hayes	67	70	71	72	280	5,171.25
Jim McGovern	71	67	67	75	280	5,171.25
David Morland	65	73	68	74	280	5,171.25
Gene Sauers	68	71	71	70	280	5,171.25
Greg Twiggs	68	70	72	70	280	5,171.25
Grant Waite	72	67	65	76	280	5,171.25
Jim Gallagher, Jr.	67	68	72	74	281	4,599
Bill Glasson	70	67	71	73	281	4,599
Jimmy Green	70	71	71	69	281	4,599
Mike Hulbert	68	70	70	73	281	4,599
Michael Long	71	67	70	73	281	4,599
Michael Muehr	68	69	70	74	281	4,599
Dave Rummells	77	64	70	70	281	4,599
Jeff Sluman	72	67	71	71	281	4,599
Stan Utley	69	69	69	74	281	4,599
Brian Watts	70	67	71	73	281	4,599
Dave Barr	73	67	70	72	282	4,263
Brad Bryant	69	72	71	70	282	4,263
Barry Cheesman	69	70	72	71	282	4,263
Trevor Dodds	69	71	72	70	282	4,263
Edward Fryatt	74	67	72	69	282	4,263
Craig Stadler	73	65	72	72	282	4,263
Mathew Goggin	74	66	73	70	283	4,053
Mike Heinen	70	70	74	69	283	4,053
Jerry Smith	71	69	74	69	283	4,053
Fred Wadsworth	71	70	72	70	283	4,053
Paul Goydos	70	70	74	70	284	3,927
Steve Pate	72	69	73	70	284	3,927
Mark Carnevale	72	69	74	70	285	3,822
Jason Hill	72	68	71	74	285	3,822
Boo Weekley	70	70	75	70	285	3,822
Mike Sposa	73	68	71	74	286	3,738
Mike Deuel	72	69	75	73	289	3,696

John Deere Classic

TPC at Deere Run, Silvis, Illinois
Par 35-36–71; 7,183 yards

July 25-28
purse, $3,000,000

	SCORES				TOTAL	MONEY
J.P. Hayes	67	61	67	67	262	$540,000
Robert Gamez	65	64	66	71	266	324,000
Kirk Triplett	68	67	66	66	267	204,000
Pat Perez	68	65	69	66	268	144,000
Briny Baird	67	64	68	70	269	109,500
Mike Heinen	63	69	66	71	269	109,500
Chris Riley	69	64	66	70	269	109,500
Peter Jacobsen	66	67	69	68	270	90,000
J.L. Lewis	67	69	66	68	270	90,000
Notah Begay	69	65	72	65	271	69,000

	SCORES				TOTAL	MONEY
David Gossett	65	69	67	70	271	69,000
Paul Goydos	69	67	69	66	271	69,000
Andrew Magee	70	67	70	64	271	69,000
John Rollins	69	66	70	66	271	69,000
Bob Burns	69	64	68	71	272	45,000
Joe Durant	67	66	71	68	272	45,000
Joel Edwards	69	69	66	68	272	45,000
Bob May	72	66	70	64	272	45,000
Carl Paulson	69	64	72	67	272	45,000
Dicky Pride	71	66	69	66	272	45,000
John Senden	68	68	68	68	272	45,000
Fred Funk	64	64	73	72	273	30,000
Charles Howell	71	65	70	67	273	30,000
Miguel Angel Jimenez	67	66	68	72	273	30,000
Greg Kraft	71	65	68	69	273	30,000
Pat Bates	70	62	73	69	274	20,850
Jonathan Byrd	69	67	67	71	274	20,850
Brian Henninger	71	67	69	67	274	20,850
Kent Jones	68	68	67	71	274	20,850
Neal Lancaster	69	65	67	73	274	20,850
Tim Petrovic	67	65	68	74	274	20,850
Paul Stankowski	72	64	72	66	274	20,850
Duffy Waldorf	66	68	72	68	274	20,850
Paul Claxton	71	67	71	66	275	15,150
Glen Day	70	66	68	71	275	15,150
Brad Elder	68	69	70	68	275	15,150
Tripp Isenhour	65	68	72	70	275	15,150
Steve Pate	69	70	71	65	275	15,150
Boo Weekley	69	70	69	67	275	15,150
Cameron Beckman	70	68	70	68	276	10,800
Bart Bryant	69	67	69	71	276	10,800
Robert Damron	69	69	70	68	276	10,800
Dan Forsman	68	67	69	72	276	10,800
Lucas Glover	66	66	73	71	276	10,800
Spike McRoy	66	67	74	69	276	10,800
Gene Sauers	66	66	75	69	276	10,800
Stan Utley	70	69	67	70	276	10,800
Brian Claar	70	69	72	66	277	7,457.15
Jeff Gove	66	70	74	67	277	7,457.15
Brian Bateman	68	66	70	73	277	7,457.14
David Berganio, Jr.	66	72	69	70	277	7,457.14
Jim Gallagher, Jr.	70	68	71	68	277	7,457.14
J.J. Henry	67	69	73	68	277	7,457.14
Jerry Smith	66	69	72	70	277	7,457.14
Brian Gay	68	70	69	71	278	6,840
John Riegger	71	68	69	70	278	6,840
Hidemichi Tanaka	67	66	75	70	278	6,840
Kelly Gibson	71	67	74	67	279	6,660
Steve Jones	68	66	74	71	279	6,660
Cliff Kresge	69	70	72	68	279	6,660
Chad Campbell	71	68	70	71	280	6,480
Jay Delsing	70	64	74	72	280	6,480
Robin Freeman	67	72	70	71	280	6,480
Nolan Henke	66	65	76	74	281	6,240
Franklin Langham	68	70	72	71	281	6,240
Michael Long	66	73	73	69	281	6,240
David Morland	74	65	72	70	281	6,240
Richard Zokol	68	70	76	67	281	6,240
David Frost	68	70	74	70	282	6,060
Jess Daley	69	69	74	71	283	5,970

	SCORES			TOTAL	MONEY
Joe Ogilvie	71	66	70	76	283	5,970
Steve Lowery	70	68	73	73	284	5,850
Ted Tryba	70	67	70	77	284	5,850
Pete Jordan	66	70	71	78	285	5,730
Mike Standly	72	66	75	72	285	5,730
Mike Sposa	71	68	76	71	286	5,640
Tommy Armour	70	69	73	76	288	5,550
Mark Carnevale	66	72	75	75	288	5,550

The International

Castle Pines Golf Club, Castle Rock, Colorado   August 1-4
Par 36-36–72; 7,559 yards   purse, $4,500,000

	POINTS			TOTAL	MONEY
Rich Beem	10	0	15	19	44	$810,000
Steve Lowery	8	13	6	16	43	486,000
Mark Brooks	1	14	11	7	33	306,000
Greg Norman	4	0	16	7	27	198,000
Ernie Els	8	6	6	7	27	198,000
Lee Janzen	6	4	6	10	26	162,000
Frank Lickliter	2	-1	14	10	25	145,125
Craig Barlow	7	10	11	-3	25	145,125
Tom Lehman	3	-2	11	11	23	126,000
Craig Perks	3	6	6	8	23	126,000
Ian Leggatt	1	5	12	4	22	108,000
Heath Slocum	9	-1	7	7	22	108,000
Brian Watts	-1	7	8	7	21	94,500
Craig Stadler	2	-1	9	10	20	78,750
Glen Day	3	3	8	6	20	78,750
Chris Riley	8	1	8	3	20	78,750
Geoff Ogilvy	7	4	7	2	20	78,750
Sergio Garcia	7	-5	19	-2	19	67,500
Billy Mayfair	10	1	1	6	18	60,750
Charles Howell	-1	4	9	6	18	60,750
Dudley Hart	7	-5	9	6	17	52,200
Phil Tataurangi	7	0	4	6	17	52,200
Fred Couples	4	-2	10	4	16	41,400
John Rollins	5	0	6	5	16	41,400
J.J. Henry	-1	4	9	4	16	41,400
K.J. Choi	0	1	10	5	16	41,400
Bob Tway	5	-3	13	0	15	34,650
Jerry Smith	0	2	8	4	14	33,300
Jeff Quinney	9	-1	2	2	12	31,950
Robin Freeman	4	3	4	0	11	27,945
Jay Haas	8	3	4	-4	11	27,945
Esteban Toledo	3	4	5	-1	11	27,945
Vijay Singh	5	2	3	1	11	27,945
Rory Sabbatini	3	2	6	0	11	27,945
Steve Pate	11	0	3	-5	9	24,300
Steve Stricker	3	1	16	-12	8	22,612.50
Rodney Pampling	-1	4	7	-2	8	22,612.50
Rafael Gomez	-3	5	8	-3	7	21,150

Out of Final 18 Holes

Chris DiMarco	-2	2	9	9	18,900
Tom Scherrer	1	3	5	9	18,900

	POINTS			TOTAL	MONEY
Brent Geiberger	6	-5	8	9	18,900
Stewart Cink	7	-7	9	9	18,900
Steve Jones	5	-4	7	8	16,200
Bob Burns	5	3	0	8	16,200
Duffy Waldorf	9	-8	6	7	13,545
Brian Bateman	3	-4	8	7	13,545
Hunter Haas	8	-4	3	7	13,545
Bubba Dickerson	5	-5	7	7	13,545
Ken Green	5	2	-1	6	10,995
Davis Love	5	-7	8	6	10,995
Kirk Triplett	3	3	0	6	10,995
Robert Damron	2	1	3	6	10,995
Paul Gow	-5	6	5	6	10,995
Ricardo Gonzalez	7	-8	7	6	10,995
Steve Elkington	1	-2	6	5	10,170
John Huston	-2	2	5	5	10,170
Chris Smith	0	1	4	5	10,170
Woody Austin	-4	6	3	5	10,170
John Senden	9	-8	4	5	10,170
Andrew Magee	0	-2	6	4	9,810
Jose Maria Olazabal	5	4	-5	4	9,810
Pat Bates	3	-3	4	4	9,810
Shaun Micheel	1	1	1	3	9,630
Tim Petrovic	7	-3	-2	2	9,540
Lee Porter	-2	4	-2	0	9,450
Hank Kuehne	9	-8	-2	-1	9,360
Billy Andrade	2	-2	-2	-2	9,135
Olin Browne	2	-4	0	-2	9,135
Bart Bryant	6	-7	-1	-2	9,135
Franklin Langham	5	-4	-3	-2	9,135
Greg Chalmers	5	0	-8	-3	8,865
Tim Clark	0	-1	-2	-3	8,865
Tim Herron	-2	0	-5	-7	8,730

Buick Open

Warwick Hills Golf & Country Club,
Grand Blanc, Michigan
Par 36-36–72; 7,127 yards

August 8-11
purse, $3,300,000

	SCORES				TOTAL	MONEY
Tiger Woods	67	63	71	70	271	$594,000
Fred Funk	71	66	67	71	275	217,800
Mark O'Meara	68	69	70	68	275	217,800
Esteban Toledo	68	67	67	73	275	217,800
Brian Gay	69	71	67	68	275	217,800
Paul Azinger	69	70	69	68	276	106,837.50
Tom Byrum	70	68	68	70	276	106,837.50
Bob Tway	71	65	68	72	276	106,837.50
Pat Bates	68	67	73	68	276	106,837.50
David Toms	68	68	70	71	277	79,200
Steve Flesch	72	68	66	71	277	79,200
Jim Furyk	69	67	70	71	277	79,200
J.J. Henry	67	67	76	67	277	79,200
Jay Haas	67	72	72	67	278	51,150
Jeff Sluman	70	67	71	70	278	51,150
Tommy Tolles	72	64	71	71	278	51,150

	SCORES				TOTAL	MONEY
Brian Henninger	71	70	67	70	278	51,150
Bob Burns	72	70	67	69	278	51,150
Glen Day	67	68	75	68	278	51,150
Kent Jones	65	70	70	73	278	51,150
Retief Goosen	70	67	72	69	278	51,150
Tom Pernice, Jr.	69	68	73	69	279	29,747.15
Scott Verplank	69	65	75	70	279	29,747.14
Stephen Ames	70	71	71	67	279	29,747.15
Chris DiMarco	68	72	70	69	279	29,747.14
Stuart Appleby	71	68	70	70	279	29,747.14
Luke Donald	67	69	71	72	279	29,747.14
K.J. Choi	66	74	68	71	279	29,747.14
Phil Mickelson	69	70	69	72	280	19,239
Kenny Perry	73	69	66	72	280	19,239
Brian Watts	71	68	72	69	280	19,239
Matt Peterson	73	69	68	70	280	19,239
Paul Goydos	71	70	69	70	280	19,239
Frank Lickliter	67	73	71	69	280	19,239
David Morland	70	69	71	70	280	19,239
Craig Barlow	71	71	68	70	280	19,239
John Senden	68	69	71	72	280	19,239
Geoff Ogilvy	72	70	69	69	280	19,239
Billy Andrade	68	71	72	70	281	13,860
Robin Freeman	70	69	73	69	281	13,860
Robert Damron	67	69	72	73	281	13,860
Rodney Pampling	69	66	74	72	281	13,860
Blaine McCallister	68	68	71	75	282	9,642.60
Greg Kraft	73	69	70	70	282	9,642.60
Vijay Singh	70	68	74	70	282	9,642.60
Dicky Pride	70	70	71	71	282	9,642.60
Mike Weir	72	67	74	69	282	9,642.60
Craig Perks	70	72	71	69	282	9,642.60
Carlos Franco	68	67	73	74	282	9,642.60
Jose Coceres	73	66	72	71	282	9,642.60
Brett Wetterich	74	68	67	73	282	9,642.60
Ben Crane	70	69	72	71	282	9,642.60
Bart Bryant	67	69	73	74	283	7,331.07
John Cook	69	71	73	70	283	7,331.08
Fred Couples	70	70	72	71	283	7,331.08
J.L. Lewis	70	71	74	68	283	7,331.08
Billy Mayfair	72	70	69	72	283	7,331.08
David Berganio, Jr.	68	74	70	71	283	7,331.08
Jeff Brehaut	72	66	71	74	283	7,331.07
Glen Hnatiuk	74	68	69	72	283	7,331.08
Tom Gillis	71	69	73	70	283	7,331.08
Jay Williamson	71	71	69	72	283	7,331.08
Tom Scherrer	70	72	72	69	283	7,331.08
Carl Paulson	70	70	69	74	283	7,331.07
Richie Coughlan	71	68	71	73	283	7,331.07
Russ Cochran	71	68	68	77	284	6,765
Joel Edwards	69	70	72	73	284	6,765
Corey Pavin	70	72	70	72	284	6,765
Steve Allan	72	68	71	73	284	6,765
Mark Brooks	66	74	73	72	285	6,534
Shaun Micheel	68	72	75	70	285	6,534
Kenneth Staton	74	67	73	71	285	6,534
David Peoples	72	70	74	70	286	6,336
Brad Lardon	69	71	74	72	286	6,336
Mike Heinen	72	68	71	75	286	6,336
Jeff Gallagher	68	74	74	72	288	6,171

	SCORES				TOTAL	MONEY
Heath Slocum	69	73	71	75	288	6,171
Skip Kendall	69	72	76	72	289	6,039
Tripp Isenhour	73	67	76	73	289	6,039
Franklin Langham	73	69	74	74	290	5,940
Phil Tataurangi	71	71	76	75	293	5,874
Brenden Pappas	72	69	79	78	298	5,808

PGA Championship

Hazeltine National Golf Club, Chaska, Minnesota   August 15-18
Par 36-36–72; 7,360 yards   purse, $5,500,000

	SCORES				TOTAL	MONEY
Rich Beem	72	66	72	68	278	$990,000
Tiger Woods	71	69	72	67	279	594,000
Chris Riley	71	70	72	70	283	374,000
Fred Funk	68	70	73	73	284	235,000
Justin Leonard	72	66	69	77	284	235,000
Rocco Mediate	72	73	70	70	285	185,000
Mark Calcavecchia	70	68	74	74	286	172,000
Vijay Singh	71	74	74	68	287	159,000
Jim Furyk	68	73	76	71	288	149,000
Robert Allenby	76	66	77	70	289	110,714
Stewart Cink	74	74	72	69	289	110,714
Jose Coceres	72	71	72	74	289	110,714
Pierre Fulke	72	68	78	71	289	110,714
Sergio Garcia	75	73	73	68	289	110,714
Ricardo Gonzalez	74	73	71	71	289	110,714
Steve Lowery	71	71	73	74	289	110,714
Stuart Appleby	73	74	74	69	290	72,000
Steve Flesch	72	74	73	71	290	72,000
Padraig Harrington	71	73	74	72	290	72,000
Charles Howell	72	69	80	69	290	72,000
Peter Lonard	69	73	75	73	290	72,000
Heath Slocum	73	74	75	69	291	57,000
Michael Campbell	73	70	77	72	292	44,250
Retief Goosen	69	69	79	75	292	44,250
Bernhard Langer	70	72	77	73	292	44,250
Justin Rose	69	73	76	74	292	44,250
Adam Scott	71	71	76	74	292	44,250
Jeff Sluman	70	75	74	73	292	44,250
Brad Faxon	74	72	75	72	293	33,500
Tom Lehman	71	72	77	73	293	33,500
Craig Perks	72	76	74	71	293	33,500
Kenny Perry	73	68	78	74	293	33,500
Kirk Triplett	75	69	79	70	293	33,500
David Duval	71	77	76	70	294	26,300
Ernie Els	72	71	75	76	294	26,300
Neal Lancaster	72	73	75	74	294	26,300
Phil Mickelson	76	72	78	68	294	26,300
Mike Weir	73	74	77	70	294	26,300
Chris DiMarco	76	69	77	73	295	21,500
Joel Edwards	73	74	77	71	295	21,500
John Huston	74	74	75	72	295	21,500
Scott McCarron	73	71	79	72	295	21,500
Briny Baird	79	69	73	75	296	17,000
Soren Hansen	73	69	78	76	296	17,000

	SCORES				TOTAL	MONEY
Shigeki Maruyama	76	72	75	73	296	17,000
Loren Roberts	77	70	77	72	296	17,000
Kevin Sutherland	72	75	71	78	296	17,000
Angel Cabrera	71	73	77	76	297	13,120
Steve Elkington	72	75	76	74	297	13,120
Davis Love	70	75	76	76	297	13,120
Len Mattiace	74	73	76	74	297	13,120
Tom Watson	76	71	83	67	297	13,120
Cameron Beckman	74	71	75	78	298	11,742
Tim Clark	72	74	76	76	298	11,742
Brian Gay	73	74	78	73	298	11,742
Toshimitsu Izawa	72	73	75	78	298	11,742
Lee Janzen	70	76	77	75	298	11,742
Greg Norman	71	74	73	80	298	11,742
Chris Smith	75	73	72	78	298	11,742
Joe Durant	74	71	79	75	299	11,200
Nick Faldo	71	76	74	78	299	11,200
Hal Sutton	73	73	75	78	299	11,200
J.J. Henry	78	70	77	76	301	11,000
Don Berry	76	71	80	75	302	10,750
Matt Gogel	74	73	83	72	302	10,750
J.P. Hayes	73	75	78	76	302	10,750
Joey Sindelar	77	71	78	76	302	10,750
Dave Tentis	76	72	78	78	304	10,500
Jose Maria Olazabal	73	75	77	80	305	10,400
Pat Perez	77	71	85	76	309	10,300
Thomas Levet	78	70	82	80	310	10,200

Out of Final 36 Holes

			TOTAL	
Ian Leggatt	75	74	149	
Greg Owen	76	73	149	
K.J. Choi	78	71	149	
David Gossett	72	77	149	
Paul Lawrie	75	74	149	
Larry Nelson	76	73	149	
Rory Sabbatini	74	75	149	
Scott Verplank	77	72	149	
Fuzzy Zoeller	76	73	149	
Darren Clarke	79	70	149	
Thomas Bjorn	74	75	149	
J.L. Lewis	76	73	149	
Nick Price	72	77	149	
Dean Wilson	74	76	150	
John Rollins	77	73	150	
Chad Campbell	74	76	150	
Eduardo Romero	73	77	150	
Bob Tway	74	76	150	
Duffy Waldorf	77	73	150	
Ian Woosnam	77	73	150	
Paul Azinger	76	74	150	
Jay Haas	77	73	150	
Jonathan Kaye	77	73	150	
Jerry Kelly	77	73	150	
Skip Kendall	74	76	150	
Spike McRoy	74	76	150	
Sean Farren	74	76	150	
Taichi Teshima	77	74	151	
David Toms	77	74	151	
John Cook	75	76	151	

	SCORES		TOTAL
Tim Herron	76	75	151
Mark O'Meara	75	76	151
James Blair	74	78	152
Toru Taniguchi	75	77	152
Rick Hartmann	79	73	152
Bruce Zabriski	75	77	152
Shingo Katayama	74	78	152
Anders Hansen	79	73	152
Matt Kuchar	78	74	152
Steve Stricker	74	78	152
John Daly	76	76	152
Billy Andrade	75	77	152
Robert Gamez	76	76	152
Colin Montgomerie	74	78	152
Craig Parry	75	77	152
Carl Paulson	73	79	152
Carl Pettersson	77	75	152
Rob Labritz	78	75	153
Tim Thelen	75	78	153
Frank Lickliter	77	76	153
Billy Mayfair	77	76	153
Paul McGinley	74	79	153
Peter O'Malley	79	74	153
Mike Gilmore	78	76	154
Mark Brooks	75	79	154
Robert Thompson	78	77	155
Scott Hoch	80	75	155
Jeff Maggert	78	77	155
Jesper Parnevik	82	73	155
David Peoples	79	76	155
Niclas Fasth	79	77	156
Jeffrey Lankford	80	76	156
Scott Laycock	80	76	156
Barry Evans	80	76	156
Joe Klinchock	79	77	156
*Craig Stevens	82	75	157
Curtis Strange	81	76	157
Jim Carter	74	83	157
Bob Estes	81	76	157
Dudley Hart	82	75	157
Tim Fleming	77	81	158
Lee Westwood	75	83	158
Paul Casey	85	74	159
Tim Weinhart	77	82	159
Phillip Price	76	83	159
Alan Morin	82	77	159
Buddy Harston	76	83	159
Wayne DeFrancesco	78	82	160
Steve Schneiter	86	76	162
Barry Mahlberg	80	86	166
Kim Thompson	87	80	167
Kent Stauffer	87	80	167
Tom Dolby	85	94	179
Stephen Ames	73	74	WD
Bill Porter			WD

(Professionals who did not complete 72 holes received $2,000.)

WGC NEC Invitational

Sahalee Country Club, Sammamish, Washington
Par 35-36–71; 6,949 yards

August 22-25
purse, $5,500,000

	SCORES				TOTAL	MONEY
Craig Parry	72	65	66	65	268	$1,000,000
Fred Funk	68	68	68	68	272	410,000
Robert Allenby	69	63	71	69	272	410,000
Tiger Woods	68	70	67	68	273	215,000
Justin Rose	67	67	72	68	274	187,500
Jim Furyk	70	67	68	70	275	150,000
Rich Beem	74	67	67	67	275	150,000
Steve Lowery	67	65	73	71	276	120,000
Phil Mickelson	66	69	71	71	277	105,000
Matt Gogel	68	69	68	72	277	105,000
Davis Love	66	74	69	69	278	78,750
Vijay Singh	68	69	69	72	278	78,750
Retief Goosen	65	68	74	71	278	78,750
Michael Campbell	70	69	70	69	278	78,750
David Toms	69	68	71	71	279	60,875
Ernie Els	71	67	67	74	279	60,875
Thomas Bjorn	68	69	72	70	279	60,875
Lee Westwood	68	69	72	70	279	60,875
Bob Estes	71	71	69	69	280	50,400
Darren Clarke	66	74	68	72	280	50,400
Peter Lonard	70	71	72	67	280	50,400
Angel Cabrera	72	70	70	68	280	50,400
K.J. Choi	73	67	73	67	280	50,400
Rocco Mediate	68	69	73	72	282	45,000
Kenny Perry	67	70	73	72	282	45,000
Mike Weir	69	70	71	72	282	45,000
Toshimitsu Izawa	65	73	73	71	282	45,000
John Cook	70	74	69	70	283	41,250
Nick Price	74	66	72	71	283	41,250
Loren Roberts	70	66	76	71	283	41,250
Kirk Triplett	71	69	70	73	283	41,250
Chris DiMarco	68	70	74	71	283	41,250
David Duval	72	75	71	65	283	41,250
Justin Leonard	70	74	69	70	283	41,250
Ricardo Gonzalez	71	72	68	72	283	41,250
Len Mattiace	69	72	72	71	284	38,750
Shigeki Maruyama	69	72	69	74	284	38,750
Paul Azinger	68	72	73	72	285	37,250
Bernhard Langer	70	70	75	70	285	37,250
Tom Lehman	72	70	69	74	285	37,250
Matt Kuchar	71	68	71	75	285	37,250
Hal Sutton	73	71	70	72	286	35,000
Craig Perks	68	70	73	75	286	35,000
Carlos Franco	75	72	67	72	286	35,000
Stuart Appleby	70	72	74	70	286	35,000
Pierre Fulke	69	73	73	71	286	35,000
Joel Edwards	73	73	71	70	287	32,550
Eduardo Romero	71	71	67	78	287	32,550
Jose Maria Olazabal	71	68	75	73	287	32,550
Stewart Cink	73	71	73	70	287	32,550
Padraig Harrington	72	70	73	72	287	32,550
Notah Begay	70	77	70	71	288	31,250
Soren Hansen	76	69	69	74	288	31,250
Graeme McDowell	72	69	73	74	288	31,250

	SCORES			TOTAL	MONEY
Scott Hoch	72	77	69	71	289	30,500
Greg Norman	69	74	73	73	289	30,500
Chris Smith	75	73	73	68	289	30,500
Scott Verplank	71	75	76	68	290	29,500
Kevin Sutherland	74	71	71	74	290	29,500
Niclas Fasth	73	68	79	70	290	29,500
Anders Hansen	71	76	74	69	290	29,500
Sergio Garcia	68	73	76	73	290	29,500
Brad Faxon	71	72	71	77	291	28,625
Charlie Wi	73	73	73	72	291	28,625
Paul Lawrie	73	69	81	70	293	28,125
Nobuhito Sato	74	76	73	70	293	28,125
Paul McGinley	79	69	73	74	295	27,750
Steve Elkington	76	77	74	69	296	27,250
Tobias Dier	76	75	72	73	296	27,250
Nicholas Lawrence	76	72	78	70	296	27,250
Jesper Parnevik	76	74	73	74	297	26,625
Phillip Price	73	73	73	78	297	26,625
John Daly	73	78	74	73	298	26,250
Mark Calcavecchia	74	81	75	69	299	26,000
Scott McCarron	74	74	77	75	300	25,625
Jose Coceres	69	71	76	84	300	25,625
Jerry Kelly	75	79	74	73	301	25,250
Colin Montgomerie	71				WD	

Reno-Tahoe Open

Montreux Golf & Country Club, Reno, Nevada
Par 36-36–72; 7,577 yards

August 22-25
purse, $3,000,000

	SCORES			TOTAL	MONEY
Chris Riley	71	66	67	67	271	$540,000
Jonathan Kaye	67	68	69	67	271	324,000
(Riley defeated Kaye on first playoff hole.)						
Charles Howell	65	73	73	64	275	174,000
J.J. Henry	68	69	70	68	275	174,000
Brian Gay	71	70	68	67	276	120,000
Tom Pernice, Jr.	66	68	73	70	277	97,125
Bob Tway	68	68	70	71	277	97,125
Steve Flesch	70	64	70	73	277	97,125
Ben Crane	67	67	73	70	277	97,125
David Peoples	69	68	72	69	278	78,000
Woody Austin	68	71	69	70	278	78,000
Brandel Chamblee	73	68	72	66	279	66,000
Craig Stadler	70	70	65	74	279	66,000
John Riegger	73	70	69	69	281	54,000
Glen Day	72	67	70	72	281	54,000
John Rollins	66	71	74	70	281	54,000
David Frost	71	68	77	66	282	40,600
Duffy Waldorf	68	67	73	74	282	40,600
Hidemichi Tanaka	71	67	70	74	282	40,600
Rodney Pampling	68	68	80	66	282	40,600
Harrison Frazar	71	70	68	73	282	40,600
Luke Donald	67	70	73	72	282	40,600
Tom Byrum	72	68	73	70	283	25,285.72
Peter Jacobsen	72	71	68	72	283	25,285.71
Jeff Maggert	71	70	71	71	283	25,285.71

	SCORES				TOTAL	MONEY
Esteban Toledo	69	69	74	71	283	25,285.71
Brent Geiberger	71	72	70	70	283	25,285.72
Paul Claxton	72	72	72	67	283	25,285.72
Steve Allan	67	68	76	72	283	25,285.71
Shaun Micheel	69	72	71	72	284	18,630
Spike McRoy	68	71	72	73	284	18,630
Franklin Langham	73	67	73	71	284	18,630
Michael Long	70	67	76	71	284	18,630
Kaname Yokoo	72	72	67	73	284	18,630
Jay Don Blake	71	70	74	70	285	13,550
Olin Browne	71	72	71	71	285	13,550
Lee Janzen	70	70	70	75	285	13,550
Dennis Paulson	69	72	73	71	285	13,550
Bob May	72	70	73	70	285	13,550
Tom Scherrer	73	70	73	69	285	13,550
Kent Jones	72	68	71	74	285	13,550
Greg Chalmers	76	68	68	73	285	13,550
Boo Weekley	67	72	70	76	285	13,550
Bradley Hughes	72	68	76	70	286	9,600
Michael Clark	73	68	72	73	286	9,600
Chad Campbell	69	71	75	71	286	9,600
Aaron Baddeley	76	67	70	73	286	9,600
Mark O'Meara	74	70	75	68	287	7,740
Paul Goydos	72	71	72	72	287	7,740
Jeff Brehaut	76	68	74	69	287	7,740
Heath Slocum	75	69	72	71	287	7,740
J.L. Lewis	66	73	75	74	288	7,080
Blaine McCallister	68	73	75	72	288	7,080
Gary Nicklaus	68	72	71	77	288	7,080
Steve Pate	72	72	74	71	289	6,840
Deane Pappas	76	68	74	71	289	6,840
Bryce Molder	70	72	73	74	289	6,840
Mark Brooks	68	72	73	77	290	6,660
Mark Wurtz	73	69	75	73	290	6,660
Frank Nobilo	73	71	76	70	290	6,660
J.P. Hayes	71	71	78	71	291	6,450
Per-Ulrik Johansson	69	73	78	71	291	6,450
Michael Muehr	71	71	73	76	291	6,450
Geoff Ogilvy	71	68	77	75	291	6,450
Peter O'Malley	70	74	76	72	292	6,300
Jay Williamson	69	73	77	74	293	6,210
Garrett Willis	71	70	77	75	293	6,210
Matt Peterson	73	71	76	74	294	6,090
Jonathan Byrd	72	70	79	73	294	6,090
Tommy Tolles	71	71	81	72	295	6,000
Eduardo Herrera	67	73	82	78	300	5,940

Air Canada Championship

Northview Golf & Country Club, Surrey,
British Columbia, Canada
Par 36-35–71; 7,069 yards

August 29-September 1
purse, $3,500,000

	SCORES				TOTAL	MONEY
Gene Sauers	69	65	66	69	269	$630,000
Steve Lowery	67	67	68	68	270	378,000
Vijay Singh	70	69	67	65	271	182,000

	SCORES			TOTAL	MONEY
Robert Allenby	71	62	68	70	271	182,000
Craig Barlow	67	65	71	68	271	182,000
Tom Scherrer	68	69	70	65	272	126,000
Peter Lonard	66	67	68	72	273	112,875
David Gossett	67	66	72	68	273	112,875
Darren Clarke	72	67	66	69	274	94,500
John Senden	68	70	70	66	274	94,500
Harrison Frazar	68	68	72	66	274	94,500
Kevin Sutherland	67	67	69	72	275	77,000
Frank Nobilo	69	71	70	65	275	77,000
Fred Funk	68	69	70	69	276	61,250
Per-Ulrik Johansson	68	69	69	70	276	61,250
Michael Clark	71	68	72	65	276	61,250
Greg Chalmers	69	71	68	68	276	61,250
Joel Edwards	68	69	69	71	277	45,640
Mike Standly	71	68	67	71	277	45,640
Stephen Ames	68	67	72	70	277	45,640
Matt Peterson	70	67	69	71	277	45,640
Ben Crane	67	71	70	69	277	45,640
Blaine McCallister	68	67	70	73	278	29,500
Brandt Jobe	69	71	66	72	278	29,500
Glen Hnatiuk	68	72	71	67	278	29,500
Shigeki Maruyama	66	70	71	71	278	29,500
Carlos Franco	68	68	70	72	278	29,500
Tim Clark	70	68	68	72	278	29,500
Stephen Gangluff	69	67	71	71	278	29,500
Dennis Paulson	71	70	70	68	279	21,735
Jeff Brehaut	68	71	71	69	279	21,735
Paul Stankowski	68	70	70	71	279	21,735
Rodney Pampling	72	67	71	69	279	21,735
Graeme McDowell	68	72	70	69	279	21,735
Mark Calcavecchia	68	69	70	73	280	16,525
Kelly Gibson	70	69	70	71	280	16,525
Mike Springer	73	66	74	67	280	16,525
Joe Durant	71	67	69	73	280	16,525
Gabriel Hjertstedt	69	72	69	70	280	16,525
J.J. Henry	67	71	69	73	280	16,525
Rory Sabbatini	68	67	71	74	280	16,525
John Riegger	71	70	69	71	281	10,752
Grant Waite	69	71	71	70	281	10,752
Esteban Toledo	67	71	71	72	281	10,752
Shaun Micheel	70	70	73	68	281	10,752
Tommy Tolles	67	69	73	72	281	10,752
Tripp Isenhour	71	66	71	73	281	10,752
Jonathan Kaye	68	72	69	72	281	10,752
Chris Riley	68	68	73	72	281	10,752
Michael Long	73	67	71	70	281	10,752
Bryce Molder	72	68	74	67	281	10,752
Kent Jones	70	67	72	73	282	8,400
Jay Delsing	68	72	75	68	283	7,990
David Frost	65	72	71	75	283	7,990
Scott McCarron	71	68	74	70	283	7,990
Phil Tataurangi	69	70	70	74	283	7,990
Tim Herron	71	70	71	71	283	7,990
Briny Baird	72	69	69	73	283	7,990
Steve Allan	68	70	73	72	283	7,990
Olin Browne	73	68	70	73	284	7,630
Jim McGovern	67	68	71	78	284	7,630
Dean Wilson	69	71	71	73	284	7,630
Scott Gump	66	73	73	73	285	7,420

		SCORES			TOTAL	MONEY
Mike Weir	68	72	74	71	285	7,420
Garrett Willis	72	67	74	72	285	7,420
Brian Henninger	69	69	77	71	286	7,280
Robert Gamez	71	69	75	72	287	7,140
Dicky Pride	71	69	73	74	287	7,140
Ian Leggatt	70	71	75	71	287	7,140
Brian Bateman	72	67	73	76	288	6,965
Geoff Ogilvy	70	70	67	81	288	6,965
Eduardo Herrera	70	67	78	75	290	6,720
Tom Pernice, Jr.	74	67	74	75	290	6,720
Jeff Gallagher	71	70	74	75	290	6,720
Jeff Gove	67	69	78	76	290	6,720
Luke Donald	69	72	75	74	290	6,720
Dave Barr	71	70	80	73	294	6,510

Bell Canadian Open

Angus Glen Country Club, Markham, Ontario, Canada
Par 36-36–72; 7,206 yards

September 5-8
purse, $4,000,000

		SCORES			TOTAL	MONEY
John Rollins	70	71	66	65	272	$720,000
Neal Lancaster	66	67	67	72	272	352,000
Justin Leonard	69	68	66	69	272	352,000
(Rollins defeated Lancaster and Leonard on first playoff hole.)						
Steve Flesch	71	67	65	70	273	176,000
Greg Chalmers	66	71	65	71	273	176,000
Grant Waite	64	70	69	71	274	134,000
Vijay Singh	67	70	66	71	274	134,000
Geoff Ogilvy	68	74	64	68	274	134,000
Bob Estes	68	71	68	68	275	108,000
Lee Janzen	72	68	69	66	275	108,000
Jeff Sluman	71	68	66	70	275	108,000
Billy Andrade	66	67	70	73	276	81,000
Dudley Hart	71	70	68	67	276	81,000
Jay Williamson	72	70	67	67	276	81,000
Pat Perez	70	69	74	63	276	81,000
Gene Sauers	70	69	67	71	277	62,000
Ian Leggatt	69	65	72	71	277	62,000
Carlos Franco	67	68	76	66	277	62,000
Paul Gow	71	68	70	68	277	62,000
Per-Ulrik Johansson	66	71	72	69	278	50,000
John Senden	70	71	69	68	278	50,000
John Daly	71	70	69	69	279	37,133.34
Paul Stankowski	69	70	70	70	279	37,133.33
Mike Weir	69	70	73	67	279	37,133.34
Frank Nobilo	67	70	67	75	279	37,133.33
Rodney Pampling	68	70	69	72	279	37,133.33
Jonathan Byrd	71	68	70	70	279	37,133.33
Len Mattiace	71	71	69	69	280	26,028.57
Jerry Smith	71	67	72	70	280	26,028.57
Pete Jordan	74	68	66	72	280	26,028.57
Glen Hnatiuk	70	71	73	66	280	26,028.57
Jonathan Kaye	69	72	71	68	280	26,028.57
Hidemichi Tanaka	71	68	71	70	280	26,028.57
Brenden Pappas	71	70	75	64	280	26,028.58
Corey Pavin	69	66	76	70	281	20,600

	SCORES				TOTAL	MONEY
Woody Austin	70	68	71	72	281	20,600
Charles Howell	69	68	74	70	281	20,600
Richard Zokol	72	67	75	68	282	16,000
Brad Lardon	71	70	71	70	282	16,000
Kent Jones	69	71	72	70	282	16,000
Mario Tiziani	74	68	70	70	282	16,000
Brent Geiberger	71	72	67	72	282	16,000
Briny Baird	76	67	69	70	282	16,000
Bo Van Pelt	70	72	68	72	282	16,000
Derek Gillespie	72	70	68	72	282	16,000
Olin Browne	69	74	66	74	283	10,174.54
Tom Byrum	72	68	69	74	283	10,174.54
David Edwards	73	68	69	73	283	10,174.54
Jim Gallagher, Jr.	72	69	70	72	283	10,174.54
Loren Roberts	68	72	70	73	283	10,174.54
Garrett Willis	75	68	70	70	283	10,174.55
Steve Allan	71	70	72	70	283	10,174.55
Kenneth Staton	70	73	69	71	283	10,174.55
Stephen Gangluff	68	73	73	69	283	10,174.55
Luke Donald	72	67	72	72	283	10,174.55
Graeme McDowell	69	71	72	71	283	10,174.55
Mike Standly	73	68	73	70	284	8,920
Matt Gogel	73	68	67	76	284	8,920
Mike Sposa	77	66	70	71	284	8,920
Todd Doohan	77	65	70	72	284	8,920
David Morland	70	72	72	71	285	8,680
Steve Scott	72	71	71	71	285	8,680
Robin Freeman	76	67	70	73	286	8,480
Brandt Jobe	70	70	70	76	286	8,480
Lee Porter	72	71	71	72	286	8,480
J.L. Lewis	73	70	70	74	287	8,080
Tom Pernice, Jr.	72	71	69	75	287	8,080
Pat Bates	69	72	74	72	287	8,080
Jesper Parnevik	69	72	78	68	287	8,080
Notah Begay	72	69	68	78	287	8,080
Stewart Cink	70	73	71	73	287	8,080
Dave Christensen	75	67	74	71	287	8,080
Robert Gamez	70	69	78	71	288	7,560
Tom Scherrer	70	72	72	74	288	7,560
Michael Clark	70	70	75	73	288	7,560
Brian Gay	73	67	77	71	288	7,560
Iain Steel	76	67	75	70	288	7,560
Brad Elder	71	72	71	74	288	7,560
Carl Paulson	71	70	74	74	289	7,240
Brett Wetterich	71	71	71	76	289	7,240
Joey Sindelar	71	72	78	69	290	7,120
Dave Barr	71	71	78	71	291	7,040

SEI Pennsylvania Classic

Waynesboro Country Club, Paoli, Pennsylvania   September 12-15
Par 35-36–71; 7,244 yards   purse, $3,300,000

	SCORES				TOTAL	MONEY
Dan Forsman	73	68	64	65	270	$594,000
Billy Andrade	66	68	68	69	271	290,400
Robert Allenby	71	68	67	65	271	290,400

	SCORES				TOTAL	MONEY
John Huston	72	68	65	67	272	158,400
Olin Browne	73	69	65	66	273	125,400
Jeff Sluman	73	67	65	68	273	125,400
Jeff Brehaut	69	68	66	71	274	99,412.50
Ian Leggatt	70	65	69	70	274	99,412.50
Brent Geiberger	69	68	69	68	274	99,412.50
Hidemichi Tanaka	73	66	70	65	274	99,412.50
Paul Goydos	69	69	69	68	275	79,200
Tim Herron	73	70	65	67	275	79,200
Chris Smith	70	71	68	67	276	66,000
Guy Boros	72	71	66	67	276	66,000
Tom Pernice, Jr.	72	68	70	67	277	54,450
Brian Bateman	69	70	69	69	277	54,450
Michael Long	76	65	70	66	277	54,450
Mathew Goggin	68	72	69	68	277	54,450
Donnie Hammond	68	69	71	70	278	39,996
Mark O'Meara	73	67	66	72	278	39,996
Loren Roberts	71	68	69	70	278	39,996
Rodney Pampling	69	71	69	69	278	39,996
John Senden	69	71	65	73	278	39,996
Brad Faxon	73	68	67	71	279	26,117.14
J.L. Lewis	72	71	68	68	279	26,117.15
Len Mattiace	70	70	69	70	279	26,117.14
Brett Quigley	69	71	69	70	279	26,117.14
Jim Furyk	73	69	68	69	279	26,117.14
John Rollins	70	74	68	67	279	26,117.15
J.J. Henry	67	71	71	70	279	26,117.14
Blaine McCallister	71	72	68	69	280	19,140
John Riegger	74	70	65	71	280	19,140
Jim McGovern	71	67	70	72	280	19,140
Scott McCarron	72	69	69	70	280	19,140
Kent Jones	74	68	72	66	280	19,140
Bo Van Pelt	75	67	70	68	280	19,140
Jim Carter	72	70	69	70	281	14,520
Chris DiMarco	72	71	72	66	281	14,520
Michael Clark	69	71	71	70	281	14,520
Chad Campbell	71	71	71	68	281	14,520
Jonathan Kaye	72	70	73	66	281	14,520
Stuart Appleby	73	70	68	70	281	14,520
Bart Bryant	74	67	69	72	282	10,582
Robert Gamez	74	66	74	68	282	10,582
David Berganio, Jr.	71	68	73	70	282	10,582
Steve Flesch	71	69	65	77	282	10,582
Tom Scherrer	72	70	70	70	282	10,582
Steve Allan	71	71	68	72	282	10,582
Jay Don Blake	71	71	67	74	283	7,936.50
David Edwards	76	68	67	72	283	7,936.50
David Peoples	74	69	71	69	283	7,936.50
Joey Sindelar	71	69	77	66	283	7,936.50
Glen Day	72	71	67	73	283	7,936.50
Carlos Franco	69	72	71	71	283	7,936.50
Brian Gay	71	69	73	70	283	7,936.50
Edward Fryatt	70	69	72	72	283	7,936.50
Billy Mayfair	74	68	72	70	284	7,392
Charles Howell	71	71	70	72	284	7,392
Stephen Gangluff	70	74	71	69	284	7,392
Tom Byrum	75	66	72	72	285	7,227
Bryce Molder	74	65	70	76	285	7,227
Tommy Tolles	74	70	73	69	286	6,996
Mike Heinen	72	68	74	72	286	6,996

	SCORES				TOTAL	MONEY
Dicky Pride	71	71	75	69	286	6,996
Cameron Beckman	71	72	74	69	286	6,996
Jess Daley	70	73	71	72	286	6,996
Brad Lardon	70	73	70	74	287	6,732
Jay Williamson	73	67	74	73	287	6,732
Kenneth Staton	67	69	78	73	287	6,732
Jim Gallagher, Jr.	74	70	72	72	288	6,600
Pete Jordan	76	67	74	72	289	6,534
Michael Bradley	73	70	77	70	290	6,402
Mike Hulbert	77	67	72	74	290	6,402
Bradley Hughes	72	70	74	74	290	6,402
Stu Ingraham	72	72	69	79	292	6,270
Mike Springer	74	70	74	78	296	6,204
Brett Wetterich	72	70	77	78	297	6,138
Frank Nobilo	74	70	75	79	298	6,072

Tampa Bay Classic

Westin Innisbrook Resort, Copperhead Course,
Palm Harbor, Florida
Par 36-35–71; 7,295 yards

September 19-22
purse, $2,600,000

	SCORES				TOTAL	MONEY
K.J. Choi	63	68	68	68	267	$468,000
Glen Day	68	67	70	69	274	280,800
Mark Brooks	73	65	70	67	275	176,800
John Morse	74	68	67	67	276	114,400
Rodney Pampling	65	68	73	70	276	114,400
Paul Gow	68	72	69	68	277	93,600
Craig Barlow	68	73	68	69	278	83,850
Pat Perez	67	67	70	74	278	83,850
Tommy Armour	71	69	70	69	279	67,600
Donnie Hammond	70	66	69	74	279	67,600
Peter Jacobsen	68	74	67	70	279	67,600
Matt Kuchar	70	69	70	70	279	67,600
Billy Andrade	66	71	70	73	280	41,888.88
Olin Browne	68	75	67	70	280	41,888.89
Jay Haas	70	68	71	71	280	41,888.89
John Huston	69	72	70	69	280	41,888.89
Joey Sindelar	68	71	70	71	280	41,888.89
Steve Flesch	70	70	70	70	280	41,888.89
Mike Heinen	70	70	71	69	280	41,888.89
Jay Williamson	72	68	71	69	280	41,888.89
Kent Jones	71	69	70	70	280	41,888.89
Jay Don Blake	71	71	70	69	281	24,960
Tom Byrum	71	71	70	69	281	24,960
Brandel Chamblee	69	72	68	72	281	24,960
Luke Donald	72	67	72	70	281	24,960
Boo Weekley	71	67	71	72	281	24,960
Joel Edwards	69	73	70	70	282	18,850
Glen Hnatiuk	72	71	71	68	282	18,850
Brenden Pappas	71	70	68	73	282	18,850
Stephen Gangluff	71	71	73	67	282	18,850
Bart Bryant	66	74	71	72	283	15,762.50
Lee Janzen	68	70	73	72	283	15,762.50
Woody Austin	74	68	69	72	283	15,762.50
Ken Duke	71	70	71	71	283	15,762.50

	SCORES				TOTAL	MONEY
Steve Jones	73	70	72	69	284	12,545
Tim Petrovic	70	71	75	68	284	12,545
Brett Quigley	70	70	69	75	284	12,545
Brent Geiberger	71	71	72	70	284	12,545
Hidemichi Tanaka	69	68	72	75	284	12,545
John Senden	74	69	72	69	284	12,545
Hal Sutton	72	71	68	74	285	8,620.44
Duffy Waldorf	75	67	70	73	285	8,620.45
Willie Wood	73	70	69	73	285	8,620.45
Bob Burns	72	71	69	73	285	8,620.45
Tripp Isenhour	71	71	74	69	285	8,620.44
Mike Sposa	69	72	72	72	285	8,620.45
Stewart Cink	73	70	72	70	285	8,620.44
Gabriel Hjertstedt	72	71	73	69	285	8,620.44
Ty Tryon	73	65	72	75	285	8,620.44
Shaun Micheel	70	73	69	74	286	6,396
Paul Claxton	70	71	72	73	286	6,396
Mathew Goggin	70	69	73	74	286	6,396
Brad Bryant	68	73	73	73	287	5,962.67
Mike Springer	70	73	72	72	287	5,962.66
Jim McGovern	72	69	73	73	287	5,962.66
Tommy Tolles	72	70	72	73	287	5,962.67
Franklin Langham	69	74	70	74	287	5,962.67
Kenneth Staton	70	69	74	74	287	5,962.67
Michael Bradley	69	74	77	68	288	5,668
Eduardo Herrera	71	71	74	72	288	5,668
Greg Kraft	75	67	75	71	288	5,668
Heath Slocum	71	71	73	73	288	5,668
Brad Elder	70	70	71	77	288	5,668
Matt Peterson	69	71	75	74	289	5,512
Robin Freeman	74	68	73	75	290	5,330
Blaine McCallister	69	74	74	73	290	5,330
Grant Waite	73	70	69	78	290	5,330
Scott Gump	71	72	73	74	290	5,330
David Berganio, Jr.	69	73	75	73	290	5,330
Per-Ulrik Johansson	73	69	74	74	290	5,330
Carl Paulson	71	70	72	78	291	5,148
Stan Utley	70	73	75	74	292	5,070
Rory Sabbatini	72	71	75	74	292	5,070
Dan Forsman	74	69	78	72	293	4,888
Kelly Gibson	70	71	76	76	293	4,888
Michael Clark	72	71	74	76	293	4,888
Robert Damron	71	70	75	77	293	4,888
Garrett Willis	71	72	74	76	293	4,888
Brett Wetterich	72	71	75	76	294	4,732
Bo Van Pelt	75	68	77	77	297	4,680
Larry Rinker	72	71	76	81	300	4,628

Valero Texas Open

LaCantera Golf Club, San Antonio, Texas
Par 35-36–71; 7,001 yards

September 26-29
purse, $3,500,000

	SCORES				TOTAL	MONEY
Loren Roberts	67	63	67	64	261	$630,000
Fred Couples	68	67	65	64	264	261,333.34
Fred Funk	68	68	64	64	264	261,333.33

	SCORES			TOTAL	MONEY
Garrett Willis	71	61	66	66	264	261,333.33
Joel Edwards	66	68	67	65	266	118,650
J.L. Lewis	70	67	65	64	266	118,650
Shaun Micheel	68	64	70	64	266	118,650
Kenneth Staton	70	67	65	64	266	118,650
Pat Perez	68	62	69	67	266	118,650
Bob Estes	68	67	66	66	267	84,000
Bob Tway	67	64	67	69	267	84,000
Matt Peterson	69	62	67	69	267	84,000
Brian Gay	67	64	69	67	267	84,000
Kelly Gibson	70	68	65	65	268	61,250
Frank Lickliter	64	69	65	70	268	61,250
Jeff Gove	67	67	67	67	268	61,250
Steve Allan	67	67	69	65	268	61,250
John Huston	64	68	69	68	269	47,250
Tripp Isenhour	68	65	69	67	269	47,250
Phil Tataurangi	70	66	65	68	269	47,250
Luke Donald	71	64	68	66	269	47,250
Andrew Magee	67	64	68	71	270	36,400
Notah Begay	69	69	64	68	270	36,400
Brad Elder	70	67	69	64	270	36,400
Tom Kite	67	68	69	67	271	27,912.50
D.A. Weibring	65	67	71	68	271	27,912.50
Jim McGovern	70	68	67	66	271	27,912.50
Gabriel Hjertstedt	68	70	67	66	271	27,912.50
Steve Elkington	68	66	69	69	272	22,750
Dave Rummells	71	64	72	65	272	22,750
Woody Austin	69	68	69	66	272	22,750
Jeff Brehaut	67	65	70	70	272	22,750
John Senden	70	68	69	65	272	22,750
Mark Brooks	66	66	70	71	273	17,300
Robert Gamez	63	69	69	72	273	17,300
Deane Pappas	70	66	70	67	273	17,300
Jay Williamson	71	65	69	68	273	17,300
Mathew Goggin	67	70	68	68	273	17,300
J.J. Henry	70	65	68	70	273	17,300
Hank Kuehne	68	70	67	68	273	17,300
Jay Don Blake	69	67	68	70	274	13,650
Kaname Yokoo	69	67	67	71	274	13,650
Ben Crane	69	68	71	66	274	13,650
Dave Barr	72	65	71	67	275	10,581.67
Donnie Hammond	67	69	72	67	275	10,581.67
Grant Waite	69	69	64	73	275	10,581.66
Brandt Jobe	69	67	70	69	275	10,581.67
Bo Van Pelt	70	68	65	72	275	10,581.66
Jess Daley	67	70	70	68	275	10,581.67
Tommy Armour	70	67	71	68	276	8,610
John Riegger	69	65	71	71	276	8,610
David Berganio, Jr.	69	69	70	68	276	8,610
Jay Haas	70	63	71	73	277	7,953.75
Eduardo Herrera	70	68	66	73	277	7,953.75
Stan Utley	70	67	70	70	277	7,953.75
Guy Boros	68	70	67	72	277	7,953.75
Lee Porter	69	66	73	69	277	7,953.75
Chad Campbell	69	65	72	71	277	7,953.75
David Gossett	71	67	66	73	277	7,953.75
Rory Sabbatini	66	65	73	73	277	7,953.75
Tim Petrovic	72	66	71	70	279	7,490
Bob Burns	69	69	72	69	279	7,490
Paul Stankowski	67	70	68	74	279	7,490

	SCORES				TOTAL	MONEY
David Morland	66	68	71	74	279	7,490
Paul Gow	71	67	69	72	279	7,490
Spike McRoy	67	71	68	74	280	7,280
Chris Smith	70	67	72	72	281	7,140
Bradley Hughes	67	69	71	74	281	7,140
Rich Beem	69	68	74	70	281	7,140
Esteban Toledo	70	68	72	72	282	7,000
Paul Goydos	68	68	70	77	283	6,930
Brian Bateman	68	69	71	78	286	6,860

Michelob Championship at Kingsmill

Kingsmill Golf Club, River Course, Williamsburg, Virginia   October 3-6
Par 36-35–71; 6,853 yards   purse, $3,700,000

	SCORES				TOTAL	MONEY
Charles Howell	70	65	68	67	270	$666,000
Scott Hoch	66	70	67	69	272	325,600
Brandt Jobe	67	68	65	72	272	325,600
Geoff Ogilvy	70	67	66	70	273	177,600
Billy Mayfair	70	63	68	73	274	148,000
Corey Pavin	66	69	68	73	276	119,787.50
Loren Roberts	66	69	73	68	276	119,787.50
Steve Flesch	72	67	66	71	276	119,787.50
Tim Clark	70	68	71	67	276	119,787.50
Tom Byrum	72	69	68	68	277	88,800
Scott Dunlap	69	70	67	71	277	88,800
David Morland	68	69	69	71	277	88,800
Harrison Frazar	70	67	71	69	277	88,800
David Toms	70	71	69	68	278	62,900
Shaun Micheel	70	67	71	70	278	62,900
Hidemichi Tanaka	64	70	71	73	278	62,900
Jason Hill	68	70	68	72	278	62,900
Matt Kuchar	71	69	67	71	278	62,900
Lee Janzen	69	72	67	71	279	43,290
John Riegger	69	70	67	73	279	43,290
Stephen Ames	70	70	71	68	279	43,290
Steve Allan	68	72	66	73	279	43,290
Luke Donald	68	70	69	72	279	43,290
Jonathan Byrd	67	69	71	72	279	43,290
John Cook	71	67	71	71	280	28,860
Donnie Hammond	71	69	68	72	280	28,860
J.P. Hayes	68	69	74	69	280	28,860
David Duval	64	69	74	73	280	28,860
Dicky Pride	72	68	70	70	280	28,860
Mark Brooks	70	71	69	71	281	23,495
Olin Browne	70	71	70	70	281	23,495
Jeff Brehaut	67	71	72	71	281	23,495
Briny Baird	75	65	70	71	281	23,495
Peter Jacobsen	67	68	73	74	282	18,685
Mike Heinen	71	68	75	68	282	18,685
Ian Leggatt	70	68	71	73	282	18,685
Jose Coceres	66	69	71	76	282	18,685
Chris Riley	67	69	72	74	282	18,685
Brett Wetterich	68	69	73	72	282	18,685
Robert Gamez	69	70	74	70	283	12,966.45
Chip Sullivan	67	69	71	76	283	12,966.44

	SCORES				TOTAL	MONEY
Kevin Sutherland	68	72	72	71	283	12,966.44
Glen Hnatiuk	69	69	72	73	283	12,966.44
Mike Sposa	69	69	74	71	283	12,966.45
Miguel Angel Jimenez	72	65	70	76	283	12,966.44
Garrett Willis	70	71	67	75	283	12,966.44
Paul Gow	69	70	74	70	283	12,966.45
John Rollins	67	72	77	67	283	12,966.45
Bart Bryant	66	72	74	72	284	8,898.50
Guy Boros	73	66	71	74	284	8,898.50
Brian Henninger	73	68	69	74	284	8,898.50
Pat Bates	71	70	68	75	284	8,898.50
Jerry Kelly	72	68	71	73	284	8,898.50
Tripp Isenhour	72	69	71	72	284	8,898.50
Jay Williamson	69	69	71	75	284	8,898.50
Bryce Molder	70	71	68	75	284	8,898.50
Chris Smith	71	67	71	76	285	8,288
Duffy Waldorf	71	68	71	75	285	8,288
Gabriel Hjertstedt	67	72	68	78	285	8,288
Joe Ogilvie	71	70	72	73	286	8,140
Brian Bateman	68	72	77	70	287	7,992
Brett Quigley	67	74	70	76	287	7,992
Woody Austin	70	70	72	75	287	7,992
Brad Lardon	68	71	73	76	288	7,844
Robin Freeman	70	69	80	70	289	7,733
Kirk Triplett	69	70	72	78	289	7,733
Phil Tataurangi	70	71	74	75	290	7,622
Russ Cochran	70	68	76	77	291	7,511
Mike Springer	72	68	77	74	291	7,511
Ken Duke	69	71	75	78	293	7,400
Lee Porter	67	74	80	74	295	7,326
Fred Wadsworth	70	71	75	84	300	7,252

Invensys Classic at Las Vegas

TPC at Summerlin: Par 36-36–72; 7,243 yards
TPC at The Canyons: Par 36-35–71; 7,019 yards
Southern Highlands Golf Course: Par 36-36–72; 7,247 yards
Las Vegas, Nevada

October 9-13
purse, $5,000,000

	SCORES					TOTAL	MONEY
Phil Tataurangi	67	66	67	68	62	330	$900,000
Jeff Sluman	66	66	64	68	67	331	440,000
Stuart Appleby	66	68	64	67	66	331	440,000
Jim Furyk	66	65	64	69	68	332	240,000
Rory Sabbatini	69	65	70	64	65	333	200,000
Dan Forsman	65	71	66	66	66	334	167,500
David Duval	67	66	67	63	71	334	167,500
Charles Howell	67	65	66	69	67	334	167,500
John Cook	69	67	64	67	68	335	130,000
Joel Edwards	72	67	62	66	68	335	130,000
Paul Stankowski	65	70	65	67	68	335	130,000
Notah Begay	65	70	70	65	65	335	130,000
David Peoples	69	68	66	67	66	336	96,666.67
Tim Petrovic	68	66	70	67	65	336	96,666.67
Jonathan Byrd	65	68	68	64	71	336	96,666.66
Robert Gamez	67	67	67	70	66	337	80,000
John Huston	65	71	64	69	68	337	80,000

		SCORES				TOTAL	MONEY
Chris DiMarco	66	67	66	69	69	337	80,000
Billy Andrade	67	68	68	67	68	338	60,600
Esteban Toledo	68	71	63	66	70	338	60,600
Shaun Micheel	66	69	66	68	69	338	60,600
Brent Geiberger	69	65	66	67	71	338	60,600
Ben Crane	67	67	67	68	69	338	60,600
Lee Janzen	63	74	62	71	69	339	39,571.43
J.L. Lewis	64	70	69	65	71	339	39,571.43
Kirk Triplett	68	68	68	65	70	339	39,571.43
Scott McCarron	67	68	65	67	72	339	39,571.42
Michael Clark	66	67	69	71	66	339	39,571.43
Carlos Franco	68	69	67	69	66	339	39,571.43
Chris Riley	65	71	66	68	69	339	39,571.43
Bart Bryant	66	68	67	67	72	340	29,000
Bob Tway	68	68	66	68	70	340	29,000
Justin Leonard	70	66	69	69	66	340	29,000
Edward Fryatt	68	67	69	70	66	340	29,000
Steve Allan	67	67	68	68	70	340	29,000
Kenneth Staton	68	68	65	69	70	340	29,000
Craig Parry	69	68	66	67	71	341	22,500
David Berganio, Jr.	70	65	66	68	72	341	22,500
Glen Day	65	73	68	67	68	341	22,500
Mike Weir	66	73	65	70	67	341	22,500
Rich Beem	64	70	70	67	70	341	22,500
Jay Don Blake	68	66	66	73	69	342	17,000
Steve Jones	62	70	67	74	69	342	17,000
Steve Lowery	67	68	65	69	73	342	17,000
Billy Mayfair	66	68	67	69	72	342	17,000
Dudley Hart	68	67	65	70	72	342	17,000
Frank Lickliter	67	65	72	71	67	342	17,000
Olin Browne	67	67	68	70	71	343	13,100
Brandt Jobe	68	70	68	67	70	343	13,100
Tom Scherrer	69	67	65	71	71	343	13,100
Chris Smith	68	68	66	69	73	344	12,150
Scott Verplank	65	69	70	69	71	344	12,150
J.P. Hayes	67	67	69	75	67	345	11,520
Robert Allenby	67	69	70	69	70	345	11,520
Jeff Gove	68	70	67	72	68	345	11,520
John Rollins	68	67	65	73	72	345	11,520
J.J. Henry	68	68	70	69	70	345	11,520
Joe Durant	67	67	70	70	72	346	11,150
Harrison Frazar	68	69	69	73	67	346	11,150
Jeff Brehaut	69	66	70	69	73	347	10,900
Jesper Parnevik	70	70	65	73	69	347	10,900
Stewart Cink	70	66	66	71	74	347	10,900
David Frost	69	67	70	75	67	348	10,500
Andrew Magee	68	73	65	73	69	348	10,500
Matt Gogel	67	70	67	71	73	348	10,500
Hidemichi Tanaka	70	71	64	69	74	348	10,500
Brett Wetterich	67	68	69	72	72	348	10,500
Jonathan Kaye	69	69	66	73	72	349	10,200
Miguel Angel Jimenez	68	68	70	79	68	353	10,050
Heath Slocum	71	69	66	74	73	353	10,050

Disney Golf Classic

Magnolia Course: Par 36-36–72; 7,190 yards
Palm Course: Par 36-36–72; 6,957 yards
Orlando, Florida

October 17-20
purse, $3,700,000

	SCORES				TOTAL	MONEY
Bob Burns	63	68	67	65	263	$666,000
Chris DiMarco	64	63	69	68	264	399,600
Tiger Woods	66	69	67	63	265	251,600
Tim Herron	67	66	67	66	266	162,800
Hidemichi Tanaka	63	67	70	66	266	162,800
David Toms	69	68	65	65	267	119,787.50
John Rollins	66	71	64	66	267	119,787.50
Tim Clark	65	68	68	66	267	119,787.50
K.J. Choi	66	68	69	64	267	119,787.50
Scott Hoch	64	65	69	71	269	88,800
Esteban Toledo	66	69	67	67	269	88,800
Carlos Franco	66	68	68	67	269	88,800
Robert Damron	68	66	67	68	269	88,800
Dennis Paulson	67	68	67	68	270	66,600
Kirk Triplett	68	66	70	66	270	66,600
Charles Howell	66	69	68	67	270	66,600
Dan Forsman	69	68	67	67	271	42,280.91
Davis Love	71	67	68	65	271	42,280.91
David Peoples	67	68	69	67	271	42,280.91
Tom Pernice, Jr.	67	67	69	68	271	42,280.91
Joey Sindelar	71	66	69	65	271	42,280.91
Chad Campbell	64	70	67	70	271	42,280.90
Craig Barlow	71	64	68	68	271	42,280.91
Brian Gay	66	66	70	69	271	42,280.91
Stuart Appleby	65	67	69	70	271	42,280.91
Michael Long	67	69	66	69	271	42,280.91
Rodney Pampling	68	65	72	66	271	42,280.91
Joel Edwards	67	65	67	73	272	26,270
Scott Verplank	69	65	69	69	272	26,270
Joe Durant	64	71	72	65	272	26,270
Billy Mayfair	70	65	67	71	273	21,941
Craig Parry	69	67	69	68	273	21,941
Bob Tway	71	65	68	69	273	21,941
Shaun Micheel	71	64	69	69	273	21,941
Jim Furyk	70	66	67	70	273	21,941
Skip Kendall	67	65	66	76	274	17,806.25
Glen Hnatiuk	70	68	71	65	274	17,806.25
Per-Ulrik Johansson	68	69	68	69	274	17,806.25
Luke Donald	67	68	71	68	274	17,806.25
Mark Brooks	67	65	73	70	275	13,690
Bart Bryant	70	67	70	68	275	13,690
Jay Haas	68	67	71	69	275	13,690
Neal Lancaster	70	68	73	64	275	13,690
Kent Jones	69	68	70	68	275	13,690
Frank Lickliter	69	68	69	69	275	13,690
Peter Lonard	64	73	69	69	275	13,690
Jay Don Blake	66	70	70	70	276	9,503.71
Olin Browne	68	68	73	67	276	9,503.72
John Cook	67	67	70	72	276	9,503.71
Len Mattiace	68	69	67	72	276	9,503.71
Kenny Perry	72	64	71	69	276	9,503.72
Loren Roberts	67	70	70	69	276	9,503.72
Rich Beem	69	68	67	72	276	9,503.71

	SCORES				TOTAL	MONEY
John Riegger	69	69	73	66	277	8,473
Jeff Sluman	63	70	70	74	277	8,473
Bob May	67	71	67	72	277	8,473
Scott McCarron	66	72	72	67	277	8,473
Russ Cochran	67	68	72	71	278	8,140
Greg Kraft	67	70	72	69	278	8,140
Jerry Kelly	69	67	71	71	278	8,140
Ian Leggatt	68	69	70	71	278	8,140
Matt Kuchar	68	68	72	70	278	8,140
Jim Carter	71	66	71	71	279	7,844
Robin Freeman	71	67	70	71	279	7,844
Pete Jordan	72	66	72	69	279	7,844
Bernhard Langer	66	68	71	75	280	7,622
Tom Lehman	69	68	70	73	280	7,622
Briny Baird	70	67	72	71	280	7,622
Hal Sutton	67	71	73	70	281	7,474
Kevin Sutherland	69	69	71	73	282	7,363
Garrett Willis	69	67	72	74	282	7,363
Brett Quigley	71	67	72	73	283	7,215
Paul Claxton	66	71	76	70	283	7,215
Brent Geiberger	68	70	75	75	288	7,104

Buick Challenge

Callaway Gardens Resort, Mountain View Course,
Pine Mountain, Georgia
Par 36-36–72; 7,057 yards

October 24-27
purse, $3,700,000

	SCORES				TOTAL	MONEY
Jonathan Byrd	67	66	65	63	261	$666,000
David Toms	66	68	63	65	262	399,600
Phil Mickelson	65	67	70	63	265	251,600
John Huston	68	67	61	70	266	152,933.33
Craig Parry	67	64	66	69	266	152,933.33
Robert Allenby	67	71	63	65	266	152,933.34
Kenny Perry	68	68	66	65	267	115,316.67
Joey Sindelar	69	68	65	65	267	115,316.67
Stewart Cink	69	66	65	67	267	115,316.66
Billy Andrade	67	69	66	66	268	92,500
Tim Herron	63	68	65	72	268	92,500
Carlos Franco	66	71	67	64	268	92,500
Jeff Sluman	70	67	70	62	269	71,533.34
Chris Smith	69	66	63	71	269	71,533.33
Chris Riley	68	66	69	66	269	71,533.33
J.L. Lewis	68	66	67	69	270	55,500
Davis Love	70	69	64	67	270	55,500
Jay Williamson	67	69	68	66	270	55,500
Paul Gow	67	70	67	66	270	55,500
John Rollins	70	67	67	66	270	55,500
Olin Browne	69	69	64	69	271	41,440
Duffy Waldorf	68	68	70	65	271	41,440
Ben Crane	65	70	66	70	271	41,440
Lee Janzen	66	70	71	65	272	31,542.50
Rocco Mediate	65	72	65	70	272	31,542.50
Kent Jones	67	69	66	70	272	31,542.50
Tim Clark	69	67	69	67	272	31,542.50
Joel Edwards	68	70	67	68	273	25,160

	SCORES				TOTAL	MONEY
Fred Funk	71	68	69	65	273	25,160
Tim Petrovic	69	68	68	68	273	25,160
Bob May	65	70	72	66	273	25,160
Chad Campbell	69	65	70	69	273	25,160
Dan Forsman	70	69	71	64	274	18,731.25
Skip Kendall	70	69	66	69	274	18,731.25
Jeff Brehaut	71	67	70	66	274	18,731.25
Glen Day	70	67	72	65	274	18,731.25
Matt Gogel	67	70	71	66	274	18,731.25
Notah Begay	72	66	66	70	274	18,731.25
Stuart Appleby	68	70	66	70	274	18,731.25
Jeff Gove	71	68	65	70	274	18,731.25
Jim Carter	71	68	69	67	275	13,690
John Riegger	70	69	67	69	275	13,690
Vijay Singh	68	67	71	69	275	13,690
Ian Leggatt	73	64	67	71	275	13,690
David Gossett	65	72	69	69	275	13,690
Jay Don Blake	71	67	71	67	276	9,749.50
Greg Kraft	67	72	68	69	276	9,749.50
Brandt Jobe	70	68	69	69	276	9,749.50
Pat Bates	67	71	70	68	276	9,749.50
Frank Lickliter	66	72	68	70	276	9,749.50
Robert Damron	69	69	68	70	276	9,749.50
Matt Kuchar	71	68	67	70	276	9,749.50
Kenneth Staton	68	69	71	68	276	9,749.50
David Berganio, Jr.	67	70	68	72	277	8,547
Lee Porter	70	68	70	69	277	8,547
Len Mattiace	69	67	72	70	278	8,177
David Peoples	67	70	73	68	278	8,177
Scott Dunlap	70	69	72	67	278	8,177
Woody Austin	67	71	67	73	278	8,177
David Duval	73	65	69	71	278	8,177
Scott McCarron	66	71	74	67	278	8,177
Michael Long	65	72	73	68	278	8,177
Luke Donald	70	69	67	72	278	8,177
Brad Faxon	67	72	69	73	281	7,807
Curtis Strange	68	71	69	73	281	7,807
Jerry Pate	68	68	74	72	282	7,696
Matt Peterson	71	68	71	73	283	7,585
Pat Perez	70	67	72	74	283	7,585
Mike Sposa	70	69	72	74	285	7,474

Tour Championship

East Lake Golf Club, Atlanta, Georgia
Par 35-35–70; 6,980 yards

October 31-November 3
purse, $5,000,000

	SCORES				TOTAL	MONEY
Vijay Singh	65	71	65	67	268	$900,000
Charles Howell	66	69	69	66	270	540,000
David Toms	70	66	70	67	273	345,000
Jerry Kelly	71	69	67	67	274	240,000
Davis Love	72	70	68	65	275	190,000
Phil Mickelson	70	69	67	69	275	190,000
Chris DiMarco	70	68	69	69	276	165,000
Tiger Woods	71	68	67	70	276	165,000
Retief Goosen	69	69	72	67	277	146,000

	SCORES				TOTAL	MONEY
K.J. Choi	71	68	70	68	277	146,000
Bob Estes	72	69	73	64	278	131,500
Scott McCarron	70	69	69	70	278	131,500
Steve Lowery	65	71	73	70	279	111,200
Rocco Mediate	74	73	68	64	279	111,200
Ernie Els	73	69	70	67	279	111,200
Shigeki Maruyama	68	73	70	68	279	111,200
John Rollins	70	71	70	68	279	111,200
Len Mattiace	68	68	74	70	280	97,000
Kenny Perry	71	69	68	72	280	97,000
Jim Furyk	68	73	72	67	280	97,000
Justin Leonard	71	73	71	65	280	97,000
Nick Price	73	68	68	72	281	91,000
Robert Allenby	74	69	66	72	281	91,000
Fred Funk	67	71	76	68	282	87,000
Jeff Sluman	72	72	68	70	282	87,000
Chris Riley	72	69	74	68	283	83,500
Rich Beem	70	72	70	71	283	83,500
Sergio Garcia	71	73	72	69	285	82,000
Jose Maria Olazabal	74	71	71	71	287	81,000
Loren Roberts	71	71	77	70	289	80,000

Southern Farm Bureau Classic

Annandale Golf Club, Madison, Mississippi
Par 36-36–72; 7,199 yards
(Fourth round cancelled—rain.)

October 31-November 3
purse, $2,600,000

	SCORES			TOTAL	MONEY
Luke Donald	66	68	67	201	$468,000
Deane Pappas	66	68	68	202	280,800
Brad Elder	65	67	71	203	176,800
Chad Campbell	69	66	69	204	124,800
Brad Faxon	67	67	71	205	85,150
Robin Freeman	71	69	65	205	85,150
Chris Smith	67	69	69	205	85,150
Spike McRoy	69	67	69	205	85,150
Jay Williamson	71	68	66	205	85,150
Jonathan Byrd	66	68	71	205	85,150
Tom Pernice, Jr.	69	71	66	206	59,800
Cameron Beckman	66	68	72	206	59,800
Brian Gay	68	71	67	206	59,800
Kirk Triplett	66	69	72	207	42,900
Tommy Tolles	66	70	71	207	42,900
Joe Durant	71	69	67	207	42,900
Bob Heintz	68	69	70	207	42,900
Jonathan Kaye	66	71	70	207	42,900
Stewart Cink	70	68	69	207	42,900
Mark Brooks	70	69	69	208	29,224
Lee Janzen	72	68	68	208	29,224
Shaun Micheel	72	70	66	208	29,224
Brian Bateman	67	72	69	208	29,224
Frank Lickliter	70	69	69	208	29,224
Bart Bryant	69	71	69	209	17,833.64
Jeff Maggert	68	68	73	209	17,833.63
David Peoples	67	73	69	209	17,833.64
Tim Petrovic	70	69	70	209	17,833.64

	SCORES			TOTAL	MONEY
Neal Lancaster	69	70	70	209	17,833.64
Brett Quigley	69	70	70	209	17,833.64
Per-Ulrik Johansson	72	67	70	209	17,833.64
Ian Leggatt	70	71	68	209	17,833.63
Jeff Gove	70	71	68	209	17,833.63
Garrett Willis	68	71	70	209	17,833.64
Heath Slocum	70	67	72	209	17,833.63
Brandel Chamblee	73	68	69	210	10,933
Joel Edwards	70	69	71	210	10,933
Dan Forsman	73	69	68	210	10,933
Eduardo Herrera	66	70	74	210	10,933
Steve Jones	69	68	73	210	10,933
Joey Sindelar	71	70	69	210	10,933
Willie Wood	69	71	70	210	10,933
David Morland	71	70	69	210	10,933
Paul Claxton	70	70	70	210	10,933
John Senden	67	71	72	210	10,933
Greg Kraft	69	73	69	211	6,851
Tom Scherrer	71	69	71	211	6,851
Notah Begay	68	74	69	211	6,851
Jason Hill	72	69	70	211	6,851
Steve Allan	74	67	70	211	6,851
Paul Gow	69	70	72	211	6,851
Brett Wetterich	75	66	70	211	6,851
Stephen Gangluff	69	71	71	211	6,851
Russ Cochran	71	70	71	212	5,746
Skip Kendall	69	70	73	212	5,746
Blaine McCallister	68	73	71	212	5,746
Dennis Paulson	72	67	73	212	5,746
John Riegger	69	72	71	212	5,746
Scott Simpson	74	68	70	212	5,746
Brian Henninger	70	71	71	212	5,746
David Berganio, Jr.	71	71	70	212	5,746
Gary Nicklaus	72	69	71	212	5,746
Lee Porter	73	68	71	212	5,746
Mike Sposa	72	70	70	212	5,746
Peter Lonard	74	66	72	212	5,746
Jay Don Blake	71	69	73	213	5,356
Brad Lardon	67	72	74	213	5,356
David Gossett	69	69	75	213	5,356
Billy Andrade	72	69	73	214	5,148
Andrew Magee	70	67	77	214	5,148
Bob May	71	70	73	214	5,148
Carlos Franco	68	71	75	214	5,148
Harrison Frazar	71	69	74	214	5,148
Paul Stankowski	72	69	74	215	4,966
Glen Day	68	70	77	215	4,966
Rory Sabbatini	73	67	76	216	4,888

Special Events

CVS/pharmacy Charity Classic

Rhode Island Country Club, Barrington, Rhode Island   July 24-25
Par 36-35–71; 6,668 yards   purse $1,200,000

	SCORES		TOTAL	MONEY (Team)
Dudley Hart/Chris DiMarco	60	62	122	$230,000
David Toms/Stewart Cink	65	57	122	170,000
(Hart and DiMarco defeated Toms and Cink on third playoff hole.)				
Steve Elkington/Craig Stadler	65	59	124	122,500
Peter Jacobsen/David Duval	64	60	124	122,500
Nick Price/Mark Calcavecchia	60	65	125	105,000
Jeff Sluman/Stuart Appleby	63	63	126	100,000
Billy Andrade/Brad Faxon	65	63	128	92,500
Brett Quigley/Dana Quigley	63	65	128	92,500
Rocco Mediate/Justin Leonard	67	62	129	85,000
Len Mattiace/Shigeki Maruyama	67	64	133	80,000

Fred Meyer Challenge

Reserve Vineyards and Golf Club, Fought Course,   August 5-6
Aloha, Oregon   purse $1,075,000
Par 35-37–72; 7,037 yards

	SCORES		TOTAL	MONEY (Team)
Brian Henninger/Scott McCarron	60	62	122	$180,000
Stewart Cink/David Toms	63	61	124	120,000
Bob Gilder/Tom Wargo	63	63	126	88,000
Matt Kuchar/Charles Howell	63	63	126	88,000
Jack Nicklaus/Gary Nicklaus	63	63	126	88,000
David Duval/Dudley Hart	64	63	127	75,000
Steve Elkington/Craig Stadler	65	62	127	75,000
Notah Begay/Casey Martin	62	65	127	75,000
Chris DiMarco/Tom Lehman	65	63	128	73,000
Fred Couples/John Cook	66	62	128	72,000
Arnold Palmer/Peter Jacobsen	67	65	132	71,000
Billy Andrade/Brad Faxon	66	67	133	70,000

Ryder Cup

The DeVere Belfry, Brabazon Course,   September 27-29
Sutton Coldfield, England
Par 445 444 344–36, 443 435 454–36–72; 7,118 yards

FIRST DAY
Morning Fourballs

Darren Clarke and Thomas Bjorn (Europe) defeated Tiger Woods and Paul Azinger (USA), 1 up.

Clarke	3	3	4	4	3	4	3	4	4	4	4	3	3	3	5	3	5	3
Bjorn	5	3	5	4	3	4	3	4	4	3	4	2	4	3	4	3	5	3
Woods	5	3	4	4	3	4	3	3	5	4	4	3	3	4	5	4	4	3
Azinger	4	5	4	3	4	4	3	4	4	4	4	3	3	3	4	5	4	3

Sergio Garcia and Lee Westwood (Europe) defeated David Duval and Davis Love (USA), 4 and 3.

Garcia	4	5	5	4	4	4	3	4	4	4	4	3	3	3	X
Westwood	5	4	5	4	3	4	2	6	5	5	4	2	3	3	4
Duval	5	4	4	4	4	4	2	4	4	4	4	3	4	3	5
Love	5	4	4	4	4	4	3	5	4	4	4	3	4	4	5

Colin Montgomerie and Bernhard Langer (Europe) defeated Scott Hoch and Jim Furyk (USA), 4 and 3.

Montgomerie	4	4	4	5	4	4	2	3	4	4	4	2	4	2
Langer	4	3	5	4	5	3	3	4	4	3	5	3	4	2
Hoch	4	4	5	4	4	4	3	4	3	3	4	3	4	3
Furyk	4	4	5	X	3	4	2	X	4	4	4	3	4	3

Phil Mickelson and David Toms (USA) defeated Padraig Harrington and Niclas Fasth (Europe), 1 up.

Harrington	4	4	4	4	4	3	3	4	4	X	4	3	X	2	4	4	4	4
Fasth	4	4	5	4	4	3	3	3	5	3	4	3	3	2	4	4	4	4
Mickelson	4	4	5	4	3	3	3	4	4	3	4	2	4	3	4	3	5	4
Toms	3	3	5	4	4	5	3	4	3	3	4	2	4	3	4	3	5	4

TOTAL: Europe 3, United States 1

Afternoon Foursomes

Hal Sutton and Scott Verplank (USA) defeated Darren Clarke and Thomas Bjorn (Europe), 2 and 1.

Clarke/Bjorn	5	4	3	4	4	4	3	3	4	3	5	2	5	4	5	4	6	
Sutton/Verplank	4	4	4	4	4	4	3	4	4	4	4	3	4	3	5	3	5	

Sergio Garcia and Lee Westwood (Europe) defeated Tiger Woods and Mark Calcavecchia (USA), 2 and 1.

Garcia/Westwood	3	5	4	4	4	4	3	4	4	3	4	3	4	3	6	4	4	
Woods/Calcavecchia	4	3	4	4	3	4	3	4	4	4	5	4	4	4	5	4	4	

Colin Montgomerie and Bernhard Langer (Europe) halved with Phil Mickelson and David Toms (USA).

Montgomerie/Langer	4	3	5	4	3	4	3	3	4	3	4	3	4	3	5	5	5	5
Mickelson/Toms	4	4	4	4	4	5	3	4	4	3	4	3	4	3	4	3	4	5

Stewart Cink and Jim Furyk (USA) defeated Padraig Harrington and Paul McGinley (Europe), 3 and 2.

| Harrington/McGinley | 4 | 4 | 4 | 3 | 4 | 5 | 3 | 4 | 4 | 4 | 4 | 4 | 3 | 3 | 4 | 4 |
| Cink/Furyk | 4 | 4 | 4 | 3 | 4 | 4 | 3 | 4 | 4 | 3 | 3 | 3 | 4 | 2 | 5 | 4 |

TOTAL: Europe 4½, United States 3½

SECOND DAY
Morning Foursomes

Phil Mickelson and David Toms (USA) defeated Pierre Fulke and Phillip Price (Europe), 2 and 1.

| Fulke/Price | 4 | 4 | 4 | 4 | 4 | 4 | 3 | 5 | 4 | 3 | 4 | 3 | 5 | 4 | 5 | 4 |
| Mickelson/Toms | 3 | 4 | 5 | 4 | 4 | 5 | 3 | 4 | 4 | 4 | 4 | 3 | 4 | 3 | 3 | 4 |

Lee Westwood and Sergio Garcia (Europe) defeated Stewart Cink and Jim Furyk (USA), 2 and 1.

| Westwood/Garcia | 4 | 4 | 5 | 4 | 3 | 4 | 4 | 3 | 5 | 4 | 5 | 3 | 4 | 3 | 5 | 4 | 5 |
| Cink/Furyk | 4 | 4 | 5 | 5 | 3 | 4 | 4 | 5 | 4 | 4 | 5 | 3 | 4 | 3 | 5 | 5 | 5 |

Colin Montgomerie and Bernhard Langer (Europe) defeated Scott Verplank and Scott Hoch (USA), 1 up.

| Montgomerie/Langer | 3 | 4 | 4 | 4 | 4 | 4 | 3 | 4 | 4 | 3 | 4 | 3 | 4 | 3 | 5 | 4 | 4 | 4 |
| Verplank/Hoch | 3 | 4 | 4 | 5 | 4 | 4 | 3 | 4 | 4 | 4 | 3 | 3 | 4 | 3 | 4 | 4 | 5 | 4 |

Tiger Woods and Davis Love (USA) defeated Darren Clarke and Thomas Bjorn (Europe), 4 and 3.

| Clarke/Bjorn | 4 | 4 | 4 | 5 | 4 | 5 | 3 | 4 | 4 | 4 | 5 | 3 | 4 | 3 | 5 |
| Woods/Love | 5 | 3 | 4 | 4 | 4 | 4 | 3 | 4 | 4 | 4 | 4 | 3 | 4 | 3 | 4 |

TOTAL: Europe 6½, United States 5½

Afternoon Fourballs

Mark Calcavecchia and David Duval (USA) defeated Niclas Fasth and Jesper Parnevik (Europe), 1 up.

Fasth	4	3	5	4	4	3	3	4	4	5	4	2	4	3	4	4	4	4
Parnevik	4	4	4	5	4	4	2	4	4	4	4	3	4	3	4	4	5	4
Calcavecchia	4	4	5	4	4	4	3	4	4	3	4	2	3	3	4	3	X	4
Duval	4	4	8	5	4	3	3	3	5	3	4	2	4	2	4	4	5	4

Colin Montgomerie and Padraig Harrington (Europe) defeated Phil Mickelson and David Toms (USA), 2 and 1.

Montgomerie	X	3	4	X	3	4	3	3	4	4	3	3	4	2	5	5	5
Harrington	4	4	4	3	3	3	3	5	4	4	3	3	4	4	5	4	5
Mickelson	4	4	4	4	4	3	2	X	3	3	4	2	X	3	5	4	5
Toms	X	4	4	4	4	3	2	4	3	4	4	3	4	3	5	4	5

Tiger Woods and Davis Love (USA) defeated Sergio Garcia and Lee Westwood (Europe), 1 up.

Garcia	4	4	5	4	4	4	3	3	4	3	3	3	4	2	5	4	5	5
Westwood	4	3	4	4	4	3	3	4	4	3	4	4	4	2	4	3	5	5
Woods	4	3	4	3	4	3	4	4	4	4	3	3	3	3	4	3	4	4
Love	4	4	4	4	4	4	3	4	4	4	4	3	4	3	5	4	4	4

Darren Clarke and Paul McGinley (Europe) halved with Scott Hoch and Jim Furyk (USA).

Clarke	4	3	4	3	4	4	2	4	4	3	4	3	4	2	5	4	5	5
McGinley	4	4	4	3	3	4	3	4	4	3	4	3	4	3	4	3	5	4
Hoch	4	4	4	X	4	3	2	3	4	4	4	3	3	3	4	5	4	5
Furyk	4	3	4	4	3	4	3	X	4	3	4	3	3	3	4	4	5	5

TOTAL: Europe 8, United States 8

THIRD DAY
Singles

Colin Montgomerie (Europe) defeated Scott Hoch (USA), 5 and 4.

Montgomerie	3	4	5	4	4	3	2	4	4	3	4	3	3	2
Hoch	4	4	4	4	5	4	2	4	5	4	4	2	4	3

David Toms (USA) defeated Sergio Garcia (Europe), 1 up.

Garcia	4	4	4	4	4	3	2	5	4	4	4	2	4	4	5	4	5
Toms	4	4	4	5	3	4	3	5	4	3	3	3	4	2	4	4	5

Darren Clarke (Europe) halved with David Duval (USA).

Clarke	3	4	6	4	4	5	3	4	4	4	4	4	3	3	4	4	4	4
Duval	4	5	4	4	4	5	2	4	6	4	4	3	3	3	4	4	4	4

Bernhard Langer (Europe) defeated Hal Sutton (USA), 4 and 3.

Langer	4	4	4	4	3	3	3	3	4	4	4	3	4	3	5
Sutton	4	4	4	4	4	4	3	4	4	C	3	3	C	3	5

Padraig Harrington (Europe) defeated Mark Calcavecchia (Europe), 5 and 4.

Harrington	4	4	5	4	3	4	2	5	3	4	4	3	4	2
Calcavecchia	4	4	6	4	5	4	3	5	5	4	4	3	4	3

Thomas Bjorn (Europe) defeated Stewart Cink (USA), 2 and 1.

Bjorn	4	4	5	5	3	4	3	4	4	4	4	3	4	3	5	5	5
Cink	4	4	5	5	4	4	3	5	4	4	4	3	4	2	6	4	6

Scott Verplank (USA) defeated Lee Westwood (Europe), 2 and 1.

Westwood	4	5	5	3	4	4	3	3	4	4	4	3	4	3	4	4	4
Verplank	3	4	3	4	4	3	3	4	4	4	3	3	4	3	5	4	4

Niclas Fasth (Europe) halved with Paul Azinger (USA).

Fasth	3	3	4	4	4	4	3	5	4	5	4	3	3	3	5	5	5	4
Azinger	3	5	5	4	3	5	3	5	4	4	4	3	4	3	5	4	5	3

Paul McGinley (Europe) halved with Jim Furyk (USA).

McGinley	4	4	5	4	4	4	3	4	5	4	4	4	4	3	4	4	4	4
Furyk	4	3	4	5	3	4	3	6	4	5	4	3	5	3	4	4	5	4

Pierre Fulke (Europe) halved with Davis Love (USA).

Fulke	4	4	5	4	3	4	3	4	4	4	3	3	4	3	5	4	5
Love	3	4	5	4	4	4	3	3	5	4	4	3	3	2	5	5	5

Phillip Price (Europe) defeated Phil Mickelson (USA), 3 and 2.

| Price | 4 | 4 | 4 | 4 | 4 | 3 | 3 | 4 | 4 | 3 | 4 | 3 | 3 | 3 | 5 | 3 | | |
| Mickelson | 4 | 4 | 4 | 4 | 5 | 4 | 4 | 4 | 3 | 4 | 4 | 3 | 3 | 3 | 4 | 4 | | |

Jesper Parnevik (Europe) halved with Tiger Woods (USA).

| Parnevik | 4 | 5 | 4 | 5 | 5 | 4 | 2 | 5 | 4 | 4 | 3 | 3 | 3 | 3 | 6 | 4 | 5 | 4 |
| Woods | 4 | 4 | 5 | 4 | 4 | 4 | 3 | 5 | 4 | 4 | 4 | 3 | 4 | 3 | 5 | 4 | 4 | 5 |

TOTAL: Europe 15½, United States 12½

LEGEND: C–conceded hole to opponent; W–won hole by concession without holing out; X–no total score.

UBS Warburg Cup

Sea Island Golf Club, Seaside Course, St. Simons Island, Georgia   November 15-17
Par 35-35–70; 6,945 yards   purse, $3,000,000

FIRST DAY
Foursomes

Nick Faldo and Gary Player (World) defeated Curtis Strange and Arnold Palmer, 1 up.
Paul Azinger and Scott Hoch (US) halved with Bernhard Langer and Eduardo Romero.
Raymond Floyd and Tom Lehman (US) defeated Sam Torrance and Ian Woosnam, 1 up.
Isao Aoki and Seiji Ebihara (World) defeated Fred Funk and Bob Gilder, 3 and 1.
Hale Irwin and Tom Kite (US) defeated Rodger Davis and Stewart Ginn, 3 and 2.
Mark O'Meara and Tom Watson (US) defeated Barry Lane and Denis Durnian, 2 and 1.

POINTS: United States 3½, Rest of the World 2½

SECOND DAY
Fourballs

Palmer and Watson (US) defeated Player and Langer, 3 and 2.
Floyd and Lehman (US) defeated Torrance and Woosnam, 2 and 1.
Funk and Gilder (US) defeated Aoki and Ebihara, 1 up.
Romero and Faldo (World) defeated Strange and Irwin, 1 up.
Lane and Durnian (World) defeated Kite and Hoch, 4 and 3.
Davis and Ginn (World) defeated O'Meara and Azinger, 4 and 2.

POINTS: United States 3, Rest of the World 3
TWO-DAY TOTAL: United States 6½, Rest of the World 5½

THIRD DAY
Singles

Player (World) defeated Palmer, 6 and 5.
Strange (US) defeated Torrance, 4 and 3.
Azinger (US) defeated Langer, 4 and 3.
Lehman (US) defeated Romero, 2 and 1.
Lane (World) defeated Hoch, 1 up.
O'Meara (US) defeated Faldo, 3 and 2.
Woosnam (World) defeated Kite, 3 and 2.
Irwin (US) defeated Davis, 2 and 1.
Funk (US) halved with Aoki.
Gilder (US) defeated Ginn, 1 up.

Floyd (US) defeated Ebihara, 2 and 1.
Watson (US) halved with Durnian.

POINTS: United States 8, Rest of the World 4
TOTAL POINTS: United States 14½, Rest of the World 9½

(Each member of the United States team received $150,000; each member of the Rest of the World team received $100,000.)

Hyundai Team Matches

Monarch Beach Golf Links, Dana Point, California
Par 35-35–70; 6,582 yards

November 16-17
purse, $1,200,000

FIRST-ROUND MATCHES

Mark Calcavecchia and Fred Couples defeated Peter Jacobsen and Scott McCarron, 5 and 4.
Peter Lonard and Rich Beem defeated Jerry Kelly and Chris Smith, 3 and 2.

THIRD-PLACE MATCH

Kelly and Smith defeated Jacobsen and McCarron, 2 up.
(Kelly and Smith received $30,000 each; Jacobsen and McCarron received $20,000 each.)

CHAMPIONSHIP MATCH

Beem and Lonard defeated Couples and Calcavecchia, 2 and 1.
(Beem and Lonard received $100,000 each; Couples and Calcavecchia received $50,000 each.)

Callaway Golf Pebble Beach Invitational

Pebble Beach GL: Par 36-36–72; 6,840 yards
Spyglass Hills GC: Par 36-36–72; 6,859 yards
Del Monte GC: Par 36-36–72; 6,278 yards
Pebble Beach, California

November 21-24
purse, $300,000

	SCORES				TOTAL	MONEY
Mark Brooks	70	65	68	69	272	$60,000
Jeff Gove	69	68	72	66	275	32,200
Duffy Waldorf	69	67	69	72	277	13,500
Loren Roberts	67	71	71	68	277	13,500
Roger Maltbie	68	69	71	70	278	9,000
Brett Quigley	72	73	64	71	280	7,500
Matt Gogel	70	69	71	70	280	7,500
Wendy Ward	71	65	73	72	281	6,500
Jeff Brehaut	71	68	67	76	282	6,000
Kevin Sutherland	70	72	65	76	283	5,500
Sean Farren	72	68	72	71	283	5,500
Ben Crane	74	70	70	69	283	5,500
Kirk Triplett	76	70	70	67	283	5,500
Olin Browne	70	70	70	74	284	4,150
Steve Flesch	76	67	69	72	284	4,150
Gary Hallberg	70	75	72	67	284	4,150
Bruce Fleisher	70	75	68	72	285	3,600

	SCORES				TOTAL	MONEY
Jim Carter	75	69	73	68	285	3,600
Brian Mogg	72	68	68	78	286	2,566
Jill McGill	74	72	66	74	286	2,566
Todd Fischer	74	70	69	73	286	2,566
Andy North	72	72	71	71	286	2,566
Rick Hartmann	71	72	73	70	286	2,566
Scott Simpson	72	74	71	68	286	2,566
Tom Purtzer	74	66	71	76	287	2,400
Andy Miller	72	71	72	72	287	2,400
Bruce Summerhays	75	71	71	70	287	2,400
Curt Byrum	72	68	73	75	288	2,200
Ty Tryon	73	69	72	74	288	2,200
Emilee Klein	67	77	71	73	288	2,200
Jim Thorpe	69	78	67	75	289	2,070
Paul Marti	72	73	69	75	289	2,070
Spike McRoy	75	69	70	75	289	2,070
Terry Dill	71	70	74	74	289	2,070
Natalie Gulbis	74	71	70	75	290	2,000
Keith Clearwater	68	74	71	78	291	1,970
David Graham	71	73	70	77	291	1,970
Ron Skayhan	70	74	72	76	292	1,930
Tommy Masters	75	72	70	75	292	1,930
Harrison Frazar	74	70	72	79	295	1,900
Randy Marchman	75	70	72	79	296	1,870
Johnny Miller	69	74	71		WD	1,870

Franklin Templeton Shootout

Tiburon Golf Course, Naples, Florida
Par 36-36–72; 7,288 yards

November 22-24
purse, $2,250,000

	SCORES			TOTAL	MONEY
					(Each)
Lee Janzen/Rocco Mediate	65	60	60	185	$250,000
John Huston/Jeff Maggert	64	64	58	186	130,000
Matt Kuchar/David Gossett	66	64	56	186	130,000
John Cook/Mark O'Meara	65	65	58	188	85,000
Mark Calcavecchia/Andrew Magee	66	65	60	191	73,750
David Toms/Stewart Cink	67	66	58	191	73,750
Steve Elkington/Peter Jacobsen	66	65	61	192	70,000
Brad Faxon/Jeff Sluman	71	63	60	194	66,250
Dudley Hart/Scott McCarron	68	62	64	194	66,250
Scott Hoch/Jerry Kelly	68	64	63	195	62,500
Fred Couples/Greg Norman	68	69	62	199	60,000
Fred Funk/Len Mattiace	68	70	62	200	57,500

PGA Grand Slam of Golf

Poipu Bay Resort, Kauai, Hawaii
Par 36-36–72; 7,064 yards

November 26-27
purse, $1,000,000

	SCORES		TOTAL	MONEY
Tiger Woods	66	61	127	$400,000
Justin Leonard	69	72	141	225,000
Davis Love	72	69	141	225,000
Rich Beem	72	73	145	150,000

Target World Challenge

Sherwood Country Club, Thousand Oaks, California
Par 36-36–72; 7,025 yards

December 5-8
purse, $3,800,000

	SCORES				TOTAL	MONEY
Padraig Harrington	65	69	63	71	268	$1,000,000
Tiger Woods	68	65	70	67	270	$500,000
Davis Love	66	68	73	65	272	$300,000
Colin Montgomerie	68	70	68	67	273	$220,000
Bernhard Langer	72	65	67	69	273	$220,000
Jim Furyk	64	74	68	68	274	$190,000
Chris DiMarco	67	72	72	64	275	$170,000
David Toms	67	70	68	71	276	$148,750
Nick Price	65	70	70	71	276	$148,750
Phil Mickelson	68	74	68	68	278	$145,000
Retief Goosen	67	70	73	70	280	$142,500
Michael Campbell	70	72	70	69	281	$138,750
Vijay Singh	75	69	68	69	281	$138,750
Mark O'Meara	69	72	72	70	283	$135,000
Bob Estes	76	71	68	69	284	$132,500
Rich Beem	74	77	70	68	289	$130,000

WGC EMC World Cup

Vista Vallarta Club de Golf, Puerto Vallarta, Mexico
Par 36-36–72; 7,021 yards

December 12-15
purse, $3,000,000

	INDIVIDUAL SCORES				TOTAL
JAPAN—$1,000,000					
Shigeki Maruyama/Toshimitsu Izawa	64	64	58	66	252
UNITED STATES—$500,000					
Phil Mickelson/David Toms	65	67	57	65	254
KOREA—$225,000					
K.J. Choi/S.K. Ho	61	67	64	66	258
ENGLAND—$225,000					
Justin Rose/Paul Casey	65	63	62	68	258
SOUTH AFRICA—$115,000					
Rory Sabbatini/Tim Clark	62	64	62	71	259
ARGENTINA—$95,000					
Eduardo Romero/Angel Cabrera	64	68	62	66	260
AUSTRALIA—$95,000					
Craig Parry/Adam Scott	60	67	65	68	260
IRELAND—$75,000					
Padraig Harrington/Paul McGinley	64	67	62	68	261
CANADA—$75,000					
Ian Leggatt/Mike Weir	59	67	64	71	261
FIJI—$60,000					
Dinesh Chand/Vijay Singh	63	62	62	75	262

	INDIVIDUAL SCORES				TOTAL
DENMARK—$55,000 Anders Hansen/Soren Hansen	63	70	62	68	263
WALES—$47,500 Ian Woosnam/Bradley Dredge	63	68	65	69	265
SCOTLAND—$47,500 Paul Lawrie/Alastair Forsyth	63	65	62	75	265
SWEDEN—$39,500 Carl Pettersson/Niclas Fasth	62	71	64	69	266
SWITZERLAND—$39,500 Marc Chatelain/Andre Bossert	63	67	65	71	266
MYANMAR—$38,000 Soe Kyaw Naing/Kyi Hla Han	66	66	64	72	268
NEW ZEALAND—$35,500 Craig Perks/Michael Campbell	65	73	64	68	270
SINGAPORE—$35,500 Mardan Mamat/Lam Chih-bingh	70	65	65	70	270
FRANCE—$35,500 Thomas Levet/Raphael Jacquelin	61	72	64	73	270
TRINIDAD & TOBAGO—$35,500 Stephen Ames/Robert Ames	63	66	64	77	270
GERMANY—$33,500 Sven Struver/Alex Cejka	67	69	64	71	271
VENEZUELA—$32,000 Jamie Acevedo/Carlos Larrain	66	67	72	69	274
MEXICO—$31,000 Esteban Toledo/Pablo Del Olmo	68	72	66	71	277
COLOMBIA—$31,000 Jesus Amaya/Rigoberto Velasquez	66	68	69	74	277

Office Depot Father-Son Challenge

Ocean Golf Club, Paradise Island, Bahamas
Par 36-36–72; 6,907 yards

December 14-15
purse, $1,000,000

	SCORES		TOTAL	MONEY (Won by Professional)
Craig/Kevin Stadler	60	60	120	$200,000
Hale/Steve Irwin	60	60	120	80,000
(Stadlers defeated Irwins on first playoff hole.)				
Raymond/Ray Jr. Floyd	62	60	122	52,500
Johnny/John Jr. Miller	62	60	122	52,500
Hubert/Myatt Green	63	62	125	44,000
Gary/Wayne Player	64	61	125	44,000
Dave Stockton	62	63	125	44,000
Tom/David Kite	64	63	127	41,000

	SCORES				TOTAL	MONEY
						(Won by Professional)
Larry/Drew Nelson	66	61			127	41,000
Jack/Jack II Nicklaus	65	62			127	41,000
Jerry/Wesley Pate	66	63			129	40,000
Lanny/Travis Wadkins	69	60			129	40,000
Bob/David Charles	65	65			130	40,000
Tom/Eric Weiskopf	64	66			130	40,000
Tom/Michael Watson	65	67			132	40,000
Bill/Ben Rogers	67	66			133	40,000
Bernhard/Stefan Langer	66	68			134	40,000
Lee/Rick Trevino	67	68			135	40,000
Seve/Javier Ballesteros	70	70			140	40,000

Buy.com Tour

Jacob's Creek Open Championship
See Australasian Tour chapter.

Holden Clearwater Classic
See Australasian Tour chapter.

Louisiana Open

Le Triomphe Country Club, Broussard, Louisiana
Par 36-36–72; 7,004 yards

April 11-14
purse, $450,000

	SCORES				TOTAL	MONEY
Steve Alker	65	66	69	64	264	$81,000
Mike Heinen	66	69	61	68	264	48,600
(Alker defeated Heinen on second playoff hole.)						
Marco Dawson	67	65	69	65	266	30,600
Keoke Cotner	68	68	64	67	267	19,800
Wes Short	71	67	64	65	267	19,800
Jason Gore	67	68	67	66	268	15,637.50
Rob McKelvey	66	67	69	66	268	15,637.50
Andy Sanders	66	69	64	70	269	13,050
Roland Thatcher	63	71	69	66	269	13,050
Tjaart van der Walt	66	69	69	65	269	13,050
Hunter Haas	67	65	68	70	270	9,225
Spike McRoy	71	67	65	67	270	9,225
Perry Moss	65	71	68	66	270	9,225
Brenden Pappas	67	69	69	65	270	9,225
Charles Raulerson	65	64	69	72	270	9,225
Anthony Rodriguez	69	68	65	68	270	9,225
Mark Hensby	66	69	66	70	271	6,300
Jim McGovern	69	68	67	67	271	6,300
Larry Rinker	67	66	66	72	271	6,300

	SCORES				TOTAL	MONEY
Patrick Sheehan	70	68	65	68	271	6,300
Bruce Vaughan	65	68	72	66	271	6,300
Rich Barcelo	68	70	68	66	272	4,680
Kevin Johnson	70	67	67	68	272	4,680
Omar Uresti	67	70	68	67	272	4,680
Bart Bryant	71	65	70	67	273	3,690
Chris Couch	66	72	66	69	273	3,690
Paul Goydos	69	67	67	70	273	3,690
Willie Wood	73	65	67	68	273	3,690
Gene Sauers	66	69	71	68	274	3,150
Tyler Williamson	69	66	71	68	274	3,150

Arkansas Classic

Diamante Country Club, Hot Springs Village, Arkansas
Par 36-36–72; 7,519 yards

April 18-21
purse, $450,000

	SCORES				TOTAL	MONEY
Jace Bugg	66	68	72	65	271	$81,000
Jason Caron	72	64	68	68	272	48,600
Aaron Baddeley	66	70	67	70	273	30,600
Cliff Kresge	69	70	68	67	274	19,800
Tommy Tolles	69	70	68	67	274	19,800
Danny Briggs	69	69	66	72	276	16,200
James McLean	71	68	68	70	277	14,025
Bryce Molder	67	70	70	70	277	14,025
Patrick Sheehan	65	69	71	72	277	14,025
Ben Bates	68	69	70	71	278	9,975
Richie Coughlan	70	69	67	72	278	9,975
Kelly Gibson	71	68	73	66	278	9,975
Andy Sanders	68	68	69	73	278	9,975
Darron Stiles	68	70	69	71	278	9,975
Dave Stockton, Jr.	71	70	65	72	278	9,975
Doug Barron	69	66	73	71	279	6,750
Joe Ogilvie	72	68	69	70	279	6,750
Brenden Pappas	71	69	72	67	279	6,750
Omar Uresti	69	67	72	71	279	6,750
Boo Weekley	68	70	71	70	279	6,750
Steve Holmes	69	70	67	74	280	4,530
Tripp Isenhour	67	69	71	73	280	4,530
Jim McGovern	68	71	70	71	280	4,530
D.A. Points	69	72	68	71	280	4,530
Tjaart van der Walt	71	70	67	72	280	4,530
Jimmy Walker	69	71	70	70	280	4,530
Jason Gore	70	69	71	71	281	3,330
Brian Kamm	69	67	71	74	281	3,330
David Ogrin	70	71	67	73	281	3,330
Jim Rutledge	68	72	71	70	281	3,330

BMW Charity Pro-Am at The Cliffs

The Cliffs Golf & Country Club, Greenville, South Carolina
Cliffs Valley Course: Par 36-36–72; 7,023 yards
Keowee Vineyards Course: Par 36-35–71; 7,006 yards

April 25-28
purse, $525,000

	SCORES				TOTAL	MONEY
Charles Warren	67	65	64	68	264	$94,500
Todd Fischer	66	69	68	65	268	56,700
Ken Green	65	66	69	70	270	30,450
Stan Utley	64	65	71	70	270	30,450
Jeff Klauk	70	62	65	75	272	19,162.50
Andy Sanders	65	69	69	69	272	19,162.50
Scott Sterling	70	67	65	70	272	19,162.50
Todd Barranger	71	68	61	73	273	15,750
Guy Boros	66	70	70	67	273	15,750
Doug Barron	68	70	70	66	274	12,600
Shane Bertsch	67	69	68	70	274	12,600
Omar Uresti	68	71	65	70	274	12,600
Chris Wisler	70	69	68	67	274	12,600
Steve Alker	71	68	70	66	275	8,925
Jeff Freeman	70	66	64	75	275	8,925
Cliff Kresge	67	71	67	70	275	8,925
Charles Raulerson	71	69	68	67	275	8,925
Tyler Williamson	67	68	69	71	275	8,925
Doug Garwood	68	67	69	72	276	6,588.75
Hunter Haas	69	65	71	71	276	6,588.75
Ryuji Imada	68	69	70	69	276	6,588.75
Gene Sauers	69	69	71	67	276	6,588.75
Ben Ferguson	67	71	68	71	277	4,746
Grover Justice	68	68	70	71	277	4,746
Eric Meeks	69	69	70	69	277	4,746
D.A. Points	71	68	72	66	277	4,746
Ted Purdy	70	67	70	70	277	4,746
Rich Barcelo	69	68	66	75	278	3,510
Danny Briggs	67	72	69	70	278	3,510
Alex Cejka	66	73	66	73	278	3,510
Raul Fretes	68	69	71	70	278	3,510
Jason Gore	66	70	71	71	278	3,510
Jeff Hart	67	72	72	67	278	3,510
Jon Mills	70	64	72	72	278	3,510

Virginia Beach Open

TPC of Virginia Beach, Virginia Beach, Virginia
Par 36-36–72; 7,432 yards

May 2-5
purse, $425,000

	SCORES				TOTAL	MONEY
Cliff Kresge	68	71	67	71	277	$76,500
Arron Oberholser	72	67	68	70	277	45,900
(Kresge defeated Oberholser on second playoff hole.)						
Mike Heinen	70	69	71	68	278	28,900
Steve Alker	74	66	71	69	280	18,700
Jace Bugg	73	69	70	68	280	18,700
Jason Buha	74	64	73	71	282	14,237.50
Jim McGovern	71	74	70	67	282	14,237.50
Patrick Sheehan	69	68	69	76	282	14,237.50
Ben Bates	71	71	69	72	283	11,050

	SCORES				TOTAL	MONEY
Todd Fischer	75	67	71	70	283	11,050
Tag Ridings	67	72	73	71	283	11,050
Vaughn Taylor	71	70	69	73	283	11,050
Nolan Henke	73	71	71	69	284	8,500
Charles Raulerson	72	69	71	72	284	8,500
Brian Claar	71	71	73	70	285	6,800
Keoke Cotner	74	68	72	71	285	6,800
Joe Daley	68	73	74	70	285	6,800
Billy Judah	74	71	71	69	285	6,800
Omar Uresti	71	72	69	73	285	6,800
Brad Adamonis	75	68	70	73	286	4,604.17
Danny Briggs	72	67	75	72	286	4,604.17
Tom Carter	73	72	70	71	286	4,604.17
Hunter Haas	70	71	75	70	286	4,604.17
Jeff Freeman	73	72	75	66	286	4,604.16
Chad Wright	69	69	74	74	286	4,604.16
Scott Gump	75	67	77	68	287	3,400
James McLean	77	66	74	70	287	3,400
Jon Mills	74	68	73	72	287	3,400
Ronnie Black	70	68	74	76	288	2,822
Barry Cheesman	74	68	76	70	288	2,822
Daniel Chopra	75	68	72	73	288	2,822
Doug Dunakey	73	70	75	70	288	2,822
Ted Tryba	73	69	73	73	288	2,822

Richmond Open

The Dominion Club, Richmond, Virginia
Par 36-36–72; 7,089 yards

May 9-12
purse, $425,000

	SCORES				TOTAL	MONEY
Patrick Moore	66	64	67	71	268	$76,500
John Maginnes	69	64	68	68	269	45,900
Jason Buha	64	68	67	72	271	24,650
Jay Delsing	67	69	67	68	271	24,650
Jason Dufner	68	69	67	68	272	17,000
Cliff Kresge	70	66	69	68	273	13,759.38
Patrick Sheehan	68	66	70	69	273	13,759.38
Jason Caron	66	65	68	74	273	13,759.37
James Driscoll	63	66	69	75	273	13,759.37
Tom Carter	63	67	72	72	274	10,625
Andrew McLardy	69	67	69	69	274	10,625
Steve Pate	68	69	66	71	274	10,625
Keoke Cotner	67	67	68	73	275	8,925
Rich Barcelo	66	68	69	73	276	7,012.50
Todd Fanning	66	68	70	72	276	7,012.50
Jeff Freeman	67	70	72	67	276	7,012.50
Ken Green	68	67	72	69	276	7,012.50
James McLean	70	68	70	68	276	7,012.50
Darron Stiles	66	69	69	72	276	7,012.50
Ben Curtis	65	68	73	71	277	4,951.25
John Elliott	68	66	72	71	277	4,951.25
Eric Meeks	67	68	72	70	277	4,951.25
Ted Tryba	71	67	67	72	277	4,951.25
Jaxon Brigman	72	66	73	67	278	3,604
Hunter Haas	69	66	71	72	278	3,604
Rob McKelvey	70	67	69	72	278	3,604

	SCORES				TOTAL	MONEY
Tag Ridings	67	68	71	72	278	3,604
Jim Rutledge	70	69	69	70	278	3,604
Dave Barr	66	73	72	68	279	2,868.75
David Morland	69	68	72	70	279	2,868.75
Don Reese	68	67	70	74	279	2,868.75
Tyler Williamson	69	68	67	75	279	2,868.75

SAS Carolina Classic

TPC at Wakefield Plantation, Raleigh, North Carolina
Par 35-36–71; 7,257 yards

May 16-19
purse, $450,000

	SCORES				TOTAL	MONEY
Zoran Zorkic	70	67	66	71	274	$81,000
Doug Barron	72	69	68	66	275	48,600
Lucas Glover	71	69	69	68	277	26,100
Jeff Hart	69	71	67	70	277	26,100
Chris Tidland	69	68	72	69	278	18,000
Jason Buha	68	67	66	78	279	15,637.50
John Maginnes	73	68	71	67	279	15,637.50
Jim McGovern	74	67	70	69	280	13,500
Mark Wilson	71	71	68	70	280	13,500
Jaxon Brigman	68	72	72	69	281	11,250
Bobby Gage	66	70	74	71	281	11,250
Rob McKelvey	70	69	73	69	281	11,250
Tommy Biershenk	72	69	68	73	282	9,000
Keoke Cotner	68	71	72	71	282	9,000
Danny Briggs	73	69	68	73	283	7,200
Marco Dawson	74	68	68	73	283	7,200
Bob Friend	69	72	70	72	283	7,200
Matt Jones	68	75	69	71	283	7,200
Tag Ridings	75	67	68	73	283	7,200
Emlyn Aubrey	70	72	69	73	284	4,875
Tom Carter	71	70	72	71	284	4,875
Patrick Moore	73	67	74	70	284	4,875
Travis Nance	68	72	69	75	284	4,875
Anthony Painter	70	72	70	72	284	4,875
Ted Tryba	72	69	72	71	284	4,875
Steve Alker	69	69	75	72	285	3,510
Michael Bradley	73	70	71	71	285	3,510
Joel Kribel	70	67	74	74	285	3,510
Pete Morgan	70	70	69	76	285	3,510
Ben Bates	70	72	70	74	286	2,835
James Driscoll	67	70	70	79	286	2,835
Kelly Gibson	70	67	75	74	286	2,835
Billy Judah	72	68	72	74	286	2,835
Andrew McLardy	68	73	73	72	286	2,835
Omar Uresti	73	70	73	70	286	2,835

Northeast Pennsylvania Classic

Glenmaura National Golf Club, Moosic, Pennsylvania
Par 35-35–70; 6,933 yards

May 30-June 2
purse, $450,000

	SCORES				TOTAL	MONEY
Gary Hallberg	69	68	74	64	275	$81,000
Roger Tambellini	69	69	66	74	278	48,600
Todd Barranger	67	69	73	70	279	23,400
Jeff Hart	69	68	70	72	279	23,400
Darron Stiles	71	69	66	73	279	23,400
Joe Daley	66	64	71	79	280	14,085
Bob Friend	68	70	70	72	280	14,085
Ken Green	72	69	68	71	280	14,085
Steve Haskins	72	69	70	69	280	14,085
Arron Oberholser	68	71	70	71	280	14,085
Cliff Kresge	73	65	75	68	281	11,250
Danny Briggs	69	71	72	70	282	8,043.75
Jace Bugg	70	69	68	75	282	8,043.75
Doug Garwood	65	68	70	79	282	8,043.75
Don Reese	73	63	71	75	282	8,043.75
Dave Rummells	68	73	69	72	282	8,043.75
Stan Utley	70	72	66	74	282	8,043.75
Charles Warren	64	74	69	75	282	8,043.75
Tyler Williamson	68	73	65	76	282	8,043.75
Steve Alker	68	72	72	71	283	5,058
Joel Kribel	70	70	69	74	283	5,058
Anthony Painter	67	70	74	72	283	5,058
Todd Rose	68	68	72	75	283	5,058
Patrick Sheehan	68	69	71	75	283	5,058
Tommy Biershenk	68	68	71	77	284	3,600
Greg Gregory	68	71	75	70	284	3,600
Ryuji Imada	68	72	73	71	284	3,600
John Maginnes	69	72	72	71	284	3,600
Roland Thatcher	68	67	78	71	284	3,600
David Branshaw	69	70	74	72	285	2,880
Keoke Cotner	68	70	76	71	285	2,880
Jason Dufner	71	70	74	70	285	2,880
Scott Gump	65	73	70	77	285	2,880
Tjaart van der Walt	67	69	77	72	285	2,880

Samsung Canadian PGA Championship

DiamondBack Golf Club, Richmond, Ontario, Canada
Par 36-36–72; 7,079 yards

June 6-9
purse, $450,000

	SCORES				TOTAL	MONEY
Arron Oberholser	70	70	62	66	268	$81,000
Doug Barron	67	71	66	66	270	48,600
Tommy Biershenk	67	68	72	64	271	30,600
Ken Green	69	65	72	66	272	17,718.75
Zoran Zorkic	73	65	67	67	272	17,718.75
Don Reese	68	62	73	69	272	17,718.75
Pete Morgan	72	65	64	71	272	17,718.75
Dave MacKenzie	67	69	68	69	273	13,950
Jason Caron	72	65	70	68	275	9,750
Doug Garwood	70	69	68	68	275	9,750
Anthony Painter	71	70	66	68	275	9,750

	SCORES			TOTAL	MONEY
Jeff Klauk	69	71	66	69	275	9,750
Greg Gregory	68	67	70	70	275	9,750
Tom Kalinowski	70	71	63	71	275	9,750
Stiles Mitchell	67	68	68	72	275	9,750
Kelly Gibson	67	68	67	73	275	9,750
Chad Wright	69	64	69	73	275	9,750
Todd Demsey	68	71	72	65	276	5,287.50
Scott Sterling	67	68	72	69	276	5,287.50
Vic Wilk	68	69	70	69	276	5,287.50
Derek Gillespie	67	71	69	69	276	5,287.50
John Morse	70	69	68	69	276	5,287.50
Keoke Cotner	70	70	67	69	276	5,287.50
David Edwards	66	68	71	71	276	5,287.50
John Maginnes	68	70	66	72	276	5,287.50
Joe Ogilvie	68	67	72	70	277	3,690
Ben Bates	71	70	66	70	277	3,690
Tommy Tolles	71	65	73	69	278	3,172.50
Steve Alker	69	70	68	71	278	3,172.50
Wes Short	66	69	71	72	278	3,172.50
Todd Bailey	70	68	68	72	278	3,172.50

Lake Erie Charity Classic

Peek'n Peak Resort, Findley Lake, New York
Par 35-36–71; 6,888 yards

June 20-23
purse, $425,000

	SCORES			TOTAL	MONEY
Patrick Moore	71	68	68	68	275	$76,500
Hunter Haas	70	69	66	71	276	45,900
Doug Barron	69	69	67	72	277	19,167.50
Kelly Gibson	71	66	68	72	277	19,167.50
Andrew McLardy	70	69	69	69	277	19,167.50
Omar Uresti	67	67	77	66	277	19,167.50
Tyler Williamson	67	70	70	70	277	19,167.50
Ben Bates	68	68	71	71	278	12,750
Anthony Painter	72	69	66	71	278	12,750
Bobby Gage	70	70	70	69	279	11,050
Billy Judah	68	69	72	70	279	11,050
Jim McGovern	70	73	68	69	280	7,832.15
Scott Sterling	70	68	71	71	280	7,832.15
Trevor Dodds	68	70	71	71	280	7,832.14
Todd Fanning	67	71	69	73	280	7,832.14
Jeff Freeman	69	71	69	71	280	7,832.14
Bob Friend	66	70	72	72	280	7,832.14
Greg Gregory	64	71	73	72	280	7,832.14
Anthony Rodriguez	71	69	69	72	281	5,151
Roger Tambellini	74	68	70	69	281	5,151
Tommy Tolles	70	70	69	72	281	5,151
Brian Wilson	68	73	69	71	281	5,151
Mark Wurtz	71	68	69	73	281	5,151
Jimmy Green	70	70	72	70	282	3,604
Rob McKelvey	69	69	73	71	282	3,604
John Morse	74	69	71	68	282	3,604
Wes Short	67	72	68	75	282	3,604
Chris Tidland	71	69	72	70	282	3,604
Todd Barranger	72	71	70	70	283	2,644.45
David Branshaw	70	73	71	69	283	2,644.45

	SCORES				TOTAL	MONEY
Jeff Klauk	73	70	71	69	283	2,644.45
Arron Oberholser	68	69	75	71	283	2,644.45
Jace Bugg	70	70	69	74	283	2,644.44
Jason Buha	71	68	73	71	283	2,644.44
Kevin Durkin	74	68	70	71	283	2,644.44
Patrick Sheehan	70	70	69	74	283	2,644.44
Chris Wollmann	71	69	71	72	283	2,644.44

Knoxville Open

Fox Den Country Club, Knoxville, Tennessee   June 27-30
Par 36-36–72; 7,142 yards   purse, $425,000

	SCORES				TOTAL	MONEY
Darron Stiles	71	69	64	68	272	$76,500
Aaron Baddeley	71	68	68	66	273	37,400
Steve Ford	70	71	67	65	273	37,400
Todd Barranger	67	71	69	68	275	20,400
Jason Caron	71	68	65	72	276	16,150
Tag Ridings	69	71	70	66	276	16,150
Patrick Moore	68	72	69	68	277	13,706.25
Patrick Sheehan	69	68	67	73	277	13,706.25
Tommy Biershenk	68	71	70	69	278	10,625
Brad Ott	71	69	66	72	278	10,625
Scott Sterling	68	67	73	70	278	10,625
Chris Tidland	67	72	69	70	278	10,625
Stan Utley	70	68	69	71	278	10,625
Eric Meeks	71	71	69	68	279	7,862.50
Sonny Skinner	68	69	68	74	279	7,862.50
Todd Bailey	72	69	67	72	280	5,078.75
Craig Bowden	69	72	71	68	280	5,078.75
Jaxon Brigman	70	71	73	66	280	5,078.75
Daniel Chopra	68	72	72	68	280	5,078.75
John Engler	73	68	67	72	280	5,078.75
Jeff Freeman	71	71	70	68	280	5,078.75
Lucas Glover	71	70	70	69	280	5,078.75
Hunter Haas	70	68	71	71	280	5,078.75
Joel Kribel	72	69	68	71	280	5,078.75
Jin Park	71	68	69	72	280	5,078.75
Anthony Rodriguez	70	70	71	69	280	5,078.75
Brian Wilson	69	71	68	72	280	5,078.75
Ahmad Bateman	70	70	71	70	281	2,890
Todd Fischer	67	72	71	71	281	2,890
Jeff Hart	71	71	70	69	281	2,890
Andrew McLardy	71	71	67	72	281	2,890
Dave Stockton, Jr.	71	70	71	69	281	2,890
Tjaart van der Walt	72	69	71	69	281	2,890

Hershey Open

Country Club of Hershey, East Course,
Hershey, Pennsylvania
Par 36-35–71; 7,154 yards

July 4-7
purse, $425,000

	SCORES				TOTAL	MONEY
Cliff Kresge	67	71	71	67	276	$76,500
Joel Kribel	67	68	70	71	276	31,733.34
Brian Claar	70	67	68	71	276	31,733.33
Steve Ford	69	68	68	71	276	31,733.33
(Kresge won on third playoff hole.)						
Steve Haskins	71	72	70	64	277	15,512.50
Rob McKelvey	68	66	71	72	277	15,512.50
Omar Uresti	68	73	67	69	277	15,512.50
Todd Barranger	67	71	74	66	278	12,750
Scott Sterling	68	69	71	70	278	12,750
Steve Alker	69	75	65	70	279	11,050
Billy Judah	68	70	70	71	279	11,050
Tom Carter	68	70	72	70	280	9,775
Jason Buha	72	69	72	68	281	7,508.34
Chris Tidland	74	68	75	64	281	7,508.34
Jace Bugg	70	72	71	68	281	7,508.33
Kevin Johnson	72	70	69	70	281	7,508.33
D.A. Points	68	72	67	74	281	7,508.33
Darron Stiles	66	71	74	70	281	7,508.33
Michael Bradley	69	71	72	70	282	5,950
Kelly Gibson	70	74	72	67	283	5,128.34
Tag Ridings	70	71	71	71	283	5,128.33
Marc Turnesa	69	74	72	68	283	5,128.33
Ben Bates	71	69	71	73	284	3,391.50
Tommy Biershenk	68	70	75	71	284	3,391.50
Joe Daley	71	73	74	66	284	3,391.50
Marco Dawson	66	75	75	68	284	3,391.50
Doug Dunakey	71	68	75	70	284	3,391.50
Doug Garwood	71	72	70	71	284	3,391.50
Greg Gregory	70	74	69	71	284	3,391.50
Brad Ott	70	71	70	73	284	3,391.50
Jim Rutledge	69	75	71	69	284	3,391.50
Mark Wurtz	67	70	72	75	284	3,391.50

Dayton Open

Golf Club at Yankee Trace, Centerville, Ohio
Par 36-36–72; 7,159 yards

July 11-14
purse, $425,000

	SCORES				TOTAL	MONEY
Jason Buha	66	67	66	66	265	$76,500
Todd Barranger	66	66	69	67	268	37,400
Marco Dawson	68	68	66	66	268	37,400
Tom Carter	68	66	69	66	269	20,400
Roger Tambellini	71	67	64	68	270	16,150
Rocky Walcher	71	65	67	67	270	16,150
Jaxon Brigman	72	69	64	66	271	11,505.36
Todd Fischer	71	66	69	65	271	11,505.36
Steve Haskins	69	68	67	67	271	11,505.36
Stiles Mitchell	73	68	66	64	271	11,505.36
Jeff Quinney	72	67	67	65	271	11,505.36

	SCORES				TOTAL	MONEY
Daniel Chopra	70	68	66	67	271	11,505.35
Darron Stiles	67	68	67	69	271	11,505.35
Tommy Biershenk	70	68	69	65	272	7,650
Bob Friend	68	67	71	66	272	7,650
Omar Uresti	70	70	67	65	272	7,650
Billy Judah	74	66	65	68	273	6,587.50
D.A. Points	68	72	66	67	273	6,587.50
Brad Adamonis	69	66	70	69	274	4,972.50
John Maginnes	71	68	69	66	274	4,972.50
Pete Morgan	68	67	70	69	274	4,972.50
Anthony Painter	68	70	67	69	274	4,972.50
Michael Sims	73	64	70	67	274	4,972.50
Dave Stockton, Jr.	69	71	66	68	274	4,972.50
Rich Barcelo	72	69	67	67	275	3,485
Robert Garrigus	72	68	68	67	275	3,485
Eric Meeks	69	72	67	67	275	3,485
Wes Short	68	73	66	68	275	3,485
Michael Flynn	70	69	69	68	276	2,644.45
Joel Kribel	66	68	73	69	276	2,644.45
Scott Petersen	70	71	69	66	276	2,644.45
Jim Rutledge	72	68	68	68	276	2,644.45
Chris Couch	70	65	71	70	276	2,644.44
Todd Demsey	75	66	65	70	276	2,644.44
Cliff Kresge	71	69	66	70	276	2,644.44
Todd Rose	68	67	70	71	276	2,644.44
Chad Wright	69	68	69	70	276	2,644.44

Fort Smith Classic

Hardscrabble Country Club, Fort Smith, Arkansas · July 18-21
Par 35-35–70; 6,619 yards purse, $425,000

	SCORES				TOTAL	MONEY
Todd Fischer	65	67	68	69	269	$76,500
Gavin Coles	70	67	68	65	270	31,733.34
Doug Barron	67	70	68	65	270	31,733.33
Andy Sanders	66	66	71	67	270	31,733.33
Daniel Chopra	66	71	67	68	272	14,407.50
Doug Dunakey	66	71	67	68	272	14,407.50
Grover Justice	64	71	66	71	272	14,407.50
Craig Spence	65	68	67	72	272	14,407.50
Vic Wilk	66	69	67	70	272	14,407.50
Marco Dawson	66	69	67	71	273	9,775
Ben Ferguson	69	68	66	70	273	9,775
Eric Meeks	67	69	69	68	273	9,775
Victor Schwamkrug	67	68	71	67	273	9,775
Rocky Walcher	70	69	68	66	273	9,775
Scott Sterling	72	65	68	69	274	7,437.50
Omar Uresti	69	71	65	69	274	7,437.50
D.J. Brigman	66	69	69	71	275	5,950
John Engler	67	68	71	69	275	5,950
Brad Ott	67	70	70	68	275	5,950
Jin Park	71	65	69	70	275	5,950
Fran Quinn	68	66	69	72	275	5,950
Tom Carter	70	70	64	72	276	4,250
Tim O'Neal	67	72	67	70	276	4,250
Charles Raulerson	71	68	66	71	276	4,250

	SCORES				TOTAL	MONEY
Bruce Vaughan	66	71	70	69	276	4,250
Danny Briggs	68	69	68	72	277	3,400
Hunter Haas	69	67	68	73	277	3,400
Mark Wurtz	69	63	72	73	277	3,400
Todd Demsey	73	67	69	69	278	2,918.34
Jay Delsing	67	69	73	69	278	2,918.33
Richard Smith	68	66	71	73	278	2,918.33

Price Cutter Charity Championship

Highland Springs Country Club, Springfield, Missouri   July 25-28
Par 36-36–72; 7,060 yards   purse, $475,000

	SCORES				TOTAL	MONEY
Patrick Sheehan	63	68	66	72	269	$85,500
Eric Meeks	66	68	69	68	271	41,800
Brian Wilson	71	67	66	67	271	41,800
Erik Compton	67	69	69	69	274	18,703.13
Craig Spence	68	67	72	67	274	18,703.13
Todd Fischer	68	66	70	70	274	18,703.12
Rob McKelvey	66	66	70	72	274	18,703.12
Tom Carter	66	66	74	69	275	12,825
Gavin Coles	70	70	69	66	275	12,825
Kevin Johnson	70	68	69	68	275	12,825
Andy Morse	72	63	70	70	275	12,825
Scott Petersen	70	66	68	71	275	12,825
Clay Devers	68	69	68	71	276	8,391.67
Charles Raulerson	70	66	73	67	276	8,391.67
Scott Sterling	68	71	67	70	276	8,391.67
Vaughn Taylor	70	68	69	69	276	8,391.67
Jeff Freeman	67	67	70	72	276	8,391.66
Omar Uresti	69	65	74	68	276	8,391.66
Todd Barranger	68	70	71	69	278	5,757
Ahmad Bateman	69	68	69	72	278	5,757
Danny Briggs	68	70	67	73	278	5,757
Grover Justice	67	65	78	68	278	5,757
Fran Quinn	71	66	70	71	278	5,757
Tommy Biershenk	67	73	69	70	279	3,926.67
Hunter Haas	68	71	71	69	279	3,926.67
Ryan Howison	68	72	72	67	279	3,926.67
Dave Stockton, Jr.	70	70	68	71	279	3,926.67
Marco Dawson	68	70	70	71	279	3,926.66
Todd Pinneo	66	71	70	72	279	3,926.66
Barry Cheesman	71	67	69	73	280	3,087.50
Andy Sanders	74	66	67	73	280	3,087.50
Tjaart van der Walt	68	68	73	71	280	3,087.50
Bruce Vaughan	67	67	75	71	280	3,087.50

Omaha Classic

The Champions Club, Omaha, Nebraska
Par 36-36–72; 7,099 yards

August 1-4
purse, $500,000

	SCORES				TOTAL	MONEY
Jay Delsing	66	66	67	68	267	$90,000
Anthony Painter	74	65	65	64	268	54,000
Chip Beck	70	66	66	67	269	34,000
Chris Tidland	71	67	68	64	270	24,000
Craig Lile	74	64	68	65	271	20,000
Andrew McLardy	69	66	70	67	272	16,750
Tommy Biershenk	69	65	67	71	272	16,750
Lucas Glover	73	65	68	66	272	16,750
Barry Cheesman	69	65	69	70	273	13,000
Brian Wilson	71	67	71	64	273	13,000
Mike Heinen	75	65	66	67	273	13,000
Mark Hensby	69	65	70	69	273	13,000
Marco Dawson	71	71	66	66	274	10,000
Joel Kribel	67	65	70	72	274	10,000
Aaron Baddeley	72	67	69	67	275	8,750
Patrick Sheehan	71	71	70	63	275	8,750
Jeff Hart	74	66	67	70	277	6,766.66
Tommy Tolles	71	69	71	66	277	6,766.67
Jeff Freeman	72	66	69	70	277	6,766.67
Wes Short	74	63	70	70	277	6,766.67
Rich Barcelo	73	67	67	70	277	6,766.66
Jimmy Walker	72	68	71	66	277	6,766.67
Danny Briggs	67	69	70	72	278	4,400
Fran Quinn	72	67	72	67	278	4,400
Todd Demsey	73	67	67	71	278	4,400
Rob McKelvey	74	65	68	71	278	4,400
Keoke Cotner	72	67	71	68	278	4,400
Travis Perkins	74	67	67	70	278	4,400
Gary Hallberg	70	70	66	73	279	3,060
Charles Raulerson	67	68	75	69	279	3,060
Dave Stockton, Jr.	69	67	73	70	279	3,060
Cliff Kresge	72	70	66	71	279	3,060
Todd Fischer	70	70	68	71	279	3,060
Patrick Moore	69	71	69	70	279	3,060
Tjaart van der Walt	72	67	73	67	279	3,060
Mark Wilson	68	71	71	69	279	3,060
Jason Gore	74	68	70	67	279	3,060
Jason Buha	76	64	68	71	279	3,060

LaSalle Bank Open

Kemper Lakes Golf Club, Long Grove, Illinois
Par 36-36–72; 7,217 yards

August 8-11
purse, $450,000

	SCORES				TOTAL	MONEY
Marco Dawson	71	69	67	69	276	$81,000
Darron Stiles	69	73	65	72	279	48,600
Mark Wurtz	72	69	71	68	280	21,600
Doug Barron	73	70	64	73	280	21,600
Casey Martin	75	67	70	68	280	21,600
Arron Oberholser	68	72	68	72	280	21,600
Barry Cheesman	71	71	69	70	281	14,512.50

	SCORES				TOTAL	MONEY
Gene Sauers	65	74	68	74	281	14,512.50
Scott Sterling	73	69	69	71	282	12,150
Rich Barcelo	70	68	73	71	282	12,150
Nathan Green	74	68	70	70	282	12,150
Jimmy Walker	70	68	73	72	283	9,900
Lucas Glover	70	69	73	71	283	9,900
Emlyn Aubrey	69	72	71	72	284	7,650
Jay Delsing	72	72	70	70	284	7,650
Dave Stockton, Jr.	68	70	74	72	284	7,650
Tom Carter	69	73	72	70	284	7,650
Patrick Moore	72	66	77	69	284	7,650
Craig Bowden	71	68	71	75	285	5,850
Scott Petersen	74	68	72	71	285	5,850
Ben Ferguson	70	73	70	72	285	5,850
Steve Haskins	74	66	73	73	286	4,500
John Elliott	72	69	74	71	286	4,500
Ryan Howison	72	71	75	68	286	4,500
Charles Warren	72	71	75	68	286	4,500
Peter O'Malley	70	73	72	72	287	3,510
Brian Wilson	69	69	75	74	287	3,510
Todd Fischer	71	72	71	73	287	3,510
Craig Lile	69	74	73	71	287	3,510
Andy Morse	72	67	76	73	288	2,835
Wes Short	72	71	72	73	288	2,835
John Morse	72	71	71	74	288	2,835
David Dyer	71	71	73	73	288	2,835
Robert Garrigus	76	64	69	79	288	2,835
Steve Holmes	71	72	69	76	288	2,835

Preferred Health Systems Wichita Open

Crestview Country Club, Wichita, Kansas
Par 36-36–72; 6,913 yards

August 15-18
purse, $425,000

	SCORES				TOTAL	MONEY
Tyler Williamson	68	67	71	66	272	$76,500
Keoke Cotner	69	69	67	68	273	37,400
Jeff Klauk	69	67	72	65	273	37,400
Emlyn Aubrey	73	67	67	70	277	18,700
Nolan Henke	67	70	69	71	277	18,700
Chip Beck	68	72	69	69	278	14,238
Tom Carter	70	68	70	70	278	14,238
Arron Oberholser	71	67	73	67	278	14,238
Jeff Freeman	70	67	70	72	279	11,475
Patrick Moore	71	67	71	70	279	11,475
Jimmy Walker	74	65	70	70	279	11,475
Bob Friend	68	68	70	74	280	7,366.66
Ken Green	70	72	71	67	280	7,366.67
Dave Schreyer	74	67	73	66	280	7,366.67
Rocky Walcher	69	70	72	69	280	7,366.67
Dave Stockton, Jr.	72	70	69	69	280	7,366.67
John Morse	71	68	71	70	280	7,366.67
Ahmad Bateman	68	69	69	74	280	7,366.66
Jeff Sanday	69	70	70	71	280	7,366.67
D.J. Brigman	71	67	70	72	280	7,366.66
Barry Cheesman	65	73	69	74	281	3,928.89
Steve Gotsche	72	67	75	67	281	3,928.89

	SCORES				TOTAL	MONEY
Scott Petersen	71	68	69	73	281	3,928.89
Casey Martin	66	74	69	72	281	3,928.89
Rob Bradley	72	68	73	68	281	3,928.89
Todd Fanning	70	68	72	71	281	3,928.89
David Dyer	69	73	67	72	281	3,928.89
Han Lee	74	65	72	70	281	3,928.89
Andy Sanders	73	64	69	75	281	3,928.88
Keith Nolan	71	69	77	65	282	2,677.50
Victor Schwamkrug	68	74	73	67	282	2,677.50
Andrew McLardy	67	74	69	72	282	2,677.50
John Restino	71	71	69	71	282	2,677.50
Jason Buha	72	70	71	69	282	2,677.50
Kevin Durkin	70	69	75	68	282	2,677.50

Permian Basin Open

Midland Country Club, Midland, Texas
Par 36-36–72; 7,354 yards

August 22-25
purse, $425,000

	SCORES				TOTAL	MONEY
Tag Ridings	69	67	67	69	272	$76,500
Mark Hensby	65	68	68	71	272	45,900
(Ridings defeated Hensby on first playoff hole.)						
Brian Claar	72	67	67	68	274	28,900
Ken Green	67	72	68	68	275	16,734.38
Gene Sauers	67	65	74	69	275	16,734.37
Omar Uresti	69	68	66	72	275	16,734.37
Joe Daley	71	67	70	67	275	16,734.38
Mike Standly	72	65	71	68	276	12,325
Wes Short	68	72	67	69	276	12,325
Brent Winston	65	67	69	75	276	12,325
Emlyn Aubrey	70	68	74	65	277	7,692.50
Jeff Hart	69	69	68	71	277	7,692.50
Steve Haskins	71	69	67	70	277	7,692.50
Patrick Burke	69	68	73	67	277	7,692.50
Tom Carter	68	69	69	71	277	7,692.50
Keoke Cotner	70	70	70	67	277	7,692.50
Joel Kribel	70	70	68	69	277	7,692.50
Chad Wright	70	69	65	73	277	7,692.50
Brad Adamonis	68	67	71	71	277	7,692.50
Dustin Wigington	69	69	69	70	277	7,692.50
Kevin Wentworth	69	71	67	71	278	4,930
Brian Wilson	69	68	71	70	278	4,930
Stan Utley	71	69	69	70	279	3,642.85
John Elliott	75	65	72	67	279	3,642.86
Billy Judah	72	68	70	69	279	3,642.86
Greg Gregory	69	70	69	71	279	3,642.85
Nathan Green	66	71	73	69	279	3,642.86
Andy Walker	70	71	69	69	279	3,642.86
Kelsey Cline	70	68	71	70	279	3,642.86
Dave Schreyer	71	69	74	66	280	2,720
Jaxon Brigman	71	69	69	71	280	2,720
Kevin Dillen	71	68	70	71	280	2,720
Michael Flynn	69	69	68	74	280	2,720
Jimmy Walker	69	68	71	72	280	2,720

Utah Classic

Willow Creek Country Club, Sandy, Utah
Par 36-36–72; 7,007 yards
(Event reduced to 54 holes—rain.)

September 5-8
purse, $425,000

	SCORES			TOTAL	MONEY
Arron Oberholser	71	64	67	202	$76,500
Brian Claar	67	71	66	204	37,400
Doug Barron	68	67	69	204	37,400
Curt Byrum	69	66	70	205	16,022.50
Patrick Moore	70	71	64	205	16,022.50
Victor Schwamkrug	71	67	67	205	16,022.50
Andy Miller	68	68	69	205	16,022.50
Jimmy Walker	70	66	69	205	16,022.50
Mark Wurtz	73	66	67	206	11,900
Todd Fischer	70	71	65	206	11,900
Trevor Dodds	71	71	65	207	8,712.50
Eric Johnson	72	68	67	207	8,712.50
Aaron Baddeley	69	71	67	207	8,712.50
Jason Caron	72	67	68	207	8,712.50
Jeff Klauk	71	66	70	207	8,712.50
D.A. Points	69	66	72	207	8,712.50
Jeff Hart	68	72	68	208	5,561.43
Fran Quinn	69	70	69	208	5,561.42
Scott Petersen	70	67	71	208	5,561.43
Omar Uresti	68	69	71	208	5,561.43
Mark Hensby	76	65	67	208	5,561.43
Ryuji Imada	70	71	67	208	5,561.43
Steve Holmes	70	71	67	208	5,561.43
Jim Benepe	73	69	67	209	3,697.50
Chris Couch	69	68	72	209	3,697.50
Boyd Summerhays	67	71	71	209	3,697.50
Brad Adamonis	71	68	70	209	3,697.50
Ben Bates	71	67	72	210	2,841.43
Ken Green	70	70	70	210	2,841.42
Perry Moss	71	72	67	210	2,841.43
Pete Morgan	68	70	72	210	2,841.43
Brad Ott	69	74	67	210	2,841.43
Tommy Biershenk	70	71	69	210	2,841.43
Rich Barcelo	74	69	67	210	2,841.43

Oregon Classic

Shadow Hills Country Club, Junction City, Oregon
Par 36-36–72; 7,007 yards

September 12-15
purse, $425,000

	SCORES				TOTAL	MONEY
Jason Gore	67	67	65	71	270	$76,500
Marco Dawson	66	67	70	70	273	25,500
Jeff Freeman	67	67	69	70	273	25,500
Arron Oberholser	70	68	69	66	273	25,500
Patrick Moore	69	66	70	68	273	25,500
Tag Ridings	71	66	69	67	273	25,500
John Restino	67	68	71	68	274	14,237.50
Omar Uresti	70	69	67	69	275	13,175
Fran Quinn	74	64	68	70	276	9,509.38
Kevin Wentworth	71	67	68	70	276	9,509.37

	SCORES				TOTAL	MONEY
Eric Johnson	72	68	69	67	276	9,509.38
Tjaart van der Walt	69	68	67	72	276	9,509.37
Ryuji Imada	68	67	66	75	276	9,509.37
Darron Stiles	70	69	68	69	276	9,509.38
Brent Winston	66	69	68	73	276	9,509.37
Jason Buha	69	70	68	69	276	9,509.38
Todd Barranger	66	71	69	71	277	5,950
Mark Hensby	67	70	70	70	277	5,950
Ted Purdy	65	67	74	71	277	5,950
Jason Caron	65	69	74	69	277	5,950
Jimmy Walker	70	71	69	67	277	5,950
Doug Barron	68	70	71	69	278	4,250
Rob Bradley	68	71	67	72	278	4,250
Tommy Biershenk	67	71	69	71	278	4,250
Jason Dufner	69	67	69	73	278	4,250
Ben Bates	70	70	71	68	279	2,984.45
Barry Cheesman	70	70	72	67	279	2,984.45
Jim Rutledge	69	72	69	69	279	2,984.44
Kevin Johnson	69	69	69	72	279	2,984.44
Mark Wurtz	70	68	72	69	279	2,984.45
Chris Couch	67	73	68	71	279	2,984.44
Todd Fischer	67	70	74	68	279	2,984.45
Richard Johnson	70	70	70	69	279	2,984.44
Jeff Quinney	66	73	71	69	279	2,984.44

Albertson's Boise Open

Hillcrest Country Club, Boise, Idaho
Par 36-35–71; 6,698 yards

September 19-22
purse, $575,000

	SCORES				TOTAL	MONEY
Jason Gore	66	68	66	73	273	$103,500
Emlyn Aubrey	69	69	68	69	275	50,600
Barry Cheesman	67	70	69	69	275	50,600
Gavin Coles	71	65	70	70	276	27,600
Eric Meeks	66	71	69	71	277	20,987.50
Patrick Moore	68	66	69	74	277	20,987.50
D.J. Brigman	71	69	70	67	277	20,987.50
Todd Barranger	74	67	67	70	278	16,100
Mark Hensby	67	66	72	73	278	16,100
Greg Gregory	68	66	69	75	278	16,100
Hunter Haas	72	68	70	68	278	16,100
Andrew McLardy	69	69	71	70	279	12,650
Aaron Baddeley	69	72	69	69	279	12,650
Brian Claar	72	68	70	70	280	9,775
Vic Wilk	71	70	70	69	280	9,775
Dave Stockton, Jr.	70	71	71	68	280	9,775
Chris Couch	73	68	72	67	280	9,775
Steve Alker	70	70	69	71	280	9,775
Jeff Hart	70	71	72	68	281	6,095
Brian Kamm	64	72	73	72	281	6,095
Doug Barron	71	70	67	73	281	6,095
Victor Schwamkrug	70	69	75	67	281	6,095
Patrick Sheehan	68	72	71	70	281	6,095
Richard Johnson	70	72	68	71	281	6,095
Jason Caron	73	69	69	70	281	6,095
Todd Rose	69	70	69	73	281	6,095

	SCORES				TOTAL	MONEY
Jason Dufner	73	69	72	67	281	6,095
Jim Benepe	72	68	69	73	282	4,053.75
Zoran Zorkic	71	68	72	71	282	4,053.75
Shane Bertsch	74	68	73	67	282	4,053.75
Jeff Klauk	69	72	72	69	282	4,053.75

State Farm Open

Empire Lakes Golf Club, Rancho Cucamonga, California
Par 36-36–72; 6,972 yards

September 26-29
purse, $450,000

	SCORES				TOTAL	MONEY
Andy Miller	69	67	70	66	272	$81,000
Dave Stockton, Jr.	68	71	66	67	272	33,600
John Restino	63	72	68	69	272	33,600
Doug Garwood	66	69	66	71	272	33,600
(Miller won on first playoff hole.)						
Jay Delsing	72	67	66	68	273	17,100
Keoke Cotner	70	70	66	67	273	17,100
Steve Haskins	68	68	66	72	274	13,095
Tjaart van der Walt	67	69	67	71	274	13,095
Andrew McLardy	67	67	68	72	274	13,095
Joel Kribel	66	69	71	68	274	13,095
Jason Buha	66	74	65	69	274	13,095
Eric Meeks	70	69	66	70	275	9,112.50
John Elliott	69	70	66	70	275	9,112.50
Eric Johnson	65	73	70	67	275	9,112.50
Richie Coughlan	71	68	67	69	275	9,112.50
Barry Cheesman	68	68	70	70	276	5,910
Jeff Hart	70	69	66	71	276	5,910
Patrick Burke	69	70	67	70	276	5,910
John Wilson	69	66	71	70	276	5,910
Craig Bowden	71	68	70	67	276	5,910
Todd Barranger	73	66	71	66	276	5,910
Todd Fischer	69	67	69	71	276	5,910
Gavin Coles	68	70	67	71	276	5,910
Chris Anderson	72	67	66	71	276	5,910
Chip Beck	67	73	68	69	277	3,510
Ernie Gonzalez	66	68	67	76	277	3,510
Brian Wilson	70	66	68	73	277	3,510
Todd Demsey	71	69	70	67	277	3,510
Joe Daley	70	70	70	67	277	3,510
Lucas Glover	70	69	68	70	277	3,510

Bank of America Monterey Peninsula Classic

Bayonet Course, Seaside, California
Par 36-36–72; 7,117 yards

October 3-6
purse, $450,000

	SCORES				TOTAL	MONEY
Roland Thatcher	66	72	71	74	283	$81,000
Aaron Baddeley	73	71	70	71	285	48,600
Barry Cheesman	71	75	69	72	287	30,600
Charles Warren	71	74	70	73	288	21,600
Vic Wilk	74	68	74	73	289	17,100

	SCORES				TOTAL	MONEY
Anthony Painter	73	73	68	75	289	17,100
Mark Wurtz	72	71	75	72	290	14,512.50
Todd Barranger	74	71	73	72	290	14,512.50
Eric Meeks	75	70	73	73	291	12,150
Omar Uresti	69	74	73	75	291	12,150
Jason Caron	67	72	79	73	291	12,150
Emlyn Aubrey	77	72	69	74	292	9,450
John Elliott	71	76	71	74	292	9,450
John Engler	75	72	71	74	292	9,450
Wes Short	72	76	71	74	293	7,200
Cliff Kresge	70	79	72	72	293	7,200
Arron Oberholser	72	73	74	74	293	7,200
Joel Kribel	69	73	75	76	293	7,200
Jason Buha	77	71	69	76	293	7,200
Gary Hallberg	75	73	75	71	294	4,875
Dave Schreyer	71	75	70	78	294	4,875
Mike Brisky	71	76	75	72	294	4,875
Todd Demsey	74	74	72	74	294	4,875
Andrew McLardy	73	74	77	70	294	4,875
Darron Stiles	74	74	73	73	294	4,875
Marco Dawson	72	73	74	76	295	3,345
Craig Bowden	74	75	74	72	295	3,345
Shane Bertsch	75	73	73	74	295	3,345
Mark Hensby	72	76	74	73	295	3,345
Ted Purdy	75	73	77	70	295	3,345
Doug Garwood	72	76	74	73	295	3,345

Gila River Classic at Wild Horse Pass Resort

Whirlwind Golf Club, Devil's Claw Course, Chandler, Arizona
Par 36-35–71; 6,994 yards

October 10-13
purse, $425,000

	SCORES				TOTAL	MONEY
David Branshaw	65	61	64	72	262	$76,500
Charles Raulerson	67	63	68	68	266	37,400
Aaron Baddeley	67	66	65	68	266	37,400
Patrick Sheehan	62	66	67	72	267	16,734.37
Charles Warren	68	65	66	68	267	16,734.38
D.A. Points	68	65	61	73	267	16,734.37
Doug Garwood	66	65	68	68	267	16,734.38
Todd Fischer	70	67	67	64	268	13,175
Brian Wilson	69	64	65	71	269	11,050
Omar Uresti	68	67	64	70	269	11,050
Patrick Moore	65	67	68	69	269	11,050
Jason Dufner	69	63	71	66	269	11,050
Eric Meeks	66	69	68	67	270	7,508.34
Dave Schreyer	65	67	66	72	270	7,508.33
Todd Barranger	63	67	67	73	270	7,508.33
Cliff Kresge	67	66	68	69	270	7,508.34
Anthony Painter	64	66	69	71	270	7,508.33
Steven Alker	68	68	64	70	270	7,508.33
Emlyn Aubrey	67	70	65	69	271	4,796.43
Stan Utley	65	70	65	71	271	4,796.43
Todd Demsey	66	69	68	68	271	4,796.43
Rob Bradley	65	64	69	73	271	4,796.43
Joel Kribel	67	68	66	70	271	4,796.43
James McLean	65	66	66	74	271	4,796.42

	SCORES			TOTAL	MONEY
Kevin Stadler	66 67 67 71			271	4,796.43
Guy Boros	70 63 65 74			272	3,159.16
Vic Wilk	68 64 67 73			272	3,159.17
Jeff Freeman	68 68 69 67			272	3,159.17
Stiles Mitchell	65 68 65 74			272	3,159.16
Darron Stiles	69 64 67 72			272	3,159.17
Tommy Biershenk	67 70 66 69			272	3,159.17

Hibernia Southern Open

Southern Trace Country Club, Shreveport, Louisiana
Par 36-36–72; 6,916 yards
(Event shortened to 54 holes—rain.)

October 17-20
purse, $425,000

	SCORES			TOTAL	MONEY
David Morland	64	65	68	197	$76,500
John Morse	65	68	67	200	37,400
Steven Alker	65	69	66	200	37,400
Aaron Baddeley	71	65	66	202	18,700
Tag Ridings	68	67	67	202	18,700
Ben Bates	65	70	68	203	13,302.50
Joe Daley	67	68	68	203	13,302.50
David Branshaw	67	68	68	203	13,302.50
Rob Bradley	69	64	70	203	13,302.50
Jeff Klauk	68	71	64	203	13,302.50
Brad Fabel	72	69	63	204	9,350
Jeff Freeman	67	68	69	204	9,350
Dicky Pride	66	70	68	204	9,350
Tommy Biershenk	69	70	65	204	9,350
Emlyn Aubrey	64	72	69	205	5,978.33
Brian Kamm	67	71	67	205	5,978.34
Wes Short	70	70	65	205	5,978.33
Cliff Kresge	68	71	66	205	5,978.34
Ted Purdy	69	69	67	205	5,978.34
Patrick Sheehan	68	69	68	205	5,978.33
John Restino	69	68	68	205	5,978.33
Jean-Paul Herbert	69	71	65	205	5,978.33
Adam Babb	68	69	68	205	5,978.33
Chip Beck	66	71	69	206	3,424.29
Brian Claar	70	71	65	206	3,424.28
Shane Bertsch	70	70	66	206	3,424.29
Jimmy Green	67	69	70	206	3,424.28
Chris Couch	68	68	70	206	3,424.28
Tjaart van der Walt	67	70	69	206	3,424.29
D.A. Points	71	67	68	206	3,424.29

Buy.com Tour Championship

Robert Trent Jones Golf Trail, Senator Course at Capitol Hill,   October 24-27
Prattville, Alabama   purse, $600,000
Par 36-36—72; 7,656 yards
(Fourth round cancelled—rain.)

	SCORES			TOTAL	MONEY
Patrick Moore	71	69	66	206	$108,000
Mike Heinen	67	70	71	208	44,800
Steven Alker	71	69	68	208	44,800
Jeff Klauk	69	68	71	208	44,800
Eric Meeks	67	70	72	209	22,800
Arron Oberholser	70	73	66	209	22,800
Keoke Cotner	69	69	72	210	18,700
Jason Buha	71	69	70	210	18,700
Roland Thatcher	68	71	71	210	18,700
Jay Delsing	73	63	75	211	15,000
Dave Stockton, Jr.	75	66	70	211	15,000
Tyler Williamson	71	69	71	211	15,000
Brian Claar	71	70	71	212	11,430
Todd Barranger	65	73	74	212	11,430
Aaron Baddeley	68	72	72	212	11,430
Tag Ridings	70	72	70	212	11,430
David Morland	72	71	70	213	9,240
Gavin Coles	70	69	74	213	9,240
Barry Cheesman	70	71	73	214	7,485
Jeff Freeman	72	70	72	214	7,485
Anthony Painter	75	69	70	214	7,485
Jason Gore	67	73	74	214	7,485
Emlyn Aubrey	74	68	73	215	5,622.86
Ken Green	73	67	75	215	5,622.85
Scott Sterling	72	72	71	215	5,622.86
Rob McKelvey	72	70	73	215	5,622.86
Doug Barron	70	71	74	215	5,622.86
Todd Fischer	72	74	69	215	5,622.86
Charles Warren	69	71	75	215	5,622.85
Omar Uresti	75	70	71	216	4,620
Jace Bugg	76	68	72	216	4,620
Doug Garwood	73	70	73	216	4,620

Canadian Tour

Panama Open Panasonic

Coronado Resort Course, Coronado Beach, Panama
Par 36-36–72; 6,983 yards

January 17-20
purse, C$337,500

	SCORES				TOTAL	MONEY
Mario Tiziani	67	67	68	71	273	C$60,000
David Kirkpatrick	69	72	66	66	273	30,000
Chad Wright	69	72	63	69	273	30,000
(Tiziani defeated Kirkpatrick and Wright on second playoff hole.)						
Patrick Moore	68	67	72	70	277	15,000
Joe Cioe	72	70	72	64	278	12,000
Jaxon Brigman	75	66	69	69	279	9,375
Lucas Glover	70	68	72	69	279	9,375
Steve Haskins	71	67	71	70	279	9,375
Sonny Skinner	71	67	70	71	279	9,375
David Ladd	66	72	69	73	280	7,350
Mark Slawter	69	69	71	71	280	7,350
Dan Stone	73	66	71	70	280	7,350
Rafael Alarcon	68	73	69	71	281	5,888
Jesus Amaya	72	73	64	72	281	5,888
Greg Gregory	69	71	69	72	281	5,888
Roger Tambellini	71	69	72	69	281	5,888
Bob Conrad	72	70	69	71	282	5,100
Dave Christensen	67	71	73	72	283	4,350
Darren Griff	72	69	70	72	283	4,350
David Howser	76	69	71	67	283	4,350
Mike McNerney	67	72	71	73	283	4,350
Aaron Barber	68	77	75	64	284	3,050
Jace Bugg	68	74	72	70	284	3,050
Ken Duke	68	76	72	68	284	3,050
Gustavo Mendoza	72	71	70	71	284	3,050
John Engler	71	69	72	73	285	2,344
Grant Masson	72	73	70	70	285	2,344
David Morland	72	75	69	69	285	2,344
Steve Scott	70	74	72	69	285	2,344
Steve LeBrun	79	73	65	69	286	2,025
Brian Unk	70	72	72	72	286	2,025
Noah Zelnick	77	70	71	68	286	2,025

Texas Classic

Kingwood Country Club, Forest Course, Houston, Texas
Par 36-36–72; 7,058 yards

March 7-10
purse, C$225,000

	SCORES				TOTAL	MONEY
Steve Scott	71	63	71	69	274	C$36,000
Hank Kuehne	72	64	75	64	275	15,300
Jeff Quinney	64	69	71	71	275	15,300
Roger Tambellini	66	68	74	67	275	15,300

		SCORES			TOTAL	MONEY
Michael Henderson	70	70	70	66	276	9,000
Nick Cassini	69	71	68	70	278	8,100
*Bubba Dickerson	66	73	72	68	279	
Jeff Klauk	71	69	68	71	279	7,425
Alan McLean	71	71	72	66	280	6,975
Marty Schiene	70	68	72	71	281	6,525
Chris Anderson	71	66	71	75	283	5,850
Conrad Ray	72	68	75	68	283	5,850
Aaron Barber	70	66	74	74	284	4,556
David Ogrin	73	67	73	71	284	4,556
Alex Rocha	73	68	75	68	284	4,556
Mario Tiziani	75	66	71	72	284	4,556
Ken Duke	71	70	72	72	285	3,198
Brian Hull	73	68	73	71	285	3,198
Tim O'Neal	72	70	72	71	285	3,198
Ben Pettitt	70	71	69	75	285	3,198
Mikkel Reese	69	70	75	71	285	3,198
Jason Schultz	69	68	76	72	285	3,198
Bryan Wright	71	70	75	69	285	3,198
Jeff Bloom	69	68	75	75	287	2,367
Mark Johnson	71	70	74	72	287	2,367
Will Mackenzie	69	70	76	72	287	2,367
Wes Martin	72	71	74	70	287	2,367
David Mathis	69	74	74	70	287	2,367
Jason Enloe	71	71	72	74	288	1,872
Chris Greenwood	72	71	75	70	288	1,872
Chris Locker	72	70	71	75	288	1,872
Landry Mahan	68	73	76	71	288	1,872
Doug McGuigan	70	70	74	74	288	1,872
Patrick Moore	70	73	74	71	288	1,872
Chris Wall	67	70	71	80	288	1,872

Texas Challenge

Circle C Ranch, Austin, Texas
Par 36-36–72; 6,859 yards

March 14-17
purse, C$150,000

		SCORES			TOTAL	MONEY
Hank Kuehne	72	68	65	65	270	C$24,000
Jason Bohn	70	67	71	63	271	11,700
Steve Runge	69	68	70	64	271	11,700
Chris Wall	70	71	70	66	277	7,200
Todd Fanning	71	67	73	67	278	5,450
Philip Jonas	72	68	71	67	278	5,450
Jeff Quinney	68	69	71	70	278	5,450
James Driscoll	69	73	70	67	279	4,650
Jeff Klauk	70	69	69	72	280	3,750
Jon Mills	74	69	65	72	280	3,750
Kevin Na	72	69	70	69	280	3,750
Andrew Sanders	69	69	71	71	280	3,750
Jason Schultz	69	70	76	65	280	3,750
Lucas Glover	75	68	72	66	281	2,334
Darren Griff	71	70	64	76	281	2,334
Wes Heffernan	69	67	75	70	281	2,334
David Mathis	69	70	73	69	281	2,334
Brian Payne	71	68	74	68	281	2,334
Drew Scott	72	73	69	67	281	2,334

	SCORES			TOTAL	MONEY
Steve Scott	74	67	68	72	281	2,334
Jarrod Warner	70	72	70	69	281	2,334
Scott Ford	73	72	71	66	282	2,334
Scott Petersen	72	72	67	71	282	2,334
Rodney Butcher	75	70	73	65	283	1,575
Craig Matthew	73	70	73	67	283	1,575
Bryan Wright	70	72	71	70	283	1,575
Michael Kirk	69	74	72	69	284	1,338
Grant Masson	75	69	71	69	284	1,338
Patrick Moore	75	67	72	70	284	1,338
Conrad Ray	72	68	74	70	284	1,338
Mark Slawter	69	72	75	68	284	1,338

Scottsdale Swing at McCormick Ranch

McCormick Ranch, Scottsdale, Arizona
Par 36-36–72; 7,044 yards

March 28-31
purse, C$150,000

	SCORES			TOTAL	MONEY
Jeff Quinney	63	68	66	68	265	C$24,000
James Driscoll	64	72	70	65	271	14,400
Iain Steel	68	67	71	67	273	9,000
Patrick Moore	66	73	65	71	275	7,200
Hank Kuehne	67	73	70	66	276	5,700
Edward Loar	72	68	68	68	276	5,700
Scott Hend	69	69	71	68	277	4,650
Alex Rocha	70	68	73	66	277	4,650
Jim Rutledge	68	69	70	70	277	4,650
Kyle Blackman	70	68	71	69	278	3,600
Rodney Butcher	72	68	68	70	278	3,600
Mike Grob	69	70	70	69	278	3,600
Roger Tambellini	70	66	74	68	278	3,600
Todd Demsey	72	71	65	71	279	2,550
Scott Ford	68	70	72	69	279	2,550
Dan Halldorson	71	72	66	70	279	2,550
Doug McGuigan	69	72	67	71	279	2,550
Jon Mills	70	72	68	69	279	2,550
Wes Martin	74	70	67	69	280	1,975
Drew Scott	70	71	64	75	280	1,975
Chris Wisler	68	71	67	74	280	1,975
Aaron Barber	72	66	71	72	281	1,762.50
Jeff Wood	72	71	67	71	281	1,762.50
Jason Bohn	70	72	71	69	282	1,650
Doug LaBelle	67	71	73	72	283	1,446
Scott Petersen	71	68	72	72	283	1,446
Warren Schutte	70	72	67	74	283	1,446
Steve Scott	70	69	71	73	283	1,446
Kyle Voska	71	71	70	71	283	1,446
Bob Conrad	72	71	74	67	284	1,204.50
David Howser	72	72	71	69	284	1,204.50
Philip Jonas	69	73	72	70	284	1,204.50
Michael Kirk	70	72	76	66	284	1,204.50
Danny Paniccia	69	71	75	69	284	1,204.50

Scottsdale Swing at Eagle Mountain

Eagle Mountain, Scottsdale, Arizona
Par 35-35–70; 6,700 yards

April 4-7
purse, C$150,000

	SCORES				TOTAL	MONEY
Jimmy Walker	66	65	64	66	261	C$24,000
Derek Gillespie	65	66	68	64	263	14,400
Chris Greenwood	65	68	66	66	265	9,000
Hank Kuehne	65	66	69	66	266	7,200
Ken Duke	65	63	67	73	268	5,450
Rafael Gemoets	68	64	70	66	268	5,450
Chris Wisler	67	67	69	65	268	5,450
Jason Enloe	67	63	68	71	269	4,350
Edward Loar	71	64	66	68	269	4,350
Mario Tiziani	65	65	74	65	269	4,350
Michael Henderson	67	65	69	69	270	3,300
Doug McGuigan	63	69	65	73	270	3,300
Alex Quiroz	67	67	68	68	270	3,300
Tony Smith	66	66	71	67	270	3,300
Bob Conrad	65	64	74	68	271	2,260.71
Mike Grob	68	68	65	70	271	2,260.71
Brian Kontak	65	66	71	69	271	2,260.71
Rob McMillan	69	67	69	66	271	2,260.71
Danny Paniccia	69	62	69	71	271	2,260.71
Jeff Quinney	66	70	70	65	271	2,260.71
Andrew Sanders	62	68	72	69	271	2,260.71
Todd Fanning	66	69	69	68	272	1,615
Michael Harris	65	70	71	66	272	1,615
David Hearn	68	68	67	69	272	1,615
Mark Johnson	64	66	73	69	272	1,615
Rob Johnson	67	65	70	70	272	1,615
Brian Payne	66	68	70	68	272	1,615
Dave Christensen	64	69	70	70	273	1,248.21
John Davis	66	65	73	69	273	1,248.21
Scott Ford	68	65	67	73	273	1,248.21
Wes Heffernan	67	66	68	72	273	1,248.21
Will Mackenzie	67	64	74	68	273	1,248.21
Grant Masson	66	69	70	68	273	1,248.21
Bryan Wright	66	68	68	71	273	1,248.21

Michelin Ixtapa Classic

Palma Real Golf Club, Ixtapa, Guerrero, Mexico
Par 36-36–72; 6,875 yards

April 18-21
purse, C$150,000

	SCORES				TOTAL	MONEY
Pablo Del Olmo	64	68	70	65	267	C$24,000
Bryan Saltus	65	68	72	66	271	14,400
Michael Kirk	71	69	68	64	272	9,000
Steve Scott	70	68	67	68	273	7,200
Bryan DeCorso	72	69	67	66	274	5,700
David McKenzie	64	68	71	71	274	5,700
Rodney Butcher	66	71	68	70	275	4,350
Ken Duke	69	66	68	72	275	4,350
Alex Quiroz	72	65	67	71	275	4,350
Mikkel Reese	69	68	68	70	275	4,350
Jose Trauwitz	70	68	69	68	275	4,350

	SCORES			TOTAL	MONEY
Alex Munoz	69	69	64	75	277	3,150
Bob Conrad	69	67	73	69	278	2,550
Michael Harris	71	72	66	69	278	2,550
Michael Mitchell	71	69	67	71	278	2,550
Mayson Petty	68	66	73	71	278	2,550
Chris Wollmann	69	68	72	69	278	2,550
Dave Christensen	71	69	70	69	279	1,890
Eddie Maunder	68	72	68	71	279	1,890
Alan McLean	73	68	66	72	279	1,890
Cesar Perez	67	72	71	69	279	1,890
Brian Smock	70	70	70	69	279	1,890
*Dan Swanson	73	70	65	71	279	
Graham Davidson	69	70	71	70	280	1,378
Jonn Drewery	71	72	67	70	280	1,378
Brad Fritsch	71	66	73	70	280	1,378
Octavio Gonzalez	73	69	71	67	280	1,378
Chris Greenwood	70	73	68	69	280	1,378
Scott Hend	69	68	73	70	280	1,378
Davidson Matyczuk	69	71	71	69	280	1,378
Wilfredo Morales	68	69	71	72	280	1,378
James Stewart	69	72	68	71	280	1,378
Jamie Welder	73	71	68	68	280	1,378

Barefoot Classic

Barefoot Resort, Norman Course, Myrtle Beach, South Carolina April 25-28
Par 36-36–72; 7,035 yards purse, C$150,000

	SCORES			TOTAL	MONEY
Rob McMillan	68	71	66	72	277	C$24,000
Paul Scaletta	69	70	69	72	280	14,400
David Hearn	66	74	68	73	281	9,000
Sean Dougherty	73	69	68	73	283	5,425
Brian Kontak	69	69	75	70	283	5,425
Eddy Lee	73	74	67	69	283	5,425
David McKenzie	70	72	72	69	283	5,425
Mikkel Reese	69	69	73	72	283	5,425
Sal Spallone	72	70	72	69	283	5,425
Marcus Cain	75	71	70	68	284	3,600
Ryan Dillon	78	68	68	70	284	3,600
Wes Heffernan	73	69	72	70	284	3,600
Bobby Kalinowski	69	74	70	71	284	3,600
Paul Devenport	72	74	70	69	285	2,220
Todd Doohan	73	70	73	69	285	2,220
John Drewery	73	71	69	72	285	2,220
James Driscoll	76	68	71	70	285	2,220
Brad Fritsch	72	72	71	70	285	2,220
Derek Gillespie	77	67	72	69	285	2,220
Michael Henderson	75	71	70	69	285	2,220
Alex Rocha	72	70	72	71	285	2,220
Iain Steel	72	73	67	73	285	2,220
Mario Tiziani	68	77	67	73	285	2,220
Doug McGuigan	69	77	66	74	286	1,612.50
Tim O'Neal	70	74	68	74	286	1,612.50
Patrick Damron	74	71	71	71	287	1,389
Scott Hend	76	70	70	71	287	1,389
Hank Kuehne	69	72	72	74	287	1,389

	SCORES				TOTAL	MONEY
Will Mackenzie	70	73	67	77	287	1,389
Tim Turpen	70	72	69	76	287	1,389

Myrtle Beach Barefoot Championship

Barefoot Resort, Pete Dye Course, Myrtle Beach, South Carolina May 2-5
Par 35-36–71; 7,257 yards purse, C$150,000

	SCORES				TOTAL	MONEY
Derek Gillespie	69	72	69	69	279	C$24,000
Scott Hend	72	67	70	73	282	14,400
Jason Enloe	73	67	72	71	283	7,400
Michael Kirk	70	68	76	69	283	7,400
Mayson Petty	73	70	71	69	283	7,400
David McKenzie	73	70	70	71	284	5,000
Steve Scott	70	75	69	70	284	5,000
Zoltan Veress	76	67	70	71	284	5,000
Mario Tiziani	74	69	72	70	285	4,200
Tim Turpen	71	73	71	70	285	4,200
Michael Harris	73	70	72	71	286	3,450
Hank Kuehne	72	69	74	71	286	3,450
Alex Rocha	73	68	73	72	286	3,450
Ryan Dillon	71	70	73	73	287	2,775
Iain Steel	74	69	72	72	287	2,775
James Driscoll	75	71	71	71	288	2,132.14
Scott Ford	69	77	66	76	288	2,132.14
Roger Harrison	67	76	72	73	288	2,132.14
Gene Jones	70	72	72	74	288	2,132.14
Kyle Kovacs	72	73	71	72	288	2,132.14
Eddy Lee	70	74	73	71	288	2,132.14
Jimmy Walker	76	69	68	75	288	2,132.14
Mike Capone	72	71	77	69	289	1,578
Tim Conley	71	73	74	71	289	1,578
Jonn Drewery	71	72	73	73	289	1,578
Alan McLean	70	76	70	73	289	1,578
Chris Wall	76	70	70	73	289	1,578
Dan Chartrand	71	68	75	76	290	1,335
Casey Martin	76	70	72	72	290	1,335
Adam Speirs	72	74	72	72	290	1,335

Lewis Chitengwa Memorial Championship

Keswick Hall at Monticello, Charlottesville, Virginia May 9-12
Par 36-35–71; 6,307 yards purse, C$150,000

	SCORES				TOTAL	MONEY
Chris Wisler	65	65	67	73	270	C$24,000
David Hearn	65	68	71	68	272	14,400
Michael Harris	65	64	74	71	274	9,000
Scott Ford	73	66	70	66	275	6,600
Cameron Yancey	65	67	71	72	275	6,600
Brad Sutterfield	69	68	71	70	278	5,400
Aaron Barber	67	69	74	69	279	4,350
Bryn Parry	69	68	69	73	279	4,350
Jason Schultz	67	72	70	70	279	4,350

	SCORES				TOTAL	MONEY
Iain Steel	70	71	70	68	279	4,350
Jarrod Warner	70	65	74	70	279	4,350
Andrew Sanders	70	69	71	70	280	3,450
Chris Anderson	66	72	67	76	281	2,812.50
Rich Massey	68	71	70	72	281	2,812.50
Grant Masson	72	68	69	72	281	2,812.50
David Mathis	67	67	73	74	281	2,812.50
Bryan DeCorso	67	69	74	72	282	2,115
Derek Gillespie	65	72	74	71	282	2,115
Mike Grob	65	70	78	69	282	2,115
*Steve Marino	70	69	72	71	282	
David McKenzie	68	70	76	68	282	2,115
Michael Mitchell	71	70	68	73	282	2,115
Jason Enloe	69	71	73	70	283	1,687.50
Jimmy Flippen	70	70	70	73	283	1,687.50
Will Mackenzie	71	70	70	72	283	1,687.50
Paul Scaletta	76	64	72	71	283	1,687.50
Jaime Gomez	69	72	72	71	284	1,341.43
Chris Greenwood	70	69	70	75	284	1,341.43
Wes Martin	68	73	72	71	284	1,341.43
Steve Pleis	71	67	72	74	284	1,341.43
Zoltan Veress	72	67	72	73	284	1,341.43
Kyle Voska	73	66	73	72	284	1,341.43
Brennan Webb	68	67	74	75	284	1,341.43

Bay Mills Open

Wild Bluff Golf Club, Brimley, Michigan
Par 36-36–72; 7,056 yards

May 30-June 2
purse, C$150,000

	SCORES				TOTAL	MONEY
Jeff Quinney	69	74	69	70	282	C$24,000
Dave Christensen	71	70	71	71	283	11,700
Mario Tiziani	66	71	71	75	283	11,700
Dirk Ayers	70	71	73	70	284	7,200
Andy Johnson	70	73	70	72	285	6,000
Jonn Drewery	71	75	68	72	286	4,680
David Mathis	69	72	72	73	286	4,680
Rob McMillan	72	71	72	71	286	4,680
Michael Mitchell	73	71	70	72	286	4,680
Conrad Ray	66	72	72	76	286	4,680
Michael Harris	71	73	75	68	287	3,300
Roger Harrison	69	69	73	76	287	3,300
Doug LaBelle	72	73	70	72	287	3,300
Brian Unk	67	74	71	75	287	3,300
Jason Bohn	72	72	70	75	289	2,475
Derek Gillespie	75	73	70	71	289	2,475
Stephen Woodard	71	73	73	72	289	2,475
Bryan Wright	69	72	77	71	289	2,475
Chad Belbin	72	69	73	76	290	1,850
Brian Flugstad	73	74	73	70	290	1,850
Kent Fukushima	70	70	76	74	290	1,850
Chris Locker	72	77	70	71	290	1,850
Perry Parker	72	72	73	73	290	1,850
Alex Rocha	71	73	71	75	290	1,850
Davidson Matyczuk	74	72	71	74	291	1,446
Bryn Parry	71	77	67	76	291	1,446

	SCORES				TOTAL	MONEY
Mayson Petty	71	77	73	70	291	1,446
Iain Steel	73	72	74	72	291	1,446
Brennan Webb	76	71	71	73	291	1,446
Aaron Barber	71	76	74	71	292	1,185
Gord Chilton	71	72	74	75	292	1,185
Paul Devenport	74	72	67	79	292	1,185
Scott Ford	69	79	73	71	292	1,185
Mikkel Reese	71	75	72	74	292	1,185
Drew Symons	73	74	69	76	292	1,185

Ontario Open Heritage Classic

Grandview Golf Club, Mark O'Meara Course,   June 13-16
Huntsville, Ontario   purse, C$150,000
Par 36-36–72; 7,065 yards

	SCORES				TOTAL	MONEY
Mike Grob	66	70	65	73	274	C$24,000
Hank Kuehne	68	70	64	74	276	14,400
Jeff Quinney	70	72	67	68	277	9,000
Jim Rutledge	71	67	71	70	279	7,200
Alex Quiroz	68	73	69	71	281	6,000
Derek Gillespie	65	71	72	74	282	5,400
David Hearn	69	70	70	74	283	4,950
Aaron Barber	67	75	73	69	284	4,350
Mike Belbin	69	74	67	74	284	4,350
Jon Mills	71	70	70	73	284	4,350
Jason Schultz	72	74	70	69	285	3,600
Iain Steel	67	70	68	80	285	3,600
Blair Buttar	72	70	69	75	286	3,000
Robert Hamilton	69	77	69	71	286	3,000
Dave Christensen	69	74	73	71	287	2,550
Michael Harris	72	73	70	72	287	2,550
Chris Wollmann	74	70	69	74	287	2,550
Andy Johnson	70	72	73	73	288	2,100
David McKenzie	72	72	72	72	288	2,100
Stephen Woodard	71	76	70	71	288	2,100
Brad Fritsch	75	69	73	72	289	1,837.50
Todd Pence	71	73	71	74	289	1,837.50
Dirk Ayers	71	73	75	71	290	1,613
Brett Bingham	75	73	74	68	290	1,613
Chris Locker	68	72	75	75	290	1,613
Craig Marseilles	74	74	73	69	290	1,613
Pablo Del Olmo	74	74	73	70	291	1,293
Paul Devenport	68	75	74	74	291	1,293
Scott Ford	72	75	71	73	291	1,293
Doug LaBelle	72	71	74	74	291	1,293
Dave Levesque	73	74	74	70	291	1,293
David Ogrin	72	74	75	70	291	1,293
Sal Spallone	74	71	76	70	291	1,293

Greater Vancouver Classic

Swan-e-set Bay Resort, Vancouver, British Columbia
Par 36-36–72; 7,000 yards

June 27-30
purse, C$150,000

		SCORES			TOTAL	MONEY
Iain Steel	66	67	75	64	272	C$24,000
Ken Duke	65	69	70	68	272	14,400
(Steel defeated Duke on first playoff hole.)						
Aaron Barber	71	69	68	68	276	7,400
Darren Griff	71	65	70	70	276	7,400
Mike Grob	67	75	70	64	276	7,400
Jason Bohn	70	69	70	68	277	5,000
Michael Kirk	67	73	71	66	277	5,000
Eddie Maunder	71	69	67	70	277	5,000
Stuart Anderson	67	71	68	72	278	4,050
David McKenzie	70	71	69	68	278	4,050
Jason Schultz	70	68	67	73	278	4,050
Bryan DeCorso	72	70	68	69	279	2,940
John Douma	69	75	70	65	279	2,940
Andy Johnson	69	72	70	68	279	2,940
Rob McMillan	74	67	71	67	279	2,940
Bryan Wright	73	71	67	68	279	2,940
Dave Christensen	70	70	70	70	280	2,250
Kyle Kovacs	69	67	73	71	280	2,250
Drew Symons	70	69	71	70	280	2,250
David Faught	70	72	69	70	281	1,875
Chris Locker	67	71	71	72	281	1,875
Michael Mitchell	71	67	73	70	281	1,875
Chad Belbin	68	75	65	74	282	1,578
Mark Brown	65	71	76	70	282	1,578
Craig Marseilles	70	71	71	70	282	1,578
Alex Rocha	75	67	67	73	282	1,578
Jeff Wood	70	73	70	69	282	1,578
David Hearn	69	72	68	74	283	1,358
Davidson Matyczuk	71	68	72	72	283	1,358
Paul Devenport	68	75	71	70	284	1,166
Todd Doohan	73	71	71	69	284	1,166
Jonn Drewery	73	70	70	71	284	1,166
Brad Fritsch	70	72	72	70	284	1,166
Bobby Kalinowski	72	68	70	74	284	1,166
Brian McCann	74	70	70	70	284	1,166
Steve Pleis	70	72	70	72	284	1,166

Victoria Open

Uplands Golf Club, Victoria, British Columbia
Par 35-35–70; 6,315 yards

July 4-7
purse, C$150,000

		SCORES			TOTAL	MONEY
Scott Hend	65	70	65	63	263	C$24,000
Michael Harris	66	69	68	63	266	10,200
David Hearn	68	69	65	64	266	10,200
Rich Massey	68	65	66	67	266	10,200
David McKenzie	68	69	67	63	267	6,000
Michael Henderson	70	69	66	63	268	5,175
Jason Schultz	71	67	67	63	268	5,175
Aaron Barber	65	69	67	69	270	4,350

	SCORES				TOTAL	MONEY
Paul Devenport	67	67	69	67	270	4,350
*Craig Doell	68	70	64	68	270	
Rob Johnson	68	67	70	65	270	4,350
Scott Gutschewski	68	68	68	67	271	3,600
Mark Johnson	69	65	70	67	271	3,600
Jason Bohn	66	67	69	70	272	2,812
Matt Daniel	67	70	71	64	272	2,812
Mike Grob	67	68	71	66	272	2,812
Steve Pleis	70	68	65	69	272	2,812
Ken Duke	68	71	69	65	273	2,115
Jason Enloe	69	68	67	69	273	2,115
Doug McGuigan	66	69	71	67	273	2,115
Mario Tiziani	66	68	70	69	273	2,115
Bryan Wright	68	65	72	68	273	2,115
Andy Johnson	70	68	67	69	274	1,688
Philip Jonas	66	72	69	67	274	1,688
Steve Scott	68	67	67	72	274	1,688
Stephen Woodard	67	69	69	69	274	1,688
Chris Anderson	69	69	71	66	275	1,365
Dave Christensen	70	68	69	68	275	1,365
Mitch Lowe	71	70	69	65	275	1,365
Danny Paniccia	70	70	71	64	275	1,365
Alex Quiroz	68	69	69	69	275	1,365
Bryan Saltus	71	65	71	68	275	1,365

Telus Edmonton Open

Glendale Golf & Country Club, Edmonton, Alberta
Par 36-36–72; 6,918 yards

July 11-14
purse, C$150,000

	SCORES				TOTAL	MONEY
Matt Daniel	67	66	67	67	267	C$24,000
Stuart Anderson	66	68	67	66	267	14,400
(Daniel defeated Anderson on first playoff hole.)						
Alex Rocha	66	67	68	69	270	9,000
Aaron Barber	71	63	68	69	271	7,200
Alex Quiroz	70	68	67	67	272	6,000
Bryan DeCorso	70	68	66	70	274	4,837
Rafael Gemoets	68	70	68	68	274	4,837
Darren Griff	66	70	69	69	274	4,837
Mike Grob	66	72	66	70	274	4,837
Brett Bingham	69	66	71	69	275	4,050
Chris Greenwood	70	72	68	67	277	3,600
Andy Johnson	69	66	73	69	277	3,600
Jason Enloe	71	67	68	72	278	2,900
Derek Gillespie	67	70	73	68	278	2,900
Scott Hend	68	66	72	72	278	2,900
Rob McMillan	65	71	71	73	280	2,550
Jason Bohn	69	68	69	75	281	2,175
Jason Schultz	74	65	73	69	281	2,175
Tim Turpen	71	68	70	72	281	2,175
Brennan Webb	66	72	69	74	281	2,175
Philip Jonas	75	68	72	67	282	1,725
David Mathis	66	73	69	74	282	1,725
Bryn Parry	69	72	72	69	282	1,725
Steve Pleis	66	74	71	71	282	1,725
Zoltan Veress	69	72	72	69	282	1,725

	SCORES				TOTAL	MONEY
Jason Fisher	75	66	71	71	283	1,500
Todd Doohan	65	71	71	77	284	1,315
Ramiro Goti	73	68	71	72	284	1,315
Bobby Kalinowski	68	66	73	77	284	1,315
Wes Martin	74	69	68	73	284	1,315
David McKenzie	71	69	75	69	284	1,315
Jeff Wood	72	71	73	68	284	1,315

MTS Classic

Pine Ridge Golf Club, Winnipeg, Manitoba
Par 36-35–71; 6,522 yards

July 18-21
purse, C$150,000

	SCORES				TOTAL	MONEY
Alex Quiroz	68	70	68	66	272	C$24,000
Aaron Barber	70	70	63	70	273	11,700
Andy Johnson	67	69	69	68	273	11,700
Bobby Kalinowski	66	67	71	70	274	6,600
Steve Scott	68	71	67	68	274	6,600
David Mathis	69	68	71	67	275	5,175
Bryn Parry	68	69	69	69	275	5,175
David McKenzie	65	69	69	73	276	4,650
Jason Enloe	69	71	69	68	277	3,900
Ben Pettitt	68	67	66	76	277	3,900
Mario Tiziani	69	71	67	70	277	3,900
Stephen Woodard	72	68	67	70	277	3,900
Scott Ford	67	70	70	71	278	3,150
Dave Christensen	68	69	70	72	279	2,550
Rob Johnson	69	68	69	73	279	2,550
Chris Locker	69	74	68	68	279	2,550
Alex Rocha	72	68	69	70	279	2,550
Jeff Wood	73	68	67	71	279	2,550
Dirk Ayers	69	70	71	70	280	1,975
Perry Parker	73	70	70	67	280	1,975
Adam Speirs	71	70	68	71	280	1,975
Todd Fanning	68	69	73	71	281	1,615
Rafael Gemoets	69	70	70	72	281	1,615
Matthew Lane	74	66	71	70	281	1,615
Rich Massey	71	67	67	76	281	1,615
Sal Spallone	72	71	66	72	281	1,615
Drew Symons	73	66	73	69	281	1,615
Chad Belbin	67	74	72	69	282	1,228
Dan Chartrand	70	72	68	72	282	1,228
Todd Doohan	67	72	70	73	282	1,228
Darren Griff	70	67	69	76	282	1,228
Brian McCann	71	71	72	68	282	1,228
Mikkel Reese	70	69	73	70	282	1,228
Brad Sutterfield	65	72	69	76	282	1,228
Brennan Webb	72	71	68	71	282	1,228

Telus Quebec Open

Le Versant Golf Club, Terrebonne, Quebec
Par 36-36–72; 7,013 yards

August 8-11
purse, C$200,000

	SCORES				TOTAL	MONEY
Hank Kuehne	68	67	69	69	273	C$32,000
Michael Harris	70	68	66	69	273	19,200
(Kuehne defeated Harris on second playoff hole.)						
Remi Bouchard	70	68	70	66	274	10,800
Ken Duke	70	67	66	71	274	10,800
Mike Grob	69	70	70	66	275	8,000
Paul Devenport	71	69	68	68	276	6,900
David McKenzie	69	67	70	70	276	6,900
Rodney Butcher	72	67	70	68	277	5,400
Wes Martin	70	69	70	68	277	5,400
Doug McGuigan	66	71	68	72	277	5,400
Perry Parker	66	72	68	71	277	5,400
Iain Steel	70	68	68	71	277	5,400
Aaron Barber	66	70	71	71	278	3,867
Dave Christensen	68	70	72	68	278	3,867
Steve Scott	73	68	66	71	278	3,867
Carl Desjardins	71	66	71	71	279	3,400
Rob McMillan	68	69	72	71	280	3,000
Birk Nelson	70	70	70	70	280	3,000
Jeff Quinney	71	69	68	72	280	3,000
Brett Bingham	69	71	73	68	281	2,450
Jason Bohn	70	70	71	70	281	2,450
Bobby Kalinowski	73	69	71	68	281	2,450
Adam Short	71	72	68	70	281	2,450
Jason Enloe	71	72	69	70	282	2,055
Derek Gillespie	71	72	68	71	282	2,055
David Howser	75	67	68	72	282	2,055
Brian Unk	71	67	70	74	282	2,055
Rob Johnson	71	72	71	69	283	1,750
Eddy Lee	70	71	71	71	283	1,750
Mario Tiziani	73	69	68	73	283	1,750
Chris Wall	70	70	73	70	283	1,750

Greater Toronto Open

Mandarin Golf & Country Club, Markham, Ontario
Par 36-36–72; 6,722 yards

August 15-18
purse, C$150,000

	SCORES				TOTAL	MONEY
Chris Locker	71	68	64	67	270	C$24,000
Derek Gillespie	65	68	66	71	270	14,400
(Locker defeated Gillespie on first playoff hole.)						
David Hearn	70	69	66	69	274	9,000
Aaron Barber	68	71	67	69	275	6,600
Steve Scott	70	69	67	69	275	6,600
David Faught	69	69	66	73	277	5,000
Robert Hamilton	66	72	67	72	277	5,000
Stephen Woodard	68	73	69	67	277	5,000
Dave Christensen	73	68	68	69	278	4,050
Michael Kirk	65	72	71	70	278	4,050
Brian Payne	69	69	72	68	278	4,050
Matthew Abbott	72	67	72	68	279	3,038

	SCORES				TOTAL	MONEY
Michael Harris	71	72	66	70	279	3,038
David Howser	69	68	71	71	279	3,038
Paul Scaletta	71	71	65	72	279	3,038
Jason Bohn	72	71	67	70	280	2,187
Rob Johnson	71	68	68	73	280	2,187
Ben Pettitt	71	71	65	73	280	2,187
Mario Tiziani	70	72	64	74	280	2,187
Jamie Welder	67	73	68	72	280	2,187
Bryan Wright	71	68	71	70	280	2,187
Chris Wollmann	70	69	71	71	281	1,800
Kent Fukushima	70	70	70	72	282	1,545
Mike Grob	71	64	72	75	282	1,545
Roger Harrison	69	74	69	70	282	1,545
Doug LaBelle	71	72	69	70	282	1,545
David McKenzie	67	73	65	77	282	1,545
Dennis Riedel	71	69	67	75	282	1,545
Bryan DeCorso	70	71	69	73	283	1,246
Todd Doohan	71	69	69	74	283	1,246
Jerry Hinds	66	73	70	74	283	1,246
Rob McMillan	67	75	65	76	283	1,246
Birk Nelson	72	70	68	73	283	1,246

Casino de Charlevoix Cup

Le Manoir Richelieu Golf Club, Pointe-au-Pic, Quebec
Par 71; 6,225 yards

August 28-31
purse, C$100,000

FIRST DAY
Canadian Tour

Scott Ford and Davidson Matyczuk defeated Brad Fritsch and David Mathis, 1 up.
Duane Bock and Rich Massey defeated Todd Doohan and Mike Woodcock, 2 and 1.
Paul Devenport and Craig Matthew defeated Dirk Ayers and David McKenzie, 2 and 1.
Stuart Anderson and Mike Belbin defeated Bryan DeCorso and Ryan Dillon, 4 and 2.
Iain Steel and Chris Wollmann defeated Eddie Maunder and Drew Symons, 4 and 2.
Dave Christensen and Michael Harris defeated Doug McGuigan and Alan McLean, 1 up.
Aaron Barber and Rob Johnson defeated Brennan Webb and Bryan Wright, 20 holes.
Chris Anderson and Mike Grob defeated Jonn Drewery and Zoltan Veress, 1 up.

Quebec Tour

Marc Girouard and Kevin Senecal defeated Christian Manegre and Yanick Mongeau, 6 and 4.
Michel Dagenais and Darryl Lepage defeated Steve Deschenes and Marc-Andre Girard, 5 and 3.
Carl Desjardins and Serge Thivierge defeated Eric Gauthier and Yves Robillard, 3 and 2.
Michel Boyer and Stephane L'Ecuyer defeated Joey Bissegger and Alain Trudeau, 2 and 1.
Martin Bergeron and Steven Brosseau defeated Luc De Bellefeuille and Daniel Santerre, 3 and 2.
Carlo Blanchard and Benoit Morin defeated David Perry and Geoff Stewart, 2 and 1.
Michel Hins and Russell Miller defeated Remi Bouchard and Chris Learmonth 4 and 3.
Pete Bousquet and Jean-Louis Lamarre defeated Eric Landreville and Jacques Paiement, 1 up.

(Each losing team received C$1,000.)

SECOND DAY
Canadian Tour

Stuart Anderson and Belbin defeated Steel and Wollmann, 1 up.
Christensen and Harris defeated Devenport and Matthew, 2 and 1.
Bock and Massey defeated Barber and Johnson, 2 and 1.
Chris Anderson and Grob defeated Ford and Matyczuk, 3 and 1.

Quebec Tour

Bergeron and Brosseau defeated Boyer and L'Ecuyer, 19 holes.
Desjardins and Thivierge defeated Blanchard and Morin, 3 and 2.
Hins and Miller defeated Dagenais and Lepage, 1 up.
Bousquet and Lamarre defeated Girouard and Senecal, 3 and 2.

(Each losing team received C$2,000.)

QUARTER-FINALS

Chris Anderson and Grob defeated Stuart Anderson and Belbin, 1 up.
Bock and Massey defeated Christensen and Harris, 2 and 1.
Bousquet and Lamarre defeated Bergeron and Brosseau, 20 holes.
Desjardins and Thivierge defeated Hins and Miller, 6 and 5.

(Each losing team received C$4,000.)

SEMI-FINALS

Bock and Massey defeated Chris Anderson and Grob, 4 and 3.
Bousquet and Lamarre defeated Desjardins and Thivierge, 4 and 3.

(Each losing team received C$8,000.)

FINAL

Bousquet and Lamarre defeated Bock and Massey, 2 and 1.

(Bousquet and Lamarre received C$20,000; Bock and Massey received C$16,000.)

South American Tour

Corona Caribbean Open

Our Lucaya Golf Resort, Freeport, Bahamas
Par 36-36–72; 6,824 yards

January 16-19
purse, US$50,000

	SCORES				TOTAL	MONEY
Rafael Gomez	68	69	68	73	278	US$9,000
Brian Quinn	71	67	72	71	281	5,700
Grover Justice	75	67	70	70	282	3,266.66
Robert Ames	68	70	73	71	282	3,266.66
Gustavo Acosta	68	69	71	74	282	3,266.66
Tatsuaki Nakamura	73	72	70	68	283	2,100
Emalcus Hield	74	70	71	69	284	1,340
Marvin King	72	72	70	70	284	1,340
Wilfredo Morales	74	71	68	71	284	1,340
Jimmy Delancey	72	73	66	73	284	1,340
Marco Ruiz	72	69	69	74	284	1,340
Adam Adams	72	71	70	72	285	925
Michael Devlin	69	72	71	73	285	925
Markus Westerberg	72	71	69	73	285	925
Adam Spring	75	68	69	73	285	925
Brian Cooper	68	71	74	73	286	775
Brad Adamonis	74	70	69	73	286	775
Matt Mocniak	70	74	72	72	288	675
Alvaro Ortiz	69	72	74	73	288	675
Adam Armagost	73	72	73	71	289	520
Hiroshi Matsuo	73	73	72	71	289	520
Marc Pendaries	72	72	73	72	289	520
Will Burnitz	70	75	70	74	289	520
John Bloomfield	76	72	73	68	289	520
D.J. Morris	72	73	74	71	290	410
Daniel Nunez	71	70	76	73	290	410
Stephen Summers	76	66	72	76	290	410
Ruberlei Felizardo	70	72	72	76	290	410
Eduardo Pesenti	76	70	75	70	291	350
Ryan Baker	75	70	73	73	291	350
Ed Hummenik	76	73	67	75	291	350
Paul Antenucci	68	73	75	75	291	350
Brooks Roberts	75	74	73	69	291	350

TLA Los Encinos Open

Los Encinos Golf Club, Toluca, Mexico
Par 36-36–72; 7,100 yards

February 7-10
purse, US$80,000

	SCORES				TOTAL	MONEY
Roland Thatcher	71	67	68	72	278	US$14,400
Rafael Gomez	72	69	71	68	280	9,120
Miguel Guzman	72	70	68	71	281	6,400
Rafael Alarcon	77	71	69	66	283	5,120
Carlos Franco	72	71	70	71	284	3,413.33

	SCORES				TOTAL	MONEY
Sebastian Fernandez	72	68	72	72	284	3,413.33
Jose Trauwitz	70	72	70	72	284	3,413.33
Sixto Torres	75	74	67	69	285	2,000
Rodolfo Gonzalez	72	72	71	70	285	2,000
Gustavo Acosta	71	74	70	70	285	2,000
Cesar Perez	68	69	75	73	285	2,000
Jorge Perez	74	72	72	68	286	1,600
Roberto Coceres	75	74	69	69	287	1,480
Alex Quiroz	72	73	71	71	287	1,480
Salvador Hernandez	74	71	73	70	288	1,280
Alexandre Balicki	73	69	75	71	288	1,280
Travis Perkins	77	67	71	73	288	1,280
Jon Mills	74	72	72	71	289	1,040
Octavio Gonzalez	70	74	73	72	289	1,040
Juan Salazar	73	71	71	74	289	1,040
Marco Ruiz	72	76	73	69	290	800
Lou Kubisa	71	74	73	72	290	800
Mathew Abbott	73	73	72	72	290	800
Marvin King	70	72	70	78	290	800
Craig Matthew	74	71	75	71	291	704
Guadalupe Rodriguez	76	72	73	71	292	608
Fabian Montovia	72	77	72	71	292	608
Eduardo Martinez	75	74	72	71	292	608
Nicolas Wrona	74	73	72	73	292	608
Oscar Serna	74	74	71	73	292	608
Antonio Maldonado	76	70	72	74	292	608

American Express Costa Rica Open

Cariari Country Club, San Jose, Costa Rica
Par 36-35–71; 6,577 yards

February 14-17
purse, US$80,000

	SCORES				TOTAL	MONEY
Rafael Gomez	73	69	73	74	289	US$14,400
Marco Ruiz	72	72	69	76	289	9,120
(Gomez defeated Ruiz on first playoff hole.)						
Miguel Guzman	73	72	77	69	291	5,226.66
Raul Fretes	73	74	72	72	291	5,226.66
Angel Franco	71	77	71	72	291	5,226.66
Roland Thatcher	68	69	75	80	292	3,360
Ramon Franco	80	72	69	73	294	2,480
Alexandre Balicki	70	68	80	76	294	2,480
Jose Trauwitz	75	70	77	74	296	2,080
Eduardo Pesenti	79	73	73	72	297	1,920
Roberto Coceres	79	77	70	72	298	1,760
Grant Masson	74	81	74	70	299	1,520
Gustavo Acosta	78	71	77	73	299	1,520
Matt Mocniak	74	76	68	81	299	1,520
Manuel Inman	74	77	73	76	300	1,320
Allan MacDonald	76	74	71	79	300	1,320
Rodolfo Gonzalez	73	78	75	75	301	1,120
Pedro Martinez	77	75	73	76	301	1,120
Jon Mills	76	73	75	77	301	1,120
Jorge Perez	75	80	75	72	302	920
Derek Gillespie	76	75	74	77	302	920
Rigoberto Velazquez	77	73	79	74	303	792
Adam Spring	78	72	73	80	303	792

	SCORES				TOTAL	MONEY
Alvaro Ortiz	80	76	76	72	304	720
David Schuster	73	75	77	79	304	720
Sebastian Fernandez	77	73	79	76	305	617.60
Bryan DeCorso	76	76	77	76	305	617.60
Michael Devlin	79	76	74	76	305	617.60
Martin Soria	79	77	72	77	305	617.60
Cesar Perez	73	77	74	81	305	617.60

Tikal Trophy Guatemala

Mayan Golf Club, Guatemala City, Guatemala
Par 36-36–72; 7,019 yards

February 21-24
purse, US$80,000

	SCORES				TOTAL	MONEY
Sebastian Fernandez	68	71	69	70	278	US$14,400
Pablo Del Grosso	69	70	72	70	281	9,120
Marco Ruiz	69	69	76	68	282	6,400
Rafael Gemoets	71	69	74	70	284	5,120
Ruberlei Felizardo	76	68	72	69	285	3,760
Rafael Gomez	73	70	71	71	285	3,760
Pedro Martinez	70	75	73	68	286	2,346.66
Jeffrey Schmid	72	71	71	72	286	2,346.66
Ramon Franco	69	69	75	73	286	2,346.66
Rigoberto Velazquez	71	67	76	74	288	1,920
Fabian Montovia	71	73	75	70	289	1,680
Derek Gillespie	73	71	74	71	289	1,680
Alexandre Balicki	74	76	72	68	290	1,400
Gustavo Acosta	73	70	76	71	290	1,400
Rodolfo Gonzalez	69	72	77	72	290	1,400
Richard Terga	75	68	74	73	290	1,400
Alex Quiroz	69	77	71	74	291	1,160
John Drewery	73	74	70	74	291	1,160
Michael Devlin	75	70	78	70	293	866.66
Chris Moody	77	69	75	72	293	866.66
Daniel Nunez	77	70	74	72	293	866.66
Raul Fretes	72	71	77	73	293	866.66
Markus Westerberg	71	76	71	75	293	866.66
Juan Abbate	71	70	76	76	293	866.66
Tatsuaki Nakamura	75	70	79	70	294	688
Greg Petersen	73	75	70	76	294	688
Adam Armagost	74	77	73	71	295	640
Jose Trauwitz	75	70	75	76	296	592
Kotaro Asahara	76	72	72	76	296	592
Cesar Perez	72	72	75	77	296	592

LG Panama Masters

Summit Golf Course & Resort, Panama City, Panama
Par 36-35–71; 6,676 yards

February 28-March 3
purse, US$75,000

	SCORES				TOTAL	MONEY
Pedro Martinez	71	67	67	67	272	US$13,500
Chris Patton	69	70	67	67	273	8,550
Ramon Franco	71	67	66	70	274	6,000
Adam Armagost	69	70	70	68	277	4,350

	SCORES				TOTAL	MONEY
Angel Franco	69	71	68	69	277	4,350
Jorge Perez	73	67	70	69	279	2,850
Miguel Guzman	70	70	70	69	279	2,850
Ruberlei Felizardo	70	75	67	68	280	2,025
Gustavo Acosta	74	68	68	70	280	2,025
Daniel Barbetti	71	70	69	71	281	1,800
Alexandre Balicki	74	71	68	69	282	1,525
Jesus Amaya	71	73	65	73	282	1,525
Richard Terga	68	71	67	76	282	1,525
Manuel Inman	74	70	70	70	284	1,275
Raul Fretes	73	71	70	70	284	1,275
Rafael Gomez	70	69	73	72	284	1,275
Ariel Licera	70	70	77	68	285	1,050
Sebastian Fernandez	70	74	69	72	285	1,050
Roberto Coceres	68	68	74	75	285	1,050
Rafael Gemoets	73	71	74	69	287	760
Mathew Abbott	76	70	72	69	287	760
Jose Trauwitz	72	74	71	70	287	760
Will Burnitz	70	73	72	72	287	760
Corey Harris	70	74	71	72	287	760
Juan Abbate	72	69	71	75	287	760
Esteban Isasi	74	74	70	70	288	588.75
Cesar Perez	74	70	73	71	288	588.75
Eduardo Pesenti	72	75	70	71	288	588.75
Greg Petersen	75	70	70	73	288	588.75
Jeffrey Schmid	75	71	71	72	289	525
Chris Moody	72	71	71	75	289	525
Rigoberto Velazquez	70	71	72	76	289	525

TLA Players Championship Acapulco Fest

Fairmont Princess Resort, Acapulco, Mexico
Par 35-35–70; 6,355 yards

May 15-18
purse, US$70,000

	SCORES				TOTAL	MONEY
Roberto Coceres	68	64	64	67	263	US$14,000
Alex Quiroz	68	67	67	64	266	7,000
Cesar Monasterio	65	64	70	67	266	7,000
David Schuster	69	66	70	63	268	5,000
Jon Levitt	68	68	68	65	269	3,166.66
Pablo Del Olmo	64	70	68	67	269	3,166.66
Jaime Gomez	64	70	67	68	269	3,166.66
Richard Terga	70	66	71	63	270	2,200
Juan Abbate	70	69	67	65	271	1,878
Adam Armagost	68	66	67	70	271	1,878
Sebastian Fernandez	69	66	66	70	271	1,878
Rafael Gomez	71	68	65	68	272	1,572
Angel Franco	71	64	66	71	272	1,572
Hiroshi Matsuo	68	69	66	70	273	1,467
Fabian Montovia	72	66	70	66	274	1,362
Julio Zapata	69	66	67	72	274	1,362
Oscar Serna	67	67	73	68	275	1,222
Ariel Licera	70	66	69	70	275	1,222
Rodolfo Gonzalez	73	72	63	68	276	1,047
Miguel Guzman	72	68	66	70	276	1,047
Ramon Franco	68	71	69	69	277	883.66
Marvin King	69	71	67	70	277	883.66

	SCORES			TOTAL	MONEY
Victor Leoni	68	65	71	73	277	883.66
Rafael Alarcon	68	72	72	67	279	823
Pablo Del Grosso	69	73	73	65	280	752.25
Daniel Nunez	70	69	74	67	280	752.25
Adam Adams	71	71	69	69	280	752.25
Bob Jacobson	66	72	69	73	280	752.25
James Watt	73	70	69	69	281	680
Alvaro Ortiz	77	70	66	69	282	457.50
Sixto Torres	71	73	68	70	282	457.50
Chris Moody	72	68	71	71	282	457.50
Landry Mahan	68	73	69	72	282	457.50

Medellin Open

El Rodeo Golf Club, Medellin, Colombia
Par 36-36–72; 6,808 yards

November 7-10
purse, US$50,000

	SCORES				TOTAL	MONEY
Jesus Amaya	68	70	71	71	280	US$9,000
Marcelo Soria	72	71	67	70	280	5,700
(Amaya defeated Soria on second playoff hole.)						
Cesar Serna	72	73	70	66	281	3,600
Eduardo Argiro	70	73	67	71	281	3,600
Luis Posada	71	72	73	66	281	3,600
Alvaro Pinedo	70	71	69	72	282	2,350
Daniel Vancsik	71	75	71	66	282	2,350
Miguel Fernandez	73	71	70	69	283	1,490
Angel Romero	69	72	71	71	283	1,490
Gustavo Mendoza	74	67	70	72	283	1,490
Oscar Alvarez	72	68	70	73	283	
Rafael Romero	70	73	68	73	284	1,220
Pedro Martinez	70	74	71	71	286	1,120
Clodomiro Carranza	73	75	68	71	287	1,070
Mauricio Molina	73	75	73	67	288	970
Diego Vanegas	78	70	69	71	288	970
Gustavo Acosta	69	74	73	72	288	970
Jesus Osmar	73	73	71	73	290	845
Oswaldo Villada	74	75	68	73	290	845
Sergio Acevedo	70	74	77	70	291	745
Mickael Dieu	74	74	72	71	291	745
Pablo Del Grosso	74	74	76	68	292	633.33
Bernardo Gonzalez	74	74	70	74	292	633.33
Juan Abbate	75	73	70	74	292	633.33
Raul Leguizamon	70	76	75	72	293	580
Daniel Barbetti	72	76	73	72	293	580
Juan Echeverry	75	73	74	72	294	530
Rigoberto Velazquez	75	74	73	72	294	530
Roberto Serna	70	76	75	73	294	530
Luis Zapata	74	72	73	76	295	495
Rodrigo Castaneda	76	69	73	77	295	495

Serrezuela Masters

Serrezuela Golf Club, Bogata, Colombia
Par 36-36–72; 7,325 yards

November 14-17
purse, US$50,000

	SCORES				TOTAL	MONEY
Jesus Amaya	68	68	69	70	275	US$9,000
Rodrigo Castaneda	77	66	68	66	277	4,850
Gustavo Mendoza	70	68	70	69	277	4,850
Diego Vanegas	75	71	67	65	278	3,200
Jorge Murdoch	69	72	73	66	280	2,350
Pedro Martinez	71	72	69	68	280	2,350
Miguel Rodriguez	72	67	70	72	281	1,700
Juan Abbate	69	71	71	71	282	1,520
Alvaro Pinedo	74	69	73	67	283	1,320
Daniel Vancsik	78	69	68	68	283	1,320
Pablo Del Grosso	74	70	69	70	283	1,320
Raul Fretes	71	71	73	69	284	1,020
Julio Zapata	71	71	72	70	284	1,020
Angel Romero	74	71	69	70	284	1,020
Clodomiro Carranza	69	68	75	72	284	1,020
Rigoberto Velazquez	70	77	65	72	284	1,020
Fernando Posada	72	71	74	68	285	845
Eduardo Argiro	76	71	70	68	285	845
Wilson Romero	74	70	72	70	286	697.50
Sergio Acevedo	75	70	71	70	286	697.50
Miguel Fernandez	71	70	74	71	286	697.50
David Schuster	70	74	69	73	286	697.50
Cesar Serna	76	70	71	70	287	595
Mickael Dieu	71	73	71	72	287	595
Rodolfo Gonzalez	72	75	72	69	288	560
Manuel Merizalde	74	70	72	72	288	560
Claudio Machado	70	75	71	73	289	530
Daniel Escalera	73	74	75	68	290	510
Omar Hernandez	71	76	73	71	291	490
Marcelo Soria	72	74	73	72	291	490
Orlando Rojas	72	70	76	73	291	490

CANTV Venezuela Open

Lagunita Country Club, Caracas, Venezuela
Par 35-35–70; 6,909 yards

November 21-24
purse, US$60,000

	SCORES				TOTAL	MONEY
Jesus Amaya	64	67	66	69	266	US$10,800
Raul Fretes	69	66	65	70	270	6,840
Daniel Vancsik	69	71	66	65	271	4,800
Pedro Martinez	71	68	68	68	275	3,840
Andres Romero	70	71	67	68	276	3,120
Alex Rocha	70	70	69	68	277	2,280
Juan Abbate	73	69	65	70	277	2,280
Adam Armagost	69	68	70	71	278	1,824
Diego Vanegas	68	70	73	68	279	1,476
Daniel Escalera	70	72	69	68	279	1,476
Miguel Rodriguez	67	71	72	69	279	1,476
Alvaro Pinedo	72	68	70	69	279	1,476
Manuel Merizalde	69	68	69	73	279	1,476
Angel Romero	74	65	72	69	280	1,194

	SCORES			TOTAL	MONEY
Miguel Guzman	71	68 68 73		280	1,194
Alvaro Ortiz	69	70 72 70		281	1,014
Ariel Licera	71	70 70 70		281	1,014
Jeff Walker	69	71 70 71		281	1,014
Eduardo Argiro	70	65 74 72		281	1,014
Damian Hale	69	73 69 71		282	808
Rodrigo Castaneda	68	69 70 75		282	808
Rafael Alarcon	68	69 70 75		282	808
Miguel Fernandez	68	73 72 70		283	714
Gustavo Acosta	72	70 67 74		283	714
Octavio Gonzalez	72	70 73 69		284	672
Pedro Russi	71	67 73 73		284	672
Antonio Maldonado	70	71 73 71		285	636
*Alfredo Adrian	70	71 72 72		285	
Marvin King	73	69 72 72		286	594
Ramon Franco	72	70 71 73		286	594
Clodomiro Carranza	68	73 71 74		286	594
Sergio Acevedo	68	71 69 78		286	594

Argentina Open

Hurlingham Club, Buenos Aires, Argentina
Par 35-35–70; 6,452 yards

November 28-December 1
purse, US$35,000

	SCORES			TOTAL	MONEY
Angel Cabrera	70	62 68 69		269	US$6,111
Jose Coceres	72	70 68 63		273	4,027
Eduardo Argiro	68	67 70 70		275	2,222
Carlos Franco	71	64 70 72		277	1,666
Sebastian Fernandez	70	69 71 68		278	1,277
Vicente Fernandez	73	68 67 70		278	1,277
Mauricio Molina	70	65 72 72		279	916.50
Pedro Martinez	71	65 71 72		279	916.50
Eduardo Romero	72	67 69 72		280	750
Ricardo Gonzalez	70	71 69 71		281	610.66
Raul Fretes	73	69 68 71		281	610.66
Daniel Vancsik	68	66 74 73		281	610.66
Andres Romero	72	68 70 72		282	527
Juan Abbate	74	67 73 70		284	486
Ramiro Goti	71	75 68 70		284	486
Hernan Rey	73	70 65 76		284	486
Ruben Alvarez	67	72 75 71		285	451
Rodolfo Gonzalez	70	71 69 75		285	451
Fabian Montovia	74	72 71 69		286	416
Dionicio Rios	72	71 73 70		286	416
Ariel Canete	71	70 74 71		286	416
Jose Cantero	76	71 69 71		287	381.50
Miguel Fernandez	72	70 72 73		287	381.50
Cesar Monasterio	73	73 69 73		288	347
Pablo Del Grosso	74	69 71 74		288	347
Rafael Gomez	70	74 70 74		288	347
Alejandro Farias	73	71 75 70		289	292.40
Daniel Nunez	75	71 73 70		289	292.40
Gustavo Acosta	78	66 74 71		289	292.40
Antonio Maldonado	75	73 70 71		289	292.40
Clodomiro Carranza	74	70 68 77		289	292.40

European Tours

Bell's South African Open
See African Tours chapter.

Dunhill Championship
See African Tours chapter.

Johnnie Walker Classic
See Australasian Tour chapter.

Heineken Classic
See Australasian Tour chapter.

ANZ Championship
See Australasian Tour chapter.

Caltex Singapore Masters
See Asia/Japan Tours chapter.

Carlsberg Malaysian Open
See Asia/Japan Tours chapter.

Dubai Desert Classic

Emirates Golf Club, Dubai, United Arab Emirates
Par 35-37–72; 7,185 yards

March 7-10
purse, €1,664,544

	SCORES				TOTAL	MONEY
Ernie Els	68	68	67	69	272	€273,335.70
Niclas Fasth	68	69	69	70	276	182,229.30
Carl Pettersson	70	73	65	69	277	102,669
Brian Davis	71	70	71	67	279	82,004
Charlie Wi	68	67	77	69	281	63,471.09
Gary Evans	70	71	72	68	281	63,471.09
Andrew Oldcorn	75	66	69	72	282	37,984.25
Mathias Gronberg	72	70	71	69	282	37,984.25
Darren Clarke	72	73	68	69	282	37,984.25
Bradley Dredge	74	70	69	69	282	37,984.25
Simon Dyson	71	68	73	70	282	37,984.25
Anders Forsbrand	74	66	75	68	283	24,320.04
Sam Torrance	68	71	75	69	283	24,320.04
Klas Eriksson	72	74	66	71	283	24,320.04
Soren Kjeldsen	74	70	69	70	283	24,320.04
Paul Broadhurst	69	70	71	73	283	24,320.04
Rolf Muntz	70	75	67	71	283	24,320.04
Greg Owen	71	70	70	72	283	24,320.04
*Michael Hoey	74	68	70	71	283	
Padraig Harrington	70	75	68	71	284	18,603.19
Raphael Jacquelin	71	71	68	74	284	18,603.19
Gregory Havret	69	71	74	70	284	18,603.19

	SCORES			TOTAL	MONEY
Olle Karlsson	68	73	73 70	284	18,603.19
Pierre Fulke	69	73	74 68	284	18,603.19
Ricardo Gonzalez	71	67	74 72	284	18,603.19
Thomas Bjorn	67	73	71 73	284	18,603.19
Richard Green	70	72	72 71	285	15,580.76
Richard Bland	70	72	74 69	285	15,580.76
Fredrik Jacobson	75	70	71 69	285	15,580.76
John Bickerton	69	68	73 75	285	15,580.76
Thongchai Jaidee	74	70	71 70	285	15,580.76
Mark Foster	72	72	72 70	286	12,587.61
Jose Manuel Lara	71	70	74 71	286	12,587.61
Anders Hansen	72	72	74 68	286	12,587.61
Steve Webster	74	70	73 69	286	12,587.61
Trevor Immelman	72	72	68 74	286	12,587.61
Soren Hansen	71	72	73 70	286	12,587.61
Robert Karlsson	67	76	72 71	286	12,587.61
Lucas Parsons	72	71	73 70	286	12,587.61
Roger Chapman	73	73	70 71	287	10,168.50
Nick Faldo	72	73	72 70	287	10,168.50
Barry Lane	73	73	71 70	287	10,168.50
Tom Gillis	75	71	72 69	287	10,168.50
Desvonde Botes	71	73	73 70	287	10,168.50
David Carter	73	70	74 70	287	10,168.50
Eduardo Romero	70	74	71 73	288	7,544.37
Ian Woosnam	73	68	74 73	288	7,544.37
Anthony Wall	70	70	74 74	288	7,544.37
Jean Hugo	73	71	72 72	288	7,544.37
Phillip Price	73	71	72 72	288	7,544.37
Roger Wessels	75	69	71 73	288	7,544.37
Tobias Dier	72	68	75 73	288	7,544.37
Nick Dougherty	71	71	72 74	288	7,544.37
Adam Scott	73	72	71 72	288	7,544.37
Scott Gardiner	72	73	72 71	288	7,544.37
Sven Struver	69	72	70 78	289	4,899.74
Justin Rose	72	71	72 74	289	4,899.74
Carlos Rodiles	72	70	70 77	289	4,899.74
Gary Emerson	74	71	71 73	289	4,899.74
Ignacio Garrido	73	72	69 75	289	4,899.74
David Park	70	70	76 73	289	4,899.74
Raymond Russell	74	72	70 73	289	4,899.74
Christopher Hanell	72	71	77 69	289	4,899.74
David Howell	74	69	72 75	290	3,772.18
Ian Poulter	71	69	75 75	290	3,772.18
Stephen Dodd	70	76	73 71	290	3,772.18
Stephen Scahill	70	74	73 73	290	3,772.18
Johan Skold	72	74	70 74	290	3,772.18
Paul Eales	72	74	73 72	291	3,198.16
Christophe Pottier	73	73	77 68	291	3,198.16
Marten Olander	70	72	77 73	292	3,001.35
Peter Baker	74	71	73 75	293	2,460
Andrew Pitts	73	71	77 73	294	2,452.50
Jamie Spence	72	72	78 72	294	2,452.50
Jarmo Sandelin	71	73	80 70	294	2,452.50
Markus Brier	72	74	76 72	294	2,452.50
Marc Farry	73	73	76 73	295	2,442
Henrik Bjornstad	72	72	76 75	295	2,442
Andrew Butterfield	70	76	72 77	295	2,442
Andrew Coltart	73	73	75 75	296	2,436
Ian Hutchings	73	71	76 77	297	2,433

Qatar Masters

Doha Golf Club, Doha, Qatar
Par 36-36–72; 7,110 yards

March 14-17
purse, €1,713,903

	SCORES				TOTAL	MONEY
Adam Scott	67	66	69	67	269	€285,650.50
Jean-Francois Remesy	68	69	68	70	275	148,858.20
Nick Dougherty	69	69	68	69	275	148,858.20
Eduardo Romero	71	67	72	67	277	58,501.22
Joakim Haeggman	66	73	72	66	277	58,501.22
Mark Pilkington	69	69	71	68	277	58,501.22
Henrik Nystrom	69	72	67	69	277	58,501.22
John Bickerton	69	70	68	70	277	58,501.22
Stephen Gallacher	69	68	69	71	277	58,501.22
David Howell	68	72	71	67	278	32,906.94
Anders Hansen	68	68	71	71	278	32,906.94
Miguel Angel Martin	70	68	68	73	279	25,965.63
Peter Fowler	70	69	69	71	279	25,965.63
Jose Manuel Lara	67	69	73	70	279	25,965.63
Soren Hansen	67	71	72	69	279	25,965.63
Benoit Teilleria	72	71	68	68	279	25,965.63
Charlie Hoffman	70	73	69	67	279	25,965.63
Ian Woosnam	69	69	70	72	280	20,338.32
Warren Bennett	70	69	69	72	280	20,338.32
Trevor Immelman	70	72	67	71	280	20,338.32
Colin Montgomerie	68	69	69	74	280	20,338.32
Ricardo Gonzalez	69	72	70	69	280	20,338.32
Rolf Muntz	74	68	70	68	280	20,338.32
Mark Roe	66	75	71	69	281	17,310.42
Charlie Wi	69	70	72	70	281	17,310.42
Darren Clarke	70	70	70	71	281	17,310.42
Bradley Dredge	68	74	69	70	281	17,310.42
Christopher Hanell	75	67	69	70	281	17,310.42
Tony Johnstone	68	70	69	75	282	14,739.57
Ian Garbutt	67	71	74	70	282	14,739.57
Fredrik Jacobson	70	73	73	66	282	14,739.57
Thongchai Jaidee	69	70	72	71	282	14,739.57
Diego Borrego	73	69	68	72	282	14,739.57
Santiago Luna	68	71	72	72	283	11,997.32
Soren Kjeldsen	70	71	69	73	283	11,997.32
Stuart Little	71	69	71	72	283	11,997.32
Carl Suneson	73	70	68	72	283	11,997.32
Phillip Price	72	69	69	73	283	11,997.32
Gary Orr	69	69	73	72	283	11,997.32
Paul Lawrie	71	72	68	72	283	11,997.32
Martin Maritz	69	71	71	72	283	11,997.32
Des Smyth	69	70	74	71	284	9,426.47
Christophe Pottier	72	69	71	72	284	9,426.47
Stephen Dodd	70	72	72	70	284	9,426.47
Robert Coles	69	73	73	69	284	9,426.47
Markus Brier	70	73	67	74	284	9,426.47
Mikael Lundberg	72	70	70	72	284	9,426.47
Sam Walker	68	72	73	71	284	9,426.47
Klas Eriksson	66	70	74	75	285	7,198.39
Brian Davis	68	73	74	70	285	7,198.39
Raphael Jacquelin	71	72	70	72	285	7,198.39
Andrew Coltart	73	69	72	71	285	7,198.39
David Carter	70	71	71	73	285	7,198.39
Matthew Cort	68	73	72	72	285	7,198.39

	SCORES				TOTAL	MONEY
Malcolm Mackenzie	74	67	72	73	286	5,655.88
Richard Bland	71	72	69	74	286	5,655.88
Carl Pettersson	74	68	73	71	286	5,655.88
Mathias Gronberg	70	70	74	73	287	4,884.62
Brett Rumford	70	73	75	69	287	4,884.62
Scott Gardiner	70	72	73	72	287	4,884.62
Kyle Thompson	71	71	74	71	287	4,884.62
Thomas Levet	73	68	73	74	288	4,284.76
Russell Claydon	70	68	76	74	288	4,284.76
Iain Pyman	73	69	71	75	288	4,284.76
Steve Webster	70	72	74	74	290	3,770.59
Erol Simsek	69	70	78	73	290	3,770.59
Lucas Parsons	72	70	71	77	290	3,770.59
Ian Hutchings	76	65	75	77	293	3,342.11
Gustavo Rojas	69	73	76	75	293	3,342.11
Gary Evans	72	71	73	78	294	3,130.73

Madeira Island Open

Santo da Serra Golf Club, Madeira, Portugal
Par 36-36–72; 6,664 yards

March 21-24
purse, €550,000

	SCORES				TOTAL	MONEY
Diego Borrego	72	68	72	69	281	€91,660
Maarten Lafeber	74	64	71	73	282	47,770
Ivo Giner	73	66	70	73	282	47,770
Roger Winchester	73	74	69	67	283	27,500
Santiago Luna	69	70	75	70	284	21,285
Charley Hoffman	70	70	73	71	284	21,285
Massimo Florioli	70	65	75	75	285	15,125
Paul Dwyer	71	70	69	75	285	15,125
Andrew Sherborne	71	76	66	73	286	10,725
Philip Walton	70	73	68	75	286	10,725
Didier de Vooght	71	67	73	75	286	10,725
David Drysdale	71	69	71	75	286	10,725
Pehr Magnebrant	73	69	72	73	287	8,277.50
Des Terblanche	70	74	68	75	287	8,277.50
Lee James	75	68	74	70	287	8,277.50
John Bickerton	72	68	71	76	287	8,277.50
Mathew Blackey	70	74	69	75	288	7,425
Andrew Oldcorn	70	65	78	76	289	6,622
Des Smyth	69	74	73	73	289	6,622
Bradford Vaughan	75	72	69	73	289	6,622
Philip Golding	73	70	72	74	289	6,622
David Lynn	73	66	74	76	289	6,622
Peter Malmgren	72	76	71	71	290	5,802.50
Steve Webster	74	70	70	76	290	5,802.50
Ilya Goroneskoul	69	74	69	78	290	5,802.50
Mikko Ilonen	76	71	70	73	290	5,802.50
Peter Fowler	70	76	74	71	291	5,142.50
Olivier David	66	71	80	74	291	5,142.50
Jesus Maria Arruti	73	74	70	74	291	5,142.50
Emanuele Canonica	71	73	72	75	291	5,142.50
Mark James	77	68	72	75	292	4,411
Henrik Stenson	71	73	72	76	292	4,411
Ian Hutchings	74	68	78	72	292	4,411
Massimo Scarpa	72	74	74	72	292	4,411

	SCORES				TOTAL	MONEY
Sion Bebb	76	70	74	72	292	4,411
Mark Mouland	74	70	76	73	293	3,795
Peter Baker	77	70	71	75	293	3,795
Christophe Pottier	70	70	78	75	293	3,795
Benn Barham	70	74	71	78	293	3,795
Benoit Teilleria	68	70	79	76	293	3,795
Euan Little	74	73	73	74	294	3,190
Chris Gane	74	74	74	72	294	3,190
Mattias Nilsson	71	77	71	75	294	3,190
Anthony Kang	75	73	72	74	294	3,190
Simon Wakefield	74	71	75	74	294	3,190
Sam Walker	76	71	70	77	294	3,190
Niels Kraaij	75	68	73	79	295	2,805
Magnus Persson Atlevi	70	76	76	74	296	2,310
Sam Little	74	73	75	74	296	2,310
Nicolas Vanhootegem	73	73	75	73	296	2,310
Robert Coles	70	78	74	74	296	2,310
Johan Skold	74	73	73	76	296	2,310
Marcus Knight	75	72	74	75	296	2,310
David Higgins	73	73	72	78	296	2,310
Ben Mason	78	69	73	76	296	2,310
Seve Ballesteros	70	76	78	73	297	1,546.11
Yngve Nilsson	73	69	75	80	297	1,546.11
Shaun Webster	74	69	78	76	297	1,546.11
Hennie Otto	70	74	74	79	297	1,546.11
Joao Pedro Carvalhosa	75	72	71	79	297	1,546.11
Carl Suneson	74	74	75	74	297	1,546.11
Miles Tunnicliff	70	74	74	79	297	1,546.11
Tomas Jesus Munoz	74	72	75	76	297	1,546.11
Oskar Bergman	75	68	78	76	297	1,546.11
Greig Hutcheon	73	74	73	78	298	1,182.50
Marcello Santi	74	72	74	78	298	1,182.50
Jorge Berendt	73	72	72	81	298	1,182.50
Kariem Baraka	74	74	73	77	298	1,182.50
Marc Pendaries	72	74	77	76	299	960
Gary Clark	76	71	76	76	299	960
Scott Kammann	73	71	76	79	299	960
Wolfgang Huget	69	79	76	76	300	822
Neil Cheetham	72	74	76	79	301	817.50
Van Phillips	76	70	75	80	301	817.50
Jeremy Robinson	72	76	71	83	302	811.50
Anssi Kankkonen	74	72	81	75	302	811.50
Michele Reale	75	72	81	78	306	807

Algarve Open de Portugal

Vale do Lobo Golf Club, Faro, Portugal
Par 37-35–72; 7,108 yards
(Shortened to 36 holes—rain, wind.)

April 4-7
purse, €750,000

	SCORES		TOTAL	MONEY
Carl Pettersson	66	76	142	€125,000
David Gilford	70	72	142	83,330
(Pettersson defeated Gilford on first playoff hole.)				
Miguel Angel Martin	73	70	143	38,750
Greg Owen	72	71	143	38,750
Henrik Nystrom	72	71	143	38,750

	SCORES		TOTAL	MONEY
Rolf Muntz	71	73	144	26,250
Diego Borrego	77	68	145	20,625
Bradley Dredge	70	75	145	20,625
Steve Webster	74	72	146	14,115
Gary Emerson	74	72	146	14,115
Emanuele Canonica	70	76	146	14,115
Mikko Ilonen	70	76	146	14,115
Alastair Forsyth	72	74	146	14,115
Mikael Lundberg	79	68	147	11,025
Roger Chapman	74	73	147	11,025
Stephen Dodd	71	76	147	11,025
Andrew Sherborne	71	77	148	8,212.50
Sam Torrance	75	73	148	8,212.50
Brian Davis	73	75	148	8,212.50
Mattias Eliasson	72	76	148	8,212.50
Justin Rose	76	72	148	8,212.50
Thomas Levet	73	75	148	8,212.50
Joakim Haeggman	73	75	148	8,212.50
Russell Claydon	76	72	148	8,212.50
Michele Reale	72	76	148	8,212.50
Ian Garbutt	73	75	148	8,212.50
Adam Mednick	74	74	148	8,212.50
Ignacio Garrido	75	73	148	8,212.50
Van Phillips	72	76	148	8,212.50
Sam Walker	75	73	148	8,212.50
Des Smyth	75	74	149	5,756.25
Anders Hansen	74	75	149	5,756.25
Soren Kjeldsen	76	73	149	5,756.25
Steen Tinning	76	73	149	5,756.25
Peter Baker	77	72	149	5,756.25
Marcel Siem	75	74	149	5,756.25
Jonathan Lomas	79	70	149	5,756.25
Gary Orr	76	73	149	5,756.25
Marc Farry	80	70	150	4,650
Raphael Jacquelin	76	74	150	4,650
Gary Evans	70	80	150	4,650
David Park	77	73	150	4,650
Jarmo Sandelin	77	73	150	4,650
David Carter	75	75	150	4,650
*Zane Scotland	74	76	150	
Malcolm Mackenzie	81	70	151	3,155.36
Mark Mouland	76	75	151	3,155.36
Mark Foster	76	75	151	3,155.36
Kenneth Ferrie	75	76	151	3,155.36
Trevor Immelman	76	75	151	3,155.36
Chris Gane	73	78	151	3,155.36
Dennis Edlund	77	74	151	3,155.36
Jorge Berendt	77	74	151	3,155.36
Gary Clark	73	78	151	3,155.36
David Drysdale	74	77	151	3,155.36
Michael Jonzon	75	76	151	3,155.36
Daren Lee	77	74	151	3,155.36
Benoit Teilleria	76	75	151	3,155.36
Stephen Gallacher	79	72	151	3,155.36
Costantino Rocca	75	77	152	1,800
Wayne Riley	75	77	152	1,800
Robert-Jan Derksen	78	74	152	1,800
Warren Bennett	76	76	152	1,800
Maarten Lafeber	79	73	152	1,800
Phillip Price	74	78	152	1,800

	SCORES		TOTAL	MONEY
Nicolas Vanhootegem	74	78	152	1,800
Markus Brier	75	77	152	1,800
Nicolas Kalouguine	73	79	152	1,800
Andrew Coltart	76	76	152	1,800
Raymond Russell	76	76	152	1,800
Gordon Brand, Jr.	80	73	153	1,145.50
Santiago Luna	77	76	153	1,145.50
Mark Roe	80	73	153	1,145.50
Jose Manuel Lara	78	75	153	1,145.50
Gregory Havret	81	72	153	1,145.50
Stuart Little	81	72	153	1,145.50
Olle Karlsson	79	74	153	1,145.50
Johan Skold	75	78	153	1,145.50
Matthew Cort	78	75	153	1,145.50
Graham Fox	77	76	153	1,145.50

The Seve Trophy

Druids Glen, Wicklow, Ireland
Par 35-36–71; 6,439 yards

April 19-21
purse, €2,400,000

FIRST DAY
Greensomes

Robert Karlsson and Thomas Bjorn (Continental Europe) defeated Paul Lawrie and Colin Montgomerie, 2 and 1.
Ian Woosnam and Steve Webster (Great Britain & Ireland) defeated Jose Maria Olazabal and Miguel Angel Jimenez, 3 and 2.
Padraig Harrington and Paul McGinley (GB&I) defeated Mathias Gronberg and Alex Cejka, 1 up.
Raphael Jacquelin and Thomas Levet (Cont.) defeated Lee Westwood and Darren Clarke, 2 and 1.

POINTS: Great Britain & Ireland 2, Continental Europe 2

Foursomes

Montgomerie and Andrew Oldcorn (GB&I) defeated Niclas Fasth and Karlsson, 2 and 1.
Olazabal and Jimenez (Cont.) defeated Webster and Paul Casey, 1 up.
Harrington and McGinley (GB&I) defeated Jacquelin and Levet, 1 up.
Clarke and Westwood (GB&I) defeated Cejka and Bjorn, 3 and 2.

POINTS: Great Britain & Ireland 3, Continental Europe 1

SECOND DAY
Fourballs

Lawrie and Casey (GB&I) defeated Bjorn and Fasth, 2 and 1.
Woosnam and Montgomerie (GB&I) defeated Karlsson and Gronberg, 4 and 3.
Seve Ballesteros and Olazabal (Cont.) defeated Harrington and McGinley, 2 and 1.
Westwood and Clarke (GB&I) defeated Jimenez and Jacquelin, 1 up.

POINTS: Great Britain & Ireland 3, Continental Europe 1

Foursomes

Bjorn and Karlsson (Cont.) halved with Woosnam and Webster.

Levet and Jacquelin (Cont.) halved with Lawrie and Oldcorn.
Harrington and McGinley (GB&I) defeated Cejka and Fasth, 1 up.
Olazabal and Jimenez (Cont.) defeated Clarke and Montgomerie, 1 up.

POINTS: Great Britain & Ireland 2, Continental Europe 2

THIRD DAY
Singles

Ballesteros (Cont.) defeated Montgomerie, 1 up.
Clarke (GB&I) defeated Bjorn, 4 and 3.
Jimenez (Cont.) defeated Casey, 4 and 3.
Karlsson (Cont.) defeated Lawrie, 1 up.
Fasth (Cont.) halved with Oldcorn.
Westwood (GB&I) defeated Jacquelin, 3 and 2.
Harrington (GB&I) defeated Olazabal, 3 and 2.
McGinley (GB&I) defeated Gronberg, 4 and 3.
Levet (Cont.) defeated Webster, 2 and 1.
Cejka (Cont.) defeated Woosnam, 5 and 4.

POINTS: Great Britain & Ireland 4½, Continental Europe 5½

TOTAL POINTS: Great Britain & Ireland 14½, Continental Europe 11½

(Each member of the Great Britain & Ireland team received €150,000; each member of the Continental Europe team received €90,000.)

Canarias Open de Espana

El Cortijo Club de Campo, Gran Canaria   April 25-28
Par 36-36–72; 6,899 yards   purse, €1,722,000

	SCORES				TOTAL	MONEY
Sergio Garcia	67	68	67	73	275	€287,000
Emanuele Canonica	68	69	70	72	279	191,330
Greg Owen	67	69	72	72	280	107,797.20
Carl Pettersson	68	72	69	72	281	86,100
*Rafael Cabrera	69	72	67	73	281	
Anders Forsbrand	70	74	68	71	283	66,641.40
Ricardo Gonzalez	68	75	70	70	283	66,641.40
David Gilford	66	77	71	70	284	47,355
Retief Goosen	73	73	71	67	284	47,355
Kenneth Ferrie	69	71	72	73	285	29,747.55
Ian Poulter	70	72	71	72	285	29,747.55
Steen Tinning	71	73	68	73	285	29,747.55
Stuart Little	68	72	70	75	285	29,747.55
Marcel Siem	67	71	72	75	285	29,747.55
Ian Hutchings	70	71	69	75	285	29,747.55
Didier de Vooght	70	69	71	75	285	29,747.55
David Drysdale	72	72	69	72	285	29,747.55
Gordon Brand, Jr.	70	72	70	74	286	22,271.20
Jose Manuel Carriles	69	73	72	72	286	22,271.20
Miguel Angel Jimenez	71	72	72	71	286	22,271.20
Mark Roe	68	73	69	77	287	19,493.04
Warren Bennett	69	69	72	77	287	19,493.04
Carl Suneson	68	70	73	76	287	19,493.04
Des Terblanche	69	72	69	77	287	19,493.04
Fredrik Jacobson	71	73	70	73	287	19,493.04
Soren Kjeldsen	69	71	73	75	288	16,875.60

	SCORES				TOTAL	MONEY
Ian Garbutt	68	75	73	72	288	16,875.60
Stephen Scahill	72	69	76	71	288	16,875.60
David Lynn	73	73	72	70	288	16,875.60
Jarmo Sandelin	68	77	69	74	288	16,875.60
Tony Johnstone	73	70	71	75	289	13,849.80
Klas Eriksson	72	72	74	71	289	13,849.80
Carlos Rodiles	68	75	72	74	289	13,849.80
Michele Reale	70	74	73	72	289	13,849.80
Fernando Roca	71	75	70	73	289	13,849.80
Bradley Dredge	72	74	71	72	289	13,849.80
Mark Pilkington	69	75	74	71	289	13,849.80
Roger Chapman	73	72	72	73	290	10,848.60
Mark Foster	71	72	77	70	290	10,848.60
Marc Farry	70	69	75	76	290	10,848.60
Anders Hansen	71	71	72	76	290	10,848.60
Soren Hansen	66	78	72	74	290	10,848.60
Jarrod Moseley	71	71	75	73	290	10,848.60
Ignacio Garrido	73	73	71	73	290	10,848.60
Daren Lee	75	69	73	73	290	10,848.60
Jamie Donaldson	72	74	71	73	290	10,848.60
Andrew Oldcorn	69	71	75	76	291	8,437.80
Peter Baker	72	67	76	76	291	8,437.80
Iain Pyman	72	74	73	72	291	8,437.80
Sam Walker	69	72	69	81	291	8,437.80
Nick Dougherty	71	74	72	74	291	8,437.80
Jamie Spence	67	73	74	78	292	7,232.40
Henrik Bjornstad	74	72	74	72	292	7,232.40
Henrik Stenson	72	73	73	75	293	6,371.40
Christophe Pottier	69	73	75	76	293	6,371.40
Eduardo De La Riva	73	73	73	74	293	6,371.40
Shaun Webster	68	77	73	76	294	5,510.40
Adam Mednick	70	74	75	75	294	5,510.40
Peter Fowler	71	74	78	72	295	4,735.50
Robert-Jan Derksen	73	71	76	75	295	4,735.50
Massimo Scarpa	71	74	72	78	295	4,735.50
Gary Orr	68	72	76	79	295	4,735.50
Markus Brier	71	72	74	78	295	4,735.50
Andrew Coltart	72	73	71	79	295	4,735.50
Chris Gane	72	72	73	79	296	3,788.40
Grant Hamerton	71	74	73	78	296	3,788.40
Raymond Russell	74	67	75	80	296	3,788.40
Benoit Teilleria	69	75	72	80	296	3,788.40
Mikko Ilonen	70	76	74	76	296	3,788.40
Marten Olander	72	71	72	82	297	2,998.67
Andrew Marshall	74	72	72	79	297	2,998.67
Gary Evans	71	72	75	79	297	2,998.67
Sam Torrance	71	75	75	77	298	2,577
Nicolas Vanhootegem	72	73	76	77	298	2,577
Roger Wessels	72	72	78	76	298	2,577
Jose Rivero	75	69	76	79	299	2,569.50
Jean Hugo	70	74	76	79	299	2,569.50
Van Phillips	71	73	74	82	300	2,563.50
Matthew Cort	70	75	75	80	300	2,563.50
Santiago Luna	76	70	78	77	301	2,557.50
Roger Winchester	73	73	79	76	301	2,557.50
Gregory Havret	71	72	80	80	303	2,553
Richard Bland	71	73	80	79	303	2,553
*Alfredo Garcia	73	73	81	81	308	

Novotel Perrier Open de France

Le Golf National, Paris, France
Par 36-36–72; 7,089 yards

May 2-5
purse, €2,000,000

	SCORES				TOTAL	MONEY
Malcolm Mackenzie	68	69	65	72	274	€333,330
Trevor Immelman	68	64	71	72	275	222,220
Ian Woosnam	69	71	66	70	276	103,333.30
Anders Hansen	69	70	65	72	276	103,333.30
Kenneth Ferrie	68	72	67	69	276	103,333.30
Eduardo Romero	70	66	71	70	277	60,000
Jose Maria Olazabal	69	67	67	74	277	60,000
Andrew Coltart	71	66	71	69	277	60,000
Jean-Francois Remesy	67	69	69	75	280	42,400
Gary Evans	71	67	67	75	280	42,400
Klas Eriksson	76	66	69	70	281	33,500
Mark Davis	69	70	72	70	281	33,500
Nick O'Hern	71	71	67	72	281	33,500
Ricardo Gonzalez	71	68	69	73	281	33,500
Marten Olander	67	71	72	72	282	27,040
Soren Kjeldsen	72	69	70	71	282	27,040
Thomas Levet	72	70	70	70	282	27,040
Soren Hansen	69	72	70	71	282	27,040
Robert Karlsson	69	71	70	72	282	27,040
Stuart Little	74	69	72	68	283	23,266.67
Gary Orr	72	69	68	74	283	23,266.67
Christopher Hanell	75	69	71	68	283	23,266.67
Mark James	72	68	73	71	284	20,800
Colin Montgomerie	67	72	71	74	284	20,800
David Drysdale	77	64	70	73	284	20,800
Stephen Gallacher	68	75	70	71	284	20,800
Nick Dougherty	71	70	69	74	284	20,800
Emanuele Canonica	75	65	73	72	285	18,100
Markus Brier	70	72	71	72	285	18,100
Daren Lee	73	69	69	74	285	18,100
Carl Pettersson	70	68	70	77	285	18,100
Roger Chapman	72	68	71	75	286	14,875
Santiago Luna	69	71	71	75	286	14,875
Mark Mouland	72	68	71	75	286	14,875
Alexandre Balicki	77	65	70	74	286	14,875
Henrik Bjornstad	70	72	75	69	286	14,875
Erol Simsek	75	66	71	74	286	14,875
Mikael Lundberg	70	70	74	72	286	14,875
Jamie Donaldson	69	70	74	73	286	14,875
Barry Lane	69	74	70	74	287	11,800
Raphael Jacquelin	71	73	70	73	287	11,800
Richard Green	68	73	72	74	287	11,800
Paul Eales	70	72	68	77	287	11,800
Jonathan Lomas	71	69	71	76	287	11,800
Christophe Pottier	74	70	71	72	287	11,800
David Carter	72	71	69	75	287	11,800
David Gilford	72	71	72	73	288	9,600
David Lynn	71	70	72	75	288	9,600
Patrik Sjoland	70	73	76	69	288	9,600
Simon Dyson	73	69	74	72	288	9,600
Richard Johnson	73	69	72	75	289	8,000
Stephen Scahill	72	65	70	82	289	8,000
Mark Pilkington	69	71	73	76	289	8,000
John Bickerton	69	71	70	79	289	8,000

		SCORES			TOTAL	MONEY
Ian Poulter	71	73	68	78	290	5,975
Gary Emerson	72	71	74	73	290	5,975
Thomas Bjorn	70	71	75	74	290	5,975
Bertrand Cornut	74	70	71	75	290	5,975
Sebastien Delagrange	70	73	73	74	290	5,975
Henrik Nystrom	73	68	76	73	290	5,975
Benoit Teilleria	74	70	73	73	290	5,975
Alastair Forsyth	69	74	72	75	290	5,975
Costantino Rocca	73	69	73	76	291	4,900
Raymond Russell	71	72	75	73	291	4,900
Matthew Cort	72	69	74	77	292	4,600
Philip Golding	72	72	73	76	293	4,100
Stephen Dodd	71	72	77	73	293	4,100
Didier de Vooght	73	68	76	76	293	4,100
Gary Clark	72	69	75	77	293	4,100
Magnus Persson Atlevi	70	74	73	77	294	3,650
Tom Gillis	71	71	74	79	295	2,997
Peter O'Malley	72	71	75	77	295	2,997
Fredrik Jacobson	70	70	76	79	295	2,997
Desvonde Botes	71	71	76	79	297	2,989.50
Jeremy Robinson	74	70	77	76	297	2,989.50
Anthony Wall	72	72	77	79	300	2,985
Ignacio Garrido	70	72	77	83	302	2,982

Benson and Hedges International Open

The De Vere Belfry, Sutton Coldfield, England
Par 36-36–72; 7,118 yards

May 9-12
purse, €1,766,171

		SCORES			TOTAL	MONEY
Angel Cabrera	68	73	68	69	278	€294,356.50
Barry Lane	69	72	65	73	279	196,237.70
Padraig Harrington	71	70	70	69	280	91,252.17
Colin Montgomerie	71	67	73	69	280	91,252.17
Michael Campbell	70	69	71	70	280	91,252.17
Peter Baker	71	68	70	72	281	61,815.98
Peter Fowler	71	69	73	69	282	48,569.70
Steve Webster	73	68	74	67	282	48,569.70
Greg Owen	66	72	70	75	283	37,442.82
John Daly	70	69	74	70	283	37,442.82
Nick Faldo	72	72	69	71	284	28,199.86
Tom Gillis	72	72	73	67	284	28,199.86
Olle Karlsson	78	68	70	68	284	28,199.86
Phillip Price	71	70	70	73	284	28,199.86
Roger Wessels	69	69	73	73	284	28,199.86
David Lynn	73	70	68	73	284	28,199.86
Raphael Jacquelin	71	70	72	72	285	23,313.46
David Drysdale	71	69	77	68	285	23,313.46
Peter Senior	71	72	71	72	286	20,593.55
Richard Green	73	69	77	67	286	20,593.55
David Carter	68	78	69	71	286	20,593.55
Retief Goosen	73	72	73	68	286	20,593.55
Adam Scott	74	71	76	65	286	20,593.55
Bernhard Langer	72	70	73	72	287	17,043.55
Malcolm Mackenzie	72	70	72	73	287	17,043.55
Ian Woosnam	67	72	78	70	287	17,043.55
Jeev Milkha Singh	70	74	72	71	287	17,043.55

	SCORES				TOTAL	MONEY
Ian Poulter	70	75	70	72	287	17,043.55
Charlie Wi	70	74	76	67	287	17,043.55
Rolf Muntz	71	71	75	70	287	17,043.55
Paul Lawrie	73	70	73	71	287	17,043.55
Eduardo Romero	71	72	72	73	288	12,951.92
Sam Torrance	72	72	71	73	288	12,951.92
Jean-Francois Remesy	72	73	70	73	288	12,951.92
Stuart Little	71	73	77	67	288	12,951.92
Michael Hoey	73	73	70	72	288	12,951.92
Stephen Scahill	72	71	74	71	288	12,951.92
Raymond Russell	73	71	74	70	288	12,951.92
Alastair Forsyth	71	72	72	73	288	12,951.92
Carl Pettersson	73	71	71	73	288	12,951.92
Richard Johnson	73	70	77	69	289	10,420.41
Peter O'Malley	70	70	73	76	289	10,420.41
Gary Orr	74	71	74	70	289	10,420.41
Bradley Dredge	74	70	73	72	289	10,420.41
Daren Lee	70	71	74	74	289	10,420.41
David Gilford	73	73	72	72	290	8,654.24
Soren Kjeldsen	75	70	71	74	290	8,654.24
Richard Bland	75	69	74	72	290	8,654.24
Russell Claydon	71	74	74	71	290	8,654.24
John Bickerton	72	68	80	70	290	8,654.24
Santiago Luna	72	70	75	74	291	6,711.45
Anthony Wall	68	71	75	77	291	6,711.45
Nick O'Hern	77	68	71	75	291	6,711.45
Trevor Immelman	72	71	75	73	291	6,711.45
Emanuele Canonica	75	71	70	75	291	6,711.45
Thomas Bjorn	71	70	80	70	291	6,711.45
Jose Maria Olazabal	74	72	77	69	292	5,298.51
Brian Davis	73	73	73	73	292	5,298.51
Henrik Stenson	73	73	71	75	292	5,298.51
Mark Foster	71	72	74	77	294	4,768.66
Paul Eales	72	72	76	74	294	4,768.66
Lucas Parsons	72	73	76	73	294	4,768.66
Sandy Lyle	69	74	74	78	295	4,327.12
Mark Pilkington	75	70	81	69	295	4,327.12
Des Smyth	73	70	77	76	296	3,973.88
Jarmo Sandelin	69	77	76	74	296	3,973.88
Andrew Marshall	74	72	77	74	297	3,532.34
Ian Garbutt	70	76	75	76	297	3,532.34
Mads Vibe-Hastrup	72	73	74	78	297	3,532.34
Benoit Teilleria	75	71	73	79	298	3,227.28
Eamonn Darcy	75	71	80	74	300	2,647.50
Carlos Rodiles	73	72	76	79	300	2,647.50
Jose Manuel Lara	73	73	79	77	302	2,643
Mark Roe	73	71	76	84	304	2,640

Deutsche Bank - SAP Open

St. Leon-Rot, Heidelberg, Germany
Par 36-36–72; 7,255 yards

May 17-20
purse, €2,700,000

	SCORES				TOTAL	MONEY
Tiger Woods	69	67	64	68	268	€450,000
Colin Montgomerie	66	68	65	69	268	300,000

(Woods defeated Montgomerie on third playoff hole.)

	SCORES				TOTAL	MONEY
Justin Rose	71	65	66	67	269	169,020
Greg Owen	68	68	68	67	271	135,000
Ricardo Gonzalez	71	67	67	68	273	114,480
Ian Woosnam	68	67	73	67	275	81,000
Marten Olander	69	69	69	68	275	81,000
Thomas Bjorn	73	65	71	66	275	81,000
Anders Hansen	72	68	71	65	276	54,720
Richard Green	68	67	70	71	276	54,720
Angel Cabrera	69	69	70	68	276	54,720
Santiago Luna	72	70	65	70	277	42,727.50
Padraig Harrington	71	70	66	70	277	42,727.50
Pierre Fulke	69	70	66	72	277	42,727.50
Bradley Dredge	70	69	70	68	277	42,727.50
Robert Karlsson	71	69	67	71	278	35,707.50
Alex Cejka	64	70	71	73	278	35,707.50
Darren Clarke	67	68	73	70	278	35,707.50
Michael Campbell	71	72	69	66	278	35,707.50
Soren Kjeldsen	72	68	70	69	279	30,982.50
Carlos Rodiles	71	69	68	71	279	30,982.50
Rolf Muntz	70	73	71	65	279	30,982.50
Adam Scott	70	73	68	68	279	30,982.50
Eduardo Romero	67	70	69	74	280	27,270
Steve Webster	73	67	70	70	280	27,270
Henrik Bjornstad	67	70	73	70	280	27,270
Mark Pilkington	71	64	72	73	280	27,270
David Carter	71	67	72	70	280	27,270
Greg Turner	65	74	71	71	281	23,625
Paul Lawrie	72	71	68	70	281	23,625
Fredrik Jacobson	73	68	69	71	281	23,625
Niclas Fasth	71	72	72	66	281	23,625
Trevor Immelman	67	74	70	71	282	19,748.57
Steen Tinning	70	73	70	69	282	19,748.57
Soren Hansen	73	71	70	68	282	19,748.57
Joakim Haeggman	71	70	68	73	282	19,748.57
Gary Orr	71	67	71	73	282	19,748.57
Gary Clark	68	72	72	70	282	19,748.57
John Bickerton	70	71	71	70	282	19,748.57
Gordon Brand, Jr.	72	70	70	71	283	17,280
Jean Van de Velde	69	70	69	75	283	17,280
Sven Struver	72	71	70	71	284	15,120
Richard Johnson	68	76	70	70	284	15,120
Olle Karlsson	72	70	72	70	284	15,120
Markus Brier	72	71	69	72	284	15,120
Andrew Coltart	72	71	72	69	284	15,120
Patrik Sjoland	72	68	72	72	284	15,120
Mark Foster	71	71	70	73	285	12,690
Maarten Lafeber	73	69	71	72	285	12,690
Jean Hugo	71	70	72	72	285	12,690
Marc Farry	71	73	69	73	286	10,530
Stephen Scahill	74	68	73	71	286	10,530
Sebastien Delagrange	71	73	68	74	286	10,530
Alastair Forsyth	69	70	69	78	286	10,530
Nick Dougherty	74	69	74	69	286	10,530
Darren Fichardt	67	75	74	71	287	8,302.50
Nick O'Hern	73	70	71	73	287	8,302.50
Gary Emerson	70	72	74	71	287	8,302.50
Raymond Russell	67	74	72	74	287	8,302.50
Bernhard Langer	73	71	71	73	288	6,885
Emanuele Canonica	70	73	72	73	288	6,885
Ian Garbutt	71	69	74	74	288	6,885

	SCORES				TOTAL	MONEY
David Lynn	71	73	71	73	288	6,885
Daren Lee	72	72	73	71	288	6,885
Retief Goosen	72	69	74	73	288	6,885
Carl Pettersson	74	70	72	73	289	5,940
Andrew Oldcorn	72	70	72	76	290	5,400
Jamie Spence	71	73	72	74	290	5,400
Stephen Gallacher	75	69	75	71	290	5,400
David Drysdale	71	73	76	71	291	4,265.25
Mads Vibe-Hastrup	70	74	74	73	291	4,265.25
Jamie Donaldson	71	71	72	77	291	4,265.25
Nick Cassini	74	70	71	76	291	4,265.25
Stephen Leaney	75	69	75	74	293	4,039.50
Diego Borrego	70	74	77	72	293	4,039.50
Philip Golding	70	72	76	77	295	4,035
Anthony Wall	72	72	76	77	297	4,032

Volvo PGA Championship

Wentworth Club, Surrey, England
Par 35-37–72; 7,072 yards

May 23-26
purse, €3,172,280

	SCORES				TOTAL	MONEY
Anders Hansen	68	65	66	70	269	€528,708.10
Eduardo Romero	67	68	71	68	274	275,528.40
Colin Montgomerie	64	71	72	67	274	275,528.40
Nick Faldo	71	68	68	69	276	134,716.20
Carlos Rodiles	69	67	68	72	276	134,716.20
Michael Campbell	68	70	71	67	276	134,716.20
Jarrod Moseley	71	73	70	63	277	87,237.70
Darren Clarke	70	71	69	67	277	87,237.70
David Gilford	68	71	70	70	279	67,252.34
Peter O'Malley	69	71	69	70	279	67,252.34
Maarten Lafeber	71	70	67	72	280	53,135.69
Stephen Leaney	68	71	73	68	280	53,135.69
Peter Baker	70	70	68	72	280	53,135.69
Niclas Fasth	71	71	71	67	280	53,135.69
Sam Torrance	71	68	72	70	281	43,777.46
Greg Turner	68	71	69	73	281	43,777.46
Gregory Havret	73	69	70	69	281	43,777.46
Gary Evans	68	75	67	71	281	43,777.46
Barry Lane	71	71	69	71	282	35,000.82
Mark McNulty	67	69	71	75	282	35,000.82
Steen Tinning	67	76	70	69	282	35,000.82
Phillip Price	72	72	68	70	282	35,000.82
Ricardo Gonzalez	73	70	69	70	282	35,000.82
Ignacio Garrido	69	71	69	73	282	35,000.82
Thomas Bjorn	71	69	73	69	282	35,000.82
John Bickerton	71	68	73	70	282	35,000.82
Nick Dougherty	72	70	71	69	282	35,000.82
David J. Russell	68	76	73	66	283	29,184.98
Soren Hansen	75	69	71	68	283	29,184.98
Alastair Forsyth	71	68	73	71	283	29,184.98
Robert Karlsson	68	75	70	71	284	26,329.92
Gary Clark	69	72	73	70	284	26,329.92
Greg Owen	71	72	75	66	284	26,329.92
Andrew Oldcorn	68	75	72	70	285	22,840.42
Marc Farry	71	72	73	69	285	22,840.42

	SCORES				TOTAL	MONEY
Tom Gillis	68	74	71	72	285	22,840.42
Andrew Marshall	72	70	72	71	285	22,840.42
Paul Lawrie	73	70	68	74	285	22,840.42
Patrik Sjoland	71	71	71	72	285	22,840.42
Jean Van de Velde	71	69	74	72	286	18,716.45
Henrik Bjornstad	72	71	72	71	286	18,716.45
Angel Cabrera	70	71	70	75	286	18,716.45
Roger Wessels	72	71	71	72	286	18,716.45
Sebastien Delagrange	70	73	71	72	286	18,716.45
David Carter	71	72	72	71	286	18,716.45
Brett Rumford	72	70	74	70	286	18,716.45
Darren Fichardt	72	72	69	74	287	15,544.17
Jorge Berendt	73	71	74	69	287	15,544.17
Stephen Gallacher	71	71	72	73	287	15,544.17
Miguel Angel Martin	70	73	75	70	288	12,689.12
Jose Rivero	71	72	71	74	288	12,689.12
Mark Davis	69	75	72	72	288	12,689.12
Sion Bebb	71	71	75	71	288	12,689.12
Lucas Parsons	68	74	72	74	288	12,689.12
Mikael Lundberg	71	71	73	73	288	12,689.12
Gordon Brand, Jr.	70	73	77	69	289	9,580.29
Robert-Jan Derksen	74	70	71	74	289	9,580.29
Diego Borrego	68	74	76	71	289	9,580.29
Jarmo Sandelin	69	71	73	76	289	9,580.29
Andrew Coltart	67	73	77	72	289	9,580.29
Richard Green	71	73	75	71	290	8,089.31
Jamie Spence	72	72	76	70	290	8,089.31
Gary Emerson	73	69	73	75	290	8,089.31
Christopher Hanell	72	72	72	74	290	8,089.31
Trevor Immelman	69	74	73	75	291	7,137.63
Yeh Wei-tze	73	71	73	74	291	7,137.63
Mark Foster	69	75	74	74	292	6,503.17
Brian Davis	72	70	76	74	292	6,503.17
Desvonde Botes	70	74	73	76	293	5,908.37
Gary Marks	71	70	77	75	293	5,908.37
Jose Maria Olazabal	68	73	75	78	294	4,756.50
Rolf Muntz	69	75	77	73	294	4,756.50
Ronan Rafferty	68	72	79	76	295	4,750.50
Markus Brier	71	72	78	74	295	4,750.50
Paul Casey	71	72	74	79	296	4,746
Murray Urquhart	73	71	82	75	301	4,743

Victor Chandler British Masters

Woburn Golf & Country Club, Milton Keynes, England
Par 36-36–72; 7,214 yards

May 30-June 2
purse, €1,976,275

	SCORES				TOTAL	MONEY
Justin Rose	70	69	65	65	269	€329,373.90
Ian Poulter	68	67	67	68	270	219,572.10
Phillip Price	68	65	68	72	273	123,714.80
Colin Montgomerie	70	69	68	67	274	98,813.75
Gary Evans	69	69	66	71	275	83,794.06
Mark Roe	71	68	70	68	277	52,331.76
Soren Hansen	68	69	67	73	277	52,331.76
Greg Owen	73	67	68	69	277	52,331.76
Fredrik Andersson	70	70	69	68	277	52,331.76
David Carter	72	70	67	68	277	52,331.76

	SCORES			TOTAL	MONEY
Roger Chapman	75	68	71 64	278	30,187.60
Padraig Harrington	73	70	65 70	278	30,187.60
Peter Hanson	72	67	69 70	278	30,187.60
Trevor Immelman	72	67	68 71	278	30,187.60
Jamie Spence	72	68	67 71	278	30,187.60
Carlos Rodiles	71	69	72 66	278	30,187.60
Roger Wessels	70	70	70 68	278	30,187.60
Paul Lawrie	70	71	68 69	278	30,187.60
Sandy Lyle	72	65	70 72	279	23,715.30
Barry Lane	69	74	68 68	279	23,715.30
John Bickerton	69	71	70 69	279	23,715.30
Nick O'Hern	71	71	66 72	280	20,256.82
Philip Golding	69	67	71 73	280	20,256.82
Stuart Little	72	72	65 71	280	20,256.82
Jarrod Moseley	74	70	71 65	280	20,256.82
Paul McGinley	72	72	65 71	280	20,256.82
Jorge Berendt	70	73	68 69	280	20,256.82
Rolf Muntz	70	74	69 67	280	20,256.82
Gary Orr	71	71	70 68	280	20,256.82
Santiago Luna	67	71	72 71	281	15,001.72
Malcolm Mackenzie	73	70	69 69	281	15,001.72
Mark Foster	70	70	73 68	281	15,001.72
Jose Manuel Lara	74	70	68 69	281	15,001.72
Thomas Levet	68	70	73 70	281	15,001.72
Chris Gane	69	75	69 68	281	15,001.72
Bradley Dredge	71	73	69 68	281	15,001.72
Simon Khan	72	65	72 72	281	15,001.72
Robert Coles	69	72	67 73	281	15,001.72
Benoit Teilleria	71	71	68 71	281	15,001.72
Simon Dyson	70	72	72 67	281	15,001.72
Steve Webster	70	71	71 70	282	11,857.65
Paul Broadhurst	72	68	74 68	282	11,857.65
Paul Eales	70	71	69 72	282	11,857.65
Olle Karlsson	69	71	69 73	282	11,857.65
Costantino Rocca	71	70	72 70	283	10,079
Raphael Jacquelin	71	72	69 71	283	10,079
Robert Karlsson	69	69	75 70	283	10,079
Lee Westwood	71	70	71 71	283	10,079
Nick Dougherty	72	72	70 69	283	10,079
Andrew Oldcorn	74	70	73 67	284	7,905.10
Sam Torrance	71	68	69 76	284	7,905.10
Marc Farry	69	73	75 67	284	7,905.10
Sven Struver	69	72	72 71	284	7,905.10
Jean Hugo	69	72	73 70	284	7,905.10
Joakim Haeggman	73	70	72 69	284	7,905.10
Jean-Francois Remesy	72	71	71 71	285	6,077.05
Henrik Stenson	72	72	74 67	285	6,077.05
Ian Garbutt	75	67	71 72	285	6,077.05
Patrik Sjoland	72	70	70 73	285	6,077.05
Des Smyth	69	74	72 71	286	4,940.69
Brian Davis	70	74	71 71	286	4,940.69
Jean Van de Velde	71	68	76 71	286	4,940.69
Steen Tinning	71	72	71 72	286	4,940.69
Charlie Wi	70	72	71 73	286	4,940.69
Peter Hedblom	69	71	72 74	286	4,940.69
Jamie Donaldson	70	74	68 74	286	4,940.69
Darren Fichardt	75	68	71 73	287	3,363.13
Shaun Webster	76	68	69 74	287	3,363.13
Ignacio Garrido	76	68	71 72	287	3,363.13
Gary Clark	72	72	72 71	287	3,363.13

	SCORES				TOTAL	MONEY
Raymond Russell	68	70	73	76	287	3,363.13
Stephen Gallacher	73	69	70	75	287	3,363.13
Mikael Lundberg	75	69	72	71	287	3,363.13
Tobias Dier	72	67	79	69	287	3,363.13
Yeh Wei-tze	71	71	73	72	287	3,363.13
Gordon Brand, Jr.	70	74	74	70	288	2,943
Ian Woosnam	72	71	74	71	288	2,943
Elliot Boult	74	70	72	72	288	2,943
Kenneth Ferrie	71	72	70	75	288	2,943
Darren Clarke	73	70	70	75	288	2,943
Adam Mednick	72	71	72	74	289	2,934
*Barry Hume	69	74	71	75	289	
Gustavo Rojas	71	73	74	72	290	2,928
Henrik Nystrom	74	68	76	72	290	2,928
Carl Pettersson	72	70	73	75	290	2,928
Robert-Jan Derksen	67	74	75	75	291	2,920.50
Arjun Atwal	70	72	76	73	291	2,920.50
Carl Suneson	75	69	72	76	292	2,916

Compass Group English Open

Marriott Forest of Arden Hotel, Warwickshire, England
Par 36-36–72; 7,213 yards

June 6-9
purse, €1,252,816

	SCORES				TOTAL	MONEY
Darren Clarke	65	70	68	68	271	€208,797.50
Soren Hansen	72	68	64	70	274	139,187.90
Raphael Jacquelin	70	68	65	73	276	70,533.54
Phillip Price	68	68	70	70	276	70,533.54
Yeh Wei-tze	68	72	69	68	277	53,119.40
Sandy Lyle	71	70	66	71	278	37,584.48
Justin Rose	68	69	68	73	278	37,584.48
Sam Walker	68	71	66	73	278	37,584.48
Bradley Dredge	69	72	69	69	279	28,063.08
Mark Roe	67	70	70	73	280	21,235.23
Sam Torrance	70	72	65	73	280	21,235.23
Steve Webster	72	67	65	76	280	21,235.23
Gregory Havret	71	69	70	70	280	21,235.23
Dennis Edlund	68	70	69	73	280	21,235.23
David Drysdale	68	67	73	72	280	21,235.23
Robert-Jan Derksen	69	73	65	74	281	16,261.55
Ian Poulter	68	72	69	72	281	16,261.55
Carl Suneson	69	72	69	71	281	16,261.55
Didier de Vooght	67	71	72	71	281	16,261.55
Nick Dougherty	70	73	68	70	281	16,261.55
Barry Lane	71	70	67	74	282	13,593.05
Chris Gane	73	69	70	70	282	13,593.05
Christophe Pottier	75	66	73	68	282	13,593.05
Niclas Fasth	70	72	68	72	282	13,593.05
Simon Dyson	69	74	67	72	282	13,593.05
Jamie Donaldson	68	71	70	73	282	13,593.05
Brian Davis	72	71	73	67	283	10,962.14
Nick O'Hern	73	68	68	74	283	10,962.14
Shaun Webster	69	74	69	71	283	10,962.14
Alberto Binaghi	67	74	73	69	283	10,962.14
Charlie Wi	70	70	70	73	283	10,962.14
Grant Hamerton	67	72	71	73	283	10,962.14
Graeme Storm	67	73	72	71	283	10,962.14

	SCORES			TOTAL	MONEY
Paul Casey	69	71	70	73	283	10,962.14
Gordon Brand, Jr.	74	68	72	70	284	9,020.27
David Gilford	71	71	72	70	284	9,020.27
Hennie Otto	71	71	72	70	284	9,020.27
Jarrod Moseley	65	73	74	72	284	9,020.27
Peter Fowler	68	74	68	75	285	7,767.46
Marten Olander	70	73	69	73	285	7,767.46
Joakim Haeggman	70	73	71	71	285	7,767.46
Pierre Fulke	74	68	70	73	285	7,767.46
Adam Mednick	71	72	69	73	285	7,767.46
Johan Skold	71	68	70	76	285	7,767.46
Santiago Luna	70	72	70	74	286	5,637.67
David Howell	69	73	71	73	286	5,637.67
Paul Broadhurst	71	71	69	75	286	5,637.67
Russell Claydon	70	71	72	73	286	5,637.67
Emanuele Canonica	69	71	69	77	286	5,637.67
Ian Garbutt	71	71	70	74	286	5,637.67
Gary Evans	71	68	73	74	286	5,637.67
Roger Wessels	70	72	73	71	286	5,637.67
Robert Coles	71	69	70	76	286	5,637.67
Benn Barham	72	68	71	75	286	5,637.67
David Carter	71	70	69	76	286	5,637.67
Wayne Riley	71	70	67	79	287	3,783.50
David J. Russell	70	71	71	75	287	3,783.50
Marc Pendaries	72	68	72	75	287	3,783.50
Michael Archer	70	73	74	70	287	3,783.50
Stephen Dodd	71	70	68	78	287	3,783.50
Philip Walton	71	72	72	73	288	3,132.04
Peter Baker	69	72	75	72	288	3,132.04
Jeremy Robinson	71	72	73	72	288	3,132.04
Darren Prosser	69	68	75	76	288	3,132.04
Gary Orr	67	73	73	75	288	3,132.04
Peter Hanson	71	71	70	77	289	2,568.27
Paul McGinley	72	71	72	74	289	2,568.27
Fredrik Andersson	69	72	74	74	289	2,568.27
Lucas Parsons	74	68	74	73	289	2,568.27
Malcolm Mackenzie	72	69	73	76	290	2,090.53
Hennie Walters	69	73	73	75	290	2,090.53
Andrew Oldcorn	72	70	74	75	291	1,871.50
Andrew Marshall	72	71	72	76	291	1,871.50
David Lynn	72	71	75	73	291	1,871.50
Mark Pilkington	68	75	74	74	291	1,871.50
Roger Chapman	69	71	72	80	292	1,861
Simon Khan	71	72	77	72	292	1,861
Greg Owen	70	71	71	80	292	1,861
Eamonn Darcy	74	68	73	78	293	1,853.50
Sebastien Delagrange	71	71	76	75	293	1,853.50
Van Phillips	70	71	72	84	297	1,849

Great North Open

De Vere Slaley Hall, Northumberland, England
Par 36-36–72; 7,088 yards

June 20-23
purse, €935,760

	SCORES			TOTAL	MONEY
Miles Tunnicliff	72	70	68	69	279	€155,960
Sven Struver	71	65	74	73	283	103,962.90
Malcolm Mackenzie	72	72	69	71	284	52,683.29

		SCORES			TOTAL	MONEY
Bradley Dredge	68	71	75	70	284	52,683.29
Brian Davis	75	68	68	75	286	30,973.66
Jean Hugo	72	73	69	72	286	30,973.66
Diego Borrego	66	71	78	71	286	30,973.66
Nicolas Vanhootegem	68	73	71	74	286	30,973.66
Rolf Muntz	72	69	71	75	287	20,961.02
David Gilford	73	70	67	78	288	17,342.75
Roger Wessels	69	69	74	76	288	17,342.75
David Lynn	74	68	69	77	288	17,342.75
Garry Houston	73	70	72	74	289	13,793.10
Ian Garbutt	73	72	73	71	289	13,793.10
Jon Bevan	72	67	78	72	289	13,793.10
Simon Dyson	71	75	71	72	289	13,793.10
Paul Casey	70	69	74	76	289	13,793.10
Gordon Brand, Jr.	70	75	71	74	290	11,266.55
Gary Murphy	72	69	71	78	290	11,266.55
Gary Emerson	71	73	72	74	290	11,266.55
Stephen Gallacher	74	72	73	71	290	11,266.55
Brett Rumford	70	70	73	77	290	11,266.55
Darren Fichardt	75	72	72	72	291	10,293.36
Santiago Luna	73	73	73	73	292	9,451.18
Mark McNulty	75	72	74	71	292	9,451.18
Yngve Nilsson	74	73	71	74	292	9,451.18
Paul Broadhurst	72	75	73	72	292	9,451.18
Jesus Maria Arruti	73	74	69	76	292	9,451.18
Peter Fowler	70	74	74	75	293	7,907.17
Dennis Edlund	72	71	73	77	293	7,907.17
Gianluca Baruffaldi	71	70	76	76	293	7,907.17
Johan Skold	76	71	74	72	293	7,907.17
Andrew Coltart	73	72	70	78	293	7,907.17
Martin Maritz	73	74	72	74	293	7,907.17
Des Smyth	69	76	73	76	294	6,550.32
Richard Green	70	75	72	77	294	6,550.32
Elliot Boult	71	69	81	73	294	6,550.32
Peter Baker	72	73	74	75	294	6,550.32
Gregory Havret	69	78	71	76	294	6,550.32
Adam Mednick	71	73	76	74	294	6,550.32
Greig Hutcheon	74	68	75	78	295	5,240.26
Nick O'Hern	73	74	71	77	295	5,240.26
Hennie Otto	70	73	73	79	295	5,240.26
Alberto Binaghi	74	73	73	75	295	5,240.26
Jonathan Lomas	75	70	70	80	295	5,240.26
Paul Dwyer	71	73	76	75	295	5,240.26
Sion Bebb	77	70	72	76	295	5,240.26
Gary Clark	74	71	78	72	295	5,240.26
Roger Chapman	72	74	76	74	296	4,304.50
Benn Barham	74	67	78	77	296	4,304.50
Shaun Webster	73	73	77	74	297	3,743.04
Gustavo Rojas	73	72	75	77	297	3,743.04
Fredrik Andersson	73	72	77	75	297	3,743.04
Matthew Blackey	72	75	76	74	297	3,743.04
Peter Lawrie	71	73	79	75	298	3,181.58
Graeme Storm	73	72	76	77	298	3,181.58
Magnus Persson Atlevi	70	75	78	76	299	2,760.49
Ilya Goroneskoul	72	72	75	80	299	2,760.49
Stuart Little	71	70	77	81	299	2,760.49
Marc Cayeux	72	73	75	79	299	2,760.49
Mark Davis	73	71	79	77	300	2,479.76
Neil Cheetham	73	74	77	76	300	2,479.76
Kenneth Ferrie	72	74	76	79	301	2,245.82

	SCORES				TOTAL	MONEY
Stephen Scahill	73	73	75	80	301	2,245.82
David Drysdale	74	73	72	82	301	2,245.82
Andrew Beal	74	72	75	81	302	2,058.67
Barry Lane	71	76	80	76	303	1,965.10
Raphael Jacquelin	75	72	76	83	306	1,871.52
Joakim Rask	73	74	77	83	307	1,777.94

Murphy's Irish Open

Fota Island Golf Club, Cork, Ireland
Par 36-35–71; 6,927 yards

June 27-30
purse, €1,600,000

	SCORES				TOTAL	MONEY
Soren Hansen	69	69	64	68	270	€266,660
Darren Fichardt	71	68	64	67	270	119,310
Richard Bland	69	71	63	67	270	119,310
Niclas Fasth	72	67	63	68	270	119,310
(Hansen won on fourth playoff hole.)						
Thomas Bjorn	71	68	63	70	272	67,840
Eamonn Darcy	69	68	68	69	274	38,400
Eduardo Romero	66	71	66	71	274	38,400
Padraig Harrington	71	68	69	66	274	38,400
Soren Kjeldsen	69	70	65	70	274	38,400
Stuart Little	68	71	66	69	274	38,400
Joakim Haeggman	66	69	69	70	274	38,400
Alex Cejka	69	65	69	71	274	38,400
Peter O'Malley	66	67	73	69	275	24,586.67
Gary Evans	69	70	66	70	275	24,586.67
Paul Casey	69	69	68	69	275	24,586.67
Des Smyth	67	68	72	69	276	21,600
Phillip Price	71	70	66	69	276	21,600
Paul Lawrie	72	69	68	67	276	21,600
Sandy Lyle	73	66	66	72	277	18,920
Peter Fowler	69	70	68	70	277	18,920
Klas Eriksson	71	70	71	65	277	18,920
Lee Westwood	67	68	72	70	277	18,920
Malcolm Mackenzie	68	73	66	71	278	16,880
Fred Funk	66	70	69	73	278	16,880
Peter Hanson	70	70	67	71	278	16,880
Colin Montgomerie	67	67	74	70	278	16,880
David Gilford	68	70	71	70	279	14,000
Mark McNulty	68	69	75	67	279	14,000
Nick O'Hern	72	69	69	69	279	14,000
Henrik Bjornstad	71	68	67	73	279	14,000
Darren Clarke	71	70	65	73	279	14,000
Nick Dougherty	66	74	64	75	279	14,000
Adam Scott	70	66	74	69	279	14,000
Graeme McDowell	70	71	65	73	279	14,000
Miguel Angel Martin	68	70	72	70	280	10,720
Anders Hansen	71	70	69	70	280	10,720
Steen Tinning	68	71	67	74	280	10,720
Richard Johnson	68	67	71	74	280	10,720
Jarrod Moseley	72	69	69	70	280	10,720
Mark Pilkington	69	66	72	73	280	10,720
Raymond Russell	70	67	74	69	280	10,720
Patrik Sjoland	69	68	69	74	280	10,720
Carl Pettersson	67	67	72	74	280	10,720

	SCORES				TOTAL	MONEY
Tony Johnstone	71	68	72	70	281	7,840
Ian Woosnam	71	66	73	71	281	7,840
Barry Lane	69	70	71	71	281	7,840
Kenneth Ferrie	70	68	73	70	281	7,840
Jamie Spence	70	69	71	71	281	7,840
Gary Emerson	70	67	68	76	281	7,840
Andrew Marshall	68	69	70	74	281	7,840
Chris Gane	70	69	67	75	281	7,840
Tobias Dier	71	69	70	71	281	7,840
Philip Walton	71	69	70	72	282	5,600
Arjun Atwal	71	68	70	73	282	5,600
Justin Rose	72	69	69	72	282	5,600
Jonathan Lomas	68	72	72	70	282	5,600
Stephen Dodd	69	72	68	73	282	5,600
Gordon Brand, Jr.	67	73	72	71	283	4,320
Mark James	69	70	67	77	283	4,320
Peter Baker	70	68	75	70	283	4,320
Jeremy Robinson	70	71	70	72	283	4,320
Carl Suneson	68	72	70	73	283	4,320
Russell Claydon	69	72	76	66	283	4,320
Diego Borrego	69	71	70	73	283	4,320
Costantino Rocca	71	70	70	73	284	3,520
Henrik Nystrom	71	68	72	73	284	3,520
Christopher Hanell	72	68	70	74	284	3,520
Andrew Coltart	70	71	73	71	285	3,200
Roger Chapman	71	66	76	73	286	2,790
Didier de Vooght	69	69	76	72	286	2,790
Andrew Butterfield	69	71	72	74	286	2,790
Paul Eales	72	67	78	72	289	2,397
Johan Skold	71	69	79	77	296	2,394

Smurfit European Open

The K Club, Dublin, Ireland
Par 35-37–72; 7,337 yards

July 4-7
purse, €3,102,816

	SCORES				TOTAL	MONEY
Michael Campbell	68	71	70	73	282	€515,584.80
Padraig Harrington	72	69	69	73	283	205,805.50
Paul Lawrie	70	71	69	73	283	205,805.50
Bradley Dredge	71	71	73	68	283	205,805.50
Retief Goosen	71	72	72	68	283	205,805.50
Colin Montgomerie	69	75	68	72	284	92,806.20
Angel Cabrera	72	71	71	70	284	92,806.20
Niclas Fasth	69	77	68	70	284	92,806.20
Barry Lane	69	71	71	74	285	54,844.04
Darren Fichardt	67	74	76	68	285	54,844.04
Jarrod Moseley	67	75	73	70	285	54,844.04
Joakim Haeggman	68	73	71	73	285	54,844.04
Patrik Sjoland	71	70	73	71	285	54,844.04
Paul Casey	71	73	69	72	285	54,844.04
Carl Pettersson	71	71	74	69	285	54,844.04
Soren Kjeldsen	75	72	72	67	286	40,912.07
Nick O'Hern	77	69	71	69	286	40,912.07
Peter O'Malley	74	72	69	71	286	40,912.07
Lee Westwood	72	71	72	71	286	40,912.07
Mark Mouland	70	76	71	70	287	34,073.13

		SCORES			TOTAL	MONEY
Ian Woosnam	73	74	67	73	287	34,073.13
Fred Funk	72	75	67	73	287	34,073.13
Robert Karlsson	70	72	72	73	287	34,073.13
Darren Clarke	74	70	76	67	287	34,073.13
Rolf Muntz	72	73	72	70	287	34,073.13
Mark Pilkington	71	69	75	72	287	34,073.13
Mark James	73	72	71	72	288	29,388.63
Richard Johnson	71	72	73	72	288	29,388.63
Sebastien Delagrange	69	73	74	72	288	29,388.63
Roger Chapman	73	73	71	72	289	24,163.98
Eamonn Darcy	75	72	73	69	289	24,163.98
Santiago Luna	71	73	73	72	289	24,163.98
Eduardo Romero	74	69	71	75	289	24,163.98
Gary Murphy	72	73	74	70	289	24,163.98
Richard Green	74	70	75	70	289	24,163.98
Paul Broadhurst	73	73	70	73	289	24,163.98
Steen Tinning	70	74	74	71	289	24,163.98
Ignacio Garrido	73	72	71	73	289	24,163.98
Markus Brier	75	71	74	70	290	20,417.36
Henrik Nystrom	70	77	72	71	290	20,417.36
Jean-Francois Remesy	71	76	70	74	291	17,633.18
Sven Struver	70	73	76	72	291	17,633.18
Maarten Lafeber	73	72	75	71	291	17,633.18
Peter Hanson	75	72	74	70	291	17,633.18
Andrew Marshall	74	72	74	71	291	17,633.18
Jorge Berendt	68	73	76	74	291	17,633.18
David Carter	73	74	70	74	291	17,633.18
Marc Farry	74	72	73	73	292	13,302.22
Brian Davis	73	72	76	71	292	13,302.22
Marten Olander	73	72	75	72	292	13,302.22
Anders Hansen	71	73	75	73	292	13,302.22
Richard Bland	75	72	76	69	292	13,302.22
Roger Wessels	72	73	73	74	292	13,302.22
Jarmo Sandelin	74	71	70	77	292	13,302.22
Warren Bennett	75	70	75	73	293	10,518.04
Paul Eales	77	70	76	70	293	10,518.04
Greg Norman	69	76	72	77	294	8,971.27
Sam Torrance	71	74	74	75	294	8,971.27
Mark McNulty	70	74	73	77	294	8,971.27
Emanuele Canonica	71	75	74	74	294	8,971.27
Ian Garbutt	72	71	80	71	294	8,971.27
Peter Fowler	76	71	76	72	295	7,733.85
Ricardo Gonzalez	73	71	75	76	295	7,733.85
Gary Clark	73	74	80	68	295	7,733.85
Lucas Parsons	70	75	76	75	296	6,960.47
Jamie Donaldson	70	71	77	78	296	6,960.47
Chris Gane	69	78	77	73	297	6,341.76
Raymond Russell	75	70	75	77	297	6,341.76
David Howell	72	72	79	75	298	5,877.73
Andrew Coltart	72	70	77	80	299	5,142.85
John Dwyer	69	75	77	78	299	5,142.85
Gregory Havret	77	70	78	75	300	4,637

Barclays Scottish Open

Loch Lomond Golf Club, Glasgow, Scotland
Par 36-35–71; 7,083 yards

July 11-14
purse, €3,458,770

	SCORES				TOTAL	MONEY
Eduardo Romero	72	66	65	70	273	€573,016.30
Fredrik Jacobson	66	65	71	71	273	382,010.80
(Romero defeated Jacobson on first playoff hole.)						
Roger Chapman	70	70	66	68	274	193,568.40
Tim Clark	71	68	67	68	274	193,568.40
Justin Rose	65	71	68	71	275	145,778
Jean-Francois Remesy	70	72	67	67	276	91,042.48
Stephen Leaney	72	65	67	72	276	91,042.48
Ricardo Gonzalez	72	70	69	65	276	91,042.48
Tom Lehman	69	69	71	67	276	91,042.48
Michael Campbell	72	67	66	71	276	91,042.48
Warren Bennett	67	70	68	72	277	59,250.96
John Bickerton	67	73	67	70	277	59,250.96
Paul Casey	72	69	65	71	277	59,250.96
Barry Lane	74	66	69	69	278	46,611.63
Marc Farry	71	69	70	68	278	46,611.63
Jamie Spence	70	69	67	72	278	46,611.63
Colin Montgomerie	72	71	69	66	278	46,611.63
Paul McGinley	69	73	68	68	278	46,611.63
Retief Goosen	72	69	69	68	278	46,611.63
Carl Pettersson	70	66	73	69	278	46,611.63
Maarten Lafeber	74	68	69	68	279	38,851.21
Nick O'Hern	72	69	69	69	279	38,851.21
Richard Bland	68	71	71	69	279	38,851.21
*Barry Hume	67	70	72	70	279	
Ian Woosnam	72	67	70	71	280	33,693.97
Rodney Pampling	74	67	68	71	280	33,693.97
Peter Hanson	76	65	68	71	280	33,693.97
Soren Hansen	72	68	70	70	280	33,693.97
Jonathan Lomas	69	70	70	71	280	33,693.97
Darren Clarke	70	73	66	71	280	33,693.97
Nick Dougherty	72	69	70	69	280	33,693.97
David Howell	68	71	67	75	281	26,015.41
Michael Hoey	68	72	72	69	281	26,015.41
Dean Wilson	68	73	70	70	281	26,015.41
Gary Evans	73	66	71	71	281	26,015.41
Jose Coceres	71	70	66	74	281	26,015.41
Bradley Dredge	72	70	70	69	281	26,015.41
Jeff Maggert	71	72	68	70	281	26,015.41
Alastair Forsyth	72	70	69	70	281	26,015.41
Rory Sabbatini	69	71	68	73	281	26,015.41
Sandy Lyle	67	68	75	72	282	19,597.51
Klas Eriksson	74	68	71	69	282	19,597.51
Cameron Beckman	71	68	72	71	282	19,597.51
Raphael Jacquelin	73	70	70	69	282	19,597.51
Soren Kjeldsen	69	74	68	71	282	19,597.51
Fred Funk	71	71	71	69	282	19,597.51
Stephen Dodd	69	71	74	68	282	19,597.51
Phillip Price	73	69	69	71	282	19,597.51
Niclas Fasth	70	68	79	65	282	19,597.51
Richard Johnson	71	65	75	72	283	15,471.72
Ernie Els	68	74	69	72	283	15,471.72
Gary Orr	73	67	72	71	283	15,471.72
Gordon Brand, Jr.	68	74	74	68	284	11,345.93

	SCORES				TOTAL	MONEY
Miguel Angel Martin	72	70	74	68	284	11,345.93
Sam Torrance	68	73	74	69	284	11,345.93
Robert-Jan Derksen	69	72	72	71	284	11,345.93
Brad Faxon	68	72	70	74	284	11,345.93
Henrik Bjornstad	72	71	68	73	284	11,345.93
Peter O'Malley	69	71	74	70	284	11,345.93
Mathias Gronberg	73	69	69	73	284	11,345.93
Paul Lawrie	69	73	72	70	284	11,345.93
Simon Dyson	68	74	75	67	284	11,345.93
Arjun Atwal	74	69	72	70	285	8,251.58
Thomas Levet	73	70	73	69	285	8,251.58
Miguel Angel Jimenez	74	69	69	73	285	8,251.58
Per-Ulrik Johansson	69	73	71	72	285	8,251.58
Joakim Haeggman	71	71	71	72	285	8,251.58
Jorge Berendt	72	68	72	74	286	7,220.14
Diego Borrego	75	68	74	70	287	6,704.41
Matt Gogel	69	68	76	74	287	6,704.41
Philip Golding	72	70	74	72	288	6,282.46
Miles Tunnicliff	66	70	76	77	289	5,155.50
Mark Pilkington	71	67	79	72	289	5,155.50
Costantino Rocca	71	72	76	71	290	5,151
Tony Johnstone	68	71	76	75	290	5,151

British Open Championship

The Honourable Company of Edinburgh Golfers,
Muirfield, East Lothian, Scotland
Par 36-35–71; 7,034 yards

July 18-21
purse, €6,080,102

	SCORES				TOTAL	MONEY
Ernie Els	70	66	72	70	278	€1,095,514
Steve Elkington	71	73	68	66	278	448,639.10
Stuart Appleby	73	70	70	65	278	448,639.10
Thomas Levet	72	66	74	66	278	448,639.10
(Els defeated Elkington and Appleby in four-hole playoff, Levet on first hole of sudden-death.)						
Padraig Harrington	69	67	76	67	279	219,102.80
Shigeki Maruyama	68	68	75	68	279	219,102.80
Gary Evans	72	68	74	65	279	219,102.80
Sergio Garcia	71	69	71	69	280	121,289
Soren Hansen	68	69	73	70	280	121,289
Peter O'Malley	72	68	75	65	280	121,289
Scott Hoch	74	69	71	66	280	121,289
Thomas Bjorn	68	70	73	69	280	121,289
Retief Goosen	71	68	74	67	280	121,289
Nick Price	68	70	75	68	281	77,859.74
Justin Leonard	71	72	68	70	281	77,859.74
Davis Love	71	72	71	67	281	77,859.74
Peter Lonard	72	72	68	69	281	77,859.74
Greg Norman	71	72	71	68	282	64,165.82
Scott McCarron	71	68	72	71	282	64,165.82
Bob Estes	71	70	73	68	282	64,165.82
Duffy Waldorf	67	69	77	69	282	64,165.82
Corey Pavin	69	70	75	69	283	50,080.64
Mark O'Meara	69	69	77	68	283	50,080.64
David Duval	72	71	70	70	283	50,080.64
Toshimitsu Izawa	76	68	72	67	283	50,080.64

	SCORES				TOTAL	MONEY
Justin Rose	68	75	68	72	283	50,080.64
Chris Riley	70	71	76	66	283	50,080.64
Bernhard Langer	72	72	71	69	284	37,560.48
Des Smyth	68	69	74	73	284	37,560.48
Tiger Woods	70	68	81	65	284	37,560.48
Loren Roberts	74	69	70	71	284	37,560.48
Jesper Parnevik	72	72	70	70	284	37,560.48
Jerry Kelly	73	71	70	70	284	37,560.48
Pierre Fulke	72	69	78	65	284	37,560.48
Bradley Dredge	70	72	74	68	284	37,560.48
Niclas Fasth	70	73	71	70	284	37,560.48
Ian Woosnam	72	72	73	68	285	26,474.92
Stephen Leaney	71	70	75	69	285	26,474.92
Scott Verplank	72	68	74	71	285	26,474.92
Darren Clarke	72	67	77	69	285	26,474.92
Andrew Coltart	71	69	74	71	285	26,474.92
Neal Lancaster	71	71	76	67	285	26,474.92
Trevor Immelman	72	72	71	71	286	21,519.03
Steve Jones	68	75	73	70	286	21,519.03
Esteban Toledo	73	70	75	68	286	21,519.03
Carl Pettersson	67	70	76	73	286	21,519.03
Paul Eales	73	71	76	67	287	18,780.24
Rocco Mediate	71	72	74	70	287	18,780.24
Jeff Maggert	71	68	80	68	287	18,780.24
Warren Bennett	71	68	82	67	288	16,067.54
Barry Lane	74	68	72	74	288	16,067.54
Ian Poulter	69	69	78	72	288	16,067.54
Bob Tway	70	66	78	74	288	16,067.54
Ian Garbutt	69	70	74	75	288	16,067.54
Fredrik Andersson	74	70	74	70	288	16,067.54
Mikko Ilonen	71	70	77	70	288	16,067.54
Shingo Katayama	72	68	74	74	288	16,067.54
Craig Perks	72	70	71	75	288	16,067.54
Nick Faldo	73	69	76	71	289	14,554.69
Steve Stricker	69	70	81	69	289	14,554.69
Richard Green	72	72	75	70	289	14,554.69
Stewart Cink	71	69	80	69	289	14,554.69
Joe Durant	72	71	73	73	289	14,554.69
Paul Lawrie	70	70	78	71	289	14,554.69
Kenichi Kuboya	70	73	73	73	289	14,554.69
Jarrod Moseley	70	73	75	72	290	13,772.18
Phil Mickelson	68	76	76	70	290	13,772.18
Chris DiMarco	72	69	75	74	290	13,772.18
Mike Weir	73	69	74	75	291	13,328.76
Toru Taniguchi	71	73	76	71	291	13,328.76
Jim Carter	74	70	73	74	291	13,328.76
Stephen Ames	68	70	81	72	291	13,328.76
Matthew Cort	73	71	78	69	291	13,328.76
Len Mattiace	68	73	77	73	291	13,328.76
Sandy Lyle	68	76	73	75	292	13,302.67
Chris Smith	74	69	71	78	292	13,302.67
Anders Hansen	71	72	79	71	293	13,302.67
Roger Wessels	72	71	73	77	293	13,302.67
David Park	73	67	74	80	294	13,302.67
Mark Calcavecchia	74	66	81	74	295	13,302.67
Lee Janzen	70	69	84	72	295	13,302.67
Colin Montgomerie	74	64	84	75	297	13,302.67
David Toms	67	75	81	75	298	13,302.67

Out of Final 36 Holes

Magnus Persson Atlevi	72	73	145	4,623.93
Eduardo Romero	72	73	145	4,623.93
Marc Farry	70	75	145	4,623.93
Jean-Francois Remesy	68	77	145	4,623.93
Brad Faxon	70	75	145	4,623.93
Jose Maria Olazabal	73	72	145	4,623.93
Matt Kuchar	75	70	145	4,623.93
Lee Westwood	72	73	145	4,623.93
John Bickerton	73	72	145	4,623.93
Michael Campbell	74	71	145	4,623.93
Adam Scott	77	68	145	4,623.93
John Senden	76	70	146	3,859.20
K.J. Choi	73	73	146	3,859.20
Taichi Teshima	69	77	146	3,859.20
Craig Parry	72	74	146	3,859.20
Robert Karlsson	72	74	146	3,859.20
Billy Mayfair	71	75	146	3,859.20
Alexander Cejka	73	73	146	3,859.20
Paul McGinley	72	74	146	3,859.20
Scott Henderson	78	68	146	3,859.20
Tom Lehman	70	76	146	3,859.20
Tim Clark	70	76	146	3,859.20
Tom Whitehouse	75	71	146	3,859.20
Tim Petrovic	73	73	146	3,859.20
David Howell	73	74	147	3,859.20
Raphael Jacquelin	74	73	147	3,859.20
Tsuneyuki Nakajima	75	72	147	3,859.20
Scott Laycock	73	74	147	3,859.20
Jim Furyk	71	76	147	3,859.20
Vijay Singh	72	75	147	3,859.20
Mathias Gronberg	75	72	147	3,859.20
Robert Allenby	73	74	147	3,859.20
Luke Donald	73	74	147	3,859.20
*Simon Young	76	71	147	
Andrew Oldcorn	79	69	148	3,521.30
Ian Stanley	76	72	148	3,521.30
Miguel Angel Jimenez	73	75	148	3,521.30
Ricardo Gonzalez	76	72	148	3,521.30
Jose Coceres	70	78	148	3,521.30
Greg Owen	76	72	148	3,521.30
*John Kemp	74	74	148	
Hal Sutton	74	75	149	3,521.30
Phillip Price	75	74	149	3,521.30
Adam Mednick	75	74	149	3,521.30
Benn Barham	76	73	149	3,521.30
Mattias Eliasson	78	72	150	3,521.30
Darren Fichardt	80	70	150	3,521.30
Dean Wilson	71	79	150	3,521.30
John Cook	74	76	150	3,521.30
Raymond Russell	71	79	150	3,521.30
Frank Lickliter	74	76	150	3,521.30
Paul Casey	72	78	150	3,521.30
Toru Suzuki	79	72	151	3,130.04
Gary Emerson	75	76	151	3,130.04
Dudley Hart	74	77	151	3,130.04
Peter Baker	75	76	151	3,130.04
Fredrik Jacobson	78	73	151	3,130.04
Patrik Sjoland	75	76	151	3,130.04
John Daly	74	77	151	3,130.04

	SCORES				TOTAL	MONEY
Kevin Sutherland	73	78			151	3,130.04
Malcolm Mackenzie	76	76			152	3,130.04
Billy Andrade	77	75			152	3,130.04
*Alejandro Larrazabal	77	75			152	
Angel Cabrera	73	79			152	3,130.04
John Riegger	78	74			152	3,130.04
Tom Watson	77	78			155	3,130.04
Jamie Spence	77	78			155	3,130.04
James Kingston	76	81			157	3,130.04
Paul Mayoh	84	73			157	3,130.04
Kiyoshi Miyazato	77	82			159	3,130.04
Roger Chapman	74				DQ	3,130.04
Jonathan Kaye	74				DQ	3,130.04
Thongchai Jaidee	80				WD	3,130.04

TNT Open

Hilversumsche Golf Club, Hilversum, Netherlands
Par 35-35–70; 6,617 yards

July 25-28
purse, €1,800,000

	SCORES				TOTAL	MONEY
Tobias Dier	60	67	67	69	263	€300,000
Jamie Spence	66	64	69	65	264	200,000
Padraig Harrington	66	67	64	68	265	101,340
Peter Lonard	67	63	68	67	265	101,340
Jarrod Moseley	66	67	67	67	267	76,320
Justin Rose	67	67	67	67	268	50,580
Ian Poulter	67	69	66	66	268	50,580
Pierre Fulke	68	65	65	70	268	50,580
Alastair Forsyth	68	69	68	63	268	50,580
Kenneth Ferrie	68	67	65	69	269	33,360
Gary Evans	69	64	69	67	269	33,360
Raymond Russell	65	70	64	70	269	33,360
Nick Faldo	68	68	67	67	270	27,660
Andrew Oldcorn	68	69	68	65	270	27,660
Steen Tinning	70	66	67	67	270	27,660
Mark Roe	67	64	66	74	271	22,577.14
Klas Eriksson	69	68	67	67	271	22,577.14
Greg Turner	70	69	68	64	271	22,577.14
Trevor Immelman	70	67	64	70	271	22,577.14
Russell Claydon	68	71	68	64	271	22,577.14
Roger Wessels	68	72	64	67	271	22,577.14
Matthew Cort	69	69	64	69	271	22,577.14
Jean-Francois Remesy	68	71	66	67	272	18,720
Nick O'Hern	71	66	69	66	272	18,720
Peter O'Malley	71	65	71	65	272	18,720
Robert Coles	68	70	66	68	272	18,720
David Lynn	68	67	68	69	272	18,720
David Gilford	65	69	70	69	273	16,560
Peter Hedblom	68	66	73	66	273	16,560
Ignacio Garrido	69	70	66	68	273	16,560
Maarten Lafeber	66	70	70	68	274	14,436
Matt Kuchar	69	66	69	70	274	14,436
Retief Goosen	69	68	67	70	274	14,436
Scott Gardiner	69	70	65	70	274	14,436
Jamie Donaldson	70	67	68	69	274	14,436
Santiago Luna	71	69	71	64	275	12,240

	SCORES				TOTAL	MONEY
Warren Bennett	68	69	68	70	275	12,240
Stuart Little	72	68	68	67	275	12,240
Richard Johnson	70	69	69	67	275	12,240
Ian Garbutt	68	69	67	71	275	12,240
Fredrik Andersson	68	72	67	68	275	12,240
Gordon Brand, Jr.	69	70	75	62	276	10,080
Raphael Jacquelin	73	66	68	69	276	10,080
Anders Hansen	69	68	71	68	276	10,080
Marcel Siem	71	67	66	72	276	10,080
Markus Brier	69	70	69	68	276	10,080
Yeh Wei-tze	69	71	66	70	276	10,080
Stephen Leaney	68	71	68	70	277	8,280
Philip Golding	69	71	68	69	277	8,280
Jonathan Lomas	70	67	71	69	277	8,280
Andrew Coltart	69	69	67	72	277	8,280
*Jamie Elson	69	69	67	72	277	
Bernhard Langer	71	69	69	69	278	6,480
Marc Farry	67	72	69	70	278	6,480
James Kingston	68	71	69	70	278	6,480
Andrew Butterfield	68	71	70	69	278	6,480
John Daly	70	67	70	71	278	6,480
Christopher Hanell	66	73	71	68	278	6,480
Ronan Rafferty	65	72	74	68	279	5,040
David Howell	66	73	69	71	279	5,040
Chris Gane	68	71	71	69	279	5,040
Jerry Pate	68	69	74	68	279	5,040
Gary Orr	71	65	66	77	279	5,040
Gary Emerson	76	64	68	72	280	4,230
Paul Eales	69	70	70	71	280	4,230
John Bickerton	67	69	70	74	280	4,230
Guido Van Der Valk	68	72	68	72	280	4,230
Darren Fichardt	69	71	67	74	281	3,600
Carl Suneson	72	68	74	67	281	3,600
Rory Sabbatini	69	70	68	74	281	3,600
Lee Westwood	70	66	72	75	283	2,990
Lucas Parsons	69	69	72	73	283	2,990
Mattias Eliasson	70	70	70	74	284	2,695.50
Carlos Rodiles	67	69	74	74	284	2,695.50
Mark Mouland	68	72	75	70	285	2,691
Joakim Rask	69	71	72	75	287	2,688

Volvo Scandinavian Masters

Kungsangen Golf Course, Stockholm, Sweden
Par 36-35–71; 6,761 yards

August 1-4
purse, €1,900,000

	SCORES				TOTAL	MONEY
Graeme McDowell	64	73	66	67	270	€316,660
Trevor Immelman	70	67	67	67	271	211,110
Jeff Sluman	69	69	65	69	272	106,970
Henrik Bjornstad	70	69	66	67	272	106,970
Carl Pettersson	68	69	68	68	273	80,569
Gary Evans	71	69	68	66	274	53,390
Niclas Fasth	67	71	65	71	274	53,390
Matthew Cort	66	73	68	67	274	53,390
Adam Scott	65	74	68	67	274	53,390
Peter Lonard	72	69	66	68	275	36,480

	SCORES				TOTAL	MONEY
David Drysdale	74	68	65	68	275	36,480
Warren Bennett	66	70	69	71	276	31,635
Alastair Forsyth	74	70	66	66	276	31,635
Fredrik Andersson	71	66	68	72	277	27,930
David Carter	71	71	67	68	277	27,930
Mikael Lundberg	72	71	68	66	277	27,930
Jesper Parnevik	67	73	68	70	278	22,657.50
Richard Green	74	71	66	67	278	22,657.50
Peter Hedblom	71	69	67	71	278	22,657.50
Joakim Haeggman	71	70	66	71	278	22,657.50
Adam Mednick	72	68	68	70	278	22,657.50
David Lynn	67	74	68	69	278	22,657.50
Christopher Hanell	70	68	71	69	278	22,657.50
Jamie Donaldson	72	68	67	71	278	22,657.50
Mark Foster	70	68	69	72	279	18,905
Colin Montgomerie	70	69	74	66	279	18,905
Marcel Siem	67	72	68	72	279	18,905
Ignacio Garrido	67	70	73	69	279	18,905
Barry Lane	70	68	69	73	280	17,480
Maarten Lafeber	70	71	67	73	281	15,057.50
Thomas Levet	69	73	72	67	281	15,057.50
Soren Hansen	71	71	73	66	281	15,057.50
Charlie Wi	68	75	69	69	281	15,057.50
Thomas Bjorn	69	72	71	69	281	15,057.50
Simon Khan	69	71	73	68	281	15,057.50
Iain Pyman	74	70	72	65	281	15,057.50
Brett Rumford	71	71	71	68	281	15,057.50
Santiago Luna	68	70	71	73	282	12,350
Olle Nordberg	74	70	65	73	282	12,350
Per-Ulrik Johansson	70	74	63	75	282	12,350
Robert Karlsson	71	74	68	69	282	12,350
Robert Coles	70	71	68	73	282	12,350
Mattias Eliasson	75	70	68	70	283	10,260
Anthony Wall	69	72	71	71	283	10,260
Grant Hamerton	66	73	74	70	283	10,260
Markus Brier	70	71	73	69	283	10,260
Michael Campbell	67	74	70	72	283	10,260
Mads Vibe-Hastrup	71	74	68	70	283	10,260
Ian Poulter	68	76	72	68	284	8,550
David Park	68	74	70	72	284	8,550
Fredrik Widmark	75	70	68	71	284	8,550
Paul Broadhurst	72	71	71	71	285	7,220
Rolf Muntz	73	70	70	72	285	7,220
Mark Pilkington	73	72	71	69	285	7,220
John Bickerton	71	69	69	76	285	7,220
Ronan Rafferty	67	71	75	73	286	5,537.14
Fredrik Orest	69	73	71	73	286	5,537.14
Marc Farry	72	73	70	71	286	5,537.14
Jarrod Moseley	73	70	71	72	286	5,537.14
Emanuele Canonica	70	73	67	76	286	5,537.14
Fredrik Jacobson	71	73	73	69	286	5,537.14
Raymond Russell	72	69	73	72	286	5,537.14
Raimo Sjoberg	72	71	73	71	287	4,655
Graeme Storm	72	70	69	76	287	4,655
Jonathan Lomas	68	76	73	71	288	4,370
Gary Emerson	70	72	76	71	289	4,085
Nick Dougherty	71	68	75	75	289	4,085
Stuart Little	71	73	74	72	290	3,626.67
Paul Eales	71	73	69	77	290	3,626.67
Benoit Teilleria	70	70	78	72	290	3,626.67

	SCORES			TOTAL	MONEY
Andrew Oldcorn	71	73 74 73		291	2,848.50
Pierre Fulke	73	72 75 71		291	2,848.50
Mark Mouland	71	73 74 74		292	2,842.50
Jamie Spence	73	72 67 80		292	2,842.50
Joakim Rask	73	72 75 74		294	3,838
Sebastien Delagrange	72	71 78 75		296	2,835
Andrew Butterfield	70	74 79 75		298	2,832
Arjun Atwal	69	73 78 80		300	2,829
Robert-Jan Derksen	71	73 83 77		304	2,826

Celtic Manor Resort Wales Open

Celtic Manor Resort, Newport, Wales
Par 36-36–72; 7,355 yards

August 8-11
purse,€1,753,869

	SCORES			TOTAL	MONEY
Paul Lawrie	67	65 70 70		272	€291,432.40
John Bickerton	67	67 73 70		277	194,288.30
Mikko Ilonen	70	68 70 70		278	109,464
Lucas Parsons	71	69 67 72		279	80,786.52
Martin Maritz	71	69 67 72		279	80,786.52
Trevor Immelman	68	70 71 71		280	52,458.78
Ian Poulter	71	71 69 69		280	52,458.78
Paul McGinley	69	71 69 71		280	52,458.78
Jean-Francois Remesy	73	68 70 70		281	32,909.14
Richard Green	65	69 73 74		281	32,909.14
Jarrod Moseley	71	70 69 71		281	32,909.14
Robert Karlsson	70	67 73 71		281	32,909.14
Bradley Dredge	66	74 70 71		281	32,909.14
Peter Fowler	72	70 69 71		282	26,229.39
Jamie Donaldson	70	73 66 73		282	26,229.39
Maarten Lafeber	71	72 71 69		283	21,595.53
Elliot Boult	68	75 69 71		283	21,595.53
Shaun Webster	72	71 71 69		283	21,595.53
Jeremy Robinson	69	68 73 73		283	21,595.53
Adam Mednick	70	72 69 72		283	21,595.53
Fredrik Andersson	74	68 70 71		283	21,595.53
Henrik Nystrom	70	75 71 67		283	21,595.53
Graeme McDowell	73	69 71 70		283	21,595.53
Barry Lane	69	72 72 71		284	16,874.24
David Gilford	72	73 69 70		284	16,874.24
Sven Struver	69	74 71 70		284	16,874.24
Joakim Haeggman	74	69 69 72		284	16,874.24
Ian Garbutt	71	71 70 72		284	16,874.24
Roger Wessels	67	70 72 75		284	16,874.24
Fredrik Jacobson	71	71 70 72		284	16,874.24
Christopher Hanell	71	73 70 70		284	16,874.24
Ronan Rafferty	70	75 71 69		285	12,642.57
Des Smyth	68	74 73 70		285	12,642.57
Greg Turner	71	72 70 72		285	12,642.57
Steve Webster	70	73 69 73		285	12,642.57
Anthony Wall	69	73 71 72		285	12,642.57
Didier de Vooght	67	74 72 72		285	12,642.57
Darren Clarke	68	74 72 71		285	12,642.57
David Lynn	71	73 70 71		285	12,642.57
David Drysdale	68	72 69 76		285	12,642.57
Ashley Roestoff	72	71 69 73		285	12,642.57

		SCORES			TOTAL	MONEY
Henrik Stenson	73	68	71	74	286	10,316.89
Charlie Wi	71	70	70	75	286	10,316.89
Lee Westwood	72	70	71	73	286	10,316.89
Mark Roe	70	71	72	74	287	8,743.13
Sam Torrance	66	73	76	72	287	8,743.13
Gary Emerson	71	72	74	70	287	8,743.13
Stuart Little	72	71	70	74	287	8,743.13
Stephen Dodd	72	70	70	75	287	8,743.13
Nick Dougherty	69	72	68	78	287	8,743.13
Emanuele Canonica	71	74	68	75	288	6,819.64
Rolf Muntz	67	71	72	78	288	6,819.64
Sion Bebb	70	73	72	73	288	6,819.64
James Kingston	65	75	74	74	288	6,819.64
Mark Wiggett	71	71	72	74	288	6,819.64
Malcolm Mackenzie	71	74	73	71	289	5,377.02
Magnus Persson Atlevi	70	74	70	75	289	5,377.02
Ian Woosnam	70	74	72	73	289	5,377.02
Richard Bland	74	70	72	73	289	5,377.02
Miguel Angel Martin	71	73	73	73	290	4,721.29
Paul Eales	73	71	71	75	290	4,721.29
Nicolas Vanhootegem	69	72	72	77	290	4,721.29
Robert-Jan Derksen	71	72	75	73	291	4,284.13
Stephen Scahill	68	72	74	77	291	4,284.13
Phillip Price	73	72	75	73	293	3,846.98
Barry Hume	69	74	75	75	293	3,846.98
Marc Warren	73	72	73	75	293	3,846.98
Costantino Rocca	73	70	73	78	294	3,159.47
Philip Golding	73	70	74	77	294	3,159.47
Mark Pilkington	74	68	79	73	294	3,159.47
Alastair Forsyth	70	75	72	77	294	3,159.47
Iain Ferrie	72	73	74	76	295	2,620

North West of Ireland Open

Ballyliffin Golf Club, Co Donegal, Ireland
Par 35-37–72; 7,222 yards

August 15-18
purse, €350,000

		SCORES			TOTAL	MONEY
Adam Mednick	76	68	69	68	281	€58,330
Costantino Rocca	71	69	74	72	286	30,395
Andrew Coltart	76	66	77	67	286	30,395
Anders Forsbrand	71	73	75	68	287	16,170
Jean-Francois Lucquin	75	67	74	71	287	16,170
Philip Walton	75	70	71	72	288	10,500
Massimo Florioli	71	70	71	76	288	10,500
Adam Crawford	77	68	75	68	288	10,500
Joakim Rask	75	72	75	68	290	7,840
Michele Reale	78	68	73	73	292	7,000
Titch Moore	73	74	75	71	293	5,588.33
Paul Broadhurst	76	72	74	71	293	5,588.33
Jesus Maria Arruti	71	72	78	72	293	5,588.33
David Park	75	72	77	69	293	5,588.33
Mark Sanders	72	72	79	70	293	5,588.33
Allan Hogh	71	72	79	71	293	5,588.33
Andrew Oldcorn	77	69	75	73	294	4,620
Per Nyman	76	69	80	69	294	4,620
Nicolas Colsaerts	75	71	78	72	296	4,081

		SCORES			TOTAL	MONEY
Pehr Magnebrant	72	73	78	73	296	4,081
Didier de Vooght	78	69	80	69	296	4,081
Iain Pyman	76	70	78	72	296	4,081
Ciaran McMonagle	74	72	80	70	296	4,081
Euan Little	74	73	77	73	297	3,692.50
Alexander Renard	77	71	80	69	297	3,692.50
Hennie Walters	77	74	78	69	298	3,377.50
Michael Archer	78	71	82	67	298	3,377.50
James Kingston	77	70	76	75	298	3,377.50
Regis Gustave	79	71	76	72	298	3,377.50
Damien McGrane	72	73	80	74	299	2,815
Mattias Nilsson	80	70	79	70	299	2,815
Ian Hutchings	78	72	76	73	299	2,815
Sion Bebb	78	72	81	68	299	2,815
Van Phillips	83	68	78	70	299	2,815
Marco Bernardini	76	71	78	74	299	2,815
Oskar Bergman	80	70	78	71	299	2,815
Kristofer Svensson	76	73	81	70	300	2,450
Simon Khan	74	72	83	71	300	2,450
Andrew Sherborne	78	72	80	71	301	2,170
Knud Storgaard	76	73	80	72	301	2,170
Denny Lucas	76	71	82	72	301	2,170
Gianluca Baruffaldi	81	69	78	73	301	2,170
Andrew Butterfield	81	69	80	71	301	2,170
Graham Fox	81	69	77	74	301	2,170
Tomas Jesus Munoz	76	73	83	70	302	1,715
Alan McLean	78	72	76	76	302	1,715
Francis Howley	75	73	78	76	302	1,715
James Hepworth	76	74	81	71	302	1,715
Kariem Baraka	78	71	85	68	302	1,715
Tino Schuster	79	69	81	73	302	1,715
John Dwyer	75	75	82	70	302	1,715
Michael Hoey	77	71	83	72	303	1,295
Carl Suneson	76	72	79	76	303	1,295
David Geall	81	69	80	73	303	1,295
Simon Hurd	79	71	79	74	303	1,295
Benn Barham	74	76	80	73	303	1,295
Fredrik Henge	75	75	83	71	304	1,032.50
Sam Little	76	74	80	74	304	1,032.50
Olivier Edmond	77	69	77	81	304	1,032.50
Richard Dinsdale	77	71	82	74	304	1,032.50
Marc Pendaries	79	72	81	73	305	875
Bradford Vaughan	77	74	80	74	305	875
Grant Hamerton	75	75	82	73	305	875
Andreas Ljunggren	79	72	83	71	305	875
Richard Sterne	77	73	80	75	305	875
Michael Welch	74	73	84	75	306	717.50
Luis Claverie	76	74	81	75	306	717.50
Thomas Norret	79	72	82	73	306	717.50
David Dixon	78	73	84	71	306	717.50
Jamie Little	77	74	87	69	307	540.83
Federico Bisazza	76	75	82	74	307	540.83
Marcus Knight	77	70	80	80	307	540.83
Ivo Giner	78	73	85	71	307	540.83
Fredrik Widmark	75	76	83	73	307	540.83
David Patrick	75	76	83	73	307	540.83
Gustavo Rojas	79	72	85	72	308	510
Stefano Reale	81	70	82	76	309	505.50
Raimo Sjoberg	79	72	87	71	309	505.50
Gary Murphy	78	73	85	74	310	495

	SCORES			TOTAL	MONEY
Kalle Brink	78	71	91	70	310	495
Andre Bossert	76	72	86	76	310	495
Guido Van Der Valk	78	73	83	76	310	495
Scott Gardiner	76	74	86	74	310	495
Francesco Guermani	80	70	85	76	311	486
Niels Kraaij	72	79	86	75	312	481.50
Joakim Gronhagen	78	73	82	79	312	481.50
Thomas Besancenez	77	74	87	76	314	477

Diageo Scottish PGA Championship

Gleneagles Hotel, Perthshire, Scotland   August 22-25
Par 36-36–72; 7,060 yards   purse, €1,590,759

	SCORES				TOTAL	MONEY
Adam Scott	67	65	67	63	262	€260,461.30
Raymond Russell	67	71	66	68	272	173,646
Sam Torrance	69	68	69	67	273	97,833.16
Scott Gardiner	67	72	65	72	276	78,141.50
Marcel Siem	70	66	73	68	277	66,263.99
Ignacio Garrido	67	71	73	67	278	54,699.05
Andrew Oldcorn	67	71	72	69	279	38,054.91
Henrik Bjornstad	68	72	70	69	279	38,054.91
Ian Garbutt	67	74	71	67	279	38,054.91
Matthew Cort	67	71	70	71	279	38,054.91
Raphael Jacquelin	67	75	69	69	280	25,536.64
Richard Green	65	71	72	72	280	25,536.64
Mathias Gronberg	70	70	72	68	280	25,536.64
Paul Casey	72	74	68	66	280	25,536.64
Marc Warren	71	70	72	67	280	25,536.64
David Gilford	69	74	69	69	281	20,668.43
David Lynn	69	73	70	69	281	20,668.43
Greg Owen	74	72	66	69	281	20,668.43
Fredrik Andersson	66	72	70	73	281	20,668.43
Santiago Luna	69	74	69	70	282	17,213.46
Peter Fowler	70	71	69	72	282	17,213.46
Nick O'Hern	71	76	67	68	282	17,213.46
Alex Cejka	69	74	69	70	282	17,213.46
Stephen Dodd	67	73	69	73	282	17,213.46
Rolf Muntz	70	75	64	73	282	17,213.46
Fredrik Jacobson	76	69	71	66	282	17,213.46
David Howell	68	74	71	70	283	14,378.04
Richard Bland	71	73	71	68	283	14,378.04
Jeremy Robinson	68	70	71	74	283	14,378.04
Olivier Edmond	73	70	71	69	283	14,378.04
Brett Rumford	69	73	70	71	283	14,378.04
Stephen Leaney	71	71	70	72	284	12,307.29
Jean Hugo	72	74	67	71	284	12,307.29
David Park	68	69	74	73	284	12,307.29
Patrik Sjoland	67	78	71	68	284	12,307.29
Mark Roe	69	68	74	74	285	11,096.09
Maarten Lafeber	68	76	68	73	285	11,096.09
Michele Reale	75	72	69	69	285	11,096.09
Jamie Spence	67	77	69	73	286	10,002.11
Adam Mednick	72	73	66	75	286	10,002.11
Gary Orr	69	73	74	70	286	10,002.11
Martin Maritz	75	72	72	67	286	10,002.11

	SCORES				TOTAL	MONEY
Mark James	70	73	75	69	287	8,283
Des Smyth	71	72	71	73	287	8,283
Philip Walton	68	70	76	73	287	8,283
Klas Eriksson	71	71	73	72	287	8,283
Warren Bennett	73	70	73	71	287	8,283
Colin Gillies	71	71	71	74	287	8,283
Miles Tunnicliff	72	73	69	73	287	8,283
Greg Turner	72	73	70	73	288	6,251.32
Shaun Webster	73	72	73	70	288	6,251.32
Stuart Little	70	74	71	73	288	6,251.32
Alastair Forsyth	68	78	73	69	288	6,251.32
Simon Dyson	74	73	69	72	288	6,251.32
Craig Lee	68	75	71	74	288	6,251.32
Roger Chapman	73	71	71	74	289	4,805.70
Robert-Jan Derksen	74	73	70	72	289	4,805.70
Van Phillips	72	69	77	71	289	4,805.70
Barry Hume	73	68	72	76	289	4,805.70
Jean-Francois Remesy	71	74	74	71	290	4,063.36
Massimo Scarpa	70	77	72	71	290	4,063.36
Didier de Vooght	73	74	71	72	290	4,063.36
Stephen Scahill	68	78	72	72	290	4,063.36
John Bickerton	68	79	73	70	290	4,063.36
Peter Senior	69	75	73	74	291	3,438.23
Anthony Wall	72	71	75	73	291	3,438.23
Stephen Gallacher	71	75	71	74	291	3,438.23
Mattias Eliasson	73	74	76	69	292	2,663
Gregory Havret	71	75	72	74	292	2,663
Scott Henderson	73	73	73	73	292	2,663
David Drysdale	76	70	74	72	292	2,663
Andrew Coltart	70	77	73	72	292	2,663
Lucas Parsons	74	73	72	73	292	2,663
Jonathan Lomas	72	75	74	72	293	2,333.50
Benoit Teilleria	69	74	73	77	293	2,333.50
Robert Coles	69	76	70	79	294	2,329
Dennis Edlund	73	73	74	75	295	2,326
Gary Emerson	70	77	76	73	296	2,321.50
Gary Evans	73	73	73	77	296	2,321.50
Iain Pyman	74	73	75	77	299	2,317
Nick Dougherty	72	74	78	77	301	2,314
Simon Khan	71	76	80	78	305	2,311

BMW International Open

Golfclub Munchen Nord-Eichenreid,
Munich, Germany
Par 36-36–72; 6,963 yards

August 29-September 1
purse, €1,800,000

	SCORES				TOTAL	MONEY
Thomas Bjorn	68	64	66	66	264	€300,000
Bernhard Langer	64	69	67	68	268	156,340
John Bickerton	67	69	66	66	268	156,340
Ian Poulter	65	66	70	70	271	83,160
David Park	68	67	69	67	271	83,160
Richard Bland	65	66	69	72	272	63,000
Philip Golding	69	65	69	70	273	46,440
David Lynn	67	67	68	71	273	46,440
Paul Casey	72	63	71	67	273	46,440

		SCORES			TOTAL	MONEY
Trevor Immelman	66	72	65	71	274	33,360
Miguel Angel Jimenez	68	68	69	69	274	33,360
John Daly	70	70	65	69	274	33,360
Anthony Wall	70	69	65	71	275	27,090
Jamie Spence	67	64	70	74	275	27,090
Joakim Haeggman	69	67	67	72	275	27,090
Robert Coles	65	73	71	66	275	27,090
Peter Senior	70	68	67	71	276	23,280
Padraig Harrington	70	70	68	68	276	23,280
Barry Lane	68	69	71	68	276	23,280
Marten Olander	69	67	71	70	277	20,655
Steen Tinning	68	67	73	69	277	20,655
Mathias Gronberg	70	67	68	72	277	20,655
Mikael Lundberg	70	69	68	70	277	20,655
Mark Roe	71	69	69	69	278	16,830
David Howell	70	65	68	75	278	16,830
Darren Fichardt	67	71	72	68	278	16,830
Justin Rose	70	67	71	70	278	16,830
Paul McGinley	70	68	66	74	278	16,830
Rolf Muntz	70	65	70	73	278	16,830
Simon Khan	68	71	66	73	278	16,830
Simon Dyson	70	67	71	70	278	16,830
Nick Dougherty	70	67	70	71	278	16,830
Carl Pettersson	71	69	65	73	278	16,830
Richard Green	71	69	66	73	279	13,320
Marcel Siem	72	67	71	69	279	13,320
Ian Garbutt	71	68	69	71	279	13,320
Alastair Forsyth	68	67	75	69	279	13,320
Santiago Luna	71	69	65	75	280	11,160
Warren Bennett	72	66	69	73	280	11,160
Thomas Levet	69	71	66	74	280	11,160
Jean Hugo	71	68	69	72	280	11,160
Emanuele Canonica	67	67	76	70	280	11,160
Gary Evans	68	72	72	68	280	11,160
Bradley Dredge	70	68	71	71	280	11,160
Gary Clark	70	67	72	71	280	11,160
Andrew Marshall	69	69	69	74	281	9,360
Fredrik Jacobson	69	65	73	74	281	9,360
Henrik Bjornstad	69	66	76	71	282	7,920
Gary Orr	70	68	73	71	282	7,920
Markus Brier	69	70	74	69	282	7,920
Andrew Coltart	70	68	68	76	282	7,920
Mikko Ilonen	70	69	67	76	282	7,920
Thongchai Jaidee	69	70	70	73	282	7,920
Jeev Milkha Singh	71	69	71	72	283	6,300
Klas Eriksson	67	72	70	74	283	6,300
Robert Karlsson	70	69	71	73	283	6,300
*Christian Reimbold	72	68	70	73	283	
David Gilford	70	70	74	70	284	5,220
Russell Claydon	67	72	73	72	284	5,220
Jorge Berendt	69	70	70	75	284	5,220
Adam Mednick	72	65	72	75	284	5,220
Scott Gardiner	71	68	69	76	284	5,220
Sven Struver	68	72	71	75	286	4,410
Gary Emerson	69	71	74	72	286	4,410
Greg Owen	69	69	73	75	286	4,410
Tino Schuster	73	67	73	73	286	4,410
Robert-Jan Derksen	73	67	73	74	287	3,780
David Geall	70	68	73	76	287	3,780

	SCORES				TOTAL	MONEY
Daren Lee	68	68	78	73	287	3,780
Gordon Brand, Jr.	68	72	78	72	290	3,420
Alex Cejka	68	72			WD	3,280

Omega European Masters

Crans-sur-Sierre Golf Club, Crans-sur-Sierre, Switzerland
Par 36-35–71; 6,857 yards

September 5-8
purse, €1,500,000

	SCORES				TOTAL	MONEY
Robert Karlsson	65	66	68	71	270	€250,000
Trevor Immelman	70	67	65	72	274	130,280
Paul Lawrie	66	70	66	72	274	130,280
Bradley Dredge	73	66	69	67	275	69,300
Simon Dyson	69	70	68	68	275	69,300
Emanuele Canonica	68	68	65	75	276	42,150
Alex Cejka	67	69	68	72	276	42,150
Jarrod Moseley	72	68	69	67	276	42,150
Stephen Leaney	68	70	68	70	276	42,150
Jeev Milkha Singh	71	70	66	70	277	27,800
Paul Casey	68	69	76	64	277	27,800
Michael Campbell	71	69	67	70	277	27,800
Fredrik Andersson	68	70	70	70	278	23,550
Barry Lane	70	68	64	76	278	23,550
Marc Farry	70	71	71	67	279	21,150
David Park	67	72	66	74	279	21,150
Sam Walker	73	65	67	74	279	21,150
Carl Pettersson	67	70	70	73	280	18,060
Jamie Donaldson	69	71	69	71	280	18,060
Mark Roe	73	66	70	71	280	18,060
Nick Faldo	66	72	69	73	280	18,060
Carlos Rodiles	70	66	73	71	280	18,060
Thomas Levet	69	71	71	70	281	15,600
Jean Hugo	70	71	68	72	281	15,600
David Howell	71	70	71	69	281	15,600
Thomas Bjorn	69	74	68	70	281	15,600
Ernie Els	70	71	66	74	281	15,600
Phillip Price	69	68	73	72	282	12,693.75
Fredrik Jacobson	72	68	69	73	282	12,693.75
Sebastien Delagrange	72	70	70	70	282	12,693.75
Mikko Ilonen	74	68	69	71	282	12,693.75
Klas Eriksson	68	67	73	74	282	12,693.75
Andrew Marshall	72	68	69	73	282	12,693.75
Ian Garbutt	70	71	69	72	282	12,693.75
Miles Tunnicliff	73	68	71	70	282	12,693.75
Dennis Edlund	72	71	71	69	283	10,050
Soren Hansen	72	69	69	74	283	10,050
Henrik Bjornstad	69	69	72	73	283	10,050
Mikael Lundberg	71	70	71	71	283	10,050
Brett Rumford	67	73	76	67	283	10,050
Matthew Cort	72	65	69	77	283	10,050
Andrew Coltart	70	65	70	78	283	10,050
Patrik Sjoland	69	71	71	73	284	7,650
Francis Valera	72	71	73	68	284	7,650
Mathias Gronberg	66	76	70	72	284	7,650
Robert Coles	72	68	73	71	284	7,650
Scott Gardiner	70	73	71	70	284	7,650

		SCORES			TOTAL	MONEY
Retief Goosen	70	73	69	72	284	7,650
Henrik Nystrom	71	67	74	72	284	7,650
Stephen Gallacher	71	72	70	71	284	7,650
Brian Davis	68	72	73	71	284	7,650
Raphael Jacquelin	70	72	65	78	285	5,156.25
Mark Foster	68	71	74	72	285	5,156.25
Chris Gane	72	70	73	70	285	5,156.25
Olle Karlsson	69	69	74	73	285	5,156.25
David Drysdale	70	73	70	72	285	5,156.25
Ignacio Garrido	72	70	69	74	285	5,156.25
Gary Orr	68	71	72	74	285	5,156.25
Stephen Scahill	73	70	70	72	285	5,156.25
Marcel Siem	71	67	69	79	286	4,125
Marten Olander	72	70	72	72	286	4,125
Santiago Luna	70	73	68	76	287	3,900
Miguel Angel Jimenez	67	73	71	77	288	3,750
Markus Brier	72	71	76	70	289	3,600
Ian Poulter	70	72	71	77	290	3,375
Peter Hanson	70	72	70	78	290	3,375
Craig Stadler	71	72	67	81	291	3,150
Stuart Little	70	71	78	73	292	3,000
Christopher Hanell	72	68	75	77	292	3,000
Jarmo Sandelin	77	66	78		WD	2,740

Linde German Masters

Gut Larchenhof, Cologne, Germany
Par 36-36–72; 7,289 yards

September 12-15
purse, €3,000,000

		SCORES			TOTAL	MONEY
Stephen Leaney	64	69	66	67	266	€500,000
Alex Cejka	68	68	63	68	267	333,330
Ian Woosnam	68	64	68	68	268	155,000
Nick Dougherty	68	65	69	66	268	155,000
Paul Casey	68	67	62	71	268	155,000
Gary Evans	67	68	65	69	269	105,000
Mathias Gronberg	67	69	66	68	270	82,500
Ricardo Gonzalez	68	69	66	67	270	82,500
Colin Montgomerie	71	66	68	67	272	67,200
Bernhard Langer	68	70	66	69	273	57,600
Warren Bennett	67	66	70	70	273	57,600
Padraig Harrington	69	66	71	68	274	49,950
Pierre Fulke	69	71	66	68	274	49,950
Maarten Lafeber	69	67	71	68	275	45,000
David Lynn	70	69	65	71	275	45,000
Eduardo Romero	70	68	64	74	276	37,628.57
Peter O'Malley	67	72	68	69	276	37,628.57
Emanuele Canonica	68	68	69	71	276	37,628.57
Thomas Bjorn	67	70	70	69	276	37,628.57
Mark Pilkington	65	69	70	72	276	37,628.57
Patrik Sjoland	71	68	66	71	276	37,628.57
Alastair Forsyth	69	71	73	63	276	37,628.57
Nick Faldo	71	70	69	67	277	29,850
Brian Davis	68	72	68	69	277	29,850
Anthony Wall	70	65	71	71	277	29,850
Miguel Angel Jimenez	72	69	67	69	277	29,850
Robert Karlsson	68	72	69	68	277	29,850

	SCORES			TOTAL	MONEY
Ernie Els	69	70	68	70	277	29,850
Bradley Dredge	69	69	71	68	277	29,850
Retief Goosen	65	70	69	73	277	29,850
David Howell	70	69	72	67	278	23,700
Steve Webster	70	68	68	72	278	23,700
Gary Emerson	71	70	66	71	278	23,700
Jarrod Moseley	70	71	70	67	278	23,700
Jonathan Lomas	67	72	71	68	278	23,700
Fredrik Jacobson	74	67	70	67	278	23,700
Barry Lane	72	70	67	70	279	18,900
Marc Farry	74	66	68	71	279	18,900
Darren Fichardt	67	69	73	70	279	18,900
Richard Bland	67	70	71	71	279	18,900
Jean Hugo	72	69	67	71	279	18,900
Angel Cabrera	71	65	74	69	279	18,900
Raymond Russell	71	70	71	67	279	18,900
David Carter	68	67	70	74	279	18,900
Jamie Donaldson	67	71	69	72	279	18,900
Soren Hansen	67	72	71	70	280	15,000
Trevor Immelman	68	72	71	69	280	15,000
Jamie Spence	71	71	68	70	280	15,000
Anders Hansen	69	71	72	68	280	15,000
Miguel Angel Martin	71	67	70	73	281	11,700
Henrik Bjornstad	70	69	69	73	281	11,700
Michele Reale	68	74	66	73	281	11,700
Ignacio Garrido	70	70	69	72	281	11,700
Niclas Fasth	70	71	75	65	281	11,700
Lee Westwood	70	67	73	71	281	11,700
Tobias Dier	73	69	69	70	281	11,700
Peter Fowler	68	73	72	69	282	8,850
Jeev Milkha Singh	72	70	68	72	282	8,850
Richard Green	71	67	72	72	282	8,850
Ian Poulter	72	68	71	71	282	8,850
Mark James	72	69	70	72	283	7,500
Costantino Rocca	70	72	71	70	283	7,500
Richard Johnson	71	71	68	73	283	7,500
Carl Suneson	70	70	72	71	283	7,500
Henrik Nystrom	70	70	72	71	283	7,500
Raphael Jacquelin	70	69	69	77	285	6,150
Stephen Dodd	71	70	68	76	285	6,150
Stephen Scahill	70	72	70	73	285	6,150
Graeme McDowell	73	68	70	74	285	6,150
Paul McGinley	70	70	71	75	286	4,985
Jorge Berendt	74	68	68	76	286	4,985
Christopher Hanell	75	67	76	70	288	4,497
Carl Pettersson	71	69	75	75	290	4,494
Anders Forsbrand	68	71	75	77	291	4,491

WGC American Express Championship

Mount Juliet, Kilkenny, Ireland
Par 36-36–72; 7,246 yards

September 19-22
purse, €5,645,078

	SCORES			TOTAL	MONEY
Tiger Woods	65	65	67	66	263	€1,026,378
Retief Goosen	67	67	68	62	264	554,244.10
Vijay Singh	67	69	66	65	267	377,193.90

		SCORES			TOTAL	MONEY
David Toms	66	67	69	66	268	241,198.80
Jerry Kelly	67	65	70	66	268	241,198.80
Scott McCarron	71	67	64	67	269	184,748
Sergio Garcia	69	69	70	62	270	159,088.60
Davis Love	69	67	68	67	271	133,429.10
Bob Estes	68	68	69	67	272	113,928
Michael Campbell	71	66	71	64	272	113,928
Justin Leonard	68	68	69	68	273	86,472.34
Stuart Appleby	69	66	70	68	273	86,472.34
Niclas Fasth	68	69	72	64	273	86,472.34
Chris DiMarco	67	69	70	67	273	86,472.34
Nick Price	68	71	69	66	274	66,714.56
Steve Lowery	66	67	69	72	274	66,714.56
Mike Weir	67	70	68	69	274	66,714.56
Scott Verplank	68	72	68	66	274	66,714.56
Gary Evans	67	68	73	66	274	66,714.56
Rocco Mediate	69	67	67	71	274	66,714.56
Padraig Harrington	69	70	67	69	275	59,529.92
Kenny Perry	68	71	68	69	276	57,477.16
Stephen Leaney	69	67	71	70	277	53,884.84
Ernie Els	68	67	72	70	277	53,884.84
Scott Hoch	71	68	67	71	277	53,884.84
Phil Mickelson	70	72	71	64	277	53,884.84
Jose Maria Olazabal	68	72	69	69	278	49,779.33
Trevor Immelman	71	71	67	69	278	49,779.33
Thomas Bjorn	72	68	66	72	278	49,779.33
Kevin Sutherland	69	68	70	71	278	49,779.33
Colin Montgomerie	72	70	69	68	279	46,700.20
Robert Allenby	72	70	67	70	279	46,700.20
Bernhard Langer	72	68	70	70	280	44,134.25
Jim Furyk	69	69	69	73	280	44,134.25
Mark Calcavecchia	72	70	71	67	280	44,134.25
Eduardo Romero	70	71	70	70	281	41,055.12
Jose Coceres	68	72	71	70	281	41,055.12
Angel Cabrera	71	66	73	71	281	41,055.12
Soren Hansen	75	68	65	74	282	38,232.57
Tom Lehman	73	72	67	70	282	38,232.57
Chris Riley	73	68	70	71	282	38,232.57
Adam Scott	70	70	69	73	282	38,232.57
Jeff Sluman	69	69	72	73	283	36,436.42
Paul Azinger	73	73	71	66	283	36,436.42
John Rollins	73	72	67	71	283	36,436.42
David Duval	71	65	72	76	284	34,896.85
Justin Rose	73	70	72	69	284	34,896.85
Len Mattiace	70	73	69	72	284	34,896.85
Brad Faxon	70	77	67	71	285	32,844.09
Fred Funk	69	70	72	74	285	32,844.09
John Cook	75	71	71	68	285	32,844.09
Craig Parry	68	71	74	72	285	32,844.09
Rich Beem	70	69	74	72	285	32,844.09
Paul Lawrie	71	70	74	71	286	30,791.34
Peter Lonard	71	69	72	74	286	30,791.34
Carl Pettersson	72	72	68	74	286	30,791.34
Anders Hansen	71	72	72	74	289	29,251.77
Peter O'Malley	75	73	71	70	289	29,251.77
Thongchai Jaidee	72	74	73	70	289	29,251.77
Scott Laycock	74	72	72	72	290	28,225.39
Craig Perks	74	74	75	68	291	27,712.20
Tim Clark	74	69	76	73	292	27,199.02
Darren Clarke	75	76	70	74	295	26,685.83

	SCORES				TOTAL	MONEY
Kenichi Kuboya	77	72	73	76	298	26,172.64
Shigeki Maruyama	75				WD	25,659.45

Dunhill Links Championship

St. Andrews Old Course: Par 36-36–72; 7,115 yards
Carnoustie Championship Course: Par 36-36–72; 7,361 yards
Kingsbarns Golf Links: Par 36-36–72; 7,126 yards
St. Andrews, Scotland

October 3-6
purse, €5,124,000

	SCORES				TOTAL	MONEY
Padraig Harrington	66	66	68	69	269	€818,662.20
Eduardo Romero	65	68	67	69	269	545,771.40
(Harrington defeated Romero on second playoff hole.)						
Sandy Lyle	69	67	67	68	271	253,785.30
Colin Montgomerie	70	69	69	63	271	253,785.30
Vijay Singh	70	67	64	70	271	253,785.30
Jyoti Randhawa	66	69	69	68	272	171,919.10
Brian Davis	70	69	69	65	273	135,079.30
Thomas Bjorn	67	68	73	65	273	135,079.30
Rolf Muntz	68	74	66	66	274	104,133.80
Adam Scott	68	70	68	68	274	104,133.80
Ignacio Garrido	70	66	67	72	275	87,433.23
Mikael Lundberg	67	67	73	68	275	87,433.23
Santiago Luna	67	69	70	70	276	77,117.98
David Gilford	72	69	67	68	276	77,117.98
Mark McNulty	68	72	70	67	277	67,785.23
Angel Cabrera	73	70	70	64	277	67,785.23
Fredrik Jacobson	70	73	67	67	277	67,785.23
Nic Lawrence	66	70	72	69	277	67,785.23
Peter Fowler	70	73	65	70	278	58,084.09
Jose Maria Olazabal	71	71	69	67	278	58,084.09
Trevor Immelman	73	67	67	71	278	58,084.09
Carlos Rodiles	70	70	67	71	278	58,084.09
Jean-Francois Remesy	68	75	68	68	279	52,558.11
Maarten Lafeber	71	69	72	67	279	52,558.11
Ricardo Gonzalez	74	69	68	68	279	52,558.11
Stephen Leaney	75	71	66	68	280	43,716.56
Justin Rose	70	71	70	69	280	43,716.56
Gary Emerson	75	69	68	68	280	43,716.56
Paul Eales	72	67	68	73	280	43,716.56
Jonathan Lomas	68	75	71	66	280	43,716.56
Phillip Price	69	68	73	70	280	43,716.56
Greg Owen	76	68	70	66	280	43,716.56
Andrew Coltart	73	67	70	70	280	43,716.56
Simon Dyson	71	68	69	72	280	43,716.56
Nick Faldo	75	68	66	72	281	34,875.01
Ian Poulter	74	73	67	67	281	34,875.01
Stephen Dodd	75	71	66	69	281	34,875.01
Darren Clarke	72	72	69	68	281	34,875.01
Retief Goosen	70	67	73	71	281	34,875.01
Gordon Brand, Jr.	71	67	72	72	282	27,015.85
Warren Bennett	78	70	66	68	282	27,015.85
Steve Elkington	73	70	70	69	282	27,015.85
Soren Kjeldsen	70	72	70	70	282	27,015.85
Joakim Haeggman	74	69	68	71	282	27,015.85
Paul Lawrie	74	68	71	69	282	27,015.85

	SCORES				TOTAL	MONEY
James Kingston	76	66	72	68	282	27,015.85
Niclas Fasth	71	71	70	70	282	27,015.85
Lee Westwood	76	68	70	68	282	27,015.85
Brett Rumford	75	69	68	70	282	27,015.85
Barry Hume	74	67	68	73	282	27,015.85
Richard Green	71	70	70	72	283	19,156.70
Paul Broadhurst	72	68	71	72	283	19,156.70
Alan McLean	76	65	73	69	283	19,156.70
Tobias Dier	75	71	68	69	283	19,156.70
Mikko Ilonen	74	69	71	69	283	19,156.70
Andrew Oldcorn	73	73	68	70	284	15,718.31
Mathias Gronberg	76	70	68	70	284	15,718.31
David Howell	79	67	67	72	285	13,262.33
Raphael Jacquelin	73	71	70	71	285	13,262.33
Scott Drummond	74	68	70	73	285	13,262.33
Paul McGinley	73	72	69	71	285	13,262.33
David Lynn	73	71	67	74	285	13,262.33
Gary Clark	71	73	66	75	285	13,262.33
John Bickerton	74	68	71	72	285	13,262.33
Richard Johnson	71	71	72	72	286	10,806.34
Amandeep Johl	70	72	72	72	286	10,806.34
Jamie Donaldson	70	74	70	72	286	10,806.34
Marc Farry	71	74	68	74	287	9,578.35
Richard Lee	72	73	67	75	287	9,578.35
Raymond Russell	70	72	71	75	288	8,954.12
Henrik Stenson	70	70	74	75	289	7,368

Trophee Lancome

Saint-Nom-La-Breteche, Paris, France
Par 36-35–71; 6,903 yards

October 10-13
purse, €1,450,736

	SCORES				TOTAL	MONEY
Alex Cejka	64	68	72	68	272	€239,640
Carlos Rodiles	67	69	72	66	274	159,760
Jean-Francois Lucquin	69	72	68	66	275	80,950.39
Angel Cabrera	69	68	71	67	275	80,950.39
Gordon Brand, Jr.	68	69	70	69	276	37,815.19
Sergio Garcia	67	70	70	69	276	37,815.19
Ian Poulter	68	71	70	67	276	37,815.19
Steen Tinning	70	70	67	69	276	37,815.19
Thomas Levet	67	69	73	67	276	37,815.19
Paul Eales	68	69	69	70	276	37,815.19
Robert Karlsson	68	69	69	70	276	37,815.19
Bradley Dredge	68	67	70	71	276	37,815.19
Ian Woosnam	70	70	65	72	277	19,950.03
Greg Turner	70	68	67	72	277	19,950.03
Maarten Lafeber	65	65	74	73	277	19,950.03
Jonathan Lomas	68	69	70	70	277	19,950.03
Ian Garbutt	68	69	68	72	277	19,950.03
Mark Pilkington	70	71	74	62	277	19,950.03
Simon Dyson	68	70	67	72	277	19,950.03
Paul Casey	68	71	67	71	277	19,950.03
Jean-Francois Remesy	70	69	69	70	278	16,463.27
Joakim Haeggman	69	67	73	69	278	16,463.27
Eduardo Romero	70	70	70	69	279	14,953.54
Anders Hansen	71	70	71	67	279	14,953.54

		SCORES			TOTAL	MONEY
Jean Hugo	70	70	70	69	279	14,953.54
Mathias Gronberg	66	73	68	72	279	14,953.54
Ricardo Gonzalez	70	65	77	67	279	14,953.54
Soren Kjeldsen	70	67	72	71	280	12,796.78
Trevor Immelman	74	66	69	71	280	12,796.78
Chris Gane	70	68	71	71	280	12,796.78
Fredrik Jacobson	65	77	71	67	280	12,796.78
Dean Robertson	65	72	72	71	280	12,796.78
Nick Faldo	65	74	68	74	281	10,812.56
Marc Farry	71	69	73	68	281	10,812.56
Colin Montgomerie	69	71	72	69	281	10,812.56
Gary Orr	69	69	74	69	281	10,812.56
Patrik Sjoland	71	70	68	72	281	10,812.56
Des Smyth	70	68	73	71	282	9,058.39
Steve Webster	66	70	70	76	282	9,058.39
Gary Emerson	71	70	72	69	282	9,058.39
Miles Tunnicliff	70	67	71	74	282	9,058.39
Paul McGinley	67	69	76	70	282	9,058.39
Andrew Coltart	74	66	72	70	282	9,058.39
Lucas Parsons	70	69	73	70	282	9,058.39
Mark Roe	68	72	73	70	283	7,620.55
Peter Hanson	69	70	71	73	283	7,620.55
David Carter	71	66	75	71	283	7,620.55
Sam Torrance	72	68	71	73	284	6,757.85
David Lynn	68	71	74	71	284	6,757.85
Markus Brier	68	73	73	70	284	6,757.85
Sandy Lyle	70	71	76	68	285	5,751.36
Warren Bennett	69	70	73	73	285	5,751.36
Brian Davis	69	74	70	72	285	5,751.36
Richard Johnson	65	73	71	76	285	5,751.36
Darren Fichardt	70	69	72	75	286	4,744.87
Daren Lee	67	73	75	71	286	4,744.87
Christopher Hanell	73	70	71	72	286	4,744.87
David Gilford	74	69	74	70	287	3,954.06
Tom Gillis	65	74	75	73	287	3,954.06
Paul Broadhurst	71	72	69	75	287	3,954.06
Gregory Havret	68	75	73	71	287	3,954.06
Gary Clark	71	69	74	73	287	3,954.06
John Bickerton	70	71	75	71	287	3,954.06
*Francois Illouz	71	68	72	77	288	
Andrew Marshall	68	74	75	71	288	3,378.92
Roger Wessels	70	72	73	73	288	3,378.92
Graeme McDowell	71	69	78	71	289	3,163.25
Justin Rose	70	73	73	74	290	2,947.57
Greg Owen	67	74	72	77	290	2,947.57
Richard Bland	70	70	75	76	291	2,502.99
Stephen Scahill	66	77	76	72	291	2,502.99
Raymond Russell	70	70	75	76	291	2,502.99
*Philippe Lima	70	73	70	78	291	
Nick O'Hern	76	67	75	75	293	2,154
Christian Cevaer	74	69	76	75	294	2,151
Philip Golding	72	71	76	76	295	2,148
Henrik Bjornstad	72	69	81	76	298	2,145

Cisco World Match Play

Wentworth Club, West Course, Surrey, England
Par 434 534 444–35; 345 434 455–37–72; 7,072 yards

October 17-20
purse, £1,000,000

FIRST ROUND

Michael Campbell defeated Nick Faldo, 43 holes

Campbell	6	3	4	4	3	4	4	3	3	34	3	4	4	3	3	5	C	4	4	X	X
Faldo	4	3	4	4	3	4	4	4	4	34	3	4	4	4	3	6	3	5	4	36	70

Campbell leads, 3 up

Campbell	4	4	4	4	2	4	4	4	6	36	3	4	4	5	3	3	4	5	6	37	73
Faldo	4	3	5	3	3	4	4	4	4	34	2	4	4	4	4	4	4	4	5	35	69

Match all-square

Campbell	4	3	4	4	4	3	4
Faldo	4	3	4	4	4	3	5

Padraig Harrington defeated Mike Weir, 4 and 3

Harrington	4	3	5	5	3	3	4	4	4	35	4	4	4	4	3	4	4	6	4	37	72
Weir	4	4	4	3	3	4	4	3	4	33	3	4	5	5	3	4	4	5	5	38	71

Match all-square

Harrington	4	3	5	4	3	4	4	3	3	33	3	3	4	4	2	4
Weir	4	4	4	4	3	4	4	4	3	34	3	4	4	5	2	5

Vijay Singh defeated Justin Rose, 1 up

Singh	4	3	4	4	2	4	4	4	4	33	3	4	4	4	3	4	3	5	4	34	67
Rose	4	3	4	4	3	4	4	4	4	34	4	4	4	4	3	4	4	5	4	36	70

Singh leads, 3 up

Singh	4	3	5	5	3	3	4	3	5	35	3	4	4	4	2	4	3	5	5	34	69
Rose	4	3	4	5	2	4	5	3	4	34	2	4	4	4	3	3	4	4	5	33	67

Colin Montgomerie defeated Fred Funk, 3 and 2

Montgomerie	4	4	4	4	2	4	4	4	4	34	2	5	3	4	2	4	4	5	4	33	67
Funk	4	2	4	4	3	4	4	4	5	34	3	3	4	4	3	4	4	4	4	33	67

Montgomerie leads, 2 up

Montgomerie	5	3	4	4	3	4	4	4	4	35	4	4	4	4	3	5	4
Funk	4	2	4	4	3	5	4	5	5	36	2	4	6	4	3	5	4

SECOND ROUND

Michael Campbell defeated Ian Woosnam, 3 and 2

Woosnam	4	2	4	4	3	4	4	4	5	34	2	4	4	5	4	5	3	4	4	35	69
Campbell	4	2	4	4	3	4	4	4	4	33	2	4	4	4	2	4	4	5	4	33	66

Campbell leads, 2 up

Woosnam	4	2	3	3	3	4	3	4	4	30	3	5	5	4	3	4	3
Campbell	4	3	4	4	2	4	3	4	4	32	3	4	3	4	2	4	3

Sergio Garcia defeated Padraig Harrington, 2 and 1

Garcia	4	3	5	5	3	4	3	3	4	34	3	4	5	4	3	4	4	4	3	34	68
Harrington	4	2	4	4	3	4	3	4	5	33	3	3	3	4	3	4	3	6	4	33	66

Harrington leads, 2 up

Garcia	4	2	4	4	3	3	3	4	3	30	3	4	4	4	3	4	4	4
Harrington	4	3	4	4	3	5	5	4	4	36	3	4	5	4	3	3	3	6

Vijay Singh defeated Retief Goosen, 4 and 3

Goosen	4 2 3	4 3 4	4 4 4	32	3 3 4	4 3 6	4 4 4	35	67
Singh	4 2 5	4 3 4	4 3 4	33	3 4 4	4 4 3	4 4 3	33	66

Match all-square

Goosen	4 3 4	4 2 4	3 4 5	33	2 5 4	4 3 X
Singh	4 2 3	4 2 3	4 4 5	31	2 4 4	4 2 X

Ernie Els defeated Colin Montgomerie, 6 and 5

Els	4 2 3	3 3 4	4 4 3	30	2 4 5	3 2 4	3 3 4	30	60
Montgomerie	5 3 3	5 2 3	4 3 4	32	2 5 4	3 3 5	3 4 4	33	65

Els leads, 4 up

Els	5 3 4	3 3 5	3 4 4	34	3 4 4	3
Montgomerie	4 3 5	5 3 4	3 4 5	36	3 4 4	C

SEMI-FINALS

Sergio Garcia defeated Michael Campbell, 2 and 1

Campbell	4 2 4	3 3 3	4 4 4	31	3 4 4	4 3 4	4 6 4	36	67
Garcia	5 3 4	3 3 4	3 4 4	33	3 3 5	4 2 4	4 4 4	33	66

Match all-square

Campbell	4 3 4	4 3 3	4 C 4	X	3 4 6	5 3 4	4 3
Garcia	5 2 4	4 3 4	4 3 4	33	3 4 4	4 3 5	3 3

Ernie Els defeated Vijay Singh, 3 and 2

Singh	5 4 5	4 3 3	4 4 4	36	2 4 5	4 3 4	6 5 4	37	73
Els	4 3 4	4 2 4	4 4 4	33	3 4 5	4 3 5	4 4 4	36	69

Els leads, 3 up

Singh	5 3 4	4 3 4	4 3 4	34	3 4 3	4 3 4	4
Els	4 3 4	4 2 4	4 4 4	33	3 5 6	3 3 4	4

FINAL

Ernie Els defeated Sergio Garcia, 2 and 1

Garcia	4 3 4	3 3 4	4 4 4	33	3 4 4	4 3 4	4 5 4	35	68
Els	4 2 3	4 3 4	3 4 3	30	3 3 3	4 3 5	5 5 4	35	65

Els leads, 3 up

Garcia	3 3 4	5 3 3	5 3 5	34	3 4 4	4 3 4	C X
Els	4 3 4	5 3 4	4 4 3	34	2 4 4	6 4 4	3 X

PRIZE MONEY: Els £250,000; Garcia £120,000; Campbell, Singh £85,000 each; Goosen, Harrington, Montgomerie, Woosnam £65,000 each; Faldo, Funk, Rose, Weir £50,000 each.

LEGEND: C—conceded hole to opponent; W—won hole by concession without holing out; X—no total score.

Telefonica Open de Madrid

Club de Campo, Madrid, Spain
Par 36-35–71; 6,967 yards

October 24-27
purse,€1,400,000

	SCORES				TOTAL	MONEY
Steen Tinning	68	68	62	67	265	€233,330
Brian Davis	65	72	66	63	266	104,396.70

	SCORES				TOTAL	MONEY
Andrew Coltart	66	68	68	64	266	104,396.70
Adam Scott	67	65	66	68	266	104,396.70
Bradley Dredge	71	65	67	64	267	59,360
Paul Lawrie	70	64	69	65	268	49,000
Padraig Harrington	65	66	66	72	269	36,120
Trevor Immelman	66	65	68	70	269	36,120
Retief Goosen	66	69	67	67	269	36,120
Des Smyth	69	63	69	69	270	25,946.67
Jean-Francois Remesy	70	66	65	69	270	25,946.67
Soren Kjeldsen	69	68	65	68	270	25,946.67
Maarten Lafeber	65	65	72	69	271	22,540
Santiago Luna	69	67	68	68	272	20,160
Anders Hansen	68	67	69	68	272	20,160
Nick O'Hern	66	70	65	71	272	20,160
Lee Westwood	64	70	66	72	272	20,160
David Howell	72	68	68	65	273	16,380
Marten Olander	67	66	70	70	273	16,380
Ian Poulter	70	69	67	67	273	16,380
Miguel Angel Jimenez	70	69	67	67	273	16,380
Miles Tunnicliff	70	63	70	70	273	16,380
Markus Brier	66	69	69	69	273	16,380
Paul Casey	70	65	67	71	273	16,380
Andrew Oldcorn	69	71	66	68	274	14,140
Sam Torrance	67	66	71	70	274	14,140
Mark Foster	74	67	65	68	274	14,140
David Gilford	72	68	71	64	275	12,460
Darren Fichardt	70	72	65	68	275	12,460
Ignacio Garrido	71	66	69	69	275	12,460
John Bickerton	73	68	69	65	275	12,460
Jamie Donaldson	69	68	69	69	275	12,460
Steve Webster	70	68	66	72	276	10,675
Jorge Berendt	68	73	70	65	276	10,675
Tomas Jesus Munoz	68	69	70	69	276	10,675
Fredrik Jacobson	68	66	69	73	276	10,675
Miguel Angel Martin	69	66	68	74	277	9,240
Jose Manuel Carriles	69	68	70	70	277	9,240
Anthony Wall	69	67	70	71	277	9,240
Joakim Haeggman	72	67	70	68	277	9,240
Rolf Muntz	71	67	69	70	277	9,240
Stephen Scahill	66	72	69	70	277	9,240
Roger Chapman	67	70	67	74	278	7,420
Mark Mouland	69	70	70	69	278	7,420
Soren Hansen	69	73	68	68	278	7,420
Diego Borrego	67	70	70	71	278	7,420
Gary Orr	68	68	69	73	278	7,420
Patrik Sjoland	67	70	71	70	278	7,420
Brett Rumford	72	70	68	68	278	7,420
Robert-Jan Derksen	70	68	70	71	279	5,880
Warren Bennett	70	68	69	72	279	5,880
Chris Gane	71	69	69	70	279	5,880
Ian Garbutt	73	67	69	70	279	5,880
Daren Lee	73	69	69	69	280	4,648
Henrik Nystrom	68	72	71	69	280	4,648
Stephen Gallacher	72	70	70	68	280	4,648
Christopher Hanell	67	71	71	71	280	4,648
Simon Dyson	69	70	74	67	280	4,648
Grant Hamerton	70	72	68	71	281	3,990
Lucas Parsons	70	72	72	67	281	3,990
Mark James	71	67	73	71	282	3,290
Peter Fowler	71	71	72	68	282	3,290

	SCORES				TOTAL	MONEY
Alvaro Salto	71	66	70	75	282	3,290
Paul Eales	72	70	68	72	282	3,290
Johan Rystrom	71	69	69	73	282	3,290
Stephen Dodd	71	69	73	69	282	3,290
Gary Evans	69	72	70	71	282	3,290
Carlos Balmaseda	67	72	70	73	282	3,290
Raphael Jacquelin	70	70	73	70	283	2,440
Henrik Stenson	69	68	76	70	283	2,440
Sebastien Delagrange	74	66	70	73	283	2,440
Malcolm Mackenzie	69	73	73	69	284	2,095.50
Jose Rivero	68˙	73	69	74	284	2,095.50
Carlos Rodiles	76	65	77	67	285	2,091
Gordon Brand, Jr.	69	72	74	71	286	2,088
Greg Owen	70	72	75	73	290	2,085
Gregory Havret	73	69	72	80	294	2,082
Olle Karlsson	71	71	77	77	296	2,079

Italian Open Telecom Italia

Olgiata Golf Club, Rome, Italy
Par 36-36–72; 6,967 yards
(Tournament reduced to 54 holes—rain.)

October 31-November 3
purse, €1,100,000

	SCORES			TOTAL	MONEY
Ian Poulter	61	67	69	197	€183,330
Paul Lawrie	66	63	70	199	122,220
Anders Hansen	64	71	66	201	56,833.33
Anthony Wall	69	67	65	201	56,833.33
Emanuele Canonica	66	65	70	201	56,833.33
Padraig Harrington	71	68	63	202	30,910
Barry Lane	69	67	66	202	30,910
Jarrod Moseley	66	66	70	202	30,910
Angel Cabrera	72	61	69	202	30,910
Nick O'Hern	71	69	63	203	20,386.67
Henrik Nystrom	67	66	70	203	20,386.67
Stephen Gallacher	69	69	65	203	20,386.67
Philip Golding	66	75	63	204	17,270
Andrew Marshall	69	67	68	204	17,270
Mark Mouland	68	68	69	205	14,093.75
Robert-Jan Derksen	71	68	66	205	14,093.75
Brian Davis	69	69	67	205	14,093.75
Maarten Lafeber	68	67	70	205	14,093.75
Thomas Levet	69	66	70	205	14,093.75
Jean Hugo	70	69	66	205	14,093.75
Miles Tunnicliff	64	70	71	205	14,093.75
Markus Brier	70	68	67	205	14,093.75
Peter Fowler	70	67	69	206	11,110
Jean-Francois Remesy	71	66	69	206	11,110
Raphael Jacquelin	76	62	68	206	11,110
Trevor Immelman	70	68	68	206	11,110
*Francesco Molinari	70	66	70	206	
Robert Karlsson	70	68	68	206	11,110
Gary Orr	66	69	71	206	11,110
Niclas Fasth	68	69	69	206	11,110
Steve Webster	71	68	68	207	8,847.14
Peter Hanson	68	69	70	207	8,847.14
Paul Eales	72	69	66	207	8,847.14

	SCORES			TOTAL	MONEY
Soren Hansen	70	68	69	207	8,847.14
Joakim Haeggman	69	69	69	207	8,847.14
Christopher Hanell	69	69	69	207	8,847.14
Alastair Forsyth	69	68	70	207	8,847.14
Mark Roe	69	69	70	208	7,260
Marten Olander	70	71	67	208	7,260
Massimo Florioli	72	68	68	208	7,260
Ignacio Garrido	74	67	67	208	7,260
Sebastien Delagrange	71	68	69	208	7,260
Graeme McDowell	71	70	67	208	7,260
Gordon Brand, Jr.	68	71	70	209	5,830
Darren Fichardt	69	70	70	209	5,830
Jamie Spence	68	71	70	209	5,830
Gary Emerson	74	67	68	209	5,830
Peter Baker	69	71	69	209	5,830
Gary Clark	72	68	69	209	5,830
Brett Rumford	67	73	69	209	5,830
Anders Forsbrand	72	67	71	210	4,730
Tony Johnstone	71	69	70	210	4,730
Eduardo Romero	72	68	70	210	4,730
David Howell	69	72	70	211	3,960
Mark McNulty	71	69	71	211	3,960
Diego Borrego	69	72	70	211	3,960
Patrik Sjoland	66	74	71	211	3,960
Roger Chapman	70	68	74	212	3,135
Alberto Binaghi	69	69	74	212	3,135
Jonathan Lomas	71	70	71	212	3,135
Rolf Muntz	71	70	71	212	3,135
Mikael Lundberg	70	71	71	212	3,135
Mikko Ilonen	71	70	71	212	3,135
Stephen Dodd	69	72	72	213	2,585
Mark Pilkington	71	70	72	213	2,585
Daren Lee	70	70	73	213	2,585
Mads Vibe-Hastrup	71	69	73	213	2,585
Ricardo Gonzalez	67	74	73	214	2,310
Alessandro Tadini	71	68	77	216	2,145
Jorge Berendt	67	74	75	216	2,145
Marco Bernardini	69	72	76	217	2,010

Volvo Masters Andalucia

Club de Golf, Valderrama, Spain
Par 35-36–71; 6,945 yards

November 7-10
purse, €3,136,700

	SCORES				TOTAL	MONEY
Bernhard Langer	71	71	72	67	281	€435,648.42
Colin Montgomerie	70	69	72	70	281	435,648.42
(Langer and Montgomerie remained tied when event called due to darkness after two playoff holes.)						
Bradley Dredge	68	71	71	73	283	196,357.40
Peter O'Malley	72	69	75	69	285	144,915.50
Angel Cabrera	63	72	76	74	285	144,915.50
Jarmo Sandelin	69	74	77	66	286	109,784.50
Sergio Garcia	69	70	75	73	287	86,259.25
Adam Scott	72	73	70	72	287	86,259.25
Robert Karlsson	72	67	77	72	288	66,498.04
Darren Clarke	73	69	75	71	288	66,498.04

	SCORES			TOTAL	MONEY
Alex Cejka	69	75	71	74	289	56,460.60
Anders Hansen	76	70	73	71	290	52,382.89
Ian Woosnam	73	72	73	73	291	46,297.69
Maarten Lafeber	69	72	75	75	291	46,297.69
Richard Green	70	74	78	69	291	46,297.69
Thomas Levet	70	75	75	71	291	46,297.69
Niclas Fasth	71	77	69	74	291	46,297.69
Jose Maria Olazabal	73	69	76	74	292	41,090.77
Justin Rose	71	69	73	79	292	41,090.77
Ian Poulter	73	75	73	71	292	41,090.77
David Gilford	72	71	79	71	293	36,134.79
Stephen Leaney	73	68	77	75	293	36,134.79
Steen Tinning	68	80	72	73	293	36,134.79
Thomas Bjorn	77	74	71	71	293	36,134.79
Fredrik Jacobson	68	72	74	79	293	36,134.79
Gary Evans	76	74	74	70	294	32,464.85
Alastair Forsyth	75	73	74	72	294	32,464.85
Brian Davis	68	81	72	74	295	28,700.80
Soren Hansen	71	71	82	71	295	28,700.80
Jarrod Moseley	71	74	80	70	295	28,700.80
Joakim Haeggman	76	74	72	73	295	28,700.80
Phillip Price	67	73	75	80	295	28,700.80
Paul Lawrie	72	73	79	71	295	28,700.80
Sandy Lyle	76	76	75	69	296	24,936.77
Retief Goosen	73	74	78	71	296	24,936.77
Eduardo Romero	71	71	75	80	297	22,584.24
Padraig Harrington	74	76	74	73	297	22,584.24
Carl Pettersson	70	77	73	77	297	22,584.24
Henrik Bjornstad	75	72	74	77	298	18,327.29
Miguel Angel Jimenez	81	70	72	75	298	18,327.29
Richard Johnson	74	67	79	78	298	18,327.29
Ignacio Garrido	70	77	76	75	298	18,327.29
Rolf Muntz	75	74	72	77	298	18,327.29
Greg Owen	74	68	79	77	298	18,327.29
Simon Dyson	68	74	76	80	298	18,327.29
Malcolm Mackenzie	71	73	76	79	299	15,369.83
Barry Lane	73	73	79	74	299	15,369.83
Costantino Rocca	72	73	75	80	300	13,315.29
Emanuele Canonica	75	71	77	77	300	13,315.29
Andrew Coltart	72	78	75	75	300	13,315.29
John Bickerton	75	77	77	71	300	13,315.29
Tobias Dier	75	76	77	72	300	13,315.29
Peter Fowler	77	75	73	76	301	11,801.83
Trevor Immelman	72	77	77	75	301	11,801.83
Jamie Spence	72	76	78	76	302	10,978.45
Paul Casey	81	71	76	74	302	10,978.45
Graeme McDowell	72	81	69	80	302	10,978.45
Carlos Rodiles	73	83	76	71	303	10,351.11
Jean-Francois Remesy	75	73	78	78	304	10,037.44
Tony Johnstone	78	78	71	78	305	9,143.48
Paul McGinley	76	77	78	74	305	9,143.48
Ricardo Gonzalez	78	76	79	72	305	9,143.48
Nick Dougherty	76	76	76	77	305	9,143.48
David Gleeson	74	81	75	75	305	9,143.48
Lee Westwood	76	73	81	78	308	8,390.67
Pierre Fulke	75				WD	8,233.84

BMW Asian Open
See Asia/Japan Tours chapter.

Omega Hong Kong Open
See Asia/Japan Tours chapter.

Challenge Tour

Sameer Kenya Open

Muthaiga Golf Club, Nairobi, Kenya
Par 36-35–71; 6,825 yards

February 28-March 3
purse, €122,481

	SCORES				TOTAL	MONEY
Lee James	66	65	70	64	265	€20,413.63
Titch Moore	66	68	68	66	268	13,603.64
Ben Mason	63	68	69	69	269	7,651.03
Benn Barham	68	69	68	65	270	5,658.66
Gary Birch, Jr.	69	67	68	66	270	5,658.66
Greig Hutcheon	74	65	67	65	271	4,397.10
Simon Wakefield	68	71	65	67	271	4,397.10
Simon Hurd	69	67	67	68	271	4,397.10
Anil Ashok Shah	68	69	69	66	272	3,576.47
Omar Sandys	64	74	70	64	272	3,576.47
Graham Rankin	69	69	67	68	273	3,025.30
Philip Worthington	71	65	70	67	273	3,025.30
Dismas Indiza	67	72	69	66	274	1,859
Erol Simsek	66	72	69	67	274	1,859
Jaco Van Zyl	71	64	70	69	274	1,859
Jacob Okello	68	69	67	70	274	1,859
James du Plessis	69	69	68	68	274	1,859
Martin Maritz	64	71	72	67	274	1,859
Paul Dwyer	69	71	67	67	274	1,859
Sean Farrell	67	68	67	72	274	1,859
Sion Bebb	71	69	69	65	274	1,859
Steven O'Hara	66	73	69	67	275	1,335.05
Josef Fourie	67	70	68	71	276	1,241.15
Roger Beames	69	71	67	69	276	1,241.15
Yngve Nilsson	72	66	70	68	276	1,241.15
Andrew Sherborne	72	68	71	66	277	1,044.16
Benjamin Nicolay	69	69	71	68	277	1,044.16
Jamie Little	71	68	69	69	277	1,044.16
Jean-Francois Lucquin	68	70	70	69	277	1,044.16
Kenneth Ferrie	67	70	73	67	277	1,044.16
Marcel Siem	69	71	71	66	277	1,044.16
Neil Reilly	69	68	69	71	277	1,044.16
Sandeep Grewal	64	70	71	72	277	1,044.16

Stanbic Zambia Open
See African Tours chapter.

Panalpina Banque Commerciale du Maroc Classic

Royal Golf Dar-es-Salam, Rabat, Morocco
Par 36-37–73; 7,359 yards

April 11-14
purse, €130,000

		SCORES			TOTAL	MONEY
Jean-Francois Lucquin	74	69	71	69	283	€21,660
Peter Lawrie	74	69	76	69	288	14,440
Andrew Raitt	75	71	72	72	290	7,313
Iain Pyman	71	71	74	74	290	7,313
Simon Wakefield	74	74	72	71	291	5,512
Simon Hurd	72	76	72	72	292	4,667
James Hepworth	71	73	75	73	292	4,667
Gary Birch, Jr.	77	72	70	73	292	4,667
Sam Little	74	71	72	76	293	3,648.67
Sebastien Branger	77	70	71	75	293	3,648.67
Christophe Pottier	75	75	71	72	293	3,648.67
Euan Little	75	74	72	73	294	2,227.88
Stefano Reale	76	74	71	73	294	2,227.88
Marcello Santi	75	74	73	72	294	2,227.88
Miles Tunnicliff	75	70	75	74	294	2,227.88
Dominique Nouailhac	70	77	74	73	294	2,227.88
Matthew Blackey	73	71	76	74	294	2,227.88
Richard Sterne	74	75	72	73	294	2,227.88
Martin Maritz	74	73	74	73	294	2,227.88
Alberto Binaghi	76	74	69	76	295	1,395.33
Olivier David	71	74	76	74	295	1,395.33
Nicolas Colsaerts	73	74	74	74	295	1,395.33
Olivier Edmond	77	72	75	71	295	1,395.33
Didier de Vooght	73	74	73	75	295	1,395.33
David Dixon	67	78	78	72	295	1,395.33
Damien McGrane	73	71	77	75	296	1,196
Hennie Walters	74	69	76	77	296	1,196
Marcel Siem	75	72	74	75	296	1,196
Amine Joudar	71	73	79	74	297	1,083.33
Massimo Florioli	73	76	71	77	297	1,083.33
Paul Dwyer	75	74	72	76	297	1,083.33

Tessali Open del Sud

Riva dei Tessali Golf Club, Taranto, Italy
Par 35-36–71; 6,502 yards

April 25-28
purse, €90,000

		SCORES			TOTAL	MONEY
Simon Wakefield	67	70	71	66	274	€15,000
Andrew Raitt	77	64	66	68	275	10,000
Jean-Francois Lucquin	64	69	72	71	276	5,618
Sam Little	66	67	74	72	279	3,939
Dominique Nouailhac	71	72	67	69	279	3,939
Federico Bisazza	71	66	70	72	279	3,939
Jamie Little	70	72	71	67	280	2,862
Massimo Florioli	68	69	68	75	280	2,862
Ben Mason	68	70	73	69	280	2,862

	SCORES				TOTAL	MONEY
Steven O'Hara	70	70	70	70	280	2,862
Emmanuele Lattanzi	69	75	71	66	281	2,127
Stefano Reale	73	69	70	69	281	2,127
Francois Delamontagne	71	72	70	68	281	2,127
Mark Hilton	72	72	65	73	282	1,432.80
Olivier David	70	68	74	70	282	1,432.80
Sion Bebb	71	68	72	71	282	1,432.80
Kariem Baraka	72	70	73	67	282	1,432.80
David Patrick	74	69	69	70	282	1,432.80
Silvio Grappasonni	72	69	71	71	283	1,044
Leif Westerberg	72	68	70	73	283	1,044
Hampus Von Post	73	68	74	68	283	1,044
Ciaran McMonagle	73	68	70	72	283	1,044
Marco Bernardini	75	67	70	72	284	945
Ralf Geilenberg	74	69	70	72	285	882
Nicolas Colsaerts	72	72	68	73	285	882
Andreas Ljunggren	71	66	74	74	285	882
Alberto Binaghi	75	69	71	71	286	775.80
Craig Cowper	75	69	72	70	286	775.80
Nicolas Marin	76	67	71	72	286	775.80
Tino Schuster	73	68	72	73	286	775.80
Ariel Canete	73	70	73	70	286	775.80

Izki Challenge de Espana

Izki Golf Urturi, Vitoria, Spain
Par 36-37–73; 7,192 yards

May 23-26
purse, €135,000

	SCORES				TOTAL	MONEY
Fredrik Widmark	67	70	73	66	276	€22,500
Raimo Sjoberg	71	69	69	68	277	15,000
Gareth Paddison	70	71	70	68	279	8,427
Hennie Otto	69	72	67	72	280	5,908.50
Iain Pyman	70	71	68	71	280	5,908.50
Oskar Bergman	73	70	67	70	280	5,908.50
Gary Murphy	70	69	73	69	281	4,464
Julien Van Hauwe	68	71	72	70	281	4,464
Mark Sanders	71	69	68	73	281	4,464
Lee James	67	70	71	74	282	3,361.50
Bjorn Pettersson	71	69	69	73	282	3,361.50
Dominique Nouailhac	68	71	72	72	283	3,186
Alvaro Salto	73	70	70	71	284	2,497.50
Jesus Maria Arruti	71	72	71	70	284	2,497.50
Ignacio Feliu	70	74	70	70	284	2,497.50
Tomas Jesus Munoz	72	70	73	69	284	2,497.50
Jamie Little	71	71	72	71	285	1,777.50
Benn Barham	74	68	73	70	285	1,777.50
Oscar Sanchez	70	70	75	70	285	1,777.50
Federico Bisazza	67	72	73	74	286	1,593
Elliot Boult	69	71	73	74	287	1,420.20
Knud Storgaard	71	74	72	70	287	1,420.20
Marc Cayeux	69	72	72	74	287	1,420.20
Frederic Cupillard	72	73	70	72	287	1,420.20
David Higgins	70	71	72	74	287	1,420.20
Patrik Gottfridson	72	70	71	75	288	1,150.88
Iestyn Taylor	72	70	71	75	288	1,150.88
Nicolas Colsaerts	68	71	74	75	288	1,150.88

	SCORES			TOTAL	MONEY
Carlos Quevedo	70	71 73 74		288	1,150.88
Lee Thompson	72	72 73 71		288	1,150.88
Neil Turley	71	73 71 73		288	1,150.88
Steven O'Hara	73	71 72 72		288	1,150.88
Allan Hogh	72	73 71 72		288	1,150.88

Austrian Golf Open

Steiermarkischer Golf Club Murhof, Graz, Austria   May 30-June 2
Par 36-36–72; 6,883 yards   purse, €110,000

	SCORES			TOTAL	MONEY
Markus Brier	67	67 62 71		267	€18,330
Gary Birch, Jr.	66	65 68 69		268	12,220
Hennie Otto	69	70 65 65		269	5,678.67
Ilya Goroneskoul	69	64 67 69		269	5,678.67
Simon Hurd	70	65 67 67		269	5,678.67
Scott Drummond	66	69 67 68		270	4,279
Massimo Scarpa	70	65 71 65		271	3,938
Marcello Santi	70	68 66 68		272	3,351.33
Andrew Raitt	69	68 69 66		272	3,351.33
Kariem Baraka	66	67 66 73		272	3,351.33
Martin Erlandsson	67	69 70 68		274	2,599.67
Richard Dinsdale	68	68 69 69		274	2,599.67
Lee James	70	67 69 68		274	2,599.67
Alberto Binaghi	69	69 71 66		275	1,751.20
Michael Archer	70	67 69 69		275	1,751.20
Robin Byrd	74	67 65 69		275	1,751.20
Nicolas Colsaerts	67	71 69 68		275	1,751.20
Joakim Gronhagen	70	69 67 69		275	1,751.20
Peter Lawrie	72	69 67 68		276	1,331
Gareth Paddison	72	67 67 70		276	1,331
Titch Moore	72	69 68 68		277	1,177
Massimo Florioli	70	65 70 72		277	1,177
Fredrick Mansson	72	69 67 69		277	1,177
Jesper Nielsen	71	69 71 66		277	1,177
Stefano Reale	72	68 70 68		278	1,028.50
Jean Louis Guepy	72	69 69 68		278	1,028.50
Matthew Blackey	70	69 70 69		278	1,028.50
Ivo Giner	66	68 66 78		278	1,028.50
Gary Murphy	64	73 73 69		279	893.20
Alessandro Tadini	72	67 71 69		279	893.20
Sam Little	66	68 72 73		279	893.20
Garry Houston	69	70 69 71		279	893.20
Hennie Walters	74	62 73 70		279	893.20

Nykredit Danish Open

Horsens Golf Club, Jutland, Denmark   June 6-9
Par 36-36–72; 7,035 yards   purse, €120,000

	SCORES			TOTAL	MONEY
Ed Stedman	71	74 70 70		285	€20,000
Lee James	71	72 74 69		286	13,330
Jean Louis Guepy	74	72 69 72		287	6,747

	SCORES				TOTAL	MONEY
Richard Sterne	77	72	71	67	287	6,747
Peter Malmgren	69	71	77	71	288	4,878
Leif Westerberg	71	74	76	67	288	4,878
Titch Moore	75	74	70	70	289	4,128
Tim Milford	75	71	67	76	289	4,128
Christian Nilsson	73	74	72	71	290	3,648
Fredrik Henge	77	74	71	69	291	2,841.60
Gary Marks	76	75	70	70	291	2,841.60
Massimo Florioli	77	74	72	68	291	2,841.60
Andrew Raitt	73	71	79	68	291	2,841.60
Simon Wakefield	74	76	74	67	291	2,841.60
Neil Price	75	77	73	67	292	2,100
Robin Byrd	75	73	73	72	293	1,704
Raimo Sjoberg	77	73	71	72	293	1,704
Mark Sanders	75	77	69	72	293	1,704
Gary Murphy	77	72	68	77	294	1,420
Mikael Piltz	76	74	71	73	294	1,420
Matthew Blackey	77	74	71	72	294	1,420
Charles Challen	76	76	67	76	295	1,284
Allan Hogh	71	79	74	71	295	1,284
Jakob Borregaard	74	78	73	71	296	1,194
Michael Jonzon	74	74	71	77	296	1,194
Viktor Gustavsson	75	77	74	71	297	1,068
Garry Houston	75	75	76	71	297	1,068
Paul Nilbrink	74	74	74	75	297	1,068
Paul Streeter	71	80	71	75	297	1,068
Thomas Norret	74	77	77	69	297	1,068

Aa Saint Omer Open

Aa Saint Omer Golf Club, France
Par 36-35–71; 6,711 yards

June 13-16
purse, €330,000

	SCORES				TOTAL	MONEY
Nicolas Vanhootegem	75	70	67	65	277	€55,000
Gustavo Rojas	72	68	69	72	281	28,633
Lee James	70	71	71	69	281	28,633
Mattias Eliasson	72	69	72	70	283	16,500
Kalle Vainola	74	70	72	68	284	11,467.50
Hennie Walters	72	68	71	73	284	11,467.50
Jean-Francois Lucquin	69	70	72	73	284	11,467.50
Didier de Vooght	74	71	70	69	284	11,467.50
Paul Dwyer	74	69	70	71	284	11,467.50
Benn Barham	72	71	69	72	284	11,467.50
Simon Hurd	73	67	73	72	285	8,514
Wayne Riley	71	71	74	70	286	6,138
Damien McGrane	72	70	72	72	286	6,138
Sam Little	71	71	77	67	286	6,138
Richard Dinsdale	71	68	76	71	286	6,138
Andrew Raitt	74	71	70	71	286	6,138
Ed Stedman	71	74	71	70	286	6,138
Alvaro Salto	72	71	70	74	287	3,927
Marc Pendaries	72	69	72	74	287	3,927
Raimo Sjoberg	75	70	72	70	287	3,927
Tim Milford	73	71	73	70	287	3,927
Jean Pierre Cixous	70	74	74	69	287	3,927
Jean Marc De Polo	75	70	76	67	288	3,139.71

	SCORES				TOTAL	MONEY
Miles Tunnicliff	75	69	74	70	288	3,139.71
Massimo Scarpa	71	73	70	74	288	3,139.71
Des Terblanche	74	69	75	70	288	3,139.71
Frederic Cupillard	73	70	74	71	288	3,139.71
Marco Bernardini	72	73	73	70	288	3,139.71
David Dupart	73	71	70	74	288	3,139.71
Sebastien Branger	73	71	73	72	289	2,607
Massimo Florioli	72	66	75	76	289	2,607
Francesco Guermani	70	75	75	69	289	2,607
Martin Maritz	76	69	73	71	289	2,607
Gareth Paddison	69	71	70	79	289	2,607

Galeria Kaufhof Pokal Challenge

Rittergut Birkhof Golf Club, Dusseldorf, Germany
Par 36-36–72; 6,807 yards

June 13-16
purse, €90,000

	SCORES				TOTAL	MONEY
Alex Cejka	66	69	68	68	271	€15,000
Marcel Siem	68	71	68	68	275	7,809
John Morgan	68	65	72	70	275	7,809
Garry Houston	70	67	69	70	276	4,158
Martin Erlandsson	70	70	69	67	276	4,158
Michael Jonzon	70	70	66	71	277	3,361.50
Linus Petersson	72	69	69	67	277	3,361.50
Alessandro Tadini	71	68	70	69	278	2,337.43
Carlos Quevedo	73	67	69	69	278	2,337.43
Charles Challen	69	65	71	73	278	2,337.43
Alan Michell	70	70	66	72	278	2,337.43
Amandeep Johl	72	68	67	71	278	2,337.43
Tom Whitehouse	71	69	66	72	278	2,337.43
Steven O'Hara	69	71	68	70	278	2,337.43
Neil Price	69	71	71	68	279	1,485
Philip Worthington	69	68	72	70	279	1,485
Viktor Gustavsson	71	71	72	66	280	1,126.80
Hampus Von Post	70	70	71	69	280	1,126.80
Jesper Nielsen	72	67	73	68	280	1,126.80
Frederic Schoettel	68	71	71	70	280	1,126.80
Nicolas Wrona	68	69	72	71	280	1,126.80
David Salisbury	72	71	68	70	281	981
Grant Dodd	71	70	71	70	282	912
Denny Lucas	72	70	69	71	282	912
Carl Richardson	72	68	71	71	282	912
Philip Archer	76	66	72	69	283	777.86
Jochen Lupprian	69	72	71	71	283	777.86
Craig Cowper	69	69	72	73	283	777.86
Alan McLean	70	73	68	72	283	777.86
Ari Pasanen	76	65	71	71	283	777.86
Chris Rodgers	69	71	73	70	283	777.86
Sandeep Grewal	68	71	71	73	283	777.86

Clearstream International Luxembourg Open

Kikuoka Country Club, Canach, Luxembourg   June 20-23
Par 36-36–72; 7,067 yards   purse, €115,000

	SCORES				TOTAL	MONEY
Lee James	66	65	68	65	264	€19,169
Mark Sanders	70	66	66	65	267	12,770
Jean-Francois Lucquin	68	72	64	65	269	7,193
Simon Hurd	64	72	69	65	270	5,750
Peter Jespersen	70	70	71	62	273	4,315.38
Juan Vizcaya	68	71	71	63	273	4,315.38
Marco Bernardini	67	68	70	68	273	4,315.38
Ben Mason	69	68	70	66	273	4,315.38
Nicolas Colsaerts	69	63	73	69	274	3,496
Jamie Little	70	69	66	70	275	2,723.20
Paul Streeter	65	69	68	73	275	2,723.20
Charles Challen	67	69	71	68	275	2,723.20
Sandeep Grewal	70	67	69	69	275	2,723.20
Ed Stedman	71	67	68	69	275	2,723.20
Grant Dodd	66	73	70	67	276	1,727.88
Alexandre Balicki	66	70	69	71	276	1,727.88
Stefano Reale	68	73	69	66	276	1,727.88
Hampus Von Post	73	66	69	68	276	1,727.88
Robert McGuirk	69	70	69	69	277	1,360.83
Sebastien Branger	69	69	69	70	277	1,360.83
John Morgan	70	70	69	68	277	1,360.83
Titch Moore	68	67	69	74	278	1,168.40
Robin Byrd	66	70	72	70	278	1,168.40
Tim Milford	69	71	69	69	278	1,168.40
Clemens Conrad-Prader	71	70	67	70	278	1,168.40
Tuomas Tuovinen	72	69	68	69	278	1,168.40
Niki Zitny	69	67	74	69	279	1,058
Jean Marc De Polo	67	70	72	71	280	936.43
Knut Ekjord	69	69	72	70	280	936.43
Wolfgang Huget	67	69	73	71	280	936.43
Nicolas Marin	69	68	70	73	280	936.43
Guido Van Der Valk	67	68	74	71	280	936.43
David Dixon	70	68	68	74	280	936.43
Ariel Canete	72	69	68	71	280	936.43

Open des Volcans

Golf des Volcans, Clermont-Ferrand, France   June 27-30
Par 36-35–71; 7,015 yards   purse, €110,000

	SCORES				TOTAL	MONEY
Scott Kammann	70	64	69	67	270	€18,330
Nicolas Colsaerts	66	66	68	71	271	12,220
Marcello Santi	72	68	63	69	272	6,872
Ilya Goroneskoul	71	65	70	68	274	5,500
Alberto Binaghi	67	69	71	68	275	4,664
Renaud Guillard	68	69	69	70	276	3,797.75
Michael Archer	71	67	69	69	276	3,797.75
Gianluca Baruffaldi	68	70	70	68	276	3,797.75
David Dupart	66	70	67	73	276	3,797.75
Nicolas Vanhootegem	68	70	67	72	277	2,838

	SCORES				TOTAL	MONEY
John Morgan	70	69	67	71	277	2,838
Nicolas Wrona	66	68	74	69	277	2,838
Niki Zitny	72	68	70	68	278	1,783.57
Grant Dodd	65	73	70	70	278	1,783.57
Stefano Soffietti	69	70	68	71	278	1,783.57
Stefano Reale	71	67	72	68	278	1,783.57
Benn Barham	70	69	72	67	278	1,783.57
Jean Louis Guepy	69	69	73	67	278	1,783.57
Marco Bernardini	72	69	68	69	278	1,783.57
Damien McGrane	70	69	70	70	279	1,201.20
Stefano Maio	71	67	71	70	279	1,201.20
Pehr Magnebrant	71	65	70	73	279	1,201.20
Paul Dwyer	70	68	71	70	279	1,201.20
Pascal Edmond	66	71	70	72	279	1,201.20
Peter Lawrie	75	65	70	70	280	1,061.50
Frederic Cupillard	67	70	73	70	280	1,061.50
Julien Van Hauwe	72	67	69	73	281	962.50
Francesco Guermani	72	68	69	72	281	962.50
Franck Aumonier	70	67	71	73	281	962.50
Steven Parry	70	67	74	70	281	962.50

Golf Montecchia - PGA Triveneta Terme Euganee Open

Golf Club Montecchia, Padova, Italy
Par 36-36–72; 6,909 yards

July 4-7
purse, €115,000

	SCORES				TOTAL	MONEY
Wolfgang Huget	69	70	63	66	268	€19,160
Francois Delamontagne	67	64	70	69	270	12,770
Alessandro Tadini	68	67	68	68	271	6,471.50
Richard Sterne	66	68	69	68	271	6,471.50
Ben Mason	68	66	69	69	272	4,674.75
Steven Parry	70	69	68	65	272	4,674.75
Marco Bernardini	66	72	67	68	273	3,956
David Ryles	70	71	65	67	273	3,956
Garry Houston	67	67	69	71	274	2,852
Sion Bebb	70	70	65	69	274	2,852
Simon Hurd	69	72	71	62	274	2,852
Iain Pyman	67	68	69	70	274	2,852
Guido Van Der Valk	69	69	69	67	274	2,852
David Dixon	70	70	72	62	274	2,852
Marc Pendaries	72	70	67	66	275	1,727.88
Nicolas Colsaerts	69	71	70	65	275	1,727.88
Massimo Florioli	69	72	71	63	275	1,727.88
Gianluca Baruffaldi	72	70	68	65	275	1,727.88
Ulrich van den Berg	69	71	66	70	276	1,308.70
Federico Bisazza	68	72	66	70	276	1,308.70
Matthew Blackey	70	68	69	69	276	1,308.70
Ivo Giner	71	71	67	67	276	1,308.70
Martin Maritz	70	71	69	66	276	1,308.70
Roberto Zappa	69	72	69	67	277	1,109.75
Michael Archer	71	71	68	67	277	1,109.75
Massimo Scarpa	69	73	68	67	277	1,109.75
Andre Bossert	72	67	69	69	277	1,109.75
Andrew Sherborne	69	69	71	69	278	936.43
Knud Storgaard	73	67	70	68	278	936.43
Stefano Reale	68	74	70	66	278	936.43

	SCORES				TOTAL	MONEY
Michele Reale	68	74	69	67	278	936.43
Van Phillips	72	69	69	68	278	936.43
Richard Dinsdale	72	69	69	68	278	936.43
John Morgan	71	68	69	70	278	936.43

Volvo Finnish Open

Espoo Golf Club, Helsinki, Finland
Par 36-36–72; 6,734 yards

July 11-14
purse, €100,000

	SCORES				TOTAL	MONEY
Thomas Norret	68	68	72	65	273	€16,660
Gary Birch, Jr.	70	73	67	64	274	11,110
Greig Hutcheon	69	71	69	66	275	6,250
Ilya Goroneskoul	71	72	65	68	276	4,620
Mikael Piltz	72	66	71	67	276	4,620
*Wilhelm Schauman	71	71	63	71	276	
Johan Edfors	69	71	65	72	277	3,735
Simon Wakefield	66	70	74	67	277	3,735
Alessandro Tadini	69	71	67	71	278	3,170
Thomas Besancenez	68	73	70	67	278	3,170
Julien Van Hauwe	69	71	70	69	279	2,472.50
Sion Bebb	66	72	71	70	279	2,472.50
Francois Delamontagne	68	72	68	71	279	2,472.50
Mark Sanders	72	70	70	67	279	2,472.50
Damien McGrane	71	67	74	68	280	1,662.50
Craig Cowper	70	69	71	70	280	1,662.50
Tony Edlund	74	68	68	70	280	1,662.50
Anssi Kankkonen	69	71	73	67	280	1,662.50
Raimo Sjoberg	74	69	68	70	281	1,190
Lee James	73	68	72	68	281	1,190
Linus Petersson	69	70	74	68	281	1,190
Neil Price	71	70	70	70	281	1,190
John Morgan	72	71	70	68	281	1,190
Viktor Gustavsson	69	70	73	70	282	982
Daniel Westermark	68	72	76	66	282	982
Patrik Gottfridson	73	68	71	70	282	982
Jamie Little	68	71	72	71	282	982
Tuomas Tuovinen	68	74	70	70	282	982
Fredrik Orest	69	71	73	70	283	814.29
Bradford Vaughan	67	74	70	72	283	814.29
Jean-Francois Lucquin	74	67	73	69	283	814.29
Nicolas Colsaerts	69	71	73	70	283	814.29
Paul Dwyer	72	68	70	73	283	814.29
Michael Jonzon	68	73	73	69	283	814.29
David Ryles	72	70	70	71	283	814.29

Golf Challenge

Brunstorf Golf & Country Club, Hamburg, Germany
Par 36-36–72; 7,458 yards
(Event reduced to 54 holes—rain.)

July 18-21
purse, €100,000

	SCORES			TOTAL	MONEY
Iain Pyman	66	66	72	204	€16,660
Graeme McDowell	69	68	70	207	11,110

	SCORES			TOTAL	MONEY
Hennie Walters	71	69	68	208	5,625
Denny Lucas	67	68	73	208	5,625
Jean Pierre Cixous	68	69	72	209	4,240
Mark Sanders	71	71	68	210	3,890
Peter Lawrie	72	67	72	211	3,440
Robin Byrd	70	71	70	211	3,440
Greig Hutcheon	73	69	71	213	2,806.67
Michael Jonzon	71	68	74	213	2,806.67
Martin Maritz	71	67	75	213	2,806.67
Gustavo Rojas	71	69	74	214	2,255
John Morgan	69	73	72	214	2,255
Niki Zitny	74	68	73	215	1,750
Jean-Francois Lucquin	74	69	72	215	1,750
Jesus Maria Arruti	77	69	69	215	1,750
Richard Gillot	78	68	70	216	1,176.25
Pasi Purhonen	71	74	71	216	1,176.25
Olivier David	74	68	74	216	1,176.25
Raimo Sjoberg	70	73	73	216	1,176.25
Richard Dinsdale	72	73	71	216	1,176.25
Dominique Nouailhac	72	70	74	216	1,176.25
Fredrik Widmark	76	71	69	216	1,176.25
Steven Parry	68	72	76	216	1,176.25
Nicolas Marin	73	72	72	217	980
Uli Weinhandl	70	73	75	218	876.67
Philip Archer	76	70	72	218	876.67
Garry Houston	74	70	74	218	876.67
Renaud Guillard	78	68	72	218	876.67
Alan McLean	72	71	75	218	876.67
Tino Schuster	75	72	71	218	876.67

Charles Church Challenge Tour Championship

Bowood Golf & Country Club, Wiltshire, England
Par 36-36–72; 7,317 yards

July 25-28
purse, €250,000

	SCORES				TOTAL	MONEY
John Morgan	66	68	73	71	278	€41,660
David Geall	70	67	76	65	278	27,770
(Morgan defeated Geall on first playoff hole.)						
Matthew Blackey	73	68	71	67	279	15,620
Andrew Sherborne	69	71	67	73	280	10,941.67
Peter Lawrie	71	69	70	70	280	10,941.67
Jean-Francois Lucquin	69	72	68	71	280	10,941.67
Gary Murphy	67	73	66	75	281	8,266.67
Titch Moore	70	69	73	69	281	8,266.67
Simon Hurd	68	72	73	68	281	8,266.67
Greig Hutcheon	69	68	68	77	282	5,662.50
Hennie Otto	68	72	70	72	282	5,662.50
Denny Lucas	68	72	72	70	282	5,662.50
Stefano Reale	73	69	72	68	282	5,662.50
Gustavo Rojas	70	68	75	69	282	5,662.50
Martin LeMesurier	70	71	69	72	282	5,662.50
Van Phillips	72	69	73	69	283	3,875
Knud Storgaard	70	73	71	70	284	3,206.25
Lee Thompson	72	72	71	69	284	3,206.25
Richard Sterne	69	70	74	71	284	3,206.25
Graeme McDowell	71	73	66	74	284	3,206.25

	SCORES				TOTAL	MONEY
Bjorn Pettersson	69	74	69	73	285	2,825
Damien McGrane	71	69	73	73	286	2,675
Mark Smith	71	71	72	72	286	2,675
Sam Little	70	74	71	72	287	2,375
Simon Wakefield	70	72	71	74	287	2,375
Michael Jonzon	74	70	73	70	287	2,375
Oskar Bergman	73	71	71	72	287	2,375
Tino Schuster	73	70	74	70	287	2,375
Marc Pendaries	69	70	73	76	288	2,004.17
Philip Archer	72	69	68	79	288	2,004.17
Olivier David	77	67	69	75	288	2,004.17
Paul Dwyer	74	70	74	70	288	2,004.17
Ivo Giner	72	71	77	68	288	2,004.17
Jon Herbert	71	72	68	77	288	2,004.17

Talma Finnish Challenge

Talma Golf Club, Talma, Finland
Par 36-36–72; 6,747 yards

August 1-4
purse, €150,000

	SCORES				TOTAL	MONEY
Lee James	64	67	70	68	269	€25,000
Matthew Blackey	65	68	67	71	271	16,660
David Ryles	70	69	71	64	274	9,370
Marcello Santi	69	71	66	69	275	6,565
Oskar Bergman	73	68	69	65	275	6,565
Allan Hogh	71	70	64	70	275	6,565
Hennie Otto	65	70	70	71	276	4,415
Ilya Goroneskoul	68	68	70	70	276	4,415
Pasi Purhonen	70	67	70	69	276	4,415
Nicolas Colsaerts	66	68	69	73	276	4,415
Andrew Raitt	67	69	70	70	276	4,415
Guido Van Der Valk	69	70	68	69	276	4,415
Euan Little	69	71	68	70	278	3,075
Alan McLean	70	68	68	72	278	3,075
Marc Chatelain	69	66	74	70	279	2,253.75
Julien Van Hauwe	72	69	67	71	279	2,253.75
James Hepworth	67	68	72	72	279	2,253.75
Steven O'Hara	71	69	67	72	279	2,253.75
Craig Cowper	68	72	71	69	280	1,707
Ivo Giner	75	62	74	69	280	1,707
Nicolas Marin	72	69	68	71	280	1,707
Paddy Gribben	68	67	71	74	280	1,707
Jani Saari	67	71	70	72	280	1,707
Grant Dodd	69	70	74	68	281	1,380
Michael Archer	69	72	69	71	281	1,380
Panu Kylliainen	69	69	71	72	281	1,380
Simon Wakefield	71	69	70	71	281	1,380
Bjorn Pettersson	69	72	67	73	281	1,380
Thomas Norret	72	69	68	72	281	1,380
Ben Mason	67	74	71	69	281	1,380

BMW Russian Open

Moscow Golf & Country Club, Moscow, Russia
Par 36-36–72; 7,066 yards

August 8-11
purse, €180,000

	SCORES				TOTAL	MONEY
Iain Pyman	62	67	71	69	269	€30,000
Benn Barham	66	66	65	73	270	15,618
Guido Van Der Valk	68	70	67	65	270	15,618
Damien McGrane	69	67	70	67	273	9,000
Denny Lucas	69	69	69	68	275	7,632
Peter Lawrie	67	70	67	72	276	6,723
Tim Milford	70	70	67	69	276	6,723
Jean-Francois Lucquin	70	70	70	68	278	5,706
Julien Van Hauwe	71	66	67	74	278	5,706
Michael Welch	73	68	64	74	279	4,262.40
Alessandro Tadini	70	67	73	69	279	4,262.40
Jamie Little	67	72	70	70	279	4,262.40
Luis Claverie	69	72	70	68	279	4,262.40
Ed Stedman	72	67	68	72	279	4,262.40
Bradford Vaughan	67	72	71	70	280	2,529
Hennie Otto	72	68	70	70	280	2,529
Nicolas Colsaerts	68	71	69	72	280	2,529
Mark Sanders	71	67	69	73	280	2,529
David Dixon	70	67	72	71	280	2,529
Stephen Browne	72	70	69	69	280	2,529
Martin Erlandsson	71	70	69	71	281	1,926
Paul Nilbrink	72	68	69	72	281	1,926
Simon Wakefield	69	69	71	72	281	1,926
Adam Crawford	69	70	71	71	281	1,926
Renaud Guillard	71	70	71	70	282	1,737
Alexandre Balicki	68	67	71	76	282	1,737
Titch Moore	67	70	73	73	283	1,575
Michael Archer	68	72	71	72	283	1,575
Gary Birch, Jr.	69	72	70	72	283	1,575
Richard McEvoy	70	70	71	72	283	1,575

North West of Ireland Open
See PGA European Tour section.

Skandia PGA Open

Halmstad Golf Club, Sweden
Par 36-36–72; 6,909 yards

August 22-25
purse, €95,000

	SCORES				TOTAL	MONEY
Thomas Besancenez	75	67	69	68	279	€15,830
Gary Murphy	72	68	73	68	281	10,550
Fredrik Orest	71	67	72	72	282	4,603.13
Kalle Brink	68	74	71	69	282	4,603.13
Carlos Quevedo	71	72	73	66	282	4,603.13
Michael Jonzon	69	72	72	69	282	4,603.13
Julien Van Hauwe	71	70	72	70	283	2,907
Markus Westerberg	68	76	69	70	283	2,907
Linus Petersson	72	72	71	68	283	2,907
Regis Gustave	69	75	69	70	283	2,907

	SCORES				TOTAL	MONEY
Richard McEvoy	72	69	70	72	283	2,907
Neil Reilly	71	70	71	72	284	2,142.25
Fredrick Mansson	73	71	68	72	284	2,142.25
Craig Cowper	72	73	66	74	285	1,852.50
Knud Storgaard	71	68	73	74	286	1,297.43
Johan Edfors	74	70	69	73	286	1,297.43
Marcus Knight	72	70	73	71	286	1,297.43
Andreas Ljunggren	72	70	70	74	286	1,297.43
Allan Hogh	69	72	74	71	286	1,297.43
Ariel Canete	72	70	75	69	286	1,297.43
Bjorgvin Sigurbergsson	71	71	72	72	286	1,297.43
Peter Malmgren	73	72	70	72	287	980.88
Joakim Rask	72	72	71	72	287	980.88
Bjorn Pettersson	71	69	72	75	287	980.88
Christopher Svarvar	72	70	73	72	287	980.88
Fredrik Henge	72	71	71	74	288	859.75
Tim Milford	70	71	71	76	288	859.75
Leif Westerberg	70	73	73	72	288	859.75
Kariem Baraka	69	71	71	77	288	859.75
Ola Eliasson	74	71	75	69	289	750.50
Knut Ekjord	73	70	75	71	289	750.50
Johan Bjerhag	72	71	73	73	289	750.50
Johan Moller	75	67	76	71	289	750.50
Niklas Bruzelius	75	70	73	71	289	750.50

Rolex Trophy

Geneve Golf Club, Geneva, Switzerland
Par 36-36–72; 6,875 yards

August 22-25
purse, €137,691

	SCORES				TOTAL	MONEY
Simon Hurd	68	65	70	65	268	€14,996.14
Gustavo Rojas	66	69	69	68	272	9,883.82
Fredrik Widmark	69	70	67	67	273	7,498.07
Gary Birch, Jr.	70	72	68	63	273	7,498.07
Wolfgang Huget	71	68	69	66	274	6,134.79
Nicolas Colsaerts	67	72	68	68	275	5,089.60
Massimo Florioli	72	66	67	70	275	5,089.60
Matthew Blackey	73	64	68	70	275	5,089.60
Ilya Goroneskoul	68	72	68	68	276	4,567.01
Denny Lucas	70	65	68	74	277	4,362.52
David Geall	71	68	69	69	277	4,362.52
Benn Barham	67	69	69	73	278	4,089.86
Richard Sterne	70	67	70	71	278	4,089.86
Andrew Sherborne	68	67	73	71	279	3,626.34
Peter Lawrie	71	67	72	69	279	3,626.34
Jean-Francois Lucquin	70	72	68	69	279	3,626.34
Andrew Raitt	72	68	69	70	279	3,626.34
Mark Sanders	68	66	76	69	279	3,626.34
Ben Mason	68	68	70	74	280	3,305.97
Ed Stedman	73	68	68	71	280	3,305.97
Andre Bossert	72	68	68	73	281	3,203.72
Francois Delamontagne	71	67	72	74	284	3,135.56

Formby Hall Challenge

Formby Hall Golf Club, Merseyside, England
Par 35-37–72; 7,002 yards

September 5-8
purse, €123,478

		SCORES			TOTAL	MONEY
Matthew Blackey	70	69	69	67	275	€19,727.63
Damien McGrane	72	68	71	65	276	10,270.20
David Dixon	72	66	67	71	276	10,270.20
Hampus Von Post	74	71	67	65	277	5,918.29
Raimo Sjoberg	69	67	70	73	279	4,811.57
David Griffiths	71	67	73	68	279	4,811.57
Paul Dwyer	72	69	72	67	280	3,913.96
Frederic Cupillard	71	69	71	69	280	3,913.96
Simon Griffiths	70	69	74	67	280	3,913.96
Peter Lawrie	76	69	70	66	281	2,802.90
Andrew Raitt	72	68	69	72	281	2,802.90
Ivo Giner	69	71	67	74	281	2,802.90
Linus Petersson	74	69	71	67	281	2,802.90
John Wells	69	72	74	66	281	2,802.90
Kalle Brink	73	71	70	68	282	1,575.74
Shaun Webster	71	72	74	65	282	1,575.74
Nicolas Colsaerts	71	70	69	72	282	1,575.74
Pehr Magnebrant	72	73	70	67	282	1,575.74
Steven Richardson	75	69	69	69	282	1,575.74
Paddy Gribben	75	66	70	71	282	1,575.74
Ben Mason	75	70	70	67	282	1,575.74
Gary Birch, Jr.	72	68	72	70	282	1,575.74
Michael Hoey	69	70	75	69	283	1,199.44
Adam Crawford	70	69	73	71	283	1,199.44
Stuart Davis	70	67	73	73	283	1,199.44
Peter Malmgren	69	71	76	68	284	1,071.21
Carlos Quevedo	73	66	74	71	284	1,071.21
Michael Jonzon	68	74	70	72	284	1,071.21
Mark Sanders	71	72	71	70	284	1,071.21
Francesco Guermani	72	71	71	71	285	970.60
Neil Price	73	71	71	70	285	970.60

Telia Grand Prix

Ljunghusens Golf Club, Stockholm, Sweden
Par 35-37–72; 6,791 yards

September 12-15
purse, €119,273

		SCORES			TOTAL	MONEY
Matthew Blackey	72	65	69	70	276	€19,878.54
Jean-Francois Lucquin	70	68	74	66	278	13,252.36
Tuomas Tuovinen	69	71	73	67	280	7,445.92
Peter Gustafsson	72	69	73	67	281	5,963.67
Euan Little	68	71	72	71	282	4,655.64
Dennis Edlund	66	65	78	73	282	4,655.64
Joakim Rask	67	67	72	76	282	4,655.64
Greig Hutcheon	66	68	75	74	283	3,226.35
Nicolas Colsaerts	68	70	73	72	283	3,226.35
Nicolas Vanhootegem	67	72	70	74	283	3,226.35
James Hepworth	67	70	73	73	283	3,226.35
Simon Wakefield	71	65	74	73	283	3,226.35
Iain Pyman	68	71	68	76	283	3,226.35
Kalle Brink	70	65	76	73	284	1,768.65

	SCORES				TOTAL	MONEY
Peter Hanson	72	68	72	72	284	1,768.65
Massimo Florioli	67	65	76	76	284	1,768.65
Richard Dinsdale	66	66	80	72	284	1,768.65
Andrew Raitt	69	70	71	74	284	1,768.65
Graeme Storm	72	67	70	75	284	1,768.65
David Dixon	69	70	72	73	284	1,768.65
Mattias Eliasson	69	72	69	75	285	1,276.23
Martin Erlandsson	71	70	67	77	285	1,276.23
Michael Archer	71	70	73	71	285	1,276.23
Fredrik Widmark	70	68	73	74	285	1,276.23
Simon Hurd	68	70	73	75	286	1,150.99
Scott Kammann	69	71	74	72	286	1,150.99
Gary Murphy	65	71	77	74	287	1,079.42
Jesus Maria Arruti	67	70	75	75	287	1,079.42
Magnus Persson Atlevi	68	69	74	77	288	993.95
David Geall	71	68	75	74	288	993.95
Fredrick Mansson	72	67	73	76	288	993.95

Fortis Bank Challenge Open

Van Nymegen Golf Club, Groesbeek, Netherlands
Par 36-36–72; 6,647 yards

October 17-20
purse, €135,000

	SCORES				TOTAL	MONEY
Didier de Vooght	71	67	67	65	270	€22,500
Robert-Jan Derksen	68	67	68	69	272	8,230.50
Peter Lawrie	69	68	69	66	272	8,230.50
Jesus Maria Arruti	70	65	69	68	272	8,230.50
Fredrik Widmark	68	71	69	64	272	8,230.50
Peter Gustafsson	73	66	68	65	272	8,230.50
Michael Archer	66	67	69	71	273	4,833
Julien Van Hauwe	65	71	71	67	274	4,113
Per Nyman	74	68	64	68	274	4,113
Guido Van Der Valk	69	67	67	71	274	4,113
Marcel Haremza	68	67	72	68	275	3,483
Shaun Webster	70	70	69	68	277	2,907
Dennis Edlund	69	68	69	71	277	2,907
Ben Mason	73	66	69	69	277	2,907
Nicolas Colsaerts	67	70	69	72	278	1,896.75
Neil Cheetham	68	72	67	71	278	1,896.75
James Hepworth	72	67	68	71	278	1,896.75
Iain Pyman	71	69	71	67	278	1,896.75
Oskar Bergman	70	67	70	71	278	1,896.75
Thomas Norret	67	74	70	67	278	1,896.75
Scott Drummond	72	66	70	71	279	1,397.25
Greig Hutcheon	72	69	71	67	279	1,397.25
Gianluca Baruffaldi	68	74	69	68	279	1,397.25
Matthew Blackey	65	71	71	72	279	1,397.25
Ivo Giner	69	69	73	68	279	1,397.25
David Dixon	70	70	68	71	279	1,397.25
Titch Moore	73	69	70	68	280	1,181.25
Massimo Florioli	71	70	69	70	280	1,181.25
Van Phillips	69	72	69	70	280	1,181.25
Andrew Raitt	67	73	72	68	280	1,181.25

Challenge Tour Grand Final

Golf du Medoc, Bordeaux, France
Par 35-36–71; 6,918 yards

October 24-27
purse, €200,000

	SCORES				TOTAL	MONEY
Peter Lawrie	71	67	69	65	272	€34,260
Julien Van Hauwe	72	65	72	67	276	22,830
Jesus Maria Arruti	67	73	70	70	280	10,625.27
Simon Wakefield	74	65	69	72	280	10,625.27
David Dixon	67	70	72	71	280	10,625.27
Titch Moore	70	73	69	69	281	7,681.20
Wolfgang Huget	71	73	68	69	281	7,681.20
Andrew Sherborne	72	71	70	69	282	5,341.17
Gary Murphy	68	74	71	69	282	5,341.17
Nicolas Colsaerts	74	69	72	67	282	5,341.17
Simon Hurd	72	68	72	70	282	5,341.17
Fredrik Widmark	69	70	73	70	282	5,341.17
Francois Delamontagne	75	69	69	69	282	5,341.17
Scott Kammann	72	67	72	71	282	5,341.17
Ilya Goroneskoul	71	69	72	71	283	2,889.47
Michael Archer	69	72	70	72	283	2,889.47
Massimo Florioli	67	73	68	75	283	2,889.47
Gustavo Rojas	65	71	73	74	283	2,889.47
Benn Barham	72	73	71	67	283	2,889.47
Mark Sanders	72	72	67	72	283	2,889.47
Iain Pyman	67	79	70	68	284	2,324
Lee James	72	73	66	74	285	2,200.50
Ivo Giner	70	71	71	73	285	2,200.50
Denny Lucas	70	70	76	70	286	2,046.30
John Morgan	70	71	71	74	286	2,046.30
Sam Little	73	71	71	72	287	1,922.90
Marcello Santi	72	70	72	73	287	1,922.90
Matthew Blackey	73	72	72	71	288	1,799.50
Ben Mason	73	71	71	73	288	1,799.50
Jean-Francois Lucquin	68	76	75	70	289	1,707

Asian PGA Davidoff Tour

Johnnie Walker Classic

See Australasian Tour chapter.

London Myanmar Open

Yangon Golf Club, Yangon, Myanmar
Par 36-36–72; 7,011 yards

February 7-10
purse, US$200,000

	SCORES				TOTAL	MONEY
Thongchai Jaidee	69	70	69	69	277	US$32,300
Edward Loar	65	71	70	71	277	22,260
(Thongchai defeated Loar on first playoff hole.)						
Thammanoon Sriroj	71	70	70	67	278	12,400
Arjun Atwal	70	66	70	73	279	10,000
Jyoti Randhawa	70	72	71	67	280	8,000
Aung Win	68	67	72	74	281	6,500
Thaworn Wiratchant	71	70	70	70	281	6,500
Boonchu Ruangkit	71	69	68	74	282	5,000
Kyi Hla Han	72	70	70	71	283	4,230
Andrew Pitts	74	72	70	67	283	4,230
Prayad Marksaeng	71	70	72	71	284	3,345
Danny Zarate	72	71	69	72	284	3,345
Jim Johnson	73	72	71	68	284	3,345
Simon Yates	70	72	71	71	284	3,345
Zaw Paing Oo	78	67	70	70	285	2,653.33
Rick Gibson	72	70	68	75	285	2,653.33
Rodrigo Cuello	71	72	71	71	285	2,653.33
James Oh	72	73	70	70	285	2,653.33
Akio Sadakata	73	73	68	71	285	2,653.33
Robert Jacobson	69	73	71	72	285	2,653.33
Sushi Ishigaki	71	71	72	72	286	2,250
Arjun Singh	70	74	71	71	286	2,250
Anthony Kang	71	76	69	70	286	2,250
Lu Wen-teh	69	76	70	71	286	2,250
Hiroaki Iijima	73	69	70	75	287	2,040
Harmeet Kahlon	74	70	68	75	287	2,040
Olle Nordberg	65	77	74	71	287	2,040
Terry Pilkadaris	75	70	73	70	288	1,830
Daisuke Maruyama	73	73	71	71	288	1,830
Chris Kamin	72	74	71	71	288	1,830
Felix Casas	72	75	68	73	288	1,830

Hero Honda Masters

DLF Golf and Country Club, New Delhi, India
Par 36-35–71; 7,151 yards

February 14-17
purse, US$300,000

	SCORES				TOTAL	MONEY
Harmeet Kahlon	69	68	70	70	277	US$48,450
Prayad Marksaeng	68	66	72	72	278	22,330
James Oh	73	68	72	65	278	22,330

	SCORES				TOTAL	MONEY
Thammanoon Sriroj	72	69	70	67	278	22,330
Steve Jurgensen	70	72	67	70	279	11,250
Arjun Atwal	65	74	70	70	279	11,250
Vijay Kumar	71	64	71	74	280	8,250
Daniel Chopra	67	71	70	72	280	8,250
Chung Joon	70	70	72	69	281	6,065
Clay Devers	69	70	72	70	281	6,065
Gaurav Ghei	68	71	69	73	281	6,065
Thaworn Wiratchant	73	68	70	71	282	4,855
Tatsuhiko Takahashi	67	69	74	72	282	4,855
Craig Kamps	68	71	68	75	282	4,855
Jeev Milkha Singh	68	65	76	74	283	4,056
Jyoti Randhawa	71	69	71	72	283	4,056
Greg Hanrahan	73	71	69	70	283	4,056
Lam Chih-bing	67	72	72	72	283	4,056
Rodrigo Cuello	70	72	69	72	283	4,056
Anthony Kang	72	68	73	71	284	3,465
Rick Gibson	69	69	74	72	284	3,465
Brad Kennedy	73	71	71	69	284	3,465
Simon Yates	73	73	68	70	284	3,465
Shiv Prakash	73	68	74	70	285	3,195
David Bransdon	76	70	70	69	285	3,195
Olle Nordberg	75	70	68	73	286	3,015
Edward Loar	69	72	71	74	286	3,015
Zaw Moe	72	70	74	71	287	2,835
Troy Kennedy	72	72	72	71	287	2,835
Arjun Singh	68	71	77	72	288	2,610
Ross Bain	74	71	73	70	288	2,610
Robert Pactolerin	71	73	70	74	288	2,610

Caltex Singapore Masters

Laguna National Golf & Country Club, Singapore   February 21-24
Par 36-36–72; 7,112 yards   purse, US$900,000

	SCORES				TOTAL	MONEY
Arjun Atwal	70	69	67	68	274	US$150,030
Richard Green	69	72	68	70	279	99,990
Nick Faldo	68	69	73	70	280	56,340
Thaworn Wiratchant	73	69	72	67	281	41,580
Ted Purdy	69	69	73	70	281	41,580
Jim Johnson	69	67	72	74	282	25,290
James Kingston	70	70	72	70	282	25,290
Richard Johnson	72	70	69	71	282	25,290
Chris Williams	67	71	73	71	282	25,290
Andrew Pitts	73	69	73	68	283	14,888.57
Gaurav Ghei	69	70	74	70	283	14,888.57
Stephen Leaney	70	71	74	68	283	14,888.57
Eduardo Romero	69	71	75	68	283	14,888.57
Nick O'Hern	64	71	72	76	283	14,888.57
Unho Park	67	73	74	69	283	14,888.57
Anthony Kang	69	73	71	70	283	14,888.57
Charlie Wi	70	67	72	75	284	12,150
Sushi Ishigaki	72	68	69	76	285	10,383.75
Chris Gane	71	69	74	71	285	10,383.75
Christopher Hanell	69	69	75	72	285	10,383.75
Patrik Sjoland	73	70	70	72	285	10,383.75

	SCORES				TOTAL	MONEY
Anders Hansen	71	72	72	70	285	10,383.75
Henrik Nystrom	71	72	71	71	285	10,383.75
Terry Pilkadaris	70	72	70	73	285	10,383.75
Brett Rumford	67	74	72	72	285	10,383.75
Stephen Dodd	71	70	73	72	286	8,685
Ricardo Gonzalez	71	71	75	69	286	8,685
Prayad Marksaeng	68	71	73	74	286	8,685
Brad Kennedy	70	73	70	73	286	8,685
Grant Hamerton	73	70	74	70	287	7,132.50
Mark Mouland	73	70	73	71	287	7,132.50
Bradley Dredge	69	72	73	73	287	7,132.50
Thongchai Jaidee	67	74	71	75	287	7,132.50
Jyoti Randhawa	67	75	74	71	287	7,132.50
Mardan Mamat	67	75	74	71	287	7,132.50
Jean Van de Velde	67	75	71	74	287	7,132.50
Maarten Lafeber	67	76	70	74	287	7,132.50
Ignacio Garrido	72	70	74	72	288	5,940
Mike Cunning	67	70	77	74	288	5,940
Wang Ter-chang	67	71	82	68	288	5,940
Zhang Lian-wei	69	74	69	76	288	5,940
Gary Clark	72	66	77	74	289	5,040
Peter Senior	72	69	74	74	289	5,040
Raphael Jacquelin	73	70	73	73	289	5,040
Daniel Chopra	71	71	74	73	289	5,040
Steen Tinning	68	72	76	73	289	5,040
Carlos Rodiles	66	72	72	79	289	5,040
Peter Hanson	71	69	79	71	290	3,960
Soren Hansen	71	69	78	72	290	3,960
Des Terblanche	72	70	76	72	290	3,960
Andrew Marshall	72	70	73	75	290	3,960
Hsieh Yu-shu	71	71	74	74	290	3,960
David Drysdale	71	72	72	75	290	3,960
Paul Broadhurst	70	72	75	74	291	3,060
Hong Chia-yuh	69	72	73	77	291	3,060
Simon Dyson	70	73	70	78	291	3,060
Mikael Lundberg	69	74	73	75	291	3,060
Liang Wen-chong	74	69	74	75	292	2,475
Stephen Scahill	73	70	75	74	292	2,475
Harmeet Kahlon	69	71	77	75	292	2,475
Lin Keng-chi	69	71	76	76	292	2,475
Danny Zarate	72	71	73	76	292	2,475
Christophe Pottier	65	74	74	79	292	2,475
Robert-Jan Derksen	71	72	76	74	293	2,115
Madasaamy Murugiah	69	74	76	74	293	2,115
Lucas Parsons	73	70	70	81	294	1,725
Chawalit Plaphol	70	72	78	74	294	1,725
David Park	70	72	78	74	294	1,725
Ross Bain	71	72	76	75	294	1,725
Ted Oh	68	74	75	77	294	1,725
Shigemasa Higaki	67	74	75	78	294	1,725

Carlsberg Malaysian Open

Royal Selangor Golf Club, Kuala Lumpur, Malaysia
Par 36-35–71; 6,935 yards

February 28-March 3
purse, US$1,000,000

	SCORES				TOTAL	MONEY
Alastair Forsyth	63	65	69	70	267	US$161,450
Stephen Leaney	67	67	66	67	267	111,250
(Forsyth defeated Leaney on second playoff hole.)						
Alex Cejka	68	65	70	65	268	61,950
Miguel Angel Martin	66	63	71	70	270	44,952.50
Ignacio Garrido	65	67	67	71	270	44,952.50
Des Terblanche	70	67	68	66	271	26,418
John Bickerton	70	67	68	66	271	26,418
Prayad Marksaeng	69	67	67	68	271	26,418
Ian Woosnam	68	69	66	68	271	26,418
Ricardo Gonzalez	65	69	68	69	271	26,418
Anthony Kang	66	65	71	70	272	16,682.75
Maarten Lafeber	66	67	72	67	272	16,682.75
Arjun Singh	67	67	70	68	272	16,682.75
Padraig Harrington	70	67	66	69	272	16,682.75
Jyoti Randhawa	66	70	70	67	273	14,658
Brad Kennedy	68	67	69	70	274	13,758
Richard Johnson	68	67	66	73	274	13,758
Joakim Haeggman	72	65	68	70	275	12,391.33
Christian Pena	70	71	71	63	275	12,391.33
Barry Lane	63	71	71	70	275	12,391.33
Andrew Pitts	69	66	71	70	276	10,908
Michael Campbell	69	66	69	72	276	10,908
Steen Tinning	69	68	72	67	276	10,908
Ted Purdy	71	68	68	69	276	10,908
Henrik Nystrom	71	69	68	68	276	10,908
Carlos Rodiles	67	69	69	71	276	10,908
Thongchai Jaidee	73	68	69	67	277	9,108
Andrew Coltart	69	68	71	69	277	9,108
Desvonde Botes	68	70	72	67	277	9,108
Jorge Berendt	70	70	65	72	277	9,108
Eduardo Romero	68	70	66	73	277	9,108
Harmeet Kahlon	65	72	68	72	277	9,108
Philip Golding	66	67	73	72	278	7,758
Thomas Levet	68	69	71	70	278	7,758
Daisuke Maruyama	69	69	70	70	278	7,758
Kim Felton	69	70	68	71	278	7,758
Yeh Wei-tze	68	72	69	69	278	7,758
Mike Cunning	69	65	69	76	279	6,658
Liang Wen-chong	72	68	69	70	279	6,658
Soren Kjeldsen	71	69	69	70	279	6,658
Gary Rusnak	69	70	70	70	279	6,658
Brett Rumford	69	72	70	68	279	6,658
Thaworn Wiratchant	66	72	67	74	279	6,658
Olle Nordberg	73	67	71	69	280	4,958
Thammanoon Sriroj	71	69	71	69	280	4,958
Sushi Ishigaki	68	69	73	70	280	4,958
Zhang Lian-wei	68	69	71	72	280	4,958
Charlie Wi	72	69	68	71	280	4,958
Simon Dyson	69	70	70	71	280	4,958
Patrik Sjoland	68	70	70	72	280	4,958
Christopher Hanell	69	70	67	74	280	4,958
Nick O'Hern	67	71	72	70	280	4,958
Warren Bennett	68	71	71	70	280	4,958

	SCORES				TOTAL	MONEY
Danny Zarate	70	71	69	70	280	4,958
Robert-Jan Derksen	72	67	71	71	281	3,558
Chris Williams	70	71	72	68	281	3,558
Kenny Druce	69	71	70	71	281	3,558
Periasamy Gunasegaran	70	68	73	71	282	3,008
Lin Keng-chi	69	70	71	72	282	3,008
Anders Hansen	69	71	71	71	282	3,008
Chawalit Plaphol	68	73	68	73	282	3,008
Mark Mouland	72	69	69	73	283	2,708
Jarrod Moseley	66	73	72	72	283	2,708
Roger Wessels	70	69	72	73	284	2,458
Jarmo Sandelin	69	69	70	76	284	2,458
Olle Karlsson	70	71	71	72	284	2,458
Kang Wook-soon	70	69	73	73	285	2,204
Mark Pilkington	69	69	72	75	285	2,204
Gerald Rosales	71	70	72	73	286	1,833.33
Craig Kamps	71	70	71	74	286	1,833.33
Chris Gane	69	72	69	76	286	1,833.33
Andrew Marshall	70	69	74	74	287	1,496.14
Gregory Havret	69	70	76	72	287	1,496.14
Ahmad Bateman	71	69	70	78	288	1,492.20
Raphael Jacquelin	68	73	74	74	289	1,489.57
Scott Kammann	71	70	72	77	290	1,485.63
Peter Senior	70	71	73	76	290	1,485.63

Casino Filipino Philippine Open

Wack Wack Golf & Country Club, Manila, Philippines
Par 36-36–72; 7,053 yards

March 7-10
purse, US$175,000

	SCORES				TOTAL	MONEY
Rick Gibson	68	69	73	73	283	US$29,172.50
Robert Jacobson	78	74	68	67	287	19,250
Pablo Del Olmo	72	72	76	68	288	10,850
Anthony Kang	74	69	73	73	289	8,050
Tony Lascuna	71	70	75	73	289	8,050
Danny Chia	73	73	72	73	291	5,950
Greg Hanrahan	70	68	81	73	292	4,900
*Angelo Que	69	73	78	72	292	
Kang Wook-soon	75	71	71	76	293	3,955
Chris Kamin	78	73	73	70	294	3,325
Sushi Ishigaki	73	73	76	72	294	3,325
Gerald Rosales	74	73	74	74	295	2,905
Mo Joong-kyung	73	73	75	74	295	2,905
Hsu Mong-nan	70	75	79	71	295	2,905
Chawalit Plaphol	72	70	74	80	296	2,590
Amandeep Johl	74	75	75	72	296	2,590
Jim Johnson	72	75	76	73	296	2,590
Kim Sang-ki	69	75	77	75	296	2,590
Tatsuya Shiraishi	73	76	74	73	296	2,590
Elmer Salvador	75	75	75	72	297	2,310
Joon Choi	74	75	74	74	297	2,310
Kyi Hla Han	70	78	77	72	297	2,310
Kim Sung-yoon	74	72	81	71	298	2,030
Frankie Minoza	70	72	81	75	298	2,030
Saneh Saengsui	71	74	78	75	298	2,030
Richie Sinfuego	72	77	79	70	298	2,030

	SCORES				TOTAL	MONEY
Terry Pilkadaris	73	77	72	76	298	2,030
Alex Oh	83	67	78	71	299	1,645
James Stewart	75	73	77	74	299	1,645
Kim Jong-myung	72	73	75	79	299	1,645
Carito Villaroman	75	75	75	74	299	1,645
*Marlon Dizon	72	75	76	76	299	
Dominique Boulet	71	77	75	76	299	1,645
Steve Jurgensen	74	78	74	73	299	1,645

Royal Challenge Indian Open

Delhi Golf Club, New Delhi, India
Par 36-36–72; 6,802 yards

March 14-17
purse, US$300,000

	SCORES				TOTAL	MONEY
Vijay Kumar	70	66	68	71	275	US$50,000
Rick Gibson	69	71	67	70	277	33,090
Digvijay Singh	72	69	69	71	281	18,325
Liang Wen-chong	71	76	67	68	282	13,262.50
Mo Joong-kyung	68	78	68	68	282	13,262.50
Soe Kyaw Naing	72	67	70	74	283	7,838
Thammanoon Sriroj	70	68	75	70	283	7,838
Dean Alaban	69	69	72	73	283	7,838
Andrew Pitts	67	70	74	72	283	7,838
Mardan Mamat	66	73	70	74	283	7,838
Craig Kamps	68	71	74	71	284	5,505
Chris Wilson	73	72	71	69	285	4,855
Jeff Burns	70	72	74	69	285	4,855
Danny Zarate	71	72	70	72	285	4,855
Shiv Prakash	78	68	73	67	286	4,140
Clay Devers	75	68	71	72	286	4,140
Mike Cunning	71	69	74	72	286	4,140
Uttam Singh Mundy	75	70	69	72	286	4,140
Unho Park	73	68	74	72	287	3,288
Thaworn Wiratchant	70	71	68	78	287	3,288
Amandeep Johl	73	72	74	68	287	3,288
Akio Sadakata	68	72	72	75	287	3,288
Chris Rodgers	73	73	72	69	287	3,288
Anthony Kang	70	73	73	71	287	3,288
Scott Taylor	73	73	70	71	287	3,288
Arjun Singh	69	74	74	70	287	3,288
Hendrik Buhrmann	70	74	71	72	287	3,288
Steve Jurgensen	69	75	70	73	287	3,288
Robert Jacobson	76	67	74	71	288	2,545.71
Lin Chie-hsiang	72	71	71	74	288	2,545.71
Chen Yuan-chi	74	72	70	72	288	2,545.71
Marciano Pucay	72	74	69	73	288	2,545.71
Pablo Del Olmo	66	74	73	75	288	2,545.71
Harmeet Kahlon	70	75	74	69	288	2,545.71
Vinod Kumar	67	77	67	77	288	2,545.71

SK Telecom Open

Lakeside Golf Club, South Course, Seoul, Korea
Par 36-36–72; 7,317 yards

April 25-28
purse, US$400,000

	SCORES				TOTAL	MONEY
Charlie Wi	67	69	67	69	272	US$68,078.67
Kevin Na	69	65	73	67	274	32,148.26
Kim Felton	68	68	71	67	274	32,148.26
Kim Dae-sub	70	70	68	68	276	18,910.74
Chris Williams	70	68	72	67	277	12,291.98
Chung Joon	72	69	67	69	277	12,291.98
Simon Yates	68	70	72	67	277	12,291.98
David Gleeson	71	70	69	67	277	12,291.98
Scott Kammann	71	70	68	70	279	8,320.73
Kim Tae-hoon	72	69	66	76	283	6,713.31
Amandeep Johl	74	70	71	68	283	6,713.31
Hendrik Buhrmann	72	70	73	68	283	6,713.31
Lee Jun-young	69	72	74	68	283	6,713.31
*Kim Byung-kwan	72	67	75	70	284	
Ahmad Bateman	73	70	71	70	284	5,276.10
Kang Wook-soon	71	74	69	70	284	5,276.10
Chawalit Plaphol	70	74	68	72	284	5,276.10
Taimur Hussain	67	75	72	70	284	5,276.10
Robert Jacobson	66	74	70	75	285	4,841.15
Mike Cunning	73	70	71	72	286	4,614.22
Wang Ter-chang	75	71	69	71	286	4,614.22
Anthony Kang	73	68	73	73	287	4,027.99
*Kang Kyung-nam	74	68	71	74	287	
Lee In-woo	74	70	71	72	287	4,027.99
*Hyun Jung-hyub	70	70	71	76	287	
Boonchu Ruangkit	73	71	74	69	287	4,027.99
Lee Boo-young	72	71	73	71	287	4,027.99
Gerry Norquist	69	71	73	74	287	4,027.99
Clay Devers	70	73	74	70	287	4,027.99
Mardan Mamat	67	74	73	73	287	4,027.99
James Kingston	67	74	72	74	287	4,027.99

Maekyung LG Fashion Open

Nam Seoul Country Club, Seoul, Korea
Par 36-36–72; 6,796 yards

May 2-5
purse, US$350,000

	SCORES				TOTAL	MONEY
*Lee Seung-yong	70	64	69	65	268	
Thammanoon Sriroj	69	66	66	68	269	US$76,569
Park Do-kyu	66	67	72	67	272	47,856
Ahmad Bateman	67	66	71	69	273	21,056
Brad Kennedy	73	68	67	65	273	21,056
Park Nam-sin	68	68	69	69	274	12,225
Kevin Na	73	69	68	64	274	12,225
Hsieh Yu-shu	72	71	66	65	274	12,225
Choi Gwang-soo	71	66	68	70	275	8,116
Yeh Wei-tze	70	68	67	70	275	8,116
Scott Kammann	69	67	73	67	276	6,278
Choi Sang-ho	70	69	70	67	276	6,278
Chawalit Plaphol	72	70	66	68	276	6,278
Edward Loar	71	67	70	69	277	5,206

	SCORES				TOTAL	MONEY
Rick Gibson	71	68	70	68	277	5,206
Kim Dae-sub	71	71	66	69	277	5,206
Kang Wook-soon	65	71	70	71	277	5,206
Hong Chia-yuh	72	69	70	67	278	4,670
Anthony Kang	75	69	65	69	278	4,670
Taimur Hussain	69	72	68	69	278	4,670
David Gleeson	73	68	69	69	279	4,230
*Choi Joon-woo	73	69	68	69	279	
Simon Yates	71	69	69	70	279	4,230
Lu Wen-teh	69	70	70	70	279	4,230
Yang Yong-eun	70	70	69	70	279	4,230
Jim Johnson	72	71	69	68	280	3,943
*Chung Ji-ho	73	68	70	70	281	
Aaron Meeks	74	70	70	67	281	3,771
*Kang Kyung-nam	71	71	69	70	281	
Daisuke Maruyama	70	74	69	68	281	3,771

Mercuries Masters

Taiwan Golf & Country Club, Taipei, Taiwan
Par 36-36–72; 6,950 yards

August 22-25
purse, US$300,000

	SCORES				TOTAL	MONEY
Tsai Chi-huang	68	69	68	69	274	US$71,005.92
Lu Wen-teh	69	65	73	72	279	42,603.55
Hsieh Yu-shu	70	66	72	72	280	16,863.91
Hong Chia-yuh	71	68	69	72	280	16,863.91
Hsieh Chin-sheng	70	69	69	72	280	16,863.91
Aaron Meeks	65	70	75	70	280	16,863.91
Lin Keng-chi	76	68	69	68	281	8,372.78
Lee Lien-fu	71	75	67	68	281	8,372.78
Thammanoon Sriroj	70	69	72	71	282	7,100.59
Kevin Na	72	71	70	70	283	5,307.69
Boonchu Ruangkit	69	72	72	70	283	5,307.69
Danny Zarate	73	72	68	70	283	5,307.69
Kim Felton	68	72	69	74	283	5,307.69
Hsu Mong-nan	72	74	71	66	283	5,307.69
Jyoti Randhawa	76	69	70	69	284	4,207.10
Gerald Rosales	73	70	74	67	284	4,207.10
Stephen Lindskog	70	70	73	71	284	4,207.10
Prayad Marksaeng	71	71	71	72	285	3,767.26
Pablo Del Olmo	72	72	70	71	285	3,767.26
Unho Park	72	75	71	67	285	3,767.26
Brad Kennedy	70	72	72	72	286	3,529.59
Yeh Yeou-tsai	71	74	68	73	286	3,529.59
David Gleeson	70	69	75	73	287	3,301.78
Chung Chun-hsing	72	70	71	74	287	3,301.78
Gary Rusnak	72	71	74	70	287	3,301.78
Yeh Wei-tze	69	76	71	71	287	3,301.78
Chen Tsang-te	73	70	71	74	288	3,076.92
Chris Rodgers	73	72	70	73	288	3,076.92
Chen Liang-hsi	73	72	74	70	289	2,934.91
Gerry Norquist	74	72	69	74	289	2,934.91
Gaurav Ghei	71	75	73	70	289	2,934.91

Shinhan Donghae Open

Jae Il Country Club, Seoul, Korea
Par 36-36–72

August 29-September 1
purse, US$400,000

	SCORES				TOTAL	MONEY
Hur Suk-ho	65	67	72	72	276	US$81,566
Simon Yates	72	65	70	69	276	48,939
(Hur defeated Yates on second playoff hole.)						
Choi Sang-ho	66	68	74	69	277	30,995
Park Boo-won	67	67	75	69	278	22,022
Choi Gwang-soo	67	66	72	74	279	19,575
Kim Jong-duck	70	68	70	72	280	16,313
Unho Park	71	67	73	71	282	13,866
Park Young-soo	71	66	69	77	283	10,603
Song Byung-keun	67	68	75	73	283	10,603
Jang Ik-Jae	70	69	71	73	283	10,603
Chris Williams	72	68	75	69	284	7,748
Gerald Rosales	72	70	70	72	284	7,748
*Kim Seung-hyuk	67	73	74	70	284	
Jyoti Randhawa	68	70	73	74	285	5,519
Kang Wook-soon	66	70	74	75	285	5,519
Daniel Chopra	67	71	76	71	285	5,519
Lee Boo-young	69	72	74	70	285	5,519
Thammanoon Sriroj	70	72	71	72	285	5,519
Andrew Pitts	66	74	74	71	285	5,519
Yang Yong-eun	70	72	73	71	286	4,404
Amandeep Johl	70	69	73	75	287	3,853
*Kwon Ki-taek	71	70	72	74	287	
Brad Kennedy	70	71	75	71	287	3,853
Clay Devers	71	71	72	73	287	3,853
Jun Tae-hyun	70	73	74	70	287	3,853
Kim Tae-hoon	73	65	75	75	288	3,371
Stephen Lindskog	73	66	78	71	288	3,371
Kang Ji-man	67	69	76	76	288	3,371
*Sung Si-woo	67	72	78	71	288	
Kong Young-joon	69	68	79	73	289	3,066
Kim Hong-sik	70	70	78	71	289	3,066
David Gleeson	71	71	73	74	289	3,066
*Hyun Jung-hyub	70	72	75	72	289	
Kim Dae-sub	68	72	73	76	289	3,066
Cho Chul-sang	68	73	77	71	289	3,066

Kolon Cup Korean Open

Seoul Hanyang Country Club, Seoul, Korea
Par 36-36–72; 6,374 yards

September 5-8
purse, US$350,000

	SCORES				TOTAL	MONEY
Sergio Garcia	67	65	66	67	265	US$81,900
Kang Wook-soon	66	67	66	69	268	40,950
Choi Gwang-soo	70	72	67	66	275	21,021
Park Nam-sin	68	71	64	72	275	21,021
Kim Jong-duck	71	69	67	68	275	21,021
Jun Tae-hyun	70	73	68	66	277	13,022
K.J. Choi	69	66	73	69	277	13,022
Sushi Ishigaki	66	72	66	73	277	13,022
Anthony Kang	67	71	75	66	279	9,029

	SCORES				TOTAL	MONEY
Shin Yong-jin	66	73	74	66	279	9,029
Kevin Na	69	69	72	69	279	9,029
Thammanoon Sriroj	69	71	68	71	279	9,029
Kim Hyung-tae	70	70	71	69	280	6,592
Jyoti Randhawa	70	73	67	71	281	5,184
Choi Sang-ho	66	76	69	70	281	5,184
Brad Kennedy	70	70	71	70	281	5,184
Craig Kamps	71	67	71	72	281	5,184
Adam Scott	70	73	65	73	281	5,184
Amandeep Johl	72	70	70	70	282	4,627
*Chung Ji-ho	73	68	73	69	283	
*Lee Seung-yong	67	75	70	71	283	
Park Boo-won	69	73	71	70	283	4,299
Rafael Ponce	70	74	68	71	283	4,299
Chung Joon	69	70	69	75	283	4,299
Hendrik Buhrmann	69	73	73	69	284	3,685
Mo Joong-kyung	70	73	71	70	284	3,685
Park Young-soo	70	72	71	71	284	3,685
Mike Cunning	71	69	70	74	284	3,685
Alex Oh	71	69	70	74	284	3,685
Park No-seok	70	71	70	73	284	3,685

Volvo China Open

Shanghai Silport Golf Club, Shanghai, China
Par 36-36–72; 7,062 yards

September 12-15
purse, US$500,000

	SCORES				TOTAL	MONEY
David Gleeson	65	67	69	71	272	US$90,000
Pablo Del Olmo	68	65	72	68	273	55,500
James Kingston	67	70	64	73	274	30,900
Brad Kennedy	68	66	75	69	278	24,000
Zhang Lian-wei	70	69	70	70	279	19,000
Scott Hend	70	66	72	72	280	15,250
Kim Felton	67	69	70	74	280	15,250
Chris Kamin	72	73	71	66	282	9,644
Arjun Singh	72	73	67	70	282	9,644
Kyi Hla Han	69	72	70	71	282	9,644
Kevin Na	66	73	72	71	282	9,644
Liang Wen-chong	69	72	69	72	282	9,644
Lin Chien-bing	72	67	69	76	284	7,890
Des Terblanche	66	71	74	74	285	6,978
Wang Ter-chang	72	69	70	74	285	6,978
Clay Devers	71	70	69	75	285	6,978
Jyoti Randhawa	69	67	72	77	285	6,978
Sushi Ishigaki	66	71	71	77	285	6,978
Gary Rusnak	71	71	75	69	286	6,000
Ross Bain	70	69	74	73	286	6,000
Hong Chia-yuh	73	66	73	74	286	6,000
Danny Zarate	69	71	74	73	287	5,600
Lam Chih-bing	71	73	70	73	287	5,600
Simon Yates	67	77	74	70	288	5,080
Chris Rodgers	72	72	71	73	288	5,080
Amandeep Johl	74	69	72	73	288	5,080
Craig Kamps	71	70	73	74	288	5,080
Aaron Meeks	69	72	72	75	288	5,080
Dean Alaban	73	74	72	70	289	4,175
Tsai Chi-huang	69	72	76	72	289	4,175

	SCORES				TOTAL	MONEY
Taimur Hussain	71	72	74	72	289	4,175
Michael Wright	75	69	72	73	289	4,175
Jamnian Chitprasong	71	71	72	75	289	4,175
Stephen Lindskog	71	70	73	75	289	4,175
Chris Williams	69	73	72	75	289	4,175
Mardan Mamat	74	67	72	76	289	4,175

Acer Taiwan Open

Sunrise Golf & Country Club, Taipei, Taiwan
Par 36-36–72; 7,062 yards

September 19-22
purse, US$300,000

	SCORES				TOTAL	MONEY
Danny Chia	76	70	77	68	291	US$50,000
Lin Chie-hsiang	74	74	79	66	293	25,707.50
Hsieh Yu-shu	75	72	69	77	293	25,707.50
Gareth Paddison	80	74	73	67	294	12,275
Chang Tse-peng	79	72	73	70	294	12,275
Anthony Kang	75	75	74	70	294	12,275
James Kingston	80	67	76	72	295	8,100
Chris Williams	78	70	74	73	295	8,100
Hong Chia-yuh	81	74	73	68	296	5,836.50
Clay Devers	72	79	74	71	296	5,836.50
Chung Chun-hsing	75	74	74	73	296	5,836.50
*Kao Bo-song	73	70	80	73	296	
Andrew Pitts	75	72	73	76	296	5,836.50
Peter Senior	78	73	76	70	297	4,707
Pablo Del Olmo	78	72	73	74	297	4,707
*Hung Yu-lin	77	77	74	70	298	
Aaron Meeks	80	73	74	71	298	4,230
*Sung Mao-chang	79	73	74	72	298	
Hendrik Buhrmann	77	72	76	73	298	4,230
Thammanoon Sriroj	75	73	74	76	298	4,230
Boonchu Ruangkit	78	69	82	70	299	3,624
Craig Kamps	81	74	73	71	299	3,624
Greg Hanrahan	77	76	75	71	299	3,624
Edward Loar	78	67	79	75	299	3,624
Hsu Mong-nan	73	79	70	77	299	3,624
Mardan Mamat	78	78	77	67	300	3,060
Michael Christensen	77	72	80	71	300	3,060
Lin Wen-tang	75	71	82	72	300	3,060
Chou Hung-nam	75	77	75	73	300	3,060
Jeff Burns	78	77	71	74	300	3,060
Adrian Percey	78	72	73	77	300	3,060
Brad Kennedy	78	69	74	79	300	3,060

Macau Open

Macau Golf & Country Club, Macau
Par 35-36–71; 6,622 yards

October 17-20
purse, US$250,000

	SCORES				TOTAL	MONEY
Zhang Lian-wei	71	69	67	70	277	US$40,375
Nick Price	66	71	71	69	277	27,825

(Zhang defeated Price on fifth playoff hole.)

	SCORES				TOTAL	MONEY
Tsai Chi-huang	71	71	68	68	278	14,000
Stephen Lindskog	69	67	70	72	278	14,000
Wang Ter-chang	73	68	68	70	279	9,375
Yang Yong-eun	71	71	68	69	279	9,375
Zaw Moe	70	66	73	71	280	7,500
Ahmad Bateman	75	69	66	71	281	6,250
Lu Wen-teh	70	75	66	71	282	5,287.50
Liang Wen-chong	75	68	68	71	282	5,287.50
Hendrik Buhrmann	72	66	74	71	283	4,300
Gary Rusnak	70	70	71	72	283	4,300
Yeh Wei-tze	70	70	70	73	283	4,300
Thaworn Wiratchant	75	72	68	69	284	3,675
James Kingston	71	70	72	71	284	3,675
Simon Yates	70	75	69	70	284	3,675
Danny Chia	70	71	76	68	285	3,233.33
Rafael Ponce	67	71	78	69	285	3,233.33
Danny Zarate	71	73	69	72	285	3,233.33
Craig Kamps	73	73	70	70	286	2,662.50
Chen Yuan-chi	74	70	72	70	286	2,632.50
Kim Sang-ki	80	66	69	71	286	2,662.50
Jamnian Chitprasong	72	70	73	71	286	2,662.50
Greg Hanrahan	73	71	70	72	286	2,662.50
Mo Joong-kyung	75	67	72	72	286	2,662.50
Rick Gibson	71	71	72	72	286	2,662.50
Gerald Rosales	75	70	69	72	286	2,662.50
Hsieh Yu-shu	73	71	68	74	286	2,662.50
Justin Hobday	71	70	69	76	286	2,662.50
Hsu Mong-nan	72	71	73	71	287	2,115
Wayne Bradley	72	70	74	71	287	2,115
Mahal Pearce	75	71	70	71	287	2,115
Jim Johnson	73	73	69	72	287	2,115
Chang Tse-peng	70	70	72	75	287	2,115

TCL Classic

Harbour Plaza Golf Club, Dongguan, China
Par 36-36–72; 7,084 yards

November 14-17
purse, US$1,000,000

	SCORES				TOTAL	MONEY
Colin Montgomerie	70	68	67	67	272	US$161,500
Thongchai Jaidee	68	67	68	71	274	111,300
Liang Wen-chong	78	66	65	69	278	62,000
Bob May	71	67	73	68	279	45,000
Michael Campbell	73	70	67	69	279	45,000
Hendrik Buhrmann	70	68	74	68	280	28,075
Ted Purdy	70	71	71	68	280	28,075
Andrew Coltart	71	68	72	69	280	28,075
Wang Ter-chang	69	71	71	69	280	28,075
Jyoti Randhawa	70	73	69	70	282	20,000
Simon Yates	71	72	73	67	283	16,725
Lee Westwood	68	70	74	71	283	16,725
Paul McGinley	71	69	71	72	283	16,725
Zhang Lian-wei	70	70	71	72	283	16,725
Fran Quinn	71	71	72	70	284	13,800
Chung Joon	68	73	72	71	284	13,800
Craig Kamps	70	70	73	71	284	13,800
Charlie Wi	68	72	70	74	284	13,800

	SCORES				TOTAL	MONEY
Kyi Hla Han	70	70	73	72	285	11,720
Zaw Moe	68	73	71	73	285	11,720
Carlos Franco	73	68	71	73	285	11,720
Prayad Marksaeng	69	71	70	75	285	11,720
Ted Oh	67	71	70	77	285	11,720
Yeh Wei-tze	74	71	72	69	286	10,500
Jon Levitt	72	69	73	72	286	10,500
Thammanoon Sriroj	71	71	70	74	286	10,500
Rick Gibson	69	70	74	74	287	9,750
Danny Zarate	69	71	72	75	287	9,750
Mardan Mamat	73	70	75	70	288	8,720
Des Terblanche	73	70	73	72	288	8,720
Chawalit Plaphol	71	72	73	72	288	8,720
Rafael Ponce	70	73	72	73	288	8,720
Boonchu Ruangkit	72	73	70	73	288	8,720

BMW Asian Open

Ta Shee Golf & Country Club, Taipei, Taiwan   November 21-24
Par 36-36–72; 7,104 yards   purse, US$1,500,000

	SCORES				TOTAL	MONEY
Padraig Harrington	66	70	68	69	273	US$250,000
Jyoti Randhawa	65	75	70	64	274	166,660
Andrew Pitts	67	70	69	70	276	77,500
Maarten Lafeber	66	66	71	73	276	77,500
Trevor Immelman	69	67	68	72	276	77,500
Thongchai Jaidee	71	67	70	69	277	52,500
Daniel Chopra	71	73	67	67	278	36,525
Rick Gibson	72	69	69	68	278	36,525
Soren Hansen	71	68	70	69	278	36,525
Ian Woosnam	71	69	68	70	278	36,525
Arjun Atwal	72	73	69	65	279	26,700
Kang Wook-soon	74	68	68	69	279	26,700
Gregory Hanrahan	73	72	68	67	280	22,575
Ted Oh	71	71	68	70	280	22,575
Simon Yates	67	71	71	71	280	22,575
Henrik Nystrom	67	75	67	71	280	22,575
Dean Robertson	70	74	71	66	281	19,050
Tony Johnstone	71	70	72	68	281	19,050
Kim Felton	69	72	70	70	281	19,050
James Kingston	68	70	71	72	281	19,050
Barry Lane	70	69	74	69	282	16,950
Sam Torrance	73	67	72	70	282	16,950
Adrian Percey	68	69	73	72	282	16,950
Simon Hurd	71	70	75	67	283	14,925
Yeh Wei-tze	69	71	74	69	283	14,925
Kenneth Ferrie	71	70	73	69	283	14,925
David Park	69	74	71	69	283	14,925
Marc Farry	70	73	70	70	283	14,925
Jarmo Sandelin	67	74	70	72	283	14,925
Des Terblanche	67	75	73	69	284	12,250
Jean-Francois Lucquin	69	73	72	70	284	12,250
Andrew Coltart	72	71	71	70	284	12,250
John Daly	70	74	70	70	284	12,250
Tobias Dier	71	70	72	71	284	12,250
Arjun Singh	68	70	73	73	284	12,250

The Johnnie Walker Classic was the first of Retief Goosen's three 2002 victories and he won $3.8 million worldwide. Goosen also won the Dimension Data Pro-Am and BellSouth Classic.

Padraig Harrington was second to Goosen on the European Order of Merit.

Ernie Els had six worldwide victories.   Eduardo Romero won at Loch Lomond.

Colin Montgomerie needed a tie with Bernhard Langer in the Volvo Masters to win for the 10th consecutive year. He later won in Asia.

Michael Campbell took the European title.

Justin Rose came of age with four wins.

Sergio Garcia won three times worldwide and earned over $3.8 million.

Adam Scott had two victories.

Thomas Bjorn won the BMW.

Stephen Leaney ranked 15th in Europe.

Jose Maria Olazabal won in Asia.

Trevor Immelman was 14th in Europe.

Soren Hansen took the Irish title.

European Tour winners, from left, Angel Cabrera (Benson & Hedges), Anders Hansen (Volvo PGA) and Paul Lawrie (Wales).

Ian Poulter was the Italian victor.

Niclas Fasth was 17th in Europe.

Darren Clarke fell to 22nd in Europe.

Alex Cejka had a victory in France.

Bernhard Langer shared one title.

Carl Pettersson won in Portugal.

Cisco World Match Play

Phil Inglis

Ernie Els won his fourth Cisco World Match Play title, one victory short of the record shared by Gary Player and Seve Ballesteros.

Ross Kinnaird/Getty Images

Warren Little/Getty Images

Vijay Singh lost to Els in the semi-finals.

Andrew Redington/Getty Images

Sergio Garcia was defeated in the final.

Michael Campbell was beaten by Garcia.

Ryder Cup

Captain Sam Torrance's European squad gathers around the Ryder Cup after their 15½-14½ victory over the United States.

Colin Montgomerie posted a 4-0-1 record.

Bernhard Langer went 3-0-1 for Europe.

Lee Westwood (left) and Sergio Garcia formed an effective European partnership, and each finished with a 3-2 record.

Tiger Woods went 2-2-1 after starting with two losses.

David Toms finished at 3-1-1.

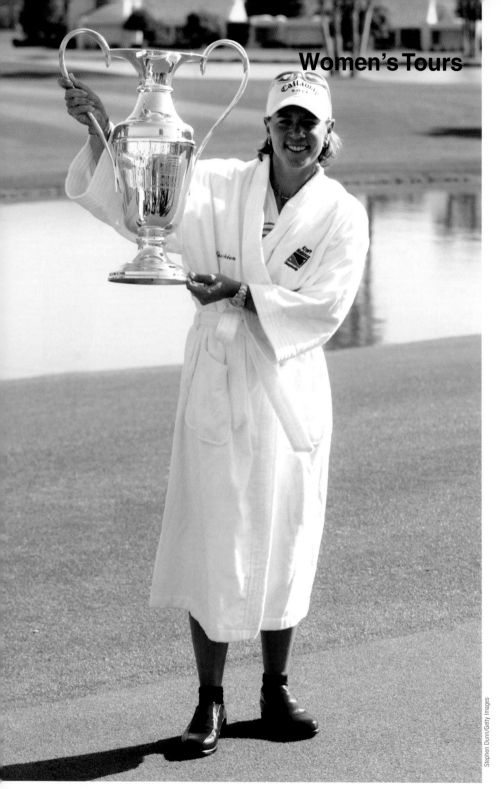

Annika Sorenstam, still wearing her red shoes after diving in the lake, won the Kraft Nabisco Championship, one of 11 LPGA victories and 13 worldwide, which earned her $3.3 million.

Se Ri Pak's five wins included the McDonald's.

Juli Inkster claimed the U.S. Women's Open.

Mi Hyun Kim had two victories in three weeks.

Karrie Webb won on three continents.

Laura Diaz posted victories in the Welch's/Circle K and Corning Classic events.

Carin Koch finished eighth on the money list.

Cristie Kerr won the Longs Drugs Challenge.

Grace Park won the Cisco Match Play.

Rachel Teske started with a victory.

Nancy Lopez completed her final year.

Paula Marti was the European money leader.

Sophie Gustafson won in Europe.

Yuri Fudoh posted four victories in Japan.

Senior Tours

Hale Irwin had four Senior PGA Tour victories and $3.3 million in total earnings.

Bob Gilder twice won back-to-back to have four victories and $2.7 million overall.

Bruce Lietzke won three times.

Tom Kite was fourth on the money list.

Bruce Fleisher took the RJR title.

Tom Watson was Senior Tour champion.

Don Pooley took the Senior Open.

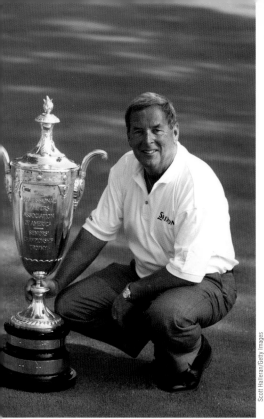

Fuzzy Zoeller claimed the Senior PGA.

Stewart Ginn won the Senior Players.

Seiji Ebihara won in Europe, Japan.

Noboru Sugai was British champion.

	SCORES			TOTAL	MONEY
Soren Kjeldsen	71	70	73	71	285	10,350
Patrik Sjoland	72	71	71	71	285	10,350
Alastair Forsyth	73	71	70	71	285	10,350
Anthony Wall	70	72	71	72	285	10,350
Sven Struver	66	74	72	73	285	10,350
Julien Van Hauwe	68	74	76	68	286	8,400
Lu Wen-teh	73	72	73	68	286	8,400
Jamie Spence	71	73	73	69	286	8,400
Jonathan Lomas	72	71	73	70	286	8,400
Pablo Del Olmo	72	71	72	71	286	8,400
Derek Fung	71	73	71	71	286	8,400
Vijay Kumar	71	74	70	71	286	8,400
Jose Maria Olazabal	73	72	70	71	286	8,400
Miguel Angel Jimenez	73	69	77	68	287	6,750
Fran Quinn	68	74	71	74	287	6,750
Kevin Na	71	67	74	75	287	6,750
Charlie Wi	70	72	77	69	288	5,850
Peter Baker	71	71	75	71	288	5,850
Anthony Kang	69	71	75	73	288	5,850
Wang Ter-chang	73	72	74	70	289	4,837.50
Mikko Ilonen	71	70	77	71	289	4,837.50
Ted Purdy	71	72	74	72	289	4,837.50
Rafael Ponce	70	72	75	72	289	4,837.50
John Morgan	74	70	79	67	290	4,125
Danny Zarate	74	71	74	71	290	4,125
Thaworn Wiratchant	70	72	76	72	290	4,125
Chung Chun-hsing	73	72	73	72	290	4,125
Chen Tze-chung	72	73	72	74	291	3,600
Peter Lawrie	71	72	72	76	291	3,600
Sushi Ishigaki	71	72	72	76	291	3,600
Stephen Dodd	71	73	76	72	292	3,300
Gary Rusnak	73	72	77	71	293	2,935
Fredrik Jacobson	75	70	75	73	293	2,935
Clay Devers	71	72	75	75	293	2,935
Ahmad Bateman	72	72	73	76	293	2,935
Gustavo Rojas	72	73	74	76	295	2,248.79
Thammanoon Sriroj	73	71	73	78	295	2,248.79
Mike Cunning	72	72	79	77	300	2,244.25

Omega Hong Kong Open

Hong Kong Golf Club, Hong Kong
Par 35-36–71; 6,697 yards

November 28-December 1
purse, US$700,000

	SCORES			TOTAL	MONEY
Fredrik Jacobson	68	65	63	64	260	US$113,000
Jorge Berendt	68	65	62	67	262	60,615
Henrik Nystrom	64	68	63	67	262	60,615
Soren Kjeldsen	65	70	63	65	263	29,126.67
Gary Orr	67	66	63	67	263	29,126.67
Stephen Dodd	64	65	66	68	263	29,126.67
Tony Johnstone	64	65	67	68	264	20,960
Thomas Levet	65	65	69	66	265	15,663.33
Jyoti Randhawa	67	62	69	67	265	15,663.33
Craig Kamps	68	63	66	68	265	15,663.33
Nicolas Colsaerts	68	64	69	65	266	10,643.13
Rick Gibson	67	65	68	66	266	10,643.13

		SCORES			TOTAL	MONEY
Marten Olander	65	64	70	67	266	10,643.13
Nick Faldo	68	65	66	67	266	10,643.13
Matthew Blackey	66	67	65	68	266	10,643.13
Jamie Spence	68	65	64	69	266	10,643.13
Arjun Singh	65	66	65	70	266	10,643.13
Boonchu Ruangkit	65	69	62	70	266	10,643.13
Gerald Rosales	70	64	68	66	268	8,383.33
Andrew Marshall	68	64	68	68	268	8,383.33
Henrik Bjornstad	67	62	69	70	268	8,383.33
Adrian Percey	66	67	70	66	269	7,625
Jean-Francois Lucquin	68	67	66	68	269	7,625
Maarten Lafeber	67	64	69	69	269	7,625
Dean Robertson	65	68	67	69	269	7,625
Clay Devers	66	64	73	67	270	6,470
Lu Wen-teh	68	69	65	68	270	6,470
Kevin Na	69	64	68	69	270	6,470
Anders Hansen	72	65	64	69	270	6,470
Barry Lane	66	67	67	70	270	6,470
Zhang Lian-wei	67	66	67	70	270	6,470
Kang Wook-soon	67	64	68	71	270	6,470
Chris Williams	68	66	70	67	271	5,280
Simon Yates	67	69	68	67	271	5,280
Vivek Bhandari	68	67	68	68	271	5,280
Danny Chia	68	66	69	68	271	5,280
Gary Rusnak	66	67	69	69	271	5,280
Pablo Del Olmo	64	71	66	70	271	5,280
Johan Rystrom	69	66	65	71	271	5,280
Marc Farry	70	65	68	69	272	4,230
Stephen Gallacher	69	66	67	70	272	4,230
Park Do-kyu	68	68	66	70	272	4,230
Wang Ter-chang	65	64	72	71	272	4,230
Peter Lawrie	68	65	68	71	272	4,230
Adam Mednick	67	67	67	71	272	4,230
Soren Hansen	66	65	66	75	272	4,230
Mikko Ilonen	69	65	64	74	272	4,230
Amandeep Johl	63	71	71	68	273	3,110
Thammanoon Sriroj	67	67	70	69	273	3,110
Peter Hedblom	72	63	68	70	273	3,110
Thongchai Jaidee	67	70	66	70	273	3,110
Ahmad Bateman	67	66	69	71	273	3,110
Rafael Ponce	66	71	65	71	273	3,110
Thomas Bjorn	68	64	68	73	273	3,110
Klas Eriksson	65	64	69	75	273	3,110
Massimo Florioli	71	64	67	72	274	2,340
Tsai Chi-huang	70	65	66	73	274	2,340
Jose Maria Olazabal	69	65	67	73	274	2,340
Chawalit Plaphol	68	69	68	70	275	2,095
Mike Cunning	68	69	66	72	275	2,095
Lee James	70	67	68	71	276	1,850
Jarmo Sandelin	69	66	69	72	276	1,850
Matthew Cort	66	71	66	73	276	1,850
Peter Baker	66	69	68	73	276	1,850
Yang Yong-eun	70	62	70	74	276	1,850
Ted Oh	69	68	72	68	277	1,535
James Kingston	65	70	71	71	277	1,535
Jose Manuel Lara	67	69	70	71	277	1,535
Aaron Meeks	72	65	68	72	277	1,535
Simon Wakefield	66	69	69	74	278	1,204.46
Alessandro Tadini	71	66	67	74	278	1,204.46

	SCORES				TOTAL	MONEY
Ross Bain	66	70	69	74	279	1,045.94
Danny Zarate	69	68	71	73	281	1,042.94
David Dixon	69	66	75	72	282	1,039.94
Taimur Hussain	70	67	72	74	283	1,036.94

Volvo Masters of Asia

Kota Permai Golf and Country Club,
Kuala Lumpur, Malaysia
Par 36-36–72; 6,962 yards

December 5-8
purse, US$500,000

	SCORES				TOTAL	MONEY
Kevin Na	69	66	71	66	272	US$90,000
Simon Yates	69	68	70	67	274	30,875
Anthony Kang	68	68	70	68	274	30,875
Craig Kamps	66	68	69	71	274	30,875
Arjun Singh	70	65	68	71	274	30,875
Edward Loar	69	69	71	66	275	14,000
Chawalit Plaphol	69	67	70	69	275	14,000
Mardan Mamat	73	66	66	70	275	14,000
Patrik Sjoland	68	70	70	68	276	9,100
Boonchu Ruangkit	69	69	69	69	276	9,100
Clay Devers	69	70	68	69	276	9,100
Jim Johnson	69	67	68	72	276	9,100
Ted Oh	68	69	72	68	277	7,375
Danny Zarate	69	68	71	69	277	7,375
Ahmad Bateman	70	71	67	69	277	7,375
Kang Wook-soon	68	71	67	71	277	7,375
Liang Wen-chong	72	71	70	65	278	6,116.67
Kyi Hla Han	72	68	70	68	278	6,116.67
Wang Ter-chang	71	69	68	70	278	6,116.67
Gary Rusnak	70	66	71	71	278	6,116.67
Mo Joong-kyung	69	70	68	71	278	6,116.67
Gerald Rosales	71	68	66	73	278	6,116.67
Daniel Chopra	71	71	71	66	279	5,400
Prayad Marksaeng	69	68	71	71	279	5,400
Danny Chia	68	72	67	72	279	5,400
Lee James	69	73	70	68	280	4,883.33
Andrew Pitts	73	67	72	68	280	4,883.33
Lin Chie-hsiang	75	72	65	68	280	4,883.33
Rafael Ponce	68	75	68	69	280	4,883.33
James Oh	69	72	69	70	280	4,883.33
Digvijay Singh	67	72	69	72	280	4,883.33

Japan Tour

Token Corporation Cup

Kedoin Golf Club, Kedoin, Kagoshima
Par 36-36–72; 7,135 yards

March 14-17
purse, ¥100,000,000

	SCORES				TOTAL	MONEY
Toru Taniguchi	71	73	67	61	272	¥20,000,000
Hirofumi Miyase	70	70	66	68	274	10,000,000
Taichi Teshima	70	69	69	67	275	5,800,000
Chen Tze-chung	69	68	69	69	275	5,800,000
Tateo Ozaki	69	67	73	67	276	3,354,000
Kiyoshi Murota	67	70	68	71	276	3,354,000
Takashi Kanemoto	72	67	70	67	276	3,354,000
Katsumasa Miyamoto	73	70	67	66	276	3,354,000
Yano Azuma	70	70	72	64	276	3,354,000
Hideki Kase	75	67	68	67	277	2,420,000
Tsukasa Watanabe	71	69	71	66	277	2,420,000
Nobuhito Sato	70	71	69	67	277	2,420,000
Anthony Gilligan	73	70	68	67	278	1,920,000
Katsunori Kuwabara	74	69	69	66	278	1,920,000
Hajime Meshiai	72	69	70	68	279	1,524,000
Toshimitsu Izawa	67	70	72	70	279	1,524,000
Shigeru Nonaka	73	71	69	66	279	1,524,000
Kazuyoshi Yonekura	72	69	69	69	279	1,524,000
Brendan Jones	69	70	70	70	279	1,524,000
Katsuyoshi Tomori	73	69	69	69	280	1,220,000
Dean Wilson	67	71	70	72	280	1,220,000
Masashi Ozaki	70	72	68	71	281	940,000
Gregory Meyer	71	72	70	68	281	940,000
Hiroyuki Fujita	73	67	71	70	281	940,000
Taku Sugaya	72	73	66	70	281	940,000
Frankie Minoza	71	73	69	68	281	940,000
Zhang Lian-wei	75	69	67	70	281	940,000
Naomichi Ozaki	69	72	71	70	282	702,000
Satoshi Higashi	74	68	71	69	282	702,000
Keiichiro Fukabori	73	71	73	65	282	702,000
Lin Keng-chi	73	69	70	70	282	702,000
Hirokazu Kuniyoshi	71	69	71	71	282	702,000

Dydo Drinco Shizuoka Open

Shizuoka Country Club, Hamaoka, Shizuoka
Par 36-36–72; 6,918 yards

March 21-24
purse, ¥100,000,000

	SCORES				TOTAL	MONEY
Kiyoshi Murota	67	68	72	69	276	¥20,000,000
Masashi Ozaki	68	70	73	67	278	8,400,000
Kim Jong-duck	69	69	71	69	278	8,400,000
Toru Taniguchi	65	72	73	69	279	4,800,000
Hideki Kase	68	69	72	71	280	4,000,000

	SCORES				TOTAL	MONEY
Hirokazu Kuniyoshi	72	68	69	72	281	3,450,000
Zhang Lian-wei	69	70	69	73	281	3,450,000
Koki Idoki	71	72	71	68	282	3,050,000
Naomichi Ozaki	71	69	73	70	283	2,820,000
Shinichi Yokota	70	69	72	73	284	2,420,000
Katsumune Imai	66	72	75	71	284	2,420,000
Tomohiro Kondou	67	70	75	72	284	2,420,000
Tsuyoshi Yoneyama	71	72	74	68	285	1,740,000
Mitsuo Harada	70	71	75	69	285	1,740,000
Hsieh Chin-sheng	71	67	74	73	285	1,740,000
Taichi Teshima	68	71	75	71	285	1,740,000
S.K. Ho	70	71	71	73	285	1,740,000
Katsuyoshi Tomori	69	72	70	75	286	1,340,000
Masashi Shimada	70	70	77	69	286	1,340,000
Dean Wilson	70	66	73	77	286	1,340,000
Hajime Meshiai	70	72	74	71	287	1,028,000
Masahiro Kuramoto	75	68	72	72	287	1,028,000
Toru Suzuki	71	69	75	72	287	1,028,000
Nobuhito Sato	72	71	71	73	287	1,028,000
Masanori Kobayashi	71	68	76	72	287	1,028,000
Yoshinori Mizumaki	71	72	70	75	288	780,000
Shoichi Yamamoto	71	69	74	74	288	780,000
Mamoru Osanai	72	69	75	72	288	780,000
Shusaku Sugimoto	72	72	76	68	288	780,000
Kiyoshi Miyazato	68	71	72	77	288	780,000

Tsuruya Open

Sports Shinko Country Club, Kawanishi, Hyogo
Par 35-36–71; 6,759 yards

April 25-28
purse, ¥100,000,000

	SCORES				TOTAL	MONEY
Dean Wilson	69	67	69	68	273	¥20,000,000
Toru Taniguchi	71	68	69	67	275	10,000,000
Katsumasa Miyamoto	67	72	68	69	276	6,800,000
Hiroyuki Fujita	67	66	74	70	277	4,400,000
Taichi Teshima	70	71	67	69	277	4,400,000
Toru Suzuki	71	72	68	67	278	3,192,500
Katsunori Kuwabara	73	71	68	66	278	3,192,500
Kazumasa Sakaitani	67	68	74	69	278	3,192,500
David Smail	72	70	70	66	278	3,192,500
Naomichi Ozaki	72	73	68	66	279	2,220,000
Shingo Katayama	70	71	69	69	279	2,220,000
Hirodai Kawai	73	72	68	66	279	2,220,000
Kiyoshi Miyazato	71	73	68	67	279	2,220,000
Scott Laycock	73	68	71	67	279	2,220,000
Koki Idoki	71	69	71	69	280	1,524,000
Tsuyoshi Yoneyama	72	72	67	69	280	1,524,000
Masashi Shimada	74	68	69	69	280	1,524,000
Tetsuji Hiratsuka	69	69	75	67	280	1,524,000
Yano Azuma	69	69	69	73	280	1,524,000
Kiyoshi Maita	72	68	71	70	281	1,066,666
Masayuki Kawamura	72	65	72	72	281	1,066,666
Hirofumi Miyase	68	70	71	72	281	1,066,666
Katsumune Imai	70	74	68	69	281	1,066,666
Jeev Milkha Singh	69	68	70	74	281	1,066,666
Brendan Jones	76	69	68	68	281	1,066,666

	SCORES				TOTAL	MONEY
Hideki Kase	70	73	68	71	282	780,000
Hsieh Chin-sheng	70	67	72	73	282	780,000
Shinobu Ishi	71	70	73	68	282	780,000
Tomohiro Kondou	69	76	71	66	282	780,000
Frankie Minoza	72	73	67	70	282	780,000

Chunichi Crowns

Nagoya Golf Club, Wago Course, Togo, Aichi
Par 35-35–70; 6,580 yards

May 2-5
purse, ¥120,000,000

	SCORES				TOTAL	MONEY
Justin Rose	64	70	63	69	266	¥24,000,000
Prayad Marksaeng	69	66	69	67	271	12,000,000
Dean Wilson	70	64	69	69	272	8,160,000
Taichi Teshima	69	71	64	69	273	5,760,000
*Yusaku Miyazato	67	68	66	72	273	
Shigemasa Higaki	68	69	70	67	274	4,560,000
Scott Laycock	67	71	68	68	274	4,560,000
Toru Suzuki	67	68	72	68	275	3,688,000
Katsunori Kuwabara	66	69	68	72	275	3,688,000
Dinesh Chand	68	70	67	70	275	3,688,000
Naomichi Ozaki	67	71	72	66	276	2,784,000
Hirofumi Miyase	68	70	70	68	276	2,784,000
Lin Keng-chi	68	69	69	70	276	2,784,000
Shingo Katayama	68	69	72	67	276	2,784,000
Masashi Ozaki	65	72	71	69	277	2,004,000
Steve Conran	70	71	67	69	277	2,004,000
Tomohiro Kondou	70	72	67	68	277	2,004,000
Todd Hamilton	68	71	72	66	277	2,004,000
Shinichi Yokota	67	75	68	68	278	1,658,000
Katsumune Imai	70	70	69	69	278	1,658,000
Hideki Kase	70	69	70	70	279	1,320,000
Tsuneyuki Nakajima	69	71	70	69	279	1,320,000
Koki Idoki	65	75	68	71	279	1,320,000
Anthony Gilligan	68	73	67	71	279	1,320,000
Toshiaki Odate	68	72	70	69	279	1,320,000
Kiyoshi Maita	71	68	69	72	280	960,000
Toshimitsu Izawa	72	68	72	68	280	960,000
Nobuhito Sato	71	70	70	69	280	960,000
Yasuharu Imano	73	70	67	70	280	960,000
Frankie Minoza	69	70	69	72	280	960,000
Jeev Milkha Singh	70	65	72	73	280	960,000

Fujisankei Classic

Kawana Hotel Golf Course, Fuji Course, Ito, Shizuoka
Par 35-36–71; 6,694 yards

May 9-12
purse, ¥140,000,000

	SCORES				TOTAL	MONEY
Nobuhito Sato	67	70	68	71	276	¥28,000,000
Scott Laycock	74	69	66	67	276	14,000,000
(Sato defeated Laycock on second playoff hole.)						
Toru Suzuki	69	71	67	70	277	8,120,000
Lin Keng-chi	65	74	68	70	277	8,120,000

	SCORES				TOTAL	MONEY
Gregory Meyer	67	73	66	72	278	5,086,666
Katsunori Kuwabara	70	73	70	65	278	5,086,666
Hidemasa Hoshino	71	70	66	71	278	5,086,666
Kiyoshi Miyazato	70	73	68	68	279	4,270,000
Tetsuji Hiratsuka	72	71	67	70	280	3,808,000
Kim Jong-duck	70	71	70	69	280	3,808,000
Takenori Hiraishi	68	71	70	72	281	2,758,000
Yoshimitsu Fukuzawa	68	73	71	69	281	2,758,000
Craig Warren	72	73	68	68	281	2,758,000
Yasuharu Imano	69	72	70	70	281	2,758,000
Tajima Soushi	67	73	68	73	281	2,758,000
David Ishii	69	71	71	70	281	2,758,000
Tsuneyuki Nakajima	74	70	65	73	282	2,058,000
Masayuki Kawamura	70	73	69	70	282	2,058,000
Katsunari Takahashi	71	72	70	70	283	1,596,000
Keiichiro Fukabori	70	73	72	68	283	1,596,000
Steve Conran	73	72	69	69	283	1,596,000
Katsumune Imai	72	71	70	70	283	1,596,000
Zhang Lian-wei	71	72	71	69	283	1,596,000
Dean Wilson	68	73	67	75	283	1,596,000
Naomichi Ozaki	70	72	68	74	284	1,232,000
Mitsuhiro Tateyama	72	70	71	71	284	1,232,000
Yoshinori Kaneko	70	71	74	70	285	986,000
Hajime Meshiai	69	74	71	71	285	986,000
Mitsuo Harada	72	74	75	64	285	986,000
Shigeru Nonaka	68	76	70	71	285	986,000
Shigemasa Higaki	70	72	72	71	285	986,000
Mamoru Osanai	68	72	69	76	285	986,000
Go Higaki	74	69	70	72	285	986,000

Japan PGA Championship

Koma Country Club, Tsukigase, Nara
Par 36-36–72; 7,048 yards

May 16-19
purse, ¥110,000,000

	SCORES				TOTAL	MONEY
Kenichi Kuboya	74	70	68	67	279	¥22,000,000
Shingo Katayama	73	72	68	66	279	11,000,000
(Kuboya defeated Katayama on second playoff hole.)						
Masashi Ozaki	72	68	71	69	280	6,380,000
S.K. Ho	73	70	66	71	280	6,380,000
Tsuyoshi Yoneyama	71	73	70	68	282	4,400,000
Todd Hamilton	72	73	68	70	283	3,795,000
Dean Wilson	73	70	71	69	283	3,795,000
Naomichi Ozaki	72	73	67	72	284	3,113,000
Toru Taniguchi	71	69	72	72	284	3,113,000
Yano Azuma	73	75	68	68	284	3,113,000
Koki Idoki	73	72	67	73	285	2,244,000
Hirofumi Miyase	73	74	69	69	285	2,244,000
Richard Backwell	69	72	71	73	285	2,244,000
Nozomi Kawahara	76	69	71	69	285	2,244,000
Prayad Marksaeng	74	70	73	68	285	2,244,000
Hiroshi Goda	74	74	70	68	286	1,529,000
Yoshinori Mizumaki	76	71	71	68	286	1,529,000
Hajime Meshiai	73	71	69	73	286	1,529,000
Mitsutaka Kusakabe	74	72	70	70	286	1,529,000
Takeshi Sakiyama	78	69	70	69	286	1,529,000

	SCORES				TOTAL	MONEY
Kohei Ban	76	72	66	72	286	1,529,000
Hideyuki Sato	69	74	71	73	287	937,200
Nobuo Serizawa	72	74	69	72	287	937,200
Kiyoshi Murota	74	69	73	71	287	937,200
Hsieh Chin-sheng	72	73	72	70	287	937,200
Shigeru Nonaka	76	67	72	72	287	937,200
Nobuhito Sato	74	73	70	70	287	937,200
Zaw Moe	75	73	68	71	287	937,200
Yasuharu Imano	70	74	68	75	287	937,200
Takashi Kamiyama	71	75	70	71	287	937,200
Christian Pena	73	72	72	70	287	937,200

Munsingwear Open KSB Cup

Ayutaki Country Club, Kagawa
Par 35-36–71; 6,697 yards

May 23-26
purse, ¥120,000,000

	SCORES				TOTAL	MONEY
Kenichi Kuboya	66	70	68	69	273	¥24,000,000
Yoshimitsu Fukuzawa	67	71	69	66	273	10,080,000
Todd Hamilton	67	68	72	66	273	10,080,000
(Kuboya defeated Fukuzawa on second and Hamilton on fourth playoff hole.)						
Kim Jong-duck	70	68	69	67	274	5,760,000
Kiyoshi Maita	68	72	70	65	275	4,185,000
Nobuhito Sato	66	69	72	68	275	4,185,000
Taichi Teshima	67	68	70	70	275	4,185,000
Tetsuji Hiratsuka	69	68	68	70	275	4,185,000
Mamoru Osanai	72	69	71	64	276	3,264,000
Hideto Tanihara	70	65	74	67	276	3,264,000
Naomichi Ozaki	67	70	69	71	277	2,904,000
Nozomi Kawahara	65	74	72	67	278	2,424,000
Tomoaki Ueda	64	73	68	73	278	2,424,000
S.K. Ho	70	69	69	70	278	2,424,000
Satoshi Oide	70	71	69	69	279	1,776,000
Jun Kikuchi	70	69	71	69	279	1,776,000
Mitsuhiro Tateyama	69	70	72	68	279	1,776,000
Masanori Kobayashi	69	72	68	70	279	1,776,000
Nobuhiro Masuda	65	74	69	71	279	1,776,000
Dean Wilson	66	68	68	77	279	1,776,000
Katsuyoshi Tomori	73	69	69	69	280	1,368,000
Gregory Meyer	69	67	76	68	280	1,368,000
Tsuyoshi Yoneyama	69	70	71	71	281	1,064,000
Shigeru Nonaka	66	74	71	70	281	1,064,000
Lin Keng-chi	71	68	73	69	281	1,064,000
Kazumasa Sakaitani	68	73	72	68	281	1,064,000
Rick Gibson	72	70	70	69	281	1,064,000
Prayad Marksaeng	65	69	75	72	281	1,064,000
Hirofumi Miyase	72	69	69	73	283	864,000
Shingo Katayama	69	67	74	73	283	864,000

Diamond Cup

Sayama Golf Club, Iruma, Saitama
Par 36-36–72; 7,110 yards

May 30-June 2
purse, ¥100,000,000

	SCORES				TOTAL	MONEY
Tsuneyuki Nakajima	67	66	68	68	269	¥20,000,000
Hirofumi Miyase	67	65	70	69	271	7,200,000
Tomohiro Kondou	64	65	74	68	271	7,200,000
Christian Pena	64	67	70	70	271	7,200,000
Shinichi Yokota	64	68	71	71	274	3,800,000
Katsumasa Miyamoto	69	69	65	71	274	3,800,000
Yoshinori Mizumaki	70	66	67	72	275	2,842,000
Nobumitsu Yuhara	67	68	68	72	275	2,842,000
Gregory Meyer	68	69	67	71	275	2,842,000
Tetsuji Hiratsuka	72	66	68	69	275	2,842,000
S.K. Ho	67	66	68	74	275	2,842,000
Hsieh Chin-sheng	66	69	68	73	276	2,220,000
Shingo Katayama	69	71	69	68	277	1,820,000
David Smail	69	68	71	69	277	1,820,000
Katsuyoshi Tomori	70	64	71	73	278	1,620,000
Katsumune Imai	68	70	69	71	278	1,620,000
Prayad Marksaeng	70	71	68	69	278	1,620,000
Nobuo Serizawa	70	70	65	74	279	1,113,333
Koki Idoki	69	69	71	70	279	1,113,333
Takuya Ogawa	69	69	66	75	279	1,113,333
Zaw Moe	67	71	70	71	279	1,113,333
Taku Sugaya	69	66	72	72	279	1,113,333
Masanori Kobayashi	67	72	73	67	279	1,113,333
Takashi Iwamoto	67	67	74	71	279	1,113,333
Takayama Tadahiro	67	70	71	71	279	1,113,333
Yang Yong-eun	71	67	69	72	279	1,113,333
Hideki Kase	69	69	72	70	280	760,000
Kiyoshi Murota	67	69	69	75	280	760,000
Nobuhito Sato	70	71	70	69	280	760,000
Dinesh Chand	72	68	71	69	280	760,000

JCB Classic Sendai

Omotezao Kokusai Golf Club, Shibata, Miyagi
Par 36-35–71; 6,659 yards

June 6-9
purse, ¥100,000,000

	SCORES				TOTAL	MONEY
Toru Suzuki	69	67	65	70	271	¥20,000,000
Tsuneyuki Nakajima	67	65	71	68	271	10,000,000
(Suzuki defeated Nakajima on second playoff hole.)						
Nobuhito Sato	68	68	68	71	275	6,800,000
Katsunori Kuwabara	72	66	65	73	276	3,925,000
Zaw Moe	67	71	65	73	276	3,925,000
Rick Gibson	69	67	67	73	276	3,925,000
Christian Pena	64	68	70	74	276	3,925,000
Masanori Kobayashi	69	71	65	72	277	3,050,000
Hideki Kase	69	68	66	75	278	2,520,000
Tsuyoshi Yoneyama	65	69	73	71	278	2,520,000
Kenichi Kuboya	70	67	64	77	278	2,520,000
Chen Tze-chung	70	69	66	73	278	2,520,000
Yoshinori Mizumaki	71	66	70	72	279	2,020,000
Kiyoshi Murota	74	65	67	74	280	1,620,000

	SCORES			TOTAL	MONEY
Hajime Meshiai	69	67 68 76		280	1,620,000
Takayama Tadahiro	67	67 72 74		280	1,620,000
Zhang Lian-wei	72	69 68 71		280	1,620,000
Brendan Jones	74	67 64 75		280	1,620,000
Masashi Ozaki	71	71 66 73		281	1,105,714
Kazuhiko Hosokawa	68	69 69 75		281	1,105,714
Taichi Teshima	72	70 66 73		281	1,105,714
Taku Sugaya	71	66 69 75		281	1,105,714
Yano Azuma	66	70 69 76		281	1,105,714
Hidemasa Hoshino	72	67 68 74		281	1,105,714
S.K. Ho	73	69 69 70		281	1,105,714
Takeshi Sakiyama	67	72 70 73		282	820,000
Shigeru Nonaka	69	68 70 75		282	820,000
Shigemasa Higaki	68	72 64 78		282	820,000
Koki Idoki	68	71 69 75		283	700,000
Brad Andrews	71	69 69 74		283	700,000
Dinesh Chand	68	70 67 78		283	700,000

Tamanoi Yomiuri Open

Yomiuri Country Club, Nishinomiya, Hyogo
Par 36-36–72; 7,030 yards

June 20-23
purse, ¥90,000,000

	SCORES			TOTAL	MONEY
Toru Taniguchi	65	69 67 69		270	¥18,000,000
Daisuke Maruyama	68	69 68 67		272	7,560,000
Satoru Hirota	72	69 66 65		272	7,560,000
Naomichi Ozaki	73	69 66 65		273	3,720,000
Hiroyuki Fujita	69	70 65 69		273	3,720,000
Kenichi Kuboya	73	63 70 67		273	3,720,000
Tsukasa Watanabe	75	68 65 66		274	2,970,000
Tatsuo Takasaki	69	67 71 68		275	2,454,750
Shinichi Akiba	70	65 74 66		275	2,454,750
Lin Keng-chi	66	69 72 68		275	2,454,750
Mitsuhiro Tateyama	68	68 70 69		275	2,454,750
Hirofumi Miyase	66	68 71 71		276	1,692,000
Shinichi Yokota	68	69 68 71		276	1,692,000
Tetsuji Hiratsuka	72	67 71 66		276	1,692,000
Takashi Kamiyama	69	67 69 71		276	1,692,000
Kiyoshi Miyazato	67	71 69 69		276	1,692,000
Hsieh Chin-sheng	71	69 71 66		277	1,368,000
Satoshi Higashi	69	70 72 67		278	1,030,500
Kiyoshi Maita	69	69 73 67		278	1,030,500
Fumio Noji	71	66 70 71		278	1,030,500
Kazumasa Sakaitani	71	67 71 69		278	1,030,500
Tomonori Takahashi	69	70 70 69		278	1,030,500
Tomohiro Kondou	68	71 68 71		278	1,030,500
Rick Gibson	73	66 70 69		278	1,030,500
Thongchai Jaidee	70	73 66 69		278	1,030,500
Masashi Ozaki	70	65 72 72		279	738,000
Jun Kikuchi	68	68 71 72		279	738,000
Koushi Yokoyama	70	68 70 71		279	738,000
Tsuneyuki Nakajima	70	70 71 69		280	574,714
Yoshinori Mizumaki	71	69 69 71		280	574,714
Hajime Meshiai	71	68 72 69		280	574,714
Katsunori Kuwabara	72	68 72 68		280	574,714
Yui Ueda	69	71 70 70		280	574,714

	SCORES				TOTAL	MONEY
Tajima Soushi	72	69	71	68	280	574,714
Chen Tze-chung	68	68	75	69	280	574,714

Mizuno Open

Setonaikai Golf Club, Kasaoka, Okayama
Par 36-36–72; 7,256 yards

June 27-30
purse, ¥100,000,000

	SCORES				TOTAL	MONEY
Dean Wilson	71	69	70	67	277	¥20,000,000
Kiyoshi Miyazato	68	72	71	67	278	10,000,000
Hajime Meshiai	73	70	71	68	282	5,800,000
Toru Taniguchi	68	69	74	71	282	5,800,000
Takenori Hiraishi	70	72	72	70	284	3,354,000
Hirofumi Miyase	66	69	77	72	284	3,354,000
Hiroyuki Fujita	70	69	75	70	284	3,354,000
Katsumasa Miyamoto	72	68	74	70	284	3,354,000
Steve Conran	72	71	73	68	284	3,354,000
Toshimitsu Izawa	68	68	79	70	285	2,136,666
Nobuhito Sato	68	71	75	71	285	2,136,666
Taichi Teshima	70	71	72	72	285	2,136,666
Daisuke Maruyama	70	73	72	70	285	2,136,666
Lin Keng-chi	74	70	70	71	285	2,136,666
Zhang Lian-wei	69	75	74	67	285	2,136,666
Hiroshi Goda	73	68	74	71	286	1,348,571
Katsunori Kuwabara	68	70	76	72	286	1,348,571
Masanori Kobayashi	69	70	76	71	286	1,348,571
Takayama Tadahiro	72	72	71	71	286	1,348,571
Tomohiro Kondou	71	68	78	69	286	1,348,571
Brian Watts	73	66	74	73	286	1,348,571
Thongchai Jaidee	72	69	75	70	286	1,348,571
Tsuneyuki Nakajima	69	70	76	72	287	753,076
Koki Idoki	72	72	71	72	287	753,076
Shigemasa Higaki	74	69	75	69	287	753,076
David Smail	70	74	72	71	287	753,076
Mitsuhiro Tateyama	71	72	72	72	287	753,076
Go Higaki	71	69	74	73	287	753,076
Tomoaki Ueda	73	69	72	73	287	753,076
Yui Ueda	74	68	72	73	287	753,076
Hidemasa Hoshino	66	72	76	73	287	753,076
Todd Hamilton	70	72	72	73	287	753,076
Brendan Jones	72	72	73	70	287	753,076
Charlie Wi	69	74	75	69	287	753,076
Scott Laycock	70	74	71	72	287	753,076

Japan Tour Championship Iiyama Cup

Hourai Country Club, Nishinasuno, Tochigi
Par 36-36–72; 7,090 yards

July 4-7
purse, ¥120,000,000

	SCORES				TOTAL	MONEY
Nobuhito Sato	67	66	71	64	268	¥24,000,000
Kenichi Kuboya	67	69	67	71	274	12,000,000
David Smail	71	69	68	68	276	8,160,000
Naomichi Ozaki	72	68	70	67	277	4,710,000

	SCORES				TOTAL	MONEY
Toru Taniguchi	67	71	67	72	277	4,710,000
Shingo Katayama	72	68	68	69	277	4,710,000
Kiyoshi Miyazato	71	69	66	71	277	4,710,000
Tomohiro Kondou	68	69	69	72	278	3,522,000
Charlie Wi	71	72	65	70	278	3,522,000
Katsumune Imai	72	69	70	68	279	3,144,000
Masashi Ozaki	71	65	74	70	280	2,904,000
Takenori Hiraishi	74	65	70	72	281	2,424,000
Daisuke Maruyama	72	68	70	71	281	2,424,000
Mamoru Osanai	69	71	71	70	281	2,424,000
Hideki Kase	68	69	77	68	282	1,828,800
Hirofumi Miyase	75	69	68	70	282	1,828,800
Hsieh Chin-sheng	69	68	75	70	282	1,828,800
Jun Kikuchi	68	74	69	71	282	1,828,800
Chen Tze-chung	71	72	68	71	282	1,828,800
Lin Keng-chi	69	72	70	72	283	1,464,000
Dean Wilson	71	70	71	71	283	1,464,000
Gregory Meyer	74	69	68	73	284	1,156,800
Katsunori Kuwabara	70	71	73	70	284	1,156,800
Taichi Teshima	74	71	70	69	284	1,156,800
Tatsuhiko Ichihara	71	72	72	69	284	1,156,800
Prayad Marksaeng	70	74	68	72	284	1,156,800
Brian Watts	71	72	68	74	285	960,000
Andre Stolz	71	70	71	73	285	960,000
Shigemasa Higaki	74	70	65	77	286	766,285
Tatsuya Shiraishi	72	71	72	71	286	766,285
Toshimitsu Izawa	69	69	74	74	286	766,285
Hiroyuki Fujita	73	70	74	69	286	766,285
Steve Conran	70	73	71	72	286	766,285
Hidemasa Hoshino	70	70	72	74	286	766,285
Kim Jong-duck	72	69	75	70	286	766,285

Juken Sangyo Open Hiroshima

Hiroshima Country Club, Higashi, Hiroshima
Par 36-36–72; 6,950 yards

July 11-14
purse, ¥90,000,000

	SCORES				TOTAL	MONEY
Hur Suk-ho	64	70	71	69	274	¥18,000,000
Mamoru Osanai	68	71	69	69	277	9,000,000
David Smail	66	69	70	73	278	5,220,000
Tomohiro Kondou	70	69	70	69	278	5,220,000
Nobuhito Sato	66	73	69	71	279	3,420,000
Shigemasa Higaki	65	72	70	72	279	3,420,000
Tatsuya Shiraishi	71	66	74	69	280	2,751,000
Katsuya Nakagawa	70	69	68	73	280	2,751,000
Hideto Tanihara	63	73	72	72	280	2,751,000
Yoshinori Mizumaki	71	65	72	73	281	1,998,000
Hsieh Chin-sheng	73	69	68	71	281	1,998,000
Daisuke Maruyama	70	70	68	73	281	1,998,000
Tetsuji Hiratsuka	68	71	65	77	281	1,998,000
Yoshinobu Tsukada	68	73	70	70	281	1,998,000
Hajime Meshiai	72	68	71	71	282	1,371,600
Yasunori Ida	70	68	71	73	282	1,371,600
Katsunori Kuwabara	74	69	68	71	282	1,371,600
Mitsuhiro Tateyama	65	69	78	70	282	1,371,600
Brendan Jones	66	71	69	76	282	1,371,600

	SCORES			TOTAL	MONEY
Hirofumi Miyase	68	71	75	69	283	960,000
Kazuhiko Hosokawa	69	74	68	72	283	960,000
Lin Keng-chi	70	70	71	72	283	960,000
Yasuharu Imano	69	70	71	73	283	960,000
Chen Tze-chung	72	69	71	71	283	960,000
Charlie Wi	71	68	72	72	283	960,000
Naomichi Ozaki	71	72	70	71	284	684,000
Nobumitsu Yuhara	68	71	70	75	284	684,000
Mitsuo Harada	68	73	70	73	284	684,000
Shigeru Nonaka	74	68	66	76	284	684,000
Brad Andrews	66	74	72	72	284	684,000
Takayama Tadahiro	71	72	68	73	284	684,000

Sato Foods NST Niigata Open

Nakamine Golf Club, Toyoura, Niigata
Par 36-36–72; 6,973 yards

July 25-28
purse, ¥50,000,000

	SCORES			TOTAL	MONEY
Yasuharu Imano	70	64	70	66	270	¥10,000,000
Katsumasa Miyamoto	66	69	68	71	274	5,000,000
Kazuhiko Hosokawa	67	68	69	71	275	2,600,000
Daisuke Maruyama	69	70	70	66	275	2,600,000
Craig Jones	67	67	72	69	275	2,600,000
Jun Kikuchi	68	72	67	69	276	1,725,000
Yutaka Horinouchi	70	69	68	69	276	1,725,000
Katsuyoshi Tomori	68	69	73	67	277	1,467,500
Hidehisa Shikada	68	70	69	70	277	1,467,500
Hideki Kase	68	70	69	71	278	1,260,000
Hiroyuki Fujita	68	68	71	71	278	1,260,000
Lin Keng-chi	67	73	71	68	279	1,010,000
Dinesh Chand	70	71	68	70	279	1,010,000
Zhang Lian-wei	68	70	71	70	279	1,010,000
Satoshi Higashi	68	71	72	69	280	740,000
Yasunori Ida	71	71	69	69	280	740,000
Fumio Noji	69	72	68	71	280	740,000
Shinichi Yokota	70	68	70	72	280	740,000
Richard Lee	70	67	73	70	280	740,000
S.K. Ho	68	69	73	70	280	740,000
Koki Idoki	74	68	71	68	281	514,000
Hirofumi Miyase	69	71	70	71	281	514,000
Hideto Tanihara	68	72	71	70	281	514,000
Shigemasa Higaki	69	72	69	71	281	514,000
Seiji Iwatate	74	66	70	71	281	514,000
Takashi Iwamoto	70	68	72	72	282	400,000
Takayama Tadahiro	71	71	71	69	282	400,000
Kunichika Iha	72	71	68	71	282	400,000
Ryuichi Oda	67	74	72	69	282	400,000
Tomohiro Maruyama	71	72	69	71	283	305,000
Kosaku Makisaka	73	70	70	70	283	305,000
Tetsuji Hiratsuka	73	67	70	73	283	305,000
Kazumasa Sakaitani	68	70	73	72	283	305,000
Mitsuhiro Tateyama	70	69	71	73	283	305,000
Hidemasa Hoshino	71	71	71	70	283	305,000
Nobuhiro Masuda	71	72	68	72	283	305,000

Aiful Cup

Twinfields Golf Club, Komatsu, Ishikawa
Par 36-36–72; 7,125 yards

August 1-4
purse, ¥120,000,000

		SCORES			TOTAL	MONEY
Yasuharu Imano	64	66	66	72	268	¥24,000,000
Toshimitsu Izawa	69	65	66	69	269	12,000,000
Tateo Ozaki	69	65	70	66	270	6,960,000
Tetsuji Hiratsuka	69	66	66	69	270	6,960,000
Naomichi Ozaki	68	67	64	72	271	4,360,000
Yui Ueda	72	66	67	66	271	4,360,000
S.K. Ho	71	66	65	69	271	4,360,000
Shigemasa Higaki	70	67	66	69	272	3,522,000
Takayama Tadahiro	71	67	66	68	272	3,522,000
Katsunori Kuwabara	65	72	70	67	274	2,664,000
Jun Kikuchi	68	68	67	71	274	2,664,000
Katsumasa Miyamoto	70	71	68	65	274	2,664,000
Tomohiro Kondou	69	68	71	66	274	2,664,000
Zhang Lian-wei	68	65	68	73	274	2,664,000
Tatsuo Takasaki	70	68	67	70	275	1,884,000
Mitsuo Harada	66	68	73	68	275	1,884,000
Hsieh Chin-sheng	69	67	71	68	275	1,884,000
Brendan Jones	71	67	69	68	275	1,884,000
Masashi Ozaki	66	69	72	69	276	1,560,000
Hirofumi Miyase	67	71	69	69	276	1,560,000
*Masaru Hasegawa	68	70	70	68	276	
Yoshitaka Yamamoto	67	70	67	73	277	1,272,000
Craig Warren	74	64	69	70	277	1,272,000
Keiichiro Fukabori	72	67	69	69	277	1,272,000
Shingo Katayama	69	69	68	71	277	1,272,000
Toru Taniguchi	71	66	74	67	278	984,000
Kazuhiko Hosokawa	70	66	69	73	278	984,000
Munehiro Chuzenji	72	68	73	65	278	984,000
Koushi Yokoyama	71	68	68	71	278	984,000
Kim Jong-duck	70	69	71	68	278	984,000

Sun Chlorella Classic

Sapporo Bay Golf Club, Ishikari, Hokkaido
Par 36-36–72; 7,039 yards

August 8-11
purse, ¥120,000,000

		SCORES			TOTAL	MONEY
Christian Pena	67	67	66	69	269	¥24,000,000
Naomichi Ozaki	67	67	68	67	269	10,080,000
Brendan Jones	66	68	70	65	269	10,080,000
(Pena defeated Ozaki and Jones on first playoff hole.)						
Brad Andrews	65	72	69	64	270	4,960,000
Tetsuji Hiratsuka	68	68	69	65	270	4,960,000
Yasuharu Imano	71	70	64	65	270	4,960,000
Toru Taniguchi	67	69	68	67	271	3,980,000
Tsuneyuki Nakajima	67	69	67	69	272	3,660,000
Tateo Ozaki	70	68	66	69	273	3,264,000
Zhang Lian-wei	67	68	70	68	273	3,264,000
Shinichi Yokota	70	68	66	70	274	2,904,000
Hirofumi Miyase	70	70	64	71	275	2,184,000
David Smail	68	73	67	67	275	2,184,000
Chen Tze-chung	69	66	69	71	275	2,184,000

	SCORES			TOTAL	MONEY
Kim Jong-duck	68	70	66	71	275	2,184,000
Prayad Marksaeng	70	69	66	70	275	2,184,000
Richard Lee	71	68	69	67	275	2,184,000
Naoya Sugiyama	68	71	69	68	276	1,656,000
Jeev Milkha Singh	66	71	70	69	276	1,656,000
Hideki Kase	70	63	69	75	277	1,320,000
Hiroyuki Fujita	70	72	65	70	277	1,320,000
Nobuhito Sato	74	67	66	70	277	1,320,000
Daisuke Maruyama	70	71	68	68	277	1,320,000
Thongchai Jaidee	68	73	67	69	277	1,320,000
Anthony Gilligan	69	72	67	70	278	1,008,000
Mitsunori Harakawa	70	71	68	69	278	1,008,000
Kazuhiro Shimizu	70	72	67	69	278	1,008,000
Takayama Tadahiro	69	72	69	68	278	1,008,000
Toru Suzuki	69	67	71	72	279	782,000
Yoshimitsu Fukuzawa	67	68	73	71	279	782,000
Taichi Teshima	68	71	68	72	279	782,000
Dinesh Chand	73	68	70	68	279	782,000
Hideto Tanihara	71	70	73	65	279	782,000
Lin Chien-bing	66	72	73	68	279	782,000

Hisamitsu-KBC Augusta

Keya Golf Club, Shima, Fukuoka
Par 36-36–72; 7,154 yards
(Third round cancelled—rain.)

August 29-September 1
purse, ¥100,000,000

	SCORES			TOTAL	MONEY
Nobumitsu Yuhara	68	69	72	209	¥15,000,000
Katsunori Kuwabara	73	65	72	210	4,380,000
Shigemasa Higaki	74	66	70	210	4,380,000
Toshimasa Nakajima	71	67	72	210	4,380,000
Christian Pena	71	67	72	210	4,380,000
Zhang Lian-wei	70	70	70	210	4,380,000
Katsumasa Miyamoto	70	70	71	211	2,381,250
Yasuharu Imano	69	71	71	211	2,381,250
Hiroyuki Fujita	68	72	72	212	1,740,000
Takashi Kanemoto	72	68	72	212	1,740,000
Daisuke Maruyama	69	72	71	212	1,740,000
Kazumasa Sakaitani	73	69	70	212	1,740,000
Hidemasa Hoshino	74	70	68	212	1,740,000
Tajima Soushi	69	71	72	212	1,740,000
Satoshi Oide	71	71	71	213	1,077,857
Taichi Teshima	73	70	70	213	1,077,857
Masashi Shimada	68	69	76	213	1,077,857
Dinesh Chand	70	69	74	213	1,077,857
Yano Azuma	74	69	70	213	1,077,857
Frankie Minoza	68	71	74	213	1,077,857
Scott Laycock	71	70	72	213	1,077,857
Satoshi Higashi	69	72	73	214	705,000
Tsukasa Watanabe	74	68	72	214	705,000
Hisayuki Sasaki	70	71	73	214	705,000
Keiichiro Fukabori	72	70	72	214	705,000
Hidezumi Shirakata	70	69	75	214	705,000
Masanori Kobayashi	69	73	72	214	705,000
Shoichi Yamamoto	74	68	73	215	473,250
Tsuyoshi Yoneyama	72	70	73	215	473,250

	SCORES			TOTAL	MONEY
Toru Suzuki	73	71	71	215	473,250
Anthony Gilligan	70	73	72	215	473,250
Masayoshi Yamazoe	70	74	71	215	473,250
Hideki Haraguchi	75	69	71	215	473,250
Kazuhiro Kinjo	68	74	73	215	473,250
Shinichi Yokota	71	72	72	215	473,250
Yoshiaki Mano	71	71	73	215	473,250
Yoshinobu Tsukada	74	68	73	215	473,250

Japan PGA Match Play

Nidom Classic Course, Tomakomai, Hokkaido
Par 36-36–72; 6,957 yards

September 5-8
purse, ¥80,000,000

FIRST ROUND

Toshimitsu Izawa defeated Shigemasa Higaki, 19 holes.
Hirofumi Miyase defeated Katsunori Kuwabara, 2 and 1.
Kazuhiko Hosokawa defeated Lin Keng-chi, 2 and 1.
Dinesh Chand defeated Katsumasa Miyamoto, 4 and 2.
Nobuhito Sato defeated Shinichi Yokota, 2 up.
Tetsuji Hiratsuka defeated Yasuharu Imano, 1 up.
Todd Hamilton defeated Taichi Teshima, 3 and 2.
David Smail defeated Naomichi Ozaki, 1 up.
Dean Wilson defeated Katsuyoshi Tomori, 19 holes.
Tomohiro Kondou defeated Toru Suzuki, 3 and 1.
Hiroyuki Fujita defeated Kenichi Kuboya, 4 and 3.
Kiyoshi Murota defeated S.K. Ho, 20 holes.
Toru Taniguchi defeated Tsuyoshi Yoneyama, 2 and 1.
Takenori Hiraishi defeated Christian Pena, 1 up.
Shingo Katayama defeated Hideki Kase, 4 and 3.
Hajime Meshiai defeated Scott Laycock, 1 up.

(Each losing player received ¥400,000.)

SECOND ROUND

Miyase defeated Izawa, 5 and 4.
Hosokawa defeated Chand, 1 up.
Sato defeated Hiratsuka, 5 and 4.
Smail defeated Hamilton, 1 up.
Kondou defeated Wilson, 1 up.
Fujita defeated Murota, 3 and 2.
Hiraishi defeated Taniguchi, 4 and 3.
Katayama defeated Meshiai, 2 and 1.

(Each losing player received ¥800,000.)

QUARTER-FINALS

Miyase defeated Hosokawa, 1 up.
Sato defeated Smail, 1 up.
Kondou defeated Fujita, 2 and 1.
Katayama defeated Hiraishi, 2 and 1.

(Each losing player received ¥1,800,000.)

SEMI-FINALS

Sato defeated Miyase, 1 up.
Kondou defeated Katayama, 2 and 1.

THIRD-FOURTH PLACE PLAYOFF

Katayama defeated Miyase, 19 holes.

(Katayama received ¥9,000,000; Miyase received ¥6,000,000.)

FINAL

Sato defeated Kondou, 5 and 4.

(Sato received ¥30,000,000; Kondou received ¥15,000,000.)

Suntory Open

Sobu Country Club, Inzai, Chiba
Par 35-36–71; 7,155 yards

September 12-15
purse, ¥100,000,000

	SCORES				TOTAL	MONEY
Shingo Katayama	68	68	68	65	269	¥20,000,000
Koki Idoki	73	67	66	67	273	8,400,000
Yasuharu Imano	65	70	69	69	273	8,400,000
Toru Taniguchi	73	68	65	69	275	4,400,000
Scott Laycock	69	73	68	65	275	4,400,000
Nobuhito Sato	70	69	68	69	276	3,600,000
Hiroyuki Fujita	65	72	68	73	278	3,300,000
Hiroshi Goda	70	70	68	71	279	2,727,500
Takenori Hiraishi	71	68	71	69	279	2,727,500
Keiichiro Fukabori	70	66	69	74	279	2,727,500
S.K. Ho	69	71	68	71	279	2,727,500
Steven Conran	68	74	69	69	280	2,120,000
David Gossett	75	69	67	69	280	2,120,000
Masashi Ozaki	72	72	68	69	281	1,670,000
Gregory Meyer	70	72	70	69	281	1,670,000
Yoshinobu Tsukada	72	71	67	71	281	1,670,000
Dean Wilson	72	71	66	72	281	1,670,000
Nobumitsu Yuhara	71	71	66	74	282	1,260,000
Shinichi Yokota	71	70	68	73	282	1,260,000
Kenichi Kuboya	71	72	67	72	282	1,260,000
Prayad Marksaeng	69	69	69	75	282	1,260,000
Brendan Jones	73	71	66	72	282	1,260,000
Hideki Kase	70	70	70	73	283	845,000
Tsuneyuki Nakajima	76	66	69	72	283	845,000
Katsuyoshi Tomori	71	67	71	74	283	845,000
Katsumi Kubo	72	71	70	70	283	845,000
Taisuke Kitajima	72	70	70	71	283	845,000
Kazuhiko Hosokawa	71	70	72	70	283	845,000
Yano Azuma	73	70	68	72	283	845,000
Richard Lee	72	69	70	72	283	845,000

ANA Open

Sapporo Golf Club, Wattsu Course,
Kitahiroshima, Hokkaido
Par 36-36–72; 7,063 yards

September 19-22
purse, ¥100,000,000

	SCORES				TOTAL	MONEY
Masashi Ozaki	67	66	69	69	271	¥20,000,000
Hiroyuki Fujita	68	69	66	69	272	10,000,000
Tsuneyuki Nakajima	71	69	67	66	273	6,800,000
Jun Kikuchi	66	70	70	68	274	4,400,000
S.K. Ho	71	68	67	68	274	4,400,000
Toru Taniguchi	68	70	67	70	275	3,450,000
Todd Hamilton	70	71	65	69	275	3,450,000
*Yusaku Miyazato	69	68	69	69	275	
Tateo Ozaki	72	67	66	71	276	2,727,500
Katsunori Kuwabara	68	71	69	68	276	2,727,500
Tadahiro Takayama	68	69	72	67	276	2,727,500
Dean Wilson	69	70	67	70	276	2,727,500
Yoshitaka Yamamoto	69	69	68	71	277	2,020,000
Kazuhiko Hosokawa	71	69	69	68	277	2,020,000
Masanori Kobayashi	67	72	71	67	277	2,020,000
Tsukasa Watanabe	70	69	69	70	278	1,670,000
Toshimitsu Izawa	69	67	70	72	278	1,670,000
Koki Idoki	74	67	69	69	279	1,385,000
Nobuhito Sato	71	70	67	71	279	1,385,000
Shinichi Yokota	73	70	66	70	279	1,385,000
Lin Keng-chi	72	71	68	68	279	1,385,000
Naomichi Ozaki	70	68	73	69	280	1,000,000
Satoshi Higashi	67	74	72	67	280	1,000,000
Shigeru Nonaka	71	71	67	71	280	1,000,000
Daisuke Maruyama	71	71	71	67	280	1,000,000
Dinesh Chand	68	74	70	68	280	1,000,000
Chen Tze-chung	70	71	71	68	280	1,000,000
Seiki Okuda	71	69	73	68	281	780,000
Keiichiro Fukabori	71	67	69	74	281	780,000
Katsumune Imai	72	71	70	68	281	780,000

Acom International

Ishioka Golf Club, Ogawa, Ibaraki
Par 36-35–71; 7,045 yards
(Third round cancelled—rain.)

September 26-29
purse, ¥120,000,000

	SCORES			TOTAL	MONEY
Toru Taniguchi	64	63	70	197	¥18,000,000
Zhang Lian-wei	67	63	68	198	9,000,000
Tsuneyuki Nakajima	68	65	66	199	6,120,000
Dean Wilson	69	67	64	200	4,320,000
Gregory Meyer	66	66	70	202	3,420,000
Katsunori Kuwabara	68	68	66	202	3,420,000
Shigemasa Higaki	72	64	67	203	2,970,000
Toru Suzuki	66	70	68	204	2,454,750
Shingo Katayama	68	67	69	204	2,454,750
Jun Kikuchi	65	64	75	204	2,454,750
Hirokazu Kuniyoshi	68	70	66	204	2,454,750
Tatsuo Takasaki	66	66	73	205	1,750,500
Hsieh Chin-sheng	71	65	69	205	1,750,500

	SCORES			TOTAL	MONEY
Kazuhiko Hosokawa	70	65	70	205	1,750,500
Richard Lee	66	73	66	205	1,750,500
Takenori Hiraishi	68	68	70	206	1,288,800
Keiichiro Fukabori	66	71	69	206	1,288,800
Nobuhito Sato	68	69	69	206	1,288,800
David Smail	71	65	70	206	1,288,800
Brendan Jones	74	66	66	206	1,288,800
Masashi Ozaki	68	69	70	207	925,200
Hideki Kase	71	70	66	207	925,200
Kiyoshi Murota	68	73	66	207	925,200
Frankie Minoza	69	67	71	207	925,200
David Ishii	67	72	68	207	925,200
Tateo Ozaki	71	65	72	208	623,700
Hajime Meshiai	72	70	66	208	623,700
Tsukasa Watanabe	70	70	68	208	623,700
Koki Idoki	69	71	68	208	623,700
Hiroyuki Fujita	72	66	70	208	623,700
Kenichi Kuboya	67	73	68	208	623,700
Yasuharu Imano	71	68	69	208	623,700
Mitsuhiro Tateyama	72	68	68	208	623,700
Tomoaki Ueda	72	68	68	208	623,700
Prayad Marksaeng	73	68	67	208	623,700

Georgia Tokai Classic

Miyoshi Country Club, Miyoshi, Aichi
Par 36-36–72; 7,095 yards

October 10-13
purse, ¥120,000,000

	SCORES				TOTAL	MONEY
Toru Taniguchi	72	69	69	68	278	¥24,000,000
Zaw Moe	72	70	70	68	280	10,080,000
Nozomi Kawahara	72	69	68	71	280	10,080,000
Nobuhito Sato	70	69	71	71	281	5,280,000
Shingo Katayama	68	71	73	69	281	5,280,000
Hiroyuki Fujita	71	69	72	71	283	4,320,000
Toshimitsu Izawa	70	70	71	75	286	3,537,000
Hsieh Chin-sheng	70	73	73	70	286	3,537,000
Shigeru Nonaka	69	73	73	71	286	3,537,000
Yano Azuma	70	75	71	70	286	3,537,000
Dean Wilson	76	71	66	74	287	2,904,000
Masashi Ozaki	73	68	69	78	288	1,992,000
Kiyoshi Murota	73	68	72	75	288	1,992,000
Tsukasa Watanabe	69	75	75	69	288	1,992,000
Daisuke Maruyama	72	72	71	73	288	1,992,000
Shigemasa Higaki	73	68	72	75	288	1,992,000
Satoru Hirota	66	76	72	74	288	1,992,000
Tadahiro Takayama	74	68	73	73	288	1,992,000
Richard Lee	69	72	76	71	288	1,992,000
Charlie Wi	71	70	71	76	288	1,992,000
Katsunori Kuwabara	70	74	71	74	289	1,320,000
Takashi Kanemoto	72	74	72	71	289	1,320,000
Zhang Lian-wei	69	72	76	72	289	1,320,000
Takenori Hiraishi	75	71	71	73	290	1,080,000
Keiichiro Fukabori	74	68	76	72	290	1,080,000
Katsumune Imai	75	71	69	75	290	1,080,000
Yoshinori Mizumaki	72	73	73	73	291	888,000
Tatsuya Shiraishi	76	69	75	71	291	888,000

	SCORES			TOTAL	MONEY
Dinesh Chand	75	72	70	74	291	888,000
Masanori Kobayashi	73	71	74	73	291	888,000
Hikaru Sudo	72	72	73	74	291	888,000

Japan Open

Shimonoseki Golf Club, Toyoura, Yamaguchi
Par 35-35–70; 6,867 yards

October 17-20
purse, ¥120,000,000

	SCORES			TOTAL	MONEY
David Smail	71	66	67	67	271	¥24,000,000
Kim Jong-duck	65	69	70	71	275	13,200,000
Katsunori Kuwabara	68	70	71	67	276	7,710,000
Katsuya Nakagawa	70	72	67	67	276	7,710,000
Masashi Ozaki	68	71	72	66	277	4,560,000
Nobuhito Sato	62	71	72	72	277	4,560,000
Kiyoshi Miyazato	66	72	73	68	279	3,444,000
Keiichiro Fukabori	70	67	72	71	280	2,734,000
Yasuharu Imano	69	70	67	74	280	2,734,000
Hidemasa Hoshino	69	73	70	68	280	2,734,000
Hiroyuki Fujita	70	68	71	72	281	1,956,000
Katsumasa Miyamoto	69	73	70	69	281	1,956,000
Naomichi Ozaki	71	71	69	71	282	1,500,000
Kazuhiko Hosokawa	66	73	70	73	282	1,500,000
Shingo Katayama	70	72	72	68	282	1,500,000
Dinesh Chand	71	71	71	69	282	1,500,000
Takao Shimada	69	72	72	69	282	1,500,000
*Yusaku Miyazato	71	72	69	70	282	
Tsuneyuki Nakajima	69	73	72	69	283	1,183,600
Takenori Hiraishi	71	72	73	67	283	1,183,600
Toru Taniguchi	73	72	68	70	283	1,183,600
Mitsuhiro Tateyama	70	71	71	71	283	1,183,600
Dean Wilson	74	70	66	73	283	1,183,600
Hajime Meshiai	69	74	69	72	284	1,070,000
Shinichi Akiba	68	73	72	71	284	1,070,000
Hideyuki Sato	69	67	74	75	285	972,000
Nobumitsu Yuhara	74	70	70	71	285	972,000
Naoki Hattori	71	72	75	67	285	972,000
Shinichi Yokota	73	71	72	69	285	972,000
Tomohiro Kondou	71	70	75	69	285	972,000
Ichihara Koudai	67	72	77	69	285	972,000
S.K. Ho	70	72	75	68	285	972,000

Bridgestone Open

Sodegaura Country Club, Chiba
Par 36-36–72; 7,208 yards

October 24-27
purse, ¥110,000,000

	SCORES			TOTAL	MONEY
Scott Laycock	66	66	69	71	272	¥22,000,000
Toru Taniguchi	67	67	67	72	273	9,240,000
Shingo Katayama	66	69	71	67	273	9,240,000
Shinichi Yokota	68	68	69	70	275	4,840,000
Dean Wilson	67	68	72	68	275	4,840,000
Kenichi Kuboya	70	73	66	68	277	3,511,750

	SCORES				TOTAL	MONEY
Yasuharu Imano	68	69	68	72	277	3,511,750
Hirokazu Kuniyoshi	73	66	70	68	277	3,511,750
S.K. Ho	67	70	70	70	277	3,511,750
Hajime Meshiai	72	67	71	68	278	2,552,000
Toshimitsu Izawa	68	70	69	71	278	2,552,000
Keiichiro Fukabori	71	64	72	71	278	2,552,000
Lin Keng-chi	73	70	69	66	278	2,552,000
Kiyoshi Murota	71	69	69	70	279	1,837,000
Tsukasa Watanabe	71	69	69	70	279	1,837,000
Zhang Lian-wei	67	70	69	73	279	1,837,000
Brendan Jones	68	72	71	68	279	1,837,000
*Taichiro Kiyota	73	68	69	69	279	
Naomichi Ozaki	72	69	73	66	280	1,474,000
Satoshi Higashi	71	70	70	69	280	1,474,000
Hiroyuki Fujita	74	70	69	67	280	1,474,000
Hideki Kase	69	73	74	65	281	1,130,800
Takenori Hiraishi	69	69	74	69	281	1,130,800
Gregory Meyer	70	71	68	72	281	1,130,800
Kazuhiro Kinjo	71	72	69	69	281	1,130,800
Hideto Tanihara	70	69	73	69	281	1,130,800
Richard Backwell	69	70	71	72	282	902,000
Tetsuji Hiratsuka	73	70	69	70	282	902,000
Tomohiro Kondou	75	67	70	70	282	902,000
Hisayuki Sasaki	66	68	72	77	283	732,600
Hidezumi Shirakata	68	73	73	69	283	732,600
Kazuhiko Hosokawa	72	69	72	70	283	732,600
Toyokazu Hioki	72	69	70	72	283	732,600
Kiyoshi Miyazato	70	71	71	71	283	732,600

Philip Morris Championship

ABC Golf Club, Tojo, Hyogo
Par 36-36–72; 7,176 yards

October 31-November 3
purse, ¥200,000,000

	SCORES				TOTAL	MONEY
Brendan Jones	65	67	67	70	269	¥40,000,000
Toshimitsu Izawa	66	66	69	70	271	20,000,000
Hiroyuki Fujita	69	69	70	66	274	11,800,000
Dean Wilson	68	68	68	70	274	11,800,000
Mamoru Osanai	70	68	66	71	275	7,266,666
Prayad Marksaeng	68	67	69	71	275	7,266,666
Scott Laycock	72	64	70	69	275	7,266,666
Shinichi Yokota	67	71	70	68	276	5,252,000
Shingo Katayama	65	70	68	73	276	5,252,000
Kenichi Kuboya	69	70	68	69	276	5,252,000
Dinesh Chand	65	70	71	70	276	5,252,000
Zhang Lian-wei	72	68	68	68	276	5,252,000
Toru Taniguchi	67	72	66	72	277	3,590,000
Zaw Moe	69	69	71	68	277	3,590,000
Tetsuji Hiratsuka	70	70	68	69	277	3,590,000
Katsumasa Miyamoto	70	69	70	68	277	3,590,000
Naomichi Ozaki	70	70	68	70	278	2,940,000
Satoshi Higashi	68	69	67	74	278	2,940,000
Masashi Ozaki	67	69	72	71	279	2,211,428
Tsuneyuki Nakajima	69	70	72	68	279	2,211,428
Tsukasa Watanabe	70	67	69	73	279	2,211,428
Masahiro Kuramoto	76	66	66	71	279	2,211,428

	SCORES				TOTAL	MONEY
Hirofumi Miyase	70	71	70	68	279	2,211,428
Nobuhito Sato	71	66	71	71	279	2,211,428
Yui Ueda	69	70	71	69	279	2,211,428
Kiyoshi Miyazato	70	69	71	70	280	1,720,000
Katsunori Kuwabara	67	70	70	74	281	1,600,000
Tomohiro Kondou	70	72	68	71	281	1,600,000
Keiichiro Fukabori	72	70	72	68	282	1,385,000
Masashi Shimada	68	74	69	71	282	1,385,000
Yasuharu Imano	70	70	67	75	282	1,385,000
David Smail	71	72	68	71	282	1,385,000

Mitsui Sumitomo Visa Taiheiyo Masters

Taiheiyo Club, Gotemba Course, Gotemba, Shizuoka
Par 36-36–72; 7,246 yards

November 14-17
purse, ¥150,000,000

	SCORES				TOTAL	MONEY
Tsuneyuki Nakajima	69	66	67	70	272	¥30,000,000
Hidemichi Tanaka	67	70	67	69	273	15,000,000
Aaron Baddeley	69	68	68	69	274	10,200,000
Shingo Katayama	69	70	67	69	275	6,600,000
Justin Rose	70	68	69	68	275	6,600,000
Katsuyoshi Tomori	72	67	72	65	276	5,400,000
Charles Howell	70	70	68	69	277	4,950,000
Toshimitsu Izawa	71	69	69	70	279	4,245,000
Katsunori Kuwabara	74	68	67	70	279	4,245,000
Kiyoshi Miyazato	71	65	72	71	279	4,245,000
Kazuhiko Hosokawa	74	67	69	70	280	3,480,000
Dean Wilson	74	67	66	73	280	3,480,000
Taichi Teshima	69	67	69	76	281	2,780,000
Brendan Jones	65	69	73	74	281	2,780,000
Scott Laycock	72	68	71	70	281	2,780,000
Hiroyuki Fujita	75	68	67	72	282	2,355,000
Takashi Kanemoto	68	72	70	72	282	2,355,000
Tsuyoshi Yoneyama	70	70	71	72	283	1,950,000
Shigeru Nonaka	73	68	69	73	283	1,950,000
Katsumune Imai	74	67	73	69	283	1,950,000
Kim Jong-duck	70	66	73	74	283	1,950,000
*Yusaku Miyazato	73	70	67	73	283	
Masashi Ozaki	71	67	72	74	284	1,530,000
Kazumasa Sakaitani	73	73	70	68	284	1,530,000
Hidemasa Hoshino	71	69	74	70	284	1,530,000
Kiyoshi Murota	75	70	69	71	285	1,290,000
Tsukasa Watanabe	77	69	70	69	285	1,290,000
David Smail	73	68	70	74	285	1,290,000
Shigemasa Higaki	78	69	68	71	286	1,110,000
Jun Kikuchi	73	72	73	68	286	1,110,000
Todd Hamilton	72	71	70	73	286	1,110,000

Dunlop Phoenix

Phoenix Country Club, Miyazaki
Par 36-35–71; 6,917 yards

November 21-24
purse, ¥200,000,000

	SCORES				TOTAL	MONEY
Kaname Yokoo	66	65	69	69	269	¥40,000,000
Sergio Garcia	67	68	69	66	270	20,000,000
K.J. Choi	72	69	66	64	271	13,600,000
Darren Clarke	64	72	65	71	272	8,800,000
Justin Rose	66	69	70	67	272	8,800,000
Hiroyuki Fujita	68	68	71	66	273	6,900,000
David Duval	69	69	67	68	273	6,900,000
Tiger Woods	71	68	69	67	275	6,100,000
Yasuharu Imano	70	69	71	66	276	5,640,000
Zaw Moe	68	67	68	74	277	5,040,000
David Smail	72	70	70	65	277	5,040,000
Dean Wilson	73	68	68	69	278	4,240,000
Thomas Bjorn	71	69	72	66	278	4,240,000
Hidemichi Tanaka	70	72	67	70	279	3,540,000
Toru Taniguchi	73	70	70	66	279	3,540,000
Naomichi Ozaki	67	71	75	67	280	2,864,000
Katsuyoshi Tomori	71	70	68	71	280	2,864,000
Hirofumi Miyase	67	71	71	71	280	2,864,000
Nozomi Kawahara	68	68	77	67	280	2,864,000
Kim Jong-duck	68	70	70	72	280	2,864,000
Tsukasa Watanabe	66	70	70	75	281	2,120,000
Shigeru Nonaka	69	72	69	71	281	2,120,000
Taichi Teshima	72	68	70	71	281	2,120,000
Shingo Katayama	70	68	73	70	281	2,120,000
Tateo Ozaki	68	70	76	68	282	1,720,000
Toshimitsu Izawa	71	67	73	71	282	1,720,000
Katsunori Kuwabara	70	72	70	70	282	1,720,000
Masashi Ozaki	67	72	72	72	283	1,480,000
Kiyoshi Miyazato	73	72	69	69	283	1,480,000
Prayad Marksaeng	70	74	72	67	283	1,480,000

Casio World Open

Ibusuki Golf Club, Kaimon, Kagoshima
Par 36-36–72; 7,151 yards
(Event shortened to 54 holes—rain.)

November 28-December 1
purse, ¥140,000,000

	SCORES			TOTAL	MONEY
David Smail	68	68	64	200	¥21,000,000
Brendan Jones	68	64	70	202	10,500,000
Tsukasa Watanabe	67	72	66	205	7,140,000
Tateo Ozaki	69	66	71	206	5,040,000
Saburo Fujiki	72	68	68	208	3,661,875
Hajime Meshiai	70	66	72	208	3,661,875
Eduardo Herrera	68	73	67	208	3,661,875
Zaw Moe	70	68	70	208	3,661,875
Takashi Kanemoto	71	71	67	209	2,646,000
Shingo Katayama	70	70	69	209	2,646,000
Tadahiro Takayama	74	63	72	209	2,646,000
Jeev Milkha Singh	71	70	68	209	2,646,000
Kazuhiko Hosokawa	67	70	73	210	2,016,000
Nozomi Kawahara	70	67	73	210	2,016,000

	SCORES			TOTAL	MONEY
Hideki Kase	69	72	70	211	1,509,000
Gregory Meyer	71	70	70	211	1,509,000
Mitsuhiro Tateyama	74	69	68	211	1,509,000
Tomohiro Kondo	70	70	71	211	1,509,000
Hidemasa Hoshino	68	72	71	211	1,509,000
Richard Lee	72	72	67	211	1,509,000
Trevor Immelman	71	69	71	211	1,509,000
Yoshinori Kaneko	74	67	71	212	1,012,200
Koki Idoki	71	68	73	212	1,012,200
Hirofumi Miyase	70	73	69	212	1,012,200
Hiroyuki Fujita	69	72	71	212	1,012,200
Kazuhiro Kinjo	72	72	68	212	1,012,200
Toshimitsu Izawa	69	70	74	213	840,000
Hideto Tanihara	71	69	73	213	840,000
Nobumitsu Yuhara	71	72	71	214	716,625
Mitsutaka Kusakabe	71	71	72	214	716,625
Tomoaki Ueda	69	72	73	214	716,625
Chen Tze-chung	74	71	69	214	716,625

Nippon Series JT Cup

Tokyo Yomiuri Country Club, Tokyo
Par 35-35–70; 6,961 yards

December 5-8
purse, ¥100,000,000

	SCORES				TOTAL	MONEY
Shingo Katayama	62	66	66	67	261	¥30,000,000
David Smail	65	68	69	68	270	14,800,000
Masashi Ozaki	62	71	67	71	271	8,000,000
Katsunori Kuwabara	68	66	70	68	272	5,150,000
Kim Jong-duck	64	65	72	71	272	5,150,000
Katsumasa Miyamoto	65	71	68	70	274	4,100,000
Hirofumi Miyase	71	67	70	68	276	3,300,000
Hiroyuki Fujita	70	68	70	68	276	3,300,000
Yasuharu Imano	68	73	69	66	276	3,300,000
Zhang Lian-wei	70	66	67	73	276	3,300,000
Toru Suzuki	69	74	67	67	277	2,600,000
Kaname Yokoo	68	70	72	67	277	2,600,000
Nobumitsu Yuhara	67	70	70	71	278	2,200,000
Brendan Jones	72	69	68	69	278	2,200,000
Naomichi Ozaki	67	73	70	69	279	1,900,000
Tsuneyuki Nakajima	66	70	71	72	279	1,900,000
Toshimitsu Izawa	70	68	71	71	280	1,600,000
Terry Price	70	72	70	68	280	1,600,000
Tomohiro Kondo	73	66	70	71	280	1,600,000
Kiyoshi Murota	69	76	71	72	288	1,400,000

Asia/Japan Okinawa Open

Southern Links Golf Club, Naha
Par 36-36–72, 6,982 yards
(Event shortened to 54 holes—rain.)

December 19-22
purse, ¥100,000,000

	SCORES			TOTAL	MONEY
Hiroyuki Fujita	67	68	67	202	¥15,000,000
*Yusaku Miyazato	68	70	67	205	

	SCORES			TOTAL	MONEY
Ted Purdy	65	70	70	205	7,500,000
Tetsuji Hiratsuka	68	67	73	208	4,350,000
Tomohiro Kondo	66	69	73	208	4,350,000
Taichi Teshima	69	71	69	209	2,850,000
James Oh	70	67	72	209	2,850,000
Masashi Ozaki	68	68	74	210	2,475,000
Nozomi Kawahara	71	71	69	211	1,818,214
Hideki Kase	69	72	70	211	1,818,214
Akinori Tani	72	68	71	211	1,818,214
Daisuke Maruyama	69	70	72	211	1,818,214
Toru Suzuki	70	69	72	211	1,818,214
Unho Park	69	67	75	211	1,818,214
Dinesh Chand	70	66	75	211	1,818,214
Thongchai Jaidee	70	71	71	212	1,292,857
Kenichi Kuboya	70	70	72	212	1,292,857
Katsumune Imai	71	69	72	212	1,292,857
Chawalit Plaphol	71	70	71	212	1,292,857
Kang Wook-soon	72	68	72	212	1,292,857
Taimur Hussain	71	69	72	212	1,292,857
Katsuya Nakagawa	71	66	75	212	1,292,857
Takenori Hiraishi	69	73	71	213	671,250
Nobumitsu Yuhara	72	70	71	213	671,250
Amandeep Johl	71	71	71	213	671,250
Shigemasa Higaki	72	69	72	213	671,250
Paul Sheehan	71	70	72	213	671,250
Zhang Lian-wei	69	72	72	213	671,250
Steve Jurgensen	71	67	75	213	671,250
Greg Hanrahan	67	70	76	213	671,250

Australasian Tour

Telstra Hyundai New Zealand Open

Paraparaumu Beach Golf Club, Wellington, New Zealand
Par 35-36–71; 6,556 yards

January 10-13
purse, NZ$1,000,000

	SCORES				TOTAL	MONEY
Craig Parry	67	69	69	68	273	A$147,977.64
Michael Campbell	67	72	66	69	274	59,602.10
Steve Alker	66	70	68	70	274	59,602.10
Stephen Leaney	68	67	68	71	274	59,602.10
*Adam Groom	69	67	74	67	277	
Stephen Scahill	67	75	69	68	279	29,595.53
Tiger Woods	70	73	67	69	279	29,595.53
Nick O'Hern	68	71	70	70	279	29,595.53
Scott Hend	71	71	71	67	280	23,840.84
Steve Conran	71	71	69	70	281	21,374.55
Marcus Norgren	71	69	70	71	281	21,374.55
*Brad Heaven	70	72	67	72	281	
Wayne Smith	70	69	72	71	282	15,825.38
Brett Rumford	66	71	71	74	282	15,825.38
Justin Cooper	69	70	68	75	282	15,825.38
James McLean	65	70	71	76	282	15,825.38
*Tim Wilkinson	70	72	70	71	283	
Eddie Barr	71	68	72	72	283	12,495.89
Craig Perks	74	68	69	72	283	12,495.89
Andrew Bonhomme	70	68	70	76	284	10,276.22
Jon Riley	69	69	70	76	284	10,276.22
Peter O'Malley	70	71	73	71	285	8,367.78
Patrick Burke	70	71	72	72	285	8,367.78
Neil Kerry	69	71	72	73	285	8,367.78
Terry Price	70	72	70	73	285	8,367.78
Andre Stolz	72	70	74	69	285	8,367.78
Anthony Painter	68	71	72	74	285	8,367.78
Stuart Malcolmson	68	73	68	76	285	8,367.78
Chris Downes	73	71	71	71	286	6,182.17
Andrew Tschudin	69	71	72	74	286	6,182.17
David McKenzie	68	73	71	74	286	6,182.17
Adrian Percey	69	72	71	74	286	6,182.17
Martin Doyle	69	70	71	76	286	6,182.17

Johnnie Walker Classic

Lake Karrinyup Country Club, Perth, Australia
Par 36-36–72; 6,974 yards

January 24-27
purse, A$2,700,000

	SCORES				TOTAL	MONEY
Retief Goosen	70	68	63	73	274	A$450,000
Pierre Fulke	72	70	74	66	282	255,000
Sergio Garcia	69	73	72	69	283	168,750
Ernie Els	72	71	71	72	286	120,000
Raphael Jacquelin	75	72	72	68	287	90,000

	SCORES				TOTAL	MONEY
Simon Dyson	71	74	70	72	287	90,000
Anthony Wall	71	75	69	72	287	90,000
Mathias Gronberg	73	73	71	71	288	70,000
Nick Dougherty	74	76	68	70	288	70,000
Wayne Riley	77	70	69	73	289	53,125
Thongchai Jaidee	67	72	78	72	289	53,125
Nick Faldo	71	73	74	71	289	53,125
Peter Fowler	71	77	70	71	289	53,125
Craig Parry	78	69	71	72	290	39,500
Trevor Immelman	75	72	70	73	290	39,500
Jamie Donaldson	73	75	70	72	290	39,500
Steve Alker	75	65	77	74	291	29,406.25
David Howell	75	71	71	74	291	29,406.25
Justin Rose	78	71	68	74	291	29,406.25
Soren Kjeldsen	77	73	69	72	291	29,406.25
Scott Gardiner	75	76	69	72	292	26,000
Peter Lonard	79	68	74	72	293	23,650
James McLean	78	70	72	73	293	23,650
Thomas Levet	75	70	76	72	293	23,650
Santiago Luna	74	75	75	69	293	23,650
Yeh Wei-tze	71	76	72	74	293	23,650
Craig Jones	71	72	74	77	294	16,444.44
Adam Crawford	74	72	73	75	294	16,444.44
Jarrod Moseley	76	72	72	74	294	16,444.44
Niclas Fasth	72	72	78	72	294	16,444.44
Greg Turner	74	73	76	71	294	16,444.44
Charlie Wi	70	76	73	75	294	16,444.44
Nick O'Hern	73	76	72	73	294	16,444.44
Roger Wessels	74	76	73	71	294	16,444.44
Brett Rumford	71	77	73	73	294	16,444.44
Brendan Jones	79	72	70	74	295	12,250
David Lynn	78	72	72	73	295	12,250
Prayad Marksaeng	77	73	70	75	295	12,250
Mark Allen	77	74	71	73	295	12,250
Jean-Francois Remesy	73	76	73	73	295	12,250
Ian Garbutt	74	77	72	72	295	12,250
Masanori Kobayashi	82	69	74	71	296	8,500
Richard Green	73	72	75	76	296	8,500
Steve Webster	75	72	75	74	296	8,500
Robert Karlsson	76	72	74	74	296	8,500
Hirokazu Kuniyoshi	75	73	76	72	296	8,500
Ed Stedman	74	74	71	77	296	8,500
Christopher Hanell	74	74	72	76	296	8,500
Markus Brier	73	75	75	73	296	8,500
Michael Campbell	69	80	74	73	296	8,500
Anders Forsbrand	78	69	79	71	297	5,617.85
Steen Tinning	78	72	72	75	297	5,617.85
Jonathan Lomas	76	72	75	74	297	5,617.85
Carl Pettersson	74	73	72	78	297	5,617.85
Anthony Kang	74	75	76	72	297	5,617.85
David Carter	73	76	76	72	297	5,617.85
Scott Laycock	73	78	74	72	297	5,617.85
Andrew Bonhomme	73	73	76	76	298	5,175
Jarmo Sandelin	77	73	74	74	298	5,175
Lee Westwood	72	74	76	76	298	5,175
Anthony Painter	73	76	75	74	298	5,175
Dean Robertson	72	78	76	72	298	5,175
Wang Ter-chang	72	79	72	75	298	5,175
John Bickerton	76	75	76	72	299	4,950
Daniel Chopra	71	77	72	79	299	4,950

	SCORES				TOTAL	MONEY
Andrew Coltart	74	77	73	75	299	4,950
Barry Lane	75	74	73	78	300	4,800
Adam Scott	72	76	77	75	300	4,800
Gary Emerson	72	79	72	77	300	4,800
Scott Hend	77	73	73	78	301	4,650
Nathan Gatehouse	76	74	76	75	301	4,650
James Kingston	74	76	76	75	301	4,650
Tobias Dier	75	71	77	79	302	4,525
David Armstrong	77	74	75	76	302	4,525
Terry Price	80	70	78	75	303	4,325
David Smail	75	75	74	79	303	4,325
Peter Senior	75	75	76	77	303	4,325
Martin Doyle	74	75	78	76	303	4,325
Lucas Parsons	75	76	75	77	303	4,325
Craig Spence	71	80	76	76	303	4,325
Stephen Gallacher	72	75	81	77	305	4,150
Kenny Druce	79	72	78	77	306	4,075
Arjun Atwal	77	74	81	74	306	4,075
Vivek Bhandari	78	73	81	80	312	4,000

Heineken Classic

Royal Melbourne Golf Club, Melbourne, Victoria
Par 36-36–72; 6,981 yards

January 31-February 3
purse, A$2,000,000

	SCORES				TOTAL	MONEY
Ernie Els	64	69	69	69	271	A$360,000
Peter Fowler	69	70	70	67	276	145,000
David Howell	68	70	70	68	276	145,000
Peter O'Malley	68	68	70	70	276	145,000
Michael Campbell	68	72	68	69	277	80,000
Greg Norman	69	67	73	69	278	64,666.66
Nick Faldo	67	73	69	69	278	64,666.66
Stephen Leaney	70	66	72	70	278	64,666.66
Greg Owen	73	70	68	69	280	52,000
Craig Parry	68	71	71	70	280	52,000
Trevor Immelman	69	69	77	66	281	40,000
Scott Laycock	73	68	71	69	281	40,000
Anthony Wall	72	70	69	70	281	40,000
Fredrik Jacobson	71	73	72	66	282	28,960
Jarrod Moseley	70	70	71	71	282	28,960
Adam Scott	67	72	70	73	282	28,960
Richard Lee	75	62	71	74	282	28,960
Barry Lane	67	73	68	74	282	28,960
David Smail	69	71	74	69	283	20,750
Greg Turner	72	72	70	69	283	20,750
Jarmo Sandelin	75	66	72	70	283	20,750
*Lee Seung-yong	67	75	71	70	283	
Mark Allen	70	70	72	71	283	20,750
Scott Hend	71	72	68	72	283	20,750
Philip Golding	72	67	70	74	283	20,750
Aaron Baddeley	70	71	73	70	284	15,920
Joakim Haeggman	72	68	73	71	284	15,920
Patrik Sjoland	68	71	73	72	284	15,920
Steen Tinning	71	72	68	73	284	15,920
Peter Lonard	67	71	72	74	284	15,920
John Bickerton	76	68	73	68	285	11,875

	SCORES			TOTAL	MONEY
Andre Stolz	71	72	72	70	285	11,875
Sven Struver	73	68	73	71	285	11,875
Steve Conran	76	68	70	71	285	11,875
Daren Lee	73	70	70	72	285	11,875
Mark Foster	70	73	70	72	285	11,875
Gary Orr	70	71	70	74	285	11,875
Niclas Fasth	73	68	69	75	285	11,875
Gavin Coles	73	67	77	69	286	8,600
Jamie Spence	72	72	73	69	286	8,600
Yeh Wei-tze	74	66	76	70	286	8,600
John Daly	71	73	71	71	286	8,600
Miguel Angel Martin	73	71	71	71	286	8,600
Carl Pettersson	71	68	74	73	286	8,600
Mark Pilkington	66	70	75	75	286	8,600
Marc Farry	68	74	69	75	286	8,600
Ian Garbutt	71	70	75	71	287	5,833.33
Robert Karlsson	70	70	75	72	287	5,833.33
Gary Evans	75	68	72	72	287	5,833.33
Doug LaBelle	70	70	74	73	287	5,833.33
Stephen Gallacher	72	70	71	74	287	5,833.33
Alastair Forsyth	70	71	71	75	287	5,833.33
Terry Price	70	73	73	72	288	4,500
Steve Collins	71	72	72	73	288	4,500
Jamie Donaldson	72	72	71	73	288	4,500
Marcus Norgren	72	71	75	71	289	4,220
Gregory Havret	71	72	74	72	289	4,220
Jeev Milkha Singh	69	73	74	73	289	4,220
Stephen Scahill	71	72	73	73	289	4,220
Richard Backwell	71	71	73	74	289	4,220
Soren Hansen	72	69	73	75	289	4,220
Thomas Levet	74	70	69	76	289	4,220
Robert Allenby	70	68	71	80	289	4,220
Costantino Rocca	72	70	75	73	290	4,000
Andrew Coltart	71	70	74	75	290	4,000
Richard Green	70	72	73	75	290	4,000
Paul Sheehan	73	71	77	70	291	3,860
Alex Cejka	70	73	77	71	291	3,860
Markus Brier	72	70	77	72	291	3,860
Marcus Cain	69	72	74	76	291	3,860
Simon Dyson	74	69	78	71	292	3,720
Soren Kjeldsen	74	70	77	71	292	3,720
Zhang Lian-wei	70	74	75	73	292	3,720
Matthew Ecob	72	72	75	74	293	3,600
Mark Wilson	71	72	75	75	293	3,600
Raphael Jacquelin	71	70	75	77	293	3,600
Andrew Tschudin	69	75	80	74	298	3,520

ANZ Championship

The Lakes Golf Club, Sydney, New South Wales
Par 36-37–73; 6,904 yards

February 7-10
purse, A$1,750,000

	POINTS			TOTAL	MONEY
Richard Johnson	3	16	16	11	46	A$315,000
Scott Laycock	11	16	7	10	44	148,321.50
Craig Parry	10	18	9	7	44	148,321.50
Andre Stolz	11	19	9	4	43	84,000

	POINTS				TOTAL	MONEY
Stephen Gallacher	10	12	13	4	39	70,000
Ian Garbutt	6	6	7	19	38	63,000
Jonathan Lomas	20	1	9	7	37	56,000
Greg Turner	10	8	12	6	36	47,250
Trevor Immelman	10	19	3	4	36	47,250
Thomas Levet	8	4	10	14	36	47,250
Nick O'Hern	4	13	15	3	35	35,000
Geoff Ogilvy	7	16	1	11	35	35,000
Niclas Fasth	3	11	10	11	35	35,000
Peter Senior	8	6	8	12	34	25,340
Jean-Francois Remesy	11	6	9	8	34	25,340
Anders Hansen	9	11	7	7	34	25,340
John Bickerton	5	13	11	5	34	25,340
Nick Dougherty	7	8	5	14	34	25,340
David Howell	10	3	4	16	33	18,156.25
Brad Andrews	8	8	7	10	33	18,156.25
Mathias Gronberg	9	13	1	10	33	18,156.25
Fredrik Jacobson	3	9	7	14	33	18,156.25
Andrew Coltart	5	11	4	13	33	18,156.25
Patrik Sjoland	11	10	0	12	33	18,156.25
Sven Struver	7	4	12	9	32	12,971.87
Steve Alker	7	13	4	8	32	12,971.87
David Bransdon	3	13	5	11	32	12,971.87
Anthony Painter	4	13	9	6	32	12,971.87
David Lynn	12	7	11	2	32	12,971.87
Johan Skold	5	11	8	8	32	12,971.87
Markus Brier	4	10	4	14	32	12,971.87
Christopher Hanell	9	5	4	14	32	12,971.87
Mark Foster	2	10	14	5	31	9,975
Marcus Norgren	11	3	10	7	31	9,975
Carlos Rodiles	10	15	5	1	31	9,975
Gregory Havret	5	19	1	6	31	9,975
David Smail	11	7	4	8	30	8,575
Mark Pilkington	3	8	8	11	30	8,575
Brendan Jones	5	6	6	13	30	8,575
Carl Pettersson	13	6	6	5	30	8,575
Jean Hugo	3	9	8	9	29	7,350
Matthew Cort	7	19	19	2	29	7,350
Brad Kennedy	-2	15	8	8	29	7,350
Raphael Jacquelin	15	4	6	3	28	5,775
Gavin Coles	7	9	2	10	28	5,775
Alex Cejka	7	9	2	10	28	5,775
Peter O'Malley	9	9	15	-5	28	5,775
Gary Orr	10	5	8	5	28	5,775
Nathan Green	-1	12	6	11	28	5,775
Euan Walters	12	8	5	2	27	4,462.50
Adam Crawford	4	12	7	4	27	4,462.50
Yeh Wei-tze	10	6	3	7	26	4,025
Tim Elliott	5	8	6	6	25	3,893.75
Aaron Baddeley	2	9	1	13	25	3,893.75
Grant Dodd	3	8	4	9	24	3,762.50
Daren Lee	7	5	5	7	24	3,762.50
James McLean	4	8	8	4	24	3,762.50
Ed Stedman	5	6	5	8	24	3,762.50
David Gilford	7	11	-3	8	23	3,622.50
Matthew Ecob	4	10	6	3	23	3,622.50
Roger Wessels	5	9	4	5	23	3,622.50
Greg Owen	9	2	2	10	23	3,622.50
Peter Fowler	1	10	6	5	22	3,517.50
Alastair Forsyth	3	13	-5	11	22	3,517.50

		POINTS			TOTAL	MONEY
Lucas Parsons	3	9	10	-1	21	3,465
Richard Lee	4	7	2	7	20	3,430
Paul Broadhurst	6	11	-2	4	19	3,395
Pierre Fulke	5	6	3	4	18	3,342.50
Ben Ferguson	2	11	-2	7	18	3,342.50
John Wade	6	12	-8	7	17	3,272.50
Scott Gardiner	8	6	-5	8	17	3,272.50
Andrew Marshall	7	4	3	2	16	3,220
Jarmo Sandelin	-7	20	-1	3	15	3,167.50
Simon Dyson	4	8	1	2	15	3,167.50
Joakim Haeggman	10	5	-2	1	14	3,115
Mark Wilson	7	6	-5	1	9	3,080
Jeev Milkha Singh	6	5	-1	-2	8	3,045

New South Wales Masters

Longyard Golf Club, Tamworth, New South Wales
Par 36-36–72; 6,771 yards

February 28-March 3
purse, A$100,000

	SCORES				TOTAL	MONEY
Steve Collins	67	67	66	68	268	A$18,000
Leigh McKechnie	68	69	64	67	268	10,200
(Collins defeated McKechnie on first playoff hole.)						
Scott Hend	69	66	69	65	269	6,750
Paul Devenport	69	66	70	65	270	4,800
Brad Andrews	63	69	71	68	271	4,000
David McKenzie	67	67	68	70	272	2,980
David Armstrong	62	72	67	71	272	2,980
Adam Crawford	68	65	68	71	272	2,980
Andrew Tschudin	65	70	67	70	272	2,980
Doug LaBelle	67	70	62	73	272	2,980
Michael Clayton	71	68	68	66	273	1,860
Ben Burge	70	64	72	67	273	1,860
Andrew Bonhomme	68	66	71	68	273	1,860
Kenichi Ryu	66	68	70	69	273	1,860
Euan Walters	66	71	68	68	273	1,860
Mark Allen	67	68	72	67	274	1,370
Anthony Painter	66	70	69	69	274	1,370
Justin Cooper	67	72	69	67	275	1,200
Jonathon Tomlinson	71	69	70	66	276	996.87
Ed Stedman	68	70	71	67	276	996.87
Brett Ogle	69	71	69	67	276	996.87
Ricky Schmidt	68	71	70	67	276	996.87
John Sutherland	68	73	68	67	276	996.87
Ewan Porter	68	70	70	68	276	996.87
Craig Jones	69	67	70	70	276	996.87
Peter Cliff	66	71	67	72	276	996.87
Lucien Tinkler	67	74	69	67	277	743.33
Grant Dodd	67	73	66	71	277	743.33
Paul Sheehan	69	71	66	71	277	743.33
Neil Sarkies	69	70	73	66	278	593.75
Chris Downes	67	71	71	69	278	593.75
Ryan Haller	68	69	72	69	278	593.75
David Bransdon	67	72	69	70	278	593.75

Jacob's Creek Open

Kooyonga Golf Club, Adelaide
Par 37-35–72; 6,732 yards

March 7-10
purse, A$1,000,000

	SCORES				TOTAL	MONEY
Gavin Coles	71	69	67	72	279	A$180,000
Bryce Molder	69	72	67	73	281	102,000
Peter Fowler	70	72	68	73	283	67,500
Stephen Leaney	70	71	74	70	285	44,000
Peter O'Malley	68	68	76	73	285	44,000
Paul Sheehan	72	72	73	69	286	29,800
Terry Price	74	71	72	69	286	29,800
Jason Gore	75	71	71	69	286	29,800
Trevor Dodds	71	73	71	71	286	29,800
Mark Hensby	75	68	70	73	286	29,800
Andre Stolz	72	70	71	74	287	22,000
Anthony Painter	76	71	73	68	288	17,080
Ahmad Bateman	76	71	72	69	288	17,080
Marcus Norgren	76	69	71	72	288	17,080
Joel Kribel	71	73	71	73	288	17,080
Scott Laycock	71	74	69	74	288	17,080
Jason Caron	76	70	73	70	289	12,083.33
Brad Kennedy	70	73	75	71	289	12,083.33
James McLean	73	70	72	74	289	12,083.33
Mathew Goggin	75	71	72	72	290	10,000
Paul Devenport	71	72	72	75	290	10,000
Doug LaBelle	72	69	73	76	290	10,000
Richard Johnson	68	74	72	76	290	10,000
Alex Cejka	70	72	70	78	290	10,000
Matthew Ecob	78	67	66	79	290	10,000
Scott Sterling	71	77	73	70	291	7,350
Jim Rutledge	72	75	73	71	291	7,350
Doug Dunakey	76	72	72	71	291	7,350
David Smail	73	74	71	73	291	7,350
Jeff Freeman	73	75	69	74	291	7,350
Chad Wright	73	73	70	75	291	7,350

Holden Clearwater Classic

Clearwater Resort, Christchurch, New Zealand
Par 36-36–72; 7,137 yards

March 14-17
purse, A$1,000,000

	SCORES				TOTAL	MONEY
Peter O'Malley	67	69	67	68	271	A$180,000
Brad Ott	69	67	72	68	276	102,000
Rich Barcelo	71	68	69	69	277	67,500
Alex Cejka	71	70	68	70	279	48,000
Nick O'Hern	67	70	75	68	280	36,000
Andrew McLardy	69	70	66	75	280	36,000
Joel Kribel	66	69	69	76	280	36,000
Jason Caron	72	70	70	69	281	24,600
Craig Jones	71	71	70	69	281	24,600
Tjaart van der Walt	68	72	71	70	281	24,600
Darron Stiles	73	69	68	71	281	24,600
Anthony Painter	70	66	72	73	281	24,600
Charles Warren	71	66	75	70	282	15,066.66
Steve Alker	67	73	72	70	282	15,066.66

	SCORES				TOTAL	MONEY
Steve Haskins	69	73	70	70	282	15,066.66
David Smail	71	71	70	70	282	15,066.66
Trevor Dodds	73	70	69	70	282	15,066.66
Scott Sterling	70	71	70	71	282	15,066.66
Ed Stedman	69	72	72	70	283	10,375
Stephen Leaney	68	69	75	71	283	10,375
Todd Fischer	71	70	71	71	283	10,375
Mark Hensby	69	73	70	71	283	10,375
Terry Price	71	70	69	73	283	10,375
Nathan Green	70	71	69	73	283	10,375
Tim Elliott	72	71	70	71	284	8,433.33
James McLean	71	72	69	72	284	8,433.33
Wayne Grady	73	70	68	73	284	8,433.33
Jeff Freeman	69	73	71	72	285	7,100
Andre Stolz	69	70	73	73	285	7,100
Jason Gore	70	72	70	73	285	7,100

Scenic Circle Hotels Dunedin Classic

Chisolm Links Golf Club, Dunedin, New Zealand
Par 35-36–71; 6,710 yards

March 21-24
purse, A$100,000

	SCORES				TOTAL	MONEY
Gareth Paddison	66	69	68	64	267	A$18,000
Brad Andrews	64	70	68	68	270	10,200
Tony Carolan	69	70	73	62	274	5,775
Andrew Bonhomme	66	74	63	71	274	5,775
Kim Felton	68	74	66	67	275	4,000
Shane Tait	66	69	73	68	276	2,850
Martin Doyle	68	69	71	68	276	2,850
Wayne Smith	68	72	68	68	276	2,850
Michael Cocking	68	73	67	68	276	2,850
Ben Burge	67	68	72	69	276	2,850
Nathan Green	66	70	68	72	276	2,850
Grant Dodd	70	70	71	66	277	1,775
Euan Walters	67	73	68	69	277	1,775
Craig Jones	67	71	69	70	277	1,775
Jeff Wagner	70	69	68	70	277	1,775
Matthew Lane	67	74	71	66	278	1,313.33
Greg Turner	72	70	67	69	278	1,313.33
Wayne Perske	67	70	69	72	278	1,313.33
Martin Pettigrew	69	76	71	63	279	996.87
David Gleeson	66	72	76	65	279	996.87
David Armstrong	73	69	72	65	279	996.87
Reon Sayer	70	72	70	67	279	996.87
Ed Stedman	66	72	73	68	279	996.87
Anthony Summers	68	70	72	69	279	996.87
David Podlich	66	73	70	70	279	996.87
Richard Lee	70	67	71	71	279	996.87
Terry Price	70	72	73	65	280	712
Paul Sheehan	67	77	70	66	280	712
Scott Hend	74	68	70	68	280	712
Marcus Wheelhouse	68	69	73	70	280	712
Justin Cooper	69	69	71	71	280	712

Volvo Trucks Golf Klassik

Bonville International Golf Resort, Coffs Harbour
New South Wales
Par 35-38–73; 6,301 yards

April 4-7
purse, A$100,000

	SCORES				TOTAL	MONEY
Terry Price	68	70	67	70	275	A$18,000
Brad Kennedy	68	72	71	65	276	10,200
David van Raalte	69	68	67	73	277	6,750
Ricky Schmidt	70	69	71	69	279	4,133.33
Jason Dawes	70	69	71	69	279	4,133.33
Steve Collins	68	69	71	71	279	4,133.33
David Diaz	70	73	69	68	280	3,050
Adam Le Vesconte	69	67	72	72	280	3,050
Scott Gardiner	73	69	70	69	281	2,466.66
Matthew Ballard	68	72	71	70	281	2,466.66
Wade Ormsby	67	70	72	72	281	2,466.66
Anthony Painter	73	70	69	71	283	1,708
Matthew Millar	68	70	73	72	283	1,708
Craig Jones	68	72	71	72	283	1,708
Dean Alaban	71	70	70	72	283	1,708
Adrian Percey	65	74	68	76	283	1,708
Wayne Rostron	72	70	74	68	284	1,090.62
Steven Bowditch	74	71	71	68	284	1,090.62
Wayne Perske	73	72	70	69	284	1,090.62
Andre Stolz	73	71	70	70	284	1,090.62
Thomas de Wit	75	70	69	70	284	1,090.62
Aaron Byrnes	70	71	71	72	284	1,090.62
Martin Doyle	69	69	73	73	284	1,090.62
Grant Dodd	65	73	73	73	284	1,090.62
Brad Lamb	74	68	72	71	285	843.33
Anthony Gilligan	72	66	75	72	285	843.33
Craig Carmichael	70	70	70	75	285	843.33
Alan Patterson	69	72	73	72	286	695
Paul Sheehan	73	71	70	72	286	695
Sam Egger	69	71	73	73	286	695
Andrew Tschudin	71	70	69	76	286	695

South Australian PGA Championship

The Vines of Reynella Golf Club, Adelaide, South Australia
Par 36-35–71; 6,643 yards

April 25-28
purse, A$100,000

	SCORES				TOTAL	MONEY
Richard Ball	67	64	65	68	264	A$18,000
Adrian Percey	68	66	68	67	269	10,200
Chris Downes	63	67	71	69	270	6,750
Euan Walters	68	73	67	64	272	4,133.33
Gary Simpson	70	67	68	67	272	4,133.33
Brad Andrews	67	69	67	69	272	4,133.33
Westley Rudel	67	72	69	65	273	2,825
Craig Carmichael	70	72	65	66	273	2,825
Craig Warren	69	69	68	67	273	2,825
Adam Fraser	76	65	65	67	273	2,825
Justin Cooper	70	68	69	68	275	1,925
Matthew Millar	71	70	66	68	275	1,925
Justin Hooper	67	69	70	69	275	1,925

	SCORES			TOTAL	MONEY
Paul Sheehan	69	67	68	71	275	1,925
Jeff Wagner	68	71	69	68	276	1,520
Martin Doyle	68	71	68	69	276	1,520
Martin Peterson	70	69	70	68	277	1,149
Jason Dawes	68	68	71	70	277	1,149
Shane Robinson	66	70	70	71	277	1,149
David Podlich	71	64	70	72	277	1,149
Nigel Spence	69	67	69	72	277	1,149
John Wade	70	72	71	65	278	918.33
Nathan Green	70	69	73	66	278	918.33
Adam Le Vesconte	67	70	74	67	278	918.33
Jens Nilsson	69	73	68	68	278	918.33
Jon Riley	72	66	69	71	278	918.33
Ed Stedman	68	70	67	73	278	918.33
Mark Allen	68	70	74	67	279	654.28
Dion Stevens	68	69	74	68	279	654.28
Wade Ormsby	71	70	70	68	279	654.28
Martin Walsh	71	69	69	70	279	654.28
Brendon Allanby	68	69	71	71	279	654.28
David Elliott	71	68	69	71	279	654.28
Stuart Bouvier	66	71	70	72	279	654.28

Western Australian PGA Championship

Gosnells Golf Club, Perth, Western Australia
Par 34-36–70; 6,443 yards

May 23-26
purse, A$100,000

	SCORES			TOTAL	MONEY
Kim Felton	70	68	66	69	273	A$18,000
Euan Walters	72	65	68	68	273	10,200
(Felton defeated Walters on first playoff hole.)						
Michael Long	69	71	66	68	274	5,775
Adrian Percey	66	67	68	73	274	5,775
Gary Simpson	70	66	74	65	275	3,425
Steve Collins	69	71	69	66	275	3,425
Nathan Gatehouse	69	72	68	66	275	3,425
Craig Carmichael	69	68	71	67	275	3,425
Justin Cooper	67	68	70	71	276	2,600
Scott Strange	69	66	68	73	276	2,600
Matthew Ballard	70	70-	70	67	277	2,100
Martin Doyle	75	63	65	74	277	2,100
Westley Rudel	69	67	70	73	279	1,800
Andrew Bonhomme	69	71	73	67	280	1,448
Craig Jones	69	69	74	68	280	1,448
Brad Lamb	66	69	74	71	280	1,448
Danny Willersdorf	69	71	69	71	280	1,448
David Diaz	69	71	67	73	280	1,448
Shane Tait	72	69	70	70	281	1,125
Dean Alaban	75	70	67	70	282	1,060
Matthew Millar	70	70	70	72	282	1,060
Ewan Porter	67	73	73	70	283	1,020
David Bransdon	70	74	71	69	284	927.50
Nigel Spence	73	71	70	70	284	927.50
Cameron Percy	71	70	72	71	284	927.50
Andrew Webster	70	70	69	75	284	927.50
Richard Ball	75	70	70	70	285	682.50
Robert Mitchell	74	71	70	70	285	682.50

	SCORES				TOTAL	MONEY
Daniel Stevenson	70	70	74	71	285	682.50
Christopher Gibson	72	68	73	72	285	682.50
Ed Stedman	74	69	70	72	285	682.50
Stuart Bouvier	69	73	70	73	285	682.50
Kenichi Ryu	67	72	71	75	285	682.50

Queensland PGA Championship

Gold Coast Country Club, Helensvale, Gold Coast
Par 36-36–72; 6,859 yards

June 13-16
purse, A$100,000

	SCORES				TOTAL	MONEY
Andre Stolz	64	66	68	68	266	A$18,000
Paul Sheehan	69	66	61	72	268	10,200
Anthony Summers	70	66	65	70	271	6,750
Jon Riley	67	66	72	69	274	4,800
Jeff Wagner	69	67	71	68	275	4,000
Wayne Perske	71	72	66	67	276	3,233.33
Stuart Bouvier	69	70	66	71	276	3,233.33
Scott Hend	68	66	68	74	276	3,233.33
Steven Jeffress	70	65	74	68	277	2,466.66
Scott Gardiner	65	69	73	70	277	2,466.66
Matthew Millar	70	68	69	70	277	2,466.66
Adam Crawford	66	74	69	69	278	1,775
Justin Hooper	71	72	66	69	278	1,775
Craig Carmichael	67	69	72	70	278	1,775
Martin Doyle	70	68	69	71	278	1,775
Matthew Ecob	69	72	70	68	279	1,440
Christopher Gibson	73	67	72	68	280	1,090.62
Leigh McKechnie	71	72	67	70	280	1,090.62
John Sutherland	70	73	67	70	280	1,090.62
Cameron Percy	69	68	72	71	280	1,090.62
Aaron Byrnes	69	70	70	71	280	1,090.62
Brad Andrews	68	67	73	72	280	1,090.62
Dean Alaban	70	71	67	72	280	1,090.62
Tom Arnott	69	70	68	73	280	1,090.62
Ewan Porter	71	71	69	70	281	875
Andrew Bonhomme	72	71	68	70	281	875
Westley Rudel	71	71	74	66	282	646
Gary Simpson	72	70	73	67	282	646
Brad Kennedy	71	68	75	68	282	646
Gavin Vearing	72	68	74	68	282	646
David Podlich	70	68	75	69	282	646
Kenny Druce	69	71	73	69	282	646
Marcus Cain	71	70	70	71	282	646
Michael Wright	71	70	70	71	282	646
Kenichi Ryu	73	70	68	71	282	646
Justin Cooper	73	67	68	74	282	646

Victorian PGA Championship

Kew Golf Club, Melbourne, Victoria
Par 37-35–72; 6,687 yards

October 10-13
purse, A$100,000

	SCORES				TOTAL	MONEY
Craig Carmichael	70	73	69	66	278	A$18,000
Craig Jones	70	66	72	70	278	10,200
(Carmichael defeated Jones on first playoff hole.)						
*Craig Scott	69	72	71	69	281	
Andrew Webster	67	71	73	70	281	5,775
Paul Sheehan	71	72	68	70	281	5,775
Tony Carolan	72	68	73	69	282	3,280
Marcus Cain	68	71	71	72	282	3,280
Adam Fraser	69	67	73	73	282	3,280
Martin Doyle	72	67	69	74	282	3,280
Steven Bowditch	70	70	67	75	282	3,280
Andrew Bonhomme	71	74	70	68	283	1,966.66
David Diaz	68	76	72	67	283	1,966.66
Peter Wilson	69	71	72	71	283	1,966.66
Jeff Wagner	71	71	69	72	283	1,966.66
Carl Brooking	70	72	69	72	283	1,966.66
Gary Simpson	66	69	70	78	283	1,966.66
Lee Eagleton	72	70	71	71	284	1,370
Matthew Millar	68	70	71	75	284	1,370
David Bransdon	73	71	71	70	285	1,077.50
Cameron Percy	73	71	70	71	285	1,077.50
Scott Laycock	70	67	76	72	285	1,077.50
Jason Dawes	72	67	74	72	285	1,077.50
Justin Cooper	70	70	72	73	285	1,077.50
Scott Strange	70	67	74	74	285	1,077.50
Michael Wright	71	72	72	71	286	802.85
Wade Ormsby	71	69	74	72	286	802.85
Christopher Gibson	73	68	73	72	286	802.85
David Van Raalte	70	72	72	72	286	802.85
Wayne Perske	68	68	80	70	286	802.85
Shane Tait	72	70	76	68	286	802.85
Nathan Gatehouse	77	67	74	68	286	802.85

Victorian Open

Sorrento Golf Club: Par 36-34–70; 6,183 yards
Portsea Golf Club: Par 36-36–72; 6,522 yards
Melbourne, Victoria

October 24-27
purse, A$100,000

	SCORES				TOTAL	MONEY
Andre Stolz	69	72	65	68	274	A$18,000
David Bransdon	73	71	63	67	274	10,200
(Stolz defeated Bransdon on second playoff hole.)						
Andrew Bonhomme	67	67	68	73	275	6,750
Michael Light	70	69	70	68	277	4,800
David Gleeson	66	75	69	68	278	3,425
Andrew Webster	68	71	70	69	278	3,425
Craig Carmichael	67	70	71	70	278	3,425
Scott Hend	69	71	68	70	278	3,425
*Marc Leishman	69	68	65	76	278	
Matt Costigan	69	74	70	66	279	2,600
Steve Collins	69	72	66	72	279	2,600

	SCORES				TOTAL	MONEY
Mahal Pearce	67	76	71	66	280	1,925
Adrian Percey	64	70	77	69	280	1,925
John Sutherland	72	69	70	69	280	1,925
Jason Dawes	69	70	69	72	280	1,925
Stuart Leong	72	71	70	68	281	1,600
Aaron Rayson	66	75	74	67	282	1,266.25
Nathan Gatehouse	70	74	69	69	282	1,266.25
*Marcus Both	68	76	69	69	282	
Gary Simpson	66	73	73	70	282	1,266.25
Grant Dodd	67	74	71	70	282	1,266.25
*Luke Hickmott	73	69	70	70	282	
*Craig Scott	71	69	71	71	282	
Leith Wastle	69	75	70	69	283	1,046.66
Craig Jones	73	71	68	71	283	1,046.66
*Andrew Tampion	68	74	70	71	283	
Euan Walters	70	72	70	71	283	1,046.66
Tim Elliott	73	70	71	70	284	898
Ewan Porter	67	71	74	72	284	898
Alastair Sidford	65	73	74	72	284	898
Matthew Hazelden	71	74	73	66	284	898
Wade Ormsby	72	68	71	73	284	898

Queensland Open

Ipswich Golf Club, Ipswich, Queensland
Par 36-36–72; 6,696 yards

October 31-November 3
purse, A$100,000

	SCORES				TOTAL	MONEY
Andrew Buckle	71	67	68	68	274	A$18,000
Ryan Haller	70	69	69	68	276	7,250
Craig Warren	72	68	68	68	276	7,250
Paul Sheehan	69	66	69	72	276	7,250
Craig Jones	70	71	70	66	277	4,000
Shane Tait	69	67	73	70	279	2,980
Andre Stolz	71	68	70	70	279	2,980
Jason Norris	72	68	68	71	279	2,980
Brad Andrews	69	70	68	72	279	2,980
Tony Carolan	67	70	68	74	279	2,980
Paul Marantz	68	75	70	67	280	1,925
Craig Woodbridge	69	70	72	69	280	1,925
Martin Pettigrew	69	69	70	72	280	1,925
Craig Carmichael	70	69	67	74	280	1,925
Grant Dodd	69	69	74	69	281	1,446.66
*Richard Moir	67	71	72	71	281	
Peter Senior	68	66	73	74	281	1,446.66
Adam Fraser	68	71	68	74	281	1,446.66
Byron Clarkson	73	68	71	70	282	1,077.50
Neil Kerry	70	71	71	70	282	1,077.50
David Bransdon	73	70	66	73	282	1,077.50
Matthew Hazelden	68	73	66	75	282	1,077.50
Terry Price	74	67	66	75	282	1,077.50
Leith Wastle	68	71	67	76	282	1,077.50
Cameron Percy	72	71	70	70	283	872.50
Mahal Pearce	73	66	73	71	283	872.50
Nigel Spence	67	74	71	71	283	872.50
*Marcus Both	72	68	70	73	283	
Alan Patterson	69	71	70	73	283	872.50
Michael Wright	68	72	76	68	284	654.28

	SCORES				TOTAL	MONEY
Eddie Barr	69	72	74	69	284	654.28
*Rowan Beste	72	69	73	70	284	
Leigh McKechnie	73	68	73	70	284	654.28
Wayne Grady	66	70	77	71	284	654.28
Martin Peterson	67	73	73	71	284	654.28
Adam Le Vesconte	69	69	74	72	284	654.28
Jason King	72	69	69	74	284	654.28

New South Wales Open

Horizons Golf Resort, Port Stephens
Par 36-36–72; 6,764 yards

November 7-10
purse, A$200,000

	SCORES				TOTAL	MONEY
Terry Price	66	71	72	70	279	A$36,000
Mahal Pearce	73	70	70	67	280	11,740
Adam Groom	72	71	70	67	280	11,740
Andre Stolz	69	71	71	69	280	11,740
Wayne Grady	73	67	70	70	280	11,740
Jason Norris	67	69	71	73	280	11,740
Andrew Tschudin	73	70	70	68	281	5,866.66
Aaron Byrnes	75	68	68	70	281	5,866.66
Michael Wright	69	68	71	73	281	5,866.66
*Richard Moir	72	68	71	71	282	
Matthew Hazelden	70	68	70	74	282	4,700
Tony Carolan	72	69	65	76	282	4,700
Nathan Green	72	73	68	70	283	3,666.66
Adam Fraser	71	69	69	74	283	3,666.66
Jens Nilsson	72	67	69	75	283	3,666.66
Alastair Sidford	72	69	73	70	284	2,510
Adam Le Vesconte	75	69	70	70	284	2,510
*Andrew Partridge	71	71	71	71	284	2,510
Scott Strange	71	68	73	72	284	
Gary Simpson	73	72	67	72	284	2,510
Justin Welsford	69	69	72	74	284	2,510
Nigel Spence	72	69	69	74	284	2,510
Marcus Cain	69	68	71	76	284	2,510
Eddie Barr	72	72	71	70	285	1,740
Anthony Summers	72	69	71	73	285	1,740
Brendan Chant	71	68	72	74	285	1,740
Danny Vera	72	69	70	74	285	1,740
Brad Lamb	70	69	71	75	285	1,740
Shane Tait	69	68	72	76	285	1,740
Craig Carmichael	68	70	71	76	285	1,740
Jon Riley	69	72	65	79	285	1,740

Holden Australian Open

Victoria Golf Club, Melbourne
Par 34-36–70; 6,619 yards
(First round cancelled—greens unplayable.)

November 21-24
purse, A$1,500,000

	SCORES			TOTAL	MONEY
Steve Allan	66	64	68	198	A$270,000
Aaron Baddeley	70	64	65	199	108,750

	SCORES			TOTAL	MONEY
Craig Parry	66	65	68	199	108,750
Rich Beem	66	64	69	199	108,750
Gavin Coles	68	64	68	200	60,000
Robert Allenby	71	65	65	201	48,500
Adam Crawford	67	68	66	201	48,500
Charles Howell	65	66	70	201	48,500
Adam Scott	69	64	69	202	40,500
Geoff Ogilvy	66	70	67	203	37,500
Richard Green	71	69	64	204	31,500
Chris Downes	66	71	67	204	31,500
Scott Laycock	69	72	64	205	26,250
Phil Tataurangi	73	67	65	205	26,250
*Richard Moir	72	68	66	206	
Craig Carmichael	70	69	67	206	20,775
James McLean	69	69	68	206	20,775
Peter Lonard	69	68	69	206	20,775
Craig Jones	70	67	69	206	20,775
Greg Chalmers	73	69	65	207	15,562.50
Paul Sheehan	74	66	67	207	15,562.50
Mathew Goggin	72	67	68	207	15,562.50
Gareth Paddison	70	68	69	207	15,562.50
Peter O'Malley	71	65	71	207	15,562.50
Jason King	70	65	72	207	15,562.50
Jarrod Moseley	74	67	67	208	12,262.60
Peter Fowler	71	70	67	208	12,262.60
Alan Patterson	70	70	68	208	12,262.60
Jens Nilsson	67	70	71	208	12,262.60
Scott Hend	70	70	69	209	9,780
John Senden	68	70	71	209	9,780
Rodney Pampling	70	67	72	209	9,780
Andrew Tschudin	68	68	73	209	9,780
Stuart Appleby	67	68	74	209	9,780

Australian PGA Championship

Hyatt Regency Coolum Resort, Coolum, Queensland
Par 36-36–72; 6,918 yards

November 28-December 1
purse, A$1,000,000

	SCORES				TOTAL	MONEY
Peter Lonard	65	68	70	68	271	A$141,000
Jarrod Moseley	65	66	67	73	271	141,000

(Lonard and Moseley declared co-winners when event called due to darkness after one playoff hole.)

Stuart Appleby	74	67	66	67	274	67,500
Greg Norman	72	67	67	69	275	48,000
Greg Chalmers	67	70	69	70	276	40,000
Aaron Baddeley	67	65	72	73	277	36,000
Adam Scott	72	65	69	72	278	32,000
Scott Gardiner	70	72	70	67	279	24,600
Peter O'Malley	72	70	69	68	279	24,600
Greg Turner	66	71	71	71	279	24,600
Nick O'Hern	70	66	71	72	279	24,600
Adam Le Vesconte	68	68	69	74	279	24,600
Jason King	71	74	67	68	280	18,000
Cameron Percy	69	69	71	72	281	16,500
Brad King	70	68	70	73	281	16,500
Andre Stolz	67	77	70	69	283	13,133.33

	SCORES			TOTAL	MONEY
Mark Brown	68	73 73	69	283	13,133.33
Rodney Pampling	73	71 67	72	283	13,133.33
Phil Tataurangi	74	69 71	70	284	10,375
Brad Kennedy	70	72 72	70	284	10,375
Matthew Ecob	71	74 68	71	284	10,375
John Senden	74	71 71	68	284	10,375
Craig Parry	68	73 69	74	284	10,375
Craig Jones	71	71 68	74	284	10,375
Michael Long	69	74 69	73	285	8,433.33
Anthony Painter	71	72 69	73	285	8,433.33
Tony Carolan	70	66 71	78	285	8,433.33
Steve Collins	69	74 70	73	286	6,542.85
Scott Hend	71	72 72	71	286	6,542.85
Jason Dawes	71	70 71	74	286	6,542.85
Aaron Byrnes	69	73 73	71	286	6,542.85
Chris Downes	70	70 70	76	286	6,542.85
Matthew Hazelden	69	72 69	76	286	6,542.85
Nathan Gatehouse	70	72 68	76	286	6,542.85

MasterCard Masters

Huntingdale Golf Club, Melbourne, Victoria
Par 36-36–72; 6,933 yards

December 5-8
purse, A$1,250,000

	SCORES			TOTAL	MONEY
Peter Lonard	70	72 71	66	279	A$225,000
Gavin Coles	71	69 69	70	279	105,937.50
Adam Scott	70	69 69	71	279	105,937.50
(Lonard defeated Scott on first and Coles on third playoff hole.)					
Robert Allenby	72	73 65	70	280	60,000
Richard Green	73	74 67	68	282	42,812.50
Adam Crawford	71	75 67	69	282	42,812.50
Steve Collins	68	68 75	71	282	42,812.50
Craig Parry	72	73 66	71	282	42,812.50
Aaron Baddeley	75	75 64	69	283	32,500
Nick O'Hern	72	74 65	72	283	32,500
Steve Conran	71	73 76	64	284	25,000
John Senden	77	72 67	68	284	25,000
Greg Turner	73	71 70	70	284	25,000
Stuart Appleby	74	74 65	72	285	21,250
Peter Fowler	73	74 68	71	286	19,000
Nick Faldo	74	74 67	71	286	19,000
Gary Simpson	74	73 73	67	287	15,104.16
Andrew Tschudin	73	73 70	71	287	15,104.16
Nathan Green	76	74 66	71	287	15,104.16
Tony Carolan	71	76 70	71	288	12,937.50
Paul Sheehan	74	73 70	71	288	12,937.50
David Bransdon	75	74 68	71	288	12,937.50
Greg Chalmers	72	75 68	73	288	12,937.50
Ty Tryon	74	71 74	70	289	10,906.25
Mark Allen	72	72 74	71	289	10,906.25
Geoff Ogilvy	78	72 68	71	289	10,906.25
Scott Gardiner	72	70 72	75	289	10,906.25
David Diaz	75	73 73	69	290	8,875
Cameron Percy	73	72 71	74	290	8,875
Jarrod Moseley	71	75 68	76	290	8,875

African Tours

Bell's South African Open

Durban Country Club, Durban, South Africa
Par 36-36–72; 6,733 yards

January 10-13
purse, £500,000

		SCORES			TOTAL	MONEY
Tim Clark	66	70	68	65	269	R1,334,363.95
Steve Webster	68	70	69	64	271	968,150.50
James Kingston	66	67	74	68	275	497,545.17
Jonathan Lomas	68	67	71	69	275	497,545.17
David Park	71	68	73	64	276	272,344.94
Simon Dyson	67	73	69	67	276	272,344.94
Alastair Forsyth	66	71	70	69	276	272,344.94
Retief Goosen	67	70	69	70	276	272,344.94
Doug McGuigan	71	69	71	66	277	162,200.28
Martin Maritz	72	64	72	69	277	162,200.28
Roger Wessels	68	71	68	70	277	162,200.28
Jean Hugo	68	71	68	71	278	139,750.42
Dean van Staden	71	70	69	69	279	127,122.37
Ernie Els	73	69	68	69	279	127,122.37
Des Terblanche	66	74	74	66	280	112,389.64
*Charl Schwartzel	71	67	73	69	280	
Andre Cruse	71	68	71	70	280	112,389.64
Andrew Butterfield	66	69	74	71	280	112,389.64
Jamie Donaldson	69	73	66	72	280	112,389.64
Andrew McLardy	75	67	72	67	281	95,636.43
Grant Muller	72	66	75	68	281	95,636.43
Ashley Roestoff	66	71	73	71	281	95,636.43
Philip Golding	70	71	69	71	281	95,636.43
Marc Cayeux	67	75	68	71	281	95,636.43
Michael Kirk	69	69	76	68	282	87,554.48
Mark McNulty	73	71	73	66	283	77,572.30
Paul Lawrie	68	70	76	69	283	77,572.30
Mark Mouland	70	71	73	69	283	77,572.30
Arjun Atwal	70	67	76	70	283	77,572.30
Christian Cevaer	69	70	73	71	283	77,572.30
Malcolm Mackenzie	71	69	72	71	283	77,572.30
Jeremy Robinson	71	70	71	71	283	77,572.30
Russell Claydon	73	70	73	68	284	64,823.99
Nicolas Vanhootegem	72	72	72	68	284	64,823.99
Don Gammon	73	70	72	69	284	64,823.99
Marco Gortana	73	67	74	70	284	64,823.99
Carl Pettersson	64	77	73	70	284	64,823.99
Warren Bennett	70	74	68	72	284	64,823.99
Andrew Marshall	71	71	75	68	285	55,563.42
Jamie Spence	71	69	74	71	285	55,563.42
Amandeep Johl	72	71	71	71	285	55,563.42
Jeev Milkha Singh	69	69	74	73	285	55,563.42
Nick Dougherty	69	71	72	73	285	55,563.42
Chris Williams	72	71	74	69	286	47,986.59
Anthony Wall	73	70	72	71	286	47,986.59
Gavin Levenson	75	69	71	71	286	47,986.59
Tjaart van der Walt	70	73	69	74	286	47,986.59
Desvonde Botes	68	70	79	70	287	42,935.37
Hendrik Buhrmann	69	74	73	71	287	42,935.37

	SCORES			TOTAL	MONEY
Magnus Persson Atlevi	73	70	74 71	288	39,567.89
Mark Hilton	70	74	73 71	288	39,567.89
*Michael Hoey	72	72	76 69	289	
Darren Fichardt	69	71	79 70	289	35,358.54
Andrew Pitts	71	72	75 71	289	35,358.54
Mikael Lundberg	76	68	71 74	289	35,358.54
Michael Archer	68	75	79 68	290	29,465.45
Hennie Walters	73	71	74 72	290	29,465.45
Simon Hurd	70	70	77 73	290	29,465.45
Bradley Davison	71	71	73 75	290	29,465.45
Keith Horne	74	70	75 72	291	23,993.29
Schalk van der Merwe	70	72	76 73	291	23,993.29
David Gilford	72	71	75 73	291	23,993.29
Trevor Dodds	73	71	73 74	291	23,993.29
Sean Pappas	75	65	76 75	291	23,993.29
Marten Olander	70	73	73 75	291	23,993.29
Stephen Dodd	73	71	74 74	292	21,046.75
Simon Lilly	73	71	78 71	293	19,783.94
Steve van Vuuren	70	74	75 74	293	19,783.94
Derek Crawford	71	73	79 71	294	18,100.20
Simon Khan	74	70	74 76	294	18,100.20
Didier de Vooght	71	71	77 77	296	16,837.40
Michael Green	73	69	75 82	299	15,995.53
Miguel Angel Martin	74	70	80	WD	14,732.72
David Drysdale	72	70		WD	14,732.72

Dunhill Championship

Houghton Golf Club, Johannesburg, South Africa
Par 36-36–72; 7,284 yards

January 17-20
purse, £500,000

	SCORES			TOTAL	MONEY
Justin Rose	71	66	66 65	268	R1,296,105.60
Retief Goosen	68	67	70 65	270	638,482.40
Mark Foster	69	67	65 69	270	638,482.40
Martin Maritz	72	64	63 71	270	638,482.40
Anthony Wall	68	67	71 65	271	290,666.72
Mark Mouland	68	69	67 67	271	290,666.72
Paul McGinley	66	71	66 68	271	290,666.72
Sandeep Grewal	70	64	68 70	272	201,798.72
Ernie Els	68	72	63 70	273	177,189.12
Alan McLean	71	70	69 64	274	153,810
Roger Wessels	68	66	69 71	274	153,810
Mark Pilkington	68	68	73 66	275	125,714.04
Jamie Donaldson	67	72	68 68	275	125,714.04
Arjun Atwal	72	64	70 69	275	125,714.04
Andrew Coltart	68	69	69 69	275	125,714.04
Jean-Francois Remesy	67	70	73 66	276	108,282.24
Richard Bland	73	68	67 68	276	108,282.24
Grant Muller	69	69	69 69	276	108,282.24
Doug McGuigan	74	67	71 65	277	96,797.76
Ian Garbutt	70	72	69 66	277	96,797.76
Darren Fichardt	73	67	66 71	277	96,797.76
Carl Pettersson	68	70	74 66	278	82,442.16
Mark McNulty	73	70	69 66	278	82,442.16
David Howell	71	69	70 68	278	82,442.16
James Kingston	67	71	71 69	278	82,442.16
Justin Hobday	73	70	66 69	278	82,442.16

	SCORES				TOTAL	MONEY
Bradley Dredge	69	72	67	70	278	82,442.16
Andrew Marshall	69	72	66	71	278	82,442.16
Daren Lee	70	68	68	72	278	82,442.16
Simon Dyson	73	65	73	68	279	67,266.24
Paul Eales	73	67	71	68	279	67,266.24
Simon Hurd	70	70	70	69	279	67,266.24
Stephen Dodd	66	71	72	70	279	67,266.24
Wallie Coetsee	70	69	69	71	279	67,266.24
Christian Cevaer	70	67	68	74	279	67,266.24
Nick Dougherty	70	71	72	67	280	55,781.76
Mark Roe	67	72	73	68	280	55,781.76
Jonathan Lomas	71	71	70	68	280	55,781.76
Rolf Muntz	71	71	70	68	280	55,781.76
Jaco Van Zyl	70	69	71	70	280	55,781.76
Alastair Forsyth	68	72	70	70	280	55,781.76
Gary Clark	70	72	68	70	280	55,781.76
Don Gammon	70	71	68	71	280	55,781.76
Andre Cruse	72	71	70	68	281	42,656.64
Marten Olander	71	67	73	70	281	42,656.64
Sammy Daniels	69	71	71	70	281	42,656.64
Maarten Lafeber	69	71	70	71	281	42,656.64
Michael Kirk	72	68	70	71	281	42,656.64
Christopher Hanell	71	70	69	71	281	42,656.64
David Lynn	72	71	66	72	281	42,656.64
Sam Walker	70	67	71	73	281	42,656.64
Tim Clark	69	69	73	71	282	34,453.44
Charlie Wi	74	68	69	71	282	34,453.44
Stephen Scahill	73	69	71	70	283	28,875.26
Gary Emerson	70	71	71	71	283	28,875.26
Sven Struver	69	69	73	72	283	28,875.26
Malcolm Mackenzie	71	66	73	73	283	28,875.26
Paul Broadhurst	74	67	68	74	283	28,875.26
Stephen Gallacher	73	69	71	72	285	23,789.28
Matthew Cort	71	69	72	73	285	23,789.28
Marco Gortana	72	71	69	73	285	23,789.28
David Dixon	71	71	69	74	285	23,789.28
Marc Cayeux	68	74	68	75	285	23,789.28
David Gilford	69	73	72	72	286	20,918.16
Jaco Olver	73	69	72	72	286	20,918.16
Titch Moore	71	71	74	71	287	18,867.36
David Park	70	73	70	74	287	18,867.36
Greg Owen	67	74	70	76	287	18,867.36
David Higgins	72	69	74	73	288	16,816.56
Philip Golding	72	71	69	76	288	16,816.56
Hendrik Buhrmann	67	74	81	69	291	12,290.44
Bradley Davison	70	73	77	71	291	12,290.44
Joachim Backstrom	73	69	80	74	296	12,245.74

Telkom PGA Championship

Woodhill Country Club, Pretoria, South Africa
Par 36-36–72; 7,382 yards

January 24-27
purse, R1,000,000

	SCORES				TOTAL	MONEY
Chris Williams	74	64	65	68	271	R158,500
Hennie Otto	70	68	68	67	273	115,000
Martin du Toit	70	73	66	65	274	59,100

	SCORES				TOTAL	MONEY
Bruce Vaughan	66	71	70	67	274	59,100
Mark McNulty	71	68	72	65	276	32,350
Andrew McLardy	66	71	73	66	276	32,350
Tjaart van der Walt	69	69	70	68	276	32,350
Tim Clark	66	67	73	70	276	32,350
Martin Maritz	74	69	67	67	277	20,100
Grant Muller	71	66	71	69	277	20,100
Jaco Van Zyl	68	69	73	68	278	15,700
Michael Archer	70	67	73	68	278	15,700
Lee Slattery	73	70	67	68	278	15,700
Darren Fichardt	68	70	71	69	278	15,700
Douglas McCabe	70	68	68	72	278	15,700
Tyrol Auret	73	71	69	66	279	12,620
Warren Abery	72	68	70	69	279	12,620
Dean Lambert	69	70	70	70	279	12,620
Justin Hobday	68	72	69	70	279	12,620
Marco Gortana	68	68	72	71	279	12,620
Nic Henning	69	72	73	66	280	10,700
Desvonde Botes	70	74	68	68	280	10,700
Gary Birch, Jr.	73	70	68	69	280	10,700
Michiel Bothma	69	69	72	70	280	10,700
Titch Moore	72	68	66	74	280	10,700
Peter Lawrie	76	69	68	68	281	8,942.85
Hendrik Buhrmann	71	71	70	69	281	8,942.85
Andre Cruse	69	68	74	70	281	8,942.85
Doug McGuigan	72	67	72	70	281	8,942.85
Marc Cayeux	70	69	72	70	281	8,942.85
Paul Dwyer	71	67	72	71	281	8,942.85
David Higgins	66	72	69	74	281	8,942.85

Dimension Data Pro-Am

Gary Player Country Club: Par 36-36–72; 6,958 yards
Lost City Golf Course: Par 36-36–72; 6,983 yards
Sun City, South Africa

January 31-February 3
purse, R2,000,000

	SCORES				TOTAL	MONEY
Retief Goosen	63	70	69	66	268	R317,000
Scott Drummond	66	67	69	69	271	230,000
Jaco Van Zyl	73	67	64	69	273	138,200
Tjaart van der Walt	67	69	71	67	274	98,200
David Park	71	70	65	69	275	82,200
Michael Kirk	69	71	69	67	276	70,200
Don Gammon	70	71	67	70	278	58,200
Darren Clarke	73	68	68	70	279	42,866.66
Tim Clark	68	69	71	71	279	42,866.66
Craig Lile	67	68	71	73	279	42,866.66
Titch Moore	68	73	72	68	281	32,200
Nicholas Lawrence	69	69	71	72	281	32,200
Mark McNulty	71	67	70	73	281	32,200
Michael Archer	69	68	71	73	281	32,200
Simon Hurd	69	73	68	72	282	27,700
Nick Price	69	72	67	74	282	27,700
Bruce Vaughan	69	72	71	71	283	24,320
Hennie Walters	71	68	71	73	283	24,320
Bradford Vaughan	70	72	68	73	283	24,320
Hendrik Buhrmann	70	75	67	71	283	24,320

	SCORES				TOTAL	MONEY
Grant Muller	72	72	72	67	283	24,320
Leonard Loxton	72	64	76	72	284	20,800
Paul McGinley	75	70	69	70	284	20,800
Warrick Druian	68	69	71	76	284	20,800
David Drysdale	71	68	69	76	284	20,800
Paddy Gribben	68	68	71	77	284	20,800
Neil Price	71	71	71	72	285	17,600
Andrew McLardy	66	75	72	72	285	17,600
Sam Little	70	72	71	72	285	17,600
Kevin Stone	73	69	72	71	285	17,600
Andre Cruse	70	70	71	74	285	17,600
Doug McGuigan	73	71	72	69	285	17,600

Nashua Masters

Wild Coast Sun Country Club, Port Edward, Natal
Par 35-35–70; 5,807 yards

February 7-10
purse, R1,000,000

	SCORES				TOTAL	MONEY
Justin Rose	64	68	65	68	265	R158,500
Titch Moore	62	69	66	69	266	115,000
Andre Cruse	70	67	67	63	267	69,100
Grant Muller	71	64	66	67	268	41,766.66
Tim Clark	70	66	64	68	268	41,766.66
Richard Sterne	66	66	65	71	268	41,766.66
Sean Pappas	72	69	65	64	270	23,350
Ashley Roestoff	71	68	64	67	270	23,350
Mark Murless	65	68	65	72	270	23,350
Scott Drummond	68	64	65	73	270	23,350
Marco Gortana	70	70	66	65	271	17,600
Chris Davison	68	69	67	68	272	16,100
James Kingston	69	61	67	75	272	16,100
Justin Hobday	68	70	69	66	273	13,850
Michael du Toit	69	68	69	67	273	13,850
Derek Crawford	67	69	68	69	273	13,850
Ryan Reid	71	67	64	71	273	13,850
Marc Cayeux	70	69	67	68	274	11,740
Bradford Vaughan	70	69	66	69	274	11,740
Bobby Lincoln	68	67	69	70	274	11,740
Michael Green	66	69	67	72	274	11,740
Ian Palmer	66	68	67	73	274	11,740
Andre Bossert	73	67	68	67	275	10,550
Ulrich van den Berg	71	67	65	72	275	10,550
Brett Liddle	71	70	68	67	276	9,214.28
Paul Dwyer	68	72	68	68	276	9,214.28
Warrick Druian	69	71	68	68	276	9,214.28
Jon Bevan	71	67	69	69	276	9,214.28
Darren Fichardt	69	67	70	70	276	9,214.28
Bruce Vaughan	70	69	67	70	276	9,214.28
Alan McLean	67	71	66	72	276	9,214.28

Southern Africa Tour Championship

Leopard Creek Country Club, Malelane, South Africa
Par 35-36–71; 6,473 yards

February 14-17
purse, R2,000,000

	SCORES				TOTAL	MONEY
Nicholas Lawrence	68	68	67	71	274	R317,000
Bruce Vaughan	67	68	71	69	275	184,100
Tim Clark	69	68	67	71	275	184,100
Nic Henning	66	71	71	68	276	90,200
Andrew McLardy	71	67	69	69	276	90,200
Hennie Otto	69	70	71	72	282	70,200
Martin Maritz	73	72	68	70	283	58,200
Doug McGuigan	66	72	74	72	284	45,200
Mark Murless	70	70	72	72	284	45,200
Richard Sterne	73	71	72	69	285	33,400
Roger Wessels	74	69	71	71	285	33,400
Trevor Immelman	67	76	71	71	285	33,400
Scott Drummond	71	70	71	73	285	33,400
Lee Slattery	67	75	67	76	285	33,400
Nico van Rensburg	74	72	71	69	286	27,700
Sean Pappas	68	71	75	72	286	27,700
Dean van Staden	72	68	73	74	287	25,700
Des Terblanche	72	73	68	74	287	25,700
Dean Lambert	77	76	68	67	288	23,050
Marc Cayeux	73	73	73	69	288	23,050
Mark McNulty	70	69	75	74	288	23,050
Bradford Vaughan	65	77	71	75	288	23,050
Justin Rose	69	74	71	75	289	21,400
Michael Kirk	73	77	72	68	290	18,725
Jaco Olver	71	75	75	69	290	18,725
Sean Farrell	72	76	73	69	290	18,725
Don Gammon	69	75	75	71	290	18,725
Andre Cruse	72	75	72	71	290	18,725
Bradley Davison	72	75	71	72	290	18,725
Michael Green	68	69	77	76	290	18,725
Steve van Vuuren	72	71	71	76	290	18,725

Royal Swazi Sun Open

Royal Swazi Sun Country Club, Mbabane, Swaziland
Par 36-36–72; 6,745 yards

February 21-24
purse, R500,000

	SCORES				TOTAL	MONEY
Andrew McLardy	69	72	63	64	268	R79,000
Nic Henning	68	66	68	68	270	57,500
James Loughnane	67	66	71	68	272	34,600
Bradford Vaughan	71	68	70	67	276	22,600
Marc Cayeux	69	71	69	67	276	22,600
Guy Woodman	71	72	68	66	277	13,070
Keith Horne	72	70	68	67	277	13,070
Bafana Hlophe	72	67	70	68	277	13,070
Titch Moore	69	70	69	69	277	13,070
Andre Cruse	68	69	68	72	277	13,070
Kyron Sullivan	70	69	69	70	278	8,383.33
Gerry Coetzee	73	67	68	70	278	8,383.33
Bradley Davison	67	69	69	73	278	8,383.33
Simon Hurd	70	69	72	68	279	6,725

	SCORES				TOTAL	MONEY
Jaco Van Zyl	67	72	71	69	279	6,725
Darren Fichardt	70	70	69	70	279	6,725
Mike Lamb	67	75	67	70	279	6,725
Alan Michell	70	71	67	71	279	6,725
Richard Sterne	71	70	64	74	279	6,725
John Mashego	68	71	72	69	280	5,637.50
Ian Kennedy	72	68	70	70	280	5,637.50
Colin Sorour	69	70	70	71	280	5,637.50
Dean Lambert	69	71	68	72	280	5,637.50
Grant Muller	75	68	71	67	281	5,025
Marco Gortana	73	71	69	68	281	5,025
Frankie Young	68	70	73	70	281	5,025
Steve van Vuuren	70	70	70	71	281	5,025
Henk Alberts	73	71	69	69	282	4,380
Michiel Bothma	73	68	71	70	282	4,380
Andy Bean	71	70	70	71	282	4,380
Warrick Druian	75	66	68	73	282	4,380
Derek Crawford	68	68	72	74	282	4,380

Stanbic Zambia Open

Lusaka Golf Club, Lusaka, Zambia
Par 35-38–73; 7,230 yards

March 7-10
purse, R927,362

	SCORES				TOTAL	MONEY
Marc Cayeux	69	66	65	70	270	R143,496.95
Andre Cruse	67	71	68	66	272	88,099.34
Richard Sterne	69	67	69	67	272	88,099.34
Simon Hurd	68	72	68	66	274	46,368.07
Simon Wakefield	69	68	69	68	274	46,368.07
Kariem Baraka	68	70	65	71	274	46,368.07
Rudy Whitfield	66	71	72	67	276	23,647.72
Benn Barham	70	69	69	68	276	23,647.72
Ben Mason	70	66	69	71	276	23,647.72
Titch Moore	68	69	68	71	276	23,647.72
Ashley Roestoff	70	68	71	68	277	18,083.55
Greig Hutcheon	69	69	70	69	277	18,083.55
Gary Birch, Jr.	68	69	69	72	278	16,228.83
Mark Murless	65	72	69	72	278	16,228.83
Hennie Otto	67	72	72	68	279	13,910.42
Thabang Simon	68	71	71	69	279	13,910.42
Sandeep Grewal	70	69	71	69	279	13,910.42
Jaco Van Zyl	72	71	72	65	280	11,592.30
Paul Nilbrink	72	68	70	70	280	11,592.30
Craig Cowper	67	74	72	68	281	9,737.30
Kyron Sullivan	69	71	72	69	281	9,737.30
Fredrik Widmark	69	72	71	70	282	8,995.40
Denny Lucas	67	70	73	72	282	8,995.40
Steven Parry	72	68	72	71	283	8,531.72
Ian Kennedy	69	73	70	71	283	8,531.72
Johan Edfors	70	70	71	72	283	8,531.72
Neil Cheetham	74	70	74	66	284	7,418.89
Robert McGuirk	74	70	70	70	284	7,418.89
Olivier David	72	68	73	71	284	7,418.89
Tim Milford	74	68	71	71	284	7,418.89
Jean Pierre Cixous	69	73	71	71	284	7,418.89
Clinton Whitelaw	72	72	69	71	284	7,418.89

	SCORES				TOTAL	MONEY
Brett Liddle	68	72	72	72	284	7,418.89
Lee James	69	71	71	73	284	7,418.89
Martin du Toit	72	72	65	75	284	7,418.89

FNB Botswana Open

Gaborone Golf Club, Gaborone, Botswana
Par 36-35–71; 6,814 yards

March 21-23
purse, R268,380

	SCORES			TOTAL	MONEY
Hendrik Buhrmann	63	65	66	194	R43,193.84
Brett Liddle	66	64	65	195	31,638.80
Douglas McCabe	64	66	67	197	22,009.60
Shane Pringle	69	60	71	200	16,232.08
Schalk van der Merwe	70	69	63	202	11,004.80
Tyrol Auret	68	67	67	202	11,004.80
Keith Horne	69	68	66	203	7,244.82
Bradley Davison	68	68	67	203	7,244.82
Nico van Rensburg	67	69	67	203	7,244.82
Justin Hobday	69	70	65	204	5,309.81
Lindani Ndwandwe	64	74	66	204	5,309.81
Vaughn Groenewald	72	65	67	204	5,309.81
Steve van Vuuren	69	67	68	204	5,309.81
Nasho Kamungeremu	68	70	67	205	4,493.62
Ashley Roestoff	66	70	69	205	4,493.62
Langley Perrins	67	68	70	205	4,493.62
Grant Muller	67	73	66	206	3,927.33
Wayne Bradley	71	68	67	206	3,927.33
Bafana Hlophe	67	71	68	206	3,927.33
Michael Green	68	69	69	206	3,927.33
Jason Lipshitz	69	70	68	207	3,203.18
Leonard Loxton	72	66	69	207	3,203.18
Sean Farrell	68	69	70	207	3,203.18
Gerry Coetzee	66	70	71	207	3,203.18
Irvin Mosate	69	65	73	207	3,203.18
Bobby Lincoln	68	66	73	207	3,203.18
Callie Swart	67	66	74	207	3,203.18
James Loughnane	70	69	69	208	2,503.59
John Bele	70	69	69	208	2,503.59
Craig Kamps	69	70	69	208	2,503.59
Dean van Staden	69	69	70	208	2,503.59
Colin Sorour	67	71	70	208	2,503.59
Gareth Davies	70	68	70	208	2,503.59
Werner Geyer	68	68	72	208	2,503.59

Limpopo Industrelek Classic

Pietersburg Golf Club, Pietersburg, South Africa
Par 36-36–72; 7,090 yards

May 9-11
purse, R225,000

	SCORES			TOTAL	MONEY
Hennie Otto	66	67	69	202	R35,325
Des Terblanche	67	67	69	203	25,875
Sean Farrell	70	69	66	205	15,637.50
Thabang Simon	69	70	66	205	15,637.50

	SCORES			TOTAL	MONEY
Nic Henning	73	68	65	206	8,250
Jaco Rall	71	67	68	206	8,250
Bobby Lincoln	69	65	72	206	8,250
Ashley Roestoff	72	69	66	207	5,512.50
Marc Cayeux	67	74	66	207	5,512.50
Keith Horne	68	72	68	208	4,455
Craig Kamps	66	73	69	208	4,455
Sammy Daniels	68	69	71	208	4,455
Rudy Whitfield	67	73	69	209	3,915
Callie Swart	70	65	74	209	3,915
Leonard Loxton	70	72	69	211	3,465
Douglas McCabe	69	72	70	211	3,465
Ryan Dreyer	71	69	71	211	3,465
Bafana Hlophe	71	67	73	211	3,465
James Kingston	75	67	70	212	3,150
Tyrol Auret	72	73	68	213	2,817
John Mashego	70	73	70	213	2,817
Vaughn Groenewald	71	71	71	213	2,817
Omar Sandys	69	69	75	213	2,817
Steve van Vuuren	68	70	75	213	2,817
Wayne Bradley	71	72	71	214	2,269.28
Steve Basson	71	71	72	214	2,269.28
Wayne de Haas	73	69	72	214	2,269.28
Ulrich van den Berg	70	71	73	214	2,269.28
Chris Williams	72	69	73	214	2,269.28
Justin Hobday	72	68	74	214	2,269.28
Nicholas Lawrence	72	68	74	214	2,269.28

Royal Swazi Sun Classic

Royal Swazi Sun Country Club, Mbabane, Swaziland
Par 36-36–72; 6,745 yards

May 17-19
purse, R200,000

	SCORES			TOTAL	MONEY
James Kingston	70	70	64	204	R31,400
Keith Horne	69	70	66	205	19,500
Bobby Lincoln	70	66	69	205	19,500
Steve Basson	71	69	66	206	10,400
Marc Cayeux	68	69	69	206	10,400
Nic Henning	72	70	65	207	7,000
Brett Liddle	70	70	68	208	5,600
Ulrich van den Berg	71	69	68	208	5,600
Ashley Roestoff	71	71	67	209	4,246.66
Wayne de Haas	67	73	69	209	4,246.66
Bafana Hlophe	70	64	75	209	4,246.66
Craig Kamps	72	72	66	210	3,288.57
Ryan Reid	72	70	68	210	3,288.57
Des Terblanche	69	72	69	210	3,288.57
Hendrik Buhrmann	68	72	70	210	3,288.57
Warren Abery	70	70	70	210	3,288.57
Mark Murless	75	64	71	210	3,288.57
Michiel Bothma	69	68	73	210	3,288.57
Richard Fulford	73	69	69	211	2,750
Damian Dunford	68	72	71	211	2,750
Mawonga Nomwa	70	74	68	212	2,328.57
Steve van Vuuren	67	75	70	212	2,328.57
Sean Farrell	68	74	70	212	2,328.57

	SCORES			TOTAL	MONEY
Titch Moore	69	72	71	212	2,328.57
Lindani Ndwandwe	66	74	72	212	2,328.57
Jaco Olver	71	68	73	212	2,328.57
Dean Nysschen	72	67	73	212	2,328.57
Justin Hobday	71	69	73	213	1,940
Omar Sandys	68	70	75	213	1,940
Werner Geyer	67	70	76	213	1,940

Vodacom Golf Classic

Royal Johannesburg & Kensington Golf Club,
Johannesburg, South Africa
Par 36-36–72; 7,416 yards

September 26-28
purse, R200,000

	SCORES			TOTAL	MONEY
Ashley Roestoff	67	67	71	205	R31,400
Chris Williams	68	68	69	205	23,000
(Roestoff defeated Williams on first playoff hole.)					
Richard Sterne	72	68	67	207	13,900
Jaco Van Zyl	66	72	69	207	13,900
Brett Liddle	70	69	69	208	8,000
Keith Horne	68	70	70	208	8,000
Craig Kamps	69	70	70	209	5,600
Vaughn Groenewald	67	68	74	209	5,600
Wallie Coetsee	70	71	69	210	4,120
Ian Hutchings	69	71	70	210	4,120
Michiel Bothma	67	72	71	210	4,120
Dean van Staden	69	69	72	210	4,120
Wayne Bradley	71	70	70	211	3,340
Des Terblanche	70	71	70	211	3,340
Ted Hendriks	69	71	71	211	3,340
Werner Geyer	72	68	71	211	3,340
Sean Pappas	69	72	71	212	2,906.66
Ulrich van den Berg	65	74	73	212	2,906.66
Tyrol Auret	73	64	75	212	2,906.66
Bafana Hlophe	67	74	72	213	2,600
Nic Henning	74	65	74	213	2,600
Hendrik Buhrmann	69	70	74	213	2,600
Bradford Vaughan	70	73	71	214	2,280
Steve Basson	71	71	72	214	2,280
John Bele	69	72	73	214	2,280
Michael Green	72	69	73	214	2,280
Adilson da Silva	70	75	70	215	1,913.33
Bobby Lincoln	71	73	71	215	1,913.33
Schalk van der Merwe	73	71	71	215	1,913.33
Henk Alberts	71	71	73	215	1,913.33
Michael du Toit	70	71	74	215	1,913.33
Grant Muller	70	70	75	215	1,913.33

Bearing Man Highveld Classic

Witbank Golf Club, Witbank, South Africa
Par 36-36–72; 6,702 yards

October 4-6
purse, R200,000

	SCORES			TOTAL	MONEY
Titch Moore	64	65	67	196	R31,400
Ashley Roestoff	67	69	65	201	23,000
Hanno de Weerd	63	69	70	202	16,000
Tyrol Auret	75	67	62	204	9,266.66
Ulrich van den Berg	71	69	64	204	9,266.66
Ryan Reid	67	68	69	204	9,266.66
Wayne Bradley	67	72	66	205	6,000
Brett Liddle	72	69	66	207	5,200
Adilson da Silva	70	71	67	208	3,651.11
Sean Ludgater	70	70	68	208	3,651.11
Michael Green	70	70	68	208	3,651.11
Mark Murless	70	69	69	208	3,651.11
Vaughn Groenewald	67	72	69	208	3,651.11
John Mashego	66	72	70	208	3,651.11
Des Terblanche	69	69	70	208	3,651.11
Henk Alberts	70	68	70	208	3,651.11
Bafana Hlophe	72	65	71	208	3,651.11
Andy Bean	72	71	66	209	2,750
Hendrik Buhrmann	72	68	69	209	2,750
Keith Horne	67	72	70	209	2,750
Bradford Vaughan	69	68	72	209	2,750
Justin Hobday	71	71	68	210	2,500
Jaco Van Zyl	70	74	67	211	2,280
Richard Sterne	74	68	69	211	2,280
Sean Farrell	68	74	69	211	2,280
Douglas McCabe	71	69	71	211	2,280
Sean Pappas	71	74	67	212	2,006.66
Dean van Staden	75	70	67	212	2,006.66
Chris Davison	71	73	68	212	2,006.66
Michiel Bothma	74	71	68	213	1,820
Richard Fulford	70	73	70	213	1,820
Richard Kaplan	69	70	74	213	1,820

Platinum Classic

Mooi Nooi Golf Club, Rustenburg, South Africa
Par 36-36–72; 6,936 yards

November 1-3
purse, R500,000

	SCORES			TOTAL	MONEY
Titch Moore	65	66	67	198	R79,000
Doug McGuigan	65	68	70	203	57,500
Des Terblanche	67	69	68	204	34,600
Grant Muller	68	66	71	205	24,550
Sean Farrell	71	68	67	206	20,650
Nico van Rensburg	66	76	66	208	13,070
Sammy Daniels	72	68	68	208	13,070
Richard Sterne	68	70	70	208	13,070
Alan Michell	70	67	71	208	13,070
Nic Henning	66	70	72	208	13,070
Henk Alberts	70	70	69	209	8,383.33
Bobby Lincoln	70	69	70	209	8,383.33
Chris Davison	70	68	71	209	8,383.33

	SCORES			TOTAL	MONEY
Eddie Lombard	73	71	66	210	6,607.14
Callie Swart	72	69	69	210	6,607.14
Bradford Vaughan	71	69	70	210	6,607.14
Roger Wessels	70	70	70	210	6,607.14
Ulrich van den Berg	68	71	71	210	6,607.14
James Kingston	69	70	71	210	6,607.14
Andre Cruse	66	71	73	210	6,607.14
Hennie Otto	69	73	69	211	5,475
Justin Hobday	70	72	69	211	5,475
Sean Pappas	72	69	70	211	5,475
Tyrol Auret	69	71	71	211	5,475
Hanno de Weerd	73	72	67	212	4,725
Thomas Aiken	71	73	68	212	4,725
Chris Williams	71	71	70	212	4,725
Wayne Bradley	71	69	72	212	4,725
Omar Sandys	70	70	72	212	4,725
Craig Kamps	71	67	74	212	4,725

Telkom PGA Championship

Woodhill Country Club, Pretoria, South Africa
Par 36-36–72; 7,382 yards

November 14-17
purse, R1,250,000

	SCORES				TOTAL	MONEY
Michiel Bothma	67	69	69	68	273	R198,125
Mark Murless	64	68	72	69	273	143,750
(Bothma defeated Murless on second playoff hole.)						
Simon Hurd	68	69	69	69	275	86,375
Keith Horne	69	68	70	69	276	52,208.33
Ashley Roestoff	71	67	69	69	276	52,208.33
Nic Henning	68	72	66	70	276	52,208.33
Mike Lamb	70	68	71	68	277	36,375
Jaco Olver	71	68	71	68	278	28,250
Lewis Atkinson	70	71	69	68	278	28,250
Desvonde Botes	69	73	74	63	279	19,421.87
Adilson da Silva	70	69	71	69	279	19,421.87
Jaco Rall	68	68	73	70	279	19,421.87
Roger Wessels	68	69	72	70	279	19,421.87
Martin Maritz	70	67	72	70	279	19,421.87
Tyrol Auret	71	69	69	70	279	19,421.87
Grant Muller	68	67	72	72	279	19,421.87
Mark McNulty	71	70	63	75	279	19,421.87
Joachim Backstrom	73	70	68	69	280	14,458.33
Craig Lile	72	71	68	69	280	14,458.33
Travis Fraser	73	69	68	70	280	14,458.33
Bradford Vaughan	72	68	69	71	280	14,458.33
Andy Bean	69	69	70	72	280	14,458.33
Steve van Vuuren	74	68	65	73	280	14,458.33
Henk Alberts	71	71	72	67	281	12,062.50
Tim Rice	74	69	69	69	281	12,062.50
Andrew McLardy	72	69	70	70	281	12,062.50
Sean Ludgater	72	70	69	70	281	12,062.50
Mark Hilton	66	71	73	71	281	12,062.50
Stefaan van den Heever	70	68	71	72	281	12,062.50
Sean Farrell	73	69	73	67	282	10,375
Ivano Ficalbi	70	74	69	69	282	10,375
David Faught	71	69	71	71	282	10,375
Marc Cayeux	70	70	71	71	282	10,375

Nashua Masters

Wild Coast Sun Country Club, Port Edward, Natal
Par 35-35–70; 5,807 yards

November 21-24
purse, R1,000,000

	SCORES				TOTAL	MONEY
Hennie Otto	67	70	73	69	279	R158,500
Gavin McNeil	69	71	71	70	281	68,575
Ciaran McMonagle	70	68	72	71	281	68,575
Roger Wessels	67	70	71	73	281	68,575
Mark McNulty	68	69	70	74	281	68,575
Tyrol Auret	67	72	77	67	283	35,100
Marc Cayeux	70	75	69	70	284	29,100
Bradford Vaughan	69	72	76	68	285	20,475
Doug McGuigan	67	69	76	73	285	20,475
Andrew McLardy	68	70	74	73	285	20,475
Nic Henning	69	70	72	74	285	20,475
Grant Muller	70	67	74	75	286	16,600
Mike Lamb	67	74	75	71	287	14,766.66
Henk Alberts	69	75	72	71	287	14,766.66
Craig Lile	68	73	72	74	287	14,766.66
Fulton Allem	71	68	78	71	288	13,600
Ashley Roestoff	68	71	78	72	289	12,600
Gary Sabbatini	74	70	73	72	289	12,600
Leonard Loxton	73	72	71	73	289	12,600
Louis Oosthuizen	69	73	73	75	290	11,700
Alan Michell	75	69	75	72	291	11,300
Sean Farrell	69	74	76	73	292	10,700
Mark Murless	77	69	73	73	292	10,700
Bradley Davison	71	70	77	74	292	10,700
Barry Painting	70	72	76	75	293	9,500
Tim Rice	77	68	73	75	293	9,500
Padraig Dooley	72	72	73	76	293	9,500
Keith Horne	73	72	70	78	293	9,500
Jaco Van Zyl	72	68	74	79	293	9,500
Roux Burger	71	73	77	73	294	8,300
Steven Parry	73	70	77	74	294	8,300
Steve Basson	75	68	76	75	294	8,300
Greg Garcia	69	73	74	78	294	8,300

Nedbank Golf Challenge

Gary Player Country Club, Sun City, South Africa
Par 36-36–72; 7,738 yards

November 28-December 1
purse, US$4,060,000

	SCORES				TOTAL	MONEY
Ernie Els	70	65	69	63	267	$2,000,000
Colin Montgomerie	74	69	65	67	275	300,000
Chris DiMarco	68	68	72	70	278	250,000
Retief Goosen	68	72	70	71	281	212,500
Jim Furyk	69	71	72	69	281	212,500
Sergio Garcia	70	73	70	70	283	175,000
Nick Price	71	70	73	70	284	160,000
Bob Estes	73	69	72	71	285	150,000
Robert Allenby	70	71	74	70	285	150,000
Darren Clarke	72	67	71	75	285	150,000
Padraig Harrington	72	70	69	77	288	150,000
Michael Campbell	71	71	69	78	289	150,000

Vodacom Players Championship

Royal Cape Golf Club, Cape Town, South Africa
Par 36-36–72; 6,693 yards

December 5-8
purse, R2,000,000

	SCORES				TOTAL	MONEY
Mark McNulty	70	66	66	70	272	R317,000
Scott Dunlap	72	72	67	64	275	230,000
Hennie Otto	70	72	69	66	277	118,200
Darren Fichardt	63	72	70	72	277	118,200
Titch Moore	69	73	66	70	278	76,200
Alan McLean	70	69	68	71	278	76,200
Ian Keenan	72	65	75	67	279	53,200
Craig Lile	69	68	70	72	279	53,200
Marc Cayeux	72	71	70	68	281	42,200
Tim Rice	74	66	75	67	282	31,771
Guy Woodman	70	73	72	67	282	31,771
Simon Hurd	72	70	72	68	282	31,771
Shaun Norris	71	71	72	68	282	31,771
Trevor Fisher	74	70	68	70	282	31,771
Omar Sandys	68	74	68	72	282	31,771
Jaco Van Zyl	68	72	69	73	282	31,771
Peter Wilson	74	70	70	69	283	24,750
Andrew McLardy	72	69	71	71	283	24,750
Tyrol Auret	73	72	67	71	283	24,750
Nic Henning	71	67	72	73	283	24,750
Ulrich van den Berg	74	71	71	68	284	19,618
Steve van Vuuren	72	68	74	70	284	19,618
Lewis Atkinson	69	71	74	70	284	19,618
Don Gammon	69	71	73	71	284	19,618
Fulton Allem	72	68	73	71	284	19,618
Michiel Bothma	67	76	69	72	284	19,618
Louis Oosthuizen	69	72	70	73	284	19,618
Brett Liddle	72	70	69	73	284	19,618
Wayne Bradley	70	69	71	74	284	19,618
Chris Davison	69	70	71	74	284	19,618
Desvonde Botes	72	67	69	76	284	19,618

Hassan II Trophy

Dar-es-Salam Golf Club, Red Course, Rabat, Morocco
Par 36-37–73; 7,600 yards

December 12-15
purse, US$490,000

	SCORES				TOTAL	MONEY
Santiago Luna	69	70	69	70	278	US$73,000
Steve Lowery	70	68	73	70	281	33,000
Olivier Edmond	77	68	69	69	283	26,500
Joakim Haeggman	73	66	69	75	283	26,500
Jean-Francois Remesy	73	71	72	68	284	21,000
Gregory Havret	75	73	67	69	284	21,000
Paul Broadhurst	69	66	75	74	284	21,000
Clay Devers	70	73	72	70	285	18,500
Ian Poulter	70	71	72	72	285	18,500
Mark Roe	76	73	73	66	288	17,000
Ignacio Garrido	73	77	69	70	289	16,000
Peter Baker	67	74	75	73	289	16,000
Mark McNulty	72	75	68	74	289	16,000

	SCORES				TOTAL	MONEY
Mustapha El Kherraz	73	75	73	69	290	15,300
Jean-Francois Lucquin	72	74	71	73	290	15,300
Robin Byrd	72	73	72	73	290	15,300
Sam Torrance	77	78	68	69	292	15,000
Roger Chapman	72	73	76	75	296	15,000
Boujemaa Assali	72	74	79	72	297	15,000
Henrik Nystrom	74	73	82	69	298	15,000
Amine Joudar	76	73	80	70	299	15,000
Younes El Hassani	76	74	76	75	301	15,000
Nicolas Colsaerts	72	75	78	77	302	15,000
Stephane Talbot	80	74	75	77	306	15,000

Ernie Els Invitational

Fancourt Golf Club, Outeniqua Course,
George, South Africa
Par 36-36–72; 6,911 yards

December 18-19
purse, R200,000

	SCORES		TOTAL	MONEY
Louis Oosthuizen	66	64	130	R25,000
Des Terblanche	65	69	134	20,000
Ulrich van den Berg	68	69	137	20,000
Richard Sterne	74	64	138	9,333
Ian Hutchings	65	73	138	9,333
Alan McLean	69	69	138	9,333
Marc Cayeux	72	67	139	5,000
Ernie Els	72	68	140	5,000
Sammy Daniels	72	68	140	5,000
Grant Muller	71	69	140	5,000
Ashley Roestoff	70	70	140	5,000
Bradford Vaughan	71	69	140	5,000
Fulton Allem	74	67	141	5,000
Dean van Staden	72	69	141	5,000
Don Gammon	71	71	142	5,000
Justin Hobday	69	73	142	5,000
Nicholas Lawrence	72	70	142	5,000
Doug McGuigan	68	74	142	5,000
Mark Murless	70	72	142	5,000
Ian Palmer	74	68	142	5,000
Desvonde Botes	70	73	143	5,000
Wayne Bradley	71	72	143	5,000
Nic Henning	72	71	143	5,000
Charl Schwartzel	71	72	143	5,000
John Bland	72	72	144	5,000
Simon Hobday	71	73	144	5,000
Richard Kaplan	72	72	144	5,000

Senior Tours

MasterCard Championship

Hualalai Golf Club, Kaupulehu-Kona, Hawaii
Par 36-36–72; 7,053 yards

January 18-20
purse, $1,500,000

	SCORES			TOTAL	MONEY
Tom Kite	63	69	67	199	$258,000
John Jacobs	70	67	68	205	154,000
Bobby Wadkins	68	70	68	206	126,000
Dana Quigley	71	68	69	208	103,000
Allen Doyle	72	68	69	209	65,750
Bruce Fleisher	68	71	70	209	65,750
Walter Hall	68	69	72	209	65,750
Larry Nelson	66	73	70	209	65,750
Mike McCullough	69	71	70	210	44,000
Doug Tewell	67	74	69	210	44,000
Lanny Wadkins	69	69	72	210	44,000
Tom Watson	71	71	70	212	34,333.34
Bob Gilder	67	70	75	212	34,333.33
Gil Morgan	71	70	71	212	34,333.33
Tom Wargo	70	70	73	213	30,000
Jim Colbert	67	72	75	214	24,750
Tom Jenkins	71	70	73	214	24,750
Bruce Lietzke	68	75	71	214	24,750
Graham Marsh	72	72	70	214	24,750
John Schroeder	73	70	71	214	24,750
Jim Thorpe	70	69	75	214	24,750
Jose Maria Canizares	70	75	70	215	19,500
Dave Eichelberger	68	74	73	215	19,500
George Archer	70	74	72	216	17,500
Hale Irwin	73	68	75	216	17,500
Lee Trevino	74	71	73	218	16,000
Sammy Rachels	75	71	73	219	15,000
Hubert Green	74	72	74	220	13,750
Gary Player	75	69	76	220	13,750
Steven Veriato	72	70	79	221	13,000
Ed Dougherty	74	72	76	222	12,750
Joe Inman	74	77	73	224	12,125
Leonard Thompson	78	74	72	224	12,125

Royal Caribbean Classic

Crandon Park Golf Course, Key Biscayne, Florida
Par 35-36–71; 6,913 yards
(Event reduced to 36 holes—rain.)

February 1-3
purse, $1,450,000

	SCORES		TOTAL	MONEY
John Jacobs	67	66	133	$217,500
Isao Aoki	70	64	134	106,333.34
Bruce Fleisher	66	68	134	106,333.33
Tom Watson	68	66	134	106,333.33
Tom Kite	67	68	135	63,800

	SCORES		TOTAL	MONEY
Jay Overton	65	70	135	63,800
Bob Gilder	66	70	136	42,340
Ted Goin	69	67	136	42,340
Walter Hall	67	69	136	42,340
Tom Purtzer	67	69	136	42,340
Sammy Rachels	67	69	136	42,340
Dick Mast	66	71	137	30,450
John Schroeder	68	69	137	30,450
Mike McCullough	70	68	138	26,100
Dana Quigley	66	72	138	26,100
Doug Tewell	69	69	138	26,100
Al Geiberger	70	69	139	19,326.43
Larry Nelson	68	71	139	19,326.43
Don Pooley	71	68	139	19,326.43
Dave Stockton	71	68	139	19,326.43
Jim Thorpe	68	71	139	19,326.43
Tom Wargo	70	69	139	19,326.43
George Archer	67	72	139	19,326.42
Ed Dougherty	70	70	140	12,959.38
Gil Morgan	72	68	140	12,959.38
Christy O'Connor, Jr.	71	69	140	12,959.38
Bruce Summerhays	71	69	140	12,959.38
John Bland	66	74	140	12,959.37
Gibby Gilbert	69	71	140	12,959.37
Stewart Ginn	69	71	140	12,959.37
Jack Spradlin	68	72	140	12,959.37
Hugh Baiocchi	73	68	141	8,142.31
Jim Dent	71	70	141	8,142.31
Bob Eastwood	73	68	141	8,142.31
Raymond Floyd	70	71	141	8,142.31
David Graham	73	68	141	8,142.31
Hubert Green	72	69	141	8,142.31
Joe Inman	72	69	141	8,142.31
Mark McCumber	74	67	141	8,142.31
Mike Smith	70	71	141	8,142.31
Bobby Wadkins	71	70	141	8,142.31
Vicente Fernandez	68	73	141	8,142.30
Harold Henning	68	73	141	8,142.30
Jack Sommers	68	73	141	8,142.30

ACE Group Classic

Twin Eagles Golf Club, Naples, Florida
Par 36-36–72; 7,124 yards

February 8-10
purse, $1,500,000

	SCORES			TOTAL	MONEY
Hale Irwin	68	64	68	200	$225,000
Tom Watson	64	66	71	201	132,000
Jim Dent	69	67	66	202	99,000
Jim Thorpe	66	68	68	202	99,000
Allen Doyle	67	67	69	203	62,000
Dana Quigley	65	68	70	203	62,000
Sammy Rachels	68	68	67	203	62,000
Mike Hill	70	65	70	205	48,000
Tom Jenkins	68	68	70	206	40,500
Jay Overton	69	68	69	206	40,500
Gil Morgan	69	67	71	207	36,000

	SCORES			TOTAL	MONEY
Stewart Ginn	69	72	67	208	27,214.29
Larry Nelson	75	67	66	208	27,214.29
Tom Purtzer	71	68	69	208	27,214.29
Bobby Wadkins	70	70	68	208	27,214.29
Bruce Lietzke	70	67	71	208	27,214.28
Don Pooley	68	69	71	208	27,214.28
Mike Smith	69	70	69	208	27,214.28
John Bland	69	72	68	209	19,850
Raymond Floyd	73	66	70	209	19,850
Doug Tewell	73	66	70	209	19,850
Ed Dougherty	74	67	69	210	16,162.50
Bruce Fleisher	72	67	71	210	16,162.50
Tom Wargo	70	71	69	210	16,162.50
Fuzzy Zoeller	71	71	68	210	16,162.50
Hubert Green	75	68	68	211	13,050
Jim Holtgrieve	72	68	71	211	13,050
Graham Marsh	72	69	70	211	13,050
Jay Sigel	69	69	73	211	13,050
Dave Stockton	72	70	69	211	13,050
Bob Gilder	75	66	71	212	11,250
Rodger Davis	71	64	78	213	10,125
Dick Mast	68	73	72	213	10,125
Bruce Summerhays	71	70	72	213	10,125
Leonard Thompson	73	65	75	213	10,125
Isao Aoki	72	68	74	214	7,971.43
Jose Maria Canizares	71	71	72	214	7,971.43
Doug Johnson	72	72	70	214	7,971.43
J.C. Snead	74	69	71	214	7,971.43
Jack Spradlin	72	69	73	214	7,971.43
Howard Twitty	73	70	71	214	7,971.43
Steven Veriato	72	68	74	214	7,971.42

Verizon Classic

TPC of Tampa Bay, Lutz, Florida
Par 35-36–71; 6,783 yards

February 15-17
purse, $1,500,000

	SCORES			TOTAL	MONEY
Doug Tewell	67	67	69	203	$225,000
Hale Irwin	70	68	66	204	132,000
Bruce Fleisher	66	65	75	206	99,000
Dave Stockton	68	70	68	206	99,000
Tom Kite	66	66	75	207	66,000
Bruce Lietzke	67	70	70	207	66,000
Mike Hill	64	71	73	208	43,800
Mike McCullough	70	71	67	208	43,800
Mark McCumber	68	73	67	208	43,800
Dana Quigley	64	71	73	208	43,800
Bruce Summerhays	65	68	75	208	43,800
Rodger Davis	68	68	73	209	28,800
Ed Dougherty	68	68	73	209	28,800
Allen Doyle	73	70	66	209	28,800
Tom Jenkins	68	69	72	209	28,800
Lee Trevino	68	70	71	209	28,800
Hugh Baiocchi	69	68	73	210	20,575
John Bland	68	69	73	210	20,575
Jose Maria Canizares	70	73	67	210	20,575

	SCORES			TOTAL	MONEY
Morris Hatalsky	71	71	68	210	20,575
Bob Murphy	68	69	73	210	20,575
Leonard Thompson	68	70	72	210	20,575
Isao Aoki	69	72	70	211	15,375
Jim Colbert	68	70	73	211	15,375
Jim Thorpe	70	69	72	211	15,375
Tom Wargo	68	71	72	211	15,375
Jim Dent	71	69	72	212	13,050
Dave Eichelberger	71	71	70	212	13,050
Gil Morgan	71	72	69	212	13,050
John Jacobs	69	73	71	213	10,600
John Mahaffey	70	70	73	213	10,600
Dick Mast	69	69	75	213	10,600
Don Pooley	71	70	72	213	10,600
Butch Sheehan	69	71	73	213	10,600
Bobby Wadkins	69	68	76	213	10,600
Graham Marsh	68	70	76	214	8,280
Andy North	71	73	70	214	8,280
Tom Purtzer	73	75	66	214	8,280
Jay Sigel	68	76	70	214	8,280
Howard Twitty	70	72	72	214	8,280

Audi Senior Classic

Club de Golf Chapultepec, Naucalpan, Mexico
Par 36-36–72; 7,204 yards

February 22-24
purse, $1,700,000

	SCORES			TOTAL	MONEY
Bruce Lietzke	75	66	67	208	$255,000
Hale Irwin	73	69	67	209	136,000
Gary McCord	74	66	69	209	136,000
Jose Maria Canizares	74	69	68	211	73,440
Ed Dougherty	71	65	75	211	73,440
Danny Edwards	72	71	68	211	73,440
Bruce Fleisher	72	66	73	211	73,440
Dana Quigley	69	73	69	211	73,440
Graham Marsh	73	71	68	212	47,600
Morris Hatalsky	72	72	69	213	42,500
Dan O'Neill	72	71	70	213	42,500
Vicente Fernandez	74	73	67	214	33,575
Stewart Ginn	77	68	69	214	33,575
Hubert Green	71	72	71	214	33,575
Jerry McGee	76	68	70	214	33,575
Bob Gilder	77	71	67	215	24,848.34
Steven Veriato	73	72	70	215	24,848.34
Hugh Baiocchi	73	68	74	215	24,848.33
Rodger Davis	71	72	72	215	24,848.33
Walter Hall	70	74	71	215	24,848.33
Jack Spradlin	73	69	73	215	24,848.33
Walter Morgan	72	68	76	216	19,210
John Schroeder	77	70	69	216	19,210
Joe Inman	72	72	73	217	17,850
Christy O'Connor, Jr.	72	74	73	219	16,206.67
Bobby Walzel	77	71	71	219	16,206.67
John Jacobs	73	72	74	219	16,206.66
Jim Colbert	71	73	76	220	13,175
Bob Eastwood	76	72	72	220	13,175

	SCORES			TOTAL	MONEY
Fred Gibson	75	70	75	220	13,175
Tony Jacklin	76	74	70	220	13,175
Tom Jenkins	76	73	71	220	13,175
Leonard Thompson	75	70	75	220	13,175
John Bland	76	71	74	221	10,965
Lon Hinkle	71	77	73	221	10,965
Rex Caldwell	73	76	73	222	8,861.25
Frank Conner	79	72	71	222	8,861.25
Bob Dickson	79	73	70	222	8,861.25
Mark Hayes	76	71	75	222	8,861.25
Dick Mast	72	72	78	222	8,861.25
Mark Pfeil	79	73	70	222	8,861.25
Gary Player	76	71	75	222	8,861.25
Butch Sheehan	74	70	78	222	8,861.25

SBC Senior Classic

Valencia Country Club, Valencia, California
Par 36-36–72; 6,905 yards

March 1-3
purse, $1,450,000

	SCORES			TOTAL	MONEY
Tom Kite	74	69	69	212	$217,500
Tom Watson	72	69	71	212	127,600
(Kite defeated Watson on second playoff hole.)					
Gil Morgan	71	72	70	213	95,700
Tom Purtzer	70	74	69	213	95,700
Bob Gilder	75	72	70	217	69,600
George Archer	75	71	72	218	55,100
Gary McCord	72	75	71	218	55,100
Allen Doyle	76	72	71	219	38,280
Dave Eichelberger	74	71	74	219	38,280
Gibby Gilbert	73	72	74	219	38,280
Doug Johnson	73	70	76	219	38,280
Doug Tewell	74	72	73	219	38,280
Bruce Fleisher	73	75	72	220	27,550
John Mahaffey	78	71	71	220	27,550
Sammy Rachels	74	72	74	220	27,550
Dave Stockton	77	72	72	221	23,925
Lee Trevino	77	74	70	221	23,925
Bob Charles	75	75	72	222	19,227
Ed Dougherty	80	68	74	222	19,227
Larry Nelson	73	73	76	222	19,227
Bruce Summerhays	76	75	71	222	19,227
Howard Twitty	72	76	74	222	19,227
Jim Albus	74	77	72	223	13,291.67
Hubert Green	75	75	73	223	13,291.67
John Jacobs	77	73	73	223	13,291.67
Bruce Lietzke	74	76	73	223	13,291.67
Mark McCumber	75	76	72	223	13,291.67
Jerry Tucker	74	76	73	223	13,291.67
Raymond Floyd	77	75	71	223	13,291.66
Chi Chi Rodriguez	76	74	73	223	13,291.66
Larry Ziegler	75	73	75	223	13,291.66
Ben Crenshaw	74	74	76	224	9,570
Tom Jenkins	75	77	72	224	9,570
Don Pooley	75	74	75	224	9,570
Dana Quigley	79	75	70	224	9,570

	SCORES			TOTAL	MONEY
Bobby Wadkins	75	72	77	224	9,570
Hugh Baiocchi	75	74	76	225	7,105
John Bland	75	75	75	225	7,105
Dale Douglass	74	75	76	225	7,105
David Graham	75	79	71	225	7,105
Wayne Levi	79	72	74	225	7,105
Mike McCullough	75	77	73	225	7,105
Mike Smith	78	73	74	225	7,105
Jack Spradlin	78	75	72	225	7,105
Tom Wargo	76	74	75	225	7,105

Toshiba Senior Classic

Newport Beach Country Club, Newport Beach, California
Par 35-36–71; 6,584 yards

March 8-10

purse, $1,500,000

	SCORES			TOTAL	MONEY
Hale Irwin	67	64	65	196	$225,000
Allen Doyle	66	68	67	201	132,000
Dave Stockton	68	68	66	202	99,000
Michael Zinni	69	66	67	202	99,000
Dana Quigley	69	68	66	203	72,000
Bobby Wadkins	68	69	67	204	60,000
Morris Hatalsky	70	69	66	205	48,000
John Jacobs	70	67	68	205	48,000
Gil Morgan	68	66	71	205	48,000
Walter Hall	68	67	71	206	33,300
Tom Jenkins	70	67	69	206	33,300
Wayne Levi	71	69	66	206	33,300
Don Pooley	70	65	71	206	33,300
Tom Watson	68	72	66	206	33,300
Bruce Fleisher	72	68	67	207	25,500
Larry Nelson	70	64	73	207	25,500
Fuzzy Zoeller	70	70	67	207	25,500
Bob Eastwood	70	67	71	208	19,325
Stewart Ginn	69	67	72	208	19,325
Gary McCord	70	72	66	208	19,325
Mark McCumber	74	69	65	208	19,325
J.C. Snead	73	70	65	208	19,325
Doug Tewell	70	70	68	208	19,325
John Bland	76	68	65	209	14,662.50
Ben Crenshaw	70	71	68	209	14,662.50
Jim Dent	67	71	71	209	14,662.50
Rocky Thompson	73	67	69	209	14,662.50
George Archer	68	71	71	210	12,150
Raymond Floyd	73	70	67	210	12,150
Terry Mauney	74	67	69	210	12,150
Mike McCullough	68	71	71	210	12,150
Vicente Fernandez	74	67	70	211	8,754.55
Bob Gilder	68	74	69	211	8,754.55
Ted Goin	73	70	68	211	8,754.55
Joe Inman	74	68	69	211	8,754.55
Sammy Rachels	70	71	70	211	8,754.55
Jay Sigel	73	71	67	211	8,754.55
Charles Coody	72	70	69	211	8,754.54
Andy North	73	73	65	211	8,754.54
Chi Chi Rodriguez	71	72	68	211	8,754.54

	SCORES			TOTAL	MONEY
Mike Smith	74	69	68	211	8,754.54
Steven Veriato	73	70	68	211	8,754.54

Siebel Classic in Silicon Valley

Coyote Creek Golf Club, San Jose, California
Par 37-35–72; 6,828 yards

March 15-17
purse, $1,400,000

	SCORES			TOTAL	MONEY
Dana Quigley	67	75	70	212	$210,000
Bob Gilder	67	75	71	213	112,000
Fuzzy Zoeller	70	73	70	213	112,000
Tom Wargo	67	76	71	214	84,000
Hale Irwin	70	79	67	216	61,600
John Jacobs	69	79	68	216	61,600
Bruce Fleisher	72	73	72	217	39,199.98
Mike Smith	70	74	73	217	39,199.98
Bobby Wadkins	74	72	71	217	39,199.98
Lanny Wadkins	70	75	72	217	39,199.98
Vicente Fernandez	71	74	72	217	39,199.97
Rocky Thompson	71	73	73	217	39,199.97
Ed Dougherty	70	72	76	218	27,300
Dave Stockton	72	74	72	218	27,300
Dave Barr	72	74	73	219	23,800
Tom Jenkins	69	76	74	219	23,800
Steven Veriato	72	75	72	219	23,800
Lon Hinkle	71	78	71	220	19,145
Wayne Levi	70	74	76	220	19,145
John Schroeder	69	76	75	220	19,145
Jay Sigel	68	73	79	220	19,145
Tom Purtzer	69	78	74	221	14,727.98
George Archer	68	74	79	221	14,727.97
Frank Conner	72	75	74	221	14,727.97
Bob Eastwood	71	75	75	221	14,727.97
Andy North	69	77	75	221	14,727.97
Rodger Davis	69	78	75	222	12,180
Stewart Ginn	70	78	74	222	12,180
Dan O'Neill	73	77	72	222	12,180
Jim Dent	73	74	76	223	10,325
Hubert Green	75	75	73	223	10,325
Butch Sheehan	68	78	77	223	10,325
Jack Spradlin	74	79	70	223	10,325
Terry Dill	77	75	72	224	8,610
Gary McCord	72	76	76	224	8,610
Sammy Rachels	67	85	72	224	8,610
Jim Thorpe	73	77	74	224	8,610
Walter Hall	78	72	75	225	7,139.98
Dave Eichelberger	73	77	75	225	7,139.97
Ted Goin	72	77	76	225	7,139.97
Jim Holtgrieve	75	77	73	225	7,139.97
Don Pooley	72	77	76	225	7,139.97

Emerald Coast Classic

The Moors Golf Club, Milton, Florida
Par 35-35–70; 6,832 yards
(Third round cancelled—rain.)

March 29-31
purse, $1,450,000

	SCORES		TOTAL	MONEY
Dave Eichelberger	65	65	130	$217,500
Doug Tewell	69	63	132	127,600
Lanny Wadkins	71	63	134	104,400
Hubert Green	69	66	135	87,000
Dana Quigley	63	73	136	59,933.34
Dale Douglass	73	63	136	59,933.33
Tom Jenkins	68	68	136	59,933.33
John Bland	71	66	137	34,256.25
Frank Conner	67	70	137	34,256.25
Allen Doyle	67	70	137	34,256.25
Bob Eastwood	67	70	137	34,256.25
Vicente Fernandez	68	69	137	34,256.25
Joe Inman	71	66	137	34,256.25
John Jacobs	69	68	137	34,256.25
Dick Mast	68	69	137	34,256.25
Wayne Levi	72	66	138	19,462.23
Larry Nelson	67	71	138	19,462.23
Ben Crenshaw	70	68	138	19,462.22
Bruce Fleisher	71	67	138	19,462.22
Fred Gibson	66	72	138	19,462.22
David Graham	70	68	138	19,462.22
Graham Marsh	70	68	138	19,462.22
Butch Sheehan	71	67	138	19,462.22
Bobby Walzel	71	67	138	19,462.22
Gibby Gilbert	71	68	139	12,929.17
Don Pooley	68	71	139	12,929.17
Sammy Rachels	68	71	139	12,929.17
Dave Stockton	71	68	139	12,929.17
Walter Hall	70	69	139	12,929.16
Mike Hill	71	68	139	12,929.16
Ted Goin	72	68	140	8,499.24
Jim Colbert	70	70	140	8,499.23
Charles Coody	69	71	140	8,499.23
Terry Dill	68	72	140	8,499.23
Harold Henning	70	70	140	8,499.23
Bruce Lietzke	72	68	140	8,499.23
John Mahaffey	70	70	140	8,499.23
Mike McCullough	68	72	140	8,499.23
Gil Morgan	69	71	140	8,499.23
Jay Sigel	70	70	140	8,499.23
Jack Spradlin	68	72	140	8,499.23
Rocky Thompson	70	70	140	8,499.23
Fuzzy Zoeller	70	70	140	8,499.23

Liberty Mutual Legends of Golf

World Golf Village, The King & The Bear Course,
St. Augustine, Florida
Par 36-36–72; 7,048 yards

April 5-7
purse, $2,505,000

	SCORES			TOTAL	MONEY
Doug Tewell	69	66	70	205	$306,000
Bobby Wadkins	73	67	66	206	181,000
Bob Gilder	68	70	70	208	134,500
Stewart Ginn	69	67	72	208	134,500
Gary McCord	69	70	70	209	98,000
Hale Irwin	67	70	73	210	74,000
Tom Jenkins	72	65	73	210	74,000
Larry Nelson	76	67	67	210	74,000
Hugh Baiocchi	73	74	64	211	53,333.34
Vicente Fernandez	68	71	72	211	53,333.33
Hubert Green	69	71	71	211	53,333.33
Bruce Fleisher	70	73	69	212	45,000
Tom Kite	72	71	70	213	37,625
Wayne Levi	68	70	75	213	37,625
Graham Marsh	70	71	72	213	37,625
Gil Morgan	71	71	71	213	37,625
Dave Eichelberger	74	73	67	214	28,820
Andy North	71	72	71	214	28,820
Jay Sigel	69	73	72	214	28,820
Larry Ziegler	73	71	70	214	28,820
Fuzzy Zoeller	72	67	75	214	28,820
George Archer	73	72	70	215	23,100
Bob Eastwood	71	72	72	215	23,100
Jim Ahern	71	74	71	216	19,560
Jim Colbert	75	69	72	216	19,560
Jim Dent	68	73	75	216	19,560
Sammy Rachels	71	67	78	216	19,560
Leonard Thompson	70	72	74	216	19,560
Walter Hall	69	72	76	217	15,420
Simon Hobday	73	71	73	217	15,420
John Jacobs	73	73	71	217	15,420
John Mahaffey	73	74	70	217	15,420
Mike McCullough	74	72	71	217	15,420
Jose Maria Canizares	71	74	73	218	12,116.67
John Schroeder	74	74	70	218	12,116.67
Jim Thorpe	76	72	70	218	12,116.67
Tom Watson	73	75	70	218	12,116.67
Ed Dougherty	66	73	79	218	12,116.66
Allen Doyle	68	75	75	218	12,116.66
Tom Purtzer	72	72	75	219	10,300
Steven Veriato	73	70	76	219	10,300

The Countrywide Tradition

Superstition Mountain, Prospector Course, Superstition, Arizona
Par 36-36–72; 7,196 yards

April 25-28
purse, $2,000,000

	SCORES				TOTAL	MONEY
Jim Thorpe	67	70	70	70	277	$300,000
John Jacobs	68	72	66	71	277	176,000

(Thorpe defeated Jacobs on first playoff hole.)

	SCORES				TOTAL	MONEY
Bob Gilder	69	68	71	70	278	132,000
Bruce Summerhays	70	70	70	68	278	132,000
Tom Watson	72	70	70	68	280	96,000
Hale Irwin	71	72	68	70	281	80,000
Tom Kite	67	72	72	71	282	68,000
Tom Purtzer	72	72	68	70	282	68,000
Bruce Fleisher	68	73	74	68	283	50,000
John Mahaffey	70	72	72	69	283	50,000
Dick Mast	67	73	71	72	283	50,000
Don Pooley	67	73	73	70	283	50,000
David Graham	72	71	70	71	284	38,000
Tom Jenkins	74	66	73	71	284	38,000
Bobby Wadkins	69	72	72	71	284	38,000
Ed Dougherty	70	71	75	69	285	32,000
Allen Doyle	66	74	73	72	285	32,000
Bruce Lietzke	75	74	70	66	285	32,000
Mike McCullough	75	70	71	70	286	27,300
Fuzzy Zoeller	68	70	73	75	286	27,300
Wayne Levi	70	77	69	71	287	21,666.67
Sammy Rachels	70	74	72	71	287	21,666.67
Doug Tewell	71	76	68	72	287	21,666.67
Leonard Thompson	73	75	70	69	287	21,666.67
Raymond Floyd	71	74	70	72	287	21,666.66
Butch Sheehan	69	72	73	73	287	21,666.66
Fred Gibson	70	75	74	69	288	17,000
Simon Hobday	75	72	69	72	288	17,000
Gary McCord	72	73	71	72	288	17,000
Dana Quigley	70	77	72	69	288	17,000
Jim Colbert	73	72	71	73	289	14,100
Bob Eastwood	71	66	76	76	289	14,100
Ted Goin	71	72	70	76	289	14,100
Jim Holtgrieve	70	74	73	72	289	14,100
Rodger Davis	71	76	72	71	290	11,085.72
Jack Spradlin	74	76	68	72	290	11,085.72
Dave Stockton	69	76	74	71	290	11,085.72
Isao Aoki	78	71	71	70	290	11,085.71
Gil Morgan	73	71	75	71	290	11,085.71
Walter Morgan	71	72	70	77	290	11,085.71
Andy North	75	73	71	71	290	11,085.71

Bruno's Memorial Classic

Greystone Golf & Country Club, Birmingham, Alabama
Par 36-36–72; 6,992 yards

May 3-5
purse, $1,400,000

	SCORES			TOTAL	MONEY
Sammy Rachels	70	64	67	201	$210,000
Dana Quigley	66	69	66	201	123,200
(Rachels defeated Quigley on second playoff hole.)					
Larry Nelson	66	66	70	202	100,800
Hale Irwin	70	63	70	203	84,000
Jim Ahern	71	67	66	204	67,200
John Jacobs	67	69	69	205	53,200
Bruce Lietzke	68	69	68	205	53,200
Bob Charles	67	69	70	206	35,466.67
Tom Jenkins	66	74	66	206	35,466.67
Tom Kite	69	67	70	206	35,466.67

	SCORES			TOTAL	MONEY
Bobby Wadkins	68	68	70	206	35,466.67
George Archer	67	67	72	206	35,466.66
Bruce Fleisher	64	71	71	206	35,466.66
Rodger Davis	68	69	70	207	26,600
Allen Doyle	69	68	71	208	23,100
David Graham	70	66	72	208	23,100
Hubert Green	69	70	69	208	23,100
Gil Morgan	71	67	70	208	23,100
John Bland	72	66	71	209	17,444
Jose Maria Canizares	69	70	70	209	17,444
Vicente Fernandez	69	70	70	209	17,444
Bob Gilder	71	65	73	209	17,444
Doug Tewell	71	69	69	209	17,444
Jim Albus	72	68	70	210	13,384
Isao Aoki	68	69	73	210	13,384
Andy North	71	68	71	210	13,384
J.C. Snead	72	71	67	210	13,384
Jack Spradlin	70	69	71	210	13,384
Ed Dougherty	70	68	73	211	9,922.50
Simon Hobday	71	69	71	211	9,922.50
Gary McCord	74	66	71	211	9,922.50
Mike McCullough	71	68	72	211	9,922.50
Don Pooley	69	72	70	211	9,922.50
Chi Chi Rodriguez	72	72	67	211	9,922.50
Leonard Thompson	71	70	70	211	9,922.50
Jim Thorpe	73	68	70	211	9,922.50
Stewart Ginn	74	67	71	212	7,420
Wayne Levi	71	72	69	212	7,420
Graham Marsh	71	68	73	212	7,420
Tom Purtzer	73	67	72	212	7,420
Tom Watson	73	67	72	212	7,420

TD Waterhouse Championship

Tiffany Greens Golf Club, Kansas City, Missouri
Par 36-36–72; 6,929 yards
(Final round cancelled—rain.)

May 10-12
purse, $1,600,000

	SCORES		TOTAL	MONEY
Bruce Lietzke	69	64	133	$240,000
Larry Nelson	69	66	135	140,800
Walter Hall	69	68	137	96,000
Hale Irwin	69	68	137	96,000
Tom Wargo	72	65	137	96,000
Bruce Fleisher	69	69	138	60,800
Tom Purtzer	69	69	138	60,800
Isao Aoki	71	68	139	45,866.67
Tom Kite	70	69	139	45,866.67
Sammy Rachels	70	69	139	45,866.66
Hubert Green	74	66	140	36,800
Jim Thorpe	72	68	140	36,800
Jose Maria Canizares	73	68	141	24,334.55
Jim Dent	74	67	141	24,334.55
Allen Doyle	72	69	141	24,334.55
Morris Hatalsky	71	70	141	24,334.55
J.C. Snead	69	72	141	24,334.55
Larry Ziegler	70	71	141	24,334.55

	SCORES			TOTAL	MONEY
Rodger Davis	72	69		141	24,334.54
Graham Marsh	72	69		141	24,334.54
Mike McCullough	73	68		141	24,334.54
Dana Quigley	73	68		141	24,334.54
Dave Stockton	72	69		141	24,334.54
Ed Dougherty	68	74		142	15,296
Gibby Gilbert	72	70		142	15,296
John Jacobs	72	70		142	15,296
John Schroeder	68	74		142	15,296
Lanny Wadkins	70	72		142	15,296
Jim Ahern	73	70		143	12,360
Bob Eastwood	68	75		143	12,360
Jay Sigel	69	74		143	12,360
Jack Spradlin	72	71		143	12,360
Mike Hill	70	74		144	9,866.67
John Mahaffey	75	69		144	9,866.67
Scott Masingill	74	70		144	9,866.67
Butch Sheehan	72	72		144	9,866.67
Stewart Ginn	72	72		144	9,866.66
Don Pooley	72	72		144	9,866.66
Vicente Fernandez	71	74		145	8,160
Howard Twitty	72	73		145	8,160
Bobby Walzel	73	72		145	8,160

Instinet Classic

TPC at Jasna Polana, Princeton, New Jersey
Par 36-36–72; 6,941 yards

May 17-19
purse, $1,500,000

	SCORES			TOTAL	MONEY
Isao Aoki	69	67	65	201	$225,000
John Jacobs	65	70	70	205	132,000
Allen Doyle	69	67	71	207	99,000
Mike Hill	69	68	70	207	99,000
Hale Irwin	69	68	71	208	62,000
Tom Jenkins	68	72	68	208	62,000
Dana Quigley	68	71	69	208	62,000
Jim Thorpe	65	69	75	209	45,000
Bobby Wadkins	72	68	69	209	45,000
Jose Maria Canizares	69	72	70	211	33,300
Ed Dougherty	67	73	71	211	33,300
Morris Hatalsky	72	71	68	211	33,300
Mike Smith	68	73	70	211	33,300
Dave Stockton	70	71	70	211	33,300
Gil Morgan	73	69	70	212	24,750
Jay Sigel	72	71	69	212	24,750
Bruce Summerhays	71	71	70	212	24,750
Lee Trevino	71	68	73	212	24,750
Jim Colbert	71	70	73	214	20,475
Fred Gibson	71	71	72	214	20,475
Hugh Baiocchi	73	71	71	215	16,650
John Bland	73	69	73	215	16,650
Doug Tewell	74	75	66	215	16,650
Howard Twitty	68	75	72	215	16,650
Bobby Walzel	69	74	72	215	16,650
George Archer	71	74	71	216	13,050
Charles Coody	69	73	74	216	13,050

	SCORES			TOTAL	MONEY
Rodger Davis	78	69	69	216	13,050
Jim Dent	74	70	72	216	13,050
Andy North	75	69	72	216	13,050
Jim Holtgrieve	70	75	72	217	10,800
Terry Mauney	70	72	75	217	10,800
Don Pooley	68	72	77	217	10,800
Walter Hall	73	71	74	218	8,850
Wayne Levi	71	72	75	218	8,850
John Mahaffey	74	69	75	218	8,850
Graham Marsh	78	72	68	218	8,850
Mike McCullough	76	68	74	218	8,850
DeWitt Weaver	71	73	74	218	8,850
Jim Ahern	75	72	72	219	7,050
David Eger	74	72	73	219	7,050
Ted Goin	73	73	73	219	7,050
Walter Morgan	76	73	70	219	7,050
Mark Pfeil	75	70	74	219	7,050

Farmers Charity Classic

Egypt Valley Country Club, Ada, Michigan
Par 36-36–72; 6,960 yards

May 24-26
purse, $1,500,000

	SCORES			TOTAL	MONEY
Jay Sigel	67	69	67	203	$225,000
Morris Hatalsky	71	66	68	205	132,000
Rodger Davis	69	67	70	206	108,000
Wayne Levi	70	68	69	207	74,000
Jim Thorpe	69	69	69	207	74,000
Tom Wargo	69	69	69	207	74,000
R.W. Eaks	69	72	67	208	51,000
Sammy Rachels	74	70	64	208	51,000
Dan O'Neill	69	67	74	210	39,000
Gary Player	72	68	70	210	39,000
Bobby Wadkins	69	72	69	210	39,000
Jose Maria Canizares	71	72	68	211	27,214.29
Allen Doyle	71	70	70	211	27,214.29
Dick Mast	69	73	69	211	27,214.29
Jay Overton	71	71	69	211	27,214.29
David Eger	67	72	72	211	27,214.28
Bob Gilder	70	68	73	211	27,214.28
John Jacobs	68	72	71	211	27,214.28
Walter Hall	72	70	70	212	19,237.50
Mike Hill	72	70	70	212	19,237.50
Larry Nelson	69	74	69	212	19,237.50
Howard Twitty	71	73	68	212	19,237.50
Ted Goin	75	70	68	213	14,700
David Graham	72	74	67	213	14,700
Jim Holtgrieve	70	71	72	213	14,700
Dave Stockton	71	73	69	213	14,700
Bruce Summerhays	71	72	70	213	14,700
Bobby Walzel	71	69	73	213	14,700
Jim Ahern	74	72	68	214	11,850
Randy Erskine	71	69	74	214	11,850
Butch Sheehan	73	70	71	214	11,850
George Archer	70	74	71	215	9,281.25
Jim Colbert	74	71	70	215	9,281.25
Jim Dent	69	73	73	215	9,281.25

	SCORES			TOTAL	MONEY
Danny Edwards	77	71	67	215	9,281.25
Mark Pfeil	71	73	71	215	9,281.25
Jack Spradlin	76	70	69	215	9,281.25
Rocky Thompson	71	70	74	215	9,281.25
Lee Trevino	72	70	73	215	9,281.25
Charles Coody	71	76	69	216	7,350
Tony Jacklin	72	74	70	216	7,350
Mike Smith	75	70	71	216	7,350

NFL Golf Classic

Upper Montclair Country Club, Clifton, New Jersey   May 31-June 2
Par 36-36–72; 6,801 yards   purse, $1,300,000

	SCORES			TOTAL	MONEY
James Mason	65	73	69	207	$195,000
Morris Hatalsky	72	70	67	209	95,333.34
Dave Eichelberger	66	71	72	209	95,333.33
Bruce Fleisher	71	71	67	209	95,333.33
Walter Hall	76	65	69	210	57,200
Jay Sigel	68	68	74	210	57,200
Hugh Baiocchi	74	68	69	211	44,200
Tom Jenkins	72	69	70	211	44,200
Don Pooley	73	68	71	212	36,400
Dave Barr	68	71	74	213	31,200
John Bland	67	69	77	213	31,200
Mark Pfeil	71	72	70	213	31,200
Lon Hinkle	73	68	73	214	24,700
Tom Kite	70	74	70	214	24,700
Paul Parajeckas	72	70	72	214	24,700
Jim Albus	72	69	74	215	18,441.43
Vicente Fernandez	71	72	72	215	18,441.43
Fred Gibson	76	68	71	215	18,441.43
Mike McCullough	72	69	74	215	18,441.43
Walter Morgan	69	71	75	215	18,441.43
Mike Smith	73	72	70	215	18,441.43
Bruce Summerhays	71	68	76	215	18,441.42
Jose Maria Canizares	71	71	74	216	13,650
Dick Mast	71	74	71	216	13,650
Butch Sheehan	73	67	76	216	13,650
Rodger Davis	77	69	71	217	11,570
Allen Doyle	76	72	69	217	11,570
Hubert Green	73	72	72	217	11,570
Larry Ziegler	73	69	75	217	11,570
Jim Dent	79	69	70	218	9,386
Raymond Floyd	70	72	76	218	9,386
Doug Johnson	72	71	75	218	9,386
Leonard Thompson	74	71	73	218	9,386
Jim Thorpe	74	74	70	218	9,386
R.W. Eaks	72	78	69	219	6,933.34
David Eger	74	73	72	219	6,933.34
Wayne Levi	72	77	70	219	6,933.34
Rex Caldwell	74	72	73	219	6,933.33
Jim Colbert	69	70	80	219	6,933.33
Ed Dougherty	73	71	75	219	6,933.33
Graham Marsh	73	70	76	219	6,933.33
John Schroeder	73	70	76	219	6,933.33
Howard Twitty	73	73	73	219	6,933.33

Senior PGA Championship

Firestone Country Club, Akron, Ohio
Par 35-35–70; 6,927 yards

June 6-9
purse, $2,000,000

	SCORES				TOTAL	MONEY
Fuzzy Zoeller	69	71	70	68	278	$360,000
Hale Irwin	71	70	71	68	280	176,000
Bobby Wadkins	70	70	69	71	280	176,000
Jim Thorpe	69	71	72	69	281	86,000
Roy Vucinich	70	72	68	71	281	86,000
Bruce Fleisher	70	72	71	70	283	60,000
Wayne Levi	69	68	75	71	283	60,000
Gil Morgan	76	70	69	68	283	60,000
Larry Nelson	70	68	72	73	283	60,000
Bob Gilder	71	69	72	73	285	42,600
Walter Hall	70	68	73	74	285	42,600
Morris Hatalsky	72	72	74	67	285	42,600
Jay Overton	70	70	71	74	285	42,600
Dana Quigley	72	71	70	72	285	42,600
Allen Doyle	71	71	72	72	286	32,000
Raymond Floyd	71	70	72	73	286	32,000
Tom Kite	68	73	72	73	286	32,000
Jim Ahern	70	76	70	72	288	20,666.67
Jose Maria Canizares	72	72	72	72	288	20,666.67
Bob Charles	73	71	72	72	288	20,666.67
Seiji Ebihara	73	75	75	65	288	20,666.67
Doug Tewell	70	73	73	72	288	20,666.67
Tom Watson	69	76	72	71	288	20,666.67
Dan O'Neill	71	70	72	75	288	20,666.66
Don Pooley	74	70	69	75	288	20,666.66
John Schroeder	71	70	71	76	288	20,666.66
Jim Colbert	75	69	72	73	289	13,000
Ben Crenshaw	78	67	72	72	289	13,000
Bob Eastwood	77	72	68	72	289	13,000
J.C. Snead	73	70	75	71	289	13,000
Lanny Wadkins	72	74	71	72	289	13,000
Rodger Davis	74	72	71	73	290	10,750
Ed Dougherty	74	74	73	69	290	10,750
Gary McCord	78	70	70	72	290	10,750
Pete Oakley	73	71	73	73	290	10,750
Tom Jenkins	76	68	76	71	291	8,620
Butch Sheehan	76	72	73	70	291	8,620
Jack Spradlin	72	69	77	73	291	8,620
Leonard Thompson	75	69	70	77	291	8,620
Larry Ziegler	70	68	75	78	291	8,620

BellSouth Senior Classic at Opryland

Springhouse Golf Club, Nashville, Tennessee
Par 36-36–72; 6,783 yards

June 14-16
purse, $1,600,000

	SCORES			TOTAL	MONEY
Gil Morgan	67	68	67	202	$240,000
Mike McCullough	69	68	68	205	117,333.34
Bruce Fleisher	72	64	69	205	117,333.33
Dana Quigley	66	70	69	205	117,333.33
Morris Hatalsky	67	70	69	206	70,400

	SCORES			TOTAL	MONEY
Leonard Thompson	68	71	67	206	70,400
Rodger Davis	68	72	67	207	48,800
Butch Sheehan	68	70	69	207	48,800
Bobby Wadkins	68	71	68	207	48,800
Fuzzy Zoeller	67	68	72	207	48,800
John Mahaffey	68	72	68	208	34,000
J.C. Snead	69	71	68	208	34,000
Jim Thorpe	69	70	69	208	34,000
Bobby Walzel	71	72	65	208	34,000
John Bland	68	73	68	209	24,880
Jose Maria Canizares	70	68	71	209	24,880
Allen Doyle	70	68	71	209	24,880
Dave Eichelberger	67	75	67	209	24,880
Vicente Fernandez	70	67	72	209	24,880
Bob Gilder	68	69	72	209	24,880
Terry Dill	71	71	68	210	16,195.56
R.W. Eaks	70	72	68	210	16,195.56
Bob Eastwood	68	73	69	210	16,195.56
Sammy Rachels	68	73	69	210	16,195.56
Mike Smith	72	70	68	210	16,195.56
Jim Ahern	67	71	72	210	16,195.55
Walter Hall	66	72	72	210	16,195.55
Tom Jenkins	71	68	71	210	16,195.55
Jay Sigel	64	70	76	210	16,195.55
Charles Coody	70	69	72	211	11,552
David Eger	67	72	72	211	11,552
Don Pooley	70	73	68	211	11,552
Dave Stockton	70	69	72	211	11,552
Howard Twitty	72	71	68	211	11,552
Ted Goin	73	69	70	212	9,400
Bruce Lietzke	72	67	73	212	9,400
Terry Mauney	73	67	72	212	9,400
Lee Trevino	67	74	71	212	9,400
Stewart Ginn	70	68	75	213	7,680
Jim Holtgrieve	68	71	74	213	7,680
James Mason	74	71	68	213	7,680
Dan O'Neill	72	70	71	213	7,680
Tom Purtzer	70	73	70	213	7,680
Bruce Summerhays	72	72	69	213	7,680

Greater Baltimore Classic

Hayfields Country Club, Hunt Valley, Maryland
Par 36-36–72; 7,031 yards

June 21-23
purse, $1,450,000

	SCORES			TOTAL	MONEY
J.C. Snead	69	64	70	203	$217,500
Bobby Wadkins	68	70	66	204	106,333.34
John Mahaffey	65	69	70	204	106,333.33
Doug Tewell	68	69	67	204	106,333.33
Jim Ahern	65	71	69	205	53,360
Bob Charles	70	68	67	205	53,360
Rodger Davis	65	68	72	205	53,360
Bruce Fleisher	67	70	68	205	53,360
Wayne Levi	69	69	67	205	53,360
Mike McCullough	67	71	69	207	37,700
Bob Gilder	69	70	69	208	34,800

	SCORES			TOTAL	MONEY
John Bland	70	71	68	209	27,840
Dale Douglass	68	71	70	209	27,840
Vicente Fernandez	69	69	71	209	27,840
John Jacobs	67	69	73	209	27,840
Jim Thorpe	71	70	68	209	27,840
Stewart Ginn	71	69	70	210	22,475
Joe Inman	69	72	69	210	22,475
Isao Aoki	71	70	70	211	17,151.43
Jim Dent	72	70	69	211	17,151.43
David Eger	71	71	69	211	17,151.43
Tom Jenkins	72	70	69	211	17,151.43
Gary McCord	74	70	67	211	17,151.43
Dave Stockton	70	69	72	211	17,151.43
Doug Johnson	70	68	73	211	17,151.42
Allen Doyle	70	69	73	212	12,325
Ted Goin	70	72	70	212	12,325
James Mason	70	73	69	212	12,325
Mark McCumber	69	73	70	212	12,325
Mark Pfeil	70	70	72	212	12,325
Dana Quigley	73	72	67	212	12,325
Ed Dougherty	76	69	68	213	10,005
Jay Overton	74	65	74	213	10,005
Jimmy Powell	71	74	68	213	10,005
Dave Eichelberger	71	68	75	214	8,192.50
Walter Hall	69	71	74	214	8,192.50
Clyde Hughey	71	76	67	214	8,192.50
Walter Morgan	69	71	74	214	8,192.50
Bruce Summerhays	75	72	67	214	8,192.50
Bobby Walzel	68	69	77	214	8,192.50

U.S. Senior Open

Caves Valley Golf Club, Baltimore, Maryland
Par 35-36–71; 7,005 yards

June 27-30
purse, $2,500,000

	SCORES				TOTAL	MONEY
Don Pooley	71	70	63	70	274	$450,000
Tom Watson	67	71	69	67	274	265,000
(Pooley defeated Watson on fifth playoff hole.)						
Tom Kite	69	67	73	68	277	171,182
Ed Dougherty	71	69	68	70	278	119,609
Fred Gibson	69	69	73	69	280	91,597
Morris Hatalsky	73	72	68	67	280	91,597
Jose Maria Canizares	68	68	76	69	281	71,689
Allen Doyle	70	69	71	71	281	71,689
Larry Nelson	71	71	72	67	281	71,689
Bob Gilder	71	71	70	71	283	60,792
Walter Hall	70	65	72	77	284	48,635
Hale Irwin	73	74	69	68	284	48,635
Gil Morgan	72	69	75	68	284	48,635
Doug Tewell	75	69	69	71	284	48,635
Jim Thorpe	70	72	72	70	284	48,635
Bobby Wadkins	72	73	71	68	284	48,635
John Schroeder	74	69	68	74	285	39,469
Isao Aoki	69	69	72	76	286	35,205
Stewart Ginn	72	73	71	70	286	35,205
Terry Mauney	72	69	71	74	286	35,205

	SCORES				TOTAL	MONEY
John Bland	75	73	70	69	287	28,731
Raymond Floyd	73	68	74	72	287	28,731
Bruce Lietzke	74	72	70	71	287	28,731
Jay Sigel	74	72	69	72	287	28,731
Vicente Fernandez	71	70	75	72	288	23,792
Dana Quigley	73	73	67	75	288	23,792
Jim Dent	73	70	74	72	289	19,993
Jay Overton	71	70	74	74	289	19,993
Roy Vucinich	72	70	73	74	289	19,993
Graham Marsh	75	72	72	71	290	17,733
Jim Ahern	69	75	74	73	291	15,994
Dave Barr	73	73	72	73	291	15,994
Jim Colbert	74	70	77	70	291	15,994
David Graham	76	73	71	71	291	15,994
Tom Jenkins	75	72	71	73	291	15,994
Christy O'Connor, Jr.	74	74	73	70	291	15,994
R.W. Eaks	64	73	78	77	292	13,522
Hubert Green	75	69	75	73	292	13,522
James Mason	68	76	74	74	292	13,522
Lanny Wadkins	73	68	79	72	292	13,522

AT&T Canada Senior Open

Essex Golf & Country Club, LaSalle, Ontario, Canada
Par 35-36–71; 6,850 yards

July 5-7
purse, $1,600,000

	SCORES			TOTAL	MONEY
Tom Jenkins	63	68	64	195	$240,000
Walter Morgan	73	60	65	198	117,333.34
Morris Hatalsky	67	64	67	198	117,333.33
Bruce Lietzke	70	62	66	198	117,333.33
Bob Gilder	73	63	64	200	76,800
Tom Kite	69	66	66	201	64,000
Allen Doyle	67	68	68	203	42,971.43
Walter Hall	68	69	66	203	42,971.43
Gar Hamilton	65	69	69	203	42,971.43
Hale Irwin	68	68	67	203	42,971.43
Bruce Summerhays	68	65	70	203	42,971.43
Doug Tewell	69	68	66	203	42,971.43
Butch Sheehan	68	66	69	203	42,971.42
Hubert Green	70	68	66	204	30,400
Ed Dougherty	68	68	69	205	24,160
Vicente Fernandez	71	66	68	205	24,160
Norm Jarvis	70	68	67	205	24,160
Wayne McDonald	69	68	68	205	24,160
Larry Nelson	69	69	67	205	24,160
Dana Quigley	70	70	65	205	24,160
John Schroeder	68	68	69	205	24,160
Mark Pfeil	67	69	70	206	18,560
Stewart Ginn	67	72	68	207	16,400
Jerry McGee	72	67	68	207	16,400
Don Pooley	70	68	69	207	16,400
Lanny Wadkins	72	67	68	207	16,400
Dave Barr	70	69	69	208	12,440
Rodger Davis	69	69	70	208	12,440
Doug Johnson	70	70	68	208	12,440
Tom Purtzer	72	69	67	208	12,440

	SCORES			TOTAL	MONEY
Jay Sigel	70	68	70	208	12,440
Mike Smith	72	68	68	208	12,440
Bobby Wadkins	67	69	72	208	12,440
Tom Wargo	67	70	71	208	12,440
Jim Ahern	67	73	69	209	9,400
Bob Eastwood	68	69	72	209	9,400
Ted Goin	71	69	69	209	9,400
Mark McCumber	72	68	69	209	9,400
Isao Aoki	68	71	71	210	7,360
Jose Maria Canizares	69	71	70	210	7,360
Ben Crenshaw	74	66	70	210	7,360
Mike McCullough	71	64	75	210	7,360
Gary Player	71	68	71	210	7,360
Sammy Rachels	73	67	70	210	7,360
Bob Ralston	69	70	71	210	7,360
Jim Thorpe	72	68	70	210	7,360

Ford Senior Players Championship

TPC of Michigan, Dearborn, Michigan
Par 36-36–72; 7,057 yards

July 11-14
purse, $2,500,000

	SCORES				TOTAL	MONEY
Stewart Ginn	66	72	70	66	274	$375,000
Jim Thorpe	74	69	67	65	275	183,333.34
Hubert Green	71	63	71	70	275	183,333.33
Mike McCullough	68	69	67	71	275	183,333.33
Doug Tewell	73	68	68	69	278	120,000
Ed Dougherty	70	72	70	67	279	95,000
Hale Irwin	64	73	72	70	279	95,000
Larry Nelson	71	69	69	71	280	75,000
Dave Stockton	72	68	71	69	280	75,000
Tom Kite	71	72	70	68	281	62,500
Fuzzy Zoeller	70	73	69	69	281	62,500
Allen Doyle	75	68	69	70	282	48,000
Bruce Fleisher	76	69	69	68	282	48,000
Bruce Lietzke	71	70	70	71	282	48,000
Bobby Wadkins	73	71	72	66	282	48,000
Tom Wargo	71	68	73	70	282	48,000
Raymond Floyd	71	73	65	74	283	36,437.50
Tom Jenkins	67	71	76	69	283	36,437.50
Tom Purtzer	74	69	71	69	283	36,437.50
Jay Sigel	71	67	73	72	283	36,437.50
Isao Aoki	74	73	70	67	284	31,000
Danny Edwards	74	72	72	67	285	26,300
Wayne Levi	68	78	70	69	285	26,300
Graham Marsh	71	74	70	70	285	26,300
Mark McCumber	67	71	74	73	285	26,300
Don Pooley	75	70	73	67	285	26,300
Vicente Fernandez	74	72	67	73	286	21,750
Ted Goin	72	69	72	73	286	21,750
Dana Quigley	72	73	74	67	286	21,750
Walter Hall	73	74	71	69	287	18,833.34
Jim Albus	77	72	69	69	287	18,833.33
J.C. Snead	72	71	73	71	287	18,833.33
Morris Hatalsky	79	73	69	67	288	15,107.15
Jim Ahern	75	71	69	73	288	15,107.15

	SCORES				TOTAL	MONEY
Hugh Baiocchi	71	73	71	73	288	15,107.14
Jose Maria Canizares	74	75	67	72	288	15,107.14
Dave Eichelberger	77	68	74	69	288	15,107.14
John Mahaffey	75	74	71	68	288	15,107.14
Gary McCord	75	73	66	74	288	15,107.14
Bob Eastwood	72	73	69	76	290	11,000
Bob Gilder	79	71	71	69	290	11,000
Terry Mauney	75	70	71	74	290	11,000
Gil Morgan	73	71	72	74	290	11,000
Walter Morgan	80	70	73	67	290	11,000
Bob Murphy	78	64	68	80	290	11,000
Bruce Summerhays	70	76	74	70	290	11,000
Roy Vucinich	72	70	72	75	290	11,000

SBC Senior Open

Harborside International Golf Center, Port Course,
Chicago, Illinois
Par 36-36–72; 6,970 yards

July 19-21
purse, $1,450,000

	SCORES			TOTAL	MONEY
Bob Gilder	70	63	71	204	$217,500
Hale Irwin	67	71	66	204	127,600
(Gilder defeated Irwin on first playoff hole.)					
Bruce Fleisher	71	69	66	206	104,400
Rodger Davis	68	69	70	207	87,000
John Mahaffey	71	65	72	208	56,550
Dick Mast	72	64	72	208	56,550
Terry Mauney	68	69	71	208	56,550
Tom Wargo	67	69	72	208	56,550
Jim Ahern	68	72	69	209	34,800
David Eger	68	70	71	209	34,800
Ted Goin	66	73	70	209	34,800
J.C. Snead	72	68	69	209	34,800
Doug Tewell	68	71	70	209	34,800
John Harris	75	67	68	210	23,262.15
Mark Pfeil	74	70	66	210	23,262.15
R.W. Eaks	71	69	70	210	23,262.14
Mike Hill	71	68	71	210	23,262.14
John Jacobs	72	68	70	210	23,262.14
Gary McCord	70	69	71	210	23,262.14
Bobby Wadkins	69	65	76	210	23,262.14
Walter Hall	70	70	71	211	16,493.75
Tom Jenkins	73	69	69	211	16,493.75
Jay Sigel	68	70	73	211	16,493.75
Bruce Summerhays	69	72	70	211	16,493.75
Jim Dent	70	70	72	212	13,224
Raymond Floyd	70	70	72	212	13,224
Jim Holtgrieve	70	72	70	212	13,224
Dave Stockton	71	70	71	212	13,224
Howard Twitty	70	73	69	212	13,224
Hugh Baiocchi	69	73	71	213	10,469
Frank Conner	73	70	70	213	10,469
Morris Hatalsky	72	69	72	213	10,469
Wayne Levi	73	70	70	213	10,469
Jerry McGee	70	69	74	213	10,469
Ben Crenshaw	71	73	70	214	8,192.50

	SCORES			TOTAL	MONEY
Bob Eastwood	67	74	73	214	8,192.50
Dan Halldorson	74	70	70	214	8,192.50
Scott Masingill	73	73	68	214	8,192.50
Walter Morgan	71	71	72	214	8,192.50
Jimmy Powell	69	69	76	214	8,192.50

FleetBoston Classic

Nashawtuc Country Club, Concord, Massachusetts
Par 36-36–72; 6,757 yards

July 26-28
purse, $1,500,000

	SCORES			TOTAL	MONEY
Bob Gilder	66	67	70	203	$225,000
John Mahaffey	70	68	65	203	132,000
(Gilder defeated Mahaffey on third playoff hole.)					
Dave Eichelberger	67	68	69	204	99,000
Jim Thorpe	69	65	70	204	99,000
Wayne Levi	67	70	68	205	66,000
Larry Nelson	67	73	65	205	66,000
Tom Kite	73	65	68	206	48,000
Don Pooley	69	70	67	206	48,000
Jack Spradlin	67	70	69	206	48,000
Terry Dill	70	69	68	207	37,500
Ted Goin	69	66	72	207	37,500
George Archer	69	71	68	208	28,800
Allen Doyle	68	69	71	208	28,800
Bruce Fleisher	72	67	69	208	28,800
Hale Irwin	71	71	66	208	28,800
Tom Jenkins	67	70	71	208	28,800
Clyde Hughey	73	68	68	209	23,250
Jay Sigel	69	70	70	209	23,250
Jim Dent	71	65	74	210	19,850
Hubert Green	69	70	71	210	19,850
Sammy Rachels	72	68	70	210	19,850
Rodger Davis	68	71	72	211	16,162.50
Mike McCullough	71	70	70	211	16,162.50
Jerry McGee	72	73	66	211	16,162.50
Dana Quigley	72	70	69	211	16,162.50
Jim Albus	71	71	70	212	12,750
Dale Douglass	72	70	70	212	12,750
Walter Hall	69	72	71	212	12,750
Andy North	72	69	71	212	12,750
Dan O'Neill	73	70	69	212	12,750
Butch Sheehan	74	69	69	212	12,750
Jim Ahern	71	70	72	213	9,675
Bob Eastwood	72	69	72	213	9,675
Morris Hatalsky	71	71	71	213	9,675
Walter Morgan	73	67	73	213	9,675
Bob Murphy	73	72	68	213	9,675
Howard Twitty	73	71	69	213	9,675
Jim Colbert	69	72	73	214	7,650
Terry Mauney	72	74	68	214	7,650
Mike Smith	74	69	71	214	7,650
Dave Stockton	71	72	71	214	7,650
Steven Veriato	74	71	69	214	7,650

Lightpath Long Island Classic

Meadow Brook Club, Jericho, New York
Par 36-36–72; 6,842 yards

August 2-4
purse, $1,700,000

	SCORES			TOTAL	MONEY
Hubert Green	67	64	68	199	$255,000
Hale Irwin	64	67	68	199	149,600
(Green defeated Irwin on seventh playoff hole.)					
Morris Hatalsky	67	65	70	202	112,200
Allen Doyle	68	68	66	202	112,200
Bruce Fleisher	66	67	70	203	81,600
Tom Purtzer	69	65	70	204	68,000
Doug Tewell	70	67	68	205	61,200
Dale Douglass	68	67	71	206	41,528.57
Mike Hill	69	65	72	206	41,528.57
Tom Jenkins	68	70	68	206	41,528.57
Tom Kite	67	71	68	206	41,528.57
Wayne Levi	71	69	66	206	41,528.58
Gil Morgan	65	73	68	206	41,528.57
Jay Sigel	68	70	68	206	41,528.57
Bruce Lietzke	69	69	69	207	27,234
Dana Quigley	68	68	71	207	27,234
Bobby Wadkins	71	68	68	207	27,234
Walter Morgan	72	65	70	207	27,234
Vicente Fernandez	69	71	67	207	27,234
Ed Dougherty	70	71	67	208	20,485
Mike Smith	69	70	69	208	20,485
Dave Stockton	70	68	70	208	20,485
Howard Twitty	66	69	73	208	20,485
Jose Maria Canizares	68	71	70	209	16,252
Graham Marsh	68	69	72	209	16,252
Jay Overton	67	72	70	209	16,252
Bruce Summerhays	69	68	72	209	16,252
Jim Holtgrieve	70	69	70	209	16,252
Rodger Davis	68	73	69	210	12,852
Dick Mast	67	73	70	210	12,852
Mike McCullough	73	67	70	210	12,852
Lee Trevino	66	70	74	210	12,852
Larry Ziegler	68	69	73	210	12,852
Jack Spradlin	72	68	71	211	10,710
Jim Thorpe	69	69	73	211	10,710
Dan O'Neill	71	69	71	211	10,710
Jim Dent	69	72	71	212	8,330
Terry Dill	68	74	70	212	8,330
Bob Eastwood	71	71	70	212	8,330
Mark McCumber	76	70	66	212	8,330
Christy O'Connor, Jr.	68	76	68	212	8,330
John Schroeder	67	70	75	212	8,330
John Bland	69	72	71	212	8,330
Stewart Ginn	67	74	71	212	8,330
Walter Hall	66	70	76	212	8,330

3M Championship

TPC of the Twin Cities, Blaine, Minnesota
Par 36-36–72; 7,100 yards

August 9-11
purse, $1,750,000

	SCORES			TOTAL	MONEY
Hale Irwin	66	70	68	204	$262,500
Hubert Green	67	73	67	207	154,000
Doug Tewell	72	69	67	208	115,500
James Mason	64	72	72	208	115,500
Bob Gilder	71	68	70	209	77,000
Allen Doyle	68	71	70	209	77,000
Bruce Fleisher	71	68	71	210	53,375
Jerry McGee	69	71	70	210	53,375
Andy North	71	70	69	210	53,375
Walter Morgan	71	72	67	210	53,375
Jim Albus	71	71	69	211	37,187.50
R.W. Eaks	72	71	68	211	37,187.50
Danny Edwards	72	72	67	211	37,187.50
Rocky Thompson	68	71	72	211	37,187.50
Rodger Davis	73	71	68	212	26,425
Graham Marsh	72	72	68	212	26,425
Larry Nelson	69	71	72	212	26,425
Jack Spradlin	73	70	69	212	26,425
Leonard Thompson	68	71	73	212	26,425
Fuzzy Zoeller	68	73	71	212	26,425
Vicente Fernandez	73	72	67	212	26,425
Jim Colbert	71	74	68	213	17,995.84
Wayne Levi	69	71	73	213	17,995.83
Terry Mauney	71	71	71	213	17,995.83
Mike McCullough	70	72	71	213	17,995.84
Don Pooley	74	66	73	213	17,995.83
Sammy Rachels	68	73	72	213	17,995.83
Ted Goin	73	74	67	214	14,175
Tom Kite	71	75	68	214	14,175
Bruce Lietzke	69	76	69	214	14,175
Bobby Wadkins	72	73	69	214	14,175
Ed Dougherty	71	71	73	215	11,812.50
Jim Holtgrieve	72	73	70	215	11,812.50
Stewart Ginn	73	72	70	215	11,812.50
John Harris	74	72	69	215	11,812.50
Terry Dill	73	74	69	216	9,479.17
David Eger	73	72	71	216	9,479.17
Fred Gibson	71	73	72	216	9,479.16
David Graham	75	70	71	216	9,479.17
Bill Brask	72	72	72	216	9,479.16
Hugh Baiocchi	69	78	69	216	9,479.17

Uniting Fore Care Classic

Park Meadows Country Club, Park City, Utah
Par 36-36–72; 7,327 yards

August 23-25
purse, $1,500,000

	POINTS			TOTAL	MONEY
Morris Hatalsky	19	11	12	42	$225,000
Jay Sigel	6	13	11	30	132,000
Hale Irwin	7	9	13	29	82,500
Mike McCullough	12	7	10	29	82,500

	POINTS			TOTAL	MONEY
Jerry McGee	10	7	12	29	82,500
John Bland	5	13	11	29	82,500
John Jacobs	6	24	-2	28	54,000
Jay Overton	8	3	16	27	45,000
Jim Thorpe	11	5	11	27	45,000
Dale Douglass	9	5	12	26	36,000
Gil Morgan	8	9	9	26	36,000
Tom Watson	14	12	0	26	36,000
Danny Edwards	6	11	8	25	28,500
Tom Jenkins	8	1	16	25	28,500
Jim Holtgrieve	10	6	9	25	28,500
Bob Gilder	10	8	6	24	24,000
Andy North	6	8	10	24	24,000
Don Pooley	11	10	3	24	24,000
Terry Dill	12	4	7	23	20,475
Butch Sheehan	2	11	10	23	20,475
David Eger	8	5	9	22	18,000
Hugh Baiocchi	12	6	4	22	18,000
Charles Coody	8	4	9	21	15,030
Jack Spradlin	6	8	7	21	15,030
Larry Ziegler	4	0	17	21	15,030
Walter Morgan	4	13	4	21	15,030
Stewart Ginn	4	13	4	21	15,030
John Mahaffey	5	9	6	20	11,880
Leonard Thompson	10	2	8	20	11,880
Rafael Navarro	6	5	9	20	11,880
John Harris	12	5	3	20	11,880
Clyde Hughey	5	9	6	20	11,880
Dana Quigley	4	7	8	19	9,450
John Schroeder	8	1	10	19	9,450
Doug Tewell	5	6	8	19	9,450
Dan O'Neill	2	11	6	19	9,450
Jim Ahern	11	7	1	19	9,450
Ted Goin	3	8	7	18	7,950
Dick Mast	6	3	9	18	7,950
Kermit Zarley	5	3	10	18	7,950

Allianz Championship

Glen Oak Country Club, West Des Moines, Iowa
Par 36-36–72; 7,327 yards

August 30-September 1
purse, $1,850,000

	SCORES			TOTAL	MONEY
Bob Gilder	67	66	67	200	$277,500
John Bland	68	63	70	201	162,800
Hale Irwin	66	68	69	203	122,100
Bruce Lietzke	68	68	67	203	122,100
Jose Maria Canizares	68	66	70	204	81,400
Allen Doyle	67	69	68	204	81,400
Bruce Fleisher	69	66	70	205	59,200
Gil Morgan	69	66	70	205	59,200
Stewart Ginn	69	69	67	205	59,200
R.W. Eaks	71	68	67	206	46,250
Bobby Wadkins	69	69	68	206	46,250
Ben Crenshaw	71	67	69	207	32,629.37
Ed Dougherty	70	68	69	207	32,629.37
Dale Douglass	69	66	72	207	32,629.37

	SCORES			TOTAL	MONEY
Morris Hatalsky	69	71	67	207	32,629.38
Gary McCord	74	66	67	207	32,629.38
Larry Nelson	67	71	69	207	32,629.38
Don Pooley	68	70	69	207	32,629.38
Dave Stockton	68	69	70	207	32,629.37
Hubert Green	70	71	67	208	21,719
Tom Jenkins	69	70	69	208	21,719
Tom Kite	69	71	68	208	21,719
Dana Quigley	70	70	68	208	21,719
Jim Thorpe	71	69	68	208	21,719
Bob Charles	69	70	70	209	15,771.25
Ted Goin	70	70	69	209	15,771.25
Wayne Levi	68	70	71	209	15,771.25
John Mahaffey	72	68	69	209	15,771.25
Mike McCullough	69	67	73	209	15,771.25
Sammy Rachels	73	72	64	209	15,771.25
Butch Sheehan	70	69	70	209	15,771.25
Hugh Baiocchi	68	69	72	209	15,771.25
Mark McCumber	69	70	71	210	11,932.50
Mike Smith	73	67	70	210	11,932.50
James Mason	69	66	75	210	11,932.50
Jay Sigel	71	70	69	210	11,932.50
Jim Colbert	75	68	68	211	9,805
Doug Tewell	72	70	69	211	9,805
Steven Veriato	70	67	74	211	9,805
Jim Holtgrieve	67	72	72	211	9,805
Walter Hall	70	74	67	211	9,805

Kroger Senior Classic

TPC at River's Bend, Maineville, Ohio
Par 36-36–72; 7,145 yards

September 6-8
purse, $1,500,000

	SCORES			TOTAL	MONEY
Bob Gilder	66	65	69	200	$225,000
Tom Jenkins	70	68	62	200	132,000
(Gilder defeated Jenkins on second playoff hole.)					
Hale Irwin	72	65	64	201	108,000
Tom Kite	69	64	70	203	81,000
Bruce Lietzke	71	70	62	203	81,000
Ed Dougherty	67	65	72	204	57,000
Larry Nelson	69	68	67	204	57,000
Ben Crenshaw	70	65	70	205	39,600
Bruce Fleisher	69	68	68	205	39,600
Gil Morgan	67	68	70	205	39,600
Andy North	64	68	73	205	39,600
Jim Thorpe	70	71	64	205	39,600
Hubert Green	67	68	71	206	27,000
Morris Hatalsky	70	67	69	206	27,000
Gary McCord	70	69	67	206	27,000
Doug Tewell	71	67	68	206	27,000
Jay Sigel	71	66	69	206	27,000
Jim Colbert	69	69	69	207	19,325
Dana Quigley	68	69	70	207	19,325
Sammy Rachels	70	70	67	207	19,325
Mike Smith	66	72	69	207	19,325
James Mason	70	66	71	207	19,325

	SCORES			TOTAL	MONEY
Walter Hall	73	70	64	207	19,325
Isao Aoki	68	70	70	208	15,000
Wayne Levi	70	70	68	208	15,000
Mike McCullough	72	69	67	208	15,000
Don Pooley	69	68	72	209	12,750
Tom Purtzer	71	72	66	209	12,750
Tom Wargo	71	68	70	209	12,750
Dan O'Neill	73	68	68	209	12,750
Stewart Ginn	70	69	71	210	11,250
John Schroeder	76	68	67	211	10,575
Leonard Thompson	71	71	69	211	10,575
Ted Goin	72	73	67	212	9,675
Jack Spradlin	76	70	66	212	9,675
Jose Maria Canizares	70	68	75	213	8,280
Rodger Davis	75	67	71	213	8,280
Gibby Gilbert	76	70	67	213	8,280
Allen Doyle	68	72	73	213	8,280
John Harris	68	72	73	213	8,280

RJR Championship

Tanglewood Park, Clemmons, North Carolina
Par 35-35–70; 6,600 yards

September 13-15
purse, $1,600,000

	SCORES			TOTAL	MONEY
Bruce Fleisher	60	64	67	191	$240,000
Hale Irwin	65	64	67	196	140,800
Don Pooley	66	64	68	198	115,200
Ed Dougherty	66	66	69	201	78,933.33
Mike McCullough	63	69	69	201	78,933.33
Larry Nelson	66	66	69	201	78,933.34
Morris Hatalsky	69	63	70	202	51,200
Jim Thorpe	66	66	70	202	51,200
Steven Veriato	66	68	68	202	51,200
Hubert Green	69	67	67	203	36,800
Doug Tewell	67	67	69	203	36,800
Jim Holtgrieve	67	69	67	203	36,800
Allen Doyle	66	68	69	203	36,800
Jim Dent	68	69	67	204	29,600
Bobby Wadkins	72	65	67	204	29,600
Isao Aoki	67	68	70	205	24,840
Jose Maria Canizares	68	65	72	205	24,840
Gary McCord	69	66	70	205	24,840
Tom Purtzer	66	69	70	205	24,840
Tom Kite	66	72	68	206	18,784
Wayne Levi	69	67	70	206	18,784
Graham Marsh	66	68	72	206	18,784
Jack Spradlin	67	69	70	206	18,784
Vicente Fernandez	67	71	68	206	18,784
R.W. Eaks	68	72	67	207	13,942.86
Jerry McGee	68	70	69	207	13,942.86
Gil Morgan	69	69	69	207	13,942.86
Mark Pfeil	72	65	70	207	13,942.85
Jay Sigel	67	73	67	207	13,942.85
Hugh Baiocchi	68	72	67	207	13,942.86
Walter Hall	71	67	69	207	13,942.86
Danny Edwards	70	66	72	208	10,102.85

	SCORES			TOTAL	MONEY
Bob Gilder	69	68	71	208	10,102.85
Ted Goin	65	73	70	208	10,102.86
Joe Inman	68	70	70	208	10,102.86
Bruce Lietzke	70	70	68	208	10,102.86
Sammy Rachels	72	66	70	208	10,102.86
Walter Morgan	70	69	69	208	10,102.86
Dale Douglass	69	69	71	209	7,840
Tom Jenkins	74	68	67	209	7,840
Dana Quigley	70	70	69	209	7,840
Leonard Thompson	68	70	71	209	7,840
Jim Ahern	67	73	69	209	7,840

SAS Championship

Prestonwood Country Club, Cary, North Carolina
Par 36-36–72; 7,137 yards

September 20-22
purse, $1,700,000

	SCORES			TOTAL	MONEY
Bruce Lietzke	72	63	67	202	$255,000
Gil Morgan	72	67	67	206	124,666.67
Sammy Rachels	69	70	67	206	124,666.67
Tom Watson	71	66	69	206	124,666.66
Tom Purtzer	69	68	70	207	81,600
Wayne Levi	67	71	70	208	61,200
John Bland	72	68	68	208	61,200
Jim Ahern	72	67	69	208	61,200
Bruce Fleisher	69	71	69	209	45,900
Don Pooley	70	67	72	209	45,900
Isao Aoki	74	66	70	210	36,125
Tom Jenkins	68	73	69	210	36,125
Andy North	68	66	76	210	36,125
Allen Doyle	71	68	71	210	36,125
Rodger Davis	73	68	70	211	26,435
Hubert Green	70	70	71	211	26,435
Hale Irwin	70	74	67	211	26,435
Dana Quigley	66	71	74	211	26,435
Doug Tewell	69	71	71	211	26,435
Jim Thorpe	64	73	74	211	26,435
Bobby Wadkins	70	73	69	212	19,833.34
Jim Holtgrieve	69	71	72	212	19,833.33
Vicente Fernandez	67	74	71	212	19,833.33
Jose Maria Canizares	69	72	72	213	16,252
Ed Dougherty	68	73	72	213	16,252
John Schroeder	70	71	72	213	16,252
Jay Sigel	71	70	72	213	16,252
Walter Hall	73	70	70	213	16,252
Dick Mast	72	67	75	214	13,132.50
Bill Rogers	72	68	74	214	13,132.50
Bruce Summerhays	72	71	71	214	13,132.50
Butch Sheehan	70	76	68	214	13,132.50
George Archer	72	71	72	215	10,710
Jim Colbert	72	68	75	215	10,710
Ben Crenshaw	70	74	71	215	10,710
Larry Nelson	70	73	72	215	10,710
Mike Smith	72	71	72	215	10,710
Jack Spradlin	76	71	69	216	9,180
James Mason	72	72	72	216	9,180

	SCORES			TOTAL	MONEY
Bob Eastwood	74	68	75	217	7,650
Bob Gilder	72	71	74	217	7,650
David Graham	76	73	68	217	7,650
Morris Hatalsky	72	76	69	217	7,650
Joe Inman	71	70	76	217	7,650
John Jacobs	75	73	69	217	7,650
Roy Vucinich	73	73	71	217	7,650

Turtle Bay Championship

The Links at Turtle Bay, Kahuku, Hawaii
Par 36-36–72; 7,008 yards

October 4-6
purse, $1,500,000

	SCORES			TOTAL	MONEY
Hale Irwin	69	69	70	208	$225,000
Gary McCord	69	70	69	208	132,000
(Irwin defeated McCord on first playoff hole.)					
Dick Mast	71	67	71	209	90,000
Mike Smith	69	69	71	209	90,000
John Bland	70	70	69	209	90,000
Isao Aoki	73	67	70	210	54,000
Morris Hatalsky	69	69	72	210	54,000
Steven Veriato	70	71	69	210	54,000
Sammy Rachels	70	71	70	211	42,000
Andy North	71	72	69	212	39,000
Rodger Davis	69	72	72	213	31,875
Bob Gilder	74	66	73	213	31,875
Mark Pfeil	69	72	72	213	31,875
Dana Quigley	71	70	72	213	31,875
Jose Maria Canizares	69	75	70	214	25,500
John Schroeder	70	73	71	214	25,500
Jim Ahern	72	70	72	214	25,500
R.W. Eaks	68	73	74	215	21,150
Bob Eastwood	74	71	70	215	21,150
Bruce Summerhays	69	74	72	215	21,150
Bruce Fleisher	73	71	72	216	15,878.57
Hubert Green	73	72	71	216	15,878.57
Tom Jenkins	72	73	71	216	15,878.57
Mike McCullough	70	74	72	216	15,878.57
Jay Overton	74	71	71	216	15,878.58
Roy Vucinich	70	73	73	216	15,878.57
Allen Doyle	71	72	73	216	15,878.57
Danny Edwards	72	74	71	217	12,150
Rik Massengale	70	74	73	217	12,150
John Harris	75	72	70	217	12,150
Walter Hall	72	74	71	217	12,150
Jim Albus	68	72	78	218	10,575
Clyde Hughey	72	73	73	218	10,575
Dave Barr	73	71	75	219	9,900
Bob Dickson	70	74	76	220	8,156.25
Terry Dill	75	74	71	220	8,156.25
Wayne Levi	73	77	70	220	8,156.25
Terry Mauney	70	75	75	220	8,156.25
Don Pooley	70	72	78	220	8,156.25
Tom Purtzer	76	75	69	220	8,156.25
Steve Stull	68	73	79	220	8,156.25
Hugh Baiocchi	74	72	74	220	8,156.25

Napa Valley Championship

Silverado Resort, South Course, Napa, California
Par 36-36–72; 6,640 yards

October 11-13
purse, $1,300,000

	SCORES			TOTAL	MONEY
Tom Kite	66	66	72	204	$195,000
Bruce Fleisher	65	73	67	205	104,000
Fred Gibson	71	68	66	205	104,000
Jim Thorpe	68	69	69	206	78,000
Bob Gilder	69	67	71	207	50,700
Hubert Green	71	72	64	207	50,700
Jay Overton	71	69	67	207	50,700
Tom Purtzer	68	70	69	207	50,700
Dave Barr	69	72	67	208	31,200
Lee Trevino	70	69	69	208	31,200
Fuzzy Zoeller	69	69	70	208	31,200
Allen Doyle	64	70	74	208	31,200
Stewart Ginn	68	69	71	208	31,200
Wayne Levi	69	73	67	209	24,050
Sammy Rachels	65	74	70	209	24,050
Don Pooley	69	69	72	210	20,182.50
Doug Tewell	68	69	73	210	20,182.50
Kermit Zarley	66	73	71	210	20,182.50
Walter Hall	68	70	72	210	20,182.50
Danny Edwards	69	72	70	211	15,665
Morris Hatalsky	70	71	70	211	15,665
Andy North	71	68	72	211	15,665
Jim Ahern	67	72	72	211	15,665
Bob Charles	70	72	70	212	11,367.78
Rodger Davis	70	72	70	212	11,367.78
Gibby Gilbert	70	69	73	212	11,367.77
Roger Maltbie	71	73	68	212	11,367.78
Dana Quigley	69	71	72	212	11,367.78
John Schroeder	74	70	68	212	11,367.78
Mike Smith	75	69	68	212	11,367.77
James Mason	74	70	68	212	11,367.78
Hugh Baiocchi	71	69	72	212	11,367.78
Jim Albus	71	69	73	213	8,016.67
Ed Dougherty	68	73	72	213	8,016.67
Tom Jenkins	74	68	71	213	8,016.67
Graham Marsh	75	73	65	213	8,016.66
Howard Twitty	72	72	69	213	8,016.67
Butch Sheehan	76	71	66	213	8,016.66
Bob Eastwood	71	72	71	214	6,240
Mike McCullough	73	74	67	214	6,240
Gary Player	68	72	74	214	6,240
J.C. Snead	68	77	69	214	6,240
Leonard Thompson	73	69	72	214	6,240
Jay Sigel	69	70	75	214	6,240

SBC Championship

Oak Hills Country Club, San Antonio, Texas
Par 35-36–71; 6,800 yards

October 18-20
purse, $1,450,000

	SCORES			TOTAL	MONEY
Dana Quigley	68	64	69	201	$217,500
Bob Gilder	71	67	64	202	127,600

	SCORES			TOTAL	MONEY
Vicente Fernandez	66	67	70	203	104,400
Tom Watson	69	66	70	205	87,000
Gil Morgan	69	66	71	206	69,600
Fuzzy Zoeller	69	67	71	207	52,200
Bruce Summerhays	68	71	68	207	52,200
John Jacobs	70	70	67	207	52,200
Jose Maria Canizares	69	73	66	208	37,700
Rodger Davis	67	67	74	208	37,700
Don Pooley	71	68	69	208	37,700
Tom Kite	70	67	72	209	30,450
Jim Thorpe	72	68	69	209	30,450
Dale Douglass	70	70	71	211	23,262.14
Ted Goin	71	70	70	211	23,262.14
Mike Hill	68	70	73	211	23,262.14
Hale Irwin	72	72	67	211	23,262.15
Dick Mast	69	70	72	211	23,262.14
John Schroeder	72	69	70	211	23,262.15
Jim Holtgrieve	69	70	72	211	23,262.14
Jim Dent	71	68	73	212	16,095
Hubert Green	71	73	68	212	16,095
Bruce Lietzke	70	68	74	212	16,095
Dave Stockton	75	72	65	212	16,095
Walter Hall	75	69	68	212	16,095
Jim Albus	71	71	71	213	10,838.75
Ben Crenshaw	70	70	73	213	10,838.75
Dave Eichelberger	70	69	74	213	10,838.75
Bruce Fleisher	69	68	76	213	10,838.75
Raymond Floyd	70	73	70	213	10,838.75
Gary McCord	73	67	73	213	10,838.75
Mike McCullough	71	71	71	213	10,838.75
Bobby Wadkins	69	75	69	213	10,838.75
Lanny Wadkins	71	68	74	213	10,838.75
James Mason	76	72	65	213	10,838.75
John Bland	68	74	71	213	10,838.75
Stewart Ginn	68	73	72	213	10,838.75
Rex Caldwell	74	72	68	214	6,960
Tom Jenkins	70	72	72	214	6,960
Graham Marsh	75	68	71	214	6,960
Larry Nelson	70	72	72	214	6,960
Tom Purtzer	69	73	72	214	6,960
Mike Smith	74	69	71	214	6,960
Doug Tewell	69	72	73	214	6,960
Hugh Baiocchi	72	71	71	214	6,960

Senior Tour Championship at Gaillardia

Gaillardia Golf & Country Club, Oklahoma City, Oklahoma
Par 36-36–72; 7,012 yards

October 24-27
purse, $2,500,000

	SCORES				TOTAL	MONEY
Tom Watson	74	67	66	67	274	$440,000
Gil Morgan	71	67	69	69	276	254,000
Bob Gilder	70	68	73	68	279	213,000
Hale Irwin	70	67	73	71	281	176,000
Morris Hatalsky	72	72	67	71	282	107,400
Larry Nelson	70	69	72	71	282	107,400
Tom Purtzer	73	70	70	69	282	107,400
Fuzzy Zoeller	72	69	69	72	282	107,400

	SCORES				TOTAL	MONEY
John Bland	75	68	71	68	282	107,400
Ed Dougherty	70	71	73	69	283	73,000
Bruce Lietzke	70	73	71	69	283	73,000
Wayne Levi	76	68	70	70	284	59,333.34
Allen Doyle	71	70	70	73	284	59,333.33
Stewart Ginn	71	70	73	70	284	59,333.33
Jim Thorpe	72	72	69	72	285	50,500
Walter Hall	69	72	72	72	285	50,500
Tom Jenkins	74	70	69	73	286	44,500
John Jacobs	73	72	72	69	286	44,500
Bruce Fleisher	77	70	69	72	288	39,250
Hubert Green	73	74	70	71	288	39,250
Tom Kite	70	72	72	75	289	31,333.34
Gary McCord	73	70	75	71	289	31,333.33
Mike McCullough	77	67	69	76	289	31,333.34
Dana Quigley	72	72	75	70	289	31,333.33
Doug Tewell	72	72	69	76	289	31,333.33
Jay Sigel	73	74	71	71	289	31,333.33
Don Pooley	73	73	71	74	291	26,000
Sammy Rachels	71	76	73	74	294	25,000
Bobby Wadkins	76	74	73	74	297	24,500
Rodger Davis	70	71	75		WD	

Senior Slam

Superstition Mountain Golf & Country Club,
Superstition Mountain, Arizona
Par 36-36–72; 6,911 yards

November 9-10
purse, $600,000

	SCORES		TOTAL	MONEY
Fuzzy Zoeller	67	71	138	$300,000
Don Pooley	70	69	139	150,000
Stewart Ginn	70	71	141	100,000
Jim Thorpe	72	73	145	50,000

Hyundai Team Matches

Monarch Beach Golf Links, Dana Point, California
Par 35-35–70; 6,548 yards

November 16-17
purse, $1,200,000

FIRST-ROUND MATCHES

Jim Thorpe and John Jacobs defeated Doug Tewell and Bruce Lietzke, 2 and 1.
Allen Doyle and Dana Quigley defeated Bruce Fleisher and David Graham, 3 and 1.

THIRD-PLACE MATCH

Tewell and Lietzke defeated Fleisher and Graham, 4 and 3.
(Tewell and Lietzke received $30,000 each; Fleisher and Graham received $20,000 each.)

CHAMPIONSHIP MATCH

Quigley and Doyle defeated Thorpe and Jacobs, 2 and 1.
(Quigley and Doyle received $100,000 each; Thorpe and Jacobs received $50,000 each.)

European Seniors Tour

Royal Westmoreland Barbados Open

Royal Westmoreland Golf Club, St. James, Barbados
Par 36-36–72; 6,756 yards

March 14-16
purse, €203,197

	SCORES			TOTAL	MONEY
Peter Townsend	71	71	70	212	€31,893.88
Guillermo Encina	68	72	73	213	21,262.59
Bernard Gallacher	72	73	69	214	14,906.57
Tommy Horton	70	76	69	215	10,680.06
Alberto Croce	73	75	67	215	10,680.06
Barry Vivian	76	71	69	216	8,524.54
Noel Ratcliffe	75	74	70	219	5,710.66
Bob Shearer	72	76	71	219	5,710.66
Malcolm Gregson	75	70	74	219	5,710.66
Eddie Polland	73	76	70	219	5,710.66
Jim Rhodes	74	73	72	219	5,710.66
Jerry Bruner	71	76	72	219	5,710.66
David Creamer	75	71	73	219	5,710.66
John Grace	71	75	75	221	4,039.57
Nick Job	77	71	74	222	3,614.75
Craig Defoy	76	72	74	222	3,614.75
Jeff Van Wagenen	76	73	73	222	3,614.75
Denis Durnian	72	75	76	223	2,599.30
Keith MacDonald	72	78	73	223	2,599.30
David Oakley	71	78	74	223	2,599.30
Denis O'Sullivan	75	75	73	223	2,599.30
Ross Metherell	73	74	76	223	2,599.30
Bobby Verwey	74	72	77	223	2,599.30
Delroy Cambridge	78	74	71	223	2,599.30
Steve Stull	76	75	72	223	2,599.30
David Good	72	75	77	224	2,020.60
Tony Jacklin	81	74	70	225	1,892.18
Peter Dawson	75	72	78	225	1,892.18
Ian Stanley	75	78	73	226	1,765.38
Terry Gale	77	77	73	227	1,601.74
Paul Leonard	75	78	74	227	1,601.74
George Burns	74	77	76	227	1,601.74

Tobago Plantations Seniors Classic

Tobago Plantations Golf & Beach Resort, Tobago
Par 36-36–72; 6,752 yards

March 20-22
purse, €201,716

	SCORES			TOTAL	MONEY
Steve Stull	68	68	69	205	€30,741.55
John Chillas	69	67	72	208	17,420.21
Barry Vivian	71	67	70	208	17,420.21
Denis Durnian	69	69	73	211	11,263.83
John Morgan	70	75	67	212	8,272.52
Simon Owen	72	65	75	212	8,272.52

	SCORES			TOTAL	MONEY
Bill Brask	72	69	71	212	8,272.52
Bernard Gallacher	69	70	74	213	5,875.05
Tommy Horton	72	71	70	213	5,875.05
David Ojala	69	70	74	213	5,875.05
Bob Lendzion	73	69	72	214	4,918.65
Tony Jacklin	69	71	75	215	4,508.76
David Oakley	72	75	69	216	3,996.40
John McTear	73	71	72	216	3,996.40
Terry Gale	71	72	74	217	3,484.04
Bobby Verwey	72	73	72	217	3,484.04
John Grace	75	68	74	217	3,484.04
Nick Job	77	71	70	218	2,505.52
Mike Miller	71	73	74	218	2,505.52
Noel Ratcliffe	73	71	74	218	2,505.52
Alan Tapie	73	72	73	218	2,505.52
Bill Hardwick	74	73	71	218	2,505.52
Jim Rhodes	76	71	71	218	2,505.52
Jerry Bruner	74	72	72	218	2,505.52
David Creamer	72	73	73	218	2,505.52
Keith MacDonald	71	74	74	219	1,824.32
Peter Dawson	74	69	76	219	1,824.32
Malcolm Gregson	73	74	72	219	1,824.32
Jeff Van Wagenen	70	72	77	219	1,824.32
Alberto Croce	75	70	75	220	1,543.80
Priscillo Diniz	73	72	75	220	1,543.80
Delroy Cambridge	74	71	75	220	1,543.80

AIB Irish Seniors Open

Adare Manor Hotel & Golf Resort, Ireland — May 17-19
Par 36-36–72; 6,706 yards — purse, €310,000

	SCORES			TOTAL	MONEY
Seiji Ebihara	66	72	70	208	€46,500
Denis Durnian	72	69	69	210	31,000
Christy O'Connor, Jr.	73	68	71	212	17,587.33
Jim Rhodes	70	70	72	212	17,587.33
John Grace	68	71	73	212	17,587.33
Mike Miller	70	67	76	213	11,780
Bob Lendzion	77	70	66	213	11,780
Keith MacDonald	72	71	72	215	8,886.67
Alan Tapie	69	71	75	215	8,886.67
Joe McDermott	69	69	77	215	8,886.67
Guillermo Encina	71	69	76	216	6,587.50
Jay Horton	72	73	71	216	6,587.50
Jeff Van Wagenen	70	74	72	216	6,587.50
Steve Stull	70	72	74	216	6,587.50
David Oakley	71	72	74	217	5,270
David Jones	72	69	76	217	5,270
Delroy Cambridge	73	73	71	217	5,270
Noel Ratcliffe	70	74	74	218	4,239.25
Terry Gale	72	72	74	218	4,239.25
Alberto Croce	73	71	74	218	4,239.25
Jerry Bruner	75	70	73	218	4,239.25
Neil Coles	74	72	73	219	2,854.82
John Morgan	73	70	76	219	2,854.82
Russell Weir	72	73	74	219	2,854.82

	SCORES			TOTAL	MONEY
Ray Carrasco	74	72	73	219	2,854.82
Eddie Polland	71	73	75	219	2,854.82
Denis O'Sullivan	68	75	76	219	2,854.82
John Chillas	75	72	72	219	2,854.82
David Good	70	73	76	219	2,854.82
Hank Woodrome	68	74	77	219	2,854.82
Bruce Fleisher	74	73	72	219	2,854.82
Barry Vivian	72	71	76	219	2,854.82

Flanders Nippon presents Legends in Golf

Flanders-Nippon Golf Club, Hasselt, Belgium
Par 36-36–72; 6,525 yards

June 6-8
purse, €170,000

	SCORES			TOTAL	MONEY
Gary Wintz	68	68	69	205	€25,500
Nick Job	71	64	71	206	17,000
David Creamer	69	71	69	209	10,625
Dragon Taki	67	75	67	209	10,625
Silvano Locatelli	72	68	70	210	7,242
Denis O'Sullivan	70	72	68	210	7,242
Martin Gray	70	73	68	211	6,120
Mike Miller	72	70	72	214	4,873.33
John Chillas	72	70	72	214	4,873.33
Hank Woodrome	67	75	72	214	4,873.33
Neil Coles	70	71	75	216	3,302.86
Ian Mosey	78	67	71	216	3,302.86
David Vaughan	71	68	77	216	3,302.86
Bill Hardwick	69	72	75	216	3,302.86
T.R. Jones	69	68	79	216	3,302.86
David Huish	76	69	71	216	3,302.86
Ross Metherell	71	73	72	216	3,302.86
Renato Campagnoli	78	69	70	217	2,324.75
Ray Carrasco	70	76	71	217	2,324.75
David Jones	69	74	74	217	2,324.75
Jeff Van Wagenen	72	72	73	217	2,324.75
Antonio Garrido	70	72	76	218	1,672.38
Malcolm Gregson	72	71	75	218	1,672.38
Paul Leonard	71	74	73	218	1,672.38
Bill Brask	75	73	70	218	1,672.38
Steve Wild	75	74	69	218	1,672.38
Martin Foster	69	75	74	218	1,672.38
Jay Dolan	74	69	75	218	1,672.38
Mike Ferguson	72	73	73	218	1,672.38
Keith MacDonald	73	72	74	219	1,309
Manuel Velasco	70	73	76	219	1,309

Microlease Jersey Seniors Masters

La Moye Golf Club, Jersey
Par 36-36–72; 6,581 yards

June 14-16
purse, €155,110

	SCORES			TOTAL	MONEY
Delroy Cambridge	70	68	67	205	€23,551.24
Tommy Horton	66	70	71	207	13,345.14

	SCORES			TOTAL	MONEY
Ian Mosey	68	69	70	207	13,345.14
John Morgan	67	70	71	208	7,866.13
Seiji Ebihara	67	68	73	208	7,866.13
Bernard Gallacher	68	70	71	209	6,279.61
Denis Durnian	75	68	67	210	5,338.36
Gary Wintz	71	69	70	210	5,338.36
John Irwin	68	74	69	211	4,395.57
Joe McDermott	69	68	75	212	3,768.07
David Good	72	70	70	212	3,768.07
Steve Stull	74	72	66	212	3,768.07
Ray Carrasco	70	71	72	213	3,061.75
Denis O'Sullivan	69	71	73	213	3,061.75
Alan Tapie	70	71	73	214	2,748.01
Martin Foster	74	72	68	214	2,748.01
Martin Gray	75	71	69	215	2,220.04
Peter Townsend	69	72	74	215	2,220.04
Malcolm Gregson	72	73	70	215	2,220.04
Ross Metherell	72	70	73	215	2,220.04
Dragon Taki	70	74	71	215	2,220.04
David Oakley	73	74	69	216	1,773.53
John Chillas	76	71	69	216	1,773.53
David Huish	72	73	72	217	1,609.70
Jeff Van Wagenen	71	74	72	217	1,609.70
Nick Job	73	74	71	218	1,334.59
Keith MacDonald	72	74	72	218	1,334.59
Peter Dawson	70	69	79	218	1,334.59
John McTear	70	75	73	218	1,334.59
David Creamer	72	73	73	218	1,334.59
John Grace	74	71	73	218	1,334.59

Lawrence Batley Seniors Open

Huddersfield Golf Club, West Yorkshire, England   June 27-29
Par 36-35–71; 6,447 yards   purse, €196,893

	SCORES			TOTAL	MONEY
Neil Coles	72	67	70	209	€30,919.17
David Creamer	67	69	73	209	17,521.17
Steve Stull	74	67	68	209	17,521.17
(Coles defeated Stull on fourth and Creamer on fifth playoff hole.)					
Denis O'Sullivan	71	69	70	210	11,336.41
Alberto Croce	66	74	71	211	9,316.52
Denis Durnian	72	69	72	213	6,678
Liam Higgins	73	74	66	213	6,678
Simon Owen	72	69	72	213	6,678
Malcolm Gregson	74	71	68	213	6,678
Delroy Cambridge	72	73	68	213	6,678
David Jones	69	68	77	214	4,741.65
John Grace	72	75	67	214	4,741.65
Bill Hardwick	70	73	72	215	3,916.76
Jeff Van Wagenen	74	70	71	215	3,916.76
Seiji Ebihara	72	73	70	215	3,916.76
Mike Miller	69	70	77	216	3,298.03
David Oakley	72	71	73	216	3,298.03
David Huish	73	70	73	216	3,298.03
Terry Gale	69	74	74	217	2,813.64
Jerry Bruner	72	72	73	217	2,813.64

	SCORES			TOTAL	MONEY
Peter Townsend	71	73	74	218	2,555.75
Tommy Horton	75	72	72	219	2,220.26
Jay Horton	73	79	67	219	2,220.26
Priscillo Diniz	74	69	76	219	2,220.26
David Good	74	76	69	219	2,220.26
Tony Jacklin	72	76	72	220	1,793.19
John Morgan	72	76	72	220	1,793.19
Keith MacDonald	73	68	79	220	1,793.19
David Snell	74	74	72	220	1,793.19
John Fourie	75	75	70	220	1,793.19

Wales Seniors Open

Royal St. David's Golf Club, Harlech, Wales
Par 36-33–69; 6,475 yards

July 5-7
purse, €773,385

	SCORES			TOTAL	MONEY
Seiji Ebihara	68	69	66	203	€116,007.80
Denis Durnian	68	70	68	206	65,737.73
Christy O'Connor, Jr.	67	73	66	206	65,737.73
Tony Jacklin	69	71	67	207	38,746.59
Ian Stanley	71	67	69	207	38,746.59
Nick Job	68	69	71	208	30,935.40
John Morgan	69	69	71	209	26,295.09
Martin Foster	71	70	68	209	26,295.09
Bob Charles	70	67	73	210	19,334.63
Malcolm Gregson	72	72	66	210	19,334.63
Eddie Polland	72	66	72	210	19,334.63
Alberto Croce	73	68	69	210	19,334.63
Noel Ratcliffe	68	72	71	211	13,920.93
Jim Rhodes	72	69	70	211	13,920.93
Ross Metherell	73	70	68	211	13,920.93
Priscillo Diniz	72	70	69	211	13,920.93
John Irwin	72	71	68	211	13,920.93
David Good	70	74	68	212	11,600.77
Ian Mosey	70	72	71	213	9,918.66
Simon Owen	72	74	67	213	9,918.66
Lawrence Farmer	72	67	74	213	9,918.66
John McTear	74	69	70	213	9,918.66
Brian Huggett	73	70	71	214	7,749.32
Terry Gale	71	72	71	214	7,749.32
David Oakley	71	71	72	214	7,749.32
David Jones	75	70	69	214	7,749.32
John Chillas	73	68	73	214	7,749.32
Neil Coles	73	70	72	215	5,866.68
Bernard Gallacher	73	69	73	215	5,866.68
Russell Weir	78	70	67	215	5,866.68
Peter Dawson	70	74	71	215	5,866.68
Jay Horton	67	78	70	215	5,866.68
Barry Vivian	75	67	73	215	5,866.68
Delroy Cambridge	70	73	72	215	5,866.68

The Mobile Cup

Stoke Park, Buckinghamshire, England
Par 36-35–71; 6,720 yards

July 12-14
purse,€195,357

	SCORES			TOTAL	MONEY
Bernard Gallacher	67	68	66	201	€30,474.60
Delroy Cambridge	67	70	68	205	20,316.40
John Morgan	70	66	70	206	14,221.48
Ian Stanley	69	68	71	208	10,177.74
Barry Vivian	67	71	70	208	10,177.74
Bob Shearer	70	67	72	209	7,720.23
David Oakley	69	72	68	209	7,720.23
Ian Mosey	70	70	70	210	6,094.92
Noel Ratcliffe	68	75	67	210	6,094.92
Bill Brask	71	73	68	212	4,875.94
Jerry Bruner	70	74	68	212	4,875.94
Steve Stull	73	69	70	212	4,875.94
Craig Defoy	73	70	70	213	3,961.70
David Creamer	68	73	72	213	3,961.70
Tony Jacklin	69	74	71	214	3,254.69
Nick Job	72	72	70	214	3,254.69
Guillermo Encina	71	73	70	214	3,254.69
Jeff Van Wagenen	70	71	73	214	3,254.69
Gary Wintz	74	69	71	214	3,254.69
Peter Townsend	72	71	72	215	2,384.83
Alan Tapie	72	72	71	215	2,384.83
Bill Hardwick	73	71	71	215	2,384.83
Denis O'Sullivan	73	72	70	215	2,384.83
Martin Foster	73	72	70	215	2,384.83
Mike Miller	71	73	72	216	1,852.86
Keith MacDonald	74	71	71	216	1,852.86
Eddie Polland	73	72	71	216	1,852.86
Alberto Croce	69	69	78	216	1,852.86
John Grace	76	71	69	216	1,852.86
Jim Rhodes	68	78	71	217	1,529.98
Ross Metherell	73	74	70	217	1,529.98
Victor Garcia	70	73	74	217	1,529.98

Senior British Open

Royal County Down Golf Club, Newcastle, N. Ireland
Par 35-36–71; 6,634 yards

July 25-28
purse, €736,714

	SCORES				TOTAL	MONEY
Noboru Sugai	67	67	73	74	281	€122,785.80
John Irwin	71	68	74	70	283	78,023.35
Christy O'Connor, Jr.	73	70	73	70	286	45,384.10
John Chillas	69	69	77	72	287	36,835.73
Katsunari Takahashi	71	69	77	72	289	27,562.03
Seiji Ebihara	72	71	77	69	289	27,562.03
Barry Vivian	71	72	78	68	289	27,562.03
Nick Job	76	67	75	72	290	22,342.34
John McTear	71	78	71	70	290	22,342.34
John Bland	71	70	73	77	291	19,428.13
Mike Miller	74	72	74	72	292	17,718.45
John Morgan	72	70	77	74	293	15,153.94
David Oakley	76	68	74	75	293	15,153.94

		SCORES			TOTAL	MONEY
Maurice Bembridge	72	73	76	73	294	10,840.89
Bob Charles	73	72	77	72	294	10,840.89
Tom Watson	70	69	76	79	294	10,840.89
Priscillo Diniz	74	72	74	74	294	10,840.89
Neil Coles	74	70	78	73	295	8,237.52
Keith MacDonald	74	70	79	72	295	8,237.52
Malcolm Gregson	72	71	77	75	295	8,237.52
David Huish	76	70	74	76	296	7,201.36
Ross Metherell	75	69	76	76	296	7,201.36
Martin Foster	71	77	78	70	296	7,201.36
Russell Weir	68	72	79	78	297	6,838.70
Denis Durnian	73	72	81	72	298	6,294.71
Noel Ratcliffe	77	71	81	69	298	6,294.71
Bill Brask	76	72	75	75	298	6,294.71
Alberto Croce	76	70	78	74	298	6,294.71
Denis O'Sullivan	77	72	75	74	298	6,294.71
Bobby Verwey	72	71	82	73	298	6,294.71

De Vere PGA Seniors Championship

De Vere Carden Park, Cheshire, England
Par 36-36–72; 6,583 yards

August 1-4
purse, €318,955

		SCORES			TOTAL	MONEY
Seiji Ebihara	69	67	65	66	267	€52,733.73
George Burns	72	66	66	73	277	26,469.71
Steve Stull	71	69	71	66	277	26,469.71
Jim Rhodes	73	70	67	68	278	15,821.70
Ian Mosey	70	69	69	71	279	11,760.80
Guillermo Encina	71	71	69	68	279	11,760.80
John Chillas	68	69	71	71	279	11,760.80
Jerry Bruner	71	69	71	70	281	9,572.13
Mike Ferguson	66	70	72	73	281	9,572.13
Noel Ratcliffe	67	71	72	72	282	7,989.96
Ross Metherell	73	70	69	70	282	7,989.96
John Morgan	71	68	70	75	284	5,221.16
Malcolm Gregson	70	74	71	69	284	5,221.16
Bill Brask	69	71	73	71	284	5,221.16
David Jones	67	77	71	69	284	5,221.16
Brian Jones	69	72	73	70	284	5,221.16
Tony Allen	67	73	76	68	284	5,221.16
Alan Tapie	74	70	70	71	285	3,484.73
Bobby Verwey	72	72	69	72	285	3,484.73
David Good	67	72	72	74	285	3,484.73
Delroy Cambridge	70	70	70	75	285	3,484.73
Russell Weir	72	70	70	74	286	3,148.52
Craig Defoy	69	70	73	74	286	3,148.52
Bob Lendzion	73	69	71	73	286	3,148.52
Tommy Horton	71	72	71	73	287	2,792.53
David Oakley	70	72	72	73	287	2,792.53
Joe McDermott	75	70	72	70	287	2,792.53
Ian Stanley	70	69	73	75	287	2,792.53
Martin Foster	74	71	73	69	287	2,792.53
Wayne McDonald	77	68	72	70	287	2,792.53

Bad Ragaz PGA Seniors Open

Bad Ragaz Golf Club, Zurich, Switzerland
Par 35-35–70; 6,098 yards
(Third round cancelled—rain.)

August 9-11
purse, €230,000

	SCORES		TOTAL	MONEY
Dragon Taki	67	63	130	€34,500
Denis O'Sullivan	66	64	130	23,000
(Taki defeated O'Sullivan on third playoff hole.)				
David Creamer	66	65	131	16,100
Ian Mosey	67	65	132	10,748.67
Noel Ratcliffe	66	66	132	10,748.67
John Chillas	65	67	132	10,748.67
Steve Stull	67	66	133	8,280
John Morgan	68	66	134	6,900
Seiji Ebihara	67	67	134	6,900
Keith MacDonald	69	66	135	4,797.14
Jim Rhodes	68	67	135	4,797.14
Ian Stanley	66	69	135	4,797.14
Helmuth Schumacher	68	67	135	4,797.14
Ross Metherell	69	66	135	4,797.14
Bobby Verwey	66	69	135	4,797.14
Barry Vivian	68	67	135	4,797.14
Jay Horton	71	65	136	3,457.67
John Grace	67	69	136	3,457.67
Delroy Cambridge	67	69	136	3,457.67
Tommy Horton	68	69	137	2,509.88
Ray Carrasco	66	71	137	2,509.88
Alan Tapie	69	68	137	2,509.88
Brian Jones	68	69	137	2,509.88
Martin Foster	70	67	137	2,509.88
John Mashego	71	66	137	2,509.88
David Good	65	72	137	2,509.88
John Irwin	68	69	137	2,509.88
Denis Durnian	68	70	138	1,821.60
Mike Miller	71	67	138	1,821.60
Russell Weir	68	70	138	1,821.60
Guillermo Encina	70	68	138	1,821.60
Joe McDermott	68	70	138	1,821.60

Travis Perkins Senior Masters

Wentworth Club, Edinburgh Course, Surrey, England
Par 36-36–72; 6,723 yards

August 16-18
purse, €352,878

	SCORES			TOTAL	MONEY
Ray Carrasco	66	71	69	206	€52,931.81
Seiji Ebihara	67	70	70	207	35,287.88
David Good	68	71	69	208	24,701.51
John Grace	68	73	69	210	19,408.33
Denis Durnian	66	72	73	211	15,950.12
Guillermo Encina	70	68	74	212	12,703.63
Jerry Bruner	69	71	72	212	12,703.63
Barry Vivian	72	69	71	212	12,703.63
Maurice Bembridge	66	77	70	213	7,914.57
John Morgan	75	69	69	213	7,914.57
Ian Mosey	68	75	70	213	7,914.57

	SCORES			TOTAL	MONEY
Christy O'Connor, Jr.	74	68	71	213	7,914.57
David Jones	69	73	71	213	7,914.57
Dragon Taki	70	75	68	213	7,914.57
Gary Wintz	72	73	68	213	7,914.57
Neil Coles	73	71	70	214	5,005.84
Malcolm Gregson	69	74	71	214	5,005.84
Alan Tapie	68	75	71	214	5,005.84
David Huish	73	72	69	214	5,005.84
John Chillas	70	74	70	214	5,005.84
David Creamer	73	72	69	214	5,005.84
Steve Stull	72	74	68	214	5,005.84
Keith MacDonald	70	73	72	215	3,535.84
Russell Weir	72	74	69	215	3,535.84
Joe McDermott	72	72	71	215	3,535.84
Denis O'Sullivan	70	72	73	215	3,535.84
Brian Jones	74	70	71	215	3,535.84
Mike Miller	71	69	76	216	2,928.89
Bob Lendzion	72	74	70	216	2,928.89
Tommy Price	77	69	70	216	2,928.89

De Vere Hotels Seniors Classic

De Vere Slaley Hall, Hexham, England
Par 36-36–72; 6,769 yards

August 30-September 1
purse, €234,654

	SCORES			TOTAL	MONEY
Brian Jones	70	68	69	207	€35,198.10
Tommy Horton	73	69	72	214	23,465.40
Neil Coles	73	72	70	215	13,312.70
Denis Durnian	75	71	69	215	13,312.70
John Morgan	72	74	69	215	13,312.70
Guillermo Encina	74	72	71	217	7,978.24
Agim Bardha	70	75	72	217	7,978.24
Martin Foster	72	72	73	217	7,978.24
Delroy Cambridge	73	72	72	217	7,978.24
Noel Ratcliffe	73	75	70	218	5,397.04
Bob Shearer	71	78	69	218	5,397.04
Jim Rhodes	75	75	68	218	5,397.04
Mike Ferguson	74	73	71	218	5,397.04
Nick Job	74	74	71	219	4,223.77
Russell Weir	74	75	70	219	4,223.77
David Oakley	78	73	68	219	4,223.77
Mike Miller	73	70	77	220	3,218.67
Ian Mosey	72	76	72	220	3,218.67
Peter Dawson	77	73	70	220	3,218.67
Denis O'Sullivan	71	78	71	220	3,218.67
John Mashego	75	71	74	220	3,218.67
John Benda	75	76	69	220	3,218.67
Keith MacDonald	76	73	72	221	2,463.87
Malcolm Gregson	75	74	72	221	2,463.87
Bill Brask	73	76	72	221	2,463.87
Bernard Gallacher	79	71	72	222	1,994.56
David Jones	72	79	71	222	1,994.56
Alberto Croce	76	71	75	222	1,994.56
Jerry Bruner	77	73	72	222	1,994.56
John McTear	76	74	72	222	1,994.56
Jeff Van Wagenen	74	75	73	222	1,994.56

GIN Monte Carlo Invitational

Monte Carlo Golf Club, France
Par 34-35–69; 6,187 yards

September 5-7
purse, €220,949

	SCORES			TOTAL	MONEY
Terry Gale	62	67	68	197	€34,681.16
Keith MacDonald	66	63	69	198	23,120.78
Manuel Pinero	68	67	66	201	14,452.46
Jerry Bruner	69	64	68	201	14,452.46
Denis Durnian	68	68	67	203	9,345.63
Nick Job	70	65	68	203	9,345.63
Barry Vivian	67	68	68	203	9,345.63
Malcolm Gregson	69	70	65	204	6,940.18
Ian Stanley	68	69	67	204	6,940.18
John Irwin	68	70	68	206	6,014.56
John Morgan	71	68	68	207	4,765.88
Simon Owen	67	70	70	207	4,765.88
Denis O'Sullivan	69	69	69	207	4,765.88
Brian Jones	70	69	68	207	4,765.88
Steve Stull	69	69	69	207	4,765.88
Noel Ratcliffe	74	64	70	208	3,592.01
Peter Townsend	71	68	69	208	3,592.01
David Creamer	70	71	67	208	3,592.01
John Grace	71	68	69	208	3,592.01
Russell Weir	71	69	69	209	2,869.19
Jim Rhodes	68	73	68	209	2,869.19
Gary Wintz	69	66	74	209	2,869.19
Priscillo Diniz	76	67	67	210	2,429.39
David Good	70	71	69	210	2,429.39
Dragon Taki	69	73	68	210	2,429.39
Mike Miller	68	72	71	211	2,059.56
Ian Mosey	68	74	69	211	2,059.56
Gary Player	73	68	70	211	2,059.56
David Oakley	74	67	70	211	2,059.56
Maurice Bembridge	73	67	73	213	1,781.80
Jay Horton	72	70	71	213	1,781.80

Bovis Lend Lease European Senior Masters

Woburn Golf & Country Club, Milton Keynes, England
Par 35-37–72; 6,796 yards

September 13-15
purse, €356,871

	SCORES			TOTAL	MONEY
Delroy Cambridge	69	70	68	207	€53,479.57
Eamonn Darcy	68	71	70	209	30,305.09
Seiji Ebihara	71	70	68	209	30,305.09
Neil Coles	71	67	73	211	16,661.86
Ross Metherell	70	70	71	211	16,661.86
David Good	70	70	71	211	16,661.86
Keith MacDonald	77	68	68	213	12,835.10
Christy O'Connor, Jr.	73	69	72	214	10,220.54
David Oakley	66	75	73	214	10,220.54
Jerry Bruner	71	73	70	214	10,220.54
John Morgan	68	72	75	215	6,926.88
Paul Leonard	72	72	71	215	6,926.88
Joe McDermott	69	72	74	215	6,926.88
Jim Rhodes	71	72	72	215	6,926.88

	SCORES			TOTAL	MONEY
John Mashego	71	70	74	215	6,926.88
Priscillo Diniz	72	70	73	215	6,926.88
John Grace	72	69	74	215	6,926.88
Manuel Pinero	75	71	70	216	4,875.36
Malcolm Gregson	72	71	73	216	4,875.36
John Chillas	71	72	73	216	4,875.36
Brian Jones	70	73	73	216	4,875.36
Ray Carrasco	71	74	72	217	3,841.42
Alan Tapie	71	68	78	217	3,841.42
John Irwin	71	73	73	217	3,841.42
Steve Stull	74	68	75	217	3,841.42
Simon Owen	72	70	76	218	3,172.33
Guillermo Encina	71	72	75	218	3,172.33
Steve Wild	70	72	76	218	3,172.33
Gary Wintz	74	72	72	218	3,172.33
Maurice Bembridge	74	73	72	219	2,573.68
Mike Miller	75	72	72	219	2,573.68
Peter Townsend	75	72	72	219	2,573.68
Eddie Polland	71	75	73	219	2,573.68
Hank Woodrome	71	76	72	219	2,573.68

Charles Church Scottish Seniors Open

The Roxburghe, Kelso, Scotland
Par 36-36–72; 6,845 yards

September 20-22
purse, €240,165

	SCORES			TOTAL	MONEY
Denis Durnian	67	68	71	206	€35,991.22
Neil Coles	67	69	76	212	16,208.05
Tommy Horton	70	72	70	212	16,208.05
Martin Gray	72	69	71	212	16,208.05
Alan Tapie	73	66	73	212	16,208.05
Russell Weir	73	69	71	213	9,117.78
Denis O'Sullivan	66	71	76	213	9,117.78
Eamonn Darcy	73	69	72	214	6,334.46
Bill Brask	70	70	74	214	6,334.46
John Mashego	74	71	69	214	6,334.46
David Good	72	69	73	214	6,334.46
Steve Stull	69	74	71	214	6,334.46
Noel Ratcliffe	75	71	69	215	4,318.95
Keith MacDonald	74	69	72	215	4,318.95
David Oakley	71	67	77	215	4,318.95
David Creamer	71	71	73	215	4,318.95
Gary Wintz	74	73	68	215	4,318.95
Nick Job	71	72	73	216	3,181.62
John Morgan	72	71	73	216	3,181.62
Peter Dawson	72	69	75	216	3,181.62
Guillermo Encina	72	69	75	216	3,181.62
Jim Rhodes	73	70	73	216	3,181.62
Ian Mosey	74	73	70	217	2,152.28
Peter Townsend	71	73	73	217	2,152.28
Malcolm Gregson	73	72	72	217	2,152.28
Ray Carrasco	76	72	69	217	2,152.28
Joe McDermott	72	73	72	217	2,152.28
Ian Stanley	75	71	71	217	2,152.28
John Chillas	72	71	74	217	2,152.28
Brian Jones	73	76	68	217	2,152.28

	SCORES			TOTAL	MONEY
John Grace	71	74	72	217	2,152.28
Delroy Cambridge	77	70	70	217	2,152.28

Daily Telegraph/Sodexho Seniors Match Play

Los Flamingos, Marbella, Spain
Par 36-36–72; 6,386 yards

October 9-12
purse, €159,760

FIRST ROUND

John Chillas defeated Ian Stanley, 5 and 4.
Antonio Garrido defeated David Oakley, 1 up.
Priscillo Diniz defeated Jerry Bruner, 1 up.
Eddie Polland defeated John Irwin, 1 up.
Denis Durnian defeated John McTear, 1 up.
Peter Townsend defeated Gary Wintz, 4 and 3.
Noel Ratcliffe defeated Alberto Croce, 1 up.
Denis O'Sullivan defeated Simon Owen, 2 and 1.
Tommy Horton defeated Ray Carrasco, 2 and 1.
Brian Evans defeated Maurice Bembridge, 4 and 3.
Ian Mosey defeated Jim Rhodes, 24 holes.
Delroy Cambridge defeated David Good, 5 and 4.
John Morgan defeated Malcolm Gregson, 22 holes.
Mike Miller defeated Keith MacDonald, 5 and 4.
Joe McDermott defeated Bernard Gallacher, 2 and 1.
Nick Job defeated David Creamer, 1 up.

(Each losing player received €1,797.)

SECOND ROUND

Garrido defeated Chillas, 5 and 4.
Polland defeated Diniz, 3 and 2.
Durnian defeated Townsend, 19 holes.
O'Sullivan defeated Ratcliffe, 3 and 2.
Evans defeated Horton, 2 and 1.
Cambridge defeated Mosey, 5 and 4.
Miller defeated Morgan, 4 and 3.
Job defeated McDermott, 4 and 3.

(Each losing player received €3,994.)

QUARTER-FINALS

Polland defeated Garrido, 4 and 3.
O'Sullivan defeated Durnian, 3 and 2.
Cambridge defeated Evans, 1 up.
Job defeated Miller, 4 and 3.

(Each losing player received €7,988.)

SEMI-FINALS

Polland defeated O'Sullivan, 1 up.
Cambridge defeated Job, 2 and 1.

(Each losing player received €11,982.)

FINAL

Cambridge defeated Polland, 1 up.

(Cambridge received €25,561; Polland received €17,573.)

Tunisian Seniors Open

Port El Kantaoui Golf Club, Tunisia
Par 36-36–72; 6,536 yards

October 17-19
purse, €158,363

	SCORES			TOTAL	MONEY
Denis O'Sullivan	68	66	68	202	€24,625.45
John Morgan	69	66	69	204	16,414.32
Noel Ratcliffe	67	66	72	205	11,489.24
Priscillo Diniz	71	69	68	208	8,223
Steve Stull	68	70	70	208	8,223
Denis Durnian	68	69	72	209	5,317.20
Mike Miller	67	69	73	209	5,317.20
Craig Defoy	68	71	70	209	5,317.20
John McTear	70	69	70	209	5,317.20
David Good	70	69	70	209	5,317.20
Simon Owen	70	70	70	210	3,941.66
Nick Job	70	67	74	211	3,243.27
Russell Weir	70	71	70	211	3,243.27
Bill Brask	70	67	74	211	3,243.27
John Chillas	70	66	75	211	3,243.27
Bob Lendzion	70	72	70	212	2,709.59
John Mashego	69	69	74	212	2,709.59
Ray Carrasco	70	74	69	213	2,389.70
Jerry Bruner	72	73	68	213	2,389.70
Liam Higgins	74	68	72	214	2,102.27
Bill Hardwick	71	66	77	214	2,102.27
Antonio Garrido	73	71	71	215	1,651.95
Keith MacDonald	73	72	70	215	1,651.95
Steve Wild	74	70	71	215	1,651.95
Norman Wood	75	69	71	215	1,651.95
Alberto Croce	74	70	71	215	1,651.95
Jim Rhodes	69	69	77	215	1,651.95
John Irwin	69	71	75	215	1,651.95
Peter Townsend	70	74	72	216	1,269.28
Manuel Velasco	73	70	73	216	1,269.28
Delroy Cambridge	71	70	75	216	1,269.28
Gary Wintz	69	73	74	216	1,269.28

Estoril Seniors Tour Championship

Quinta da Marina Golf Club, Cascais, Portugal
Par 35-36–71; 6,392 yards

October 25-27
purse, €240,000

	SCORES			TOTAL	MONEY
Denis Durnian	68	68	72	208	€37,320
Eamonn Darcy	69	69	70	208	24,880
(Durnian defeated Darcy on first playoff hole.)					
Delroy Cambridge	71	67	71	209	17,415
John Morgan	71	70	69	210	10,958.50
Keith MacDonald	73	69	68	210	10,958.50

	SCORES			TOTAL	MONEY
Malcolm Gregson	70	70	70	210	10,958.50
John Chillas	68	72	70	210	10,958.50
Steve Wild	74	70	67	211	7,963
Ray Carrasco	70	71	71	212	6,719
Bill Brask	70	71	71	212	6,719
Maurice Bembridge	74	68	71	213	5,475
Christy O'Connor, Jr.	70	74	69	213	5,475
Priscillo Diniz	74	68	71	213	5,475
Ian Mosey	72	70	72	214	4,479.67
Alan Tapie	70	69	75	214	4,479.67
John Irwin	72	71	71	214	4,479.67
Mike Miller	69	67	79	215	3,627.25
Jerry Bruner	72	72	71	215	3,627.25
David Creamer	71	75	69	215	3,627.25
David Good	70	75	70	215	3,627.25
Neil Coles	71	75	70	216	2,831
Bill Hardwick	72	73	71	216	2,831
Jim Rhodes	76	69	71	216	2,831
John McTear	71	70	75	216	2,831
Simon Owen	72	69	76	217	2,269.80
Bob Lendzion	76	72	69	217	2,269.80
Denis O'Sullivan	71	72	74	217	2,269.80
John Mashego	72	75	70	217	2,269.80
Gary Wintz	72	70	75	217	2,269.80
Antonio Garrido	73	72	73	218	1,875
Joe McDermott	74	74	70	218	1,875
Jeff Van Wagenen	70	76	72	218	1,875

Japan Senior Tour

Castle Hill Open

Castle Hill County Club, Hoi-gun, Aichi
Par 36-36–72; 6,730 yards

May 24-26
purse, ¥30,000,000

	SCORES			TOTAL	MONEY
Namio Takasu	74	67	71	212	¥5,400,000
Toshiki Matsui	76	68	68	212	2,250,000
Norihiko Matsumoto	73	69	70	212	2,250,000
(Takasu defeated Matsui and Matsumoto in playoff.)					
Takayoshi Nishikawa	72	70	71	213	1,350,000
Fujio Kobayashi	72	74	68	214	1,050,000
Hisao Inoue	70	72	72	214	1,050,000
Toshiharu Morimoto	71	71	72	214	1,050,000
Seiichi Kanai	76	72	68	216	648,000
Katsunari Takahashi	73	72	71	216	648,000
Tadami Ueno	71	74	71	216	648,000
Toru Nakamura	69	76	71	216	648,000
Yoshitaka Yamamoto	77	69	70	216	648,000
Koichi Uehara	77	69	71	217	465,000

	SCORES			TOTAL	MONEY
Seiji Ebihara	74	72	71	217	465,000
Shuichi Sano	70	73	74	217	465,000
Fumio Tanaka	73	70	74	217	465,000
Hsieh Min-nan	77	70	71	218	390,000
*Tetsuo Sakata	77	70	71	218	
Yukio Noguchi	74	73	72	219	298,500
Katsuji Hasegawa	71	73	75	219	298,500
Hiroshi Ishii	71	76	72	219	298,500
Ryosuke Ota	71	73	75	219	298,500
Toyotake Nakao	74	74	71	219	298,500
Takashi Miyoshi	76	71	72	219	298,500
Tadao Furuichi	72	79	69	220	249,000
Seiji Ogawa	77	68	76	221	234,000
Shoichi Sato	73	77	71	221	234,000
Yasuzo Hagiwara	75	74	72	221	234,000
*Motohide Yanagi	74	75	72	221	
Seiji Kusakabe	77	75	70	222	216,000
Akira Yabe	73	78	71	222	216,000
Yasuo Sone	74	69	79	222	216,000

Asahi Ryokken Cup

Ito Golf Club, Fukuoka
Par 36-36–72; 6,787 yards

June 1-2
purse, ¥10,000,000

	SCORES		TOTAL	MONEY
Hisao Inoue	71	67	138	¥2,000,000
Noboru Sugai	69	69	138	600,000
Tetsuhiro Ueda	70	68	138	600,000
(Inoue defeated Sugai and Ueda in playoff.)				
Hsieh Min-nan	68	71	139	350,000
Motomasa Aoki	67	73	140	300,000
Takaaki Kono	70	71	141	240,000
Noboru Shibata	71	70	141	240,000
Yasuhiro Miyamoto	70	71	141	240,000
Koichi Uehara	72	70	142	206,000
Seiichi Kanai	72	70	142	206,000
Shuichi Sano	71	71	142	206,000
Tadao Nakamura	70	72	142	206,000
Katsuji Hasegawa	71	71	142	206,000
Hiroshi Ishii	74	69	143	200,000
Tadao Furuichi	69	74	143	200,000
Namio Takasu	72	72	144	180,000
Toru Nakayama	75	69	144	180,000
Teruo Sugihara	72	72	144	180,000
Norihiko Matsumoto	75	69	144	180,000
Kenichi Tsurumoto	70	74	144	180,000
Kiyokuni Kimoto	71	74	145	157,500
Koji Nakajima	70	75	145	157,500
Yukio Noguchi	70	75	145	157,500
Kanae Nobechi	71	74	145	157,500
Yurio Akitomi	72	73	145	157,500
Tadami Ueno	74	71	145	157,500
Kunio Koike	71	74	145	157,500
Teruo Suzumura	73	72	145	157,500
*Takuya Tsukane	74	71	145	
Shingaku Maeda	74	72	146	150,000

	SCORES		TOTAL	MONEY
*Masaaki Ueki	72 74		146	
*Keiichi Shimoda	74 72		146	

Aderans Wellness Open

Nakajo Golf Club, Nakajo, Niigata
Par 36-36–72; 6,813 yards

July 12-14
purse, ¥60,000,000

	SCORES			TOTAL	MONEY
Yukio Noguchi	68	66	70	204	¥12,000,000
Katsuji Hasegawa	71	71	65	207	6,000,000
Kenjiro Iwama	69	66	73	208	4,080,000
Fumio Tanaka	69	70	71	210	2,490,000
Toshiharu Morimoto	71	69	70	210	2,490,000
Masaru Amano	71	71	69	211	1,466,571
Seiji Ebihara	70	69	72	211	1,466,571
Toru Nakayama	68	72	71	211	1,466,571
Hiroshi Ishii	69	71	71	211	1,466,571
Toru Nakamura	72	70	69	211	1,466,571
Takashi Miyoshi	69	73	69	211	1,466,571
Yoshitaka Yamamoto	74	71	66	211	1,466,571
Shoichi Sato	69	68	75	212	913,500
Katsunari Takahashi	71	70	71	212	913,500
Noboru Shibata	69	74	69	212	913,500
Toyotake Nakao	69	70	73	212	913,500
Hisao Inoue	73	68	72	213	810,000
Tadaaki Uehara	70	72	72	214	705,000
Yurio Akitomi	73	67	74	214	705,000
Toshihiko Kikuichi	72	71	71	214	705,000
Hisashi Suzumura	71	74	69	214	705,000
Teruo Nakamura	71	70	73	214	705,000
Terry Gale	72	67	75	214	705,000
Motomasa Aoki	71	71	73	215	475,800
Fujio Kobayashi	68	76	71	215	475,800
Sadao Sakashita	71	69	75	215	475,800
Renkyoku Sugiyama	69	73	73	215	475,800
Junji Hashizoe	69	73	73	215	475,800
Akira Yabe	69	74	72	215	475,800
Koji Okuno	68	73	74	215	475,800
Eitaro Deguchi	69	73	73	215	475,800
Takeshi Matsukawa	75	68	72	215	475,800
Kinpachi Yoshimura	67	76	72	215	475,800

Fancl Senior Classic

Susono Country Club, Shizuoka
Par 36-36–72; 6,851 yards

August 23-25
purse, ¥60,000,000

	SCORES			TOTAL	MONEY
Katsunari Takahashi	71	70	70	211	¥15,000,000
Teruo Nakamura	73	71	70	214	6,900,000
Yoshitaka Yamamoto	74	73	68	215	3,600,000
Sadao Sakashita	73	76	67	216	2,120,000
Koji Okuno	73	70	73	216	2,120,000
Terry Gale	70	75	71	216	2,120,000

	SCORES			TOTAL	MONEY
Katsuji Hasegawa	75	73	69	217	1,515,000
Hisao Inoue	71	73	73	217	1,515,000
Motomasa Aoki	71	75	72	218	1,093,200
Noboru Sugai	74	72	72	218	1,093,200
Eiichi Itai	76	72	70	218	1,093,200
Yukio Noguchi	74	72	72	218	1,093,200
Toru Nakamura	73	72	73	218	1,093,200
Seiji Ogawa	72	74	73	219	697,333
Fujio Kobayashi	76	71	72	219	697,333
Namio Takasu	73	76	70	219	697,333
Fumio Tanaka	74	72	73	219	697,333
Haruo Yasuda	73	74	72	219	697,333
Hiroshi Ishii	68	80	71	219	697,333
Yasuo Tanabe	73	71	75	219	697,333
Takashi Miyoshi	71	78	70	219	697,333
Tadanao Takeshita	70	74	75	219	697,333
Teiji Sano	75	72	73	220	504,000
Yasuzou Hagiwara	72	78	70	220	504,000
Toshihiko Kikuichi	72	74	74	220	504,000
Tadao Furuichi	74	74	72	220	504,000
Koichi Uehara	71	75	75	221	414,000
Seiji Ebihara	72	74	75	221	414,000
Seiji Kusakabe	78	72	71	221	414,000
Junji Hashizoe	78	70	73	221	414,000
Tomitake Nakao	74	73	74	221	414,000

HTD Senior Classic

Mitsui Kanko Iris Golf Club, Hokkaido
Par 36-36–72; 6,492 yards

September 14-15
purse, ¥10,000,000

	SCORES		TOTAL	MONEY
Noboru Sugai	72	65	137	¥2,500,000
Tadao Nakamura	67	71	138	1,200,000
Hisao Inoue	67	72	139	750,000
Toru Nakayama	70	70	140	550,000
Koichi Uehara	68	73	141	375,000
Katsunari Takahashi	70	71	141	375,000
Seiji Ogawa	71	71	142	260,000
Seiichi Kanai	70	73	143	210,000
Masaji Kusakabe	75	68	143	210,000
Shuichi Sano	72	71	143	210,000
Kunio Koike	71	72	143	210,000
Norihiko Matsumoto	72	71	143	210,000
Katsuji Hasegawa	73	72	145	182,500
Tetsuhiro Ueda	74	71	145	182,500
Fujio Kobayashi	73	73	146	174,000
Takaaki Fukuzawa	74	72	146	174,000
Kikuo Arai	77	70	147	170,000
Namio Takasu	77	70	147	170,000
Takaaki Kono	74	74	148	166,000
Yasuzo Hagiwara	74	74	148	166,000
Ichiro Ino	76	73	149	162,000
Tadao Furuichi	74	75	149	162,000
*Kazuo Nishikawa	70	80	150	
Shigeru Takeuchi	80	71	151	158,000
Kanae Nobechi	75	76	151	158,000

	SCORES				TOTAL	MONEY
Kinoshi Tahara	75	77			152	154,000
Yasuhiro Miyamoto	80	72			152	154,000
*Masaru Kiyonobu	78	75			153	
*Mayashi Tadahiko	77	76			153	
*Kazutaka Kayou	75	78			153	

Japan PGA Senior Championship

Caledonian Golf Club, Yokoshima, Chiba
Par 36-36–72; 6,877 yards

October 2-5
purse, ¥30,000,000

	SCORES				TOTAL	MONEY
Chen Tze-ming	68	68	63	68	267	¥5,400,000
Teruo Nakamura	70	69	73	65	277	2,700,000
Takeru Shibata	72	66	72	69	279	1,800,000
Katsuji Hasegawa	73	72	69	67	281	1,350,000
Kiyoshi Hinata	73	68	69	72	282	1,200,000
Koichi Uehara	70	73	69	71	283	900,000
Katsunari Takahashi	76	68	71	68	283	900,000
Hisao Inoue	73	73	69	68	283	900,000
Fujio Kobayashi	73	69	73	69	284	600,000
Tadami Ueno	71	75	69	69	284	600,000
Yasuo Sone	74	70	72	68	284	600,000
Toru Nakamura	73	68	74	69	284	600,000
Yoshitaka Yamamoto	72	74	71	67	284	600,000
Seiji Ebihara	70	70	76	69	285	465,000
Yasuzo Hagiwara	72	75	69	69	285	465,000
Dragon Taki	71	73	72	70	286	390,000
Masami Morishita	71	76	70	69	286	390,000
Toyotake Nakao	70	71	75	70	286	390,000
Kikuo Arai	70	72	75	70	287	279,500
Toru Kurihara	73	70	72	72	287	279,500
Hsieh Min-nan	73	70	72	72	287	279,500
Koji Nakajima	71	76	69	71	287	279,500
Takaaki Fukuzawa	74	71	68	74	287	279,500
Akira Yabe	71	70	73	73	287	279,500
Shoichi Sato	71	70	76	71	288	222,000
Eitaro Deguchi	72	70	73	73	288	222,000
Ichiro Teramoto	76	71	73	68	288	222,000
Mitoshi Tomita	75	69	73	71	288	222,000
Takashi Miyoshi	70	73	73	72	288	222,000
Motomasa Aoki	72	68	74	75	289	201,000
Tadao Furuichi	72	74	72	71	289	201,000

PGA Philanthropy Biglayzac Senior

Biglayzac Country Club, Miyagi
Par 36-36–72; 6,754 yards

October 10-13
purse, ¥30,000,000

	SCORES				TOTAL	MONEY
Seiji Ebihara	74	70	67	68	279	¥5,400,000
Haruo Yasuda	74	67	71	72	284	2,250,000
Chen Tze-ming	71	70	71	72	284	2,250,000
Fujio Kobayashi	68	74	71	72	285	1,200,000
Wataru Horiguchi	71	76	72	66	285	1,200,000

		SCORES			TOTAL	MONEY
Brian Jones	72	73	71	69	285	1,200,000
Takaaki Fujisawa	74	71	73	68	286	780,000
Tadami Ueno	72	70	73	71	286	780,000
Koji Okuno	73	68	71	74	286	780,000
Hiroshi Fujita	71	71	72	74	288	645,000
Katsunari Takahashi	75	70	75	69	289	555,000
Takeshi Matsukawa	75	72	68	74	289	555,000
Takashi Miyoshi	75	72	70	72	289	555,000
Takayoshi Nishikawa	71	73	75	71	290	465,000
Terry Gale	73	72	73	72	290	465,000
Toru Nakayama	68	74	74	75	291	347,000
Toshiaki Namiki	72	74	74	71	291	347,000
Yoshimi Watanabe	68	77	74	72	291	347,000
Yurio Akitomi	71	72	77	71	291	347,000
Yasuo Sone	76	72	70	73	291	347,000
Toru Nakamura	72	70	74	75	291	347,000
Yoshikazu Iwase	73	73	74	72	292	261,000
Toshiharu Morimoto	73	72	71	76	292	261,000
Akira Yabe	77	72	70	74	293	235,000
Toshiki Matsui	77	71	70	75	293	235,000
Keizo Yamada	77	70	72	74	293	235,000
Yasuzo Hagiwara	73	76	73	72	294	219,000
Mitsuo Iwata	74	74	76	70	294	219,000
Tamotsu Ito	73	72	76	74	295	193,285
Kiyokuni Kimoto	76	74	72	73	295	193,285
Tadao Nakamura	73	75	72	75	295	193,285
Hisao Inoue	75	74	74	72	295	193,285
Eitaro Deguchi	75	75	76	69	295	193,285
Kinpachi Yoshimura	74	74	73	74	295	193,285
Tadanao Takeshita	76	71	75	73	295	193,285

Japan Senior Open Championship

Abiko Golf Club, Fukuoka
Par 36-36–72; 6,774 yards

October 31-November 3
purse, ¥50,000,000

		SCORES			TOTAL	MONEY
Takaaki Fukuzawa	69	71	69	70	279	¥10,000,000
Isao Aoki	70	71	69	70	280	5,500,000
Seiji Ebihara	71	70	69	73	283	3,875,000
Chen Tze-ming	73	70	75	66	284	2,550,000
Motomasa Aoki	67	80	69	69	285	1,900,000
Fujio Kobayashi	71	71	75	68	285	1,900,000
Toshiharu Morimoto	71	72	74	69	286	1,435,000
Katsunari Takahashi	71	75	71	70	287	1,305,000
Koichi Uehara	70	73	71	74	288	1,056,500
Takashi Miyoshi	71	73	73	71	288	1,056,500
Shuichi Sano	70	75	75	70	290	815,000
Kinpachi Yoshimura	76	71	73	70	290	815,000
Shoichi Sato	71	77	73	70	291	625,000
Yurio Akitomi	74	72	73	72	291	625,000
Tadami Ueno	75	73	71	72	291	625,000
Koji Okuno	68	74	77	72	291	625,000
Hiroshi Fujita	70	72	73	76	291	625,000
Noboru Sugai	73	71	71	77	292	493,000
Yasuzo Hagiwara	71	75	77	69	292	493,000
Toyotake Nakao	74	73	72	73	292	493,000

	SCORES				TOTAL	MONEY
Toru Nakamura	73	74	71	74	292	493,000
Denis Dernian	76	72	72	72	292	493,000
Takao Kage	73	78	71	71	293	428,666
Sadao Sakashita	75	73	75	70	293	428,666
Tadao Nakamura	74	74	73	72	293	428,666
Yukio Noguchi	72	76	73	72	293	428,666
Hiroaki Uenishi	73	75	74	71	293	428,666
Terry Gale	70	76	73	74	293	428,666
Takeru Shibata	76	75	72	71	294	385,000
Yoshitaka Yamamoto	74	72	74	74	294	385,000
Ian Stanley	74	73	70	77	294	385,000
*Makoto Kamido	72	73	72	77	294	

Takanosu Senior Open

Takanosu Golf Club, Hiroshima
Par 36-36–72; 6,630 yards

November 15-16
purse, ¥10,000,000

	SCORES		TOTAL	MONEY
Takashi Miyoshi	68	68	136	¥2,000,000
Mitsuo Iwata	69	68	137	800,000
Yasuzo Hagiwara	69	69	138	500,000
Ichiro Teramoto	73	66	139	400,000
Kiyoshi Hinata	75	66	141	250,000
Wataru Horiguchi	70	71	141	250,000
Namio Takasu	71	71	142	140,000
Yoshio Fumiyama	69	73	142	140,000
Koji Okuno	70	72	142	140,000
Toyotake Nakao	70	72	142	140,000
Toru Nakamura	71	71	142	140,000
Takayoshi Nishikawa	73	69	142	140,000
Toshiharu Morimoto	73	69	142	140,000
Teiji Sano	72	71	143	110,000
Yukio Noguchi	72	72	144	110,000
Masaru Amano	75	70	145	109,166
Fumio Tanaka	72	73	145	109,166
Yurio Akitomi	67	78	145	109,166
Takafumi Ogawa	76	69	145	109,166
Kazuo Kanayama	75	70	145	109,166
Kenichi Tsurumoto	72	73	145	109,166
Kikuo Arai	72	74	146	105,000
*Yukio Saiki	72	74	146	
Motomasa Aoki	79	68	147	105,000
Toru Kurihara	73	74	147	105,000
Shuichi Sano	75	72	147	105,000
Yoshimi Watanabe	75	72	147	105,000
Hiroshi Taninaka	71	76	147	105,000
Norihiko Matsumoto	72	75	147	105,000
*Toranobu Mukusege	75	72	147	
*Tatsuo Anoo	75	72	147	

N. Cup Senior Open

Central Golf Club, Ibaragi
Par 37-36–73; 6,931 yards

November 28-29
purse, ¥15,000,000

	SCORES		TOTAL	MONEY
Isao Aoki	68	71	139	¥2,500,000
Koichi Uehara	69	72	141	1,250,000
Seiji Ebihara	72	70	142	775,000
Fujio Kobayashi	72	70	142	775,000
Toru Nakayama	71	71	142	775,000
Katsuji Hasegawa	73	69	142	775,000
Kikuo Arai	71	72	143	500,000
Fumio Tanaka	75	69	144	400,000
Yukio Noguchi	73	71	144	400,000
Norihiko Matsumoto	76	68	144	400,000
Seiji Ogawa	73	72	145	254,000
Shoichi Sato	73	72	145	254,000
Hisao Jitsukata	75	70	145	254,000
Toshimoto Houri	74	71	145	254,000
Akira Yabe	72	73	145	254,000
*Toru Ogawa	72	73	145	
Masaru Amano	73	73	146	195,000
Shigeru Kawamata	71	75	146	195,000
Wataru Horiguchi	71	75	146	195,000
Mitsuhiro Kitta	71	75	146	195,000
Teiji Sano	75	72	147	145,000
Dragon Taki	78	69	147	145,000
Tadao Nakamura	72	75	147	145,000
Mitoyoshi Maruyama	74	73	147	145,000
Haruo Yasuda	73	74	147	145,000
Akira Yatabe	76	71	147	145,000
*Shigeuji Shiboya	74	73	147	
Nanoru Kondo	73	75	148	110,000
Toshiyuki Kisawa	76	72	148	110,000
Mutsumi Yamazaki	72	76	148	110,000

Women's Tours

Takefuji Classic

Waikoloa Beach Resort, Waikoloa, Hawaii
Par 35-35–70; 6,164 yards

February 28-March 2
purse, $900,000

	SCORES			TOTAL	MONEY
Annika Sorenstam	64	66	66	196	$135,000
Lorie Kane	63	66	67	196	82,192
(Sorenstam defeated Kane on first playoff hole.)					
Heather Bowie	68	65	65	198	52,875
Gloria Park	66	67	65	198	52,875
Kasumi Fujii	66	61	72	199	37,125
Suzanne Strudwick	66	67	68	201	26,025
Carin Koch	67	69	65	201	26,025
Grace Park	71	64	66	201	26,025
Catriona Matthew	64	71	68	203	18,375
Mhairi McKay	67	67	69	203	18,375
Liselotte Neumann	64	69	70	203	18,375
Tina Barrett	67	70	67	204	14,790
Mi Hyun Kim	64	71	69	204	14,790
Michele Redman	65	69	70	204	14,790
Tracy Hanson	71	68	66	205	12,360
Candie Kung	67	68	70	205	12,360
Tina Fischer	66	68	71	205	12,360
Cristie Kerr	75	64	67	206	10,185
Nancy Scranton	70	69	67	206	10,185
Natalie Gulbis	68	70	68	206	10,185
Denise Killeen	67	70	69	206	10,185
Charlotta Sorenstam	67	68	71	206	10,185
Jill McGill	66	68	72	206	10,185
Silvia Cavalleri	67	68	72	207	8,122
Laura Diaz	71	68	68	207	8,122
Donna Andrews	68	70	69	207	8,122
Kristal Parker-Manzo	70	67	70	207	8,122
Hee-Won Han	70	66	71	207	8,122
Stephanie Keever	67	69	71	207	8,122
Jenny Lidback	69	70	69	208	6,930
Beth Bauer	68	68	72	208	6,930

Ping Banner Health

Moon Valley Country Club, Phoenix, Arizona
Par 36-36–72; 6,473 yards

March 14-17
purse, $1,000,000

	SCORES				TOTAL	MONEY
Rachel Teske	70	69	71	71	281	$150,000
Annika Sorenstam	67	70	68	76	281	91,325
(Teske defeated Sorenstam on second playoff hole.)						
Mi Hyun Kim	75	70	67	72	284	52,916
Cristie Kerr	70	69	70	75	284	52,916
Akiko Fukushima	68	70	71	75	284	52,916

	SCORES				TOTAL	MONEY
Jeong Jang	72	70	75	68	285	31,000
Juli Inkster	72	71	71	71	285	31,000
Kris Tschetter	76	69	73	68	286	20,700
Leta Lindley	71	74	70	71	286	20,700
Laurel Kean	69	74	71	72	286	20,700
Emilee Klein	67	73	74	72	286	20,700
Lorie Kane	70	73	69	74	286	20,700
Kelly Robbins	67	73	79	68	287	16,400
Shani Waugh	67	76	75	70	288	14,150
Sophie Gustafson	70	71	74	73	288	14,150
Tina Barrett	70	71	74	73	288	14,150
Rosie Jones	70	71	72	75	288	14,150
Beth Daniel	73	73	76	67	289	11,316
Carin Koch	76	72	72	69	289	11,316
Se Ri Pak	74	69	77	69	289	11,316
Maria Hjorth	73	72	72	72	289	11,316
Mhairi McKay	72	72	73	72	289	11,316
Grace Park	74	69	74	72	289	11,316
Hee-Won Han	73	72	76	69	290	9,200
Wendy Ward	72	72	74	72	290	9,200
Catriona Matthew	68	75	75	72	290	9,200
Yu Ping Lin	71	73	73	73	290	9,200
Vicki Goetze-Ackerman	72	73	69	76	290	9,200
Jennifer Rosales	74	73	75	69	291	7,850
Kelli Kuehne	70	72	79	70	291	7,850
Kim Saiki	70	67	78	76	291	7,850

Welch's/Circle K Championship

Randolph North Golf Course, Tucson, Arizona
Par 35-37–72; 6,222 yards

March 21-24
purse, $800,000

	SCORES				TOTAL	MONEY
Laura Diaz	67	67	68	68	270	$120,000
Juli Inkster	66	64	70	71	271	73,060
Grace Park	71	67	71	64	273	47,000
Kelly Robbins	71	67	68	67	273	47,000
Karrie Webb	68	69	70	67	274	33,000
*Lorena Ochoa	70	67	69	68	274	
Heather Daly-Donofrio	70	71	68	66	275	20,680
Denise Killeen	68	72	66	69	275	20,680
Laura Davies	70	66	70	69	275	20,680
Annika Sorenstam	72	66	67	70	275	20,680
Dorothy Delasin	65	68	69	73	275	20,680
Meg Mallon	73	68	71	64	276	13,610
Janice Moodie	67	70	71	68	276	13,610
Maria Hjorth	69	67	72	68	276	13,610
Rosie Jones	68	68	70	70	276	13,610
Liselotte Neumann	70	70	69	68	277	10,986
Marisa Baena	69	67	70	71	277	10,986
Nancy Scranton	65	68	72	72	277	10,986
Leta Lindley	70	70	69	69	278	9,380
Cristie Kerr	69	68	72	69	278	9,380
Mhairi McKay	66	70	72	70	278	9,380
Akiko Fukushima	71	65	70	72	278	9,380
Tammie Green	68	72	72	67	279	7,800
Smriti Mehra	70	71	72	66	279	7,800

	SCORES				TOTAL	MONEY
Beth Bauer	72	69	69	69	279	7,800
Beth Daniel	69	72	69	69	279	7,800
Kris Tschetter	70	70	70	69	279	7,800
Lorie Kane	72	70	66	71	279	7,800
Wendy Doolan	69	69	75	67	280	6,045
Dawn Coe-Jones	71	66	75	68	280	6,045
Helen Alfredsson	75	66	70	69	280	6,045
Ashli Bunch	64	76	71	69	280	6,045
Jean Bartholomew	70	72	68	70	280	6,045
Michelle McGann	68	68	74	70	280	6,045
Jeong Jang	71	68	70	71	280	6,045

Kraft Nabisco Championship

Mission Hills Country Club, Rancho Mirage, California   March 28-31
Par 36-36–72; 6,520 yards   purse, $1,500,000

	SCORES				TOTAL	MONEY
Annika Sorenstam	70	71	71	68	280	$225,000
Liselotte Neumann	69	70	73	69	281	136,987
Cristie Kerr	74	70	70	68	282	88,125
Rosie Jones	72	69	72	69	282	88,125
Akiko Fukushima	73	76	68	66	283	56,250
Carin Koch	73	73	71	66	283	56,250
Karrie Webb	75	70	67	72	284	42,375
*Lorena Ochoa	75	69	71	70	285	
Grace Park	75	73	70	68	286	31,050
Se Ri Pak	74	71	71	70	286	31,050
Leta Lindley	72	72	72	70	286	31,050
Lorie Kane	73	72	70	71	286	31,050
Becky Iverson	71	74	68	73	286	31,050
Heather Bowie	75	71	72	69	287	21,900
Kris Tschetter	74	69	73	71	287	21,900
Beth Daniel	71	70	75	71	287	21,900
Vicki Goetze-Ackerman	74	73	68	72	287	21,900
Dorothy Delasin	72	73	69	73	287	21,900
Juli Inkster	73	76	71	68	288	18,225
Mhairi McKay	73	72	73	70	288	18,225
Wendy Doolan	78	70	72	69	289	16,350
Laura Davies	75	75	69	70	289	16,350
Janice Moodie	73	73	73	70	289	16,350
Mi Hyun Kim	75	74	69	71	289	16,350
Laurel Kean	79	74	71	66	290	13,800
Hee-Won Han	74	74	73	69	290	13,800
Suzann Pettersen	74	71	73	72	290	13,800
Sophie Gustafson	77	69	71	73	290	13,800
Michele Redman	75	70	72	73	290	13,800
Laura Diaz	74	73	73	71	291	12,225
*Aree Song Wongluekiet	71	74	73	73	291	

The Office Depot Hosted by Amy Alcott

El Caballero Country Club, Tarzana, California
Par 36-36–72; 6,493 yards

April 5-7
purse, $1,000,000

	SCORES			TOTAL	MONEY
Se Ri Pak	68	68	73	209	$150,000
Annika Sorenstam	71	68	71	210	91,325
Laura Diaz	71	69	73	213	66,250
Jackie Gallagher-Smith	73	72	70	215	42,083
Kelli Kuehne	71	76	68	215	42,083
Wendy Doolan	69	74	72	215	42,083
Vicki Goetze-Ackerman	73	73	70	216	22,850
Val Skinner	76	71	69	216	22,850
Laura Davies	75	72	69	216	22,850
Heather Daly-Donofrio	76	70	70	216	22,850
Kristal Parker-Manzo	70	74	72	216	22,850
Liselotte Neumann	76	73	68	217	15,950
Mi Hyun Kim	73	74	70	217	15,950
Karen Stupples	71	74	72	217	15,950
Michelle Estill	71	70	76	217	15,950
Tammie Green	72	72	74	218	12,750
Sophie Gustafson	72	75	71	218	12,750
Dawn Coe-Jones	70	77	71	218	12,750
Karrie Webb	74	71	73	218	12,750
Amy Fruhwirth	72	71	76	219	9,261
Leta Lindley	77	71	71	219	9,261
Michele Redman	76	72	71	219	9,261
Catriona Matthew	76	72	71	219	9,261
Rosie Jones	75	73	71	219	9,261
Tina Barrett	77	70	72	219	9,261
A.J. Eathorne	73	73	73	219	9,261
Beth Daniel	74	71	74	219	9,261
Meg Mallon	74	71	74	219	9,261
Maria Hjorth	73	72	74	219	9,261
Sherri Turner	76	68	75	219	9,261
Jean Bartholomew	73	71	75	219	9,261
Tonya Gill	69	75	75	219	9,261

Longs Drugs Challenge

Twelve Bridges Golf Club, Lincoln, California
Par 36-36–72; 6,388 yards

April 18-22
purse, $900,000

	SCORES				TOTAL	MONEY
Cristie Kerr	66	72	67	75	280	$135,000
Hee-Won Han	74	70	67	70	281	82,192
Heather Bowie	70	73	68	71	282	52,875
Jane Crafter	69	71	70	72	282	52,875
Grace Park	76	74	69	65	284	33,750
Mi Hyun Kim	71	69	71	73	284	33,750
Vicki Goetze-Ackerman	73	71	70	71	285	25,425
Carin Koch	71	74	74	67	286	19,350
Marnie McGuire	75	73	69	69	286	19,350
Se Ri Pak	73	70	72	71	286	19,350
Juli Inkster	72	70	70	74	286	19,350
Charlotta Sorenstam	72	74	74	68	288	14,790
Sophie Gustafson	69	80	68	71	288	14,790

	SCORES				TOTAL	MONEY
Jenny Lidback	72	72	71	73	288	14,790
Michele Redman	78	72	70	69	289	12,060
Helen Alfredsson	70	76	72	71	289	12,060
Maria Hjorth	74	71	70	74	289	12,060
Shani Waugh	74	71	70	74	289	12,060
Stephanie Keever	73	74	74	69	290	10,170
Tracy Hanson	72	74	72	72	290	10,170
Brandie Burton	74	71	71	74	290	10,170
Donna Andrews	73	71	70	76	290	10,170
A.J. Eathorne	72	74	74	71	291	9,090
Sherri Steinhauer	73	73	70	75	291	9,090
Yu Ping Lin	73	76	71	72	292	8,122
Leta Lindley	75	71	72	74	292	8,122
Mhairi McKay	72	71	75	74	292	8,122
Karen Weiss	70	74	73	75	292	8,122
Leslie Spalding	75	71	76	71	293	6,930
Silvia Cavalleri	72	75	74	72	293	6,930
Jung Yeon Lee	73	75	72	73	293	6,930
Suzanne Strudwick	74	70	75	74	293	6,930

Chick-fil-A Charity Championship

Eagle's Landing Country Club, Stockbridge, Georgia
Par 36-36–72; 6,254 yards
(Event reduced to 36 holes—rain.)

May 3-5
purse, $1,250,000

	SCORES		TOTAL	MONEY
Juli Inkster	66	66	132	$187,500
Kelly Robbins	64	70	134	114,156
Laura Diaz	66	69	135	82,812
Se Ri Pak	69	67	136	57,812
Grace Park	67	69	136	57,812
Hee-Won Han	71	66	137	36,145
Kelli Kuehne	68	69	137	36,145
Rachel Teske	67	70	137	36,145
Mi Hyun Kim	72	66	138	25,520
Mhairi McKay	67	71	138	25,520
Karrie Webb	67	71	138	25,520
Michelle Estill	71	68	139	20,541
Catriona Matthew	71	68	139	20,541
Wendy Ward	69	70	139	20,541
Michele Redman	72	68	140	15,732
Janice Moodie	71	69	140	15,732
Natalie Gulbis	70	70	140	15,732
Carin Koch	70	70	140	15,732
Dina Ammaccapane	69	71	140	15,732
Becky Morgan	69	71	140	15,732
Jennifer Rosales	67	73	140	15,732
Joanne Mills	72	69	141	11,113
Patricia Meunier-Lebouc	71	70	141	11,113
Laura Davies	71	70	141	11,113
Audra Burks	70	71	141	11,113
Donna Andrews	70	71	141	11,113
Jane Geddes	70	71	141	11,113
Heather Bowie	69	72	141	11,113
Akiko Fukushima	69	72	141	11,113
Luciana Bemvenuti	69	72	141	11,113

	SCORES		TOTAL	MONEY
Denise Killeen	68	73	141	11,113
Shani Waugh	67	74	141	11,113

Aerus Electrolux USA Championship

Legends Club of Tennessee, Franklin, Tennessee
Par 36-36–72; 6,425 yards

May 9-12
purse, $800,000

	SCORES				TOTAL	MONEY
Annika Sorenstam	65	72	70	64	271	$120,000
Pat Hurst	70	69	67	66	272	73,060
Grace Park	69	71	67	67	274	53,000
Donna Andrews	71	70	69	65	275	41,000
Brandie Burton	67	69	70	70	276	33,000
Hee-Won Han	70	71	69	67	277	27,000
Betsy King	71	70	68	69	278	22,000
Natalie Gulbis	70	69	66	74	279	19,800
Ashli Bunch	68	76	66	70	280	17,000
Danielle Ammaccapane	69	69	70	72	280	17,000
Patricia Baxter-Johnson	72	70	71	68	281	13,610
Michelle Ellis	68	71	71	71	281	13,610
Se Ri Pak	72	71	66	72	281	13,610
Laura Diaz	70	68	70	73	281	13,610
Catrin Nilsmark	71	71	71	69	282	11,600
Maria Hjorth	70	70	76	67	283	8,963
Denise Killeen	70	72	73	68	283	8,963
Helen Alfredsson	72	74	68	69	283	8,963
Cristie Kerr	69	75	69	70	283	8,963
Jane Crafter	70	72	71	70	283	8,963
Kelli Kuehne	71	69	73	70	283	8,963
Kris Tschetter	67	74	71	71	283	8,963
Angela Stanford	72	74	65	72	283	8,963
Mhairi McKay	67	73	71	72	283	8,963
Mi Hyun Kim	70	71	69	73	283	8,963
Sherri Turner	69	73	67	74	283	8,963
Sophie Gustafson	69	76	71	68	284	6,175
Juli Inkster	71	74	70	69	284	6,175
Angela Buzminski	70	75	70	69	284	6,175
Catriona Matthew	70	73	71	70	284	6,175
Kristi Albers	72	70	71	71	284	6,175
Laurie Rinker-Graham	70	74	68	72	284	6,175
Kelly Robbins	69	71	72	72	284	6,175
Rosie Jones	69	71	71	73	284	6,175

Asahi Ryokuken International

Mount Vintage Plantation Golf Club,
North Augusta, South Carolina
Par 36-36–72; 6,366 yards

May 16-19
purse, $1,250,000

	SCORES				TOTAL	MONEY
Janice Moodie	70	66	67	70	273	$187,500
Laura Davies	67	71	69	73	280	114,156
Rosie Jones	71	71	72	67	281	73,437
Annika Sorenstam	72	70	67	72	281	73,437

	SCORES				TOTAL	MONEY
Carin Koch	70	73	71	69	283	51,562
Amy Fruhwirth	75	71	68	70	284	34,062
Kim Williams	71	72	72	69	284	34,062
Grace Park	69	72	70	73	284	34,062
Catriona Matthew	72	71	67	74	284	34,062
Marnie McGuire	73	73	70	69	285	22,074
Nancy Scranton	75	70	71	69	285	22,074
Mi Hyun Kim	71	74	71	69	285	22,074
Wendy Doolan	72	70	74	69	285	22,074
Dawn Coe-Jones	70	70	73	72	285	22,074
Jill McGill	73	70	72	71	286	18,125
Leta Lindley	74	71	72	70	287	15,937
Helen Alfredsson	79	68	69	71	287	15,937
Beth Bauer	73	73	70	71	287	15,937
Hee-Won Han	73	71	71	72	287	15,937
Sherri Steinhauer	76	73	72	68	289	12,901
Yu Ping Lin	71	74	73	71	289	12,901
Ashli Bunch	77	70	70	72	289	12,901
Jeong Jang	70	76	71	72	289	12,901
Charlotta Sorenstam	76	69	71	73	289	12,901
Cristie Kerr	74	71	71	73	289	12,901
Brandie Burton	75	70	69	75	289	12,901
Emilee Klein	71	71	73	75	290	10,625
Karen Stupples	73	74	68	75	290	10,625
Stephanie Keever	71	71	72	76	290	10,625
Heather Bowie	72	72	72	75	291	9,062
Candie Kung	74	71	74	72	291	9,062
Karen Pearce	74	73	72	72	291	9,062
Kathryn Marshall	75	71	71	74	291	9,062
Joanne Morley	72	75	73	71	291	9,062

Corning Classic

Corning Country Club, Corning, New York
Par 36-36–72; 6,062 yards

May 23-26
purse, $1,000,000

	SCORES				TOTAL	MONEY
Laura Diaz	66	69	69	70	274	$150,000
Rosie Jones	69	69	67	71	276	91,325
Marnie McGuire	70	72	68	67	277	58,750
Silvia Cavalleri	69	68	70	70	277	58,750
Jung Yeon Lee	67	69	72	70	278	41,250
Pamela Kerrigan	72	70	70	67	279	28,916
Michele Redman	69	71	70	69	279	28,916
Beth Bauer	68	68	74	69	279	28,916
Carin Koch	74	71	67	68	280	20,416
Leslie Spalding	68	70	74	68	280	20,416
Alison Nicholas	68	70	71	71	280	20,416
Diana D'Alessio	74	67	73	67	281	17,500
Michelle McGann	71	71	71	69	282	14,600
Becky Morgan	69	71	72	70	282	14,600
Fiona Pike	75	69	67	71	282	14,600
Barb Mucha	71	71	69	71	282	14,600
Sherri Steinhauer	66	72	71	73	282	14,600
Pearl Sinn	71	73	70	69	283	11,933
Joanne Mills	70	75	69	69	283	11,933
Heather Daly-Donofrio	68	72	72	71	283	11,933

	SCORES				TOTAL	MONEY
Becky Iverson	72	69	74	69	284	10,900
Meg Mallon	74	71	69	70	284	10,900
Jill McGill	67	75	74	69	285	8,710
Nicole Jeray	72	69	73	71	285	8,710
Stephanie Keever	70	71	72	72	285	8,710
Mhairi McKay	73	69	70	73	285	8,710
Catriona Matthew	72	69	71	73	285	8,710
Beth Daniel	69	68	75	73	285	8,710
Namika Omata	71	70	70	74	285	8,710
Marilyn Lovander	71	68	72	74	285	8,710
Allison Finney	71	70	69	75	285	8,710
Michelle Estill	69	70	70	76	285	8,710

Kellogg-Keebler Classic

Stonebridge Country Club, Aurora, Illinois
Par 36-36–72; 6,327 yards

May 31-June 2
purse, $1,200,000

	SCORES			TOTAL	MONEY
Annika Sorenstam	63	67	65	195	$180,000
Michele Redman	64	74	68	206	83,529
Mhairi McKay	71	65	70	206	83,529
Danielle Ammaccapane	65	70	71	206	83,529
Kris Tschetter	70	69	68	207	45,000
Candie Kung	71	66	70	207	45,000
Hee-Won Han	70	71	67	208	28,650
Akiko Fukushima	67	73	68	208	28,650
Leslie Spalding	67	72	69	208	28,650
Donna Andrews	70	68	70	208	28,650
Beth Daniel	68	74	67	209	18,728
Cindy Schreyer	72	68	69	209	18,728
Emilee Klein	69	71	69	209	18,728
Dawn Coe-Jones	67	73	69	209	18,728
Se Ri Pak	70	68	71	209	18,728
Karrie Webb	68	68	73	209	18,728
Vicki Goetze-Ackerman	67	69	73	209	18,728
Jackie Gallagher-Smith	65	77	68	210	14,319
Joanne Morley	72	68	70	210	14,319
Alison Nicholas	69	70	71	210	14,319
Kelli Kuehne	69	75	67	211	11,500
Joanne Mills	71	71	69	211	11,500
Tonya Gill	73	68	70	211	11,500
Kathryn Marshall	73	68	70	211	11,500
Carin Koch	72	69	70	211	11,500
Tracy Hanson	69	72	70	211	11,500
Yu Ping Lin	67	74	70	211	11,500
Amy Alcott	71	69	71	211	11,500
Anna Acker-Macosko	70	69	72	211	11,500
Karen Stupples	70	73	69	212	8,365
Jeanne-Marie Busuttil	70	73	69	212	8,365
Jane Geddes	69	74	69	212	8,365
Silvia Cavalleri	74	67	71	212	8,365
Juli Inkster	72	69	71	212	8,365
Jan Stephenson	67	73	72	212	8,365
Grace Park	72	64	76	212	8,365

McDonald's LPGA Championship

DuPont Country Club, Wilmington, Delaware
Par 35-36–71; 6,408 yards

June 6-9
purse, $1,500,000

		SCORES			TOTAL	MONEY
Se Ri Pak	71	70	68	70	279	$225,000
Beth Daniel	67	70	68	77	282	136,987
Annika Sorenstam	70	76	73	65	284	99,375
Juli Inkster	69	75	70	71	285	69,375
Karrie Webb	68	71	72	74	285	69,375
Carin Koch	68	73	73	72	286	46,500
Michele Redman	74	69	70	73	286	46,500
Catriona Matthew	70	73	75	70	288	37,125
Kristi Albers	74	73	73	70	290	30,625
Karen Stupples	75	70	70	75	290	30,625
Michelle McGann	71	72	72	75	290	30,625
Meg Mallon	73	72	76	70	291	24,650
Karen Weiss	70	74	75	72	291	24,650
Kim Saiki	71	71	69	80	291	24,650
Kelli Kuehne	71	75	74	72	292	19,650
Rachel Teske	72	71	77	72	292	19,650
Natalie Gulbis	72	72	75	73	292	19,650
Grace Park	72	73	73	74	292	19,650
Akiko Fukushima	71	71	76	74	292	19,650
Barb Mucha	70	73	75	75	293	16,950
Laura Diaz	73	71	71	78	293	16,950
Maria Hjorth	78	70	75	71	294	15,450
Kelly Robbins	70	75	74	75	294	15,450
Silvia Cavalleri	72	73	73	76	294	15,450
Brandie Burton	74	76	74	71	295	12,543
Kris Tschetter	74	75	75	71	295	12,543
Danielle Ammaccapane	73	76	73	73	295	12,543
Tammie Green	70	78	73	74	295	12,543
Leta Lindley	72	77	71	75	295	12,543
Gloria Park	75	72	73	75	295	12,543
Kathryn Marshall	73	73	72	77	295	12,543
Vicki Goetze-Ackerman	72	72	74	77	295	12,543

Evian Masters

See Evian Ladies European Tour section.

Wegmans Rochester LPGA

Locust Hill Country Club, Rochester, New York
Par 35-37–72; 6,190 yards

June 20-23
purse, $1,200,000

		SCORES			TOTAL	MONEY
Karrie Webb	64	72	72	68	276	$180,000
Mi Hyun Kim	69	67	67	74	277	109,590
Se Ri Pak	72	72	67	70	281	79,500
Kristal Parker-Manzo	68	75	72	69	284	61,500
Helen Alfredsson	72	71	70	72	285	38,400
Beth Daniel	70	68	74	73	285	38,400
Juli Inkster	71	72	67	75	285	38,400

		SCORES			TOTAL	MONEY
Jennifer Rosales	74	75	68	68	285	38,400
Rachel Teske	70	72	72	72	286	26,700
Danielle Ammaccapane	73	70	73	71	287	21,870
Meg Mallon	67	73	75	72	287	21,870
Joanne Morley	68	74	74	71	287	21,870
Gloria Park	69	71	72	75	287	21,870
Maria Hjorth	72	73	68	75	288	18,480
Dawn Coe-Jones	72	73	73	71	289	16,480
Chris Johnson	70	74	75	70	289	16,480
Rosie Jones	73	71	72	73	289	16,480
Nanci Bowen	73	74	70	73	290	14,320
Candie Kung	73	72	71	74	290	14,320
Fiona Pike	70	71	76	73	290	14,320
Eva Dahllof	73	72	71	75	291	13,080
Kelly Robbins	71	71	73	76	291	13,080
Jane Crafter	74	74	69	75	292	11,260
Dorothy Delasin	73	74	68	77	292	11,260
Yu Ping Lin	72	73	71	76	292	11,260
Angela Stanford	75	69	72	76	292	11,260
Sherri Turner	74	74	72	72	292	11,260
Wendy Ward	75	71	76	70	292	11,260
Jean Bartholomew	74	72	77	70	293	8,542
Silvia Cavalleri	75	73	68	77	293	8,542
Laura Davies	71	69	69	84	293	8,542
Amy Fruhwirth	73	74	75	71	293	8,542
Shiho Katano	71	74	74	74	293	8,542
Marilyn Lovander	71	78	71	73	293	8,542
Jill McGill	76	73	73	71	293	8,542
Shani Waugh	74	70	75	74	293	8,542
*Naree Song Wongluekiet	69	74	73	77	293	

ShopRite Classic

Marriott Seaview Resort, Bay Course,
Galloway Township, New Jersey
Par 36-35–71; 6,051 yards

June 28-30
purse, $1,200,000

		SCORES		TOTAL	MONEY
Annika Sorenstam	68	67	66	201	$180,000
Carin Koch	71	66	67	204	83,530
Kate Golden	64	69	71	204	83,530
Juli Inkster	65	67	72	204	83,530
Hiromi Kobayashi	71	69	65	205	45,000
Natalie Gulbis	68	71	66	205	45,000
Becky Morgan	71	70	65	206	30,100
Helen Alfredsson	70	67	69	206	30,100
Lorie Kane	65	70	71	206	30,100
Ashli Bunch	74	69	64	207	21,192
Shani Waugh	71	70	66	207	21,192
Laura Davies	70	68	69	207	21,192
Johanna Head	67	70	70	207	21,192
Nanci Bowen	68	68	71	207	21,192
Emilee Klein	72	71	65	208	16,080
Kim Saiki	73	68	67	208	16,080
Rosie Jones	69	69	70	208	16,080
Julie Piers	67	70	71	208	16,080
Heather Bowie	70	73	66	209	13,320

	SCORES			TOTAL	MONEY
Karen Stupples	72	69	68	209	13,320
Betsy King	68	71	70	209	13,320
Jung Yeon Lee	69	69	71	209	13,320
Stephanie Keever	67	69	73	209	13,320
Angela Stanford	74	69	67	210	10,830
Karen Weiss	73	68	69	210	10,830
Tina Barrett	70	71	69	210	10,830
Karen Pearce	72	68	70	210	10,830
Tracy Hanson	66	72	72	210	10,830
Pat Hurst	69	65	76	210	10,830
Charlotta Sorenstam	74	69	68	211	8,365
Kristi Albers	70	72	69	211	8,365
Nancy Scranton	73	68	70	211	8,365
Jennifer Rosales	73	67	71	211	8,365
Laurie Brower	72	68	71	211	8,365
Alison Nicholas	69	70	72	211	8,365
Jackie Gallagher-Smith	72	66	73	211	8,365

U.S. Women's Open

Prairie Dunes Country Club, Hutchinson, Kansas
Par 35-35–70; 6,267 yards

July 4-7
purse, $3,000,000

	SCORES				TOTAL	MONEY
Juli Inkster	67	72	71	66	276	$535,000
Annika Sorenstam	70	69	69	70	278	315,000
Shani Waugh	67	73	71	72	283	202,568
Raquel Carriedo	75	71	72	66	284	141,219
Se Ri Pak	74	75	68	68	285	114,370
Mhairi McKay	70	75	71	70	286	101,421
Jennifer Rosales	73	72	74	68	287	78,016
Kelli Kuehne	70	76	72	69	287	78,016
Beth Daniel	71	76	71	69	287	78,016
Laura Diaz	67	72	77	71	287	78,016
Janice Moodie	71	72	71	73	287	78,016
Kelly Robbins	71	74	74	69	288	54,201
Joanne Morley	78	68	73	69	288	54,201
Rachel Teske	75	71	72	70	288	54,201
Stephanie Keever	72	71	73	72	288	54,201
Lynnette Brooky	73	73	69	73	288	54,201
Jill McGill	71	70	69	78	288	54,201
Grace Park	71	77	71	70	289	40,738
Donna Andrews	74	74	70	71	289	40,738
Beth Bauer	74	72	71	72	289	40,738
Lorie Kane	69	77	69	74	289	40,738
Meg Mallon	73	75	73	69	290	26,894
Stacy Prammanasudh	75	74	72	69	290	26,894
Catriona Matthew	69	80	72	69	290	26,894
Jeong Jang	73	73	74	70	290	26,894
Danielle Ammaccapane	74	71	73	72	290	26,894
Michelle Ellis	71	71	75	73	290	26,894
Rosie Jones	71	77	69	73	290	26,894
Susan Ginter-Brooker	74	72	70	74	290	26,894
Mi Hyun Kim	74	72	70	74	290	26,894
Michele Redman	71	69	73	77	290	26,894

Jamie Farr Kroger Classic

Highland Meadows Golf Club, Sylvania, Ohio
Par 34-37–71; 6,408 yards

July 11-14
purse, $1,000,000

	SCORES				TOTAL	MONEY
Rachel Teske	67	73	64	66	270	$150,000
Beth Bauer	69	67	67	69	272	91,325
Laura Diaz	70	64	72	67	273	58,750
Karrie Webb	72	65	66	70	273	58,750
Amy Fruhwirth	70	70	68	66	274	37,500
Kelli Kuehne	71	66	69	68	274	37,500
Danielle Ammaccapane	73	68	72	62	275	23,875
Mhairi McKay	71	71	68	65	275	23,875
Natalie Gulbis	73	67	70	65	275	23,875
Se Ri Pak	72	67	68	68	275	23,875
Mi Hyun Kim	70	71	68	67	276	18,750
Tracy Hanson	72	67	75	63	277	15,500
Jackie Gallagher-Smith	70	71	70	66	277	15,500
Jeanne-Marie Busuttil	68	68	74	67	277	15,500
Jeong Jang	69	71	68	69	277	15,500
Vicki Goetze-Ackerman	70	68	70	69	277	15,500
Michelle Ellis	71	73	70	64	278	11,980
Barb Mucha	71	68	73	66	278	11,980
Maria Hjorth	71	69	70	68	278	11,980
Hee-Won Han	69	70	71	68	278	11,980
Shani Waugh	70	70	67	71	278	11,980
Catriona Matthew	72	71	70	66	279	9,750
Kelly Robbins	70	73	69	67	279	9,750
Janice Moodie	71	69	71	68	279	9,750
Dawn Coe-Jones	74	70	66	69	279	9,750
Jill McGill	72	70	68	69	279	9,750
Donna Andrews	69	69	72	69	279	9,750
Karen Stupples	75	67	69	69	280	7,708
Laura Davies	70	71	70	69	280	7,708
Luciana Bemvenuti	72	70	68	70	280	7,708
Brandie Burton	73	68	69	70	280	7,708
Gloria Park	69	71	70	70	280	7,708
Heather Bowie	69	70	66	75	280	7,708

Giant Eagle Classic

Squaw Creek Country Club, Vienna, Ohio
Par 37-35–72; 6,454 yards

July 19-21
purse, $1,000,000

	SCORES			TOTAL	MONEY
Mi Hyun Kim	65	68	69	202	$150,000
Kelly Robbins	64	68	71	203	91,325
Grace Park	72	66	67	205	58,750
Dorothy Delasin	69	69	67	205	58,750
Tammie Green	76	65	65	206	34,416
Natalie Gulbis	67	71	68	206	34,416
Beth Bader	64	71	71	206	34,416
Michele Redman	72	67	68	207	23,500
Pat Hurst	69	69	69	207	23,500
Fiona Pike	70	71	67	208	17,660
Joanne Morley	71	69	68	208	17,660
Gail Graham	71	68	69	208	17,660

	SCORES			TOTAL	MONEY
Jennifer Rosales	69	70	69	208	17,660
Danielle Ammaccapane	65	70	73	208	17,660
Jeong Jang	71	69	69	209	14,100
Beth Daniel	68	69	72	209	14,100
Beth Bauer	69	72	69	210	11,150
Emilee Klein	70	70	70	210	11,150
Kris Tschetter	70	70	70	210	11,150
Helen Alfredsson	70	70	70	210	11,150
Stefania Croce	68	72	70	210	11,150
Kristal Parker-Manzo	70	69	71	210	11,150
Patricia Meunier-Lebouc	70	69	71	210	11,150
Jackie Gallagher-Smith	68	71	71	210	11,150
Janice Moodie	68	70	72	210	11,150
Candie Kung	71	73	67	211	7,450
Audra Burks	71	73	67	211	7,450
Diane Irvin	72	70	69	211	7,450
Marilyn Lovander	71	71	69	211	7,450
Karrie Webb	71	71	69	211	7,450
Dawn Coe-Jones	71	70	70	211	7,450
Catriona Matthew	70	71	70	211	7,450
Ara Koh	70	71	70	211	7,450
Barb Mucha	69	71	71	211	7,450
Namika Omata	69	71	71	211	7,450
Tina Barrett	68	72	71	211	7,450
Mhairi McKay	72	66	73	211	7,450

Sybase Big Apple Classic

Wykagyl Country Club, New Rochelle, New York
Par 35-36–71; 6,161 yards

July 25-28
purse, $950,000

	SCORES				TOTAL	MONEY
Gloria Park	71	67	63	69	270	$142,500
Hee-Won Han	70	67	66	67	270	86,758
(Park defeated Han on first playoff hole.)						
Annika Sorenstam	71	66	64	70	271	62,937
Karrie Webb	70	69	66	67	272	48,687
Beth Daniel	73	65	69	67	274	39,187
Michele Redman	71	72	65	67	275	29,449
Diana D'Alessio	72	69	66	68	275	29,449
Kelli Kuehne	69	65	73	69	276	23,512
Kim Saiki	71	67	71	68	277	19,395
Sherri Steinhauer	69	69	71	68	277	19,395
Candie Kung	70	72	66	69	277	19,395
Ara Koh	72	70	68	69	279	16,102
Kelly Robbins	71	70	69	69	279	16,102
Jennifer Rosales	70	74	67	69	280	14,630
Rachel Teske	71	71	69	70	281	12,445
Janice Moodie	74	70	66	71	281	12,445
Natalie Gulbis	71	69	70	71	281	12,445
Chris Johnson	71	65	74	71	281	12,445
Nancy Scranton	71	68	68	74	281	12,445
Shiho Katano	71	74	71	66	282	9,982
Moira Dunn	72	72	69	69	282	9,982
Meg Mallon	70	71	71	70	282	9,982
Dorothy Delasin	71	69	71	71	282	9,982
Rosie Jones	75	67	68	72	282	9,982

	SCORES				TOTAL	MONEY
Silvia Cavalleri	69	71	70	72	282	9,982
Tracy Hanson	72	73	70	68	283	8,084
Lorie Kane	72	69	74	68	283	8,084
Kris Tschetter	69	75	70	69	283	8,084
Kathryn Marshall	68	76	70	69	283	8,084
Maria Hjorth	75	68	71	69	283	8,084

Wendy's Championship for Children

Tartan Fields Golf Club, Dublin, Ohio
Par 37-35–72; 6,517 yards

August 2-4
purse, $1,000,000

	SCORES			TOTAL	MONEY
Mi Hyun Kim	68	67	73	208	$150,000
Hee-Won Han	73	66	70	209	91,325
Danielle Ammaccapane	73	65	72	210	66,250
Lorie Kane	68	73	70	211	46,250
Michele Redman	68	72	71	211	46,250
Rosie Jones	66	75	71	212	33,750
Barb Mucha	71	73	69	213	25,083
Betsy King	71	71	71	213	25,083
Candie Kung	73	68	72	213	25,083
Donna Andrews	73	73	69	215	18,225
Mhairi McKay	65	80	70	215	18,225
Juli Inkster	73	71	71	215	18,225
Yu Ping Lin	70	72	73	215	18,225
Gloria Park	77	68	71	216	15,400
Beth Bauer	74	74	69	217	12,350
Kelli Kuehne	76	70	71	217	12,350
Amy Fruhwirth	73	73	71	217	12,350
Wendy Ward	72	74	71	217	12,350
Hilary Homeyer	71	75	71	217	12,350
Tonya Gill	74	71	72	217	12,350
Suzanne Strudwick	70	72	75	217	12,350
Pat Hurst	69	72	76	217	12,350
Nanci Bowen	76	72	70	218	9,560
Allison Finney	75	71	72	218	9,560
Tammie Green	75	70	73	218	9,560
Eva Dahllof	70	74	74	218	9,560
Tina Barrett	68	75	75	218	9,560
Vickie Odegard	73	74	72	219	8,012
Giulia Sergas	73	73	73	219	8,012
Patricia Baxter-Johnson	72	72	75	219	8,012
*Virada Nirapathpongporn	69	75	75	219	
Anna Acker-Macosko	71	71	77	219	8,012

Weetabix Women's British Open

See Evian Ladies European Tour section.

Bank of Montreal Canadian Women's Open

Summerlea Golf & Country Club, Vaudreuil-Dorian
Quebec, Canada
Par 36-36–72; 6,435 yards

August 15-18
purse, $1,200,000

		SCORES			TOTAL	MONEY
Meg Mallon	71	71	69	73	284	$180,000
Michele Redman	69	74	72	72	287	83,530
Michelle Ellis	69	71	73	74	287	83,530
Catriona Matthew	70	70	70	77	287	83,530
Se Ri Pak	73	72	68	75	288	49,500
Charlotta Sorenstam	74	70	70	75	289	37,200
Gloria Park	69	71	73	76	289	37,200
Lorie Kane	74	75	70	71	290	26,900
Susan Ginter-Brooker	76	75	67	72	290	26,900
Laura Diaz	71	76	70	73	290	26,900
Marisa Baena	70	74	76	71	291	21,060
Kelli Kuehne	72	75	71	73	291	21,060
Beth Daniel	74	71	72	74	291	21,060
Karrie Webb	72	70	72	78	292	18,480
Wendy Ward	73	77	71	72	293	15,720
Leta Lindley	72	74	74	73	293	15,720
Mi Hyun Kim	68	74	76	75	293	15,720
Hee-Won Han	69	77	71	76	293	15,720
Cristie Kerr	72	74	70	77	293	15,720
Patti Rizzo	76	73	73	72	294	13,080
Dorothy Delasin	70	76	75	73	294	13,080
Kelly Robbins	69	78	72	75	294	13,080
Ara Koh	73	71	74	76	294	13,080
Nanci Bowen	71	80	72	72	295	10,830
Natalie Gulbis	75	72	76	72	295	10,830
Wendy Doolan	76	75	71	73	295	10,830
Dawn Coe-Jones	75	76	70	74	295	10,830
Moira Dunn	70	76	74	75	295	10,830
Kate Golden	67	74	75	79	295	10,830
Heather Bowie	73	75	76	72	296	9,060
Rosie Jones	70	78	74	74	296	9,060
Janice Moodie	72	74	72	78	296	9,060

First Union Betsy King Classic

Berkleigh Country Club, Kutztown, Pennsylvania
Par 35-37–72; 6,278 yards

August 22-25
purse, $1,200,000

		SCORES			TOTAL	MONEY
Se Ri Pak	70	68	66	63	267	$180,000
Angela Stanford	68	70	66	66	270	109,590
Karrie Webb	71	65	67	69	272	79,500
Catriona Matthew	73	69	66	65	273	61,500
Wendy Doolan	67	68	72	67	274	49,500
Joanne Morley	71	66	69	69	275	37,200
Michelle Ellis	67	69	65	74	275	37,200
Beth Bauer	72	66	71	67	276	26,900
Rachel Teske	69	67	72	68	276	26,900
Kelli Kuehne	71	69	67	69	276	26,900
Moira Dunn	68	72	69	68	277	21,750
Kelly Robbins	72	67	65	73	277	21,750

		SCORES			TOTAL	MONEY
Dorothy Delasin	71	70	68	69	278	19,080
Lorena Ochoa	72	68	68	70	278	19,080
Barb Mucha	73	65	71	70	279	16,920
Jackie Gallagher-Smith	70	69	69	71	279	16,920
Yu Ping Lin	69	72	71	68	280	14,920
Jeong Jang	69	70	73	68	280	14,920
Hee-Won Han	72	70	69	69	280	14,920
Michele Redman	73	69	71	68	281	13,080
Kris Tschetter	71	67	72	71	281	13,080
Dina Ammaccapane	71	70	68	72	281	13,080
Carri Wood	67	73	69	72	281	13,080
Smriti Mehra	69	71	72	70	282	11,250
Jung Yeon Lee	71	72	68	71	282	11,250
Vicki Goetze-Ackerman	70	70	70	72	282	11,250
Natalie Gulbis	72	68	68	74	282	11,250
Maggie Will	75	68	71	69	283	8,895
Jill McGill	66	77	71	69	283	8,895
Pat Hurst	70	72	72	69	283	8,895
Michelle McGann	67	72	75	69	283	8,895
Kristi Albers	71	72	70	70	283	8,895
Tammie Green	69	73	70	71	283	8,895
Kim Saiki	70	71	71	71	283	8,895
Giulia Sergas	70	71	71	71	283	8,895

State Farm Classic

Rail Golf Course, Springfield, Illinois
Par 36-36–72; 6,558 yards

August 29-September 1
purse, $1,100,000

		SCORES			TOTAL	MONEY
Patricia Meunier-Lebouc	64	67	72	67	270	$165,000
Se Ri Pak	70	69	68	65	272	86,666
Mi Hyun Kim	67	68	68	69	272	86,666
Laura Davies	73	68	65	67	273	46,291
Beth Bauer	71	70	65	67	273	46,291
Emilee Klein	68	69	67	69	273	46,291
Cristie Kerr	67	69	69	69	274	31,075
Angela Stanford	68	69	68	70	275	27,225
Pat Hurst	71	66	68	71	276	24,475
Karen Stupples	71	70	69	67	277	21,450
Shani Waugh	67	70	67	73	277	21,450
Heather Bowie	74	67	70	67	278	17,545
Catriona Matthew	70	69	68	71	278	17,545
Grace Park	68	69	69	72	278	17,545
Akiko Fukushima	67	67	71	73	278	17,545
Jennifer Rosales	70	70	74	65	279	14,025
Tammie Green	69	72	69	69	279	14,025
Moira Dunn	70	72	67	70	279	14,025
Laura Diaz	66	71	67	75	279	14,025
Danielle Ammaccapane	70	70	70	70	280	11,559
Leta Lindley	70	70	68	72	280	11,559
Kim Saiki	71	65	72	72	280	11,559
Jill McGill	68	69	70	73	280	11,559
Candie Kung	68	69	70	73	280	11,559
Nancy Scranton	67	69	68	76	280	11,559
Penny Hammel	72	70	72	67	281	9,185
Cindy Schreyer	68	74	70	69	281	9,185

	SCORES			TOTAL	MONEY
Joanne Mills	73	68	70 70	281	9,185
Donna Andrews	68	72	71 70	281	9,185
Vicki Goetze-Ackerman	70	67	74 70	281	9,185
Wendy Ward	67	70	72 72	281	9,185

Williams Championship

Tulsa Country Club, Tulsa, Oklahoma
Par 35-35–70; 6,269 yards

September 6-8
purse, $1,000,000

	SCORES			TOTAL	MONEY
Annika Sorenstam	68	66	65	199	$150,000
Lorie Kane	71	64	68	203	91,325
Joanne Mills	69	68	67	204	58,750
Cristie Kerr	65	70	69	204	58,750
Meg Mallon	74	68	64	206	37,500
Beth Bauer	69	68	69	206	37,500
Liselotte Neumann	66	74	67	207	25,083
Moira Dunn	71	68	68	207	25,083
Catriona Matthew	66	70	71	207	25,083
Becky Iverson	70	71	67	208	18,225
Shani Waugh	71	66	71	208	18,225
Pamela Kerrigan	69	68	71	208	18,225
Candie Kung	70	66	72	208	18,225
Emilee Klein	72	72	65	209	13,483
Kim Saiki	71	71	67	209	13,483
Jennifer Rosales	70	71	68	209	13,483
Patricia Meunier-Lebouc	66	74	69	209	13,483
Brandie Burton	70	68	71	209	13,483
Grace Park	66	72	71	209	13,483
Jamie Hullett	72	72	66	210	11,300
Rachel Teske	71	70	69	210	11,300
Diana D'Alessio	71	72	68	211	9,222
Nancy Scranton	72	69	70	211	9,222
Jean Bartholomew	71	70	70	211	9,222
Suzanne Strudwick	70	71	70	211	9,222
Beth Bader	72	68	71	211	9,222
Wendy Doolan	72	68	71	211	9,222
Marilyn Lovander	69	70	72	211	9,222
Kristi Albers	70	68	73	211	9,222
Kris Tschetter	68	69	74	211	9,222

Safeway Classic

Columbia Edgewater Country Club, Portland, Oregon
Par 36-36–72; 6,318 yards

September 13-15
purse, $1,000,000

	SCORES			TOTAL	MONEY
Annika Sorenstam	69	62	68	199	$150,000
Kate Golden	70	65	65	200	91,325
Rosie Jones	67	69	68	204	58,750
Karen Stupples	68	66	70	204	58,750
Michele Redman	69	72	66	207	37,500
Emilee Klein	69	70	68	207	37,500
Akiko Fukushima	70	71	67	208	22,850

	SCORES			TOTAL	MONEY
Donna Andrews	67	73	68	208	22,850
Karrie Webb	67	71	70	208	22,850
Jamie Hullett	69	68	71	208	22,850
Penny Hammel	68	68	72	208	22,850
Michelle Ellis	70	69	70	209	17,500
Leta Lindley	71	71	68	210	14,600
Barb Mucha	72	68	70	210	14,600
Cristie Kerr	73	66	71	210	14,600
Kelly Robbins	68	70	72	210	14,600
Heather Bowie	70	67	73	210	14,600
Sophie Gustafson	73	72	66	211	10,540
Rachel Teske	73	69	69	211	10,540
Beth Bader	72	70	69	211	10,540
Maggie Will	72	69	70	211	10,540
Kim Saiki	72	68	71	211	10,540
Chris Johnson	72	67	72	211	10,540
Dawn Coe-Jones	71	68	72	211	10,540
Joanne Mills	70	69	72	211	10,540
Laura Davies	69	69	73	211	10,540
Beth Bauer	69	69	73	211	10,540
Diana D'Alessio	73	72	67	212	7,708
Grace Park	70	73	69	212	7,708
Becky Iverson	70	71	71	212	7,708
Liselotte Neumann	70	71	71	212	7,708
Patricia Meunier-Lebouc	71	68	73	212	7,708
Juli Inkster	67	71	74	212	7,708

Solheim Cup

Interlachen Country Club, Edina, Minnesota   September 20-22
Par 36-36–72; 6,545 yards

FIRST DAY
Morning Foursomes

Laura Davies and Paula Marti (Europe) defeated Juli Inkster and Laura Diaz (USA), 2 up.
Beth Daniel and Wendy Ward (USA) defeated Iben Tinning and Raquel Carriedo (Europe), 1 up.
Helen Alfredsson and Suzann Pettersen (Europe) defeated Kelly Robbins and Pat Hurst (USA), 4 and 2.
Annika Sorenstam and Carin Koch (Europe) defeated Meg Mallon and Kelli Kuehne (USA), 3 and 2.

TOTAL: United States 1, Europe 3

Afternoon Fourballs

Rosie Jones and Cristie Kerr (USA) defeated Laura Davies and Paula Marti (Europe), 1 up.
Laura Diaz and Emilee Klein (USA) defeated Sophie Gustafson and Karine Icher (Europe), 4 and 3.
Michele Redman and Meg Mallon (USA) defeated Annika Sorenstam and Maria Hjorth (Europe), 2 and 1.
Mhairi McKay and Carin Koch (Europe) defeated Juli Inkster and Kelli Kuehne (USA), 3 and 2.

TOTAL: United States 4, Europe 4

SECOND DAY
Morning Foursomes

Annika Sorenstam and Carin Koch (Europe) defeated Cristie Kerr and Michele Redman (USA), 4 and 3.
Emilee Klein and Wendy Ward (USA) defeated Iben Tinning and Mhairi McKay (Europe), 3 and 2.
Meg Mallon and Juli Inkster (USA) defeated Laura Davies and Paula Marti (Europe), 2 and 1.
Laura Diaz and Kelly Robbins (USA) defeated Helen Alfredsson and Suzann Pettersen (Europe), 3 and 1.

TOTAL: United States 7, Europe 5

Afternoon Fourballs

Annika Sorenstam and Carin Koch (Europe) defeated Beth Daniel and Wendy Ward (USA), 4 and 3.
Maria Hjorth and Iben Tinning (Europe) defeated Pat Hurst and Kelli Kuehne (USA), 1 up.
Karine Icher and Raquel Carriedo (Europe) defeated Rosie Jones and Cristie Kerr (USA), 1 up.
Laura Davies and Sophie Gustafson (Europe) defeated Kelly Robbins and Emilee Klein (USA), 1 up.

TOTAL: United States 7, Europe 9

THIRD DAY
Singles

Juli Inkster (USA) defeated Raquel Carriedo (Europe), 4 and 3.
Laura Diaz (USA) defeated Paula Marti (Europe), 5 and 3.
Emilee Klein (USA) defeated Helen Alfredsson (Europe), 2 and 1.
Iben Tinning (Europe) defeated Kelli Kuehne (USA), 3 and 2.
Michele Redman (USA) halved with Suzann Pettersen (Europe).
Wendy Ward (USA) halved with Annika Sorenstam (Europe).
Kelly Robbins (USA) defeated Maria Hjorth (Europe), 5 and 3.
Sophie Gustafson (Europe) defeated Cristie Kerr (USA), 3 and 2.
Meg Mallon (USA) defeated Laura Davies (Europe), 3 and 2.
Pat Hurst (USA) defeated Mhairi McKay (Europe), 3 and 2.
Beth Daniel (USA) halved with Carin Koch (Europe).
Rosie Jones (USA) defeated Karine Icher (Europe), 3 and 2.

TOTAL: United States 15½, Europe 12½

Samsung World Championship

Hiddenbrooke Golf Club, Vallejo, California
Par 36-36–72; 6,359 yards

October 3-6
purse, $775,000

	SCORES				TOTAL	MONEY
Annika Sorenstam	66	67	68	65	266	$162,000
Cristie Kerr	68	64	69	71	272	97,000
Michele Redman	65	70	70	68	273	71,000
Rosie Jones	68	66	70	71	275	48,500
Se Ri Pak	69	69	67	70	275	48,500
Lorie Kane	70	67	70	70	277	33,000
Rachel Teske	72	73	67	65	277	33,000
Juli Inkster	70	67	70	71	278	26,500

	SCORES				TOTAL	MONEY
Carin Koch	73	67	69	69	278	26,500
Dorothy Delasin	72	72	68	67	279	21,000
Mi Hyun Kim	69	68	71	71	279	21,000
Laura Diaz	68	74	70	69	281	17,550
Paula Marti	69	73	68	71	281	17,550
Grace Park	67	75	70	70	282	16,000
Hee-Won Han	73	68	72	71	284	15,500
Karrie Webb	75	71	68	71	285	15,000
Beth Daniel	75	73	72	68	288	14,500
Kelly Robbins	77	70	72	70	289	14,000
Mi Na Lee	74	72	74	73	293	13,500
Mikino Kubo	73	74	73	77	297	13,000

Mobile Tournament of Champions

Robert Trent Jones Golf Trail, The Crossings,
Semmes, Alabama
Par 36-36–72; 6,253 yards

October 10-13
purse, $750,000

	SCORES				TOTAL	MONEY
Se Ri Pak	65	70	67	66	268	$122,000
Catriona Matthew	68	66	70	68	272	64,875
Carin Koch	62	67	70	73	272	64,875
Wendy Ward	68	68	69	68	273	34,916
Rosie Jones	70	68	66	69	273	34,916
Annika Sorenstam	66	70	67	70	273	34,916
Laura Diaz	71	66	70	67	274	22,825
Emilee Klein	66	68	67	73	274	22,825
Laura Davies	71	68	66	71	276	18,550
Janice Moodie	66	70	69	71	276	18,550
Nancy Scranton	72	68	68	69	277	15,840
Cristie Kerr	70	63	69	75	277	15,840
Michele Redman	67	74	68	69	278	14,345
Meg Mallon	68	69	70	71	278	14,345
Beth Daniel	70	72	70	68	280	13,240
Karrie Webb	68	72	71	70	281	12,246
Charlotta Sorenstam	68	69	72	72	281	12,246
Patricia Meunier-Lebouc	66	72	70	73	281	12,246
Lorie Kane	68	73	69	72	282	11,600
Wendy Doolan	70	70	70	74	284	11,320
Pat Hurst	71	73	66	75	285	10,970
Dorothy Delasin	73	69	67	77	286	10,620
Juli Inkster	73	70	70	74	287	10,100
Rachel Teske	72	70	71	74	287	10,100
Kate Golden	72	70	74	72	288	9,750
Betsy King	69	73	69	78	289	9,500
Grace Park	73	73	71	73	290	9,120
Sophie Gustafson	67	76	74	73	290	9,120
Laurel Kean	74	72	74	71	291	8,770
Heather Daly-Donofrio	71	79	71	74	295	8,530

Sports Today CJ Nine Bridges Classic

The Club at Nine Bridges, Jeju Island, South Korea
Par 36-36–72; 6,306 yards

October 25-27
purse, $1,500,000

	SCORES			TOTAL	MONEY
Se Ri Pak	65	76	72	213	$225,000
Carin Koch	70	76	73	219	139,638
Lorie Kane	70	75	76	221	90,576
Mhairi McKay	70	75	76	221	90,576
Annika Sorenstam	73	73	76	222	58,497
Danielle Ammaccapane	72	74	76	222	58,497
Woo-Soon Ko	73	77	73	223	44,534
Suzanne Strudwick	73	76	75	224	35,475
Rachel Teske	73	76	75	224	35,475
Jill McGill	70	79	75	224	35,475
Leta Lindley	74	76	76	226	26,098
Mi Hyun Kim	70	75	81	226	26,098
Grace Park	73	71	82	226	26,098
Gloria Park	74	77	76	227	22,158
Joanne Morley	71	77	79	227	22,158
Jennifer Rosales	73	77	78	228	19,574
Catriona Matthew	71	77	80	228	19,574
Kim Saiki	72	80	77	229	17,726
Dorothy Delasin	71	81	77	229	17,726
Hee-Won Han	72	78	79	229	17,726
Sherri Steinhauer	79	75	76	230	15,234
Emilee Klein	72	78	80	230	15,234
Il Mi Chung	71	77	82	230	15,234
Jackie Gallagher-Smith	69	76	85	230	15,234
Patricia Meunier-Lebouc	74	76	81	231	13,664
Silvia Cavalleri	71	79	81	231	13,664
Sophie Gustafson	79	78	76	233	12,113
Barb Mucha	75	81	77	233	12,113
Young Kim	74	81	78	233	12,113
Tracy Hanson	74	80	79	233	12,113
Becky Morgan	73	81	79	233	12,113

Cisco World Ladies Match Play

See Japan LPGA Tour section.

Mizuno Classic

See Japan LPGA Tour section.

Hyundai Team Matches

Monarch Beach Golf Links, Dana Point, California
Par 35-35–70; 6,094 yards

November 16-17
purse, $1,200,000

FIRST-ROUND MATCHES

Dottie Pepper and Juli Inkster defeated Laura Diaz and Heather Bowie, 2 and 1.
Lorie Kane and Janice Moodie defeated Beth Bauer and Grace Park, 4 and 3.

THIRD-PLACE MATCH

Diaz and Bowie defeated Bauer and Park, 1 up.
(Diaz and Bowie received $30,000 each; Bauer and Park received $20,000 each.)

CHAMPIONSHIP MATCH

Kane and Moodie defeated Inkster and Pepper, 3 and 2.
(Kane and Moodie received $100,000 each; Inkster and Pepper received $50,000 each.)

ADT Championship

Trump International Golf Club, West Palm Beach, Florida
Par 36-36–72; 6,506 yards

November 21-24
purse, $1,000,000

	SCORES				TOTAL	MONEY
Annika Sorenstam	67	70	70	68	275	$215,000
Rachel Teske	72	66	68	72	278	115,000
Karrie Webb	69	70	68	74	281	86,000
Patricia Meunier-Lebouc	69	71	71	71	282	57,000
Rosie Jones	69	70	73	71	283	46,500
Meg Mallon	67	71	73	72	283	46,500
Se Ri Pak	67	73	77	68	285	33,000
Carin Koch	73	71	70	71	285	33,000
Lorie Kane	69	69	74	74	286	26,500
Grace Park	70	73	73	71	287	24,000
Beth Bauer	70	74	73	71	288	20,250
Kelly Robbins	69	74	70	75	288	20,250
Maria Hjorth	72	76	72	69	289	16,750
Cristie Kerr	74	68	77	70	289	16,750
Catriona Matthew	75	70	73	73	291	14,000
Mhairi McKay	73	72	73	73	291	14,000
Juli Inkster	72	73	72	74	291	14,000
Dorothy Delasin	70	75	72	74	291	14,000
Michele Redman	74	75	72	71	292	12,250
Jennifer Rosales	74	73	76	70	293	11,375
Janice Moodie	80	69	69	75	293	11,375
Laura Diaz	76	70	79	71	296	11,000
Shani Waugh	71	71	83	72	297	10,650
Laura Davies	73	74	82	70	299	10,300
Mi Hyun Kim	74	75	74	77	300	9,666
Michelle Ellis	71	77	74	78	300	9,666
Danielle Ammaccapane	73	74	74	79	300	9,666
Beth Daniel	74	79	76	75	304	8,925
Gloria Park	79	74	74	77	304	8,925
Kelli Kuehne	73	78	82	73	306	8,700

Evian Ladies European Tour

Australasian Ladies Masters

See Australian Women's Tour section.

AAMI Women's Australian Open

See Australian Women's Tour section.

Ladies Tenerife Open

Golf del Sur, Tenerife, Canary Islands
Par 36-36–72; 6,123 yards

May 2-5
purse, €200,000

	SCORES				TOTAL	MONEY
Raquel Carriedo	73	71	77	71	292	€30,000
Johanna Head	72	74	79	68	293	20,300
Marine Monnet	76	72	77	71	296	12,400
Elisabeth Esterl	77	72	72	75	296	12,400
Lynnette Brooky	76	75	74	73	298	8,480
Diana Luna	73	75	79	72	299	5,296
Sophie Sandolo	79	72	76	72	299	5,296
Asa Gottmo	78	73	76	72	299	5,296
Veronica Zorzi	72	73	81	73	299	5,296
Cherie Byrnes	77	74	75	73	299	5,296
Iben Tinning	78	75	78	69	300	3,213.33
Georgina Simpson	74	74	82	70	300	3,213.33
Karine Icher	79	77	73	71	300	3,213.33
Stephanie Arricau	77	76	74	73	300	3,213.33
Valerie Van Ryckeghem	76	77	71	76	300	3,213.33
Ana Belen Sanchez	75	74	72	79	300	3,213.33
Caroline Hall	77	76	77	71	301	2,800
Suzann Pettersen	71	83	77	71	302	2,553.33
Marieke Zelsmann	75	75	84	68	302	2,553.33
Marie Hedberg	76	78	80	68	302	2,553.33
Laurette Maritz	77	76	73	76	302	2,553.33
Lora Fairclough	76	72	77	77	302	2,553.33
Regine Lautens	78	75	72	77	302	2,553.33
Marina Arruti	76	78	77	72	303	2,160
Valerie Michaud	79	76	78	70	303	2,160
Nicola Moult	79	72	78	74	303	2,160
Paula Marti	76	77	81	69	303	2,160
Diane Barnard	77	74	77	75	303	2,160
Kirsty Taylor	77	74	77	75	303	2,160
Samantha Head	78	75	74	76	303	2,160

Ladies Irish Open

Killarney Golf & Fishing Club, County Kerry, Ireland
Par 36-36—72; 6,101 yards

May 10-12
purse, €165,000

	SCORES			TOTAL	MONEY
Iben Tinning	71	70	73	214	€24,750
Suzann Pettersen	71	71	72	214	16,747.50
(Tinning defeated Pettersen on first playoff hole.)					
Maria Boden	75	70	70	215	11,550
Marina Arruti	74	73	70	217	6,657.75
Kirsty Taylor	75	71	71	217	6,657.75
Corinne Dibnah	72	72	73	217	6,657.75
Trish Johnson	71	71	75	217	6,657.75
Pernilla Sterner	75	73	70	218	3,707
Raquel Carriedo	71	75	72	218	3,707
Stephanie Arricau	74	70	74	218	3,707
Nadina Taylor	76	70	73	219	2,843.50
Georgina Simpson	72	73	74	219	2,843.50
Marine Monnet	72	69	78	219	2,843.50
Ludivine Kreutz	72	74	74	220	2,499.75
Laurette Maritz	77	68	75	220	2,499.75
Karine Icher	76	70	75	221	2,247.30
Karolina Andersson	72	73	76	221	2,247.30
Alexandra Armas	76	69	76	221	2,247.30
Cecilie Lundgreen	74	71	76	221	2,247.30
Gina Scott	68	76	77	221	2,247.30
Patricia Sota	76	72	74	222	2,054.25
Ana Larraneta	75	70	77	222	2,054.25
Asa Gottmo	75	76	72	223	1,782
Diane Barnard	76	74	73	223	1,782
Amanda Moltke-Leth	75	75	73	223	1,782
Valerie Michaud	75	74	74	223	1,782
Caroline Hall	77	72	74	223	1,782
Rachel Kirkwood	73	75	75	223	1,782
Ana Belen Sanchez	75	73	75	223	1,782
Sara Jelander	76	71	76	223	1,782
Lesley Nicholson	74	71	78	223	1,782

La Perla Italian Open

Poggio dei Medici Golf Club, Florence, Italy
Par 37-36—73; 6,252 yards

May 16-19
purse, £117,000

	SCORES				TOTAL	MONEY
Iben Tinning	69	69	70	70	278	€28,575
Silvia Cavalleri	68	70	69	72	279	19,335.75
Gina Scott	67	74	73	69	283	13,335
Karen Lunn	77	71	64	72	284	10,287
Samantha Head	74	72	70	69	285	6,819.90
Trish Johnson	73	72	69	71	285	6,819.90
Asa Gottmo	71	70	72	72	285	6,819.90
Nicola Moult	72	69	73	72	286	4,086.22
Cecilie Lundgreen	73	69	71	73	286	4,086.22
Cecilia Ekelundh	69	75	69	73	286	4,086.22
Lora Fairclough	67	72	73	74	286	4,086.22
Kirsty Taylor	75	69	71	72	287	3,171.82
Marine Monnet	71	71	71	74	287	3,171.82

	SCORES				TOTAL	MONEY
Elisabeth Esterl	71	75	71	71	288	2,795.58
Maria Boden	69	72	75	72	288	2,795.58
Raquel Carriedo	73	70	71	74	288	2,795.58
Paula Marti	71	78	65	74	288	2,795.58
Alison Munt	74	75	72	68	289	2,461.26
Marie-Laure de Lorenzi	73	72	72	72	289	2,461.26
Suzann Pettersen	67	76	73	73	289	2,461.26
Riikka Hakkarainen	72	70	73	74	289	2,461.26
Kirsty Taylor	74	72	68	75	289	2,461.26
Alison Nicholas	71	68	79	72	290	2,200.27
Julie Forbes	72	70	76	72	290	2,200.27
Karine Icher	70	72	74	74	290	2,200.27
Georgina Simpson	70	76	70	74	290	2,200.27
Erica Steen	70	74	78	69	291	1,971.67
Lynnette Brooky	72	73	75	71	291	1,971.67
Caroline Hall	74	74	69	74	291	1,971.67
Nicole Stillig	72	72	72	75	291	1,971.67

Ladies Open of Costa Azul

Aroeira Golf Club, Aroeira, Portugal
Par 36-36–72; 6,113 yards

May 25-26
purse, €70,000

	SCORES		TOTAL	MONEY
Kanna Takanashi	69	70	139	€10,500
Julie Forbes	72	68	140	8,000
Lynnette Brooky	71	70	141	5,375
Nicola Moult	71	70	141	5,375
Catherine Knight	71	71	142	3,083.33
Nienke Nijenhuis	70	72	142	3,083.33
Nina Karlsson	69	73	142	3,083.33
Ana Larraneta	72	71	143	1,916.66
Corinne Dibnah	71	72	143	1,916.66
Sachie Yoshida Lavoie	71	72	143	1,916.66
Jehanne Jail	76	68	144	1,320
Cherie Byrnes	72	72	144	1,320
Karen Lunn	72	72	144	1,320
Dale Reid	71	73	144	1,320
Tamara Johns	72	73	145	1,030
Wendy Dicks	72	73	145	1,030
Mette Hageman	70	75	145	1,030
Patricia Sota	75	71	146	867.50
Alison Munt	73	73	146	867.50
Nadina Taylor	73	73	146	867.50
Elisabeth Esterl	72	74	146	867.50
Silvana Kali	76	71	147	757.50
Mandy Adamson	74	73	147	757.50
Marieke Zelsmann	73	74	147	757.50
Milagros Ingaramo	72	75	147	757.50
Marina Arruti	74	74	148	695
Gina Scott	74	74	148	695
Virginie Roques	73	75	148	695
Naima Ghilain	73	75	148	695
Anne-Marie Knight	72	76	148	695
Sara Beautell	72	76	148	695

Caja Duero Open de Espana

Campo de Golf de Salamanca, Salamanca, Spain
Par 36-36–72; 6,201 yards

May 30-June 2
purse,€250,000

	SCORES				TOTAL	MONEY
Karine Icher	69	69	68	71	277	€37,500
Raquel Carriedo	70	68	70	70	278	25,375
Paula Marti	70	72	71	67	280	15,500
Lynnette Brooky	66	73	69	72	280	15,500
Kirsty Taylor	75	69	68	69	281	10,600
Marina Arruti	71	70	69	72	282	7,500
Marine Monnet	74	68	68	72	282	7,500
Sara Beautell	69	71	69	73	282	7,500
Corinne Dibnah	71	67	75	70	283	5,600
Sandrine Mendiburu	73	70	75	66	284	5,000
*Emma Cabrera	68	70	78	69	285	
*Tania Elosegui	68	73	71	73	285	
Nicola Moult	73	72	74	68	287	4,193.75
Asa Gottmo	73	72	70	72	287	4,193.75
Laura Navarro	70	70	74	73	287	4,193.75
Iben Tinning	70	71	71	75	287	4,193.75
Lara Tadiotto	71	76	71	70	288	3,330.55
Elaine Ratcliffe	73	70	74	71	288	3,330.55
Malin Burstrom	69	74	73	72	288	3,330.55
Nadina Taylor	75	72	72	69	288	3,330.55
Ludivine Kreutz	76	70	70	72	288	3,330.55
Trish Johnson	73	71	71	73	288	3,330.55
Cecilia Ekelundh	73	70	71	74	288	3,330.55
Cecilie Lundgreen	73	71	70	74	288	3,330.55
Elisabeth Esterl	72	73	68	75	288	3,330.55
*Carmen Alonso	76	72	69	72	289	
Sara Jelander	74	73	69	73	289	2,775
Ana Belen Sanchez	72	68	74	75	289	2,775
Diane Barnard	72	76	72	69	289	2,775
Anne-Marie Knight	76	69	69	75	289	2,775
Julie Forbes	69	71	71	78	289	2,775

Evian Masters

Evian Masters Golf Club, Evians-les-Bains, France
Par 36-36–72; 6,110 yards

June 12-15
purse, US$2,100,000

	SCORES				TOTAL	MONEY
Annika Sorenstam	68	67	65	69	269	US$315,000
Maria Hjorth	71	68	70	64	273	177,912
Mi Hyun Kim	66	70	68	69	273	177,912
Laura Diaz	68	73	68	65	274	104,440
Se Ri Pak	71	64	70	69	274	104,440
Vicki Goetze-Ackerman	68	71	67	69	275	76,200
Grace Park	68	69	71	70	278	56,650
Karine Icher	68	66	73	71	278	56,650
Leta Lindley	69	66	70	73	278	56,650
Cristie Kerr	70	68	67	74	279	45,730
Lorie Kane	72	73	70	65	280	38,411
Rosie Jones	73	73	67	67	280	38,411
Betsy King	73	68	71	68	280	38,411
Kirsty Taylor	72	70	68	70	280	38,411

	SCORES				TOTAL	MONEY
Dorothy Delasin	70	71	73	67	281	30,259
Gloria Park	68	74	71	68	281	30,259
Yu Ping Lin	71	74	67	69	281	30,259
Kathryn Marshall	69	74	67	71	281	30,259
Hiromi Kobayashi	73	70	69	70	282	25,065
Beth Bauer	71	70	71	70	282	25,065
Jackie Gallagher-Smith	69	71	69	73	282	25,065
Mhairi McKay	67	72	70	73	282	25,065
Wendy Ward	73	68	67	74	282	25,065
Kate Golden	74	72	70	67	283	20,775
Catriona Matthew	71	68	75	69	283	20,775
Jeong Jang	72	71	70	70	283	20,775
Wendy Doolan	72	67	72	72	283	20,775
Carin Koch	67	72	72	72	283	20,775
Lynnette Brooky	71	71	71	71	284	18,404
Hee Won Han	74	72	69	70	285	17,387
Catrin Nilsmark	70	71	73	71	285	17,387

Open de France Dames Credit Mutuel Nord

Le Golf d'Arras, Aubin, France
Par 36-36–72; 5,800 yards

June 20-23
purse, €275,000

	SCORES				TOTAL	MONEY
Lynnette Brooky	69	69	68	66	272	€41,250
Paula Marti	69	71	69	68	277	27,912.50
Karine Icher	70	68	71	70	279	15,253.33
Marine Monnet	72	70	67	70	279	15,253.33
Iben Tinning	72	71	66	70	279	15,253.33
Ana Belen Sanchez	73	69	71	68	281	9,625
Nicola Moult	70	72	71	71	284	7,562.50
Karen Lunn	68	75	70	71	284	7,562.50
Cecilia Ekelundh	75	69	71	70	285	5,573.33
Kirsty Taylor	68	72	74	71	285	5,573.33
Joanne Mills	69	72	70	74	285	5,573.33
Alison Munt	73	70	76	68	287	4,464.16
Corinne Dibnah	74	74	70	69	287	4,464.16
Suzanne O'Brien	73	71	71	72	287	4,464.16
Valerie Michaud	71	75	72	70	288	3,804.16
Nina Karlsson	70	70	77	71	288	3,804.16
Riikka Hakkarainen	72	71	74	71	288	3,804.16
Suzann Pettersen	74	72	71	71	288	3,804.16
Gina Scott	76	70	69	73	288	3,804.16
Nadina Taylor	72	68	71	77	288	3,804.16
Elisabeth Esterl	75	71	72	71	289	3,300
Sachie Yoshida Lavoie	72	72	73	72	289	3,300
Lara Tadiotto	73	73	70	73	289	3,300
Raquel Carriedo	70	68	76	75	289	3,300
Nienke Nijenhuis	72	72	70	75	289	3,300
Trish Johnson	74	71	75	70	290	2,887.50
Lisa Hed	73	75	71	71	290	2,887.50
Samantha Head	72	74	72	72	290	2,887.50
Dale Reid	74	72	70	74	290	2,887.50
Diana Luna	72	72	71	75	290	2,887.50

P4 Norwegian Masters

Oslo Golf Club, Oslo, Norway
Par 36-36–72; 7,351 yards

August 1-4
purse, £220,000

	SCORES				TOTAL	MONEY
Laura Davies	73	69	68	73	283	€52,800
Ana Larraneta	68	69	78	68	283	35,728
(Davies defeated Larraneta on second playoff hole.)						
Marine Monnet	71	72	71	70	284	21,824
Karine Icher	70	70	71	73	284	21,824
Shani Waugh	76	69	74	66	285	13,622.40
Sophie Gustafson	69	73	72	71	285	13,622.40
Kirsty Taylor	68	74	69	75	286	10,560
Liselotte Neumann	71	71	72	73	287	8,342.40
Mia Lojdahl	71	70	71	75	287	8,342.40
Elisabeth Esterl	73	72	74	69	288	5,984
Lora Fairclough	74	71	74	69	288	5,984
Silvia Cavalleri	74	74	71	69	288	5,984
Samantha Head	66	72	78	72	288	5,984
Nina Karlsson	72	71	73	72	288	5,984
Lynnette Brooky	71	73	71	73	288	5,984
Suzann Pettersen	75	74	72	68	289	4,857.60
Nicola Moult	77	71	71	70	289	4,857.60
Sara Eklund	73	73	69	74	289	4,857.60
Riikka Hakkarainen	72	73	69	75	289	4,857.60
Raquel Carriedo	78	70	72	70	290	4,276.80
Sara Beautell	71	73	74	72	290	4,276.80
Mandy Adamson	72	73	73	72	290	4,276.80
Stephanie Arricau	74	74	70	72	290	4,276.80
Caroline Hall	74	75	68	73	290	4,276.80
Alison Munt	73	73	70	74	290	4,276.80
Veronica Zorzi	75	73	73	70	291	3,748.80
Vibeke Stensrud	71	73	75	72	291	3,748.80
Corinne Dibnah	73	72	72	74	291	3,748.80
Marlene Hedblom	71	68	75	77	291	3,748.80
Paula Marti	72	75	75	70	292	3,326.40
Asa Gottmo	71	72	78	71	292	3,326.40
Federica Dassu	71	73	76	72	292	3,326.40
Sophie Sandolo	71	73	74	74	292	3,326.40

Weetabix Women's British Open

Turnberry Golf Club, Ailsa Course, Ayrshire, Scotland
Par 36-36–72; 6,407 yards

August 8-11
purse, €1,580,110

	SCORES				TOTAL	MONEY
Karrie Webb	66	71	70	66	273	€249,007.43
Michelle Ellis	69	70	68	68	275	136,552.46
Paula Marti	69	68	69	69	275	136,552.46
Jeong Jang	73	69	66	69	277	67,975.01
Catrin Nilsmark	70	69	69	69	277	67,975.01
Candie Kung	65	71	71	70	277	67,975.01
Jennifer Rosales	69	70	65	73	277	67,975.01
Meg Mallon	69	71	68	70	278	40,430.24
Beth Bauer	70	67	70	71	278	40,430.24
Carin Koch	68	68	68	74	278	40,430.24
Sophie Gustafson	69	73	69	68	279	31,728.36

	SCORES				TOTAL	MONEY
Se Ri Pak	67	72	69	71	279	31,728.36
Angela Stanford	69	70	69	72	280	26,641.12
Pat Hurst	69	70	69	72	280	26,641.12
Natalie Gulbis	69	70	67	74	280	26,641.12
Beth Daniel	73	68	68	74	283	23,053.27
Tina Barrett	67	70	70	76	283	23,053.27
Fiona Pike	72	73	67	72	284	19,438.64
Jean Bartholomew	71	72	72	69	284	19,438.64
Marine Monnet	71	70	70	73	284	19,438.64
Jane Geddes	71	69	70	74	284	19,438.64
Wendy Doolan	70	69	71	74	284	19,438.64
Rachel Teske	67	74	68	75	284	19,438.64
Suzann Pettersen	72	71	72	70	285	16,466.62
Patricia Meunier-Lebouc	69	71	69	76	285	16,466.62
Dorothy Delasin	70	71	70	75	286	15,047.55
Emilee Klein	68	71	72	75	286	15,047.55
Elisabeth Esterl	67	71	72	76	286	15,047.55
Yu Ping Lin	73	69	74	71	287	12,771.67
Kelli Kuehne	75	67	71	74	287	12,771.67
Cristie Kerr	72	71	69	75	287	12,771.67
Brandie Burton	71	70	71	75	287	12,771.67
Iben Tinning	71	69	71	76	287	12,771.67

Compaq Open

Vasatorps Golf Club, Helsingborg, Sweden
Par 36-36–72; 6,364 yards

August 15-18
purse, €537,555

	SCORES				TOTAL	MONEY
Annika Sorenstam	67	66	68	70	271	€77,122.50
Sophie Gustafson	67	70	72	66	275	52,186.23
Ana Belen Sanchez	70	72	68	68	278	35,990.50
Mhairi McKay	71	74	65	69	279	24,782.03
Johanna Head	68	70	70	71	279	24,782.03
Nadina Taylor	70	68	74	70	282	17,995.25
Laura Davies	70	71	66	76	283	15,424.50
Suzann Pettersen	71	68	74	71	284	11,028.51
Catrin Nilsmark	70	71	71	72	284	11,028.51
Sara Beautell	72	72	68	72	284	11,028.51
Elisabeth Esterl	71	67	72	74	284	11,028.51
Asa Gottmo	70	73	73	69	285	7,756.32
Liselotte Neumann	69	71	75	70	285	7,756.32
Marine Monnet	72	71	71	71	285	7,756.32
Raquel Carriedo	72	72	70	71	285	7,756.32
Diana Luna	72	70	71	72	285	7,756.32
Kathryn Marshall	73	71	69	72	285	7,756.32
Carin Koch	70	77	66	72	285	7,756.32
Paula Marti	69	74	72	71	286	6,632.53
Corinne Dibnah	71	71	72	72	286	6,632.53
Cecilia Ekelundh	73	69	68	76	286	6,632.53
Joanne Mills	70	71	75	71	287	6,169.80
Federica Dassu	72	74	70	71	287	6,169.80
Lynnette Brooky	73	73	69	72	287	6,169.80
Jane Leary	69	74	74	71	288	5,552.82
Marieke Zelsmann	69	73	74	72	288	5,552.82
*Mikaela Parmlid	75	69	72	72	288	
Nicole Stillig	71	71	73	73	288	5,552.82

	SCORES				TOTAL	MONEY
Marlene Hedblom	73	72	70	73	288	5,552.82
Alison Munt	72	73	69	74	288	5,552.82

Wales WPGA Championship of Europe

Royal Porthcawl Golf Club, Bridgend, Wales
Par 36-37–73; 6,183 yards

August 22-25
purse, €661,600

	SCORES				TOTAL	MONEY
Asa Gottmo	76	69	69	71	285	€94,740
Maria Hjorth	74	73	68	72	287	64,107.40
Kirsty Taylor	75	72	70	71	288	44,212
Helen Alfredsson	72	77	71	69	289	30,442.12
Nicola Moult	78	73	68	70	289	30,442.12
Claire Duffy	67	76	76	71	290	17,747.96
Becky Morgan	73	72	72	73	290	17,747.96
Virginie Auffret	71	72	73	74	290	17,747.96
Johanna Head	72	68	71	79	290	17,747.96
Iben Tinning	70	69	78	74	291	11,705.65
Laura Davies	74	72	71	74	291	11,705.65
Elisabeth Esterl	78	68	70	75	291	11,705.65
Caroline Hall	71	71	77	73	292	9,947.70
Shani Waugh	69	73	74	76	292	9,947.70
Marine Monnet	77	73	74	69	293	8,518.70
Loraine Lambert	75	73	75	70	293	8,518.70
Joanne Mills	71	78	72	72	293	8,518.70
Paula Marti	73	72	75	73	293	8,518.70
Alison Nicholas	72	74	74	73	293	8,518.70
Nina Karlsson	73	74	73	73	293	8,518.70
Corinne Dibnah	73	78	69	73	293	8,518.70
Natascha Fink	72	70	75	76	293	8,518.70
Suzann Pettersen	68	75	79	72	294	7,294.98
Lynnette Brooky	77	70	73	74	294	7,294.98
Alison Munt	75	72	73	74	294	7,294.98
Veronica Zorzi	74	73	73	74	294	7,294.98
Raquel Carriedo	71	74	76	74	295	6,726.54
Marieke Zelsmann	80	69	71	75	295	6,726.54
Gina Scott	72	79	74	72	297	6,158.10
Ana Belen Sanchez	69	74	81	73	297	6,158.10
Sophie Sandolo	76	70	78	73	297	6,158.10
Lora Fairclough	73	77	74	73	297	6,158.10

Solheim Cup

See U.S. LPGA Tour section.

Biarritz Ladies Classic

Biarritz Le Phare Golf Club, Biarritz, France
Par 35-35–70; 5,688 yards

October 3-5
purse, €165,000

	SCORES			TOTAL	MONEY
Sophie Gustafson	69	67	64	200	€24,750
Mhairi McKay	67	67	66	200	16,747.50
(Gustafson defeated McKay on first playoff hole.)					
Riikka Hakkarainen	67	65	69	201	10,230
Helen Alfredsson	65	65	71	201	10,230
Laurette Maritz	69	68	67	204	6,996
*Virginie Beauchet	68	68	68	204	
Joanne Morley	69	70	66	205	4,950
Silvia Cavalleri	70	68	67	205	4,950
Corinne Dibnah	67	70	68	205	4,950
Johanna Head	68	71	67	206	3,217.50
Cecilia Ekelundh	70	68	68	206	3,217.50
Samantha Head	70	66	70	206	3,217.50
Nicola Moult	67	68	71	206	3,217.50
Marine Monnet	69	70	68	207	2,598.75
Vibeke Stensrud	67	71	69	207	2,598.75
Virginie Auffret	72	68	68	208	2,458.50
Alison Munt	69	72	68	209	2,247.30
Nicole Stillig	70	70	69	209	2,247.30
Diana Luna	70	70	69	209	2,247.30
Suzann Pettersen	70	68	71	209	2,247.30
Sara Eklund	66	72	71	209	2,247.30
Diane Barnard	70	73	67	210	1,980
Suzanne O'Brien	69	74	67	210	1,980
Karen Lunn	69	73	68	210	1,980
Lisa Hed	70	71	69	210	1,980
Johanna Westerberg	65	72	73	210	1,980
Shani Waugh	73	70	68	211	1,782
Ana Larraneta	71	72	68	211	1,782
Karen Margrethe Juul	68	71	72	211	1,782
Cecilia Sjoblom	71	71	70	212	1,608.75
Jessica Lindbergh	72	69	71	212	1,608.75
Wendy Dicks	70	71	71	212	1,608.75
Lara Tadiotto	67	70	75	212	1,608.75

Japan LPGA Tour

Daikin Orchid Ladies

Ryukyu Golf Club, Tamagusuku, Okinawa
Par 36-36–72; 6,270 yards

March 8-10
purse, ¥60,000,000

	SCORES			TOTAL	MONEY
Kasumi Fujii	68	68	72	208	¥10,800,000
Junko Omote	70	70	69	209	4,740,000
Mikino Kubo	68	69	72	209	4,740,000
Ji-Hee Lee	72	72	66	210	3,300,000
Aki Takamura	77	66	67	210	3,300,000
Kaori Higo	75	69	67	211	2,100,000
Norimi Terasawa	73	70	68	211	2,100,000
Yuri Fudoh	71	71	69	211	2,100,000
Ok-Hee Ku	72	70	70	212	1,159,200
Natsuko Noro	71	70	71	212	1,159,200
Michie Ohba	70	69	73	212	1,159,200
Riko Higashio	70	69	73	212	1,159,200
Hiromi Kobayashi	70	69	73	212	1,159,200
Orie Fujino	71	72	70	213	852,000
Oh-Soon Lee	73	68	72	213	852,000
Mihoko Takahashi	70	69	74	213	852,000
Rie Murata	72	72	70	214	582,000
Chikayo Yamazaki	71	74	69	214	582,000
Toshimi Kimura	67	76	71	214	582,000
Shiho Ohyama	71	71	72	214	582,000
Kayo Fukumoto	70	71	73	214	582,000
Fuki Kido	72	69	73	214	582,000
Kozue Azuma	67	73	74	214	582,000
Masaki Maeda	69	71	74	214	582,000
Yun-Jye Wei	76	70	69	215	486,000
Miho Koga	68	74	73	215	486,000
Hsiao-Chuan Lu	73	72	71	216	450,000
Man-Soo Kim	73	70	73	216	450,000
Mitsuko Kawasaki	73	70	73	216	450,000
Hisako Ohgane	69	78	69	216	450,000

Promise Ladies

Tomisato Golf Club, Shibayama, Chiba
Par 36-36–72; 6,225 yards

April 12-14
purse, ¥60,000,000

	SCORES			TOTAL	MONEY
Mayumi Inoue	69	71	71	211	¥10,800,000
Michiko Hattori	72	69	71	212	5,280,000
Kaori Higo	70	71	73	214	3,600,000
Hsiu-Feng Tseng	72	69	73	214	3,600,000
Yu-Chen Huang	72	69	73	214	3,600,000
Mayumi Murai	72	73	70	215	2,250,000
Ji-Hee Lee	73	68	74	215	2,250,000
Nayoko Yoshikawa	73	69	74	216	1,650,000
Yuri Fudoh	72	73	71	216	1,650,000

	SCORES			TOTAL	MONEY
Midori Yoneyama	73	73	71	217	1,108,000
Michie Ohba	72	73	72	217	1,108,000
Yuri Kawanami	70	73	74	217	1,108,000
Chieko Amanuma	76	72	70	218	882,000
Keiko Arai	73	72	73	218	882,000
Nahoko Hirao	74	71	73	218	882,000
Woo-Soon Ko	73	71	74	218	882,000
Ai Ogawa	73	76	70	219	572,000
Hikaru Kobayashi	75	74	70	219	572,000
Yun-Jye Wei	76	72	71	219	572,000
Norimi Terasawa	76	71	72	219	572,000
Hisako Ohgane	70	76	73	219	572,000
Kozue Azuma	73	73	73	219	572,000
Kayo Yamada	71	73	75	219	572,000
Mayumi Ishii	71	72	76	219	572,000
Kuniko Maeda	73	70	76	219	572,000
Chihiro Nakajima	72	75	73	220	456,000
Yuko Motoyama	76	71	73	220	456,000
Oh-Soon Lee	72	73	75	220	456,000
Rie Murata	70	73	77	220	456,000
Hiroko Yamaguchi	71	72	77	220	456,000

Saishunkan Ladies Hinokuni Open

Kumamoto Kuukou Country Club, Kikuyo, Kumamoto   April 19-21
Par 36-36–72; 6,433 yards   purse, ¥60,000,000

	SCORES			TOTAL	MONEY
Ai-Yu Tu	75	71	69	215	¥10,800,000
Mikino Kubo	74	72	70	216	4,360,000
Kyoko Ono	72	72	72	216	4,360,000
Shiho Ohyama	73	71	72	216	4,360,000
Kaori Harada	75	73	69	217	2,160,000
Akiko Fukushima	78	69	70	217	2,160,000
Kasumi Fujii	72	74	71	217	2,160,000
Kaori Higo	73	73	71	217	2,160,000
Ok-Hee Ku	73	72	72	217	2,160,000
Yuri Fudoh	75	73	70	218	1,120,000
Junko Yasui	74	74	70	218	1,120,000
Fuki Kido	73	73	72	218	1,120,000
Miho Koga	74	74	71	219	900,000
Mayumi Inoue	75	73	71	219	900,000
Shoko Asano	73	73	73	219	900,000
Yoko Tsuchiya	74	72	73	219	900,000
Momoyo Yamazaki	75	73	72	220	564,000
Mikiyo Nishizuka	74	74	72	220	564,000
Kayo Yamada	76	72	72	220	564,000
Young-Me Lee	73	72	75	220	564,000
Hikaru Kobayashi	72	75	73	220	564,000
Kayo Fukumoto	74	73	73	220	564,000
Yukiyo Haga	76	71	73	220	564,000
Kozue Azuma	75	71	74	220	564,000
Ji-Hee Lee	75	73	72	220	564,000
Hisako Ohgane	75	70	75	220	564,000
Ayako Okamoto	71	73	76	220	564,000
Chieko Amanuma	73	71	76	220	564,000
Toshimi Kimura	74	74	73	221	438,000

	SCORES	TOTAL	MONEY
Mitsuko Kawasaki	74 74 73	221	438,000
Eika Ohtake	72 76 73	221	438,000
Yu-Chen Huang	73 74 74	221	438,000
Kyoko Namikawa	75 72 74	221	438,000

Katokichi Queens

Yashima Country Club, Mure, Kagawa
Par 36-36–72; 6,160 yards

May 3-5
purse, ¥60,000,000

	SCORES	TOTAL	MONEY
Chieko Nishida	73 71 71	215	¥10,800,000
Orie Fujino	70 70 76	216	5,280,000
Rena Yamazaki	73 73 71	217	3,600,000
Mineko Nasu	75 71 71	217	3,600,000
Mikiyo Nishizuka	77 68 72	217	3,600,000
Eriko Moriyama	74 72 72	218	2,100,000
Kayo Yamada	75 71 72	218	2,100,000
Rie Murata	73 72 73	218	2,100,000
Nayoko Yoshikawa	73 71 75	219	1,188,000
Yuri Fudoh	75 74 70	219	1,188,000
Mikino Kubo	75 73 71	219	1,188,000
Kaori Harada	72 72 75	219	1,188,000
Kaori Higo	74 70 75	219	1,188,000
Bie-Shyun Huang	71 77 72	220	810,000
Junko Omote	72 76 72	220	810,000
Ayako Okamoto	74 73 73	220	810,000
Mihoko Takahashi	75 72 73	220	810,000
Ok-Hee Ku	76 70 74	220	810,000
Michiko Hattori	74 68 78	220	810,000
Mayumi Hirase	71 78 72	221	570,000
Kumiko Hiyoshi	74 73 74	221	570,000
Kasumi Fujii	75 75 71	221	570,000
Yuka Tonsho	71 75 75	221	570,000
Nahoko Hirao	74 72 75	221	570,000
Kozue Azuma	73 72 76	221	570,000
Young-Me Lee	75 74 73	222	504,000
Hiroko Yamaguchi	71 76 75	222	504,000
Midori Yoneyama	79 71 72	222	504,000
Emi Hyodoh	74 72 76	222	504,000
Chieko Amanuma	75 70 77	222	504,000

Nichirei Cup World Ladies

Yomiuri Country Club, Tokyo
Par 36-36–72; 6,424 yards

May 9-12
purse, ¥60,000,000

	SCORES	TOTAL	MONEY
Yuri Fudoh	65 69 70 67	271	¥10,800,000
Karrie Webb	69 70 65 70	274	5,280,000
Chieko Amanuma	71 69 68 70	278	4,200,000
Rie Murata	71 68 69 72	280	3,600,000
Midori Yoneyama	71 70 70 72	283	3,000,000
Woo-Soon Ko	69 74 72 69	284	2,400,000
Chikako Matsuzawa	70 69 74 72	285	1,800,000

	SCORES				TOTAL	MONEY
Mikiyo Nishizuka	69	71	73	72	285	1,800,000
Mineko Nasu	67	75	71	72	285	1,800,000
Hsiao-Chuan Lu	73	74	72	67	286	1,158,000
Laura Davies	74	72	68	72	286	1,158,000
Mikino Kubo	72	75	73	67	287	1,026,000
Ok-Hee Ku	71	74	69	73	287	1,026,000
Ikuyo Shiotani	70	71	73	74	288	906,000
Mayumi Hirase	70	74	70	74	288	906,000
Kayo Yamada	69	76	75	69	289	726,000
Yu-Chen Huang	74	72	72	71	289	726,000
Kaori Suzuki	71	71	74	73	289	726,000
Michie Ohba	72	72	71	74	289	726,000
Yuri Kawanami	70	73	77	70	290	564,000
Kyoko Ono	69	73	73	75	290	564,000
Toshimi Kimura	67	72	75	76	290	564,000
Hiroko Yamaguchi	70	76	72	73	291	540,000
Ji-Hyun Suh	69	72	77	74	292	516,000
Miyuki Shimabukuro	74	71	73	74	292	516,000
Ayako Okamoto	72	72	73	75	292	516,000
Rie Fujiwara	72	71	77	73	293	474,000
Yun-Jye Wei	74	73	73	73	293	474,000
Yuka Shiroto	71	71	78	73	293	474,000
Hisako Ohgane	69	77	73	74	293	474,000

Vernal Ladies

Fukuoka Century Golf Club, Amagi, Fukuoka
Par 36-36–72; 6,476 yards

May 17-19
purse, ¥100,000,000

	SCORES			TOTAL	MONEY
Mikino Kubo	71	67	75	213	¥18,000,000
Toshimi Kimura	74	72	67	213	7,900,000
Rena Yamazaki	71	70	72	213	7,900,000
(Kubo defeated Yamazaki on first and Kimura on seventh playoff hole.)					
Yuri Fudoh	70	74	70	214	5,500,000
Ikuyo Shiotani	74	68	72	214	5,500,000
Yun-Jye Wei	72	66	77	215	4,000,000
Mihoko Takahashi	71	76	69	216	2,750,000
Fuki Kido	78	69	69	216	2,750,000
Kasumi Fujii	73	69	74	216	2,750,000
Kumiko Hiyoshi	67	72	77	216	2,750,000
Yu-Chen Huang	76	74	67	217	1,900,000
Michie Ohba	74	74	71	219	1,600,000
Kyoko Ono	74	73	72	219	1,600,000
Ayako Okamoto	72	74	73	219	1,600,000
Kozue Azuma	73	71	75	219	1,600,000
Riko Higashio	68	75	76	219	1,600,000
Chieko Amanuma	71	75	74	220	1,250,000
Young-Me Lee	74	76	70	220	1,250,000
Atsuko Ueno	75	73	73	221	983,333
Rie Murata	75	73	73	221	983,333
Midori Yoneyama	73	74	74	221	983,333
Rie Mitsuhashi	73	73	75	221	983,333
Hikaru Kobayashi	73	73	75	221	983,333
Shiho Ohyama	74	71	76	221	983,333
Mayumi Hirase	77	71	74	222	870,000
Kaori Harada	73	76	73	222	870,000

	SCORES			TOTAL	MONEY
Hiroko Yamaguchi	75	75	72	222	870,000
Yuri Kawanami	70	73	79	222	870,000
Woo-Soon Ko	73	75	75	223	750,000
Ok-Hee Ku	75	74	74	223	750,000
Hiroko Fujishima	72	75	76	223	750,000
Fumiko Muraguchi	76	74	73	223	750,000
Junko Omote	71	75	77	223	750,000
Kayo Yamada	73	73	77	223	750,000
Yuka Shiroto	71	79	73	223	750,000
Mayumi Murai	74	70	79	223	750,000

Chukyo TV Bridgestone Ladies

Chukyo Golf Club, Toyota, Aichi
Par 36-36–72; 6,354 yards

May 24-26
purse, ¥50,000,000

	SCORES			TOTAL	MONEY
Shin Sora	73	72	67	212	¥9,000,000
Mikino Kubo	71	71	71	213	4,400,000
Shiho Ohyama	71	70	73	214	3,500,000
Ae-Sook Kim	78	69	69	216	3,000,000
Hsiu-Feng Tseng	73	73	71	217	1,800,000
Hiroko Yamaguchi	75	71	71	217	1,800,000
Orie Fujino	76	70	71	217	1,800,000
Kaori Harada	72	73	72	217	1,800,000
Mayumi Hirase	77	68	72	217	1,800,000
Kyoko Ono	74	71	73	218	955,000
Toshimi Kimura	74	70	74	218	955,000
Aki Takamura	77	73	69	219	860,000
Mitsuko Kawasaki	79	72	69	220	785,000
Hsiao-Chuan Lu	71	74	75	220	785,000
Mihoko Takahashi	75	75	71	221	585,000
Chieko Nishida	76	73	72	221	585,000
Michie Ohba	77	72	72	221	585,000
Yukiyo Haga	71	75	75	221	585,000
Kasumi Fujii	75	71	75	221	585,000
Woo-Soon Ko	76	67	78	221	585,000
Jeanne Kei	77	74	71	222	440,000
Bie-Shyun Huang	78	71	73	222	440,000
Kasumi Adachi	74	74	74	222	440,000
Yun-Jye Wei	77	74	72	223	410,000
Kyoko Namikawa	77	71	75	223	410,000
Yuko Motoyama	75	76	72	223	410,000
Harumi Sakagami	75	75	74	224	365,000
Junko Omote	76	73	75	224	365,000
Kumi Yamashita	71	77	76	224	365,000
Natsuko Noro	75	73	76	224	365,000
Mei-Chi Cheng	78	70	76	224	365,000
Midori Yoneyama	74	73	77	224	365,000

Kosaido Ladies Golf Cup

Chiba Kosaido Country Club, Ichihara, Chiba
Par 36-36–72; 6,260 yards

May 31-June 2
purse, ¥60,000,000

	SCORES			TOTAL	MONEY
Orie Fujino	76	70	66	212	¥10,800,000
Toshimi Kimura	67	68	77	212	5,280,000
(Fujino defeated Kimura on second playoff hole.)					
Mihoko Takahashi	72	73	69	214	3,900,000
Michiko Hattori	72	67	75	214	3,900,000
Fumiko Muraguchi	75	70	70	215	2,500,000
Yuri Fudoh	75	70	70	215	2,500,000
Natsuko Noro	72	72	71	215	2,500,000
Yun-Jye Wei	75	72	69	216	1,408,500
Atsuko Ueno	72	74	70	216	1,408,500
Ae-Sook Kim	74	69	73	216	1,408,500
Shin Sora	72	70	74	216	1,408,500
Yuko Motoyama	75	73	69	217	924,000
Hsiu-Feng Tseng	72	74	71	217	924,000
Kasumi Fujii	76	69	72	217	924,000
Junko Yasui	75	69	73	217	924,000
Yasuko Satoh	72	71	74	217	924,000
Kaori Suzuki	74	69	74	217	924,000
Yuka Shiroto	75	74	69	218	594,000
Woo-Soon Ko	78	69	71	218	594,000
Kasumi Adachi	76	71	71	218	594,000
Riko Higashio	73	73	72	218	594,000
Yu-Chen Huang	77	69	72	218	594,000
Mikiyo Nishizuka	77	68	73	218	594,000
Jae-Sook Won	73	71	74	218	594,000
Rie Mitsuhashi	73	70	75	218	594,000
Harumi Sakagami	74	74	71	219	480,000
Young-Me Lee	75	73	71	219	480,000
Kyoko Ono	74	73	72	219	480,000
Chieko Amanuma	74	73	72	219	480,000
Mikino Kubo	75	72	72	219	480,000
Chihiro Nakajima	71	75	73	219	480,000
Momoyo Yamazaki	75	71	73	219	480,000
Kyoko Isoda	73	71	75	219	480,000

Resort Trust Ladies

Grandee Naruto Golf Club, Naruto, Tokushima
Par 36-36–72; 6,514 yards

June 7-9
purse, ¥50,000,000

	SCORES			TOTAL	MONEY
Kozue Azuma	70	71	72	213	¥9,000,000
Michie Ohba	71	70	72	213	4,400,000
(Azuma defeated Ohba on first playoff hole.)					
Kaori Harada	69	72	73	214	3,000,000
Toshimi Kimura	73	68	73	214	3,000,000
Mikino Kubo	70	70	74	214	3,000,000
Yu-Chen Huang	71	71	73	215	2,000,000
Mei-Chi Cheng	74	72	71	217	1,500,000
Aki Takamura	68	74	75	217	1,500,000
Rie Murata	71	71	75	217	1,500,000
Mitsuko Kawasaki	73	73	72	218	925,000

	SCORES			TOTAL	MONEY
Chihiro Nakajima	74	72	72	218	925,000
Yuri Fudoh	72	72	74	218	925,000
Kayo Yamada	70	73	75	218	925,000
Man-Soo Kim	74	75	70	219	700,000
Natsuko Noro	75	73	71	219	700,000
Young-Me Lee	72	75	72	219	700,000
Yuka Shiroto	74	73	72	219	700,000
Hsiao-Chuan Lu	75	71	73	219	700,000
Kaori Higo	76	73	71	220	505,000
Junko Omote	75	74	71	220	505,000
Shiho Ohyama	74	73	73	220	505,000
Midori Yoneyama	75	72	73	220	505,000
Kyoko Ono	74	74	73	221	445,000
Masaki Maeda	74	73	74	221	445,000
Kuniko Maeda	75	72	74	221	445,000
Junko Yasui	72	74	75	221	445,000
Momoyo Yamazaki	73	73	75	221	445,000
Mari Nishi	74	70	77	221	445,000
Rie Mitsuhashi	75	73	74	222	390,000
Takayo Bandoh	76	71	75	222	390,000
Chieko Amanuma	75	72	75	222	390,000
Yuriko Ohtsuka	73	73	76	222	390,000
Michiko Hattori	72	73	77	222	390,000

We Love Kobe Suntory Ladies Open

Japan Memorial Golf Club, Yokawa, Hyogo
Par 36-36–72; 6,488 yards

June 13-16
purse, ¥60,000,000

	SCORES				TOTAL	MONEY
Takayo Bandoh	70	69	74	67	280	¥10,800,000
Hiroko Yamaguchi	69	69	69	73	280	5,280,000
(Bandoh defeated Yamaguchi on first playoff hole.)						
Hisako Takeda	72	70	73	67	282	3,600,000
Orie Fujino	72	69	72	69	282	3,600,000
Mihoko Takahashi	70	73	69	70	282	3,600,000
*Ai Miyazato	71	71	67	73	282	
Fuki Kido	69	70	72	72	283	2,400,000
Kayo Yamada	71	73	71	69	284	1,800,000
Misayo Fujisawa	71	69	74	70	284	1,800,000
Eriko Moriyama	69	72	71	72	284	1,800,000
Shiho Ohyama	73	71	72	69	285	1,074,000
Kasumi Fujii	71	73	72	69	285	1,074,000
Yoko Yamagishi	69	75	69	72	285	1,074,000
Yu-Chen Huang	66	67	77	75	285	1,074,000
Harumi Sakagami	72	74	75	65	286	792,000
Kaori Higo	70	73	73	70	286	792,000
Mikino Kubo	66	73	75	72	286	792,000
Toshimi Kimura	69	69	74	74	286	792,000
Woo-Soon Ko	70	68	73	75	286	792,000
Kaori Yamamoto	70	71	75	71	287	582,000
Kumiko Hiyoshi	72	72	71	72	287	582,000
Miyuki Shimabukuro	69	75	74	70	288	504,000
Riyo Fukuroi	70	72	75	71	288	504,000
Mie Nakata	73	69	75	71	288	504,000
Norimi Terasawa	69	75	73	71	288	504,000
Michie Ohba	66	72	77	73	288	504,000

	SCORES			TOTAL	MONEY
Yoko Inoue	68	71	74	75	288	504,000
Yuri Fudoh	69	70	74	75	288	504,000
Kuniko Maeda	72	72	75	70	289	444,000
Hsiu-Feng Tseng	71	73	74	71	289	444,000
Nayoko Yoshikawa	71	70	72	76	289	444,000

Apita Circle K Sankus Ladies

U Green Golf Club, Nakatsugawa, Gifu
Par 36-36–72; 6,361 yards

June 21-23
purse, ¥50,000,000

	SCORES			TOTAL	MONEY
Mihoko Takahashi	70	71	68	209	¥9,000,000
Takayo Bandoh	68	71	71	210	4,400,000
Miyuki Shimabukuro	74	69	68	211	3,500,000
Kasumi Fujii	70	71	71	212	2,750,000
Midori Yoneyama	70	70	72	212	2,750,000
Mitsuko Kawasaki	73	71	69	213	1,875,000
Mikiyo Nishizuka	74	70	69	213	1,875,000
Mikino Kubo	74	68	72	214	1,375,000
Kaori Yamamoto	69	72	73	214	1,375,000
Kaori Harada	73	69	73	215	1,000,000
Woo-Soon Ko	76	71	70	217	835,000
Yu-Chen Huang	73	73	71	217	835,000
Hisako Ohgane	76	69	72	217	835,000
Toshimi Kimura	72	72	73	217	835,000
Yuri Fudoh	76	71	71	218	660,000
Michie Ohba	73	75	70	218	660,000
Rie Murata	69	71	78	218	660,000
Masaki Maeda	76	70	73	219	475,000
Kayo Yamada	74	74	71	219	475,000
Yuriko Ohtsuka	73	71	75	219	475,000
Shoko Asano	73	71	75	219	475,000
Rena Yamazaki	72	76	71	219	475,000
Nobuko Kizawa	74	69	76	219	475,000
Junko Yasui	71	75	74	220	400,000
Norimi Terasawa	74	73	73	220	400,000
Kaori Suzuki	73	72	75	220	400,000
Chieko Amanuma	76	72	72	220	400,000
Yun-Jye Wei	71	77	72	220	400,000
Kyoko Ono	74	73	74	221	350,000
Ok-Hee Ku	75	72	74	221	350,000
Fuki Kido	76	71	74	221	350,000
Aki Nakano	74	72	75	221	350,000
Mizue Igarashi	74	72	75	221	350,000

Belluna Ladies Cup

Obatago Golf Club, Kanra, Gunma
Par 36-36–72; 6,339 yards

July 5-7
purse, ¥60,000,000

	SCORES			TOTAL	MONEY
Orie Fujino	71	66	69	206	¥10,800,000
Hsiu-Feng Tseng	70	68	70	208	5,280,000
Natsuko Noro	67	71	71	209	4,200,000

	SCORES			TOTAL	MONEY
Young-Me Lee	71	72	67	210	3,000,000
Takayo Bandoh	68	71	71	210	3,000,000
Yu-Chen Huang	71	67	72	210	3,000,000
Mayumi Ishii	71	71	69	211	1,350,000
Yasuko Satoh	72	70	69	211	1,350,000
Chihiro Nakajima	71	70	70	211	1,350,000
Yuriko Ohtsuka	68	72	71	211	1,350,000
Rena Yamazaki	69	71	71	211	1,350,000
Kaori Harada	73	67	71	211	1,350,000
Yun-Jye Wei	72	68	71	211	1,350,000
Midori Yoneyama	69	70	72	211	1,350,000
Mitsuko Kawasaki	73	70	69	212	780,000
Eika Ohtake	72	71	69	212	780,000
Mikino Kubo	72	70	70	212	780,000
Jae-Sook Won	73	67	72	212	780,000
Atsuko Ueno	69	70	73	212	780,000
Mayumi Itagaki	69	73	71	213	582,000
Misako Toba	69	73	71	213	582,000
Mikiyo Nishizuka	74	68	71	213	582,000
Yoko Yamagishi	73	67	73	213	582,000
Yuri Kawanami	73	71	70	214	516,000
Junko Omote	70	73	71	214	516,000
Masaki Maeda	70	73	71	214	516,000
Riko Higashio	73	70	71	214	516,000
Toshimi Kimura	71	71	72	214	516,000
Eriko Moriyama	71	69	74	214	516,000
Hsiao-Chuan Lu	66	73	75	214	516,000

Toyo Suisan Ladies Hokkaido

Sapporo Kitahiroshima Prince Golf Course, Hokkaido   July 12-14
Par 36-36–72; 6,405 yards   purse, ¥50,000,000

	SCORES			TOTAL	MONEY
Chihiro Nakajima	68	70	70	208	¥9,000,000
Ok-Hee Ku	67	74	67	208	4,400,000
(Nakajima defeated Ku on first playoff hole.)					
Kasumi Fujii	67	75	69	211	3,250,000
Mihoko Takahashi	71	69	71	211	3,250,000
Ji-Hee Lee	72	72	68	212	2,500,000
Mikino Kubo	71	73	69	213	1,875,000
Young-Me Lee	71	70	72	213	1,875,000
Yun-Jye Wei	72	72	70	214	1,375,000
Orie Fujino	68	73	73	214	1,375,000
Michie Ohba	71	75	70	216	888,000
Woo-Soon Ko	70	75	71	216	888,000
Rie Fujiwara	69	75	72	216	888,000
Junko Omote	69	73	74	216	888,000
Yuka Shiroto	72	70	74	216	888,000
Kyoko Isoda	73	73	71	217	685,000
Aki Takamura	68	77	72	217	685,000
Masaki Maeda	68	75	74	217	685,000
Eika Ohtake	70	74	74	218	585,000
Junko Yasui	72	75	72	219	490,000
Man-Soo Kim	73	73	73	219	490,000
Akane Ohshiro	73	73	73	219	490,000
Mikiyo Nishizuka	69	74	76	219	490,000

	SCORES			TOTAL	MONEY
Momoyo Kawakubo	73	75	72	220	435,000
Yuri Kawanami	73	73	74	220	435,000
Mie Nakata	72	73	75	220	435,000
Kayo Yamada	74	70	76	220	435,000
Chie Yoshida	72	71	77	220	435,000
Shiho Ohyama	69	80	72	221	380,000
Yoko Yamagishi	73	75	73	221	380,000
Toshimi Kimura	72	75	74	221	380,000
Natsuko Noro	73	74	74	221	380,000
Hiroko Yamaguchi	71	74	76	221	380,000
Yuriko Ohtsuka	73	71	77	221	380,000

Golf 5 Ladies

Mizunami Country Club, Mizunami, Gifu
Par 36-36–72; 6,471 yards

July 26-28
purse, ¥50,000,000

	SCORES			TOTAL	MONEY
Ikuyo Shiotani	70	67	69	206	¥9,000,000
Hikaru Kobayashi	67	70	70	207	4,400,000
Mikiyo Nishizuka	71	69	69	209	3,500,000
Kozue Azuma	71	71	70	212	2,750,000
Yuri Fudoh	71	68	73	212	2,750,000
Aki Takamura	73	71	69	213	1,875,000
Shiho Ohyama	71	69	73	213	1,875,000
Orie Fujino	73	72	69	214	1,175,000
Hsiu-Feng Tseng	73	71	70	214	1,175,000
Mikino Kubo	73	70	71	214	1,175,000
Chieko Amanuma	69	72	73	214	1,175,000
Michiko Hattori	70	73	72	215	875,000
Toshimi Kimura	73	69	73	215	875,000
Atsuko Ueno	74	73	69	216	725,000
Mayumi Hirase	70	72	74	216	725,000
Kyoko Ono	70	72	74	216	725,000
Masaki Maeda	71	68	77	216	725,000
Yuriko Ohtsuka	72	74	71	217	515,000
Eika Ohtake	72	73	72	217	515,000
Nobuko Kizawa	73	72	72	217	515,000
Junko Omote	71	73	73	217	515,000
Seiko Satoh	71	73	73	217	515,000
Yun-Jye Wei	71	70	76	217	515,000
Hsiao-Chuan Lu	73	73	72	218	445,000
Hisako Takeda	74	72	72	218	445,000
Midori Yoneyama	72	73	73	218	445,000
Woo-Soon Ko	70	73	75	218	445,000
Mayumi Ishii	75	72	72	219	400,000
Kaori Harada	74	73	72	219	400,000
Yuka Irie	75	70	74	219	400,000
Harumi Sakagami	73	72	74	219	400,000
Kasumi Fujii	71	71	77	219	400,000

Vernal Open

Masters Golf Club, Miki, Hyogo
Par 36-36–72; 6,433 yards

August 2-4
purse, ¥80,000,000

	SCORES			TOTAL	MONEY
Yuri Fudoh	72	70	68	210	¥14,400,000
Chieko Amanuma	73	72	70	215	6,320,000
Hsiao-Chuan Lu	75	70	70	215	6,320,000
Yoko Tsuchiya	73	72	71	216	4,000,000
Shin Sora	72	70	74	216	4,000,000
Yun-Jye Wei	70	70	76	216	4,000,000
Hiroko Yamaguchi	76	71	70	217	1,949,333
Ikuyo Shiotani	73	72	72	217	1,949,333
Mikino Kubo	73	71	73	217	1,949,333
Mayumi Hirase	68	75	74	217	1,949,333
Chihiro Nakajima	70	73	74	217	1,949,333
Ae-Sook Kim	69	72	76	217	1,949,333
Mineko Nasu	77	70	71	218	1,248,000
Orie Fujino	77	69	72	218	1,248,000
Ai Kikuchi	69	72	77	218	1,248,000
Midori Yoneyama	75	73	71	219	1,048,000
Mayumi Murai	71	71	77	219	1,048,000
Michiko Hattori	76	73	71	220	768,000
Natsuko Noro	75	74	71	220	768,000
Chieko Nishida	71	76	73	220	768,000
Kaori Higo	72	75	73	220	768,000
Momoyo Kawakubo	74	73	73	220	768,000
Ji-Hee Lee	75	71	74	220	768,000
Young-Me Lee	65	78	77	220	768,000
Aki Nakano	70	73	77	220	768,000
Junko Omote	79	70	72	221	664,000
Chiharu Yamaguchi	72	74	75	221	664,000
Yuka Shiroto	75	74	73	222	592,000
Toshimi Kimura	74	73	75	222	592,000
Yu-Chen Huang	76	71	75	222	592,000
Woo-Soon Ko	72	74	76	222	592,000
Emi Hyodoh	73	72	77	222	592,000
Fuki Kido	76	69	77	222	592,000
Masaki Maeda	73	71	78	222	592,000

NEC Karuizawa 72

Karuizawa 72 Golf Club, Nagano
Par 36-36–72; 6,511 yards

August 16-18
purse, ¥60,000,000

	SCORES			TOTAL	MONEY
Akiko Fukushima	68	68	66	202	¥10,800,000
Masaki Maeda	72	69	65	206	4,740,000
Woo-Soon Ko	69	68	69	206	4,740,000
Kasumi Fujii	70	69	68	207	2,580,000
Misayo Fujisawa	68	70	69	207	2,580,000
Toshimi Kimura	69	67	71	207	2,580,000
Yuri Fudoh	70	66	71	207	2,580,000
Yu-Chen Huang	69	65	73	207	2,580,000
Orie Fujino	70	71	67	208	1,500,000
Eriko Moriyama	69	71	69	209	1,161,000
Kyoko Ono	71	68	70	209	1,161,000

	SCORES			TOTAL	MONEY
Yun-Jye Wei	67	73	70	210	942,000
Mineko Nasu	69	71	70	210	942,000
Seiko Watanabe	70	70	70	210	942,000
Chihiro Nakajima	68	70	72	210	942,000
Aki Nakano	70	68	72	210	942,000
Young-Me Lee	73	68	70	211	732,000
Kaori Suzuki	68	69	74	211	732,000
Mihoko Takahashi	68	73	71	212	579,600
Yoko Inoue	72	70	70	212	579,600
Midori Yoneyama	71	70	71	212	579,600
Yuka Arita	70	70	72	212	579,600
Harumi Sakagami	70	69	73	212	579,600
Yuka Shiroto	68	73	72	213	504,000
Ok-Hee Ku	70	71	72	213	504,000
Tomo Sakakibara	70	70	73	213	504,000
Natsuko Noro	70	70	73	213	504,000
Yoshie Suzuki	74	65	74	213	504,000
Hiroko Yamaguchi	70	69	74	213	504,000
Shin Sora	72	70	72	214	432,000
Mayumi Murai	70	72	72	214	432,000
Kayo Yamada	71	72	71	214	432,000
Yuriko Ohtsuka	70	73	71	214	432,000
Atsuko Ueno	67	71	76	214	432,000
Kumiko Hiyoshi	68	70	76	214	432,000

New Caterpillar Mitsubishi Ladies

Daihakone Country Club, Hakone, Kanagawa
Par 36-37–73; 6,648 yards

August 23-25
purse, ¥60,000,000

	SCORES			TOTAL	MONEY
Kaori Higo	72	72	68	212	¥10,800,000
Toshimi Kimura	73	75	67	215	4,740,000
Woo-Soon Ko	73	70	72	215	4,740,000
Kasumi Fujii	73	74	70	217	3,600,000
Nobuko Kizawa	71	74	74	219	3,000,000
Mayumi Murai	76	77	67	220	1,800,000
Michie Ohba	72	77	71	220	1,800,000
Ayako Okamoto	75	74	71	220	1,800,000
Kaori Harada	75	72	73	220	1,800,000
Yun-Jye Wei	70	76	74	220	1,800,000
Kyoko Ono	71	77	73	221	1,074,000
Ikuyo Shiotani	72	76	73	221	1,074,000
Rie Mitsuhashi	73	77	72	222	894,000
Hsiao-Chuan Lu	73	76	73	222	894,000
Masaki Maeda	75	74	73	222	894,000
Midori Yoneyama	73	73	76	222	894,000
Ji-Hee Lee	74	79	70	223	618,000
Chikako Matsuzawa	79	72	72	223	618,000
Aki Nakano	73	77	73	223	618,000
Yu-Chen Huang	74	76	73	223	618,000
Harumi Sakagami	72	77	74	223	618,000
Chieko Amanuma	73	74	76	223	618,000
Kozue Azuma	75	79	70	224	498,000
Momoyo Kawakubo	75	78	71	224	498,000
Mayumi Hirase	75	77	72	224	498,000
Mihoko Takahashi	77	74	73	224	498,000

	SCORES			TOTAL	MONEY
Yuri Fudoh	76	74	74	224	498,000
Chihiro Nakajima	73	76	75	224	498,000
Yuka Sakaguchi	76	76	73	225	438,000
Yuka Shiroto	77	75	73	225	438,000
Mitsuko Kawasaki	71	80	74	225	438,000
Yuriko Ohtsuka	73	76	76	225	438,000

Yonex Ladies Open

Yonex Country Club, Teradomari, Niigata
Par 36-36–72; 6,302 yards

August 30-September 1
purse, ¥60,000,000

	SCORES			TOTAL	MONEY
Yuri Fudoh	64	69	68	201	¥10,800,000
Kaori Higo	66	71	71	208	5,280,000
Yuka Shiroto	73	71	66	210	3,300,000
Yuka Sakaguchi	73	68	69	210	3,300,000
Woo-Soon Ko	72	68	70	210	3,300,000
Ikuyo Shiotani	67	70	73	210	3,300,000
Midori Yoneyama	73	70	68	211	1,540,800
Norimi Terasawa	74	69	68	211	1,540,800
Aki Nakano	73	69	69	211	1,540,800
Michie Ohba	72	69	70	211	1,540,800
Yu-Chen Huang	68	72	71	211	1,540,800
Momoyo Kawakubo	72	73	67	212	894,000
Ayako Okamoto	71	71	70	212	894,000
Hisako Takeda	72	70	70	212	894,000
Atsuko Ueno	70	71	71	212	894,000
Kotomi Akiyama	70	71	71	212	894,000
Michiko Hattori	68	69	75	212	894,000
Toshimi Kimura	75	69	69	213	606,000
Ji-Hee Lee	71	70	72	213	606,000
Kasumi Fujii	71	70	72	213	606,000
Kayo Yamada	71	69	73	213	606,000
Fuki Kido	73	73	68	214	504,000
Yumi Kubota	73	71	70	214	504,000
Ji-Yeon Han	73	71	70	214	504,000
Rena Yamazaki	71	72	71	214	504,000
Kayo Fukumoto	74	69	71	214	504,000
Kozue Azuma	74	68	72	214	504,000
Mayumi Hirase	70	71	73	214	504,000
Kyoko Ono	72	71	72	215	450,000
Hikaru Kobayashi	72	70	73	215	450,000

Fujisankei Ladies Classic

Fujizakura Country Club, Kawaguchiko, Yamanashi
Par 35-36–71; 6,297 yards

September 6-8
purse, ¥60,000,000

	SCORES			TOTAL	MONEY
Ok-Hee Ku	73	66	67	206	¥10,800,000
Midori Yoneyama	67	70	72	209	5,280,000
Kasumi Fujii	68	71	71	210	4,200,000
Yuri Kawanami	74	71	68	213	3,600,000
Laura Davies	74	71	69	214	2,500,000

	SCORES			TOTAL	MONEY
Yuri Fudoh	73	71	70	214	2,500,000
Kayo Yamada	72	70	72	214	2,500,000
Nobuko Kizawa	74	72	69	215	1,329,600
Akane Ohshiro	76	69	70	215	1,329,600
Yu-Chen Huang	73	69	73	215	1,329,600
Misayo Fujisawa	73	69	73	215	1,329,600
Aki Nakano	74	68	73	215	1,329,600
Fuki Kido	72	74	70	216	954,000
Kozue Azuma	70	74	72	216	954,000
Kaori Suzuki	69	73	75	217	744,000
Mihoko Takahashi	74	73	70	217	744,000
Norimi Terasawa	77	69	71	217	744,000
Chieko Amanuma	72	73	72	217	744,000
Miyuki Shimabukuro	72	72	73	217	744,000
Yoshie Suzuki	75	73	70	218	552,000
Kotomi Akiyama	74	71	73	218	552,000
Woo-Soon Ko	71	72	75	218	552,000
Michiko Hattori	72	74	73	219	492,000
Tomo Sakakibara	72	74	73	219	492,000
Toshimi Kimura	73	73	73	219	492,000
Shin Sora	74	72	73	219	492,000
Junko Omote	72	73	74	219	492,000
Mizue Igarashi	74	71	74	219	492,000
Mayumi Hirase	74	71	74	219	492,000
*Ai Miyazato	71	71	77	219	

Japan LPGA Championship Konica Cup

Taiheiyo Club, Rokko Course, Hyogo
Par 36-36–72; 6,480 yards

September 12-15
purse, ¥70,000,000

	SCORES				TOTAL	MONEY
Ok-Hee Ku	68	71	71	73	283	¥12,600,000
Toshimi Kimura	69	69	73	73	284	6,160,000
Mikiyo Nishizuka	69	73	69	74	285	4,900,000
Woo-Soon Ko	73	70	72	71	286	3,850,000
Orie Fujino	70	67	72	77	286	3,850,000
Hiromi Kobayashi	71	71	73	72	287	2,800,000
Hiroko Yamaguchi	75	73	70	70	288	2,275,000
Yuri Kawanami	73	70	71	74	288	2,275,000
Michiko Hattori	71	71	72	75	289	1,575,000
Yuri Fudoh	73	71	69	76	289	1,575,000
Junko Omote	75	70	74	71	290	1,078,000
Mikino Kubo	74	71	73	72	290	1,078,000
Aki Takamura	72	75	71	72	290	1,078,000
Kasumi Fujii	72	71	73	74	290	1,078,000
Yuka Shiroto	72	74	68	76	290	1,078,000
Ji-Hee Lee	73	71	72	75	291	868,000
Shiho Ohyama	75	72	73	72	292	669,200
Rie Murata	74	72	72	74	292	669,200
Mayumi Inoue	74	73	71	74	292	669,200
Kotomi Akiyama	73	70	74	75	292	669,200
Midori Yoneyama	74	69	72	77	292	669,200
Harumi Sakagami	77	70	75	71	293	539,000
Riko Higashio	72	72	75	74	293	539,000
Keiko Arai	78	69	71	75	293	539,000
Nobuko Kizawa	76	69	71	77	293	539,000

	SCORES				TOTAL	MONEY
Kaori Yamamoto	78	71	75	70	294	483,000
Fuki Kido	76	73	75	70	294	483,000
Michiko Mitsui	75	72	73	74	294	483,000
Yu-Chen Huang	76	71	72	75	294	483,000
Mitsuyo Hirata	76	69	77	73	295	395,500
Hikaru Kobayashi	75	72	75	73	295	395,500
Nayoko Yoshikawa	75	74	73	73	295	395,500
Hsiao-Chuan Lu	71	75	75	74	295	395,500
Rika Tsubaki	74	72	74	75	295	395,500
Yuriko Ohtsuka	75	72	73	75	295	395,500
Kayo Yamada	74	72	73	76	295	395,500
Chieko Amanuma	74	75	69	77	295	395,500
Mayumi Hirase	76	70	71	78	295	395,500
Mihoko Takahashi	74	71	71	79	295	395,500

Munsingwear Ladies Tokai Classic

Ryosen Golf Club, Inabe, Mie
Par 36-36–72; 6,400 yards

September 20-22
purse, ¥60,000,000

	SCORES			TOTAL	MONEY
Kasumi Fujii	66	69	69	204	¥10,800,000
Kyoko Ono	67	66	73	206	5,280,000
Junko Yasui	68	69	70	207	4,200,000
Toshimi Kimura	69	73	66	208	3,600,000
Yu-Chen Huang	71	69	69	209	3,000,000
Tomo Sakakibara	73	66	71	210	2,250,000
Yuriko Ohtsuka	70	67	73	210	2,250,000
Michiko Hattori	67	71	73	211	1,650,000
Mineko Nasu	70	68	73	211	1,650,000
Hikaru Kobayashi	72	72	68	212	1,041,600
Kayo Yamada	71	72	69	212	1,041,600
Shiho Ohyama	72	71	69	212	1,041,600
Hiroko Yamaguchi	69	70	73	212	1,041,600
Mihoko Takahashi	69	69	74	212	1,041,600
Ji-Hee Lee	71	74	68	213	702,000
Young-Me Lee	70	72	71	213	702,000
Yuka Shiroto	73	69	71	213	702,000
Midori Yoneyama	70	71	72	213	702,000
Aki Takamura	71	70	72	213	702,000
Hsiu-Feng Tseng	71	70	72	213	702,000
Takayo Bandoh	71	72	71	214	534,000
Yun-Jye Wei	72	69	73	214	534,000
Nobuko Kizawa	72	72	71	215	480,000
Rie Fujiwara	73	71	71	215	480,000
Mikino Kubo	69	74	72	215	480,000
Kaori Suzuki	71	72	72	215	480,000
Rie Mitsuhashi	73	70	72	215	480,000
Hiromi Kobayashi	73	70	72	215	480,000
Kotomi Akiyama	70	71	74	215	480,000
Yuri Kawanami	69	76	71	216	384,000
Ae-Sook Kim	74	71	71	216	384,000
Ai-Yu Tu	72	73	71	216	384,000
Mayumi Inoue	70	74	72	216	384,000
Woo-Soon Ko	74	70	72	216	384,000
Mikiyo Nishizuka	73	71	72	216	384,000
Chihiro Nakajima	72	71	73	216	384,000

	SCORES			TOTAL	MONEY
Junko Omote	70	72	74	216	384,000
Miyuki Shimabukuro	71	71	74	216	384,000

Miyagi TV Cup Dunlop Ladies Open

Rainbow Hills Golf Club, Tomiya, Miyagi
Par 36-36–72; 6,453 yards

September 27-29
purse, ¥60,000,000

	SCORES			TOTAL	MONEY
Mihoko Takahashi	70	72	69	211	¥10,800,000
Woo-Soon Ko	72	71	70	213	5,280,000
Nobuko Kizawa	77	69	68	214	3,600,000
Young-Me Lee	72	73	69	214	3,600,000
Hsiu-Feng Tseng	71	69	74	214	3,600,000
Kaori Harada	70	76	70	216	2,250,000
Yuri Kawanami	73	72	71	216	2,250,000
Laura Davies	71	74	72	217	1,650,000
Kotomi Akiyama	72	69	76	217	1,650,000
Aki Nakano	74	77	68	219	1,110,000
Shiho Ohyama	74	74	71	219	1,110,000
Kasumi Fujii	73	74	72	219	1,110,000
Yuri Fudoh	72	73	74	219	1,110,000
Ji-Hee Lee	77	72	71	220	930,000
Misayo Fujisawa	71	75	74	220	930,000
Toshimi Kimura	76	74	71	221	698,000
Orie Fujino	70	79	72	221	698,000
Hisako Ohgane	73	76	72	221	698,000
Mitsuko Kawasaki	71	77	73	221	698,000
Kyoko Ono	75	73	73	221	698,000
Fumiko Muraguchi	72	74	75	221	698,000
Harumi Sakagami	75	75	72	222	552,000
Ok-Hee Ku	74	76	72	222	552,000
Hiromi Kobayashi	72	77	73	222	552,000
Chieko Amanuma	77	74	71	222	552,000
Mayumi Hirase	77	72	73	222	552,000
Atsuko Ueno	75	76	72	223	492,000
Akane Ohshiro	73	76	74	223	492,000
Yuriko Ohtsuka	76	73	74	223	492,000
Kaori Higo	75	73	75	223	492,000
Hikaru Kobayashi	72	73	78	223	492,000

Japan Women's Open

Hakone Country Club, Hakone, Kanagawa
Par 36-37–73; 6,418 yards

October 3-6
purse, ¥70,000,000

	SCORES				TOTAL	MONEY
Woo-Soon Ko	69	73	69	67	278	¥14,000,000
Yu-Chen Huang	69	70	70	72	281	7,700,000
Yuri Fudoh	69	74	71	71	285	3,978,333
Yuka Shiroto	70	72	71	72	285	3,978,333
Lorena Ochoa	65	72	73	75	285	3,978,333
Aki Takamura	72	78	67	70	287	2,340,000
Shiho Ohyama	69	73	70	76	288	2,114,000
Kaori Higo	72	71	73	73	289	1,640,666

	SCORES				TOTAL	MONEY
Misayo Fujisawa	69	72	74	74	289	1,640,666
Junko Omote	67	71	75	76	289	1,640,666
Midori Yoneyama	74	72	74	70	290	1,104,000
Akiko Fukushima	73	69	76	72	290	1,104,000
Ok-Hee Ku	72	74	72	72	290	1,104,000
Kayo Yamada	68	73	69	80	290	1,104,000
Harumi Sakagami	71	73	75	72	291	832,333
Toshimi Kimura	73	75	69	74	291	832,333
Kasumi Fujii	68	74	73	76	291	832,333
Masaki Maeda	74	70	75	73	292	716,500
Laura Davies	72	74	73	73	292	716,500
Miho Koga	75	74	74	70	293	635,500
Chieko Amanuma	71	74	76	72	293	635,500
Mihoko Takahashi	74	76	69	74	293	635,500
Michie Ohba	69	74	74	76	293	635,500
Mieko Takano	71	77	73	73	294	579,000
Hiromi Kobayashi	72	74	73	75	294	579,000
Akane Ohshiro	68	73	74	79	294	579,000
Kyoko Ono	72	75	71	77	295	561,000
*Izumi Narita	72	71	73	79	295	
Ji-Hee Lee	71	78	73	74	296	524,500
Hiroko Yamaguchi	72	77	73	74	296	524,500
Rie Mitsuhashi	77	72	73	74	296	524,500
Junko Yasui	71	74	76	75	296	524,500

Sankyo Ladies Open

Akagi Country Club, Niisato, Gunma
Par 36-36–72; 6,387 yards

October 11-13
purse, ¥60,000,000

	SCORES			TOTAL	MONEY
Toshimi Kimura	70	65	72	207	¥10,800,000
Kasumi Fujii	70	67	73	210	5,280,000
Kyoko Ono	73	70	68	211	3,300,000
Mayumi Hirase	70	72	69	211	3,300,000
Misayo Fujisawa	73	69	69	211	3,300,000
Yu-Chen Huang	68	72	71	211	3,300,000
Yuriko Ohtsuka	73	69	70	212	1,650,000
Ikuyo Shiotani	73	69	70	212	1,650,000
Mayumi Inoue	71	70	71	212	1,650,000
Takayo Bandoh	69	70	73	212	1,650,000
Hisako Ohgane	70	72	71	213	1,122,000
Ji-Hee Lee	70	74	70	214	1,002,000
Tomo Sakakibara	73	71	70	214	1,002,000
Ok-Hee Ku	70	71	73	214	1,002,000
Junko Omote	73	72	70	215	882,000
Michiko Hattori	75	69	72	216	732,000
Chieko Amanuma	74	70	72	216	732,000
Mieko Takano	72	71	73	216	732,000
Hsiu-Feng Tseng	68	74	74	216	732,000
Mihoko Takahashi	73	72	72	217	570,000
Bie-Shyun Huang	73	72	72	217	570,000
Woo-Soon Ko	73	72	72	217	570,000
Kozue Azuma	75	71	72	218	510,000
Ayako Okamoto	74	71	73	218	510,000
Maki Sasayama	71	73	74	218	510,000
Mizue Igarashi	75	69	74	218	510,000

	SCORES	TOTAL	MONEY
Hiroko Yamaguchi	73 71 74	218	510,000
Yuko Motoyama	71 72 75	218	510,000
Rie Mitsuhashi	74 69 75	218	510,000
Young-Me Lee	72 74 73	219	432,000
Rika Tsubaki	76 70 73	219	432,000
Mineko Nasu	73 73 73	219	432,000
Fusako Nagata	77 68 74	219	432,000
Nobuko Kizawa	73 71 75	219	432,000
Kayo Yamada	72 71 76	219	432,000

Fujitsu Ladies

Tokyu Seven Hundred Club, Chiba
Par 36-36–72; 6,520 yards

October 18-20
purse, ¥60,000,000

	SCORES	TOTAL	MONEY
Chihiro Nakajima	65 69 70	204	¥10,800,000
Kyoko Ono	71 66 68	205	4,740,000
Hsiu-Feng Tseng	67 65 73	205	4,740,000
Ok-Hee Ku	69 71 66	206	3,000,000
Masaki Maeda	70 69 67	206	3,000,000
Toshimi Kimura	68 70 68	206	3,000,000
Woo-Soon Ko	71 68 68	207	2,100,000
Rie Mitsuhashi	71 71 66	208	1,500,000
Yuri Fudoh	70 68 70	208	1,500,000
Akiko Fukushima	67 70 71	208	1,500,000
Michie Ohba	70 72 67	209	984,000
Ayako Okamoto	73 69 67	209	984,000
Yun-Jye Wei	67 73 69	209	984,000
Midori Yoneyama	68 71 70	209	984,000
Mayumi Hirase	66 72 71	209	984,000
Yu-Chen Huang	69 72 69	210	744,000
Yuka Shiroto	74 67 69	210	744,000
Mayumi Murai	67 70 73	210	744,000
Aki Nakano	69 72 70	211	554,000
Aki Takamura	69 71 71	211	554,000
Kayo Yamada	68 71 72	211	554,000
Eriko Moriyama	69 70 72	211	554,000
Yoko Inoue	70 69 72	211	554,000
Tatsuko Morimoto	68 70 73	211	554,000
Mikino Kubo	69 74 69	212	474,000
Keiko Sasaki	70 73 69	212	474,000
Takayo Bandoh	71 71 70	212	474,000
Junko Omote	69 72 71	212	474,000
Yoshie Suzuki	70 71 71	212	474,000
Ji-Hee Lee	71 70 71	212	474,000

Hisako Higuchi Classic

Taiheiyo Club, Minori, Ibaraki
Par 36-36–72; 6,399 yards

October 25-27
purse, ¥60,000,000

	SCORES	TOTAL	MONEY
Kasumi Fujii	68 68 73	209	¥10,800,000
Mayumi Hirase	68 73 71	212	5,280,000

	SCORES			TOTAL	MONEY
Yuri Fudoh	70	75	68	213	3,600,000
Hisako Ohgane	70	72	71	213	3,600,000
Ikuyo Shiotani	71	70	72	213	3,600,000
Aki Nakano	70	76	70	216	2,100,000
Hiromi Kobayashi	72	75	69	216	2,100,000
Yuka Shiroto	72	72	72	216	2,100,000
Nobuko Kizawa	74	73	70	217	1,500,000
Namika Omata	74	73	71	218	1,046,400
Midori Yoneyama	74	73	71	218	1,046,400
Akiko Fukushima	68	78	72	218	1,046,400
Miho Koga	74	72	72	218	1,046,400
Toshimi Kimura	71	73	74	218	1,046,400
Riko Higashio	72	78	69	219	768,000
Chieko Amanuma	72	76	71	219	768,000
Aki Takamura	74	72	73	219	768,000
Ai Nishikawa	75	69	75	219	768,000
Yuka Arita	72	75	73	220	520,800
Mie Nakata	69	77	74	220	520,800
Hsiu-Feng Tseng	71	75	74	220	520,800
Ok-Hee Ku	76	73	71	220	520,800
Kyoko Ono	75	74	71	220	520,800
Fuki Kido	75	71	74	220	520,800
Yun-Jye Wei	74	75	71	220	520,800
Junko Omote	72	76	72	220	520,800
Eriko Moriyama	73	75	72	220	520,800
Kaori Harada	72	75	73	220	520,800
Kumiko Fuchi	75	75	71	221	414,000
Hiroko Yamaguchi	77	72	72	221	414,000
Yu-Chen Huang	76	73	72	221	414,000
Yasuko Satoh	70	76	75	221	414,000
Michie Ohba	74	72	75	221	414,000
Orie Fujino	71	74	76	221	414,000
Eika Ohtake	70	72	79	221	414,000

Cisco World Ladies Match Play

Narita Golf Club, Narita, Chiba
Par 36-36–72; 6,467 yards

October 31-November 3
purse, ¥107,100,000

FIRST ROUND

Chieko Amanuma defeated Annika Sorenstam, 2 and 1.
Rosie Jones defeated Mihoko Takahashi, 5 and 4.
Hee-Won Han defeated Woo-Soon Ko, 20 holes.
Laura Diaz defeated Kyoko Ono, 1 up.
Midori Yoneyama defeated Mi Hyun Kim, 1 up.
Lorie Kane defeated Orie Fujino, 7 and 6.
Kelly Robbins defeated Kasumi Fujii, 3 and 2.
Cristie Kerr defeated Kaori Higo, 1 up.
Takayo Bandoh defeated Se Ri Pak, 1 up.
Michele Redman defeated Ok-Hee Ku, 1 up.
Catriona Matthew defeated Toshimi Kimura, 19 holes.
Carin Koch defeated Ikuyo Shiotani, 3 and 2.
Karrie Webb defeated Hsiu-Feng Tseng, 3 and 2.
Grace Park defeated Mikino Kubo, 4 and 3.
Yuri Fudoh defeated Beth Bauer, 3 and 2.
Rachel Teske defeated Yu-Chen Huang, 28 holes.

(Each losing player received ¥1,260,000.)

SECOND ROUND

Jones defeated Amanuma, 5 and 4.
Han defeated Diaz, 3 and 2.
Yoneyama defeated Kane, 1 up.
Robbins defeated Kerr, 1 up.
Redman defeated Bandoh, 4 and 3.
Koch defeated Matthew, 5 and 3.
Park defeated Webb, 1 up.
Fudoh defeated Teske, 3 and 1.

(Each losing player received ¥2,415,000.)

QUARTER-FINALS

Han defeated Jones, 5 and 4.
Yoneyama defeated Robbins, 4 and 3.
Koch defeated Redman, 2 and 1.
Park defeated Fudoh, 6 and 5.

(Each losing player received ¥4,725,000.)

SEMI-FINALS

Yoneyama defeated Han, 19 holes.
Park defeated Koch, 5 and 4.

PLAYOFF FOR THIRD-FOURTH PLACE

Koch defeated Han, 1 up.

(Koch received ¥8,400,000; Han received ¥7,213,500.)

FINAL

Park defeated Yoneyama, 22 holes.

(Park received ¥16,065,000; Yoneyama received ¥10,080,000.)

Mizuno Classic

Seta Golf Club, Otsu, Shiga
Par 36-36–72; 6,450 yards

November 8-10
purse, ¥138,990,000

	SCORES			TOTAL	MONEY
Annika Sorenstam	69	65	67	201	¥20,182,025
Grace Park	66	69	68	203	12,512,825
Se Ri Pak	68	69	67	204	9,130,958
Gloria Park	66	69	71	206	7,101,909
Lorie Kane	67	73	67	207	5,241,769
Kasumi Fujii	68	70	69	207	5,241,769
Liselotte Neumann	74	66	68	208	3,381,748
Maria Hjorth	71	69	68	208	3,381,748
Woo-Soon Ko	67	72	69	208	3,381,748
Rosie Jones	69	69	70	208	3,381,748
Ji -Hee Lee	71	70	68	209	2,468,688
Catriona Matthew	70	69	70	209	2,468,688
Jennifer Rosales	69	73	68	210	1,927,584
Beth Bauer	68	74	68	210	1,927,584

	SCORES			TOTAL	MONEY
Rachel Teske	68	73	69	210	1,927,584
Midori Yoneyama	68	71	71	210	1,927,584
Mayumi Hirase	68	71	71	210	1,927,584
Yuri Fudoh	70	68	72	210	1,927,584
Toshimi Kimura	72	70	69	211	1,521,727
Jill McGill	69	70	72	211	1,521,727
Sophie Gustafson	69	70	72	211	1,521,727
Mi Hyun Kim	65	73	73	211	1,521,727
Orie Fujino	70	72	70	212	1,252,305
Junko Omote	69	73	70	212	1,252,305
Hee-Won Han	69	72	71	212	1,252,305
Michele Redman	70	70	72	212	1,252,305
Janice Moodie	69	70	73	212	1,252,305
Jeong Jang	69	69	74	212	1,252,305
Heather Bowie	70	75	68	213	1,068,527
Vicki Goetze-Ackerman	68	71	74	213	1,068,527
Akiko Fukushima	69	68	76	213	1,068,527

Itoen Ladies

Great Island Club, Chonan, Chiba
Par 36-36–72; 6,364 yards

November 15-17
purse, ¥60,000,000

	SCORES			TOTAL	MONEY
Yuri Fudoh	65	71	68	204	¥10,800,000
Akiko Fukushima	68	65	72	205	5,280,000
Kasumi Fujii	65	70	71	206	4,200,000
Woo-Soon Ko	67	69	71	207	3,600,000
Fuki Kido	73	68	68	209	2,700,000
Midori Yoneyama	70	73	66	209	2,700,000
Toshimi Kimura	74	66	70	210	1,800,000
Hikaru Kobayashi	71	67	72	210	1,800,000
Ji-Yeon Han	72	69	69	210	1,800,000
Junko Yasui	69	66	76	211	1,200,000
Ae-Sook Kim	72	73	67	212	984,000
Ikuyo Shiotani	72	72	68	212	984,000
Mayumi Nakajima	68	70	74	212	984,000
Mayumi Hirase	70	68	74	212	984,000
Yu-Chen Huang	70	70	72	212	984,000
Shin Sora	72	71	69	212	984,000
Young-Me Lee	72	70	71	213	663,600
Ok-Hee Ku	75	70	68	213	663,600
Rie Murata	70	70	73	213	663,600
Yun-Jye Wei	70	72	71	213	663,600
Laura Davies	69	69	75	213	663,600
Harumi Sakagami	68	74	72	214	534,000
Hisako Takeda	71	71	72	214	534,000
Natsuko Noro	69	73	72	214	534,000
Kaori Harada	73	68	73	214	534,000
Kaori Higo	67	70	77	214	534,000
Eika Ohtake	72	67	75	214	534,000
Junko Omote	77	67	70	214	534,000
Michiko Hattori	74	70	71	215	468,000
Momoyo Kawakubo	71	70	74	215	468,000
Tomo Sakakibara	73	69	73	215	468,000
Eriko Moriyama	71	71	73	215	468,000

Daio Seishi Elleair Ladies Open

Elleair Golf Club, Saita, Kagawa
Par 36-36–72; 6,337 yards

November 22-24
purse, ¥80,000,000

	SCORES			TOTAL	MONEY
Hiromi Kobayashi	66	69	70	205	¥14,400,000
Yun-Jye Wei	68	72	67	207	7,040,000
Midori Yoneyama	72	67	69	208	5,600,000
Keiko Sasaki	73	71	65	209	4,800,000
Ji-Hee Lee	72	69	69	210	4,000,000
Yu-Chen Huang	72	70	69	211	3,000,000
Yuka Irie	73	69	69	211	3,000,000
Natsuko Noro	71	72	69	212	1,880,000
Ok-Hee Ku	77	68	67	212	1,880,000
Orie Fujino	70	71	71	212	1,880,000
Misayo Fujisawa	71	68	73	212	1,880,000
Mayumi Murai	74	70	69	213	1,200,000
Mayumi Ishii	68	75	70	213	1,200,000
Hisako Takeda	71	71	71	213	1,200,000
Yuriko Ohtsuka	73	69	71	213	1,200,000
Oh-Soon Lee	72	74	67	213	1,200,000
Mikino Kubo	73	68	72	213	1,200,000
Hiroko Yamaguchi	67	73	73	213	1,200,000
Junko Omote	73	71	70	214	796,800
Michiko Hattori	69	73	72	214	796,800
Kasumi Adachi	70	72	72	214	796,800
Tomo Sakakibara	71	71	72	214	796,800
Kaori Harada	72	69	73	214	796,800
Hsiao-Chuan Lu	72	72	71	215	712,000
Suzuka Kanazawa	77	68	70	215	712,000
Hisako Ohgane	73	70	72	215	712,000
Kayo Yamada	73	70	72	215	712,000
Mayumi Inoue	73	72	71	216	672,000
Woo-Soon Ko	73	71	73	217	632,000
Kasumi Fujii	73	72	72	217	632,000
Hsiu-Feng Tseng	72	73	72	217	632,000
Mineko Nasu	70	76	71	217	632,000

Japan LPGA Tour Championship

Hibiscus Golf Club, Sadowara, Miyazaki
Par 35-36–71; 6,445 yards

November 28-December 1
purse, ¥60,000,000

	SCORES				TOTAL	MONEY
Woo-Soon Ko	70	70	67	71	278	¥15,000,000
Kaori Higo	70	70	69	71	280	8,700,000
Yuri Fudoh	71	74	68	68	281	6,000,000
Ji-Hee Lee	71	70	71	70	282	4,800,000
Kasumi Fujii	68	70	74	72	284	4,020,000
Chieko Amanuma	70	71	70	76	287	3,456,000
Toshimi Kimura	72	71	76	69	288	2,556,000
Yun-Jye Wei	69	71	76	72	288	2,556,000
Orie Fujino	75	74	71	69	289	1,374,000
Ok-Hee Ku	70	73	74	72	289	1,374,000
Kyoko Ono	74	72	76	68	290	912,000
Hsiu-Feng Tseng	70	75	73	72	290	912,000
Akiko Fukushima	74	73	73	71	291	678,000

	SCORES				TOTAL	MONEY
Chihiro Nakajima	72	73	74	72	291	678,000
Mikino Kubo	73	73	72	74	292	510,000
Hiromi Kobayashi	76	74	73	70	293	426,000
Takayo Bandoh	73	71	76	73	293	426,000
Yu-Chen Huang	74	77	71	72	294	324,000
Mihoko Takahashi	69	75	77	73	294	324,000
Kozue Azuma	73	72	78	72	295	297,000
Shin Sora	74	73	75	73	295	297,000
Ikuyo Shiotani	78	71	75	72	296	288,000
Chieko Nishida	72	76	77	74	299	279,000
Midori Yoneyama	73	74	75	77	299	279,000
Ai-Yu Tu	78	78	74	75	305	270,000
Mayumi Inoue	74	75	77	80	306	264,000

Australian Women's Tour

Educom ALPG Players' Championship

Horizons Golf Resort, Port Stephens, Australia
Par 36-37–73; 6,243 yards

February 14-16
purse, A$100,000

	SCORES			TOTAL	MONEY
Paula Marti	68	76	72	216	A$15,000
Karen Pearce	73	71	72	216	10,000
(Marti defeated Pearce on third playoff hole.)					
Judith Van Hagen	75	71	71	217	5,900
Diane Barnard	72	78	67	217	5,900
Marnie McGuire	74	74	70	218	3,730
Sarah Carbon	72	75	71	218	3,730
Michelle Ellis	75	75	69	219	2,350
Lara Tadiotto	71	74	74	219	2,350
Elisabeth Esterl	76	72	71	219	2,350
Alison Munt	76	73	70	219	2,350
Kathryn Marshall	70	76	74	220	1,650
Fiona Pike	71	74	76	221	1,310
Corinne Dibnah	76	70	75	221	1,310
Marie-Josee Rouleau	73	75	73	221	1,310
Karine Icher	72	73	76	221	1,310
Jane Leary	71	75	75	221	1,310
Anne-Marie Knight	73	74	75	222	1,128
Simi Mehra	73	72	77	222	1,128
Joanne Mills	76	77	69	222	1,128
Pernilla Sterner	77	75	70	222	1,128
Becky Morgan	77	72	73	222	1,128
Iben Tinning	79	74	70	223	1,020
Lynnette Brooky	71	77	75	223	1,020
Sara Sanders	79	71	74	224	945
Marieke Zelsmann	74	78	72	224	945
Joanne Morley	74	70	80	224	945

	SCORES			TOTAL	MONEY
Nicola Moult	70	76	78	224	945
Julie Forbes	76	74	75	225	705
Helen Beatty	71	80	74	225	705
Catrin Nilsmark	72	80	73	225	705
Silvia Cavalleri	75	74	76	225	705
Laura Davies	77	74	74	225	705
Rachel Kirkwood	75	78	72	225	705
Rachel Teske	76	75	74	225	705
Melissa Fraser	76	76	73	225	705
Jennifer Sevil	76	78	71	225	705
Tanya Holl	78	72	75	225	705
Christine Greatrex	76	77	72	225	705
Jane Crafter	76	74	75	225	705

Australasian Ladies Masters

Royal Pines Golf Club, Gold Coast, Queensland
Par 37-35–72; 6,397 yards

February 21-24
purse, A$750,000

	SCORES				TOTAL	MONEY
Annika Sorenstam	74	64	71	69	278	A$112,500
Karrie Webb	69	69	68	72	278	75,000
(Sorenstam defeated Webb on fourth playoff hole.)						
Michelle Ellis	68	70	70	72	280	52,500
Laura Davies	75	72	68	66	281	31,125
Helen Alfredsson	71	71	71	68	281	31,125
Charlotta Sorenstam	69	71	70	71	281	31,125
Rachel Teske	71	70	71	70	282	20,062.50
Elisabeth Esterl	66	69	71	76	282	20,062.50
Paula Marti	68	73	71	71	283	14,875
Cherie Byrnes	71	69	71	72	283	14,875
Silvia Cavalleri	70	67	72	74	283	14,875
Soo-Yun Kang	73	68	72	71	284	11,625
Marnie McGuire	70	74	72	69	285	9,600
Iben Tinning	70	70	75	70	285	9,600
Maria Hjorth	72	72	69	72	285	9,600
Kelly Robbins	72	74	67	72	285	9,600
Wendy Doolan	74	66	71	74	285	9,600
Natascha Fink	73	70	73	70	286	8,550
Marine Monnet	76	70	70	70	286	8,550
Smriti Mehra	71	71	73	71	286	8,550
Pernilla Sterner	69	71	78	69	287	7,987.50
Johanna Head	72	73	68	74	287	7,987.50
Raquel Carriedo	73	73	74	68	288	6,733.30
Mhairi McKay	70	74	74	70	288	6,733.30
Julie Forbes	75	71	72	70	288	6,733.30
Dodie Mazzuca	72	72	73	71	288	6,733.30
Rachel Kirkwood	70	74	73	71	288	6,733.30
Joanne Mills	71	76	70	71	288	6,733.30
Laurette Maritz	71	70	73	74	288	6,733.30
Jane Leary	75	67	72	74	288	6,733.30
Suzann Pettersen	72	73	67	76	288	6,733.30

AAMI Women's Australian Open

Yarra Yarra Golf Club, Melbourne, Victoria
Par 36-36–72; 6,054 yards

February 28-March 3
purse, A$500,000

	SCORES				TOTAL	MONEY
Karrie Webb	68	72	69	69	278	A$49,291.16
Suzann Pettersen	70	70	69	69	278	32,860.77
(Webb defeated Pettersen on first playoff hole.)						
Michelle Ellis	70	73	73	70	286	19,716.46
Becky Morgan	73	70	72	71	286	19,716.46
Sophie Gustafson	74	73	67	73	287	13,472.92
Karen Pearce	75	70	71	72	288	11,008.36
Elisabeth Esterl	72	73	75	69	289	8,269.96
Johanna Head	74	73	73	69	289	8,269.96
Jane Crafter	76	68	70	75	289	8,269.96
Ana Belen Sanchez	74	75	69	72	290	5,038.65
Rachel Teske	71	72	74	73	290	5,038.65
Wendy Doolan	70	75	72	73	290	5,038.65
Gina Scott	70	75	72	73	290	5,038.65
Marine Monnet	75	71	71	73	290	5,038.65
Tamara Johns	73	76	66	75	290	5,038.65
*Nikki Campbell	71	71	78	71	291	
Kelly Robbins	77	74	73	68	292	3,831.56
Iben Tinning	72	76	74	70	292	3,831.56
Nicola Moult	73	77	70	72	292	3,831.56
Samantha Head	73	73	73	73	292	3,831.56
Lynnette Brooky	71	75	73	73	292	3,831.56
Jane Leary	76	72	71	74	293	3,548.96
*Rebecca Coakley	76	72	73	73	294	
*Carlie Butler	76	72	76	71	295	
Corinne Dibnah	73	73	74	75	295	3,401.09
Sophie Sandolo	70	74	75	76	295	3,401.09
Valerie Van Ryckeghem	70	76	78	72	296	3,132.73
Dale Reid	74	77	72	73	296	3,132.73
Raquel Carriedo	76	74	72	74	296	3,132.73
*Vicky Uwland	74	73	74	75	296	

South African Women's Tour

Vodacom SA Ladies Players Championship

Parkview Golf Club, Cape Town
Par 35-37–72; 6,100 yards

March 22-24
purse, R150,000

	SCORES			TOTAL	MONEY
Mandy Adamson	75	68	70	213	R22,500
Laurette Maritz	70	72	72	214	16,500
Cherry Moulder	70	75	74	219	12,000
Eva-Lotta Stromlid	73	71	76	220	9,150
Cecilie Lundgreen	69	77	75	221	7,350
Maria Boden	77	75	70	222	6,225
Andrea Hirschhorn	76	76	71	223	4,950
Amanda Moltke-Leth	75	75	73	223	4,950
Anna Becker	77	76	71	224	3,975
*Cas Bridge	72	79	74	225	
Johanna Westerberg	81	70	74	225	3,525
Karen Fries	74	74	78	226	3,112.50
Karen Pringle	78	77	71	226	3,112.50
Caryn Louw	78	76	73	227	2,925
Sara Jelander	74	75	79	228	2,850
Annerie Wessels	81	78	70	229	2,737.50
Letitia Moses	78	72	79	229	2,737.50
*Jo Corkish	79	78	72	229	
Anna Tybring	74	80	77	231	2,625
Susanne Westling	81	76	75	232	2,550
Elsabe Hefer	81	79	74	234	2,400
Pia Josefsson	80	77	77	234	2,400
Joanne Norton	79	78	77	234	2,400
Vanessa Smith	81	76	78	235	2,220
Sanet Marais	79	82	75	236	2,100
Rae Hast	76	79	82	237	2,025
*Kim Brooks	81	78	78	237	
Natou Soro	76	84	78	238	1,950
Morgana Robbertze	78	84	77	239	1,875
Denise Woodard	78	83	81	242	1,800

Kyocera-Mita South African Women's Open

Devondale Golf Club, Stellenbosch
Par 35-36–71; 5,650 yards

April 5-7
purse, R100,000

	SCORES			TOTAL	MONEY
Mandy Adamson	69	68	68	205	R15,000
Morgana Robbertze	74	69	67	210	9,500
Annerie Wessels	72	71	67	210	9,500
Carina Vagner	70	72	69	211	5,050
Cecilie Lundgreen	70	73	68	211	5,050
Andrea Hirschhorn	69	75	67	211	5,050
Maria Boden	71	72	69	212	3,550
Sanet Marais	71	70	72	213	3,050

	SCORES			TOTAL	MONEY
Cecilia Ekelundh	71	72	71	214	2,500
Johanna Westerberg	69	74	71	214	2,500
Caryn Louw	70	73	72	215	2,150
Laurette Maritz	72	76	68	216	1,975
Anna Becker	73	72	71	216	1,975
*Cas Bridge	78	70	69	217	
Cherry Moulder	76	72	70	218	1,900
Karolina Andersson	70	75	74	219	1,825
Amanda Moltke-Leth	72	77	70	219	1,825
Sara Jelander	72	77	71	220	1,725
Anna Tybring	70	75	75	220	1,725
Elsabe Hefer	72	74	75	221	1,650
Charlaine Coetzee-Hirst	78	72	72	222	1,575
Eva-Lotta Stromlid	75	73	74	222	1,575
*Gilly Tebbutt	76	77	70	223	
Yvonne Cassidy	78	71	74	223	1,480
Isabelle Rosberg	75	74	75	224	1,400
*Francis Botha	76	75	74	225	
Karen Fries	78	74	73	225	1,300
Susanne Westling	72	77	76	225	1,300
Letitia Moses	77	74	74	225	1,300
Pia Josefsson	74	76	76	226	1,200

Telkom Ladies Classic

Randpark Golf Club, Johannesburg
Par 36-36–72; 6,139 yards

April 12-14
purse, R140,000

	SCORES			TOTAL	MONEY
Riikka Hakkarainen	70	70	70	210	R21,000
Cecilia Ekelundh	72	70	70	212	13,300
Amanda Moltke-Leth	73	67	72	212	13,300
Mandy Adamson	73	73	67	213	7,700
Eva-Lotta Stromlid	69	74	70	213	7,700
Caryn Louw	70	70	74	214	5,390
Anna Becker	74	67	73	214	5,390
Cecilie Lundgreen	71	75	69	215	4,270
Laurette Maritz	76	71	70	217	3,710
Andrea Hirschhorn	69	75	74	218	3,290
Charlaine Coetzee-Hirst	75	72	72	219	2,905
Karolina Andersson	73	71	75	219	2,905
Annerie Wessels	75	73	72	220	2,660
Anna Tybring	70	75	75	220	2,660
Maria Boden	72	75	73	220	2,660
Camilla Bergh	76	72	73	221	2,415
Mariette Language	73	76	72	221	2,415
Vanessa Smith	72	73	76	221	2,415
Pia Josefsson	70	74	77	221	2,415
Johanna Westerberg	76	70	76	222	2,240
Cherry Moulder	73	75	75	223	2,121
Sara Jelander	74	74	75	223	2,121
*Esme Behrens	77	68	79	224	
Joanne Norton	76	75	73	224	1,960
*Cas Bridge	74	74	76	224	
*Jo Corkish	79	74	72	225	
Zoe Grimbeek	78	75	72	225	1,750
Morgana Robbertze	77	73	75	225	1,750

	SCORES			TOTAL	MONEY
Carina Vagner	75	73	77	225	1,750
Sanet Marais	77	75	73	225	1,750
Rae Hast	77	74	74	225	1,750

Nedbank Ladies South African Masters

Houghton Golf Club, Johannesburg
Par 36-36–72; 5,846 yards

April 17-19
purse, R125,000

	SCORES			TOTAL	MONEY
Mandy Adamson	69	64	71	204	R18,750
Cecilie Lundgreen	68	69	68	205	13,750
Amanda Moltke-Leth	69	68	69	206	10,000
Eva-Lotta Stromlid	73	69	65	207	7,625
Carina Vagner	68	68	72	208	6,125
Sanet Marais	71	71	67	209	4,812.50
Anna Becker	69	72	68	209	4,812.50
Johanna Westerberg	69	71	71	211	3,812.50
*Cas Bridge	70	72	69	211	
Andrea Hirschhorn	68	73	72	213	3,125
Karin Fries	70	72	71	213	3,125
Cecilia Ekelundh	74	70	70	214	2,541.67
Karolina Andersson	73	70	71	214	2,541.67
Riikka Hakkarainen	75	71	68	214	2,541.66
Laurette Maritz	70	71	75	216	2,312.50
Isabelle Rosberg	72	72	72	216	2,312.50
Caryn Louw	67	76	73	216	2,312.50
Charlaine Coetzee-Hirst	72	72	73	217	2,187.50
Anna Tybring	74	73	71	218	2,093.75
Camilla Bergh	72	76	70	218	2,093.75
Sara Jelander	71	72	76	219	2,000
Karen Pringle	70	78	73	221	1,937.50
*Jo Corkish	75	72	74	221	
Letitia Moses	75	73	74	222	1,800
Zoe Grimbeek	72	77	73	222	1,800
Susanne Westling	72	79	72	223	1,593.75
Pia Josefsson	70	74	79	223	1,593.75
Rae Hast	70	76	77	223	1,593.75
Morgana Robbertze	73	77	73	223	1,593.75
Annerie Wessels	76	73	76	225	1,406.25
Elsabe Hefer	72	75	78	225	1,406.25